THE ATHENIAN AGORA

VOLUME XVI

INSCRIPTIONS: THE DECREES

THE ATHENIAN AGORA
RESULTS OF EXCAVATIONS CONDUCTED BY
THE AMERICAN SCHOOL OF CLASSICAL STUDIES AT ATHENS

* *Out of print*

THE ATHENIAN AGORA

RESULTS OF EXCAVATIONS

CONDUCTED BY

THE AMERICAN SCHOOL OF CLASSICAL STUDIES AT ATHENS

VOLUME XVI

INSCRIPTIONS: THE DECREES

BY

A. GEOFFREY WOODHEAD

THE AMERICAN SCHOOL OF CLASSICAL STUDIES AT ATHENS

PRINCETON, NEW JERSEY

1997

Library of Congress Cataloging-in-Publication Data
Woodhead, A. G. (Arthur Geoffrey)
    Inscriptions : the decrees / by A. Geoffrey Woodhead.
      p.   cm. — (Athenian Agora ; v. 16)
    Includes bibliographical references and index.
    ISBN 0-87661-216-8 (alk. paper)
    1. Agora (Athens), Greece. 2. Inscriptions, Greek–Greece–Athens. 3. Athens
(Greece)–Antiquities. I. Title. II. Series.
DF287.A23A5 vol. 16
938′.5–dc21   97-898
                                                            CIP

TYPOGRAPHY BY THE AMERICAN SCHOOL OF CLASSICAL STUDIES PUBLICATIONS OFFICE
6–8 CHARLTON STREET, PRINCETON, NEW JERSEY
PLATES BY THE STINEHOUR PRESS, LUNENBURG, VERMONT
PRINTED IN THE UNITED STATES OF AMERICA
BY PRINCETON ACADEMIC PRESS, LAWRENCEVILLE, NEW JERSEY

To the memory of
BENJAMIN DEAN MERITT
1899–1989

for more than forty years
teacher, counsellor, colleague, companion, and friend
this volume is dedicated
in gratitude and affection

PREFACE

As foreshadowed more than twenty years ago in the preface to *Agora* XV, the present work is concerned with the decrees of the Athenian body politic (and subdivisions of it) other than those dealing with councillors and their officers (the subject of *Agora* XV itself) and, it may be added, those listing and honoring the young men (epheboi) who had completed their higher education and military training. Its aim is to offer a republication, or in a few cases a first publication, of all such decrees discovered in the Agora in the course of the first thirty-six years of the American School's work there, in other words during the Directorships of T. Leslie Shear (1931–1945) and Homer A. Thompson (1946–1967). Thus the latest inscriptional inventory number to be included is I 7029, although it has been possible and indeed essential to introduce later finds that have proved to belong to stelai discovered at an earlier date. To the republished texts are added commentaries intended to draw together such discussions and conclusions as were elicited by their first publication.

The material spans more than six and a half centuries of Athenian history and has for convenience been divided into five sections. Of these, sections 2 and 3 are by far the most substantial. They cover, almost exactly, the 4th and 3rd centuries B.C., the period when the Athenian system of government was, theoretically at least, at its most democratic and when the machinery of administration was in its most, and best, developed form. That this does not coincide entirely with the pattern of *Agora* XV, or at all with the yet-to-be-presented ephebic texts, is itself of interest.

Although 1967/68 forms a "cut-off" date for the volume, continuing work in the Agora has inevitably resulted in the discovery and publication of new material distinct from those additions to the old already mentioned. References to these, without texts, have been assembled at the end of each section to which they are relevant, in the belief that they will add to the usefulness of the collection.

It must also be noted that, although firm groundwork for this volume was laid soon after it was commissioned, a variety of other obligations both personal and professional impeded its progress for a number of years, and the manuscript was not finally complete until the last months of 1991. This delay, though in many respects regrettable, brought in the event unexpected and compensating advantages, for in the course of it a number of scholarly works were published which dealt with, or derived argument from, the material under review. Without the possibility of referring to and discussing the matters they raised the volume would have been infinitely the poorer, and to that extent what has been described as its long period of gestation has been of inestimable benefit to the final product.

But research and controversy do not cease and, in the words of the Preacher, of making many books there is no end. During the five years that have elapsed between the delivery of the typescript and the final publication of the volume further contributions to the issues with which it deals have been published, and these, had opportunity offered, would have been called into service where applicable. Thanks to the understanding and indulgence of a generous editor-in-chief it has been possible, here and there, to insert brief references to this most recent material, chiefly in citations of their treatment in *SEG*, and even to withdraw one complete item (no. 196). Nevertheless, there is much more. Where reliance in this work is placed on J. Kirchner's great *Prosopographia Attica* of 1901, readers will now wish to consult also volume II (Attica) of the British Academy's *A Lexicon of Greek Personal Names* (1994), edited by M. J. Osborne and S. G. Byrne. C. Habicht's *Athen:*

die Geschichte der Stadt in hellenistischer Zeit (1995) replaces W. S. Ferguson's *Hellenistic Athens* of 1911 and will be the future focus of reference concerning that subject. In *Athenian Democracy in Transition* (also 1995) S. V. Tracy applies to the period 340–290 B.C. the techniques that earlier proved so valuable (and are here fully utilized) for the years between 229 and 86 B.C. Those who have occasion to study nos. 64–173 among the texts of the present volume, no small proportion of the whole, will need to take this work into account for possible additions and corrections to what is written here. Finally it may be added that a fourth edition (1990) of the *Agora Guide* has replaced the third edition cited in these pages; and it is reported that a revised and enlarged edition of J. K. Davies' *Athenian Propertied Families*, to which frequent reference is made here, is currently in production.

All this conveys a general lesson which the users of this work should bear constantly in mind. In a sense, any *Corpus Inscriptionum* or similar collection of material is an interim statement, as it were a still photograph extracted from a process of discovery, discussion, and reevaluation constantly in motion. Thus this volume should be understood as a representation of the *status rerum*, in these particular matters, at the end of 1991, as that *status* presented itself to the author; for, on many a detail, others might well have seen the same material in another light and interpreted it differently.

The dissertations on the archonships to which many of the texts are assigned, interspersed at the appropriate chronological points, should be regarded similarly. They attempt on each occasion an historical review, of independent interest as a facet of that same process of discovery, discussion, and reevaluation, in order to show how opinion took shape concerning the date of the archon's year of office, the calendric character of that year, and how, by 1991, these had come to be determined as they are stated here. However, in this area too, and in particular for certain parts of the 3rd and 2nd centuries B.C., conclusions remain open to revised interpretation and fresh evidence, and continuing controversy is to be expected.[1]

The introductory data that describe the physical characteristics of the inscribed stelai have used the conventional "shorthand" in identifying the type of marble employed to which M. B. Walbank has drawn helpful attention. In his work on proxeny decrees of the 5th century he discussed in detail what is conventionally intended by the terms "Pentelic" and "Hymettian", and the reader may be referred to his account of them.[2] It is indeed true, as N. Herz and W. K. Pritchett long ago pointed out,[3] that the distinctions may be purely subjective; but the scientific rigor they prescribed, difficult to achieve at the outset and even more difficult to practice in the field, is likely to prove in the event no more than marginally helpful, and that only in occasional cases. For present purposes the conventions may suffice.

The commentaries that follow the texts fall for the most part into two sections. The first deals with the textual problems, if any, presented by the legibility of the inscription; matters of more general historical, social, or procedural interest then follow. At this point it may also be appropriate to repeat the paragraph that concludes the preface to *Agora* XV, for the practice adopted by B. D. Meritt and J. S. Traill there has been exactly followed here. "Inscriptions in the Epigraphical Museum are recorded with their inventory numbers, designated with the letters E.M. Inscriptions found in the American Excavations of the Athenian Agora are also recorded with their inventory numbers, designated by the letter I. Places of discovery are noted with reference to the standard grid of the Agora excavations, reprinted here [before Plate 1]."

In an ideal world, with expense no object and the resources of intending subscribers limitless, every inscription in the volume would be accompanied by a photograph. A compromise with

---

[1] Cf. J. N. Morgan, *AJA* 100, 1996, p. 395.

[2] M. B. Walbank, *Athenian Proxenies of the Fifth Century B.C.*, 1978, pp. 52–55.

[3] N. Herz and W. K. Pritchett, *AJA* 57, 1953, pp. 71–83.

practicality is, however, unavoidable; in reaching it the assumption has perforce been made that readers seeking illustrations will have access to the volumes of *Hesperia* in which they are chiefly to be found, usually in connection with the *editio princeps* of the stone under discussion. On that basis it has been possible to limit the illustrative material at the end of the book to certain categories. The first priority, obviously enough, has been given to the illustration of inscriptions hitherto unpublished, and the next to inscriptions published elsewhere than in *Hesperia*. In the early years of *Hesperia* the photographs, though admirable for their time, lacked the quality of those of more recent decades; moreover, some texts were illustrated not by photographs but by line drawings. These where possible have been photographed anew, and they make up a third category. Other inclusions serve to illustrate lettering styles of a particular character or period as well as a few texts of special artistic or historical interest which, one may justly feel, demand a place here despite their availability elsewhere.

It remains to express the author's gratitude to those who have done so much over the years to assist him in his labors. Of their number two claim preeminence. It was at the request of, and by the encouragement of, Homer A. Thompson and Benjamin D. Meritt that this work was first set in hand, and to them the debt throughout a now-lengthy epigraphical career remains the greatest and the most deeply felt. The dedication of this volume to the memory of the latter, who died in 1989, is appropriate and right, but even so a sense of understatement remains.

As the work began to take shape, the advice and timely correction of those who saw drafts of all or part of it proved invaluable. Where Malcolm F. McGregor (who also died in 1989), Alan S. Henry, John S. Traill, and Michael B. Walbank are concerned the thanks they deserve can hardly be measured by this brief expression of it. In particular, the many citations of Alan Henry and Michael Walbank in matters of detail will convey their own grateful message. John Camp, the present Director of the Agora excavations, and his staff have been constantly helpful: and no-one who has written for an Agora publication can fail to appreciate what is meant when gratitude is expressed to Marian H. McAllister, the editor-in-chief, for so much care, patience, tolerance, and editorial wisdom. To work with the A.S.C.S. editorial office is always a pleasure and at times an education. On the technical and production side, all who have been concerned with the putting into print of this exceptionally difficult material have well earned the thanks and congratulations that must assuredly find a rightful place in this record.

Finally, two special debts extending over the whole period of the work remain to be gratefully acknowledged. Lucy Shoe Meritt's constant encouragement has meant a great deal to the author, and his thanks for it demand inclusion as his task ends; and lastly, and most notably, his wife's patient support through so many years when that end seemed so remote has been vital to the whole endeavor.

That this volume will meet general welcome and approval is a hope but not an expectation. Reviewers, if any there be, will emphasize inadequacies and occasions for disagreement, that being their function; and readers consulting its material for their particular purposes will often be more liable to be irritated by what they do not find than appreciative of what they do. *Tantum docet experientia.* Nevertheless, taken as a personal summation of the past history of the inscriptions with which it deals and as a point of departure for their future use as discovery and debate proceed, it will offer a useful and, possibly, even a lasting contribution. If it so proves, it will have served its purpose.

A. GEOFFREY WOODHEAD

SUTTON-ON-THE-FOREST
North Yorkshire
England

November 1996

CONTENTS

Illustrations

LIST OF ILLUSTRATIONS

BIBLIOGRAPHICAL ABBREVIATIONS

BOOKS

These titles, which are cited frequently in the text, appear there in abbreviated form.

AbhAkadBerlin = *Abhandlungen der Deutschen Akademie der Wissenschaften zu Berlin*
Agora = *The Athenian Agora: Results of Excavations Conducted by the American School of Classical Studies at Athens*, Princeton
   III = R. E. Wycherley, *Literary and Epigraphical Testimonia*, 1957
   XIV = H. A. Thompson and R. E. Wycherley, *The Agora of Athens*, 1972
   XV = Benjamin D. Meritt and John S. Traill, *Inscriptions: The Athenian Councillors*, 1974
   XVII = Donald W. Bradeen, *Inscriptions: The Funerary Monuments*, 1974
   XIX = G. V. Lalonde, M. K. Langdon, and M. B. Walbank, *Inscriptions: Horoi. Poletai Records. Leases of Public Lands*, 1991
*Agora Guide*³ = H. A. Thompson, *The Athenian Agora: A Guide to the Excavation and Museum*, Athens 1976
Alessandri, S., *Annali della Scuola Normale di Pisa*, ser. 3, 12, 1982
Ancient Macedonian Studies in Honor of Charles F. Edson, H. Dell, ed., Thessaloniki 1981
ANRW = *Aufstieg und Niedergang der römischen Welt*, H. Temporini, ed., Berlin 1972–
A.P.B. = Excavations of the Athenian Agora Picture Books
ATL = B. D. Meritt, H. T. Wade-Gery, and M. F. McGregor, *The Athenian Tribute Lists* I–IV, Cambridge, Mass. 1939–1953
Behrend, D., *Attische Pachturkunden* (*Vestigia* 12), Munich 1970
Bengtson, H., *Die Staatsverträge des Altertums*, II, *Die Verträge der griechische-römischen Welt von 700 bis 338 v. Chr.*, Munich 1962
Busolt-Swoboda = G. Busolt, *Griechische Staatskunde*, 2nd ed., revised by H. Swoboda, Munich 1926
CAH = *Cambridge Ancient History*, Cambridge
Camp, J. M., *The Athenian Agora*, London 1986
CIG = *Corpus Inscriptionum Graecarum*, A. Boeckh, ed., Berlin 1828–1877
Davies, J. K., *Athenian Propertied Families, 600–300 B.C.*, Oxford 1971
Deubner, L., *Attische Feste*, Berlin 1932
Develin, R., *Athenian Officials, 684–321 B.C.*, Cambridge/New York 1989
Dinsmoor, W. B., *The Archons of Athens in the Hellenistic Age*, Cambridge, Mass. 1931
————. *The Athenian Archon List in the Light of Recent Discoveries*, New York 1939
Dow, S., *Prytaneis* (*Hesperia*, Supplement I), Athens 1937
Ferguson, W. S., *The Athenian Secretaries*, New York 1898
————. *Athenian Tribal Cycles in the Hellenistic Age*, Cambridge, Mass. 1932
————. *Hellenistic Athens: An Historical Essay*, London 1911
Geagan, D. J., *The Athenian Constitution after Sulla* (*Hesperia*, Supplement XII), Princeton 1967
Habicht, C., *Studien zur Geschichte Athens in hellenisticher Zeit* (*Hypomnemata* 73), Göttingen 1982
————. *Untersuchungen zur politischen Geschichte Athens im 3. Jahrhundert v. Chr.* (*Vestigia* 30), Munich 1979
Hansen, M. H., *The Athenian Ecclesia*, Copenhagen 1983
————. *The Athenian Ecclesia II*, Copenhagen 1989
Henry, A. S., *Honours and Privileges in Athenian Decrees*, Hildesheim/New York 1983
————. *The Prescripts of Athenian Decrees* (*Mnemosyne*, Supplement 49), Leiden 1977
ID = *Inscriptions de Délos*, F. Durrbach, P. Roussel, and M. Launey, edd., Paris 1926–
IG = *Inscriptiones Graecae*, Berlin
   I = *Inscriptiones Atticae Euclidis anno vetustiores*, A. Kirchhoff, ed., 1873
   I² = *Inscriptiones Atticae Euclidis anno anteriores, editio minor*, F. Hiller von Gaertringen, ed., 1924
   I³ = *Inscriptiones Atticae Euclidis anno anteriores, editio tertia*, D. M. Lewis, ed., 1981
   II = *Inscriptiones Atticae aetatis quae est inter Euclidis annum et Augusti tempora*, U. Koehler, ed., indices by J. Kirchner, 1877–1895

II^2 = *Inscriptiones Atticae Euclidis anno posteriores*, II–III, *editio minor*, J. Kirchner, ed., 1913–1940

VII = *Inscriptiones Megaridis et Boeotiae*, W. Dittenberger, ed., 1892

XI = *Inscriptiones Deli*, F. Dürrbach *et al.*, edd., 1912–1927

XII = *Inscriptiones insularum maris Aegaei praeter Delum*, F. Hiller von Gaertringen *et al.*, edd., 1895–1915

IIA[2] = J. Kirchner, *Imagines Inscriptionum Atticarum*, 2nd ed., Berlin 1948

Inscriptiones Creticae, M. Guarducci, ed., 4 vols., Rome 1935–1950

Jacoby, *FGrHist* = F. Jacoby, *Die Fragmente der griechischen Historiker*, Berlin/Leiden 1923–1958

Judeich, W., *Topographie von Athen*, 2nd ed., Munich 1931

Lambrechts, A., *Tekst en uitzicht van de Atheense proxeniedecreten tot 323 v. C.*, Brussels 1958

LSJ = *Greek-English Lexicon*, H. G. Liddell, R. Scott, and H. S. Jones, edd., Oxford 1968

McDonald, W. A., *The Political Meeting-Places of the Greeks*, Baltimore 1943

Meiggs, R., *The Athenian Empire*, Oxford 1972

Meiggs-Lewis = R. Meiggs and D. M. Lewis, *A Selection of Greek Historical Inscriptions to the End of the Fifth Century B.C.*, Oxford 1969

Meisterhans-Schwyzer[3] = K. Meisterhans, *Grammatik der attischen Inschriften*, 3rd ed., revised by E. Schwyzer, Berlin 1900

Meritt, B. D., *The Athenian Year*, Berkeley 1961

Mikalson, J. D., *The Sacred and Civil Calendar of the Athenian Year*, Princeton 1975

Moretti, L., *Iscrizioni storiche ellenistiche* I, Florence 1967

OCD[2] = *Oxford Classical Dictionary*, 2nd ed., N. G. L. Hammond and H. H. Scullard, edd., Oxford 1970

OGIS = *Orientis Graeci inscriptiones selectae*, W. Dittenberger, ed., Leipzig 1903–1905

Osborne, M. J., *Naturalization in Athens* I, Brussels 1981, II, Brussels 1982, III/IV, Brussels 1983

PA = J. Kirchner, *Prosopographia Attica*, Berlin 1901–1903

Pečírka, J., *The Formula for the Grant of Enktesis in Attic Inscriptions*, Prague 1966

Phoros = Φόρος: *Tribute to Benjamin Dean Meritt*, D. W. Bradeen and M. F. McGregor, edd., Locust Valley, N.Y. 1974

PIR[2] = *Prosopographia Imperii Romani saec. I. II. III.*, 2nd ed., E. Groag and A. Stein, edd., Berlin 1933–

Pouilloux, J., *La forteresse de Rhamnonte*, Paris 1954

P. Oxy. = *Oxyrhynchus Papyri*, B. P. Grenfell and A. S. Hunt, edd., London 1898–

Pritchett, W. K., *Ancient Athenian Calendars on Stone* (University of California Publications in Classical Archaeology IV, iv, pp. 267–402), Berkeley 1963

Pritchett, W. K., and B. D. Meritt, *The Chronology of Hellenistic Athens*, Cambridge, Mass. 1940

Pritchett, W. K., and O. Neugebauer, *The Calendars of Athens*, Cambridge, Mass. 1947

RE = *Paulys Realencyclopädie der classischen Altertumswissenschaft*, Neue Bearbeitung, revised by G. Wissowa, Stuttgart 1893–1980

Rhodes, P. J., *The Athenian Boule*, Oxford 1972

SbAkadBerlin = *Sitzungsberichte der Deutschen Akademie der Wissenschaften zu Berlin, Klasse für Sprachen, Literatur und Kunst*

SbAkadWien = *Sitzungsberichte, Österreichische Akademie der Wissenschaften [Wien], Philosophisch-historische Klasse*

Schmitt, H. H., *Die Staatsverträge des Altertums*, III, *Die Verträge der griechisch-römischen Welt von 338 bis 200 v. Chr.*, Munich 1969

Schwenk, C. J., *Athens in the Age of Alexander: The Dated Laws and Decrees of "the Lykourgan Era", 338–322 B.C.*, Chicago 1985

SEG = *Supplementum Epigraphicum Graecum*

SGDI = *Sammlung der griechischen Dialekt-Inschriften*, H. Collitz *et al.*, edd., Göttingen 1884–1915

Shear, T. L., *Kallias of Sphettos and the Revolt of Athens in 286 B.C.* (*Hesperia*, Supplement XVII), Princeton 1978

Sokolowski, F., *Lois sacrées des cités grecques (Supplément)*, Paris 1962

———. *Lois sacrées des cités grecques*, Paris 1969

Syll.[3] = W. Dittenberger, *Sylloge Inscriptionum Graecarum*, 3rd ed., Leipzig 1915

TAPS = *Transactions of the American Philosophical Society*

Threatte, L., *The Grammar of Attic Inscriptions*, I, *Phonology*, Berlin/New York 1980

Tod, *GHI* = M. N. Tod, *A Selection of Greek Historical Inscriptions*, 2nd ed., Oxford 1946; II, Oxford 1948

Tracy, S. V., *Attic Letter-Cutters of 229 to 86 B.C.*, Berkeley 1990

Traill, J. S., *The Political Organization of Attica* (*Hesperia*, Supplement XIV), Princeton 1975

Walbank, M. B., *Athenian Proxenies of the Fifth Century B.C.*, Toronto 1978

Woodhead, A. G., *The Study of Greek Inscriptions*, 2nd ed., Cambridge 1981

PERIODICALS

AAA = Athens Annals of Archaeology
AJA = American Journal of Archaeology
AJAH = American Journal of Ancient History
AJP = American Journal of Philology
ArchAnz = Archäologischer Anzeiger (JdI)
ArchCl = Archeologia Classica
᾿Αρχ. ᾿Εφ.= ᾿Αρχαιολογικὴ ᾿Εφημερίς
AthMitt = Mitteilungen des Deutschen Archäologischen Instituts, Athenische Abteilung
BCH = Bulletin de correspondance hellénique
BSA = Annual of the British School at Athens
CJ = Classical Journal
CP = Classical Philology
CQ = Classical Quarterly
CR = Classical Review
CSCA = California Studies in Classical Antiquity
Δελτ. = ᾿Αρχαιολογικὸν Δελτίον
GRBS = Greek, Roman, and Byzantine Studies
HarvThRev = Harvard Theological Review
HSCP = Harvard Studies in Classical Philology
JdI = Jahrbuch des Deutschen Archäologischen Instituts
JHS = Journal of Hellenic Studies
ÖJh = Jahreshefte des Österreichischen Archäologischen Instituts in Wien
RA = Revue archéologique
REA = Revue des études anciennes
REG = Revue des études grecques
RendAccArchNapoli = Rendiconti dell'Accademia di archeologia, lettere e belle arti, Napoli
RevPhil = Revue de philologie, de littérature et d'histoire anciennes
RhMus = Rheinisches Museum für Philologie
RivFil = Rivista di filologia e d'istruzione classica
TAPA = Transactions of the American Philological Association
ZPE = Zeitschrift für Papyrologie und Epigraphik

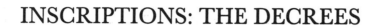

INSCRIPTIONS: THE DECREES

SECTION 1

TO THE FALL OF ATHENS IN 404 B.C.

(1–28)

SECTION 1

TO THE FALL OF ATHENS IN 404 B.C.: **1–28**

In the course of the work of the first thirty-seven years (1931–1968), the Agora Excavations turned up fragments of twenty-eight public decrees dating to the Periklean Age and the period of the Peloponnesian War, exclusive of the four small items briefly mentioned on p. 36 and the two more recent discoveries (**28A** and **28B**) recorded in the appendix. None provided a complete text, and seven were so fragmentary that the character of the enactment concerned could not be assessed. Nine, nearly one-third of the total, proved to form part of documents already known and published, and in some cases the new contribution added significantly to an understanding of them. Since the already known sections of eight of them had been discovered on the Akropolis itself, or in one instance on the South Slope, it is apparent that much of the "Agora" material had been thrown or brought down from the citadel as debris or for reuse, and this must apply also to the "new" documents known for the first time as the result of the Agora undertaking: indeed four of them, in what survives of their texts, provide or may be regarded as providing for their own deposit on the Akropolis.

With the exception of the *incerta*, one-quarter of the total, the largest group among the decrees (also one-quarter of the total) is represented by expressions of gratitude and grants of honors and privileges to individual non-Athenian benefactors; three others of similar character (**1, 3, 15**) are concerned with communities rather than individuals, and three more fragments form part of treaties with other cities (**4, 16, 19**). A further three (**2, 7**, and very probably **24**) record regulations dealing with an ally or a colony overseas. Thus sixteen out of twenty-one identifiable decrees deal with "external relations", whether with allied or with "foreign" communities. One more text (**17**), dealing with currency, will also have affected the allies. For all these matters, permanent record guaranteed by the tutelage of Athena in her sanctuary was appropriate.

Four decrees only (**6, 8, 9, 12**) are concerned with "internal" arrangements, such as public works, public property, or state ceremonial. Internal requirements as far as inscribed records are concerned more usually extended to the public accountability of officials, in the form of accounts, inventories, and the like, which are not in point here. To that extent, the 5th-century decrees considered alone may show an imbalance in suggesting that the interest of the βουλή and the δῆμος was strongly concentrated on foreign affairs. Nevertheless, the role of Athens as an imperial power, organizing her ἀρχή and fighting a long and ultimately disastrous war, must surely have meant that a large proportion of public enactments were indeed concerned with external matters; and as the practice of public documentation developed it is likely to have been thought advisable for a correspondingly large proportion of these to achieve the permanence of an inscribed stele.

PRAISE OF THE PEOPLE OF SIGEION

1 (Pl. 1). Two nonjoining fragments of a stele of Pentelic marble, of which the upper and small fragment (*a*, I 1276) preserves the left side, original back, and part of the upper molding of the monument. This fragment was discovered on January 31, 1934, in a modern context over the Southwest Fountain House (H 15). Fragment *b* (E.M. 6800) is complete except at the top and was discovered long since on the South Slope of the Akropolis.

   a: H. 0.21 m.; W. 0.16 m.; Th. 0.112 m.

   b: H. 0.332 m.; W. 0.361 m.; Th. 0.116 m.

   LH. 0.01 m. (line 1, 0.015 m.).
   Στοιχ. (lines 2 and following) Hor. 0.0167 m.; Vert. 0.014 m.

Ed. *b*: *IG* I², 32, with earlier references. *a* and *b*: B. D. Meritt, *Hesperia* 5, 1936, pp. 360–362, no. 3, with photograph (see also *SEG* X, 13 and XXI, 9); *IG* I³, 17, with further references. Photograph of *a* only, Meritt, *Inscriptions from the Athenian Agora* (A.P.B. 10), no. 12.

a. 451/50 *a.*   ΣΤΟΙΧ. 23 (lines 2 and following)

Σιγ[ειέον].   (*a*)
[Ἔ]δοχσεν τε͂[ι βολε͂ι καὶ το͂ι δέ]
[μ]οι· Οἰνε[ὶ]ς [ἐπρυτάνευε, . .⁴. .]
[ς] ἐγραμμάτ[ευε, ...⁹. . . . ἐ]
5   πεστάτε, Ἀν[τίδοτος ε͂ρχε, . . .]
[.]χίδες ε[ἴ]π[ε· ἐπαινέσαι τοῖς]
[Σι]γειεῦ[σ]ιν [ὃς ὅσιν ἀνδράσι]
[ν ἀγ]αθοῖς ἐς [τὸν δε͂μον τὸν Ἀθ]
[εναίον . . . . . . .¹⁷. . . . .]
                lacuna
10   [. . . . . .²⁰. . . . . ἐν σ]   (*b*)
[τέλει λιθί]νει τ[έλεσι τοῖς Σ]
ιγε[ιο͂]ν καὶ καταθέτο ἐμ πό[λε]
ι καθάπερ αὐτοὶ δέονται, ὅπο
ς ἂν ε͂ι γεγραμμένον καὶ με͂ ἀδ
15   ικο͂νται μεδὲ ὑφ’ἑνὸς το͂ν ἐν τ
ε͂ι ἐπείροι.   *vacat*
                vacat

The hand is regarded by M. B. Walbank (*Athenian Proxenies*, p. 97; cf. *Hesperia* 42, 1973, p. 334 with note 4) as the same as, or closely related to, that of **4**, *IG* I³, 20, and several other texts to be dated in the later 450's or early 440's. The Attic lettering is characteristic of the mid-5th century, including tailed rho and sigma with three strokes (four however in line 1). The aspirate, H, is not expressed.

The text is that of Meritt, except in line 6 (ε[ἴ]π[ε· ᵛ ἐπαινέσαι μὲν]): the present restoration, adopted in *IG* I³, was also followed by H. B. Mattingly (*AJP* 95, 1974, pp. 282–284). Lines 5–6. Mattingly (*Historia* 12, 1963, pp. 267–270; see *SEG* XXI, *loc. cit.*) restored Ἀν[τιφο͂ν ε͂ρχεν, Ἀντι|ο]χίδες ε[ἴ]πε[ν, but on the ephelkystic nu see A. S. Henry, *CSCA* 11, 1978, pp. 87–88. Mattingly urged that the decree be dated to 418/17 B.C., later arguing that the presence of the archon's name necessitated a dating later than 421/20 (*Atti del I Convegno del Centro Internazionale di Studi Numismatici, 1967*, 1969, p. 217, note 55; see *SEG* XXV, 4). But cf. Walbank, *Athenian Proxenies*, p. 94. Mattingly maintained his contention on other grounds (*AJP, loc. cit.*) and reiterated it in *AJP* 105, 1984, pp. 346 and 348–349, this time proposing in lines 5–6 Ἀν[τιφο͂ν ε͂ρχε, Λυσιμ|α]χίδες ε[ἴ]π[ε: cf. *SEG* XXXIV, 6, XLII, 5. But arguments for the later date remain unconvincing in the face of those to be derived from the character of the writing. For these see R. Meiggs, *JHS* 86, 1966, pp. 86–97 (esp. pp. 94–95). Meiggs suggested Μορ|υ]χίδες as the name of the proposer; cf. the archon of 440/39 B.C. On the preamble as a whole see Henry, *Prescripts*, p. 7.

Lines 11–12. The cost of inscribing the stele is borne by the Sigeians themselves: on the formula see Henry, *Vindex Humanitatis: Essays in Honour of John Huntly Bishop*, 1980, pp. 17–33 (this text, p. 21).

For the historical circumstances see *ATL* III, p. 255; N. G. L. Hammond, *A History of Greece to 322 B.C.*, 2nd ed., 1967, p. 305; Meiggs, *Athenian Empire*, p. 117; M. F. McGregor, *The Athenians and Their Empire*, 1987, p. 64.

REGULATIONS FOR THE GOVERNMENT OF AN ALLIED CITY

2. Two nonjoining fragments of a stele of Pentelic marble, of which the first (fragment *a*, I 5172 a) preserves the left side of the monument and possibly the original back; its inscribed face is badly blackened and corroded. This fragment was discovered on January 26, 1937, in the wall of a late bothros west of the Panathenaic Way and west of the Eleusinion (R 19). Fragment *b* (I 5172 b) is broken all around and was discovered on April 11, 1939, in a marble pile in the area west of the Eleusinion. The relationship between the two fragments remains uncertain.

a: H. 0.36 m.; W. 0.205 m.; Th. 0.093 m.

b: H. 0.13 m.; W. 0.06 m.; Th. 0.105 m.

LH. 0.011 m.
Στοιχ. (square) 0.018 m.

Ed. B. D. Meritt, *Hesperia* 14, 1945, pp. 82–83, no. 2, with photograph; *IG* I³, 16. See also Meritt, *Hesperia* 15, 1946, pp. 246–249, no. 77; *SEG* X, 11.

ca. a. 450 *a., vel paullo ante* ΣΤΟΙΧ.

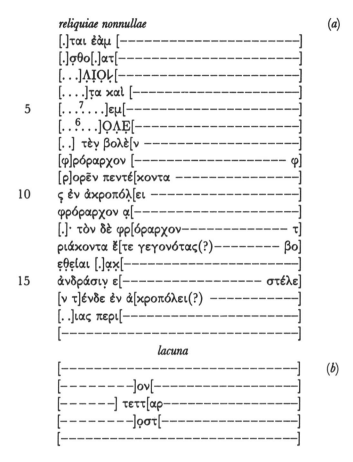

reliquiae nonnullae

```
                                                              (a)
        [.]ται ἐὰμ [---------------------]
        [.]σθο[.]ατ[---------------------]
        [...]ΛΙΟ[---------------------]
        [....]τα καὶ [---------------------]
    5   [...⁷...]εμ[---------------------]
        [..⁶...]ΟΛΕ[---------------------]
        [..] τὲγ βολὲ[ν ---------------------]
        [φ]ρόραρχον [--------------------- φ]
        [ρ]ορὲν πεντέ[κοντα ---------------]
   10   ς ἐν ἀκροπόλ[ει ---------------------]
        φρόραρχον α[---------------------]
        [.]· τὸν δὲ φρ[όραρχον------------- τ]
        ριάκοντα ἔ[τε γεγονότας(?)-------- βο]
        εθεῖαι [.]αχ[---------------------]
   15   ἀνδράσιν ε[-------------------- στέλε]
        [ν τ]ένδε ἐν ἀ[κροπόλει(?) ------------]
        [..]ιας περι[---------------------]
        [---------------------]
```

lacuna

```
                                                              (b)
        [---------------------]
        [-------]ον[--------------]
        [------] τεττ[αρ--------------]
        [-------]ροτ[--------------]
        [---------------------]
```

Among those who have studied fragment *a* confidence has varied in the evaluation of letters as certainly read or to be underdotted, but in no case is this of real consequence. Line 2 *init.* [. .]θο Meritt; [.]σθο *IG* I³. Line 3. ΛΛΟΤ Meritt. Line 7. τὲς βολὲ[ς--] Meritt; τὲγ βολὲ[ν --] *IG* I³. Lines 15–16. The suggestion is Meritt's, not however included in *IG* I³. That πόλις is used for ἀκρόπολις at this epoch in instructions for the setting up of stelai in that location in Athens may or may not be relevant in this particular turn of phrase. That fragment *b* is to be placed at a point lower on the stele than fragment *a* is suggested by the greater thickness of the former, not (like that of fragment *a*?) fully preserved.

The character of the lettering, which includes Ϟ, closely resembles that of the surviving part of the "Erythrai dossier" (*IG* I³, 14–15), and in the *editio princeps* Meritt attributed these two fragments to that group of texts. But the thickness of the stones does not correspond, and, even though this may not be original on fragment *a* (and certainly is not on fragment *b*), he withdrew the attribution in the following year. Cf. Meiggs-Lewis, p. 94. Moreover, despite the close resemblance doubt remains concerning the positive identity of the lettering with that of the Erythrai documents; cf. *IG* I³, 16 *comm.*

Line 8 *et seq.* The presence of a phrourarchos with, presumably, a garrison on the acropolis of the city in question suggests that, as in the texts dealing with Erythrai and Miletos (*IG* I³, 21), where garrisons are referred to, there had been defection from the Athenian alliance, or at least some wavering of loyalty. For disaffection in the alliance in the later 450's see R. Meiggs, *HSCP* 67, 1963, pp. 4–11 (esp. pp. 4–6) and *Athenian Empire*, pp. 109–118; and cf. **3**. On phrourarchs see Meiggs, *Athenian Empire*, p. 214; J. M. Balcer, *Historia* 25, 1976, pp. 277–282 (where lines 7–17 of this text are quoted *in extenso*).

Lines 12–13. For the requirement of a minimum age of thirty years cf. *IG* I², 22, lines 4–5.

GOOD RELATIONS WITH AN ALLIED CITY CONFIRMED

3. Three nonjoining fragments of a stele of Pentelic marble, two of which (fragments *b* and *c*) were found in the Agora (I 4546 a and b, in corrected numeration) and shown to belong with the long-known fragment E.M. 6565, now fragment *a*, originally found on the Akropolis. Fragment *a* preserves the right side and original back of the stele; fragment *b*, broken on all sides, was discovered on February 27, 1937, in a late context under Akropolis Street, west of the Post-Herulian Wall (R 25); fragment *c*, also broken on all sides, was discovered on March 9, 1938, in a modern house wall outside the Market Square to the southeast, west of the Panathenaic Way (O 19).

a: H. 0.20 m.; W. 0.375 m.; Th. 0.166 m.

b: H. 0.052 m.; W. 0.081 m.; Th. 0.033 m.

c: H. 0.095 m.; W. 0.08 m.; Th. 0.07 m.

LH. 0.011–0.012 m.
Στοιχ. Hor. 0.0122 m.; Vert. 0.019 m.

Ed. *a* only: *IG* I², 29, with earlier references. *a–c*: B. D. Meritt, *Hesperia* 14, 1945, pp. 83–85, no. 3, with photographs (see also *SEG* X, 21); *IG* I³, 29. Photograph of *a*, D. W. Bradeen and M. F. McGregor, *Studies in Fifth-Century Attic Epigraphy*, 1973, pl. XVI.

ca. a. 450 a.   ΣΤΟΙΧ. 56

[῎Εδοχσεν κτλ.--]
[----------------------------· ἐπειδὲ οἱ ----------------------------πρ]
[ότερον ἄνδρες ἀγαθοὶ ἔσαν περὶ τὲν π]όλι[ν τὲ]ν ᾿Αθεναίον, καὶ νῦν ἐ[μπε]δ   (a)
[όσαντες τὲν χσυμμαχίαν καὶ τὸν ὅρκ]ον περὶ τὲν πόλιν τὲν ᾿Αθεναίον φσ
[έφισμα αἰτōσι παρὰ τō δέμο ὅστε τυχε͂]ν ὅν δέονται αὐτοὶ καὶ χσυγ[θ]έσθ
[αι τὲν χσυμμαχίαν, λαβε͂ν μὲν αὐτὸς παρὰ τō] δέμο τō ᾿Αθεναίον ὅν δέοντα
5   [ι ἀβλαβο͂ς καὶ ἀδόλος, ἔχοντας τὰ νόμιμα τὰ σ]φέτερα αὐτōν καὶ ἄρχοντα
[ς καὶ βολὲν καὶ δίκας ὅπος καὶ πρὸ τō· ἄρχοντα] δὲ ἄλλον μεδένα [χ]αθιστά
[ναι μεδὲ ....²²......... ἐὰν μὲ τοῖς ᾿Α]θεναίοις [δοκεῖ· ....]
[----------------------------------]τονι [......¹²......]

lacuna

[--]   (b, c)
[....¹⁰....· περὶ δὲ τούτο]ν διχ[άσαι τέν τε] βολὲν [.......¹⁷.......]
10   [....¹⁰....· ἐὰν δέ τις πα]ρὰ ταῦ[τα εἴπει ἒ] ἐπιφσε[φίσει .....¹².....]
[----------------------------------] τὲμ [-------------]
[----------------------------]Ε[-------------]
[--]

The distinctive lettering, which includes Ϟ, is particularly characterized by the angled "upright" stroke of lambda. M. B. Walbank (*Athenian Proxenies*, p. 115) compares the hand of *IG* I³, 30 (I², 31) and 37 (I², 14/15, *ATL* II, D 15). See also R. Meiggs, *JHS* 86, 1966, p. 94. For the nature of the marble see Walbank, *op. cit.*, pp. 54 and 59, note 6. The aspirate (H) is not expressed. The text is that of *IG* I³; for the reading of the end of line 6 see Bradeen and McGregor, *op. cit.*, p. 118. In *IG* I², Hiller von Gaertringen posited a line of 53 letters in length, with other restorations.

Lines 6–7. Officials are to be local and not imposed from outside. On the Athenian archons in allied cities see *ATL* III, pp. 145–146; Meiggs, *Athenian Empire*, pp. 213–215; J. M. Balcer, *Historia* 25, 1976, pp. 271–277. Line 10. On the "entrenchment clause" prohibiting, or at least making difficult, any attempt to alter or negate the decree see D. M. Lewis in *Phoros*, pp. 81–89.

For the disaffection within the alliance in the later 450's, in the context of which this decree might have its historical place, see **2** and references there cited.

TREATY BETWEEN ATHENS AND HERMIONE

4. The upper part of a stele of Pentelic marble, broken below and with the inscribed surface to right and left worn smooth (I 317), discovered on November 27, 1932, in a wall of a modern house east of the Temple of Apollo Patroos (I 8).

H. 0.22 m.; W. 0.47 m.; Th. (at lines 1–2) 0.115 m., (lower) 0.105 m.
LH. (lines 1–2) 0.013 m., (lines 3 and following) 0.008 m.
Στοιχ. (lines 3 and following) Hor. 0.011 m.; Vert. 0.0127 m.

Ed. J. H. Oliver, *Hesperia* 2, 1933, pp. 494–497, no. 12, with photograph (see also *SEG* X, 15); *IG* I³, 31. Text also in A. S. Arvanitopoulos, Ἐπιγραφική, 1937, pp. 123–124 (where it is dated to 457 B.C.); H. Bengtson, *Staatsverträge* II, p. 59, no. 150; A. S. Henry, *Prescripts*, p. 8 (lines 1–6 only). Photographs also in Arvanitopoulos, *op. cit.*, fig. 90; M. Lang, *The Athenian Citizen* (A.P.B. 4, 1960), ill. 10; B. D. Meritt, *Inscriptions from the Athenian Agora* (A.P.B. 10, 1966), no. 9.

ca. a. 450 *a.*   ΣΤΟΙΧ. 35 (lines 3 and following)

```
[Θ] ε ό δ ο ρ ο ς  Π ρ α σ ι ε ὺ ς  ἐ γ ρ α μ μ ά τ ε υ ε.
                        vacat
[χ σ] υ ν θ ε̃ κ α ι ⋮ ῾Ε ρ μ ι ο ν έ ο ν ⋮ κ α ὶ  ᾿Α θ ε ν α ῖ ο [ν].
                        vacat
[῎Ε]δοχσεν τε̃ι βολε̃ι καὶ το̃ι δέμοι· ᾿Αντιοχ[ὶς ἐ]
[π]ρυτάνευε, Θεόδορος ἐγραμμάτευε, Σι[..⁵..]
[.] ἐπεστάτε               vacat
[Λ]έον ε[ἴ]π[ε]· χσυνθέσθαι hὰ hοι ῾Ερμιο[νε̃ς ....]
[...............¹⁶.......]ρ[..⁵..]ου[....¹¹....]
[------------------------]
```

The lettering bears some resemblance to that of **1** (cf. M. B. Walbank, *Athenian Proxenies*, p. 97); but rho lacks a tail, the aspirate is expressed (other than in the name ῾Ερμιονε̃ς), upsilon in line 2 has the form V. The text of lines 1–6 is that of Oliver. Line 7. [......¹³......]Ο[------------] Oliver: M. H. Jameson (*per ep.*) has read N in the 15th space and Ḅ in the 17th and suggests for lines 6–7 ῾Ερμιο[νέες καὶ| hοι ᾿Αθεναῖοι χσυ]ν̣[έ]β̣[αλον].

The date of the treaty has been much disputed. For the arguments see references in *SEG* XIX, 5, XXI, 11, XXV, 9, XXXIV, 9. H. B. Mattingly (*Historia* 10, 1961, p. 173; in *Ancient Society and Institutions: Studies Presented to Victor Ehrenberg on His 75th Birthday*, 1966, p. 211; *BCH* 92, 1968, pp. 484–485; *AJP* 105, 1984, pp. 348–349) urged that it be assigned to 425/4 B.C. (*SEG* XXXIV, 9, in reporting the 1984 article, erroneously stated that he wished to attribute it to 422/1.) *Contra*, Meritt and H. T. Wade-Gery, *JHS* 83, 1963, pp. 103–104; R. Meiggs, *HSCP* 67, 1963, p. 26 and *JHS* 86, 1966, pp. 94–95. They supported Oliver's original dating, here retained. Cf. also R. Develin, *Athenian Officials*, p. 110, with a listing of the individuals named in lines 4–6.

The historical circumstances of the treaty are not known, but "a date in the fifties suits the pattern of the first Peloponnesian War" (Meiggs). Mattingly advanced the parallels of the Athenian treaties with Troizen (Thucydides 4.118.4) and Halieis (*IG* I³, 75) in the same region, which he claimed were slightly preceded by that with Hermione. For his continued advocacy of 425/4 as the date of the treaty see further *SEG* XLII, 7.

FRAGMENT OF A DECREE(?)

5. Fragment of a stele of Pentelic marble (I 779), preserving the original left side (which is smooth) and perhaps the original back but elsewhere broken and much battered at the edges, discovered on May 2, 1933, in a late context over the southeast corner of the Stoa of Zeus (I 7).

H. 0.145 m.; W. 0.077 m.; Th. 0.07 m.
LH. 0.009 m.
Στοιχ. (square) 0.012 m.

Ed. B. D. Meritt, *Hesperia* 29, 1960, pp. 50–51, no. 63, with photograph pl. 13 (cf. *SEG* XIX, 3); *IG* I³, 22.

ca. a. 450 *a.*   ΣΤΟΙΧ.

```
[------------------------------]
[..]ọ[--------------------------]
αι τοῖς [------------------------]
[.] το̃ι δέ[μοι --------------------]
[.]καχρ[------------------------]
περὶ δ[------------------------]
τον σọ[------------------------]
```

```
[.]εχε[––––––––––––––––––––––––––––––]
[.]νδε[––––––––––––––––––––––––––––––]
[.]οφ[––––––––––––––––––––––––––––––]
10      vacat
```

Line 2. τõι λ[– – – –] Meritt, *SEG* XIX; τοῖς *IG* I³. Line 5. [π]ερὶ Meritt, *SEG* XIX; περὶ δ[ὲ – – –] *IG* I³.
Line 8. [.]νδ[– – –] *IG* I³. Lines 8–9. [– – ἐν Κο|λ]οφ[õνι(?) – – –] *IG* I³.

The lettering is large, rather irregular, and not of the best quality. The shape of some letters varies in different
examples (delta, nu); the tall rho with narrow loop is distinctive; sigma has three strokes. There is some similarity with
the lettering of *IG* I³, 21 (I², 22), the "Miletos regulations" of 450/49 B.C.

The text is evidently concerned with a public matter (line 3), but its character cannot be more precisely
determined. The suggestion of Kolophon in line 9 is arbitrary. References might be to money (χρ[έματα], line 4) and
debts (ὀφ[ειλόμενα] *vel sim.*, line 9) and would suggest a decree concerned with (internal?) financial matters.

DECREE(?) CONCERNING THE LEASE OF PUBLIC PROPERTY

6 (Pl. 2). Two nonjoining fragments of a stele of Pentelic marble, of which fragment *a* (I 3611) preserves the original
thickness of the monument but is otherwise broken all around. On the small fragment *b* (I 4829) the left edge of the
stele is preserved (although the first letter or two of the preserved lines have been rubbed away), but it is broken
elsewhere. Fragment *a* was discovered on February 26, 1936, in the foundation of a modern house northeast of
the Eleusinion (T 18), fragment *b* on April 28, 1937, in a modern context in the area west of the Stoa of Attalos.

a: H. 0.375 m.; W. 0.20 m.; Th. 0.143 m.

b: H. 0.067 m.; W. 0.069 m.; Th. 0.036 m.

LH. 0.01 m.
Στοιχ. Hor. 0.016 m.; Vert. 0.0165 m.

Ed. B. D. Meritt, *Hesperia* 14, 1945, pp. 85–86, no. 4, with photographs of fragment *a* and of a squeeze of
fragment *b* (cf. *SEG* X, 26); *IG* I³, 44; *Agora* XIX, L1 (M. B. Walbank). Summary account without text, D. Behrend,
Attische Pachturkunden, p. 55, no. 5.

ca. a. 450 *a.*   ΣΤΟΙΧ.

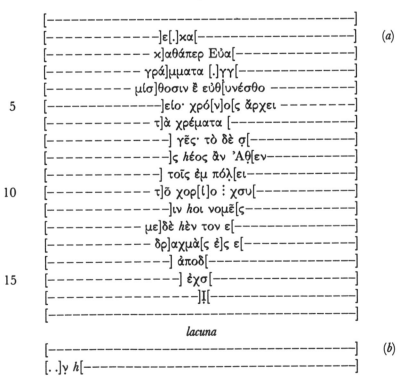

```
        [––––––––––––––––––––––––––––––––––––––]
        [–––––––––––––––]ε[.]χα[–––––––––––––––––]    (a)
        [––––––––––– χ]αθάπερ Εὐα[–––––––––––––]
        [––––––––––– γρά]μματα [.]γγ[–––––––––––––]
        [––––––––– μισ]θοσιν ε̃ εὐθ[υνέσθο –––––––––]
   5    [––––––––––––––]ειο· χρό[ν]ο[ς ἄρχει ––––––––]
        [––––––––––– τ]ὰ χρέματα [––––––––––––––]
        [––––––––––––] γε̃ς· τὸ δὲ σ[––––––––––––––]
        [––––––––––––]ς hέος ἂν ’Αθ[εν–––––––––––]
        [–––––––––––] τοῖς ἐμ πόλ[ει–––––––––––––]
   10   [––––––––––– τ]õ χορ[ί]ο ⁚ χου[–––––––––––]
        [–––––––––––]ιν hοι νομε̃[ς–––––––––––––]
        [––––––––– με]δὲ hὲν τον ε[––––––––––––––]
        [––––––––– δρ]αχμὰ[ς ἐ]ς ε[––––––––––––]
        [––––––––––] ἀποδ[–––––––––––––––––––]
   15   [––––––––––––] ἐχσ[–––––––––––––––––––]
        [–––––––––––]Ι[––––––––––––––––––––––]
        [––––––––––––––––––––––––––––––––––––]
                        lacuna
        [––––––––––––––––––––––––––––––––––––]    (b)
        [. .]ν h[––––––––––––––––––––––––––––––––]
```

```
[.]αι ε[----------------------------------------]
[. .]ο̣δε[--------------------------------------]
[. . .]Ị[---------------------------------------]
[---------------------------------------------]
```

As in **2**, the inscribed surface of the major fragment is ill preserved, and the visibility of some letters has been assert-ed with varying confidence by the editors. Line 1 *ad fin.* καΛ[-----] *IG* I³, Walbank. Line 3 *ad fin.* [. .]γ[------] Meritt. Line 6. τ̣ὰ *IG* I³, Walbank. Line 12. δὲ *h*έντον ἐ[---] Meritt; the version of *IG* I³ and of Walbank is as shown except for τὸν. Line 14. Some traces before A are indicated by *IG* I³; [---]ε ἀποδ[----] Walbank. The above text in other respects concords with that of *IG* I³. Fragment *b*, line 3. [.]οδε[---] Meritt; [. .]ο̣δε[----] Walbank; [. .]δε [----] *IG* I³.

Line 2 suggested to Meritt the formula of amendment of a decree, [τὰ μὲν ἄλλα κ]αθάπερ ---, Εὐα--- being thus a proper name in this context, and in that case the decree was of some length, since the amendment would amend a preceding amendment and not the original *probouleuma*. In *IG* I³, there is no commitment to a descriptive title. Whatever the precise nature of the document, it is evidently concerned with land (lines 7, 10), lease (line 4), regulations or written agreements (line 3), revenue or funds (lines 6, 13), repayment (line 14?, where Walbank suggests a possible reference to the *apodektai*), a penalty (for a public official?, line 4), and perhaps some ultimate decision by the Athenian assembly (line 8). In line 5 the phrase χρόνος ἄρχει reflects the customary phraseology for the starting date of a loan or lease (e.g., *IG* I³, 402, lines 14, 16, 21; *SEG* XXIV, 203, line 27). For these reasons the text properly figures also in *Agora* XIX, as noted above.

Line 9. Meritt adduced *IG* I³, 32 (*SEG* X, 24), line 12, where the complete phrase οἱ ἐπὶ τοῖς ἐμ πόλει ἔργοις concerns the commissioners of public works on the Akropolis who also have charge of the temple and statue of Athena. Its relevance here remains obscure.

DECREE REGULATING AN ATHENIAN FOUNDATION AT BREA

7. A small fragment of a stele of Pentelic marble (I 3972), on which the left side of the monument is preserved but which is otherwise broken, discovered on April 6, 1936, in a Byzantine context west of the Post-Herulian Wall, southeast of the Market Square (R–S 17).

H. 0.062 m.; W. 0.056 m.; Th. 0.02 m.
LH. 0.011 m.
Στοιχ. Hor. 0.0125 m.; Vert. 0.017 m.

Ed. B. D. Meritt, *Hesperia* 14, 1945, pp. 86–87, no. 5, with photograph of a squeeze. In showing that the fragment forms part of *IG* I³, 46 (I², 45), Meritt suggested that it be closely attached at the upper left of lines 1–2 of the main text of that inscription (cf. *SEG* X, 34), but he subsequently withdrew the suggestion, *Hesperia* 21, 1952, p. 380; cf. *SEG* XII, 15. It is now described as *IG* I³, 46, fragment c, to be located at an uncertain distance above fragment a.

a. 439/8 *a.* (?)   ΣΤΟΙΧ. 35

```
[-----------------------]
νε[.............33.............]
ελι[............32............]
αρχ[............32............]
νδε̣[............32............]
[-----------------------]
```

Line 4. ναε Meritt; ΝΛ *IG* I³. The second letter might equally well be gamma or alpha. For the lettering see *IG* I³ and Meiggs-Lewis, no. 49. Rho has a tail; sigma has four strokes. Tailed rho is not attested after 438/7 B.C. (R. Meiggs, *JHS* 86, 1966, p. 93; M. B. Walbank in *Phoros*, p. 168). The fragment is intentionally omitted in Meiggs-Lewis, no. 49 without prejudice to its attribution. The other two fragments were found in the Erechtheion in 1833 and 1837.

The text of the remainder of the "Brea foundation decree" is for convenience given below. Discussion has concen-trated upon (a) its date and (b) the colony's location. The dating generally accepted is "*ca.* 445 B.C.": so A. W. Gomme, *A Historical Commentary on Thucydides* I, 1945, pp. 373–374; M. N. Tod, *GHI* I², no. 44; *ATL* III, pp. 286–289; Meiggs-Lewis, *loc. cit.*, with other references, as also *IG* I² and I³. A. G. Woodhead argued for the date here retained, *CQ* n.s. 2, 1952, pp. 57–62. The slightly later date also better accommodates the apparent career of Phantokles (*b*, line 1), whose name (*PA* 14114; cf. H. B. Mattingly, *CQ* n.s. 16, 1966, p. 187) is unusual in Attic prosopography. Mattingly withdrew (*BSA* 65, 1970, p. 135, note 35) his earlier suggestion (*Historia* 12, 1963, pp. 257–261; *CQ* n.s. 16, 1966, pp. 172–192) that the decree be dated to 426/5 B.C., on which see also *SEG* XXI, 29, XXIII, 14, and Meiggs-Lewis, p. 132.

As to location, the colony is sited by most commentators in the territory of the Bisaltai (Plutarch, *Perikles* 11). Cf. Gomme, *ATL*, and Meiggs-Lewis, *locc. citt.*, as well as Meiggs, *Athenian Empire*, pp. 158–159, 260 and N. G. L. Hammond, *A History of Greece to 322 B.C.*, 2nd ed., 1967, p. 313. Woodhead's proposal (*loc. cit.*) that it was founded at a site on the inner Thermaic Gulf and that it was mentioned in a passage of Thucydides (1.61.4) has not been retracted (*pace* D. Kagan, *The Outbreak of the Peloponnesian War*, 1969, pp. 389–390, where a useful summary of the controversy is provided, with other references accepting the revised location). See also Hammond and G. T. Griffith, *A History of Macedonia* II, 1979, p. 118; D. Asheri, *AJP* 90, 1969, pp. 337–340, with bibliography in note 1; J. A. Vartsos, *Ancient Macedonia* II, 1977, pp. 13–16.

On the expression of the amendment in fragment *b* and the reference to a previous year by the citation of the name of its first secretary of the boule (*a*, lines 15–16) cf. P. J. Rhodes, *Athenian Boule*, pp. 226, 259. For the foundation in the context of Athenian colonization, and Greek colonization generally, see A. J. Graham, *Colony and Mother-City in Ancient Greece*, 1964, pp. 34–35 and *passim*; P. A. Brunt in *Ancient Society and Institutions: Studies Presented to Victor Ehrenberg on His 75th Birthday*, 1966, pp. 71–92 (esp. pp. 71, 77).

Fragments *a* and *b*:

          [. . . . . . . .¹⁸. . . . .]ε πρὸς hὲν ἂν φα[ίνει ἒ]

(*a*, face) [γράφεται, ἐσ]αγέτο. ἐὰν δὲ ἐσάγει ἐνεχ[.⁵..]

          [..⁷..] ho φένας ἒ ho γραφσάμενος. πο[.⁵..]

          [..⁶..]ν αὐτοῖς παρασχόντον hοι ἀπ[οικιστ]

5   [αἱ καλλ]ιερέσαι hυπὲρ τἔς ἀποικίας, [hοπόσα]

          [ἂν αὐτο]ῖς δοκεῖ. γεονόμος δὲ hελέσθ[αι δέκα]

          [ἄνδρας], ἕνα ἐχ φυλἔς· hοῦτοι δὲ νεμάντ[ον τὲν]

          [γἔν. Δεμ]οχλείδεν δὲ καταστἔσαι τὲν ἀ[ποικί]

          [αν αὐτο]χράτορα, καθότι ἂν δύνεται ἄ[ριστα. τ]

10   [ὰ δὲ τεμ]ένε τὰ ἐχσειρεμένα ἐᾶν καθά[περ ἐστ]

          [ί, καὶ ἄλ]λα μὲ τεμενίζεν. βοῦν δὲ καὶ π[ανhοπλ]

          [ίαν ἀπά]γεν ἐς Παναθέναια τὰ μεγάλ[α καὶ ἐς Δ]

          [ιονύσι]α φαλλόν. ἐὰν δέ τις ἐπιστρα[τεύει ἐπ]

          [ὶ τὲν γἔ]ν τὲν τὸν ἀποίκον, βοεθἔν τὰ[ς πόλες h]

15   [ος ὀχσύ]τατα κατὰ τὰς χσυγγραφὰς hα[ὶ ἐπι..]

          [..⁶..]το γραμματεύοντος ἐγένον[το περὶ τ]

          [ὸν πόλε]ον τὸν ἐπὶ Θράικες. γράφσαι δ[ὲ ταῦτα]

          [ἐν στέλ]ει καὶ καταθἔναι ἐμ πόλει· πα[ρασχόν]

          [τον δὲ τ]ὲν στέλεν hοι ἄποικοι σφὸν α[ὐτὸν τέ]

20   [λεσιν. ἐ]ὰν δέ τις ἐπιφσεφίζει παρὰ τὲ[ν στέλ]

          [εν ἒ ῥέ]τορ ἀγορεύει ἒ προσκαλἔσθα[ι ἐγχερ]

          [ἒ ἀφαι]ρἔσθαι ἒ λύεν τι τὸν hεφσεφι[σμένον],

          [ἄτιμον] ἔναι αὐτὸν καὶ παῖδας τὸς ἐχς [ἐκένο]

          [καὶ τὰ χ]ρέματα δεμόσια ἔναι καὶ τἔς [θεὅ τὸ ἐ]

25   [πιδέκα]τον, ἐὰμ μέ τι αὐτοὶ hοι ἄποικ[οι....]

          [.... δέ]ονται∷hόσοι δ'ἂν γράφσοντα[ι ἐποικ]

          [έσεν τὅ]ν στρατιοτὅν, ἐπειδὰν hέκοσ[ι Ἀθένα]

          [ζε, τριά]κοντα ἐμερὅν ἐμ Βρέαι ἔναι ἐπ[οικέσ]

          [οντας. ἐ]χσάγεν δὲ τὲν ἀποικίαν τριάχ[οντα ἐ]

30   [μερὅν. Α]ἰσχίνεν δὲ ἀκολουθὅντα ἀπο[διδόνα]

          [ι τὰ χρέ]ματα. *vacat*

    (*b*, side) [Φ]αντοκλἔς εἶπε· περὶ

          [μ]ὲν τἔς ἐς Βρέαν ἀποι

          [κ]ίας καθάπερ Δεμοχλ

```
     [ε]ῖδες εἶπε· Φαντοκλέ
  5  [α] δὲ προσαγαγεν τὲν ’Ε
     [ρ]εχθείδα πρυτανεία
     [ν] πρὸς τὲν βολὲν ἐν τε̄
     [ι] πρότει hέδραι· ἐς δὲ
     [Β]ρέαν ἐχ θετο̄ν χαὶ ζε
 10  [υ]γῖτο̄ν ἰέναι τὸς ἀπο
     [ί]χος.
```

On the decree and its details see further the references in *SEG* XXXIV, 15, XXXVI, 1527, XXXVII, 9.

DECREE REGULATING PROCEDURES AT CERTAIN RELIGIOUS CEREMONIES

8. Part of a stele of Pentelic marble (I 568), preserving the right side of the original monument but otherwise broken save that the smooth back (which is almost totally eroded) bears traces of an inscription. It was discovered on March 17, 1933, in a modern wall in an area east of the Tholos (H 11).

H. 0.28 m.; W. 0.22 m.; Th. 0.093 m.
LH. 0.01 m. (reverse face, 0.007 m.).
Στοιχ. Hor. 0.0142 m.; Vert. 0.0145 m.

Ed. J. H. Oliver, *Hesperia* 4, 1935, pp. 32–34, no. 3 (where the inventory number is erroneously printed as I 588), with photograph (cf. *SEG* X, 42); F. Sokolowski, *TAPA* 90, 1959, pp. 253–255 (*SEG* XVIII, 4) and *Lois sacrées (Supplément)*, pp. 24–25, no. 7 (*SEG* XXI, 32); *IG* I³, 129.

a. 440–430 a.   ΣΤΟΙΧ.

```
                                               vacat
     [----------------------------------] δεμο
     [------------------------------τὸς π]ολετὰς χ
     [------------------------- ἐπὶ τε̄ς ––] πρυτανεί
     [ας --------------------- hιε]ρὸν hέχαστ
  5  [ον --------------------------] ἐς χσύλα χαὶ τ
     [ἄλλα ----------------------]ρματι λαμβάνε
     [ν ------------------- χ]ατὰ τὸγ χοῖρον h
     [έχαστον --------------] δὲ τὰ χαθάρματα ε
     [--------------------- τ]ὸς ἐπενέγχοντ
 10  [ας ------------------· ἐὰν] δὲ μέ, χαταχε
     [-------------------------· ἀ]ποτίνεν δὲ
     [----------------------------hέχ]αστον
     [-------------------------------------]
```

On the reverse face, the letters Τ̣, Ḥ, Σ, at the beginning of three lines. That the text of the enactment covered both faces is made unlikely by the difference in the lettering; but the lettering of the reverse face is of a date comparable with that of the obverse, and its text might have been purposely deleted because of its replacement (fairly soon) with what stands on the front face. Or, of course, the two texts may have presented different regulations, operative concurrently, with the text of the reverse face destroyed through later adaptation to other purposes. The lettering of the principal text is slim, with narrow loops to rho and beta; nu leans slightly forward.

If the thickness of the stele is original, the length of line is unlikely to have been greater than *ca.* 38–40 letters. The above text is substantially that of *IG* I³ (M. H. Jameson), where a full *apparatus criticus* makes repetition of full detail unnecessary here. Traces of letters at the edge of the break remain a matter of opinion but in the present state of the document are of no real consequence.

Line 1. Oliver supposed the formula [ἔδοχσεν τε̄ι βολε̄ι χαὶ το̄ι] δέμο||ι but did not indicate either that it began the text or that the rest of a regular prescript could be accommodated. This was adjusted by Sokolowski (*locc. citt.*), who supposed a line of 25 letters, equally without accounting for the absence of the other customary elements of the prescript. The text was not discussed by A. S. Henry (*Prescripts*). Jameson (*IG* I³) hesitantly discerned omicron before delta. Line 4. χατὰ τὸ hιερ]ὸν Oliver, comparing *IG* I³, 255 B, line 18; τὸ hιε]ρὸν *IG* I³. Line 6. δέ]ρματι

Oliver. Line 7. τὰ δέρμ]ατα *SEG* X, 42. Lines 10–11. εἰ] δὲ μέ, καταχέ‖[φαλα λούσεται Oliver, with reference to *IG* II², 1365, lines 23–24, 1366, line 4.

Both *IG* I³ and the present text eschew restorations, for an example of which the text of Sokolowski (*TAPA, loc. cit.*) is added below: his version in *Lois Sacrées (Supplément)* was less fully restored. Cf. J. and L. Robert, *REG* 74, 1961, p. 161, no. 275. Except in the most general terms, that it contains instructions for the provision (and disposal?) of materials for certain religious ceremonies, with penalties for noncompliance, and that it seems to be a public enactment, the nature of the document cannot be further determined.

Sokolowski's (1959) text:

ΣΤΟΙΧ. 25

```
     ["Εδοχσεν τῆι βολῆι καὶ τõι] δέμο
     [ι· ἀποδιδόναι μὲν τὸς π]ολετὰς χ
     [ατὰ τὸν νόμον ἐν ταῖς] πρυτανεί
     [αις τὰ κατὰ τὸ hιερεῖ]ον hέκαστ
  5  [ον διατεταγμένα] ἐς χσύλα καὶ τ
     [ἄλλα τὰ ἐπὶ καθά]ρματι· λαμβάνε
     [ν δὲ δύο ὀβολὸ] κατὰ τὸγ χοῖρον h
     [έκαστον· πρὸς δ]ὲ τὰ καθάρματα ἐ
     [μβαλῆν ὀβολὸν τ]ὸς [ἐ]πενεγχόντ
 10  [ας πάντα hõν δεῖ· εἰ] δὲ μέ, κατὰ χε
     [φαλὲν καὶ ...⁷... ἀ]ποτίνεν δέ
     [χα δραχμὰς ...⁸.... hέχα]στον
     [--------------------]
```

DECREE CONCERNING PUBLIC WORKS

9. Two nonjoining fragments of a large block of Pentelic marble, of which fragment *a* (I 3745 a) provides the upper left corner of the block and is broken below, to the right, and at the back. This fragment was discovered on October 9, 1935, in a wall of a modern house west of the Odeion (K 10). Fragment *b* (I 3745 b) preserves the left side and original back but is broken elsewhere; it was discovered on March 13, 1936, in a wall of a modern house south of the Church of the Holy Apostles (O 16).

a: H. 0.253 m.; W. 0.18 m.; Th. 0.148 m.

b: H. 0.255 m.; W. 0.162 m.; Th. 0.218 m.

LH. 0.011 m.

Στοιχ. Hor. 0.0133 m.; Vert. 0.0172 m.

Ed. B. D. Meritt, *Hesperia* 14, 1945, pp. 87–93, no. 6, with photographs of squeezes (*SEG* X, 44 [incorporating revised restorations by Meritt]); *IG* I³, 50. Photograph of fragment *a*, U. K. Duncan, *BSA* 56, 1961, pl. 31:c.

a. 435/4 a.(?)   ΣΤΟΙΧ. 62(?)

```
     Θεοί.
     "Εδοχσεν τῆ[ι βολῆι καὶ τõι δέμοι· ...⁸.... ἐπρυτάνευε, ...⁷... ἐγραμμάτευε],   (a)
     Προιναύτες [ἐπεστάτε, Καλλίας (?) εἶπε· χσυγγραφὰς ποιῆν καθότι ἂν ὁρισθῆι χα]
     ὶ θυροθῆι τὸ ['Ελευσίνιον hος ἐχυρότατα· τõ δὲ ἔργο hοι ἐπιστάται ἐπιμελέσθο]
  5  ν hος ἂν ἐ βολ[ὲ χρίνει· συνεπιμέλεσθαι δὲ αὐτοῖς καὶ τὸς ἐπιμελετὰς καὶ τὸν ἀ]
     ρχιτέκτονα[----------------------------------------]
     σθαι hοῖον τ[----------------------------------------]
     ἐγ Διὸς ὁ[πόσον----------------------------------]
     ι γραφ[------------------------------------------]
 10  οσ[---------------------------------------------]
```
lacuna non minus quattuor versuum
```
 15  ρες ὄντον[----------------------------------------]   (b)
     αὐτὸν hοι[----------------------------------------]
     ν περὶ αὐτ[---------------------------------------]
     ροντες h[-----------------------------------------]
```

```
        ἐς ταῦτα [--------------------------------------------------------]
   20   ἐχσειρ[---------------------------------------------------------------]
        οι καὶ h[---------------------------------------------------------------]
        ς καὶ το[---------------------------------------------------------------]
        [.]μενο[----------------------------------------------------------------]
        [...]ε[------------------------------------------------------------------]
   25   [-------------------------------------------------------------------------]
```

The craftsman who worked on this text was also responsible for the "Springhouse Decree" (*IG* I³, 49; I², 54), as Meritt observed. The identity usefully corroborates the historical circumstances (see below). M. B. Walbank (*Athenian Proxenies*, p. 158; cf. p. 51, note 21) regards the hand as comparable with *IG* I³, 131 (I², 77) and 173 (I², 148), which are likely to be dated to the later 430's; see on **13**. On the circular letters of this text see Duncan, *op. cit.*, p. 187 (*SEG* XXI, 34). The thickness of the monument is worth remark. The *editio princeps* referred to a stele, but it may be that the block formed part of the structure the authority for which it records.

That structure may have been the Eleusinion itself, on which see *Agora* XIV, pp. 150–155; *Agora Guide*³, pp. 143–147. The size of the fragments and the proximity of their places of finding to the site of the precinct are alike indicative, as Meritt emphasized. This text, with quotation of lines 3–4, is listed among testimonia for the Eleusinion in *Agora* III, p. 81, no. 220. Some provision for the completion of work in this area, especially if Kallias were the proposer of it, would fit the pattern of enactments such as the "Kallias Decrees" (*IG* I³, 52) and the "Springhouse Decree" mentioned above. On this series of documents, slightly antedating the Peloponnesian War, see A. G. Woodhead, *ArchCl* 25–26, 1973–1974, p. 759 and in *Mélanges helléniques offerts à Georges Daux*, 1974, pp. 375–388 (on this text pp. 385–386).

The document was dated to 432/1 B.C. by H. B. Mattingly (*Proceedings of the African Classical Associations* 9, 1966, pp. 69–73), who argued that it formed part of a second copy of *IG* I³, 32 (*SEG* X, 24); cf. *SEG* XXV, 23 and 15. This depends on his dating of the latter text, which is, however, generally accepted as being of *ca.* 450 B.C. In *AJP* 105, 1984, p. 354, without reiterating that contention, Mattingly urged that the present text is a second copy of *IG* I³, 58 (I², 185; *SEG* X, 60) and that, since the latter was evidently enacted after the outbreak of the Archidamian War, it must be dated similarly. Cf. *SEG* XXXIV, 18.

Line 2. The name Proinautes is otherwise unattested in Attic epigraphy. Kallias is presumed to be he of the "Kallias Decrees" (see above), identified in *PA* 7827 as Καλλίας Καλλιάδου: on the identification see *ATL* III, pp. 276–277. The restoration here fits the lacuna and is attractive but should not be pressed. The two are listed by R. Develin (*Athenian Officials*, p. 111).

On the hand at work see further Mattingly, *ZPE* 83, 1990, pp. 113–114; *SEG* XL, 5.

DECREE OF UNCERTAIN CHARACTER PROPOSED BY CHROMON

10. Two joining fragments of Pentelic marble, both of which preserve part of the top of the stele with the remains of an upper molded band and probably also the original back but which are otherwise broken. The Agora fragment (*a*, I 658, now E.M. 13370) was discovered on April 6, 1933, near the surface at a late level, southeast of the Tholos (I 12), and was connected by B. D. Meritt with *IG* I², 141/142, fragments b–e, and 174. D. M. Lewis subsequently suggested, and E. Vanderpool confirmed, a join with *IG* I², 141, fragment d (now fragment b of the combined text, E.M. 5197), the place of discovery of which is not recorded but may have been the Akropolis. The inscription composed of these two fragments may now be dissociated from the other fragments mentioned.

a: H. 0.245 m.; W. 0.146 m.; Th. (at upper molding) 0.075 m., (below) 0.065 m.

b: H. 0.22 m.; W. 0.11 m.; Th. as fragment *a*.

LH. 0.01–0.012 m.

Στοιχ. Hor. 0.014 m.; Vert. 0.0214 m.

Ed. *b*: *IG* I², 141, d; *a*, separately from but in association with *IG* I², 141, b–e + 174: B. D. Meritt, *Hesperia* 14, 1945, pp. 94–97, no. 8, with photographs of squeezes (*SEG* X, 51); *a* and *b*: *IG* I³, 145. Photograph of stones as joined, A. P. Bridges, *JHS* 100, 1980, pl. IV:e.

a. 440–430 *a*.   ΣΤΟΙΧ. (not less than 48)

```
[Ἔδοχσεν τῖ βολῖ καὶ τῖ δέμοι, ---ὶς ἐπ]ρυτά[νευε, .]α[----]     (a, b)
[---- ἐγραμμάτευε, ------ ἐπεστάτ]ε, Χρόμον [εἴ]πε· το[---]
[-----------------------------]δέμο hὸ hεύροντ[ο (?)---]
```

[— — — — — — — — — — — — — — — — — — — —] μέτε hυπ[ὀ] τοῖς τ[— — —]
5   [— — — — — — — — — — — — — — — — — — —]ς καὶ τ[. .]ι̣γ[— — — — —]
    [— — — — — — — — — — — — — — — — —]τεσ[— — — — — — —]
    [— —]

Line 4. hō hευρōντ[αι — — —] *IG* I³. Line 5. [— —]ς καὶ τ[. . .]ι̣[— — —] *ibid.* The lettering was regarded by Lewis as identical with that of the treaty with Samos of 439/8 B.C. (*IG* I³, 48; I², 50); it is certainly close to it, but differences may be discerned: see Bridges, *op. cit.*, pp. 187–188. (Cf. *SEG* XXX, 6.) M. B. Walbank identified it with the work of "a mason whose public career lasted from the 430s to the early 410s" (in *Phoros*, pp. 168–169, note 21 and *Athenian Proxenies*, p. 51, note 21). Cf. **9**. Doubtless there was at this period a general similarity in the work of the various craftsmen commissioned to inscribe public documents, and over-nice attributions should perhaps be treated with hesitation. The letters have a squat and somewhat irregular appearance, the former feature probably accounted for by the greater space between the lines; upsilon is especially distinctive. The stoichedon pattern is not punctiliously executed.

Meritt suggested that the document might be a treaty, but too little remains for its character to be determined. The name of the proposer (line 2) is unusual; he could well be identical with that Chromon found on a public funeral monument to be dated post-445 B.C. and with some probability before 430 B.C. (*Agora* XVII, 19, line 24). It may be added that the writing on that stele is also comparable with that of this document, upsilon again being noteworthy.

DECREE CONFERRING THE TITLE OF PROXENOS ON KRISON AND OTHERS

11. A fragment of a stele of Pentelic marble (I 4977), of which the left side and original rough-picked back are preserved, but which is otherwise broken: the break above the first preserved line of text is evidently not far below the original top of the monument. It was discovered on June 15, 1937, in the filling of the Post-Herulian Wall over the paved court below Klepsydra (T 26–27), close under the Akropolis.

H. 0.20 m.; W. 0.187 m.; Th. 0.079 m. (0.193 m.; 0.20 m.; 0.083 m. Walbank).
LH. 0.01 m.
Στοιχ. Hor. 0.0135 m.; Vert. 0.018 m. (0.0132 m.; 0.0179 m. Walbank).

Ed. W. K. Pritchett, *Hesperia* 11, 1942, pp. 230–231, no. 42, with photograph (cf. *SEG* X, 54); revised version of lines 4–5 and 9 by B. D. Meritt, *Hesperia* 21, 1952, pp. 348–351 (cf. *SEG* XII, 22 and J. and L. Robert, *REG* 67, 1954, p. 120, no. 76); *IG* I³, 155; M. B. Walbank, *Athenian Proxenies*, pp. 146–151, no. 24, *et passim*, with photograph pl. 9:b.

See also A. Lambrechts (*De Atheense Proxeniedecreten*, p. 150, no. 10, *et alibi*), who uses the text of the *editio princeps*. Lines 4–9 are quoted by R. E. Wycherley (*Agora* III, 1957, p. 136, no. 429). U. K. Duncan discusses the technique of the inscription (*BSA* 56, 1961, p. 186, with photograph pl. 31:b). Further references collected in *SEG* XXI, 39, XXV, 28, XXX, 7.

ca. a. 435–430 *a.*   ΣΤΟΙΧ. 28

["Ἔδοχσεν τῖ βολῖ καὶ τ õι δέμοι· . .]
[. . . .]ι̣[ς ἐ]πρυτ[άνευε, . . .⁷. . . ἔγραμ]
μά[τε]υε, Μέλετ[ος ἐπεστάτε, . . .⁷. . . .]
ν εἶπε· Κρίσονα̣ [. . . . . . .¹⁶. . . . . . .]
5   δελφος καὶ Δεχ[. . . . ἀναγράφσαι (*vel* Δεχ[. . .⁷. . . γράφσαι) πρ]
οχσένος καὶ εὐ[εργέτας ἐν στέλει λ]
ιθίνει ἐμ πόλει [καὶ ἐν τõι βολευτε]
ρίοι ἐς σανίδα τ[ὸν γραμματέα τ ῖς β]
ολῖς τέλεσι το[ῖς . . . . . .¹⁴. . . . . . .]·
10   ὀμόσαι δέ κα[ὶ τὸς στρατεγὸς καὶ τ ὲ]
     [μ] βολὲν [— — — — — — — — — — — — — —]
     [— — — — — — — — — — — — — — — — — — —]

Walbank's full analysis of the lettering, and his commentary on the text and subject matter, make it unnecessary to undertake here a discussion of any length. The above text concords (save in two minor details) with that of *IG* I³ and begs no questions of interpretation.

Lines 1–2. Κε|χροπ]ι̣[ς](?) Pritchett, *SEG* X, and accepted by Mattingly (see below). Line 2. [. . . .]ι̣ς ἐπρυτ[άνευε κτλ.] Walbank. Line 3. Μέλετ[ος Pritchett *et omnes nisi* Walbank, who prefers Μελετ[. . (drawing attention to the existence of a name Μελέτων: cf. *IG* II², 956, line 45). The hesitation is proper, but the name Meletos is so likely as to be reasonably acceptable. Lines 4–5. [τὸν ..⁶... καὶ τὸς ἀ]||δελφὸς καὶ Δεχ[.... ἀναγράφσαι (possibly Κρῖσον ἀ[ναγράφσαι καὶ τὸς ἀ]||δελφὸς καὶ Δέχ[ελον) Pritchett; [τὸν Δελφὸν κτλ.] A. E. Raubitschek in *SEG* X; [καὶ ....¹⁰.... τὸς]|| Δελφὸς καὶ δὲ Κ[ιρραῖος γράφσαι Meritt; Walbank follows Pritchett, suggesting also Δεχ[...⁷... γράφσαι. For the name in line 5 A. Wilhelm (in *SEG* X) considered Δέχ[ατον, Walbank Δεχ[άμνιχον, a Macedonian name (cf. Aristotle, *Politics* 1311b30; N. G. L. Hammond and G. T. Griffith, *A History of Macedonia* II, 1979, p. 167). Lines 9–10. τέλεσι το[ῖς τὸν ..⁶... *vacat*] (possibly το[ῖς Κρίσο καὶ Δεχέλο]) Pritchett; τέλεσι το[ῖς αὐτὸν· ..⁵... εἶπε·] Wilhelm in *SEG* X; τ[οῖς ......¹⁴.......] *IG* I³. τέλεσι το[ῖς σφετέροις αὐτὸν Meritt, followed by Walbank; this use of the reflexive is doubted by A. S. Henry (in *Vindex Humanitatis: Essays in Honour of John Huntly Bishop*, 1980, pp. 23–24), but see Meritt and M. F. McGregor, *AAA* 13, 1981, pp. 351–353. Line 11. [μ] βολὲν [------] Pritchett, *cett., nisi* μ βολὲν [------] *IG* I³; [μ] βολὲν χ[αὶ τὸς πρυτάνες(?) ----] Walbank.

This decree, which is the earliest "proxeny" decree yet found among the Agora texts, appears to belong to the first years of the Archidamian War (or just before it), whether or not Walbank's contention that the honorands are Macedonian be accepted. If they are Macedonians, Athens' involvement in that region provides a context appropriate for the time (Walbank, *loc. cit.*, pp. 150–151). H. B. Mattingly (*BCH* 92, 1968, pp. 482–483) argued for a date of 423/2 on the basis of the names of the phyle and the officials postulated in lines 1–3, regarding as plausible Pritchett's suggestion that the name of the epistates was Meletos and that he was the tragic poet of that name (*PA* 9829), the father of Sokrates' accuser. P. J. Rhodes (*Athenian Boule*, p. 44) accepts "about 430"; so also Meritt, *ZPE* 25, 1977, pp. 290–291. The details of chairman and proposer are briefly listed by R. Develin (*Athenian Officials*, p. 112).

DECREE CONCERNING DUTIES OF THE HIEROPOIOI

12. Two fragments of a stele of Pentelic marble, of which the larger, fragment *a* (E.M. 6627), broken all around except for the original back, has long been known and was discovered, apparently, in the area of the Agora at the north end of the Odeion of Agrippa (L–M 8–9). The small fragment *b* (I 4103, now E.M. 13371), broken on all sides, was discovered on May 1, 1936, in a modern context west of the Stoa of Attalos and near its northern end (O 8).

a: H. 0.295 m.; W. 0.107 m.; Th. 0.075 m.

b: H. 0.123 m.; W. 0.07 m.; Th. 0.039 m.

LH. 0.011 m.

Στοιχ. Hor. 0.014 m.; Vert. 0.021 m.

Ed. *a* only: *IG* I², 130, with earlier references; both *a* and *b*: B. D. Meritt, *Hesperia* 14, 1945, p. 127, no. 13, with photograph of squeezes showing the join (cf. *SEG* X, 62); *IG* I³, 139.

a. 435–410 *a*.   ΣΤΟΙΧ.

```
                              [----------] vestigia [--------------------]       (a)
         (b)          [--------- θ]ύετα[ι τõι ἱε[ρõι -----------]
                      [---- ἀναγρ]αφεν τ[ο ἀ]ργυρ[ιο-----------]
                      [---------]εται· τὲν δὲ οἰ[κίαν ----------]
      5               [---- hοι hιε]ροποιοὶ μετα[--------------]
                      [--------]ς κατὰ τὸ φσέ[φισμα ---------]
                      [-------] ἐκ ταύτες τẽς [--------------]
                      [-------]πε τõ[ι] θεõι τ[--------------]
                      [-------]τον hοι νέοι [--------------]
     10               [----- παρ]αδόγτον αὐτ[-------------]
                      [-------]γεται ἀργυρ[ιο-------------]
                      [----- ἐπ]ειδὰν ἐχσα[-------------]
                      [----- εὐθ]υνεσθο[------------------]
                      [--------] vestigia [------------------]
     15               [------------------------------------]
```

The lettering is a good, regular example of standard later-5th-century craftsmanship, which may fall within the space of a quarter of a century or even more (440–405, *IG* I³). The Agora fragment attaches to the upper left corner of the larger piece. The text is that of Meritt except where indicated.

Line 1. [--]I/[----] Meritt, *IG* I³. Line 2. [---]υεται[ι τõι ἱε[ρ----] *IG* I³. Line 3. Either [---- ἀναγρ]αφεν τ[õ ἀ]ργυρ[ιο ----] (Meritt) or [---- ἀναγρ]άφεν τ[ὸ ἀ]ργύρ[ιον (M. N. Tod, in a letter to Meritt);

IG records both options. Line 5. [--- *hoι hιε*]ροποιοὶ Meritt; [--- *hοι δὲ ἱε*]ροποιοὶ *IG* I³. Line 7. τε͂[ς στέλες ----]Meritt; τε͂ς [-----] *IG* I³. Line 8. [----ε͂]πε· τõ[ι] θεõι τ[----] *IG* I², Meritt, *IG* I³. Line 11. [---γ*ίγ*]νεται *IG* I³; ἀργύρ[ιον ---] Meritt. Line 12. ἐχσα[λείφσοσι ---] *IG* I², Meritt; ἐχσα[ιφ----] *IG* I³. Line 13. Meritt restored δραχμαῖς towards the end of the line, after εὐθ]υνέσθο[ν --.

The sequence in line 8 is unclear. If εἶπε is correct, it is surely not the introduction to an amendment but may be the truncated preamble of a fresh enactment, as in decrees of phylai, phratriai, and the like. The lack of connective with τõι θεõι is perhaps of significance. Or there may be a general reference to a decree (this one?) whereby action is to be taken (lines 6–8) κατὰ τὸ ψήφισμα δ *x* εἶπε; cf. Meiggs-Lewis, no. 45 (*ATL* II, D 14), §12. Too little remains of the text for any of its provisions to emerge with clarity. It is not given a descriptive title in *IG* I³.

FRAGMENT OF A DECREE

13. Fragment of a stele of Pentelic marble (I 2545), broken all around except perhaps at the top, discovered on February 28, 1935, in a modern context east of the South Square at its northeast corner (P 13).

H. 0.109 m.; W. *ca.* 0.095 m.; Th. 0.079 m.
LH. 0.011 m.
Στοιχ. (lines 2 and following) Hor. 0.014 m.; Vert. 0.0175 m.

Ed. D. M. Lewis, *Hesperia* 44, 1975, pp. 379–380, no. 1, with photograph pl. 85; *IG* I³, 187.

ca. a. 430 *a.*   ΣΤΟΙΧ. 37(?) (lines 2 and following)

```
        [.........16–17....... ἐγρ]αμ[μάτευε].
        ["Εδοχσεν τε͂ι βολε͂ι καὶ τõι δέμ]οι· Κε[κροπὶς ἐπρ]
        [υτάνευε, .........17........]σερ/[----]
        [...........23...........]ν hιπ[-----]
    5   [...........23...........]ρι[------]
        [------------------------]
```

The letters in line 1 are slightly larger, and more widely spaced, than those in the body of the text. The number of letters to be restored makes it likely that the name of the secretary was accompanied by his demotic, as in **4** (the first-known instance in Attic decrees: cf. A. S. Henry, *Prescripts*, p. 107). This may be confirmed by line 3, where it is necessary to restore ἐγραμμάτευε preceded by a short name, if, as Lewis observed, ΣΕΡ/ forms part of the name of the epistates. Even so, ΣΕΡ/ is not easily accommodated as part of a name, and [*nomen, demoticum*]ς ἐ⟨γ⟩ρα[μμάτευε ---] is worth a thought.

Lewis noted B. D. Meritt as having attributed this piece to the craftsman identified by H. T. Wade-Gery as the "three-chisel hand": cf. M. B. Walbank in *Phoros*, pp. 168–169, note 21 and *Athenian Proxenies*, p. 51, note 21; **9**.

DECREE HONORING ACHILLEUS(?), PHILIPPOS, AND ONE OTHER

14. A fragment of a stele of Pentelic marble (I 5826), which preserves the original left side and back of the monument but is broken elsewhere, discovered on May 9, 1939, in a late 2nd- or 3rd-century A.D. context in a brick drain and shaft south of the Eleusinion (U 22). The inscribed surface is much worn, and a considerable part of the text, especially that on the lower part of the fragment, is beyond decipherment.

H. 0.33 m.; W. 0.20 m.; Th. 0.14 m.
LH. 0.009–0.01 m.

Ed. B. D. Meritt, *Hesperia* 14, 1945, pp. 115–119, no. 10, with photograph (see *SEG* X, 76, where suggestions by A. Wilhelm and M. N. Tod, as well as by A. E. Raubitschek, were included); *IG* I³, 70; M. B. Walbank, *Athenian Proxenies*, pp. 123–129, no. 19, with photograph pl. 7:b.

ca. a. 430 *a.*   NON-ΣΤΟΙΧ. *ca.* 45–50(?)

```
        [-----------------------------------]
        [.ca. 9....]Σ[-------------------------------]
        [.ca. 6..]ιτασθαι ρ[--------------------------]
        [...] ἔστω· τὸ δὲ ψή[φισμα τόδε ---------------]
        [..] ἐμ πόληι τὸγ [γραμματέα ------------------]
    5   [Κ]λ[εώ]νυμος εἶπ[ε· τὰ μὲν ἄλλα καθάπερ τῆι βολῆι, -- δὲ ---]
        ἐξεῖναι ζημιõν [-----------------------------]
```

```
        τõ δήμο τõ ’Αθηναί[ων·  ————————————————————  τῶν]
        πίσ[τ]εων τὴν ζημ[ίαν  ——————————————————  χαὶ τὰ χρή]
        [μα]τα δημόσια χ[αὶ  ——————————————————·  πρόσο]
   10   δον δὲ εἶναι ’Αχ[————————————  πρὸς τὴμ βολὴν χαὶ τὸν δῆμ]
        ον χαθάπερ Χίω[ν————————————————————————————]
        ἑα χαὶ Φίλιπ[π]ο[ν  ————————————————————————·  ἡ δὲ]
        Αἰαντὶς πρ[υτανεία  ——————————————————————]
        [——————————————————————————————————————]
   15   [——————————————————————————————————————]
        [——————————————————————————————————————]
        [. ᶜᵃ·⁶ .]τωδ[————————————————————————————]
        [——————————————————————————————————————]
```

As in **11**, Walbank's full study, together with the publication in *IG* I³ and the *apparatus criticus* in both, makes extended commentary unnecessary. The differing opinions on the date and reference of the decree, as well as on the details of the text, are best illustrated by a brief account of the progress of the study of it.

The Ionic lettering is crowded, with a rather old-fashioned appearance; but Meritt noted a resemblance to (though not an identity with) the hand of *IG* I³, 63, of *ca.* 426 B.C. The main part of the surviving text consists of an amendment proposed by Kleonymos (line 5), adding to the privileges given to Ach——— and to Philippos and containing, as it appeared, a reference to the people of Chios. Meritt identified Kleonymos with the proposer of *IG* I³, 61 II (I², 57) and 68 (I², 65), the well-known victim of Aristophanes' wit (*PA* 8680); for the Chians he referred to Thucydides 4.51. These criteria conspired to suggest a date of 425/4 B.C. He did not include the traces now shown as line 1, and his proposals for lines 3–13 were the following:

```
           τὸ δὲ [ψ]ή[φισμα τόδε γράψαι χαὶ χαταθεῖν]
           [αι] ἐμ πόληι τὸν [γραμματέα τέλεσι τοῖς Χίων. ᵛᵛᵛ]
      5    [Κ]λ[εώ]νυμος εἶπ[ε· περὶ μὲν οὖν ’Αχ.ᶜᵃ·⁶.. τõ Χίο μὴ]
           [ἐ]ξεῖναι ζημιõν [αὐτὸν μήτε τὸν υἱὸν μηδενὶ ἄνευ]
           τõ δήμο τõ ’Αθηνα[ίων· ἐὰν δέ τις παραβαίνηι τι τῶν]
           πίσ[τ]εων τὴν ζημ[ίαν αὐτõ θάνατον εἶναι χαὶ τὰ χρή]
           [μα]τα δημόσια χ[αὶ τῆς θεõ τὸ ἐπιδέχατον· πρόσο]
      10   δον δὲ εἶναι ’Αχ[.ᶜᵃ·⁶.. πρὸς τὴν βολὴν χαὶ τὸν δῆμ]
           ον χαθάπερ Χίω[ν τοῖς ἥχοσι· ἀναγράψαι δὲ ’Αχ...]
           ἑ[α] χαὶ Φίλιπ[π]ο[ν τὸν υἱὸν εὐεργέτας ’Αθηναίων· ἡ δὲ]
           Αἰαντὶς [πρυτανεία  ——————————————————]
```

This text was reproduced in *SEG* X, *loc. cit.*, with added suggestions for lines 3–4: τὸ δὲ [ψ]ή[φισμα τόδε ἀναγράψαι ἐν στήληι λιθίν|ηι] ἐμ πόληι τὸν [γραμματέα τέλεσι τοῖς τῶν Χίων] (Wilhelm *ad init.* and Raubitschek *ad fin.*). Meritt hesitantly suggested the name Achilleus for the honorand who is partially recorded in line 10 and restored elsewhere.

Meritt's restoration in line 5 did not follow the usual formula of an amendment to a decree, and the more customary phrase was adopted in *IG* I³, with the observation that this would require a length of line longer than that (*ca.* 39) assumed by Meritt's text. Nevertheless the text of *SEG* X was reproduced for lines 3 and 7–13. In line 4 τὸν [γραμματέα τῆς βολῆς ————] and in line 12 Φίλιπ[π]ο[ν ———— (?) εὐεργέτας χτλ.] were preferred, and line 6 was left unrestored except for final ἄνευ. The editor (D. M. Lewis) did not agree with Meritt's reference to events in Chios in 425/4 but regarded the appearance of Kleonymos as the most significant item for dating purposes, giving the decree a date 430–420 B.C. The *manus satis negligens* was considered a less certain criterion. Cf. Lewis, *Phoenix* 33, 1979, p. 268.

Walbank, however, elevated this last to the main consideration, requiring a date 440–430 B.C., which did not in his view necessarily involve the rejection of a connection with the well-known Kleonymos. He interpreted Χίων (line 11) not as an ethnic but as a proper name, in fact that of the father of Achilleus (whose name he saw more fully in line 10) and Philippos, and the supplements proposed in his commentary accommodate this interpretation to the longer line already mentioned as preferable. He saw, with some confidence and with a minimum of subscript dots, more letters on this difficult surface than his predecessors discerned or his contemporaries have been able to discern, and his text as it stands must be viewed with some reservation. In most cases, however, his readings either confirm what was previously surmised or in no way affect the issue, by adding a few letters of no real consequence, but in line 4 (*ad init.*) AI would require Tod's rather than Wilhelm's rendering of the publication formula (see above). In line 1 Walbank's ΣΥΑΙ is totally at variance with the ΑΣΒΟ of *IG* I³: the sigma alone may be confidently accepted. The remains in lines 16–18, where he saw a few more letters, are hardly worth transcription, but he correctly attributes the ΤΩΔ read by Meritt (and still acceptably legible) to line 17 rather than line 16.

The text presented above, like that of Walbank, refrains from all but minimal restorations and accepts only what the present editor sees, without denying the perhaps keener perception of others. In the present state of historical and epigraphical understanding, a date near the beginning of the Archidamian War reconciles the effective criteria.

Walbank's version of lines 5–12, compounded from his commentary, runs as follows:

5 Κλεώνυμος εἶπ[ε· τὰ μὲν ἄλλα καθάπερ τῆι βολῆι, μηδενὶ δὲ μὴ]
ἐξεῖναι ζημιῶν [μήτε Χίωνα μήτε Ἀχιλλέα μήτε Φίλιππον ἄνευ]
τõ δήμο τõ Ἀθηναί[ων· ἐὰν δέ τις Ἀθηναίων παραβαίνηι τι τῶν]
πίσ[τ]εων, τὴν ζημ[ίαν αὐτõ ἀτιμίαν εἶναι καὶ φυγὴν καὶ τὰ χρή]
ματα δημόσια κα[ὶ τῆς θεõ τὸ ἐπιδέκατον τῶν χρημάτων· πρόσο]
10 δον δὲ εἶναι Ἀχιλ[λε͂ι καὶ Φιλίπποι πρὸς τὴμ βολὴν καὶ τὸν δῆμ]
ον καθάπερ Χίω[νι· πρόξενος δὲ καὶ εὐεργέτας γράψαι Ἀχιλλ]
έα καὶ Φίλιππον [τὸς Χίωνος (*vel ethnicum*) τὸγ γραμματέα τὸν τῆς βολῆς].

The decree is briefly considered by R. Develin (*Athenian Officials*, p. 190). On its interpretation see further J. P. Barron in *Chios: A Conference at the Homereion in Chios, 1984*, J. Boardman and C. E. Vaphopoulou-Richardson, edd., 1986, pp. 115–119; cf. *SEG* XXXVI, 10. *SEG* XXXIX, 61 summarizes additional discussion relevant to this text.

RELATIONS WITH APHYTIS IN CHALKIDIKE

15. Three fragments of a stele of Pentelic marble, of which two (*a* and *b*) found in the Agora (I 5147) join closely down a vertical break, while the third (*c*) is to be located *ca.* 0.01 m. to their right. Fragment *a* was discovered on November 30, 1937, in a wall of a modern house outside the Market Square, in the area south of the Church of the Holy Apostles (N–O 19); fragment *b* was discovered on January 28, 1938, in a similar context nearby (N 19). Together they preserve the left edge and original back of the stele, but the former is so worn that one stoichos of the lettering has been lost at the beginning of even the best-preserved lines. The entire surface is corroded, and a large hole for the insertion of a door hinge interrupts lines 16–21. Fragment *c* (E.M. 6953), discovered on the Akropolis and first transcribed by U. Koehler, is broken all around except for the original back.

a+b: H. 0.33 m.; W. 0.26 m.; Th. 0.092 m.

c: H. 0.20 m.; W. 0.19 m.; Th. 0.092 m.

LH. 0.007 m.

Στοιχ. Hor. 0.0084 m.; Vert. 0.0124 m.

Ed. *c* only: *IG* II², 55, b, with earlier references. *a–c*: B. D. Meritt, *Hesperia* 13, 1944, pp. 211–224, no. 2, with photograph (see *SEG* X, 67); text with bibliography, *ATL* II, p. 75, D 21, with photographs pls. XII, XIII; revisions to lines 11–12 and 19, *ATL* IV, p. x, nos. 18, 19 (see *SEG* XIII, 7); *IG* I³, 62; further bibliography collected in *SEG* XXVIII, 7, XXX, 10.

(*IG* II², 55, a, was ascribed to this text by A. Wilhelm, and the ascription was accepted by Meritt, *loc. cit.*; but he subsequently concluded that that piece, showing the relief of a standing female figure with the word Ἀφυταίων, is not to be considered as forming a part of the monument, and it is left out of account here. See Meritt, *Hesperia* 36, 1967, pp. 57–58, no. 3, with photograph pl. 19, and *SEG* XXIV, 6.)

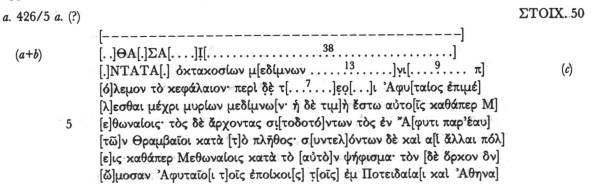

a. 426/5 a. (?) ΣΤΟΙΧ. 50

(a+b)

[--]
[. .]ΘΑ[.]ΣΑ[. . . .]Ι̣[. . . . . .³⁸. . . . .]
[.]ΝΤΑΤΑ[.] ὀκτακοσίων μ[εδίμνων . . . . . .¹³. . . . . .]υι[. . . .⁹. . . . π̣]
[ό]λεμον τὸ κεφάλαιον· περὶ δὲ τ[. . .⁷. . .]ε̣ρ[. . .]ι Ἀφυ[ταῖος ἐπιμέ]
[λ]εσθαι μέχρι μυρίων μεδίμνω[ν· ἡ δὲ τιμ]ὴ ἔστω αὐτο[ῖς καθάπερ Μ]
5 [ε]θωναίοις· τὸς δὲ ἄρχοντας σι̣[τοδοτό]ντων τὸς ἐν Ἄ[φυτι παρ'ἑαυ]
[τῶ]ν Θραμβαῖοι κατὰ [τ]ὸ πλῆθος· σ[υντελ]όντων δὲ καὶ α[ἱ ἄλλαι πόλ]
[ε]ις καθάπερ Μεθωναίοις κατὰ τὸ [αὐτὸ]ν ψήφισμα· τὸν [δὲ ὅρκον ὃν]
[ὤ]μοσαν Ἀφυταῖο[ι τ]οῖς ἐποίκοι[ς] τ̣[οῖς ἐμ Ποτειδαία[ι καὶ Ἀθηνα]

(c)

[ί]οις καὶ τόδε τὸ [ψή]φισμα ἀναγράψ[ας ὁ] γραμματεὺ[ς ὁ τῆς βολῆς ἐ]

10 [ν] στήληι λιθίνη[ι x]α[τ]αθέτω ἐμ πό[λει τ]έλεσι το[ῖς σφετέροις αὐ]

[τ]ῶν· ὅ [τ]ι δ'ἄν τις τούτων τῶν ψηφισθ[έντ]ων τῶι δήμ[ωι περὶ Ἀφυταί]

[ος μὴ] πειθαρχῆι, [ἢ] οἱ Ἑλληνοταμί[αι ἢ ἄλ]λη τις ἀ[ρχή, ἐνεχέσθων τ]

[οῖς ἐν] τῶι ψηφίσματι· ἐπαινέσαι [δὲ Ἀφυ]ταίος ὅ[τι ἄνδρες ἀγαθο]

[ὶ ἐ]σι[ν] καὶ νῦν καὶ ἐν τῶι πρόσθεν [χρόνω]ι περὶ Ἀ[θη]ν[αίος καὶ ἀπο]

15 [πεφά]νθαι ἐς τ[ὸν δῆμ]ο[ν ε]ὑρήσοντ[ας ὅτο ἄ]ν δέω[νται παρὰ Ἀθηναί]

[ων]· ᵛᵛ ἔδοξεν [τῶι δήμωι] ἀποδιδόν[αι Ἀφυταίος ἀπαρχὴν τῆι θεῶι]

[ᴾ δ]ραχμάς. ᵛ [vacat]   vacat

[Τ]όνδε τὸν ὅρ[κον ὤμοσαν] Ἀφυταῖοι [τοῖς ἐμ Ποτειδαίαι· ἐάν τις ἴ]

[ηι π]ολέμιος [ἐπὶ τὴν πό]λιν τὴν Ἀθη[ναίων ἢ ἐπὶ τὸς ἐποίκος τὸς Ἀ]

20 [θηναίων τ]ὸ[ς Ποτείδ]αιαν ἔχοντ[ας, βοηθήσω Ἀθηναίοις κατὰ τὸ δ]

[υνατὸν καὶ λόγωι x]αὶ ἔργωι Ἰ[.]Μ[..............²⁵..........]

[.......¹⁵......]οι[..]ιον κατ[..........²⁵............]

[..⁵.. οὔτε λόγωι ο]ὔτε ἔργωι [.............²⁷............]

[...........¹⁸.......]Ε[..............³¹............]

25 [⎯⎯⎯⎯⎯⎯⎯⎯⎯⎯⎯⎯⎯⎯⎯⎯⎯⎯⎯⎯⎯⎯⎯⎯]

The lettering is, like that of **14**, in Ionic characters but (unlike that text) follows a stoichedon pattern. The forms of sigma and omega, the latter consistently raised above the base line of the writing, are distinctive. The text is that of Meritt, as modified in *ATL* IV and (for lines 15–16) by Wilhelm in *SEG* X, 67, and is adopted also in *IG* I³. Lines 2–4. See H. B. Mattingly, *CQ* n.s. 28, 1978, p. 85 (*SEG* XXVIII, 7). Lines 6–7. σ[υντελ]όντων δὲ καὶ Α[ἰγάντιοι . |.]ις Mattingly, *loc. cit.*

The decree concerns the city of Aphytis on the peninsula of Pallene in Chalkidike; for the site see *ATL* I, p. 474. Restorations as shown are generally acceptable to the overall sense and give little room for maneuver. The surviving part of the text (1) gives to the people of Aphytis favorable terms presumably in regard to grain supply, on a pattern already established in the case of Methone; (2) regulates the supply of provisions to the Athenian archons at Aphytis, again on a pattern obtaining at Methone; (3) requires the inscription of the decree and of the oath already taken by the people of Aphytis; (4) guarantees sanctions against any official who fails to abide by the terms of the decree; (5) expresses Athenian gratitude to the people of Aphytis and promises favorable reception of further requests.

A decision by the demos that Aphytis is henceforward to pay only the *aparche* (one-sixtieth) of the *phoros* to Athens, and not the whole amount assessed, is appended, and the oath, the inscribing of which has been provided for, then follows.

The historical circumstances were discussed by Meritt in the *editio princeps* and again in Στήλη: Τόμος εἰς μνήμην Νικολάου Κοντολέοντος, 1977, pp. 21–25. The reference to the precedents available in the case of Methone are crucial to the dating of the decree, as is the mention of the colonists at Poteidaia, sent there by the Athenians after the recapture of that city in 430/29 (Thucydides 2.70.4). Another decree concerning Aphytis, *IG* I³, 63 (I², 58), is of uncertain contextual relationship with this one.

Meritt's discussions established and reiterated the date as 428/7 B.C., by which time the colony at Poteidaia was surely well settled and Methone had already received the privilege of paying the *aparche* instead of the full amount of *phoros*; cf. *IG* I³, 61 I (*IG* I², 57), lines 29–32, and the accepted dating of the relevant decree in that Methone dossier. This date is retained in *IG* I³, 62. The precedent for the special dispensation in regard to the importation of grain supplies apparently occurs, however, in the second decree of the Methone dossier, securely dated to 426/5 B.C., and this decree concerning Aphytis is therefore, perhaps, to be dated later (probably no more than slightly later) than that. Meritt nevertheless urged that the precedent is likely to have been established at an earlier date and is not necessarily reflected in the extant decree about Methone (Στήλη, pp. 22–23). The privilege of paying the *aparche* only need not (*pace ATL* III, p. 70, and Meritt, Στήλη, p. 24) be tied to an assessment year. The other provisions concerning Methone to which reference is made do not occur in *IG* I³, 61. Cf. F. A. Lepper, *JHS* 82, 1962, p. 52 with note 83.

Mattingly (*CQ* n.s. 11, 1961, pp. 161–163; *CQ* n.s. 16, 1966, p. 179; *CQ* n.s. 28, 1978, pp. 84–85; *BSA* 65, 1970, pp. 134–135) in his attempt to establish and defend a reverse order for Tribute Lists nos. 25 and 26 (*IG* I³, 281, 282) dated the first Methone decree to 427/6 and the present text to 426/5 as part of the sequence of his argument. The possible date of 426/5 for this Aphytis text does not however depend on acceptance of his contentions in general (on which see *IG* I³, *locc. citt.* and R. Meiggs, *Athenian Empire*, pp. 531–537). In any case, the privilege accorded to Aphytis may not have outlived the great reassessment of 425/4, *IG* I³, 71, where the city is assessed in the normal way (col. III, line 168); but the absence of a rubric for special cases in that document may not, on the other hand, imply that their privileges were not maintained. Cf. Meritt, *GRBS* 8, 1967, pp. 51–52.

Lines 5–8. The provisions are not clearly explicable. Whatever is precisely to be restored in lines 5–6, the sense seems to be that the cities in the area had already joined in contributing to the maintenance of the Athenian officials in Methone and that this system was to be applied in the case of Aphytis. The town of Therambos on the tip of Pallene was to be included as a contributor in proportion to its population. Its position in relation to "the other cities" had presumably been in doubt, and this doubt is now resolved. Cf. Meritt, *Hesperia* 13, 1944, p. 217 and Στήλη, pp. 24–25. On the archons in the cities see **3**, note on lines 6–7.

Line 10. A. S. Henry (in *Vindex Humanitatis: Essays in Honour of John Huntly Bishop*, 1980, pp. 24–25) discusses and rejects the restoration το[ῖς σφετέροις αὐτ]ῶν, preferring the το[ῖς τῶν ὁρκισθέντ]ων of Meritt's original version. But see Meritt and M. F. McGregor, *AAA* 13, 1981, p. 353, where it is reasserted (*SEG* XXX, 10). Lines 16–17. For decisions reserved to the discretion of the assembly by the *probouleuma* see P. J. Rhodes, *Athenian Boule*, p. 280 (type 1).

A TREATY WITH CERTAIN CITIES IN BOTTIKE

16. Eight fragments of a large stele of Pentelic marble, all of which save one (fragment *h*) were discovered on the Akropolis and are now in the Epigraphical Museum (fragments *a–f*, E.M. 6599; fragment *g*, E.M. 5392). Fragment *h* (I 1218), broken on all sides, was discovered on January 23, 1934, in a marble pile in the southwest corner of the Market Square: it is a mere chip, containing parts of seven lines, and has a width of four letters at most. Fragments *a–f* have long been known; four (*a–d*) join and together provide part of the left side and bottom of the stele; two more (*e* and *f*) also join and preserve part of the right side. Fragments *g* (identified by E. Schweigert) and *h* are located between these larger groups.

Whole surviving monument: H. 1.021 m.; W. 0.651 m.; Th. 0.126 m.

h only: H. 0.16 m.; W. 0.064 m.; Th. 0.088 m.

LH. 0.014 m.

Στοιχ. Hor. 0.0148 m.; Vert. 0.0187–0.0195 m.

Ed. *a–f*: *IG* I², 90, with earlier bibliography (see also M. N. Tod, *GHI* I², pp. 166–168, no. 68). *g+h*, in the context of lines 11–25: B. D. Meritt, *Hesperia* 7, 1938, pp. 80–81, no. 8, with photograph, *h* only (see also *SEG* X, 89, and Tod, *GHI* I², p. 264); full text with brief commentary, H. Bengtson, *Staatsverträge* II, pp. 113–115, no. 187; *IG* I³, 76.

a. 422 a.   ΣΤΟΙΧ. 42

```
                [----------------------------- τὰς τά]
      (b)        χσες ἔγ[αι .................... 34 ...................]
                 ντες ho[ι] εἰ[................ 27 ........ · διδόντ]
                 ο[ν] δὲ τὰς δί[κας ................ 30 .................]
      5          [.]ι ἐπειδὰν [................. 33 ................]
                 [h]ετέραι πα[.................. 32 ........ h]
                 εκατερον ε[................. 33 ................]
                 ος· τὸν δὲ hό[ρκον ὀμόσαι hεκατέρος, Ἀθεναῖον μὲν τὲν]
                 βολὲν καὶ τ[ὸς στρατεγὸς καὶ τὰς ἄλλας ἀρχάς, Βοττια]
      10         ίον δὲ τὲν βο[λὲν καὶ τὸς στρατεγὸς] κα[ὶ τὸς λοιπὸς ἄρ]            (e)
                 χοντας τὸς ἐ[ν ταῖς πόλεσι ταῖς Βοτ]τια[ίον· ho δὲ hόρχ]
      (g)        ος ἔστο Ἀθεν[αί]οι[ς hόδε· ἀμυνῶ τοῖς] Βοττιαίοις τοῖς
                 χσυντιθεμέ[νοι]ς [τὲν χσυμμαχίαν, κ]αὶ τὲν χσ[υμμαχία]
                 ν πιστὸς καὶ [ἀδ]όλο[ς φυλάχσο Βοττι]αίοις προ[θυμόμε]
      15         [ν]ος κατὰ τὰ χ[συ]νκε[ίμενα· καὶ οὐ μνε]σικακέσο τõ[ν παρ]
                 οιχομένον ἔ[νε]κα· [Βοττιαῖοι δὲ ὀμν]υόντον κατὰ [τάδε·]
                 φίλοι ἐσόμε[θα Ἀθεναίοις καὶ χσύμ]μαχοι πιστὸ[ς] κα[ὶ]            (f)
      (h)        ἀδόλος καὶ τ[ὸς αὐ]τὸ[ς φίλος καὶ ἐχθ]ρὸς νομιόμε[ν] hόσ
                 περ ἀν Ἀθενα[ῖοι], καὶ ο[ὐκ ὀφελέσο τὸ]ς ἐχθρὸς τὸς Ἀθεν
      20         αίον οὔτε χρ[έμα]σιν h[απλõς οὔτε δυ]νάμει οὐδεμιᾶι, ο
                 ὐδὲ μνεσικ[ακέσο] τõν [παροιχομέν]ον ἕνεκα· τὰς δὲ χσυ
```

νθέκας τά[σδε καὶ] τὸγ [hόρκον κατα]θε͂ναι Ἀθεναίος μὲ

ν ἐμ πόλε[ι ἀναγρά]φσ[αντας ἐστέλει] λιθίνει καὶ τὰ ὀν

(a)

[ὀ]ματα τὸν [πόλεον] τõ[ν Βοττιαίον τ]õν χσυντιθεμένον

25   τὲν φιλία[ν καὶ τὲν χσυμμαχίαν, καὶ] ἐπιγράφσαι ἐν τ[ε͂]

ι στέλει τõ ἄ[ρχοντος τὸ ὄνομα ἐφ'õ] ἐγένοντο αἱ χσ[υ]ν[θ]

ε͂και· Βοττια[ῖοι δ'ἐν στέλαις λιθί]ναις ἀναγράφ[σαντ]

ες καταθέντ[ον ἐν τοῖς hιεροῖς κ]ατὰ πόλες, ἐπι[γράφσ]

αντες ἐν ταῖ[ς στέλαις τõν ἀρχόν]τον τὰ ὀνόμα[τα τõν Β]

30   οττιαίον ἐφ'[õν ἐγένοντο hαι χσυνθε͂]κ[α]ι· τὸς δὲ [ὄρχος]

hοίτινες λέ[φσονται παρὰ Βοττιαίον ἐλέσθαι τὸν δε͂]

μον πέντε ἄν[δρας αὐτίκα μάλα ἐκ πάντον Ἀθεναίον· τὸ]

ς δὲ ὁμέρος h[ὸς ἔχοσι . . . . .25. . . . .]

[. .] Εὐκράτες [εἶπεν· τὰ μὲν ἄλλα καθάπερ τε͂ι βολε͂ι· τὰ δ]

(d)   35   ὲ ὀν[όματα] κ[. . . . . .33. . . . .]

ἀποδ[— —]

ν hοι σ[τρατ]ε[γοὶ . . . . .29. . . . .]

ἐπειδὰ[ν τὸ]ς hόρ[κος . . . . .26. . . . .]

ον ἀποδõ[σι] Βοττια[ῖοι . . . . .24. . . . .]

40   μὲ δόχσε[ι] ἀποδõνα[ι . . . . .26. . . . .]

ὅτι ἀποκρίνονται α[. . . . . .25. . . . . ο]

ὐδὲ [γ]νόμας χορὶς κα[. . . . . .26. . . . .]

ον καθὰ παραινõσιν Β[οττιαῖοι . . .17. . . . .]   *(c)*

Αἵδε πόλε[ς] ἐσίν·   *vacat*

45   Καλίνδοι[α]   *vacat*

Τριποιαί   *vacat*

[Κ]εμαχαί   *vacat*

reliquiae versuum   *vacat*

saltem quinque   *vacat*

(*In latere dextro stelae, prope vs. 21 lateris antici*)

vacat

53   ḥαιό[λειον]

vacat

Although the contribution of the Agora to this text is small, it is desirable to show it in its complete context. Except in line 24 (τõν [πόλεον ἐγγράφσαντας τ]õν χσυντιθεμένον *priores*), the Agora fragment vindicated the supplements previously advanced. The above version, that also of *IG* I³, unites the text of *IG* I² with that of Meritt, new readings being added in lines 43, 46, and 53. Lines 33–34. h[ὸς ἔχοσι Ἀθεναῖοι, ἀποδõναι Βοττιαίοις ᵛ] Tod. Line 43. παραινõσι *IG* I², Tod, Bengtson; παραινõσιν E. Erxleben *apud IG* I³.

The tidy lettering is distinctive especially for its circular letters (including phi) and a tall tau. The same craftsman was at work on the small fragment *IG* I³, 197.

For the date and historical circumstances see in particular Meritt, *AJA* 29, 1925, pp. 29–31, A. G. Woodhead, *Mnemosyne*, ser. 4, 13, 1960, pp. 3–5, note 1. The treaty may be linked to the activities of Kleon and Nikias in the Thraceward area towards the close of the Archidamian War (Thucydides 4.129–5.3). The absence of Spartolos from the list of cities (which as the leading polis in Bottike it might have been expected to head) is indicative that it remained outside Athenian control; cf. Thucydides 5.18. The cities here named, since Thucydides does not specify them in that context, must have been brought back into the Athenian alliance by the time of the "Peace of Nikias". The Aiolitai (line 53) were indeed assessed in the sum of 500 drachmai in the *phoros* assessment of 422/1 B.C. (*IG* I³, 77 = *ATL* II, A 10, col. V, line 17); Tripoai and Kemakai (or Kamakai) are recorded in List 34 (*IG* I³, 285), col. III, lines 8 and 11, as paying a quota of 13⅓ and 10 drachmas respectively (representing *phoros* of 800 and 600 dr.). These were small places, of uncertain location. Kalindoia does not appear elsewhere in Athenian records; see *ATL* I, p. 494.

The date 422 had previously been advocated by G. Busolt (*Griechische Geschichte* III, ii, 1904, p. 1171), but a later date (417/16) had been preferred by E. Meyer and K. J. Beloch; for further references, see Tod and Bengtson, *locc. citt.* A. W. Gomme (*A Historical Commentary on Thucydides* I, 1945, p. 207) suggested "*ca.* 420" but later (II, 1956,

p. 633) regarded 422, "accepted by many", as apparently "as probable as any other." Cf. also R. Meiggs, *Athenian Empire*, p. 211; W. Schuller, *Die Herrschaft der Athener im ersten attischen Seebund*, 1974, p. 60.

Lines 33–34. *SEG* XXIX, 13 drew attention to A. Panagopoulos, *Captives and Hostages in the Peloponnesian War*, 1978, pp. 202–203, concerning the identity of the hostages.

A DECREE CONCERNING CURRENCY

17 (Pl. 3). A fragment of a monument in Pentelic marble (I 5879), of which the original back may be preserved, discovered on June 17, 1937, in the original filling of the Post-Herulian Wall over the southwest corner of the Library of Pantainos (R 15). The right side of the fragment also appears to be original, but this straight edge is probably the result of a later reworking; it is, however, convenient for the transcription of the text to treat it as the right margin, and the inscription has appeared in this form in modern publications. The upper part of the inscribed surface is badly worn.

H. 0.38 m.; W. 0.215 m.; Th. 0.25 m.
LH. 0.01 m.
Στοιχ. Hor. 0.01 m.; Vert. 0.014 m.

Ed. B. D. Meritt, *Hesperia* 14, 1945, pp. 119–122, no. 11, with photograph (cf. *SEG* X, 87); *IG* I³, 90; R. Stroud, *CSCA* 6, 1974, pp. 283–290, no. II, with photographs pls. 2, 3 (cf. *SEG* XXVI, 13).

a. 435–415 *a.*   ΣΤΟΙΧ.

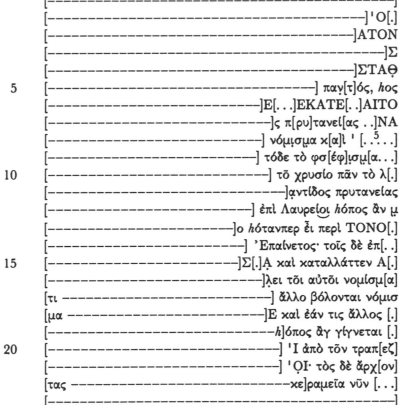

The thickness of the fragment suggests that it may have formed part of a building block of a larger monument rather than a piece of a conventional stele. Such a thickness, even in a stele, could accommodate a text of greater width than the line of 52 letters postulated by Meritt or that of *ca.* 50–56 letters to which the text of *IG* I³ points. Stroud regarded the length of line as impossible to determine, a conclusion here endorsed in the acceptance of his text.

This fragment of what must have been a lengthy document was thought to preserve parts of two amendments to a preceding *probouleuma*, the first by Epainetos and the second by a proposer whose name is lost. But, as Stroud observed, the assumption though tempting is not justified, and the proper name in line 14 is not necessarily to be construed as concluding a formula of amendment. The tidy but rather crowded lettering closely resembles that of *IG* I³, 89 (I², 71), also a wide text, and has been regarded as the work of the same craftsman. This is a treaty between the Athenians and Perdikkas II, king of Macedon, and the dating of the present decree is therefore affected to some degree by the date given to the treaty (see below). Identity of year need not however be assumed. H. B. Mattingly (*BCH* 92, 1968, pp. 466–467) attributed *SEG* X, 215 (*IG* I³, 467, there dated *ca.* 430/29 B.C.) to the same hand. M. B. Walbank extended the list (in *Phoros*, pp. 168–169, note 21 and *Athenian Proxenies*, p. 51, note 21). The career of the mason could have been sufficiently long to make any date within two decades acceptable for either the Perdikkas treaty or the present document independently. Stroud's date of 440–420 has a lower limit too high to accommodate the possible latest date of the treaty.

The above text follows Stroud's conservative presentation, which adds a new line 1 and more traces in line 2 to previous versions but avoids restorations. The readings elsewhere are in general those of Meritt, whose text, with a line of 52 letters, was substantially restored. In lines 7 and thereafter it ran as follows:

$$
\begin{aligned}
&[-------------- \text{καθάπερ κελεύει } ho] \text{ νόμος } h[o] \text{ Κ}[α]λλ[..\overset{5}{.}..] \\
&[. \text{ τὸν δὲ γραμματέα τες βολες ἀναγράφσαντα] τόδε τὸ φσ[έφι]σ[μα ἐν σ]} \\
&[\text{τέλει καταθεναι ἐμ πόλει· καταλλάττεν δὲ καὶ] τὸ χρυσίο πᾶν τὸ λο}} \\
10 \quad &[\text{ιπὸν ἐάν τις βόλεται· τὸς δὲ πρυτάνες τες Αἰ]αντίδος πρυτανείας} \\
&[\text{γνόμεν ἐχσενεγκεν περὶ τον μετάλλον τὸν ἐ]πὶ Λαυρείοι hόπος ἂν [φ]} \\
&[\text{σεφίσεται } ho \text{ δεμος ἐν τει πρότει } h\acute{ε}δραι \text{ } h]\text{ότανπερ εἰ περὶ τὸ νο[μ]}} \\
&[\text{ίσματος. ..}\overset{6}{...} \text{ εἶπε· τὰ μὲν ἄλλα καθάπερ ᾿Ε]παίνετος· τοῖς δὲ ἐπ[ισ]}} \\
&[\text{τάταις ἔστο χρυσᾶ νομίσματα παραδέχεσθα]ι καὶ καταλλάττεν ἀ[π]}} \\
15 \quad &[\text{αριθμεσαμένοις ἐναντίον τες βολες ἐμ πό]λει τοι αὐτοι νομίσμ[α]}} \\
&[\text{τι χρομένοις } hoίοι \text{ καὶ ἐς τὰ ἀργυρᾶ· ἐὰν δὲ] ἄλλο βόλονται νόμισ}} \\
&[\text{μα ....}\overset{21}{.........} \text{ κρινέτο } he \text{ βολ]έ· καὶ ἐάν τις ἄλλος [.]}} \\
&\text{κτλ.}
\end{aligned}
$$

In lines 20–21 Meritt restored τραπ[εζιτον – –] and in line 22 νῦν [δέ .].

The text of *IG* I³ accepts that of Meritt, largely shorn of its restorations, with minor variants in lines 8, 14, and 21.

This inscription was discussed on several occasions by Mattingly (*Historia* 12, 1963, p. 267; *Proceedings of the African Classical Associations* 7, 1964, pp. 49–53; *BCH* 92, 1968, pp. 470–471; *BSA* 65, 1970, p. 142; *Klio* 59, 1977, pp. 83–100), chiefly to support his contentions (a) that it formed part of or was an independent supplement to the great "Coinage Decree" of Klearchos (*ATL* II, D 14; *SEG* XXVI, 6) and (b) that both decrees are to be dated, together with the Perdikkas treaty, to the later 420's. Meritt's original dating for this text had been "*ca.* 423/2 B.C.", which was derived from the then-accepted date of the Perdikkas treaty. When the revised date of *ca.* 436 was proposed for the latter (*ATL* III, p. 313, note 61; cf. R. Meiggs, *Athenian Empire*, pp. 428–430), this decree was similarly adjusted. A date at or near the beginning of the Archidamian War would still suit it (A. G. Woodhead in *Mélanges helléniques offerts à Georges Daux*, 1974, pp. 384–385; R. J. Hoffmann, *GRBS* 16, 1975, pp. 359–377; and cf. Stroud's dating), irrespective of the date of the treaty, which opinion has latterly preferred to place *ca.* 416/15 (so *IG* I³, 89; N. G. L. Hammond and G. T. Griffith, *A History of Macedonia* II, 1979, pp. 134–136). The preference of others for retaining 423/2 as the year of the treaty (H. Bengtson, *Staatsverträge* II, pp. 109–113, no. 186; J. W. Cole, *Phoenix* 28, 1974, pp. 55–72 and *GRBS* 18, 1977, pp. 29–32) has supported Mattingly's contention concerning the present decree; cf. also P. J. Rhodes, *Athenian Boule*, p. 259. Mattingly further drew attention to the Kall– – in Meritt's text (line 8 of the present text), in whom he saw the Kallias of the "Kallias Decrees" and indeed a reference to those very decrees, for which he also sought a date in the later 420's.

All the arguments so ingeniously deployed, whether historical or epigraphical, are inconclusive. Despite much speculation, constructed mainly on the basis of the restorations, this text remains without firm date or context, and it is advisable not to build theoretical reconstructions upon such insecure foundations unless or until better evidence is forthcoming. So also Stroud, *loc. cit.*, p. 290. For the collected bibliography see *SEG* XXI, 45, XXII, 10, XXV, 33, and cf. XXXVI, 6, XXXVII, 6.

ANTIOCHIDES, PHANOSTHENES, AND OTHERS HONORED

18. Four nonjoining fragments (*a–d*) of a stele of marble, perhaps Hymettian, to which a fifth fragment (*e*) may possibly be added; of these the Agora excavations supplied only fragment *b* (I 419, now E.M. 13374), broken on all sides except for the original rough-picked back, which was discovered on February 10, 1933, in a modern foundation wall east of the Temple of Apollo Patroos (I 7). It was closely associated with fragment *a* (E.M. 6616) by A. E. Raubitschek; a direct join (below the inscribed surface) has been postulated but remains doubtful. Fragment *d* (E.M. 12948), broken on all sides, was found in a late fill on the North Slope of the Akropolis on April 12, 1937, in the area northwest of the sanctuary of Eros and Aphrodite. It was, on publication, not associated with the fragments already mentioned but with E.M. 6847, now fragment *c*, which preserves the left edge of the stele and the bottom of the text but is broken elsewhere. The attribution of the fifth fragment, *e* (E.M. 2505), was suggested by D. M. Lewis (in *IG* I³) and accepted by M. B. Walbank (see below) but remains dubious: it is of uncertain provenance and is broken on all sides.

b only: H. 0.335 m.; W. 0.358 m.; Th. 0.13 m.

a–e: LH. 0.01–0.011 m.
Στοιχ. Hor. 0.0133–0.0137 m.; Vert. 0.0145 m.

For the measurements of separate fragments Walbank, *locc. citt. infra*, and *IG* I³, 182. Walbank assessed the total height of the stele (excluding fragment *e*) as now surviving at *ca.* 0.65 m. and the width at *ca.* 0.62 m.

Ed. *a*: *IG* I², 122, with earlier bibliography. *a+b*: B. D. Meritt, *Hesperia* 14, 1945, pp. 129–132, no. 16, with photographs of squeezes (cf. *SEG* X, 131). *c*: *IG* I², 156, with earlier bibliography. *c+d*: E. Schweigert, *Hesperia* 7, 1938, pp. 269–270, no. 4, with photograph (see *SEG* X, 79, with references also to A. Wilhelm, *Attische Urkunden* IV [= *SbAkadWien* 217, 5], 1939, pp. 83–87, no. XXXV and Meritt, *Hesperia* 10, 1941, pp. 331–332). *a–e*: M. B. Walbank, *Hesperia* 45, 1976, pp. 289–295, with photographs pl. 68, and *Athenian Proxenies*, pp. 313–324, no. 60, with photograph pl. 36 (see *SEG* XXVI, 21); *IG* I³, 182. Fragment *e* was unpublished in this context before Walbank's study of it. It should be noted that Walbank's tabulation of the fragments varies from that adopted here, which follows the series preferred in *IG* I³.

ca. a. 420–414 *a.* ΣΤΟΙΧ. 46

```
                    [------------------------------------]
(b)        [....10....]A[.............35.............]
           [....10....]γ]ρ[α]μμα[τε ..........28..........]
           [...7....  Ἀν]τιοχίδει καὶ [Φανοσθένει ......16......]
           [...9.....]ις Ἀθεναίοις καὶ [..........23..........]
    5      [....10.....]ορας καὶ τὰ ἄλλα ℎότ[.........20.........]
           [...9....] τὸν δῆμον τὸν Ἀθεναί[ον ........18........]
           [....13.........] καὶ νῦν αὐτὸς καὶ [.........19.........]
           [ℎόπος ἂν ℎο δῆμο]ς ℎος περὶ πολλõ ποιõ[ν φαίνεται τὸς ἐσάγ]
(a)        [οντας χο]πέας [κα]ὶ χάριν ἀποδόσον τὸ λ[οιπόν· ἀζέμιος δὲ τό]
    10     [χο ℎεχ]ατοστõ τ[ὸς] χοπέας ℎὸς ἔγαγον ο[ἴκοθεν δόντον τοῖς]
           [τρι]εροποιοῖς κ[αὶ] ℎοι τριεροποιοὶ ε[ὐθὺς παραλαβόντες]
           [τιθ]έντον ἐς τὸ να[υ]πέγιον καὶ ἐὰν δέ[ονται ἄλλο τινὸς ℎοι]
           [στ]ρατεγοὶ χρόσθο[ν φρ]άζοντες τῆι β[ολῆι καὶ ℎάμα ἀποδιδ]
           [όν]τες τὲν τεταγμέν[εν] τιμὲ[ν]· καὶ ℎο[ι ναυπεγοὶ λογιζόσθο]
    15     [ν το]ῖς τριεροποιο[ῖς τὰ τε]ταγμέν[α· ἐπειδὲ οὖν Ἀντιοχίδε]
           [ς καὶ] Φανοσθένες τὸ[ν δῆμον τὸν Ἀθεναῖον εὖ ποιῆτον καὶ π]
           [ερὶ αὐ]τõ ℎο ℎελλενοτ[αμίας .............24.............]
           [...6...]ς χρῆσθαι ἐς τ[ὸν πόλεμον ........20........]
           [.... αὐτ]οῖν ἀγαγόντ[οιν .............26............]
    20     [...8....]ορᾳ, ἐπαιν[έσαι μὲν Ἀντιοχίδεν καὶ Φανοσθένε]
           [ν ℎότι ἐδι]ᾳκονεσάτε[ν τὰ τεταγμένα· ἐὰν δέ τινος δεέσθον]
           [παρὰ τõ δέμο], προσάγ[εν αὐτὸ τὸς πρυτάνες ἐς τὸν δῆμο]ν [ἐς τ]
           [ἐν πρότεν ἐκ]κλεσίᾳ[ν· πρόσοδον δὲ ἔναι αὐτοῖν ἐς τὲ]ν βολὲ[ὲ]
(d)        [ν ἐὰν δεέσθον ἄ]λλο [τινὸς πρότοιν μετὰ τὰ ℎιερά· τὸ] δ(ὲ) φσέ[φ]
    25     [ισμα τόδε ἀναγράφσαι τὸν γραμματέα τὸν τῆς βολ]ῆς ἐν στ[έ]
           [λει λιθίνει καὶ καταθῆναι ἐμ πόλει· ....10....]ι δὲ τὸς [.]
           [------------------------------------]

                              lacuna

           [------------------------------------]
(c)        τιεπαι[...................40...................]
           ι εὐεργέτας· ἔν[αι δὲ αὐτοῖς ℎευρέσθαι ἄλλο τινὸς ℎõ ἂν δέ]
           ονται παρὰ Ἀθεν[αίον· ἀναγράφσαι δὲ .....12..... ἐν στέ]
```

30   λει εὐεργέτας Ἀθ[εναίον . . . . .¹¹. . . . . τὸν γραμματέα τες]
        βολες. ✕   *vacat*
                          vacat

The lettering is regular and characteristic of the last two decades of the 5th century. Phi with two loops in place of a continuous oval is noteworthy. Walbank claims that the same craftsman worked on *IG* I³, 176 and that the hands of *IG* I³, 99, 115, and 121 are very similar; to the craftsman of 115 are attributed also 114 and 116. All these are dated between 410 and 406 B.C., with the exception of *IG* I³, 176, which is assigned more generally to the period 420–405. The concluding mark of punctuation, a cross with circles at the points and the center, is a peculiar feature of the inscription.

The stoichedon pattern of fragment *e* differs slightly from that of the other fragments; if it belongs (as is to be supposed) to a different enactment, this is of no significance. Walbank places it high on the stele and calls it "Decree I".

The above text as far as line 24 is that of Walbank, whose association of the fragments and fresh treatment of the whole document have transformed the study of this monument. He has added two fragmentary lines at the beginning of fragment *b* and has discerned a number of letters at the edges of the stones not read by previous editors; whether or not these additions are to be accepted, they do not affect the overall tenor of the text. His line of 46 letters confirms that tentatively established by Meritt, from whose study the restorations in what are now lines 8–23 are derived. The Agora fragment, although only one element in what has emerged as a much larger complex, was instrumental in establishing the sense and character of the enactment. The readings of *IG* I³, using a 42-letter line and regarding fragment *d* as of uncertain location, are not here repeated. Also omitted here are the five lines of fragment *e*, offering no more than thirteen letters, which (as noted above) are interpreted by Walbank as the preamble to a preceding decree.

Line 4. το]ῖς Ἀθεναίοις Meritt. Line 5. hότι – – – Meritt. Lines 7–8. καὶ π[αῖδας αὐτο̄|ν hύστερον hόπος ἂν ho δε̄μο]ς κτλ. Meritt. Lines 25–27. τὸν τες βολ]ες ἐν στ[έ|λει λιθίνει καὶ θε̄ναι ἐν ἀκροπόλει· ἀπομισθο̄σα]ι δὲ τὸς [π|ολετάς· ἀποδο̄ναι δὲ τὸς κολακρέτας τὸ ἀργύριον· Walbank. Walbank assumed a gap of no more than one further line before the first surviving line of fragment *c* and included in his main text in *Athenian Proxenies* a proposal for lines 27 and preceding, which in 1977 he reserved for a footnote: τὸ ἀργύριον· . . .⁷. . .| εἶπε· τὰ μὲν ἄλλα καθάπερ τε̄ι βολε̄ι· hότι δὲ ἀνὲρ ἀγαθός ἐσ]|τι Ἐπαι[νέτος(?) περὶ τὸν δε̄μον αὐτὸν καὶ τὸς παῖδας γράφσα]|ι εὐεργέτας ἐν [στέλει. He continued (in both editions), ε̄ναι δὲ αὐτοῖς heυρέσθαι ho̅ν ἂν δέ]|ονται παρὰ Ἀθεν[αίον· γράφσαι δὲ Ἀνδρίος(?) ἐν τε̄ι αὐτε̄ι στέ]||λει εὐεργέτας Ἀθ[εναίον ἐν ἀκροπόλει τὸν γραμματέα τες]| βολες.

Walbank's reconstruction of lines 21–24 is open to the criticism expressed by A. S. Henry (*Honours*, pp. 192–193, 201, notes 10, 11) that the πρόσοδος clause always precedes the instructions for implementing the grant of it and never *vice versa*: his restorations must on that account be treated with some reserve. Cf. *SEG* XXXIII, 11.

The date, to which the lettering gives only a general guide, may be more narrowly defined by the content. The one-percent harbor tax (lines 9–10) existed from about 425 to 414, when it was apparently replaced by the five-percent duty levied in place of the *phoros* (Thucydides 7.28.3–4) and may not have been restored when the *phoros* was reimposed in 410. B. R. McDonald (*Hesperia* 50, 1981, pp. 141–146; cf. *SEG* XXXI, 21), however, has denied that the tax offers a guide to the dating, suggesting rather that the two taxes just mentioned need not be mutually exclusive and that in any case there were various one-percent duties (cf. Aristophanes, *Vespae* 658–659) that might be involved. While there is some attraction in an association of this decree with the circumstances in which honors were voted to King Archelaos of Macedon in 407/6 (*IG* I³, 117; I², 105), as Meritt (*Hesperia* 14, 1945, p. 130) suggested and McDonald has reemphasized, a connection with preparations for the Sicilian expedition is no less in point. It is not necessary to interpret the decree as implying that shipbuilding material was in positively short supply.

H. B. Mattingly (in *Ancient Society and Institutions: Studies Presented to Victor Ehrenberg on His 75th Birthday*, 1966, pp. 198–200) called for a date *ca.* 420 B.C. on the grounds of the spelling χρόσθον in line 13, which, he claimed, should not have survived much later than that date. On this point see Meritt, *GRBS* 8, 1967, pp. 131–132.

Phanosthenes may have been the Andrian who came to Athens *ca.* 411 and, having become an Athenian citizen, served as στρατηγός in 407/6 (*PA* 14083). Hence Walbank's suggestion for the ethnic in line 31. The terms of the decree are such that, if the identification be accepted, Phanosthenes was clearly not a citizen at the time of its enactment and presumably was not even resident in Athens. The name is unusual and perhaps to be associated with the islands (cf. a Tenian in *SEG* XIV, 553, II, line 20, of *s.* II/I *a.*): it seems not to occur otherwise in Athenian prosopography. Phanosthenes' personal history was given particular emphasis by M. J. Osborne (*Naturalization* III/IV, pp. 31–33), who reproduced the text of *IG* I³, fragments *a–c*, as T9 (pp. 31–32), with accompanying testimonia, and regarded the date of the decree as "best set in the years 410–407."

On Walbank's restoration of lines 26–27 see also Henry, *ZPE* 78, 1989, pp. 249–250 (cf. *SEG* XXXIX, 308).

TREATY BETWEEN ATHENS AND ARGOS

19. Seven fragments of a stele of Pentelic marble, of which only one, now fragment *g* (I 5026), comes from the Agora; this fragment is broken on all sides and was discovered on October 9, 1937, in a modern house wall west of the Panathenaic Way where it passes west of the Eleusinion (R 19). The other six fragments, *a–f* (E.M. 6588 and 6588α–ε), were all discovered on the Akropolis and have long been known: fragments *a* and *b* go back to the first half of the 19th century and the period of Pittakys and Rangabé; fragments *c–f* were identified and added by A. Wilhelm. Fragment *g* makes a direct join with fragments *a+b* to its left; fragments *e* and *f* remain of uncertain location.

g only: H. 0.17 m.; W. 0.065 m.; Th. 0.128 m.

(For the dimensions of the remaining fragments see *IG* I³, 86.)

a–g: LH. 0.011 m. (line 1, 0.017 m.).
Στοιχ. Hor. 0.0136 m. above, diminishing to 0.0115 m.; Vert. 0.017–0.0185 m.

Ed. *a+b* only: *IG* I, 50, with earlier references. *a–f*: *IG* I², 96, with addenda p. 302; *a–g*: B. D. Meritt, *Hesperia* 14, 1945, pp. 122–127, no. 12, with photographs of fragments *d* (squeeze) and *g* (stone) (see also *SEG* X, 104); H. Bengtson, *Staatsverträge* II, pp. 134–136, no. 196 (cf. *SEG* XXI, 49); *IG* I³, 86.

a. 417/16 a. ΣΤΟΙΧ. 76 (lines 3 and following)

(c)
[..]όδορος Πολυχάρος Ἀμ[φιτροπῆθεν(?) ἐγραμμάτευεν].
[Ἔδοχσεν τῆι] βολῆι καὶ τῶι δέμοι· Αἰαν[τὶς ἐπρυτάνευε, ..όδορος ἐγραμμάτευε],
[....¹⁰.... ἐπεσ]τάτε, Εὔφεμος ἔρχε· ΧΣΥ[.............³⁹.................
Ἀθενα]
[ίοις καὶ Ἀργείοις πε]ντέχοντα ἔτε· περὶ [μὲν τὸν hιερὸν
............³²............]

(a)

5   [........¹⁸........ Ἀθ]εναῖος καὶ Ἀργ[εῖος ....¹⁷........]ι περ[ὶ
.........¹⁸.........]
[..........²³..........]ν ἐὰν ἐσβά[λλοσιν ἐς τὲγ γῆν τὲν Ἀργ]εῖον ἐπὶ πο[λέμοι ἒ
Λακεδαιμόν]
[ιοι ἒ ἄλλος τις, βοεθῆν Ἀργείοις Ἀ]θενα[ίος hοπόσοις ἂν ἐπαγγέ]λλοσιν·
τούτον [δὲ .....¹²......]
[------------------------------ πρ]ὸς τὸς ἐπιστρατεύ[οντας ...⁸....]
[-----------------------------] μέχρι hεχσακοσίον [.....¹².....]

10 [..............................⁴⁷.............................]ς· χρέμασι δὲ hόπος ἂν [Ἀργεῖοι
χρõντ]

(d)
[αι hικανοῖς ἐχσελῆν ἐ[κ τ]õ φόρο μ[ὲ ἔλαττον ἒ .....¹².....] τάλαντα ἐς τὸν πόλε[μον
κατ'ἐνιαυτὸ]
[ν hέκαστον· ἐὰν δὲ] ἐρένεν βόλον[ται ποῖσθαι Λακεδαιμόνιοι] Ἀργείοις καὶ Ἀθε[ναί]ο[ις
καὶ τοῖς ἀ]
[μφοτέρον συμμάχ]οις, Ἀργεῖο[ι] Λ[ακεδαιμονίος ἐς τὲν βολὲν χα]ὶ τὸν δῆμον τὸν
[Ἀθε]ναί[ον Ἀθέναζε]
[ἐφιέντον· ἐὰν δὲ] ἐσβάλλοσιν [ἐς τὲγ γῆν τὲν Ἀθεναῖον ἒ Λακε]δαιμόνιοι ἒ ἄλλος τις
ἐ[πὶ πολέμοι β]

(g)

15 [οεθόντον Ἀργεῖο]ι Ἀθεναῖο[ις αὐτίκα καθάπερ ἂν Ἀθεναῖοι] ἐπαγγέλλοσιν μ[έ]χρι δι[
μένο
καὶ στρ]
[ατιόταις μὲ ὀλεζο]ν δισχιλ[ίον· τοῖς δὲ χρέμασι τοῖς ὑπάρ]χοσι χρῆσθαι ἐπὶ [τ]ὸς
ἐπ[....¹¹.....]
[.....¹⁵...... το]ῦτο [...........²⁶...........] δέονται πρὸς τού[το]ις
[.....¹².....]
[------------------------------]αι αὐτοῖς τέ[ν]δε
τ[ὲν(?) ....¹¹.....]

(b)
[------------------------------] ἐχσῆν[αι ἒ τὸ]ν
[π]όλεμ[ον ....¹¹.....]

20 [------------------------------ τὸ]ν πρὸς
Λακε[δαιμ]ον[ίος ....¹¹.....]

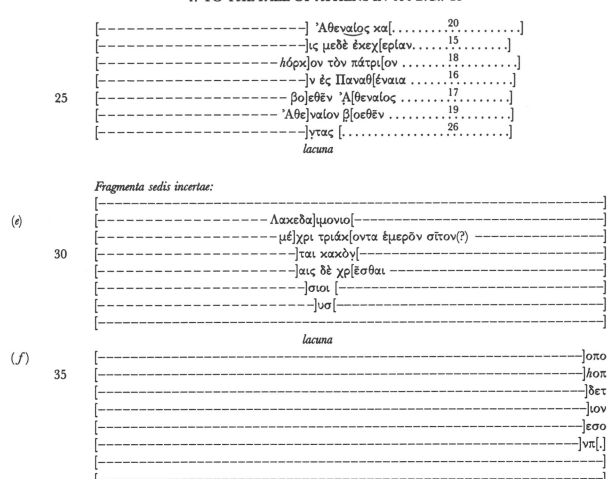

```
[------------------------------] ’Αθεναῖος χα[..........20..........]
[-----------------------------]ις μεδὲ ἐχεχ[ερίαν.......15........]
[---------------------------- hόρχ]ον τὸν πάτρι[ον.......18.......]
[---------------------------]ν ἐς Παναθ[έναια......16.......]
[-------------------------- βο]εθε͂ν ’Α[θεναῖος.......17.......]
[------------------------- ’Αθε]ναῖον β[οεθε͂ν.......19.......]
[-------------------------]γτας [.........26........]
```
                                    lacuna

Fragmenta sedis incertae:

```
[--------------------------------------------------------------------]
[---------------- Λαχεδα]ιμονιο[-------------------------------------]
[-------------- μέ]χρι τριάχ[οντα ἐμερο͂ν σῖτον(?) ------------------]
[-----------------]ται χαχὸγ[------------------------------------]
[----------------]αις δὲ χρ[ε͂σθαι --------------------------------]
[---------------]σιοι [-------------------------------------------]
[---------------]υσ[---------------------------------------------]
[--------------------------------------------------------------------]
```
                                    lacuna

```
[------------------------------------------------------------]οπο
[------------------------------------------------------------]hοπ
[------------------------------------------------------------]δετ
[------------------------------------------------------------]ιον
[------------------------------------------------------------]εσο
[------------------------------------------------------------]υπ[.]
[------------------------------------------------------------]
[------------------------------------------------------------]
```

The stele was surmounted by a relief, the remains of which appear on fragment *a*, showing Zeus, seated and accompanied by his eagle, and Hera (representing Argos), who extends her hand to Athena. Below the relief, a taenia carries line 1 of the inscription, and a cyma-reversa molding then provides a transition to the inscribed surface. On the relief see J. N. Svoronos, *Das Athener Nationalmuseum*, 1908, pl. CCVII; O. Walter, *Beschreibung der Reliefs im kleinen Akropolismuseum*, 1923, pp. 1–3, no. 2; R. Binneboessel, *Studien zu den attischen Urkundenreliefs des 5. und 4. Jahrhunderts*, 1932, pp. 4–5 and 32–33, no. 9; *SEG* XXXIX, 324 and the reference there given. D. M. Lewis (cf. *IG* I³) believes that more letters may be missing on the left of line 1 than are here shown. This, if so, would affect the restoration of lines 2–3.

The lettering is in the best Attic style of the later 5th century B.C. A. E. Raubitschek (*Hesperia* 12, 1943, p. 27, note 57) regarded *IG* I³, 167 (I², 149) as by the same hand; on this see D. W. Bradeen and M. F. McGregor, *Studies in Fifth-Century Attic Epigraphy*, 1973, p. 102, note 2. M. B. Walbank (*Athenian Proxenies*, p. 231; cf. p. 51, note 21) has added *IG* I³, 1042 and 1180 (I², 852 and 944), 1445 (*SEG* X, 112*d*), and probably, but less certainly, 168 (I², 28); he is also inclined to assign **20** and *IG* I³, 165 to the same craftsman (*op. cit.*, p. 348). The date is assured by the name of the archon (line 3).

Although the contribution of the Agora to this text is comparatively small, the effect of its discovery was considerable, for it enabled the length of line, provisionally reckoned as *ca.* 72 letters, to be determined as 76 letters. The above text is that of Meritt, with restorations that must give the general if not the exact wording of the original, and was followed in *IG* I³; but there are two variations. In lines 3–4, where Meritt restored ἔρχε· χσυ[μμαχίαν χαὶ χσυνθέχας ἀδόλος χαὶ ἀβλαβε͂ς ε͂ναι ’Αθεναί|οις χαὶ ’Αργείοις πε]ντέχοντα ἔτε, Wilhelm's Χσύ[μμαχος(?) εἶπε· χσυμμαχίαν ε͂ναι ἄδολον χαὶ ἀβλαβε͂ ’Αθεναί|οις χτλ., proposed in *SEG* X, 104, has been more recently advocated by A. S. Henry (*Prescripts*, p. 14), who points to the unlikelihood that the preamble would lack the name of the proposer. The coincidence that Symmachos should propose a *symmachia* may be matched by the proposal of a *proxenia* for a man named Proxenos in *IG* I³, 181 (I², 146) but might be regarded as optimistic. The correct solution might be even more radical; cf., for instance, *IG* II², 225. Secondly, in line 11, where Meritt restored τετταράχοντα, the amount πέντε χαὶ δέχα may be preferable; cf. *ATL* III, p. 357, note 45. Bengtson (*Staatsverträge* II, *loc. cit.*) preferred an unrestored text. Lines 10–12 were quoted by H. B. Mattingly (*BCH* 92, 1968, p. 460) in the course of a study (pp. 460–464) of the financial recovery of Athens in the years 421–415 B.C.

For the historical circumstances, which need not be entered into here, see Thucydides 5.82.5 and 6.29; Diodorus Siculus 12.81.2; Plutarch, *Alkibiades* 15. The events have been well studied by G. Busolt (*Griechische Geschichte* III, ii, 1904, p. 1265); W. S. Ferguson in *CAH* 5, 1924, p. 277; *ATL* III, p. 357. A. Andrewes' note in A. W. Gomme, A. Andrewes, and K. J. Dover, *A Historical Commentary on Thucydides* IV, 1970, p. 151, was revised and amplified by him in V, 1981, pp. 261–263, where the terms and date of this text are particularly taken into account. Those attested as performing official functions during this year are listed in R. Develin, *Athenian Officials*, pp. 146–147 (this text cited, p. 147).

PROXENIDES OF KNIDOS HONORED

20. Eight fragments of a stele of Pentelic marble, all except one discovered on the Akropolis, the exception being fragment *g*, the sole contribution of the Agora excavations to this text (I 2806). Fragment *g* was discovered on April 19, 1935, in a modern pit west of the East Building between the Middle and South Stoas (O 14). It preserves part of the left side and original back of the stele but is broken elsewhere; it also makes direct joins, however, with fragment *d* to the left, with fragment *f* above it, and (below the inscribed surface) with fragment *a* on the right. Fragment *a* may be joined with fragment *b* on its right, and, since the latter preserves the right edge of the stele, the total width of the monument is thereby recovered. Fragment *f* is a small piece joining fragment *d* to the upper right of the latter and is sometimes not distinguished from fragment *d* but assumed as part of it (e.g., *IG* I², 144, and B. D. Meritt's *editio princeps* of the Agora fragment). Fragments *e* and *c*, from a lower part of the monument, together preserve part of its left side and original back. The attribution to this text of fragment *e*, the bottom of which joins the top of fragment *c*, was made by Meritt at the time of his edition of fragment *g* and restudy of the whole stele.

Fragment *h* is generally omitted from editions of this inscription, together with the invocation [Θ]εο[ὶ] appearing on the taenia surmounting it. It joins the top of fragments *a–d* and *f* and consists of a relief showing a male figure (Proxenides) flanked by two goddesses, Aphrodite (of Knidos) on the left and Athena on the right. Its inclusion here (as by M. B. Walbank; see below) adds a new line 1 and in consequence alters the numeration of the lines as they are customarily reckoned. It should be noted that Walbank's designation of the fragments differs from that adopted here, which, to avoid confusion, is the same as that of *IG* I³, 91.

The stele is wider and thicker in its lower section. The body of the text (lines 3 and following) is surmounted by a simple ovolo molding supporting a projecting taenia on which line 2 is inscribed. This taenia represents the widest part of the monument, and the relief above it is narrower than the inscribed face.

g only: H. 0.242 m.; W. 0.198 m.; Th. 0.083 m.

a–g: LH. (line 3 and following) 0.012–0.013 m.
Στοιχ. Hor. 0.0222 m.; Vert. 0.0225 m.

For the measurements of the other fragments separately and in combination, see *IG* I³, 91, and Walbank, *loc. cit. infra*, the latter with a very full physical description of each fragment.

Ed. *a–d*, *f*: *IG* I², 144, with earlier bibliography (*d+f* also *IG* II², 66, a and b). *e*: *IG* I², 155, with earlier bibliography. *a–g*: B. D. Meritt, *Hesperia* 8, 1939, pp. 65–69, no. 22, with photographs pp. 66 and 68; see A. Wilhelm, *Attische Urkunden* IV (= *SbAkadWien* 217, 5), 1939, pp. 35–36 (on lines 13–17), on the basis of which Meritt revised part of his original text, *Hesperia* 10, 1941, pp. 328–330 (cf. *SEG* X, 108, with further suggestions by Wilhelm for lines 13, 22, 25–28); *IG* I³, 91. *a–h*: M. B. Walbank, *Athenian Proxenies*, pp. 336–349, no. 64, with photographs pls. 40–43. Text also in *ATL* II, D 23, with photographs pls. XIV, XV; photograph of *a+b+d+f*, J. N. Svoronos, *Das Athener Nationalmuseum*, 1908, pl. CCVI.

Minor references are collected in *SEG* XII, 33 (Meritt, *Hesperia* 21, 1952, p. 344, on the restoration of line 8); XIV, 40; XXI, 50 (H. B. Mattingly, *JHS* 81, 1961, p. 128); XXV, 37 (Mattingly, *Proceedings of the African Classical Associations* 7, 1964, p. 53 and *BCH* 92, 1968, pp. 478–479). See also A. Lambrechts, *De Atheense Proxeniedecreten*, pp. 78–79, 151, *et alibi*; Mattingly in *Phoros*, pp. 91, notes 8–10, and 92–93; D. W. Bradeen and M. F. McGregor, *Studies in Fifth-Century Attic Epigraphy*, 1973, pp. 128–129 (readings in lines 3, 5–6, 10, 14, 33–38, incorporated in the text below).

For fragment *h* (the surmounting relief, with line 1) see O. Walter, *Beschreibung der Reliefs im kleinen Akropolismuseum in Athen*, 1923, pp. 10–12, no. 11; R. Binneboessel, *Studien zu den attischen Urkundenreliefs des 5. und 4. Jahrhunderts*, 1932, pp. 4, no. 6, and 29; J. Frel and B. M. Kingsley, *GRBS* 11, 1970, p. 208, note 14. It appears with fragments *a+b+d+f* in Lambrechts, *op. cit.*, pl. I.

ca. a. 416/15 *a.* (*nisi potius a.* 422/1 *a.*)   ΣTOIX. 27 (lines 4 and following)

```
(h)                        [Θ] ε ο [ι].
(d+f+a+b)   Π ρ ο ξ ε [ν ι δ] ο  Π ρ ο ξ έ ν ο  τ ō  Κ ν ι δ [ί ο].
(g)              Ἀρχικλῆ[ς] Ἁλαιεὺς ἐγραμμάτευεν.
                 Ἔδ[ο]χσε[ν τε͂ι βολε͂ι καὶ το͂ι δέμ]οι· Ἀ
       5         χα[μ]αντ[ὶς ἐπρυτάνευ]ε, [Ἀρχικλ]ε͂ς [ἐ]
                 [γ]ραμμά[τευε, Ἀντικράτες] ἐ[πε]στά[τ]
                 [ε], Δεμόσ[τρατος εἶπε· ἐπειδὲ εὔ ποι]
                 εῖ Προχ[σενίδες hό τι ἂν δυνατὸς ε͂]
                 [ι] Ἀθεναΐ[ος καὶ νῦν καὶ ἐν το͂ι πρόσ]
      10         [θε]ν χρόγ[οι, ἐπαινέσαι τε αὐτο͂ι χα]
                 [ὶ ἀνα]γρ[άφσαι αὐτὸν ἐστέλει λιθί]
                 [νει πρόχσενον καὶ εὐεργέτεν Ἀθε]
                 [ναῖον καὶ καταθε͂ναι ἐμ πόλει ...]
                                lacuna
(e)              τὸν δὲ [ἀποκτείναντα ἐνέχεσθαι τ]
      15         οῖς αὐ[τοῖς hάπερ hυπὲρ Ἀθεναίον]
                 ἐφσέφ[ισται ἐάν τις ἀποθάνει βια]
                 ίοι θαν[άτοι· τὲν δὲ τιμορίαν κατὰ]
                 τὸ αὐτὸ [ε͂ναι ἐάν τις δέσει ε͂ ἀπάγε]
                 ι Προχσ[ενίδεν hέπερ Ἀθεναίον το]
      20         ῖς πολί[ταις ἐν το͂ν πόλεον προείρ]
                 εται· ἐὰ[ν δὲ ἀδικε͂ι τις ε͂ Ἀθεναίον]
(c)              ε͂ τὸ[ν σ]υ[μμάχον τὸν Ἀθεναίον κατὰ]
                 [τ]ούτον λ[αγχανέτο Ἀθένεσιν πρὸς]
                 [τ]ὸμ πολέ[μαρχον τὰς δίκας ἄνευ πρ]
      25         υτανείο[ν· ἄλλον δὲ ἀτελὲς ἔστο, τὰ]
                 δὲ τέλε τ[οῖς ἐγλογεῦσι τελέτο hὰ]
                 δεῖ Κνιδ[ίος ἐς τὸμ φόρον τελε͂ν χα]
                 θάπερ ho[ὶ ἄλλοι Κνίδιοι· καλέσαι]
                 δὲ αὐτὸν χ[αὶ ἐπὶ χσένια ἐς τὸ πρυτ]
      30         ανεῖον ἐ[ς αὔριον. ᵛ .... ¹⁰ .... εἶ]
                 πε· τὰ μὲν [ἄλλα καθάπερ .... ⁹ ....]
                 [.], hοι [δ]ὲ̣ τ[......... ²⁰ .........]
                 ΣΑΣΣΤΕΣ[......... ²⁰ .........]
                 [.]ΛΣΚ[.]ΕΤ[......... ²⁰ .........]
      35         ΕΤΟΝ[......... ²³ .........]
                 [...]Ν[...]Μ[......... ²⁰ .........]
                 [..]Ι[......... ²⁴ .........]
                 [..]Ι[......... ²⁴ .........]
                 [––––––––––––––––––––]
```

Lines 2 and 3 are in Ionic characters, the remainder of the text in Attic. The lettering is, as Walbank observes, "appropriate to a date between 430 and 415 B.C." There is some carelessness and inconsistency; strokes that should be parallel, as in epsilon, are not always so; the angles formed by the strokes of nu and sigma vary, while those formed by the "arms" of upsilon offer a notable idiosyncrasy. Walbank noted a similarity to, if not identity with, the hand of **19** and *IG* I³, 167 (I², 149) and claimed for the same craftsman also *IG* I³, 165 and 168 (I², 85 and 28). Cf. commentary on **19**. Meritt observed that the γραμματεύς in office and the phyle in prytany recur in *IG* I³, 92 (II², 27), and he restored from that text the name of the chairman (epistates): thus both decrees were passed on the same day. He also restored the proposer's name (line 7) as that of the Demostratos (*PA* 3611) on whose motion in the assembly the great expedition to Sicily was voted in 415 B.C. Meritt's dating of *ca. a.* 416/15 *a.* appeared also in *IG* I³, as complying with all these indications, and was originally accepted in the present context (which accounts for its place in the numerical order); but a new text dating to 422/1, unpublished as of 1989, was said to reveal that Archikles was γραμματεύς in that year, with the result that the present decree and *IG* I³, 92 are to be redated accordingly (information provided by D. M. Lewis to R. Develin, who quoted it, *Athenian Officials*, p. 429; cf. p. 191).

Mattingly argued from the presence of the ἐγλογεῖς (line 26) that the decree should be dated soon after 426/5, when this board was instituted (*SEG* XXI, 50), later refining his proposal to 422/1 (*SEG* XXV, 37) and subsequently to 425/4 (in *Phoros*, *loc. cit.*). On the ἐγλογεῖς see *ATL* III, p. 148, and R. Meiggs, *Athenian Empire*, p. 241. Frel and Kingsley gave a date of "*ca.* 412" without comment.

The above text is that of Meritt as revised in 1941, with the improved readings of Bradeen and McGregor; except for the inclusion of line 1 and a minor change in line 3, it is also that of *IG* I³, prepared by Meritt and McGregor. For lines 7–9 Mattingly (*BCH* 92, 1968, *loc. cit.*) proposed Δεμοσ[θένες εἶπε· ἐπειδὲ διατελ]|εῖ Προχ[σενίδες ὁ Κνίδιος εὖ ποιõ|ν] Ἀθεναῖ[ος κτλ.]. Meritt in 1952 suggested for lines 8–9 Προχ[σενίδες ho Κνίδιος ἀεὶ τὸ|ς] κτλ. The ethnic may however be omitted in the body of the decree if it occurs in the heading, even though the latter is not technically part of the decree. Cf. **21**.

Walbank has seen evidence for letters partly or wholly surviving that make no real difference to the substance of the text but deserve to be shown separately. His variants are as follows: Line 2. Προξε[νί]δο. Line 4. ἔδοχσεν [τ]ε̄ι βολε̄ι χα[ὶ] τõι δέμοι, Ἀ. Line 7. ε, Δεμοσ[........²¹..........]. Line 8. No restoration after Προχσ[ενίδες. Line 10 *init.* [θ]ε̣ν. After line 13 he gives an undecipherable line 14, a line 15 reading [.....¹².....]ε̣ρ [.....¹³......], and four more undecipherable lines (16–19), resuming on fragment *e* (*g* in his designation) after the *lacuna* with line 20 rather than the 14 of the text given above. His subsequent line numeration is therefore six in advance of other versions. Lines 23–24. The positions of Ἀθένεσιν and τὰς δίκας are reversed. Walbank's version of lines 32 to the end differs markedly from that of Bradeen and McGregor:

$$
\begin{array}{ll}
& \varsigma \cdot \ hοι\ δὲ\ τ[........^{20}........] \\
& σας\ στε̣σ[........^{20}........] \\
& θας\ χαὶ\ τ[........^{20}........] \\
35 & ντον[........^{20}........\ προ] \\
& χσενο[.]\ δ[ὲ........^{19}........] \\
& [.]h[..........^{25}..........] \\
& [.]ι[..........^{25}..........]
\end{array}
$$

Line 3. For the citation of the name of the γραμματεύς separately above the prescript, cf. **4** and A. S. Henry, *Prescripts*, p. 8. Line 20. ἐν τὸν πόλεον. Cf. Meisterhans-Schwyzer, *Grammatik*³, pp. 214–215, §18, with notes 1720–1722. Lines 26–30. For the formula of invitation to public entertainment in the Prytaneion, see W. A. McDonald, *AJA* 59, 1955, pp. 151–155 and Lambrechts, *De Atheense Proxeniedecreten*, pp. 101–103. The details were later more fully explored by M. J. Osborne (*ZPE* 41, 1981, pp. 153–170; on this text esp. p. 157 with note 10) and by Henry (*Antichthon* 15, 1981, pp. 100–110 and *Chiron* 13, 1983, pp. 61–67; on this text esp. pp. 63 and 66). See also Walbank, *Athenian Proxenies*, pp. 5 and 26, note 13.

The character of Proxenides' services to Athens and the occasion for the grant of the honors and privileges here recorded remain unknown. The former must have been substantial, for the latter, as expressed on this imposing monument, were considerable. The *probouleuma* was amended in the assembly at least twice, for the remains of lines 31–32 preclude the restoration τε̄ι βολε̄ι in the amendment formula.

For further material relevant to this text see *SEG* XXXIX, 324.

AN– – – –S AND HIS SONS HONORED

21. A fragment of a stele of Pentelic marble (I 1674), preserving the smooth-picked left side and original rough-picked back of the monument as well as the top of the inscribed text but otherwise broken; discovered on March 25, 1934, in a wall of a Late Roman building east of the Tholos (H 11). The blank space above the inscription may well have carried painted decoration. Since the decree appears to give no room for the ethnic of the honorand, which is a customary feature in such cases (cf. A. S. Henry, *Honours*, p. 120), there may have been an upper molding bearing a heading with this information, as in **20**; cf. (e.g.) *IG* I³, 92. But the supposition is not inevitable: cf. **30** and B. D. Meritt, *Hesperia* 21, 1952, p. 343.

H. 0.245 m.; W. 0.23 m.; Th. 0.073 m.
LH. 0.008–0.009 m.
Στοιχ. (square) 0.0119 m.

Ed. B. D. Meritt, *Hesperia* 5, 1936, pp. 381–382, no. 5, with photograph (cf. *SEG* X, 111, incorporating a suggestion for lines 2–3 by A. Wilhelm, *Attische Urkunden* IV [= *SbAkadWien* 217, 5], 1939, p. 39); *IG* I³, 95; M. B. Walbank, *Athenian Proxenies*, pp. 367–370, no. 69, with photograph pl. 46:b. See also A. Lambrechts, *De Atheense Proxeniedecreten*, pp. 27, 56, 70, 151; A. S. Henry, *Vindex Humanitatis: Essays in Honour of John Huntly Bishop*, 1980, pp. 26–27, no. 5, with citation of lines 5–10 (*SEG* XXX, 14). Photograph also in Meritt, *Inscriptions from the Athenian Agora* (A.P.B. 10, 1966), no. 15.

a. 415/14 *a.*   ΣTOIX. 23

vacat

["Ε]δοξεν τῆι βολῆι καὶ [τῶι δήμ]

ωι· 'Αντιοχὶς ἐπρυτάν[ευε, . . .]

οφράδης ἐγραμμάτευ[ε, ..⁵..]

άδης ἐπεστάτε, Χαρία[ς ἦρχε, Κ]

5   αλλισθένης εἶπε· 'Αν/[..⁶...]

ν καὶ τὸς παῖδας, ἐπε[ιδὴ εὖ πο]

[ι]εῖ τὴν πόλιν καὶ 'Αθ[ηναῖος, ἀ]

γαγράψαι πρόξενον [καὶ εὐερ]

[γ]έτην 'Αθηναίων ἐν [στήληι λι]

10 [θί]νηι τε[λ]ε[σ]ι[ν το]ῖ[ς ...⁷....]

[------------------]

The lettering is in Ionic characters, plain and with some awkwardnesses (beta, sigma) as well as inconsistent treatment of the same letter (alpha, nu); the extended lower stroke of kappa is distinctive. The use of Ionic may well indicate that the honorand was an Ionian (Meritt gave reasons for suggesting that he may have been an Ephesian) and that he bore the cost of the inscription (line 10). The date is fixed by the reference to the archon in line 4. The restorations are those of Meritt, adopted also in *IG* I³.

Lines 2–3. Κλε]οφράδης Wilhelm, *IG* I³: the restoration is highly likely. Line 5. 'Αν/[--- Meritt; 'Ανα[ξι(?)--- *IG* I³; 'Ανδ[--- Walbank. Line 10. [θί]νηι τε[λεσ]ι[ν το]ῖ[ς ἑαυτō ..] Meritt, *IG* I³; [θ]ίνηι τέλεσιν [το]ῖ[ς ἑαυτō ..] Walbank. Henry (*loc. cit.*) regards the use of the reflexive as grammatically unjustified and prefers to restore (*exempli gratia*) the name of the honorand in the genitive case. Walbank has discerned evidence of other extra letters on the right of the fragment (τ[ῶι in line 1, σ[τήληι in line 9). For the singular verb and accusatives (lines 6–9) with plural reference cf. M. J. Osborne, *BSA* 67, 1972, p. 156, note 105.

On the historical circumstances cf. A. G. Woodhead, *Hesperia* 17, 1948, p. 57. The γραμματεύς and proposer are otherwise unknown, unless (as Walbank suggested) the latter is possibly to be identified with *PA* 8088; but the name is not uncommon. Cf. R. Develin, *Athenian Officials*, p. 151.

FRAGMENT OF AN HONORARY DECREE

22. Two nonjoining fragments of a stele of Pentelic marble, the larger of which (I 6923, now fragment *a*) is broken all around save on the right, where the right side seems to be preserved even though the edge of the inscribed face has been worn at its corner; that the right side is original has however been doubted by D. M. Lewis *apud IG* I³, 122. This fragment was discovered on June 12, 1959, in a late fill in the Eleusinion behind the western part of the South Stoa (T 21). The smaller fragment (E.M. 12577, now fragment *b*: *non vidimus*) was identified by Lewis and is recorded as broken on all sides; its provenance is not stated.

a: H. 0.115 m.; W. 0.085 m.; Th. 0.045 m.

b: H. 0.095 m.; W. 0.085 m.; Th. 0.06 m.

LH. (lines 1–11) variable between 0.007 and 0.009 m.; (lines 12–13) 0.016–0.023 m.
Στοιχ. (lines 1–11) Hor. 0.0085 m.; Vert. *ca.* 0.015 m.

Ed. *a*: B. D. Meritt, *Hesperia* 32, 1963, p. 39, no. 38, with photograph pl. 2 (cf. *SEG* XXI, 57); M. B. Walbank, *Athenian Proxenies*, pp. 373–375, no. 71, with photograph pl. 47; Meritt's text reprinted by H. B. Mattingly in *Ancient Society and Institutions: Studies Presented to Victor Ehrenberg on His 75th Birthday*, 1966, pp. 204–205. *a*+*b*: *IG* I³, 122.

a. 413–405 *a.*   ΣTOIX. 25 (lines 1–11)

(a)
```
[------------------]
[........16........]ον· καὶ ḥ[όπο]
[ς ἂν μὲ ἀδικõνται, ἐπι]μέλεσθαι
[αὐτὸν τέν τε βουλὲν] τὲν 'Αθεναί
[ον καὶ τὸς στρατεγὸς] τὸς ἀεὶ στ
```
5
```
[ρατεγõντας καὶ τὸς ἄ]ρχοντας τ
[ὸς .......14...... ἐν] 'Ιονίαι· τ
[ὸ δὲ φσέφισμα τόδε ἀνα]γράφσαι
[τὸν γραμματέα τẽς βου]λẽς ἐγ [στ]
[έλει λιθίνει ........14......]
```
                        lacuna
10
```
[....10....] ιΑ ι[.....12.....]
```
(b)
```
[..6...] δ'ἐς τὲν ḥα[ύριον ἐμέραν].
[-------]Ο [ΜΕṬ[-------] ]
[[-------]ΥΟΡ[---------] ]
[----------------------]
```

Fragment *a* is a clumsy piece of work, but its style is so distinctive that the association with it of fragment *b* could be confidently made. The same craftsman worked on *IG* I³, 101 (I², 108), lines 48–64, of 410/09 B.C., and Walbank attributed to him *IG* I³, 475 (I², 372), the Erechtheion building accounts of 409/8. The vertical stoichoi are not well aligned, and the letters are crowded and inconsistently formed: sigma is tall and awkward, rather as in **21**.

The text of fragment *a* is that of Meritt, except as follows: Line 1. ḥọ[. .] Walbank, which would make more probable the restoration shown above for lines 1–3, suggested in *IG* I³, *in comm.*; καὶ ι[. . .] Meritt, *IG* I³ (*in textu*). Lines 2–3. [......14...... ἐπι]μέλεσθαι | [δὲ αὐτõ τέν τε βολὲν] Meritt, Walbank, *IG* I³ (*in textu*); but the evident inclusion of upsilon in βου]λẽς in line 8 suggests its inclusion also in line 3. Walbank, who also made this observation, proposed for line 3 [δὲ αὐτὸν τὲν βουλέν]. On the order within the phraseology cf. Henry, *Honours*, pp. 173 and 175. Line 6. So also *IG* I³; τ[ὸς ἐκ τõν πόλεον τõν ἐν] 'Ιονίαι Meritt, Walbank (the latter reading ἐ]γ). Line 8. βουλ]ẽς ἐ[ν στ] Meritt; βου]λẽς ἐγ ọṭ Walbank; βου]λẽς ἐ[ν στ] *IG* I³.

In fragment *b*, shown here as in *IG* I³, the *rasura* may or may not extend beyond the letters shown, which do not certainly belong to the original enactment. The line division in lines 10–11 is uncertain and may invalidate the restoration.

Meritt's publication gave to the text a general date "*s.* V *a.*". Mattingly (*loc. cit.*) envisaged a date of 415–410 on the basis of the spelling ἀεί (line 4) and βουλῆς (line 8), to match the archons in the Ionian cities (line 5–6); on these officials see R. Meiggs, *Athenian Empire*, pp. 213–215, and **3**, commentary on lines 6–7. The specific reference to Ionia seems to make the period of the Ionian War more likely (cf. A. G. Woodhead, *Hesperia* 17, 1948, p. 57), and the floruit of the mason appears to give a similar indication. The date shown here is also that of *IG* I³ (420–405 Walbank). The honorands (or honorand) will in all probability have been Ionian.

FRAGMENT OF AN HONORARY DECREE

23. A fragment of a stele of Pentelic marble (I 5296), broken all around save that the back is probably original, discovered on March 8, 1938, in a Byzantine context west of the Panathenaic Way and northwest of the Eleusinion (S 18).

H. 0.156 m.; W. 0.12 m. (inscribed face, 0.07 m.); Th. 0.058 m.
LH. 0.01 m.
Στοιχ. (square) 0.014 m.

Ed. B. D. Meritt, *Hesperia* 14, 1945, pp. 132–133, no. 17, with photograph (see also *SEG* X, 140); M. B. Walbank, *Athenian Proxenies*, pp. 418–421, no. 84, with photograph pl. 56; *IG* I³, 121. Lines 1–3 considered by D. M. Lewis, *BSA* 49, 1954, p. 32. The decree listed by A. Lambrechts, *De Atheense Proxeniedecreten*, p. 151.

a. 410–405 *a.* ΣΤΟΙΧ. 28 (?)

["Εδοχσεν τε̑ι βολε̑ι καὶ το̑ι δέμοι· . .]
[— — — — ἐπρυτάνευε, — —]ΑΙΙ[. .⁶. . .]
[— — — ἐγραμμάτευε, — — — 'Α]ναχα[ιεὺς ἐ]
[πεστάτε, . . .⁸. . . . εἶπ]ε· 'Αρχι[. .⁵. .]
5 [. . .⁷. . . ἀναγράφσαι πρ]όχ[σ]εν[ον κα]
[ὶ εὐεργέτεν 'Αθεναῖον ἐ]πειδ[ὲ περὶ]
[τὲν πόλιν τὲν 'Αθεναῖον ἐ]στὶ[ν ἀνὲρ]
[ἀγαθὸς καὶ πρόθυμος κατ]ὰ τὸ [δυνατ]
[ὸν . . . . .¹⁹. . . . .]Ρ[. .⁶. . .]
10 [— — — — — — — — — — — — — — — — — — —]

The lettering is rather thin and fine. Walbank suggested that the forms of the letters are close to those of **18** and of *IG* I³, 99 (I², 109), 115 (I², 123), and 176, all attributable to the later stages of the Peloponnesian War. The use of Attic lettering makes a date beyond 406/5 unlikely, but the introduction of a demotic into the preamble argues for as late a dating as may be acceptable. Cf. A. S. Henry, *Prescripts*, pp. 11–12.

Meritt's tentative establishment of a line of 28 letters, comparing *IG* I³, 110 (I², 118) of 408/7 B.C. for the restorations, causes difficulty if the demotic in line 3 is that of the chairman (epistates). Lewis (*loc. cit.*) pointed out that the phyle to be restored in lines 1–2 would in consequence be Hippothontis and that Meritt's suggestion for the name of the secretary, Πάτ]αιχ[ος, could not be accommodated. He himself proposed Αἰγ[έας as the secretary's name, and the version of the end of line 2 in *IG* I³ is Αἰγ[. .⁶. . .]. The tenuous remains do indeed suggest N as preferable to K at the crucial point, but Walbank's text reads [— — —]αιχ[. .⁶. . .] without hesitation, and the difficulty remains. His resolution of it is achieved only by the introduction of the name Καῖχος, otherwise unattested in Attic prosopography, and by the abandonment of the expressed rough breathing, thus ῾Ιπ|ποθοντὶς ἐπρυτάνευε, Κ]αῖχ[ος *demoticum* ἐγραμμάτευε κτλ. This too is unsatisfactory, and the reading in line 2 cannot be regarded as assured. It seems preferable in consequence to leave the text with the minimum of restoration: doubt concerning the spelling of the phyle name precludes its insertion even though its identity may be regarded as certain (on the assumption that lines 3–4 have been correctly interpreted).

The text is mainly that of Meritt, followed also in *IG* I³. Line 1. το̑ι δ[έμοι Walbank. Line 4. [. . . . . . . .¹⁸. . . . .]ε· Walbank, who sees ἔρχ]ε also as a possibility; εἶπε] Meritt, *IG* I³. Line 5. [. . . .¹⁰. . . . . γράφσαι is also possible. Line 9. [ὸν εὖ ποε̑ν . . . . .¹³. . . . . .]ρ[. .⁶. . .] Meritt, *IG* I³; [ὸν . . . . .¹⁹. . . . .] βο[λε . . .] Walbank, who suggested that these lines might contain the relics of a clause requiring the Athenian officials to give special protection to the honorand, *viz.*

[ὸν εὖ ποε̑ν τὲν πόλιν· τὲν δὲ] βο[λὲν κα]
10 [ὶ τὸς πρυτάνες καὶ τὸς στρατεγὸς ἐ]
[πιμέλεσθαι αὐτο̑ ὅπος ἂν μὲ ἀδικε̑τ]
[αι κτλ.]

The honors voted to Archi— — — may fit into the context mentioned in the commentaries to **21** and **22**, but beyond that nothing can be said as to the content or historical reference of the fragment. The details of the officers and proposer (lines 2–4) are briefly noted by R. Develin (*Athenian Officials*, p. 192).

FRAGMENT OF A REGULATION

24 (Pl. 3). A fragment of a stele of Pentelic marble (I 4442), broken all around save at the (smooth-dressed) back, discovered on January 23, 1937, in a modern house wall south of the Eleusinion (T 22). The fragment has been reworked on its upper surface in more modern times, with a cutting on the left side. The inscribed face is very battered.

H. 0.108 m.; W. 0.138 m.; Th. 0.093 m.
LH. 0.008 m.
Στοιχ. Hor. 0.012 m.; Vert. 0.013 m.

Ed. B. D. Meritt, *Hesperia* 14, 1945, pp. 128–129, no. 15, with photograph of the squeeze (cf. *SEG* X, 123); *IG* I³, 135.

ca. a. 430–405 *a.* ΣΤΟΙΧ.

```
[------------------------------------------]
[.....12.....κέρ]υχα τὰ τ[ε]τα[γμένα -------]
[......13.......εὐ]θύνεσθαι.        vacat
                    vacat
[γνόμε τὸν χσυγγ]ραφέον· τõι ℎερ[----------]
[.......14........]τος τὸς ἄρχο[ντας --------]
5   [.......12.......ελ]ευθέροις ℎι[-------------]
[......16..........]ον πραττε[-------------]
[......16..........]τατα[--------------------]
[------------------------------------------]
```

The lettering is in the developed Attic style of the later 5th century, without distinctive feature. The above text is in general that of Meritt's *editio princeps*.

Line 1. τ[ετ]α[γμένα – – –] Meritt; τετα[γμένα – – –] *IG* I³. Line 3. ℎεο[θινõι (?) – – –] *IG* I³. Line 5. [– – – ἐλ]ευθέροις Meritt; [– – – ελ]ευθέροις *IG* I³, where ἀπελ]ευθέροις is suggested *in comm.* Line 6. πράττε[ν – – –] *IG* I³.

Meritt restored line 3 on the basis of *IG* I³, 99 (I², 109; *ATL* II, D 9), line 8. The commissioners might be supposed to be concerned with the codification of sacral law, and in *SEG* X the fragment was entitled "lex sacra". *IG* I³, *in comm.*, makes the suggestion that a procession of some kind is under consideration. But the text was not included by F. Sokolowski in his volumes, *Lois sacrées des cités grecques* and its *Supplément*, and all that may be derived from it (especially lines 1–2 and 4) concerns procedure which may be secular no less than sacred. Nor are the syngrapheis attested for 410/09 the sole candidates for consideration. There is evidence for various boards so designated at other times within the general period to which this text may be assigned: cf. A. S. Henry, *Prescripts*, p. 4, note 12. A wider dating span, adopted also in *IG* I³, is therefore preferred to the more precise "*ca.* 410 B.C.(?)" of the *editio princeps* and *SEG* X.

FRAGMENT OF A DECREE

25. A fragment of a stele of bluish white marble (I 1611) acknowledged as "very micaceous", broken on all sides, discovered on March 16, 1934, in a marble pile in the southeast part of the Market Square (L–M 13–14).

H. 0.177 m.; W. 0.14 m.; Th. 0.085 m.

LH. 0.01–0.011 m.

Στοιχ. Hor. 0.014 m.; Vert. 0.0155 m.

Ed. B. D. Meritt, *Hesperia* 14, 1945, p. 128, no. 14, with photograph (cf. *SEG* X, 120); M. B. Walbank, *Athenian Proxenies*, pp. 393–395, no. 76, with photograph pl. 50:a; *IG* I³, 225.

ca. a. 420–405 *a.* ΣΤΟΙΧ.

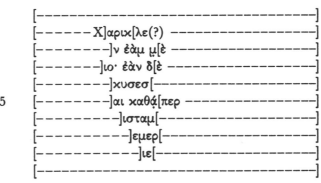

```
[------------------------------------------]
[------X]αριϰ[λε(?) ----------------------]
[--------]ν ἐὰμ μ̣[ὲ -----------------------]
[-------]ιο· ἐὰν δ[ὲ ----------------------]
[-------]ϰυσεσ[---------------------------]
5   [-------]αι ϰαθά[περ --------------------]
[--------]ισταμ[------------------------]
[---------]εμερ[-----------------------]
[----------]ιε[------------------------]
[------------------------------------------]
```

The lettering is in the developed Attic style of the later 5th century. The diameter of the circular letters is less than the height of the remaining letters; the shape of nu is inconsistent in the two examples extant; upsilon occurs only once, but its misplaced upright is noteworthy. Walbank suggested that the hand is close to that of *IG* I³, 100 (*ATL* II, A 13), the assessment of *phoros* of 410/09 B.C., and that the type of marble indicates a date later than *ca.* 420.

Line 1. [– – –]αριϰ[– – –] Meritt, *IG* I³; [– – – X]αριϰ[λε̃ς – – –] A. E. Raubitschek *apud SEG* X. Line 3. [– – –]το Meritt, Walbank; [– – –]ΙΟ *IG* I³. Line 4. The reading is clear, but the interpretation of it has eluded scholars. "Nec ὅρ]ϰυς nec ἐλ]ϰύσες placet", *IG* I³; Walbank thought in terms of "a name, apparently Asiatic". Line 5. [– – ἔν]αι Walbank. Line 6. [– – ℎ]ισταμ[εν – –] Meritt; [– – –]ισταμ[– – –] *IG* I³, where [– – – το]ῖς ταμ[ίαις – –] is also suggested *in comm.;* [−−−]ις· τὰ μὲν [−−−] Walbank. Line 7. ἐμερō̄[ν −−−] Walbank; [−−− h]εμερ[−−−] Meritt; [−−−] ἐμερ[−−−] *IG* I³. Line 9. Evidence of a tau, presumably underneath the iota of line 8, has been discerned by Walbank. It remains an open question whether or not the rough breathing was expressed.

That this fragment forms part of a decree is universally agreed, but its nature cannot be determined. Meritt had "no good suggestion for its restoration," and refrained "from giving several dubious ones." Walbank suggested that it was a proxeny decree for two honorands, probably from Asia Minor, and was prepared to hazard a restoration of lines 3–6 which provides for a stoichedon line of 28 letters: ἐὰν δ[ὲ βιαίοι θανάτοι | ἀποθάνει . .]χυσες [ἒ . . . ., τὲν ‖ τιμορίαν ἔν]αι καθά[περ ἐὰν ἀποθάν|ει ’Αθεναῖον τ]ις· τὰ μ[ὲν κτλ.].

FRAGMENT OF A DECREE

26 (Pl. 3). A fragment of a stele of Pentelic marble (I 207), broken on all sides, discovered on April 6, 1932, in a Byzantine context at the southwest corner of the Market Square (G 14).

H. 0.20 m.; W. 0.11 m.; Th. 0.12 m.
LH. *ca.* 0.01 m.
Στοιχ. Hor. 0.0113 m.; Vert. 0.0117 m.

Ed. B. D. Meritt, *Hesperia* 3, 1934, p. 1, no. 1, with drawing (cf. *SEG* X, 145a [a brief mention, without text]); *IG* I³, 202.

a. 445–405 *a.*   ΣΤΟΙΧ.

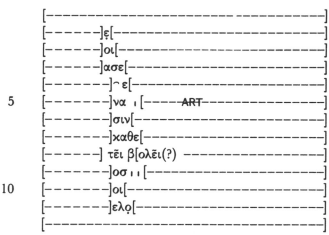

Line 9. [−−−]ος χε[−−−] *IG* I³. Line 11. [−−−]ελ[−−−] *IG* I³. The writing is clear and developed, in good style, but without distinguishing feature save in epsilon, which gives the impression, particularly in lines 4 and 8, of dominating its neighbors. Despite the concentration of epigraphical attention on Attic 5th-century texts, as well as the fact that so many Agora fragments have been matched together or with inscriptions already known, this piece, discovered early in the work of excavation, remains isolated. That it forms part of a decree has been generally presumed, probably from line 8 as restored, but cannot be regarded as certain.

FRAGMENT OF THE END OF A DECREE

27. A small fragment of a stele of Pentelic marble (I 4816), broken on all sides, discovered on May 7, 1937, in a late road packing west of Klepsydra (S–T 27).

H. 0.057 m.; W. 0.062 m.; Th. 0.036 m.
LH. 0.009 m.

Ed. D. M. Lewis, *Hesperia* 44, 1975, pp. 380–381, no. 3, with photograph pl. 85; *IG* I³, 196.

ca. a. 430–405 *a.*

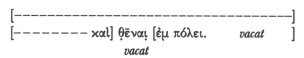

vacat

As in **28**, the lettering suggests a general reference to the later part of the 5th century. The diameter of the circular letter is markedly smaller than the full height of the others: the line of break betrays the final iota. θε̄ναι Lewis; θε̄ναι *IG* I³.

Since the fragment appears to show the end of the document, Lewis' restoration of the formula for permanent display of the stele on the Akropolis is reasonable.

FRAGMENT OF A DECREE

28. A small fragment of a stele of Pentelic marble (I 4813), broken on all sides, discovered on May 7, 1937, in a late context below Klepsydra (S–T 27).

H. *ca.* 0.06 m.; W. *ca.* 0.145 m.; Th. 0.006 m.
LH. 0.009 m.
Στοιχ. (square) 0.012 m.
Ed. D. M. Lewis, *Hesperia* 44, 1975, p. 380, no. 2, with photograph pl. 85; *IG* I³, 210.

ca. a. 430–405 *a.*ΣΤΟΙΧ.

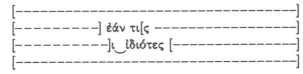

The lettering is not distinctive; on the basis of it, as in **27**, the date must be expressed in general terms. The diameter of omicron is less than the full height of the other letters.

The restoration of an "entrenchment clause" here, for which see **3**, line 10 and note, is tempting but proves beyond the possibility of accommodation to the requirements of the surviving evidence, meager though that is. In the *editio princeps* Lewis favored something on the lines of *IG* I³, 102 (I², 110), lines 44–47; in *IG* I³ this suggestion is incorporated into the definitive text (with a stoichedon line of 40 letters) as

[καὶ] ἐὰν τί[ς τι ἄλλο εἰδέι περὶ τούτον· ἀποφαινέτο]
[δὲ κα]ὶ ἰδιότες [ἐάν τις βόλεται ....¹⁶........].

D. M. Lewis (*Hesperia* 44, 1975, pp. 394–395, nos. 23–25, with photographs pl. 88) published three small fragments (I 6743, I 6999, and I 5964), all of them broken on all sides and all four or five lines in length and no more than two or three letters in width. Lewis suggested that they might be parts of decrees, and all belong to the 5th century B.C., but there is no real indication of their character, and one (I 6743) has appeared in the context of *IG* I³, 416 as a likely *traditio*. It has not seemed worthwhile to devote space to them here.

Also omitted from extended treatment is the small fragment I 3617 (Lewis, *op. cit.*, pp. 392–393, no. 20, with [inverted] photograph pl. 88; *IG* I³, 26) of *ca.* 450 B.C., which Lewis regarded as possibly part of a preamble to a decree. It is broken all around, and the reading is no more than

[----------]
[---]ΡΧ[---]
[---]ϟΥ[----]
vacat

APPENDIX: MATERIAL DISCOVERED SINCE 1967

28A. Epikerdes of Kyrene honored, *a.* 405/4 *a.* The discovery of the fragment I 7065 added a third to the two existing fragments published as *IG* II², 174. It was discovered on September 19, 1969, built into the northern retaining wall of the cutting for the Athens–Piraeus railway on the north side of the Agora (J 5), and preserves the right side and original rough-picked back of the stele.

For the text see the *editio princeps* by B. D. Meritt, *Hesperia* 39, 1970, pp. 111–114, with photographs of all three fragments pl. 31; *IG* I³, 125 (full *apparatus criticus* and text less fully restored). See also M. B. Walbank, *Athenian Proxenies*, p. 488. For further discussion see *SEG* XXXIII, 17, XXXIX, 324 (on the relief sculpture), XLI, 8.

The new fragment (*c*) preserves the name of the archon, Alexias, and resolves the controversy concerning the date of the text. See *IG* II², 174, *in comm.*; *SEG* XXIV, 13. Even so, the Ionic lettering shows the first signs of the enlargement into a wedge shape of the "free ends" of strokes, and in this particular anticipates a style favored from the middle of the 4th century onward.

28B. A fragment of a decree showing the remains of the first three lines of a prescript (I 7382), discovered on April 27, 1972, in a modern fill (T 14). Edited by M. B. Walbank, *Hesperia* 51, 1982, pp. 41–42, no. 1, with photograph pl. 19. Walbank suggests that the decree may be an honorary decree and that the date is near to the end of the 5th century if the lettering is Attic rather than Ionic. Cf. *SEG* XXXII, 16.

SECTION 2

FROM ONE RESTORATION OF DEMOCRACY TO ANOTHER
403/2–307/6 B.C.
(29–106)

SECTION 2

FROM ONE RESTORATION OF DEMOCRACY TO ANOTHER

403/2–307/6 B.C.: **29–106**

The eighty-seven texts of this section (a number which includes **106A–106J** more briefly treated in the appendix) roughly triple the 5th-century survivals dealt with in Section 1. This owes something, but perhaps less than may be thought, to that general archaeological "law" relating to a long-inhabited site, that later material tends to drive out the earlier, a law perhaps more influential in the context of Sections 3 and 4. Although the 5th century is properly regarded as the high-water mark of democratic Athens, it was not until the 4th century that administrative procedures were really matured and chancery practice fully developed.

This may be seen not only in a tendency to commit more business of state to stone-cut record, even at a time when the Athenian role on the Hellenic stage was radically different from what it had once been, and when, ultimately, Macedonian domination of the Greek world completely transformed that stage and Athens' place on it. It is observable also, more narrowly, in the detail of the prescripts of Athenian decrees: the preoccupation with careful detail, for example, or the introduction of the *tria nomina* for all but the eponymous archon, or the record of proedroi and symproedroi. It is evident in the crystalization of formulas for grants of citizenship or of stephanoi or of other honors, in the long-lasting expression of reference of a given piece of business between boule and demos, in the appearance of the "hortatory intention" and of stock phraseology for the merits of the various honorands, and finally in the assignment of responsibility for expenditure and the amount to be expended (on stelai and on stephanoi).

As in the 5th century, the emphasis is very largely upon what may be generally called "foreign affairs". Ten texts among these Agora decrees involve the more parochial units of deme, phratry, or genos and may be set on one side. Of the remaining seventy-seven, twenty-three are fragments the reference of which cannot be determined. Among the other fifty-four, the three (perhaps four) treaties, four or five "symbolai" agreements, six proxeny decrees, and five decrees conferring citizenship manifestly involve external relations; and five more texts (**41, 43, 48, 51, 72**) may be loosely defined as having an extraterritorial reference. No less than twenty-four texts are, or appear to be, decrees conferring honors of some kind, insufficiently preserved for sure attribution; but of these, twelve clearly concern noncitizens, and only five reward citizens of Athens itself.

One important feature of Athenian administration in the 4th century was a new procedure for *nomothesia*. The Agora excavations have been fortunate in turning up three highly significant texts (**73, 75, 106C**) to document this. Of no less interest has been the new contribution to knowledge concerning the city's regulation of the Eleusinian Mysteries (**56, 57**); and helpful light on intercity relations has been shed by the discovery of the *symbolai* documents already referred to.

It is of interest to note the distribution of this material through the period, where this can be safely established. Twenty-six decrees clearly belong to the years between the battle of Chaironeia in 338 and the beginning of the regime of Demetrios of Phaleron in 317; yet no more than ten are to be attributed to the important period between 350 and 338, when the literary sources reveal that Athenian politics and policies were being conducted at a high level of intensity and of significance for the future of the city and for "free" Hellas as a whole. During the first half of the century the distribution of the twenty-one reliably dated decrees is more even, although the emphasis is on the 375–350 period.

Finally, that nineteen of the documents discovered were already represented by fragments previously known and published in *IG* II² suggests that the number of decrees available for discovery, so to speak, was and is limited. Much that is importantly new has been brought to light, and with continuing excavation this may be expected to happen in the future: but when some new discovery was made during past work there was at least one chance in four or five that it would relate to evidence already in the epigraphical record. Moreover, among the *nova* there is also a one-in-four probability that it will be in so fragmentary a state that it can tell us little or nothing of real substance. Such, at any rate for the 4th century, seems to have been the Agora's message.

A FRAGMENT OF A DECREE AND A SET OF REGULATIONS

29. A fragment of a stele of Pentelic marble (I 6755), with the left side preserved but otherwise broken all around, discovered on June 29, 1956, among stones removed from the walls of modern houses near the southeast corner of the Market Square (N–O 15).

H. 0.135 m.; W. 0.088 m.; Th. 0.047 m.
LH. 0.008 m.
Στοιχ. (square) 0.014 m.

Ed. B. D. Meritt, *Hesperia* 32, 1963, p. 39, no. 39, with photograph pl. 10. See also *SEG* XXI, 219.

s. V/IV*a*.   ΣΤΟΙΧ. 30

```
        [————————————————————]
        [. . . . . . . . . .²². . . . . . . . . . προς την β]
        [ο]υλην κ[αι τον δημον τον Ἀθηναιων· ανα]
        γραψα[ι δε τον γραμματεα της βουλης τ]
        οδε το [ψηφισμα εν στηλη λιθινηι και]
        τας συγ[γραφας . . . . . . . . .¹⁸. . . . . . . .]
   5    εσθαι ε[. . . . . . . . . . .²⁴. . . . . . . . . . .]
        εργαζε[. . . . . . . . . . .²⁴. . . . . . . . . .]
        οφειλε[. . . . . . . . . . .²⁴. . . . . . . . . .]
        [.]ηναια[. . . . . . . . . . .²³. . . . . . . . .]
        [————————————————————]
```

The lettering is plain, regular, and straightforward in style. It could be accommodated anywhere within the last ten years of the 5th century or the first quarter of the 4th. Upsilon is present in the word βουλή (cf. **22**). The estimated length of line depends on the formulaic phraseology of lines 1–3.

Meritt noted in the συγγραφαί of line 4 (if correctly restored) and in the part of the verb ἐργάζεσθαι in line 6 points of contact with *IG* I³, 84 (I², 94; *SEG* XIX, 18, XXV, 36, XXXVI, 15), of 418/17 B.C., in which regulations are laid down for the leasing of cultivable land in the precinct of Kodros, Neleus, and Basile. This text may be part of a document of similar character.

Lines 4–5. τὰς συγ[γραφὰς τὰς γεγενημένας(?) καὶ θ]||έσθαι Meritt. Line 6. ἐργάζε[σθαι – – –] Meritt. Line 8. [.]ιναι / [– – – – –] Meritt. Possibly, in case of noncompliance with the regulations, a fine was prescribed as due to the treasury of Athena (e.g., εἰ δὲ μή], | ὀφειλέ[τω πεντακοσίας δραχμὰς τῆι Ἀ|θ]ηναία[ι). The hasta of the supposed iota before the nu in the last surviving line stands well to the right in its stoichos, and a break obscures possible traces of the cross-stroke of the eta which its position suggests. For the spelling Ἀθηναία (replaced in the 4th century by Ἀθηνᾶ) see L. Threatte, *Grammar*, pp. 272–274.

32 (*q.v.*) may provide a small fragment of the top of this stele; at least it appears to be the work of the same craftsman. M. B. Walbank has identified him as the man who worked also on *IG* II², 43, 105, and 144 (**47**). If this identification is to be accepted, the date of this present fragment must be lowered by two or three decades. But it may be a matter of the vernacular of an epigraphical generation rather than of the absolute identity of the hand of a single person.

A DECREE IN PRAISE OF AN EMBASSY

30. Three nonjoining fragments of a stele of Pentelic marble, of which one (I 4639; here fragment *b*) was discovered in the excavations of the Agora on March 19, 1937, at the north foot of the Areopagos (K 17), in a Byzantine context. Fragment *a*, now in the Epigraphical Museum (E.M. 6883), has long been known; fragment *c*, discovered on the Akropolis (Akr. 7018), remains unpublished at the time of writing and is not included here. The left side of the monument is preserved on fragment *a*, with the first letter of each line abraded; fragment *b* forms part of the right side.

a: H. 0.10 m.; W. 0.095 m.; Th. 0.065 m.

b: H. 0.07 m.; W. 0.058 m.; Th. 0.032 m.

LH. 0.007–0.008 m.

Στοιχ. Hor. 0.014 m.; Vert. 0.0135 m.

Ed. *a* only: *IG* II², 11, with earlier bibliography. *a* + *b*, with reference also to *c*: M. B. Walbank, *Hesperia* 58, 1989, pp. 71–72, no. 1, with photograph of *b* pl. 17. For a photograph of *c*, see Ἔργον 1960, p. 12, pl. 13. See also *SEG* XXXIX, 62.

a. 400/399 a.   ΣΤΟΙΧ. 26 (lines 4 and following)

           (a)   [³⁻⁴.]μοτ[. . . . . . . *ca.* 20–21 . . . .]
                           [᾽Ε]πὶ Λάχη[τος ἄρχοντος, ... *ca.* 17 . . . .]
                           [.]ο ῾Αλαιεὺ[ς ἐγραμμάτευεν·   *vacat*   ]
                           [ἔ]δοξεν [τῆι βολῆι· Λάχης ἦρχε, Λεω(?)]
        5   [ν]τὶς [ἐπρυτάνευε, ... ¹² . . . . .]
                           [——————————————————]
                                lacuna
                           [——————————————————]
                         [. . . . . ²⁴ . . . .]ον   (b)
                         [. . . . . ²⁴ . . . .]μο
                         [. . . . . ²⁴ . . . .]υο
                         [. . . . . ²⁵ . . . .]β
                         [——————————————————]

The above text is that of Walbank, who added that the data of fragment *c* reveal that the body of the document carried a stoichedon text of 26 letters per line and that its subject concerned praise of an embassy.

Line 1. Perhaps parts of a superscript naming the honorand(s), as in **33** and in *IG* II², 3, 6, etc. Lines 3–5. [.]ο ῾Αλαιεὺ[ς ἐγραμμάτευε, – – –ις ἐπρυτάνευε. | ῎Εδοξεν [τ– – – – – – –||.]τιμ– – – – – – *IG* II². A. S. Henry (*Prescripts*, p. 11) noted that lines 2–3 should represent a heading rather than part of the opening formula, proposing an uninscribed space after ἐγραμμάτευε. In line 4 he suggested [ἔ]δοξεν [τῆι βουλῆι καὶ τῶι δήμωι· – – – – ἐπρυτάνευε κτλ.].

Line 5. Henry interpreted τιμ as part of the name of the γραμματεύς. If Walbank's reading of sigma for mu is correct, this should rather form part of the name of the phyle in prytany: but this involves the location of the archon's name at an unusual place in the formula as well as the omission of ephelkystic nu in ἦρχε.

The decree is postulated by Walbank as an enactment of the council only, for which, at this period, see **33**, commentary on line 3. But τῶι δήμωι is an equally possible restoration. On the craftsman who worked on this text see Walbank, *Classical Views* 26, 1982, pp. 259–274, and cf. *SEG* XXXII, 38. Walbank further suggested (*Hesperia*, *loc. cit.*) that he also inscribed *IG* II², 56 and 81 (neither securely dated) and that he may have inscribed *IG* II², 17 (394/3), 97 (375/4), and 1392 (398/7).

For a full list of those attested as having held public office during Laches' archonship see R. Develin, *Athenian Officials*, pp. 203–204.

FRAGMENT OF AN HONORARY DECREE

31. A fragment of a stele of Pentelic marble (I 5520), discovered on June 7, 1938, in a Classical context over the west wall of the antechamber of Klepsydra (T 27). The rough-picked original back and the left and right sides of the monument are preserved, but the surface is badly abraded.

H. 0.48 m.; W. 0.37 m.; Th. 0.10 m.

LH. 0.01 m.

Στοιχ. Hor. 0.0105 m.; Vert. 0.017 m.

Ed. M. B. Walbank, *Hesperia* 58, 1989, pp. 72–74, no. 2, with photograph pl. 18. See also *SEG* XXXIX, 63.

ca. a. 400–390 *a.*   ΣΤΟΙΧ. 31

```
           [------------------------]
           [....]E[.............26.............]
           [.]E[...............29...............]
           [.................31.................]
           [.................31.................]
      5    [................30................]Σ
           [..]O[...........23...........]Λ[..]T[.]
           [.]X[...............29...............]
           [.................31.................]
           [...............29...............]ΣO
      10   [...............27...............]Σ[..]Υ
           [.]E[...........22...........]Φ[...]ΩΣΤ
           [............25............]O[..]EAT
           [..........18..........· τὸ δὲ ψήφι]σ[μ]α τό
           [δε ἀναγράψαι ἐν στήλῃ λιθί]ν[ῃι] τὸγ γρ
      15   [αμματέα τῆς βολῆς ...6...]· ἐς δὲ τὴν ἀνά
           θεσι[ν τῆς εἰκόνο]ς δ[ō]ναι : XΓΡ: δραχμὰς χ
           [................22................]Ω[.]Ạ ἐς τὸ π[ρ]
           [υτανεον ἐς αὔριον· ἐ]ς δὲ [τ]ὴν ἀναγραφὴ[ν]
           [τῆς σ]τή[λης δō]ν[αι ........17........]
      20   [------------------------]
```

Walbank, whose readings are here reproduced, observed that the craftsman at work on this stone seems also to have inscribed *IG* II², 8 + 65 (*SEG* XXXII, 10, XXXIII, 12, XXXIV, 21, XXXVI, 11, XXXIX, 9).

Line 16. The sum voted raises also the question of the nature of the honors voted: hence Walbank's restoration of the line. Any suggestion that one of the "liberators" (after the overthrow of the Thirty Tyrants) or a hero such as Konon after the battle of Knidos in 394 is concerned must remain purely speculative. Line 18. So Walbank; L. Threatte however quotes only one text (*IG* II², 1, of 403/2) in which the spelling πρυτανεον occurs (thrice; even so, two of the instances are restored), although the word is common (*Grammar*, pp. 312 and 317, no. 37). There appear in fact to be no more than four certain and two probable instances. Other alleged examples occur in restorations or are otherwise open to doubt. A. S. Henry, who has dealt with this matter at length (*Honours*, pp. 282–284, note 33), concluded that there is less evidence for this spelling without the intervocalic iota "than one might have been led to suppose" and that "we should not unnecessarily introduce the phenomenon into fragmentary texts where it can be avoided."

FRAGMENT OF A DECREE(?)

32. A small fragment of a stele of Pentelic marble (I 5487), broken on all sides and at the back, discovered on June 4, 1938, in a Late Roman context south of the Eleusinion (U 22).

H. 0.062 m.; W. 0.043 m.; Th. 0.03 m.
LH. 0.008 m.

Ed. M. B. Walbank, *Hesperia* 58, 1989, pp. 78–79, no. 5, with photograph pl. 17. See also *SEG* XXXIX, 68.

ca. a. 400 *a., vel paullo post*   ΣΤΟΙΧ. 30(?)

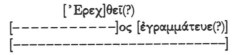

```
              ['Ερεχ]θεῖ(?)
    [----------]ος [ἐγραμμάτευε(?)]
    [------------------------]
```

Walbank identified the hand as that of the craftsman who produced **29** and is inclined to believe that this fragment forms part of (the top of) that monument. If that is so, the heading in line 1 may well indicate the cult in question, and Walbank suggested the supplements shown above, in consequence. The vertical spacing of the letters on this fragment (0.028 m.) is twice that of the horizontal interval (0.014 m.), presumably to offset the heading:

on the hypothesis that **29** continues the text, a square pattern of stoichoi has there taken over for the body of the inscription.

For discussion of the date of this fragment see the commentary on **29**.

FRAGMENT OF AN HONORARY DECREE

33. A fragment of a stele of Pentelic marble (I 788), with the smooth right side and original rough-picked back preserved but otherwise broken all around except at the top, which (while preserving the top line of the inscribed text) appears to have been squared off in a later reworking of the stone, discovered on May 11, 1933, in a modern wall east of the Tholos (H 11). The left and bottom edges of the fragment are much battered.

H. 0.144 m.; W. 0.135 m.; Th. 0.079 m.

LH. 0.009 m. (omicron 0.007 m., nu and sigma 0.011 m.).

Στοιχ. (almost square) Hor. 0.013 m.; Vert. 0.0125 m.

Ed. B. D. Meritt, *Hesperia* 7, 1938, pp. 91–92, no. 11, with photograph. Brief references by A. Lambrechts, *De Atheense Proxeniedecreten*, pp. 52 and 153, no. 48.

ca. a. 398–390 a.   ΣΤΟΙΧ. 23

$$
\begin{array}{l}
[\ldots\ldots\overset{14}{\ldots\ldots\ldots}\ \pi]\rho\acute{o}\xi[\epsilon\nu]o\varsigma\ ^{v} \\
[\text{'}A\theta\eta\nu\alpha\acute{\iota}\omega\nu\ \varkappa\alpha\grave{\iota}\ \epsilon\dot{\upsilon}\epsilon]\rho\gamma\acute{\epsilon}\tau\eta\varsigma.\ ^{vvv} \\
[\text{"}E\delta o\xi\epsilon\nu\ \tau\tilde{\eta}\iota\ \beta o\upsilon\lambda\tilde{\eta}\iota]\cdot\ K\epsilon\varkappa\rho o\pi\grave{\iota}\varsigma \\
[\dot{\epsilon}\pi\rho\upsilon\tau\acute{\alpha}\nu\epsilon\upsilon\epsilon,\ ..\overset{5}{.}..]\varkappa\lambda\epsilon\acute{\iota}\delta\eta\varsigma\ \dot{\epsilon} \\
[\gamma\rho\alpha\mu\mu\acute{\alpha}\tau\epsilon\upsilon\epsilon,\ [..\overset{6}{.}...]\epsilon\mu o\varsigma\ \dot{\epsilon}\pi\epsilon \\
[\sigma\tau\acute{\alpha}\tau\epsilon,\ ....\overset{9}{....}\ \epsilon\tilde{\iota}\pi\epsilon]\cdot\ \dot{\epsilon}\pi\alpha\iota\nu \\
[\acute{\epsilon}\sigma\alpha\iota\ \mu\grave{\epsilon}\nu\ ...\overset{7}{...}\ \dot{\omega}\varsigma\ \acute{o}\nu\tau]\iota\ \dot{\alpha}\nu\delta \\
[\rho\grave{\iota}\ \dot{\alpha}\gamma\alpha\theta\tilde{\omega}\iota\ \pi\epsilon\rho\acute{\iota}\ \tau\epsilon\ \tau\grave{\eta}\nu\ \pi\acute{o}\lambda]\iota\nu\ \tau \\
[\grave{\eta}\nu\ \text{'}A\theta\eta\nu\alpha\acute{\iota}\omega\nu\ \varkappa\alpha\grave{\iota}\ ....\overset{10}{.}....] \\
[-------------------]
\end{array}
$$

5

10

The lettering is competent but by no means artistically outstanding. There is some clumsiness, especially in the inscribing of sigma. It is, however, amply characteristic of the later 5th and early 4th centuries. There is some irregularity in the horizontal spacing of the letters. Meritt estimated the date not only on the style of the writing (which by itself might permit a date within the 5th century) but also by the appearance of the boule alone in the enactment formula (ἔδοξεν τῆι βουλῆι), on which see further below. The date cannot be 399/8, as in that year Kekropis, during its period in office as prytanizing phyle, had a γραμματεύς whose name was six or seven letters in length (*IG* I³, 98 [II², 12], line 31).

The length of line may be determined by lines 2–3. For line 2 Meritt compared (e.g.) *IG* II², 49 (*SEG* XXI, 224), line 2, where there is a similar heading *extra decretum ipsum*, and 79, lines 7–8. For the actual order of words, *IG* II², 78, lines 6–7 offer a better example. There was at this period a good deal of flexibility and perhaps some insouciance in the formulation and consistency of these documents, and the planning of the text could to a certain extent depend upon the secretary's choice and assiduity. Cf. (from the mid-5th century on) *IG* I³, 28 (I², 143), 74 (I², 145), 181 (I², 146), *IG* II², 2, 6 (*SEG* XV, 83), etc. The length of the names in lines 5 and 6 is variable by one letter, absence of ephelkystic nu having been assumed in the text. A. S. Henry's study of "movable nu" in the 5th century (*CSCA* 11, 1978, pp. 83–91) and Hellenistic period (*CQ* n.s. 17, 1967, pp. 277–284) leaves a gap for the eighty years from 403 to 323; but it may be judged that in the first decade of the 4th century it might well have been added to εἶπε, less surely to ἐγραμμάτευε, but not to ἐπρυτάνευε.

Line 3. Βουλή must be restored in place of βολή if this line is to conform to the requirements of line 2. The usage had already crept into documents of the 5th century (see **22**) but remains rare in the first quarter of the 4th century; cf. L. Threatte, *Grammar*, pp. 241–246. According to the prescript, the enactment was the work of the council alone, rather than of the council and assembly. Cf. **36**. This sets it beside a number of other decrees of the early years of the 4th century and, in this case, is a criterion of date (see above). For the list of these and full discussion of the possible competence of the boule in passing decrees at this time, see P. J. Rhodes, *Athenian Boule*, pp. 82–85 (list, p. 83, note 1) and Henry, *Prescripts*, pp. 15–16. Cf. also Lambrechts, *De Atheense Proxeniedecreten*, pp. 52–53; R. A. de Laix, *Probouleusis at Athens*, 1973, pp. 125–126, 138; M. H. Hansen, *GRBS* 22, 1981, p. 353, note 24. The best explanation (cf. A. H. M. Jones, *Athenian Democracy*, 1957, pp. 114 and 157, note 101) seems to lie in the flexibility or indifference already mentioned. Rhodes notes the uncertainty in the use of formulas in the early 4th century, and to this may be added the suspicion that modern scholars are more worried by such inconsistencies and their implications than were the ancient draftsmen. The examples occur mostly, but not entirely, in proxeny decrees; this may be no more than an index of the comparative frequency of that type of decree at the time and does not require the inferences Lambrechts drew from it. The rapid succession of monthly γραμματεῖς doubtless did not discourage inconsistency or skimped work, and the appearance of the annual γραμματεύς between 370 and 360 (see Rhodes, *Athenian Boule*, pp. 134–136) represented a tightening up of the system in this as in other respects.

Line 5. Meritt suggested [Τληπόλ]εμος. Line 7. The inclusion of μέν seems guaranteed by two factors: (1) its common appearance after ἐπαινέσαι in decrees of this date and character; cf. *IG* II², 2, line 9, 7, line 4, 23 (*SEG* XIV, 37), line 6, 26, line 7, 28, line 4, 31, line 5, etc.; (2) its omission would require that the honorand be credited with a name of ten letters, but line 1 indicates that his name and ethnic together comprise no more than fourteen letters. Although his ethnic might indeed have been Χῖος (cf. *IG* II², 23), the possibilities are so limited that the likelihood of the inclusion of μέν in line 7 is proportionately greater. The omission of the ethnic in the body of the decree is unusual and may be doubted in some places where it has been assumed. See Meritt, *Hesperia* 21, 1952, pp. 343–349, where **21**, *IG* II², 133, and the present text are cited among the few indisputable examples. In **20**, *IG* II², 95 and 133, as here, the ethnic was included in the heading. Meritt argued that that was not part of the decree as such and is therefore without significance, but it remains possible that the γραμματεύς felt himself at liberty to improvise to the extent of suppressing the ethnic in the body of the text if he extracted it for special prominence in the heading. Even so, the pattern of **21**, *q.v.*, remains to be explained; it may be supposed that the long uninscribed space above that text perhaps contained a painted heading, or more likely that the information was carried on the (now lost) upper part of the monument. Henry has argued (*Honours*, pp. 12–13, note 2[2]) that the ethnic may be omitted "in cases where it is self-evident" and has discussed ἐπαινέσαι μέν, *op. cit.*, pp. 13–14, note 4.

TREATY OF ALLIANCE BETWEEN ATHENS AND THE BOIOTIANS

34. Two nonjoining fragments of a stele of Pentelic marble, one of which (fragment *a*) was found on the Akropolis and has long been known; the other (I 4352), fragment *b*, which preserves the right side and original back of the monument but is otherwise broken, was discovered on December 18, 1936, in a wall of a modern house over the area of the southwestern part of the Eleusinion (S–T 20). Fragment *b* is badly battered at the edges, but, while making no join with fragment *a*, it can be precisely aligned to the right of it at an average distance of eight letter spaces.

b only: H. 0.28 m.; W. 0.19 m.; Th. 0.106 m.

a and *b*: LH. (lines 2–3) 0.011 m. (theta and omicron 0.008 m.), (lines 1 and 4–12) 0.008 m. (theta and omicron 0.0065 m., omega 0.0045 m.).

Στοιχ. (lines 4–12) Hor. 0.0125 m.; Vert. 0.0185 m.

Ed. *a* only: *IG* II², 14, with earlier bibliography. *a* + *b*: E. Schweigert, *Hesperia* 8, 1939, pp. 1–3, no. 1, with photograph of *b*. See also M. N. Tod, *GHI* II, pp. 14–15, no. 101; H. Bengtson, *Staatsverträge* II, pp. 168–170, no. 223; cf. *SEG* XXI, 220.

a. 395 a. ΣTOIΧ. 30 (lines 4–12)

```
              [---------------------------]
    (a)       [. .]οι[--------------------]
                        vacat
              [Συμ]μαχία Βοιω[τῶν καὶ ᾿Α]θηναί[ων ἐς τὸ]    (b)
              [ν ἀεὶ] χρόνον.      vacat
              [ἐάν τ]ις ἴηι ἐπ᾿ ᾿Αθηναίος] ἐπ[ὶ] πολέμω[ι ἢ]
    5         [κατὰ] γῆν ἢ κατ[ὰ θάλαττ]αν, βοηθὲν Βοι[ω]
              [τὸς π]αντὶ σθέ[νει καθ]ότι ἂν ἐπαγγέλλ
              [ωσιν] ᾿Αθηναῖ[οι κατὰ τὸ] δυνατόν, καὶ ἐ[ὰ]
              [ν τις ἴ]ηι ἐπὶ [Βοιωτὸς ἐ]πὶ πολέμωι ἢ [κα]
              [τὰ γῆν ἢ] κατὰ [θάλατταν], βοηθὲν ᾿Αθηνα[ί]
    10        [ος παντὶ σθένει καθότι] ἂν ἐπαγγέλλ[ω]
              [σι Βοιωτοὶ κατὰ τὸ δυνα]τόν· ἐὰν δέ τ[ι δ]
              [οκῆι ἢ προσθεῖναι ἢ ἀφελεῖ]ν ᾿Αθην[αίο]
              [ις καὶ Βοιωτοῖς κοινῆι βουλευομένο]
              [ις ---------------------------]
    15        [---------------------------]
```

The date depends upon the historical circumstances of this alliance, which are well known through the literary sources. See Xenophon, *HG* 3.5.16; Andokides 3.25; Lysias 16.13; Diodorus Siculus 14.81.2; and Bengtson, *loc. cit.* For modern accounts see, e.g., N. G. L. Hammond, *History of Greece to 322 B.C.*, 2nd ed., 1967, p. 455; and S. Accame, *La lega ateniese del secolo IV a.C.*, 1941, pp. 17–18, *idem, Ricerche intorno alla guerra Corinzia*, 1951, pp. 45–46, *idem, L'Imperialismo ateniese all'inizio del secolo IV a.C. e la crisi della Polis*, 1966, pp. 130–131; P. Cloché, *Thèbes de Béotie*, 1951, p. 104; D. Kagan, *La Parola del Passato* 16, 1961, pp. 321–341; S. Perlman, *CQ* n.s. 14, 1964, pp. 72–73; R. Seager, *JHS* 87, 1967, pp. 95–99; S. Perlman, *CP* 63, 1968, pp. 258–261; D. H. Kelly, "Sources and Interpretations of Spartan History in the Reigns of Agesilaus II, Archidamus II and Agis III" (diss. Cambridge University, 1975), pp. 107–112; G. T. Griffith in *Imperialism in the Ancient World*, P. D. A. Garnsey and C. R. Whittaker, edd., 1978, p. 129 with note 8. For earlier bibliography see Schweigert and Tod, *locc. citt.*

The treaty was not abrogated by the Peace of Antalkidas of 386, in which the independence of the constituent Boiotian cities was recognized, but Schweigert urged that it was unilaterally denounced by the Thebans between spring 386 and winter 383, drawing on the indications of Lysias 26.23 and Aelius Aristeides, *Panathenaicus* 173, with scholia.

The lettering of the text is described in *IG* II² as "volg. init. s. IV"; this indeed accounts for its general character, but certain features deserve comment. The "square" and "angled" letters are inconsistently formed; the horizontal strokes of epsilon, usually of equal length in the same example, vary in length from one instance to another and are sometimes inaccurately joined to the vertical stroke. The circular letters tend to become oval, and beta is, as often, clumsily executed. The flat, wide omega is notable, and the right vertical of pi is long in proportion to the horizontal. E is used for EI twice in βοηθε͂ν (lines 6 and 9), and O for OY in the words Ἀθηναῖος and Βοιωτός (lines 4, 6, 8, 10): on this see L. Threatte, *Grammar*, pp. 177–178 and 241–242.

The larger lettering of the heading in lines 2–3 is preceded by an uninscribed interval of 0.03 m. and, on fragment *a*, by the letters [. .]οι. Above and to the right of these letters the stone is abraded and broken. There is no indication that this was the top of the inscribed face, and from the appearance of the fragment one would judge the reverse. The restoration [Θε]οί, adopted by Schweigert and Tod, would however assume that the inscription began at this point: it is taken to represent the invocations made before the business of the assembly, or of this particular measure, was embarked upon (cf., among numerous examples, **9** and **20**). It should properly be followed by the enactment formula, ἔδοξεν τῆι βουλῆι καὶ τῶι δήμωι or its equivalent, and the customary preamble. Moreover, nearly all treaties of this kind contain such a formula in guarantee of the assent of the Athenian people, before the terms or the oaths are detailed; cf. for example *IG* I³, 11 (I², 19), **19**, and *IG* II², 16 and 225 (*SEG* XXI, 222 and 264); see also A. S. Henry, *Prescripts*, p. 44 with note 60. *IG* II², 97, the *exceptio quae probat regulam*, begins without Θεοί and embarks immediately on the detail of the treaty terms; but this constitutes a plain statement in amplification, in the case of Kerkyra, of an enabling decree which comprehended treaties with Kephallenia and Akarnania as well and which exists on a separate stele (*IG* II², 96; *SEG* XXI, 234); see **46** for the less well preserved treaty with the Kephallenians. If such a separate stele existed for the enabling decree of the treaty with the Boiotians, the word Θεοί would properly precede that text rather than this one. Otherwise, it is remarkable to begin a document of the present kind, in a comparatively developed (even though still fluid) period of governmental procedure, without the proper preamble by which the measure is defined and registered. Further, since Θεοί regularly begins the record, the present text should begin with line 2 at the head of the inscribed face, which it evidently does not.

Two further points may be suggested: (1) The uninscribed interval between Θεοί and the heading remains unexplained; (2) the word Θεοί is customarily spread across the inscribed face in a symmetrical or tolerably symmetrical plan or is centered relative to the text beneath. The former practice is too frequent to need documentation; for the latter, cf., e.g., *IG* I³, 66, II², 6 and 111. The compression of the word to the extreme left edge of the stele is not only unusual in itself (cf. **9**) but is sometimes wrongly shown when the printed texts show it. For example, in *IG* I³, 84 and 110 (I², 94 and 118) the printed text of *IG* I² compressed Θεοί to the left in just this manner, an error corrected in *IG* I³, where the letters are spaced out across the stelai.

The suppositions that [. .]οι and the line in which it stands end an earlier part of the inscription, probably representing the decree that recorded agreement to the terms set out in what survives, will account for the position of the letters, for their size and character (that of the body of the lower text), and for the uninscribed interval that will thus divide the enabling decree from the record of the terms. There is a precise parallel in *IG* II², 15, although without the uninscribed interval, for that text is less generously set out on its stele. It ended, according to the restored text, with the words καθάπερ] τοῖς [Κορινθίοις, and the [. .]οι of the present text (perhaps [. .]οι[ς *vacat*]) could well have formed part of a similar phrase.

The discovery of fragment *b* made changes in the text as previously restored necessary only in lines 4 and 8, where the conjectured provisions had placed the prepositional phrases in the reverse order as ἐπὶ πολέμωι ἐπ᾽ Ἀθεναίος and ἐπὶ πολέμωι ἐπὶ Βοιωτός. For the phraseology of the treaty terms cf. *IG* II², 15, lines 4–10, and 16, b, lines 1–3.

Tod observed, "this is the earliest appearance of the phrase ἐς τὸν ἀεὶ (or ἅπαντα) χρόνον in an alliance, in place of the previous limitation to a specified number of years." But it is now known that such "unlimited" treaties may be traced back not only into the 5th century (*IG* I³, 53 and 54) but into the 6th, where the earliest Greek treaty yet known (*SEG* XXII, 336 and XL, 381; Meiggs-Lewis, no. 10) contains such a provision, though expressed in a different way.

AGREEMENT BETWEEN ATHENS AND TROIZEN

35. Twenty fragments of an opisthographic stele of Pentelic marble, of which one preserves both inscribed faces, and of which three were discovered in the course of the Agora excavations. All the Agora fragments are broken all around: two of them were joined immediately on discovery (I 4985, now fragment *q*), being found on June 3 and June 18, 1937, respectively, in a Late Hellenistic to Early Roman context near Klepsydra (T 26). The third Agora fragment (I 5351, now fragment *r*) was discovered on March 22, 1938, in a context of the 2nd to 3rd centuries A.D., in a cutting in line with the East Stair parapet on the North Slope of the Akropolis (T 22–23). Among the other fragments, three (*b*, *d*, *m*) may be joined, and the total of separate pieces of the stele is thus reduced to seventeen. All fragments previously known were discovered on the Akropolis or are of uncertain provenance. The measurements and text of the Agora fragments alone are detailed here.

q (as joined): H. 0.25 m.; W. 0.14 m.; Th. 0.112 m.

r: H. 0.067 m.; W. 0.09 m.; Th. 0.06 m.

(All fragments): LH. 0.007–0.008 m.

Στοιχ. Hor. *ca.* 0.008 m.; Vert. *ca.* 0.014 m.

Ed. *a–p*: *IG* II², 46, with earlier bibliography. *q* and *r*: A. G. Woodhead, *Hesperia* 26, 1957, pp. 225–229, no. 85, with photographs pls. 58, 59 (see also *SEG* XVII, 17, with suggestions for the text of fragment *q* by A. N. Oikonomides, not here reproduced); discussion of all fragments and some revised readings by D. M. Lewis, *Hesperia* 28, 1959, pp. 248–250. See also H. Bengtson, *Staatsverträge* II, p. 183, no. 235; P. Gauthier, *Symbola: Les étrangers et la justice dans les cités grecques*, 1972, pp. 166–167 (discussions of content and date, without text).

ca. a. 390–370 *a.*ΣΤΟΙΧ. (*ca.* 90?)

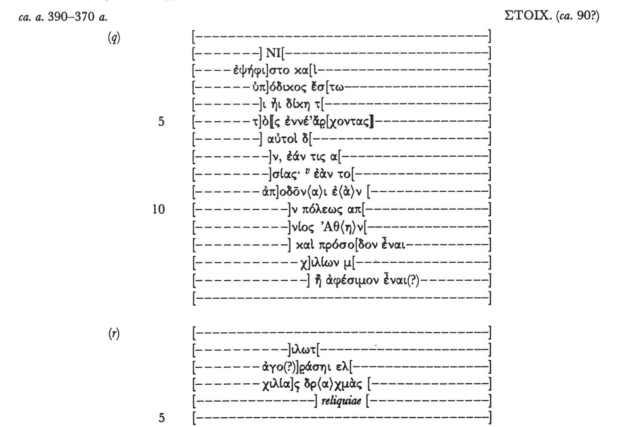

q: line 3. [--- ὑπ]όδικος Lewis; [--- πρ(?)]οδικος *ed. princ.* Line 13. [--- 'Αθη]γ(α)ίων Lewis. On both fragments omission of cross-strokes in alpha (once also in eta) is to be noted. Despite the evident size and comprehensiveness of the document or documents on the two faces of this monument, the *disiecta membra* are so fragmentary as to permit little to be said. Arguing from the likely restoration of the "title" or "heading" on fragment *a*, Lewis suggested that the inscription on that face (A) "had nearly 90 letters to the line," giving the monument a width of some 0.85 m. In this it would be comparable with the analogous agreement between Athens and the people of Stymphalos in Arkadia (**47**).

Discussion has centered upon (1) the attribution of the fragments to the two faces, only fragment *a* preserving both; (2) the date of the texts (which appear to be contemporary); (3) the character of the contents.

(1) Attribution is difficult and, in the present state of the monument, is to some degree a matter of subjective judgment. In *IG* II², 46, fragments *aB, f, i, l, m*, and *p* were assigned to face B, the remainder to face A. Fragment *m*, now joined with *b* and *c*, belongs therefore to face A, and the transfer is eloquent of the problem. The *editio princeps* assigned both *q* and *r* to face B: the carelessness with cross-strokes unites them in character, and the same feature, though to be found indeed on both faces, is more frequent on the other fragments assigned to face B. What prompted Lewis to regard all the fragments save *f* and *i* (with *aB*) as belonging to face A was the *penchant* of the "Face B hand" for double cutting of letters. Face B was, however, corrected (on fragment *aB*) by the hand of face A, which might imply that it was the "prior" face (see further below); nor is double cutting absent from face A. The two hands are in any case extremely similar, and, since the writing of face A seems to "improve" (Lewis, p. 248), both are likely to be the work of the same craftsman on "on" and "off" days. Here too **47** offers an interesting parallel as an opisthographic monument on which the attribution of numerous fragments to one face or the other, despite editorial ingenuity, remains equally uncertain. Its writer, himself described as "none-too-careful", was nevertheless more competent than the inscriber of the present text.

Other criteria, such as the location of the *rasurae* that occur on several fragments and on both faces, or the "tilt" of omega, which rises to the left on some fragments and to the right on others, are insufficient to be of positive help. Lewis noted (p. 249) that fragment *b* (A) preserves the top of the stele and that there is no prescript. Fragment *a* (A), however, which he described as "of course from the bottom of the stone", preserves the "heading" in larger lettering restored in *IG* II², 46 as [Σύμβολα ᾿Αθηναίων καὶ Τρο]ζηνίω[ν], and above it is the end of a list of names, partly preserved also on fragment *o*. For the implications of this see further below.

(2) In *IG* II², the inscription is dated before 378 or, more specifically, "paullo post a. 400", with the note "Monumentum c. a. 400 lapidi incisum esse indicavit Wilhelm per colloquium." *IG* II², 85, attributed to the "prima decennia saeculi", is comparable in respect of its irregular and often crowded lettering. On these stylistic grounds Lewis also preferred a date early in the century. Bengtson gave the date as "um 390"; see also J. Cargill, *The Second Athenian League*, 1981, p. 94.

However, the agreement or agreements here entered into are of the character generally described as *symbolai* or *symbola* (see below), of which a number seem to have been concluded in the period following the establishment of the Second Athenian Confederacy in 378/7, especially perhaps in the early 360's. The Agora has provided the remains of several of them (**47, 50, 51**, and perhaps **58**). A rapprochement between Athens and a city in the northern Peloponnese would be well suited to the pattern of events in this period, after the battle of Leuktra and in the context of known Athenian interest in the area (cf. Xenophon, *HG* 6.5.1–3). The Troizenians bestowed honors on the boule and demos of the Athenians in 368/7 (*IG* II², 1425, lines 227–231). Argument for a date not earlier than *ca.* 375 was therefore advanced by Woodhead (*op. cit.*, pp. 227–228) and accepted by Gauthier (*op. cit.*, pp. 166–167, "vers 370"). Lewis acknowledged the force of the argument but nevertheless (see above) preferred a date of 395–390: M. B. Walbank's "400–375" (*Hesperia* 55, 1986, pp. 319–354, esp. p. 350, note 41) also noted the later possibility. The alternatives remain, and the dating here given has intentionally reflected them.

(3) For the nature and number of the *symbolai* or *symbola* known from literary as well as from epigraphical sources, see in particular Gauthier, *op. cit.* (esp. pp. 157–173); D. M. MacDowell, *The Law in Classical Athens*, 1978, pp. 220–221; G. E. M. de Ste Croix, *CQ* n.s. 11, 1961, pp. 108–110; Walbank, *op. cit.*, pp. 349–353. These agreements were concerned, as it appears, with judicial and civil procedures, regulating the status in law of citizens of the contracting parties, should a national of the one community become involved in litigation or in charges arising in the city of, or in conflict with a national of, the other community. The treaties in question were evidently lengthy and detailed: their provisions showed certain similarities (as might be expected); note especially fragment *b* (A) of this document and fragment *j* of **47**. It is the more regrettable that they survive in too fragmentary a state to provide more than generalized and conjectural evidence. Walbank (pp. 320–321, note 8, 348–349, note 37) has suggested that a number of them, including perhaps this one and **47**, were inscribed on an opisthographic wall on the Akropolis, comparable in character with that in the Stoa Basileios on which the law code of Nikomachos (*SEG* XV, 114) was recorded.

Fragment *a* (A) should perhaps be particularly reconsidered in the light of this possibility. It is notable that the style of the lettering of the "heading" on that fragment is more careful and sophisticated than that of the rest of the text and would support the "later" rather than the "earlier" dating on that score. But its acknowledged position near the foot of the monument, with wide uninscribed spaces above and below, raises a doubt whether it "heads" anything at all or whether it characterizes, in the style of a caption, that part of the monument below which it is inscribed, thus differentiating that section from other, unrelated sections of the same total record. The "heading" is apparently concluded at this point, and the list of names partly preserved above it (and on fragment *o*) is thus likely to have concluded the record to which it belongs. If this, then, represents the "bottom right-hand corner" of the Troizenian *symbola*, the possibility of its forming part of a more continuous collection of *symbolai* may be enhanced.

The supposition of a "continuous collection" does however also allow the possibility to remain that, if this small piece of *scriptura monumentalis* is after all a "heading" to precede the Troizenian record, the list of names may be the conclusion of a totally different agreement, unconnected with Troizen.

However that may be, it is to be accepted that the two faces of the document as we have it dealt with Troizen (cf. Lewis, p. 250): the name of that city appears clearly on fragments of both. The references on face B might, indeed, use Troizen as a point of reference for an agreement with another city (cf. **51**), but this seems the less likely alternative; cf. *IG* II², 46, *comm.* If both faces refer to Troizen and form parts of a single enactment, it may be that face B represents the "obverse" and face A, concluding with the list of names and the "caption", the "reverse". Walbank, on other grounds, reached a similar conclusion (*op. cit.*, p. 338) and regarded these *symbolai* with Troizen as the model for the later compact with Stymphalos (**47**). Cf. *SEG* XXXVI, 141, XLI, 39.

STHORYS OF THASOS HONORED

36. Eight fragments of a stele of Pentelic marble, one of which, fragment *h* (I 4633), was discovered in the excavations of the Athenian Agora; the other seven (fragments *a–g*) were already long known and with the exception of fragment *b* are in the Epigraphical Museum in Athens (E.M. 6900, 6900α+390, 6900β). Fragment *b*, which makes a direct join with *a*, is in the National Museum, Copenhagen (no. ABb 254). Fragment *h*, which makes no join with any other fragment, provides part of the lower right-central section of the stele at lines 23–29 and was discovered on March 20, 1937, at the surface on the North Slope of the Akropolis, west of the Post-Herulian Wall (S 25–26). It is broken on all sides except the back (the original back is preserved also on the other fragments except *b*).

h only: H. 0.134 m.; W. 0.095 m.; Th. 0.102 m.

a–h: LH. 0.009–0.01 m.

Στοιχ. (roughly square, but irregular in execution) Hor. *ca.* 0.016 m.; Vert. *ca.* 0.015 m.

For the details of the other fragments see M. J. Osborne (*BSA*, *loc. cit.* below), who assessed the overall dimensions of the stele as H. *ca.* 0.654 m., W. *ca.* 0.635 m., Th. 0.075–0.102 m., and M. B. Walbank, *loc. cit.* below.

Ed. *a–g* only: *IG* II², 17 with references to earlier literature; W. Dittenberger, *Syll.*³, no. 127. See also A. Wilhelm (*Attische Urkunden* V [= *SbAkadWien* 220, 5], 1942, pp. 87–96, no. XLIII), whose conjectures were largely confirmed by the discovery of fragment *h*; J. Pouilloux, *Recherches sur l'histoire et les cultes de Thasos* I, 1954, pp. 196, 203; *SEG* XV, 84. *h* only, with full text of lines 22–40 as here numbered: B. D. Meritt, *Hesperia* 26, 1957, pp. 51–52, no. 8, with photograph pl. 8 (see also *SEG* XVI, 42). *a–h*: M. J. Osborne, *BSA* 65, 1970, pp. 151–174, with photographs of all fragments except *a* and *h*, pl. 42; M. B. Walbank, *Athenian Proxenies*, 1978, pp. 398–405, no. 78, with photographs of all fragments pls. 51–54:a; Osborne, *Naturalization* I, pp. 43–45, no. D 8, *Naturalization* II, pp. 45–48.

a. 394/3 *a*. ΣΤΟΙΧ. 37–39

(a+b)

```
        Ἔδοξεν τῆι βολῆι· Αἰγηὶς [ἐπρυτάνευε, Ἀριστοχρ]
        άτης ἐγραμμάτευε, Ἀμειψ[ίας ἐπεστάτε, ...⁷⁻⁸...]
        εἶπε· ἐπαινέσαι Σθόρυν [τὸν μάντιν, ὅτι πρόθυμό]
        ς ἐστι ποεῖν ὅ τι δύναται [ἀγαθὸν τὴν στρατιὰν καὶ]
   5    τὴν πόλιν τὴν Ἀθηναίων· [περὶ δὲ ὧν λέγει Σθόρυς],
        ἐπειδὴ αὐτῶ ἦσαν οἱ πρόγο[νοι πρόξενοί τε καὶ εὐ]
        εργέται τῆς πόλεως τῆς Ἀθη[ναίων, αὐτὸν δὲ καὶ πο]
        λίτην ἐποιήσαντο Ἀθηναῖοι, [ἀναγράψαι Σθόρυι]
        τὸν γραμματέα τῆς βολῆς ἐν σ[τήλαιν λιθίναιν ἐν]
   10   πόληι καὶ ἐν Πυθίο τὰ ἐψηφι[σμένα περὶ Σθόρυος]
        τ[ῶ]ι δήμωι· καλέσαι δὲ Σθόρυ[ν ⟦καὶ ἐπὶ δεῖπνον⟧]
        [εἰς α]ὔριον ⟦ἐς τὸ πρυτανεῖο[ν.⟧    vacat    ]
        [Ἀρι]στοχράτης Αἰσχίνο Κεφ[αλῆθεν ἐγραμμάτευε],
        [Εὐ]βολίδης Ἐ[λ]ευσίνιος ἦρ[χεν, ἐπὶ τῆς Αἰγηΐδος]
```

15   [πρυτα]ν̣ε̣ι̣α̣[ς. *vv*]   *vacat*   [*vacat*   ]

[*vacat*   ]   *vacat*   [*vacat*   ]

[*vacat*   ]   *vacat*   [*vacat*   ]

[*vacat*   ]   *vacat*   [*vacat*   ]

[——————————————————————]

20   [. . . . . 37 . . . .]ν   (*f*)

[. . . . . 34 . . . . εἶ]πε·

[κύρια μὲν ἔναι Σθόρυι τὰ ψηφίσματα τὰ ἐψη]φισμέ

[να αὐτῶι πρότερον ὑπὸ τõ δήμο τõ ᾿Αθηναίω]ν καὶ τὸ

[νυνὶ ψηφισθέν· ἐπαινέσαι δ'αὐτὸν ἐπει]δὴ πρότε

25   [ρόν τε διετέλει Σθόρυς πρόθυμος ὢν] ᾿Αθηναίοις

(*c*)   [καὶ ὅ]τι προ[εῖπε(?) . . . .8. . . . τὰ γενόμ]ενα περὶ τῆς

ναυμαχίας [μαντευσάμενος ἐκ τῶν ἱ]ερῶν τῶν εἰσι

τητηρίων ὥ[νπερ ἔθυσεν καὶ τὰ] ἄλ[λα ἐσ]τὶ ἀνὴρ ἀγα   (*h*)

(*d*)   θὸς περὶ τὴ[ν πόλιν τὴν ᾿Α]θην[αί]ων χ[αὶ ο]ἱ̈ πρόγονο[ι]

30   πρότερον, χα[ὶ ἔναι αὐ]τὸν ᾿Αθ[ην]αῖο[ν· γρά]⟨ψ⟩ασθαι δ[ὲ]

αὐτὸν εἰς φυ[λὴν χα]ὶ δῆμον ἵ[ν'ἂ]ν βόλ[ηται]· τὸς δὲ [στ]

ρατηγὸς τὸς [ἐνθ]άδε ἀποδõνα[ι] αὐτῶ[ι τὸν μι]σθὸ̣ν [ὅ]   (*g*)

σομπερ πέρυ[σι]ν ἔφερε· τὸν δὲ [γ]ραμμ[ατέα τ]ῆς βολ[ῆ]

ς ἀναγράψαι τὸ ψήφισμα τόδε [τέ]λε[σι τοῖ]ς Σθόρυ[ο]

35   ς ἐν στήληι ἵναπερ αὐτῶι τὰ π[ρ]ότερ[α ψηφί]σματα [ἃ]   (*e*)

ναγέγραπται· ἐὰν δέ τις ταῦ[τ]α ἄκυρ[α ποι]ῆι, ὀφε[λέ]

τω χιλίας [δ]ραχμὰς ἱερ[ὰς τῆ]ι ᾿Αθηνάα[ι καὶ] τῶι ᾿Α[πό]

λλωνι τῶ[ι] Πυθίωι ἑτέρα[ς]· ἔναι δὲ ταῦ[τα κ]αὶ τοῖς [ἐ]

χγόνοις τοῖς Σθόρυος· καλέσαι δὲ αὐ[τὸν] ἐπὶ δε[ῖπ]

40   νον εἰς [τ]ὸ πρυτανεῖον εἰς αὔριον.   *vacat*

The lettering represents competent but somewhat idiosyncratic work of the early 4th century, and the text was evidently set out with artistic pretensions; but its execution falls short of its aims. The vertical stoichoi slope forward; letters rise and fall along the horizontal lines, varying in height and in the exactitude of their relationship to their neighbors and varying also within their vertical stoichoi. Cf. Osborne, *ZPE* 10, 1973, pp. 255–256. The forward tilt to alpha and lambda is particularly noteworthy, as are the varied renderings of upsilon, as well as a noticeable tendency to flatten the lowest stroke of sigma. Some ends of "free strokes" show the beginnings of an emphasis later to become fashionable. Part of the text in line 12 is written *in rasura* (with an erasure postulated also in line 11), and the letters there are larger and clumsier than elsewhere. Unusually, the entire inscription is enclosed by a raised, flat band, like a picture in a frame. In lines 22–23 and 27–39 an extra letter is crowded up against it to the right, and the same must be supposed elsewhere in the restoration of certain line endings. Line 8 evidently contained only 37 letters, and the revised line 11, 36. The tenon by which the stele was sunk into a separate base survives complete. On these features, and on the lettering in general, see Osborne, *BSA, op. cit.*, pp. 152–154 and *ZPE* 19, 1975, p. 175; Osborne has further deduced that a relief attachment, "set in a good way from the sides of the stele," surmounted the ensemble.

This is the earliest decree conferring full citizenship on a foreigner for which the Agora has provided material. Osborne's full account of the readings of the text (*BSA, op. cit.*, pp. 158–160), as well as that of Walbank, makes detailed commentary of the whole unnecessary. Where fragment *h* is concerned, the following may be noted: Line 28. ὥ[ν ἔθυσεν καὶ ὅτι τὰ] ἄλ[λα Osborne (*BSA*, but not *Naturalization*), Walbank; ὥ[ν ἀπέθυσεν καὶ ἐμ π]ᾶσ[ιν Meritt. Line 29.]ΩΝ[Meritt;]ΩΝΚ[Osborne, Walbank; but the mark of the supposed kappa on the stone may be casual. Line 31. βόλ[ηται Meritt; βόλ[ηται Osborne, Walbank. Line 34. [τέ]λε[σι Meritt, Walbank; [τέ]λε[σι Osborne. The readings otherwise are those of Meritt. In lines 36–39 Walbank has read ἄκυρα, χα]ὶ̣ τῶι, ἑτέρας and αὐτ[ὸν]. The relationship between the first fifteen lines and the remainder of the text has been redefined by Osborne, who showed that a blank space of three or four lines intervened between the two decrees which the stele records: cf. Osborne, *ZPE* 10, 1973, p. 265, note 30. The lines have been renumbered in consequence.

The "first decree" at least was a decree of the boule alone, not of the boule and demos. See **33**, commentary on line 3. This instance ill accords with explanations of the phenomenon that have been advanced with regard to the competence of the boule; but it may be supposed that the "first decree" represents a fairly simple piece of executive action, a matter, as Osborne expresses it (*Naturalization* II, p. 45), of "minor clarification", embodying confirmation that there were to be two stelai and specifying their location. It also included a further general compliment (lines 3–5) and a repeated invitation to dinner. That the decrees are indeed to be inscribed on two stelai, without mention of Sthorys' responsibility for the cost (which may have remained unaffected, since the amended provisions followed representations on his part), suggests that the detail of a decree might be varied in a matter of minor importance; cf. P. J. Rhodes, *Athenian Boule*, pp. 83, note 6, and 271.

For the occasion of the decrees and the career of Sthorys see Osborne, *BSA, op. cit.*, pp. 163–168 and *Naturalization* II, *loc. cit.*; Pouilloux, *op. cit.*, p. 196. Both agree with Wilhelm that the naval battle of lines 26–27 is the battle of Knidos (August 394 B.C.), and it is Osborne's view that the preliminary sacrifices (lines 27–28) are those preceding the battle and not those which would accompany the entry upon office of the generals of 394/3, these latter being the province of citizen ἱερεῖς and not of a foreign μάντις. The prevalent assumption that Sthorys was a Thasian in exile (cf. *IG* II², 24 and 36; **40**) has been questioned by Walbank. For the circumstances in Thasos affecting all these documents see Pouilloux, *op. cit.*, pp. 195–203.

Lines 1–3. The officials are recorded in the 5th-century style, without patronymic or demotic; but practice was already becoming variable. The γραμματεύς (with patronymic and demotic) is repeated, and the archon (with demotic only) is introduced in lines 13–15 as a remarkable and unique tailpiece to the "first decree": cf. Osborne, *BSA, op. cit.*, pp. 156, 161–162; A. S. Henry, *Prescripts*, p. 9, note 34. Line 10. πόληι. For the form see L. Threatte, *Grammar*, pp. 381–382. For its continuing use as the designation of the Akropolis cf. **39** and **40**, commentary on line 16. Ἐν Πυθίο. See **20**, commentary on line 20. Sthorys was a μάντις of Apollo Pythios; cf. lines 37–38.

Lines 30–31. For the phraseology in connection with the grant of citizenship see Osborne, *BSA, op. cit.*, pp. 171–173, with references to other literature, and *Naturalization* II, p. 47, and cf. **40**. Here there is no reference to enrolment in a phratry, which was a customary element of citizenship. This is probably no more than a matter of careless drafting, but it is an additional reminder that formulas at this period were fluid and subject to variations of detail. See further Osborne, *BSA* 66, 1971, p. 305 with note 51, and 67, 1972, pp. 146–147; Henry, *Honours*, pp. 69–71.

Lines 34–35. See **37**, note on line 13. Line 37. Ἀθηνάα[ι]. See Threatte, *Grammar* pp. 271–274. Lines 39–40. Sthorys' newly acquired citizenship makes ἐπὶ δεῖπνον rather than ἐπὶ ξένια the appropriate invitation, even though the distinction between the two, generally maintained, is sometimes disregarded. For the formula see **20**, note on lines 28–30 and references there. The phrase is here expressed in its regular form: at its earlier appearance (lines 11–12) Osborne supposed that an initial confusion on the part of the stonecutter caused the erasure and correction, although even so the regular phraseology was not fully regained.

References to further discussions of elements of this text are to be found in *SEG* XXIX, 85, XXXIII, 72, and XXXVI, 140. For Euboulides (line 14) and other officials of his year see also R. Develin, *Athenian Officials*, pp. 208–210.

CITIZENS OF IALYSOS HONORED

37. A fragment of a stele of Pentelic marble (I 5896), with the right side preserved but otherwise broken all around, discovered on November 29, 1943, among marbles in the area just southeast of the Market Square and west of the Panathenaic Way.

H. 0.247 m.; W. 0.19 m.; Th. 0.07–0.075 m.

LH. 0.01–0.012 m. (omega 0.007 m., xi and omicron 0.009 m.).

Στοιχ. Hor. 0.0164 m.; Vert. 0.016 m.

Ed. A. G. Woodhead, *Hesperia* 17, 1948, pp. 54–57, no. 65, with photograph pl. 24; M. B. Walbank, *Athenian Proxenies*, pp. 376–378, no. 72, with photograph pl. 47:b (= *SEG* XXVIII, 48). See also J. and L. Robert, *REG* 62, 1949, pp. 103–104, no. 42; A. Lambrechts, *De Atheense Proxeniedecreten*, pp. 27, 31, 69, 74, 125–127, 153; P. Funke, *ZPE* 53, 1983, pp. 169–174 (*SEG* XXXIII, 68).

paullo post a. 394 a.   ΣΤΟΙΧ. 20

```
                    [----------------]
                    [.........17........ εἶ]π
                    [εν· ἐπαινέσαι μὲν ...]λλι
                    [........14....... Ἰη]λυσί
                    [ωι, ἐπειδὴ φίλος ἐν] τῶι πρ
              5     [όσθεν χρόνωι ἦν, κ]αὶ τοῖς
                    [ἀδελφοῖς ..5..]κωι Ἰηλυ
                    [σ....9...., ἐπ]ειδὴ καὶ ὁ
                    [πατὴρ αὐτῶν ἦ]ν πρόξενος
```

```
        [καὶ εὐεργέτ]ης καὶ ἐπὶ τῶ
10      [ν τριάκοντα] καθηιρέθη ἡ
        [στήλη· ἀναγρά]ψαι δὲ αὐτὸ
        [ν καὶ τὸς ἀδελ]φὸς τὸν γρα
        [μματέα τῆς βολῆ]ς τέλεσι
        [τοῖς ....8.... πρ]οξένος
15      [καὶ εὐεργέτας ᵛᵛᵛᵛ]ᵛᵛᵛᵛ
        [            vacat           ]
```

The writing is well cut and of good quality: omega is open and rather squat; xi and omicron are (in some instances) pendent from the upper line of the lettering.

The restorations are slightly modified from those of the *editio princeps* (which was followed also by Walbank). The general purport of the decree is to honor a citizen of Ialysos and his brothers, one of whose forebears (probably their father) had been named proxenos and benefactor at an earlier date, in all likelihood before 412/11 B.C. The stele carrying the record of that earlier decree had, like a number of others (for which see *IG* I³, p. 196), been destroyed during the brief oligarchical regime of the "Thirty Tyrants". The renewal of the family honors may be held to postdate the battle of Knidos in 394. Funke, however, *loc. cit.*, prefers to place the restored grant soon after the restoration of the Athenian democracy in 403/2. The city of Rhodes had been established by the synoecism of Lindos, Ialysos, and Kameiros in 408/7, but the honorands here retain the ethnic of the original grant without modification. The phraseology of lines 8–13 leaves no doubt of the length of line in this brief statement.

Lines 5–7. [ὅσθεν χρόνωι ἦν, κ]αὶ τοῖς ‖[ἀδελφοῖς ὧν καὶ τ]ῶι Ἰηλυ‖[σίων κήρυκι(?), ἐπ]ειδὴ κτλ. *ed. princ.*; but in line 6 kappa may be seen to precede omega, and the suggestion, in any case difficult, must be abandoned. Proper names may be concerned. *IG* II², 6 (*SEG* XV, 83) offers a general guide to the presumed character of the text as well as an exact parallel to its stoichedon pattern. Line 10. Cf. **39**. Line 13. In *IG* II², 6, the cost of the stele was defrayed by one of the several honorands (although not the first named among them), and the same is likely to have been the case here. For the formula τέλεσι τοῖς τοῦ δεῖνος in relation to grants of *proxenia*, see A. S. Henry, *Vindex Humanitatis: Essays in Honour of John Huntly Bishop*, 1980, pp. 17–33 (examples of the present type, pp. 20–21); cf. **1**, **11**, and **21**. The latest example, *IG* II², 289 (*SEG* XXI, 300, XXIII, 60) is to be dated a little before or a little after the middle of the 4th century. *IG* II², 411 (*SEG* XIII, 41; D. Behrend, *Attische Pachturkunden*, pp. 71–72, no. 18), in which the formula is used in a *pactio*, is dated *ca.* 330.

FRAGMENT OF AN HONORARY(?) DECREE

38. A fragment of the upper part of a stele of Pentelic marble (I 4663), with the worn remains of a sculptured representation in shallow relief surviving above the first line of the inscription, and with the left edge and perhaps the original back of the monument preserved, but otherwise broken and much battered all around, discovered on March 29, 1937, in a Turkish pit of late date on the North Slope of the Akropolis, below Klepsydra (T 26). In the sculptured relief, on the left, is the lower part of a standing draped figure facing right; confronting this figure appear the forehooves of a prancing horse and the booted foot of a second human figure. The inscribed surface is considerably worn.

H. 0.227 m.; W. 0.283 m.; Th. 0.095 m.

LH. 0.009 m. (nu 0.0115 m.).

Στοιχ. Hor. 0.014 m.; Vert. 0.016 m.

Ed. B. D. Meritt, *Hesperia* 26, 1957, p. 207, no. 53, with photograph pl. 52. See also *SEG* XVII, 16.

init. saec. IV *a.*　　　　　　　　　　　　　　　　　　　　　　　　　ΣΤΟΙΧ. 25

```
                Θ     [ε     ο     ι].
        [Ἔ]δοξεν τῆι βολ[ῆ]ι [καὶ τῶι δήμωι]·
        [Ἐρ]εχθηὶς ἐπρυτάγ[ευε, ...7....]
        [..] ἐγραμμάτευ[ε, ...6... ἐπεστά]
5       [τε], Γνάθων εἶπε[ν· .....12.....]
        [..]αχίδην καὶ [......14......]
        [————————————————]
```

In the appreciation of the lettering the poor state of the stone permits less than justice to be done: but the inscription does not seem to be well executed. The lower preserved lines slope away to the right, and the letters are inconsistently set in their stoichoi. The horizontal strokes of epsilon and the center strokes of mu are all short; omega has a "wishbone" shape with very short horizontals. Parallels for some of the features of this text appear in *IG* II², 32, 34, and 37, all datable to the second half of the second decade of the 4th century; the present inscription could well belong to the same period.

Line 1. Meritt regarded it as possible that a theta was preserved above the tau of τῆι in the first line of the decree. The traces are reasonable enough for the inclusion of Θ[εοί] in the text. The epsilon (if the word was symmetrically spaced) should have stood slightly to the right of omicron in βολ[ῆ]ι, and the damage to the stone at the point appears briefly to follow a vertical line where its upright stroke should be. Line 5. The name Gnathon is very rare in Attic prosopography, but the examples of it are spread through four centuries from the 6th to the 3rd. A possible identification for the proposer of this decree is Γνάθων Ἐλευσίνιος (*PA* 3050), whose daughter Philoumene is commemorated on the stele *IG* II², 6054 (dated 365–340 B.C.), and whose son E[. .⁵. . .] proposed the Eleusinian decree *IG* II², 1188 (dated "med. s. IV"). For Γνάθων Λακιάδης see M. B. Walbank, *Hesperia* 52, 1983, p. 129. Γνάθων Χολλείδης (*PA* 3051) belongs later in the century. Line 6. [. .]α[.]ίδην Meritt. Between the alpha and iota appear cuts at the edge of the break which are certainly intentional, that is, parts of a cut letter, and can only be the tips of the vertical and upper oblique strokes of kappa, the oblique stroke of which rises high in the only other examples of the same letter on this stone (in the same line). The name [Αἰ]ακίδης would answer the indications, with, for example, εἶπε[ν· ἐπαινέσαι μέν] in the previous line. It may be worth remarking that Aiakides is a name particularly associated with central and northern Greece and that the appearance of a horse in the relief may suggest a connection with Thessaly. Cf. *IG* II², 116 (*SEG* XXI, 243); R. Binneboessel, *Studien zu den attischen Urkundenreliefs des 5. und 4. Jahrhunderts*, 1932, p. 10, no. 38. But other names, for example Φυλακίδης, and other hypotheses may come into consideration.

FRAGMENT OF A REINSCRIBED DECREE

39 (Pl. 4). A small fragment of a stele of Pentelic marble (I 4768), broken on all sides, discovered on April 21, 1937, in a late context southeast of the Market Square, east of the Post-Herulian Wall (U 23–24).

H. 0.09 m.; W. 0.115 m.; Th. 0.049 m.
LH. 0.009 m.
Στοιχ. Hor. 0.0175 m.; Vert. 0.0165 m.

Ed. E. Schweigert, *Hesperia* 9, 1940, pp. 313–314, no. 30, with photograph.

init. saec. IV *a.*   ΣΤΟΙΧ. 23

```
        [--------------------]
        [. . . .]ης χ[αὶ ἀναγράψαι τὸ ψήφ]
        [ισμα] ἐν στ[ήληι λιθίνηι τὸγ γ]
        [ραμμ]ατέα [τῆς βολῆς ἐμ πόλει]
        [ἐπει]δὴ χα[θηιρέθη ἡ στήλη ἡ α]
   5    [ὐτῶι πρ]ότ[ερον ἀναχειμένη ἐ]
        [πὶ τῶν τριάχοντα . . . .⁹. . . .]
        [-------------------]
```

The lettering is clear, well cut, and orderly in the best style of the early 4th century. It has no special characteristic save that sigma is particularly neat and compact and that the central horizontal stroke of epsilon slightly projects beyond its neighbors above and below. The position ascribed to the fragment in relation to the edges of the stele and the resulting division of lines shown in the text are purely arbitrary.

The restoration calls for the use of the word πόλις for the Akropolis, and on this criterion the decree must be dated within the first quarter of the century. The last dated instance of πόλις possibly occurs in 379/8 in an honorary decree (*SEG* XXXII, 50), where it is a proposed restoration; but this does not represent a *terminus ante quem*. See **40**, commentary on line 16 and A. S. Henry, *Chiron* 12, 1982, p. 92. Lines 4–6. The decree reenacted an earlier measure, probably an honorary decree, which had been inscribed on a stele demolished during the regime of the "Thirty Tyrants" in 404/3; cf. **37**. In all these cases the fact of demolition underscores the thoroughness of that regime in dealing with what displeased it, as well as the significance attached to the inscribed record. The phraseology on which the text of these lines is based occurs in *IG* II², 9 (*SEG* XIV, 35, XXXII, 41); see also, in addition to **37**, *IG* II², 6 and 66, fragment c (*SEG* XV, 83 and XIV, 40). Another form of words is used in *IG* II², 52.

ATHENIAN CITIZENSHIP BESTOWED ON ARCHIPPOS AND HIPPARCHOS OF THASOS

40. A fragment of a stele of Pentelic marble (I 4954, hereafter fragment *a*), a larger section of which is provided by *IG* II², 25 (now fragment *b*), broken on all sides although evidently preserving part of the initial line of the inscribed text, discovered on June 7, 1937, in a Byzantine well in the north wall of the paved court below Klepsydra (T 26–27). The two fragments make no join with each other but are separated by a lacuna of indeterminate length.

  a: H. 0.14 m.; W. 0.135 m.; Th. 0.07 m.

  b: H. 0.29 m.; W. 0.37 m.; Th. 0.10 m.

  LH. 0.012 m. (beta 0.016 m., nu 0.0145 m., omicron 0.009 m., omega 0.007 m.).

  Στοιχ. Hor. 0.022 m.; Vert. 0.02 m., with variations.

  Ed. *b* only: *IG* II², 25. *a* + *b*: W. K. Pritchett, *Hesperia* 10, 1941, pp. 262–263, no. 66, with photographs (cf. *SEG* XV, 86); see also W. B. Dinsmoor, *AJA* 36, 1932, pp. 157–160 (especially p. 159, note 6), on the date of *IG* II², 25. Photograph of fragment *b*, J. Pouilloux, *Recherches sur l'histoire et les cultes de Thasos* I, 1954, pl. XVI: 4. Brief references by M. J. Osborne, *BSA* 65, 1970, p. 169, with note 103, and 67, 1972, pp. 146–147, 150, 156; P. J. Rhodes, *Athenian Boule*, p. 247 (in the list of "probouleumatic decrees"). See further Osborne, *Naturalization* I, pp. 45–46, no. D 9, *Naturalization* II, pp. 48–57 (cf. *SEG* XXXI, 58).

  a. 388/7 a. vel 375/4 a.   ΣΤΟΙΧ. 18

(a)
```
      ["Εδοξεν τῆι βο]λῆι χα[ὶ τ]
      [ῶι δήμωι· ....]ις ἐπρ[υτ]
      [άνευε, ...⁷...]ς Πε[ιρα]
      [ιεὺς ἐγραμμάτ]ε[υε, ...]
  5   [...........¹⁸...........]
                    lacuna
```
(b)
```
      [...........¹⁷........ "Α]
      [ρ]χ[ι]π[πο]ν τὸ[ν] Θάσιο[ν χα]
      ι ῞Ιππαρχον ᾿Αθηναίο[ς ἐν]
      αι ἀνδραγαθίας ἕν[εχα]
  10  τῆς ἐς ᾿Αθηναίος, χ[αὶ φυ]
      λὴν χαὶ δῆμον χαὶ [φρατ]
      ρίαν ἐλέσθαι, ἥντ[ιν'ἀν]
      βόλωνται· χα[ὶ] ἀνα[γράψ]
      αι αὐτὸς ἐστήλη[ι λιθί]-
  15  νηι τὸγ γραμμ[ατέα τῆς]
      βολῆς ἐν ἀχ[ροπόλει, ἐς]
      δὲ τὴν ἀν[αγραφὴν δõνα]
      ι τὸν τα[μίαν εἴχοσι δρ]
      αχμάς.    [vacat]
                [vacat]
```

The lettering of *IG* II², 25 is referred to in its context as "volg. init. s. IV", which does not reflect its stylistic quality and general precision; the letters are well spaced, well formed, and well cut, without notable idiosyncrasies; all three horizontals of epsilon are of equal length; omega is distinctive enough to be useful in any search for work by the same craftsman.

  Line 2. Αἰγη]ὶς or Οἰνη]ὶς. Lines 6–7. ῎Αρ]χ[ιππον] τὸ[ν] Θάσιο[ν Pritchett; [... ῎Αρχιππον(?)] Θάσιο[ν *IG* II²; ῎Α]ρχιπ[πο]ν τὸν Θάσιο[ν Osborne. Line 8. The two iotas at the beginning of the line are inscribed in a single letter space. Traces of extra letters have been noted in lines 15–19: the text is otherwise that of Pritchett.

  For the developing situation in Thasos during this period, variously interpreted, on which the date of the decree is to some extent dependent, see Pouilloux, *op. cit.*, pp. 195–203, with references, Osborne, *Naturalization* II, *loc. cit.*, and **36**. The comparable text *IG* II², 24 (*SEG* XXXI, 58) is also relevant. There the same two Thasians receive honors, and the phrase ὅτε [Θρασ]ύβολος ἦρ[χεν (line 6) is most likely to refer to a date preceding the death of Thrasyboulos in 389; cf. M. B. Walbank, *Athenian Proxenies*, pp. 328, 405. The occasion of the present decree must also be related to the use of ἐν ἀχ[ροπόλει in line 16 and the appearance of ὁ τα[μίας, *tout court*, in line 18, on both of which see further below: for both have been held, in the past, to offer decisive support for the later of the dates proposed.

If that were so, the honors here recorded would belong not just after the expulsion of the Spartan garrison from Thasos (cf. Xenophon, *HG* 5.1.7), the date favored by earlier opinion (references in Pritchett, *op. cit.*, p. 263, note 1), but to the time when Chabrias was active in extending the Second Athenian Confederacy in the north (cf. *IG* II^2, 43, line 100; M. N. Tod, *GHI* II, p. 67; F. H. Marshall, *The Second Athenian Confederacy*, 1905, p. 61; A. G. Woodhead, *AJA* 61, 1957, p. 371 and *Phoenix* 16, 1962, pp. 258–259). *IG* II^2, 24 perhaps belongs to the earlier occasion, while the later date would suit the present text in that it shows a greater and more extraordinary generosity to the same honorands in the award of full citizenship. Pouilloux, preferring to leave the issue open, gave to both texts the general date 388–375 (*op. cit.*, p. 203). Osborne argued on general grounds, notwithstanding the single treasurer and the reference to the Akropolis, for the earlier date. See also A. S. Henry (*Chiron* 14, 1984, p. 50, note 4), who favoured a date "shortly before 387/6" in an earlier article, *Chiron* 12, 1982, p. 114.

Line 9. Ἀνδραγαθία is less usually cited as a quality in these circumstances than εὔνοια or ἀρετή, with which it is sometimes associated, being particularly relevant, as it appears, to merit displayed in war or civil strife. In the late 5th century it is found in *IG* I^3, 97 (I^2, 103; Walbank, *Athenian Proxenies*, pp. 378–384, no. 73), joined with (restored) φιλοτιμία; see also *IG* II^2, 1, line 70 (honors for the Samians in 403/2), where it is joined with ἀρετή, and R. S. Stroud, *Hesperia* 40, 1971, pp. 280–301, no. 7, lines 8–9 (in reference to men killed in the civil conflict of 404/3), joined with εὐεργεσία. It is restored (by itself, as here) in *IG* II^2, 23, of 388/7. The evidence suggests that its use at Athens antedates 336 b.c. It was also used in honors awarded to Athenian citizens; cf., for example, Hypereides, ὑπὲρ Λυκόφρονος 16. At this period, however, the formula of the type ὅτι (or ἐπειδὴ) ἀνὴρ ἀγαθός ἐστι preponderates in citations of this kind (cf. **36**, lines 28–29). Cf. also Henry, *Honours*, p. 65.

Line 10. For the variations of formula for choice of phyle, deme, and phratry see Osborne, *locc. citt.* and **36**, note on lines 30–31. Line 15. The γραμματεὺς τῆς βουλῆς, responsible for the inscription of the decree, is still the monthly official changing with the prytany. The addition of the demotic to his name in lines 3–4 (although not the patronymic; contrast **36**, line 13 and *IG* II^2, 16, line 4, of 394/3) represents a development in documentary practice emerging at the end of the 5th century (*IG* II^2, 1, lines 5–6) but at this time still followed out variably and intermittently; see Henry, *Prescripts*, pp. 31–32.

Line 16. ἐν ἀκ[ροπόλει. The significance of this, in place of the hitherto customary ἐμ πόλει, for the date of the decree has already been referred to, but its value for dating purposes cannot be precisely determined; cf. **36**, line 10 and **39**. The argument about it is also linked to the evidence concerning the disbursing officer (line 18), and both issues have been studied by Henry (*Chiron* 12, 1982, pp. 91–118 [*SEG* XXXII, 347]: on this text see particularly pp. 99 and 113–114). The view of Dinsmoor (*loc. cit.*) was that no instance of ἀκρόπολις can be shown to antedate 386 and that no instance of πόλις surely postdates 374. Despite attempts, stretching back a hundred years, to establish a firm point for the change of usage (cf. P. Foucart, *BCH* 12, 1888, pp. 161 and 166; *IG* II^2, 51, 56, and 57, *comm.*), definite dates are lacking for most of the decrees of the first quarter of the 4th century. It is not unreasonable to believe that there was a period of overlap during which either designation might be employed and that the lines may not be so nicely drawn as Dinsmoor argued. Cf. J. Pečírka, *Formula*, pp. 27–28. If that is so, the appearance of ἀκρόπολις for πόλις cannot be decisive one way or the other.

Line 18. "The Treasurer" (i.e., of the δῆμος) is responsible for defraying the cost of the stele. At this period there was some variation in the officer or officers to whom this duty fell. A. C. Johnson (*CP* 9, 1914, pp. 417–423), reviewing all the evidence, sought to define four periods down to 377, during which this treasurer functioned in the second (394–387) as well as during the remainder of the century after 377. Cf. W. S. Ferguson, *The Treasurers of Athena*, 1932, pp. 132–139. Dinsmoor (*loc. cit.*) maintained that the single treasurer did not begin to provide funds for the inscription of decrees until after 376 and that those decrees showing him as paymaster to which an earlier date had been assigned should be given a later attribution. Henry's review of the problem concluded that Johnson's and Dinsmoor's reconstructions erred on the side of neatness; he claimed that the single treasurer is to be found as early as *ca.* 390/89, the date to which he would assign *IG* II^2, 21 (*SEG* XXXII, 43). Thus both the single officer of the demos and the plural board of treasurers of the goddess were called up for disbursements between *ca.* 390 and *ca.* 364, after which the single treasurer certainly functioned as the only disbursing officer. Cf. Pečírka, *Formula, loc. cit.*; Rhodes, *Athenian Boule*, p. 103, note 7. Since this element too offers no dating criterion for this text, its date must in the last resort depend upon such historical interpretation of its circumstances as may be preferred.

A sum of twenty drachmas is restored as the intended cost, and the formula here makes its first appearance among the Agora decrees; if the earlier dating of this text be favored, it is also the earliest instance of a specified cash limit in Attic epigraphy, apart from *IG* II^2, 24, where it is also to be found. On this subject see Brian T. Nolan, "Inscribing Costs at Athens in the Fourth Century B.C." (diss. The Ohio State University, 1981). The first firmly dated such text is *IG* II^2, 31, of 386/5 b.c., where the cash amount is preserved.

RELATIONS WITH LEMNOS

41. Five nonjoining fragments of a stele of Pentelic marble, three of them (fragments *a, c, d*) long familiar as *IG* II², 30, the fourth (fragment *b*) discovered in O. Broneer's excavations on the North Slope of the Akropolis, and the fifth (fragment *e*) discovered in the excavations of the Athenian Agora; their details are as follows:

Fragment *a* (E.M. 6916) preserves the top of the stele but is otherwise broken all around; it was discovered in 1849 on the Akropolis west of the Parthenon and is now in the Epigraphical Museum.

Fragment *b* (E.M. 12964) also preserves the top of the stele and from the nature of its contents must be located to the right of fragment *a*, although it is not contiguous with it; it is otherwise broken all around. Discovered on May 6, 1938, in late fill in the main area of Broneer's excavations (for which see *Hesperia* 2, 1933, pp. 329–417, *Hesperia* 4, 1935, pp. 109–188, *Hesperia* 7, 1938, pp. 161–263), it is now in the Epigraphical Museum.

Fragment *c* (E.M. 6904), broken all around (except that the back has been dressed down obliquely to the front in a later reworking), was also found on the Akropolis and is now in the Epigraphical Museum.

Fragment *d* (E.M. 6905) similarly is broken all around, was found on the Akropolis, and is in the Epigraphical Museum. Fragments *c* and *d* had both been discovered before *IG* II went to the press in 1876 and with fragment *a* were included as no. 14 in that volume, from U. Koehler's own transcript.

Fragment *e* (I 5588), broken on all sides, was discovered on October 15, 1938, in the wall of a modern house southwest of the Eleusinion, on the west side of the Panathenaic Way (R 20).

The monument seems to have been very thoroughly shattered. Many breaks run obliquely to the surface and in a variety of directions, without any pattern helpful in the reconstruction of the stele.

a: H. 0.46 m.; W. 0.28 m.; Th. 0.15 m.

b: H. 0.192 m.; W. 0.087 m.; Th. 0.05 m.

c: H. 0.215 m.; W. 0.20 m.; Th. 0.145 m.

d: H. 0.132 m.; W. 0.154 m.; Th. 0.088 m.

e: H. 0.192 m.; W. 0.188 m.; Th. 0.153 m.

LH. 0.007–0.008 m.

Ed. *a, c, d*: *IG* II², 30, with earlier references; *SEG* III, 73. *e* only: B. D. Meritt, *Hesperia* 37, 1968, pp. 266–267, no. 2, with photograph pl. 77 (cf. SEG XXV, 63). *b*, with reedition of fragments *a* and *c–e*: R. S. Stroud, *Hesperia* 40, 1971, pp. 162–173, no. 23, with photographs of all fragments pl. 30. Discussion by V. P. Yailenko, Греческая Колонизация 7–8, 3, 1982, pp. 206–216. See further *Agora* XIX, L3 (M. B. Walbank), where the lemma includes earlier references not detailed here.

The designation of the fragments here and in *Agora* XIX differs slightly from that adopted by Stroud: Stroud's *b*, *c*, and *d* appear as *c, d*, and *b* respectively in the present text.

a. 387/6 a.   NON-ΣΤΟΙΧ. *ca.* 95–100

(a)
```
    ["Εδοξεν τῆι βολῆι καὶ τῶι δήμωι· Θεόδοτος ἦρχε, ----------------------]ις
        ἐπρυτάνευεν· [.]ρι[.ᶜᵃ·⁵. ἐγρα]μμάτευεν, [---ἐπεστάτει, ----------]          (b)
    [εἶπεν· εὔξασθαι μὲν τὸν κήρυκα αὐτίκα μάλα ...ᶜᵃ·⁹...]ι καὶ τοῖ[ς] δώδεκα θεοῖς, ἐ[ὰν
        ...ᶜᵃ·⁸...] συνενείκηι [---------------------------]
    [----------------------------θυσίαν καὶ πρόσοδον ποιήσε]σθαι καθότι ἂν
        τῶι [δ]ήμ[ωι δοκῆι· ταῦ]τα μὲν ηὖχ[θαι, ἐπειδὴ δὲ --------------]
    [-------------------------------δεδ]όχθαι τῶι δήμωι πρὸς τὸς [κλη-
        ρόχος τὸς ο]ἰκõντας ἐν [Λήμνωι -----------------]
5   [----------------------- ἐπὶ τοῦ δεῖνα ἄρ]χοντος ἐν Λήμν[ω]ι
        ἐγένετ[ο ..ᶜᵃ·⁹⁻¹⁰...]τοις τὰς αὐτ[-----------------]
    [------------------ἐὰν δέ τις --?-- παρ]ὰ ταῦτα ἢ φαίνηι ἢ, :πάγηι ἢ
        [...ᶜᵃ·¹⁰...] ἀπογραφὴ[ν -----------------]
    [------------------δημ]ευθῆι τῆς νῦν ἀπογεγραμμέ[νης γῆς ᶜᵃ·⁴.]
        τα ἐγ Λήμν[ωι -----------------]
    [--------------------] ἐκτείσωσιν ἐπὶ τῆς ἐνάτης [πρυ-
        τανείας ..]πεν ἐπι[-----------------]
```

```
      [——————————————————————————————————]αν τὸν ἐσιόντα ἐνιαυτὸν
              χα̣[.....ca. 13.....]θων[——————————————————————]
10    [—————————————————————————————] βολῆς εἴτε τρεῖς κατὰ τὼ
                δ[.....ca. 13.....]ο̣[——————————————————————]
      [———————————————————————————παρ]ὰ τῶι Θησείωι ἐν ἧιτινι
              ἂν ἡμέ[ραι ——————————————————————————————]
      [—————————————————————————————]ι πεντακοσιομεδίμνων
              του[——————————————————————————————————]
      [———————————————————————————]αι τοῖς κληρόχοις τά
              τε ἐχτεισ[ματα ——————————————————————————]
      [—————————————————————]εις τῶν οἰκιῶν τῶν δεδημε[υ-
              μένων ——————————————————————————————]
15    [——————————————————————ἐ]γ Λήμνο εἰσάγοσιν ὁπό-
              σοι ἂν [————————————————————————————]
      [————————————————————τ]ῶι δημοσίωι ὁπόσοι ἂν
              μὴ ἐχτ[είσωσι ——————————————————————]
      [—————————————————————————]ων· ὁπόσην δ’ αὐτοὶ
              ἠργάζον[το ——————————————————————————]
      [————————————————————τ]ὰ ὄρη χαὶ τὰ ἀφορίσ-
              ματα ἐσ[———————————————————————————]
      [————————————————————————]της αὐτὴ ἡ
              μίσθωσις πέπρατ[αι ——————————————————]
20    [————————————————τοῖς κλη]ρόχοις ἢ ἐν-
              οφέλεσθαί τις χ[——————————————————]
      [—————————————————————ὀφέλ]οντες τῶι
              δημοσίωι εἶχον ἐπ[————————————————————]
      [————————————————————τ]ῶν κληρόχων τὰ
              μὲν ἄλλα [————————————————————————]
      [—————————————————————] ἀμφισβητῶν τῆς
              γῆς ἢ τῆ[ς ——————————————————————]
      [————————————————————δ]ίκαις, ἐὰν δὲ μὴ
              λάχηι δὶς [——————————————————————]
25    [—————————————————————] ἡ δίκη τήν τε ἀνά-
              χρισιν π[———————————————————————]
      [————————————————————]ων ἐς τὸ δικαστήριον
              παρὰ [——————————————————————————]
      [———————————————ἀμφι]σ[β]ητῶν ἕνα λόγο̣ν
              πρι̣[————————————————————————————]
                              lacuna
```

```
(c)   [———————————]ι̣ν[————————————————————————————]
      [————————— στησ]άτω ἐν ἀκροπό[λει ———————————————]
30    [——————————]ολων χαὶ μὴ ἐξε͂να[ι ———————————————————]
      [———— μήτε ———————]ναι μήτε μισθῶσαι πλὴν [———————————]
      [————————— ὦ]νος μηνὸς τὸ͂ μετὰ Θεό[δοτον ἄρχοντα —————————]
      [—————————] γῆν τὸς κληρόχος χαὶ[————————————————————]
      [———————— χαθάπ]ερ τοῖς ἐς Σαλαμ[ῖνα —————————————————]
35    [——————————— ἀφιχ]νομένων ε[————————————————————————]
      [—————————————]⌐[.]ι[.] ∨ᴨⁱ[————————————————————————]
                              lacuna
```

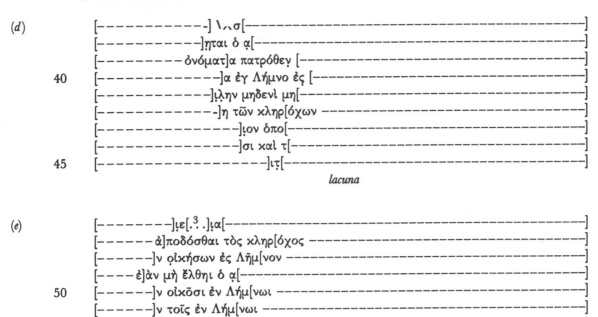

(d)
```
[------------] \˄σ[----------------------------]
[------------]ηται ὁ ᾳ[---------------------------]
[--------ὀνόματ]α πατρόθεν [---------------------------]
```
40
```
[------------]α ἐγ Λήμνο ἐς [------------------------]
[------------]ͅλην μηδενὶ μη[---------------------------]
[------------]η τῶν κληρ[όχων ------------------------]
[------------]ͅον ὁπο[---------------------------]
[------------]σι καὶ τ[---------------------------]
```
45
```
[------------]ͅτ[-------------------------------]
```
             lacuna

(e)
```
[--------]ͅε[.³.]ͅα[---------------------------]
[------ἀ]ποδόσθαι τὸς κληρ[όχος ---------------------]
[------]ν οἰκήσων ἐς Λῆμ[νον ---------------------]
[----ἐ]ὰν μὴ ἔλθηι ὁ ᾳ[---------------------------]
```
50
```
[------]ν οἰκῶσι ἐν Λήμ[νωι ---------------------]
[------]ν τοῖς ἐν Λήμ[νωι ---------------------]
[--------]σιάσαντες [---------------------------]
[--------]σηι ο[---------------------------]
```
             lacuna

Stroud's full text (reproduced above, as in *Agora* XIX, L3) and careful commentary make it unnecessary to enter into substantial detail in this context. Stroud assessed the overall width of the monument as *ca.* 0.85–0.90 m. and its probable height at not less than 1.30 m. The relationship of fragments *a* and *b* may be established with some accuracy, but the location below them of the other fragments cannot be determined. A vertical vein of discoloration on fragment *a*, which might have assisted to that end, is not reproduced on any other fragment. On the "Agora fragment", *e*, Stroud read as shown a first line (now line 46) recorded by Meritt simply as "traces"; its first letter may be nu rather than iota. Line 48 was read by Meritt as ΝΗΚΕΣΩΝ. Otherwise, his readings of this fragment were followed in the subsequent publication.

At first glance the lettering of this document may appear careless and shabby: but it is in fact reasonably tidy and by no means as poor as some of the less creditable work of the early 4th century, such as *IG* II², 110. Irregularities in the formation of single letters do not preclude an overall appearance of competence. The curved element of omega is noticeably open; its horizontal strokes are short. Delta is sometimes small (cf. *IG* II², 28, of 387/6, a less well executed piece); the angle made by the lowest stroke of sigma varies markedly. The writing appears to the worst effect on fragment *e*, the inscribed surface of which is more worn than on the other fragments.

The date depends upon the interpretation of line 32. The phrase – – –ῶ]νος μηνὸς τὸ μετὰ Θεό[δοτον ἄρχοντα– – – implies that the year of the decree immediately follows that for which Theodotos was eponymous archon, that is, 387/6: see *IG* II², 30, *comm.* The simpler and usual method of reference to 386/5 would have been in terms of the eponymous for that year, Mystichides; and Stroud preferred to see the text as itself a document of 387/6, looking forward to action to be taken in the year following, the eponymous archon for which had not at the time been determined. He therefore restored the name of Theodotos in line 1, although its position, with its verb, is unusual, for the citation of the archon is customarily the last in prescripts of this form and period before the proposer of the measure is named (or is separated from it at most by the name of the epistates): but it may be significant that *IG* II², 28, also of this year (see above), is a notable exception to this general rule. Cf. A. S. Henry, *Prescripts*, p. 22.

Walbank (*Agora* XIX) provides a full list of proposals made for the supplementation of the text, as well as a summary of the "probable" total content of the document. Where so little survives, however, analysis both of the general tenor and of detailed provisions must remain speculative. Yailenko's discussion involves similar reservations. Certain suggestions nevertheless merit record, for example that of Stroud on line 18 proposing that the ἀφορίσματα represent sacred properties, or *temene*. The "mountainous areas" define land unsuitable for agriculture by reason of geography; the "areas set aside" presumably include land unsuited for use for other reasons, of which ownership by a god was undoubtedly one.

Among tentative restorations may be mentioned the following: Line 2. ἱερέα (for κήρυκα) Yailenko. Line 6. ἢ ἀπάγηι ἢ [εἴπηι ὡς δεῖ τὴν] ἀπογραφὴν [λύειν (*vel* καταλῦσαι) – – –] Stroud. Line 22. [– – –εἶπεν· περὶ τ]ῶν κληρόχων τὰ μὲν ἄλλα [καθάπερ τῆι βολῆι – – –] Stroud. Line 23. ἢ τῆ[ς οἰκίας – – –] Stroud. Line 26. κ ἡμερ]ῶν ἐς τὸ δικαστήριον Stroud. Line 47. κλήρ[ος – – –] Yailenko. Line 52. – – –στα]σιάσαντες Yailenko. The discovery of fragment *b* invalidated some of the restorations proposed by S. Luria (*SEG* III, *loc. cit.*), which in any case bordered upon the venturesome: but his suggestion for line 12 (πλὴν ἱππέων κα]ὶ πεντακοσιομεδίμνων), with reference to *IG* I³, 46 (**7**), lines 43–46, may be noted.

That leasing of public properties is in large part the concern of the decree requires the inclusion of this text also in the *Agora* volume (XIX) devoted to this class of material. Cf. D. Behrend, *Attische Pachturkunden*, pp. 51–52, no. 2.

For the state of Lemnian affairs at this time see Stroud, *loc. cit.*, pp. 170–171. The island had received Athenian colonists or cleruchs at least on two occasions during the 5th century. The fate of their descendants during the period of Spartan ascendancy after 404 is unclear, but it is evident that at the time of the King's Peace, with Athenian possession of Lemnos firmly reestablished, some reorganization of land holdings and the terms on which they were occupied was necessary. The presence and, in the context, importance of the cleruchs is visible on every fragment of the document here reviewed. They were apparently resident, and not absentee landlords (lines 47–51), and the allocation or reallocation of their land might lead, or had already led, to dispute and litigation (lines 20–27). See also *SEG* XLII, 87.

FRAGMENT OF AN HONORARY DECREE

42 (Pl. 4). A fragment of the upper part of a stele of Pentelic marble (I 111), with flat top preserved but otherwise broken all around, discovered in 1931 (no more precise detail is available) in a wall of a modern house east of the Metroon (J 9).

H. 0.143 m.; W. 0.12 m.; Th. 0.10 m.

LH. 0.007 m.

Στοιχ. Hor. 0.014 m.; Vert. 0.0175 m.

Ed. B. D. Meritt, *Hesperia* 3, 1934, pp. 2–3, no. 3, with photograph.

ca. a. 378–372 *a.*   ΣΤΟΙΧ.

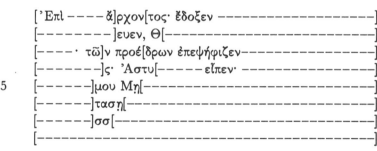

Line 5. ΝΟΥ Meritt.

The inscription was originally published with a minimum of commentary, but the following factors guide any consideration of it:

(1) The plain, tolerably correct, and rather thin style of the lettering closely resembles that of *IG* II², 96 (*SEG* XXI, 234, XXXIV, 61), 99, and other inscriptions of comparable date.

(2) The prescript indicates that the text belongs to the fluid, transitional period of the first half of the 4th century, on which see A. S. Henry, *Prescripts*, pp. 19–33. It combines the archon's name in the genitive case with ἐπί, found also in *IG* II², 96 and 99 (for the "new style" see Henry, *Prescripts*, p. 24), the formula τῶν προέδρων ἐπεψήφιζεν, and the prytanizing phyle and the γραμματεύς expressed in the nominative case with a main verb. The τῶν προέδρων formula is not attested earlier than 378/7, and the closest parallel for the combination just described is in fact the decree in which it first appears, *IG* II², 44 (= 155; *SEG* XXI, 232). Cf. D. M. Lewis, *BSA* 49, 1954, p. 32. The usual practice in the 378–340 period was to combine the τῶν προέδρων formula with the prytanizing phyle expressed in the genitive with ἐπί and to prefer the succession of nominatives and main verbs when ἐπεστάτει remained also in use. On the institution of the proedroi see Lewis, *op. cit.*, pp. 31–34; J. H. Thiel, *Mededelingen der koninklijke Nederlandse Akademie van Wetenschappen*, afd. Letterkunde, n.s. 28, no. 8, 1965, pp. 433–441; P. J. Rhodes, *Athenian Boule*, pp. 26–27; Henry, *Prescripts*, pp. 27–28, note 32. They first occur epigraphically in 379/8; see *SEG* XXXII, 50. Cf. also F. X. Ryan, *JHS* 115, 1995, pp. 167–168.

(3) At this period the *tria nomina* were not yet fully in epigraphical use; cf. **40**, commentary on line 10. Thus the simple formula of introduction ἔδοξεν τῆι βολῆι (or τῶι δήμωι) seems the preferable supposition. The full ἔδοξεν τῆι βολῆι καὶ τῶι δήμωι would make the lines awkwardly though not impossibly long and would require patronymic as well as demotic for the secretary and the presiding proedros, while one or the other would necessarily be added to the name of the proposer. *IG* II², 44 has a line of 32 letters, and other texts of the same date are comparable.

(4) If Asty––– is the name of the proposer of the decree, various names may be considered: Astydamas, Astynomos, Astychares, and the like. But an Astyphilos is a known politician of the period, and if (as is not unlikely) he may be identified with Astyphilos the son of Philagros of Halai Aixonides, there is a good deal of evidence about him (see below).

(5) This Astyphilos proposed the treaty with Methymna which survives as *IG* II², 42 (*SEG* XXI, 231) in 378/7. R. K. Sinclair has suggested (*per ep.*) that the ethnic in line 5 may be restored as Μη[θυμναῖος, and this might reinforce a hypothesis that the known Astyphilos, concerned with relations between Athens and Methymna, also proposed this decree in honor of a particular friend of Athens in that city.

On this basis the following text, relating to 378/7, may be proposed. Aiantis is given as the phyle in prytany, since Leontis, the only alternative within the framework of the restoration, had Aristoteles of Acharnai as its γραμματεύς (*IG* II², 44, lines 1–6; *PA* 2061). The names of the γραμματεύς and presiding proedros will have been accompanied by their demotics only.

a. 378/7 *a.*   ΣΤΟΙΧ. 35

       ['Επὶ Ναυσινίκου ἄ]ρχον[τος· ἔδοξεν τῶι δήμωι]·
       [Αἰαντὶς ἐπρυτάν]ευεν, Θ[......15.......ἐ]
       [γραμμάτευεν· τῶ]ν προέ[δρων ἐπεψήφιζεν ...]
       [.....13......]ς· 'Αστύ[φιλος εἶπεν· ἐπειδὴ .]
  5 [.....12.....]μου Μη[θυμναῖος κτλ.]

Meritt on the other hand used the data of *IG* II², 101 as the basis for his suggestions.

a. 373/2 *a.*   ΣΤΟΙΧ. 37

       ['Επὶ 'Αστείο ἄ]ρχον[τος· ἔδοξεν τῶι δήμωι· 'Αχαμαν]
       [τὶς ἐπρυτάν]ευεν, Θ[ουδαίτης Διομεεὺς ἐγραμμ]
       [άτευεν· τῶ]ν προέ[δρων ἐπεψήφιζεν ....10....]
       [..8....]ς· 'Αστύ[φιλος εἶπεν· ἐπειδὴ ...8....]
  5 [..6...]νου Μη[–––– κτλ.]

Other suggestions may be possible with the same length of line, but with the archons Kalleas (377/6) or Chion (365/4) substituting for Asteios.

Line 2. Nothing more is known of Thoudaites of Diomeia (*PA* 7246) than is contained in *IG* II², 101. The name is otherwise unattested in Attic epigraphy.

Line 4. Astyphilos Φιλάγρου 'Αλαιεύς (*PA* 2663 + 2664; see J. K. Davies, *Athenian Propertied Familes*, p. 230 and *PA*, addenda), if correctly identified as the proposer of this decree and of *IG* II², 42, is known from other epigraphical testimony. Cf. *Agora* XV, 31, in commentary; M. H. Hansen, *Athenian Ecclesia II*, p. 39. He served as bouleutes in this period, in the same year as his brother Leon (*PA* 9110, where a stemma of the family is provided), and is commemorated in the list *Agora* XV, 7 (*IG* II², 1743). With twenty-three others of his deme, including his son Menyllos, he was epistates overseeing the dedication of a statue to Aphrodite, for which he and his colleagues were awarded a stephanos by their fellow demesmen, in 368 B.C. (*IG* II², 2820, line 5; cf. A. Wilhelm, *Attische Urkunden* V [= *SbAkadWien* 220, 5], 1942, p. 139; W. K. Pritchett, *Hesperia* 15, 1946, p. 162). He proposed a decree of his deme which survives as *IG* II², 1175 (dated *ca.* 360 on the basis of the copy of Fourmont transcribed by Wilhelm). That the family was well-to-do is indicated by the survival of three funerary lekythoi, of about the middle of the century, which commemorate in a scene identical to all three both him and his son Menyllos (*IG* II², 5497–5499). Menyllos is shown as a ἱππεύς leading his horse and clasping the hand of his bearded father, who stands on the right facing him. Astyphilos was thus prominent at both national and local levels as an active and responsible politician, and his inclusion in the restored text of this decree of the 370's appears as the more plausible in the light of his record.

DECREE CONCERNING RELATIONS WITH ARETHOUSA

43. A fragment of a stele of Pentelic marble (I 6521), with part of the original rough-picked back preserved but otherwise broken all around, discovered on April 26, 1953, in a gravel fill of the Byzantine period northeast of the Church of the Holy Apostles (Q 15). The vertical striations of a toothed chisel are visible on the inscribed surface.

H. 0.215 m.; W. 0.13 m.; Th. 0.08 m.

LH. (lines 1–6) 0.013 m. (omicron 0.011 m.); (lines 7–11) 0.005–0.006 m.

Στοιχ. (lines 1–6) Hor. 0.0215 m.; Vert. 0.0235 m.

Ed. B. D. Meritt, *Hesperia* 32, 1963, pp. 1–2, no. 1, with photograph pl. 2. See also *SEG* XXI, 230.

```
      [————————————]
      [. . 6. . .]το[. . . . .12. . . . .]
      [. . . .]ς· ἐς δ[ὲ ἀναγραφὴν δō]
      [ναι] τριάκ[οντα δραχμάς· x]
      [αλ]έσαι δὲ [τὸς πρέσβες τὸ]
  5   [ς ἥ]κοντα[ς ἐπὶ δεῖπνον ἐς]
      [τὸ] πρυτ[ανεῖον ἐς αὔριον].
   [Τοῖς μὲν] Ἀρεθοσίοις ε[ἶναι τἆλλα πάντα καθάπερ————————————]·
   [περὶ δὲ ὦν ἀ]παγγέλλ[————————————————————————]
   [———————]ΕΙΩΝΗΜ[———————————————————————————]
  10 [———————]ΙΣΣΥ[————————————————————————————]
   [———————]ΠΕΔ[—————————————————————————————]
   [—————————————————————————————————————————]
```

This decree interestingly displays, on the same stone and doubtless in connection with a single piece of business, both the ample style and the microstyle in which *psephismata* were variously recorded at this period (cf. **54**, commentary). Frequently the microstyle is used for the body of the text, with the more ample lettering being reserved for a monumental heading. Here however the stele contains a decree in large lettering, arranged stoichedon, with an amendment to it (the work apparently of the same mason) in a nonstoichedon text of much smaller and more crowded letters. In both cases the writing is of good workmanship, with the beginning of some enlargement of the "free ends" of letters to be discerned in lines 1–6. The horizontal strokes of epsilon are of equal length or almost so; the cross-bar of alpha is set at an angle; the tiny omega is very open, with vestigial horizontal strokes.

The text and restorations above are those of Meritt. Much depends on the assumed position of the fragment in the original stele. Lines 7–11 have been held to contain a recognizable formula of amendment, but the presumed omission at its outset of the name of its proposer (ὁ δεῖνα εἶπε) is remarkable. There is no room for the phrase at the end of line 6 since, as restored in the *editio princeps*, that line is full. It could however be accommodated at the beginning of line 7 if the words ἐς αὔριον were omitted in line 6 and the position of the fragment in relation to the total width of the stele readjusted by removing it to the right by the required amount, with consequential changes to the distribution of words in the earlier lines. The formula in lines 2–3 is expressed in a truncated manner, lacking a reference to the official responsible for the disbursement of costs; see **40**, commentary on line 18. The same brevity might have been applied to the "hospitality formula" of the succeeding lines. On this basis, the following might be possible:

[. . . . .*ca.*.18. . . . . . . εἶπε· τοῖς μὲν] Ἀρεθοσίοις ε[ἶναι τἆλλα πάντα καθάπερ τῆι βολῆι],
[περὶ δὲ τῶν —————ὦν οἱ ————— ἀ]παγγέλλ[ουσι ———————————————————]

Ἐς αὔριον may be considered too regular a part of the hospitality formula to be discarded in the present context; but cf. *IG* II², 42 (*SEG* XXI, 231), lines 24–25, of 378/7. For the formula itself, see **20**, commentary on lines 28–30, and references there.

The identification of Arethousa has been the subject of controversy. An Arethousa was among the earliest members of the Second Athenian Confederacy (*IG* II², 43 [= *SEG* XXXI, 61, XLI, 40, with earlier bibliography], line 82, col. II; cf. *IG* II², 1437, lines 18–19, *SEG* XXVIII, 112), and from its position on the "Confederacy stele" has been regarded as a city of Euboia; so Meritt, *loc. cit.* and J. Cargill, *The Second Athenian League*, 1981, pp. 33–34, note 17 and 82, note 43. This separate treaty may well have been concluded just before or just after the founding of the Confederacy in 377. See F. H. Marshall, *The Second Athenian Confederacy*, 1905, p. 57; and for the site of the town O. Hirschfeld, *RE* II, i, col. 680, no. 9. On the other hand, S. Accame (*La lega ateniese del secolo IV a.C.*, 1941, pp. 71–73 and 179) contended that the Arethousa in question was that on the borders of Macedonia and Thrace, at the southeast corner of Lake Bolbe; for the location see Hirschfeld, *loc. cit.*, cols. 679–680, no. 8; S. Casson, *Macedonia, Thrace, and Illyria*, 1926, p. 86; N. G. L. Hammond, *A History of Macedonia* I, 1972, p. 196 and map 17. This view, which must discard the strong evidence of the position of the name on the stele, has also been strongly supported by D. Knoepfler, *BCH* 95, 1971, p. 239, note 43 (cf. *SEG* XXXII, 54), and M. Zahrnt, *Olynth und die Chalkidier* (*Vestigia* 14), 1971, pp. 160–161 with note 90, and is favored by Hammond, *loc. cit.*

PYRRHOS AND SOSIBIOS HONORED BY THEIR FELLOW MEMBERS OF THE PHYLE KEKROPIS

44. Two joining fragments of a stele of Pentelic marble, which preserve the left side and most of the original width of the monument. The left-hand fragment is in the Epigraphical Museum (E.M. 7741): the right-hand fragment (I 4564), broken on all sides, was known from a copy by the Abbé Fourmont (cf. *CIG* I, 85), made when the two pieces had not been broken apart, but it was subsequently lost. Later editions of the text include this portion on Fourmont's authority, sometimes but not always distinguished in some way, for instance, by a line under the relevant letters (*IG* II², 1141) or by showing it outside a line drawing of the surviving piece (*IG* II, 555). It was rediscovered on February 26, 1937, by a truck driver, who picked it up on the site of public baths northeast of the Agora, at the corner of Athena and Bysses Streets, and brought it to the Agora excavations. Some letters at the ends of lines 1–3, most of those in line 9, and all those in line 10 which Fourmont saw on this fragment have been broken away, damage reminiscent of that on the main fragment, where lines 8–10 and the initial letters of lines 5–7 have been similarly lost. The right side and probably its bottom surface suggest a reworking in ancient times.

Agora fragment only: H. 0.61 m.; W. 0.165 m.; Th. 0.122 m.
Maximum width as joined: 0.534 m.
LH. (lines 1–7) 0.013 m.; (line 8) 0.01 m.

Ed. (left fragment by autopsy and right fragment *ex schedis Fourmontii*): *IG* II², 1141, with references to earlier literature. Both fragments: W. K. Pritchett, *Hesperia* 10, 1941, pp. 263–265, no. 67, with photograph.

a. 376/5 a.   NON-ΣΤΟΙΧ.

reliquiae   *reliquiae*
coronae   *coronae*

'Εξ οὖ Κέκροπα λαὸς 'Αθηναίων ὀνομάζ[ει]
καὶ χώραν Παλλὰς τήνδ' ἔκτισε δήμωι 'Α[θηνῶν],
οὐδὲς Σωσιβίο καὶ Πύρρο μείζονα θνητ[ῶν]
φυλὴν Κεκροπιδῶν ἔργωι ἔδρασε ἀγαθά.
vacat 0.135 m.

```
 5   "Εδοξεν τῆι Κεκροπίδι φυλῆι ἐπὶ Χαρισάνδρ[ο ἄρχοντος]
     τῆι κυρίαι ἀγορᾶι κρύβδην ψηφισαμένων τῶν [φυλετῶν]
     ἐν ἀκροπόλει·                    vacat
               vacat 0.075 m.
     'Ονήτωρ Κηφισοδώρο Μελιτεὺς εἶπ[εν· ἀγαθῆι τύχ]ηι Πύρρον [ἐπαινέσαι ὅτι ἀγαθὸς]
     γεγένητα[ι] περὶ τὴμ φυλὴν καὶ τὰ κοιν[ὰ τῆς φυλῆς, κα]ὶ αὐτὸγ [στεφανῶσαι ἀρετῆς ἕνεκα(?)]
10   χρυσῶι στεφάνωι ἀπὸ πε[ν]τακοσίων [δραχμῶν· στ]εφανῶσα[ι δὲ καὶ Σωσίβιον –––––––––]
     [–––––––––––––––––––––––––––––––––––––––––––––––––––––––––––––––––––––––]
```

The letters underlined were seen by Fourmont but are now lost. Two well-cut stephanoi of olive in relief surmount the text and are in part broken away at the top; that on the right is also incomplete on the right.

Line 8. ΙΙΠΥΡΡ Fourmont *apud CIG*; ἐπειδ]ὴ Πύρρ[ης ἀγαθός] Boeckh (*CIG*), Koehler (*IG* II); Πύρρο[ς Wilhelm, after reexamining Fourmont's papers (cf. C. Michel, *Recueil d'inscriptions grecques, Supplément*, 1912, no. 1505). Pritchett's restorations, adopted here and in lines 9–10, allow for a longer line consonant with the size and location of the stephanoi and the assumed symmetry of the arrangement.

The reference to the archonship of Charisandros gives a precise date to the monument: on his year in office cf. Diodorus Siculus 15.36 and references under *PA* 15471 and *IG* II², 1410, line 4, 1411, line 1, 1445 *init.*, 1635, lines 6–7, *et alibi* (M. N. Tod, *GHI* II, p. 78). The lettering is plain, with memories of 5th-century styles, but the shapes of individual letters vary (upsilon with curved arms in lines 5–6, straight in lines 1 and 3; diverse forms of nu; central horizontal of epsilon at times markedly shorter than the rest). The "horseshoe" of omega is less open than usual at this period. In general the work seems second-class but not incompetent.

The honorands are not otherwise known. The proposer of the decree, Onetor (*PA* 11470), belonged to the important family in Melite, for which see J. K. Davies, *Athenian Propertied Families*, pp. 421–426 (for Onetor here, esp. p. 425).

Line 3. Οὐδὲς, μείζονα. See L. Threatte, *Grammar*, pp. 177–178, 180. Line 6. The κυρία ἀγορά of the phyle corresponded in importance with the ἐκκλησία κυρία of the whole δῆμος, but the definition of the latter in decrees of the people at large had not yet come into chancery usage. Cf. Busolt-Swoboda, II, p. 991, note 4, and p. 154 below. The vote is specified as having been taken by secret ballot, the procedure being thus comparable on a small scale with that required in the popular assembly for νόμοι ἐπ'ἀνδρί, grants of citizenship, etc. For the procedure in these cases see M. H. Hansen, *GRBS* 17, 1976, pp. 124–130 (= *Athenian Ecclesia*, pp. 10–18) and M. J. Osborne, *Naturalization* III/IV, pp. 161–162. Cf. also Busolt-Swoboda, II, p. 1163, note 5; E. S. Staveley, *Greek and Roman Voting and Elections*, 1972, pp. 84 and 92–93. A similar procedure in the phratry of the Demotionidai is elaborated in *IG* II², 1237, lines 78–88 (396/5 B.C.).

Line 7. The *phyletai* assembled on the Akropolis at the sanctuary of their eponymous hero Kekrops: for the Kekropion Pritchett cited A. B. Cook, *Zeus* III, 1940, p. 771, with bibliography notes 1–4, and Busolt-Swoboda, II, pp. 974–975 with note 7. See also W. Judeich, *Topographie*, p. 282; G. P. Stevens, *Hesperia* 15, 1946, pp. 93–97; I. T. Hill, *The Ancient City of Athens*, 1953, pp. 177–178 and 245, note 13; R. J. Hopper, *The Acropolis*, 1971, p. 47; N. F. Jones, *Hesperia* 64, 1995, pp. 509, 512.

A GRANT OF PROXENIA

45. Four fragments, which do not join, of a stele of Pentelic marble, the largest of which (here designated fragment *d*) has long been known and is now in the Epigraphical Museum (E.M. 2633). It was discovered on the Akropolis at an unknown date earlier than 1913 (the date of its *editio princeps*) and is broken all around. Of the three small fragments, all from the Agora excavations, fragment *a* (I 2426) was discovered on February 11, 1935, in a modern context east of the north part of the Odeion (N 10); it too is broken on all sides. Fragment *b* (I 2580), broken all around save on the right, was discovered on March 6, 1935, in a late context over the East Stoa (O 14). Fragment *c* (I 5263), similarly preserving the right side of the monument but otherwise broken, was discovered on February 24, 1938, in a marble pile west of the Stoa of Attalos (N–P 7–12).

a: H. 0.075 m.; W. 0.08 m.; Th. 0.05 m.

b: H. 0.077 m.; W. 0.058 m.; Th. 0.036 m.

c: H. 0.084 m.; W. 0.079 m.; Th. 0.048 m.

d: H. 0.113 m.; W. 0.081 m.; Th. 0.039 m.

LH. 0.007–0.008 m.
Στοιχ. (square but with some vertical irregularity) 0.0135 m.

Ed. *d* only: *IG* II², 272. *b+d*: M. B. Walbank, *Hesperia* 54, 1985, pp. 312–313, no. 2, with photographs pl. 87 (see also *SEG* XXXV, 65). All fragments: Walbank, *Hesperia* 58, 1989, pp. 75–78, no. 4, with photographs of *a* and *c* pl. 17 (see also *SEG* XXXIX, 67).

ca. a. 375–360 *a.*   ΣΤΟΙΧ.

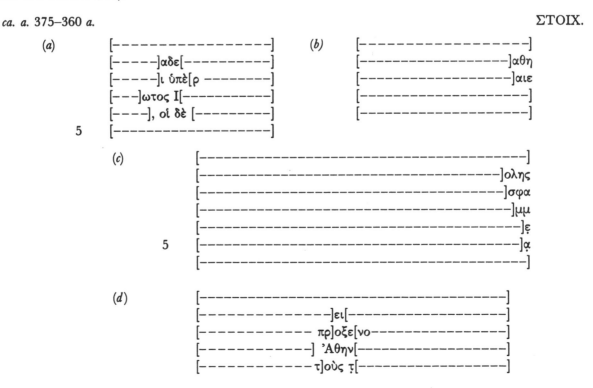

5   [――――――τὸ ψήφι]σμα τ[όδε ――――――――――]
     [――――――στήλη. λι]θίνη[――――――――――――]
     [――――――――――]τη[――――――――――――]
     [――――――――――]ω[――――――――――――]
     [―――――――――――――――――――――――――]

The fragments were associated by Walbank and justify the remark of J. Kirchner concerning fragment *d* that the letters are "bonae accurate incisae." The "free ends" of the strokes are not enlarged.

Walbank emphasized that the relationship of the fragments to each other is uncertain. Fragment *d* clearly preserves a formula for the inscription and payment resulting from the passage of the decree and presumably, by concluding the document, is to be placed below the other three. In his commentary Walbank hazarded the location of fragment *c* to its right, at lines 3–8, and attempted a restored text of 36 letters per line on this basis: but a variety of answers may be found, with slight formulaic variations, and the fragments are here presented separately.

b, line 1. Walbank's suggestion ἐπειδὴ δὲ κ]αθη[ιρέθη ἐπὶ τῶν τριάκοντα ἡ στήλη ――― (cf. **37**) might require a relatively early dating for this enactment, and on the basis of its lettering it seems to belong to the second quarter of the century. But while such a renewal is likely to be within reasonable distance of the original grant (hence Walbank's date of *ca.* 375), it remains possible that this was a long backward reference to an ancestral grant of *proxenia*. Moreover, ΑΘΗ is capable of other restorations (cf. *d*, line 3), and a wider dating is here preferred.

d, lines 4–9. Walbank's restorations in both his editions postulated a line of 43 letters and ran as follows:

ἀναγράψαι δὲ τόδε]
5   [τὸ ψήφι]σμα τ[ὸν γραμματέα τὸν κατὰ πρυτανείαν εἰς στ]
     [ήλην λι]θίνη[ν καὶ στῆσαι ἐν ἀκροπόλει· εἰς δὲ τὴν ἀναγ]
     [ραφὴν τῆς σ]τή[λης δοῦναι τὸν ταμίαν τοῦ δήμου εἴκοσι]
     [δραχμὰς ἐκ τ]ῶ[ν κατὰ ψηφίσματα ἀναλισκομένων τῶι δή]
     [μωι . . . . 40 . . . .]

This restoration involves payment for the stele from the source described as ἐκ τῶν κατὰ ψήφισματα ἀναλισκομένων τῶι δήμωι. This was the fund drawn upon by the ταμίας τοῦ δήμου (see **40**, commentary on line 18). The first firmly dated instance of its appearance in a decree occurs in *IG* II², 106, lines 18–19, of 368/7: it is found in the following year in **48**. P. J. Rhodes (*Athenian Boule*, p. 101, note 3) believed that it was set up *ca.* 376, noting that the ταμίας τοῦ δήμου was thought to have made his earliest appearance at that time as the disbursing officer.

A. S. Henry argued however (see **40**) that *IG* II², 21, the earliest context in which the ταμίας τοῦ δήμου is to be found, is preferably to be dated *ca.* 390/89. Moreover, *IG* II², 82, in which the "analiskomena fund" is mentioned for, apparently, the first time, has been dated on the basis of its lettering "earlier than 378/7", a date to which Henry subscribes; see *Chiron* 12, 1982, pp. 102 and 111 with note 76.

If that is so, the Treasurer perhaps drew from the outset on a fund at first variously described as "the ten talents" or with the "analiskomena" formula, with the latter becoming the norm: in that case its appearance here offers no obstacle to a date for this text of *ca.* 375. But *IG* II², 82 may be susceptible of a date later than 376, as W. B. Dinsmoor maintained (see **40**). It might therefore be preferable to treat 368/7 as a provisional *terminus ante quem non* for any restoration of the "analiskomena" designation until more exact knowledge is forthcoming.

TREATY OF ALLIANCE BETWEEN THE ATHENIANS AND THE KEPHALLENIANS

46. Two fragments of a stele of Pentelic marble, which make a join below the inscribed surface. The larger fragment (*a*), long known but of unrecorded provenance, preserves the left side and, apparently, the original back of the stele but is otherwise broken. The smaller fragment (*b*, I 4113), which joins fragment *a* at the latter's lowest point and is broken all around, is that found in the Agora and was discovered on May 4, 1936, in a modern context over the area of the Post-Herulian Wall, northwest of the Eleusinion (S 17).

a: H. 0.33 m.; W. 0.17 m.; Th. 0.095 m.

b: H. 0.056 m.; W. 0.105 m.; Th. 0.044 m.

LH. 0.007 m.

Στοιχ. (square but irregular) *ca.* 0.012 m.

Ed. *a* only: *IG* II², 98 (cf. *IG* II², addenda, p. 658); W. Bannier, *Philologische Wochenschrift* 48, 1928, cols. 287–288; A. Wilhelm, *Attische Urkunden* V (= *SbAkadWien* 220, 5), 1942, pp. 131–133 and 189–191, no. L. *a*+*b*: E. Schweigert, *Hesperia* 9, 1940, pp. 321–324, no. 33, with photographs of both fragments. Cf. *SEG* XXI, 237 (references to M. N.

Tod, *GHI* II, p. 86; H. Bengtson, *Staatsverträge* II, pp. 225–226, no. 267), XXXI, 66 (reference to J. Cargill, *The Second Athenian League*, 1981, pp. 74–75).

a. 372 a.(?)   ΣΤΟΙΧ. 26

```
          [....9....]Ι[........16........]              (a)
          [...8....]Ν[........17........]
          [..5.. τ]ὴν δὲ σ[......15.......]
          [....]ν μηδὲ ο[ἱ Κεφαλῆνες ἄνευ Ἀ]
   5      [θη]ναίων· ἐὰν δέ [τις ἐπὶ τὴν Ἀττικ]
          [ὴν] ἐπιστρατ[εύηται ἐναντίον τῶ]
          [ι ψ]ηφίσματι τ[ῶιδε, βοηθεῖν Κεφα]
          [λλ]ῆνας καθάπερ [οἱ ἄλλοι σύμμαχ]
          [οι]· ὁπόσοι δὲ νό[μοι εἰσὶ κατ' Ἀθην]
  10      [α]ίων κείμενο[ι ἐν Κεφαλληνίαι, κ]
          αθελόντων [οἱ ἄρχοντες καὶ ἐξαλ]
          ειψάντ[ων ἁπανταχόθεν ἐπάναγκ]
          ες· πέ[μψαι δὲ καὶ οἵτινες ἐπιμελ]
          ήσοντ[αι Ἀθηναίων τῶν ἐν τοῖς νή]
  15      σοις, κα[ὶ χρείας παρέχεσθαι τού]
          τοις, ἐάν [τινος δέωνται, τὰς φρ]
          ορὰς αἵ[περ εἰσὶν ἐν ταῖς νήσοις]·
          ἐπιμελη[τ]ὰς δ'[ἑλέσθαι ἐς Κεφαλλ]
          ηνίαν τρὲς ἄν[δρας, ἕως ἂν ὁ πόλεμ]
  20      ος ἦι, ὑπὲρ τεττα[ράκοντα ἔτη γεγ]
          ονότας, οὗτοι δ'ἐ[πιμελείσθων Κε]
          φαλληνίας, ὅπω[ς ἂν ἦι σᾶ τοῖς τε Ἀ]
          θηναίοις καὶ Κε[φαλλῆσιν· τὸ δὲ ψ]
          [ήφ]ισμα ὁ γράμματ[εὺς ἀναγραψάτ]
  25      [ω ἐν] στήληι λιθί[νηι καὶ θέτω ἐν ἀ]
          [κροπόλ]ει τέλεσ[ι τοῖς Κεφαλλήν]
          [ων· ................24..............]
          [...8....]Ο[.........17.........]              (b)
          [...7....]ν Κεφαλλ[ην....10.....]
  30      [...7....] οἱ ἐπιμε[λήται ἐπιμελε]
          [ισθων Κε]φαλλ[λ]ην[.....13......]
          [----------------------]
```

In lines 6–13 and 18–27 the above text follows that of Wilhelm, adopted also by Bengtson. Alternative restorations are possible; those of Schweigert (pronounced unsatisfactory by Wilhelm) were as follows: Lines 6–7. παρὰ τὰ ἐν τῶ|ι ψ]ηφίσματι. Lines 8–17. καθάπερ [γεγραμμένον ἐσ|τί]· ὁπόσοι δὲ ν[όμοι περὶ τῶν Ἀθην||α]ίων κείμενο[ί εἰσι ἐν στήλαις κ]|αθελόντω[ν αὐτίκα μάλα καὶ ἐξαλ]|ειψά[ντων ....9.... καὶ ἄρχοντ]|ες πέ[ντε ἰόντων οἵτινες ἐπιμελ]|ήσοντ[αι τῆς φυλακῆς τῆς τε ἐν νή]||σοις κα[ὶ ἐν ἠπείρωι· εἶναι δὲ τού]|τοις ἐὰν [βούλωνται ἔχειν τὰς φρ]|ορὰς αἵ[περ εἰσὶ ἐγ Κεφαλληνίαι]. In lines 18–27 Schweigert's text coincided with Wilhelm's save that in line 18 he preferred δ[ὲ πέμψαι and in lines 25–27 καὶ καταθέτ|ω ἐμ πόλει τέλε[σι τοῖς τῶν Κεφαλ|λήνων. The inclusion of τῶν before Κεφαλλήνων is possible (cf. *IG* I³, 10, lines 26–27), but customary usage accords with Wilhelm's omission of it; cf. A. S. Henry, *Vindex Humanitatis: Essays in Honour of John Huntly Bishop*, 1980, pp. 21–22 with note 13 (see **37**, commentary on line 13) and Meisterhans-Schwyzer³, p. 225, note 1789. Schweigert's introduction of πόλις for ἀκρόπολις also militates against the dating he preferred and which is here followed. Cf. **40**, note on line 16. Schweigert followed the payment formula with the formula of amendment τὰ μὲν ἄλλα καθάπερ τεῖ βολεῖ .....]Ο κτλ. to effect the transition to fragment *b*, but he did not explain how he envisaged such an amendment without a proposer's name and verb of proposal (x εἶπε) preceding it, assuming only that fragment *b* contained a rider to the main decree and observing that his restoration seemed "fairly certain" (*loc. cit.*, p. 322). Bengtson adopted it, but it is omitted here. The relationship between the text of fragment *b* and what precedes it remains uncertain; but it cannot be assumed that the provisions for the inscription of the decree necessarily concluded its detail (cf. *IG* I³, 40, lines 60–61 and 66, lines 20–22).

The workmanship of this inscription is poor, even though the letters individually are well and accurately formed. The horizontal line of writing rises from left to right, and the letters have a forward tilt, their upright strokes being consistently off the true vertical. The circular letters are full and round; omega is well open at the foot.

J. Kirchner's date for this treaty, given in *IG* II², was 375/4 B.C. The implication was that it provided, in the case of Kephallenia, a separate and fuller formulation to the provisions of *IG* II², 96, which records an Athenian treaty with the Kephallenians together with the Kerkyraians and Akarnanians, all three peoples having sent ambassadors to Athens at the same time: see Tod, *GHI* II, pp. 82–86, no. 126; Bengtson, *Staatsverträge* II, pp. 217–218, no. 262. This interpretation receives considerable support from the existence of such a "follow-up" treaty in the case of Kerkyra, *IG* II², 97, to which the date 375 has regularly, though perhaps too readily, been assigned. The accession of Kephallenia to the Athenian alliance was the result of the activities of Timotheos in western waters in the early part of the campaigning season of 375 (Xenophon, *HG* 5.4.64; Diodorus Siculus 15.36.5. Cf. *IG* II², 43, lines 107–108; F. R. Marshall, *The Second Athenian Confederacy*, 1905, pp. 26 and 63; S. Accame, *La lega ateniese del secolo IV A.C.*, 1941, p. 91; Cargill, *loc. cit.*). Schweigert, without arguing the matter, showed the date of this treaty as 373/2 B.C., no doubt opting for a connection with the western campaign of Iphikrates (Xenophon, *HG* 6.2.33), and was followed in this by Bengtson (who mentioned that G. Klaffenbach accepted it also).

It is to be noted that the "Confederacy Stele", *IG* II², 43, records at lines 107–108 only the Pronnoi of the Kephallenians, even though *IG* II², 96 and the literary accounts are clear that all the Kephallenians were brought into alliance. In the words of G. L. Cawkwell (*JHS* 101, 1981, p. 46), "something had gone wrong. . . . When the decree of alliance was drafted it was presumed that all would accept membership of the Confederacy, but only one city in the event did." Either alliance was possible without membership, or the other cities repented of their commitment before their names could be inscribed (so Marshall, *op. cit.*, p. 71). It was left for Iphikrates to reaffirm the Athenian position in Kephallenia in 372, and even then, according to Xenophon (*HG* 6.2.38), when he extracted money from the cities "some were willing but others recalcitrant." In those circumstances the need for a new treaty, with provisions for "overseers" and garrisons (lines 13–23), is understandable, and Schweigert's dating is therefore here accepted.

Lines 26–27. For the charging of the cost of the monument to the Kephallenians cf. W. Larfeld, *Handbuch der griechischen Epigraphik* II, 1902, p. 720. This is the last attested case in Attic epigraphy of the transfer of such a charge to another community, but in respect to individual recipients of honors it continues to appear sporadically down to *ca.* 336/5 B.C. See also Henry, *Honours*, p. 12, note 1. M. B. Walbank prefers to see in these lines the remains of an amendment formula, *exempli gratia*, Τελέσ[ιππος εἶπεν· – – –]. He has also noted (*per ep.*) that another large but ill-preserved fragment, I 5368, may perhaps be attributed to this monument and that its probable location would set it below the text discussed above, with expanded detail on the proposed duties of the overseers.

AGREEMENT BETWEEN ATHENS AND STYMPHALOS IN ARKADIA

47. Eighteen fragments, designated *a–r*, two of which (*b* and *c*) may be joined, of an opisthographic stele of bluish white Pentelic marble: five of these were discovered in the excavations of the Athenian Agora; the remainder, apparently found on the Akropolis or in debris from it, are in the Epigraphical Museum save for fragment *q*, which is lost. Six of the fragments (*a, b, c, d, h,* and *i*) preserve both inscribed faces of the monument. The Agora fragments (*d, e, g, o,* and *r*) alone are considered in full in the present context; but all fragments are listed in accordance with the edition of M. B. Walbank (see below), the text of which is reproduced entire.

Fragment *d* (I 2025) was discovered in November 1934, in a marble pile in the south central part of the Market Square (O 11). It preserves part of both inscribed faces and part also of the right edge (as of Face A) of the monument but is broken elsewhere. Fragment *e* (I 5803), broken all around save for one inscribed face, was discovered on May 6, 1939, in a Byzantine context west of the Panathenaic Way and of the Eleusinion (S 20). Fragment *g* (I 5751), discovered on March 31, 1939, in a modern wall at the foot of the Areopagos (Q 22), is similarly broken all around save for one inscribed face. Fragment *o* (I 5278), broken all around save for one inscribed face, was discovered on March 1, 1938, in a late fill west of the Post-Herulian Wall, at the foot of the North Slope of the Akropolis (T 23). Fragment *r* (I 2925) was discovered in a late context east of the Middle Stoa (P 13), on May 25, 1935. It too is broken all around save for one inscribed face.

d: H. 0.372 m.; W. 0.31 m.; Th. 0.147 m.
   LH. (Face A) 0.008 m.; (Face B) 0.007 m.
   Στοιχ. (Face A; square) 0.013 m.; (Face B) Hor. 0.018 m.; Vert. 0.016 m.

e: H. 0.204 m.; W. 0.132 m.; Th. 0.053 m.
   LH. 0.006–0.007 m.
   Στοιχ. (square) 0.012–0.013 m.

g: H. 0.112 m.; W. 0.085 m.; Th. 0.09 m.
LH. 0.006–0.007 m.
Στοιχ. (square) 0.012–0.013 m.

o: H. 0.082 m.; W. 0.047 m.; Th. 0.04 m.
LH. 0.007–0.008 m.
Στοιχ. (square) 0.015–0.016 m.

r: H. 0.074 m.; W. 0.048 m.; Th. 0.043 m.
LH. 0.006–0.007 m.
Στοιχ. (square) 0.013 m.

The correspondences between the other thirteen fragments and their designation in *IG* II², as well as their E.M. inventory numbers, are as follows:

	IG II²	E.M.
a	144, fr. *c*	64
b	144, fr. *d*	7097
c	144, fr. *a*	7098
f	144, fr. *i*	7101
h	144, fr. *b*	7099
i	305	2673
j	144, fr. *k*	7092
k	144, fr. *h*	7093
l	144, fr. *g*	7094
m	144, fr. *e*	7096
n	144, fr. *f*	7095
	(= 319)	
p	144, fr. *l*	7091
	(= 635)	
q (lost)	318	

Ed. *a–c, f, h, j–n, p*: *IG* II², 144, with earlier bibliography. *d*: A. G. Woodhead, *Hesperia* 26, 1957, pp. 221–225, no. 84, with photograph pl. 58 (see also *SEG* XVII, 18; H. Bengtson, *Staatsverträge* II, p. 236, no. 279). *a–q*: M. B. Walbank, *Hesperia* 55, 1986, pp. 319–354, with photographs (*a–p*) pls. 71–76 (see also *SEG* XXXVI, 147). *r*: Unpublished; details kindly supplied for this publication by Walbank.

Fragment *i* was attributed to the stele by Walbank, confirming previous conjectures by himself and D. M. Lewis. He also identified fragments *e, g, o*, and *r* as parts of the same stele. Fragment *q* was assigned to it by G. A. Stamires, Πολέμων 5, 1952–1955, pp. 153–157; cf. *SEG* XV, 91. There is however some doubt as to whether it, and perhaps fragment *p* also, properly belong to the monument.

Taking account of the position on the stele to which he tentatively assigned them, Walbank (*loc. cit.*, p. 324) distributed the fragments between the two faces as follows:

Face A: *a, b+c, d, e, f, r, g, h, i, j*.

Face B: *a, k, b+c, l, d, m, n, h, o, i*.

If they are to be included, fragment *p* may be attributed to Face A and fragment *q* to either face.

ca. a. 368 *a.*   ΣΤΟΙΧ.

FACE A

(a)
```
    [----------------------------------------------]
    [.....10.....]ουστρ[------------------------------]
    [.....9.....]δ]ὲ διδόνα[ι-----------------------------]
    [...8....]ν ἄρχειν δὲ[---------------------------]
    [... πρ]οξένων πρεσβ[--------------------------]
5   [... ἐπι]τίμ[ι]α(?) ἀποτινε[------------------------]
    [..5..]την ἐ[λ]ευθέραν ι[-------------------------]
    [..5.. νηι ἐκ τῆς προδοσ[------------------------]
    [..5..]τούσης τι ποιῆι π[-----------------------]
```

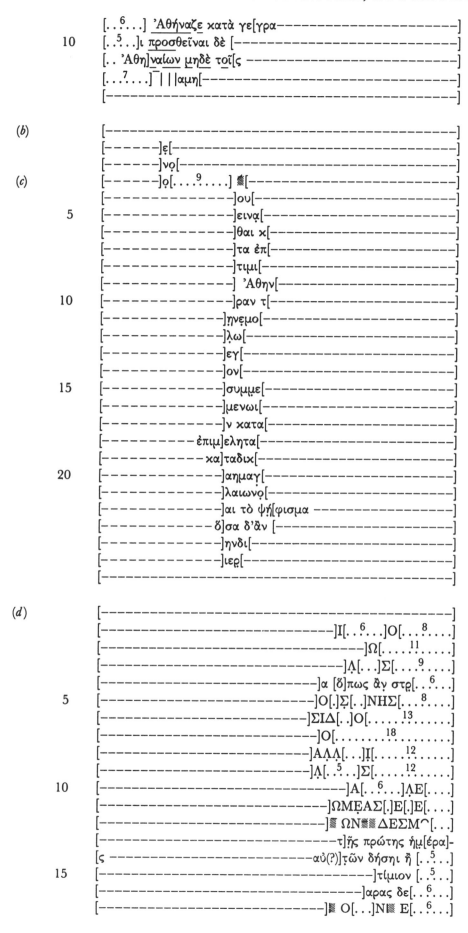

```
        [..⁶...] Ἀθήναζε κατὰ γε[γρα————————————————]
   10   [..⁵..]ι προσθεῖναι δὲ [————————————————————]
        [.. Ἀθη]ναίων μηδὲ τοῖ[ς ——————————————————]
        [...⁷...]¯ | |αμη[————————————————————————]
        [————————————————————————————————————————]


(b)     [————————————————————————————————————————]
        [—————]ε[————————————————————————————————]
        [—————]νο[———————————————————————————————]
(c)     [—————]ο[....⁹.....] ▨[————————————————————]
        [————————————]ου[————————————————————————]
   5    [————————————]εινα[——————————————————————]
        [————————————]θαι κ[——————————————————————]
        [————————————]τα ἐπ[——————————————————————]
        [————————————]τιμι[——————————————————————]
        [————————————] Ἀθην[——————————————————————]
   10   [————————————]ραν τ[——————————————————————]
        [————————————]ηνεμο[—————————————————————]
        [————————————]λω[————————————————————————]
        [————————————]εγ[————————————————————————]
        [————————————]ον[————————————————————————]
   15   [————————————]συμμε[————————————————————————]
        [————————————]μενωι[————————————————————————]
        [————————————]ν κατα[——————————————————————]
        [————— ἐπιμ]ελητα[——————————————————————]
        [————— χα]ταδιχ[————————————————————————]
   20   [————————————]αημαγ[——————————————————————]
        [————————————]λαιωνο[—————————————————————]
        [————————————]αι τὸ ψή[φισμα ——————————————]
        [————————— δ]σα δ'ἂν [——————————————————————]
        [————————————]ηνδι[——————————————————————]
        [————————————]ιερ[————————————————————————]
        [————————————————————————————————————————]


(d)     [————————————————————————————————————————]
        [————————————————————————]Ι[..⁶...]Ο[...⁸....]
        [——————————————————————————————]Ω[....¹¹....]
        [————————————————————————————]Λ[...]Σ[...⁹....]
        [————————————————————]α [δ]πως ἂν στρ[...⁶..]
   5    [———————————————————]Ο[.]Σ[..]ΝΗΣ[...⁸....]
        [———————————————————]ΣΙΔ[..]Ο[.....¹³......]
        [——————————————————————]Ο[.......¹⁸.......]
        [——————————————————]ΑΛΛ[...]Ι[.....¹²....]
        [——————————————————]Λ[..⁵..]Σ[......¹²....]
   10   [———————————————————]Α[..⁶...]ΛΕ[....]
        [——————————————————]ΩΜΕΑΣ[.]Ε[.]Ε[....]
        [————————————————]▨ ΩΝ▨▨ΔΕΣΜ^[...]
        [—————————————————τ]ῆς πρώτης ἡμ[έρα]-
   [ς —————————————————αὐ(?)]τῶν δήσηι ἢ [..⁵..]
   15   [———————————————————]τίμιον [..⁵..]
        [——————————————————]αρας δε[..⁶...]
        [————————————————]▨ Ο[...]Ν▨ Ε[..⁶...]
```

```
[———————————————————————————]Λ[..⁵..]ΔΡΑ[..⁵..]
[————————————————————————————]Λ[..⁶...]Ζ[..⁶...]
20 [—————————————————————————————]Α[..]▓[..]
[——————————————————————————————]ṬῪΦΛ[.]Σ[..]
[———————————————————————————————]οσια[.]ε[..]
[———————————————————————————————]λ̣όν[τ]ων [..]
[————————————————————————————————]
```

(e)
```
[————————————————————————————]
[———————— τοὺς] πριαμέν[ους(?)————————————]
[———————— κατ(?)]α̣ γιγνωσκ[———————————]
[———————]α τὰς πράξ[εις———————————————]
[——————— μέχρι] οὗ ἂν λυθῆ[ι——————————]
5 [———————— ἀξ]ιοχρέων τ[————————————]
[———————— ἐ]κτὸς Σου[————————————]
[———————— ἐν] θέρει στε̣[———————————]
[———————————]ισαν δρα[πετ(?)——————————]
[——————————] ἐννεοβ[———————————]
10 [————————————— τ]ὴν ἡμέ[ραν(?)——————]
[———————————————]Ω[.]Ị̣Ị[————————]
[————————————————]
```

(f)
```
[————————————————————————————]
[———————— τοὺ]ς πρακτόρ[ας——————————]
[———————— τῆ]ς Θεõ τό τε [———————————]
[———————— ὀφε]ιλόντων τὸ ὄ[γδοον(?)—————]
[——— οἱ στρατη]γοὶ κατὰ ταῦτα [—————————]
5 [———————— αὐτ]ὸς [ὁ]φειλέτω τὸ [————————]
[———————————]ον ἰδιώτην ἀπαλ[λα—————]
[———————— αὐτ]όθι ξενοδίκας υ[—————————]
[———————— ὑπ]ηκόων εἰ μ[ὴ] ἀγα̣[———————]
[————————————————————————————]
```

(r)
```
[————————————————————————————————]
[——————————]ιν[————————————————]
[——————————]ωεπ[——————————————]
[——————————]ς το[——————————————]
[——————————]ψηφ[——————————————]
5 [——————————]ηιθ[——————————————]
[——————————]υ[————————————————]
[————————————————————————————————]
```

(g)
```
[————————————————————————————————]
[——————]ẸΣ[————————————————————]
[————]ους πο[—————————————————————]
[————]του φον[————————————————————]
[————]ωι χρησ[———————————————————]
5 [————]δικαι[—————————————————————]
[————]ς ἐξε[——————————————————————]
[————]συν[———————————————————————]
[————]ωγη[———————————————————————]
[————————————————————————————————]
```

(*h*)

[————————————————————————]
[————————————————————————]Ω[. .]Λ̣
[————————————————————————]ν̣ δὲ θυ
[————————————————————————]ν ἐξέσ
[τω(?)——————————————————————]ν̣ι̣α̣τ̣
[————————————————————————]

(*i*)

[————————————————————————]
[ἐπιμέ]λειαν στ[——————————————————]
[. .5. .]λειτουργου[——————————————ἐ]
[κ τῶν] ἰδίων ἐκπε[μπ————————————————]
[. . ὅπω]ς ἂν ταφῶσι [———————————————]
[. .5. .]ν Ἀθηναίων [———————————————]
[. . . . ἐ]παίνους, ἐψ[ήφισθαι ————————————]
[. .5. .] ἣν εἶχο[ν———————————————————]
[. . . πρ]εσβεὺς [————————————————————]
[. .5. .]κηθελη[——————————————————————]
[. .5. .]ιων κεκο[μι ———————————————————]
[. . . .]αν καὶ τὴν [——————————————————]
[. .5. .]υσαν καὶ [——————————————————]
[. . ἀγα]θοῖς του[——————————————————]
[. . λο]ιπὸν χρόν[ον——————————————————]
[. . . .] τὴν ἡμέρ[αν———————————————————]
[. . . .]ο καὶ τῆς [——————————————————]
[. . τ]ρίτηι ἡμ[έραι——————————————————]
[. . . κ]αθ'ἑκασ[τ————————————————————]
[. . .6. . .]εσθαι το[——————————————————]
[. . .7. . .] τοῖς ἐν [——————————————————]
[. . . .9. . . .]ωνιω[——————————————————]
[. . . .10. . . .]οι[——————————————————]
[————————————————————————]

(*j*)

[————————————————————————]
[————————————————————————]
[————————————————————————]ε̣λ̣ι̣
[————————————————————————]κ̣ομετο
[——————————————————————]οντος ἐγ δ
[——————————————————————]οντος ἀπο
[——————————————————ἐὰν ἀποκ]τείνηι ἐκ
[προνοίας ——————————————ἀπο]κ̣τείνηι μὴ
[————————————————————————]υ̣λος τὸν ε
[————————————————————————]σεντοι[.]
[————————————————————————]Λ̣[. . .]
[————————————————————————]

FACE B

(*a*)

[————————————————————————]
[——————————————————————]ωι[. .6. .]
[————————————————————] ἐξέστω[. . . .]
[————————————————————] ἑκαστ[. .5. .]
[——————————————————]\\IIβά[λ]λ̣ηι δ[. .]
[————————————————————]σασθαι ε̣[. . . .]

[——————————————————————————————] μαρτ[υ]ρι [. . . .]
[——————————————————————————] τὸ ἐπιδέ[χατο]
[ν——————————————————]τερτο[. .⁶. . .]
[——————————————————]θαι εχ[. .⁶. . .]
10 [—————————————————]ασο[. . .⁸. .]
[—————————————————]οσ[. . . .⁹. . . .]
[—————————————————]υχ[. . . .⁹. . . .]
[—————————————————]ον[. . . .⁹. . . .]
[—————————————————]οτ[. . . .⁹. . . .]
[————————————————————————————————]

(k)
[——————————————————————————————]
[——————]υ[——————————————————————]
[——————]ον[—————————————————————]
[——————]αζ[—————————————————————]
[——————]μενε[———————————————————]
[——————————————————————————————]

(b)
[——————————————————————————————]
[————————————————]η[————————————]
[——————————————]τηρι[—————————————]
[——————————————]υοιν[—————————————]
[————————προ]διχ[ιαν(?)——————————————]
5 [——————————————]ειο[—————————————]
[——————————————]χην[—————————————]
(c)
[——————————]υ[. . .]χωι[———————————]
[——————————]ατ[—————————————————]
[——————————ʼΑ]θήνη[σι————————————]
10 [—————————δ]ραχμ[ὰς————————————]
[—————————]ουσηι[———————————————]
[—————————] τέχνηι [—————————————]
[—————————] πρῶτον [————————————]
[—————————]υτα ἢ αὐτ[————————————]
15 [—————————] ξενοδιχ[————————————]
[—————————]ληι ὀφει[λ—————————————]
[————————χατ]ὰ τὰς σ[υμβολὰς(?)——————]
[———————ʼΑθηνα]ιων[ω]—————————————]
[———————δραχμὰ]ς ἀργ[υρίου(?)——————————]
20 [———————————]γοθε[ν————————————]
[———————————]χω[————————————————]
[——————————————————————————————]

(l)
[——————————————————————————————]
[———] ὑπο[.]ν[——————————————————]
[———]τα ἑαυτ[————————————————————]
[———]α ʼΑθηνα[——————————————————]
[—————]θα[—————————————————————]
5 [——]ς χαι το[——————————————————]
[——]τονομο[————————————————————]
[——]σα[————————————————————————]
[——]στ[.]ι[——————————————————————]
[——] τῶ[ι] δή[μωι ————————————————]

10
    [– –]ατ[————————————————————]
    [– –]τ̣[————————————————————]
    [—————————————————————]

(d)
    [—————————————————————]
    [. .] ἑ[κατ]έρωθι παρ[————————————]
    [. ο]ἱ Στ[υμ]φάλιοι σ[——————————ὅπως ἀ]
    [ν ἤ]ι δ[ι]καιότατα υ[————————————]
    [οὔ]τε [αὐ]τὸς ἐγὼ οὔ[τε ————————————]

5
    [. . . .]Μ̣[.]ΑΠ[.]ΟΙΜ̣ΙΥ̣[————————————]
    [. . .⁶. . .]το[.]ς ξε[νο————————————]
    [. . . . Στ]υμφάλωι δ[————————————]
    [. . . .⁹. . . . .] δικαζ[————————————]
    [. .⁵. .]ος ἐ[π]ε[ι]δὰν η[————————————]

10
    [. . .⁷. . . Σ]τυμφαλ[————————————]
    [. .⁵. .]ερον· ἐὰν δὲ [——————————το]
    [ὺ]ς δαμιοργ[οὺς] π̣ο[————————————]
    [.]ΑΘΕΣΩΣΙ[.]Ι̣[.]Ι̣Δ[————————————]
    [. .]ιος ἐν δ[.]χα[.]οι̣[————————————]

15
    [. .⁵. .]ατ[. . .]ιερω[————————————]
    [. .⁵. .]Α̣ΘΕΣΩΣΙ̣Μ[————————————]
    [.]ο̣π[————————————————————]
    [—————————————————————]

(m)
    [—————————————————————]
    [– – – – –]νε̣[————————————————]
    [– – – – –]πα[————————————————]
    [– – – – –]ντ[————————————————]
    [– – – – –]ικα[———————————————]

5
    [– – δραχ]μῶν ε[———————————————]
    [– – – – –]ατος [———————————————]
    [– – – – –] ἡ βου[λὴ —————————————]
    [– – – – –]ηκα[———————————————]
    [– – – – –]νηι[———————————————]
    [– – – – –]υ[—————————————————]
    [—————————————————————]

(h)
    [—————————————————————]
    [.]γ[—————————————————————]
    ντω[————————————————————’Α]
    θήνη[σι ———————————————————]
    ωθηι[————————————————————]

5
    ων χα[ὶ ———————————————————]
    σαγο[————————————————————]
    ην ὀφ[ειλ————————————————————]
    τριτ[————————————————————]
    υαν δ[————————————————————]

10
    ’Αθην[————————————————————]
    ικα[—————————————————————]
    οσ[—————————————————————]
    γ[——————————————————————]
    [—————————————————————]

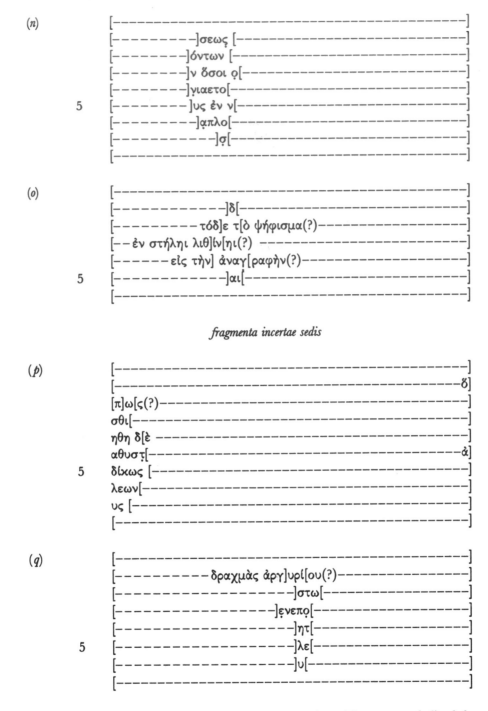

(n)

```
[-------------------------------------------------------]
[-----------]σεως [------------------------------------]
[----------]όντων [-----------------------------------]
[--------]ν ὅσοι ο[------------------------------------]
[--------]γιαετο[-------------------------------------]
[-------]υς ἐν ν[------------------------------------]
[---------]απλο[-------------------------------------]
[-----------]σ[-------------------------------------]
[-------------------------------------------------------]
```
5

(o)

```
[-------------------------------------------------------]
[-----------]δ[---------------------------------------]
[---------τόδ]ε τ[ὸ ψήφισμα(?)--------------------]
[--ἐν στήληι λιθ]ίν[ηι(?) -------------------------]
[------εἰς τὴν] ἀναγ[ραφὴν(?)--------------------]
[-----------]αι[---------------------------------------]
[-------------------------------------------------------]
```
5

fragmenta incertae sedis

(p)

```
[-------------------------------------------------------]
[--------------------------------------------------δ]
[π]ω[ς(?)-----------------------------------------------]
σθι[---------------------------------------------------]
ηθη δ[ὲ -----------------------------------------------]
αθυστ[-------------------------------------------ά]
δίκως [------------------------------------------------]
λεων[-------------------------------------------------]
υς [---------------------------------------------------]
[-------------------------------------------------------]
```
5

(q)

```
[-------------------------------------------------------]
[----------δραχμὰς ἀργ]υρί[ου(?)----------------]
[--------------]στω[----------------------------------]
[-------------]ενεπο[--------------------------------]
[-------------]ητ[------------------------------------]
[-------------]λε[------------------------------------]
[-------------]υ[-------------------------------------]
[-------------------------------------------------------]
```
5

On fragments *a* and *i* the letters underlined survive to the present time. Those not underlined depend on the readings of A. Wilhelm.

The above text is that of Walbank, with a few minor modifications. For a full account of the physical attributes of the monument and the readings hitherto advanced for each fragment, together with the details of the text now adopted, the reader is referred to his discussion, especially to pp. 333–345. It is clear that the same "none-too-skilled workman", as Walbank describes him, was engaged on both faces of the inscription, and the irregularities in his work have made it possible to propose the allocation of the fragments to various likely areas of the faces concerned.

The height of the stele when complete may be gauged as not less than 1.38 m. and its width as at least 0.69 m. Face A is calculated by Walbank (p. 348) to have contained over 100 lines, each of at least 53–55 letters: face B had room for some 85 lines of a length of 43–45 letters as a minimum. But essays of restoration have suggested the possibilities of lines of as much as 110 and 90 letters in each case, and the total text was undoubtedly of considerable extent.

That Stymphalos was the city involved first became apparent when fragment *d* was identified. The agreement between that city and Athens recorded on face B is one of the few surviving records of *symbolai* or *symbola*, already evidenced in **35** (*q.v.*), regulating the administration of justice as between nationals of the contracting cities. It remains unclear whether the treaty on face A is also part of the Stymphalian agreement, as has usually been thought, or whether it is to be regarded as a similar and contemporary agreement with a different city. Walbank, who gives a summary of the contents of both faces as far as, in his opinion, they may be assessed (p. 353), has suggested that these and other *symbolai* documents may have formed part of a continuous opisthographic wall erected on the Akropolis (pp. 320–321, note 8, and 348–349, note 37).

For bibliography on the character of these *symbolai*, see Walbank, *loc. cit.*, p. 319, note 1, and **35**; on this treaty especially see G. E. M. de Ste Croix, *CQ* n.s. 11, 1961, pp. 108–110 (cf. *SEG* XIX, 48); D. M. MacDowell, *The Law in Classical Athens*, 1978, pp. 220–221; and P. Gauthier, *Symbola: les étrangers et la justice dans les cités grecques*, 1972, p. 167. On the date see Woodhead, *loc. cit.*, pp. 223–224; Walbank, *loc. cit.*, p. 352, note 51.

THE ARCHONSHIP OF POLYZELOS, 367/6 B.C.

For the literary references to Polyzelos' year of office see *PA* 11960. His name as archon is well attested epigraphically. It appears three times in the records of the Treasurers of Athena (*IG* II², 1428, line 1, 1436, line 17, and 1438 [= *SEG* XIX, 129], line 5), twice in the records of the Treasurers of the Other Gods (*IG* II², 1450, line 5 and 1451, line 7), and twice also in the records of the Naval Commissioners (*IG* II², 1617, line 110 and 1622, line 500). It stands at the head of the earliest in series (and best preserved) of the records of the poletai detailing the leases of the mines at Laureion (M. Crosby, *Hesperia* 10, 1941, pp. 14–27, no. 1); cf. M. I. Finley, *Studi in onore di Vicenzo Arangio-Ruiz* III, 1952, pp. 473–491; *SEG* XII, 100 with full bibliography, XXXI, 128; *Agora* XIX, P5, with further references; and it dates the dedication made by the prytaneis of Erechtheis in his year (W. K. Pritchett, *Hesperia* 11, 1942, pp. 231–239, no. 43 = *Agora* XV, 14).

The important poletai record gives, in its account of month-by-month leasing of the mines, the detail of seven of the ten prytanies of the year, which are thus known to have been as follows: I Hippothontis, II Antiochis, III Oineis, IV Kekropis, V Aigeis, VII Leontis, and IX Erechtheis. This leaves the sixth, eighth, and tenth prytanies to be shared among Aiantis, Akamantis, and Pandionis. **48** is dated to the prytany of Oineis, without inclusion in the record of the number of that prytany in series. *Agora* XV, 14 may be seen to have been set up at earliest in the final prytany of the year.

The character of the year, that is, whether it was ordinary or intercalary, is not deducible from any of the evidence. It was however the ninth year of the fourth Metonic cycle and as such was scheduled as ordinary in that cycle.

The γραμματεύς was not yet an annual officer, but 367/6 was, it is generally agreed, the last year in which the old system obtained whereby the secretary changed with each prytany. See S. Alessandri, *Annali della Scuola Normale di Pisa*, pp. 46–47; P. J. Rhodes, *Athenian Boule*, pp. 135–136. The γραμματεύς while Oineis was in prytany was Demophilos, son of Theoros, of Kephale. Nothing more is certainly known of him or of his family, but it is conceivable that he was the grandfather of Demophilos, son of Timokrates, of that deme who was a βουλευτής in 303/2 (*SEG* XXIV, 162 = *Agora* XV, 62, line 89).

The number of individuals known as holding office during Polyzelos' year is quite considerable; all were listed, with references, by R. Develin (*Athenian Officials*, pp. 256–259).

DECREE REQUIRING THE SENDING OF A PROTEST TO THE AITOLIAN LEAGUE

48 (Pl. 4). Three joining fragments of a pedimental stele of Pentelic marble, of which the largest fragment (*a*, I 4384 b) preserves the center and right section of the top of the monument, complete with the low and shallowly cut pediment and the central and right akroteria, as well as the right side and original back. This fragment was discovered on April 26, 1937, in a wall of a modern house over the southern part of the Eleusinion (T 19–20). The smallest fragment (*b*, I 4384 a) preserves the left side and original back of the stele and was discovered on January 17, 1937, in a modern context southwest of the Eleusinion and west of the Post-Herulian Wall (T 20). A third fragment (*c*, I 7259), discovered on April 2, 1971, in a modern wall (Q 21), joins fragment *a* on the right and fragment *b* below: it preserves the top (including part of the pediment) and left side of the monument, as well as the original back, but it has suffered damage at the left edge of the inscribed surface.

The thickness of the stele decreases rapidly from right to left. The floor of the pediment consists of a broad taenia, below which a straight-sided ovolo molding of equal depth descends to the inscribed face, being cut back sharply at the point of junction. The taenia and ovolo taken together exceed the pedimental field itself in vertical measurement. The first line of the decree proper begins 0.061 m. below the molding, and the intervening space is filled with lines 2–3 of the text shown below, written as a heading in larger letters. These lines are however so clumsily inscribed, and so contrast with the workmanship of the rest of the stele, that it is to be presumed that they were added at a later stage, after the monument was in position. Line 1, in the regular writing of the lower lines, is inscribed asymmetrically on the horizontal cornice of the pediment.

a: H. 0.433 m.; W. 0.35 m.; Th. 0.127 m. H. of inscribed surface 0.272 m. W. of inscribed face at top 0.303 m.

b: H. 0.151 m.; W. 0.085 m.; Th. 0.101 m.

c: H. 0.30m.; W. 0.09 m.; Th. 0.094 m.

LH. 0.005–0.007 m. (lines 2–3, 0.012 m.).
Στοιχ. (lines 4 and following) Hor. 0.012 m.; Vert. 0.0125 m.

Ed. *a+b*: E. Schweigert, *Hesperia* 8, 1939, pp. 5–12, no. 3, with photograph. See A. Wilhelm, *Abhandlungen der Preussischen Akademie der Wissenschaften, philosophisch-historische Klasse*, 1939, no. 22, p. 15 (on lines 12–13); M. N. Tod, *GHI* II, pp. 110–112, no. 137; *SEG* XV, 90 (where the title "Foedus cum Communi Aetolorum" gives an inexact impression of the content of the decree), with references also to M. Sordi, *Acme* 6, 1953, pp. 419–445 and to J. and L. Robert, *REG* 68, 1955, pp. 191–192, no. 21 (on the former see in addition *SEG* XV, 357). Fragment *c* is hitherto unpublished; but cf. *SEG* XXXII, 57. Its connection with fragments *a* and *b* was first noted by J. McK. Camp.

a. 367/6 a., *pryt*. III   ΣΤΟΙΧ. 32 (lines 4 and following)

(c)   Θ [ε] ο ι.   (a)
            Δ η μ ό φ ι λ ο ς Θ ε ώ ρ ο Κ ε φ α λ ῆ
            θ ε ν ἐ γ ρ α μ μ ά τ [ε] υ ε.
            Ἔδοξεν τῆι βουλῆι καὶ τῶ[ι] δήμωι· Οἰνηὶς
      5   ἐπρυτάνε[υ]ε, Δημόφιλος Θεώρο Κεφαλῆθε
            γ ἐγραμμάτευεν, Φί[λι]ππος Σημαχίδης ἐπ
            εστάτει, [Π]ολύζηλος [ἦρχ]ε, Κηφισόδοτος ε
            [ἶ]πεν· ἐπε[ι]δὴ Αἰτωλῶν [τ]οῦ κ[ο]ινοῦ δεξαμέ
            [ν]ων τὰς μ[υ]στηριώτιδ[α]ς [σ]π[ο]νδὰς τῆς Δήμ
      10   [η]τρος τῆς ['Ε]λευσινίας καὶ τῆς Κόρης τοῦ
            [ς] ἐπαγγείλαντας τὰς σπονδὰς Εὐμολπιδ
            ῶν καὶ Κηρύκων δεδέκασι Τ[ρ]ιχονεῖς Πρ
            [ό]μαχον καὶ Ἐπιγένην παρὰ τοὺς νόμους τ
            [ο]ὺς κοι[ν]οὺς τῶν Ἑλλήνων, ἑλέσθαι τὴμ βο
      15   [υ]λὴν αὐ[τ]ίκα μάλα κήρυκα ἐξ Ἀθηναίων ἀπ
            άντων ὅσ[τ]ις ἀφικόμενος πρὸς τὸ κοινὸν
            [τὸ Αἰ]τω[λῶν] ἀ[παιτήσει τοὺς] ἄνδρας ἀφεῖ
(b)   [ναι] καὶ [.........¹⁸......... δικ]άζειν
            [ὅ]πως ἂν μ[.........²².........]ς κα
      20   ι Αἰτωλο[.........²⁴.........]ρ
            οι εἰς το[.........²⁵.........]
            αν οἳ ἂν τ[.........²¹......... Εὐμολ]
            πίδας κ[αὶ Κήρυκας.........¹⁷.........]
            ας βουλ[.........²⁶.........]
      25   ἤσοντ[αι ....²⁵.........]
            ους δώσ[ουσι(?) ....²².........]
            ἐς ἐφόδ[ια τὸν ταμίαν τοῦ δήμου ΔΔΔ δραχ]
            μὰς ἐκ τ[ῶν κατὰ ψηφίσματα ἀναλισκομέν]
            ων τῶι [δήμωι.   vacat(?)   ]
      30   [vacat(?)]

Schweigert noted that the stele was "of unusually good workmanship." The writing is small and the letters generously spaced. There are minor inconsistencies in different examples of the same letter, *exempli gratia*, the curved element in omega is drawn more closely together at the bottom of the letter in some instances than in others. The right oblique stroke of alpha and lambda is cocked up slightly higher than its counterpart on the left, causing the letters to appear as striding forward on the stone. The horizontal strokes in epsilon are all of equal length in the main text but not in lines 2–3. Phi in line 5 is of the "crossbow type": but this is no more than a casual aberration, as is the "rectangular oval" of the same letter in line 2. In line 22 NOIAN is inscribed in the space of four letters. O appears in the place of OY only in the genitive Θεώρο in lines 2 and 5.

The Athenians had sent σπονδοφόροι to the Aitolian League and its constituent cities to announce the sacred truce of the Greater Mysteries of Eleusis, and the League had accepted the truce (lines 8–10), which lasted for fifty-five days. Despite this acceptance, the σπονδοφόροι had been arrested by the inhabitants of Trichonion, one of the cities with membership of the League, and the present decree is concerned with action to make immediate representations to the League, by means of a κῆρυξ, whereby the League would be urged to bring the Trichonians into line and procure the release of the two ambassadors. For the dispatch of κήρυκες by the boule see P. J. Rhodes, *Athenian Boule*, p. 94 with note 4, and for the immediacy of the action, *ibid.*, p. 280.

Most inscribed records of the boule and the demos concern matters of long-lasting consequence or deserving of enduring commemoration: treaties, expressions of gratitude, and grants of honors. Such documents were regularly placed on the Akropolis under the care and guarantee of Athens, as a reflection of the solemnity of Athens' commitment. Ephemeral resolutions of the assembly for some immediate, short-term action, of which the greater part of Athens' public business must have been composed, were registered in archival copies, perhaps sometimes (until the action was complete) committed to σανίδες or πινάκια but not regarded as meriting the permanent record of a stone stele. In the present instance, however, a short-term probouleumatic resolution (cf. Rhodes, *Athenian Boule*, p. 248), the effective accomplishment of which within the shortest possible time would fulfill the decree's purpose and utility, is indeed given an imposing inscriptional record. This aspect of the monument, which did not attract the interest of Schweigert or of any later commentator, may perhaps be accounted for by the location in which the fragments were found and by the sacrilegious character of the Trichonians' action. The two σπονδοφόροι, Promachos and Epigenes, were members of the clans of the Eumolpidai and Kerykes, intimately associated with the Eleusinian cult. The fragments were found in the vicinity of the Eleusinion. The stele was thus probably inscribed on the initiative of the officials of the shrine of Demeter and Kore and erected within the precinct as a special record both of Aitolian conduct towards the representatives of the goddesses and of the gratifyingly prompt reaction of the demos. It may be noted that the decree does not itself contain any instruction to the γραμματεύς for its inscription and setting up.

For the μυστηριώτιδες σπονδαί and the σπονδοφόροι see the commentaries of Schweigert, *Hesperia* 8, 1939, pp. 10–11, and Tod, *GHI* II, *loc. cit.* Important references concerning the former are *IG* I³, 6 (*SEG* XXXI, 2, XXXVI, 3, with bibliography) and Aischines 2.133. On the σπονδοφόροι cf. *IG* II², 1235–1236 and K. Latte, *RE*, 2nd ser., III, ii, cols. 1849–1850.

The principal importance of the text was immediately recognized in the evidence it provides for the existence of the Aitolian League at a date more than fifty years earlier than the first reference to it in literary sources (Diodorus Siculus 19.66.2, in 314 B.C.). Schweigert pointed out that *IG* II², 358, with a reference in line 13 to τὸ κοινὸ[ν τῶν Αἰτωλῶν, was to be dated in either 333/2 or 327/6 and thus provided testimony (ignored by commentators) of the League's existence in the reign of Alexander the Great: but this decree is now preferably to be dated in 307/6 (see *SEG* XXI, 326 and p. 169 below), although both the revised date and the relevance of the document have been doubted (see *SEG* XXVI, 87). The new evidence has been integrated into the more recent historical treatments of the period, and the League is no longer considered as having come into being during or just after Alexander's reign. It is seen either as a product of the movements of the second quarter of the 4th century under Theban auspices which produced the Arkadian League and the new Messenian state (so Schweigert) or of that earlier coalescence of independent cities or *ethnê* from which the Achaian and Akarnanian *koina* developed. See Sordi, *loc. cit.* and J. A. O. Larsen, *Greek Federal States*, 1968, pp. 196–197. Cf. Larsen, *Representative Government in Greek and Roman History*, 1955, pp. 69–71; N. G. L. Hammond, *A History of Greece to 322 B.C.*, 2nd ed., 1967, p. 500.

Line 5. Φίλιππος Σημαχίδης. Schweigert hazarded that he was the proposer in 362/1 of the measure to authorize the sending of cleruchs to Potidaia (*PA* 14373; *IG* II², 114; Tod, *GHI* II, pp. 141–143, no. 146). Otherwise he has left no record in the tradition. Line 7. Kephisodotos ἐκ Κεραμέων was the gifted orator (Demosthenes 20.150) who was an ambassador to Sparta in 371 (Xenophon, *HG* 6.3.2) and who appears at intervals in the historical sources during the subsequent fifteen years. See *PA* 8331; *IG* II², 141 (*SEG* XII, 85, XXVI, 73); M. H. Hansen, *Athenian Ecclesia II*, p. 51. His father's name is unknown, but if Kephisodotos is to be restored among the διαιτηταί listed in *IG* II², 143 (*SEG* XXX, 60) at line 36 (see *Hesperia* 7, 1938, pp. 278–280, no. 13 + *IG* II², 2813; P. Roussel, *RA* 18, 1941, pp. 216–220), he will there appear as [Κηφισόδοτος Κ]ηφισοδότου ἐκ Κε[ραμέων].

Line 13. The name Promachos is assured by the discovery of fragment *c*: Πρ[οφήτην Schweigert; Πρ[οφάνην Wilhelm. The victor recorded in *IG* II², 3126 (cf. *PA* 12245) could be his son. If so, his demotic was Ἐλευσίνιος. Schweigert suggested that Epigenes might be of the same family as Ἐπιγένης Λυσανίου Ἐλευσίνιος (*PA* 4794), whose tombstone (*IG* II², 6031) was seen by A. R. Rangabé. If that stele is correctly dated to the 4th century, there is some probability that the two should be identified. That being the case, the demotics of the two κήρυκες may in the circumstances be not without significance.

Line 27. For the ταμίας τοῦ δήμου see A. S. Henry, *Chiron* 12, 1982, pp. 97–118 and **40**. It is noteworthy that, if the restorations are acceptable, traveling expenses for the κῆρυξ could also be met from the monies spent by the demos on ψηφίσματα (the "analiskomena fund") and that the use of this fund was not restricted to the expenses of the record of an enactment but might also include the incidental costs of implementing it. Cf. Henry, *Chiron* 14, 1984, p. 56, note 28. This is in any case one of the earliest clearly dated examples of the fund as the source of payment. See **45**.

AN EMBASSY FROM MACEDONIA HONORED

49. A fragment of a stele of Pentelic marble (I 5272), with the original rough-picked back preserved but otherwise broken and very battered all around, discovered on February 28, 1938, in a wall of a modern cellar west of the Panathenaic Way and west of the Eleusinion (Q 19).

H. 0.192 m.; W. 0.181 m.; Th. 0.125 m.
LH. 0.007 m.

Ed. B. D. Meritt, *Hesperia* 30, 1961, pp. 207–208, no. 2, with photograph pl. 35. See also *SEG* XXI, 246. Cf. A. G. Woodhead in *Ancient Macedonian Studies*, p. 357.

ca. a. 364 *vel* 359/8 *a.* (?)   NON-ΣΤΟΙΧ. *ca.* 22–26

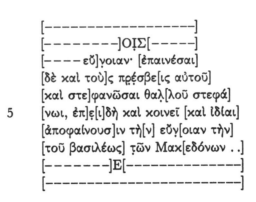

Traces indicated here of a few letters additional to those recorded in the *editio princeps* do not affect the text.

The restorations are those of Meritt, who urged that the letters MAK in line 7 almost certainly belong to an ethnic, and on the basis of the style of the writing, to which he compared *IG* II², 110 (*SEG* XXXIII, 80) of 363/2 B.C. (see J. Kirchner, *IIA*², p. 17 and pl. 25, no. 53), he attributed the honors accorded to this embassy of a Macedonian king to the beginning of the reign of Philip II (359/8). The embassy in question would in that case probably be that referred to by Demosthenes 23.121 and Diodorus Siculus 16.4.1. See also G. Glotz and R. Cohen, *Histoire grecque* III, 1936, pp. 228–229; P. Cloché, *Un fondateur d'empire: Philippe II, roi de Macédoine*, 1955, p. 50; J. R. Ellis, *Philip II and Macedonian Imperialism*, 1976, p. 51; G. L. Cawkwell, *Philip of Macedon*, 1978, p. 73; N. G. L. Hammond and G. T. Griffith, *A History of Macedonia* II, 1979, pp. 236–237.

On the other hand, the decree could refer to such an embassy sent by Philip's brother and predecessor Perdikkas III. For the occasion see Demosthenes 2.14; K. J. Beloch, *Griechische Geschichte* III, i, 1922, p. 195; M. Cary, *CAH* VI, 1933, p. 105; Cloché, *Histoire de la Macédoine jusqu'à l'avènement d'Alexandre le Grand*, 1960, p. 127; Hammond and Griffith, *op. cit.*, p. 186. Hence a tentative date as between 364 and 358 has been preferred above.

There are, however, certain considerations which may cast doubt on this dating and reference. (1) The lettering on this fragment is poor and nondescript work and, like *IG* II², 110 (which Koehler thought to have been inscribed at a date later than that of the archon whose name stands in its heading), may be adjudged a poor representative of its period. Indeed it might be attributable to the latter part of the century, for the short central horizontal of epsilon, the drawing together of the curved element in omega at the bottom of the letter, and the phi in which the upright stroke does not pass through the "oval" (see **85**) combine to point in that direction.

(2) The epsilon of κοινεῖ in line 5 and the restorations calling for ΟΥ rather than Ο in the apposite places throughout may in combination suggest a later rather than an earlier date. Cf. L. Threatte, *Grammar*, pp. 369–370 and 247–256. But the nonstoichedon arrangement can admit of some adjustments in the restored part of the text.

(3) The expression κοινῇ καὶ ἰδίᾳ is not clearly evidenced until later in the century, when it becomes a frequent turn of phrase in honorary texts (cf. *IG* II², 283, 294, etc.). *IG* II², 252 contains it and is dated in general terms " med. s. IV". This present example, as dated, would evidently provide its earliest appearance. Nevertheless it is fair to add that ἰδίᾳ καὶ δημοσίᾳ is to be met with in the 5th century (*IG* I³, 80, line 10).

(4) The reference to εὔνοια as a virtue in honorands is attested in the 330's but not earlier save in *IG* II², 196, lines 12–13 ("ante a. 353/2"): in *IG* II², 177, line 8 (also "ante a. 353/2") the adjective εὔνοι is restored in an ἐπειδή clause as part of the phrase ἀποφαίν]οσιν ὅτι [εὔνοί εἰσιν.

(5) Inscribed treaties and other dealings with monarchs usually refer to them by their personal names (e.g., *IG* II², 21, 102, 126, 127, 190); but when their function as monarch ("king of ... ") is cited the people over whom they rule are customarily not given a definite article (e.g., *IG* II², 31, 141). Literary practice is much the same, for example in Thucydides, where the article is only rarely included (e.g., 1.89.2). If he is in fact referred to in line 7, therefore, the king should be described as τοῦ βασιλέως Μακεδόνων or τοῦ βασιλέως τοῦ Μακεδόνων. Cf. J. Kalléris, *Les anciens Macédoniens* I, 1954, pp. 116–117, with references in note 7; N. G. L. Hammond, *CQ* n.s. 38, 1988, p. 386.

If these points, in sum, be adjudged to tell against the dating initially proposed, it must be admitted that a historical reference for Athenian-Macedonian relations of this character two or three decades later is hard to identify. The restoration of line 7 in particular would in that case be open to reconsideration.

TREATY BETWEEN THE ATHENIANS AND THE SIPHNIANS

50. A fragment of a stele of Pentelic marble (I 5410), with the left side and original rough-picked back preserved, discovered on April 27, 1938, in a marble pile in the area of the southern end of the Stoa of Attalos. Above the inscription are the remains of the left-hand section of a figured relief, elegantly cut within a recessed panel, which shows the lower part of a draped female figure, seated and facing to right, with the right foot extended. It is likely that a second figure, leftward facing and now lost, completed the group and that the two were representative of Athens and Siphnos. The inscribed surface of the stone has been much worn and is considerably discolored.

H. 0.267 m.; W. 0.168 m.; Th. 0.073 m.

LH. 0.007–0.01 m.

Στοιχ. Hor. 0.011 m.; Vert. 0.0135 m.

Ed. A. G. Woodhead, *Hesperia* 26, 1957, pp. 231–233, no. 87, with photograph pl. 59; see also *SEG* XVII, 19. Text and brief commentary by H. Bengtson, *Staatsverträge* II, pp. 258–259, no. 294; see also *SEG* XXI, 245. Short discussion by G. E. M. de Ste Croix, *CQ* n.s. 11, 1961, p. 109 (*SEG* XIX, 48), and consideration also by P. Gauthier, *Symbola: les étrangers et la justice dans les cités grecques*, 1972, p. 169, note 2.

ca. a. 365–355 *a.*   ΣΤΟΙΧ. 26

Θ   ε   [ο   ι].

’Ενάτης πρυτανεί[ας, ἔκτηι καὶ τρ]

ιακοστῆι· ἔδ[οξεν τῆι βολῆι καὶ τ]

ῶι δήμ[ω]ι· εἶ[ναι μὲν τὰς γραφὰς πε]

5   ρὶ ἀδικίας [κατὰ τὰς συμβολὰς ἐχ]

α[τ]έ[ρωθι Ἀθηναίοις καὶ Σιφνίοι]

ς [ἀδόλως καὶ ....¹⁶........]

[...............²⁶............]

[..⁵..]τ[.. · Ἀθηναῖον δὲ τὸν δῆμον]

10   [τ]ὸ[ν] Σιφνίων [μὴ κτένεν ἄνευ τō]

δήμο τō Ἀθηναίων [μηδὲ διώκεν]·

ὡς δ’ἀμ μηδὲς ἀποθ[άνηι Ἀθηναί]

[ω]ν ἄκριτος, ἀντισ[.....¹².....]

[....] ΤΙΝ[........¹⁸........]

15   [——————————————]

The date of this document depends upon a reconciliation of the lettering, formulaic usage, and likely historical circumstances. (1) The writing is thin, hesitant, and with some imprecision but because of the worn surface may appear to undeserved disadvantage. Omega is well spread; epsilon has equal horizontal strokes. Except in line 4, E and O appear throughout for EI and OY; cf. L. Threatte, *Grammar*, pp. 185 and 248. All this suggests a date not later than *ca.* 360–355 B.C. The presence of the relief also implies a date in the first half of the century; see the *editio princeps*, p. 232.

(2) The abridged prescript lacks any reference to the name of the phyle in prytany, to the γραμματεύς, to the πρόεδρος or ἐπιστάτης, or to the archon. These elements, or some of them, might have stood independently above the relief; but the presence of Θεοί in line 1 makes this unlikely. A fuller statement could have stood in a second text in which a proposal to make or accept this treaty was registered; cf. **34**. Yet some of the usual data are present, and it is more likely that the γραμματεύς was not concerned, nor under any obligation, to elaborate the information. The text thus belongs to a period when the formulas employed were fluid and, within limits, arbitrary. Cf. A. S. Henry, *Prescripts*, p. 33. That the date within the prytany is given implies a date not earlier than the second quarter of the century; cf. W. B. Dinsmoor, *Archons of Athens*, p. 351 and Henry, *Prescripts*, p. 107—first dated occurrence, 368/7 B.C. But the whole form is exceptional.

(3) For the Siphnians in the Second Athenian Confederacy see *IG* II², 43, line 126; M. N. Tod, *GHI* II, p. 67; F. H. Marshall, *The Second Athenian Confederacy*, 1905, p. 69; Woodhead, *AJA* 61, 1957, p. 371; *eund.*, *Phoenix* 16, 1962, pp. 259–265; J. Cargill, *The Second Athenian League*, 1981, p. 94. They seem to have been recruited in 373/2. This treaty is of a different character. Separate agreements were made by Athens with Keos and Naxos in consequence of disaffection in the late 360's (*IG* II², 111 and 179). Siphnos, in the same area, may have been affected, and the provisions of this treaty, the best surviving of which is apparently designed to ensure justice in capital cases, may reflect a previously obtaining situation in which justice had not been so ensured.

The treaty, so far as existing, relates entirely to judicial arrangements; these do not necessarily imply any military alliance or other political cooperation between the cities concerned, nor do they extend to commercial or contractual matters. However, despite the hesitations of Gauthier (*loc. cit.*), it may be included within the category of agreements collectively referred to as *symbolai*. See **35**, with references there, and M. B. Walbank, *Hesperia* 55, 1986, pp. 349–353.

The restorations shown in lines 4–7 and 9–11 suggest what is likely to have been the sense of the document but cannot be regarded as more than a hypothesis. On the relief sculpture see also *SEG* XXXIX, 324.

TREATY BETWEEN THE ATHENIANS AND A CRETAN CITY

51. A thin fragment of a stele of coarse-grained Pentelic marble (I 3055), broken on all sides and at the back, discovered on June 24, 1935, in a modern context in the central area of the Market Square (L 9).

H. 0.20 m.; W. 0.18 m.; Th. 0.028 m.
LH. 0.005–0.006 m.
Στοιχ. Hor. *ca.* 0.01 m.; Vert. 0.009 m.

Ed. A. G. Woodhead, *Hesperia* 26, 1957, pp. 229–231, no. 86, with photograph pl. 58; see also *SEG* XVII, 20. Text and brief commentary by H. Bengtson, *Staatsverträge* II, pp. 261–262, no. 296; see also *SEG* XXI, 259. Further study of the nature of the provisions by G. E. M. de Ste Croix, *CQ* n.s. 11, 1961, p. 109; P. Gauthier, *Symbola: les étrangers et la justice dans les cités grecques*, 1972, p. 168, no. XIII; S. Dušanić, *Talanta* 12/13, 1980–1981, pp. 25–27 (*SEG* XXXII, 65).

ca. a. 360 *a.* (?)   ΣΤΟΙΧ. 49(?)

```
     [------------------------------------------------]
     [----------------]ΜΗ[--------------------------]
     [----------------]ΩΛΛ[------------------------]
     [----------- ἐν]νέ’ἀρχο[ντ---------------------]
     [-------------]αι αὐτημε[---------------------]
  5  [----------- χ]ρίναντες Κυ[δωνιατ(?)-----------]
     [-------------]α καὶ εἰσαγ[γελλόντων ----------]
     [----------]αι δικαστη[ρι-------------------]
     [--------- ἐπ]ιμελείσθω καθάπ[ερ Κνωσίοις------]
     [------- οἱ ἐ]ννέ’ἄρχοντες ’Αθή[νησι------------]
 10  [-------- τῶ]ν δικῶν καθάπερ τα[ῖς Κνωσίων δίκαις -]
     [------παρό]ντος ’Αθήνησι· μετο[ικίο δὲ ἀτέλειαν (τοῖς)]
     [Κυδωνιάταις(?) δίδοσ]θαι καθάπερ Κνωσ[ίοις---------]
     [---------]ηθη ὑπὸ τὸ πρὶν μ[---------------]
```

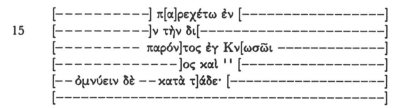

A few improved readings since the *editio princeps* make little difference to the meager message of this text. The lettering is competent work of the second quarter of the 4th century. In general terms, *IG* II², 2311 (J. Kirchner, *IIA*², p. 20 and pl. 27, no. 58) is comparable. The length of line must be in the region of 45–50 letters. M. B. Walbank (*per ep.*) has regarded the lettering as executed by the craftsman who, in his view, also worked on *IG* II², 124 and 125 (of 357/6), 254 (a text described as using "litt. volg. med. saec."), *SEG* XXI, 586 (cf. XXII, 138), and **63**.

The date cannot otherwise be determined, but within the limits already envisaged Athenian treaty relationships with Knossos and another presumably Cretan city might plausibly be assigned to a period when the Second Confederacy was still in a flourishing and expanding state. Bengtson and Gauthier hesitantly preferred a date after 360, which seems less consonant with this supposition, but 355 might surely be viewed as an acceptable *terminus ante quem*. Dušanić (*loc. cit.*) showed reason to connect it with an Athenian foreign policy particularly to be associated with Timotheos in the later 360's.

The document records an agreement between Athens and an unknown city, the provisions of which are modeled on a treaty already existing between Athens and Knossos. Good relations with the latter are indeed evidenced by the crown given by the Knossians to Athens, which appears in *IG* II², 1443 (col. II, line 121), a catalogue of 345/4 B.C. The term of reference certainly suggests that the unknown city of the present treaty was also Cretan; the remains of line 5 allow the further suggestion (regarded by Dušanić [*loc. cit.*, p. 26] as the only plausible restoration) that the city was Kydonia, an object of interest to the Athenians in the 5th century (Thucydides 2.85.5). Arrangements apparently provided for lawsuits (for the involvement of the nine archons, similarly elided, cf. **35**). These were partly in Athens (lines 3–11) and partly, perhaps, in Crete (cf. line 16). For the remission of the metic tax in Athens cf. (e.g.) *IG* II², 211, line 5. See also D. Whitehead, *The Ideology of the Athenian Metic*, 1977, p. 23, note 59. There can be no certainty about the exact formula employed here: Ἀθήνησι μετο[ικουντ––– is also possible, as A. S. Henry has pointed out (*Honours*, p. 245).

Like **50**, this text may be counted among the *symbolai* agreements regulating the status of private citizens of the contracting cities in judicial or commercial matters or both. See **35**, with references, and Walbank, *Hesperia* 55, 1986, pp. 349–353. The original back of this stone is not preserved, but it may well, like **35** and **47**, have belonged to an opisthographic stele, with the Knossian agreement on the reverse side (which would make it the more convenient as a point of reference). Walbank (*loc. cit.*, pp. 320–321, note 8; cf. pp. 348–349, note 37) has suggested that the whole series of *symbolai* may have formed a single wall of record.

Dušanić (*loc. cit.*, especially note 133) has suggested that a policy uniting Athens and the Cretan city in hostility against Maussollos of Karia was written into it. Proposing a stoichedon line of 49 letters (which would depend on the retention of τοῖς in line 11), he suggested for lines 1–3, where he claims with some hesitation to see traces of ΥΣ before ΩΛΛ, μὴ [ἐξεῖναι δὲ Κυδωνιάταις | συμμαχίαν ποιεῖσθαι (or ποιήσασθαι, if ΥΣ be accepted) πρὸς Μαύσσω]ωλλ[ον ἄνευ Ἀθηναίων(?) καὶ το|ῦ πλήθους τῶν συμμάχων· τοὺς δ'ἐνν]έ'ἄρχο[ντας ––––]. But the inclusion of such a clause, at such a point, in a document of this character at this date would be somewhat surprising.

THE ΚΗΡΥΚΕΣ EUKLES AND PHILOKLES APPOINTED

52 (Pl. 6). A fragment (I 5207, hereafter fragment *b*) of the stele of Pentelic marble of which *IG* II², 145 (hereafter fragment *a*) provides a larger section, broken on all sides, discovered on February 10, 1938, in a late context west of the Panathenaic Way and west of the Eleusinion (S 19). The Agora fragment supplies part of lines 14–20 of the text in *IG* II², correcting the restorations there given in lines 15 and 20 and confirming the remainder.

b only: H. 0.055 m.; W. 0.086 m.; Th. 0.034 m.

    LH. 0.0055 m. (omega 0.004 m., phi 0.0085 m.).

    Στοιχ. (square) 0.01 m.

Ed. W. K. Pritchett, *Hesperia* 10, 1941, p. 266, no. 68, with photograph of fragment *b loc. cit.* and of fragment *a* p. 267. The reading of line 20 of fragment *b* and of the ends of lines 1–10 in fragment *a* corrected by D. M. Lewis, *BSA* 49, 1954, pp. 36–37; see also *SEG* XIV, 50. The text of both fragments thus amended is given here for convenience, as it is also by M. J. Osborne, *Naturalization* III/IV, pp. 39–41, T 20.

a. 359/8 *a.*(?)   ΣΤΟΙΧ. 36

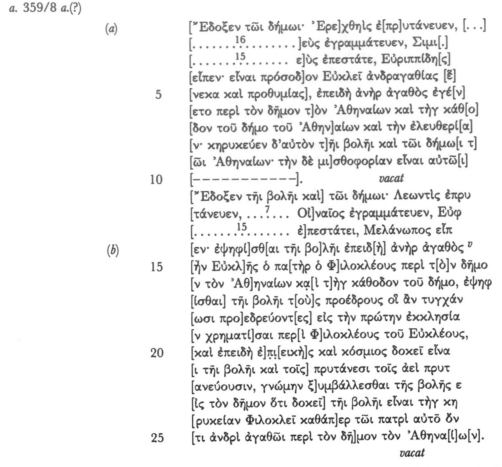

(a)

      [Ἔδοξεν τῶι δήμωι· Ἐρε]χθηὶς ἐ[πρ]υτάνευεν, [. . .]
      [. . . . . . .¹⁶. . . . .]εὺς ἐγραμμάτευεν, Σιμι[.]
      [. . . . . . .¹⁵. . . . . . ε]ὺς ἐπεστάτε, Εὐριππίδη[ς]
      [εἶπεν· εἶναι πρόσοδ]ον Εὐκλεῖ ἀνδραγαθίας [ἕ]
5   [νεκα καὶ προθυμίας], ἐπειδὴ ἀνὴρ ἀγαθὸς ἐγέ[ν]
      [ετο περὶ τὸν δῆμο τ]ὸν Ἀθηναίων καὶ τὴγ κάθ[ο]
      [δον τοῦ δήμο τοῦ Ἀθην]αίων καὶ τὴν ἐλευθερί[α]
      [ν· κηρυκεύεν δ'αὐτὸν τ]ῆι βολῆι καὶ τῶι δήμω[ι τ]
      [ῶι Ἀθηναίων· τὴν δὲ μι]σθοφορίαν εἶναι αὐτῶ[ι]
10   [— — — — — — — — —].   *vacat*
      [Ἔδοξεν τῆι βολῆι καὶ] τῶι δήμωι· Λεωντὶς ἐπρυ
      [τάνευεν, . . .⁷. . . Οἰ]ναῖος ἐγραμμάτευεν, Εὐφ
      [. . . . . . .¹⁵. . . . . . ἐ]πεστάτει, Μελάνωπος εἶπ

(b)

      [εν· ἐψηφί]σθ[αι τῆι βο]λῆι ἐπειδ[ὴ] ἀνὴρ ἀγαθὸς ᵛ
15   [ἦν Εὐκλ]ῆς ὁ πα[τὴρ ὁ Φ]ιλοκλέους περὶ τ[ὸ]ν δῆμο
      [ν τὸν Ἀθ]ηναίων κα[ὶ τ]ὴγ κάθοδον τοῦ δήμο, ἐψηφ
      [ίσθαι] τῆι βολῆι τ[οὺ]ς προέδρους οἳ ἂν τυγχάν
      [ωσι προ]εδρεύοντ[ες] εἰς τὴν πρώτην ἐκκλησία
      [ν χρηματί]σαι περ[ὶ Φ]ιλοκλέους τοῦ Εὐκλέους,
20   [καὶ ἐπειδὴ ἐ]πι[εικὴ]ς καὶ κόσμιος δοκεῖ εἶνα
      [ι τῆι βολῆι καὶ τοῖς] πρυτάνεσι τοῖς ἀεὶ πρυτ
      [ανεύουσιν, γνώμην ξ]υμβάλλεσθαι τῆς βολῆς ε
      [ἰς τὸν δῆμον ὅτι δοκεῖ] τῆι βολῆι εἶναι τὴγ κη
      [ρυκείαν Φιλοκλεῖ καθάπ]ερ τῶι πατρὶ αὐτο ὄν
25   [τι ἀνδρὶ ἀγαθῶι περὶ τὸν δῆ]μον τὸν Ἀθηνα[ί]ω[ν].
                               vacat

    The character of the lettering, although plain and regular in its general features, is distinctive in detail. A tendency to emphasize or widen the "free ends" of strokes, the "compressed" aspect of sigma, with short central strokes and modestly angled external strokes, the variable central horizontal of epsilon, the drawing in (in some instances) of the lower part of the curve of omega—all these features conspire to suggest that the stele should be dated later rather than earlier in the span of time judged on other grounds to be available for it. Beta was an awkward letter for any mason and here is clumsy but not without individual character. There is inconsistency in the substitution, in appropriate cases, of ΕΙ for Ε and ΟΥ for Ο. Βολή appears throughout. Τοῦ and Φιλοκλέους appear beside δήμο and αὐτο, and ἐπεστάτε in line 3 reflects the greater age of the first of the two recorded resolutions, as compared with line 13.

    The two decrees (lines 1–10 and 11–25) were inscribed at the same time but differ in date by a generation. Neither contains the customary instructions for ἀναγραφή and payment, and this led W. Hartel to the opinion that the monument was privately commissioned by Philokles (*IG* II², 145, *comm.*). The thesis of private commission is possibly enhanced by the unusual character of the "πρόσοδος clause" in lines 4–8, coming as it does immediately after the verb of proposal; cf. A. S. Henry, *Honours*, p. 194. The first decree must be dated between 402 and 399; cf. Lewis, *loc. cit.* Eukles was already in office as κῆρυξ τῆς βουλῆς καὶ τοῦ δήμου in the latter year (Andokides 1.112), and this text is the record of his appointment to it. The second decree was shown by Pritchett to antedate 356/5, since the γραμματεῖς of the phyle Hippothontis are known thereafter. Of earlier years, 378/7, 369/8, and the span 363/2 to 360/59 are all to be excluded as possibilities, as Lewis observed. That this text is to be dated to the year 359/8 is thus on all counts a plausible hypothesis, but a date in 364/3 or shortly beforehand is not to be excluded. Cf. R. Develin, *Athenian Officials*, p. 262.

    Eukles and Philokles of Trinemea (*PA* 5732 and 14562) were the progenitors of a long line of descendants who supplied the boule and demos with κήρυκες by an apparently well-accepted family tradition, until 140/39. See *Agora* XV, pp. 14–15 (where the first Eukles named is presumably the son of the Philokles of this text), supplemented by J. S. Traill, *Hesperia* 47, 1978, p. 281; also M. Piérart, *BCH* 100, 1976, pp. 443–447. The inscription in which that Eukles first appears (*Agora* XV, 58) is of a date later than Lewis thought, and the family succession was interrupted before his appointment by Diophon, son of Diophantos of Aphidna (*Agora* XV, 43, of 335/4), and perhaps by another appointee.

    Line 1. [ἔδοξεν τῆι βουλῆι κτλ.] *IG* II²; τῆι βολῆι Lewis; τῶι δήμωι P. J. Rhodes, *Athenian Boule*, pp. 84–85, thereby making this a nonprobouleumatic decree (*ibid.*, p. 259), on the grounds that the boule is unlikely to have had the power to make this appointment on its own authority: see also Henry, *Prescripts*, p. 17. The correction may however be unnecessary; see **33**, line 3. Lines 3–4. On Eurippides (*PA* 5949-5955-5956), son of Adeimantos of Myrrhinoutta, see J. K. Davies (*Athenian Propertied Families*, pp. 202 and 204), who discusses the evidence and describes him as a "political figure of considerable importance", and M. H. Hansen, *Athenian Ecclesia II*, p. 47.

Lines 6–7 and 16. That is, the events of 403/2. Kirchhoff, whose restorations are the basis of *IG* II², 145, held from line 4 that Eukles was not an Athenian citizen at the time of his appointment; if he was not, he was presumably given citizenship along with other metoikoi who actively supported the democrats in 403/2; cf. *IG* II², 10 (*SEG* XXXI, 57, with earlier references, XXXII, 40); D. Whitehead, *The Ideology of the Athenian Metic*, 1977, pp. 58, 155–156; Osborne, *Naturalization* III/IV, pp. 39–41.

Line 13. Melanopos, the proposer of the decree to appoint Philokles as his father's successor, was presumably the well-known rhetor Μελάνωπος Λάχητος Αἰξωνεύς lambasted by Demosthenes (24.127). See *PA* 9788 and references assembled by Hansen, *Athenian Ecclesia II*, p. 55. Lines 16–19. For the instructions to the proedroi (the probouleumatic formula), of which this is the earliest example among the "Agora decrees", cf. Rhodes, *Athenian Boule*, p. 65 (also p. 84). The phraseology is not yet in its settled "standard" form and is unusually separated from the phrase γνώμην δὲ ξυμβάλλεσθαι, which ordinarily follows it without interruption. For the retention of xi in this latter phrase see L. Threatte, *Grammar*, p. 554.

Line 20. χ]ρή[σιμο]ς(?) Pritchett; ἐπι[εικ]ής Lewis. Lines 21–22. πρυτ[ανεύσασιν *IG* II², 145, *et priores*; πρυτ[ανεύουσιν *IG* II², iv, 1, p. 61. Line 24. καθάπ]ερ τῶι πατρὶ αὐτõ, i.e., presumably (barring incapacity) for life.

THE ARCHONSHIP OF AGATHOKLES, 357/6 B.C.

Agathokles' year of office (*PA* 44 and R. Develin, *Athenian Officials*, p. 275, for the literary references to him) is epigraphically well attested. In addition to **53** and **54**, his name as archon is present or suitably restored in the decrees *IG* II², 121, 122, 123 (*SEG* XVI, 48), and 124 (*SEG* XXI, 248, XXXVII, 72), in the inventories of the Treasurers of Athena *IG* II², 1436, 1437, and 1438 (*SEG* XIX, 129), in the list of magistrates *IG* II², 1696, in the list of trierarchs who sailed with Chares to the Hellespont *IG* II², 1953, and in the dedications *IG* II², 2790, 2818, and 2839 + 2844 (*SEG* XXIV, 209). Furthermore, *IG* II², 125 and 126 (*SEG* XXXI, 72) are assigned to this year on historical grounds derived from the literary tradition, although on the former see *SEG* XXXIV, 67. The naval record *IG* II², 1611 (+ E. Schweigert, *Hesperia* 8, 1939, pp. 17–25, no. 5) is shown on internal evidence also to belong to 357/6 B.C.

The γραμματεύς of Agathokles' term of office was Διόδοτος Διοκλέους ᾽Αγγελῆθεν (Pandionis III): see *IG* II², 121–123 and **53** and **54**. J. Kirchner (*PA* 3891) suggested a family relationship between him and the trierarch Diokles (*PA* 4010) who appears in *IG* II², 1953, dated to this year (see above); both were perhaps related to Καλλιστράτη Διοκλέους ᾽Αγγελῆθεν (*PA* 8117), who shared the tomb monument *IG* II², 6707 ("post med. s. IV a."). J. K. Davies (*Athenian Propertied Families*, pp. 156–157, *s.v.* no. 4009) combined *PA* 4010 with 4009 and regarded the γραμματεύς as the son of the trierarch. For a list of those known to have held public office in this year see Develin, *Athenian Officials*, pp. 275–278.

VIII Hippothontis and IX Aigeis are the two phylai whose terms in prytany are certainly known. The phyle in office during the sixth prytany (...⁷... ίς, in *IG* II², 121) cannot have been on duty when **54** was enacted, since the restoration in that text would be too short by one letter were its name to be inserted. Nor, for similar reasons of space, was **54** enacted in the eighth or ninth prytany.

DECREE CONCERNING THE CITY OF ELAIOUS

53. A fragment of a stele of Pentelic marble (I 5030) consisting of the top central section of the monument, broken all around save that the original rough-picked back is preserved. Above the inscribed face there survive the very battered remains of a substantial crowning molding, which terminates in an abrupt horizontal cut-back immediately above the first line of the text. The fragment was discovered on October 20, 1937, in a wall of a modern house southeast of the Market Square and west of the Panathenaic Way (R 18).

H. 0.457 m.; W. 0.18 m.; Th. 0.10 m.

LH. 0.007 m. (on average, but varying between 0.005 and 0.01 m.).

Στοιχ. (almost square in design, but horizontally, at least, irregularly maintained) Hor. *ca.* 0.012 m.; Vert. 0.013 m.

Ed. E. Schweigert, *Hesperia* 8, 1939, pp. 12–17, no. 4, with photograph.

a. 357/6 *a., pryt.* VIII   ΣΤΟΙΧ. 28

```
        ['Επὶ 'Αγαθο]χλέος ἄ[ρχοντος ἐπὶ τῆς 'Ι]
        [πποθωντ]ίδος ὀγδόης [πρυτανείας ἧ]
        [ι Διόδοτο]ς Διοκλέος 'Α[γγελῆθεν ἐγ]
        [ραμμάτε]υεν· ἐνάτε[ι] χ[αὶ εἰχοστῆι τ]
  5     [ῆς πρυτα]νείας· Λυσιππ[....¹⁰....]
        [.. Μαρ]αθώνιος ἐπεστά[τει· ἔδοξεν τ]
        [ῆι βο]λῆι χαὶ τῶι δήμω[ι· ...⁷... εἶπ]
        [εν· πε]ρὶ ὧν λέγοσιν οἱ ['Ελαιόσιοι, ἐψ]
        [ηφί]σθαι τεῖ βολῆι το[ὺς μὲν προέδρ]
  10    [ους] οἳ ἂν τυγχάνωσιν [προεδρεύοντ]
        [ες] προσαγαγῆν τὸς πρ[έσβες τῶν 'Ελα]
        [ιο]σίων εἰς τὸν δῆμον [εἰς τὴν πρώτη]
        [ν ἐ]χχλησίαν πρώτου[ς μετὰ τὰ ἱερά, γ]
        [ν]ώμην δὲ συμβάλλεσ[θαι τῆς βολῆς ε]
  15    [ἰ]ς τὸν δῆμον ὅτι δο[χεῖ τῆι βολῆι, ἐπ]
        [ε]ιδὴ 'Ελαιόσ[ι]οι ε[ἰσιν ἄνδρες ἀγαθ]
        [οὶ περ]ὶ τὸ[ν δ]ῆμο[ν τὸν 'Αθηναίων ...]
        [––––––––––––––––––––––––]
```

With **54**, this text is the latest among the Agora *psephismata* to employ E for EI and O for OY in the "spurious diphthongs". The practice is maintained in some of the other texts of the same year (*IG* II², 123 and 124, for instance) but not in all. Its use here is intermittent, and it continues to appear intermittently in some inscriptions of a date later than the middle of the century; but it is never again applied with any consistency throughout an entire text of regular character. See L. Threatte, *Grammar*, pp. 184–185, 189, 251, 256–259.

The writing displays the ordinary characteristics of its period; cf. **50**. Omega is wide, with long horizontals in proportion to its size (that on the left set at an angle); the horizontal strokes of epsilon are all of equal length, but many of them are slanted upward or downward. As a whole, however, the lettering is poor in comparison with the best of the contemporary style, beta and sigma being especially clumsy. Variations in the letter height and maintenance of the lateral stoichoi suggest that the engraving was carried through in some haste and that a minimum of trouble was taken over it. M. B. Walbank (*per ep.*) suggested that the same mason worked on *IG* II², 139 and 289; cf. *eund.*, *BSA* 85, 1990, p. 440.

The preamble is of the developed type, showing the ἐπί formula with the archon's name and the prytanizing tribe, together with the relative clause introducing the γραμματεύς and adding also the date within the prytany. The chairman is however still named as ἐπιστάτης rather than as spokesman of the proedroi (contrast *IG* II², 123, which otherwise follows the same pattern), and the proposer's name is not yet accompanied by his patronymic and demotic. Cf. A. S. Henry, *Prescripts*, pp. 24–32.

Lines 4, 9. On EI in the place of HI in the dative feminine ending see Threatte, *Grammar*, p. 369. Line 8. περὶ ὧν λέγοσιν. Cf. *IG* II², 42 (*SEG* XXI, 231), lines 3–4, 44 (*SEG* XXI, 232), lines 7–8, 96 (*SEG* XXXI, 64, XXXIV, 61), line 5, 103 (M. J. Osborne, *Naturalization* I, pp. 46–48, D 10), lines 6–7, 107, lines 8–9. Lines 8–15. For the phraseology cf. **52**, commentary on lines 16–19. Πρώτους μετὰ τὰ ἱερά. Cf. (e.g.) *IG* II², 107, line 16. This grant of priority goes back to the 5th century (*IG* I³, 65, 159) and is evidenced as late as the middle part of the 3rd (*IG* II², 665, of 266/5 B.C.). Cf. Henry, *Honours*, p. 197. On the ἱερά see J. D. Mikalson, *Athenian Popular Religion*, 1983, p. 13.

The Elaiousians had joined the Second Athenian Confederacy in 373 (*IG* II², 43 = *SEG* XXXI, 61, with earlier references, and XXXII, 53, line 123; 375 is a less likely year. For alternative views on the date see A. G. Woodhead, *Phoenix* 16, 1962, pp. 258–266, with references to earlier literature). See further J. Cargill, *The Second Athenian League*, 1981, p. 185 with note 46.

On the geographical location of the city see *ATL* I, p. 484 (for additional references, *ATL* IV, p. 37). Good relations with Athens were maintained despite the effective collapse of the Confederacy after 355. Cf. Demosthenes 23.158. In 346/5 the people of Elaious presented the Athenians with a stephanos of gold (*IG* II², 1443, lines 93–95; Demosthenes 18.92), and in early 340 they were beneficiaries of a special decree safeguarding their possessions and commending them to the good offices of Chares, again strategos in those parts (*IG* II², 228; Osborne, *Naturalization* I, pp. 60–61, D 15, *Naturalization* II, p. 83).

GRANT OF ATHENIAN CITIZENSHIP TO A CERTAIN ARISTOMENES

54 (Pl. 5). A fragment of a stele of Pentelic marble (I 5560), with part of the original back apparently preserved but otherwise broken all around save for a trace of the right edge below the inscribed surface, discovered on September 12, 1938, in a wall of a modern house southeast of the Market Square and west of the Panathenaic Way (Q 22). The inscribed surface is scarred and worn, especially on the left.

H. 0.421 m.; W. 0.22 m.; Th. 0.139 m.

LH. 0.006 m.

Στοιχ. (square, with slight irregularities) *ca.* 0.011–0.012 m.

Ed. B. D. Meritt, *Hesperia* 13, 1944, pp. 229–231, no. 3, with photograph; M. J. Osborne, *Naturalization* I, pp. 55–56, D 13, *Naturalization* II, pp. 80–81.

a. 357/6 *a.*   ΣΤΟΙΧ. 32

```
        ['Ἐπὶ Ἀγαθοκλέους ἄρχοντ]ος·   vacat
        [ἔδοξεν τῆι βουλῆι καὶ τῶ]ι δήμω[ι, ἐπὶ τῆς]
        [........15........]ης [πρυ]τανεί[ας ἧι Διό]
        [δοτος Διοκλέους Ἀ]ν[γελῆ]θεν ἐγρ[αμμάτε]
   5    [υεν· ........15....... Ἀφ]ιδνα[ῖος ἐπεστ]
        [άτει· ....9.... εἶ]πεν· ἐπειδὴ Ἀρ[ιστομέ]
        [νης ὁ ...7... τὸν δῆμον τ]ὸν Ἀθη[ναίων εὖ]
        [ποεῖ ὅ τι ἂν δύνηται, ἐπ]αινέσαι [αὐτὸν χα]
        [ὶ στεφανῶσαι χρυσῶι σ]τεφάνωι [ἀπὸ : Ͱ : δρ]
   10   [αχμῶν καὶ ἀνειπεῖν] ὅταν τῶι δή[μωι δοχῆ]
        [ι· εἶναι δὲ αὐτὸν Ἀθη]ναῖον· γράψ[ασθαι δὲ]
        [φυλῆς καὶ δήμου καὶ φ]ρατριάς ἧ[ς ἂν βούλ]
        [ηται, καὶ τὴν ψῆφον] τοὺς πρυτάν[εις οἳ ἂν]
        [πρυτανεύωσιν δοῦ]ναι περὶ αὐτ[οῦ ἐν τῆι]
   15   [πρώτηι ἐκκλησίαι]· ἀναγράψαι [δὲ τὸ ψήφι]
        [σμα τόδε τὸν γραμματέα] τῆς βο[υλῆς ἐν στ]
        [ήληι λιθίνηι καὶ σ]τῆσαι ἐν ἀκρ[οπόλει· δ]
        [οῦναι δὲ τὸν ταμία]ν τοῦ δήμου τ[ῶι γραμμ]
        [ατεῖ τῆς βουλῆς : ΔΔΔ : ] δραχμὰς ἐ[κ τῶν κατ]
   20   [ὰ ψηφίσματα ἀναλισκ]ομένων τ[ῶι δήμωι. ᵛ]
                        vacat
        [....9.... εἶπεν· τὰ] μὲν ἄλλα κα[θάπερ τῆ]
        [ι βουλῆι, περὶ δὲ Ἀρι]στομένους [δεδόχθαι]
        [τῶι δήμωι· ἐπειδή] ἐστιν ἀνὴρ ἀγα[θὸς περ]
        [ὶ τὸν δῆμον τὸν Ἀθην]αίων καὶ νῦ[ν καὶ ἐν τ]
   25   [ῶι ἔμπροσθεν χρόνωι], καὶ ποε[ῖ ὅ τι δύνα]
        [ται ἀγαθόν ..........23..........]
        [––––––––––––––––––––––––]
```

The lettering of this text is very similar to that of *IG* II², 120 (*SEG* XXXII, 68) of 353/2 B.C., and the same craftsman could well have been responsible for both inscriptions. At this period, a mason's script varied between this "microstyle" of small letters (even if, as here, the letters are well separated), of which this text is a good example, better indeed than **49** or *IG* II², 123 (*SEG* XVI, 48), and on the other hand the larger and more ample style of *IG* II², 113 or 114.

M. B. Walbank's preference (*per ep.*), however, is to assign this text to the hand of *IG* II², 130 and 131, of 355/4 (two texts recognized by A. Wilhelm as the work of a single mason); and he would see the same man at work on *IG* II², 102, of 370. These suggestions do not exclude the considerations already advanced; but they may confirm that what is at issue is perhaps the general and close resemblance of a contemporary style followed by a variety of craftsmen rather than, or no less than, the style of a single individual.

The prescript is of a mixed type. It begins with the archon's name in the form ἐπί + genitive of the participle, inserts the ἔδοξεν clause immediately afterwards, and then resumes on the genitival principle with the statement of the prytanizing phyle + ordinal numeral, to which the name of the γραμματεύς is attached in what became the standard phraseology employing a relative clause. Cf. A. S. Henry, *Prescripts*, pp. 24–26. *IG* II², 117, of 361/60, may offer a parallel but is heavily restored; *IG* II² 114 and 115 come close to this example but include a double statement of the prytanizing phyle, by means of each method. In other cases where the ἔδοξεν clause is so well forward, the prytanizing phyle follows in the nominative case with a main verb, in the old formula (*IG* II², 110, 116 [*SEG* XXI, 243], 121, etc.). The chairman appears as ἐπιστάτης (cf. **53**) but was apparently given his patronymic as well as his demotic (as in **53** but unlike other surviving examples of 357/6 and most examples in preceding years). The proposer's name appeared without patronymic or demotic (cf. **53**), as did that of the mover of the amendment (line 21).

These comparisons of lettering and style of prescript suggest a date for this decree in the decade 360–350, and the possibilities may be narrowed. Indeed, the eleven letters available in line 1 for the name of the archon in the genitive case, together with the remains of the demotic in line 4, had led Meritt to assign the decree without hesitation to 357/6, the year of Agathokles, with *IG* II², 121, 122, and 123 providing the comparative material. Osborne however regarded this as "rather adventurous", even though confirming the reading in line 4, and queried whether the inscription might not belong to the period earlier than 363/2 when the γραμματεύς was not yet an annual official: his text in consequence omits the proper names in the prescript. The original dating is nevertheless more soundly based than this laudable hesitation allows and is here retained. The decree is probouleumatic; cf. P. J. Rhodes, *Athenian Boule*, p. 248. The formulas employed are mostly of a standard type but with variants interesting for their place in the overall development of the formulaic elements of the "chancery style".

The text is that of the *editio princeps* with the exception that in line 23 Osborne correctly read ἐστιν for Meritt's ἐστι. In lines 22–23 there was evidently a slight stoichedon irregularity, resolved by Osborne with the suggestion that at the end of line 22 alpha and iota were crowded into a single space ([δεδόχθα|ι Meritt). Elsewhere Osborne discerned or failed to discern letter traces that make no difference of substance to the text, as follows: Line 3. πρυ]τανεία[ς. Line 6. εἶπε]ν. Line 7. τὸν δ]ῆ[μ]ον [τ]ὸν Ἀθην[αίων. Line 9. χρυσῶ]ι στεφάνωι. Line 11. γράψα[σθαι. Line 12. καὶ] φρατρίας. Line 15. ἀναγρ[ά]ψαι. Line 21. τ]ὰ μὲν ἄλλα [κ]α[θάπερ.

Line 7. The year 357/6 saw the strengthening of relations between Athens and Andros (*IG* II², 123), and the ethnic Ἄνδριος would supply the lacuna in this line where the honorand's ethnic is in fact required. Meritt, who made the suggestion, properly observed that it was purely conjectural, but it deserves to remain in the record.

Lines 9–10. This is the earliest example in which the cost of the stephanos is indicated by a numeral, although the amount is expressed in words in *IG* II², 103 (Osborne, *Naturalization* I, pp. 46–48, D 10), of 369/8. Specification of the amount to be spent is typical of the formulation of the grant of stephanoi during the 4th century: see Henry, *Honours*, pp. 22–25. The cost here restored is a standard amount: the alternative, 1000 drachmas, is less likely, but Osborne declined to insert a figure in his text.

Lines 10–11. Reference to the occasion of the announcement of the award of a stephanos seldom occurs in the 4th century. When it does, the phraseology varies and is not otherwise found in this form. This may leave the restoration open to doubt (cf. Henry, *op. cit.*, p. 53, note 66), but there is little room for maneuver here. It became usual to specify the time and place (e.g., at the Dionysia or Panathenaia), and the custom of making the proclamation at these festivals produced a standard formula of words. Cf. **224**.

Lines 11–15. Cf. *IG* II², 103. The formula for the grant of citizenship was variable at this time. *IG* II², 251 (Osborne, *Naturalization* I, pp. 66–68, D 19), of *ca*. 350, uses phraseology close to this example and is tending towards the developed "standard" form, Type 1 (Osborne, *BSA* 67, 1972, pp. 156–157) or "Formulation A" (Henry, *Honours*, pp. 64–80).

Line 13. τοὺς πρυτάνεις οἳ ἂν πρυτανεύωσιν. Cf. Henry, *Honours*, pp. 74–75, 101, note 98 (and on the sequence beginning τὴν ψῆφον *ibid.*, pp. 77–78).

Lines 15–17. For the γραμματεὺς τῆς βουλῆς as the official responsible for the inscription and erection of the stele see **40**.

Lines 17–20. The ταμίας τοῦ δήμου was, until the end of the century, the officer instructed to meet the costs. See **120** and Henry, *Chiron* 12, 1982, p. 118, *Chiron* 14, 1984, p. 50, *ZPE* 78, 1989, pp. 256–267 (on this text, p. 257). The phraseology, in which it is laid down that he pay the money over to the γραμματεύς, is unusual and confined to this period. Cf. *IG* II², 107 (of 368/7), lines 22–24 and 117 (of 361/60), lines 16–19. On the source and the amount of the money to be expended see **40**, commentary on line 18 and **45**.

Lines 21–25. The customary formula of an amendment additionally includes the new variant of the ἔδοξεν clause in the use of the perfect passive infinitive and stresses (in the restored section) that the extra decision is the work of the demos independently of the boule. The body of the amendment, before the stone breaks off, pursues a form of words typical of the 4th century. Line 25. For the doubled sigma to be postulated, by reason of the stoichedon requirements, in ἔμπροσθεν, see L. Threatte, *Grammar*, p. 530 and **102**, line 12. Osborne, disliking this solution to the problem, preferred to restore νυ[νὶ καὶ ἐν || τῶι ἔμπροσθεν χρόνωι]. Cf. *IG* II², 237, line 11.

THE ARCHONSHIP OF THOUDEMOS, 353/2 B.C.

Thoudemos' term of office is well attested both in literary and in epigraphical sources. For the literary references see *PA* 7248, where variants Θουμήδης and Εὔδημος, which occur in places, are noted and corrected. Thoudemos' year is covered by the *tabula curatorum navalium IG* II², 1613 and by the record of the curators of the sanctuary of Brauronian Artemis *IG* II², 1524. In the inventory of the Treasurers of Athena (*IG* II², 1438 + E. Schweigert, *Hesperia* 7, 1938, pp. 281–289, no. 16) his is the last year for which acquisitions are registered, and line 14 of side B provides the name of the γραμματεύς, Philokedes, whose patronymic and demotic are attested in the two surviving decrees of the boule and demos of this year, **55** and *IG* II², 139.

Schweigert also observed, however, that *IG* II², 120, which requires the listing of treasures in the Chalkotheke, belongs to Thoudemos' year. Moreover, *IG* II², 140, an enactment of the nomothetai, enjoins it upon the boule of the years following that of Thoudemos to attend to the fulfillment of an antecedent *nomos* of Chairemonides (see **57**) and presumably is to be dated to 353/2, even though it lacks an archon-dating in a truncated prescript.

On the γραμματεύς see (apart from Schweigert, *loc. cit.*) S. Alessandri, *Annali della Scuola Normale di Pisa*, pp. 26–29, 59–60, and *SEG* XXXII, 68; cf. also P. J. Rhodes, *Athenian Boule*, pp. 136–137. R. Develin (*Athenian Officials*, pp. 288–290) provides a full list of all those known to have held office during Thoudemos' archonship. Nothing is known of the order of the prytanies in this year.

HONORS (POSSIBLY CITIZENSHIP) VOTED FOR XENNIAS

55. Two fragments, which do not join, of a stele of bluish Pentelic marble. One of these (fragment *a*) has long been known and is now in the Epigraphical Museum (E.M. 6988): it provides part of the left side of the monument, including the uppermost lines of the inscription, as well as the original back. Fragment *b* (I 4477), of which the right side and back are preserved, was discovered on February 5, 1937, in a wall of a modern house southeast of Market Square (U 22). Fragment *a* is surmounted by an olive crown carved in relief and, above that, the remains of the lower part of an inset relief panel showing two figures: symmetry would require at least one further figure to the right (or an object of equivalent size), and a second crown to the right of that which survives.

a: H. 0.365 m.; W. 0.238 m.; Th. 0.095–0.115 m.

b: H. 0.124 m.; W. 0.242 m.; Th. 0.104–0.09 m.

LH. (line 1) 0.01 m., (lines 2–11) 0.008–0.009 m.

Στοιχ. (with some inconsistencies) Hor. *ca.* 0.008 m. (lines 3–11); Vert. 0.019 m.

Ed. *a* only: *IG* II², 138, with earlier references. *a* and *b*: M. B. Walbank, *Hesperia* 54, 1985, pp. 309–312, no. 1, with photographs pl. 86; see also *SEG* XXXV, 58.

a. 353/2 *a*.   ΣΤΟΙΧ. 49 (lines 2 and following)

Anaglyphum

	Corona	[*Corona*]

(a)   Ἐπὶ Θουδήμου ἄρχ[οντος, ἐπὶ τῆς ......¹⁴......].

       Ἔδοξεν τῆι βουλῆι καὶ τ[ῶι δήμωι· ...⁷... ἐπρυτάνευεν, Φιλοχ]

       ήδης Δωροθέο Παλλην[εὺς ἐγραμμάτευεν, ...¹⁷........]

       ἐπεστ[ά]τει, Εὐθύμα[χος ....¹⁸........ εἶπεν· ἐπειδὴ Ξε]

5   γνίας ἐστὶν ἀνὴρ [ἀγαθὸς περὶ τὸν δῆμον τὸν Ἀθηναίων καὶ νῦν]

       καὶ ἐν τῶι πρόσθ[εν χρόνωι, δεδόχθαι τῶι δήμωι ἐπαινέσαι μὲν]

(b)   [Ξε]γνία[ν Ἀνδ]ρ[...............³⁴...............]α[...]

       [......¹⁴......, στεφανῶσαι δὲ αὐτὸν θαλ]λοῦ στεφάνωι δι[..]

       [...............³⁵...............δ]ὲ Ξεννίαν Ἀθ[...]

10   [...............³⁵...............] αὐτοῦ Ἀνδρογ[...]

       [...............³⁸...............]ΙΑΣ[...]ΝΒΟ[.]Λ

       [--]

The text (other than in lines 1–2) follows that of Walbank, to whose edition the reader is referred for fuller details of the monument as a whole and of the readings on fragment *b*. Fragment *a* has suffered damage since it was first recorded. Walbank describes the style of the writing as "semi-stoichedon", noting that line 2 is set more closely to line 1 (the lettering of which is larger) than to line 3. It is in any case a clumsy and untidy piece of work, and the letters have a forward tilt.

The Agora fragment revealed that the name of the honorand was Xennias (not, as previously restored, Mennias), a name more familiar in a northern or northwestern Greek context. Walbank suggests that lines 9–11 contain the traces of a formula for the grant of citizenship and proposes [εἶναι δ]ὲ Ξεννίαν ’Αθ[ηνα||ῖον αὐτὸν καὶ τοὺς ἐκγόνους τε καὶ τὸν υἱὸν] αὐτοῦ ’Ανδρογ[...| ———καὶ γράψασθαι αὐτοὺς φυλῆς καὶ δήμου καὶ φρατρ]ίας [ἧς ἂ]ν βο[ύ]λ[[ωνται ————·, which resembles though does not precisely reproduce the formula of citizenship decrees of the period. But see **66**, commentary on lines 8–9.

P. J. Rhodes (*Athenian Boule*, pp. 75–77 and 260) classed the decree as nonprobouleumatic, despite the enactment formula in line 2, under the influence of the restored motion formula in line 6. This sort of "crossbreed" is, on his argument, a "product of the evolutionary process" of the period.

Line 1. ’Επὶ Θουδήμου ἄρχ[οντος, ..⁵..ἰς ἐπρυτάνευεν] *IG* II². But, despite much variety in the framing of prescripts àt this period (cf. A. S. Henry, *Prescripts*, pp. 19–33), a mixture of the genitival phrase with ἐπὶ for the archon and the old formula of nominative + main verb for the phyle is hardly to be expected. Walbank's text omits a reference to the prytany, assuming line 1 to end midway across the stone, with a *vacat* of 19–20 letters. There is however room for mention of the phyle here if the formulation of *IG* II², 114 (of 362/1 B.C.) be admitted as a parallel. See Henry, *Prescripts*, pp. 25–26 and for the omission of πρυτανείας *IG* II², 218, 224, 348. Thus ἐπὶ Λεωντίδος (or Αἰαντίδος) ἕκτης will fulfill the requirements, since in line 2 the name of the phyle contains seven letters. If one extra letter can be accommodated in line 1, various ordinal numerals are possible. Line 4. On the proposer of the decree, Euthymachos, see *PA* 5624; M. H. Hansen, *Athenian Ecclesia II*, p. 46; and R. Develin, *Athenian Officials*, p. 289. On the relief sculpture see also *SEG* XXXIX, 324.

LAW CONCERNING THE MYSTERIES OF THE ELEUSINIAN GODDESSES

56. Nineteen fragments of an opisthographic stele of Hymettian marble, among which several joins may be made (thus reducing the total of separate pieces to fifteen), discovered between 1936 and 1963 in the area of the Agora identified as the site of the City Eleusinion (cf. J. Travlos, *Pictorial Dictionary of Ancient Athens*, 1971, pp. 198–203; *Agora* XIV, pp. 150–152; *Agora Guide*³, pp. 143–147; J. M. Camp, *Athenian Agora*, p. 88). One fragment only, I 6794 (see below), itself composed of two joining pieces, preserves both inscribed faces of the monument. All fragments save the composite I 5733 + 6974 are broken on all sides.

Nine fragments were separately edited before their united connection with the single monument was recognized. The designation, order, assignment to Face A or B, and detail of the fragments here shown reproduce that of the definitive edition by K. Clinton described below. The identification of the fragments as belonging to one stele, and the joins of fragments where it proved possible, were made by C. N. Edmonson (*apud* Clinton).

Face A

Fragment *a*, composed of two joining fragments, I 5733 and I 6974, and preserving the top and left side of the stele: I 5733 was discovered on March 23, 1939, in a Turkish lime pit at the west side of the Panathenaic Way opposite the southwest corner of the Eleusinion (S 20); I 6974 was discovered on July 10, 1963, in the same general area (S 22), reused as a door sill.

Fragment *b* (I 6794, the opisthographic fragment), composed of two joining fragments, the larger of which was discovered on July 16, 1957, in a wall dated to the 4th century A.D., just west of the Eleusinion (Q 19): the smaller fragment was discovered nearly two years later, on March 13, 1959, as part of a Byzantine work of repair outside the Market Square and northwest of the Eleusinion (T 17).

Fragment *c* (I 4007) was discovered on April 16, 1936, in an Early Byzantine context north of the Eleusinion (T 17).

Face B

Fragment *a* is the reverse side of Face A, fragment *b* (I 6794), *q.v.*

Fragment *b* (I 6877 a) was discovered on April 29, 1959, in the area of the Eleusinion (U 19).

Fragment *c* (I 6877 b) was discovered on June 6, 1959, in Late Roman fill within the Eleusinion area (U 19–20).

Fragment *d* consists of two joined pieces, I 4739 and I 6915 a. Of these, the larger, I 4739, was discovered on April 14, 1937, west of the Stoa of Attalos in fill for a road of Late Roman date (O 11); I 6915 a joins it at its upper right and was discovered on the same date and in the same location as fragment *c* (I 6877 b).

Fragment *e*, joined from two pieces, I 6915 e and I 6915 f, was discovered on the same date and in the same location as fragment *c* (I 6877 b).

Fragments *f* (I 6915 b), *g* (I 6915 c), *h* (I 6915 d), *i* (I 6915 g), *j* (I 6915 h), and *k* (I 6915 i) were all discovered on the same date and in the same location as fragment *c* above.

Fragment *l* (I 3854) was discovered on March 27, 1936, in an Early Byzantine context north of the Eleusinion (T 17); cf. fragment *c* (I 4007) of Face A.

Fragment *m* (I 4140) was discovered on May 14, 1936, in a Byzantine context over the Eleusinion (T 19).

The measurements of the fragments listed above are as follows:

Face A

    a: H. 0.59 m.; W. 0.325 m.; Th. 0.171 m.

    b: H. 0.51 m.; W. 0.43 m.; Th. 0.18 m.

    c: H. 0.065 m.; W. 0.082 m.; Th. 0.03 m.

LH. 0.006–0.007 m.

Face B

    a: see Face A, fragment *b*.

    b: H. 0.19 m.; W. 0.20 m.; Th. 0.05 m.

    c: H. 0.089 m.; W. 0.095 m.; Th. 0.028 m.

    d: H. 0.125 m.; W. 0.124 m.; Th. 0.027 m.

    e: H. 0.12 m.; W. 0.138 m.; Th. 0.02 m.

    f: H. 0.11 m.; W. 0.15 m.; Th. 0.004 m.

    g: H. 0.09 m.; W. 0.11 m.; Th. 0.045 m.

    h: H. 0.10 m.; W. 0.07 m.; Th. 0.055 m.

    i: H. 0.03 m.; W. 0.035 m.; Th. 0.008 m.

    j: H. 0.023 m.; W. 0.041 m.; Th. 0.01 m.

    k: H. 0.07 m.; W. 0.06 m.; Th. 0.058 m.

    l: H. 0.095 m.; W. 0.12 m.; Th. 0.049 m.

    m: H. 0.045 m.; W. 0.057 m.; Th. 0.016 m.

LH. 0.006–0.008 m.

Edmonson calculated from Face A that the width of the stele at the top, when complete, is likely to have been 0.924 m. The original thickness (0.18 m.) implies that the stele may have been taller than *ca.* 1.5 m.

Στοιχ. (Face A only, with the exception of the text *in rasura* at lines 17–18) *ca.* 0.01 m. (almost square, but not well maintained). Face B, though described by Clinton as "largely non-*stoichedon*", is roughly comparable.

Ed. Face A, *a* (I 5733 only): B. D. Meritt, *Hesperia* 26, 1957, pp. 52–53, no. 9, with photograph pl. 7 (see also *SEG* XVI, 50); further, F. Sokolowski, *TAPA* 88, 1957, pp. 131–134 (see also *SEG* XVII, 21), and *Lois sacrées (Supplément)*, pp. 32–33, no. 12 (see also *SEG* XXI, 257).

Face B, *b*: Meritt, *Hesperia* 32, 1963, p. 2, no. 2, with photograph pl. 1; see also *SEG* XXI, 255. *d* (I 6915 a only) and *e–j*: Meritt, *Hesperia* 32, 1963, pp. 40–41, no. 41, with photograph pl. 11; see also *SEG* XXI, 346.

Both faces and all fragments: Clinton, *Hesperia* 49, 1980, pp. 258–288, with photographs pls. 69–73; see also *SEG* XXX, 61.

ante med. saec. IV a.   ΣΤΟΙΧ. 97 (except lines 17–18)

FACE A

(*a+b*)

    [περὶ τῆς ἐ]παγγέλσεως καὶ σ[...............................75...............................
                                         ....]

    [..⁵.. γε]γονότων· ἐς μὲν τὰ μ[...............................75...............................
                                         ....]

    [...⁷...] ἱσταμέγ[ου]· ᵛ τὸς [...............................77...
                                         ....]

    [...⁷...]ται παραλαβόγ[τ...............................77...............................
                                         ....]

5 [..εἰ δὲ] μή, ὅταμ πρῶτον ο[ἷόν τε ἦι...............................71...............................
                                         ....]

    [...] δοκιμασ(θ)ῶσι θύεν τ[...............................77...............................
                                       .... τ]

[ὸν δ]ὲ ἱεροφάντην τὴν με[......................................78...................................

[. .]██ς κατευωχε̄σθαι ἐπὶ̣ [..................................72.......................................

....72..ἐπαγγέ]

[λ]λεν ἐς τὰς πόλες τὰς μ[υστηριώτιδας σπονδὰς ....67................................

10 κατὰ τὴν μαντείαν τõ [Ἀπόλλωνος ....71...............................

ἐων ἐφόδια· ᵛ ἐὰν δὲ ο̣[..................................78...................................... τοῖ]

ς θεσμοθέτα̣ις ἢ οἱ θ[εσμοθέται ....71.................................. τὰ]

γεγραμμένα, ὀφεί[λεν . . δραχμὰς ἱερὰς τοῖν Θεοῖν.................57............................

ων τοῖν Θεοῖν κα[...................63...................] τοῖς
μύστησιν καὶ τοῖς ἐπ]

15 [ό]πτηισιν καὶ τ[οῖς ἀκολούθοισιν ....62..............................
... καὶ Ἀθηνα]

ίοισιν ἅπασι[ν ....85.......................................]

[[[.]α̣λα τõ Ἑκατο[μβαιῶνος μηνὸς ....ca. 73....................
....]]]

[[[. . .]ε προσαγ[.......ca. 39.......]οδ[.........ca. 47.........
.................................]]]

[.⁵..]ΙΤ[...]██[.......36.......]νται [τ]õι̣[.........43.........
.................................]

20 [... τõ]ν σπονδ[οφόρων.......21..........τὰς μυστη]ριώτιδας σπ[ονδὰς ....33.........
..................τὸς]

[ἐννέ]α̣ ἄρχοντας [..............31..........δί]κας εἴρηται κα̣[.......34.........
..............τὰς πό]

[λεις τ]ὰς δεξαμένας [τὰς σπονδάς· οἱ δὲ σπονδοφόροι ἀπογ]ραφόντων τῶι γρα[μματεῖ τὰ ὀνόματα
τῶν πόλεων· ὁ δὲ βασιλεὺς προ]

[σαγέ]τω αὐτὸς πρὸς τ[ὴν βολήν.........23.........] ἀπογράψωσι ἀναγρα[φ.............
...............34...........]

[...]νας τῶμ πόλεων τ[..............28.............] τῶι βασιλεῖ· ὁ δὲ βασιλε[ὺς...........
.........27...... Ἀθηνα]

25 [ω]ν τῶι β[ο]λομένωι ο[ἷς ἔξεστι ....19........]ων ἐξ ὦν οὐκ ἔξεστι μυε̄σθα[ι..........
................32............]

[. .]ερομένας τὰς μυσ[τηριώτιδας σπονδὰς ...⁶... τῶν] σπονδοφόρων καὶ ἐπαγγέλλ[...........
...........33...........]

[μ]ηδένα· ἐὰν δέ τις μυῆ[ι Ε]ὑμολ[πιδῶν ἢ Κηρύκων οὐκ ὦν ε]ἰδώς, ἢ ἐὰν προσάγηι τις μυησό-
με[νον ....23.........τοῖ]

[ν] Θεοῖν, φαίνεν δὲ τὸμ βολόμε̣νο̣[ν Ἀθηναίων, καὶ ὁ βασι]λεὺς εἰσαγέτω εἰς τὴν Ἡλιαίαν
κα[.................26............ αὐ]

[τ]õ βολευέτω ἡ βολὴ ὡς ἀδικõντος· κα[ὶ τὸς ἐπιμελητὰ]ς χρὴ ἐπιμελε̄σθαι τῆς ἑορτῆς τοῖν Θ[εο]ῖν
[μετὰ τõ βασιλέως καὶ διοικε̄]

30 [ν τ]ὰ Μυστήρια κατὰ τὰ πάτρια μετὰ το[ύτου καὶ Εὐμολ]πιδῶν καὶ Κηρύκων· προσαιρε̄σθαι δὲ
[τ]ὸν δ[ῆμον ἐπιμελητὰς δύο περὶ τὴ]

[ν] ἑορτὴν ἐξ Ἀθηναίων ἁπάντων ἐκ τῶν ὑ[πὲρ τριάκοντα] ἔτη γεγονότων καὶ Κηρύκων ἕνα καὶ
[Εὐ]μολπιδ[ῶν ἕνα· τοῖς δὲ ἐπιμελητ]

[αῖ]ς ἔναι ζημιõν τὸς ἀκοσμõντας μέχρι̣ [. . δραχμῶν· ἐ]ὰν δὲ μείζονος δοκῆι ζημίας ἄξιος ε̣ῖναι,
εἰσάγε[ιν τούτος εἰς τὴν Ἡλι]

[αἱ]αν προσκαλεσαμένος κατὰ τὸν νόμον· ἐ[πιθέσθω δὲ ἡ] Ἡλιαία ὅτι ἂν δοκῆι ἄξιος εἶναι παθēν

ἢ ἀποτεῖσ[αι· ᵛ εἶναι δὲ τῶι βασ]

[ι]λεῖ τῶμ πρακτόρων ἕνα καὶ τὸγ γραμματ[έα ἀπὸ νομη]νίας ἀρξάμενον μέχρι ō ἂν μύσται λυθῶ-

σιν, καὶ γράψ[αι τούτους τὰς ζημ]

35   [ία]ς ᾶς ἂν ὁ βασιλεὺς ἐπιβάληι ἢ τῶ[ν] ἡιρ[ημένων μετὰ β]ασιλέως ἐπιμελεῖσθαι· τὸ δὲ ἀργύρ[ι]ον

ὅτι ἂν ἐπιβᾴ[ληι τούτων τις ἱε]

[ρὸν] εἶναι τοῖν Θεοῖν·ᵛ ἐὰν δὲ ὁ βασι[λ]εὺ[ς καὶ οὓς χρὴ] μετ’αὐτō ἐπιμελēσθαι μὴ ζημιῶσιν τὸς

ἀκοσμōντος κ[ατὰ τὸν νόμον ἢ ἐὰ]

[ν μὴ ἐπι]θῶσιν κατὰ τὸ εἰκός, εὐθυνέ[σθω. . . δραχμαῖς] ἱεραῖς τοῖν Θεοῖν ἕκαστος αὐτῶν·ᵛ τὰς δὲ

[δ]ίκας δι[κάζεν . . .¹⁰ . . . . . .]

[. . .⁶. . . ἐ]ννέα ἄρχοντας τὰς μετὰ τὴγ [ἑορτήν. . .⁸. . . .]ενα περὶ ἑκάστο αὐτῶν·ᵛ Εὐμολπιδῶν δὲ

τὸς ἐξηγη[τὰς . . . . .¹² . . . . . .]

[. . .⁷. . . . ἀρ]ξ[αμ]έ[νο]ς ἀπὸ νομηνίας το[. . . . . .¹⁵. . . . . . .] ἐξηγēσθαι Ἀθηναίων καὶ τῶγ ξ[έ]νων

τῶι δεομέν[ωι . . . . . . .¹⁴. . . .]

40   [. . . . . . .¹⁶. . . . . . .]ε παρὰ τὸς ἐπι[μελητάς. . .⁸. . . .]σθαι κατὰ ταὐτά· ἐὰν δὲ μὴ ποιῶσι[ν οἱ] αἱρε-

θέντες [τὰ ἀναγραφέντα, εὐθ]

[ύνεσθαι. . . δραχμαῖς]· περὶ τō ἀφ’[ἑστίας χρὴ τὸμ βασι]λέα προσαγορεύεν γράφεσθαι τὸμ β[ολ]ό-

μενον Ἀθην[αίων . . . . . .¹³. . .]

[. . . . . . . .¹⁸. . . . . . ἡ]μέραις [. . .⁷. . . · ἐκ δὲ τῶγ γρα]ψαμένων κληρούτω ὁ βασιλεὺς τῆ[ι] νο-

μηνίαι τὸ[ν ἀφ’ἑστίας . . .⁹. . . . . .]

[. . . . . .⁴¹. . . . .] τοῖς ἱερεῦσι καὶ ταῖς ἱερέαις ο[ἷς] πάτριον τη[. .

. . . . .¹⁹. . . . .]

[. . . . . .⁴¹. . . . .] ποιēσθαι ἅπαντα· ᵛ ἐάν τις ποιῆι παρὰ τὰ ἀναγρ

[αφέντα . . . . . .¹³. . . . . .]

45   [. . . . . .⁴¹. . . . .] τοῖς χαλκοῖς γραμματείοις· ἔνδειξις αὐτο[ῖς . . .

. . . . .¹⁹. . . . .]

[. . . . . .⁴¹. . . . .]όντος περὶ τὰ Μυστήρια· οἱ δὲ θεσμοθέται 🮕[. . .

. . . . .²². . . . .]

[. . . . . .³⁷. . . . .] τὸς μ]εμυημένος καὶ τὸς ἐπωπτευκότας δέκα ἡμ[ερ

. . . . .²¹. . . . .]

[. . . . . .²⁵. . . . .] τὸς ἐπιστάτας Ἐλευσι]νόθεν ἀπὸ τō ἀργυρίου τοῦ τοῖν Θεοῖ[ν. . .

. . . . .²⁴. . . . .]

[. . . . . .³⁹. . . . .] ἐὰν κατ]αγνῶι ἡ Ἡλιαία ποιēν τι παρὰ τὰ γ[εγραμ-

μένα . . . . .¹⁷. . . . . . .]

50   [. . . . . .⁴¹. . . . .] ὁ βασιλεὺς ὁ ἀ]εὶ βασιλεύων· ᵛ ἐγ δὲ τῶγ χρη

[μάτων . . . . .²². . . . .]

[. . . . . .⁵³. . . . .]σθαι δὲ τοῖγ γραματείοιν [. . . . .

. . . . .²⁸. . . . .]

[. . . . . .⁴¹. . . . .] ἐσφραγισμ]ένον τῆι δημοσίαι σφ[ραγῖδι. . . . .

. . . . .²⁴. . . . .]

[. . . . . .⁵⁰. . . . .] ἐ]κ τῶγ γενῶν τούτῳ[ν . . . .

. . . . .³¹. . . . .]

[. . . . . .⁵⁷. . . . .] ΑΣΤΟΝΤΕ[.]Π[. . . . .

. . . . .³⁵. . . . .]

[––– –––––––––––––]

(c)

[––]

[–––––––––––––––––]ΕΛΑ[––––––––––––––––––––––––––––––––––––––]

[––––––––––––––––]α τὸς ν[––––––––––––––––––––––––––––––––––]

[—————————————————]τὸμ μερο[————————————————]
[—————————————————]ων ἃ ἔστι[————————————————]
5 [————————————————ἡ ʻΗ]λιαία τ[————————————————]
[—————————————————————————————————————]

FACE B

(a)

[——]
[.................*ca. 43*.................] ⋀ [——————————*ca. 44*——————————]
[.................*ca. 42*.................]ΑΕ[——————————*ca. 44*——————————]
[................*ca. 40*................]ΣΤΟΣΕ [——————————*ca. 43*——————————]
[...............*ca. 37*...............χα]τὰ τὰ πάτ[ρια ————————*ca. 39*————————]
5 [...............*ca. 38*...............]▓ΜΙΣΗΤΑΓᴾ [——————————*ca. 42*——————————]
[...............*ca. 38*...............]νεσιν· οἱ δὲ [——————————*ca. 42*——————————]
[..............*ca. 35*..............]ὄτ[ι] ἂν δοχῆι ⋀ ▓[————————*ca. 41*————————]
[.............*ca. 33*.............]ην τοῖς ἐπιστάται[ς————————*ca. 39*————————]
[............*ca. 32*............]ις· μύστην δὲ μὴ ἐξεῖ[ναι—————*ca. 38*—————]
10 [...........*ca. 29*...........]▓ν μ[ή]δ'ἐλεῖν ἐξεῖναι δᾶιδ[α———*ca. 40*———]
[...*ca. 8*... ὀφείλειν . δραχμὰς ἱερ]ὰς τοῖν Θεοῖν· ἐὰν δὲ δοῦλος [———*ca. 41*———]
[.....*ca. 17*..........χαὶ ἐὰν ἀλ]ῶι τιμάτω περὶ αὐτὸ παραχρῆμ[α ὅτι ἂν δοχῆι ἄξιος εἶναι παθεῖν ἢ
                                                        ἀποτεῖσαι..*ca. 8*...]
[.......*ca. 23*......... τ]ῶν τὴν ἀπαρχὴν τὸ σίτο ἀπαγόντ[ων———*ca. 39*———]
[............*ca. 22*............] ὅτι ἂν ἀδίχημ[α ἐν τῆ]ισι σπονδῆσιν ▓[———*ca. 40*———]
15 [....*ca. 17*....ἐν] τούτωι τῶι χρόγω[ι μὴ ἐξ]έστω δίχας ἃς [———*ca. 40*———]
[....*ca. 15*........μη]δεμίαν χλῆσιν εἶναι ▓[..*6*..]⌒ΒΔΗΝ χαλέσ[αι ——*ca. 38*——]
[....*ca. 15*........] ὧν οὔ[τ]οι χύριοί εἰσιν τα[..*8*...]εῖναι χαθάπ[ερ——*ca. 38*——]
[....*ca. 15*........] χήρυχι ἐλθὼν ἀπαιτέτω [..*ca. 8*.. ἐὰ]μ μὴ παρ[αδῶι——*ca. 36*——]
                          vacat 0.016 m. (= *spatium unius versus*)
[....*ca. 9*..ἐὰμ μὲ]ν ὁ ἰδιώτης ὀφλῃι κατὰ ταῦ[τα· ἐὰν] δὲ ἡ πόλις το[———*ca. 40*———]
                          vacat 0.016 m. (= *spatium unius versus*)
20 [....*ca. 13*.....τ]ὸ ὕστερον ἔτος ἐὰν ἀπὼν ὀφ[λῃι· δικ]άζεν δὲ τοὺς [——*ca. 40*——]
[   ] *vacat*   τὴν ἐβδ[όμη]ν φθίνοντος ἐγ [——————*ca. 40*——————]
                          vacat 0.016 m. (= *spatium unius versus*)
[   ] *vacat*   ἁπλῆι, [τ]ὰ δὲ ἑχούσια διπ[λῆι——————*ca. 37*——————]
                          vacat 0.009 m.
[....*ca. 12*....ἐ]πιμελεῖσθαι τοῦ Ἐλευσινίου τοῦ ἐν ἄστει χαὶ το[ῦ Ἐλευσῖνι ἱεροῦ——*ca. 28*———]
[....*ca. 12*....το]ῦ τοῖν Θεοῖν ἀργυρίου· τὰς δ'εὐθύνας τούτων εἶν[αι————*ca. 39*—————]
                          vacat

(b)

[———————————————————————————————————————]
[————————————————]Ο[.]ΕΛΩ[.. ἄ]ρχοντ[————————————]
[———————————————]Ε[..] ⋮ ΕΣΤ[..]ΦΕΤΕΡ[————————————]
[——————————————μεγ]άλα Μυστήρια τ[.]ε[————————————]
[——————————————] μηνὸς ἀπὸ δι[χ]ομ[η]νίας ————————————]
5 [————————————δίχας] ἃς ἂν δικάσωσιν στε[————————————]
[———ἐὰν ——————ἀπ]ογνῶσιν ἔναι τῶι [..] ⋮ [————————————]
[——————————————ἄ]λλων δικῶν εἴρηται παθ[ε]ν ————————————]
[—————————————χ]αθάπερ εἴρηται ἐν τῶι [νόμωι ——————————]

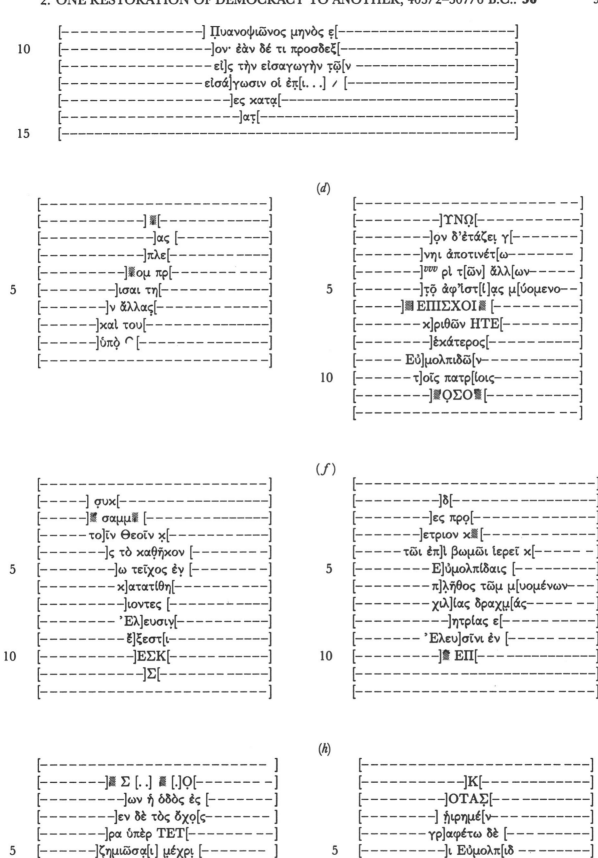

```
        [———————————————] Πυανοψιῶνος μηνὸς ε[———————————————]
10      [———————————————]ον· ἐὰν δέ τι προσδεξ[———————————————]
        [——————————— εἰ]ς τὴν εἰσαγωγὴν τῶ[ν ———————————————]
        [——————— εἰσά]γωσιν οἱ ἐπ[ι. . .] ⁄ [———————————————]
        [———————————]ες κατα[————————————————————]
        [———————————]ατ[———————————————————————]
15      [——————————————————————————————————————]
```

(c)
```
[——————————————————————————]
[—————————]▨[——————————————]
[————————]ας [————————————]
[———————]πλε[————————————]
[——————]▨ομ πρ[——————————]
[——————]ισαι τη[——————————]
[—————]ν ἄλλας[——————————]
[——————]χαὶ του[——————————]
[——————]ὑπὸ ⌒ [——————————]
[——————————————————————————]
```

(d)
```
[———————————————————————]
[————————]ΥΝΩ[——————————]
[————————]ον δ’ἐτάζει γ[———————]
[————————]νηι ἀποτινέτ[ω————————]
[————————]ᵛᵛᵛ ρι τ[ῶν] ἄλλ[ων————]
[————————]τῷ ἀφ’ἱστ[ί]ας μ[ύομενο——]
[—————]▨ ΕΠΙΣΧΟΙ▨ [————————]
[————————]χ]ριθῶν ΗΤΕ[————————]
[————————]ἑκάτερος[————————]
[————— Εὐ]μολπιδῶ[ν————————]
[————— τ]οῖς πατρ[ίοις————————]
[—————————]▨ΟΣΟ▨[————————]
[———————————————————————]
```

(e)
```
[——————————————————————————]
[—————] ουχ[——————————————]
[————]▨ σαμμ▨ [——————————]
[————— το]ῖν Θεοῖν χ[——————]
[———————]ς τὸ καθῆκον [———————]
[————————]ω τεῖχος ἐγ [———————]
[———————χ]ατατίθη[———————]
[————————]ιοντες [———————]
[————— Ἐλ]ευσιγ[——————————]
[————— ἔ]ξεστ[ι——————————]
[————————]ΕΣΚ[——————————]
[————————]Σ[——————————]
[——————————————————————————]
```

(f)
```
[——————————————————————————]
[—————————]δ[——————————]
[————————]ες πρ[ο——————————]
[————————]ετριον χ▨[——————————]
[————— τῶι ἐπ]ὶ βωμῶι ἱερεῖ χ[——————]
[————— Ε]ὐμολπίδαις [——————————]
[————— π]λῆθος τῶμ μ[υομένων———]
[————— χιλ]ίας δραχμ[άς——————————]
[————————]ητρίας ε[——————————]
[————— Ἐλευ]σῖνι ἐν [——————————]
[—————————]▨ ΕΠ[——————————]
[——————————————————————————]
```

(g)
```
[————————————————————————————]
[—————————]▨ Σ [. .] ▨ [.]Ο[————————]
[——————————]ων ἡ ὁδὸς ἐς [————————]
[—————————]εν δὲ τὸς ὄχο[ς————————]
[—————————]ρα ὑπὲρ ΤΕΤ[————————]
[—————————]ζημιῶσα[ι] μέχρι [————————]
[——— προσχα]λεσαμενος [————————]
[—————————]θειν ΗΠΟΤ[————————]
[—————————] ἢ ἰδιωτ[————————]
[————————————————————————————]
```

(h)
```
[——————————————————————————]
[—————————]Κ[——————————]
[—————————]ΟΤΑΣ[——————————]
[—————————] ἡιρημέ[ν——————————]
[————— γρ]αφέτω δὲ [——————————]
[—————————]ι Εὐμολπ[ιδ ——————]
[————— ἡι]ρημένοι ζ[ημιούντων———]
[——— τοῖς ὀ]λίζωσιν [Μυστηρίοις ———]
[—————————] ἐξ Ε[——————————]
[——————————————————————————]
```

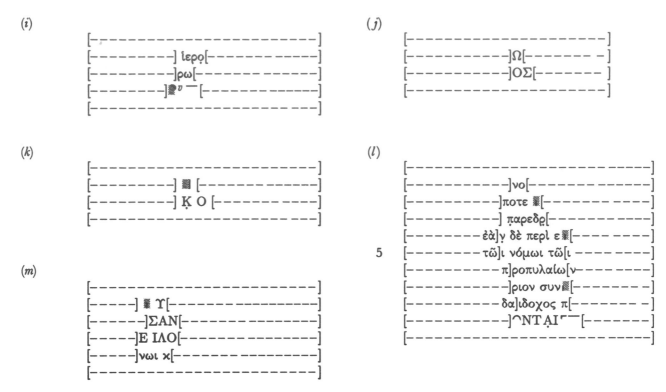

(i)

```
[----------------------------]
[-----------] ἱερο[----------------]
[----------]ρω[-----------------]
[--------]▓ᵛ ̄[------------------]
[----------------------------]
```

(j)

```
[------------------------------]
[---------------]Ω[----------- -]
[--------------]ΟΣ[-------- ]
[------------------------------]
```

(k)

```
[------------------------------]
[-----------] ▓ [-----------------]
[----------] Ḳ Ο [---------------]
[------------------------------]
```

(l)

```
[------------------------------]
[----------------]νο[----------------]
[--------------]ποτε ▓[----------------]
[------------] παρεδρ[--------------]
[---------ἐὰ]ν δὲ περὶ ε▓[---- ------]
[--------- τῶ]ι νόμωι τῶ[ι ------------]
[----------π]ροπυλαίω[ν----------]
[--------]ριον συν▓[---------]
[--------δα]ιδοχος π[-----------]
[----------]^ΝΤ ΑῙ ̄[--------]
[------------------------------]
```

5

(m)

```
[------------------------------]
[-----] ▓ Υ[------------------]
[------]ΣΑΝ[-----------------]
[-----]Ε ΙΛΟ[----------------]
[-----]νωι κ[----------------]
[------------------------------]
```

The text set out above is that of Clinton, who provided a commentary on his readings, *Hesperia* 49, 1980, pp. 269–271. Among variant readings or restorations, some of them advanced by Clinton himself in his discussion of the content of the law, the following may be particularly noted.

Face A, *a+b*: Line 1. [περὶ μὲν ἀ]παγγέλσεως καὶ σπ--- Meritt; [περὶ τῆς ἐ]παγγέλσεως καὶ σπ[ονδοφορίας Sokolowski; perhaps [καὶ περὶ ἐπ. Clinton. Lines 1–2. [---ἐκ τῶν χρησμ|ῶν τῶν γε]γονότων Sokolowski. For lines 1–3 Clinton further suggested [περὶ τῆς ἐ]παγγέλσεως καὶ συ[....¹⁰.... Εὐμολπίδας καὶ Κήρυκας αἱ-ρε̄σθαι σπονδοφόρους ἐξ ἑαυτῶν ἐκ τῶν ....|..... ἔτη γε]γονότων, ἐς μὲν τὰ Μ[εγάλα Μυστήρια ----, ἐς δὲ τὰ Μικρὰ Μυστήρια -----|.......] ἱσταμέν[ου], *loc. cit.*, p. 276. Line 5 *suppl.* Sokolowski. Line 6. *Lapis* Ο. θύεν τ[ῆι Δήμητρι καὶ Κόρηι καὶ τοῖς ἄλλοις θεοῖς ----] Sokolowski. Line 9 *suppl.* Meritt.

Lines 10–11. [---παρέχεν δὲ ἑκάστην τῶν πόλ]|εων ἐφόδια Sokolowski. Lines 13–14. [--τῶν ἱερέ]|ων Clinton, p. 277. Lines 14–16. [----σπονδὰς εἶναι τοῖσι μύστησιν καὶ τοῖς ἐπ||ό]πτηισιν καὶ τ[οῖς ἀκολούθοισιν καὶ χρήμασιν τῶν ὀθνείων καὶ ᾿Αθηνα]|ίοισιν ἅπασι[ν ---] Meritt, as a quotation from *IG* I³, 6; but the lines of the text are demonstrably of greater length than was then envisaged.

Lines 16–17. [ἄρχεν δὲ τὸν χρόνον τῶν σπονδῶν ἐς τὰ Μυστήρια τὰ Με|[γ]ά̣λα τὸ ῾Εκατ[ομβαιῶνος ἀπὸ ----καὶ τὸν Μεταγειτνιῶνα καὶ τὸν Βοηδρομιῶνα καὶ ----]], Clinton, p. 277, on the analogy of *IG* I³, 6. Line 19. χρῶ]νται [τ]ῶ̣ι ἱ[ερῶι Edmonson, who also suggested some elements of the supplements in the rest of this fragment.

Lines 28–29. κα[τὰ τὸν νόμον· ἐὰν δὲ μὴ ἐσάγηι, περὶ αὐ|τ]ο̄ κτλ. G. Stumpf, *Tyche* 3, 1988, pp. 223–228; cf. *SEG* XXXVIII, 57. Line 29. ἱεροποιοὺ]ς P. J. Rhodes, *A Commentary on the Aristotelian Athenaion Politeia*, 1981, p. 636; cf. *SEG* XXXI, 69.

Lines 37–38. τὰς δὲ [δ]ίκας δι[κάζεν τὸν βασιλέα· | καὶ τὸς ἐ]ννέα ἄρχοντας τὰς μετὰ τὴν [ἑορτὴν εἰσάγειν] ἕνα περὶ ἑκάστο αὐτῶν. Stumpf, *loc. cit.*

Face B, *a*: Line 7. αὐ[τοῖς --- Edmonson. Line 16. εἰσ]ό̣βδην καλέσ[αι R. O. Hubbe, *apud* Clinton, p. 286.

Lines 21–22 *init.* The uninscribed spaces remain a problem (so also fragment *d*, line 4 *init.*). Clinton suggested that the letters may have remained painted at these points and not incised.

b: Line 6. ἀπ]όγνωσιν Meritt. Line 10. προσδέσ[ηι Meritt. Line 11 *init.* ---]ι τὴν Meritt. Line 12 *fin.* Perhaps ΕΚ rather than ΕΓ.

d: Line 6. ἐπισχόν[τες --- Meritt. Lines 7, 9–10 *supplevit* Meritt.

e: Line 6. κ]ατατίθη[μι and line 8, ᾿Ελ]ευσῖν[ι Meritt.

f: *Supplevit* Meritt, except line 6, where he restored μ[υηθέντων.

It is notable that the law carries no prescript. Despite Clinton's useful discussion (pp. 259–260), the reason for this remarkable omission is completely obscure.

For the date and intention of the enactment see Clinton, *loc. cit.*, pp. 272–275. On grounds of spelling and of the style of the lettering, it should not postdate the middle of the 4th century. Clinton supposed (although the argument is by no means conclusive) that the γραμματεύς referred to on Face A, line 34, is the secretary of the boule and that his duties imply that he is an annual officer, not one holding office merely for the length of a single prytany. This would provide a *terminus post quem* of 367/6: see the commentary on the archonship of Polyzelos, p. 75 above. This law is not the law of Chairemonides referred to in *IG* II², 140, lines 9–10, for the stele recording that was set up in front of the Metroon, and it dealt only with the ἀπαρχή. Cf. further **57**.

The regulations set out in this document seem, as Clinton indeed described them, to be "the most extensive . . . we possess from antiquity concerning this famous cult." From such parts as may be determined in broad terms, it is clear that the announcement of the Mysteries, the choice and despatch of the σπονδοφόροι, the Sacred Truce, the reception of the σπονδοφόροι by the cities to which they came (cf. **48**), and regulations for the epimeletai, exegetai, epistatai, and initiates are all defined in considerable detail. On initiation cf. also *SEG* XL, 290.

That it was a piece of legislation entrusted to the nomothetai seems evident, and this adds one more to the list of *nomoi* provided by the Agora excavations. See D. M. MacDowell, *The Law in Classical Athens*, 1978, pp. 48–49; M. H. Hansen, *GRBS* 20, 1979, p. 33, nos. 3 and 4 (= *Athenian Ecclesia*, p. 185); and on *nomothesia* in general see the references given in the context of **73**.

FRAGMENT OF A LAW CONCERNING ELEUSINIAN FIRST FRUITS

57 (Pl. 6). Two joining fragments of a stele of Pentelic marble, which in part preserve the original back of the monument but which are otherwise broken all around. The larger piece, fragment *b* (I 5254), which joins fragment *a* (I 5283) at its upper left, was discovered on February 24, 1938, in a late wall in the Church of the Hypapanti (T 21). The smaller fragment, *a*, makes the join with fragment *b* along the lower half of its right side and was discovered on March 4, 1938, in the west wall of the same church. The marble shows evidence of fire.

Measurements as joined: H. 0.17 m.; W. 0.19 m.; Th. 0.065 m.
LH. 0.006–0.008 m.
Στοιχ. (square) 0.015 m.

Unpublished.

ante med. saec. IV a.   ΣΤΟΙΧ.

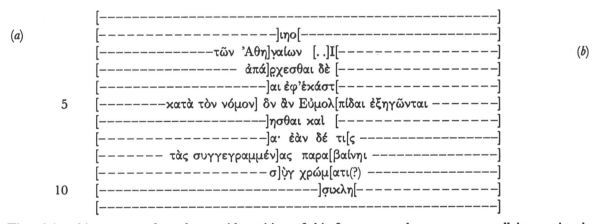

The plain, thin, apparently rather untidy writing of this fragment makes a poor overall impression but in detail is reasonably precise. Some letters, especially epsilon and eta, appear narrow in proportion to their height. Omega is "wide" in the early- and mid-4th-century manner; the horizontal strokes of epsilon are all of equal length. The general resemblance to the hand of Face A of the great opisthographic stele **56** suggests that this enactment belongs to the same date and may be part of (perhaps an addendum to) the same grand revision of "Eleusinian" law on the Mysteries and the First Fruits. It is not itself a part of **56**, for it is not opisthographic. Nor is it part of *IG* II², 140 (*SEG* XXI, 253, XXX, 62) of 353/3. It might be the νόμος Χαιρημονίδου that K. Clinton suggested (*Hesperia* 49, 1980, p. 273) as a possible amendment to **56** in respect of the ἀπαρχή, just as *IG* II², 140 in turn amended that *nomos*. But the *nomos* of Chairemonides and *IG* II², 140 stood in front of the Metroon (*Agora* III, p. 156, no. 495; cf. Meiggs-Lewis, p. 223), whereas the location in which the present fragments were found suggests that this monument, like **56**, is likely to have stood in the Eleusinion, an appropriate site for it.

The phraseology of the law in lines 3, 5, and 7–8 is reminiscent of the "lex de primitiis Eleusinem consecrandis" *IG* I³, 78 (*SEG* XXXII, 11, with earlier references), dated in *IG* I³ "*c. a.* 422(?)" but variously assessed between 435 and 416/15; it is reminiscent also of *IG* II², 140, to which reference has already been made. All the 4th-century legislation on these Eleusinian matters so far discussed took the form of enactments of the nomothetai: it is likely therefore that this present text forms part of a *nomos* rather than of a *psephisma*.

Line 3. Cf. *IG* I³, 78, lines 14, 31–34, 44. Line 5. Cf. Lysias 6.10; *IG* I³, 78, lines 36–37; *IG* II², 140, lines 18–20. Line 8. Cf. *IG* I³, 78, line 57. Line 9. The reading is not in doubt. Unless some part of the verb συγχράομαι is concerned, the reference to color in the context arouses interest: some kind of anointing may be involved. Line 10. The first preserved letter seems to be sigma rather than kappa: in either case, the remains point *prima facie*, though not necessarily, to a proper name.

FRAGMENT OF A SYMBOLA AGREEMENT(?)

58. A fragment of a stele of Pentelic marble (I 4184), broken on all sides and at the back, discovered on May 23, 1936, in a marble dump in the southeast section of the Market Square (N–O 16–17).

H. 0.145 m.; W. 0.085 m.; Th. 0.06 m.
LH. 0.006 m.
Στοιχ. (almost square) Hor. 0.009 m.; Vert. 0.0095 m.

Ed. M. B. Walbank, *Hesperia* 58, 1989, pp. 79–81, no. 6, with photograph pl. 19. See also *SEG* XXXIX, 76.

ante med. saec. IV *a.*(?)ΣΤΟΙΧ.

```
      [————————————————————————]
      [————————]Ι[——————————————]
      [——————]ομησ[————————————]
      [——————]χανθ[.]ọ[————————]
      [——————]εσθαι[——————————]
  5   [————————] κατα[——————————]
      [——————]ναλ[————————————]
      [———————]σεγ[————————————]
      [———————]ωντα[——————————]
      [———————]υνωι [—————————]
  10  [————————] ὀφειλ[————————]
      [————————]μο[.]α[—————————]
      [———————]ạπụ[——————————]
      [————————————————————————]
```

It was Walbank's opinion that the craftsman who produced this document also worked on *IG* II², 278, there dated by J. Kirchner "ante a. 336/5" and with lettering described as "volg. med. s. IV". His suggestions for the text include the following: Line 2. [– – – ἀποτ]όμης(?). Line 6. [– – ἐὰ]ν ἀλ[ῶι(?) – – –]. Line 7. [– – – αὐτὸ]ς ἐγ[ώ(?) – – –] (e.g., οὔτ'αὐτὸ]ς ἐγὼ οὔτ'ἄλλος ἐμοὶ οὔτ'ἄλλη εἰδότος ἐμοῦ). Line 10. ὀφειλ[ειν – – – *vel* ὀφειλ[έτω – – –]. If, as this might indicate, the inscription records an agreement resembling **35**, **47**, **50**, and **51**, line 3 might conceal Ἀ]χανθ[ι]ο– – –, i.e., the people of Akanthos in Chalkidike, as the name of the other contracting party: cf. *IG* II², 210, of mid-century date. The stele would in that case antedate, perhaps by a decade or so, Philip II's final defeat of the Chalkidian League in 348/7.

All this is highly speculative, but the dating is reasonable on general grounds, and the fragment seems likely to have formed part of a decree of the boule and demos.

HONORS VOTED FOR POSEIDANIOS

59. Two fragments, which do not join, of a stele of Pentelic marble. The larger of the two, fragment *a*, was discovered on the Akropolis before 1913, the date of its first publication, and is now in the Epigraphical Museum (E.M. 2604). Its right side is preserved, but it is broken elsewhere. The Agora fragment, *b* (I 5257), which is broken all around and at the back, was discovered on February 24, 1938, in a mixed Classical and Roman context south of the Eleusinion (T 23).

a: H. 0.225 m.; W. 0.176 m.; Th. 0.094 m.

b: H. 0.077 m.; W. 0.057 m.; Th. 0.076 m.

LH. 0.007–0.008 m.

Στοιχ. (square) 0.0135 m.

Ed. *a* only: *IG* II², 181 (based on the text of A. Wilhelm and including his restorations); M. B. Walbank, *Athenian Proxenies*, pp. 413–415, no. 82, with photograph pl. 55. *b* only: Walbank, *Hesperia* 58, 1989, pp. 74–75, no. 3, with photograph pl. 17. See also *SEG* XXXIX, 64.

ante med. saec. IV a.   ΣΤΟΙΧ. 25

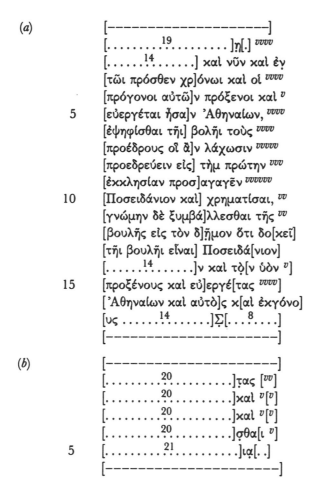

(a)

```
            [------------------]
            [........19........]η[.] vvvv
            [......14......] καὶ νῦν καὶ ἐγ
            [τῶι πρόσθεν χρ]όνωι καὶ οἱ vvvv
            [πρόγονοι αὐτῶ]ν πρόξενοι καὶ v
   5        [εὐεργέται ἦσα]ν Ἀθηναίων, vvvv
            [ἐψηφίσθαι τῆι] βολῆι τοὺς vvvv
            [προέδρους οἳ ἂ]ν λάχωσιν vvvvv
            [προεδρεύειν εἰς] τὴμ πρώτην vvv
            [ἐκκλησίαν προσ]αγαγὲν vvvvvv
   10       [Ποσειδάνιον καὶ] χρηματίσαι, vv
            [γνώμην δὲ ξυμβά]λλεσθαι τῆς vv
            [βουλῆς εἰς τὸν δ]ῆμον ὅτι δο[κεῖ]
            [τῆι βουλῆι εἶναι] Ποσειδά[νιον]
            [......14......]ν καὶ τὸ[ν ὑὸν v]
   15       [προξένους καὶ εὐ]εργέ[τας vvvv]
            [Ἀθηναίων καὶ αὐτὸ]ς κ[αὶ ἐκγόνο]
            [υς ......14......]Σ[...8....]
            [------------------]
```

(b)

```
            [------------------]
            [.........20.........]τας [vv]
            [.........20.........]καὶ v[v]
            [.........20.........]καὶ v[v]
            [.........20.........]σθα[ι v]
   5        [.........21.........]ια[..]
            [------------------]
```

b: Line 1. [–––εὐεργεσ]ίας(?) Walbank. Line 4. [–––ἐπιμελεῖ]σθα[ι(?) Walbank. Fragment *b* is evidently to be located near the right side of the stele, but it may be that a letter space or two should be added to the right and deducted from the left in the text as shown.

The attribution of fragment *b* to the same document as *IG* II², 181 was made by Walbank on the basis of the script, spacing, and type of marble, which he judged identical, together with the marked presence of syllabic division, with vacant spaces at the line ends, which is a feature of *IG* II², 181 and appears to be present on the Agora fragment (cf. M. J. Osborne, *ZPE* 10, 1973, pp. 263–264, with note 27). The relationship between the two fragments cannot be determined.

The lettering of *IG* II², 181 was described by J. Kirchner (presumably with the concurrence of Wilhelm) as of the first half of the 4th century, and he dated his edition of it "ante a. 353/2". Walbank at first (*Athenian Proxenies*, p. 415) agreed it was roughly of the second quarter of the century but later (*Hesperia* 58, 1989, pp. 74–75) detected in the letter style a similarity with that of *IG* II², 34, of 384/3 B.C.; he therefore restated his date as "*ca. a.* 390/370 a." Precision in the matter may be accounted unduly optimistic, and a more general ascription of date is here preferred.

That the document is to be dated later rather than earlier in the first half of the century may be suggested by the use of the probouleumatic formula in fragment *a*, lines 6–13, which seems not to antedate 378/7 and is otherwise first met with among Agora texts in 359/8 (**52**). The variations in the expression of O and OY to represent the "spurious diphthong" may suggest a date not later than the middle 350's; cf. commentary on **53** and references there. For this decree as probouleumatic see also P. J. Rhodes, *Athenian Boule*, p. 249. On the phraseology of lines 13–15 see A. Lambrechts, *De Atheense Proxeniedecreten*, pp. 69–72; A. S. Henry, *Honours*, pp. 130–140 (this text cited p. 136).

FRAGMENT OF THE CONCLUSION OF A DECREE

60. A fragment of a stele of Pentelic marble (I 5504), broken on all sides and at the back, discovered on June 4, 1938, in a Classical context in the antechamber of Klepsydra (T 27).

H. 0.085 m.; W. 0.09 m.; Th. 0.053 m.
LH. 0.007–0.008 m.
Στοιχ. (square) *ta.* 0.015 m. (but with larger space between lines 3 and 4).

Ed. M. B. Walbank, *Hesperia* 58, 1989, pp. 81–82, no. 7, with photograph pl. 17. See also *SEG* XXXIX, 74.

ante med. saec. IV *a.*   ΣΤΟΙΧ. 31

```
                    [――――――――――――――――――――]
                    [. . . . . . . . . . . . . . .28. . . . . . . . . . . . · ἐς δ]
                    [ἐ τὴν ἀναγραφὴν τῆς στήλης τὸν ταμίαν]
                    [τõ δήμο δõνα]ι τ[ριάκοντα δραχμὰς ἐκ τῶ]
                    [ν κατὰ ψηφί]σματ[α ἀναλισκομένων τῶι δ]
         5          [ήμωι· καλέσ]αι δὲ [ἐπὶ δεῖπνον ἐς τὸ πρυτ]
                    [ανεῖον ἐς α]ὔριον. [        vacat        ]
                                    vacat
```

The restorations are those of Walbank (save that he restored ανεον in line 6; but see L. Threatte, *Grammar*, pp. 312 and 317). The source of payment for the stele is to be the "analiskomena fund", and the reference should make unlikely a date for this document earlier than 368/7 B.C. See **45** and **54**, commentary on lines 17–20, where the ταμίας τοῦ δήμου as paymaster is also discussed. On the other hand, the "impure diphthongs" EI and OΥ are restored throughout as E and O, and the text on these grounds is unlikely to postdate *ca.* 360; cf. Threatte, *Grammar*, pp. 184–189 and 247–255.

In the light of these data must be assessed Walbank's claim that this piece belongs with *IG* II², 187, a fragment described by J. Kirchner in that context as showing lettering "volg. med. s. IV" and given the date "ante a. 353/2". Walbank himself restudied it, dating it to the second quarter of the century (*Athenian Proxenies*, pp. 415–417, no. 83, with photograph pl. 56), and (if the connection be accepted) its apparently inconsistent orthography allowed him to propose ἐπὶ ξένια ἐς τὸ πρυτανεῖον εἰς α]ὔριον in lines 5–6 of the present text. In his opinion the same craftsman cut *IG* II², 134, dated by the archon's name to 354/3 B.C. Even if the identity of hands be accepted, the same man's career will have spanned a number of years, and a date in the 360's for **60**, whether or not it carries *IG* II², 187 with it, may be preferable. Nevertheless, the flexibility of a more general dating, following the example of Kirchner, is preferred here.

As it stands, the restoration in line 5 supposes the honorand to be an Athenian citizen: cf. A. S. Henry, *Antichthon* 15, 1981, pp. 104–110 and *Honours*, pp. 271–275 (on the formulation as restored, pp. 265–266). But if Walbank's connection with *IG* II², 187 is to be seriously entertained, the restoration must be varied as proposed, for the honorand there is evidently of foreign origin. Walbank suggested, in consequence, that the combined text may have been a decree conferring citizenship (or reaffirming an earlier grant of it).

A PUBLIC OFFICIAL HONORED

61. A fragment of an apparently flat-topped stele of Pentelic marble (I 4646), with the battered top (including a crowning molding) and original rough-picked back preserved but otherwise broken all around, discovered on March 24, 1937, in a late context southeast of the Market Square and east of the Post-Herulian Wall (U 21–22).

H. 0.17 m.; W. 0.11 m.; Th. 0.10 m.
LH. 0.007 m.
Στοιχ. Hor. 0.015 m.; Vert. *ca.* 0.0135 m.

Ed. B. D. Meritt, *Hesperia* 29, 1960, pp. 1–2, no. 2, with photograph pl. 1. See also *SEG* XIX, 53.

ca. med. saec. IV *a.* (*inter a.* 352 *et* 339)   ΣΤΟΙΧ. (min. 39, max. 45)

```
                ['Επὶ ――――  ἄρχον]τος ἐπὶ [τῆς ―――――――――]
                [πρυτανείας· ――――]ων Λεωσ[――――――― εἶπεν]·
                [ἐπειδὴ ――――κατα]σταθεὶ[ς―――――――――――]
                [―― εἰς τὸν ἐνιαυτὸν τ]ὸν ἐπὶ Θ[――ἄρχοντος ἔθυ]
         5      [σεν ἁπάσας τὰς θυσ]ίας ἃς ἔδ[ει ―――――――――]
```

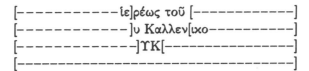

[– – – – – – – – – – ἱε]ρέως τοῦ [– – – – – – – – – – –]
[– – – – – – – – – –]υ Καλλεν[ικο – – – – – – – – – –]
[– – – – – – – – – –]ΥΚ[– – – – – – – – – – – – – – –]
[– –]

The lettering represents a piece of rather poor mid-century work. The strokes are thin and pusillanimous; while the letters are, in the main, regularly formed, there is considerable variety in the aspect of sigma, and alpha and upsilon betray clumsiness. The circle of omega is drawn in before reaching the horizontal strokes, and this together with the short central bar of epsilon suggests that the date should be later rather than earlier in the available span of time. A parallel in general terms is provided by *IG* II², 342, of a date between 350 and 320 (cf. J. Pečírka, *Formula*, p. 62 with note 2). M. B. Walbank (*per ep.*) has been so positive as to consider this piece the work of the craftsman who cut *IG* II², 261 + 216 and 217, said to be of the archonship of Archias (346/5), and to propose the same date for it. This would affect the considerations discussed in the next paragraph, and the texts adduced may well belong in 365/4 (cf. *SEG* XIV, 47). Whether or not the hand and year may be so precisely defined, the observation at least confirms the dating in more general terms shown above.

The honorand received commendation for the manner in which he had carried out certain public duties, presumably (though not beyond all doubt) in the year immediately following that of his tenure of office. Those duties had included the performance of certain prescribed sacrifices (lines 4–5), but the office need not have been that of a ἱερεύς or ἐπιμελητής of a cult. His year of office fell in the archonship of Th– – – –. If the year of Theodotos (387/6) be set aside as in all probability too early either for the script or for the preamble, the possible archonships are those of Thoudemos (353/2), Theellos (351/50), Theophilos (348/7), Themistokles (347/6), and Theophrastos (340/39). On the assumption that the restoration of lines 4–5 is acceptable, the insertion of the shortest name (Theellos) produces a line length of 39 letters, and to restore the longest (Themistokles) results in a line of 45 letters.

The prescript is truncated. In its form it is suitable to the mid-century or slightly after, a time when the formulas employed were fluid in expression and arrangement and when omissions of one sort or another were not uncommon; cf. A. S. Henry, *Prescripts*, pp. 43–45. There is no mention of the γραμματεύς, of proedroi, or alternatively of an epistates, and the enactment formula was presumably placed at the conclusion of the ἐπειδή-clause. The fragmentary name of the proposer should be added to the list of rhetores of the period discussed by M. H. Hansen, *GRBS* 25, 1984, pp. 135–140 (= *Athenian Ecclesia II*, pp. 105–110); cf. R. Develin, *Athenian Officials*, p. 354.

Line 2. Hansen (*loc. cit.*, p. 136 [= p. 106], note 33) regarded the restoration of εἶπεν as "questionable", since in his view the restoration of the proposer's name in the line immediately following the mention of the archon "presupposes a line of some 100 letters": cf. *SEG* XXXIV, 64. But the subsequent lines, even in their fragmentary state, appear to suggest that the substance of the decree immediately follows; the statement of proposition must therefore immediately precede. Further, as stated, the prescript is apparently of unusual brevity. The length of line is, in consequence, reasonably assessed as shown.

Line 7. Kallenikos is, as it happens, an unusual name in Attic prosopography. The tomb of an Ἐράσιππος Καλλενίκου Κριωεύς (*IG* II², 6548; see *PA* 7770) is dated to the early 4th century B.C. Another Kallenikos (*PA* 7769) appears as a trierarch in *IG* II², 1632 (*SEG* XXIV, 160), line 244, of 323/2 B.C. With the addition of the present text, two occurrences of the name in 4th- and 3rd-century *defixiones* (*IG* III, iii, appendix, 54, a, line 5 and 103, a, line 6) complete the roster.

FRAGMENT OF THE CONCLUSION OF A DECREE

62 (Pl. 7). A fragment of a stele of Pentelic marble (I 5173), broken on all sides but with the original thickness probably preserved, discovered on January 31, 1938, in a context of Byzantine date west of the Panathenaic Way (S 19).

H. 0.193 m.; W. 0.111 m.; Th. 0.113 m.
LH. 0.009 m.
Στοιχ. (square) 0.015 m.

Unpublished.

ca. med. saec. IV a.   ΣΤΟΙΧ. 47

[– –]
[. . . . . . .¹⁶. . . . . . .]· ἐπα[ινέσαι δὲ καὶ . . . . .¹⁷. . . . .]
[. . . . . . .¹⁶. . . . . . .]ων ἀφ[. . . . . .²⁷. . . . .]
[. . . .¹¹. . . . . .· ἀναγρ]άψαι δ[ὲ τὸ ψήφισμα τόδε τὸν γραμματέα]

[τὸν κατὰ πρυτανεί]αν ἐν στ[ήληι λιθίνηι . . . . . . ¹⁵ . . . . . .]

5   [. . . . . ¹² . . . . . ὑπ]ηρεσία[————————————————].

vacat

The formula in lines 3–4 conditions the estimate of the length of line in this stoichedon text. The position of the fragment in the total width of the stele cannot be determined, and the line division shown is purely arbitrary.

The lettering is stylish: well spaced, well cut, and neat. It suggests a date after rather than before the middle point of the century. The central horizontal stroke of epsilon is short, while the strokes of sigma, although all of equal length, are set quite closely together. The side strokes of psi are elegantly curved; cf. *IG* II², 1699, of 343/2 B.C. Omega remains relatively open in form; the "oval" of phi appears incompletely described but is not, perhaps, to be regarded as an intentional precursor of that phi showing the upper part of the oval only, which J. Kirchner indicates as a feature of the 3rd century (see **102**). In general the writing is comparable with that of *IG* II², 264 (earlier than 336/5 B.C.); but M. B. Walbank (*per ep.*) has noted a comparability with *IG* II², 572, which, although described as showing "litterae bonae volg. s. IV", is placed by Kirchner at the end of the century.

Reference to the γραμματεὺς ὁ κατὰ πρυτανείαν as responsible for the inscribing of the stele indicates that the inscription does not in any case antedate the decade before 350, when the secretary charged with this duty is first described in this manner: cf. P. J. Rhodes, *Athenian Boule*, pp. 135–137. In lines 4–5 the continuing phraseology at this period is regularly καὶ στῆσαι ἐν ἀκροπόλει, following which, in this text, δοῦναι δ'ὑπ]ηρεσία[ς ἃς αἰτοῦσι ————] might be suggested. Cf. (for the latter section) *IG* II², 212 (*SEG* XXVI, 74 with earlier references, XXXII, 75, XXXIV, 66), of 347/6 B.C., lines 59–60: δοῦναι δὲ τὰς ὑπηρεσίας ἃς αἰτοῦσι Σπάρτοκος καὶ Παιρισάδης. But occasional variations in the stock phrases for the erection and placement of the stele make it unwise to insert any supplement into the text.

The reference to ὑπηρεσία perhaps indicates that (as in *IG* II², 212) the decree concerned relations with a foreign state requesting permission to recruit rowers attached to the Athenian navy. For the meaning of ὑπηρεσία see L. J. D. Richardson, *CQ* 37, 1943, pp. 55–61; M. H. Jameson, *Historia* 12, 1963, pp. 386–391; B. Jordan, *CSCA* 2, 1969, pp. 183–207 (esp. pp. 200–201); and cf. **129**, lines 5–6.

FRAGMENT OF A TREATY(?)

63. A fragment of a stele of Pentelic marble (I 5713), with the left edge preserved though chipped, but otherwise broken all around, discovered on March 15, 1939, in a context of Turkish date over the Panathenaic Way west of the Eleusinion (T 20).

H. 0.108 m.; W. 0.078 m.; Th. 0.065 m.

LH. 0.005 m.

Στοιχ. (square) 0.0076 m.

Ed. B. D. Meritt, *Hesperia* 30, 1961, p. 257, no. 59, with photograph pl. 47. See also *SEG* XXI, 258.

ca. med. saec. IV *a.* (*fortasse paullo post*)   ΣΤΟΙΧ.

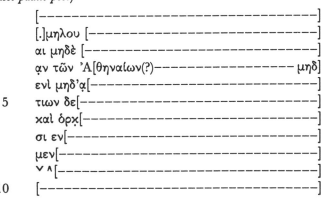

Line 5. δε/[– – –] Meritt.

Although the remains of this text are too scanty for a precise determination of its character, the reading in line 6 implies the taking of an oath. If this is so, a treaty between the Athenians (line 3) and a foreign state, or a document requiring some comparable contractual commitment, may be involved. ΜΗΛΟΥ in line 1 possibly conceals the name of the other contracting party; it would be attractive, if in the circumstances over-adventurous, to contemplate that of the Phocian leader Philomelos, with whom the Athenians entered into a compact at the beginning of the Sacred War (Diodorus Siculus 16.27.3–5). The character of the writing is indeterminate. It is not dissimilar from that of **72**, for example, of 337/6 B.C.; but a date a few years earlier than 350 would not be inappropriate to it, and indeed M. B. Walbank (*per ep.*) has seen in it the work of the same craftsman who was responsible for **51**, *q.v.*, and other documents of the period.

If a treaty is involved, a phrase such as ἐμμένου]σι ἐν [τῆι συμμαχίαι could be envisaged in lines 6–7, while in lines 4–5 provision to supply what the ally or allies may require (τι ὧν δέ[ωνται – – –]) offers itself as a suggestion. But too little survives for speculation to be profitable.

A CITIZEN OF HALIKARNASSOS HONORED

64. A fragment of a stele of bluish marble (I 2995), broken on all sides, discovered on June 7, 1935, in a late context in the northeast corner of the Market Square.

H. 0.124 m.; W. 0.089 m.; Th. 0.07 m.
LH. 0.006 m.
Στοιχ. (square) 0.012 m.

Ed. B. D. Meritt, *Hesperia* 29, 1960, pp. 5–6, no. 5, with photograph pl. 1. See also *SEG* XIX, 54.

post med. saec. IV *a.*   ΣΤΟΙΧ. 32(?)

```
           [..5..]Ν[------------------------]
           [..5..]Ị[------------------------]
           [..5..] εἶπεν· ἐπ[ειδὴ ---------------]
           [..5... Ἁ]λιϰαρνα[σσεὺς ϰαὶ νῦν ϰαὶ ἐν τῶι]
      5    [πρόσθεν] χρόνω[ι ---------------]
           [...7...]Ṇ[.]Α[.]Ε[-----------------]
           [...7...]ΚΙ[..]Ị[------------------]
           [.....11.....]ΙẸ[------------------]
           [------------------------------]
```

Epigraphically this is a jejune piece of work, with scratchy and imprecise lettering. The date (that of the *editio princeps*) reflects this impression. The location of the fragment in relation to the left edge of the stele is arbitrary, and no reconstruction of a prescript from the meager remains of lines 1–3 may be based on it.

Maussollos, the dynast of Karia, within whose satrapy Halikarnassos lay, had been instrumental in fomenting the Social War of 357–355 (Demosthenes 15.3; Diodorus Siculus 16.7.3), and the Athenians no doubt found it diplomatic to cultivate the friendship of individual Halikarnassians who might effectively support their interest in that city. *IG* II² , 136, of 354/3, provides another instance of the implementation of such a policy. Cf. S. Hornblower, *Mausolus*, 1982, pp. 214–215 with note 266. The present text may be slightly later in date but is not likely to postdate the accession of Alexander the Great. On the craftsman thought to be responsible for it see M. B. Walbank, *BSA* 84, 1989, p. 399.

FRAGMENT OF A DECREE

65. A fragment of a block of Pentelic marble (I 2719), broken on all sides, discovered on April 1, 1935, in the destruction debris of a Late Roman gymnasium west of the East Building (O 14).

H. 0.065 m.; W. *ca.* 0.20 m.; Th. 0.113 m.
LH. 0.01 m. (omicron and omega 0.007 m.).
Στοιχ. (square) 0.014 m.

Ed. B. D. Meritt, *Hesperia* 29, 1960, p. 51, no. 66, with photograph pl. 14. See also *SEG* XIX, 55.

post med. saec. IV *a.*   ΣΤΟΙΧ.

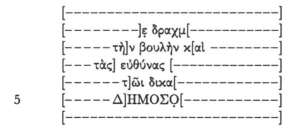

```
          [----------------------------]
          [--------]ε δραχμ[-----------]
          [-----τὴ]ν βουλὴν ϰ[αὶ --------]
          [---τὰς] εὐθύνας [-------------]
          [------τ]ῶι διϰα[-----------]
      5   [-----Δ]ΗΜΟΣỌ[-----------]
          [----------------------------]
```

Line 4. δικα[στηρίωι ---] Meritt. Line 5. [--- δ]ῆμος ο[-----] Meritt; the final letter might however be theta, thus [---- Δ]ημοσθ[εν---] *vel aliquid simile.*

The ends of the "free" strokes of the letters are slightly enlarged. The lettering much resembles, but is slightly larger than, that of *IG* II², 212, of 347/6, and the inscription is to be dated to the same general period. The view of M. B. Walbank (*per ep.*) is that the same hand was at work on *IG* II², 423, and perhaps also on *IG* II², 434 and 276: of these, 423 and 434, described as having "litt. volg. s. IV", were placed by J. Kirchner "post 336/5", while 276 was placed by him earlier than that date, with its lettering described as "volg. med. s. IV". But the present fragment is too small for precise attribution, and what this amounts to is an agreement that such lettering as it preserves is fairly standard for its generation. The thickness of the fragment suggests that it is part of what was a sizable monument.

--- MACHUS OF AL--- (?) HONORED

66. Two joining fragments of a stele of Pentelic marble (I 5464), with the right side and possibly the original back preserved but broken elsewhere, discovered on May 23, 1938, in the latest (19th century) repair to the Post-Herulian Wall, opposite the western passage to Klepsydra (T 27).

Measurements of united piece: H. 0.29 m.; W. 0.155 m.; Th. 0.039 m.

LH. 0.006–0.009 m.

Στοιχ. (square) 0.013 m. (slightly erratic towards the end of the text).

Ed. B. D. Meritt, *Hesperia* 30, 1961, pp. 208–210, no. 3, with photograph pl. 35. See also *SEG* XXI, 340.

ca. a. 350–330 *a.*   ΣΤΟΙΧ. 27

```
              [----------------------]
              [.....¹⁰..... τοὺς προέδρους] οἱ ἂ[ν]
              [εἰς τὴν πρώτην προεδρεύωσ]ιν ἐκκ
              [λησίαν προσαγαγεῖν ....]μαχον π
              [ρὸς τὸν δῆμον καὶ χρηματί]σαι, γνώ
         5    [μην δὲ ξυμβάλλεσθαι τῆς] βουλῆς ε
              [ἰς τὸν δῆμον ὅτι δοκεῖ τ]εῖ βουλεῖ
              [εἶναι ....μαχον ....κ]ράτους Ἀλ
              [..⁶... πρόξενον τοῦ δή]μου τοῦ Ἀθ
              [ηναίων καὶ αὐτόν τε καὶ ὑ]οὺς, καὶ [ἐ]
        10    [πιμελεῖσθαι αὐτῶν τοὺς σ]τ[ρατηγ]
              [οὺς καὶ τὴν βουλὴν τὴν ἀεὶ β]ουλε[ύ]
              [ουσαν ὅπως ἂν μηδ'ὑφ'ἑνὸς ἀ]δικῶν[τ]
              [αι· ἀναγράψαι δὲ τόδε τὸ ψή]φισμα [ἐ]
              [ν στήλει λιθίνει τὸν γρα]μματέια
        15    [τὸν κατὰ πρυτανείαν κα]ὶ στῆσαι [ἐ]
              [ν ἀκροπόλει· εἰς δὲ τὴν ἀ]ναγραφὴ[ν]
              [τῆς στήλης δοῦναι τὸν τ]αμίαν [τοῦ]
              [δήμου ΔΔΔ ἐκ τῶν κατὰ ψη]φίσ[ματα ἀ]
              [ναλισκομένων τῶι δήμωι.      vacat      ]
```

The formulas employed or supplied in this text, as well as the character of the script, are consonant with a date in the second half of the 4th century, preferably not later than *ca.* 320. The letters are quite widely spaced, and there is little sign of any widening of the "free ends". They are, however, clumsily cut in several instances, beta, omega, and the elongated upsilon being especially noteworthy.

In his publication of the fragmentary decree I 7134 (= **106F**; *Hesperia* 51, 1982, pp. 45–46, no. 4; *SEG* XXXII, 74), which he dated "post med. s. IV a.", M. B. Walbank expressed the opinion that the hand there employed was also at work on this text and on **67**, and perhaps also on *IG* II², 229 (dated to 341/40).

Lines 1–6. The decree is probouleumatic; cf. P. J. Rhodes, *Athenian Boule*, pp. 65, 250. The formula is now standard; cf. **52**, commentary on line 13. Lines 6 and 14. For EI in the place of HI see L. Threatte, *Grammar*, pp. 377–378: on this criterion the date of the text should be later rather than earlier in the suggested span of time. Lines 7–8. The ethnic of the honorand is Al--- or Sal---, for the preceding genitive of the patronymic may have ended in ---PATOΥ rather than as shown in the text. In neither case is there a convincing supplement. Meritt suggested Ἀλ[υζαῖον and drew attention to the adherence of the Alyzaioi to the alliance formed against Macedon by the Athenians in 323 (Diodorus Siculus 18.11).

Lines 8–9. For the formula and phraseology cf. A. S. Henry, *Honours*, pp. 140–141. *Proxenia* alone (without *euergesia*) is here involved. The normal formula calls for αὐτὸν καὶ ἐκγόνους, which falls short of the available space by one letter. The possibility Ἀθ[ηναίων, αὐτὸν καὶ τοὺς υἱ]ούς must be discounted, since in the 4th century υός is the standard form of the word. Lines 9–13. For the "protection formula" see Henry, *Honours*, pp. 176–181. The order "generals and boule" is less frequently met with than its reverse.

Line 14. On the intrusion of iota into γραμματέια see Threatte, *Grammar*, p. 152, and cf. *IG* II², 226, lines 10 and 19, where similar iotas were erased. Lines 16–20. For the ταμίας τοῦ δήμου as the disbursing officer and for the source and amount of the expenditure, see **45** and **54**, commentary on lines 17–20. As there noted, the "analiskomena fund" makes its earliest sure appearance in 368/7: and it may be added that its use continued, at any rate sporadically, through the 3rd century and is found in the late 2nd; cf. Henry, *Chiron* 14, 1984, p. 63. The numeral is restored *exempli gratia*. Numerals were not always inscribed in conformity with strict stoichedon requirements and are frequently distinguished by marks of punctuation. Cf. Threatte, *Grammar*, pp. 83–84. The cost of the stele may thus have been twenty rather than thirty drachmas.

DECREE REGULATING THE FESTIVAL DIPOLIEIA

67. A fragment of a stele of Pentelic marble (I 6421), with the smooth left side and original rough-picked back preserved but broken elsewhere, discovered on February 1, 1952, in a wall of a modern house south of the Church of the Holy Apostles (O–Q 16–17).

H. 0.17 m.; W. 0.26 m.; Th. 0.078 m.
LH. 0.008 m. (omicron and omega 0.006–0.007 m.).
Στοιχ. (square) 0.013 m.

Ed. B. D. Meritt, *Hesperia* 37, 1968, pp. 267–268, no. 3, with photograph pl. 77. See also *SEG* XXV, 82 (with additional reference to the more amply restored text of F. Sokolowski, *Lois sacrées*, p. 315, no. 179).

ca. a. 350–330 *a.*   ΣΤΟΙΧ.

```
     [------------------------------------------------]
     [....9....]ν ποεῖν [---------------------------------]
     [..5..]ιοτε[.]η νηφαλι[-----------------------------]
     [...]ιν τοῦ Θαργηλι[ῶ]ν[ος-------------Σκιροφοριῶνος]
     [μη]νὸς τετράδι ἐπὶ δέ[κα --------------------------]
  5  πομπὴν πέμπειν τοὺ[ς--------------------------ἱερ]
     οποιοὺς ἐπ[ε]ιδὰν [------------------------ἐν τῶι ἱ]
     ερῶι ὦσιν τὸ ἱερ[ὸν -------------------------------]
     τὸ ἱερὸν [-----------------------------------------]
     περι[.]Λ[-----------------------------------------]
 10  [τ]ὴν μάχ[αιραν ----------------------------------]
     [------------------------------------------------]
```

The text is in principle that of Meritt. Sokolowski, postulating a stoichedon line of 43 letters, restored lines 1–7 as follows:

```
     [. τὴν θυσία]ν ποεῖν [--------------κατὰ τὰ νόμιμα τ]
     [ἀ ἀρχα]ιότε[ρα] νηφάλι[ον -----------------------]
     [...]ιν τοῦ Θαργηλι[ῶ]ν[ος ...6... τοῦ δὲ Σκιροφοριῶνος]
     [μη]νὸς τετράδι ἐπὶ δέ[κα τὰ θύματα παριστάναι καὶ τὴν]
  5  πομπὴν πέμπειν τοὺ[ς ὑπὸ τῆς βουλῆς αἱρουμένους ἱερ]
     οποιούς· ἐπ[ε]ιδὰν [δὲ οἱ πομπεύοντες ἐν τῶι ἱ]
     ερῶι ὦσιν, τὸ ἱερ[ὸν κτλ.
```

Line 6 of this text is short by eight letters. Line 8. τὸ ἱερὸν [πῦρ ἅπτειν(?) Sokolowski. Line 9. περι[ε]λ[αύνειν Sokolowski. Line 10. Sokolowski erroneously indicates a *vacat* below this line.

The characteristics of the writing of this text, which is not susceptible of dating on other grounds, indicate a date in the latter part of the 4th century and are comparable with those of **66**. Indeed, M. B. Walbank (*Hesperia* 51, 1982, p. 46) regards both inscriptions as perhaps the work of the same craftsman; see **66**, commentary. In this text however there is some (but not too much) carelessness and some enlargement of the "free ends" of the strokes. A distinctive feature (as Walbank also noted) is that omicron appears as "suspended" from the upper line of the letter area. A date within the same span as **66** seems a reasonable conclusion. Walbank's further suggestions (*per ep.*) of connection with *IG* II², 257 and 274 (both dated in that edition "ante a. 336/5") and with two other Agora fragments, I 4034 (**98**) and 5767, as products of the same hand may also be noted. See also *SEG* XL, 68.

The date by the month in line 4 suggests that the festival, with the regulations for which the decree appears to be concerned, is most probably the Dipolieia, which took place on Skirophorion 14. This suggests the name of the month restored at the end of line 3 and requires that the mention of Thargelion in the earlier part of that line be connected with the preceding clause. The Bouphonia, in which the guilt of the knife rather than that of the man wielding it was a central feature of the ritual, formed part of the festival, and the remains of line 10 further accord with the tradition of which Pausanias (1.24.4 and 28.10) provides the chief literary authority. Cf. Porphyry, *de Abstinentia* 2.29–30 and, for the date, Schol. Aristophanes, *Pax* 419. For a fuller study see L. Deubner, *Attische Feste*, pp. 158–170; M. P. Nilsson, *Geschichte der griechischen Religion* I, 3rd ed., 1967, pp. 152–155, with bibliography p. 152, note 1.

TWO HONORARY DECREES OF THE DEME KYDATHENAION

68 (Pl. 8). A fragment of an opisthographic stele of Pentelic marble (I 5212), with the left side (as viewed on Face A) preserved but broken above, below, and to the right, discovered on February 12, 1938, in the original filling of the Post-Herulian Wall (T 22). On Face B the striations of a toothed chisel are visible, running diagonally from the upper right to the lower left.

H. *ca.* 0.55 m.; W. *ca.* 0.24 m.; Th. 0.108 m.

LH. (Face A) 0.006 m. (in the stephanoi, 0.008–0.01 m.); (Face B) 0.006 m. (in the stephanoi, 0.009 m.).

Unpublished.

FACE A

ca. a. 350–330 *a.*(?)   NON-ΣΤΟΙΧ. *ca.* 38–40

```
[------------------------------------------]
[. .]ει[----------------------------------]
[τ]ῶι χο[ί]γ[ῶι· ἀναγράψαι δὲ τόδε τὸ ψήφισμα ἐν στή]
[λ]ει λιθίνε[ι καὶ στῆσαι ἐν τῶι ἱερῶι τῶι τῶν 'Ηρακ]
[λ]ειδῶν· εἰ[ς δὲ [τὴν ἀναγραφὴν καὶ τὴν ποίησιν τῆ]
5    [ς] στήλης δοῦνα[ι ........13–16......... τῶν δημοτῶν· τα]
     ῦτα ἔδοξεν Κυδ[αθηναιεῦσιν.      vacat           ]
           (in corona)                  [(in corona)]
           'Ο δῆμος           10    ['Η βουλή]

           (in corona)                  [(in corona)]
           'Ο δῆμος                     [-----]
           ὁ ἐν Σάμ[ωι]                 [-----]
```

FACE B

ca. a. 350–330 *a.*(?)   NON-ΣΤΟΙΧ. *ca.* 40–41

```
[------------------------------------------]
[-----------------------]υσι[....11–12....]
[-----------------------]αφ[.]α[...ca. 10...]
[......13–15......· ἀναγράψαι δ]ὲ τόδε τὸ ψήφισ[μα ἐν]
[στήλει λιθίνει καὶ στῆσαι ἐν τ]ῶι ἱερῶι τῶι τῶν 'Ηρ[α]
5    [κλειδῶν· εἰς δὲ τὴν ἀναγραφὴ]ν καὶ τὴν ποίησιν τῆς
     [στήλης δοῦναι ......13–16...... τ]ῶν δημοτῶν· ταῦτα ἔ
     [δοξεν Κυδαθηναιεῦσιν.    vacat]       vacat

           [(in corona)]                    (in corona)
           ['Ο δῆμος]                       'Η βουλή
```

[(*in corona*)]   (*in corona*)

[- - - - - -]   ῾Ο δῆμος

10   [- - - - - -]   ὁ ἐν ῾Ηφαισ[τίαι]

The lettering of the two decrees was evidently executed by the same mason. His style is neat and unpretentious, with the letters somewhat "spread" (notably the wide-angled alpha and delta and the very open omega). There is slight emphasis on the "free ends" of strokes in upsilon and phi. The vertical stroke of xi is omitted. By contrast the inscriptions within the stephanoi are more clumsy, irregular in both placing and spacing, and less well cut, although showing the same idiosyncrasies. It may be surmised that they were added after the stele was erected and in place. The stephanoi themselves are elegantly carved. The arrangement shows that there were two pairs of them on either face, and it is to be presumed that in each case the upper pair consisted of citations by the demos and the boule. It is not improbable, but it cannot be regarded as sufficiently certain for inclusion in the text, that the second pair of citations was also exactly duplicated on both faces of the monument.

The date suggested by the writing is also subject to the guidance of the lower register of the stephanoi. The δῆμος in Hephaistia has reference to the long-standing Athenian cleruchy in Lemnos (cf. **41** and **335**, *IG* II², 1222–1223, and *IG* XII, viii, *Praefatio de Lemno et Imbro*, pp. 3–5). The cleruchy on the island of Samos had a shorter life, established in 365 and terminated in 322; see G. Glotz and R. Cohen, *Histoire grecque* III, 1936, p. 189 with note 48; S. Accame, *La lega ateniese del secolo IV a.C.*, 1941, p. 183 with note 1; G. L. Cawkwell, *JHS* 101, 1981, p. 51; J. Cargill, *The Second Athenian League*, 1981, pp. 148–149; *IG* II², 1437, line 20 with commentary. The stele should therefore date between these two limits, and on general grounds, for example, this type of "multiple crowning", apart from the style of the engraving, attribution to the 340's or 330's seems appropriate. A similar combination of stephanoi bestowed by cleruchs on Samos and Lesbos is found in *IG* II², 3207, which A. Wilhelm referred to a collation in 307/6 of honors decreed to the statesman Lykourgos, whose memory was then rehabilitated (cf. *IG* II², 457; Wilhelm, *Attische Urkunden* III [= *SbAkadWien* 202, 5], 1925, pp. 3–6, no. IX). It is likely that the two decrees on this stele concerned decisions by the demesmen of Kydathenaion similarly to place on record the honors bestowed by the citizens of Athens at home and abroad upon two members of the deme.

The territory of Kydathenaion (of the phyle Pandionis) comprised part of the center of Athens city, including the Akropolis. It is therefore more likely that a stele erected by its demesmen would come to light in the Agora area; but the monument was erected in the precinct of the Herakleidai, the site of which is unknown, and it presumably cannot be excluded that the deme Kydantidai rather than Kydathenaion sponsored it. Kydantidai was apparently an inland deme of Aigeis but may have had some connection with the cult of the Herakleidai. The deme Aixone (coastal deme of Kekropis) certainly had; cf. *IG* II², 1199, line 23, with commentary. No other deme decree either of Kydathenaion or of Kydantidai has hitherto been identified. For a (partial) list of deme decrees, see J. S. Traill, *Political Organization*, pp. 74–75, note 10.

The restoration of the standard formulas for the conclusion of a decree on the two faces offers mutual support for both texts, and its extent is conditioned both by the formulaic content and by the measurement and position of the stephanoi below them. The only difficulty appears to occur in line 5 of Face A and line 6 of Face B, where in the usual turn of phrase δοῦναι should require both subject (the official responsible for payment, which in the case of a deme is likely to be the demarch or the treasurer; cf. *IG* II², 1193, 1197, 1202, 1203, and **277**) and object (τὸ ἀνάλωμα or a statement of the amount). So, for instance, one might expect in Face A, line 5 some such phraseology as δοῦνα[ι :ΔΔ: δραχμὰς τὸν ταμίαν τῶν δημοτῶν. But without excessive crowding, not indicated by what survives of the lines concerned, the lacuna is too short for the restoration of both of these features. Some customary element must therefore have been omitted. It is possible that the demarch figured immediately above, in the lost sections of the two texts, and that he is thus easily to be inferred as the subject of both ἀναγράψαι and δοῦναι. Or the infinitives represent instructions by the demesmen as it were to themselves, without specific reference to an official. Some such form of words as :ΔΔ: δραχμὰς ὑπὲρ τῶν δημοτῶν, or ἀπὸ τῆς προσόδου (or τοῦ κοινοῦ), or ἐκ τῆς διοικήσεως τῶν δημοτῶν might enter into consideration. Cf. *IG* II², 1186, line 34, 1197, lines 17–18, and **277**.

The postponement of the enactment formula to the ends of the two decrees (or possibly its repetition) adds a quaintly old-fashioned note: the best parallel is to be found over a century earlier, in 485/4 (*IG* I³, 4, A, lines 14–15 and B, lines 26–27). Cf. P. J. Rhodes, *Athenian Boule*, p. 64; A. S. Henry, *Prescripts*, p. 2. In the 4th century, instances occur of such postponement (or repetition) of the record of the archon, or γραμματεύς, or both: so in *IG* II², 17 (= M. J. Osborne, *Naturalization* I, pp. 43–45, D 8), lines 13–15, 32, lines 26–27, 69, line 5. And outside Attica the postscript position was regular, for example in Argos, for the record of the name of the proposer of a decree.

This text is no. 71 in the list of deme decrees assembled by D. Whitehead (*The Demes of Attica, 507–ca. 250 B.C.*, 1986, on p. 383) and is cited *passim*, its number in quotation appearing in its unrevised form as *Agora* XVI, 54.

FRAGMENT OF AN HONORARY DECREE

69 (Pl. 6). A fragment of a stele of Pentelic marble (I 5148), with the right side and the original rough-picked back preserved but otherwise broken, discovered on November 30, 1937, in a modern house wall outside the Market Square, south of the Church of the Holy Apostles (O 17). The inscribed surface is worn (thus making much of the lettering barely legible) and abraded on the right before reaching the edge of the monument.

H. 0.223 m.; W. 0.18 m.; Th. 0.106 m.
LH. 0.005–0.006 m.
Στοιχ. (almost square) Hor. 0.0115 m.; Vert. 0.011 m.

Unpublished.

ca. a. 350–320 *a.*   ΣΤΟΙΧ.

```
[--------------------------------------]
[------------------------------Π]αλληνεῖ Η[. .⁵. .]
[----------------------------]τε πρὸς τὸν δῆ[μον]
[----------------------------]ππος ΤΟΥΣΤΕ[. . . .]
[----------------------------]ν ἐστεφάνωσ[εν . .]
5  [------------------- ἐψηφίσ]ατο ὁ δῆμος [. . . .]
[----------------------------]εγος εἰς τὴν [. . .]
[----------------------------]στέλλοντα τ[. . .]
[----------------------------]υνωσιν πρὸς τ[. .]
[----------------------προθ]υμίας [. .]υ χατ[. .]
10 [--------------------------] ταύτης τῆς [φ]ιλο
[τιμίας(?) ------------------] πολιται[. . .]Ι[. .]
[--------------------------ἀγ]αθὸν Ι[.]Ν[. . .⁶. . .]
[--------------------------]ΑΤΟΥ[.]Ι[. . .⁶. . .]
[--------------------------]ΤΕ[. .]Ι[. . . . .⁸. .]
15 [--------------------------]ΝΤ[. . . . . .¹⁰. .]
[--------------------------]νοις π[. . . .⁷. . .]
[----------------------τῆι πό]λει δι[. . . .⁷. . .]
[--------------------------] reliquiae [-----]
[--------------------------------------]
```

The decree appears to confer honors on a recipient, perhaps a citizen (line 1), who has rendered good service to the people (line 2). He or his forebears may have received honors and been the subject of a *psephisma* at some earlier date (lines 4–5). The readings are difficult throughout and become more so as the text progresses. J. S. Traill and M. B. Walbank have generously provided *per ep.* their interpretations of some of the more doubtful passages, and the possible variations in what the stone appears to offer may be judged from the reading of line 9 by Walbank as [----ἐφ]αμίλλους ὄντα[ς]. In general the text remains uninformative and, unless a further piece from the same text is identified, unrewarding.

The style of the lettering provides the only criterion of date; it gives the impression of rather poor work of the second half of the 4th century: the writing is plain, the letters well spaced, and there is no attempt at the enlargement of the "free ends" of the strokes. But a date later than the regime of Demetrios of Phaleron is not impossible.

THE ARCHONSHIP OF THEMISTOKLES, 347/6 B.C.

Themistokles (*PA* 6650) is well attested as archon both in the literature (especially Diodorus Siculus 16.56; Aischines 3.62) and in inscriptions. In addition to **70**, three *psephismata* are recorded as passed during his year of office: *IG* II², 212 (*SEG* XXVI, 74, XXXIV, 66, with other references), 213 (*SEG* XXI, 263), and perhaps 214 (*SEG* XXIV, 88). In *IG* II², 215, of 346/5, at line 11, and 505 + addendum, p. 661 (*SEG* XXIV, 113, with other references, XXXIII, 97), of 303/2, at line 17, his archonship is introduced in backward references. Other epigraphical contexts in which his name occurs as archon are as follows: in the records of the Treasurers of Athena, *IG* II², 1441, line 4, 1443 (*SEG* XV, 119, with other references), lines 92, 104, 216; in the records of the Joint Board of Treasurers of Athena and of the Other Gods, *IG* II², 1455, lines 17–18 (cf. *SEG* XXXIX, 158), *SEG* XV, 120, line 26; in the records of the Commissioners of the

Brauronian sanctuary, *IG* II², 1514 (*SEG* XXV, 176, with other references), line 12, 1515, line 6, 1519, line 10, 1521 (*SEG* XXI, 555), lines 26–27, 1524, lines 60–61; in the record of the Naval Commissioners, *IG* II², 1622, lines 446–447 (cf. *SEG* XXX, 106, XXXV, 118); in the record of victors in the dramatic competitions at the Dionysia, *IG* II², 2318 (*SEG* XIX, 168, XXVI, 202), line 283; in the dedication(?) *SEG* XIX, 51; and in the inventory of treasures in the Temple of Hera on the island of Samos, then occupied by Athenian cleruchs (C. Michel, *Recueil d'inscriptions grecques*, 1900, pp. 678–680, no. 832, line 6), where Themistokles' term of office is equated with that of the Samian archon Theokles.

The phyle Aigeis is known to have held office during the eighth prytany (*IG* II², 212), and *IG* II², 213 also belongs to this prytany, although the ordinal numeral of the prytany in its series is not expressed in the preamble. No other prytany of the year can be identified.

The γραμματεύς who served with Themistokles was Lysimachos, son of Sosidemos, of Acharnai, whose phyle (Oineis VI) fits correctly into the official sequence of the cycle of secretaries first determined by W. S. Ferguson and referred to as "Ferguson's Law". Cf. S. Alessandri, *Annali della Scuola Normale de Pisa*, p. 49; P. J. Rhodes, *Athenian Boule*, p. 136, note 1. Nothing further is known of Lysimachos (*PA* 9512) or of his father. *SEG* XXI, 839 may be his tombstone, and the Lysimachides (*PA* 9480) who was archon in 339/8 might be his son: but the names are not uncommon. Office holders attested for the archonship of Themistokles are listed in R. Develin, *Athenian Officials*, pp. 318–322.

The character of the year was discussed by D. M. Lewis (*BSA* 50, 1955, pp. 25–26, no. 26), who showed that both 346/5 and 345/4 were ordinary years and that there is, in consequence, a presumption that 347/6 was intercalary in the festival calendar at Athens. This could be supported with reference to the literary testimony concerning the date of the assembly held to discuss the proposed peace with Philip II of Macedon in Elaphebolion of this year. It may be confirmed by appeal to the Metonic system, 347/6 being the tenth year of Meton's fifth cycle. In Meton's system the tenth year was scheduled as intercalary, the eleventh and twelfth as ordinary (cf. B. D. Meritt, *TAPA* 95, 1964, p. 236).

FRAGMENT OF A DECREE

70. The upper left corner of a stele of Pentelic marble (I 5354), with a substantial flat-topped molding preserved above the inscribed face, discovered on March 23, 1938, in a modern wall in the area west of the north end of the Stoa of Attalos (P 7).

Overall measurements including the molding: H. 0.115 m.; W. 0.174 m.; Th. 0.14 m.
LH. 0.009 m.

Irregularly spaced lettering.

Ed. B. D. Meritt, *Hesperia* 29, 1960, p. 51, no. 65, with photograph pl. 13. See also *SEG* XIX, 52.

a. 347/6 *a.*

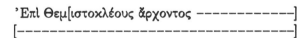

Ἐπὶ Θεμ[ιστοχλέους ἄρχοντος -----------]
[-------------------------------]

The date given by the archon (there is no other known eponymous archon in Classical or Hellenistic Athens whose name begins with these three surviving letters) is confirmed by the character and quality of the script, with which Meritt compared *IG* II², 212, of the same year.

THE ARCHONSHIP OF ARCHIAS, 346/5 B.C.

The term of office of Archias (*PA* 2449), like that of Themistokles (p. 106 above), is not only well evidenced by Diodorus Siculus (16.59) and other literary sources but is mentioned in a substantial number of epigraphical contexts. In addition to **71**, the decrees *IG* II², 215 and 218 (*SEG* XXXI, 74) were enacted when Archias held the archonship. (*IG* II², 216 and 217 belong not to his year but to that of Chion, 365/4; see *SEG* XIV, 47). *IG* II², 3201 is also evidently part of a decree in which a taxiarchos of this year was honored, although no more of it survives than the citations which concluded it. Archias' name occurs or is obviously to be restored also in the following: the record of the Treasurers of Athens, *IG* II², 1443 (*SEG* XV, 119), line 89 (in 1442, line 3, the restoration is probably erroneous); the records of the Joint Board of the Treasurers of Athena and of the Other Gods, *IG* II², 1461, line 11 and *SEG* XV, 120, line 31; the records of the

Commissioners of the Brauronian sanctuary, *IG* II², 1514 (*SEG* XXI, 555, XXV, 176), line 24, 1515, lines 16–17, 1516 (*SEG* XVIII, 35, XXI, 555), line 4; the poletai record of leases of the mines at Laureion, *Agora* XIX, P19, line 1; the record of the Naval Commissioners, *IG* II², 1622, lines 390 and 422; the record of the Delian Amphiktyons, *IG* II², 1646, line 17; the rent contract of a piece of land owned by the demesmen of Aixone, *IG* II², 2492, lines 42–43 (see *SEG* XXIV, 202; D. Behrend, *Attische Pachturkunden*, pp. 80–83, no. 25); the dedication of Xenokles, victorious gymnasiarch at the Great Panathenaia of this year, *IG* II², 3019; and the Samian inventory of the treasures in the Temple of Hera, line 1 (see under the Archonship of Themistokles, p. 107 above), in which Archias' year is equated with that of the Samian archon Peisileos.

Two prytanies of the year may be definitely attributed to the phylai then in office, VIII Hippothontis and IX Akamantis (*IG* II², 215 and 218). The other eight remain unidentified.

For Archias' term as archon the γραμματεύς (from the phyle Kekropis [VII]) was Kephisodoros, son of Athenophanes, of Phlya (*PA* 8387). Cf. S. Alessandri, *Annali della Scuola Normale di Pisa*, pp. 49, 61. Athenophanes is a very rare name in Attic prosopography, known otherwise as held only by an ephebos from the deme Aixone in 119/18 (*PA* 286; *IG* II², 1008, col. III, line 105), and by one of the bath stewards of Alexander the Great (Plutarch, *Alexander* 35; *PA* 285). Kephisodoros married Archestrate, daughter of Isonomos of Kydathenaion and his wife Myrtale (*PA* 2388; *IG* II², 6580), whose name was inscribed on the tomb monument of her parents; but beyond this detail no more is known of him, unless he is to be considered the father of the βουλευτής from Phlya listed in *Agora* XV, 73, at line 28. R. Develin (*Athenian Officials*, pp. 322–324) provides a full list with references of those known to have held official positions during Archias' archonship.

For the character of the year, which was ordinary in the Athenian festival calendar, see D. M. Lewis, *BSA* 50, 1955, pp. 25–26, no. 26 and the discussion of the archonship of Themistokles above (p. 107). A text from the Athenian settlement on Samos in the archonship of Peisileos confirms the year as ordinary by giving the earliest of that long series of equations between the festival and prytany calendars on which Athenian calendric studies have been so largely based, showing Posideon 27 (less likely 26) as the equivalent of pryt. V, 31, that is, the 175th (less likely 174th) day of the year. The first four prytanies were thus of 36 days each in length, and the lunar months alternated full and hollow, beginning the year with full Hekatombaion but with full Posideon succeeding full Maimakterion. If the day is the 174th, the year began with hollow Hekatombaion and alternation was regular, but one of the early prytanies will have contained only 35 days. See W. K. Pritchett and O. Neugebauer, *Calendars*, pp. 40–42; B. D. Meritt, *Athenian Year*, pp. 72–73. The year was the eleventh in Meton's (fifth) cycle and as such was scheduled in his system as ordinary.

A CITIZEN OF SALAMIS IN CYPRUS HONORED

71. A fragment from the right-hand section of the upper part of a pedimental stele of Pentelic marble (I 657), broken on all sides except for a portion of the raking cornice of the pediment, discovered on April 5, 1933, in a late context southeast of the Tholos (H 12).

Below the pediment and the molding supporting it, there survive the much-damaged remains of a relief showing a figure standing on the right and extending a hand towards a seated figure, evidently in the center of a composition which presumably included a further figure on the left, now lost. The right-hand figure is entitled "Salamis". It is a reasonable supposition that Athena stood on the left and that both eponymous goddesses were shown as gesturing towards the seated honorand.

Inscription *a* appears on the horizontal cornice of the pediment, inscription *b* above the head of the sculptured figure already described.

H. 0.29 m.; W. 0.245 m.; Th. 0.102 m.

LH. (*a*) 0.009 m.; (*b*) 0.005 m.

Ed. J. H. Oliver, *Hesperia* 4, 1935, pp. 34–35, no. 4, with photograph.

a. 346/5 a.

(*a*) ['Επὶ 'Αρχί]ου ἄρχοντ[ος].

(*b*) Σαλαμίς.

The restoration of the archon's name is conditioned by the measurement of the width of the stele, which may be assessed from the pediment, and by the spacing of the letters. It is also consonant with the character of the lettering, which indicates a date in the middle of the 4th century. *IG* II², 283 is also a decree in honor of a Salaminian, is of much the same workmanship, and has similar lettering; but its marble is not that of the Agora stele, and Oliver discounted any relationship between the two fragments.

On events in Cyprus at this time see Diodorus Siculus 16.26.42 and 46. Oliver suggested a possible connection between these and this monument. On the relief sculpture see *SEG* XXXIX, 324.

THE ARCHONSHIP OF PHRYNICHOS, 337/6 B.C.

A number of decrees of this year are known, and the majority to which an accurate date can be assigned were passed towards the end of it, in the tenth prytany. Apart from the two published below, these texts appear as *IG* II², 239 (M. N. Tod, *GHI* II, 180; *SEG* XXI, 267, XXXII, 78), perhaps of pryt. VI, 240 (Tod, *GHI* II, 181; *SEG* XXXI, 77), 241, 242, 243, and E. Schweigert, *Hesperia* 7, 1938, pp. 292–294, no. 19 (not an Agora text), all of pryt. X. *IG* II², 244 (*SEG* XIX, 57, XXXV, 62) and 304 + 604 (*SEG* XVIII, 11) are also attributable to 337/6. On the dated inscriptions of this year see also C. J. Schwenk, *Athens in the Age of Alexander*, pp. 27–71, nos. 4–14. On the γραμματεύς of the year, Chairestratos of Acharnai, see S. Alessandri, *Annali della Scuola Normale di Pisa*, p. 50. R. Develin (*Athenian Officials*, pp. 346–349) details those known to have held public office during Phrynichos' year.

The inscription published in *Hesperia* 7, 1938 (= Schwenk, *op. cit.*, pp. 49–51, no. 9; *SEG* XXXV, 64) and **72** are the only texts among these to include an equation between the "festival" date and the prytany date; and **72** is in fact the earliest of the decrees found in the Agora to do so.

The year 337/6 was ordinary in the Athenian calendar. The details were reconstructed by B. D. Meritt (*Athenian Year*, pp. 76–78), who quoted the first few lines of four of the relevant decrees and envisaged a regular succession of full and hollow months in the festival calendar, save that Thargelion and Skirophorion were both full months. His reconstruction was however to some extent based upon the equation for **72**, proposed by its first editor, Schweigert, which, though perfect in itself, cannot be maintained: see the commentary below on the date of that text. The succession of civil months may remain unaffected by the necessary changes, whatever choice of revised equation be accepted. As for the prytanies, a pattern showing the first four and the last to be of 36 days and the remaining five of 35 (Meritt, Schwenk) will conform to that defined by Aristotle (*Athenaion Politeia* 43.2); but it is a pattern that was varied in practice (cf. A. G. Woodhead, *Study of Greek Inscriptions*, pp. 117–120), and a sequence requiring two prytanies of 36 days in the first half of the year and the other three in the second half will accommodate the equation suggested by M. H. Hansen (*GRBS* 23, 1982, p. 342, no. 21 [= *Athenian Ecclesia*, p. 94; cf. *SEG* XXXII, 78]); his alternative suggestions (one prytany moved and an irregular succession of festival months, or the insertion of extra days into the festival calendar) have less to recommend them.

Known phylai in prytany are IX Leontis and X Pandionis. If **72** was passed in the sixth prytany, the phyle then in office was Akamantis; if in the eighth, the phyle will have been Antiochis, Erechtheis, or Kekropis.

A DECREE CONCERNING LEMNOS

72. Two nonjoining fragments of a stele of Pentelic marble, each of which has its rough-picked back preserved but is otherwise broken all around. Fragment *a* (I 5234) was discovered on February 18, 1938, in a Late Byzantine context south of the Eleusinion and east of the Post-Herulian Wall (T 22); fragment *b* (I 2409) was discovered on February 5, 1935, in a modern context in the area of the East Building (N–O 14).

    a: H. 0.144 m.; W. 0.12 m.; Th. 0.08 m.

    b: H. 0.21 m.; W. 0.071 m.; Th. 0.081 m.

    LH. 0.005–0.007 m. (omega 0.004 m.).

    Στοιχ. (square, with irregularities) *ca.* 0.011 m.

Ed. E. Schweigert, *Hesperia* 9, 1940, pp. 325–327, no. 35, with photographs; C. J. Schwenk, *Athens in the Age of Alexander*, pp. 30–33, no. 5 (cf. *SEG* XXXV, 63). Cf. B. D. Meritt, *Athenian Year*, p. 76, where lines 1–4 are cited.

a. 337/6 *a., pryt.* VI (*vel* VIII)   ΣΤΟΙΧ. 39

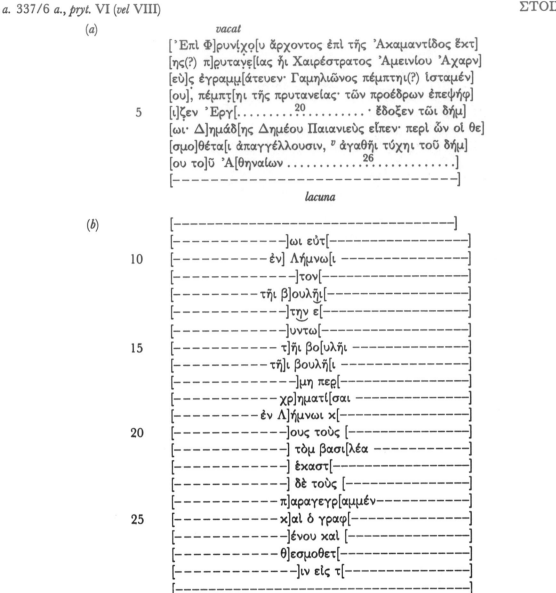

(a)   *vacat*

['Επὶ Φ]ρυνίχο[υ ἄρχοντος ἐπὶ τῆς 'Ακαμαντίδος ἕκτ]
[ης(?) π]ρυταγε[ίας ἧι Χαιρέστρατος 'Αμεινίου 'Αχαρν]
[εὺ]ς ἐγραμμ[άτευεν· Γαμηλιῶνος πέμπτηι(?) ἱσταμέν]
[ου], πέμπτ[ηι τῆς πρυτανείας· τῶν προέδρων ἐπεψήφ]
5   [ι]ζεν 'Εργ[.........20......... · ἔδοξεν τῶι δήμ]
[ωι· Δ]ημάδ[ης Δημέου Παιανιεὺς εἶπεν· περὶ ὧν οἱ θε]
[σμο]θέτα[ι ἀπαγγέλλουσιν, ᵛ ἀγαθῆι τύχηι τοῦ δήμ]
[ου το]ῦ 'Α[θηναίων ....26..............]
[–––––––––––––––––––––––––––––––––]

lacuna

(b)   [––––––––––––––––––––––––––––]
[–––––––––––––]ωι εὐτ[––––––––––––]
10   [–––––––– ἐν] Λήμνω[ι –––––––––––]
[–––––––––––]τον[––––––––––––]
[––––––––– τῆι β]ουλῆι[––––––––––]
[–––––––––––]την ε[––––––––––]
[–––––––––––]υντω[––––––––––]
15   [––––––– τ]ῆι βο[υλῆι –––––––––]
[–––––––– τῆ]ι βουλῆ[ι –––––––––]
[–––––––––––]μη περ[–––––––––]
[––––––– χρ]ηματί[σαι –––––––––]
[––––––– ἐν Λ]ήμνωι χ[–––––––––]
20   [–––––––––]ους τοὺς [–––––––––]
[–––––––––] τὸμ βασι[λέα ––––––––]
[–––––––––] ἕκαστ[–––––––––]
[–––––––––] δὲ τοὺς [–––––––––]
[––––––– π]αραγεγρ[αμμέν–––––––]
25   [––––––– χ]αὶ ὁ γραφ[–––––––––]
[–––––––––]ένου χαὶ [–––––––––]
[––––––– θ]εσμοθετ[–––––––––]
[–––––––––––]ιν εἰς τ[–––––––––]
[––––––––––––––––––––––––––]

Schwenk's text (other than in lines 1–3) follows that of Schweigert; she noted, however, that since the *editio princeps* the omicron in line 12 and the iota in line 16 had become illegible.

Line 8. [. . . .]ợα[– – – –] Schweigert; but what remains of the first letter indicates upsilon rather than sigma.

Lines 9–28. Schweigert's text placed seven letters to the right of what survives in line 9, with comparable estimates in the succeeding lines. The stone is so broken, however, as to give no indication where its edge came, nor did Schweigert note the basis for his so framing his textual arrangement.

The lettering is small, with a tendency to inexactitude. Fragment *b*, the first to be found, was on this score provisionally regarded as of the end of the century. M. B. Walbank has suggested (*per ep.*) that the inscribing of this stele was the work of the craftsman who produced *IG* II², 553, 581, and 606. The first of these was, in that context, dated by J. Kirchner "ca. a. 307", the latter two "fin. s. IV". If these dates are correct (and for *IG* II², 553 there is particularly good reason to accept a date in the last years of the century; cf. M. J. Osborne, *Naturalization* I, pp. 113–114, D 44, *Naturalization* II, pp. 117–120), the engraver survived the "Lykourgan period" and the period of Macedonian domination, to resume his activity with style unchanged under the restored democracy.

For the date, Schweigert suggested that this inscription may be taken with *IG* II², 239 (*SEG* XXXII, 78) and that both were passed on the same day. He proposed therefore in lines 3–4 Γαμηλιῶνος ἑβδόμηι ἱσταμένου, and in lines 1–2 ἐπὶ τῆς 'Ακαμαντίδος ἕκτης π]ρυταγε[ίας (Gamelion 7 = pryt. VI, 5 = 184th day). So also W. K. Pritchett and O. Neugebauer, *Calendars*, p. 42; Meritt, *Athenian Year*. J. D. Mikalson has demonstrated, however, that assemblies were not held on the seventh day of the month, this being sacred to Apollo; and he noted specifically that this equation merited revision (*Sacred and Civil Calendar*, pp. 99, 190). Revisions were attempted by Schwenk (*loc. cit.*) and by M. H. Hansen (*GRBS* 23, 1982, p. 342, no. 21 = *Athenian Ecclesia*, p. 94). For Hansen's solution, cf. the commentary above on the archonship of Phrynichos. He retained Schweigert's proposal in lines 1–2 and suggested πέμπτηι as the ordinal numeral in line 3 (Gamelion 5 = pryt. VI, 5 = 182nd day), with a reordering of the originally proposed succession of prytanies. Of the four possibilities that presented themselves to her, Schwenk preferred the restoration ὀγδόης in lines 1–2, and in lines 3–4 ᾿Ελαφηβολιῶνος ὀγδόηι ἐπὶ δέκα (18 Elaphebolion = pryt. VIII, 5 = 254th day). Slightly in favor of Hansen's proposal is the historical consideration that, in the wake of Philip II's conclusion of a peace treaty with the Athenians (see below), a revision of Athens' relations with Lemnos, in an area so vital to her interests, might plausibly be supposed to have taken place earlier rather than later, the more so since Demades the proposer had been closely involved in the treaty. If the decree, as nonprobouleumatic, arose from the assembly itself, this would further indicate early action prompted by popular demand. Schweigert's suggestion concerning *IG* II², 239 may in that case also stand.

On the preamble in general see A. S. Henry (*Prescripts*, pp. 37–38), who noted that the earliest example of an Athenian decree showing both name and day of the month is, on our evidence, *IG* II², 237, of the year previous to this.

Lines 5–6. ἔδοξεν τῶι δήμωι. As mentioned above, the decree (as restored) was nonprobouleumatic: see P. J. Rhodes, *Athenian Boule*, p. 261. Line 6. On Demades the well-known democratic politician see *PA* 3263; A. N. Oikonomides, Πλάτων 8, 1956, with this text listed among decrees proposed by him, p. 112, no. 2; Hansen, *Athenian Ecclesia II*, p. 40. On his activity in this year cf. Schwenk, *op. cit.*, pp. 29–30.

Lines 6–7. The body of the decree appears to be an implementation of recommendations by the thesmothetai, who seem to have been active in this year. Cf. *IG* II², 242. Lines 7–8. ἀγαθῆι τύχηι. This *Wunschformel* (cf. W. Larfeld, *Handbuch der griechischen Epigraphik* II, 1902, p. 665) appears as early as 378/7 (*IG* II², 43, line 7) but was now increasing in popularity. Since it was used in this year also in **73**, as well as in *IG* II², 240 and 241, its restoration in the present context is not unreasonable. Cf. A. G. Woodhead in *Ancient Macedonian Studies*, pp. 361–362.

Line 10. For a summary of Lemnian history at this period see *IG* XII, viii, *Praefatio de Lemno et Imbro*, p. 3. Lemnos was retained as an Athenian possession under the peace agreement with Philip II (who may be referred to in line 21) after the battle of Chaironeia (Diodorus Siculus 16.87; Demosthenes 18.285; cf. N. G. L. Hammond and G. T. Griffith, *A History of Macedonia* II, 1979, p. 607). Athenian involvement with Lemnos is epigraphically documented also in **41** and **68**, and, at a much later date, in **335**.

LAW OF EUKRATES CONCERNING ATTEMPTS TO ESTABLISH A TYRANNY

73. An almost complete, slightly tapering stele of white, apparently Pentelic, marble (I 6524) with a pedimental top, discovered on May 3, 1952, in the filling of the lawcourt building (the Square Peristyle) underlying the north end of the Stoa of Attalos (Q 9). The molding below the pediment retains traces of painted egg-and-dart decoration. Above the text, a sculptured group in low relief, set between antae, represents a seated, bearded male figure, to be identified as Demos, who faces left but makes a half-turn to the front and shows frontal head and shoulders, and standing behind his chair a draped frontal female figure, identified as Demokratia, who holds a wreath over his head with her right hand.

H. 1.57 m.; W. (upper) 0.41 m., (lower) 0.43 m.; Th. (upper) 0.010 m., (lower) 0.012 m.
LH. 0.005 m.
Στοιχ. (square) *ca.* 0.011 m.

Ed. B. D. Meritt, *Hesperia* 21, 1952, pp. 355–359, no. 5, with photographs pls. 89 and 90. See also *SEG* XII, 87 (with added reference to Meritt, *Hesperia* 22, 1953, p. 129).

SEG XV, 95 (R. E. Wycherley, *JHS* 75, 1955, pp. 118–121, on the topographical problem of lines 24–26); XVII, 26 (A. N. Oikonomides, Πολέμων 6, 1956/7, σύμμεικτα pp. 28–36, with photographs figs. 10, 11, on legislation against tyranny); XVIII, 12 (R. Sealey, *AJP* 79, 1958, pp. 71–73 = *Essays in Greek Politics*, 1967, pp. 183–185, on the political situation with especial reference to the Areopagos; M. Ostwald, *TAPA* 86, 1955, pp. 118–128, on the place of the law in the series of legislative attempts to prevent tyranny); XXIV, 96 (L. Braccesi, *Epigraphica* 27, 1965, pp. 110–126, on the political context, with text p. 111); XXXVI, 151; XXXVIII, 65.

Further, C. J. Schwenk, *Athens in the Age of Alexander*, pp. 33–41, no. 6 (text with bibliography, description, translation, and commentary especially on the powers of the Areopagos and on the nomothetai). Texts also in J. Pouilloux, *Choix d'inscriptions grecques*, 1960, pp. 121–124, no. 32, with translation into French; G. Pfohl, *Griechische Inschriften als Zeugnisse des privaten und öffentlichen Lebens*, 1966, pp. 114–117, no. 106, with translation into German, and p. 216 (bibliography). See in addition J. and L. Robert, *REG* 67, 1954, pp. 120–121, no. 76; M. Lang, *The Athenian Citizen* (A.P.B., no. 4), 1960, no. 29, and illustration on cover; H. Berve, *Die Tyrannis bei den Griechen*, 1967, pp. 303–304 and 676; C. Mossé, *Athens in Decline, 404–86 B.C.*, 1973, pp. 76–79 (and in *Eirene* 8, 1970, pp. 71–78); M. Guarducci,

Epigrafia Greca II, 1969, pp. 59–61; *Agora Guide*[3], p. 188, with photograph p. 187; J. M. Camp, *Athenian Agora*, pp. 154–156, with photograph fig. 128.

The stele has been frequently illustrated; see for example *AJA* 57, 1953, pl. 29, fig. 7; *BCH* 77, 1953, p. 203, fig. 10; *Fasti Archaeologici* VII, 1952, p. 111, fig. 25; *JHS* 73, 1953, pl. I:i; U. Hausmann, *Griechische Weihreliefs*, 1960, pls. 21, 22 (cf. pp. 43–44); Guarducci, *vol. cit.*, p. 60, fig. 7 (relief only); *Agora* XIV, pl. 53:a; A. G. Woodhead, *Study of Greek Inscriptions*, pl. 3.

On the Demos-Demokratia symbolism see A. E. Raubitschek, *Hesperia* 31, 1962, pp. 238–243; *Agora* XIV, p. 102.

a. 337/6 *a.*, *pryt.* IX   ΣΤΟΙΧ. 36

         Ἐπὶ Φρυνίχου ἄρχοντος ἐπὶ τῆς Λεωντίδος ἐν
         άτης πρυτανείας ἧι Χαιρέστρατος Ἀμεινίου
         Ἀχαρνεὺς ἐγραμμάτευεν· τῶν προέδρων ἐπεψή
         φιζεν Μενέστρατος Αἰξωνεύς· Εὐκράτης Ἀρισ
    5   τοτίμου Πειραιεὺς εἶπεν· ἀγαθῆι τύχηι τοῦ δ
         ήμου τοῦ Ἀθηναίων, δεδόχθαι τοῖς νομοθέται
         ς· ἐάν τις ἐπαναστῆι τῶι δήμωι ἐπὶ τυραννίδι
         ἢ τὴν τυραννίδα συνκαταστήσηι ἢ τὸν δῆμον τ
         ὸν Ἀθηναίων ἢ τὴν δημοκρατίαν τὴν Ἀθήνησιν
    10   καταλύσηι, ὃς ἂν τὸν τούτων τι ποιήσαντα ἀπο
         κτείνηι ὅσιος ἔστω· μὴ ἐξεῖναι δὲ τῶν βουλευ
         τῶν τῶν τῆς βουλῆς τῆς ἐξ Ἀρείου Πάγου καταλ
         ελυ⟨μ⟩ένου τοῦ δήμου ἢ τῆς δημοκρατίας τῆς Ἀθ
         ήνησιν ἀνιέναι εἰς Ἄρειον Πάγον μηδὲ συνκα
    15   θίζειν ἐν τῶι συνεδρίωι μηδὲ βουλεύειν μη
         δὲ περὶ ἑνός· ἐὰν δέ τις τοῦ δήμου ἢ τῆς δημοκρ
         ατίας καταλελυμένων τῶν Ἀθήνησιν ἀνίηι τῶ
         ν βουλευτῶν τῶν ἐξ Ἀρείου Πάγου εἰς Ἄρειον Π
         άγον ἢ συνκαθίζηι ἐν τῶι συνεδρίωι ἢ βολεύη
    20   ι περί τινος ἄτιμος ἔστω καὶ αὐτὸς καὶ γένος
         τὸ ἐξ ἐκείνου, καὶ ἡ οὐσία δημοσία ἔστω αὐτοῦ
         καὶ τῆς θεοῦ τὸ ἐπιδέκατον· ἀναγράψαι δὲ τόν
         δε τὸν νόμον ἐν στήλαις λιθίναις δυοῖν τὸν γ
         ραμματέα τῆς βουλῆς καὶ στῆσαι τὴμ μὲν ἐπὶ τ
    25   ῆς εἰσόδου τῆς εἰς Ἄρειον Πάγον τῆς εἰς τὸ βο
         υλευτήριον εἰσιόντι, τὴν δὲ ἐν τῆι ἐκκλησία
         ι· εἰς δὲ τὴν ἀναγραφὴν τῶν στηλῶν τὸν ταμίαν
         δοῦναι τοῦ δήμου :ΔΔ: δραχμὰς ἐκ τῶν κατὰ ψη
         φίσματα ἀναλισκομένων τῶι δήμωι.   *vacat*
                                vacat

In lines 10, 12, 13 (twice), 18, 21, 26, and 27 the cross-stroke of alpha has been omitted; in line 11 the cross-stroke of tau has been omitted in the first word; in line 13 the fourth letter was written as nu; at the beginning of line 15 ΙΕΙΝ was inscribed in five letter spaces.

The letters have a backward tilt, and the text either was not accurately planned or was executed in some haste, for the stoichedon spacing shows slight irregularities. Otherwise, the lettering by being securely dated provides a useful standard for purposes of comparison. The "free ends" of some letters tend to be emphasized; beta is less clumsily cut than in **72**. The now old-fashioned O for OY occurs as a "sporadic survival" in line 19: cf. L. Threatte, *Grammar*, p. 256.

Two unsuccessful attempts were made to dismember the stele before it was buried, but both cuttings fortunately occur above the inscribed text.

Lines 3–4. P. J. Rhodes (*Athenian Boule*, p. 28) urged that the πρόεδροι are the πρόεδροι τῶν νομοθετῶν, not the πρόεδροι of the boule and the ecclesia, but that the two sets of πρόεδροι differed was disputed by M. H. Hansen (*ZPE* 30, 1978, pp. 151–157). Lines 5–6. ἀγαθῆι τύχηι. See **72**, commentary on lines 7–8. Lines 6–7. The law was a *nomos* produced by the nomothetai. Cf. **56** and **57**, and Hansen, *GRBS* 20, 1979, p. 39 (= *Athenian Ecclesia*, p. 191). On the functions and procedures of the nomothetai in 4th-century Athens see Busolt-Swoboda, II, 1926, pp. 1011–1014;

U. Kahrstedt, *Klio* 31, 1938, pp. 1–25 (esp. pp. 1–6): Rhodes, *Athenian Boule*, pp. 49–52 and *CQ* n.s. 35, 1985, pp. 55–60; Hansen, *Classica et Medievalia* 32, 1979–1980, pp. 87–104; D. M. McDowell, *JHS* 95, 1975, pp. 62–74; Hansen, *GRBS* 26, 1985, pp. 345–371. On the enactment formula cf. Rhodes, *Athenian Boule*, p. 276.

Lines 11 *et seqq.* The Areopagos had in recent years acquired revived prestige and importance. See Ostwald, *op. cit.*, pp. 125–127; Schwenk, *Athens in the Age of Alexander*, p. 37. The precise connotations of *synedrion* and *bouleuterion* in this context have been disputed. Wycherley (*loc. cit.*; *Agora* III, p. 127) regarded *synedrion* as a flexible word appropriate to any place of meeting of the body specified, here probably the meeting place of the Areopagites on the "Hill of Mars" itself, to which in this context *bouleuterion* would also refer. H. A. Thompson (*Hesperia* 22, 1953, pp. 51–53) referred the terms to the Old Bouleuterion in the Agora, a reference that did not convince Rhodes (*Athenian Boule*, p. 32).

Eukrates, the proposer of the law (cf. Hansen, *Athenian Ecclesia II*, p. 46), was known before the discovery of the stele only from a reference in Lucian (*Demosthenis Encomium* 31); J. Kirchner (*PA* 5762) was prepared to doubt his very existence ("de Luciani fide dubitandum est"). Lucian's reliability in this detail was, however, vindicated by the present text. For the historical circumstances of the law see Ostwald, *op. cit.* and H. Bengtson, *Griechische Geschichte*, 5th ed., 1977, p. 335. There was evident apprehension among democrats that coups d'état in the Macedonian interest might take place even though participants in the League of Corinth undertook mutual guarantees to preserve existing constitutions. The author of [Demosthenes] 17 implies that fears of this nature were not without justification.

The excellent state of preservation of the stele, and the situation in which it was found, suggest that the law was not long in operation. Meritt regarded it as "quite probable that the law and the man who moved it perished simultaneously in 322 B.C." (*Hesperia* 21, 1952, p. 359).

Lines 23–24. The identity of the γραμματεὺς τῆς βουλῆς with the γραμματεὺς ὁ κατὰ πρυτανείαν, generally accepted (see Rhodes, *Athenian Boule*, pp. 136–137, and cf. p. 138, note 6), has been disputed by S. Alessandri (*Annali della Scuola Normale di Pisa*, pp. 15–32). Lines 27–29. The order of words, with δοῦναι inserted between τὸν ταμίαν and τοῦ δήμου, is of interest. On the treasurer, the "analiskomena fund", and the specified cost, see A. S. Henry, *Chiron* 12, 1982, pp. 97–118 and the commentaries on **40** and **45**.

On the historical circumstances and interpretation of the law of Eukrates see also R. W. Wallace, *The Areopagos Council to 307 B.C.*, 1989, pp. 179–184 (and on lines 16–20, p. 218) and *SEG* XXXIX, 80.

THE ARCHONSHIP OF PYTHODELOS, 336/5 B.C.

Apart from **74**, four other decrees of this year are known: *IG* II^2, 328 (*SEG* XXI, 268, XXXI, 271, XXXII, 79) of pryt. IV, 329 (*SEG* XXXV, 66, containing no date but assigned on historical grounds), 330, lines 29–46 attributed to pryt. IX and 330, lines 47–65 attributed to pryt. X. Cf. C. J. Schwenk (*Athens in the Age of Alexander*, pp. 72–94), who includes the first of these (as no. 15, pp. 72–79); but she also assigns **75** specifically to Pythodelos' year.

The year was intercalary in the Athenian calendar, beginning with a hollow month and ending with two full months according to the reconstruction of B. D. Meritt (*Athenian Year*, pp. 10–15 and 78–79). Meritt attributed 39 days to pryt. I, II, VIII, and IX, 38 to the remainder. For different interpretations see W. K. Pritchett and O. Neugebauer, *Calendars*, pp. 43–44 (discussed by Schwenk, *Athens in the Age of Alexander*, pp. 76–77) and M. H. Hansen, *GRBS* 23, 1982, p. 343, no. 24 (= *Athenian Ecclesia*, p. 95). The latter has to suppose that the omitted day in a "hollow" month was the 29th (which was also the contention of Pritchett); but this supposition cannot now be maintained. On the question of the "omitted day" see A. G. Woodhead, *Study of Greek Inscriptions*, pp. 121–122 and literature cited there; also J. A. Walsh, *ZPE* 41, 1981, pp. 107–124; Schwenk, *op. cit.*, pp. 154–156.

Known phylai in prytany are IV Akamantis and IX Aigeis or Oineis. The name of the γραμματεύς of the year, from Kekropis, remains unknown; expressed in full, it contained nineteen letters (*IG* II^2, 328, line 3). See S. Alessandri, *Annali della Scuola Normale di Pisa*, pp. 50, 63. For a detailed list of those known to have held public office during Pythodelos' archonship see R. Develin, *Athenian Officials*, pp. 363–372.

FRAGMENT OF A DECREE

74. A fragment of a stele of Pentelic marble (I 4899), broken all around except perhaps at the back, which is rough, discovered on May 19, 1937, in a context of Byzantine date over the Post-Herulian Wall on the North Slope of the Akropolis (T 26). The beginning of the spring of the crowning molding of the monument is visible above the first line of text. Later reuse has caused a rebate cut to be made below line 4, slightly damaging the letters of that line.

H. 0.11 m.; W. 0.07 m.; Th. 0.10 m.
LH. 0.006–0.007 m.

Ed. B. D. Meritt, *Hesperia* 26, 1957, pp. 207–208, no. 54, with photograph pl. 52. See also *SEG* XVII, 27. C. J. Schwenk (*Athens in the Age of Alexander*, pp. 79–80, no. 16) reproduces Meritt's text with a brief description.

a. 336/5 a.   NON-ΣΤΟΙΧ. *ca.* 37–40

$$
\begin{array}{l}
[\text{'}Ἐπὶ\ Πυ]θοδή[λου\ ἄρχοντος\ ἐπὶ\ τῆς\ \underset{ca.\ 11-13}{\ldots\ldots}.] \\
[\underset{ca.\ 5}{\ldots}.]ς\ πρυτ[ανείας\ ἧι\ \underset{19-21}{\ldots\ldots\ldots\ldots\ldots}.] \\
[ἐγραμ]μάτευ[εν\cdot\ ----\ ὦνος----------] \\
[\underset{ca.\ 5}{\ldots}.]ι\ καὶ\ εἰ[κοστεῖ\ τῆς\ πρυτανείας\cdot\ \underset{ca.\ 7-9}{\ldots\ldots}.] \\
[------------------------------]
\end{array}
$$

5

The lettering shows slight emphasis on "free ends" in upsilon but is generally somewhat poor for its period.

LAW PROVIDING REGULAR FUNDS FOR CELEBRATION OF THE LESSER PANATHENAIA

75 (Pl. 7). A fragment of a stele of Pentelic marble (I 5477), broken all around save for the rough-picked back and the top, where part of a double flat molding is preserved. It was brought into the Agora by a taxicab driver on May 27, 1938, from the neighborhood of Evangelistria Street. It forms the upper part of the substantial record of which *IG* II^2, 334 is a lower section, but there is no join between the two pieces.

H. 0.326 m.; W. 0.37 m.; Th. 0.111 m.
LH. (line 1) 0.012 m.; (line 2) 0.009 m.; (lines 3 and thereafter) 0.005 m.
Στοιχ. (except lines 1 and 2) 0.0103 m. (square).

Ed. D. M. Lewis, *Hesperia* 28, 1959, pp. 239–247, with photograph pl. 43; see also *SEG* XVIII, 13 (which includes a reference to J. and L. Robert, *REG* 73, 1960, p. 153, no. 131); C. J. Schwenk, *Athens in the Age of Alexander*, pp. 81–94, no. 17.

SEG XXI, 269 (L. Robert, *Hellenica* XI/XII, 1960, pp. 189–203, on the location of the territory described as ἡ Νέα); XXV, 65 (F. Sokolowski, *Lois sacrées*, pp. 63–66, no. 33, giving full text of both fragments, with bibliography and commentary). The full text also given by H. W. Pleket, *Epigraphica* 1, 1964, pp. 38–39, no. 25. Since this document involves the leasing of public land, the text is also included by M. B. Walbank in *Agora* XIX at L7, where its contents are discussed in that connection. See also D. Behrend, *Attische Pachturkunden*, pp. 63–67, no. 13 and *SEG* XXXVI, 152.

For the year see Lewis, *op. cit.*, p. 240, who regards 336/5 or 335/4 as best suited to the data of line 2 (Pythodelos or Euainetos as archons). The historical circumstances (cf. L. Robert, *loc. cit.*) appear to suggest a date not long after 338/7, and Schwenk opted firmly for the year 336/5. Sokolowski left the issue more open (335/4–330/29). A date between 336 and 330, perhaps earlier rather than later within that span, seems to be called for, and the law relates well with the program of Lykourgos, for which cf. F. W. Mitchel, *Greece and Rome*, ser. 2, 12, 1965, p. 196 and *Lykourgan Athens, 338–322* (Lectures in Memory of Louise Taft Semple, second series), 1970, pp. 35–36.

I 5477 is here designated fragment *a*; the text of *IG* II^2, 334 is added for convenience, and the line numeration is made continuous. Line 1 is inscribed on the upper of the two crowning moldings.

paullo post a. 337 a.   ΣΤΟΙΧ. 42

(a)

$$
\begin{array}{l}
[Θ\qquad ε]\qquad ο\qquad [ι]. \\
[\text{'}Ἐ\ π\ ὶ\ \ldots\underset{ca.\ 9}{\ldots}\ ἄ]\ ρ\ χ\ ο\ ν\ τ\ ο\ ς, \\
[\ldots\ldots\underset{16}{\ldots\ldots}\ldots\ldots]σ[\ldots]\cdot\ \text{'}Ἀριστόνικος\ \text{'}Ἀρι[στοτέλο] \\
[υς\ Μαραθώνιος\ εἶπ]εν\cdot\ τύχηι\ ἀγαθῆι\ τοῦ\ δήμου\ [τοῦ\ \text{'}Ἀθη] \\
[ναίων,\ ὅπως\ ἂν\ τῆι]\ \text{'}Ἀθηνᾶι\ ἡ\ θυσία\ ὡς\ κάλλιστ[η\ ἧι\ Πανα] \\
[θηναίοις\ τοῖς\ μ]ικροῖς\ καὶ\ πρόσοδος\ ὡς\ πλεί[στη\ \ldots] \\
[\ldots\ldots\underset{12}{\ldots\ldots}]ις,\ δεδόχθαι\ τοῖς\ νομοθέτ[α]ι[ς\cdot\ τὴν\ μὲν] \\
[Νέαν\ μισθούτω]σαν\ δέκα\ ἡμέραις\ πρότερον\ γ[\ldots\underset{7}{\ldots}.] \\
[οἱ\ πωληταὶ\ δέκ](α)\ ἔτη\ κατὰ\ διχληρίαν\ τῶι\ τὸ\ π[\ldots\underset{7}{\ldots}.] \\
[\ldots\underset{7}{\ldots}\ τῶι\ πρ]οτέρωι\ ἔτει\ ἢ\ ὧι\ ἂν\ ἡ\ ΔΑ[.]ΑΝΤΙ[\ldots\underset{7}{\ldots}.] \\
[\ldots\underset{10}{\ldots\ldots}\ μι]σθωταῖς\ ἐγγυητὰς\ λαμβάνου[σι\cdot\ τοὺς\ δ]
\end{array}
$$

5

10

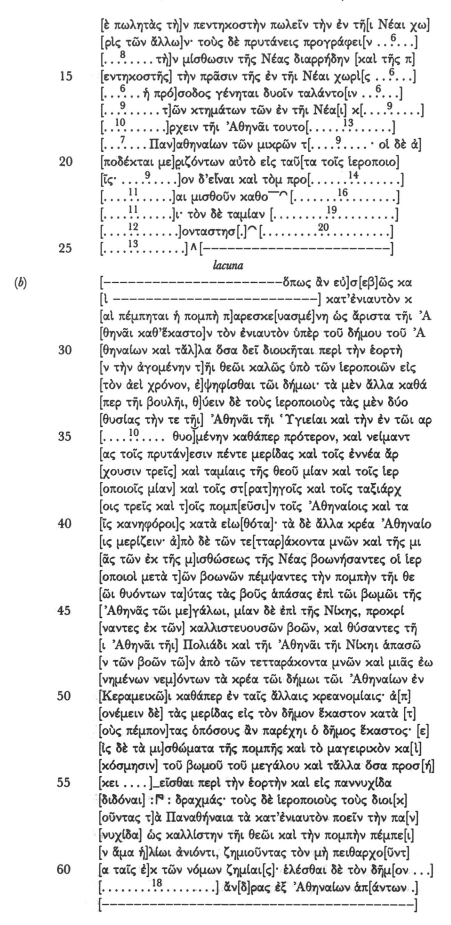

[ὲ πωλητὰς τὴ]ν πεντηκοστὴν πωλεῖν τὴν ἐν τῆ[ι Νέαι χω]

[ρὶς τῶν ἄλλω]ν· τοὺς δὲ πρυτάνεις προγράφει[ν …⁶…]

[…⁸…. τὴ]ν μίσθωσιν τῆς Νέας διαρρήδην [καὶ τῆς π]

15 [εντηκοστῆς] τὴν πρᾶσιν τῆς ἐν τῆι Νέαι χωρὶ[ς …⁶…]

[…⁶…. ἡ πρό]σοδος γένηται δυοῖν ταλάντο[ιν …⁶…]

[…⁹…. τ]ῶν κτημάτων τῶν ἐν τῆι Νέα[ι] x[….⁹….]

[..¹⁰……]ρχειν τῆι Ἀθηνᾶι τουτο[……¹³……]

[…⁷…. Παν]αθηναίων τῶν μικρῶν τ[….⁹…. · οἱ δὲ ἀ]

20 [ποδέκται με]ριζόντων αὐτὸ εἰς ταῦ[τα τοῖς ἱεροποιο]

[ῖς· …⁹…]ον δ᾽εἶναι καὶ τὸμ προ[……¹⁴……]

[….¹¹…..]αι μισθοῦν καθο⎯⌒[…….¹⁶…….]

[….¹¹…..]ι· τὸν δὲ ταμίαν […….¹⁹…….]

[….¹²….]ονταστησ[.]⌒[…….²⁰…….]

25 [….¹³……] ∧[————————————————]

lacuna

(b)   [———————————————ὅπως ἂν εὐ]σ[εβ]ῶς κα

[ι ————————————————] κατ᾽ἐνιαυτὸν x

[αὶ πέμπηται ἡ πομπὴ π]αρεσκε[υασμέ]νη ὡς ἄριστα τῆι Ἀ

[θηνᾶι καθ᾽ἕκαστο]ν τὸν ἐνιαυτὸν ὑπὲρ τοῦ δήμου τοῦ Ἀ

30 [θηναίων καὶ τἄλ]λα ὅσα δεῖ διοικῆται περὶ τὴν ἑορτὴ

[ν τὴν ἀγομένην τ]ῆι θεῶι καλῶς ὑπὸ τῶν ἱεροποιῶν εἰς

[τὸν ἀεὶ χρόνον, ἐ]ψηφίσθαι τῶι δήμωι· τὰ μὲν ἄλλα καθά

[περ τῆι βουλῆι, θ]ύειν δὲ τοὺς ἱεροποιοὺς τὰς μὲν δύο

[θυσίας τήν τε τῆι] Ἀθηνᾶι τῆι Ὑγιείαι καὶ τὴν ἐν τῶι ἀρ

35 [….¹⁰…. θυο]μένην καθάπερ πρότερον, καὶ νείμαντ

[ας τοῖς πρυτάν]εσιν πέντε μερίδας καὶ τοῖς ἐννέα ἄρ

[χουσιν τρεῖς] καὶ ταμίαις τῆς θεοῦ μίαν καὶ τοῖς ἱερ

[οποιοῖς μίαν] καὶ τοῖς στ[ρατ]ηγοῖς καὶ τοῖς ταξιάρχ

[οις τρεῖς καὶ τ]οῖς πομπ[εῦσι]ν τοῖς Ἀθηναίοις καὶ τα

40 [ῖς κανηφόροι]ς κατὰ εἰω[θότα]· τὰ δὲ ἄλλα κρέα Ἀθηναίο

[ις μερίζειν· ἀ]πὸ δὲ τῶν τε[τταρ]άκοντα μνῶν καὶ τῆς μι

[ᾶς τῶν ἐκ τῆς μ]ισθώσεως τῆς Νέας βοωνήσαντες οἱ ἱερ

[οποιοὶ μετὰ τ]ῶν βοωνῶν πέμψαντες τὴν πομπὴν τῆι θε

[ῶι θυόντων τα]ύτας τὰς βοῦς ἁπάσας ἐπὶ τῶι βωμῶι τῆς

45 [Ἀθηνᾶς τῶι με]γάλωι, μίαν δὲ ἐπὶ τῆς Νίκης, προκρί

[ναντες ἐκ τῶν] καλλιστευουσῶν βοῶν, καὶ θύσαντες τῆ

[ι Ἀθηνᾶι τῆι] Πολιάδι καὶ τῆι Ἀθηνᾶι τῆι Νίκηι ἁπασῶ

[ν τῶν βοῶν τῶ]ν ἀπὸ τῶν τετταράκοντα μνῶν καὶ μιᾶς ἑω

[νημένων νεμ]όντων τὰ κρέα τῶι δήμωι τῶι Ἀθηναίων ἐν

50 [Κεραμεικῶ]ι καθάπερ ἐν ταῖς ἄλλαις κρεανομίαις· ἀ[π]

[ονέμειν δὲ] τὰς μερίδας εἰς τὸν δῆμον ἕκαστον κατὰ [τ]

[οὺς πέμπον]τας ὁπόσους ἂν παρέχηι ὁ δῆμος ἕκαστος· [ε]

[ἰς δὲ τὰ μι]σθώματα τῆς πομπῆς καὶ τὸ μαγειρικὸν κα[ὶ]

[κόσμησιν] τοῦ βωμοῦ τοῦ μεγάλου καὶ τἄλλα ὅσα προσή]

55 [κει ….]_εῖσθαι περὶ τὴν ἑορτὴν καὶ εἰς παννυχίδα

[διδόναι] :Ϝ: δραχμάς· τοὺς δὲ ἱεροποιοὺς τοὺς διοι[κ]

[οῦντας τ]ὰ Παναθήναια τὰ κατ᾽ἐνιαυτὸν ποεῖν τὴν πα[ν]

[νυχίδα] ὡς καλλίστην τῆι θεῶι καὶ τὴν πομπὴν πέμπε[ι]

[ν ἅμα ἡ]λίωι ἀνιόντι, ζημιοῦντας τὸν μὴ πειθαρχο[ῦντ]

60 [α ταῖς ἐ]κ τῶν νόμων ζημίαι[ς]· ἑλέσθαι δὲ τὸν δῆμ[ον …]

[………¹⁸………] ἄν[δ]ρας ἐξ Ἀθηναίων ἀπ[άντων .]

[————————————————————————]

Line 2. ἄ]ρχοντος ‒‒‒‒‒ Sokolowski; but the stone is uninscribed after the sigma. Line 3. The traces in the seventeenth letter space are those of sigma rather than of any other letter, as Lewis and E. Vanderpool observed; but no plausible supplement conforms with known formulas in the prescript. Line 4. τύχηι ἀγαθῆι. See **72**, commentary on lines 7–8. Lines 6–7. ὡς πλεί[στη γέν|ηται ἱεροποιο]ῖς Lewis, Walbank, Schwenk; ὡς πλεί[στη ἐγλ|εχθῆι τοῖς θεο]ῖς Sokolowski. Lines 8–9. γ[.... οἱ π|ωληταὶ εἰς δέκ](α) ἔτη Sokolowski; in line 8 Ν[εμεσίων] was Lewis' tentative proposal. Line 9. ΛΕΤΗ on the stone; an error is to be presumed. Lewis compared Aristotle, *Athenaion Politeia* 47.4. Lines 9–10. τῶι τὸ π[λεῖστον|| διδόντι κτλ.] Lewis, Walbank, Schwenk; τῶι τὸ π[ρόδομα σ||υνθέντι κτλ.] Sokolowski. Line 10. ἡ λᾶ[ς] ἀντι[μισθωθῆ]ι Sokolowski, who cited Hypereides 3.16 and continued καὶ ἄλλοις μι]σθωταῖς.

Lines 11–13. *supplevit* Lewis. Lines 13–14. προγράφει[ν βουλῆς | ἕδραν εἰς τὴ]ν μίσθωσιν Lewis (who compared the restoration in *IG* II², 244, lines 36–37), Walbank, Schwenk; προγράφει[ν ἐν τῆι β]ουλῆι καὶ τὴ]ν μίσθωσιν A. M. Woodward *apud* Lewis; προγράφει[ν ἐν στήλ]αιν δυοῖν τὴ]ν μίσθωσιν Sokolowski. Lines 15–18. χωρὶ[ς τῶν ἄλλ|ων, ἐὰν δὲ πρό]σοδος γένηται δυοῖν ταλάντο[ιν κατὰ ἐν|ιαυτὸν ἀπὸ τ]ῶν κτημάτων τῶν ἐν τῆι Νέα[ι] κ[αὶ τῆς πεντ|ηκοστῆς, ὑπά]ρχειν τῆι Ἀθηνᾶι· τοῦτο κτλ. was Lewis' preference between two suggestions hesitantly put forward in his commentary. He urged that a full stop after Ἀθηνᾶι is to be desired, and this is included in their texts by Walbank and Schwenk. χωρὶ[ς ἑκάστην·| ὅταν δὲ ἡ πρό]σοδος γένηται δυοῖν ταλάντο[ιν ...⁶... |...⁷... ἐκ τ]ῶν κτημάτων τῶν ἐν τῆι Νέαι κ[αὶ τῆς πεντ|ηκοστῆς ὑπά]ρχειν τῆι Ἀθηνᾶι· Sokolowski, who continues τοῦτο [ἀναλῶσαι εἰς τὴ|ν θυσίαν Παν]αθηναίων κτλ. Lines 19–25. The text is that of Lewis. Line 21. [ῖς· διαλογισμ]ὸν δ'εἶναι καὶ τῶμ προ[τέρων προσόδων] Sokolowski. Line 22. μισθοῦν καθότ[ι ‒‒‒‒] Sokolowski.

Lines 26–61. The text follows *Syll.*³, 271, which is adopted also by Sokolowski and Schwenk. Both give further bibliographical references for *IG* II², 334. Lines 34–35. See *IG* II², 334, where ἐν τῶι ἀρ[χαίωι νεῶι is the adopted reading; Ἀρ[είωι Πάγωι A. R. Rangabé; Ἀρ[χηγετίδος Sokolowski; ἀρ[ρηφορείωι, although with hesitation, S. C. Humphreys in *The Craft of the Ancient Historian: Studies in Honor of Chester G. Starr*, J. W. Eadie and J. Ober, edd., 1985, pp. 228–229 (cf. *SEG* XXXV, 68). See also C. J. Herington, *Athena Parthenos and Athena Polias*, 1955, p. 10. Line 55. πρ]ονοεῖσθαι Sokolowski. "Dubito num prima littera fuerit O", J. Kirchner in *IG* II². See also the commentary of Schwenk, *loc. cit.*, p. 89.

Since this document concerns the leasing of state property, it falls within the category of material dealt with by Walbank in *Agora* XIX, where it appears as L7. Little therefore need be added here to the commentary and discussion in that context. Walbank is of the opinion (*per ep.*) that the hand at work in the inscribing of it may be that of the craftsman who also worked on **57** as well as on one of the fragments from the North Slope of the Akropolis (E.M. 13395) edited by R. S. Stroud (*Hesperia* 40, 1971, p. 192, no. 41).

Lines 3–4. Aristonikos is to be identified with the well-known politician (*PA* 2028) who was a colleague of Lykourgos (cf. *IG* II², 1623, lines 280–283) and who perished after the Lamian War together with Eukrates and others (see **73** and Lucian, *Demosthenis Encomium* 31). Cf. M. H. Hansen, *GRBS* 25, 1984, pp. 132, 147 (= *Athenian Ecclesia II*, pp. 102, 117) and *Athenian Ecclesia II*, p. 37. Lewis judged that Alexis, fragments 125–126 (Kock) refer to the same man. That his father's name is to be restored as Aristoteles, and that this Aristoteles may have been the proposer of *IG* II², 43, the so-called Charter of the Second Athenian Confederacy, was a suggestion made to Lewis by Woodward.

Line 7. The decree was primarily a *nomos* enacted by the nomothetai. On the procedure of *nomothesia* see **73**, commentary on lines 6–7 and the references cited there. In this particular case a vote of the assembly is also involved (line 33). Hansen (*GRBS* 20, 1979, pp. 34–35 [= *Athenian Ecclesia*, pp. 186–187]) suggested that the *psephisma* was inscribed below the *nomos* "because the enactment of the demos was referred to the nomothetai and ratified by them." Lines 7–8. Lewis observed in his *editio princeps* (pp. 242–243) that what is described in the text as "the Nea" was a specific area of state-owned land. L. Robert (*Hellenica* XI/XII, 1960, pp. 189–203) urged that as "New Territory" it consisted of land forming part of what had previously been the territory of Oropos, bestowed on Athens by Philip II after Chaironeia as compensation for the loss of the Thracian Chersonese and justifiably designated as new land. This determination, which found general acceptance (but see Lewis, *Hesperia* 37, 1968, p. 374, note 18), confirmed the dating of the inscription (see above). However, in his edition of **84** (*q.v.*), M. K. Langdon (*Hesperia* 56, 1987, pp. 54–58; cf. *SEG* XXXVII, 79) challenged this view of the Nea and suggested the alternative interpretation that it was the island of the same name, which Pliny the Elder (*HN* 2.89) described as having arisen out of the sea between Lemnos and the Hellespont. It subsequently disappeared and survives at the present time in the form of a reef below sea level.

For this enactment in the context of the financial administration of Lykourgos see also Humphreys, *op. cit.*, pp. 202–203, 209 and *SEG* XXXV, 238. For a suggestion that it is to be dated to 341/40 see *SEG* XXXIX, 88. The sacrifices involved have also merited further discussion; see *SEG* XLII, 92.

THE ARCHONSHIP OF EUAINETOS, 335/4 B.C.

Apart from **76**, decrees attributable to this year are *IG* II², 330 + 445, of pryt. III, 331 (*SEG* XXI, 270; cf. M. H. Hansen, *GRBS* 23, 1982, p. 343, no. 27 = *Athenian Ecclesia*, p. 95), 333 (*SEG* XVI, 53, XXI, 271, XXXI, 78), and *SEG* XXI, 272, all of pryt. X, and perhaps *IG* II², 363 (*SEG* XII, 89, XXI, 281, XXIII, 53, XXV, 66), of an unknown prytany (not III, V, or X). The first three of these were reedited with commentary by C. J. Schwenk (*Athens in the Age of Alexander*, pp. 95–128) as nos. 18, 22, and 21 respectively; the last of them she placed in 326/5 (pp. 322–333, no. 67). *IG* II², 332, placed here by J. Kirchner following G. F. Unger, is better located earlier in the century. W. K. Pritchett and O. Neugebauer (*Calendars*, p. 45) restored it *exempli gratia* in terms applicable to 353/2. Cf. Schwenk, *op. cit.*, pp. 106–108, no. 20.

The year was ordinary in the Athenian calendar, containing 355 days. See B. D. Meritt, *Athenian Year*, pp. 79–82, where the calendric data from the texts listed above are transcribed, and *TAPA* 95, 1964, pp. 213–217; Pritchett and Neugebauer, *op. cit.*, pp. 44–45. The lunar months alternated hollow and full in almost regular succession save that at some point two full months came together. The prytanies (5 × 36 and 5 × 35) followed the pattern described by Aristotle (*Athenaion Politeia* 43.2), with the variation that besides pryt. I–IV one other prytany (but not the tenth) contained 36 days.

Known prytanies of the year are III Erechtheis or Kekropis, V Akamantis, X Antiochis. On the γραμματεύς Proxenos, son of Pylagoras (*PA* 12271), see also S. Alessandri, *Annali della Scuola Normale di Pisa*, pp. 50 and 63–64. A detailed list of those known to have held office in 335/4 is provided by R. Develin (*Athenian Officials*, pp. 372–379).

FRAGMENT OF A DECREE

76 (Pl. 7). A fragment of a stele of Pentelic marble (I 3960), with rough-picked back and remains of a plain molding above the inscribed face preserved, but otherwise broken, discovered on April 2, 1936, in a modern wall in the northeast corner of the Market Square, south of the Athens–Piraeus railway tracks (O 6).

H. 0.285 m.; W. 0.36 m.; Th. 0.148 m.
LH. 0.008 m. (omicron smaller).
Στοιχ. (slightly irregular) Hor. *ca.* 0.016 m.; Vert. *ca.* 0.0164 m.

Ed. E. Schweigert, *Hesperia* 9, 1940, pp. 327–328, no. 36, with photograph: see also C. J. Schwenk, *Athens in the Age of Alexander*, pp. 105–106, no. 19 (cf. *SEG* XXXV, 67). Lines 1–5 quoted by B. D. Meritt, *Athenian Year*, pp. 79–80; the calendar equation cited by W. K. Pritchett and O. Neugebauer, *Calendars*, p. 44.

a. 335/4 *a.*, *pryt.* V   ΣΤΟΙΧ. 26

```
        ['Επὶ Εὐα]ινέτου ἄρχοντος ἐπὶ τῆ[ς]
        ['Ακαμαν]τίδος πέμπτης πρυτανε[ί]
        [ας ἧι Πρόξ]ενος Π[υλα]γόρου 'Αχερ[δ]
        [ούσιος ἐ]γραμμάτ[ευ]εν· Ποσειδε[ῶ]
   5    [νος ἐνδεκ]άτει· τῶ[ν π]ροέδρων ἐ[πε]
        [ψήφιζε Νι]κοκλ[ῆς] 'Ραμνούσιος. vv
                      vacat
        [....⁹....]η[...]υ Παιανιε[ὺς εἶπ]
        [εν· .....¹².....]εν^[....⁹....]
        [.......¹⁴.......]τ[....¹¹.....]
   10   [--------------------]
```

Line 7. [....⁹....]N[....] Παιανιε[ὺς Schweigert. Line 8. εν[....¹⁰....] Schweigert. Line 9. [.....¹¹.....] π[ρό]τ[ερον ...⁷...] Schweigert. Tau is certain in the fifteenth letter space, but the pi is more doubtful. The uninscribed space between lines 6 and 7 is less than the height of an omitted regular line of writing. Schwenk noted that she was unable to read the first two surviving letters of line 1, the initial tau in line 2, the iota in line 5, and (cf. above) Schweigert's pi in line 9.

The surface of the lower part of the text has been worn smooth, and the lettering as now surviving does not appear deeply cut. It is, however, generally well spaced and neat; omicron (which is "suspended" from the upper lettering line) is an exception in showing some clumsiness.

Lines 4–5. For Posideon 11 as a well-attested day for the meeting of the assembly cf. **78** and J. D. Mikalson, *Sacred and Civil Calendar*, pp. 89–90. The date by prytany is not given; cf. *IG* II², 333, 335 and A. S. Henry, *Prescripts*, p. 38 with note 29. Line 6. Nikokles, otherwise unknown, is listed by J. Pouilloux (*Forteresse*, p. 177). For a Rhamnousian Nikokles of later date see *SEG* XV, 104 (XXII, 108, XXV, 130, XXVI, 114), line 245. *IG* II², 7361 is the grave marker of Nikanor, son of Nikokles, of Rhamnous, dated to the Early Imperial period.

Line 7. On the proposer see M. H. Hansen, *GRBS* 25, 1984, p. 140 (= *Athenian Ecclesia II*, p. 110), no. 29. He cannot have been [Δημάδης Δ]η[μέο]υ Π. without some violation of the stoichedon order, the names being too short by one letter for the space available.

DECREE OF THE GENOS OF THE KERYKES IN HONOR OF XENOKLES OF SPHETTOS

77. Two joining fragments of a stele of Pentelic marble, both preserving the smooth-worked right side and the rough-picked back. The lower fragment (I 4439), designated *b*, was discovered on January 29, 1937, among marbles from modern house walls over the southwestern part of the Eleusinion (S–T 20); the upper fragment, *a* (I 6804), was discovered on April 23, 1958, along the Panathenaic Way north of the Eleusinion (T 18), and its connection with *b* was recognized by E. Vanderpool. Fragment *a* preserves the top of the stele, with moldings and the remains of palmette ornamentation above the inscribed face. The united piece is broken away below and to the left.

Measurements of the stone as joined: H. 0.496 m.; W. 0.177 m.; Th. 0.085–0.088 m.

LH. 0.009 m. (omicron 0.006 m., phi 0.011 m.).

Στοιχ. (square) 0.0175 m.

Ed. B. D. Meritt, *Hesperia* 29, 1960, pp. 2–4, no. 3, with photograph of the combined fragments pl. 1. See also *SEG* XIX, 119. Fragment *b* had received separate publication by Meritt, before the discovery of fragment *a*, in *Hesperia* 10, 1941, p. 42, no. 10, with photograph.

The date is determined by the known careers of Xenokles and of Lykourgos (see below), confirmed by the character of the writing and ornamentation, which do not support a dating later in Xenokles' public career.

ca. a. 334–326 *a.*   ΣΤΟΙΧ. 18

(a)
[.....10.....]ς εἶπεν· δε
[δόχθαι Κήρυ]ξιν· ἐπειδ
[ὴ Ξενοκλῆς Ξ]είνιδος Σ
[φήττιος ἀνή]ρ ἐσ[τ]ιν ἀ[γ]
5 [αθὸς περὶ τὸ] γέν[ος] τ[ὸ Κ]
(b)
[ηρύκων, ποιῶ]ν [ἀεὶ ὅ]τ[ι ἀ]
[ν δύνηται ἀ]γαθόν, χ⟨α⟩τ[α]
[σταθεὶς δ'ἐ]πὶ τῆι διοι
[κήσει τῆς π]όλεως καλῶ
10 [ς καὶ εὐσεβ]ῶς ἐμέρισε
[ν τὰ εἰς τὸ ἱ]ερὰ θῦσαι [τ]
[ὸ γένος τὸ Κ]ηρύκων ὑπ[έ]
[ρ τε τοῦ δήμ]ου τοῦ Ἀθην
[αίων καὶ ὑπ]ὲρ τοῦ γέν[ο]
15 [ς τοῦ Κηρύκ]ων, ἐπαινέ[σ]
[αι αὐτὸν κα]ὶ στεφανῶσ
[αι χρυσῶι στ]εφάνωι ἀπ
[ὸ χιλίων δρ]αχμῶν, καὶ ε
[ἶναι πρόσο]δον αὐτῶι π
20 [ρὸς τὸ γένος τ]ὸ Κηρύκ[ω]
[ν ......12......]Λ[....]
[---------------]

Line 1. The stonecutter at first wrote ΕΓΕ but at once recognized his error and erased ΓΕ, substituting the correct letters. Lines 7–8. So Meritt: perhaps χ⟨α⟩ὶ [ἡ⟨ι⟩ρημένος ἐ]πί. The crossbar of alpha is omitted. The lettering is a good piece of work, characteristic of its period, neat and well spaced, the best form of a style too often scamped. "Free ends" of strokes are rarely emphasized except in upsilon. Omega is (like omicron) smaller than the other letters and retains a very open form.

Line 2. This is the first of two decrees of the genos of the Kerykes recognized among the Agora material; the second is **271**. For others see *IG* II², 1230, 1235 (*SEG* XXVIII, 365, XXIX, 134), and 1236 (*SEG* XXXVI, 197). For a decree of the Eumolpidai, see **306**. On the Kerykes and the Attic γένη see W. S. Ferguson, *Hesperia* 7, 1938, pp. 12–47, with references to earlier literature; J. H. Oliver, *The Athenian Expounders of the Sacred and Ancestral Law*, 1950, p. 34 with note 2; C. Hignett, *A History of the Athenian Constitution*, 1952, pp. 61–67; D. MacDowell, *Andokides, "On the Mysteries"*, 1962, pp. 153 and 156.

Line 3. Xenokles, son of Xeinis, of Sphettos. For detail on this important political figure, whose career covered almost the whole of the latter half of the 4th century, see *PA* 11234; Meritt, *Hesperia* 29, 1960, p. 3; H. Schaefer, *RE* IXA, ii, 1967, cols. 1506–1508, *s.v.* Xenokles, no. 5; J. K. Davies, *APF*, pp. 414–415; C. Ampolo, *La Parola del Passato* 34, no. 186, 1979, pp. 167–178 (cf. *SEG* XXIX, 132); and C. Habicht, *Hesperia* 57, 1988, pp. 323–327. Xenokles was gymnasiarch in 346/5 (*IG* II², 3019), trierarch in 335/4 (*IG* II², 1623, line 298), epimeletes of the Eleusinian Mysteries in 321/20 (*IG* II², 1191, *SEG* XXIX, 132, *IG* II², 2840, 2841), agonothetes in 307/6 (*IG* II², 3073 and 3077, *SEG* XXVI, 222), and a member of a special commission in 306/5 (*IG* II², 1492, *SEG* XXXII, 159, line 100). J. and L. Robert pointed out (*REG* 74, 1961, p. 155, no. 264, with references to earlier commentaries) that the reference in *Anthologia Palatina* 9.147 is properly to Xenokles' activities in connection with the Mysteries. From the present text he appears to have succeeded his friend Lykourgos as financial manager of Athens, even though the latter continued to control the administration *de facto* during two quadrennia after his own tenure of that position (338–334), which could not be repeated (Plutarch, *Moralia* 841B–C). Cf. F. W. Mitchel, *Lykourgan Athens, 338–322* (Lectures in Memory of Louise Taft Semple, second series), 1970, pp. 12, 28; S. Markianos, *GRBS* 10, 1969, pp. 325–331; and also (on the career of Lykourgos in general), S. C. Humphreys in *The Craft of the Ancient Historian: Studies in Honor of Chester G. Starr*, J. W. Eadie and J. Ober, edd., 1985, pp. 199–252 (on the present text esp. p. 213).

Lines 8–9. ἐ]πὶ τῆι διοι[κήσει. See Meritt, *loc. cit.* The specific office of ὁ ἐπὶ τῇ δ. cannot be demonstrated to antedate the democratic restoration of 307/6, when it was held by Lykourgos' son Habron, unless this text be itself the demonstration. The title was more probably adopted from the phrase generally used (as perhaps here) to describe the effective position held by Lykourgos. But see P. J. Rhodes, *Athenian Boule*, pp. 107–108 with notes 1, 2 and *A Commentary on the Aristotelian Athenaion Politeia*, 1981, pp. 515–516; A. S. Henry, *Chiron* 14, 1984, p. 52, note 13 (with a reference to this inscription).

Lines 10–11. ἐμέρισε[ν. The text of this decree is reproduced by T. Eide (*Symbolae Osloenses* 69, 1984, pp. 21–22), where he discusses (pp. 21–28) the use and implications, in decrees of the 4th century, of δοῦναι and μερίσαι in the instructions to officials competent to defray the cost of inscribing and erecting stelai. Cf. *SEG* XXXIV, 263.

Lines 14–15. The use of O for OY is required by the stoichedon arrangement and would represent a "sporadic survival"; cf. L. Threatte, *Grammar*, p. 256. M. N. Tod (*SEG* XIX) regarded the supplement as doubtful after and before fully expressed τοῦ. Lines 16–18. On the stephanos and its expressed cost see Henry, *Honours*, pp. 22–26.

THE ARCHONSHIP OF NIKETES, 332/1 B.C.

No fewer than ten decrees, including **78** and **79**, are known from Niketes' year. Four of them, **79** and *IG* II², 345, 346, and 347 (*SEG* XIV, 55), were passed on the same day (Elaphebolion 19 = pryt. VIII, 7); cf. M. H. Hansen, *GRBS* 23, 1982, pp. 339 and 343, no. 37 (= *Athenian Ecclesia*, pp. 91 and 95). Of the remainder, *IG* II², 344 (*SEG* XXI, 279; cf. *IG* II², 368, lines 1–18) belongs to the second prytany, **78** to the fifth, and *IG* VII, 4252 and 4253 to the ninth. *SEG* XXVIII, 102 is a deme decree of Eitea of this year, and *SEG* XXVIII, 103 contains two decrees of the demesmen of Eleusis. An eleventh decree, *IG* II², 420 (*SEG* XXI, 322, XXII, 93), though lacking the names of both archon and γραμματεύς, may be convincingly assigned to 332/1. See also C. J. Schwenk, *Athens in the Age of Alexander*, pp. 177–219, nos. 33–43.

The year was ordinary in the Athenian festival calendar, with 354 days. B. D. Meritt (*Athenian Year*, pp. 85–88), quoting the calendric sections of the relevant texts, noted that there was no irregularity. He supposed a regular alternation of hollow and full months, with a succession of three prytanies of 36 days, six of 35, and a tenth prytany of 36. W. K. Pritchett and O. Neugebauer (*Calendars*, pp. 48–49) maintained the Aristotelian "norm" of prytany lengths (4 × 36 followed by 6 × 35) and thus advanced by one day the date of the passage of all these decrees except the earliest, assuming two successive full months in the festival calendar early in the year.

The γραμματεύς of the year was Ἀριστόνους Ἀριστόνου Ἀναγυράσιος (*PA* 2038). His name occurs in full in association with Niketes (in full or partly preserved) in *IG* II², 345 and VII, 4252 and 4253, partly preserved in *IG* II², 346 and 347. Outside the epigraphical evidence he is not otherwise known. Cf. S. Alessandri, *Annali della Scuola Normale di Pisa*, pp. 51 and 64. For details of those known to have held public office in this year, see R. Develin, *Athenian Officials*, pp. 387–390.

Known phylai in prytany are II Aiantis or Leontis, V Kekropis, VIII Antiochis, and IX Erechtheis.

FRAGMENT OF A DECREE

78. The upper right-hand corner of a pedimental stele of Pentelic marble (I 830), broken below and to the left but with the back, right side, molding above the inscribed face, and part of the pediment preserved, discovered on May 15, 1933, in the curbing of a late well in the northeast corner of the Temple of Apollo Patroos (H 7).

H. 0.175 m.; W. 0.122 m.; Th. 0.095 m.
LH. 0.006 m. (omicron 0.004 m.).
Στοιχ. (lines 2 and thereafter) Hor. (slightly irregular) *ca.* 0.0125 m.; Vert. 0.0125 m.

Ed. B. D. Meritt, *Hesperia* 5, 1936, pp. 413–414, no. 11, with photograph; C. J. Schwenk, *Athens in the Age of Alexander*, pp. 181–183, no. 34. Lines 1–6 quoted by Meritt, *Athenian Year*, p. 86; lines 2–3 and 5–6 quoted by W. K. Pritchett and O. Neugebauer, *Calendars*, p. 49. See also *SEG* XXXII, 84.

a. 332/1 a., pryt. V   ΣΤΟΙΧ. 31

```
        [Θ         ε          ο]              ι.
        ['Επὶ Νικήτου ἄρχοντος ἐπὶ τῆς] Κεκροπί
        [δος πέμπτης πρυτανείας ἧι 'Αρ]ιστόνου
        [ς 'Αριστόνου 'Αναγυράσιος ἐγρ]αμμάτε[υ]
    5   [εν· Ποσιδεῶνος ἐνδεκάτει, πέμπ]τει καὶ
        [δεκάτει τῆς πρυτανείας· τῶν πρ]οέδρων
        [ἐπεψήφιζεν .........¹⁶.......]· ᵛ ἔδ[οξ]
        [εν τῶι δήμωι· .........²¹.........]
        [----------------------------]
```

The lettering is "standard" for its time but slipshod. Omega is open and appears as a continuous curve; the central bar of epsilon varies in length; sigma is generously spread (0.0075 m.).

Line 1. The "invocation" is written on the horizontal molding of the pediment. Lines 3 and 5. The determination of the length of line in lines 2 and 4 from the archon's and secretary's names carries with it the assurance of the lunar month and date and of the prytany date. Posideon 11 is well attested as a meeting day of the assembly. See **76**, commentary on lines 4–5. The day is the 158th of the year (Meritt): Pritchett and Neugebauer saw it as the 159th (see above, on the archonship of Niketes). M. H. Hansen, *GRBS* 23, 1982, p. 349, no. 85 (= *Athenian Ecclesia*, p. 101) envisaged two other possibilities for the calendric equation, Anthesterion 20 = pryt. VII, 13 and Skirophorion 11 = pryt. X, 16. Meritt's equation retained the succession of full and hollow months in the festival calendar and is to be preferred. R. Develin (*Athenian Officials*, p. 389) left the question open.

Lines 5–6. For EI in the place of HI in the ordinal numeral see **66**, commentary on lines 6 and 14, and **89**.

A CITIZEN OF ABDERA HONORED

79. Five small joining fragments of a stele of Pentelic marble (I 3364), discovered over a short period of time on February 10 and 12 and on March 18, 1936, among the debris of the demolished Church of Christ, outside the Market Square to the southeast (T 17). The composite piece preserves the original back of the stele and the foot of the inscription (though not of the monument) but is otherwise broken.

H. 0.35 m.; W. 0.108 m.; Th. 0.05 m.
LH. 0.007 m.
Στοιχ. (almost square) Hor. 0.012–0.013 m.; Vert. 0.013 m.

Ed. E. Schweigert, *Hesperia* 8, 1939, pp. 26–27, no. 6, with photograph of composite fragment; C. J. Schwenk, *Athens in the Age of Alexander*, pp. 196–198, no. 39 (cf. *SEG* XXXV, 71). The calendric data (= those of *IG* II², 345–347) quoted by W. K. Pritchett and O. Neugebauer, *Calendars*, p. 49; lines 1–5 quoted by B. D. Meritt, *Athenian Year*, p. 87. The decree is listed by A. Lambrechts, *De Atheense Proxeniedecreten*, p. 157, no. 132; cf. pp. 51, 57, 133–134.

a. 332/1 *a., pryt.* VIII   ΣΤΟΙΧ. 29

```
        ['Επὶ Νικήτου ἄρχοντος ἐπὶ τῆς 'Αντιο]
        [χίδος ὀγδόης πρυτανείας ἧι 'Αριστό]
        [νο]υ̣[ς 'Αριστόνου 'Αναγυράσιος ἐγραμ]
        [μά]τευ[ε]ν· 'Ε[λαφηβολιῶνος ἐνάτηι ἐπὶ]
   5    [δέ]κα, ἑβδό[μηι τῆς πρυτανείας· ἐκκλη]
        [σία] ἐν Διο[νύσου· τῶν προέδρων ἐπεψή]
        [φιζ]εν Ν[ι]κ[όστρατος Κόπρειος· ἔδοξεν]
        [τῶι δ]ήμωι· Ε[.........20.........]
        [...]άσιος εἶ[πεν· ἐπειδὴ ....8....ς ὁ 'Α]
  10    [βδη]ρίτης [.........21.........]
        [...]ε προα[.........21.........]
        [...] τῶι δ[ήμωι .......15......, δεδ]
        [όχθαι] τῶ[ι δήμωι ἐπαινέσαι ...7...]
        [.]ν 'Ογ[ο]μά[ρχου 'Αβδηρίτην καὶ στεφαν]
  15    [ῶσ]αι χρυσ[ῶι στεφάνωι· εἶναι δ'αὐτὸν]
        [κ]αὶ πρόξε[νον καὶ εὐεργέτην τοῦ δήμ]
        [ο]υ τοῦ 'Αθη[ναίων αὐτὸν καὶ ἐκγόνους]
        [α]ὐτοῦ· ἀνα[γράψαι δὲ τόδε τὸ ψήφισμα]
        ⟨τὸν γραμματέα τὸν κατὰ πρυτανείαν⟩
  20    [ἐ]ν στήληι [λιθίνηι καὶ στῆσαι ἐν ἀκρ]
        [ο]πόλει· εἰ[ς δὲ τὴν ἀναγραφὴν τῆς στή]
        [λη]ς δοῦνα[ι τὸν ταμίαν τοῦ δήμου ...]
        [δρ]αχμὰς ἐ[κ τῶν κατὰ ψηφίσματα ἀναλ]
        [ισ]κομένων [τῶι δήμωι].
                    vacat
```

The writing is "standard" for its time, with slight emphasis of "free ends" and some carelessness, for example, in the inscribing of epsilon or the alignment of a stoichos. In line 9 three letters are set in the space of two, and in line 7 two are restored in the space of one. At line 19 an entire line may have been omitted (see below).

Lines 1–7. The entire prescript, including the name of the proedros who put the motion, is derived from the other decrees passed on the same day, with which, on the tenuous but sufficient surviving evidence, Schweigert was able to associate this text. This is the earliest of the decrees found in the Agora to have been passed at an assembly held in the Theater of Dionysos and is the first clear instance of this definition of the place of assembly, preceding by fourteen years that quoted by A. S. Henry, *Prescripts*, p. 39. On these meetings, more properly described as "in the precinct", see W. A. McDonald, *Political Meeting-Places*, pp. 47–51.

Lines 4–5. Elaphebolion 19 is well attested (and several times acceptably restored) as a meeting day of the assembly. See J. D. Mikalson, *Sacred and Civil Calendar*, pp. 130–131.

Lines 8–9. Schweigert restored the proposer's name as Ε[ὔβοιος Κρατιστόλεω 'Αναγυρ]άσιος, for whom see *PA* 5313 and J. K. Davies, *Athenian Propertied Families*, p. 188. The restoration must, as Davies noted, be regarded as uncertain; but it is regarded as highly likely by M. H. Hansen (*GRBS* 25, 1984, p. 140 [= *Athenian Ecclesia II*, p. 110, no. 28]) and was not questioned by Schwenk, *loc. cit.* Euboios is known to have been trierarch in 338/7 (*IG* II², 1623, line 135, 1628, lines 398–399, 1629, lines 917–918, and 1631, line 12). It may be his daughter Choirine who is commemorated by *IG* II², 5639.

Lines 9–10. The ethnic was restored (also in line 14) by Meritt. The space available in line 14 dictates its length, and alternatives are so limited (cf. F. Dornseiff and B. Hansen, *Rückläufiges Wörterbuch der griechischen Eigennamen*, English ed., 1978, pp. 174–175) that it may be regarded as all but assured.

Lines 14–18. On καί before the titles see Henry, *Honours*, p. 134, and on the extension of the honors to the descendants with the inclusion of a final αὐτοῦ, *ibid.*, p. 138. On the stephanos, for which no cost is determined, see Henry, *Honours*, pp. 22–24. Line 19. The title of the γραμματεύς exactly fills the line and may have been omitted by oversight, although Schwenk found it difficult to understand how this could have happened. There are in fact a few apparently intentional omissions of the words, e.g., *IG* II², 493 + 518, 508, 648 (= M. J. Osborne, *Naturalization* I, pp. 128–130, D 53, D 54 and pp. 148–150, D 69, respectively), **123**, and **141**.

Line 22. Schweigert restored the cost of the stele as 30 drachmas, without interruption of the stoichedon sequence, and the restoration was adopted by Schwenk. For so brief a record, 20 drachmas might have been adequate, the inscribed figure being preceded and followed by marks of punctuation (:ΔΔ:). *IG* II², 344, of comparable length, affords no parallel, for although ΔΔ[Δ was restored in the *IG* text at line 23, the repetition of the same text in *IG* II², 368 allows in line 16 for the restoration of no more than ΔΔ. Furthermore, sufficient of the stone survives in 344 to suggest that a blank space (or perhaps a single following mark of punctuation, for which compare, e.g., *IG* II², 393, line 13) stood between ΔΔ and the concluding letters of the line. On the cost of stelai cf. **40**, commentary on lines 18–19. For the paymaster and the source of the expenditure see Henry, *Chiron* 12, 1982, pp. 97–118 and the commentaries on **40** and **45**.

Line 24. Schwenk was hesitant about the restoration of the concluding τῶι δήμωι: cf. *IG* II², 344. But its inclusion represents the more usual practice.

THE PHYLE PANDIONIS HONORS ITS THREE EPIMELETAI

80. A fragment of a stele of a marble variously described as Pentelic or Hymettian (I 6842), broken on all sides except for the rough-picked back, discovered on April 6, 1959, in a wall of a modern house near the Eleusinion (U 21).

H. 0.25 m.; W. 0.20 m.; Th. 0.095 m.
LH. 0.01 m.
Στοιχ. Hor. 0.023 m.; Vert. 0.021 m.

Ed. B. D. Meritt, *Hesperia* 32, 1963, p. 41, no. 42, with photograph pl. 11 (see also *SEG* XXI, 515); J. S. Traill, *Demos and Trittys*, 1986, pp. 85–87, no. 6. On lines 3–7 see also Traill, *Studies Presented to Sterling Dow on his Eightieth Birthday*, 1984, p. 293, note 14 (*SEG* XXXIV, 101).

a. 332/1, 327/6, *vel* 324/3 *a*.   ΣΤΟΙΧ. 18

```
        ["Εδοξεν τῆι Πανδιονίδ]
        [ι φυλῆι· .....¹²......]
              lacuna
        [...⁸....]Ι[....⁹....]
        [.. Πα]ιανι : Ἀ[ντισθένην]
   5    ['Αντι]σθενο : Κυ[θήρ : Μειδ]
        [οκρ]άτην : Μει[δοκράτο : Π]
        [ροβ]αλ : δοῦνα[ι δὲ αὐτοῖ]
        [ς κα]ὶ εἰς θυ[σίαν πεντή]
        [κον]τα δραχ[μὰς τοὺς ἐπ]
  10    [ιμε]λητὰς [τοὺς ἐπὶ Νικ]
        [ήτου] ἄρχο[ντος· ἀναγρά]
        [ψαι δὲ] τό[δε τὸ ψήφισμα]
        [ἐν στή]λ[ηι λιθίνηι καὶ]
        [στῆσαι ἐν ἀκροπόλει ἐ]
  15    [ν τῶι ἱερῶι τοῦ Πανδίο]
        [νος.        vacat       ]
```

The impression of the lettering is of a less good version of "quality" work such as that of the Kleokrateia base (*SEG* XVII, 83). The shape of rho, with the lower part of the loop brought back in a reentrant curve, is particularly notable. The circular letters are not well executed.

The above text is that of Traill. In the *editio princeps*, reproduced in *SEG* XXI, 515, it began with what is now line 4. The lacuna after the present (restored) line 2 may have been of two lines at most: preambles to enactments of phylai, demes, and other sections of the body politic were customarily briefer than to those of the boule and demos; cf. **86**. The restorations follow the model of *IG* II², 1152 (= 596), Traill, *Demos and Trittys*, pp. 87–88, no. 7, a decree in which Pandionis honored another trio of epimeletai before the end of the 4th century. The length of the lines is conditioned by the content of lines 7–9 and by the formulas of lines 11–13.

Meritt's text in what are now lines 4–5 appeared as Ἀ[....⁹....|....]σθένο : Κυ[δαθ:, and he took it that Ο was being used in place of ΟΥ. This influenced his restorations in lines 9–10 (δραχ[μὰς : Ρ : τὸς ἐπ||ιμε]λητὰς [τὸς ἐπὶ ....]), as well as his general dating of the inscription in the first half of the 4th century. But the genitives are better taken as abbreviations; cf. L. Threatte, *Grammar*, pp. 100, 256–257. This interpretation suits a later date no less well (Threatte, *Grammar*, pp. 83–84), and this later dating is supported by the prosopography.

Lines 4–5. Traill noted that Κυ−−− could introduce Κυθήρριος as well as Κυδαθηναιεύς and identified that epimeletes with the Antisthenes, son of Antisthenes, active in the Lykourgan period and listed as *PA* 1195; cf. *IG* II²,

1629, lines 569–577, of 325/4. For other discussion of him and his family, see D. M. Lewis, *BSA* 50, 1955, p. 21; J. K. Davies, *Athenian Propertied Families*, pp. 38–39. Traill argued further that his inclusion here confirms Kytherros as a coastal deme and part of the coastal trittys of Pandionis.

Lines 5–6. Meidokrates of Probalinthos was βουλευτής in 336/5 (*Agora* XV, 42, line 165). Lines 9–11. With the restoration of τούς in place of τός (cf. δοῦναι in line 7), the choice among archons' names of the period evidently in question becomes limited. Apart from the restoration included in the text, ἐφ''Ηγήμονος (327/6), for which cf. **86**, and ἐπὶ 'Ηγησίου (324/3) are equally possible, and the text has been given the appropriate set of datings. For the duties of the epimeletai of the phyle, one from each component trittys, see Traill, *op. cit.*, p. 89 and bibliography on p. 79, in particular Busolt-Swoboda, II, pp. 974–975; and cf. W. S. Ferguson, *Hesperia* 17, 1948, p. 130. Other inscriptions in which they figure are discussed by Traill (*op. cit.*, pp. 79–92). See also N. F. Jones, *Hesperia* 64, 1995, pp. 521–525.

Lines 14–16. Stelai concerned with the affairs of phylai were customarily erected in the heroon of the phyle that originated the enactment. Cf., e.g., **86**, *IG* II², 1158, 1163, and (for Pandionis) 1138, 1144, 1148, 1157, etc. On the sanctuary of Pandion see W. Judeich, *Topographie*, p. 284; I. T. Hill, *The Ancient City of Athens*, 1953, pp. 146 and 239, note 17; Jones, *op. cit.*, p. 508.

HONORS FOR AN UNKNOWN BENEFACTOR

81. A fragment of a stele of Pentelic marble (I 5271), broken all around except for the smooth-dressed left side, discovered on February 28, 1938, in a marble pile in the area west of the Eleusinion (Q–R 17–19).

H. 0.164 m.; W. 0.147 m.; Th. 0.04 m.
LH. 0.005–0.006 m.
Στοιχ. (square) 0.0125 m.

Ed. M. B. Walbank, *Hesperia* 58, 1989, pp. 82–83, no. 8, with photograph pl. 19. See also *SEG* XXXIX, 78.

ca. a. 332–326 *a.*   ΣΤΟΙΧ.

```
         [––––––––––––––––––––––]
         [. . . .]ον πα[––––––––––––––––]
         [. . .] τὸν μὲ[ν –––––––––––––]
         [. .]ς ἐλευ[θερ––––––––––––––]
         [.]ς ἐπὶ τὰ τε[–––––––––––––––]
    5    [.]τας τὴν πο[–––––––––––––––]
         [.]λων καὶ με[–––––––––––––––]
         αὐτὸν ὅτε βλ[–––––––––––––––]
         [.]ρίαις ἔτι [––––––––––––––––]
         [.]ς μὲ[ν] λυτ[–––––––––––––––]
   10    [. . .]νκα[––––––––––––––––––]
         [––––––––––––––––––––––]
```

Walbank regards the lettering and workmanship as so closely resembling those of *IG* II², 346 and 356 that all three texts are likely to be by the same hand. For *IG* II², 346, of 332/1, see pp. 119–120 above under the Archonship of Niketes; for *IG* II², 356, of 327/6, see p. 128 below under the archonship of Hegemon. The date indicated above reflects these possibilities and must be in the right region even if the common identity of the craftsman be left out of account.

As suggestions for the text Walbank offered the following: Line 3. [τῆ]ς ἐλευ[θερίας – – – –]. Line 4. τε[ταγμένα – – – –]. Line 5. πό[λιν – – –]. Line 7. βλ[άβη – – – –]. Lines 7–8. [– – – ὑπερ|ο]ρίαις. Lines 8–9. [– – – το|ὺ]ς μὲ[ν] λυτ[ρωσάμενος – –]. On this basis it could be envisaged that the decree recorded gratitude to, and honors as a reward for, some person (or persons) instrumental in recovering Athenian citizens captured through piracy or in the course of the current warfare in the East: cf. *IG* II², 283 and 284.

PANDIOS OF HERAKLEA HONORED

82. Two joining fragments of a stele of Pentelic marble (I 4956), preserving the original back and right side (chipped, however, at the edge) but otherwise broken; some of the inscribed surface is lost at the junction between the two pieces. The lower fragment (*b*) was discovered on June 9, 1937, in the original fill of the Post-Herulian Wall over the paved court below Klepsydra (T 26–27); the upper fragment (*a*) was discovered on September 22, 1937, in a modern house wall southeast of the Market Square, west of the Panathenaic Way (Q–R 19–20).

Measurements of combined fragments: H. 0.212 m.; W. 0.112 m.; Th. 0.086 m.
LH. 0.007 m. (omicron 0.004 m., omega 0.0035 m.).
Στοιχ. (almost square) Hor. 0.0135 m.; Vert. 0.014 m.

Ed. E. Schweigert, *Hesperia* 9, 1940, pp. 332–333, no. 39, with photograph of composite fragment. See also
M. N. Tod, *GHI* II, 1948, p. 276.

a. 330–320 *a.*   ΣΤΟΙΧ. 24

```
                             [------------------]
     (a)     [..........18.........]μο[....]
             [...7... εἶπεν· ἐπειδὴ] Πάνδιο
             [ς διατελεῖ εὔνους ὢν τ]ῶι δήμω
             [ι τῶι Ἀθηναίων καὶ πρ]άττων κα
     5       [ὶ λέγων ὅτι δύναται ἀ]γαθὸν τὸ
             [ν σῖτον ἀπῆγε τῶι δήμ]ωι, ὅ τε πα
             [τὴρ ...7... καὶ αὐτὸ]ς σιτηγῶ
             [ν εἰς τὸ ἐμπόριον τὸ Ἀ]θηναίων
             [καὶ τῆς τοῦ σίτου πομπ]ῆς καὶ [.]
     10      [..........18.........] καὶ τ[..]
     (b)     [..........18.........]ενο[.]ιρ
             [..5... παρὰ τῶν προγόν]ων αὐτο
             [ῦ ........14....... εὔν]οιαν ἐν
             [....11.... τῶι δήμωι] τῶι Ἀθ
     15      [ηναίων, δεδόχθαι τῶι δή]μωι ἐπ
             [αινέσαι Πάνδιον ..5...ο]υ Ἡρα
             [κλεώτην ἀρετῆς ἕνεκεν καὶ φ]ι
             [λοτιμίας ........16.......]
                             [------------------]
```

The extremely small size of the "circular" letters is a particular feature of the engraving of this text, the general
features of which indicate a date in the later 4th century: cf. *IG* II², 494 (J. Kirchner, *IIA*², no. 70) of 303/2 B.C.
The decree was associated by Schweigert with others expressing gratitude to benefactors for services rendered during
the great famine of 330–326 (see Tod, *GHI* II, p. 276; J. McK. Camp, *Hesperia* 43, 1974, p. 323, and **106G–106J**).
The latest of these, *IG* II², 400, is dated to 320/19.

Lines 1–2. "The proposer may have been [Μοιροκλῆς Εὐθυδή]μο[υ Ἐλευσίνιος] or one of the seventeen
proposers for whom no patronymic or demotic is known", M. H. Hansen, *GRBS* 25, 1984, p. 140 (= *Athenian
Ecclesia II*, p. 110), no. 30. Line 2. Pandios of Heraklea, listed as "*ca.* 330" by H. Pope (*Foreigners in Attic Inscriptions*,
1947, p. 55), presumably on the basis of this text, is not otherwise known. Two other Herakleots are honored for
similar reasons in *IG* II², 408. Lines 5–9. For his restorations Schweigert compared *IG* II², 407, lines 4–7, for which
see **106J**.

Lines 13–14. [ῦ διαφυλάττων τὴν εὔν]οιαν ἐμ ||[πᾶσι καιροῖς τῶι δήμωι] Schweigert. The last letter of line 13 is
not mu but nu. Various restorations are possible, which make it inadvisable to select one of them as a definitive
suggestion, e.g., [ῦ ἀεὶ τὴν πατρικὴν εὔν]οιαν ἐν||[δεικνύμενος τῶι δήμωι], [ῦ, ἐνδείκνυται τὴν εὔν]οιαν ἐν ||[παντὶ
καιρῶι τῶι δήμωι], etc.

FRAGMENT OF THE CONCLUSION OF A DECREE

83. A fragment of a stele of Hymettian marble (I 2688), broken on all sides, discovered on March 27, 1935, in a
wall of a vaulted Byzantine chamber east of the Odeion near the Panathenaic Way (O 11).

H. 0.12 m.; W. 0.14 m.; Th. 0.085 m.
LH. 0.01 m.
Στοιχ. (square) 0.019 m.

Ed. B. D. Meritt, *Hesperia* 10, 1941, p. 41, no. 9, with photograph.

ca. a. 330 *a.*(?)   ΣΤΟΙΧ. 32

```
[------------------------------]
[....⁹....· εἰς δὲ τὴν] ἀνα[γραφὴν καὶ τὴν]
[ποίησιν τῆς στήλης δ]οῦνα[ι τὸν ταμίαν τ]
[οῦ δήμου ᵛ ΔΔΔΔ ᵛ δραχμ]ὰς ἐ[κ τῶν κατὰ ψηφ]
[ίσματα ἀναλισκομένων. ᵛ]     vacat
                    vacat
```

The writing is "standard" for its time, with "free ends" of the letters slightly emphasized; but there is some carelessness, and the junctions of the strokes are not always accurately made. There is some resemblance to *IG* II², 335, of 334/3, and this suggested the approximate date which Meritt gave to this text.

For the paymaster and source of the expenditure see A. S. Henry, *Chiron* 12, 1982, pp. 97–118 and the commentaries on **40** and **45**. The stele was evidently expensive and must have been either sizeable or elaborate, or both. For the cost compare *IG* II², 410 (*SEG* XXII, 94), of the same approximate date, with 41 lines each of 45 letters, and with ten citations within sculptured crowns, for which forty drachmas were also allotted: and cf. **121**. But B. T. Nolan (see commentary on **40**) has observed that after 332/1 there are few stelai costing as little as twenty drachmas, and the cost of the present monument may thus be interpreted as an instance of inflation rather than as an index of the character of the monument.

Line 4. The concluding words τῶι δήμωι are clearly omitted in this version of the formula. Cf. **79**, commentary on line 24.

DECREE ENACTED JOINTLY BY THE PHYLAI AIGEIS AND ANTIOCHIS

84. A complete, slightly tapered stele of Pentelic marble (I 6793), composed of two joining pieces and lacking only a small part on the right where the join occurs, discovered on July 4 and 8, 1957, as a cover for a manhole leading to an underground water channel southwest of the Hephaisteion (A 11). The inscribed surface, above which is preserved a crowning molding, has been badly corroded, and much of it has flaked away; even the lettering that remains has been considerably distorted by the same corrosive elements.

H. 1.65 m.; W. (max.) 0.49 m.; Th. 0.09–0.10 m.
LH. 0.004 m.
Στοιχ. (square) 0.0075 m.

Ed. M. K. Langdon, *Hesperia* 56, 1987, pp. 47–58, with photographs pls. 9, 10. See also *SEG* XXXVII, 100. A revised text of lines 2–16 by M. B. Walbank, *ZPE* 84, 1990, pp. 95–99. Cf. *Agora* III, p. 225. Langdon's text, with Walbank's commentary, appears also as *Agora* XIX, L8. See further *SEG* XXXIX, 145 and XL, 125.

ca. a. 330 *a.*   ΣΤΟΙΧ. 57

```
     Θεοί·
     [.]οιο[...]ι[....⁸....]ρχουι[....⁸....]η[..........²⁷..........]
     [.]α[.]ν[.]ιλ[..⁵..]ργα[.]ιν[.]ιλ[...............³⁴............. δε]
     [δ]όχθαι ται[...]λ[..]τους [....⁸....]ι[..........²⁹..........]
 5   [.]ς λιθινα[....]νο[.]λ[.]ι[...]ν[.............³⁵.............]
     [τ]ὸ κεφάλαιον [..⁵..]η[..............⁴⁰..............]
     [.] φυλῶν [...⁷...]εκ[..⁶...]γγ[....¹⁰....]ιου[.]τα[.......¹⁸.......]
     α[.]κι[..]τους [.]τησ[...]ε[...............³⁹...............]
     οι[...⁷....]ατα[....] φυλη[..⁸⁻⁹...]     vacat
10   [..]δε[...]λη[.]ο τὰ ἐδά[φη τ]ὰ ἐ[ν Ὠρ]ω[πῶι τ]ῶ[ν] Αἰγειδῶν καὶ Αἰαντιδῶν [...⁶...]
     [...⁷...]οοτο[...⁷...]δων [....]οκράτης Ἱπποκ[...]υ[..]ο[..]ρχι[...⁸....]
     [.]κ[..]λλου[..]ρα[.]α[....]ο[....¹¹....]ορος [....]αφια[......¹⁵......]
     [....]ο[...]ιφαλ[..⁵..]ν[...⁷...]λ[.]ι[...⁷...]λλ[.]λλρ[...⁸....]ραν[.]ο[...]
     [...⁷...]οταλ[..⁶...]η[.....¹³.....]λ[..]αχ[......¹⁵......]ι[..⁵..]
15   [.]α[..⁶...]ου[..]ο[..]ο[...¹⁰...]οροι[..]ιστο[.....¹².....]ο[..]ν[...]α[.]
     [Κ]αλλικράτης [-----------]     vacat
     [..⁵..]ωνεν[...................⁴³...................]οκράτ
     [η]ς [...]ο[..]λιτ[..]ο[................³⁷................ ἔδ]οξεν
```

[. . .]δ[. .]: ΗΗ; Δη[. . . . . .⁴³. . . . .]ομ[. .]

20 [.]τοσιαμ[. . .⁸. . . .]λ[. . . . . .³⁷. . . . .]ο[. . .]

75 [. . . . . .²⁶. . . . .]ταις [. . . .] Ἀ[να]φ[λ]υ[στιο. . . . .¹³. . . . . .]

[. . . . ἐ]φύλωι τόπ[ωι . . .⁷. . . .]π[. . .]τ[. . . .]ι[.]ο[. . . . . .²³. . . . .]

[. .]ατεὺς [. . . .]πα[. . . . . .⁴⁴. . . . .]

[.]εστοσιαχμο[. .]ιο[. .¹². . . .]αιτ[. . . . . .²⁷. . . . .]

[. . .] διαβὰ[ς] τὸ[ν αὐλῶνα τ]ὸ[ν . . . .]ο[. . . . . .¹². . . . . .]τατ[. . . . . . . .¹⁶. . . . . . .]

80 [. . .]ι[. .]του[. . . . . .⁴⁸. . . . .]

[. . .]ε[. . .]ρχη[. . .]το[.]η[. . . . . . .¹⁶. . . . . . . Ἀν]αφλυσ[τιο. . . . . .¹⁴. . . . . .]

[. .] διαβὰ[ς τ]ὸ[ν] αὐλῶ[να τ]ὸ[ν . . . . .³⁷. . . . .]

90 [. .]ελ[.]η[. . . . . . .¹⁶. . . . . .]ου[.]ο[. . . .⁷. . .]ε[. . . . . .¹⁸. . . . . Ῥ]α[μ]νο

ύσιος καὶ ἀμφισβητ[εῖ . .]ι[. .⁵. . .]α[.]σο[. .]ε[. .]ω[. . . . . .²⁰. . . . .]ρ[.]

πάντα τὸν [τ]όπον [. .⁵. .]ρατη[.]αφ[. .⁵. .]ο[. . . . . .²³. . . . .]η[. .]

ππαδιτος [.]ο[. . . . .¹³. . . . .]λ[. . . . . .²⁸. . . . .]ο[.]α[. .]

οντος Εὐρυ[. .⁵. .]υ[. . .]α[. .⁵. .]χ[ω]ρί[ον . . . .¹¹. . . .]τ[. . .]μ[. . . . .¹⁰. . . .]ά

95 δης ἔχει [. .⁶. . .]μ[. .]ιλ[.]ε[. . .]α[.]ομε[.] Λευκοπ[ύρ]α καὶ τὰ [π]ρ[ὸς] το[. .⁵. .] ἀπὸ

τοῦ Ἑρμαίου [τοῦ] Λευκοπυρ[α]ίου. τ[ό]π[ος .]ο[. .⁵. .]γος ἔφυλο[ς . . . .]ου[. .⁵. .]

[.]α[.]ται Καλλίστ[ρ]α[τος Ἰχ]αρι[ε]ύ[ς]. Ἀλεξίας Ὑ[βάδης] λόφον π[. . . .⁹. . . .]τ[.]

σελ[. . .] καὶ το[ύ]του [. . . .⁹. . . .]υ[.]υ[.]ο[.]ω[.]ο[. . . . . .²⁴. . . . .]

ενον καὶ τὰς [.]τηι[. . .]ηι[.]λυτο[. . . . . .²⁹. . . . .]των [ἤ]

100 νφεσβήτε[ι] Φ[ε]ρεκράτη[ς] Κολ[λυ]τεύ[ς]. πρὸς [. . . . .¹². . . . .]χ[. . . . .¹². . . . .]

ου[. . .⁷. . . .]έως [.]ι[.]υ[. . .⁷. . .]νη ὕλη [. . .]οσ[. . . .⁸. . . .]ε[.]τα[. . . . .¹². . . . .]

ενα τῶν Φ[ερ]εχράτου[ς] τόπ[ος] πολ[ὺς] ἔφυλος ἀργὸς μέ[χ]ρι τ[. .⁵. .]ο[. . .⁷. . .]

ων ἔστιν καὶ οὐκ ἠνφε[σ]βήτ[ει οὐδ]εὶς [. . . .] ὑλώνης. π[ρ]ὸ[ς τῶι λό]φωι πρ[οσκα]

τ[ε]ίργαστα[ι] καὶ ἔτερα ἐ[χ]όμενα τούτων, ὑπερβάντ[ι . . . . .¹⁷. . . . .]

105 σιν παρε[λ]θόντι τὸν λόφ[ον] οἱ αὐτοί. ἀπὸ τοῦ λό[φ]ο[υ . .]θηπ[. .]εφ[. . . .⁹. . . .]

τῶν Προξένο[υ ἐρ]γ[α]σίμων τούτου ὧν φυ[λῶν] ἔτ[ερα ἐ]ργάσιμα πολλ[ὰ . .⁶. . .]

υ[.]ητα καὶ [πεφυ]τευμένα [. . .⁸. . . .]μ[. .⁵. .]αι ἔδ[αφ]ος καὶ οἰκίαν [. . .⁸. . . .]

τα[ῦ]τα ἔφη μεμισθῶσθ[αι] Χα[ρίας Κ]ο[λ]λυτεὺς [. . . . . .²⁰. . . . . χαρ]

άδρ[α. .]ων[. . . .]ο[. . .]ειτ[. . . . ν]οτόθεν Πρόξενος [. . . . . .¹⁹. . . . .]

110 [π]ρὸς νότον [. . .]ων πρὸς ἐσπέρα[ν] οιορανοι[.]αι[. . .]ενο[.] πρὸς [ἡλί]ο[υ ἀνιόν]

τος [.]α[.]ετ[. .]ρου[.]ημενα τούτων [. . . . . .²⁸. . . . . .το]υ τ

οῦ [χ]ωρίου τούτου χαράδρα Ξυλλεχο[. . . . . .²⁵. . . . .]ορο[.]

αδα καλουμένην τόπον ἔφ[υ]λο[ν] πολ[ὺν . . . . .²⁴. . . . .] μέχρ

ι τῶν ἀμ[π]έλ[ων] τοῦτον ἐπεργασ[. . . . . .²⁹. . . . .]ηι[. .]

115 ἔτερα [ἐπ]ε[ί]ργαστο [.]τη[.] ἐφυ[λ. . . . . .³⁴. . . . .]

α βορρᾶθεν τῆι [. . .¹⁰. . . .]α[. .]ιβ[. . . . . . . .¹⁹. . . . .]υ[. .⁵. .]ν[. . . .]

131 [. . . .]το[. . . . .¹². . . . .]ι[. . . . . . . .¹⁷. . . . .]ομοσιν[. . .⁸. . . .]ητο[.] τ[ό]π

[ος .]τοη[. . .⁷. . .]ν τόπος ἐρ[γάσιμος . .⁵. .]υ[. . . .]χων τ[. .⁵. .]ο[.]θεις ἠ[ν]φη

[σ]βήτει [. .]ο[. .⁵. .]απ[.]ειου[. . . .¹¹. . . . .]ο[.]μ[.]ωπου[. . .χ]αλούμενος . .]ο[.]

[ἐργά]σιμ[ο]ς [. .]χ[.]ο[.] ἀνανφι[σβήτητος . . .]ρο[. .]ο[. . .⁸. . .]ο[. . . .] ἐρ[γάσιμ]

135 ος [. .]ωνος ἀ[ν]α[νφ]ισβήτη[τος . . . .¹¹. . . . .]α[. .]αρ[. . .⁸. . .]λο[. .⁶. .]ε[.]ο

[. . . .] τόπος ἐργάσιμος ἀν[ανφ]ισβ[ήτητος . .⁵. .]ο[. . . . . . .¹⁷. . . . . . .]ου

[. . .] τόπος πολὺς ηβα[.]λειδης ἐν τα[ῖς . .]αιοι[. . .]εγε[. .⁵. .]χα[. . .⁷. . .]ε[.]

[φ]άσκων μ[εμ]ισθῶσθαι: ͰΔΓ: δραχμῶν [. . . .]υνε[. τ]οῦτον [. . . . .¹¹. . . . .]: Ͱ: δραχ

ταῦτα ἔφη μεμισθῶσθαι παρ' Ὑβρίο[υ πρὸς τῶι λό]φωι [. .⁵. .]ηνη[.]ει[. . . . ὑ]π

140   [ε]ρσχ[ε]ῖν τούτων ἠ[ν]φεσβήτει Ὑβρί[ας Ὀτρυ]νεύς· τοῦτο[ν] τ[ὸ]ν τόπον [. . . .]ε[.]

[. . . .]ιημι[.]σι[.] τῶν ὑλωνῶν Νόθιππ[ος . . . .¹¹. . . .]ο[. . . .]ουρο[. . .⁸. . . .]

ο[. .]ς ἄπρατον τῶν φυλῶν ὕλην ε[. . . .¹⁰. . . .]εφην ὁ[δὸ]ν [εἰ]ς τὴν Βοωτί[αν] ε

[. .⁵. .] θόλος οκ[.]ιο[. χ]αλούμενο[ς . .⁵. .]του[. . . .¹⁰. . . .]ανο[. .]ε[.]ου[. . . .]

[. .⁵. .]ν τούτωι τῶι [τόπ]ωι ἐργασ[ίμωι . . . . . .¹⁵. . . . . .]α[. . .⁸. . .]ρ[. . .]

145   [. . .]νεου τῶν φυλῶν [ἔσ]τιν ἀνανφι[σ]βήτητα [. .]εορι[. . . . . . .¹⁸. . . . . . .]

ο[. .]υ λειμῶνος τοῦ τῆς αθ[. . . .]ο[.]αιπα[.]τ[. .]οιπ[. . . .]ο[. . .⁸. . . .]α[. .⁶. .]

λαν ἀνανφι[σ]β[ήτ]ητο[ν . .]ο[.]ιξε[.]τατ[. .] ἀγρι[. . .]δεορ[.]οσ[. . .⁷. . .]αο[. . . .]

ν[. .]ο λειμω[. . . .]το[. . . .]π[.]ιου[. .⁵. .] καλουμ[έν]ου [. .]ο[. . .⁸. . .]γα[. . . . τ]

ὁπος ἐργάσιμος α[. .]α[. . . .]τα[. . . .⁹. . . .]οσ[. . . . . .²³. . . . .]

156   [Φ]ιλαίδης [. . . .¹⁰. . . .]τ[. . . .]μ[. . . . . .³³. . . . .]

φλα[.]ο[.]ο[. . . .]λ[. . . . .¹². . . . .]α[. . . . . .³². . . . .]

νόσου τόπος τ[. . . . . .⁴⁶. . . . .]

170   [. .]ρευ[.]μένωι ο[.]οη[.]ε[. . . .⁹. . . .]ειλ[. .⁵. .]μοι χ[αλού]μ[ενος] τόπος ἐ[ργάσ]

[ιμ]ος χαὶ ὕλη [. .⁶. .]ο[. .⁵. .]ω[. . .]λ[.]νμε[. .] τοῦτον τὸν τ[όπ]ον ε[.]σαρ[. .]τ[. .]

[τ]όπο[ς . .]ο[.]ε[. .]ι[. . .]α[. . .χαλ]ο[ύ]μεν[ος ὁ τό]πος λ[.]χ[. .] ἐργάσιμος [.]αρ[. . . .]

[. .]α[. . .]ο[. . . .⁹. . . .]ετ[. . .⁷. . .] ὁ δρυμ[ὸς .]λ[.]ε[. . .⁶. . .]χ[. . .]ε[.]ε[. .]υ[.]νισυ

δρα[χ.]ΔΔΔ ηλ[. .⁶. .]υριτου[. . . .]ουι[. . . .]χλοη[. . . .]αο[. .]χ[. .]α[. . .]η[. . .]ι

175   ηχε[. . . .]ηνε[. .]αω[. . . .]ν[. .]οι[. . .]ολ[.]ητοις [.]ει[. . . .]ορ[. .]ο[. .]ι[. .]ρη[. .]α[.]

[.]εια[.]τ[.]ο[.]ουπαρ[. . .] χαὶ τὸ ε[.]βου[.]ολ[. . . .]λ[. .⁶. .]ο[. . . .⁹. . . .]ον[. .]ο[.]

[. .]ιο[. . .]ιοπ[. . .⁷. . .]ητ[.]ε[. .⁶. .]α[. .]χ[. .⁵. .]ε[.]δων[. .]ο[. . . . .¹³. . . . .]

[. .]οτα χαὶ [. . .]αο[. . .⁸. . .]ο[.]σα[. . . . .¹². . . . .]οιτε[.]τ[.]ι[. . . .]ιοι[. . . .]ο

[. .⁶. .]λλο[. .]ο[. .⁵. .]τουλ[.]τ[. .]ι[. . .⁸. . .] καλου[μ]έ[ν]ου [. .⁵. .]τα[. . . .]ο

180   [.]πο[.]ε[. . .⁸. . .]λ[. .]ητρια[. . . . . . .²⁶. . . . . . .]ο[. .]ν[. .]ιτα

υ[. . . . .¹². . . . .]τ[.]ι τῶι γε[. . .]γο[. .]ιο[. . . . . .¹⁴. . . . . .]ε[.] γειτονία ἧς τ

[.]να[. . . . . .¹⁴. . . . . .]επη[. .]ουγεω[. . . . . .²⁷. . . . .]ιε

[.]τηι[. . . . . .¹⁵. . . . . .]λ[. .⁵. .]ργ[. . .]ο[. .]εμ[. . .⁸. . .]α[. . . . .¹³. . . . .]

[. . . . .¹³. . . . .] ἀπράτων [. . . .¹⁰. . . .]ολ[. . . . . . .¹⁶. . . . . . .]λυ[. .⁷. .]

185   ινον[. . .⁸. . .]τ[. .⁷. .]τε[. . . . . . .¹⁷. . . . . . .]ρι[. .⁵. .]τ[. . . .¹⁰. . . .]

ασα[. . . . . .⁵⁴. . . . .]

α[. . . . . .⁴⁹. . . . .]λι[. .⁵. .]

vacat

The above text is that of Langdon, with correction of minor errors; he justifiably emphasized the difficulty of reading the stone and the uncertainties of the result. Since so much is uncertain, the use of capital letters, the placing of dots beneath what is doubtful, or both, have been dispensed with. In lines 21–74, 83–89, 117–130, 150–155, and 159–169 no more than a few scattered letters can be discerned, and these lines have been totally omitted.

Line 4. Probably not ταῖ[ς φυ]λ[αῖ]ς Langdon. Lines 4–5. Perhaps [——— ἐν δυοῖν στήλα||ι]ς λιθίνα[ις κτλ.] Langdon. Line 18 *fin*. Walbank preferred to regard ΟΞΕΝ as part of a proper name, *exempli gratia*, Πρόξενος.

The text of lines 2–16 proposed by Walbank is as follows:

Ἐπὶ Ο[. .]ι[. . . .]ιστάρχου Ι[. . .⁸. . .]η[. . . . . . .²⁷. . . . . . .]

[.]α[.]ν[.]ιλ[. .⁵. .]ργα[.]ιν[.]ιλ[. . . . . .³⁴. . . . . .δε]

[δ]όχθαι ταῖς [φ]υλαῖς θῦσ[αι(?) . .⁶. .]ι[. . . . . . .¹⁷. . . . . . .ἐ]ν δυοῖν(?) στήλα]

5   [ι]ς λιθίνα[ις . .]νο[.]λ[.]ι[. . .]ν[. . . . . .³⁵. . . . .]

[τ]ὸ χεφάλαιον [. .⁵. .]η[. . . . . .³⁸. . . . . .τῶ]

[ν] φυλῶν ἐδά[φη(?) . .⁵. .]εκ[. . .⁶. . .]γγ[. . . .¹⁰. . . .]ιου[.]τα[. . . . . .¹⁵. . . . . .]
α[.]κι[. .]τους [.]τησ[. . .]ε[. . . . . .²⁰. . . . .] τ[ῶν] φυλῶν [. . .]κα[. . .] ἐκ κ
οινῶν χρημάτων [τῶν] φυλῶν [. . .]οτη[. . . .]   *vacat*

10   [Ο]ἴδε ὡρί(σ)αντο τὰ ἐδά[φη τ]ὰ ἐ[ν] Ὠ[ρ]ωπ[ῶι τ]ῶ[ν] Αἰγειδῶν καὶ Αἰαντιδῶν [. .⁶. .]
[Β]ατ[ῆ]: [. . .]οστων[.]ς [ἐκ Κο]λων: Μ[ει]δοκράτης ἐκ Κο[λ: Φ]ο[ρ]ύ[σ]κος ['Ε]ρχι[:. .⁶. .]ιν
[.]η[ς Κ]ολλυ: Ἱεροκλῆ[ς Δι]ο[μι: . . .]α[.]κηλυουσα[. . .]κλ[. . .⁸. . . .]μ[. . .]αρχα[.]
[.]ιη[.]όνιος Φαλ[η]: Σκ[.]ιν[. .⁵. . .]τια[.]ι[.]τ[. . . Κο]λλυ[τ]: Αρ[. . .⁸. . . .]ραγιοι
[.]ι: Χρ[έ]μης Φαλ[η:] Ῥο[. . . .]ν[. . . . . . .¹⁶. . . . . . .]λινιλ[. . .⁸. . . .]λοντ[. . .]ι[.]

15   [.]α[. . .]: Λυκοῦρ[γος Κ]ο[λλυτ: . .⁵. . Τριχ]ορύσ[:] 'Α[ρ]ιστο[. . . .¹¹. . . . .]παιας [Μαρ]α[θ:]·
Καλλικράτης ['Ραμ]νο: ἐγραμμάτευε]·   *vacat*

That the decree was enacted jointly by two phylai emerges from line 10, and that Oropos is concerned seems to be plausibly indicated in the same line, assisted by line 142. This joint action, with the same connection, may be confirmed (as D. M. Lewis suggested to Langdon) by the evidence of Hypereides 4.16, whence it appears that when in 338 Athens once again assumed control of Oropian territory this was divided among the phylai in pairs. This text, insofar as sense can be made of it, suggests that a dispute had arisen between the two phylai involved or between the two jointly and a third party. For Athenian concern about Oropian land at this period see **75**.

W. Ameling (*ZPE* 77, 1989, pp. 95–96 [cf. *SEG* XXXVII, 100]) suggested that line 2 conceals the name of the archon Olympiodoros (see p. 240 below) and that the document should be dated accordingly; cf. the testimony of *SEG* III, 117, of 303/2. Walbank, on the other hand (*loc. cit.*, p. 96), argued that the remains of line 2 do not support this contention and that the style of the lettering militates against a dating in the 3rd century.

Line 95. On Leukopyra see J. S. Traill, *Political Organization*, pp. 94 and 117–118, no. 24. Lines 100, 102. For Pherekrates, son of Philokrates, of Kollytos, see *PA* 14196: he was a βουλευτής in 341/40; see *Agora* XV, 38, line 41 (= *IG* II², 1749). But another member of the same family might be involved here.

THE ARCHONSHIP OF HEGEMON, 327/6 B.C.

Two other decrees, in addition to **85** and **86**, belong with certainty to the year of Hegemon. These are *IG* II², 356 (*SEG* XXI, 286, XXIII, 57; M. N. Tod, *GHI* II, no. 199), of an uncertain prytany variously interpreted as the fourth, seventh, or eighth (of which the seventh is the most likely), and 357, restored as of the sixth prytany. In dealing with the decrees of this year, C. J. Schwenk (*Athens in the Age of Alexander*, pp. 285–307, nos. 57–62) includes also *IG* II², 113 and 358: for the former cf. M. B. Walbank, *ZPE* 76, 1989, pp. 257–261; the latter certainly belongs elsewhere.

The character of the year has been the subject of much discussion. Considered as intercalary by J. Kirchner (*IG* II², 357, *comm.*) and by W. K. Pritchett and O. Neugebauer (*Calendars*, pp. 52–54; reiterated by Pritchett, *Ancient Athenian Calendars on Stone*, pp. 273–274), it was held to have been ordinary by W. B. Dinsmoor (*Archons of Athens*, pp. 371–372) and by B. D. Meritt (*Athenian Year*, pp. 98–101; reiterated *TAPA* 95, 1964, pp. 221–226, *Historia* 26, 1977, p. 169). As the eleventh year of a Metonic cycle (the sixth) it must be expected to have been ordinary, and none of the available calendar equations contradicts the hypothesis that it was so, although all of these are fragmentary. Two of them (*IG* II², 356 and 357) omit the name of the month, and the third (**85**) presents special difficulties described below. Schwenk (*op. cit.*, p. 287) also accepts, after some discussion, that 327/6 was an ordinary year.

For an ordinary year, then, of 355 rather than 354 days Meritt (*Athenian Year*, pp. 99–100, revised in *GRBS* 17, 1976, pp. 151–152) envisaged a regular alternation of full and hollow months as far as Maimakterion, which was followed by a full Posideon and regular alternation thereafter. His suggested arrangement of prytanies reverses the Aristotelian "norm", with the first five each of 35 days and the last five of 36. The necessary restorations in *IG* II², 357 show that Aristotle's "rule" cannot in any case be maintained for this year, unless an error on the part of the stonecutter be postulated. The equation in *IG* II², 356 compels the assumption that one day was retarded in the festival calendar during Gamelion or Anthesterion. See also Schwenk (*op. cit.*, pp. 287–288), who gives a *résumé* of the problem.

Known phylai in prytany, on the assumption that ἕκτης is correctly restored in *IG* II², 357, line 3 and that ἐ]β[δόμης is correctly read and restored in *IG* II², 356, lines 2–3, are VI Aiantis, VII Hippothontis, and IX Oineis. Details of those known to have held public office in this year are listed by R. Develin (*Athenian Officials*, pp. 399–400).

FRAGMENT OF AN HONORARY DECREE

85. The upper right-hand section of a pedimental stele of Pentelic marble (I 226), broken below and to the left, and with the inscribed surface broken away also to the right, so that the inscription is complete only at the top. The raking cornice and part of the pediment are preserved, however, as well as the original rough-picked back and the right edge of the stele below the inscribed surface. It was discovered on April 28, 1932, in a late wall north of the Altar of Zeus Agoraios (J 9).

H. 0.26 m.; W. 0.25 m.; Th. 0.082 m.

LH. 0.004–0.006 m.

Στοιχ. (with slight irregularities) Hor. 0.01–0.0135 m.; Vert. *ca.* 0.012 m.

Ed. B. D. Meritt, *Hesperia* 3, 1934, pp. 3–4, no. 5, with photograph; C. J. Schwenk, *Athens in the Age of Alexander*, pp. 294–298, no. 59. See *SEG* XXI, 288 (with references to W. K. Pritchett and O. Neugebauer, *Calendars*, p. 53, where parts of lines 1–4 are quoted; Meritt, *Athenian Year*, p. 100, where lines 1–6 are quoted; Pritchett, *Ancient Athenian Calendars on Stone*, pp. 273–274, with photograph of latex squeeze pl. 20:b), XXIII, 58 (Meritt, *TAPA* 95, 1964, pp. 221–225), XXV, 69 (Meritt, ’Αρχ. ’Εφ., 1968, pp. 107–115).

a. 327/6 a., pryt. IX   ΣTOIX. 33

```
        ['Εφ''Ηγήμονος ἄρχοντ]ος ἐπὶ τῆς Οἰνηΐ[δος ἐ]
        [νάτης πρυτανείας] ἧι Αὐτοκλῆς Αὐτί[ου 'Αχ]
        [αρνεὺς ἐγραμμάτε]υεν· Μουνιχιῶνος [....]
        [......15......] δ'ἐνάτει μετ'εἰκά[δας· τ]
    5   [ῶν προέδρων ἐπεψή]φιζεν Πάμφιλος Π[αιαν]
        [ιεύς· ἔδοξεν τῶι δή]μωι·        vacat
        [..........17......] Θριά[σ]ιος εἶπ[εν· ἐπε]
        [ιδὴ ......15...... ἐπ]ὶ ['Η]γήμονο[ς ἄρχο]
        [ντος ......16........] τὰς ἐπιμ[ελείας]
   10   [------------------------]
```

The writing is of reasonable accuracy and affords a good criterion for the period. Phi in the form ⊕ is especially noteworthy (cf. J. Kirchner, *IIA*², p. 21, no. 62); omega varies between the more open form characteristic of the 4th century and the "horseshoe" shape of the future.

Line 2. Autokles' demotic is partly preserved in *IG* II², 356, line 4. He and his family are discussed by A. E. Raubitschek in *Hesperia* 11, 1942, p. 305. It is presumably his son Autias who is named in **182**, line 23 and in *IG* VII, 4266, line 3. The Demostrate, daughter of Autokles, commemorated by *IG* II², 5789 was probably his aunt, and the Autokles, son of Autias, of *IG* II², 1745 (*Agora* XV, 17), line 45 and 2408, line 3, his grandfather. Cf. *PA* 2725.

Lines 3–4. It is the first and third surviving letters of line 4 which have been the cause of major controversy in the attempt to interpret the calendric data of this inscription. In the *editio princeps* the first letter was not read and the third was seen as a certain nu, the whole passage being restored, with month name without date and with prytany date without name, as Μουνιχιῶνος· [ἐκκλ]ησία ἐν τῶι θεάτρωι]· ἐνάτει μετ'εἰκάδας.

Pritchett and Neugebauer (*loc. cit.*) read ΔEN in line 4, with the whole text as Μουνιχιῶνος [δευτ|έραι, ἡμερολεγδὸν] δ'ἐνάτει μετ'εἰκά[δας. Here δευτέραι represented δευτέραι φθίνοντος and supposed forward count in the last days of the month. 'Ημερολεγδόν, borrowed from the year 307/6 (to which it otherwise seems to be confined on the available evidence; see Meritt, ’Αρχ. ’Εφ., 1968, *loc. cit.*), with δ(έ) to point the contrast, was regarded as emphasizing an alternative means of calculation at a time agreed to have been transitional in the practice of naming the days of the last "third" of the month. See further Pritchett, *CP* 54, 1959, pp. 156–157 and for criticism of the restoration, A. W. Gomme, *CR* 63, 1949, p. 122. For the transitional period see also Meritt, *Athenian Year*, pp. 45 with note 10, 57–58.

In *Athenian Year*, p. 100, Meritt abandoned the version of the *editio princeps* and believed ≶EN to be the correct reading, restoring Μουνιχιῶνος [πέμπ|τει τῆς πρυτανεία]ς· ἐνάτει μετ'εἰκά[δας. Both the reading and the unusual formulation were strongly criticized by Pritchett (*Ancient Athenian Calendars on Stone*, pp. 273–274), who confirmed his former text; Meritt (*TAPA*, *loc. cit.*) thereafter accepted delta in the first position. For the third letter he regarded kappa as a possible alternative and, comparing *IG* XII, ix, 207, line 39, also suggested δεχάτει μετ'εἰκά[δας for consideration, the period of transition being responsible for the irregularity of phraseology. In ’Αρχ. ’Εφ., *loc. cit.*, he proposed Μουνιχιῶνος [ἐνάτ|ει φθίνοντος, νυνὶ] δ'ἐνάτει μετ'εἰκά]δας, where ὁμῶς is perhaps preferable to νυνί: cf. *eund.*, *GRBS* 17, 1976, p. 152, note 20.

Schwenk, *loc. cit.*, discussed these earlier interpretations, confirmed delta as the first visible letter in line 4, and believed that kappa was best suited by what could be seen in the third space, thus concurring with Meritt's earlier but rejected δεκάτει μετ'εἰκάδας (to be regarded as an equivalent of δεκάτει ὑστέραι which did not attain general acceptance). The draftsman will thus have given "transitional" alternatives: Μουνιχιῶνος [δεκάτει ὑστέραι, ὁμῶς δὲ] δεκάτει μετ'εἰκά[δας. But this, being too long by one letter for the stoichedon pattern, would require the assumption of an irregularity in the inscribing of the document.

The remains of the first letter in line 4 are in fact barely discernible but suggest that there is no alternative to delta. Of the third letter, traces of an upright stroke certainly survive in the left section of the available space; see Meritt, ᾽Αρχ. ᾽Εφ., 1968, p. 108, note 6. For the rest of that space nothing conclusive can really be said, and different pairs of eyes may well judge differently. Δ(ἐ), if accepted, must be regarded as indicating a contrast with an equivalent expression that precedes: ἡμερολεγδόν, "by count of days", even if acceptable beyond the confines of 307/6 B.C., would on the contrary point to a contrast with a different, that is, not equivalent, expression of time.

Any supplement at this point will be unusual if not unique among calendric formulas and should not be hazarded in a definitive text. This is, in sum, a prescript that defies any interpretation along "normal" lines. A. S. Henry, who discussed it briefly (*Prescripts*, pp. 47–48) among a series of "Problems", noted with some justification that "it is perhaps better to confess that, as yet, we do not really understand what has gone wrong with this text." Cf. M. H. Hansen, *GRBS* 23, 1982, p. 348 (= *Athenian Ecclesia*, p. 100), no. 83; R. Develin, *Athenian Officials*, p. 399.

Line 5. The demotic of the member of the proedroi who put the motion was suggested to Meritt by Gomme (*per ep.*). Cf. *PA* 11555 and J. K. Davies, *Athenian Propertied Families*, pp. 566–568, where a stemma of the family is given.

Line 6. The enactment, whatever it was, was voted by the assembly without (or in variance of) a preceding decision of the Council. Cf. P. J. Rhodes, *Athenian Boule*, p. 261 (where this text is cited twice, under different publication heads). Line 7. On the unknown rhetor from Thria who proposed the measure see Hansen, *GRBS* 25, 1984, p. 140 (= *Athenian Ecclesia II*, p. 110), no. 27.

THE PHYLE AIANTIS HONORS ITS THESMOTHETES

86 (Pl. 9). A pedimental stele of Pentelic marble (I 3625), reconstructed from seven fragments and complete with the exception of a few small pieces, discovered on February 27, 1936, in the filling of a Roman well on Kolonos Agoraios (C 9).

H. 1.065 m.; W. (top) 0.316 m., (bottom) 0.365 m.; Th. 0.07 m.
LH. 0.006–0.009 m.
Στοιχ. Hor. 0.0185 m.; Vert. 0.0175 m.

Ed. B. D. Meritt, *Hesperia* 7, 1938, pp. 94–96, no. 15, with photograph; C. J. Schwenk, *Athens in the Age of Alexander*, pp. 300–305, no. 61. Lines 27–33 quoted, as a *testimonium* for the Eurysakeion, by R. E. Wycherley in *Agora* III, p. 93, no. 255.

a. 327/6 *a.* ΣΤΟΙΧ. 16

```
            Θ   ε   o   ι.
        Δημοκράτης Δημοκλέ
        ους ᾽Αφιδναῖος εἶπε·
        ἐπειδὴ ὁ θεσμοθέτη
    5   ς ὁ τῆς Αἰαντίδος ἐπ
        ιμεμέληται τῆς τε κ
        ληρώσεως τῶν ἀρχῶν
        καὶ τῶν δικαστηρίω
        ν τῆς πληρώσεως καὶ
   10   τῶν ἄλλων ἁπάντων τ
        ῶν περὶ τὴν Αἰαντίδ
        α φυλήν, ἐπαινέσαι Τ
        ηλέσκοπον ᾽Αριστοχ
        ρίτου ῾Ραμνούσιον κ
   15   αὶ στεφανῶσαι αὐτ[ὸ]
        ν χρυσ[ῶ]ι στεφάνωι ἀ
        πὸ : Χ : δραχμῶν δικα
        ιοσύνης ἕνεκα καὶ φ
```

ιλοτιμίας τῆς περὶ
20   τὴν Αἰαντίδα φυλήν,
ὅπως ἂν καὶ οἱ ἄλλοι
θεσμοθέται οἱ θεσμ
οθετοῦντες φ[ι]λοτι
μῶνται περὶ τὴν φυλ
25   ὴν εἰδότες ὅτ[ι] χάρι
τας ἀπολήψονται πα
ρὰ τῆς φυλῆς· τὸ δὲ ψή
φισμα τόδε ἀναγρά[ψ]
αι τοὺς ἐπιμελητὰς
30   τοὺς ἐφ᾽ Ἡγήμονος ἄρ
χοντος ἐν στήληι λι
θίνηι καὶ στῆσαι ἐν
τῶι Εὐρυσακείωι.

(*corona*)

Line 23. [φι]λοτι. Meritt, Schwenk. Line 24. [τ]ὴν *eidem.* Line 28. ἀναγράψ. *eidem.* In line 2 three letters are inscribed in the space of two. The writing is otherwise regular. Upsilon has strongly emphasized "free ends": for the form of phi see **85**. Omega remains open and rather flat and is the smallest in height of the letters.

Lines 2–3. The truncated prescript is characteristic of the inscribed texts of decrees passed by phylai, demes, and other subdivisions of the Athenian body politic. See the commentary on **80**. Demokrates, whose patronymic was first made known by the discovery of this text, appears in the sources as a contemporary of Demosthenes. See *PA* 3521 and J. K. Davies, *Athenian Propertied Families*, p. 475. His was a branch of the extensive family tree formed by the genos of the Gephyraioi, and he could count the tyrannicides Harmodios and Aristogeiton among his ancestors. Cf. Schwenk, *op. cit.*, p. 304; M. H. Hansen, *Athenian Ecclesia II*, p. 41.

Line 4. The honorand is not named until line 12. An ephebe of the same name, recorded in 267/6 (*PA* 13567; *IG* II², 665, col. III, line 55), was presumably his grandson. Both men are listed by J. Pouilloux (*Forteresse*, p. 179). The name Teleskopos is otherwise unique in Attic prosopography. Lines 4–9. On these aspects of the duties of the thesmothetai, see Busolt-Swoboda, II, p. 1071; U. Kahrstedt, *Untersuchungen zur Magistratur in Athen*, 1936, pp. 56–57. On the thesmothetai in more general terms see the references listed in Busolt-Swoboda, II, index p. 32.

Lines 15–20. On the expression of the award of the gold crown and the cost formula employed see A. S. Henry, *Honours*, pp. 22–27; the phyle followed the practice of the time evident in decrees of the people at large. For the clause expressing Teleskopos' virtues see Henry, *op. cit.*, pp. 42–44 and (for the terms here employed) *IG* II², 488, of 303/2.

Lines 21–24. This is the earliest instance, among decrees found in the Agora, of a formula indicating the wider purpose of the inscription in the general sense of encouraging others to emulate the honorand or to publicize the community's readiness to show gratitude to those who serve it well. For earlier instances (in the 340's) cf. *IG* II², 222, lines 11–16, 223A, lines 13–14. This hortatory intention was enhanced by the location of the stele (lines 32–33). See also G. Klaffenbach, *Griechische Epigraphik*, 2nd ed., 1966, p. 77; M. B. Walbank, *Hesperia* 49, 1980, p. 255, note 14.

Line 29. For the epimeletai of the phyle and their duties, see **80** and the references there cited. Lines 32–33. For the location of the Eurysakeion see *Agora* III, pp. 90–93; J. Travlos, *Pictorial Dictionary of Ancient Athens*, 1971, pp. 261–262; N. F. Jones, *Hesperia* 64, 1995, p. 509.

ANOTHER THESMOTHETES HONORED

87. A fragment of a stele of Pentelic marble (I 409), with the left side and original rough-picked back preserved, but otherwise broken, discovered on February 8, 1933, in a modern wall south of the Tholos (H 12).

H. 0.155 m.; W. 0.203 m.; Th. 0.077 m.
LH. 0.01 m.
Στοιχ. (square) 0.019–0.02 m.

Ed. B. D. Meritt, *Hesperia* 3, 1934, pp. 43–44, no. 32, with photograph; revised with better text, Meritt, *Hesperia* 15, 1946, p. 189, no. 35.

ca. a. 325 *a.*   ΣΤΟΙΧ. 18

[——————————————]
[ο]υ̣ Π[οτάμιος(?) εἶπε· ἐπεὶ]
δὴ Τιμοκ[ράτης ὁ θεσμο]
θέτης καλῶ[ς καὶ φιλοτ]
ἱμως ἄρχει [τὴν ἀρχὴν κ]
5   αἱ ἐπιμελε[ῖται τῶν πε]
ρὶ τὴν φυλὴ[ν κατὰ τοὺς]
[νό]μους, ἐψη[φίσθαι Λεω(?)]
[ντίδ]αις ἐπ[αινέσαι Τι]
[μοκράτη]ν Τ[....⁹....]
10 [——————————————]

The writing is of very high quality, except that vertical strokes have a tendency to lean forward. Meritt compares *IG* II², 660, a (*SEG* XXXIII, 84), of the second half of the 4th century, and *Hesperia* 3, 1934, pp. 66–67, no. 60, of 325/4. "Free ends" of letters are slightly enlarged and depressed into wedge shapes. Nu and omega are slightly archaic for the time; the upright stroke of phi is continued through the oval but strongly emphasized above and below it.

Line 1. If, as is likely, the prescript was in the form of that surviving in full on **86**, a text which in width and character this decree evidently resembles, one full line of text, and perhaps an additional line reading Θεοί, are to be supposed above this first extant line. The second surviving letter is Γ, Π, or Ρ. If the upsilon concludes the patronymic, this is the initial letter of the demotic; and if the phyle is correctly identified as Aiantis or Leontis, the only choices in fact permitted by the stoichedon pattern, the demotic can on the evidence hardly have been other than Potamios (Leontis). Therefore, unless the stoichedon order was violated, ephelkystic nu was omitted from εἶπε, as in **86**, line 3. [Θ]υρ[γωνίδης (attributed to Aiantis by Harpokration, *s.v.*) would have the same effect, but neither this nor ῾Υπ[ωρειεύς (probably however of Aigeis) appears to be a possibility at this period. See Meritt, in *The Classical Tradition: Literary and Historical Studies in Honor of Harry Caplan*, 1966, pp. 32–34; J. S. Traill, *Political Organization*, pp. 87–88, 115, 121.

Line 2. Timokrates, son of T———, cannot otherwise be identified. On the duties of the thesmothetes see **86**, lines 4–9, and references there. Lines 7–8. Not φυλέτ]αις as in the *editio princeps*. Sufficient of the surface of the stone remains to ensure that part of the tau would be visible. For the use of the name of the phyle in the formula Meritt compared *IG* II², 1163, line 15.

FRAGMENT OF THE CONCLUSION OF A DECREE

88. A small fragment of a stele of Pentelic marble (I 4902 a), with the right side partly preserved but otherwise broken, discovered on May 21, 1937, at the surface on the North Slope of the Akropolis (no grid reference).

H. 0.105 m.; W. 0.09 m.; Th. 0.04 m.
LH. 0.01 m.
Στοιχ. (almost square, but with slight irregularity) Hor. 0.0165 m.; Vert. 0.016 m.

Ed. E. Schweigert, *Hesperia* 9, 1940, pp. 333–334, no. 40, with photograph.

ca. a. 325 *a.*   ΣΤΟΙΧ. 20

[———————————]
[..⁵.. ἐν στήληι λιθί]νηι
[καὶ στῆσαι ἐν ἀκροπ]όλει·
[εἰς δὲ τὴν ἀναγραφὴ]ν τῆς
[στήλης δοῦναι τὸν τ]αμία
5   [ν τοῦ δήμου ....δρα]χμὰ[ς]
[ἐκ τῶν εἰς τὰ κατὰ ψη]φίσ[μ]
[ατα ἀναλισκομένων τῶι δ]
[ήμωι.   *vacat*   ]

The writing has a tendency to be inexact (epsilon, sigma) but is in general very characteristic of the period to which, on the basis also of the formulas employed, Schweigert (with minimal commentary) assigned it. It is very similar in style to that of **89**, with which (as the inventory numbers imply) it seems to have been at first associated, and the same craftsman may well have been at work. M. B. Walbank (*per ep.*), in sharing that opinion, tentatively associated with the same hand *IG* II², 306, the lettering of which J. Kirchner, giving a date "ante a. 336/5", described as "volg. med. s. IV".

For the disbursing officer and the source of the expenditure see A. S. Henry, *Chiron* 12, 1982, pp. 97–118 and **40**, **45**, and **54**. The exact cost of the stele (line 5) should remain unrestored. So narrow a text is unlikely, perhaps, to have been lengthy, but usage in the inscribing of numerals is variable, and : ΔΔΔ : would fill the available space no less than Schweigert's ᵛ ΔΔ ᵛ. It should also be noted that at this period 30 drachmas appear to represent the minimum expenditure: see **83**.

Lines 7–8. The text could have ended after ἀναλισχομένων. See **79**, commentary on line 24 and **83**, line 4.

FRAGMENT OF A DECREE

89. A small fragment of a stele of Pentelic marble (I 4902 b), broken on all sides, discovered on June 15, 1937, in the original filling of the Post-Herulian Wall over the paved court below Klepsydra (T 26–27).

H. 0.14 m.; W. 0.11 m.; Th. 0.074 m.

LH. 0.008 m.

Στοιχ. (square) 0.017 m.

Ed. E. Schweigert, *Hesperia* 9, 1940, pp. ⁀4–335, no. 41, with photograph.

ca. a. 325 *a.*   ΣΤΟΙΧ. 26

```
          [--------------------]
          [...⁷...]αστε[..., ἀγαθῆι τύχηι]
          [δεδόχ]θαι τεῖ [βουλεῖ τοὺς προέδ]
          [ρους ο]ἵτινες [ἂν λάχωσιν προεδρ]
          [εύειν] ἐν τῶι [δήμωι εἰς τὴν πρώτη]
     5    [ν ἐκκλ]ησίαν [προσαγαγεῖν ..⁵...]
          [...⁶...]τους [.....¹³...... πρὸ]
          [ς τὸν δῆμ]ον κ[αὶ χρηματίσαι περὶ]
          [αὐτοῦ, γνώμ]η[ν δὲ ξυμβάλλεσθαι τ]
          [ῆς βουλῆς ...........¹⁸........]
    10    [--------------------]
```

On the character of the writing see **88**. In the present case it may be further noted that the lettering and the nature of the stone are precisely those of **94**, the Agora fragments of which were discovered in the same location: but for the difference of two letters in the stoichedon pattern it would be tempting to associate this fragment with that text. At least the two inscriptions may be attributed to the same mason.

Line 1. Ι≼Ι Schweigert: the stone appears to have ∨≼Ι⌐. Line 6. ΤΟΥ≼ rather than Schweigert's ΝΟΥ≼.

Line 1. ἀγαθῆι τύχηι. See **72**, lines 7–8. The decree is probouleumatic; cf. P. J. Rhodes, *Athenian Boule*, p. 250. The formula of lines 2–9 offers an example of the standard pattern on which, as Rhodes noted (*ibid.*, p. 65), many variations are possible. Cf. **52**, commentary on line 16, **66**, commentary on lines 1–6.

Line 2. τεῖ [βουλεῖ. For EI present and restored in place of HI, see **66**, commentary on lines 6 and 14. It should not be restored in line 1: cf. A. S. Henry, *CQ* n.s. 14, 1964, pp. 241–242. As for example in **101**, the two forms frequently coexist within the same text; where they do so, the preference seems to be for the EI form to stand in the ordinal numeral of the date, even if not elsewhere. The dative feminine singular of the relative almost always shows the HI form; see Henry, *loc. cit.*, pp. 244–245.

FRAGMENT OF THE CONCLUSION OF A DECREE

90. A fragment of a stele of Pentelic marble (I 6434), with part of the smooth right side and perhaps the original back preserved but otherwise broken all around, discovered on February 13, 1952, in a wall of a modern house northwest of the Church of the Holy Apostles (O 15).

H. 0.12 m.; W. 0.11 m.; Th. 0.068 m.

LH. 0.005–0.006 m.

Στοιχ. Hor. 0.0125 m.; Vert. 0.013 m.

Ed. B. D. Meritt, *Hesperia* 32, 1963, pp. 39–40, no. 40, with photograph pl. 11. See also *SEG* XXI, 345.

vix post a. 325 *a.*ΣΤΟΙΧ. 25

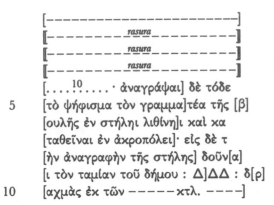

[----------------]
[------ *rasura* ------]
[------ *rasura* ------]
[------ *rasura* ------]
[. . . . .¹⁰. . . . . ⸱ ἀναγράψαι] δὲ τόδε
5 [τὸ ψήφισμα τὸν γραμμα]τέα τῆς [β]
[ουλῆς ἐν στήληι λιθίνη]ι καὶ κα
[ταθεῖναι ἐν ἀκροπόλει]⸱ εἰς δὲ τ
[ὴν ἀναγραφὴν τῆς στήλης] δοῦν[α]
[ι τὸν ταμίαν τοῦ δήμου : Δ]ΔΔ : δ[ρ]
10 [αχμὰς ἐκ τῶν -----κτλ. ----]

The first three surviving lines of the text have been erased, leaving a shallow depression. The writing is indicative of the second half of the 4th century, accurately set out but careless in detail, with strokes negligently joined. Forms of nu and sigma are variable, and the angled "horizontal" of delta is distinctive. There is some enlargement or indentation of "free ends" of strokes, especially in epsilon, kappa, and upsilon. M. B. Walbank (*per ep.*) has suggested that the craftsman at work here may also have produced *IG* II², 450 (*SEG* XXV, 75; M. J. Osborne, *Naturalization* I, pp. 109–112, D 42), securely dated to 314/13, and 392 + 586 (*SEG* XXVI, 83), assigned to the period 321–318.

The restorations demanded by the formulas of inscription and payment impose some limit upon the period within which this text is to be set. The ταμίας τοῦ δήμου as disbursing officer does not outlast the 4th century: see A. S. Henry, *Chiron* 12, 1982, p. 118, *Chiron* 14, 1984, pp. 51–56, *ZPE* 78, 1989, pp. 256–267. The γραμματεὺς τῆς βουλῆς as responsible for the inscribing of the stele is not attested under that title later than 318/17 (*IG* II², 448, lines 68–69; cf. P. J. Rhodes, *Athenian Boule*, pp. 136–137). The use of καταθεῖναι for the erection of the monument, in place of the more usual στῆσαι, seems to have gone out of use during the third quarter of the century, having in an earlier period been the regular term. *IG* II², 226 (= M. N. Tod, *GHI* II, pp. 214–218, no. 173), of *ca.* 343/2, is the latest example susceptible to a close dating (although the word is restored in *IG* II², 571, which must belong to the end of the 4th century or even the early years of the 3rd). It has a stoichedon line of 21 letters, runs to 46 lines, is written in a monumental script with generous spacing, and is adorned with an ambitious piece of relief sculpture. Nevertheless it cost no more than the thirty drachmas allotted to the present stele. By the 320's, however, this seems to have become the "regular" minimum price; see **83**.

The reason for the erasure of lines 1–3 (and perhaps also the first ten letter spaces of line 4?) can only be guessed at. The *damnatio memoriae* of an honorand, if such were the case, would have been followed by the destruction of the whole record, not merely the deletion of part of it. The rasura is shallow and suggests the correction of some element included by mistake. It may be not unlikely that a clause of the probouleuma was rejected by the assembly but not excised from the working copy handed to the mason for inscription and that the work was completed before the error was realized.

THE ARCHONSHIP OF HEGESIAS, 324/3 B.C.

Five decrees of the Athenian assembly are extant which were passed during Hegesias' year. Of these, two (**91** and **92**) were discovered in the course of the Agora excavations. The others were previously known: they are *IG* II², 362 (*SEG* XXI, 291), of the ninth prytany, 454 (*SEG* XXI, 293), and 547 (*SEG* XXI, 292, XXXII, 88), both of the tenth prytany. In addition, **93** is a decree of a deme (Peiraieus), *IG* II², 1257 represents a dedication to the Mother of the Gods accompanied by a decree of the city's *syllogeis* of the year, and *IG* II², 1258 preserves an enactment of the *koinon* of Eikadeis which is also identified as to date by reference to Hegesias as archon eponymos. These eight texts have all been dealt with by C. J. Schwenk (*Athens in the Age of Alexander*, pp. 355–380, nos. 71–78).

The year is agreed to have been ordinary in the Athenian festival calendar, with no irregularities (W. B. Dinsmoor, *Archons of Athens*, pp. 372–373; W. K. Pritchett and O. Neugebauer, *Calendars*, pp. 40, 56–57; B. D. Meritt, *Athenian Year*, pp. 104–106). Meritt envisaged a year of 354 days, with alternation of hollow and full months as far as Posideon, followed by a full Gamelion and regular alternation thereafter. The prytany calendar was that of the Aristotelian "norm", four prytanies of 36 days each, followed by six of 35.

Phylai known or presumed on the available evidence to have held identifiable prytanies are V Aiantis, VI Pandionis, IX Akamantis, and X Erechtheis. On the γραμματεύς of the year see commentary on **91** and S. Alessandri, *Annali della Scuola Normale di Pisa*, pp. 51, 66–67. For others attested as office holders see R. Develin, *Athenian Officials*, pp. 404–407.

FRAGMENT OF A DECREE

91. The upper right-hand corner of a pedimental stele of Pentelic marble (I 4071), with the right side and original back preserved, as well as a wide double molding and part of the pediment above the inscribed face, but broken elsewhere (including the raking cornice of the pediment and the right-hand akroterion); discovered on April 27, 1936, in a wall of the Church of Christ north of the Eleusinion (T 17).

H. 0.21 m.; W. 0.147 m.; Th. 0.104 m.
LH. 0.007 m. (omicron 0.004 m.).
Στοιχ. (square) 0.0146 m.

Ed. B. D. Meritt, *Hesperia* 10, 1941, pp. 49–50, no. 12, with photograph; Meritt, *Athenian Year*, p. 105, with more complete restorations (see also *SEG* XXI, 290); C. J. Schwenk, *Athens in the Age of Alexander*, pp. 355–356, no. 71. Parts of lines 1–6 quoted by W. K. Pritchett and O. Neugebauer, *Calendars*, p. 57.

a. 324/3 a., pryt. V   ΣΤΟΙΧ. 25

```
      ['Επὶ 'Ηγησίου ἄρχοντος ἐπ]ὶ τῆς Ἀ
      [ιαντίδος πέμπτης πρυτα]νείας
      [ἧι Εὐφάνης Φρύνωνος 'Ραμ]νούσι
      [ος ἐγραμμάτευεν· Ποσιδε]ῶνος ᵛ
  5   [τρίτηι μετ'εἰκάδας, μιᾶι χ]αὶ τρ
      [ιακοστῆι τῆς πρυτανείας· ἐ]χχλ
      [ησία .........²¹.........]
      [———————————————]
```

The writing well suits its period but does not represent the best class of work, displaying little finesse and some clumsiness (e.g., in variable sigma and in the ill-positioned tau of line 5).

The length of line is conditioned by lines 1 and 3, but the restorations elsewhere depend upon the assumed presence of ephelkystic nu in ἐγραμμάτευεν (line 4), for which Meritt argued in *Athenian Year*, loc. cit. By this date the inclusion of nu in this context had become regular: cf. A. S. Henry, *CQ* n.s. 17, 1967, p. 278; L. Threatte, *Grammar*, p. 641. See also **33**. The result of this is that the month must be Posideon or Gamelion and the prytany the fifth, with Aiantis therefore as the phyle in prytany. See Meritt, *Hesperia* 10, 1941, p. 50, and cf. Schwenk, *loc. cit.* R. Develin (*Athenian Officials*, p. 406) regarded the reconstruction as speculative.

Line 3. Euphanes, son of Phrynon, of Rhamnous, appears as Εὐφάνης Φ[ρύνωνος] 'Ραμνούσιος on the dedicatory base I 5512 (*Hesperia* 10, 1941, pp. 42–49, no. 11). The patronymic appears in full in *IG* II², 362, line 3, and the whole name may be restored conformably in the other texts of the year where apposite. Cf. J. Pouilloux, *Forteresse*, p. 173. The recognition of his demotic in this text confirmed the restoration of the name of the archon in line 1 and thus the date of the document. Phrynon is doubtless to be identified with the Φρύνων 'Ραμνούσιος who was an ambassador to Philip II of Macedon at the time of the Peace of Philokrates and whom Demosthenes (19.230) describes as ὁ μιαρός. See *PA* 15032; *IG* II², 4351.

FRAGMENT OF AN HONORARY DECREE

92. Three fragments, which do not join, of a stele of Pentelic marble (I 4224) surmounted by a sculptured relief with flat top. The largest fragment (*a*) preserves the upper left-hand section of the stele, with the left side, original back, and remains of the relief, but is broken below and to the right; it was discovered on March 6, 1939, in a Turkish context in Grave XXXI in the north peristyle of the Hephaisteion (E 7). Fragment *b*, broken on all sides, was discovered on June 1, 1936, in a Turkish context in a well in the Hellenistic Building on Kolonos Agoraios (F 6). Fragment *c*, also broken all around, was discovered on the same day and in the same context as fragment *a*.

The relief, which is very battered, appears to show Athena, with helmet and spear, leaning on her shield and facing to the right. She looks towards the figure of a man, presumably the honorand, partly preserved in the center of the composition. A further figure now lost may be presumed to have existed farther to the right. For this compositional arrangement cf. **71**. On the sculpture see also *SEG* XXXIX, 324.

a: H. 0.65 m.; W. 0.26 m.; Th. 0.16 m.

b: H. 0.17 m.; W. 0.13 m.; Th. 0.12 m.

c: H. 0.076 m.; W. 0.162 m.; Th. 0.15 m.

LH. 0.007–0.008 m.

Στοιχ. (square) 0.0158 m.

Ed. B. D. Meritt, *Hesperia* 10, 1941, pp. 50–52, no. 13, with photographs of all the fragments; C. J. Schwenk, *Athens in the Age of Alexander*, pp. 356–358, no. 72 (cf. *SEG* XXXV, 75).

a. 324/3 *a.*, *pryt.* VI   ΣTOIΧ. 31

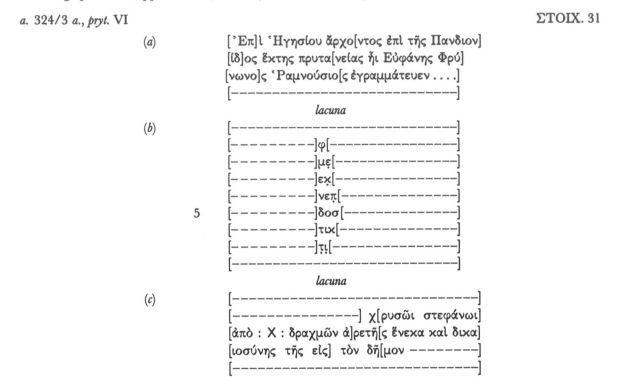

(*a*)
[ʼΕπ]ὶ Ἡγησίου ἄρχο[ντος ἐπὶ τῆς Πανδιον]
[ίδ]ος ἕκτης πρυτα[νείας ἧι Εὐφάνης Φρύ]
[νωνο]ς Ῥαμνούσιο[ς ἐγραμμάτευεν . . . .]
[------------------------]
lacuna

(*b*)
[------------------------]
[- - - - - - - -]φ[----------------]
[- - - - - - - -]με[---------------]
[- - - - - - - -]εχ[---------------]
[- - - - - - - -]νεπ[--------------]
5 [- - - - - - - -]δοσ[--------------]
[- - - - - - - -]τιχ[--------------]
[- - - - - - - -]τι[---------------]
[------------------------]
lacuna

(*c*)
[-------------------------------]
[----------------] χ[ρυσῶι στεφάνωι]
[ἀπὸ : Χ : δραχμῶν ἀ]ρετῆ[ς ἕνεκα καὶ δικα]
[ιοσύνης τῆς εἰς] τὸν δῆ[μον ---------]
[-------------------------------]

Fragment *b*: Line 4. An upright is preserved at the left of the stoichos after the epsilon: the letter is pi, gamma, or possibly nu, but cannot be kappa or rho. The readings on this and the other fragments are otherwise those of Meritt, followed also by Schwenk. Fragment *c*: There is no clue concerning the position of the fragment within the latitude of the stele, and the lines are divided arbitrarily.

The writing is regular and well ordered, with considerable artistic sensibility. "Free ends" of strokes are carefully widened. Certain letters, for example epsilon and nu, appear unusually wide in proportion to their height: also characteristic of this text is a rather stocky kappa, with its lower stroke angled at twenty degrees from the horizontal and the two angled strokes meeting at a slight interval from the upright.

Fragment *a*: Lines 1–2. Pandionis is a mandatory restoration, since the only alternative, Akamantis, is shown by *IG* II², 362 to have been the ninth prytany of the year. Lines 2–3. For detail on Euphanes, son of Phrynon, see **91**. Fragment *c*: Lines 1–2. On the cost of the stephanos and the formula here restored see A. S. Henry, *Honours*, pp. 22–27, 42–44; and cf. **86**, lines 15–20.

M. B. Walbank (*Hesperia* 58, 1989, p. 85) regards **132** as the work of the same craftsman who was responsible for this inscription, and he dates it accordingly; but there is no sound argument for any closer association of that fragment with these. He further sees *IG* II², 416 (*SEG* XXVI, 78), of *ca.* 331–324, as the handiwork of the same man and suggests that *SEG* XVIII, 85, a statue base with the "signature" of the sculptor Praxiteles, to be dated within the third quarter of the 4th century, may be by his hand also.

A RENT AGREEMENT AND AN HONORARY DECREE VOTED BY THE DEME PEIRAIEUS

93 (Pl. 10). Four fragments of a stele of bluish gray Hymettian marble, two of which were discovered in the excavations of the Agora. Of these two the uppermost fragment (I 2440), here designated *a*, preserves the left edge of the stele but is otherwise broken all around: it was discovered on February 15, 1935, in a wall of a modern house over the East Building (O 14).

The bottom edge of this fragment makes a direct join with the upper left-hand section of the upper fragment of *IG* II², 1176 (hereafter fragment *b*), a piece similarly preserving the left edge of the stele and identified by A. Wilhelm in the Epigraphical Museum, under the number E.M. 7719, as part of the same inscription as the lower and larger fragment of *IG* II², 1176 (hereafter fragment *d*), which is now in the British Museum.

A fourth fragment (*c*), the second of the two found in the American excavations (I 6439), was published separately but is to be attributed to this stele. This preserves part of the right edge of the monument but is broken above, below, and to the left. It was discovered on February 15, 1952 (coincidentally, seventeen years later to the day than the discovery of fragment *a*), in the foundation of a modern house northwest of the Church of the Holy Apostles (O 14, the same area as fragment *a*). The rough back of this fragment was reported as original in the *editio princeps*. It makes a direct join with the right edge of fragment *b* and (below the inscribed surface) with fragment *a*. Both Agora fragments are now in the Epigraphical Museum (E.M. 13447 and E.M. 13446 respectively).

The stele evidently tapered both in width and in thickness from bottom to top.

a + *b* +*c*, as joined: H. 0.174 m.; W. 0.208–0.215 m.; Th. 0.038–0.06 m.

d: H. 0.227 m.; W. 0.219–0.229 m.; Th. 0.06–0.065 m.

LH. 0.005–0.006 m.

Ed. *b* + *d* only: *IG* II², 1176, with earlier bibliography: for Wilhelm's identification of fragment *b* see *Urkunden dramatischer Aufführungen in Athen*, 1906, pp. 235–237 and for his dating, *Beiträge zur griechischen Inschriftenkunde*, 1909, p. 297. *a*, with reference to *b* only: B. D. Meritt, *Hesperia* 29, 1960, p. 1, no. 1, with photograph of fragments *a* + *b*, as joined, pl. 1. See also *SEG* XIX, 117 and (for mention of a reference to *IG* II², 1176 by D. D. Feaver, *Yale Classical Studies* 15, 1957, pp. 153–154) XXI, 516. *c* only: Meritt, *Hesperia* 32, 1963, pp. 12–13, no. 10, with photograph pl. 4; see also *SEG* XXI, 521. An incomplete version of this text, with some false readings, was published by N. C. Conomis from a transcript by A. N. Oikonomides, *Klio* 39, 1961, pp. 82–83. Cf. J. and L. Robert, *REG* 77, 1964, p. 149, no. 117.

All fragments: R. S. Stroud, *CSCA* 7, 1974, pp. 290–298, no. III, with photograph pl. 4 (see also SEG XXXIII, 143); C. J. Schwenk, *Athens in the Age of Alexander*, pp. 366–370, no. 76, who follows Stroud's text. Since this inscription contains a lease document, it appears also as Agora XIX, L13 (ed. M. B. Walbank), and the details of its content are more appropriately considered there.

Fragments *a* + *b* and *d* were discussed and their details utilized by D. Behrend (*Attische Pachturkunde*, pp. 86–88, no. 30; see also p. 155), whose suggestion for line 9 was vital in the fresh determination of the date of the document. He further studied fragment *c* (*op. cit.*, p. 88, no. 31; see also p. 155) but did not make a connection between this and his no. 30. Their juxtaposition in that context, however, was conducive to the association which Stroud's edition established (where cf. p. 279, note 1). *IG* II², 1176, as it existed at the time of their respective publications, was further briefly cited by Wilhelm (*Griechische Inschriften rechtlicher Inhalts*, 1951, pp. 80–81) and M. I Finley (*Studies in Land and Credit in Ancient Athens, 500–200 B.C.*, 1952, pp. 216, note 68, 295, note 10).

a. 324/3 *a.*   NON-ΣΤΟΙΧ. *ca.* 31–43

```
(a, c)      [—————————————————————————]
            [τὴν(?)] σκηνὴν προ[.4–5.]ασι[....].//[..ca.7..]
            [ἐ]άν τι βο[ύ]λωντ[αι πε]ρὶ τὴν οἰκοδομίαν·
            ἐξεῖναι δὲ αὐ[τοῖς χ]ρῆσθαι λίθοις καὶ
            γῆι ἐκ τοῦ τεμ[ένους] τοῦ Διονύσου· ὅταν δ'
       5    ἐξίωσιν, παρα[διδόναι(?)] ἅπαντα ὀρθὰ καὶ ἑ
            στηκότα· ἐὰ[ν δὲ .4–5..]ειψωσιν πρὸς τῆι σκη
            νεῖ, κέρα[μον καὶ ξ]ύλα ἀπίτω λαβὼν πα
(b)         ρὰ(?) [..ca.7..]λι[.· ὁ δὲ χ]ρόνος ἄρχει τῆς μι
            σθώσεως ʽΗγησίας ἄρχων· τοὺς δὲ δημό
      10    τας θεωρεῖν ἀργύριο[ν] διδόντας πλὴν ὅ
            σοις οἱ δημόται προ[εδρίαν δ]εδώκασι·
            τούτους δ' ἀπογράψα[ι πρὸς τοὺς π]ρια[μέ]
            νους τὸ θέατρον· εἶν[αι δὲ καὶ προεδρίαν]
            καὶ τῶι δημάρχωι κα[ὶ τῶι ταμίαι καὶ τῶι κή]
      15    ρυκι καὶ εἴ τωι ἄλλωι [δεδώκασιν οἱ δημόται]
            [τὴ]ν προεδρίαν· ὅσοι δ[ὲ —————————]
            [————————]νι[—————————]
                                lacuna
```

(d)

[------τοὺς πριαμένους τὸ θέ]ατρ[ο]ν πα[ρέ]

[χειν τοῖς δημότ]αις ἡδ[ω]λιασμένην τὴν θέαν [κα]

20 [τὰ τ]ὰ πάτρια· ἐὰν δὲ μὴ ποήσωσιν κατὰ τὰς συνθή[ή]

κας τὰς περὶ τὸ θέατρον, οἰκοδομῆσαι μὲν Πειρα

έας τὰ δεόμενα, τὰ δ' ἀναλώματα τοῖς πριαμένοις

εἶναι· ἐπιτιμητὰς δὲ αἱρεῖσθαι Πειραέας ὅταν πα

ραδιδῶσι τὸ θέατρον τρεῖς ἄνδρας ἐκ Πειραέων·

25 ἀναγράψαι δὲ τὸν δήμαρχον καὶ τοὺς ταμίας ἀντί

γραφα τῶν συνθηκῶν εἰς στήλην λιθίνην καὶ στῆσα

ι ἐν τῆι ἀγορᾶι τῶν δημοτῶν· παραγράψαι δὲ καὶ τὸ

ὄνομα, παρ'ὧι ἂν κείωνται αἱ συνθῆκαι· ὠνηταὶ Ἀρι

στοφάνης Σμικύθο :ΓΗ: Μελησίας Ἀριστοκράτο : ΧΗ

30 Ἀρεθούσιος Ἀριστόλεω Πήληξ :Γ: Οἰνοφῶν Εὐφι

λήτου Πειραιεύς : ΧΗ.　　　vacat

Καλλιάδης εἶπεν· ἐψηφίσθαι Πειραεῦσι· ἐπειδὴ Θεαῖος

φιλοτιμεῖται πρὸς τοὺς δημότας καὶ νῦν καὶ ἐν τῶι

ἔμπροσθε χρόνωι, καὶ πεπόηκεν τριακοσίαις δρα

35 χμαῖς πλέον εὑρεῖν τὸ θέατρον, στεφανῶσαι αὐτ

ὸν θαλλῶ στεφάνωι ἀρετῆς ἕνεκα καὶ δικαιο

σύνης τῆς εἰς τοὺς δημότας· στεφανῶσαι δὲ

καὶ τοὺς πριαμένους τὸ θέατρον Ἀριστοφάνην

Πειραέα, Μελησίαν Λαμπτρέα, Οἰνοφῶντα

40 Πειραιέα, Ἀρεθούσιον Πήληκα.

The text of lines 1–8 is basically composed of Meritt's two texts fitted together: lines 9–12 are similarly a compound of the first lines of *IG* II², 1176 and Meritt's text of what is now fragment *c*. In lines 8–9 Behrend, during his survey of fragments *a* + *b*, suggested χρόνος ἄρχει τῆς μι]|σθώσεω[ς· Ἡ]γησίας [ἄρχων· καταβάλλειν δὲ κτλ. in place of the ---τῆς μι]|σθώσεω[ς· Ἡ]γησίας [εἶπεν· καταβάλλειν δὲ κτλ. of Wilhelm (followed by J. Kirchner in *IG* II² and by Meritt). This admirably accorded with the evidence of fragment *c* and led to the revision of this part of the text.

The evidence of line 9 now dates the document to 324/3. The date hitherto accepted for *IG* II², 1176 was "*ca.* 360 B.C.", a dating which originated with Wilhelm (see above), although his *en passant* remark about it did not make his grounds clear. It is possible that the use of O for OΥ in the genitives of line 29 influenced him; but sporadic survivals of this continued throughout the 4th century (see **77**, lines 14–15): or it may be a matter of simple abbreviation (see **80**, lines 4–5). The lettering of the inscription is undoubtedly poor and *prima facie* would not support a "high" date. E. L. Hicks in his edition of fragment *d* (*British Museum Inscriptions*, no. XII) had considered the inscription as of the 3rd century. It is also to be noted that fragment *c*, when published separately, was attributed to the middle of that century. These variations of date, on the basis of the letter forms, of what prove to be pieces of the same stele are not uninstructive as an index of the reliability of this criterion. Even so, it is fair to add that the writing is perfunctory and hasty (though not careless), and the diminutive circular letters add to its untidy appearance. Not all epigraphical work even of the mid 4th century had the regularity and distinction commonly regarded as characteristic of it. Cf. **49** and (for the craftsman) **143**.

For an analysis of the lease and the decree see Stroud, *loc. cit.* and *Agora* XIX, L13. The major part of the document is apparently concerned with the conditions of lease of the theater in the Peiraieus and (particularly in lines 9–16) with rights of free admission reserved by the demesmen for those to whom they have granted *proedria*. In the last nine lines is added a decree in honor of one Theaios, not mentioned in what remains of the earlier section but through whose good offices the deme evidently made a favorable bargain. With him are joined the four lessees, named this time without their patronymics. J. J. Buchanan (*Theorika*, 1962, p. 86, note 1) referred to "the ἀρχιτέκτων" as being granted the lease. If, more correctly, the plural πριάμενοι are to be regarded as joint ἀρχιτέκτονες of the theater, the assumption must be based on lines 20–23, but the supposition is unnecessary and probably mistaken.

The theater in Mounychia in the Peiraieus already existed in the 5th century. See W. Judeich, *Topographie*, p. 451, with further references; T. Lenschau, *RE* XIX, i, 1937, col. 90, *s.v.* Peiraieus; E. Fiechter, *Das Theater im Piraeus*, 1950; L. Moretti, *Iscrizioni storiche ellenistiche* I, p. 79, note 3; C. T. Panagos, *Le Pirée*, 1968, p. 221.

Lines 5–6. On the obligation to return the property in good order and in the state in which it was originally leased, cf. Finley, *Political Science Quarterly* 68, 1953, pp. 262–263; Behrend, *Attische Pachturkunden*, pp. 121–124. Line 6. In the separate publication of this fragment Meritt restored ἀλ]είψωσιν, and this, or some compound of it, may indeed be acceptable. The change in the main clause to a singular subject is awkward but may be attributable to imperfect drafting based on well-known but mutually incompatible formulas. Lines 6–7. τῆι σκηνεῖ. For the variation HI–EI in the dative feminine singular see L. Threatte, *Grammar*, p. 378 and **89**, commentary on line 2. Line 8. For the formula χρόνος ἄρχει, establishing the initial date of the operation of a lease, see *SEG* XXIV, 203, lines 27–28; *IG* II², 2492, 2493, 2499, and elsewhere: cf. also Wilhelm, *Archiv für Papyrusforschung* 11, 1935, pp. 203–204.

Lines 25–26. On the designation of the inscription as an ἀντίγραφον of the contract see G. Klaffenbach, *Bemerkungen zum griechischen Urkundenwesen* (= *SbAkadBerlin* 1960, 6), pp. 28–29. The original of the συνθῆκαι was to be deposited with an individual, and it is ordered that his name be appended, an order not explicitly carried out, although Theaios may have been the man concerned. Behrend made the assumption, perhaps unnecessary and cumbersome, that the original should have been in the public archives and that what we have is "die Abschrift des Sitzungsprotokolls" (*op. cit.*, p. 87, with note 175). He also drew attention to the point that the ἀντίγραφον was not erected in the agora of the demesmen, as prescribed in lines 26–27, but in the Agora of Athens itself, if, that is to say, its place of discovery is to be directly related to the place in which it anciently stood, as one is tempted to presume.

Lines 29 and 39. For the family of Melesias of Lamptrai (*PA* 9814) see J. K. Davies, *Athenian Propertied Families*, p. 59. Aristophanes (*PA* 2094) also contributed to the setting up of a cult statue and the repair of a sanctuary in his neighborhood (*IG* II², 2329, the date of which may be more narrowly defined in the light of the present text). Oinophon and Arethousios (*PA* 11368 and 1588) are otherwise unknown.

For the variations in spelling of Πειρα(ι)εύς (lines 21, 23, 24, 31, 32, 39, 40) cf. Threatte, *Grammar*, pp. 282–284.

This text is no. 86 in the list of deme decrees assembled by D. Whitehead, *The Demes of Attica, 507–ca. 250 B.C.*, 1986, on p. 385, and is quoted *passim* in the course of his study. See also R. Garland, *The Piraeus from the Fifth to the First Century B.C.*, 1987, pp. 76, 227 (nos. 2, 3); for the theater itself see p. 221, note 161, with further references.

THE ARCHONSHIP OF KEPHISODOROS, 323/2 B.C.

IG II², 343 (*SEG* XXIV, 103), 365 (*SEG* XXXVI, 157, with earlier references), 366, 367 (*SEG* XXI, 295, XXVI, 81, XXXII, 91), 368, lines 19–24 (*SEG* XXI, 296, XXXII, 92), and 448, lines 1–34 (*SEG* XXI, 297, XXIII, 59, XXVI, 82, XXXI, 79, XXXII, 90) constitute with **94** the seven decrees attributable to the year of Kephisodoros, with the reservation that the attribution of the first of these, based on the restoration, remains uncertain even if acceptable. All have been restudied (although not in the order just listed) by C. J. Schwenk (*Athens in the Age of Alexander*, pp. 381–432, nos. 79–85).

Of these seven, 365 (pryt. I), 367 (pryt. III), 368 (pryt. V), and 448 (also pryt. V) preserve calendric data that help to determine the character of the year; but that character has been disputed and the texts so restored as to support rival contentions in the matter. To J. Kirchner (*IG* II², 365, *comm.*) the year was ordinary in the Athenian festival calendar; to W. B. Dinsmoor (*Archons of Athens*, p. 373) it was intercalary, and it was regarded as intercalary also by W. K. Pritchett and O. Neugebauer (*Calendars*, pp. 57–59). B. D. Meritt (*Athenian Year*, pp. 106–110, 133) returned to the supposition that it was ordinary, which Pritchett countered by a reaffirmation (*Ancient Athenian Calendars on Stone*, pp. 285–286) that it could indeed be intercalary. See also C. W. Fornara, *CJ* 57, 1961–1962, pp. 370–371. The contentions in each case centered round the reading and restoration of *IG* II², 448 (see *SEG*, *locc. citt.*), and Meritt repeated his position in *TAPA* 95, 1964, pp. 226–228. Cf. Schwenk, *Athens in the Age of Alexander*, pp. 397–398, 403–405.

As the fifteenth year of a Metonic cycle (the sixth), the year may be expected to have been ordinary (see Meritt, *TAPA* 95, 1964, p. 236). Meritt supposed it to have contained 355 days, beginning with a full Hekatombaion but with one day intercalated into Posideon, so that it also ended with a full month. Prytanies I, II, III, IX, and X he considered to have contained 36 days, the remainder 35.

Four of the phylai in prytany are known, and for one other there are three possibilities: I Hippothontis, II Aigeis, III Antiochis, Erechtheis, or Kekropis, V Pandionis, and VIII Oineis. The γραμματεύς of the year was Archias, son of Pythodoros of Alopeke, on whom see **94** and S. Alessandri, *Annali della Scuola Normale di Pisa*, pp. 52, 67. For a detailed list of known office holders in Kephisodoros' archonship see R. Develin, *Athenian Officials*, pp. 407–410.

HONORS (INCLUDING ONE GRANT OF CITIZENSHIP) FOR VARIOUS FOREIGN BENEFACTORS

94. Eleven fragments of a tall, comparatively narrow stele of Pentelic marble, of which two join, one preserves the left side of the stele, and one preserves the original back and right side. Eight of them were found in the Agora excavations and were associated with *IG* II², 369 and 414, b and c (no longer themselves to be connected with *IG* II², 414, a and d). Above the inscribed face of the stele was a double molding (cyma reversa, similar in type to L. T. Shoe, *Profiles of Greek Mouldings*, 1936, pl. XXVII:7, but with a heavier lower member) and surmounting relief sculpture (cf. the *lemma* of *IG* II², 369). All the fragments, including those discovered before the excavations in the Agora, are detailed separately.

a: I 4935 e, a fragment preserving the left side of the stele and part of the upper molding but otherwise broken, discovered between June 6 and 9, 1938, in a context of (probably) Early Roman times over the paved court below Klepsydra (T 26–27).

H. 0.10 m.; W. 0.10 m.; Th. 0.042 m.

b: *IG* II² 369, now in the Epigraphical Museum (E.M. 7333). This fragment preserves a complete section of the upper molding and a small piece of the surmounting decoration but is otherwise broken. It was apparently discovered on the North Slope of the Akropolis.

H. 0.18 m.; W. 0.125 m.; Th. 0.105 m.

c: I 4935 b, a fragment broken all around, which joins with its right side the left side of fragment *j*; discovered on June 6, 1938, a little north of the point at which fragment *a* was found.

H. 0.127 m.; W. 0.095 m.; Th. 0.075 m.

d: I 4935 a, a fragment broken all around, discovered on June 3, 1937, in the same area.
H. 0.14 m.; W. 0.105 m.; Th. 0.075 m.

e: I 4935 c, a fragment broken all around, discovered on June 9, 1938, in the same location as fragment *a*.
H. 0.09 m.; W. 0.048 m.; Th. 0.067 m.

f: I 4935 d, a fragment broken all around, discovered on June 7, 1938, in the filling of the Klepsydra antechamber (T 27).

H. 0.127 m.; W. 0.085 m.; Th. 0.06 m.

g: I 5496, a fragment broken all around, discovered on June 2, 1938, in a Classical context in the Klepsydra antechamber (T 27).

H. 0.20 m.; W. 0.045 m.; Th. 0.075 m.

h: I 4935 f, a fragment preserving the original rough-picked back and lightly toothed right side of the stele but otherwise broken, discovered on October 12, 1938, in a wall of a modern house south of the Market Square (O–P 22–23).

H. 0.21 m.; W. 0.127 m.; Th. 0.145 m.

i: I 2752, a fragment from the upper right corner of the inscribed face and preserving the spring of the surmounting molding but broken all around, discovered on April 8, 1935, in a late wall east of the Odeion (N 11).

H. 0.09 m.; W. 0.07 m.; Th. 0.06 m.

j: *IG* II², 414, c, a fragment broken all around but making on its left side a join with fragment *c*, *q.v.*; discovered on the North Slope of the Akropolis and now in the Epigraphical Museum (E.M. 12572).

H. 0.125 m.; W. 0.087 m.; Th. 0.055 m.

k: *IG* II², 414, b, a fragment broken all around, discovered near the Cave of Pan and now in the Epigraphical Museum (E.M. 7332).

H. 0.255 m.; W. 0.165 m.; Th. 0.125 m.

LH. 0.007–0.008 m.

Στοιχ. (almost square) Hor. 0.017 m.; Vert. 0.018 m.

Ed. *a–f* only: E. Schweigert, *Hesperia* 8, 1939, pp. 27–30, no. 7, with photographs of all fragments. (The subsequent identification of fragments *g–k* necessitated a complete reedition in the following year, also by Schweigert [*Hesperia* 9, 1940, pp. 335–339, no. 42], with photographs of fragments *c + j*, *g*, *h*, *i*, and *k*); M. J. Osborne, *Naturalization* I, pp. 80–85, D 25, *Naturalization* II, p. 95, with a revised order (though not a revised identification) of the fragments; C. J. Schwenk, *Athens in the Age of Alexander*, pp. 426–432, no. 85, whose text is based on that of Schweigert as revised. See *SEG* XXI, 298 (Schweigert's revised text, with additional references to M. Rostovtzeff, *The Social and Economic History of the Hellenistic World* III, 1941, p. 1627, note 189; J. B. Brashinsky, Краткие Сообщения о Докладах и Полевых Исследованиях Института Материальной Културы, Академия Наук СССР 74, 1959, pp. 3–8, with photograph and drawing of fragment *f* fig. 2; J. and L. Robert, *REG* 75, 1962, pp. 146–147, no. 108); *SEG* XXIV, 102 (reference to Brashinsky, *ibid.*, 109, 1967, pp. 49–51, who adjusted his previous article, which had taken account only of Schweigert's first publication, and urged that the recipients of the honors were certain Bosporan citizens, officials specifically charged by the king of the Bosporan kingdom with the duty of assisting Athenian merchants). Cf. *IG* II^2, 212 and Brashinsky in *Acta of the Fifth International Congress of Greek and Latin Epigraphy, Cambridge, 1967*, 1971, pp. 119–121.

a. 323/2 *a., pryt.* VIII   ΣΤΟΙΧ. 28

```
(a, b, i)        Θ        ε        [ο]        ι.
            ᾽Επὶ Κη[φισοδ]ώρου [ἄρχοντος ἐπὶ] τῆς
            [Ο]ἰνεῖ[δος ὀγ]δόης [πρυτανείας ἧ]ι ᾽Αρ
            [χίας Πυθοδώρου ᾽Αλωπεκῆθεν ἐγρ]α[μ]
      5     [μάτευεν· . . . . . . . . .²¹. . . . . . . . . .]
                          lacuna
  (d)       [– – – – ἐπειδὴ – – – – – – – – –πρότερόν]
            [τε ἐπιδέδω]χεν τῶ[ι δήμωι . . .⁸. . . .]
            [. . . .⁹. . . .], χαὶ νῦν [ἐπιδέδωχεν εἰς]
            [τὸν πόλεμον] τῶι δή[μωι . . . .¹⁰. . . . .],
     10     [δεδόχθαι τῶι] δήμω[ι ἐπαινέσαι . . .]
            [. . .⁷. . . Δημη]τρίο[υ εὐνοίας ἕνεχα]
            [χαὶ φιλοτιμί]ας τ[ῆς εἰς τὸν δῆμον τ]
            [ὸν ᾽Αθηναίων, χ]αὶ στ[εφανῶσαι αὐτὸν]
            [χρυσῶι στεφά]νωι [ἀπὸ – – – δραχμῶν]
                          lacuna
  (f)  15   [. . . . . . . . . . . . . .²⁶. . . . . . . . . . . . . ., χα]
            [ὶ δοῦν]α[ι περὶ αὐτοῦ τὴν ψῆφον τοὺς]
            [πρυτ]άνει[ς τῆς Οἰνεῖδος εἰς τὴν πρ]
            [ώτην] ἐχχλ[ησίαν . . . . . .¹⁵. . . . . . .]
            [. . .]αιος ε[. . . . . . . .²⁰. . . . . . . . .]
     20     [. . .] προγ[. . . . . . . .²¹. . . . . . . . .]
            [. . .]ονα[. . . . . . . . . .²¹. . . . . . . . .]
                          lacuna
  (g)       [– – – – – – – – – – – – –]ι[– – – – – – – – – –]
            [– – – – – – – – – –]εστ[– – – – – – – – – –]
            [– – – – – – – – – –]ου[– – – – – – – – – –]
     25     [– – – – – – – – – –] vacat [– – – – – – – – – –]
            [– – – – – – – – – –]ρ[– – – – – – – – – –]
                          lacuna
 (c +j)    [. . . . .¹⁰. . . . . ᾽Αθ]ην[αί]ων χα[. . .⁸. . . .]
            [. . . .¹¹. . . . . .] ὅτι δ[ύ]ναντ[αι ἀγαθὸν]
     30     [δημοσίαι τε χ]αὶ ἰδ[ί]αι τ[οῖς τε ἀφιχ]
            [νουμένοις εἰ]ς Βόσπορο[ν, ἐπαινέσα]
            [ι δὲ χαὶ . .⁵. . . χ]αὶ ᾽Αστυμ[. . . .⁹. . . .]
            [χαὶ . .⁶. . . χαὶ] Πολ[υ]οσθέν[ην . .⁶. . .]
            [. . .⁷. . ., χαὶ στ]εφ[αν]ῶ[σαι ἑχάστους]
     35     [τούτων χρυσῶι] σ[τεφάνωι . . .⁸. . . .]
                          lacuna
  (e)       [. . . .]ω[. . . . . . . . .²³. . . . . . . . . .]
            [. . . .]επ[. . . . . . . .²². . . . . . . . .]
            [. . . .]τε[. . . . . . . .²². . . . . . . . .]
            [. . . .]λε[. . . . . . . .²². . . . . . . . .]
     40     [. . . .] traces [. . . . . . . . .²². . . . . . . . . .]
                          lacuna
```

(h)

[. . . . . .²⁴. . . . .]η[. . .]
[. . . . . .²². . . . .]αιει[. .]
[. . . . . .²². . . . . .α]ὐτῶν [.]
[. . . . . .²³. . . . . σ]τρατ

45   [. . . . . .²³. . . . . δ]πως ἃ
[ν . . . . .²³. . . . . τ]ὴν ἐ
[κκλησίαν . . . .¹⁸. . . . .]ολ

lacuna

(k)

[. . . . ᾿Α]θηναι[. . . . . .¹⁸. . . . .]
[κεχ]ειροτο[νημέν. . . . . . .¹¹. . . ᾿Α]

50   [θηναί]ων εἰδό[τες ὅτι . . .¹¹. . . . . . .]
[. . τὰς] δωρεὰς κ[. . . . . .¹⁶. . . . .]
[. .⁵. .]ου ἐκ τῶν [. . . . . .¹⁶. . . . . .]
[. .⁵. .]αι αὐτοι[. . . . . . . .¹⁶. . . . . .]
[. . δημ]όσιον αγ[. . . . . .¹⁶. . . . . .]

55   [. γρα]φομένας [. . . . . . . .¹⁷. . . . . .]
[. .⁵. .]α καὶ το[. . . . . . .¹⁷. . . . . .]
[. .⁵. .]ας τῆς [. . . . . .¹⁸. . . . . . .]
[. . . . τῶ]ι δή[μωι . . . . . .¹⁶. . . . . .]
[————————————————]

Osborne discerned the remains of a letter at the foot of fragment *e*, below the last line as recorded by Schweigert, and this adds an extra unit to the line numeration. But he also omitted a line in fragments *h* (here line 44) and *k* (here line 56), and his subsequent line numeration is understated by one, finally by two, to the end of the document. Fragments *e*, *h*, and *k* are to be regarded as of uncertain location in the sequence of the text: the position of *e* in relation to the width of the stele is arbitrary. The above text follows that of Osborne's study (see below).

Lines 6–8. [– – – – – – – – | . . ἐπιδέδω]κεν τῶ[ι δήμωι XXX μεδίμ|νους πυρῶν(?)], καὶ νῦν κτλ. Schweigert. Lines 15–16. [. . . . . .²⁷. . . . ., δ|οῦναι δὲ περὶ αὐτοῦ τὴν ψῆφον τοὺς] Schweigert. Lines 19–21. [. . .]αιος ε[. . . .· στῆσαι δὲ καὶ παρὰ τ||οὺς] προγ[όνους Σάτυρον καὶ Λεύκω|να εἰκ]όνα [αὐτοῦ χαλκῆν ἐν τῆι ἀγορᾶ|ι – – – –] (or εἰκ]όνα[ς αὐτῶν χαλκᾶς κτλ.]) Brashinsky. Lines 33–34. [καὶ . . .⁸. . . .] Πολ[υ]οσθέν[ην. .⁶. .|. . .⁷. . ., καὶ στ]εφ[αν]ῶ[σαι ἕκαστον] Schweigert.

The writing is clean and clear, with some enlargement of the "free ends" of the strokes. The spacing of the text is generous, and as the width is comparatively narrow and the numerous fragments for the most part defy close association, the stele must have been tall. It was evidently demolished with some thoroughness. The lettering closely resembles that of *IG* II², 414, a (*SEG* XXI, 276), **89**, and the deme decree from Halai Araphenides (now in the Epigraphical Museum [E.M. 12807]) published by P. D. Stavropoullos (᾿Αρχ. ᾿Εφ., 1932, ᾿Αρχαιολογικὰ Χρονικά, pp. 30–32), for all of which the same stonemason could well have been responsible.

Schweigert published the fragments in the order of their present alphabetical designation (but with *a*, *b*, *i*, and *c* + *j* as shown). This arrangement was followed by Schwenk. Osborne however suggested that two decrees are embodied here, the first containing the grant of a crown and of citizenship (the last clause of which appears on fragment *f*) and the second beginning at line 26 following a blank line, which contained a grant of honors for a number of recipients. This suggestion, which is here adopted, caused him to move fragments *c* + *j* into the context of the second decree. The honorands were all doubtless connected with the kingdom of Bosporos and the grain trade, the successful maintenance of which through famine (cf. **82**) and war (lines 8–9), presumably the Lamian War, was of such vital importance to the Athenians.

Line 3. On EI in the place of HI in the name of the phyle, see L. Threatte, *Grammar*, pp. 374–377. The spelling with epsilon-iota becomes common after *ca.* 330, but at this period the version with eta-iota is still the more frequent. Lines 3–5. This text supplied the correct name of the secretary of this year, previously interpreted as Eukles. His patronymic and demotic survive on the joint evidence of *IG* II², 365 and 367. His name was wholly restored by Schweigert in *IG* II², 343 (*Hesperia* 9, 1940, pp. 342–343), but the restorations and attribution to this year remain uncertain (*SEG* XXIV, 103). See above under the Archonship of Kephisodoros, p. 139.

Lines 13–14 (and 34–35). On the cost of the stephanos and the formula of the grant see A. S. Henry, *Honours*, pp. 22–27, 42–44, and cf. **86** and **92**.

Lines 19–21. Brashinsky's suggestion (accepted in Schwenk's text) would connect this inscription with the erection of honorary statues of members of the Bosporan dynastic house referred to by Deinarchos as decreed at the instigation of Demosthenes, *In Demosthenem* 43. Cf. *Agora* III, p. 211, no. 700 and *IG* II², 653, lines 40–42. On the kingdom of Bosporos and the dynasty of the Spartokidai see M. Cary, *CAH* VI, p. 71; R. Werner, *Historia* 4, 1955, pp. 412–444; M. N. Tod, *GHI* II, pp. 42–45, with further references. But it is difficult to accommodate Brashinsky's hypothesis to the nature and content of this text. Osborne's view, that the individual of Decree I was "a state leader" but not "one of the known Bosporan kings", and that Decree II honors local Bosporan citizens, represents the most reasonable conclusion from the evidence.

The decree was nonprobouleumatic; cf. **85** and P. J. Rhodes, *Athenian Boule*, p. 262. The enactment was complex and dealt with benefactors in an area of particular political concern. The assembly may therefore have given the council's proposals substantial debate and amendment. It is hard to envisage either that the council would have handed down an "open" *probouleuma* or that the honors here bestowed were voted in defiance of its advice (cf. Rhodes, *op. cit.*, p. 68).

THE ARCHONSHIP OF PHILOKLES, 322/1 B.C.

Of the six enactments of the boule and demos that survived to modern times from the year of Philokles, two (*IG* II², 375 [for which cf. *SEG* XXI, 302] and *IG* II², 377) have disappeared since they were first published: the former was passed in the last prytany of the year; the latter lacks a date. A third decree is dealt with below as **95**. The remainder are *IG* II², 308 + 371 (*SEG* III, 82), of the seventh prytany, 373 (*SEG* XXI, 301, XXIV, 105) of the ninth, and 376, which, with an incomplete prescript, seems to belong to the middle of the year. All have been restudied, in the order of their numbering in *IG* II², by C. J. Schwenk (*Athens in the Age of Alexander*, pp. 433–454, nos. 86–91).

W. B. Dinsmoor (*Archons of Athens*, pp. 373–374) and W. K. Pritchett and O. Neugebauer (*Calendars*, pp. 59–60), who had argued that the year of Kephisodoros was intercalary (see p. 139 above), regarded that of Philokles as ordinary. But there can be little doubt that 322/1 was intercalary in the Athenian festival calendar (cf. *IG* II², 372, *comm.*; B. D. Meritt, *Athenian Year*, pp. 110–112, *Historia* 26, 1977, p. 170), for it is best interpreted as having been preceded by two ordinary years and followed by another one, while 320/19 was again intercalary. However, because of errors in the drafting or engraving of *IG* II², 373 and 375, precision of its detail is hard to come by, while **95** contains a problem of its own, considered below in its context.

The year 322/1 was the sixteenth of the sixth Metonic cycle and as such was intercalary in that cycle as currently understood; cf. Meritt, *TAPA* 95, 1964, p. 236. Nevertheless, more recent commentators have remained divided in their interpretation; thus Schwenk (*Athens in the Age of Alexander*, p. 438) followed Meritt, while M. H. Hansen (*GRBS* 23, 1982, p. 345 [= *Athenian Ecclesia*, p. 97]) preferred to see the year as ordinary.

Meritt's proposed arrangement of months and prytanies, advanced as no more than a possibility in the light of the evidence, consisted of regular alternation of hollow and full months, with the final (thirteenth) month also full, and four prytanies of 39 days followed by six of 38, the Aristotelian "norm" revised for a year of 384 days. Four prytanies may be definitely associated with phylai known to have been in office: VII Akamantis, VIII Aiantis or Leontis, IX Oineis, X Pandionis.

The γραμματεύς of the year was Euthydemos, son of Hephaistodemos, of Kephisia: *IG* II², 373 and 375 preserve his name more or less in full. See S. Alessandri, *Annali della Scuola Normale di Pisa*, pp. 52, 67. He may have belonged to the same family as the Euthydemos of Kephisia whose death in the early 4th century is commemorated by *IG* II², 6415; and the man of the same name and deme active in the middle of the century (see J. K. Davies, *Athenian Propertied Families*, p. 191) could well have been his grandfather. He and others known to have held office during Philokles' archonship are listed by R. Develin (*Athenian Officials*, pp. 410–412).

A DECREE PROPOSED BY DEMADES, 322/1 B.C.

95. Two fragments, which do not join, of a stele of Hymettian marble, of which the smaller fragment (*b*, I 4421), broken all around save that it preserves the left side of the monument, was discovered on January 14, 1937, in a wall of a modern house outside the Market Square to the southeast, east of the Post-Herulian Wall (U 22). The upper fragment (*a*) has long been known and is in the Epigraphical Museum (E.M. 7184).

    a: H. 0.125 m.; W. 0.126 m.; Th. 0.085 m.

    b: H. 0.115 m.; W. 0.05 m.; Th. 0.046 m.

LH. 0.005 m.
Στοιχ. (square) 0.0124 m.

Ed. *a*: *IG* II², 372, with earlier bibliography; E. Schweigert, *Hesperia* 8, 1939, pp. 173–175, no. 4, with photograph
p. 174, fig. 3; C. J. Schwenk, *Athens in the Age of Alexander*, pp. 436–440, no. 87. *b* only: M. B. Walbank, *Hesperia* 58,
1989, pp. 85–86, no. 11, with photograph pl. 19. Fragment *a* quoted in full by B. D. Meritt, *Athenian Year*, pp. 110–111
(see also *SEG* XXI, 300). Photograph of fragment *a* also in J. Pečírka, *Listy Filologické* 89, 1966, pl. 1.

a. 322/1 a., *pryt.* VIII   ΣΤΟΙΧ. 27

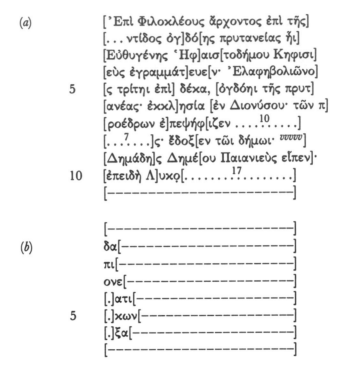

(*a*)
[Ἐπὶ Φιλοκλέους ἄρχοντος ἐπὶ τῆς]
[... ντίδος ὀγ]δό[ης πρυτανείας ἧι]
[Εὐθυγένης Ἡφ]αισ[τοδήμου Κηφισι]
[εὺς ἐγραμμάτ]ευε[ν· Ἐλαφηβολιῶνο]
5   [ς τρίτηι ἐπὶ] δέκα, [ὀγδόηι τῆς πρυτ]
[ανέας· ἐκκλ]ησία [ἐν Διονύσου· τῶν π]
[ροέδρων ἐ]πεψήφ[ιζεν ....¹⁰....]
[...⁷...]ς· ἔδοξ[εν τῶι δήμωι· ᵛᵛᵛᵛ]
[Δημάδη]ς Δημέ[ου Παιανιεὺς εἶπεν]·
10   [ἐπειδὴ Λ]υκο[.......¹⁷........]
[————————————————]

(*b*)
[————————————————]
δα[————————————————]
πι[————————————————]
ονε[————————————————]
[.]ατι[————————————————]
5   [.]κων[————————————————]
[.]ξα[————————————————]
[————————————————]

Small as fragment *b* is, Walbank's firm suggestion of its association with fragment *a* (although the relationship
between the two cannot be determined) makes it appropriate for both texts to be shown in full. Schweigert (*loc. cit.*)
associated *IG* II², 372 with *IG* II², 289; but this association, although maintained in *SEG* XXXII, 93, was convincingly
refuted by Pečírka (*op. cit.*, pp. 262–266). See also *SEG* XXIII, 60, Pečírka, *Formula*, pp. 57–58, and P. J. Rhodes,
Athenian Boule, p. 72, note 2. Fragment *b* is shown by itself, and rejected as a decree, in *SEG* XXXIX, 94.

Line 5. ἐνάτηι ἐπὶ] δέκα, [ἐνάτηι κτλ. *IG* II²; ἐνάτηι ἐπὶ] δέκα, [ἕκτηι Schweigert, i.e., the 255th day of an
ordinary year. In *Calendars*, pp. 59–60, W. K. Pritchett and O. Neugebauer advanced the idea of τρίτηι ἐπὶ] δέκα,
[ὀγδόηι κτλ.: but this would be the 278th day of an intercalary year, and they believed Philokles' year to have been
ordinary (see above). It was an idea adopted by Meritt (*loc. cit.*), whose interpretation of the year as intercalary
has been followed here and appears in the text shown. An objection to it is that it requires the unusual spelling
in lines 5–6 of πρυτανέας for πρυτανείας: but an example of this occurs in a text of this very year (*IG* II², 373, line 17);
another is to be found in **104**. Thus the supposition is not unreasonable. Cf. L. Threatte, *Grammar*, pp. 316–317.

More recently, M. H. Hansen (*GRBS* 23, 1982, p. 345, no. 56 [= *Athenian Ecclesia*, p. 97]) has preferred to
see 322/1 as an ordinary year and to revert to a festival date of 18 or 19 Elaphebolion; cf. *SEG* XXXII, 93. For
Elaphebolion 13 as a meeting day of the assembly, see J. D. Mikalson, *Sacred and Civil Calendar*, pp. 128–129 (for
Elaphebolion 18 and 19 *ibid.*, pp. 130–131, and cf. **79**). Schwenk, who briefly discussed the calendric problem,
accepted Meritt's equation in her commentary but printed that of *IG* II² in her text.

Line 6. The proximity of the festival of Dionysos no doubt affected the location of the assembly. See **79** and
references there. Line 8. The decree was nonprobouleumatic: cf. Rhodes, *Athenian Boule*, p. 262 and **94**. Line 9. For
the proposer Demades see **72**, commentary on line 6. This decree is listed among those ascribed to him by A. N.
Oikonomides (Πλάτων 8, 1956, p. 116, no. 11) and by Rhodes (*Athenian Boule*, p. 269) but is omitted by Hansen
(*Athenian Ecclesia II*, p. 40).

GRANT OF ATHENIAN CITIZENSHIP TO A CITIZEN OF PLATAIA

96 (Pl. 11). A fragment of a stele of Hymettian marble (I 5828), with the left side and the original back preserved but broken elsewhere, discovered on May 12, 1939, in a Late Roman (4th century A.D.) context, in a brick drain and shaft south of the Eleusinion (U 22).

H. 0.225 m.; W. 0.165 m.; Th. 0.057 m.
LH. 0.005–0.006 m. (the smallest omega 0.0035 m.).
Στοιχ. (with irregularities) Hor. 0.01 m.; Vert. 0.009–0.012 m.

Ed. B. D. Meritt, *Hesperia* 13, 1944, pp. 231–233, no. 5, with photograph; M. J. Osborne, *Naturalization* I, pp. 85–86, D 26, *Naturalization* II, pp. 95–96. Text quoted by A. N. Oikonomides, Πλάτων 8, 1956, pp. 127–128.

paullo ante a. 321/20 *a.*   ΣΤΟΙΧ. 24 (lines 16–18, 23; 15 and 19, 22)

```
              [----------------------]
              [-- τῶν προέδρων ἐπεψήφιζεν --]
              [...]γος Θ[ορ]αιε[ύς· ἔδοξεν τῶι δ]
              [ή]μωι· Δημέας Δημ[άδου Παιανιε]
              [ὺ]ς εἶπεν· ἐπειδὴ Τ[....⁹....Μ]
        5     [ό]σχου Πλαταιεὺς [εὔνους ἐστὶ]
              τῶι δήμωι τῶι ’Αθη[ναίων καὶ πρ]
              άτ⟨τ⟩ει ὑπὲρ τῆς πόλ[εως ὅτι ἂν δύ]
              [ν]ηται ἀγαθόν, δεδ[όχθαι τῶι δή]
              μωι εἶναι ’Αθηναῖ[ον αὐτὸν καὶ]
       10     ἐκγόνους, καὶ γρ[άψασθαι αὐτὸ]
              ν φυλῆς καὶ δήμου [καὶ φρατρία]
              ς ἧς ἂν βούληται π[λὴν ὧν οἱ νόμοι]
              ἀπαγορεύουσιν· τ[οὺς δὲ πρυτά]
              νεις τῆς ’Ακαμαντ[ίδος δοῦναι]
       15     [π]ερὶ αὐτοῦ τὴν ψ[ῆφον τῶι δή]
              μωι εἰς τὴν ἐκκ[λησίαν· ἀναγρ]
              άψαι δὲ τόδε τ[ὸ ψήφισμα τὸν γ]
              ραμματέα τὸν [κατὰ πρυτανεί]
              αν ἐν στήλη[ι λιθίνηι καὶ στ]
       20     ῆσα[ι ἐν ἀκροπόλει· -----]
              [------------------]
```

Line 2. [....]ος Meritt; [..]ιχος Osborne, which makes for an awkward patronymic.   Lines 4–5. So Meritt; Osborne does not restore the patronymic.   Line 7. The stone has ΑΤΕΙ: [ά]τ⟨τ⟩ει Osborne.   Line 15. So A. S. Henry, *Honours*, p. 102, note 105; ἐν τῶι δήμωι Meritt, Osborne.   Line 19. So also Osborne; στή[λη]ι Meritt.

The date of this text depends on the prosopography (see below) but is confirmed by the features of the writing, which reflect the characteristics of the later 4th and the early 3rd centuries. While preserving an orderly arrangement, and while not as slapdash as some later examples of the period (e.g., *IG* II², 378: for the date see *SEG* XXI, 353, XXXIII, 89), it is hasty and irregular in execution. Osborne justly described its lettering as "wretchedly cut" and the text as of "very scrappy appearance". In detail, the junctions of strokes are carelessly made and the strokes themselves often carelessly aligned, especially in epsilon. The crossbar of alpha is rarely horizontal; the right hasta of pi is lengthened. Rho and phi are expressed with economy, the former appearing in line 15 in a simple curve (Ρ), and the latter showing that cruciform shape which remained as a feature of the period; see **102**. *IG* II², 383, b (*SEG* XXI, 305) of 320/19 is almost identical in character, and *IG* II², 389 (*SEG* XXI, 354) of 293/2 is very close. Meritt compared *IG* II², 343 and 418.

Line 2. This was a nonprobouleumatic decision. Cf. P. J. Rhodes, *Athenian Boule*, p. 262 and **94**. Lines 3–4. The proposer was the son of the famous Demades and himself a budding politician, executed together with his father by Kassandros in 319 (Diodorus Siculus 18.48; Plutarch, *Phokion* 30). See M. H. Hansen, *Athenian Ecclesia II*, p. 41 and *PA* 3322, where the estimated date of his birth (*ca. a.* 355 *a.*) suggests that he could hardly appear as the proposer of a motion in the ekklesia before *ca.* 325. Cf. also J. K. Davies, *Athenian Propertied Families*, pp. 101–102. That this decree antedates 321 is shown by the instruction to the γραμματεὺς κατὰ πρυτανείαν in lines 17–19; this function was taken over in 321–318 by the ἀναγραφεύς (see p. 147 below). Meritt suggested (*op. cit.*, p. 233) that Demeas' oratorical style was parodied for its floridity by Lucian in his *Timon* (50–51), a contention vigorously denied by Oikonomides, *loc. cit.*

Lines 9–13. For the formula of decrees conferring citizenship see Osborne, *Naturalization* I, pp. 16–18, *Naturalization* III/IV, pp. 155–170; Henry, *Honours*, pp. 64–78 (for the word order εἶναι Ἀθηναῖον αὐτόν esp. p. 66). The nature of his reward suggests that the services of T———— had been unusually great, more considerable than those of his countryman Eudemos (*IG* II², 351 + 624; SEG XXI, 283, XXIV, 99). The proviso πλὴν ὧν οἱ νόμοι ἀπαγορεύουσιν is a rare addition; cf. Henry, *Honours*, p. 72. An alternative formula, ὧν οἱ νόμοι λέγουσιν, expresses the same thing more positively. It is not apparent why the legal restrictions are not more regularly inserted in these more explicit terms: κατὰ τὸν νόμον, from 319/18 onwards, seems to suffice; but even that is at times omitted.

Lines 13–16. The provision appears to indicate a need for haste. Either Akamantis was the phyle currently in prytany and it was important to complete this business before the prytany ended, or the current prytany was the ninth, with Akamantis, by a process of elimination, known to be about to become the tenth. In the latter case the concern will have been the completion of the process of enrolling T———— as a citizen before the end of the archon year. On the formulas employed see Henry, *Honours*, pp. 75–76.

THE ARCHONSHIP OF ARCHIPPOS, 321/20 B.C.

Apart from **97**, only one decree of the year 321/20 has been identified to the general satisfaction: *IG* II², 546, for which see W. K. Pritchett and B. D. Meritt, *Chronology*, p. 6 and *SEG* XXI, 304. *IG* II², 385, placed here by W. B. Dinsmoor (*Archons of Athens*, p. 25; cf. Meritt, *Athenian Year*, pp. 112–113), belongs elsewhere; see *SEG* XXI, 341 and 355.

IG II², 378 more probably belongs to the year 294/3 B.C., but it was attributed to this year by S. Dow (*HSCP* 67, 1963, pp. 44–45, *Hesperia* 32, 1963, pp. 342–346). The same possibility was considered but, on balance, rejected by Meritt (*Hesperia* 30, 1961, pp. 290–292), and he again rejected it, after further consideration of the arguments which Dow had meanwhile advanced, *Hesperia* 32, 1963, pp. 429–431. For a summary of the controversy to that point, with full texts, see *SEG* XXI, 353. The decree, passed on an uncertain day in the month Posideon and on the twenty-fourth day of an unidentified prytany, was retained in 294/3 by M. J. Osborne, *Naturalization* I, pp. 151–153, D 70, *Naturalization* II, pp. 153–154. However, M. H. Hansen (*GRBS* 23, 1982, pp. 345–346, no. 59 [= *Athenian Ecclesia*, pp. 97–98]) adopted Dow's dating (cf. *SEG* XXXII, 95), although A. S. Henry (*Honours*, pp. 76 and 102, note 110) retained that of Meritt.

Helpful information concerning the calendar survives only in **97**; but as 320/19 was undoubtedly an intercalary year and 322/1 has on the best analysis been determined as such, the year of Archippos was postulated as ordinary (Dinsmoor, *Archons of Athens*, p. 25; Meritt, *Athenian Year*, p. 113). What was preserved in the subsequently published **97** agreed with this hypothesis. By the date of the passage of that decree, the first five lunar months had evidently shown a regular succession of hollow and full months (the preceding year having ended with a full month), and among the first four prytanies were two of 36 days and two of 35: see further **97**, commentary on lines 5–6.

Leontis in the fifth prytany is the only prytanizing phyle identified. For the ἀναγραφεύς and γραμματεύς see **97**, p. 147 below. On the dates of the introduction and discontinuance of reference to the former officer see *SEG* XXXVII, 81.

FRAGMENT OF A DECREE

97. A fragment of the upper part of a stele of Pentelic marble (I 6496), with the right side (below the inscribed surface) and the original rough-picked back preserved but otherwise broken, discovered on April 8, 1952, in a wall of a mediaeval house above the east end of South Stoa II (O 15). Above the inscribed face and the molding surmounting it are the remains of a sculptured panel. A draped female figure, wearing a chiton folded in the manner of that of Athena on late Panathenaic vases, of whom only the feet and lower part of the dress survive, stood on the right of the composition, facing, to the left, a dolphin.

H. 0.205 m.; W. 0.19 m.; Th. 0.07 m.
LH. 0.005 m. (omicron 0.004 m.).
Στοιχ. (square) 0.0095 m.

Ed. B. D. Meritt, *Hesperia* 30, 1961, pp. 289–292, no. 184, with photograph pl. 59. See *SEG* XXI, 303 (text amplified with reference to S. Dow, *HSCP* 67, 1963, pp. 44–45, who identified the γραμματεύς and proposed the possible demotics in line 9). Cf. J. and L. Robert, *REG* 78, 1965, p. 101, no. 138.

a. 321/20 *a.*, *pryt.* V   ΣΤΟΙΧ. 33

```
                     [Θ          ε]        o          ι.
                     ['Αναγραφεὺς Θρασ]υκλῆς Ναυσικράτου[ς] Θ[ρ]
                     [ιάσιος· ἐπὶ 'Αρχίππ]ου ἄρχοντος ἐπὶ τῆς Λ[ε]
                     [ωντίδος πέμπτης π]ρυτανείας ἧι Σωκράτ[η]
              5      [ς Εὐμάχου Εὐπυρί]δης ἐγραμμάτευεν· Μαι[μ]
                     [ακτηριῶνος ἔνει] καὶ νέαι, πέμπτει τῆς [πρ]
                     [υτανείας· ἐκκλησ]ία· τ[ῶ]ν προέδρων ἐ[πεψήφ]
                     [ιζεν ...7... Παλ]ληνεύς· ἔδοξεν τ[ῶι δήμω]
                     [ι· ......13......]ήλου Πό[ριος εἶπεν· ----]

             10      [.......14.......]μου τ[--------------]
                     [.......14.......]ιδη[--------------]
                     [.......15.......]Ι[--------------]
                     [--------------------------]
```

The writing is small but orderly, regular, and well executed. "Free ends" of strokes are slightly enlarged.

H. Möbius, in a letter to E. Vanderpool (January 5, 1962), suggested on the basis of the dolphin in the relief that the decree may be concerned with a treaty with the Tarentines. On the sculpture see also *SEG* XXXIX, 324.

The *anagrapheus*, probably an elected officer, took over in this year the duties in regard to the publication of decrees hitherto the province of the γραμματεὺς κατὰ πρυτανείαν and occupied this position, though epigraphically with waning prominence, until the end of 319/18. The change is no doubt a reflection of one consequence at least of Athens' radically altered political situation. On the background and details of the "years of the *anagrapheis*", see especially Dow, *op. cit.*, pp. 38–54 (on the period 321–318 esp. pp. 40 and 44–51, with the present text considered on pp. 44–45); A. S. Henry, *Prescripts*, pp. 50–57 (the present text specifically cited pp. 52 and 54). In this inscription the *anagrapheus* takes precedence before the regular prescript but is not placed in a superscript position (here occupied by θεοί) as in some examples. This is thus an instance of Henry's Type I, b: parallel instances all belong to the following year, 320/19.

Line 2. Thrasykles, son of Nausikrates, of Thria was also the proposer of a decree in 314/13 (*IG* II², 450) and thus presumably in accord with the oligarchic regime. He may be the Thrasykles referred to in the private letter *Syll.*³, 1259, at line 11, as one of its possible recipients. See *PA* 7323 and, for a *stemma* of the family, 10562. Lines 3–4. The γραμματεύς in these years changed with the prytany, as in the 5th century. See Dow, *op. cit.*, p. 40; P. J. Rhodes, *Athenian Boule*, p. 140; Henry, *Prescripts*, p. 50. Sokrates, son of Eumachos, of Eupyridai would, as Dow's restoration with good reason supposed, be an ancestor (probably the great-grandfather) of the Eumachos, son of Sokrates, of the same deme who contributed to a national defense fund in the archonship of Diomedon in the middle 240's (see **213**, lines 51–52 and *PA* 5818 and 13107).

Lines 5–6. On the last day of Maimakterion as a meeting day for the assembly see J. D. Mikalson (*Sacred and Civil Calendar*, pp. 85–86), who quotes lines 3–7 of this text: the date will be Maimakterion 29 = pryt. V, 5 = 147th day. (Mikalson named it as Maimakterion 30; this would be the 148th day and would vary the scheme noted above, under the Archonship of Archippos, to give a succession of full and hollow months, with the first four prytanies of 3 × 36 and 1 × 35 days. But 322/1 is likely to have ended with a full month, indeed possibly with two full months in succession, and Archippos' year will in that case surely have begun with a 29-day Hekatombaion.)

Line 7. 'Εκκλησ]ία. That is, a "regular" meeting (i.e., other than an ἐκκλησία κυρία) of the assembly on the Pnyx. This designation is attested here for the first time among the decrees discovered in the Agora excavations (**91** is incomplete at lines 6–7) but is found already in 336/5 (*IG* II², 330, line 49). See W. A. McDonald, *Political Meeting-Places*, pp. 56–61; Henry, *Prescripts*, pp. 38–39. The designation of a meeting as taking place in the Theater of Dionysos has already been met with among the Agora texts in 332/1 (**79**) and is restored in **95**. Line 8. The enactment was nonprobouleumatic: see Rhodes, *Athenian Boule*, p. 262 and **94**. Line 9. Or Πο[τάμιος Dow.

FRAGMENT OF A DECREE

98. A fragment of a stele of Hymettian marble (I 4034), broken all around (including the back), discovered on April 24, 1936, in a Turkish context north of the Eleusinion, over the area of the Post-Herulian Wall (S 17).

H. 0.112 m.; W. 0.063 m.; Th. 0.006 m.
LH. 0.006 m.
Στοιχ. (square) 0.012 m.

Ed. M. B. Walbank, *Hesperia* 58, 1989, p. 84, no. 9, with photograph pl. 20.

ca. a. 321/20 *a., vel aliquanto ante*   ΣΤΟΙΧ.

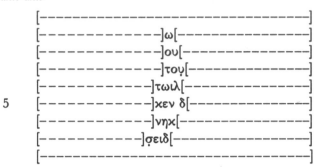

Walbank at first regarded the hand in evidence in this small fragment as so similar to that of **103** that he assigned it to a comparable date; but the differences are sufficient to ensure that it does not form part of that monument. However, he also noted that the marble type, spacing, size of letters, and general style suggest comparison with *IG* II², 257, a fragment placed by J. Kirchner "ante a. 336/5". The present text should perhaps be regarded as having been inscribed between *ca.* 335 and the end of the period of the *anagrapheis*.

Walbank suggested in line 5 [--- ἐπέδω]κεν and in line 7 [--- ὅπως δ'ἀν πάντε]ς εἰδ[ῶσιν ---], for which latter cf. **86**, commentary on lines 21–24. See further *SEG* XXXIX, 87, where the identity of this fragment as a decree is doubted. The reference to this *SEG* entry in *SEG* XL, 70 does not in fact concern the present text.

FRAGMENT OF A DECREE

99. A fragment of a stele of Pentelic marble (I 2720), broken on all sides and at the back and with the inscribed surface badly abraded, discovered on April 2, 1935, in a modern wall over the east end of the Middle Stoa (N 12).

H. 0.192 m.; W. 0.115 m.; Th. 0.062 m.
LH. 0.007–0.008 m.
Στοιχ. Hor. 0.0155 m.; Vert. (variable) 0.015–0.017 m.

Ed. M. B. Walbank, *Hesperia* 58, 1989, p. 86, no. 12, with photograph pl. 19. See also *SEG* XXXIX, 97.

ca. a. 321–318 *a.*(?)   ΣΤΟΙΧ.

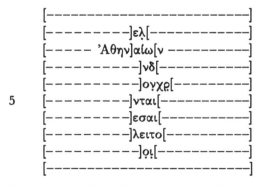

This fragment seems more likely than not to have formed part of a decree, and Walbank edited it as such. He suggested that it shows the same characteristics and hand as those of *IG* II², 397, a decree dated to "the years of the *anagrapheis*", and that it might derive from that stele. On that basis he made tentative proposals for lines 3–6, showing the same length of line as that text, on the supposition that the decree, among other honors for a benefactor of the city, awarded him a golden stephanos:

ΣΤΟΙΧ. 26 or 27

[– – –τὸ]ν δ[ῆμον – – – στεφανῶσαι]
[αὐτ]ὸν χρ[υσῶι στεφάνωι ἀπὸ Χ δρα]
5   [χμῶ]ν· ταῖ[ς δὲ(?) – – – – – – – – – ἐπα]
[ιν]έσαι [– – – – – – – – – – – – – – – – –]

(The location of the fragment within the width of the stele is purely arbitrary.) Lines 5–6. Or χαλ]έσαι.
For a further Agora decree of this period cf. **106J**.

THE ARCHONSHIP OF NEAICHMOS, 320/19 B.C.

In addition to **100**, seven decrees may be definitely assigned to this year: *IG* II², 380 (*SEG* XXI, 307, XXVI, 84, XXXIII, 90), of the second prytany, 381 and 382 (*SEG* XXI, 308), both of the fifth prytany, a decree from the North Slope of the Akropolis published by R. S. Stroud (*Hesperia* 40, 1971, pp. 174–178, no. 25), of the tenth prytany, *IG* II², 383 and 384 (*SEG* XXI, 309), both of unknown prytanies, and 383b (addenda, p. 660), the prytany of which has been the subject of controversy (*SEG* XXI, 305, and below). As the penultimate year of a Metonic cycle (the sixth), 320/19 should have been an intercalary year (cf. B. D. Meritt, *TAPA* 95, 1964, p. 236, with further references), and the epigraphical evidence (cf. *IG* II², 381, lines 5–6) has elicited general agreement that it was so (J. Kirchner, *IG* II², 380 and 381, *comm.*; W. B. Dinsmoor, *Archons of Athens*, pp. 370 and 374; W. K. Pritchett and O. Neugebauer, *Calendars*, pp. 61–62; Meritt, *Athenian Year*, pp. 113–120, *Historia* 26, 1977, p. 170).

There has however been dispute concerning the arrangement of the lunar (festival) months within the year, the evaluation of which has revolved around the differing interpretations of *IG* II², 383b. If the restoration of that text follows the strict stoichedon pattern in line 4, the prytany will necessarily be the seventh or the tenth, and either will produce a calendric irregularity. To restore ἑβδόμης calls for the retardation of the festival calendar by six days in Gamelion. Δεκάτης appeared to involve the lesser irregularity and was preferred by Pritchett and Neugebauer (*Calendars*, p. 62), who assumed the intercalation of one or two extra days in Mounichion or Thargelion, for which there was compensation in Skirophorion. Their supplement, and their understanding that the year consisted of 385 days, were discounted by Meritt (*Athenian Year*, pp. 113–120), who preferred a year of 384 days (for which there is corroboration in Babylonian chronology) on a regular pattern, that is, without official adjustments of intercalated days. But this is obtainable only at the cost of postulating as the ordinal numeral of the prytany τρίτης followed by an uninscribed space in line 4 of *IG* II², 383b, a solution criticized by S. Dow (*HSCP* 67, 1963, pp. 60–67) and Pritchett (*Ancient Athenian Calendars on Stone*, p. 375) as impermissible. The continuing controversy, for which see *SEG* XXI, 305, served to polarize the issues, each possibility being challenged and defended with equal resolution. For a summary of the calendric evidence see Stroud, *Hesperia* 40, 1971, p. 177. Meritt returned to the defense of his restoration of *IG* II², 383b, in the light of Stroud's publication (*AJP* 93, 1972, pp. 166–168, corrected in *Hesperia* 45, 1976, p. 173, note 3), but in the end preferred to place that text in the seventh prytany with the restoration of ἑβδόμης.

With *IG* II², 383b in the seventh prytany, Meritt's supposition may still be maintained that the year of thirteen months contained 384 days, beginning with full Hekatombaion and continuing in a regular succession of hollow and full months until full Anthesterion was followed by full Elaphebolion; thereafter regular succession was resumed. This pattern was interrupted by a retardation in Gamelion with compensation not long delayed. The prytany calendar would have contained three prytanies of 39 days followed by a succession of prytanies of 38 days at least through the sixth, with one more prytany of 39 among the final four. Pritchett and Neugebauer, on the other hand, required six full and four hollow months among the first ten, followed by Mounichion 29 + 2, Thargelion 30, and Skirophorion 28 (or 27 in a year of 384 days; see G. Klaffenbach, *Gnomon* 21, 1949, p. 135). This aimed to preserve the regular pattern of the prytany calendar, and it was indeed their contention that this regularity must form a basic requirement in any reconstruction of the Athenian year. But compensation for earlier retardation was never, on the evidence available, made in Skirophorion; cf. Meritt, *Athenian Year*, pp. 103 and 208, *TAPA* 95, 1964, p. 245. The evidence of *Hesperia* 40, 1971, pp. 174–178, no. 25, while not otherwise helpful in the resolution of the calendric problems, required that the tenth prytany, if it is not Pandionis, be Akamantis.

For a convenient tabulation of the year by months and the evidence for it, as he saw it at the time, see Meritt, *Hesperia* 32, 1963, p. 433; but if Pandionis is after all to be regarded as pryt. VII, adjustment to it is necessary, since *IG* II², 383b shows the equation Gamelion 28 = pryt. VII, 10 = 241st day. Known or presumed phylai in prytany are, in the light of the unfolding discussion, II Erechtheis, V Antiochis, VI Oineis, VII Pandionis, and X Akamantis.

A DECREE IN HONOR OF NIKOSTRATOS OF PHILIPPOI (?)

100 (Pl. 12). Two joining fragments of a stele of Hymettian marble (I 5626), with the original rough-picked back preserved, discovered on October 14, 1938, in a wall of a modern house at the north foot of the Areopagos (P 23). The right side of the stele survives on the lower fragment; on the upper fragment the inscription is complete at the top, and above the inscribed face are the remains of a surmounting molding which has been chipped away. Stone surviving above this point below the level of the inscribed surface suggests that the stele originally carried a pediment or other crowning decorative feature.

Measurements of combined fragments: H. 0.40 m.; W. 0.195 m.; Th. 0.075 m.

LH. (line 1) 0.005 m. (omicron)–0.014 m. (sigma); (line 2 and thereafter) 0.005 m. (omicron)–0.01 m. (phi). Στοιχ. (square) 0.0116 m.

Ed. B. D. Meritt, *Hesperia* 13, 1944, pp. 234–241, no. 6, with photograph. See *SEG* XXI, 306 (full bibliography from 1944 to 1964, with references to W. K. Pritchett and O. Neugebauer, *Calendars*, pp. 61–62; Meritt, *Athenian Year*, pp. 119–120; S. Dow, *HSCP* 67, 1963, pp. 67–75; Pritchett, *Ancient Athenian Calendars on Stone*, pp. 376–377; Meritt, *Hesperia* 32, 1963, pp. 425–432).

In the first edition Meritt suggested but rejected three possible arrangements of the text of the preamble before deciding upon a fourth as that most suited to the solution of the problems involved. Parts of lines 4–6, as presented in that fourth text, were quoted by Pritchett and Neugebauer (*Calendars*, p. 62). Meritt, who because of wartime conditions had been unable to check the stone in person on the occasion of the *editio princeps*, revised lines 1–9 after he had done so (*Athenian Year*, *loc. cit.*). This text ("Text 5") was criticized by Dow (*loc. cit.*), who substituted a fresh version ("Text 6"). Meritt made a further revision ("Text 7") in the light of this, with reasons for the rejection of Dow's text (*Hesperia* 32, 1963, *loc. cit.*).

The text here printed is that of "Text 7". "Texts 5" and "6" are added in the commentary for the reader's interest and convenience.

a. 320/19 a., *pryt.* VI   ΣΤΟΙΧ. 36 (lines 2 and following)

```
        [Ν ι κ ό σ τ ρ α τ ο ς – – –]λ ω ν ο ς  Φ ι λ [ι π π ε ύ ς(?)].
(a)     ['Επὶ Νεαίχμου ἄρχοντος] ἀναγραφέω[ς δ' Ἀρχεδί]
        [χου τοῦ Ναυχρίτου Λαμπ]τρέως, ἐπὶ τῆ[ς Οἰνεῖδ]
        [ος ἕκτης πρυτανείας ἧι ..]νων 'Οῆθ(εν) ἐγραμ[μάτε]
5       [υεν· Γαμηλιῶνος δεκάτηι ἱσ]ταμένου, τετ[άρτηι]
        [καὶ εἰκοστῆι τῆς πρυτανεί]ας· ἐκκλησί[α· τῶν π]
        [ροέδρων ἐπεψήφιζεν ..⁵..]οφῶν Στει[ρι(εύς)· ἔδοξ]
        [εν τῆι βουλῆι καὶ τῆι δήμωι]· Δημάδης Δη[μέου Π]
        [αιανιεὺς εἶπεν· ᵛ ἐπειδὴ Νι]κόστρατο[ς ..⁵...]
10      [– – – – – – – – – – – – – – –]τε τῶν ἐς Σ[..⁶...]
(b)     [– – – – – – – – – – – – – – –] Ἀθηναίων μη[....]
        [– – – – – – – – – – – – – – – –] τοὺς ἐπιβουλ[...]
        [– – – – – – – – – – – – – – – –] Ἀθηναι[..⁵...]
        [.........²⁰.......... γυναι]ξὶ καὶ παι[σὶν]
15      [– – – – – – – – – – – – – –]ε [.] ὁ μέλλων Λ[...]
        [– – – – – – – – – – – – – – χα]ταληφθῆναι [...]
        [– – – – – – – – – – – – – –]ων καὶ διΛ[..⁵..]
        [..........²⁴..........]ν αὐτὸν Ἀθ[ηναῖ]
        [ον – – – – – – – – – ἐπίστατ(?)]αι ὁ δῆμος ὁ ['Αθη]
20      [ναίων – – – – – – – – – – – – –]ο πλέον τ[....]
        [– – – – – – – – – – – – – – – –]ι μετ[....]
        [– – – – – – – – – – – – – – – –]τα[..⁵..]
```

```
[------------------------]ι[..⁵..]
[------------------------------]
```

"Text 5"   ΣTOIX. 38

```
      ['Επὶ Νεαίχμου ἄρχοντος, ἐπ'] ἀναγραφέω[ς δὲ 'Αρχε ᵛ]
      [δίχου τοῦ Ναυχρίτου Λαμπ]τρέως, ἐπὶ τῆ[ς Οἰνεῖ ᵛ]
      [δος ὀγδόης πρυτανείας ἧι ...]νων 'Οῆθ(εν) ἐγραμ[μάτ ᵛ]
  5   [ευεν· Μουνιχιῶνος ὀγδόηι ἱσ]ταμένου, τετ[άρτηι]
      [χαὶ τριαχοστῆι τῆς πρυτανεί]ας· ἐχχλησί[α χυρ ᵛ]
      [ια· τῶν προέδρων ἐπεψήφιζεν 'Ι]οφῶν Στει[ρ(ιεὺς) χαὶ σ ᵛ]
      [υμπρόεδροι· ἔδοξεν τῶι δήμωι]· Δημάδης Δη[μέου ᵛ]
      [Παιανιεὺς εἶπεν· ᵛᵛ ἐπειδὴ ..]χόστρατο[ς ..⁵..]
 10   χτλ.
```

"Text 6"   ΣTOIX. 35 (lines 3 and 5, 36)

```
      ['Επὶ Νεαίχμου ἄρχοντος], ἀναγραφέω[ς 'Αρχεδί]
      [χου τοῦ Ναυχρίτου Λαμπ]τρέως, ἐπὶ τῆ[ς Οἰνεῖδ]
      [ος ἕχτης πρυτανείας ἧι ..]νων 'Οῆθ(εν) ἐγραμ[μάτ]
  5   [ευεν· Γαμηλιῶνος ἕχτηι ἱσ]ταμένου, τετ[άρτηι]
      [χαὶ εἰχοστῆι τῆς πρυτανεί]ας· ἐχχλησί[α· τῶν]
      [προέδρων ἐπεψήφιζεν ....]οφῶν Στει[ρ(ιεύς)· ἔδοξ]
      [εν τῆι βουλῆι χαὶ τῶι δήμωι]· Δημάδης χτλ.
```

The writing is wide in proportion to its height; occasional carelessnesses in the accurate formation of individual letters suggest a competent mason in a hurry. The upright stroke of phi is unusually long; upsilon alone, save in line 1, is affected by a tendency to emphasize "free ends" of strokes (cf. **120**). Line 1 is expressed in slightly more of a *scriptura monumentalis*, and both lambda and sigma are thus decoratively treated.

Line 1. The honorand could have been cited in the genitive case. Cf. *IG* II², 385; A. S. Henry, *Prescripts*, p. 51. But the presence of the patronymic perhaps makes the nominative more probable. Lines 2–3. The *anagrapheus* of the year, Archedikos, son of Naukritos, of Lamptrai, was also the proposer of two decrees in 318/17: *IG* II², 402 (addenda, p. 660) and **104**. On the *anagrapheis* of these years see **97**, and for the formula Henry, *op. cit.*, pp. 52 and 54. The latter provides an example of Henry's Type II, a.

Lines 4 and 7. For the abbreviated demotics see **112**, line 4 and commentary and L. Threatte, *Grammar*, p. 100. On the deme Oe see also S. Dow, *AJP* 84, 1963, pp. 166–181 and J. S. Traill, *Political Organization*, p. 49. Line 5. A meeting of the assembly on Gamelion 10 is not attested other than by restoration here and in *IG* II², 239; see J. D. Mikalson, *Sacred and Civil Calendar*, p. 101. But there is nothing intrinsically objectionable to the supposition. There are objections, however, to Mounichion 8 ("Text 5") and Gamelion 6 ("Text 6"): cf. Mikalson, *op. cit.*, pp. 140–141 and **98**. M. H. Hansen (*GRBS* 23, 1982, 349, no. 96 [= *Athenian Ecclesia*, p. 101]) briefly reviewed the restorations of the calendar equation at this point hitherto proposed and, while preferring to suspend judgment, criticized adversely all except "Text 7", which he reported without comment. Cf. *SEG* XXXII, 96.

Line 6. ἐχχλησία. See **97**, line 7. Lines 7–8. As restored, the decree is probouleumatic, i.e., the assembly adopted without alteration the *probouleuma* that came to it. Cf. P. J. Rhodes (*Athenian Boule*, p. 250), who regarded the text as too unsettled for statistical use. Lines 8–9. Demades has already appeared as the proposer of **72** and **95**, *qq.v.* This decree is listed among his enactments by A. N. Oikonomides, Πλάτων 8, 1956, pp. 118–119, no. 13 and by Rhodes (*Athenian Boule*, p. 270).

The nature of Nikostratos' services cannot be determined. Lines 12 and 15–16 suggest some conspiracy against Athenian interests which had perhaps been frustrated by Nikostratos' good offices, of which the Athenian people are properly appreciative (lines 19–20).

THE ARCHONSHIP OF APOLLODOROS, 319/18 B.C.

101, 102, and **103** comprise three of the seven decrees, usefully distributed in date through the months, which are now known to belong to the year of Apollodoros. The other four are *IG* II², 386 (*SEG* XXI, 311; M. J. Osborne, *Naturalization* I, pp. 90–91, D 30, *Naturalization* II, pp. 97–98) of the sixth prytany, 387 (*SEG* XXI, 314) of the tenth, 388 (*SEG* XXI, 313, XXXII, 97) of the eighth, and 390 (*SEG* XXI, 315) also of the tenth. **101** of the fourth prytany, **102** of the seventh, and **103** of the tenth assist in spreading the calendric evidence through five of the ten prytanies. *IG* II², 385, fragment a and 389, formerly attributed to 319/18, are now recognized as belonging to 292/1 and 293/2 respectively; see *SEG* XXI, 355 and 354.

As the final year of the sixth Metonic cycle this year should have been, and was, an ordinary year (see B. D. Meritt, *TAPA* 95, 1964, p. 236, with further references). Babylonian observation (see Meritt, *Athenian Year*, p. 124) made it a year of 355 days, although this need not imply that it was so at Athens. The data concerning the year were tabulated by W. K. Pritchett (*Hesperia* 10, 1941, p. 269), on the basis of which he supposed a regular alternation of full and hollow months in a year of 354 days and a prytany year arranged exactly in accordance with Aristotle's pattern: four prytanies each of 36 days followed by six each of 35. Cf. E. Schweigert, *Hesperia* 9, 1940, p. 346. In again setting out the calendric data of the year, Pritchett and O. Neugebauer (*Calendars*, pp. 63–64) found this scheme of the lunar (festival) calendar too rigid in conception, but no change was made in the overall assessment of the year. Meritt's reconstruction (*Athenian Year*, p. 124) recognized the same arrangements as that of Pritchett. If the year was indeed of 355 days, one day would be added to Skirophorion, making it full instead of hollow, as well as to the tenth prytany.

In *IG* II², 388, an error on the part of the mason, who wrote Ἐλαφηβολιῶνος in line 5 when he should have written Μουνιχιῶνος, has been generally acknowledged since it was advanced as a hypothesis by M. Crosby (**102**) and supported by W. B. Dinsmoor (*Athenian Archon List*, p. 34, note 62). Such an error may be paralleled in *IG* II², 375 (*SEG* XXI, 302), of 322/1 (see Meritt, *Athenian Year*, pp. 111–112). The existing text of *IG* II², 388 could be accommodated to a supposition that four days were intercalated into the festival calendar in the latter part of Elaphebolion, but the assumption of an error in the engraving affords a preferable explanation for the discrepancy; see Meritt, *Athenian Year*, pp. 124–125.

Known phylai in prytany are IV Aiantis or Leontis, VI Aigeis, VII Antiochis, VIII Erechtheis, and X Oineis.

ATHENIAN CITIZENSHIP CONFERRED ON AINETOS OF RHODES

101. A squat pedimental stele of honey-colored Pentelic marble (I 5454), broken below but almost completely preserved, discovered on May 20, 1938, when it was removed from the cleft above the Klepsydra basin into which it had fallen, in ancient times, in such a way as to expose the inscribed face to the action of dripping water (T 27). The surface has been much eroded in consequence, and the inscription is in places extremely difficult to read. In addition, a semicircular area of the surface has been entirely lost on the left between lines 4 and 18, and there is considerable discoloration below this point. Cf. the description of the stone given by M. J. Osborne, *loc. cit.* (below).

H. 0.805 m.; W. 0.442 m.; Th. 0.087 m.
LH. 0.007 m. (line 2, 0.01–0.012 m.).
Στοιχ. (almost square) Hor. *ca.* 0.015 m.; Vert. 0.015 m.

Ed. E. Schweigert, *Hesperia* 9, 1940, pp. 345–348, no. 44, with photograph; M. J. Osborne, *Naturalization* I, pp. 88–89, D 29, *Naturalization* II, pp. 96–97. A preliminary reference to the discovery of the stele was made by T. L. Shear, *Hesperia* 8, 1939, pp. 223–224. See *SEG* XXI, 310 (full text with minor corrections and complete bibliography from 1940 to 1964, with references to W. K. Pritchett [*Hesperia* 10, 1941, p. 269], who discussed the calendar equation in lines 4–7; Pritchett and O. Neugebauer, *Calendars*, p. 63, where lines 4–7 are quoted; B. D. Meritt, *Athenian Year*, pp. 121–122, also with quotation of lines 1–7; S. Dow [*HSCP* 67, 1963, pp. 47–51], who studied the *anagrapheus* Eukadmos and the prescripts to the decrees of his year). Further, *SEG* XXV, 73 (L. Moretti, *Iscrizioni storiche ellenistiche* I, pp. 4–6, no. 3, who reproduced the text of *SEG* XXI, *loc. cit.*, with description, commentary, and bibliography, and added a translation into Italian).

a. 319/18 *a., pryt.* IV   ΣΤΟΙΧ. 28 (lines 4–9)
                                                                                          ΣΤΟΙΧ. 29 (lines 11–43)

Θεοί.
Πολιτεία Αἰνήτωι ʿΡοδίωι·
Ἀναγραφεὺς Εὔκαδμος Ἀναχαιεύς· *v*
Ἐπὶ Ἀπολλοδώρου ἄρχοντος ἐπὶ τῆς
5   [...]ντίδος τετάρτης πρυτανείας· Μ
[αιμα]κτηριῶνος ἑνδεκάτει, μιᾶι καὶ
[εἰκοσ]τεῖ τῆς πρυτανείας· ἐκκλησί

[α κυρία]· τῶμ προέδρων ἐπεψήφιζεν Ε

[. .⁶. .] Ἁλαιεύς· ἔδοξεν τῆι βουλῆι

10   [καὶ τῶι] δήμωι.   *vacat*

[. .⁵. .κρ]άτης Κτήσωνος ἐκ Κεραμέων

[εἶπεν· ἀγ]αθῆι τύχηι τῆς βουλῆς καὶ τ

[οῦ δήμου] τοῦ Ἀθηναίων, ἐπειδὴ Αἴνητ

[ος Δαήμ]ονος Ῥόδιος πρότερόν τε διε

15   [τέλει τ]ὰ βέλτιστα ἐπιτηδε[ύ]ων Ἀθήν

[ησιν ἀ]ποδημήσας τε μετ' Ἀλεξάνδρου

τοῦ βασιλέως εἰς τὴν Ἀσίαν διεπολέ

μησε τὸν πόλεμον καλῶς καὶ ἐνδόξ[ως]

καὶ διὰ τὰς εὐεργεσ[ίας . . .¹⁰. . . . .]

20   ΔΟΜΗ[. .]Ạ[.]ΤΟḤΚΟỊ[. . . .⁸. . . .] ἐπήινε[σέ]

ν τε καὶ ἐστεφά[νωσεν . . . .¹². . . . . .]

[.]α τούτου περι[.]θ[. . . . . .¹⁵. . . . . . .]

ουπ[. . .⁷. . . .]ṭ[. .]ψ[. . . . . . .¹⁵. . . . . . .]

τοῦ δ[ήμου τοῦ Ἀθηναίων, δεδόχθαι τῆ]

25   ι βουλῆ[ι τοὺς προέδρους οἳ ἂν λάχωσ]

ι προεδ[ρεύειν ἐν τῆι πρώτηι ἐκκλησ]

ί[α]ι χ[ρηματίσαι περὶ . . . . .¹². . . . .]

ỊṬỊΜΝỌΝ[. .]Υ[. .], γνώμην [δὲ ξυμβάλλεσ]

θαι τῆς [β]ουλῆς εἰς τὸν δῆμον ὅ[τι] δọχ

30   εῖ τῆι β[ο]υλῆι ἐπαινέσαι Αἴν[η]τον Δα

ήμονος [Ῥ]όδιον καὶ στεφανῶσαι χρυσ

ῶι στεφ[ά]νωι ἀπὸ : Χ : δραχμῶν ἀρετῆς

ἕνεκα καὶ εὐνοίας τῆς περὶ τὸν δῆμο

ν τὸν Ἀθηναίων· εἶναι δὲ Αἴνητον Δαή

35   μονος Ἀθηναῖον αὐτὸγ καὶ ἐγγόνους,

καὶ γράψασθαι αὐτὸν φυλῆς καὶ δήμο

υ καὶ φρατρίας ἧς ἂν βούληται κατ[ὰ τ]

ὸν νόμον, τοὺς δὲ πρυτάνεις δοῦν[αι π]

ερὶ αὐτοῦ τὴμ ψῆφον εἰς τὴμ π[ρώτην ἐ]

40   κκλησίαν ὅπως ἂν καὶ οἱ ἄλλ[οι πάντε]

[ς] φιλοτιμῶνται ποεῖν ἀγ[αθὸν ὅτι ἂν]

ἕκ[α]σ[τ]ος δύνηται τὸν [δῆμον· ἀναγράψ]

αι [δ]ὲ τόδε τ[ὸ ψ]ήφισ[μα ἐν στήληι λιθίν]

[ηι ————————————]

45   [————————————]

Lines 6–7. καὶ | [εἰκοσ]τεῖ Meritt; κα|[ὶ εἰκοσ]τεῖ Schweigert.   Line 14. Δαήμο]νος Schweigert; Δαήμ]ọνος Osborne.   Line 15. βέ[λτι]στ[α] Schweigert; βέλτιστα Osborne.   Line 17. το[ῦ β]ασιλέως Schweigert; τοῦ βασιλέως Osborne.   Line 19. εὐερ⟨γ⟩εσ[ίας Schweigert, Osborne; but the gamma is clear on the stone.   Line 34. Ἀθ[η]ναίων Schweigert; Ἀθηναίων Osborne.   Line 35. Ἀ[θ]ηναῖον Schweigert; Ἀθηναῖον Osborne.   Line 42. [ἕκαστ]ος Schweigert; ἕχ[α]σ[τ]ος Osborne.   Persistent study of the eroded sections of the stone has yielded few additions to Schweigert's original readings and no alterations to the substance of his text.   For what may be discerned cf. Osborne's *adnotationes criticae*.   The writing is of a "standard" character appropriate to its period and presents no special features.   There is no emphasis on the "free ends" of strokes, except in the more monumental line 2, where omega in particular is so treated.

Line 2. Ainetos of Rhodes and his exploits on the expedition of Alexander the Great are otherwise unknown. Schweigert thought it unlikely that he could be connected with the Ainetos who was general in service with Demetrios Poliorketes (Polyainos 5.19; for further references on that Ainetos see Moretti, *loc. cit.*). Noting that the honors were voted in Maimakterion, Osborne speculated that the Ainetos of the present decree was a supporter of Polyperchon and unlikely to have been a protégé of Phokion. For the historical circumstances see also W. S. Ferguson, *Hellenistic*

Athens, pp. 28–31; R. M. Errington, *Hermes*, 105, 1977, pp. 487–496; E. Will, *Histoire politique du monde hellénistique* I, 1966, pp. 43–45.

Line 3. The *anagrapheus* of the year, Eukadmos of Anakeia, is otherwise unknown. For the expression of the prescript (a standard preamble preceded by the *anagrapheus* in the nominative case), see Dow, *loc. cit.* and A. S. Henry, *Prescripts*, pp. 52 and 54. The form employed represents Henry's Type I, a. Lines 5–7. For Maimakterion 11 as a meeting day of the assembly see J. D. Mikalson (*Sacred and Civil Calendar*, pp. 81–82), who quotes lines 4–8 of this text. EI for HI in the dative feminine singular, increasingly common at this period, becomes regular after 300 B.C. (except in the relative pronoun ἧι) and requires no further comment. Cf. L. Threatte, *Grammar*, p. 378 and Henry (*CQ* n.s. 14, 1964, pp. 240–245), who gave totals of the examples subdivided by phrase and by period between 323 and 146 B.C.

Lines 7–8. ἐκκλησία κυρία. The restoration is unavoidable, and this designation of the assembly is thus attested here for the first time among the decrees discovered in the Agora excavations: but it appears as early as 334/3. Cf. W. A. McDonald, *Political Meeting-Places*, p. 56; Henry, *Prescripts*, p. 39; M. H. Hansen, *GRBS* 23, 1982, pp. 337–338 (= *Athenian Ecclesia*, pp. 89–90); **97**, commentary on line 7.

Lines 9–10. The decree was probouleumatic. Cf. **100** and P. J. Rhodes, *Athenian Boule*, p. 250. Line 11. Kteson of Kerameis was identified by Schweigert with the witness in [Demosthenes] 59.48, who testified concerning dinner parties held by Stephanos and Phrynion in company with Neaira. Cf. *PA* 8910 and, for further detail of the family, J. K. Davies, *Athenian Propertied Families*, p. 338. Line 12. ἀγαθῆι τύχηι. See **72**, commentary on lines 7–8. Lines 24–30. For the now regular probouleumatic formula cf. **89**, commentary on lines 2–9.

Lines 32–34. The grant of the stephanos, the specification of its cost, and the reasons for the grant follow the regular formulaic procedure. Cf. Henry, *Honours*, pp. 22–27, 42–44 (this decree cited, p. 42) and **92**. Lines 34–38. On the formulas employed in the award of Athenian citizenship see **96**, commentary on lines 9–13 and references there. In this instance the positive phrase κατὰ τὸν νόμον replaces the more negative concept πλὴν ὧν οἱ νόμοι ἀπαγορεύουσιν in the qualification of free choice of phyle, deme, and phratry. Lines 40–42. ὅπως ἂν κτλ. Cf. **86**, commentary on lines 21–24.

DECREE IN HONOR OF A CERTAIN APOL –––––

102. Two joining fragments of a stele of patchily discolored Hymettian marble (I 3878), of which that on the left (fragment *a*) preserves the left side and part of the original rough-picked back, and that on the right (fragment *b*) in addition to the back preserves the right side and the springing of the crowning molding above the inscribed face. Much of the join between the fragments is made below the inscribed surface, leaving a gap in the preserved text at the affected point. Fragment *a* was discovered on March 28, 1936, in a Byzantine wall north of the Odeion (M 8), fragment *b* on December 23, 1937, in a wall of a modern house southeast of the Market Square (N 19).

Measurements of combined fragments: H. 0.27 m.; W. 0.295 m.; Th. 0.075–0.08 m.

LH. 0.005–0.008 m. (omicron and omega 0.004 m.).

Στοιχ. (square but with slight irregularities) 0.01 m.

Ed. *a* only: M. Crosby, *Hesperia* 6, 1937, pp. 442–444, no. 1, with photograph. *a* + *b*: eadem, *Hesperia* 7, 1938, pp. 476–479, no. 31, with photograph of joined fragments. See *SEG* XXI, 312 (full text and complete bibliography from 1938 to 1964, with references to W. K. Pritchett and O. Neugebauer, *Calendars*, p. 63, where parts of lines 1–6 are quoted; B. D. Meritt [*Athenian Year*, p. 122], who quotes lines 1–6; S. Dow [*HSCP* 67, 1963, pp. 49–51], who analyzes the preamble in the context of a discussion of the *anagrapheus* and the method of including him in it). Further, *SEG* XXV, 74 (L. Moretti [*Iscrizioni storiche ellenistiche* I, pp. 6–7, no. 4], who provides text, bibliography, commentary, and Italian translation). The calendric data were included by Pritchett in his original tabulation of the evidence for the year of Apollodoros, *Hesperia* 10, 1941, p. 269.

a. 319/18 a., *pryt.* VII   ΣΤΟΙΧ. 26

(*b*) [᾽Επὶ ᾽Απο]λλοδ[ώρ]ου ἄρχοντος ἐπ[ὶ τ]
[ῆς ᾽Αντι]οχί[δος ἐ]βδόμης πρυτα[νε]
[ίας καὶ ἀναγραφέ]ως Εὐκάδμου ᾽Α[ν]
(*a*) [αχαι]ξέως· ᾽Ελαφ[ηβο]λιῶνος δωδεκ[ά]
5 τει, τετάρτει [καὶ τ]ριακοστεῖ τ[ῆ]
ς πρυτανείας· ἐ[κκ]λ[η]σία κατὰ ψ[ήφ]
ισμα βουλῆς· τῶν προ[έ]δρων ἐπε[ψή]
φισζεν ᾽Αμφίλοχος Ξυπετα[ι]ών· [ἔδ]
οξεν τεῖ βουλῆι καὶ τῶι δ[ήμωι· *vv*]

```
10   Τηλοκλῆς Τηλεγνώτο[υ] Ἀλ[ωπεκῆθ]
     εν εἶπεν· ἐπειδὴ Ἀπολ[...⁷.... ἐν]
     τε τῶι ἔμπροσσθεν χ[ρόνωι διετέ]
     λει εὔνους ὢν τῶι δή[μωι τῶι Ἀθην]
     αίων καὶ τὰς στρατ[είας ἁπάσας ἐ]
15   στράτευται καὶ τ[ὰς εἰσφορὰς εἰ]
     σενήνοχεν ὅσας ἀ[πήιτει ὁ δῆμος],
     καὶ νῦν οἰκεῖος [ὢν τῶν ἐλθόντων]
     μετὰ Πρωτέου [...⁷.... καὶ ....ο]
     υ τοῦ ὑοῦ αὐτ[οῦ καλῶς καὶ φιλοτί]
20   μως ἀπ[.........²¹..........]
     [————————————————]
```

Lines 17–20. Crosby's restorations are here retained. Moretti prefers οἰκεῖος [ὢν τῶν ξένων τῶν]‖ μετὰ Πρωτέου [τεταγμένων ..⁵..]‖υ τοῦ ὑοῦ αὐτ[οῦ, καλῶς καὶ φιλοτί]‖μως, but too little space is left for an adequate connection between τεταγμένων and τοῦ ὑοῦ. He notes μετὰ Πρωτέου [καὶ .....¹².....]‖υ τοῦ ὑοῦ αὐτ[οῦ ἐλθόντων, φιλοτί]‖μως κτλ. as a possible alternative: but καλῶς καὶ φιλοτίμως is so regular a phrase as almost to demand inclusion, and a 13-letter name, which would be required, must be accounted unusual.

The writing, while basically competent, is careless and badly articulated. The upright of epsilon frequently projects above the topmost or below the lowermost horizontal, and these "horizontals" often belie their name. Adjacent sigmas vary in size from 0.005 to 0.008 m. (line 12); the lower stroke of kappa is almost horizontal; the two uprights of pi are almost of equal length. Cf. **96**, which is very comparable in general style. There, as here, phi has the cruciform shape so frequently met with at this period that it may serve as a criterion of date in doubtful cases. See J. Kirchner, *IIA*², nos. 68, 73, and 77, where its first appearance is dated to 341/40 (*IG* II², 1455). However, the first phi of line 8, which is the most clearly surviving example, has a curved cross-stroke of the type claimed by Kirchner as a feature of the early 3rd century (*op. cit.*, no. 78). On the mason he considers to have been responsible for this text, see M. B. Walbank, *BSA* 84, 1989, p. 399.

Lines 1–4. For the prescript in this form, with the *anagrapheus* named in the genitive case after the archon and prytanizing phyle, see Dow, *loc. cit.* and A. S. Henry, *Prescripts*, pp. 53 and 55. This example is a variant version of Henry's Type II, b.

Lines 6–7. ἐκκλησία κατὰ ψήφισμα βουλῆς. Not appearing in *IG* II², this formula occurs in this context for the first time. Crosby compared *IG* II², 554, lines 2–3: ἐκκλησία κατὰ ψήφισμα δήμου. Cf. *IG* II², iv, 1, p. 67; Henry, *Prescripts*, p. 56. The meeting was evidently specially called and of a kind later described as an ἐκκλησία συγκλητός. Cf. M. H. Hansen, *GRBS* 18, 1977, p. 48 and *GRBS* 20, 1979, p. 152 (= *Athenian Ecclesia*, pp. 40 and 76). Its character was perhaps the occasion of its falling on a festival day, Elaphebolion 12. See J. D. Mikalson (*Sacred and Civil Calendar*, pp. 127–128), who quotes lines 1–7 of this text; Hansen, *GRBS* 23, 1982, pp. 332–333, 336, 341, no. 88 (= *Athenian Ecclesia*, pp. 84–85, 88, 93).

Lines 7–8. For the spelling ἐπεψήφισζεν see L. Threatte, *Grammar*, pp. 547–549 (where this instance is quoted from the unrevised edition of the text). Cf. also Pritchett and Meritt, *Chronology*, p. 25 with note 5. Line 8. Amphilochos of Xypete is otherwise unknown. Lines 8–9. The decree was probouleumatic. Cf. **100** and P. J. Rhodes, *Athenian Boule*, p. 250. Line 10. Telokles, son of Telegnotos, of Alopeke has been restored as the proposer of *IG* II², 453, of 310/09, by C. Habicht (*Studien*, p. 198, no. 2). Cf. *SEG* XXXII, 100. He was tentatively identified by Crosby with the chief of the Athenian naopoioi at Delphi at the beginning of the Sacred War (*PA* 13580; *Fouilles de Delphes* III, v, no. 19, lines 34 and 39); but the interval of time is too great for the identification to be upheld, and there was at least one other contemporary Telokles (Ἀγγελῆθεν), who was trierarch in *ca.* 342/1 (*PA* 13584; *IG* II², 1622, line 744). The proposer's name receives particular emphasis by appearing at the beginning of a new line of text, two spaces having been left vacant at the end of the preceding line in order to avoid division of it. See Henry, *Prescripts*, pp. 63–66 (esp. p. 64).

Line 12. ἔμπροσσθεν. For the gemination of the sibilant before theta see Threatte, *Grammar*, p. 530 (the unrevised version of the text is quoted; cf. lines 7–8 above). Lines 14–16. Cf. *IG* II², 421, lines 8–11, 554, lines 8–12; R. Thomsen, *Eisphora*, 1964, pp. 237–240.

Lines 17–20. Proteas was tentatively identified by Crosby with the officer on the staff of Alexander the Great and Antipater (H. Berve, *Das Alexanderreich auf prosopographischer Grundlage* II, 1926, p. 328, no. 664). Moretti expressed justified doubt (*op. cit.*, p. 7) but added as references to the mercenaries and their contacts with the citizens of Athens M. Launey, *Recherches sur les armées hellénistiques* II, 1950, pp. 1038–1054 and J. Pouilloux, *Forteresse, passim*.

FRAGMENT OF A DECREE

103. A fragment of a stele of Hymettian marble (I 5655), with the original rough-picked back and a small part of the left edge (below the inscribed surface) preserved but broken elsewhere, discovered on February 20, 1939, among marbles from the demolition of houses at the north foot of the Areopagos.

H. 0.18 m.; W. 0.29 m.; Th. 0.095 m.

LH. 0.007 m.

Στοιχ. (square) 0.0125 m.

Ed. W. K. Pritchett, *Hesperia* 10, 1941, pp. 268–270, no. 69, with photograph. See *SEG* XXI, 316 (text, with references also to Pritchett and O. Neugebauer, *Calendars*, p. 64, where lines 2–5 are quoted; B. D. Meritt [*Athenian Year*, p. 124], who quotes lines 1–5).

a. 319/18 a., pryt. X   ΣΤΟΙΧ. 30

```
        [ Ἐπ’ Ἀπολλοδώρου ἄρχοντος, ἀναγραφέω]
        [ς δὲ Εὐκάδμ]ου Ἀν[αχ]αέω[ς, ἐπὶ τῆς Οἰνεῖ]
        [δος δεχάτ]ης πρυτανεία[ς· Σκιροφοριῶ]
        [νος ἔνε]ι χαὶ νέαι, πέμπτ[ει χαὶ τριαχο]
    5   [στεῖ τῆ]ς πρυτανείας· ἐχ[χλησία· τῶν προ]
        [έδρων ἐ]πεψήφιζεν Ἐπι[.....¹².....]
        [.... χαὶ συμπ]ρόεδρο[ι· ......¹².....]
        [─────────────────────]
```

The stone is very battered, and in proportion to its bulk comparatively little of the inscription survives. The writing is of the same general character as that of **102**. Two letters must be assumed in the space of one in the latter part of line 5.

Lines 1–5. For the form of the prescript, with the name of the *anagrapheus* in the genitive case, following that of the archon but before the reference to the phyle in prytany, see S. Dow, *HSCP* 67, 1963, pp. 49–50 and A. S. Henry, *Prescripts*, pp. 53–54. This mode of expression corresponds to Henry's Type II, a; cf. **100**. Lines 2, 4–5. On the use of EI for HI in the name of the phyle and in the ordinal numerals, see **101**, commentary on lines 5–7. Lines 4–5. For the last day of Skirophorion as a meeting day of the assembly see J. D. Mikalson, *Sacred and Civil Calendar*, pp. 177–181, where the date should not be expressed as Skirophorion 30; in a hollow month the last day would be the 29th, as it may well have been in this instance (see above on the Archonship of Apollodoros, pp. 151–152).

Line 6. ἐχχλησία. See **97**, line 7. Line 7. The symproedroi are here mentioned for the first time among the Agora decrees. See Dow, *Hesperia* 32, 1963, pp. 335–336 and Henry, *Prescripts*, pp. 39–41. The first reference to them comes in 333/2 (*IG* II², 336, III, lines 9–13), where they are listed by name, a phenomenon occurring occasionally for a century thereafter, with the last examples slightly antedating 225/4; cf. Dow, *op. cit.*, pp. 336–365 and A. G. Woodhead in *Studies Presented to Sterling Dow on his Eightieth Birthday*, 1984, p. 317. More usually there is a simple reference to the symproedroi without a detailed list of their names, as may well have been the case in this enactment; the first example of this more usual formula appears to be *IG* II², 545, of (probably) 321/20.

THE ARCHONSHIP OF ARCHIPPOS II, 318/17 B.C.

Four decrees, of which **104** and **105** are two, survive from this year of the second Archippos when, after the interval in which the *anagrapheus* fulfilled some of the secretary's functions, the γραμματεύς was restored to his full competence in the conduct of public business. It is unfortunate that all the inscriptions of the year have presented problems that have affected the interpretation of the calendric data, the vital places on the stones being either lost or the supposed victims of scribal error, or indeed both at once. As the first year of the seventh Metonic cycle, Archippos II's year should have been ordinary (B. D. Meritt, *TAPA* 95, 1964, p. 236, with further references). It had however been supposed in *IG* II² that the year was intercalary (*IG* II², 448 and 449, *comm.*) and that this was a useful distinction between the years of the one Archippos and the other. It was so regarded initially by W. B. Dinsmoor (*Archons of Athens*, p. 375, *Athenian Archon List*, p. 212), by J. H. Oliver (*Hesperia* 4, 1935, p. 37), and by Meritt (*Hesperia* 4, 1935, p. 544), followed by E. Schweigert (*Hesperia* 8, 1939, p. 34), who set out the pattern of the prytanies and months, with a second Gamelion as the intercalated month rather than the more regular second Posideon.

This general consensus was interrupted by W. K. Pritchett and O. Neugebauer (*Calendars*, pp. 64–66), who believed that the year was ordinary and so interpreted the evidence of the texts. On that interpretation,

IG II², 448, lines 35–87 (*SEG* XXI, 317, XXII, 95, XXIII, 61; M. J. Osborne, *Naturalization* I, pp. 101–105, D 38) belonged to the fourth prytany and **104** and **105** to the sixth. *IG* II², 350 (*SEG* XXI, 320, XXII, 98; Osborne, *vol. cit.*, pp. 105–106, D 39) was also, although with some hesitation, assigned to this year and thought to belong to the seventh prytany. Dinsmoor (*Hesperia* 23, 1954, p. 313) and Meritt (*Athenian Year*, pp. 125–127) concurred in this revision. A subsequent attempt to vindicate the year as intercalary was made by S. Dušanić (*BCH* 89, 1965, pp. 128–141), chiefly in the interests of a reinterpretation of Kassandros' activity in the course of it. Apart from supposing an irregular festival calendar whereby the first five months contained 152 days, it was necessary for Dušanić to dismiss *IG* II², 350 from Archippos' year (cf. Pritchett and Neugebauer, *Calendars*, p. 66) or at the least to require an intercalation of ten days by the archon in order to assimilate it.

Whatever the merits of the historical reinterpretation, the problem of the calendar caused Meritt to return to a consideration of this year via a restudy of *IG* II², 448 (*Hesperia* 43, 1974, pp. 463–466). He became convinced that, after all, the data did point to the correctness of the earlier view that this was an intercalary year. He was further persuaded that *IG* II², 350 properly belongs to this year and can have been passed on Anthesterion 9 = pryt. VII, 18 (*Hesperia* 45, 1976, p. 173; see *SEG* XXVI, 85: for contrary opinions about the date see *SEG* XXXII, 85, XXXV, 77). The addition of one day in the festival calendar before Maimakterion, with later compensation, will suffice to account for the discrepancy in the calendar equation of *IG* II², 448. **104** and **105** can be interpreted as having been passed on the same day, the 207th of the year. The months in the festival calendar alternated as full and hollow until full Gamelion. Gamelion II was also full and was succeeded by regular alternation until hollow Skirophorion. There was a regular succession of prytanies for an intercalary year, six of 38 days being followed by four of 39, thus reversing the "Aristotelian" pattern. Osborne (*Naturalization* II, pp. 104–106) provides a useful summary of the calendric points at issue, at the end of which he accepts the interpretation followed here.

IG II², 449 (*SEG* XVI, 56, XXI, 325) is attributed to this year in *IG* II² but belongs to an unknown intercalary year between 317 and 307 (Pritchett and Meritt, *Chronology*, p. 1; Pritchett and Neugebauer, *Calendars*, pp. 66–67).

Known phylai in prytany in the year of Archippos II are two only, IV Akamantis and VI Kekropis.

HERMO– – – – OF HERAKLEIA HONORED

104. Two fragments of a stele of Pentelic marble (I 4772 a, b), one of which (fragment *a*) preserves the left side and original back, and the other (fragment *b*) the right side and original back; both fragments are otherwise broken all around. Fragment *a* was discovered on April 22, 1937, at the surface southeast of the Market Square, west of the Post-Herulian Wall (S–T 27); fragment *b* was discovered on April 29, 1937, in a modern wall south of the Eleusinion (T 21–22). Subsequent study indicated that the top of fragment *a* made a join with the bottom of a fragment (*c*) preserved in the Epigraphical Museum (E.M. 2537) and until that time unpublished; these two joined fragments are treated henceforward as a unit. *IG* II², 535, hereafter fragment *d*, was found to provide the concluding section of the same inscription. It makes no join with any other piece.

a + *c*: H. 0.238 m.; W. 0.125 m.; Th. 0.062 m.

b: H. 0.205 m.; W. 0.142 m.; Th. 0.07 m.

d: H. 0.17 m.; W. 0.165 m.; Th. 0.055 m.

LH. 0.005–0.006 m.

Στοιχ. Hor. (irregular) 0.012–0.015 m.; Vert. 0.0125 m.

Ed. E. Schweigert, *Hesperia* 8, 1939, pp. 30–34, no. 8 (all fragments), with photographs of fragments *a*–*c*. See *SEG* XXI, 318, with references also to the fuller text of A. E. Raubitschek (*TAPA* 76, 1945, pp. 105–107), who associated fragment *b* very closely with the bottom of fragment *a*; W. K. Pritchett and O. Neugebauer, *Calendars*, p. 65, where parts of lines 1–7 are quoted; B. D. Meritt, *Athenian Year*, p. 126, with quotation of lines 1–7). Further, *SEG* XXII, 96 (S. Dušanić, *BCH* 89, 1965, p. 132); Meritt, *Hesperia* 43, 1974, pp. 464–465, with quotation of lines 1–10. See also (on lines 17–29) A. Wilhelm, *Attische Urkunden* V (= *SbAkadWien* 220, 5), 1942, pp. 179–180.

The stone was subsequently reused, without erasure of the existing decree, for a commemorative inscription of the pyloroi of 15/14 B.C., which has damaged some parts of the text. See Raubitschek, *loc. cit.*, and cf. *IG* II², 492 and 2304.

a. 318/17 *a.*, *pryt.* VI   ΣΤΟΙΧ. 23

(c)
     Ἐπὶ Ἀρχίππ[ου ἄρχοντος ἐπὶ τ]
     ῆς Κεκροπίδ[ος ἕκτης ^{νν} πρυταν]
     έας ἧι Θ[έ]ρ[σιππος Ἱππο..⁵..]
     [. Κ]ολλυ[τ]ε[ὺς ἐγραμμάτευε· Γα]

5   μηλι[ῶνο]ς [ἕνει καὶ νέαι, ἑβδό]
     [μ]ει καὶ δε[κάτει τῆς πρυτανε]
     [ίας· ἐκ]κλ[ησία· τῶν προέδρων ἐ]

(a)
     [πε]ψήφιζ[εν Γλαύκιππος Δεκε(λεεύς)]·
     ἔδοξεν τῶ[ι δήμωι· Ἀρχέδικος]

10   [Ν]αυκρίτου [Λαμπτρεὺς εἶπεν]·
     ἐπειδὴ Ἑρμ[ο...⁷... ἐν τῶι ἔ]
     [μ]προσσθεν [χρόνωι διατετέλ]
     εχε εὔνου[ς ὢν τῶι δήμωι τῶι Ἀ]
     θηναίων κ[αὶ παρεδέξατο τὴν]

15   ναῦν ἀπὸ Κ[υζίκου ἥκουσαν κα]

(b)
     [ὶ στρατ]ηγ[οὺς καὶ στρα]τ[ιώτα]
     [ς φέρουσαν τά τε ἄλλ]α χρήσι[μ]
     [ον αὐτὸν παρέσχηκ]ε τοῖς ἐκ [τ]
     [ῆς ναυμαχίας ἀνασ]ῳζομέν[ο]

20   [ις, καὶ νῦν ἐλθὼν ἐπ]αγγέλλε[τ]
     [αι ἀγαθὸν ὅτι ἂν δύ]νηται ποι
     [ήσειν πρὸς τὴν εἰρή]νην [κ]αὶ ἕ
     [καστον τῶν Ἀθηναίω]ν, δεδόχθ
     [αι τῶι δήμωι ἐπαινέ]σαι Ἑρμο

25   [......¹⁴...... Ἡρ]ακ[λ]⟨ε⟩ιώτη
     [ν καὶ στεφανῶσαι αὐ]τὸν θαλ[λ]
     [οῦ στεφάνωι· εἶναι] δὲ Ἑρμο[..]
     [.... πρόξενον τοῦ δ]ήμου τ[οῦ]
     [Ἀθηναίων, καὶ ἀναγρ]αψ[άτω τὸ]

30   [ψήφισμα τόδε .....¹².....]

         lacuna

(d)
     [----------------· ε]
     [ὶς δὲ τὴν ἀναγραφὴν δοῦναι τ]
     [ὸ]ν τ[αμίαν τοῦ δήμου ⊢ δραχμὰ]
     [ς] ἐκ τῶ[ν κατὰ ψηφίσματα ἀναλ]

35   ισκομέ[νων τῶι δήμωι].
         vacat

Lines 1–10. The text is that of Meritt, *Hesperia* 43, 1974, *loc. cit.* Ἐπὶ Ἀρχίππ[ου ἄρχοντος ἐπὶ τ]‖ῆς Κεκροπίδ[ος ἕκτης πρυταν^{νν}]‖έας [ἧ]ι [Θέ]ρ[σιππος Ἱππο.....|.] Κ̣[ο]λλυτε[ὺς ἐγραμμάτευε· Γα]‖μηλι[ῶ]ν̣ο̣ς̣ ἕ[νει καὶ νέαι, πέμπ|τ]ει καὶ δε[κάτει τῆς πρυτανε|ίας· ἐκ]κλ[ησία· κτλ. Schweigert; [Γα]‖μηλι[ῶ]νος ἕ[κτει ἐπὶ δέκα, τρί|τ]ει καὶ δε[κάτει τῆς πρυτανε|ίας· κτλ. Pritchett and Neugebauer; [Γα]‖μηλι[ῶνο]ς [ὀγδόει ἐπὶ δέκα, ἔκ|τ]ει καὶ δε[κάτει τῆς πρυτανε|ίας· κτλ. Meritt (*Athenian Year*); ἐπὶ τ]‖ῆς Κεκροπίδ[ος ἑβδόμης πρυταν]‖έας [ἧ]ι [Θέ]ρ[σιππος Ἱππο.....|.] Κ̣ολλυτε[ὺς ἐγραμμάτευε· Γα]‖μηλι[ῶ]ν̣ος̣ ἕ[νει καὶ νέαι, πέμπ|τ]ει καὶ δε[κάτει τῆς πρυτανε|ίας· κτλ. Raubitschek, Dušanić.

Line 2. Four letters are inscribed near the beginning of the line in the space of two. The mason apparently began by engraving KPO but on realizing his error erased it and succeeded in crowding KEKPO into the same space. The text is elsewhere correctly inscribed. It is not to be supposed that a mason, after plotting out his work, necessarily began his engraving at the beginning and worked forward with one complete letter after another. Incompleted letters, or blank spaces destined for later completion, occur not infrequently (cf., e.g., **112**, line 2). Here the mason was in some way betrayed into faulty execution of the line when the correction of it could not be carried over into the line following, and the supposition of two empty letter spaces towards the end of the line is to that extent the more acceptable. Lines 2–3. For the spelling πρυτανέας see **95**, commentary on lines 5–6. Lines 4–5. For meetings of the assembly on the last day of Gamelion see J. D. Mikalson, *Sacred and Civil Calendar*, pp. 108–109, where the date is here correctly to be described as Gamelion 30. See **103**, commentary on lines 4–5.

Lines 9–10. The text is that of Raubitschek. ...⁸.... Π||ο]λυχρίτου [....⁹.... εἶπεν Schweigert, Meritt. Ἔδοξεν τῷ[ι δήμωι. The formula, with that of lines 23–24, places this in the category of nonprobouleumatic decrees, for which see **94** and P. J. Rhodes, *Athenian Boule*, pp. 66–68, 263.

Lines 11–14. The text is that of Schweigert.   Line 11. Ἑρμ[οχλείδης(?) Raubitschek, who supplied the name at other relevant points of the text. Lines 11–12. ἔμπροσθεν. See **102**, commentary on line 12. Lines 14–29. The text is that of Raubitschek. Wilhelm, allowing for inequalities in the stoichedon pattern, offered the following text:

καὶ] χρήσι[μ]

[ον αὐτὸν παρέσχηκ]ε τοῖς ἐκ [τ]

[ῆς ναυμαχίας(?) ἐκκο]μ[ι]ζομέν[ο]

20   [ις Ἀθηναίων καὶ ἐπ]ανγέλλε[τ]

[αι ἀγαθὸν ὅτι ἂν δύ]⟨ν⟩ηται πο⟨ή⟩

[σειν τόν τε δῆμον κοι]νῆ⟨ι⟩ [κ]αὶ ἕ

[καστον ἰδίαι Ἀθηναίω]ν, δεδόχθ

[αι τῶι δήμωι ἐπαινέ]σαι Ἑρμο

25   [κρέοντα ...⁷... Ἡρ]ακ[λε]ώτη

[ν καὶ στεφανῶσαι κτλ.]

Line 25. The stone has ΑΚ[.]ΙΩΤΗ. Lines 31–35. So Schweigert and Raubitschek. Raubitschek supplies the lacuna between fragments *b* and *d* as follows: καὶ ἀναγρ]αψ[άτω τὸ | ψήφισμα τόδε ὁ γραμματεὺς τ|ῆς βουλῆς ἐν στήλει λιθίνει | καὶ καταθέτω ἐν ἀκροπόλει· εἰ|ς δὲ τὴν ἀναγραφὴν δοῦναι τ|ὸ]ν τ[αμίαν κτλ.]. On the restoration of line 35 see **88**, commentary on lines 7–8.

Raubitschek's text in lines 14–17 and 21–23 represents the general sense of the decree but is open to the objections in detail expressed by J. and L. Robert, *REG* 59–60, 1946–1947, pp. 321–322, no. 95.

The writing is plain and "standard" for its period, showing some carelessness in execution, in that the letters are at times spread out (e.g., lambda with an almost obtuse angle) or crookedly set (e.g., omega in line 25).

Line 3. Thersippos is not otherwise known. The name occurs relatively infrequently in Attic prosopography. Line 7. ἐκκλησία. See **97**, line 7. Line 8. The presiding officer Glaukippos of Dekeleia is not otherwise known. For the abbreviated demotic see **112**, line 4 and commentary and L. Threatte, *Grammar*, p. 100. Lines 9–10. Archedikos was the *anagrapheus* of 320/19: see **100**, commentary on lines 2–3.

Lines 14–23. The battle concerned was identified by Wilhelm as that in the Hellespont, off Abydos, during the initial stages of the Lamian War, which is epigraphically commemorated as late as 303/2 in *IG* II², 493 + 518, as well as in *IG* II², 398, dated *ca.* 320/19. Wilhelm also referred *IG* II², 492 to the same occasion (*loc. cit.*, pp. 176–181). For the detail of events see W. S. Ferguson, *Hellenistic Athens*, pp. 16–17; W. W. Tarn, *CAH* VI, 1933, p. 458; G. Glotz, R. Cohen, and P. Roussel, *Histoire grecque* IV, i, 1933, pp. 271–272; and cf. J. S. Morrison, *JHS* 107, 1987, pp. 93–97. The basis of any connected account is to be found in Diodorus Siculus 18.15.

Lines 26–27. On the award of the olive stephanos to a foreigner, an honor less notable than that of the stephanos of gold, see A. S. Henry, *Honours*, pp. 38–39. Another Herakleot was so honored towards the end of the century (*IG* II², 479, lines 22–23). For Athenian good relations with Herakleia see also **82**. Line 33. Schweigert restored Δ as the sum to be expended on the inscribing of the stele: but an expenditure of ten drachmas is, at this date, impossibly small. See **83**. For the disbursing officer and the source of the funding see Henry, *Chiron* 12, 1982, pp. 97–118, *ZPE* 78, 1989, pp. 256–267, and **88**.

THE *EPILEKTOI* OF THE PHYLE KEKROPIS HONORED

105 (Pl. 11). The upper left corner of a stele of Hymettian marble (I 559) broken below, on the right, and at the back, discovered on March 6, 1933, in a wall of a modern blacksmith shop over the southwestern part of the Library of Pantainos (R 14). The surface of the inscribed face above the first line of the inscription and extending to the top edge of the stone (*ca.* 0.035 m.) has been dressed back, and this drafting is carried around the left side.

H. 0.205 m.; W. 0.295 m.; Th. 0.195 m.

LH. 0.006 m.

Στοιχ. (square) 0.013 m.

Ed. J. H. Oliver, *Hesperia* 4, 1935, pp. 35–37, no. 5, with photograph. See *SEG* XXI, 319 (with references also to W. K. Pritchett and O. Neugebauer [*Calendars*, p. 65], who quote lines 1–2; B. D. Meritt, *Athenian Year*, p. 127, with quotation of the same lines), XXII, 97 (S. Dušanić, *BCH* 89, 1965, pp. 132–133, with variant text of lines 1–2 and 7; P. Roussel, *RA* ser. 6, 18, 1941, pp. 220–222). Lines 1–3 revised by Meritt, *Hesperia* 43, 1974, p. 464.

a. 318/17 *a.*, *pryt.* VI   ΣΤΟΙΧ. 87

'Επὶ 'Αρχίππου ἄρχοντος [ἐπὶ τῆς Κεκροπίδος ἕκτης πρυτανείας ἧι Θέρσιππος
    'Ιππο..⁶... Κολλυτεὺς ἐγραμμά]
τευεν· Γαμηλιῶνος ἕνει [καὶ νέαι, ἑβδόμει καὶ δεκάτει τῆς πρυτανείας· ἐκκλησία·
    τῶν προέδρων ἐπεψήφιζεν *vvv*]
Γλαύκιππος Δεκελεεὺς [καὶ συμπρόεδροι· *v* ἔδοξεν τῶι δήμωι· *v* ....²⁷.........
    ....εἶπεν· ἐπειδὴ]
[ο]ἱ ἐπίλεκτοι Κεκροπιδῶ[ν ————————————————————τοὺς μὲν]
5 [αὐ]τῶν ἀπέκτειναν, τ[ο]ὺς δὲ [ἐξέβαλον ——————————————————]
[..α]ὐτοὺς ἐπήινεσεν κα[ὶ ——————————————————]
[..⁶...]ς τοὺς παραγεν[ομένους ἐπιλέκτους(?), δεδόχθαι τῶι δήμωι ————— ἀρετῆς]
[ἕνεκα καὶ] εὐνοίας τῆς [εἰς τὸν δῆμον τὸν 'Αθηναίων ——————————]
[..Κεκροπ]ιδῶν, δοῦναι δ[ὲ ——————————————————]
10 [....⁹....]κα[..]Ο[——————————————————]
[....⁹....]ΙΛ[——————————————————]
[——————————————————]

Lines 1–3. The text is that of Meritt (1974); [ἐπὶ τῆς —————ἑβδόμης πρυτανείας ἧι Θέρσιππος 'Ιπποθέρσους 'Αχαρνεὺς ἐγραμμά]|τευεν· Γαμηλιῶνος ἕνει [καὶ νέαι, ὀγδόηι τῆς πρυτανείας· ἐκκλησία κυρία ἐν Διονύσου· τῶν προέδρων ἐπεψήφιζεν *v*] Oliver, with a stoichedon pattern of 90 letters and regarding the year as intercalary; Γαμηλιῶνος ἕνει [καὶ νέαι, ἕκτει καὶ εἰκοστῆι τῆς πρυτανείας· κτλ.] Pritchett and Neugebauer, supposing an ordinary year and a line of 89 letters with syllabic division at the ends of lines. Their text was adopted by Meritt (*Athenian Year*) in every respect other than the day of the prytany, where he read ὀγδόει καὶ εἰκοστεῖ and omitted the iota in πρυτανείας. [ἐπὶ τῆς Κεκροπίδος ἑβδόμης πρυτανείας ἧι Θέρσιππος 'Ιππο..⁶... Κολλυτεὺς ἐγραμμά*vv*]|τευεν· Γαμηλιῶνος ἕνει [καὶ νέαι ἐμβολίμωι, ἕκτει καὶ δεκάτει τῆς πρυτανέας· ἐκκλησία· τῶν προέδρων ἐπεψήφιζεν] Dušanić, who required a stoichedon pattern of 91 letters and an intercalary year. Lines 3–11. The text is that of Oliver, except that in lines 4 and 9 Oliver's Κεκροπίδος is replaced by Roussel's readings and that a restoration by Roussel in line 5 is also included.

Lines 6–8. Dušanić restored as follows: [—————, δεδόχθαι τῶι δήμωι ἐπαινέσαι | ἅπαντα]ς τοὺς παραγεν[ομένους ἐν τῶι πολέμωι ἐπιλέκτους, καὶ στεφανῶσαι χρυσῶι στεφάνωι ἀπὸ Ⲡ δραχμῶν ἀρετῆς | ἕνεκα κτλ.]. [ἅπαντα]ς τοὺς παραγεν[ομένους ἐπιλέκτους· δεδόχθαι τῶι δήμωι ἐπαινέσαι τοὺς ἐπιλέκτους Κεκροπίδος ἀρετῆς | ἕνεκα κτλ.] Oliver (Κεκροπιδῶν Roussel).

The width of the line and the thickness of the stone alike indicate that this was a substantial monument, and one presumably not erected in haste. The writing is finely cut and of excellent craftsmanship, with many "free ends" of strokes discreetly emphasized. The later 4th century offers few texts which can outmatch this as representative of lettering of the highest artistic quality. The horizontal side strokes of omega are so modest and its circle so well formed that the letter was twice read as omicron in the *editio princeps*.

Lines 1–3. For the date and character of the assembly, and for the officials named in the prescript, see **104**. This decree, like that one, was nonprobouleumatic: see **104**, commentary on lines 9–10. The enactment formula, as restored, is isolated by single vacant spaces before and after it. The emphasis of the orator's name, now beginning to occur in the preambles of decrees, has already been noticed (**102**); the name of the chairman of the proedroi is here similarly emphasized, if the restoration be accepted. Compare A. S. Henry (*Prescripts*, pp. 65–66, note 64), who views the restorations with some hesitation but notes that, if correct, they provide the earliest example of the isolation of the enactment formula.

Line 4. The *epilektoi* were apparently a select cadre of hoplites within the contingent of each phyle, under the command of the taxiarchos, who also maintained a corporate social entity. There is evidence for their passing resolutions and making corporate dedications: see Roussel (*op. cit.*, p. 222), who referred to texts now most conveniently accessible as *IG* II², 680 (*SEG* XXI, 390, XXVII, 3), *SEG* III, 116, and XXXIII, 144 (with earlier references). A deme decree in honor of the *epilektoi* of an unknown phyle published as *IG* II², 1209, datable on general grounds to this period, may belong to the same events with which this present text is concerned. See also *SEG* XXXIX, 306.

The interpretation of the contents of the inscription depends to a great extent upon the historical circumstances of Athens in 318/17 at the time of year at which the decree was passed. The surrender of the city to Kassandros took place early in 317 (cf. W. S. Ferguson, *Hellenistic Athens*, pp. 35–37; W. W. Tarn, *CAH* VI, 1933, p. 480; G. Glotz, R. Cohen, and Roussel, *Histoire grecque* IV, i, 1938, p. 294), certainly later than Maimakterion 318/17 (*IG* II², 448, line 37). The passage of **104** (on the same day, it is judged, as the present decree) seems unlikely in the circumstances following the surrender: the ἀρετή of the *epilektoi* must therefore have been exercised in some context before the Macedonian occupation. On the other hand, the quality of the monument suggests that it was not hastily erected on the eve of Kassandros' triumph. Oliver believed that the decree postdated the fall of Athens and suggested that the *epilektoi* had put to death some public enemy of the Athenians (perhaps Epikouros or Demophilos, two of the accusers of Phokion; cf. Plutarch, *Phokion* 38.1), for which they had already been praised (line 6) by Kassandros himself. Dušanić held that both **104** and **105**, which he placed on successive days, postdated Athens' fall; that the year is to be considered intercalary suits the activities of Kassandros during the remainder of 317, which could not otherwise, in his view, be accommodated to the calendar. He supposed that after the surrender, when Kassandros went north to face and defeat Polyperchon (Diodorus Siculus 19.35.7), he took with him an Athenian contingent of which these *epilektoi* formed a part; it will thus have been in the battle against Polyperchon that they earned the distinction here recorded. These historical difficulties, made more acute by the contemporaneity of **104** and **105**, remain unresolved. But see further, on the circumstances giving rise to this decree, R. M. Errington, *Hermes* 105, 1977, pp. 493–494.

FRAGMENT OF THE CONCLUSION OF A DECREE

106. A fragment of a stele of Pentelic marble (I 2821), broken on all sides including the back, discovered on May 2, 1935, in a mixed Late Roman and Turkish context in the northeast part of the Odeion (M 10).

H. 0.18 m.; W. 0.13 m.; Th. 0.11 m.
LH. 0.007–0.008 m.
Στοιχ. (square) 0.0155 m.

Ed. M. B. Walbank, *Hesperia* 58, 1989, pp. 87–88, no. 13, with photograph pl. 21. See also *SEG* XXXIX, 98, where it is doubted if this fragment should be classed as a decree.

ca. a. 318–307 *a.*(?)   ΣΤΟΙΧ.

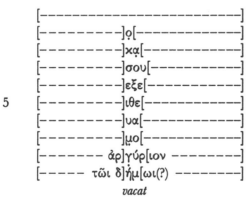

vacat

Walbank's judgment is that this fragment so closely resembles in character *IG* II², 451 (*SEG* XXI, 321, XXXII, 99) that it might be part of the same stele: if so, it would have a stoichedon line of 33 letters. He also ascribes *IG* II², 762 to the same craftsman, but in this case the marble of the fragment is of a different kind. Since *IG* II², 451 is securely dated by the name of the archon (Theophrastos) to 313/12, a comparable date is tentatively given to this text. But the lettering of that inscription, and equally of this fragment, is well described as "volg. s. IV a.", and date and attribution of the present scrap of text must remain uncertain.

Line 4. ἐξε[ῖναι(?) ---] Walbank. Line 5. [--- κα]ὶ θε[ῖναι(?) ---] Walbank (but στῆσαι is perhaps to be expected; cf. **90**, commentary). Line 6. [--- ὅπο]υ ἂ[μ βούληται(?) ---] Walbank; cf. *IG* II², 450, lines 25–34 (for which see also **90**).

Under the oligarchic regime of Demetrios of Phaleron from 317 to 307, the general forms of Athenian constitutional practice survived, albeit with modifications; but comparatively few decrees of the assembly as then constituted seem to have been committed to stone, and no more than five were firmly assigned to this period in *IG* II²: even one of these (*IG* II², 452) proved to belong elsewhere; see *SEG* XIV, 56. The present fragment may or may not add to this small number. On the texts of this period cf. A. S. Henry, *Prescripts*, p. 58 and references there.

APPENDIX: MATERIAL DISCOVERED SINCE 1967

106A. Decree proposed by Theozotides concerning the children of those killed while supporting the democratic cause during the oligarchic period that followed the surrender of Athens at the end of the Peloponnesian War, *a. 403/2 a. vel paullo post.* This tall stele (I 7169), which survives complete although the main inscribed surface is badly eroded, was discovered on August 4, 1970. It had been reused as a covering slab for the Great Drain east of the Stoa Basileios (J 5), hence the erosion. A list of names on the narrow left side, apparently added after the completion of the monument, is, however, well preserved.

The *editio princeps* is that of R. S. Stroud, *Hesperia* 40, 1971, pp. 280–301, with photographs pls. 60, 61. The text also in *SEG* XXVIII, 46, with references to subsequent literature: further references in *SEG* XXIX, 82, XXXII, 37, XXXIII, 67, XXXVII, 65, and XLII, 86. Discussion has centered around the content and character of Theozotides' proposals and upon Greek attitudes in general towards orphans.

106B. Decree in honor of Euagoras, King of Salamis in Cyprus, *a. 393 a.* A fragment (I 7121) broken on all sides except the back but preserving part of a relief sculpture above the inscribed text, discovered on May 15, 1970, in a modern context in Hadrian Street (Q 6), provided a new and important, though nonjoining, addition to *IG* II², 20 (which now becomes fragment *c* of the whole). Fragment *b* was acquired late in 1958 by the British Museum from the sale of a private collection; it preserves part of the right side of the stele and the original back but makes no join with either of the other fragments.

The whole text was reedited by D. M. Lewis and R. S. Stroud, *Hesperia* 48, 1979, pp. 180–193, with photographs pls. 60, 61 and a full bibliography of *IG* II², 20 to that date. The text was repeated as *SEG* XXIX, 86; see also *SEG* XXXIII, 72, recording revision of the prescript by P. Funke, *ZPE* 53, 1983, pp. 149–189.

106C. Law (*nomos*) proposed by Nikophon concerning the acceptability and testing of silver coinage, *a. 375/4 a.* The lengthy piece of legislation, which added one more to the number of the *nomoi* that have emerged from the Agora excavations (cf. **73**, commentary on lines 6–7), is inscribed on a completely preserved, slightly tapering stele (I 7180), discovered (like **106A**) on August 4, 1970, built into the west wall of the Great Drain in front of the Stoa Basileios (J 4–5).

The *editio princeps* is that of R. S. Stroud, *Hesperia* 43, 1974, pp. 157–188, with photographs pls. 25–27: text also in *SEG* XXVI, 72. The provisions of this significant document at once provoked discussion and differences of opinion. The beginning of the long series of studies arising from it was already documented in *SEG* XXVI: thereafter, *SEG* XXVIII, 49 was the prelude to further bibliography appearing in every subsequent volume for the next nine years: XXIX, 87, XXX, 59, XXXI, 63, XXXII, 55, XXXIII, 77, XXXIV, 62, XXXV, 57, XXXVI, 145, XXXVII, 69. *SEG* XLI, 41 and 1877 and XLII, 88 are to be added to the series.

106D. A decree, probably of a *collegium* or a *sodalitas* (and certainly not of the Athenian state) in honor of Charias, son of Hieron, of the deme Pallene, *ca. a. 350 a.* This small fragment (I 7400), preserving the top and back of the stele but otherwise broken, was discovered on June 6, 1972, in a late pithos on Poikiles Street (T 13). The text, unusually, is arranged in two columns. It was edited by M. B. Walbank, *Hesperia* 51, 1982, pp. 43–45, no. 3, with photograph pl. 19, and the text was reproduced as *SEG* XXXII, 72.

106E. Fragment of an enactment of a phyle, *ante med. s.* IV *a.* This upper left corner of a decree (I 7110), preserving the left side and back of the monument and the remains of no more than eleven visible letters, was discovered on March 31, 1970, northwest of the Stoa of Attalos (P 6). It too was edited by M. B. Walbank, *Hesperia* 51, 1982, pp. 46–47, no. 5, with photograph pl. 19, and the text was reproduced as *SEG* XXXII, 140.

106F. Decree in honor of an unknown benefactor, *post med. s.* IV *a.* A fragment of a stele (I 7134), broken all around, was discovered on June 17, 1970, north of the Stoa Basileios (I 4). It preserves a narrow sliver of text 15 lines long but at no point more than six letters in width, which was edited by M. B. Walbank, *Hesperia* 51, 1982, pp. 45–46, no. 4, with photograph pl. 19. The text also appears as *SEG* XXXII, 74.

106G. Decree in honor of a number of benefactors (including five Rhodians) at a time of grain shortage, *a. 331–324 a.*(?). A fragment of a stele of Hymettian marble (I 7360), preserving the right side and original back, was discovered on March 23, 1972, in the Roman Round Building (J 5). The *editio princeps* by M. B. Walbank appeared in *Hesperia* 49, 1980, pp. 251–255, no. 1, with photograph pl. 68; the text also appears as *SEG* XXX, 65. For other decrees in recognition of help given towards the maintenance of the Athenian grain supply during the "Lykourgan period" see **82**, **106H**, and **106J**. But the formulas employed in the text seem to be of the 3rd century rather than the 4th, and the decree may have been occasioned by a later time of dearth.

106H. Sopatros of Akragas in Sicily honored, *a.* 331–324 *a.*(?). Three joining fragments of Hymettian marble together form I 7178, a stele incomplete at top and bottom but preserving both sides and the original back, which was discovered in a Late Roman context on the North Slope of the Akropolis (Q 21). The text of the inscription is complete, apart from the prescript and a few letters elsewhere, and represents a grant of *proxenia* in recognition of services in connection with the import of grain, in a context parallel with that of **106G**, *q.v.* The *editio princeps* was that of J. McK. Camp, *Hesperia* 43, 1974, pp. 322–324, no. 3, with photograph pl. 64:c.

106J. Honors for a Milesian grain dealer, *ca. a.* 321–318 *a.* A fragment of a stele, I 7050, broken all around save at the back, was discovered on February 23, 1969, in the course of demolition of a modern house on Hadrian Street (H 4), and provided the bottom part of a decree (with an uninscribed space below the last line). M. B. Walbank, who edited it (*Hesperia* 51, 1982, pp. 47–48, no. 6, with photograph pl. 20 [text also as *SEG* XXXII, 94]), subsequently determined that it constituted the concluding section of *IG* II², 407 and republished it as such, with slight amendments to the original text, *ZPE* 67, 1987, pp. 165–166 (see also *SEG* XXXVII, 83). For recognition of benefactors during the grain shortage, see **106G** and **106H** above. The date is assured by the mention of the *anagrapheus* as responsible for the inscribing of the decree; see **97** and commentary there. A further revision of the text by Walbank is recorded in *SEG* XL, 79.

SECTION 3

THE "MACEDONIAN CENTURY"
307/6–201/200 B.C.
(107–255)

SECTION 3

THE "MACEDONIAN CENTURY"

307/6–201/200 B.C.: **107–255**

The 107 years comprehended in this section have proved by far the most fruitful period for the Agora excavation in the provision of public decrees. The 157 surveyed here (inclusive of those in the appendix) amount to a little less than half of the total number of texts in the present volume. The dictum that later material drives out the earlier, mentioned in the preface to Section 2, may be partly responsible for this imbalance but not wholly so, for there is a great tailing-off in the 2nd century B.C., which has yielded little more than half the enactments of this period (see p. 357 below). The comparative abundance of 3rd-century material seems in inverse ratio to Athens' diminished importance in the wider Greek world: but this observation must be tempered by the continuing significance of the Athenian state in the rivalry for Aegean domination between the Antigonid, Seleucid, and Ptolemaic monarchs. Indeed, its importance in that context, as well as in the context of Greek sentiment in general, warns against an underestimate of the role of the Athenians on the stage of Hellenistic history.

More important in the survival of decrees of the boule and demos may be the sheer momentum of governmental and archival procedures which, despite the changed political situation, had now got into their stride. The business transacted might carry less international weight, but the determination to record it and the niceties of the recording seem to have increased, as have the detail and comprehensiveness of the honors recorded in so many of the extant documents. The information provided by the prescripts is full, careful, and standardized; and the provisions for inscription and payment, while undergoing change, are equally explicit. This century, while by no means the high-water mark of the history of Athens, was surely the high-water mark of its bureaucracy. It may be noted *en passant* that it was in this period that the honoring of deserving prytaneis began to appear as a major element in the activity of the assembly, as the 95 texts assigned to it (*Agora* XV, 57–152) reveal. Nevertheless, it is worth observing that in *IG* II^2 the balance between the 4th century (to 307 B.C.) and the 3rd (from 307 to 200) is roughly equal, and to that extent the Agora discoveries vary the picture previously existing.

Fifty-three, or just over one third, of the decrees in this section are too fragmentary for any assessment of their likely contents to be made. Of the 104 that remain, 86 are concerned with the award of honors (including, in 11 cases, full citizenship for meritorious foreigners): as between the honoring of citizens and noncitizens, where the matter is clear, there is an equal division (31:32), the remaining 23 being inconclusive. As a particular reflection of the period, there are five occasions (**117, 122, 144, 172, 173**) on which kings or their courtiers are specially honored. The grant of *proxenia* is hardly in evidence (**111, 131, 164**). Six texts are relevant to "foreign affairs" in other respects (**115, 208, 209, 225, 238, 255J**); but Athens' place in the world clearly did not call for a great deal of inscribed record in that regard beyond a care for personal relationships with individuals who seemed to matter. Sixteen enactments of groups within the body politic, whether religious or secular, do not quite maintain the proportion noted in the previous section. Activity in the matter of *nomothesia*, so evident in the material provided by the Agora for the 4th century, has entirely abated.

Finally, no more than 11 of the Agora decrees in this period relate to inscriptions already known and presented in *IG* II^2, in marked contrast with the evidence in Section 2. There may be conclusions to be drawn from this for those inclined to draw them.

THE ARCHONSHIP OF ANAXIKRATES, 307/6 B.C.

As noted in the commentary to **106**, during the ten years of oligarchic rule in Athens, under the tutelage of Kassandros' nominee Demetrios of Phaleron and with the support of the Macedonian garrison in the Peiraieus, very few decrees of the Athenian people were, on our evidence, committed to stone; and although constitutional forms largely survived, the ordinary democratic procedures of the constitution were undoubtedly truncated. The liberation of the city by Demetrios Poliorketes in Thargelion 308/7, completed by the surrender early in 307/6 of the Macedonian troops holding out in Mounychia, resulted in the restoration of full democracy, the reestablishment (to judge from the prescripts of the decrees) of the regular officers of state in their pristine functions, and a flood of public business of which numerous epigraphical texts preserve the record.

In the course of the year the Athenians honored their "liberators" by according to Antigonos Monophthalmos and his son Demetrios the then-unparalleled distinction of having new phylai created and named for them. For the details of this reorganization, which took final effect at some time after the fifth prytany, see W. K. Pritchett, *The Five Attic Tribes after Kleisthenes*, 1943, pp. 5–12 (= *AJP* 61, 1940, pp. 186–193). From this time onwards, during the "period of twelve phylai", which lasted until 224/3 B.C., the "ideal" calendar of an ordinary year would show prytany (conciliar) months and lunar (festival) months of generally equal length. This cannot always be guaranteed in practice: cf. A. G. Woodhead, *Study of Greek Inscriptions*, p. 119.

This reorganization was not, however, suddenly conceived and as suddenly implemented. The changes envisaged were reflected in the entire calendar of what W. B. Dinsmoor called "this peculiar year", which B. D. Meritt also characterized as "most instructive". It has presented problems of great complexity and has evoked long and careful examination and discussion on the part of a number of scholars. The investigation by Pritchett and Meritt (*Chronology*, pp. 1–21) still forms the best and most fundamental basis for study, and the data it established have been generally accepted. For earlier work see in particular Dinsmoor, *Archons of Athens*, pp. 377–385, *Hesperia* 4, 1935, pp. 303–310, *Athenian Archon List*, pp. 212–222; Meritt, *Hesperia* 4, 1935, pp. 536–544, *Hesperia* 5, 1936, pp. 203–205; Pritchett, *AJP* 57, 1937, pp. 220–222 and 329–333; A. B. West in *Classical Studies Presented to Edward Capps*, 1936, pp. 356–363. For later studies of detail see Meritt, *Athenian Year*, pp. 176–178, *Hesperia* 32, 1963, pp. 435–438, *Hesperia* 33, 1964, pp. 13–15, 'Αρχ. 'Εφ., 1968, pp. 108–115 *Historia* 26, 1977, p. 171. A useful summary bibliography on the year, to the date of his writing, is also to be found in J. Pečírka, *Formula*, p. 79, note 2. The salient points that have emerged from these studies may be summarized as follows.

The year was from the outset planned as one of twelve prytanies (Pritchett and Meritt, *Chronology*, p. 21), and there was no change in the course of it (as implied by Pritchett and O. Neugebauer, *Calendars*, p. 69) from the old pattern of ten prytanies to the new pattern of twelve. During the month of Gamelion it was suddenly decided that the year was to be intercalary in the lunar (festival) calendar, although it had begun as an ordinary year and the first six months had corresponded to that form. The intercalation was effected by the insertion of a second Gamelion and by distributing the thirty additional days among the last six prytanies. The necessary rearrangement of demes, following on the decision to create the two new phylai, had been carried through during the early months of the year. For the details of the reapportionment see J. S. Traill, *Political Organization*, pp. 58–61. Thus the phylai Antigonis and Demetrias were able to play their part in the provision of prytaneis by the end of 307. The complications of all this made it necessary for the officials to be extraordinarily careful in their counting of days. The unique expression ἡμερολεγδόν is found in texts of this year and is not certainly attested anywhere else; see Meritt, 'Αρχ. 'Εφ., 1968, pp. 108–115 and **85**, commentary on lines 3–4.

In the event, the year consisted of 384 days, with thirteen months alternating hollow and full except that both Thargelion and Skirophorion were full. There were however some internal adjustments as the year went along. Two days were added to, and later subtracted from, the first Gamelion; and eleven days and then one day were added to Elaphebolion, compensation being made for them in Mounichion; see Meritt, *Hesperia* 32 and 33, *locc. citt.* The prytany calendar, according to Meritt's final revision of it (*Athenian Year*, p. 177; cf. *Hesperia* 33, 1964, p. 13), which substituted a scheme of greater regularity for that shown in Pritchett and Meritt, *Chronology*, p. 21, was made up of six prytanies each of 30 days followed by six each of 34 days.

Apart from **107**, the earliest extant decree of the year, passed in the first prytany, **107A**, evidently of the third prytany, and **108**, if indeed it forms part of *IG* II², 458, which was passed in prytany VII, the following decrees provide calendric data for Anaxikrates' archonship: *IG* II², 464, of pryt. IV; 456 (*SEG* XXI, 328), of pryt. V; 457, of pryt. VI; *Hesperia* 3, 1934, pp. 398–402, no. 16, of pryt. VIII; *IG* II², 459 (*SEG* XXI, 330, XXV, 77), of pryt. IX; 358 (*SEG* XXI, 326, XXVI, 87), 461 (= 726; *SEG* XXI, 332), and 462, all of pryt. X; 455 (*SEG* XXI, 327), of pryt. XI; and 460 (*SEG* XXI, 331), of pryt. XII. Additional material is provided by the poletai record *IG* II², 1589 (*Agora* XIX, P40, with earlier references), of the first prytany, *SEG* III, 86 (cf. *SEG* XXXIII, 103), of the tenth, and by the *traditio* of the temple treasures, *IG* II², 1487, in a reference to the month Gamelion II at lines 53–54. The testimony of *IG* II², 457 (cf. *SEG* III, 156, XXX, 67) in being referred to the sixth prytany rests on its literary counterpart in [Plutarch], *Vitae X oratorum* 852; the extant inscribed text omits the formula of dating. *IG* II², 463 (**109**) and 466 (*SEG* XXIV, 110) are also attributable to the year of Anaxikrates but contain no data helpful to the evaluation of its calendar problems. The last-named contains a reference to the "Council of the Five Hundred" and could be assigned to the last two months of 308/7, after the liberation of Athens, rather than to 307/6; at the least it must belong to the early months of the latter year.

Known or probable phylai in prytany during this complex year are as follows: I Erechtheis or Kekropis, III Akamantis(?), IV Aigeis or Oineis, V Oineis or Aigeis, VI Antiochis, VII Antigonis, VIII Demetrias, IX Akamantis(?), but, if not, Kekropis or Erechtheis, X Hippothontis, XI Pandionis, XII Aiantis or Leontis.

A CERTAIN ANDROS– – HONORED

107. A fragment of a stele of Pentelic marble (I 5884), with the right side and the original back partly preserved, as well as the spring of a crowning molding, but broken elsewhere, discovered on July 5, 1939, in the vaulting above the north wall of the Hephaisteion (E 7).

H. 0.35 m.; W. 0.182 m.; Th. 0.11 m.
LH. 0.006–0.007 m.
Στοιχ. (square, with slight irregularity) 0.015 m.

Edd. W. K. Pritchett and B. D. Meritt, *Chronology*, pp. 7–8, with photograph. See *SEG* XXI, 334 (reference also to Meritt, *Athenian Year*, p. 178, where the calendric data are listed). Cf. Meritt, *Hesperia* 33, 1964, p. 14. The text of lines 1–10 is quoted by A. S. Henry (*Prescripts*, p. 59).

a. 307/6 *a., pryt.* I   ΣΤΟΙΧ. 27

```
        ['Ἐπὶ 'Αναξικράτους ἄρχ]οντος ἐπὶ [τ]
        [ῆς ....¹⁰.... πρώτης] πρυ[τ]ανεί[α]
        [ς ἧι Λυσίας Νοθίππου Δ]ιο[μ]ειεὺ[ς ἐ]
        [γραμμάτευεν· Ἑκατομ]βα[ιῶ]νος ἐ[νδ]
   5    [εκάτει, ἐνδεκάτει τῆς] πρυταν[εία]
        [ς· ἐκκλησία κυρία· τῶν π]ροέδρω[ν ἐπ]
        [εψήφιζεν –––––––––––].     vacat
        [–––––––––––––––––––]ᵛ ἔδοξε[ν τῶ]
        [ι δήμωι· Πυθόδωρος Νικ]οστράτ[ου 'Α]
  10    [χαρνεὺς εἶπεν· ἐπει]δὴ 'Ανδροσ[...]
        [......¹⁸.........]ς ὑποδη[...]
        [......¹⁶........]δου ἐπὶ τη[...]
        [......¹⁶........]ου κατὰ τὰ [...]
        [......¹⁶........]ονυ[...]ην[...]
  15    [–––––––––––––––––––––]
```

The writing is plain and competent, without adornment and equally without evident carelessness, and is fully consistent with its dating. The stone itself has been much battered, and what little of the text survives is not set off to the best effect. The text is that of the *editio princeps*, except that M. B. Walbank, in reexamining the inscription, has discerned traces of the letters dotted in lines 2–4 and 10–13 and has added line 14. See also below, commentary on lines 9–10.

Line 1. Erechtheis or Kekropis alone will fit the space available for the name of the phyle. Line 3. The γραμματεύς of this year, Lysias, son of Nothippos, of Diomeia, is not otherwise known. His name is almost fully preserved in *IG* II², 458. See *PA* 9370. It was presumably his father Nothippos who in 331/30 proposed the decree in honor of the Thracian prince Rheboulas (*IG* II², 349; M. N. Tod, *GHI* II, 193; cf. M. H. Hansen, *Athenian Ecclesia II*, p. 56).

Line 6. ἐκκλησία κυρία. See **101**, commentary on lines 7–8. Lines 8–9. The enactment was nonprobouleumatic; cf. P. J. Rhodes, *Athenian Boule*, p. 263. Lines 9–10. The name of the proposer, which was not restored in the *editio princeps*, was the suggestion of Walbank, *Hesperia* 54, 1985, p. 318, note 25; Pythodoros will have been the son of Nikostratos, son of Pythodoros, *PA* 11026. For the family see J. K. Davies, *Athenian Propertied Families*, pp. 481–484. Walbank further noted that the honorary decree I 2173 (**144**) shows the same letter spacing and letter height as the present text and appears to be the work of the same craftsman.

FRAGMENT OF A DECREE

107A (Pl. 13). A fragment of a stele of Pentelic marble (I 4593), broken all around (including the back), discovered on March 10, 1937, in a Byzantine context south of the Eleusinion and east of the Post-Herulian Wall (U 22).

H. 0.072 m.; W. 0.118 m.; Th. 0.08 m.
LH. 0.006 m.
Στοιχ. (square) 0.0116 m.

Unpublished. Details, text, and material for comment were generously made available for this volume by M. B. Walbank.

a. 307/6 a., pryt. III   ΣΤΟΙΧ. 28 (lines 2 and following)

$$
\begin{array}{l}
[\Theta] \quad \varepsilon \quad [o \quad \iota]. \\
[\text{'Επὶ 'Αναξ}]\iota\kappa\rho\acute{\alpha}\tau[\text{ους ἄρχοντος ἐπὶ τῆ}] \\
[\varsigma \ldots^8\ldots]\text{ος τρί[της πρυτανείας}] \\
[\ddot{\eta}\iota\ \Lambda\upsilon\sigma\acute{\iota}\alpha\varsigma\ \text{No}]\theta\acute{\iota}\pi\pi\upsilon\ [\Delta\iota\text{ομεεὺς ἔγρα}] \\
5 \quad [\mu\mu\acute{\alpha}\tau\epsilon\upsilon\epsilon\nu\cdot\ \text{Βοηδ}]\rho\upsilon\mu[\iota\tilde{\omega}\nu\text{ος}\ \ldots^8\ldots] \\
[\ldots\ldots^{13}\ldots\ldots]\Lambda[\ldots\ldots^{14}\ldots\ldots] \\
[\text{------------------------}]
\end{array}
$$

Walbank identified the craftsman who inscribed this text as responsible also for *IG* II², 461 (= 726), 487, and 510.

The chief interest of the fragment lies in the name of the phyle that must be supplied in line 3, requiring nine letters in the nominative case. The possibilities are Akamantis, Pandionis, Antigonis, and Demetrias: but of these the last three are almost certainly preempted by the eleventh, seventh, and eighth prytanies respectively (see p. 169 above). This leaves Akamantis, which B. D. Meritt assigned to the ninth prytany in his reassessment of *IG* II², 459 (*SEG* XXI, 330) in 'Αρχ. 'Εφ., 1968, pp. 109–115 (*SEG* XXV, 77), where he extended the stoichedon line of 49 letters, previously accepted, to a line of 50 letters. But the revision rests on insecure grounds, and the present text, for which Akamantis seems to be the obligatory choice for association with the third prytany (unless there be some violation of the stoichedon pattern), may serve to invalidate it. That being so, *IG* II², 459 must revert to the 49-letter line formerly envisaged, and the phyle then in office will be that of eight letters in the nominative case which had not served as the first prytany of the year.

FRAGMENT OF A DECREE

108. A fragment of a stele of Pentelic marble (I 5372), broken on all sides including the back, discovered on March 31, 1938, in a late context in the northeast corner of the Church of the Hypapanti (T 21).

H. 0.09 m.; W. 0.066 m.; Th. 0.042 m.
LH. 0.007 m.
Στοιχ. (square) 0.016 m.

Ed. M. B. Walbank, *Hesperia* 58, 1989, p. 88, no. 14, with photograph pl. 20. Cf. *SEG* XXXIX, 100, where the text is considered too fragmentary for classification.

a. 307/6 *a., pryt.* VII(?)   ΣΤΟΙΧ. 25(?)

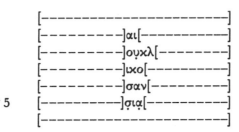

Walbank noted that the type of marble, the letter height and spacing, and the characteristics of the writing to be found on this fragment are the same as those of *IG* II², 458, of the year of Anaxikrates. In consequence, he regarded it as likely to provide part of the body of the decree of which that text is the prescript. If this judgment is correct, the date and stoichedon pattern, here marked with a query, will be confirmed as shown: if not, the fragment should at least be attributable to the closing years of the 4th century. For convenience, the text of *IG* II², 458, of particular interest for the calendar of this year (see p. 169 above), is also reproduced here. For further references on it see *SEG* XXI, 329 and XXV, 76.

ΣΤΟΙΧ. 25

'Επ' 'Αναξ[ικράτους ἄρχοντος] ἐ[π]ι
τῆς 'Αντιγονίδ[ος ἐβ]δ[όμη]ς [πρ]υτ
ανείας ἧι Λυσίας Νοθ[ιππ]ου Διο
μεεὺς ἐγρα[μμ]άτευεν· Γαμηλιῶν
5   ος δευτ[έ]ραι ἐ[μ]βολίμωι ὀγδόε[ι]
μετ' εἰκάδας ἡμερολεγδόν, μιᾶ[ι]
καὶ εἰκοστεῖ τῆς πρυτανε[ίας· ἐ]
[κκλη]σ[ί]α κυρία· τῶν προέδ[ρων ἐπ]
[εψήφιζε ....18........]
10   [—————————————————]

On the interpretation of lines 4–7 see in particular W. K. Pritchett and B. D. Meritt, *Chronology*, pp. 14–15. The date (Gamelion 24, i.e., a second intercalated Gamelion 22 in a month predicated as hollow and the 201st day of the year) is not adduced as evidence by J. D. Mikalson (*Sacred and Civil Calendar*, p. 105). For the equation see Meritt, *Hesperia* 33, 1964, pp. 13–14; A. S. Henry, *Prescripts*, pp. 60–61.

THE REPAIR OF THE FORTIFICATION WALLS OF ATHENS

109. A large fragment of a stele of Pentelic marble (I 3843), with the right side and original back preserved but broken elsewhere, discovered on March 23, 1936, below the floor of the Church of Christ, north of the Eleusinion (T 17). It was at once recognized as providing part of the lower right section of the large stele *IG* II², 463, now in the Epigraphical Museum (E.M. 10396), and it makes a join with that stele at the relevant point, adding substantially to lines 100–130 of the inscription.

I 3843: H. 0.49 m.; W. 0.48 m.; Th. 0.17 m.
LH. (lines 100–118) 0.006 m.; (line 119) 0.009 m.; (lines 120–130) 0.005 m.
Στοιχ. (lines 100–118 only; square) 0.0135 m.

Ed. B. D. Meritt, *Hesperia* 9, 1940, pp. 66–72, no. 9, with photograph. See *SEG* XIX, 58, with references (concerning the Agora fragment) to A. Wilhelm, *AbhAkadBerlin*, 1941, no. 4, pp. 3–17, and to F. G. Maier, *Griechische Mauerbauinschriften* I, 1959, pp. 48–67, no. 11, who provided a complete text and discussion of the whole enactment. The text of column IV, lines 120–130, was further discussed by Y. Garlan (*BCH* 93, 1969, pp. 152–158) in the course of a study of various texts in Maier's volume; see *SEG* XXV, 78. *SEG* XIII, 42 records the citation of column I, lines 122–123, by J. Papademetriou in Γέρας 'Αντωνίου Κεραμοπούλλου, 1953, pp. 294–297, and XXI, 333 a small correction to line 35 by Meritt.

IG II², 463 is in a bad state of preservation, and much of the text seen by earlier editors, especially in the lower part of the inscription, is no longer discernible. See Meritt, *loc. cit.*, p. 71. That section which connects with the Agora fragment is here transcribed with that fragment to give a full text of lines 100–130. For lines 1–99 the latest revision is that of Maier, *loc. cit.* For further references to the text and interpretation of the contents of the upper part of the stele see N. Kyparissis and W. Peek, *AthMitt* 66, 1941, pp. 238–239 (on line 39); L. B. Holland, *AJA* 54, 1950, pp. 337–356 and F. E. Winter, *Phoenix* 13, 1959, pp. 161–200 (especially on lines 52–74 and the καταστέγασμα for which provision is there made); R. L. Scranton, *Harvard Library Bulletin* 14, 1960, pp. 165–172. Lines 28–29 are quoted in *Agora* III, p. 156, no. 496, as a testimonium for the Metroon. Later discussion is treated in *SEG* XXXVII, 85.

a. 307/6 *a.*   ΣΤΟΙΧ. 71

```
100  [.]Α[.]ΟΝ[.]Ι̣[....¹⁰....]ΜΕΝΟ[....]ΝΑΝΜΗ[...]ΔΕΝ[.....¹³......]ΓΤΙ̣[.........¹⁹.........]
     δὲ α[ὐ]το[..⁶..]Ν̣[....] εἴ τις [...]ΑΟΙΔΕΙ[..]ΛΗΦ[.....¹¹..... τ]ῶν τει[χῶν ......¹⁵.......]
     ΡΑΣ[.]Η[....¹⁰....] τ[ὰ] ἔργα π[άντα] ἐγγ[υητὰς] Μ[...⁷... σᾶ καὶ(?)] ἐντελῆ κ[ατὰ τὰς
        συγγραφὰς το]
     ῖς ἀρχ[ιτέκτοσι ..⁶..]ΣΣ[..⁵..]ΙΑΡ[....¹⁰.... ἐπὶ τῆι δ]ι̣[ο]ικήσει πλὴ[ν(?) ...]Ι̣ΝΙ̣[...⁷...]
     ΑΥΤ[..⁵..]Α[....¹⁰....] κα[ὶ τὴν] ἔρειψ[ι]ν [...⁶... λιθολογ]ήσας καὶ τῶν πύργων [...]Γ[...⁶...]
105  ΗΝΚΟ[...]ΣΟΥ[..⁵.. τοῦ ἄ]στε[ως· τ]ῶ̣[ι] δὲ δευ[τ]έ̣[ρωι ἔτει τὰς] ὑπολογὰς καὶ τὰ
        ΕΞΕΡΡΕΙΟΔ̣[..⁵..]
     καὶ [τ]οὺ[ς ἀ]να[βασμο(ύ)]ς· [τῶι δ]ὲ [τ]ρ[ίτ]ωι ἔτει τὴν [...⁷... καὶ] τὴν ἀλιφὴν ἔνδοθεν καὶ
        ἔξω[θεν κα]
     ὶ τὴν κο[ρώ]ν[ην· τῶι δὲ ⟨[τετάρ]⟩τ[ωι] ἔτ[ε]ι [π]αρέξει ὀ[ρθὰ καὶ στ]έγοντα πάντα [κ]α̣ὶ σᾶ καὶ
        ἐντε[λῆ κατ]
     [ὰ] τὰς συ[γ]γ[ρ]α[φὰς συ]ν[τετ]ελε[σμ]ένα· ἐὰν δέ τινε[ς βούλ]ωνται τῶν μεμισθωμένων πλείω σ[υντελ]
     [εῖ]ν ἔργ[α] τῶν ἀ[ποτε]τ[αγμέ]ν[ω]ν εἰς τὸν ἐνι[α]υτόν, [ἐξεῖ]ναι αὐτοῖς πλὴν τῆς κονιάσεως, [καὶ ὁ τ]
110  [αμ]ίας μεριεῖ τἀργύ[ρι]ον σ[ύμπ]αν πρὸς τὰ ἐξῆ[ς γενό]μενα τῶν ἔργων· παρέξουσιν δὲ αὐτο[ὶ ἐα]
     [υτ]οῖς ἅ[π]αντα ὅσων ἄ[ν δ]έ̣ων[ται] εἰ[ς] τὰ ἔργα πλὴ[ν ἐά]γ τι μέχρι τοῦ λιθολογήματος πέσῃ[ι ἢ κα]
     [τὰ] πόλε[μ]ον κινηθ[ῆ]ι· ἐγγυητ[ὰς] δὲ κα[τ]αστήσαν[τε]ς λήψονται κατὰ τὸν νόμον τὸ ἀργύρι[ον κα]
     [τὰ τ]ὸν ἐνιαυτὸν ἕκαστον· ὅσ[αι δὲ] τῶν παρ[ό]δω[ν στ]ενότεραί εἰσιν καὶ γεγεισηποδι[σ]μέ[ναι]
     [λιθ]ίνωι γεισηποδίσματι ὑ[πο]ικοδομήσ[ε]ι σ[τόχ]ους λιθολογήσας ὕψος ὑπὲρ γῆς τριημ[ιπό]
115  [δια] πλάτος πενθη[μ]ιποδίου[ς δ]ιαλείπον[τα]ς [ἀπ'ἀ]λλήλων δέκα πόδας καὶ τοὺς ΑΝ̣ΑΚΛ[..⁶...]·
     [παρ]έσται δὲ καὶ [ἀ]τ̣[έ]λεια στ[ρα]τείας τοῖ[ς μισθ]ωσαμένοις τὰ ἔργα τὰ περὶ τὰ τείχη [εἰς τετ]
     [ραε]τίαν· κατὰ τάδε ἔνειμαν ο[ἱ ἀ]ρχιτέκ[τονες τ]ὰ μέρη τοῦ τείχους· πρώτ[η μ]ερὶς τοῦ̣ ν[οτίου]
     [τεί]χους.       vacat
     Κ α τ ὰ  τ ά δ ε  μ ε μ ί σ θ ω τ α ι  τ ὰ  ἔ ρ [γ α  τ ὰ  π ε]ρ ὶ  τ ὰ  τ ε ί χ η  ε ἰ ς  τ ὴ ν
        τ ε τ ρ α ε τ ί α ν.
```

Col. I

```
120  [Τοῦ β]ορείου τείχους πρώτη μερὶς
     [ἀπὸ τ]οῦ διατειχίσματος μέχρι τῶν
     [πρώτω]ν πυλῶν καὶ τὰς διόδους
     [..⁵..] ΗΗΗΗ   vacat
     [μισθωτ]ής·   vacat
125  [...⁸...]ης Χίωνος Κορυ[δα]λλ[ε]ύ[ς]
     [––––––––––––––––––––]
```

Col. II

```
     Τοῦ νοτίου [τε]ίχους π[έμ]πτ[η μερὶς ἀπὸ]
     τοῦ διατειχ[ί]σματος τ[οῦ ἐμ Πειραιεῖ]
     μέχρι τοῦ Κηφ[ι]σοῦ   vacat
                          vacat
     ἕκτη μερὶς ἀπὸ [τ]οῦ Κ[ηφισοῦ μέχρι τοῦ]
125  [.]ΡΕ[.]Ο[..]ΝΟ[––––––––––––––]
     [––––––––––––––––––––]
```

Col. III

```
120  [τοῦ ἄ]στεως πρώτη μερὶς ἀπὸ τοῦ διατει
     [χίσμ]ατος τοῦ νοτίου τείχους μέχρι τῶν
     ['Ιτων]ίδων πυλῶν ΤΤΧ μισθωταί·
     [....]τας Μενεκράτους ἰσοτελής,
     [..⁵..]ς Νικηράτου 'Ηρακλεώτης ἰσοτε(λής)·
125  [ἐγγυη]ταί· Δίκαιος Δικαιογένου Κολωνῆ(θεν),
     [..⁶...]ος Νικολό[χ]ου Φαληρεύς,
```

Col. IV

```
     Πέμπτη μερὶς ἀπὸ [–––––μέχρι τῶν]
     πυλῶν τῶν πρὸς ['Αχαρνάς(?)]·
     μισθωτής· Φιλιστίδης [Αἰ]σ[χ]ύ[λου Περιθοίδης]·
     ἐγγυηταί· Μεγακλῆς Μενίππ[ου 'Αχαρνεύς],
     Μένιππος Μεγακλέους 'Α[χ]α[ρνεύς],
125  Εὐκτήμων Αἰσ[χύ]λου Π[εριθοίδης],
     Εὐ[..]Ο[..]Ε[––––––––––].
```

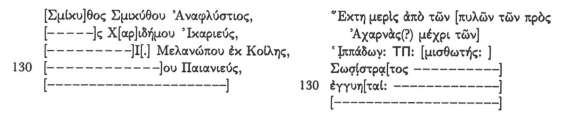

[Σμίκυ]θος Σμικύθου Ἀναφλύστιος,
[– – – – –]ς Χ[αρ]ιδήμου Ἰκαριεύς,
[– – – – – – – – –]Ι[.] Μελανώπου ἐκ Κοίλης,
130 [– – – – – – – – – – – –]ου Παιανιεύς,
[– – – – – – – – – – – – – – – – –]

Ἕκτη μερὶς ἀπὸ τῶν [πυλῶν τῶν πρὸς
Ἀχαρνὰς(?) μέχρι τῶν]
Ἱππάδων: ΤΠ: [μισθωτής:]
Σωσίστρα[τος – – – – – – – – –]
130 ἐγγυη[ταί: – – – – – – – – – – –]
[– – – – – – – – – – – – – – – – –]

Line 101. δὲ α[ὐ]το Meritt; δὲ αὐτὸ Maier.   Line 102. ἐντελῆ κτλ.   Cf. lines 107–108.   Line !03. ΠΛ[..⁵..]ΙΝΙ[...⁷....] Meritt; ΠΛΙ[....]ΙΝΙ[...⁷...] Maier. Line 104. [λιθολογ]ήσας. Cf. line 114. Line 105. Τὰς ὑπολογάς. See LSJ, s.v. ὑπολογή II (reference to this text added in LSJ, *Supplement*, 1968, p. 145). The letters on the stone towards the end of the line are clear and remain enigmatic. The context suggests that ἐξερείσματα or some equivalent noun linking with the καί of the following line may have been intended. Lines 106–107. The text is that of Meritt, except that ⟨[τετάρ]⟩τ[ωι] here replaces his [πέμπ]τ[ωι]. For line 107 see E. Schweigert, *Hesperia* 9, 1940, p. 323, note 7. Wilhelm proposed τ[ὴ]ν [κονίασιν καὶ] in line 106 and [τετά⟨ρ⟩]τ[ωι] in line 107. καὶ τ[ο]ὺς [ἀ]να[βασμοὺ⟨ύ⟩)]ς· [τῶι δ]ὲ [τ]ρ[ίτ]ωι ἔτει τὴν [πάροδον καὶ] τὴν ἀλιφὴν ἔνδοθεν καὶ ἔξω[θεν κα]ὶ τὴν κο[ν⟨ί⟩ασιν· τῶι] δὲ [τετά⟨ρ⟩]τ[ωι] ἔτει [π]αρέξει ὀ[ρθὰ καὶ στ]έγοντα πάντα [κ]α⟨ὶ⟩ ἴσα καὶ κτλ. Maier. Line 109. ἐνι[α]υτὸν and [καὶ ὁ τ] Meritt; ἐνιαυτὸν and χ[αὶ ὁ τ] Maier.   Line 110. The text is that of Meritt, followed by Maier; Wilhelm's πρὸς τὰ ⟨α⟩ίεὶ [γιγνό]μενα cannot be accepted. Line 111. ε[ἰ]ς τὰ ἔργα πλὴ[ν Meritt; εἰς τὰ ἔργα πλὴ[ν Maier. Line 113. εἰσι[ν] Meritt; εἰσιν Maier. Line 116. [παρ]έσται Meritt; both Wilhelm and Maier expressed doubt concerning the restoration. Line 117. The stonemason began work on the record of contracts at this point, but either his copy was incomplete, and he resumed at a later stage, in a different style and with the north rather than the south wall, or he realized that a different method was to be employed and began on it, with certain adjustments to his material, without erasing what he had already begun. The reading at the end of the line is that of Maier, which invalidates Wilhelm's proposed [βορέου]. Meritt read τοῦ [νοτίου].

Col. IV: The text is that of Garlan, whose reading in line 126 is also that of Maier. Elsewhere, Maier followed the readings of Meritt's edition, which were as follows: Line 121. τῶν πρὸς [– – – – – –]. Line 124. [Ἀχαρνεύς]. Line 125. Εὐκτήμων Αἰ[– – – – – –]. Line 126. Εὐ[– – –]Ε[– – – – – –]. Lines 127–129. ἕκτη μερὶς ἀπὸ τῶν [– – – – – –]ηι πυλῶν: ΤΓ: [μισθωτής]· | ΣΩ[...]ΤΟ[– – – – – –] ‖ κτλ.

For the general characteristics of the monument see *IG* II², 463. The writing throughout is untidy (despite J. Kirchner's characterization of it as "diligenter"), but it is reasonably representative of its time and despite the length and complexity of the text preserves a good overall standard of accuracy. Repair of the fortifications of Athens and the Peiraieus and the Long Walls between them was undoubtedly an important priority for the restored democracy; the date of 307/6 and the context of the Four Years' War well suit the provisions here committed to stone. See W. S. Ferguson (*AJP* 59, 1938, pp. 230–232) and Wilhelm (*Wiener Studien* 58, 1940, pp. 75–77), both of whom defended 307/6 as a date for this text against the contentions of U. Kahrstedt (*Untersuchungen zur Magistratur in Athen*, 1936, pp. 12–14) that the inscription should be assigned to 304/3. See also W. K. Pritchett, *Hesperia* 9, 1940, pp. 108–111.

Col. I, line 125. On Chion of Korydallos see *PA* 15555.

Col. III, lines 123–129. None of the persons here listed is otherwise identifiable.

Col. IV, line 122. Philistides, son of Aischylos, of Perithoidai is likely to be that Philistides (*PA* 14449) commemorated with his brother Eukles on the funerary monument *IG* II², 7219 (dated in general terms to the 4th century but no doubt susceptible of attribution to the early years of the 3rd). Eukles is recorded as a prytanis in a list dated to 303/2 (*Agora* XV, 62, line 182). Euktemon in line 125 below is presumably another brother. Lines 123–124. Megakles and Menippos, father and son, of Acharnai presumably belong to the family of which other members are listed at *PA* 3522, 10037, and 10038. Megakles' father, Menippos (*PA* 10038), is commemorated on the grave monument *IG* II², 5818, which should be dated to the second half of the 4th century. Another Menippos, son of Demokrates of Acharnai and grandson of a Megakles, who performed a λειτουργία *ca.* 340 (*IG* II², 417, line 23), is probably a collateral. On this family see J. K. Davies, *Athenian Propertied Families*, p. 391. Line 128. Garlan's discussion was mainly concerned with the location of this gate, for which in particular cf. [Plutarch], *Vitae X oratorum* 849C. His conclusion was that, on balance of argument, it may be construed as having looked northwest towards Κολωνὸς Ἵππιος.

There is another small fragment (I 4725), broken all around (including the back), of which the type of marble, letter spacing, and letter forms are identical with those of this text (Pl. 13). It was discovered on April 16, 1937, in surface fill on the line of the Post-Herulian Wall, southwest of the Eleusinion (T 20), i.e., not far distant from the location in which I 3843 came to light. Its details and text are as follows:

H. 0.76 m.; W. 0.104 m.; Th. 0.019 m.

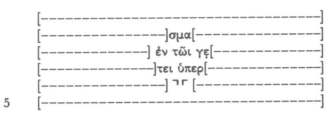

That this small piece belongs somewhere in this large inscription is not improbable, a view endorsed by M. B. Walbank (*per ep.*), who has reexamined the fragment.

FRAGMENT OF A DECREE

110. A fragment of a stele of Pentelic marble (I 5401), discovered on April 15, 1938, in a modern context south of the eastern part of the Market Square (P 21). The right side, thought in the *editio princeps* to be possibly original, seems to have been smooth trimmed and undercut for a later reuse; elsewhere the fragment is broken, save for the rough-picked back.

H. 0.10 m.; W. 0.105 m.; Th. 0.082 m.
LH. 0.006–0.007 m.
Στοιχ. (square) 0.0155 m.

Ed. W. K. Pritchett, *Hesperia* 11, 1942, pp. 241–242, no. 46, with photograph.

inter a. 307 *et* 301 *a.*   ΣΤΟΙΧ. 24

```
[---------------------]
[.....¹²..... τῆς πρυτα]νεί[α]
[ς· ἐκκλησία· τῶν προέδρ]ων ἐπεψ
[ήφιζεν ....¹¹.....]ιάδου Ἀχ
[αρνεὺς καὶ συμπρόεδρ]οι· ᵛ Στρ
[ατοκλῆς Εὐθυδήμου Διομ]εεὺς
[εἶπεν· ...........¹⁹.........]
[---------------------]
```

Apart from one epsilon in line 5, the writing is accurate and of good style at a time when there was much inscriptional work of poor quality. "Free ends" of strokes are enlarged, and in the case of sigma and omega the effect is almost that of apex writing (for which see M. Guarducci, *Epigrafia greca* I, 1967, pp. 372–377; A. G. Woodhead, *Study of Greek Inscriptions*, p. 64).

Lines 2–4. The formula of enactment ἔδοξεν τῶι δήμωι is omitted. Pritchett compared *IG* II², 456 (*SEG* XXI, 328), 460 (*SEG* XXI, 331), 467, 474, and 500, all of this period, and disputed the contention of S. Dow (*AJA* 37, 1933, pp. 413–414, in a study of *IG* II², 474), that the phrase is to be presumed lower down in the text. See further A. S. Henry, *Prescripts*, p. 61. From a variety of peculiarities in prescripts of the year 307/6 (cf. Henry, *op. cit.*, pp. 60–62) it seems that the excitement of revived democratic practice and publication led to a temporarily cavalier attitude towards precision of detail of this kind, a passing but understandable phase. The phenomenon reinforces the dating of the text, secured by the name of the proposer (see below).

Line 3. Enough of the surface of the stone is preserved on the left to make it certain that iota preceded alpha. Lines 4–5. On Stratokles, son of Euthydemos, of Diomeia see *PA* 12938, where the testimonia to the date of that publication are collected; W. S. Ferguson, *Hellenistic Athens*, pp. 119–138; W. B. Dinsmoor, *Archons of Athens*, pp. 13–15; K. Fiehn, *RE* IVA, i, 1931, cols. 263–271, *s.v.* Stratokles (5); J. K. Davies, *Athenian Propertied Families*, pp. 494–495; C. Mossé, *Athens in Decline, 404–86 B.C.*, 1973, pp. 109–111 *et alibi*. Stratokles' date of birth is estimated as "soon after 356": although politically active in 324/3, he was most prominent after the democratic restoration of 307. Of the twenty-one decrees (other than this) of reasonably certain date with which he is associated, twenty belong within the years 307–301, and the presumption must be that this fragment is to be assigned to the same period.

DECREE IN HONOR OF A SON OF ADMETOS OF PRIENE

111. Two fragments of a stele of Pentelic marble, of which the upper (fragment *a*), I 5295, was discovered on March 7, 1938, in the wall of a modern cellar west of the Post-Herulian Wall (Q 19): it preserves the left side of the monument (although part of the first stoichos of lettering has been lost) and perhaps part of the original rough-picked back but is otherwise broken all around. The lower fragment (*b*) was discovered on the Akropolis as long ago as 1836 and is in the Epigraphical Museum (E.M. 7157): it preserves the right side and original back of the stele but is broken elsewhere and badly battered.

a: H. 0.162 m.; W. 0.165 m.; Th. 0.107 m.

b: H. 0.35 m.; W. 0.25 m.; Th. 0.11 m.

LH. 0.004 m. (omega)–0.008 m. (sigma).

Στοιχ. (almost square) Hor. 0.011 m.; Vert. 0.01 m.

Ed. *a* only: A. G. Woodhead, *Hesperia* 29, 1960, pp. 81–82, no. 157, with photograph pl. 26. See also *SEG* XVIII, 18. *b* only: *IG* II², 564, with earlier references; J. Pečírka, *Formula*, pp. 89–91, with photograph pl. 16 (see also *SEG* XXIV, 112).

a. 307/6–302/1 a. (*sed vix post a.* 306/5?)   ΣΤΟΙΧ. 37

```
              [-----------------------------]
(a)   reliquiae incertae [---------------------]
              [τ]ὸν δῆμον [τὸν Ἀθηναίων, ἐπαινέσαι ....⁹....]
              [.] Ἀδμήτου Πρ[ιηνέα καὶ στεφανῶσαι χρυσῶι στε]
              [φ]άνωι ἀπὸ χιλ[ίων δραχμῶν· ἀναγράψαι δὲ πρόξε]
5             [ν]ον αὐτὸν [καὶ] εὐε[ργέτην τοῦ δήμου τοῦ Ἀθηναί]
              ων καὶ αὐ[τ]ὸ[ν] κα[ὶ ἐκγόνους, καὶ εἶναι αὐτοῖς πρ]
              όσοδον πρὸς τὴ[ν βουλὴν καὶ τὸν δῆμον πρώτοις]
              μετὰ τὰ ἱερά, [καὶ ἐάν τινος ἄλλου δέωνται, κατὰ]
              τὸν νόμον· ἐπ[αινέσαι δὲ καὶ(?) ......¹⁵......]
10            [.]ΗΝΗΣΣΑΜ[............²⁹...........]
              [-----------------------------]
                        lacuna incerta
              [-----------------------------]
(b)   [.........²⁰........].ΠΙΛ[......¹⁴......]
      [........¹³........, ἔγκτη]σιν γῆς [καὶ οἰκίας ..⁵..]
15    [........¹⁵.......· εἶνα]ι δὲ [α]ὐ[τῶι ....¹⁰....]
      [........¹⁶........δ]ῆμον καὶ τῶν σ[....⁹....]
      [........¹⁷.........]ους Ἀθήνηθεν ο[...⁸....]
      [........¹⁶........· ἀ]γα[γ]ρ[ά]ψαι δὲ τό[δε τὸ ψήᵛᵛ]
      [φισμα τὸν γραμματέα τ]ὸν κα[τὰ] πρυταγ[εί]α[ν καὶ]
20    [στῆσαι ἐν ἀκροπόλε]ι· [εἰ]ς [δ]ὲ τὴν ἀναγ[ραφὴν τῆς]
      [στήλης δοῦναι τὸν ταμίαν τοῦ] δήμ[ου :ΔΔΔ:] δρ[α]
      [χμὰς ἐκ τῶν κατὰ ψηφίσμα]τα ἀναλ[ισκομένω]ν ᵛ[ᵛ]
      [τῶι δήμωι· καλέσαι δὲ το]ὺ[ς] πρέσβε[ις τῶν Πρ]ιη[ᵛ]
      [νέων ἐπὶ ξένια εἰς τὸ πρ]υτανεῖον ε[ἰς αὔρι]ον. [ᵛ]
                        vacat
              [in corona]          in corona
25            [ἡ βουλή]            ὁ δ[ῆ]μ[ος]
              [--------(?)]        Φ[---]ην[---]
```

The lettering of this text is a useful illustration of that "careless style" (stoichedon but with careless overlapping and placement of strokes), which, as B. D. Meritt noted, "would not have been characteristic of the fourth century before Demetrios of Phaleron" (*Hesperia* 29, 1960, p. 8). It came, however, to be one of the characteristic styles of the first half of the 3rd century, coexisting nonetheless with a better tradition exemplified, for example, by **152**.

Lines 1–2. E.g., [--- ποιεῖ ὅ τι δύναται ἀγαθὸν περὶ | τ]ὸν δῆμον κτλ. M. B. Walbank (*per ep.*) has read the "*reliquiae incertae*" as [.]ΔΑΙ[---]. The text of this fragment was placed one stoichos further to the right in the *editio princeps* but is here adjusted in the light of reassessment of the left margin.

Line 8. But this restoration is entitled to some scepticism, since μετὰ τὰ ἱερά, on the evidence, always concludes the πρόσοδος formula that occupies lines 5–7. See A. S. Henry, *Honours*, pp. 191–198 and 203, note 30 (where the restoration is strongly doubted) and *SEG* XXXIII, 104. It might be claimed that the κατὰ τὸν νόμον formula, which was coming into enhanced use at this time, has been attached unusually and unwisely to a clause with which it ought not to be associated. Otherwise, the contents of lines 8–9, and their relation to "the *nomos*", must remain a matter of speculation.

Line 13. The reading is Walbank's. Lines 14–17. So *IG* II² but with the omission of the restoration for lines 15–16 there shown. Lines 18–24. Pečírka's revision of *IG* II², here adopted, is notable for his observation that the craftsman maintained syllabic division, leaving vacant letter spaces at the ends of lines 18 and 22–24.

Line 21. The marks of punctuation restored as surrounding the numeral take up a letter space each; cf. **114**, line 19. Or the spaces may have been left blank; cf. **139** and **162**. It is less likely that the cost amounted to 40 drachmas, with some dislocation of the stoichedon pattern as in line 22 of **114**.

Line 26. Walbank claims Φε[.⁴⁻⁵..]νη[έ]α here: but the state of the stone is such as to make any reading hazardous that is not absolutely clear.

That these two fragments were to be closely associated (and were surely by the same hand) became apparent soon after the publication of fragment *a* but did not find its way into print. The association was confirmed as a definite attribution to a single document by Walbank.

To add to the general grounds for dating provided by the stylistic criteria it may be noted that U. Koehler regarded the hand of what became *IG* II², 564 as close to that of *IG* II², 456 (*SEG* XXI, 328), of 307/6 b.c. Walbank claims the hands as in fact identical. But there are three further considerations: (1) The cost of the stele is to be met by the ταμίας τοῦ δήμου (lines 20–24); he appears as disbursing officer for the last time in 302/1. See Henry, *Chiron* 14, 1984, pp. 51–52. (2) The cost of the stephanos is specified (line 4). There is no example of this later than 306/5, and from 302/1 onwards such grants were described only as bestowed κατὰ τὸν νόμον. Cf. Henry (*Honours*, p. 26), who sees the change as occurring in or about 304 b.c., with possibly a brief period of overlap or confusion of the two practices. For these two criteria of date see also **112**. (3) There was an evident rapprochement between Athens and Priene in the period of the restored Athenian democracy, which resulted in several honorific enactments to be dated in this period. M. J. Osborne (*Naturalization* III/IV, p. 129, X 20) lists five such, including the present text, the other four being *IG* II², 565–567 and *SEG* III, 86 (XXXIII, 103). (The reference to *IG* II², 567 applies more precisely to fragment *b*; fragment *a* belongs to a later date and should be dissociated from its partner.) In *IG* II², 565 and 567 the ταμίας τοῦ δήμου is reasonably to be restored as the officer responsible for payment for the stele. In the other two texts the provision for payment does not survive, but *SEG* III, 86 is precisely dated by its prescript to 307/6 (see above). From these arguments, thus, is derived the dating shown at the head of the text.

Line 3. The name Admetos is scarcely found in Attic epigraphy and is more usually associated with Thessaly, Molossia, and northern Greece. An Admetos was, however, neopoios in Priene at the time of the great renaissance of the city and the building of the Temple of Athena (F. Hiller von Gaertringen, *Inschriften von Priene*, 1906, pp. 5–6, no. 3, line 24 = *Syll.*³ 282, of 333/2). This may suggest that he was a member of an important family, and his son might well have been entrusted with diplomatic duties a generation later.

Line 14. Ἔγκτησις γῆς καὶ οἰκίας. See Pečírka, *loc. cit.*, and Henry, *Honours*, pp. 207–208. The order of words here is that less frequently found: in the majority of cases the accusative noun follows rather than precedes.

Lines 21–22. On the "analiskomena fund" as the source for payment see Henry, *Chiron* 12, 1982, pp. 97–118 and the commentaries on **40** and **45**. Lines 23–24. For the formula for entertainment in the Prytaneion see **115**, commentary on fragment *c*, lines 8–9, and references there.

For the few testimonia on Prienean history of this period see Hiller von Gaertringen, *op. cit.*, pp. 206–211, nos. 485–511; G. Kleiner, *RE, Supplement* IX, 1962, col. 1187. For the grouping of texts dealing with relations between Athens and Ionia see J. J. E. Hondius, *Novae Inscriptiones Atticae*, 1925, pp. 39–46; A. Wilhelm, *Attische Urkunden* V (= *SbAkadWien* 220, 5), 1942, pp. 166–175, no. LXII; Pečírka, *op. cit.*, p. 91 with note 2. *IG* II², 456 and 470 (both concerned with Kolophon), as well as 466 (Tenos), belong to the group.

PHILEAS OF PALLENE HONORED FOR HIS WORK AS COUNCILLOR

112. A fragment of a stele of Pentelic marble (I 4534), broken on all sides, discovered on February 27, 1937, in a modern fill southeast of the Market Square, east of the Post-Herulian Wall (U 22).

B. D. Meritt observed that the fragment forms part of the same monument as *IG* II², 514, which was discovered on the Akropolis and is now in the Epigraphical Museum (E.M. 2659). There is no join between the two fragments, both of which are recorded here for convenience. The Agora fragment, hereafter fragment *a*, belongs to a point higher up the stele than *IG* II², 514, now fragment *b*, on which the formula of publication occurs.

a: H. 0.109 m.; W. 0.109 m.; Th. 0.055 m.

b: H. 0.23 m.; W. 0.185 m.; Th. 0.045 m.

LH. 0.007 m.

Στοιχ. (becoming irregular in fragment *b*): Hor. 0.0165 m.; Vert. 0.015 m.

Ed. B. D. Meritt, *Hesperia* 32, 1963, pp. 3–5, no. 4, with photographs of both fragments pl. 1. See also *SEG* XXI, 336. The text of fragment *b* is that of A. Wilhelm in *IG* II², with three slight changes of reading.

a. 307/6–302/1 *a. (sed vix post* 306/5?)   ΣΤΟΙΧ. 25 (lines 17–20, 26)

```
        [----------------χρηματίσαι]
(a)     [περὶ τούτω]γ, [γνώμην δὲ ξυμβάλλ]
        [εσθαι τῆ]ς β⟨ο⟩υλ[ῆς εἰς τὸν δῆμον]
        [ὅτι δοκ]εῖ τῆι β[ουλῆι ἐπαινέσα]
        [ι Φιλέ]αν Φιλον[αύτου Παλλη(νέα) καὶ]
   5    [στεφαν]ῶσαι χρ[υσῶι στεφάνωι ἀ]
        [πὸ . δραχ]μῶγ [ἀρετῆς ἕνεκα καὶ π]
        [ροθυμίας] τ[ῆς περὶ τὸν δῆμον . . .]
                    lacuna
(b)     [. . . . · εἰ]ς δὲ [τὴν ἀναγραφὴν τῆς σ]
        [τήλη]ς δοῦνα[ι τὸν ταμίαν τοῦ δή]
   10   [μου] ΔΔ δραχμὰς ἐ[κ τῶν κατὰ ψηφί]
        [σματ]α ἀναλισκο[μένων τῶι δήμω]
        [ι, ὅπ]ως ἂν εἰδῶσι[ν πάντες οἱ ἂν λ]
        [αγχ]άνωσι βουλε[ύειν ᵛ ὅτι τιμᾶ]
        [ι ὁ δῆ]μος τοὺς δι[καίως καὶ κατὰ]
   15   [τοὺ]ς νόμους πολ[ιτευομένους ἐ]
        [ν] τῆι βουλῆι καὶ [ἐν τῶι δήμωι, κα]
        [ὶ] ὡς πλεῖστοι φιλ[οτιμῶνται λέγε]
        [ι]ν καὶ γράφ[ε]ιν τὰ [ἄριστα τῆι βου]
        [λῆι] καὶ τῶι δήμω[ι εἰδότες ὅτι χά]
   20   [ρ]ιτας ἀπολήψον[ται ἀξίας . ⁵⁻⁶ . .]
        [----------------------]
```

Line 2. *Lapis* Βᵛ⟨Υ⟩Λ. Line 4. The demotic was probably expressed in abbreviated form, for which Meritt compared *IG* II², 336 (*SEG* XXXVI, 153, with earlier references), lines 1, 5, and 6, 360 (*SEG* XXVI, 79, with earlier references), line 2, and 399 (*SEG* XXV, 72, XXXIV, 71), line 4. See also **100**, lines 4 and 7 and **104**, line 8. The less agreeable alternative is to postulate an error on the part of the stonemason. Lines 6–7. So Meritt, supposing two letters to have been inscribed in the space of one in line 7. Cf. line 17, where this occurs visibly on the stone. The supposition could be avoided by writing ἕνεκεν καὶ | εὐνοίας] τ[ῆς κτλ. (cf. *IG* II², 1261, line 13, for the use of ἕνεκεν for ἕνεκα at this period). The horizontal stroke surviving at the top of the letter space in line 7 is probably part of tau. It rises at a slight acute angle above the strictly horizontal, as do many such strokes in this text. Conversely, however, the uppermost stroke of sigma is sometimes depressed to a similar angle, and ἕνεκα καὶ ε|ὐνοίας τῆς [περὶ τὸν δῆμον . . ⁵ . .] is a possible interpretation. Line 13. Wilhelm's restoration, to which no alternative can readily be supplied, leaves the line with 24 letters. Line 14. δ]ῆμος Wilhelm. Line 16. τ[ῆ]ι Wilhelm. Line 17. Two letters are written in the space of one, making a line of 27 letters. Line 18. γράφ[ει]ν Wilhelm.

Meritt observed the connection between the two fragments on the basis of the lettering, which is competent but careless. Strokes are badly joined together, and sigma and upsilon in particular are haphazardly done. Letters such as mu and nu are of variable width. The stoichedon order is disturbed as the text proceeds, and from line 17 onwards is indeed better described as στοιχ. 26.

Line 1. The decree was probouleumatic. See P. J. Rhodes, *Athenian Boule*, p. 251. For the enactment formula, now in its regular pattern, see **89**, lines 2–9. Line 4. Phileas, son of Philonautes, of Pallene is known from two other decrees, *IG* II², 554 (*SEG* XXIV, 111) and 585 (*SEG* XXI, 352, XXXI, 87), of which he was the proposer. The former is of the period 307–304, and the latter is now attributed to 300/299 or to 297/6. The date of the present decree (see below) requires that the vote of thanks to Phileas is likely to concern his first term of membership of the Council. *PA* 14243 and 14244 duplicate him unnecessarily, *IG* II², 554 having originally (as *IG* II, 413) been dated to the early 2nd century.

Lines 5–7. Although the numeral forms part of the restored text, the cost of the stephanos was evidently specified and probably amounted to 500 dr. The last clearly dated example of this formulation belongs to 306/5; cf. A. S. Henry, *Honours*, pp. 24, 26. In 302/1 and thereafter it was replaced by the formula prescribing the grant κατὰ τὸν νόμον. This detail, together with the necessary presence in the restored text of the ταμίας τοῦ δήμου (lines 8–10) as the disbursing officer, imposes the same criteria for the dating of this decree as in the case of **111**, *q.v.* For the formulaic procedure see **101**, commentary on lines 32–34. On both the paymaster and the source of the expenditure see **83** and references there. The present text was allotted no more than 20 drachmas for its inscription, an amount rare after *ca.* 332/1, although *IG* II², 657, of 283/2, for which the same sum was assigned, is a sizable document of more than seventy lines. **111**, it may be noted, cost half as much again as this stele.

Lines 12–20. For the "hortatory intention" of the decree see **86**, commentary on lines 21–24. In this text the encouragement to emulation of the honorand, and the proclamation of the public response to those who advise the people well, are unusually fulsome. The phraseology of lines 12–13 confirms that under the restored democracy, as earlier, the method of appointment to the Council was by sortition. Cf. Rhodes, *Athenian Boule*, pp. 6–7.

THE ARCHONSHIP OF KOROIBOS, 306/5 B.C.

Although **113** is the only decree attributable to Koroibos' year that the Agora excavations have so far yielded, it was a year prolific, like its predecessor, in public business, and it has left a substantial epigraphical record. Apart from **113**, which belongs to the seventh prytany, thirteen decrees of 306/5 are extant, of which seven provide data helpful to an evaluation of the character of the year. *IG* II², 467 (*SEG* XXXI, 81, XXXIV, 73; M. J. Osborne, *Naturalization* I, pp. 112–113, D 43), 468 (*SEG* XIX, 60), and 469 preserve sections of their respective inscriptions which do not contain that part of the prescript in which the dating formulas occur and are assigned to Koroibos' year on other grounds. R. S. Stroud, *Hesperia* 40, 1971, pp. 181–183, no. 30 is of the fourth prytany, *IG* II², 773 (S. Dow, *AJA* 37, 1933, pp. 415–416) is of the sixth, 470 (A. Wilhelm, *Anatolian Studies Presented to William Hepburn Buckler*, 1939, pp. 345–352) of the seventh, 675 + 525 (W. K. Pritchett, *AJP* 58, 1937, pp. 329–333) of the eighth (but cf. *SEG* XXXIV, 72 and references there), 471, 472 + 169 (*SEG* XXI, 335), and 473 of the tenth. *IG* II², 474 (Dow, *op. cit.*, pp. 412–414), 475, and 476 (Dow, *op. cit.*, p. 414) are fragmentary texts in which the dating formulas are insufficiently preserved. See also the *traditiones IG* II², 1484, lines 7–8, 1487, line 91, 1491, line 10, 1492B, lines 97–124, as well as the *locatio IG* II², 2499 (D. Behrend, *Attische Pachturkunden*, pp. 96–97, no. 39), line 43. Of these, only *IG* II², 1492B is materially helpful, in that it identifies the last three prytanies of the year.

Following an intercalary 307/6, the year of Koroibos was ordinary, with 355 days, an extra day being added to Mounichion (*IG* II², 471, lines 6–7). Cf. J. Kirchner, *IG* II², 470, comm.; W. B. Dinsmoor, *Archons of Athens*, pp. 385, 387–388; B. D. Meritt, *Hesperia* 7, 1938, p. 131; Pritchett and Meritt, *Chronology*, p. xv; Pritchett and O. Neugebauer, *Calendars*, p. 79; Dinsmoor, *Hesperia* 23, 1954, p. 313. It was the subject of particular investigation by Pritchett (*AJP* 58, 1937, *loc. cit.*), who envisaged a prytany calendar showing six prytanies of 30 days each, followed by five of 29 and a final prytany again of 30 days. Meritt (*Athenian Year*, pp. 138–139, *Hesperia* 33, 1964, p. 9) agreed with this formulation and, with a slight modification of Pritchett's scheme for the festival (lunar) calendar to take account of the two full months at the end of 307/6, proposed a regular alternation of hollow and full months to Pyanopsion, followed by full Maimakterion and regular alternation thereafter to full Elaphebolion, ending the year with full Mounichion, hollow Thargelion, and full Skirophorion. Two days were apparently added early in Pyanopsion to put the festival calendar in arrears vis-à-vis the prytany date by the twenty-first of that month, an insertion presumably rectified soon thereafter; cf. Meritt, *AJP* 93, 1972, pp. 164–166.

Known phylai in prytany are as follows: IV Pandionis, VI Erechtheis or Kekropis, VII Demetrias, VIII Antigonis, X Oineis, XI Akamantis, XII Antiochis.

THE EUBOIANS ONOMAKLES, ANTIPHANES, AND OTHERS HONORED

113. The upper left section of a pedimental stele of Pentelic marble (I 250), broken below, to the right, and at the back, discovered late in 1932 in a wall of a modern house southeast of the Tholos (H 12–13). The spring of the left akroterion remains, but the akroterion itself has been broken away.

H. 0.31 m.; W. 0.21 m.; Th. 0.105 m.

LH. 0.005 m. (omicron 0.004 m.).

Στοιχ. (almost square) Hor. 0.0103 m.; Vert. 0.0096 m.

Ed. B. D. Meritt, *Hesperia* 3, 1934, pp. 5–6, no. 6, with photograph. Lines 12–14 improved by Meritt (*Hesperia* 15, 1946, pp. 188–189, no. 34), with the inclusion of restored ethnics proposed by H. Pope (*Non-Athenians in Attic Inscriptions*, 1935, p. 230) and a new reading in the last preserved line by J. H. Oliver. The calendric data are cited without quotation of the text in the principal studies of the calendar of the year discussed above.

a. 306/5 a., pryt. VII   ΣΤΟΙΧ. 30

```
          Ἐπὶ Κοροίβου ἄρχον[τος ἐπὶ τῆς Δημητ]
          ριάδος ἑβδόμης πρυτ[ανείας ἧι Πάμφι]
          [λ]ος Θεογείτονος Ῥα[μνούσιος ἐγραμμ]
          [ά]τευεν· Γαμηλιῶνος· [τετάρτει καὶ δεκ]
     5    άτει τῆς πρυτανεία[ς· ἐκκλησία· τῶν πρ]
          οέδρων ἐπεψήφιζεν [....¹⁰.... Ἀρισ]
          τοκράτου Ἀφιδναῖ[ος καὶ συμπρόεδρο]
          ι· ἔδοξεν τῶι δήμωι· ᵛ [......¹⁴......]
          [Κ]ηφισογένου Ἀχαρνε[ὺς εἶπεν· ἐπειδὴ]
    10    [Ὀ]νομαχλῆς Σμικύθου [καὶ ...⁸.... Ἀσ]
          [τ]υφίλου καὶ Ἀντιφάνη[ς ....¹¹.....]
          [κ]αὶ Ἀρχέλεως Αἰσχρων[ος Χαλκιδεῖς κ]
          [α]ὶ Νικησίας Σιτ[άρχ]ου [Ἐρετριεὺς ἄνδ]
          [ρ]ες [ἀ]γα[θ]οί [εἰσιν .......¹⁶.......]
    15    [----------------------------]
```

The stone is bulky, and the pediment with its moldings heavy; the stele may well have been a substantial one. The writing is generally tidy but not of the highest quality: the "free ends" of the strokes are in some cases emphasized, especially in epsilon and upsilon (cf. **120**), but without consistency. Beta, always a difficult letter for the mason, is clumsy. The form of phi, with two horizontal strokes replacing the oval, is characteristic of the period (see **114**).

Line 2. Pamphilos, son of Theogeiton, of Rhamnous (*PA* 11557), the secretary of the year, is perhaps unlikely to be identical with that Pamphilos of Rhamnous mentioned as a creditor of Phainippos in [Demosthenes] 42.28, a speech generally dated *ca.* 330. The two are listed separately in *PA* and by J. Pouilloux (*Forteresse*, p. 178).

Line 4. The day of the month was evidently not recorded, for the data of *IG* II², 470, which is also of the seventh prytany, show that the date by prytany was at that stage three days, numerically, behind that of the festival month, and no supplement showing both dates and conforming to this requirement can be accommodated in the available space. Such omissions are rare; for comparable examples see *IG* II², 365 and 451; cf. also A. S. Henry, *Prescripts*, p. 60; A. G. Woodhead in *Ancient Macedonian Studies*, p. 364 (incorrectly reported in *SEG* XXX, 70). Where truncation of the date by the festival month occurs, it is more usually the name of the month, rather than the numeral, that is omitted. Line 5. ἐκκλησία. See **97**, line 7.

Lines 6–7. The chairman may well have been a member of that family from Aphidna in which the names Aristokrates and Lysimachos alternated and which has left scattered traces in the epigraphical record: cf. J. K. Davies, *Athenian Propertied Families*, p. 282. But the name Lysimachos is too short by one letter for the space available here. Line 8. ᵛ[ᵛᵛ−−−−−] Meritt. On the vacant letter spaces before the name of the proposer see Henry, *Prescripts*, p. 64, with note 60 (in which he was misled by Meritt's restoration; only one vacant space is visible on the stone). Line 9. A Kephisogenes of Acharnai is listed among the epheboi in a list of 330/29 (W. K. Pritchett in *Hesperia*, Supplement VIII, 1949, pp. 273–278; O. W. Reinmuth, *The Ephebic Inscriptions of the Fourth Century B.C.*, 1971, pp. 42–50, no. 12, at line 51). But he could hardly be identifiable with the father of the proposer of this decree unless the ephebic record were to be placed at least ten years earlier than the accepted date. A date as early as 345, however, although it has been suggested, is unlikely.

Lines 10–13. The persons honored, listed by Pope (*Foreigners in Attic Inscriptions*, 1947, pp. 47 and 164–165), are otherwise unknown. She suggested (*Non-Athenians in Attic Inscriptions*, 1935, p. 230) that the Aischron mentioned in line 12 is the man honored in *IG* II², 491, b, lines 9–10, although if there is any connection it may be preferable to think that the Aischron there referred to is the son rather than the father of Archeleos. It is, however, hazardous to support her further claim that the Aischron son of Proxenos who received Athenian citizenship soon after 286/5 (*IG* II², 652; M. J. Osborne, *Naturalization* I, pp. 161–163, D 75, *Naturalization* II, pp. 158–160) is to be connected with the Aischron of this text.

The Athenians seem to have been concerned in these years to repay widespread obligations incurred at the time of their "liberation" in 307. Many of the texts of this period refer either to the liberation in general terms or to specific military events, and it may be presumed that these men of Euboia had also contributed to the success of Demetrios, as did those honored in *IG* II², 491.

THE ARCHONSHIP OF PHEREKLES, 304/3 B.C.

The comparative flood of legislation committed to stone, which had characterized the years of the democratic restoration after the end of the regime of Demetrios of Phaleron, continued in 304/3, and much is known of the year. But the decrees found in the Agora have contributed little to it. Only one, formerly ascribed to the succeeding year, can now be attributed to it with certainty, and more precisely to the ninth prytany, which may be identified as that of Akamantis. For the calendar of the year see B. D. Meritt, *Hesperia* 33, 1964, pp. 7–8 and A. G. Woodhead in *Ancient Macedonian Studies*, p. 365, *Hesperia* 58, 1989, pp. 297–301. Inscriptions on which these studies are based are *IG* II², 481, of the fourth prytany, 482, of the sixth, 483, of the seventh, 484, of the eighth, *Hesperia* 58, 1989, p. 300, of the tenth, *IG* II², 485, of the eleventh, and 486 (M. J. Osborne, *Naturalization* I, pp. 115–116, D 45, *Naturalization* II, pp. 120–121; *SEG* XXXVI, 163), which, together with *Hesperia* 7, 1938, p. 297, no. 22, *IG* II², 597 (with addenda, p. 662; see also L. Robert, "Inscriptions grecques," in *Collection Froehner* I, 1937, p. 3, no. 3), and S. N. Koumanoudes, *Horos* 4, 1986, pp. 11–18 (*SEG* XXXVI, 164), belongs to the twelfth prytany. A total of eleven texts thus serves to supply what may be known of the pattern of the year in both the festival and the prytany calendars.

In the festival calendar the year was ordinary, but an extra day was added to Skirophorion at the end of it to give a total of 355 days (cf. *IG* II², 481, comm.). According to Meritt's calculation, the months alternated as hollow and full until full Anthesterion, which was followed by full Elaphebolion and then regular alternation until the last month, made full instead of hollow. On the added day see W. K. Pritchett, *Ancient Athenian Calendars on Stone*, pp. 361–363; Meritt, 'Αρχ. 'Εφ., 1968, pp. 77–80. With twelve months and twelve prytanies, the dates by festival and prytany calendars should have run closely in harmony, and they did so with minor inequalities, the one calendar at times running a day ahead or a day in arrear of the other; for the list see Woodhead, *Hesperia* 58, 1989, p. 297. The equations may be accounted for by a succession of four prytanies of 29 days followed by six of 30, with the eleventh and twelfth prytanies of 29 and 30 days respectively. For the year see also Pritchett and O. Neugebauer, *Calendars*, p. 79; and Meritt, *Historia* 26, 1977, p. 171.

Phylai identified with prytanies in Pherekles' year are, on the evidence, IV Aigeis, VI Leontis, VII Oineis, VIII Antigonis, IX Akamantis, X Erechtheis or Kekropis, and XII Aiantis. By elimination of possible restorations in *IG* II², 485 it emerges that the eleventh prytany was held by either Pandionis or Demetrias. In the festival calendar the month Mounichion was, on the motion of Stratokles, redesignated first as Anthesterion II and then as Boedromion II: see Plutarch, *Demetrios* 26 and Woodhead, *Hesperia, loc. cit.*

DECREE CONCERNING SACRIFICE AND THANKSGIVING
FOR THE SUCCESSFUL CAMPAIGN OF DEMETRIOS POLIORKETES

114 (Pl. 14). Two nonjoining fragments of a stele of Pentelic marble, the larger of which (fragment *a*, I 5972) preserves the left edge and original rough-picked back of the monument, but is broken elsewhere, and was discovered on April 23, 1947, in a context of the later 3rd or early 2nd century B.C., in a cistern in the industrial area (B 18:13). On this cistern see R. S. Young, *Hesperia* 20, 1951, p. 226. The smaller fragment (*b*, I 1441) preserves the right edge of the stele but is otherwise broken all around. It was discovered on March 3, 1934, in a late context just outside the Tholos on the north (G 11).

a: H. 0.27 m.; W. 0.207 m.; Th. 0.065 m.

b: H. 0.115 m.; W. 0.114 m.; Th. 0.055 m.

LH. 0.006 m.

Στοιχ. Hor. 0.0098 m.; Vert. 0.0105 m.

Ed. *a* only: W. S. Ferguson, *Hesperia* 17, 1948, pp. 114–136, no. 68, with photograph pl. 33. See *SEG* XXV, 141, with references to J. and L. Robert, *REG* 62, 1949, pp. 109–113, no. 51 (discussion of content, and criticism of Ferguson's text, with revised restorations); L. Moretti, *Iscrizioni storiche ellenistiche* I, pp. 8–10, no. 5 (text with commentary, bibliography, Italian translation, and some revised restorations); also E. Cavaignac, *REG* 62, 1949, pp. 233–234 and G. Daux, *REG* 63, 1950, pp. 253–254 (both on the date). *b* only: B. D. Meritt, *Hesperia* 16, 1947, p. 153, no. 46, with photograph pl. XXVI. *a* and *b*: A. G. Woodhead in *Ancient Macedonian Studies*, pp. 357–367, with photograph pl. 26. See *SEG* XXX, 69.

a. 304/3 *a.*, *pryt.* IX   ΣΤΟΙΧ. 36

(a)

[------------------------------]
[. . . ⁸ . . . .]ΗΙ[. . . . . .²⁶. . . . .]
[. . . x]ατὰ θάλ[ατταν . . . . .²¹. . . . .]
[. . .]υούσης χα[. . . . . .²⁵. . . . .]
[. το]ῦ δήμου τοῦ Ἀ[θηναίων . . . .¹⁶. . . . .]
5   [. .]ι τῶν Ἑλλήνων π[. . . . . .²². . . . .]
αι Πλείσταρχον καὶ [. . . . . .²⁰. . . . . . .]
αι πόλεις Ἑλληνίδα[ς . . . . .¹⁸. . . . . . . ἐ]
πὶ δουλείαι λαβὼν κατὰ [κράτος ἐλευθέρας χα]
ὶ αὐτονόμους πεπόηκεν· ὅ[πως ἂν οὖν καὶ τὰ λοι]
10 πὰ συντελῆται ἐπὶ τῶι συ[μφέροντι τῶι τε δήμ]
[ω]ι τῶι Ἀθηναίων καὶ τοῖς [Ἕλλησι πᾶσιν, οἵ τε σ]
[τ]ρατευόμενοι σωιζόμεν[οι ἐκ πολέμου κατιώ]
[σ]ιν εἰς τὴν πόλιν κρατήσ[αντες τῶν πολεμίων],
[β]οῦς θῦσαι τοὺς πρυτάνε[ις τῆς Ἀκαμαντίδος]
15 ὑπὲρ τῆς σωτηρίας τῶν στ[ρατευομένων τῆι τε]
Ἀθηνᾶι τῆι Νίκηι καὶ τῆι Ἀ[γαθεῖ Τύχει καὶ το]
ῖς Σωτῆρσιν· τὸν δὲ ταμίαν [τῶν στρατι]ωτικῶν   (b)
μερίσαι αὐτοῖς εἴς τε τὴν [θυσίαν χα]ὶ εἰς ἀνά
θημα τῶι ἐπωνύμωι : ΗΗΗ : [δραχμάς· πο]ρίζεσθα
20 ι δὲ αὐτοῖς καὶ εἰς τὸν με[τὰ ταῦτα χρ]όνον κατ'
ἐνιαυτὸν τοῦ Ἐλαφηβο[λιῶνος μην]ὸς εἰς θυσ[ί]
αν τοῖς Σωτῆρσιν χα[ὶ τεῖ Ἀγαθεῖ Τ]ύχει [[ΗΗ]] [δρ]
αχμὰς ὑπόμνημα τῶν [νῦν ἀγγελθέ]ντων ἀγ[ώνων]
ἐπὶ τῆς Ἀκαμαντίδ[ος πρυτανεία]ς· ἐπαι[νέσαι]
25 [δὲ χα]ὶ τοὺς γραμμ[ατεῖς τῆς βου]λῆς χα[ὶ τῆς πρ]
[υτανείας . . . . ¹⁷. . . . .]ελο[. . . ⁸. . . .]
[------------------------------]

The marble is of poor quality with bluish streaks, and the inscribed surface is rust stained in places. The writing so closely resembles that of **118**, especially in the tenuous omega, that it is undoubtedly the work of the same craftsman. There is some evidence of carelessness. Alpha frequently lacks its horizontal stroke, which, although instances of it were underdotted by Ferguson and Moretti, is a phenomenon sufficiently familiar in this and other texts to merit no distinguishing mark. The crossbar of eta varies its position (see in particular the numerals in lines 19 and 22), and epsilon is seldom cut with any exactitude. A half-looped rho (Ρ) and a phi with two horizontal strokes in place of the "oval" (Φ) are also noteworthy. The latter, like the form with the single horizontal ("cruciform" phi), is characteristic of this period; cf., e.g., **113** and *IG* II², 541 (M. J. Osborne, *Naturalization* I, pp. 127–128, D 52) and 554 (*SEG* XXIV, 111). M. B. Walbank has considered the craftsman at work here as responsible for more than thirty texts of the period: see **151**. In line 22 the two letters of the numeral are inscribed in three letter spaces in a *rasura*. Presumably the mason made an initial error at this point which he subsequently sought to correct.

Lines 11, 19–20, and 23. C. Habicht prefers to restore τοῖς [βασιλεῦσιν, με]ρίζεσθα||ι and ἀγ[αθῶν]: see *SEG* XXXII, 1705, a proposal reiterated with fuller argument in *Hesperia* 59, 1990, pp. 463–466. The restoration proposed for line 11 is too short by one letter for the available space (but Habicht later restored καὶ οἵ here); in line 23 ἀγ[ώνων] may be judged particularly apposite to the circumstances of the Four Years War (cf. Woodhead, *op. cit.*, pp. 365–366) in contrast to the more insipid alternative. Cf. also Woodhead, *Hesperia* 58, 1989, p. 301, **120**, and **150**.

The date of the decree can be settled principally on historical grounds, with reference to the activities of Demetrios Poliorketes, coupled with the requirement that Akamantis be the phyle in prytany in the month Elaphebolion (pryt. IX). For the detailed discussion see Woodhead in *Ancient Macedonian Studies*, pp. 363–365. In the light of the evidence the year of the initial celebrations here decreed must be 304/3. A résumé of the events to which the inscription refers (Athenian participation in Demetrios' Peloponnesian campaign) is to be found in Ferguson, *loc. cit.*; W. W. Tarn, *CAH* IV, 1927, pp. 501–502; G. Glotz, R. Cohen, and P. Roussel, *Histoire grecque* IV, i, 1938, pp. 338–340; C. Mossé, *Athens in Decline, 404–86 B.C.*, 1973, pp. 108–113.

Line 2. Κατὰ θάλ[ατταν. Ferguson referred to Polyainos 4.7.3 for confirmation that Demetrios invaded the Peloponnese by sea as well as by land. Line 6. Pleistarchos, son of Antipater and brother of Kassandros. See H. Schaefer, *RE* XXI, i, cols. 196–199, *s.v.* Pleistarchos (2); H. Berve, *Das Alexanderreich auf prosopographischer Grundlage* II, 1926, p. 321, no. 641. Prepelaos, whose name was restored in the same line by Ferguson, was Kassandros' commander in Corinth; see Diodorus Siculus 20.102.1; K. Ziegler, *RE* XXII, ii, cols. 1836–1838, *s.v.* Prepelaos.

Lines 15–17. Σωτηρία. Cf. **120**, commentary on lines 6–7. The cult of Antigonos and Demetrios Σωτῆρες had been introduced at Athens in 307/6, at the time when the new phylai were created in their honor, and it lasted, apparently, until 288. Cf. Plutarch, *Demetrios* 12–13; Diodorus Siculus 20.46.2; Ferguson, *op. cit.*, pp. 131–136. The cult of a military liberator as σωτήρ went back to Brasidas and the Amphipolitans (Thucydides 5.11.1); cf. A. W. Gomme, *A Historical Commentary on Thucydides* III, 1956, p. 655. The epithet as applied in the historical sources to Gelon of Syracuse (Diodorus Siculus 11.26.6), Pelopidas (Plutarch, *Pelopidas* 12.4), and Dion (Plutarch, *Dion* 46.1) may be anachronistically affected by its familiarity in the Hellenistic and Roman periods. Line 19. τῶι ἐπωνύμωι, i.e., Akamas.

Line 25. For the two γραμματεῖς cf. **120**, commentary on line 8. *Prima facie* their titles (if correctly restored) and separate identities appear to conflict with the conclusion of P. J. Rhodes (*Athenian Boule*, p. 137), following Ferguson and M. Brillant, that the supposed two officials so designated were in fact identical. Cf. **73**, commentary on lines 23–24. Indeed, it seems on the contrary to reinforce the evidence of *IG* II², 120 (of 353/2 B.C.), lines 16–19. However, cf. *Agora* XV, 58, of 305/4, where, among various secretaries, the γραμματεὺς κατὰ πρυτανείαν and the γραμματεὺς βουλῆς καὶ δήμου (given his full title) are both listed. Two γραμματεῖς are also, as it appears, named in *Agora* XV, 49, at lines 34–35. On the functions of the γραμματεὺς βουλῆς καὶ δήμου see Rhodes, *op. cit.*, p. 136, with note 3. Since the instructions for inscribing and erecting this present text do not survive, we lack the directive to the γραμματεύς (one of them, presumably), which would have done much towards the resolution of some of the difficulty and confusion concerning the elements and nomenclature of the official secretariat.

In this decree the ταμίας τῶν στρατιωτικῶν makes his first appearance (at line 17) in an Agora document, as responsible for making payment for the present and future celebrations here prescribed. Since it was a military success that was to be commemorated, the military, or "stratiotic", fund was a proper source for the expense, and its treasurer was the proper disbursing officer. For the earlier history of this fund see Rhodes, *Athenian Boule*, pp. 105–108; A. S. Henry, *Chiron* 14, 1984, pp. 52–53, note 14. The loss of the instructions for the erection of the stele (see above) robs us of the knowledge of the disbursing officer there nominated to provide funds for that element of expenditure, as well as of the source of those funds. Thus the mention of the Treasurer of the Stratiotic Fund in its present context does not affect the exposition by Henry (*op. cit.*, pp. 51–63) of the transitional and varied arrangements for payment evidenced in the texts of the years 303–301. At this time the ταμίας τῶν στρατιωτικῶν began to take over the disbursing duties hitherto exercised by the ταμίας τοῦ δήμου, who is not in evidence after 302/1: but, even so, the prime responsibility fell to other officials, as will appear in later texts, and the role of the Military Treasurer in this connection did not become predominant until after 229 B.C.

The association of the two fragments of this inscription, with the determination that the length of the line was στοιχ. 36 and not, as Ferguson had thought, στοιχ. 41, invalidates all previous texts and discussions, and an account of the various restorations hitherto proposed for fragment *a*, as well as of the separate text of fragment *b* published by Meritt, is here omitted. Ferguson believed, and subsequent commentators accepted, that fragment *a* represented a decree of the phyle Akamantis. It is clear, however, that the inscription does record a regular enactment of the boule and demos in celebration of an event closely linked with the month during which Akamantis had the good fortune to be the phyle in prytany, and the prytaneis of that phyle are consequently given special instructions governing action to be taken both now and in future years, with the inclusion of a dedication to their eponymous hero.

See further *SEG* XXXIX, 102, XL, 82, XLI, 49. On the mason responsible for the inscription see Walbank, *BSA* 84, 1989, p. 403.

TREATY OF ALLIANCE BETWEEN ATHENS AND SIKYON

115 (Pl. 13, *a* only). Seventeen fragments, most of them very small, of a stele of Hymettian marble (I 2636), discovered between March 18 and March 23, 1935, along the west edge of the Panathenaic Way, mostly in a Late Roman context (N 10). Five fragments may be joined to make one large fragment (*a*), broken on all sides. On no other fragment except perhaps fragment *c*, which may be complete below, and fragment *d*, which preserves a small part of the right edge of the stele, is more than the inscribed surface preserved.

a (I 2636 a): H. 0.27 m.; W. 0.257 m.; Th. 0.098 m.

b (I 2636 d): H. 0.19 m.; W. 0.04 m.; Th. 0.053 m.

c (I 2636 c): H. 0.152 m.; W. 0.062 m.; Th. 0.03 m.

d (I 2636 m): H. 0.065 m.; W. 0.07 m.; Th. 0.037 m.

e (I 2636 b): H. 0.125 m.; W. 0.05 m.; Th. 0.05 m.

Fragments *f–m* are mere scraps of insignificant dimensions; *f* = I 2636 l, *g* = I 2636 e, *h* = I 2636 h, *i* = I 2636 g, *j* = I 2636 k, *k* = I 2636 f, *l* = I 2636 j, *m* = I 2636 i. Fragment *m* consists of one letter only, and that uncertain.

LH. *ca.* 0.005 m.
Στοιχ. (square, with irregularities) *ca.* 0.01 m.

Ed. E. Schweigert, *Hesperia* 8, 1939, pp. 35–41, no. 9, with photographs of all fragments except *m*. See also H. H. Schmitt, *Staatsverträge* III, 1969, pp. 61–63, no. 445.

a. 303 *a.*   ΣΤΟΙΧ.

(a)
```
[------------------------------------------]
[----------------------]Σ/[----------------]
[-------------- Δ]ημητρίωι του[------------]
[------------ τοῖς Σω]τῆρσιν καὶ γ[--------]
[----------- τὴν συμ]μαχίαν ἥνπερ [--------]
[----------------] εἰς ἄπ[α]ντα τὸ[ν χρόνον ------------]
[ὀμνύω Δία, Γῆν], Ἥλιον, Ἀθηνᾶν [---------]
[---------- ἔ]σομαι φίλος [καὶ σύμμαχος -----------]
[--------- τῆ]ς πόλε[ω]ς εὐγ[--------------]
[-----------]ων καὶ τὴν φιλί[αν ------------]
[---- τὸν δῆμο]ν τὸν Σικυωνίων δ[ιαφυλάξω(?) ----------]
[------- · ἐλέσθα]ι δὲ τὸν δῆμον τρ[εῖς ἄνδρας ---------]
[-- οἵτινες ἀφικό]μενοι εἰ⟨ς⟩ Σικυῶν[α -----------]
[---------] ἐγ τῶι ἔμπροσ[θεν χρόνωι -----------]
[-------- το]ὺς ὅρκους ἀπολήψ[ονται(?) ---------------]
[---------] τὰ ἄλλα το[ῖ]ς Σικυων[ίοις -------------]
[------]ν τοὺς ταμίας Ε[..]Σ[-------------]
[παρασ(?)]κευὴν [κ]εχειροτον[ημέν-----------]
[--------]τι[....]γατων ἐπει[δὴ ---------------]
[------]ειπ[..]υ[.] καθὰ ἐψη[φισ----------]
[-----]ατασ[..]κα καὶ πει[--------]
[-----]κατα[....]ικα καὶ τ[-----------]
[----]π[.]ρ[.⁵..]ονοπι[-------]
[----]τ[...⁷...]γ· ᵛ τάδ[ε --------]
[---]αν[.]ο[..⁶...]ν του[----------]
[---]ιρον[..⁵...]ιτω[-----------]
[----]ν[-----------------]
[------------------------------------------]
```

(b)
```
[------------------------------------------]
[--------------------]ενοι ει[-------------]
[------------- Σικυων]ίων καὶ Ἀ[θηναίων(?) ----------]
[-------------]ς Ἀθήνησιν κα[ὶ -----------]
[------------ σύ]γπασιν ἐπαινέ[σαι ----------]
[--- καὶ στεφανῶσαι χρυ]σῶι στεφάνωι [------------]
[--------------]της [-------------]
[------------------------------------------]
```

(c)

[――――――――――――――――――――――――――――]
[―――――――――――――――]λο[――――――――――――]
[―――――――――――――――]νο[――――――――――――]
[―――――――――――――――]ισ[――――――――――――]
[―――――――――――――――]\ους [――――――――――]
5 [――――――――――――δ]υοῖν [―――――――――――]
[―――――――――――――――]ρατο[―――――――――――]
[――――――――――――――] καὶ κ[――――――――――]
[――――――――― · ἀναγρά(?)]ψαι δ[ὲ ―――――――――]
[――――――――――――――]ιαει[――――――――――――]
10 [――――――――――――――]λονο[―――――――――――]
[――――――――――――――]\εφαν[――― · ἀναγράψαι δὲ ―――――――τὸ]
[ν γραμματέα ――――――――] ἐν στή[ληι λιθίνηι ――――――――]
[――――――――――――――― · εἰ]ς δὲ τὴ[ν ἀναγραφὴν τῆς στήλης δοῦναι τὸ]
[ν ταμίαν τοῦ δήμου ―――――] δραχ[μὰς ἐκ τῶν εἰς τὰ κατὰ ψηφίσματα]
15 [ἀναλισκομένων τῶι δήμωι · ―――――――――――――――――(?)]

(d)

[――――――――――――――――――――――――――――]
[―――――――――――――――――――――――――――] Σικυ
[ωνι ――――――――――――――――――――――τ]ὸν στέ
[φανον ――――――――――――――――――――――]λου
[―――――――――――――――――――――――――――]ον
5 [――――――――――――――――――――――――――――]
[――――――――――――――――――――――――――――]

(e)

[――――――――――――――――――――――――――――]
[―――――――――――――――]νο[――――――――――――]
[―――――――――――――――]νφι[―――――――――――]
[―――――――――――――――]ρονα[――――――――――]
[―――――――――――――――]ιον[――――――――――――]
5 [―――――――――――――――]θαι [―――――――――――]
[―――――――――――――――] στε[φαν――――――――]
[―――――――――――――――]ρα[――――――――――――]
[―――――――――――――――]λον[――――――――――――]
[―――――――――――――――]φευ[――――――――――――]
10 [―――――――――――――――]ομε[――――――――――――]
[―――――――――τοῦ δήμου το]ῦ Ἀθη[ναίων ――――――――]
[―――――――――――ἔδ(?)]οξεν [――――――――――――]
[―――――――――――――]ονα ἐν[――――――――――]
[―――――――――Χο(?)]λαργ[――――――――――――]
15 [―――――――――――]τι χρ[――――――――――――]
[――――――――――――――――――――――――――――]

(f)

[――――――――――――――――――――]
[―――――――――]ο[―――――――――]
[―――――――――]λ[―――――――――]
[―――――――――]ο[―――――――――]
[―――――――――]ε[―――――――――]
5 [―――――――――]να[―――――――――]
[―――――――――]ιξ[―――――――――]
[―――――――――]υμ[―――――――――]
[―――――――――]ρισι[―――――――――]
[―――――――――]ους [―――――――――]

(g)

[――――――――――――――――――――]
[―――――――――]α[―――――――――]
[―――――――――]ντ[―――――――――]
[―――――――――]οις [―――――――――]
[―――――――――]εν[―――――――――]
5 [―――――――――]οσοτ[―――――――――]
[―――――――――]αιπ[―――――――――]
[―――――――――]ργ[―――――――――]
[―――――――――]ω[―――――――――]
[――――――――――――――――――――]

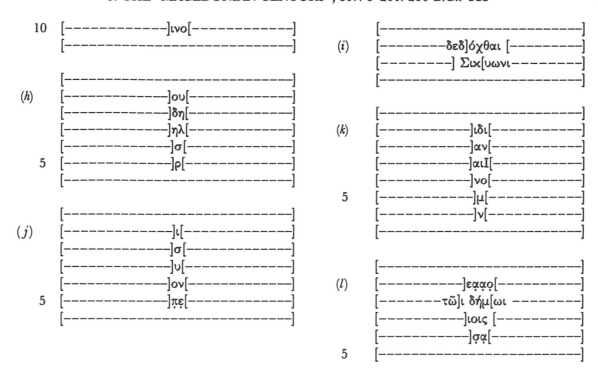

The concluding part of fragment *c*, lines 4–5 of fragment *b*, and the oath in fragment *a*, lines 5–7, led Schweigert to postulate a stoichedon pattern of 50 letters per line. This, or a figure approaching it, is likely to be correct, but Schweigert's restorations, though attractive, lack certainty. It is therefore preferable to leave the length of line without precise definition. Schmitt incorporates Schweigert's restorations into his own text (of fragments *a–c* only), with a few minor changes, but describes them as "weithin hypothetisch". Fragments *a–c* are given in what appears to be their correct relative order on the stele; the position of the other fragments in relation to them and to each other cannot be determined.

Fragment *a*: Lines 4–7. [..⁵.. τὴν συμ]μαχίαν ἥνπερ [ἐποιήσαντο οἱ Ἀθηναῖοι πρὸς τοὺς ‖ Σικυωνίους] εἰς ἅπ[α]ντα τὸ[ν χρόνον· ᵛ ὁ δὲ ὅρκος ἔστω κατὰ τάδε· ὀ|μνύω· Δία, Γῆν], Ἥλιον, Ἀθηνᾶν [Ἀρείαν, Ποσειδῶ, Ἄρη, καὶ θεοὺς πάντα]ς καὶ πάσας· ἔ]σομαι φίλος [καὶ σύμμαχος κτλ. Schweigert.

Lines 8–10. εὐγ[..........²¹.......... τὸν δῆμον τ|ὸν Σικυωνί(?)]ων καὶ τ[ὴ]ν φιλί[αν καὶ τὴν συμμαχίαν τὴν προτέραν ε‖ἰς τὸν δῆμο]ν τὸν Σικυωνίων δ[ιαφυλάξω(?) ....¹⁹.........] Schweigert; τὴν συμμαχίαν τὴν ...⁷... πρ‖ὸς(?) τὸν δῆμο]ν Schmitt. Lines 11–12. [....· ἑλέσθα]ι δὲ τὸν δῆμον τρ[εῖς ἄνδρας ἐξ Ἀθηναίων ἁπάντων ο|ἵτινες ἀφικό]μενοι εἰ⟨ς⟩ Σικυων[ίους Schweigert; εἰ⟨ς⟩ Σικυῶν[α G. Klaffenbach *apud* Schmitt; *lapis* ΕΙΣΙΚΥΩΝ. Line 14. ἀπολήψ[ονται παρὰ τῶν Σικυωνίων ...⁷....] Schweigert. Lines 16–17. [...]ν τοὺς ταμία[ς .]ε[.]μ[...]ε[..⁵.. τὸν στρατηγὸν τὸν ἐπὶ τὴν πα|ρασ(?)]κευὴν κτλ. Schweigert. Lines 18–25. Several minor adjustments have been made to Schweigert's readings.

Fragment *b*: Lines 4–5. [......¹⁴...... σύ]νπασιν ἐπαινέ[σαι τὸν δῆμον τὸν Σικυωνίω‖]ν καὶ στεφανῶσαι χρυ]σῶι στεφάνωι [..........²².........] Schweigert.

Fragment *c*: Lines 8–9. [.......¹⁵.......· ἀναγρά]ψαι δ[ὲ καὶ τὰ ὀνόματα τῶν πρέσβεων κ|αὶ καλέσαι αὐτοὺς ἐπὶ ξέν]ια εἰ[ς τὸ πρυτανεῖον εἰς αὔριον ....] Schweigert. Lines 11–13. [........²⁰.........]\εφαν[..· ἀναγράψαι δὲ τὴν συμμαχίαν(?)| τὸν γραμματέα τοῦ δήμου] ἐν στή[λῃ λιθίνηι καὶ στῆσαι ἐν ἀκρο|πόλει παρὰ τὴν Ἀθηνᾶν(?), εἰ]ς δὲ τὴ[ν ἀναγραφὴν κτλ. Schweigert.

The writing of this text is, like much of the work of this period, imprecise and indeed careless. Schweigert justifiably drew attention to the slovenliness of its arrangement and execution, comparing in particular *IG* II², 497 of 303/2 and 504 (*SEG* XXI, 339) of 302/1. **114** and **118** exhibit better workmanship but display the same tendencies in, for example, the "narrowing" of the letters mu, nu, and omega. Characteristic of this mason are his use of the cruciform phi (see **102**) and of rho in the form F, as well as a neglect to make accurate joins of the strokes of a letter. Schweigert correctly noted that on epigraphical grounds, without the support of the historical data, the inscription could be dated "with considerable certainty" to the close of the 4th century. On the hand at work here see further **151**.

a: Lines 2–3. The reference to Demetrios (Poliorketes) and to the Soteres is not necessarily conclusive for a dating before 301 and Antigonos' death at Ipsos, as Schweigert believed. Cf. W. S. Ferguson, *Hesperia* 17, 1948, p. 126, note 39. On the cult of the two "savior-kings" see **114**, commentary on lines 15–17. Line 6. For a pattern of the oath cf. *IG* II², 236 (*SEG* XXX, 63, XXXI, 75, with other bibliography; M. N. Tod, *GHI* II, p. 224, no. 177, with note p. 225), lines 2–3, which, as in *IG* IV², i, 68, V, lines 139–140, inspire the greatest part of the restorations. For the replacement of the 'Αθηνᾶ of that text by 'Αθηνᾶ 'Αρεία in Schweigert's text, compare *IG* II², 686 + 687 (*SEG* XXXIII, 112, with earlier references), lines 54–55.

c: Lines 8–9. For the formula as restored by Schweigert see W. A. McDonald, *AJA* 59, 1955, pp. 151–155 and particularly A. S. Henry, *Honours*, pp. 262–275. Lines 11–15. If the title of the disbursing officer is correctly restored, the treaty must antedate 301. See **111** and **112**. For the formula of payment and the source of the funding see **83** and references there.

The relationship between Athens and Sikyon to which *IG* II², 448 bears witness was presumably invalidated by the events of 317 and thereafter. From 309 until 303 the troops of Ptolemy I Soter were in occupation of Sikyon, and it is to be presumed that the new treaty is to be dated after their surrender of the city to Demetrios (Diodorus Siculus 20.102; Polyainos 4.7.3) at some time in the summer of 303. It is uncertain whether it took place before or after the beginning of the new Athenian year; see A. G. Woodhead in *Ancient Macedonian Studies*, p. 366. Demetrios persuaded the Sikyonians to rebuild their city on a different site, and they renamed it Demetrias in his honor (Plutarch, *Demetrios* 25; cf. Strabo 8.6.25, Pausanias 2.7.1). In this treaty it is, however, referred to throughout as Sikyon, and although Diodorus expressly notes that the new name did not last long, it would be surprising if it were so soon ignored, and ignored in an official document of this character. This argument against a date in 303 for the treaty has more force than Schweigert was inclined to allow. Correspondingly, and if the name of the disbursing official(s) can be differently restored, a date between 294 and 288, when Demetrios had reestablished himself in Greece, remains a reasonable possibility, even though Schweigert argued that the changed character of his rule made free associations of this kind between individual Greek cities unlikely. Nevertheless, the revived Hellenic League and its circumstances remains an attractive context for this treaty, and the issue cannot on the evidence be proved either way. For a résumé of Sikyonian history at this period, see C. H. Skalet, *Ancient Sikyon*, 1928, pp. 80–82.

[Addendum: The text of Schweigert as corrected by Schmitt appears as *SEG* XLI, 50. A large fragment, which provides the upper right corner of the stele and reveals that it is pedimental, has been identified since this commentary was completed but remains as yet unpublished. Mentioned here by permission, it apparently confirms, in some fifteen lines of surviving text, Schweigert's dating and general conclusions. A superscription on the taenia below the pediment identifies the contents as a record of alliance. Fragment *d* fits closely beneath this new fragment.]

THE ARCHONSHIP OF LEOSTRATOS, 303/2 B.C.

Like its predecessor, the year of Leostratos saw much activity on the part of the Athenian assembly that has survived in the inscriptional record. Apart from two decrees, **115** and **122**, which may or may not belong to it and should be left out of account, and several others for which "*ca.* 303/2" or "303–301" must remain the acceptable dating (even if Leostratos' year might seem the attractive option), fifteen extant enactments provide the basis for the study of this archonship. Two of the fifteen, **117** and **118**, offer no detail that helps to determine the year's calendric character. Of the remainder, all are to be assigned to the latter part of the year. No fewer than six of them (*IG* II², 493 + 518, 494, 495 [*SEG* XXV, 79; M. J. Osborne, *Naturalization* I, pp. 136–137, D 60], 496 + 507 [Osborne, *op. cit.*, pp. 137–139, D 61], 497, and **116**) were passed in the twelfth prytany. Cf. M. H. Hansen, *GRBS* 28, 1987, p. 47, note 33.

Two pieces of evidence evaluated in the 1970's established that, among the material previously existing, an error on the part of the mason or of the γραμματεύς had provided a false detail to be corrected. A fragmentary decree published by J. Threpsiades ('Αρχ. 'Εφ., 1971, Χρονικά, p. 26) showed that the phyle Kekropis was in office in the ninth prytany, whereas in the long-known *IG* II², 489 it was evidently the eighth prytany (*IG* II², 490 also having been suitably restored to conform with the indication of 489). B. D. Meritt (*AAA* 5, 1972, pp. 292–293) recognized that either Threpsiades' decree or *IG* II², 489/490 must be in error, and the dilemma was resolved soon thereafter when *IG* II², 734 (for which see *SEG* XXVI, 90, XXX, 71; Osborne, *Naturalization* I, pp. 116–118, D 46) was augmented by a small unpublished fragment in the Epigraphical Museum and shown to belong to this year. It became clear that Kekropis was indeed in office in prytany IX and that the phyle holding the eighth prytany in *IG* II², 489 could no longer be restored on the basis of the extant text of 490. Cf. *SEG* XXX, 70. A further fragmentary decree of the prytany of Kekropis was published in 1972 by W. K. Pritchett (*CSCA* 5, 1972, p. 169), with ὀγδόης restored as the ordinal numeral: the restoration there too must now be ἐνάτης.

The two decrees among the fifteen that have not been accounted for in the preceding paragraphs are *IG* II², 491 and 498 (*SEG* XXI, 338), the former apparently and the latter very probably of the tenth prytany. For a useful account of the developing evaluation of the year see also Osborne, *Naturalization* II, pp. 121–123.

These more recent determinations make earlier discussions of the year for the most part of interest only for the bibliographical record. The material known at the time of writing was listed by Pritchett and O. Neugebauer, *Calendars*, p. 69. That the year was intercalary, as there shown, has not been disputed (see *IG* II², 489, in comm.; W. B. Dinsmoor, *Archons of Athens*, p. 386; Pritchett and Meritt, *Chronology*, p. xv); and the evidence of **116** served only as further confirmation of this (Meritt, *Athenian Year*, pp. 150–151). This was the sixteenth year of the seventh Metonic cycle, and in that cycle Year 16 should indeed be intercalary (Meritt, *TAPA* 95, 1964, p. 236, with additional references). See also Meritt in *Historia* 26, 1977, p. 171.

Meritt considered the year more fully, with particular reference to the text of *IG* II², 498, in *Hesperia* 33, 1964, pp. 4–7 (*SEG* XXI, 338), where for a year of 384 days he proposed a regular succession of hollow and full months in the festival calendar, with one day added at the end (cf. *IG* II², 495, 496, 497), and twelve prytanies each of 32 days. On the added day see p. 180 above, on the archonship of Pherekles, and p. 268 below, on that of Pytharatos. There was retardation of the festival calendar in Elaphebolion, apparently rectified soon afterwards. See A. G. Woodhead in *Ancient Macedonian Studies*, pp. 364–365, note 22.

Known phylai in prytany are VIII Erechtheis or Antiochis, IX Kekropis, X Antigonis, and XII Aiantis. Hypothetical restorations of *IG* II², 498 produce the possibilities of V Demetrias, Pandionis, or Akamantis or of XI Leontis; but on balance that text seems best assigned to prytany X.

THE PRESCRIPT OF A DECREE

116. Two joining fragments of the upper part of a pedimental stele of Pentelic marble, the larger of which (I 6516, hereafter fragment *a*) was discovered on April 22, 1952, in a Byzantine context east of the Church of the Holy Apostles (Q 15). Its original rough-picked back is preserved, but it is otherwise broken all around; much stone survives above the first line of the text that it carries (line 2), below the level of the inscribed surface. That the stele was pedimental, as this suggested, was confirmed by the identification of the small fragment *b* (I 5215), discovered on February 10, 1938, in a Late Roman context northeast of the Odeion (N 9). On this the top and right side of the monument are preserved, but it is broken elsewhere. It joins fragment *a* at the upper right of the latter. Line 1 is inscribed on a projecting fascia missing on fragment *a*.

a: H. 0.145 m.; W. 0.08 m.; Th. 0.043 m.

b: H. 0.069 m.; W. 0.097 m.; Th. 0.02 m.

LH. 0.005 m.

Στοιχ. (square) 0.0112 m.

Ed. *a* only: B. D. Meritt, *Hesperia* 21, 1952, pp. 367–368, no. 8, with photograph pl. 92. See also *SEG* XII, 91; lines 2–7 quoted by Meritt, *Athenian Year*, pp. 150–151. *b*, with the first three lines of *a* in order to illustrate the connection: M. B. Walbank, *Hesperia* 58, 1989, p. 89, no. 16, with photograph pl. 22. See also *SEG* XXXIX, 105.

a. 303/2 a., *pryt.* XII   ΣΤΟΙΧ. 29

```
                    [Θ        ε          ο]        ι.       (b)
         (a)       ['Επὶ Λεωστράτου ἄρ]χοντ[ος ἐπ]ὶ τῆς Αἰ
                   [αντίδος δωδεκάτ]ης πρυτ[ανείας ἧι Δ]
                   [ιόφαντος Διονυσ]οδώρου Φ[ηγούσιος]
         5         [ἐγραμμάτευεν· Σχ]ιροφορ[ιῶνος ἔνει]
                   [χαὶ νέαι, δευτέρα]ι χαὶ τρ[ιαχοστεῖ τ]
                   [ῆς πρυτανείας· βο]υλὴ ἐμ βο[υλευτηρί]
                   [ωι· τῶν προέδρων ἐ]πεψήφιζ[εν ..6...]
                   [.........17.........] Ἀχαρ[νεὺς χαὶ σ]
         10        [υμπρόεδροι ........19........]
                   [——————————————————]
```

Fragment *b* was identified and the join made by Walbank. The lettering of this text is careful and reasonably precise, although with some bad junctions of strokes in places. Some "free ends" of strokes are slightly enlarged.

Lines 3–4. The name of the γραμματεύς of this year survives in full in *IG* II², 493, lines 4–5. He is not otherwise known (cf. Meritt, *Hesperia* 13, 1944, p. 245). The remains of his patronymic and demotic in line 4 were sufficient guide to the date and restoration of the whole fragment. Lines 5–6. For assemblies held on the last day of Skirophorion, of which the evidence is abundant, see J. D. Mikalson, *Sacred and Civil Calendar*, pp. 177–181.

Line 7. Mention of the place of meeting of the boule occurs as early as 336/5; see *IG* II², 330, II, lines 30–31: but this happens to be its first occurrence among decrees discovered in the Agora excavations. See further A. S. Henry, *Prescripts*, p. 39.

HONORS FOR A FRIEND OF DEMETRIOS POLIORKETES

117. Two nonjoining fragments of a stele of micaceous Pentelic marble, of which the larger (I 7070, hereafter fragment *a*) was discovered on September 29, 1969, in the basement of a modern house beside the Athens–Peiraieus railway (M 5–6). It preserves the right side and original rough-picked back of the monument but is broken elsewhere; its configuration indicates that the stele increased in thickness towards the foot. The smaller fragment *b* (I 5463), broken all around and at the back, is really no more than a flake providing a dozen letters in lines 11–13 to the left of fragment *a*. It was discovered on May 23, 1938, in the latest repair of the Post-Herulian Wall, opposite the west passage of Klepsydra (T 27).

a: H. 0.294 m.; W. 0.19 m.; Th. 0.102–0.12 m.

b: H. 0.06 m.; W. 0.076 m.; Th. 0.026 m.

LH. 0.007 m.

Στοιχ. Hor. 0.015 m.; Vert. 0.014 m.

Ed. *a* only: M. B. Walbank, *Hesperia* 49, 1980, pp. 255–257, no. 2, with photograph pl. 68. See also *SEG* XXX, 72; M. J. Osborne, *Naturalization* I, pp. 139–140, D 62, *Naturalization* II, p. 137, with text, brief details of the monument, and short commentary. *b* only, with repetition of *a*, lines 10–15, to demonstrate the comparative location: Walbank, *Hesperia* 58, 1989, pp. 88–89, no. 15, with photographs pl. 21. See also *SEG* XXXIX, 103.

a. 303/2 *a.*, *pryt.* XII   ΣΤΟΙΧ. 25

```
                              [------------------]
        (a)                   [..........22..........]ι[..]
                              [...........19......... κα]ι εἶν
                              [αι αὐτὸν ᾿Αθηναῖον καὶ ἐγγ]όνου
                              [ς αὐτοῦ, καὶ γράψασθαι αὐτ]ὸν φυ
              5               [λῆς καὶ δήμου καὶ φρατρία]ς ἧς ἂ
                              [ν βούληται κατὰ τὸν νόμο]γ· δοῦν
                              [αι δὲ καὶ τὴν ψῆφον περ]ὶ αὐτοῦ [τ]
                              [οὺς πρυτάνεις εἰς τὴν] π⟨ρ⟩ώτην [ἐ]
                              [κκλησίαν καὶ τοὺς θε]σμοθέτα[ς]
             10               [τοὺς ἐπὶ Νικοκλέους] ἄρχον[τ]ος
        (b)                   [προγρ]άψαι [αὐτῶι τὴ]ν δοκιμασ[ί]
                              [αν ἐν τ]ῶι Μετ[αγειτν]ιῶνι μηνί, [ὅ]
                              [πως ἂν ο]ἱ δ[ιατρίβο]γ[τ]ες πα[ρὰ τῶ]
                              [ι βασιλεῖ ἅπαντες] ἐ[ν]δειχ[νύων]
             15               [ται τὴν εὔνοιαν τῶ]ι δήμω[ι εἰδό]
                              [τες ὅτι τιμηθήσον]ται ὑπ[ὸ τοῦ δ]
                              [ήμου ἀξίως τῆς εὐνο]ίας· [ἀναγρά]
                              [ψαι κτλ. ------------------]
                              [------------------------]
```

Lines 7 and 16. The crossbar of alpha is omitted. Line 8. *Lapis* ΠΙΩΤΗΝ.

Walbank observed that the decree, although for a different honorand, follows exactly the wording of *IG* II², 495 and 496 + 507 (Osborne, *Naturalization* I, pp. 136–138, D 60–61), in which Alkaios of Ainos and Solon of Bargylia, also friends of Demetrios Poliorketes helpful to Athenians both individually and collectively in their dealings with the king, were honored with Athenian citizenship. Cf. *JHS* 104, 1984, p. 243 and *SEG* XXXIV, 76. Like the second of these (the first is not preserved as far as that point), this enactment shows an awareness of the name of the eponymous archon in the year to come and was thus presumably, like them, passed in the twelfth prytany on its last and "busy day", as Osborne describes it: and indeed *IG* II², 497 and **116** were also passed at that assembly.

The formula for the grant of citizenship is that of Osborne's "Formulation A" (*Naturalization* I, p. 16), with all the elements identifiable, including the scrutiny clause not in evidence in the procedure between 307/6 and the early part of Leostratos' year. For the formula in general see **96**, commentary on lines 9–13, with references there.

Lines 12–17. For the "hortatory intention" see **86**, commentary on lines 21–24.

FRAGMENT OF A DECREE

118. The upper left corner of a pedimental stele of Hymettian marble (I 937), with the apex, left akroterion, and major part of the pediment preserved, together with the original rough-picked back and part of the left side, discovered on June 6, 1933, in a modern context at the surface in front of the Propylon to the New Bouleuterion (H 11).

H. 0.185 m.; W. 0.185 m.; Th. 0.065 m.
LH. 0.005 m.
Στοιχ. (almost square) Hor. 0.007 m.; Vert. 0.0065 m.

Ed. E. Schweigert, *Hesperia* 9, 1940, p. 351, no. 46, with photograph.

a. 303/2 *a.*   ΣΤΟΙΧ. 19

Θ   ε   ο   [ι].
['Ε]πὶ Λεωστρ[άτου ἄρχοντ]
[ος] ἐπὶ τῆ[ς ....¹¹.....]
[————————————]

Line 1 is inscribed on the horizontal cornice of the pediment. The stele was narrow (original width *ca.* 0.24 m.) and thin, features that seem to be reflected in the thin and pusillanimous writing. The very narrow omega with barely discernible horizontal strokes is especially distinctive. *IG* II², 497 offers a less exaggerated parallel for this idiosyncrasy, but the parallel of **114** is so close as to make it certain that the stonemason of this text inscribed that text also. That being so, this stele may be added to those listed by M. B. Walbank (*BSA* 84, 1989, pp. 399–405) as inscribed by the "Mason of *I.G.*, II², 497". See **151** and, for other texts attributed by Walbank to the same hand, **114**, **115**, **120**, **122**, **129**, and **155**.

FRAGMENT OF A DECREE

119. A fragment of a stele of bluish Pentelic marble (I 4988), with the original left side preserved but otherwise broken all around, including the back, discovered on June 23, 1937, east of the Post-Herulian Wall north of Akropolis Street (T 24).

H. 0.11 m.; W. 0.089 m.; Th. 0.077 m.
LH. 0.005–0.007 m.
Στοιχ. (square) 0.012 m.

Ed. M. B. Walbank, *Hesperia* 58, 1989, pp. 90–91, no. 18, with photograph pl. 23. See also *SEG* XXXIX, 104.

ca. a. 303 *a.*   ΣΤΟΙΧ.

[————————————————]
[.]ΛΟΔ[————————————ε]
ὺς εἶπ[εν· ————————————]
ροστατ[————————————]
οντες α[————————————]
5   ντι καὶ [————————————]
[. .]νησι[————————————]
[. . .]υο[————————————]
[————————————————]

Walbank regarded the hand at work here as close to that of the craftsman who inscribed *IG* II², 484, of 304/3. A date in the context of the abundant legislation of this period would therefore be appropriate.

He further interpreted the verb of proposal (line 2), which establishes the fact that this is an enactment of some kind, as indicative of an amendment to a main decree, and he restored τὰ μὲν ἄλλα καθάπερ – – – to follow it. But so little of the text survives that any suggestion about it must remain speculative.

A GRANT OF ATHENIAN CITIZENSHIP

120. A fragment of a stele of Pentelic marble (I 1541), broken on all sides, discovered on March 8, 1934, in a modern wall south of the central part of the Middle Stoa (M 13).

H. 0.19 m.; W. 0.12 m.; Th. 0.10 m.
LH. 0.006–0.007 m.
Στοιχ. (square) 0.0125 m.

Ed. B. D. Meritt, *Hesperia* 10, 1941, pp. 55–56, no. 19, with photograph; M. J. Osborne, *Naturalization* I, pp. 140–141, D 63, *Naturalization* II, p. 137. See also *SEG* XXXIII, 96.

a. 303/2–302/1 *a.*   ΣΤΟΙΧ. 29

```
      [----------------------]
      [---------------------· τ]
      [οὺς δὲ θεσμοθέτας εἰσαγαγεῖν αὐτῶ]
      [ι τὴν] δοκιμ[ασίαν ὅταν πρῶτον δικασ]
      [τήρ]ιον πληρ[ῶσι, ὅπως ἂν ἐφάμιλλον ἦ]
   5  [ι κα]ὶ πᾶσιν ἀγ[ωνίζεσθαι ὑπὲρ τοῦ δή]
      [μο]υ τοῦ Ἀθη[ναίων καὶ τῆς τῶν ἄλλων Ἑ]
      [λλ]ήνων σωτ[ηρίας· ἀναγράψαι δὲ τόδε]
      [τὸ ψ]ήφισμα [τὸν γραμματέα τοῦ δήμου]
      [εἰσ]τήλην λι[θίνην καὶ στῆσαι ἐν ἀκρ]
  10  [οπό]λει· εἰς δ[ὲ τὴν ἀναγραφὴν τῆς στή]
      [λης] δοῦναι τ[ὸν ταμίαν τοῦ δήμου εἴκ]
      [οσι] δραχμὰς [ἐκ τῶν εἰς τὰ κατὰ ψηφί ᵛ]
      [σματ]α ἀναλι[σκομένων τῶι δήμωι].
                          vacat
```

The text, except where noted in the following commentary, is that of Meritt. Lines 1–3. [– – – καὶ τοὺς θεσμοθέτας εἰσαγαγεῖν αὐτῶι εἰς τὸ δικαστήριον τὴν] δοκιμ[ασίαν κτλ.] A. S. Henry, *Honours*, p. 105, note 131. Line 4. [τήρι]ον Meritt. Sufficient of the surface of the stone remains to make iota certain at this point. πλη- ρῶ[σι Osborne. Line 7. [λλή]νων Meritt; [λλ]ήνων Osborne. The right *hasta* of eta is detectable at the break. Line 8. ψήφισμα Osborne. The characteristics of the writing closely resemble those of **121**, and the two stelai could well be the work of the same craftsman. Osborne's differentiation of the qualities of the two pieces of work does less than justice to the one and more than justice to the other. There is the same tendency to emphasize the "free ends" of the strokes of upsilon; this letter, more than others, is liable to be so treated (cf., for example, **77, 86**, and **100**). Phi has the cruciform shape which is a feature of this period (see **102**). Other letters, principally eta, mu, and nu, appear narrow in proportion to the width of epsilon and sigma (on this last see the comment of W. K. Pritchett, *Hesperia* 10, 1941, pp. 272–273). Meritt also compared *IG* II², 464, of 307/6, which is of the same general character. Since on other grounds this text is best attributed to the limited period between later 303/2 and 301, the high reward both here and in **121** of full Athenian citizenship, suggesting deserts of a high order, implies a connection either with the Four Years' War of 307–303 or with the revived Hellenic League of 303/2. On the hand identified here see **151**.

The citizenship grant, of which only the concluding section survives, is that of Osborne's "Formulation A" (*Naturalization* I, p. 16). Cf. **117**. Lines 1–4 contain the "scrutiny clause", missing from the formulas of grant between 307/6 and the earlier part of 303/2; cf. Osborne, *Naturalization* II, p. 136. The responsibility of the thesmothetai for instituting the procedure of scrutiny is emphasized first in *IG* II², 398b, dated to 318; see Osborne, *Naturalization* I, pp. 98–99, D 36, *Naturalization* II, p. 102. Its presence in *IG* II², 336 (*SEG* XXI, 273), of 333/2, is to be regarded as extremely doubtful (cf. Osborne, *Naturalization* I, p. 77). See Busolt-Swoboda, II, p. 946, with note 3 summarizing earlier conflicts of opinion. On the thesmothetai see further **86**, commentary on lines 4–9.

This is immediately followed (lines 4–7) by the "hortatory intention", for which see **86**, commentary on lines 21–24. For the restoration here Meritt compared *IG* II², 466 (*SEG* XXIV, 110), line 35 and 558 (Osborne, *Naturalization* I, pp. 118–119, D 47), lines 11–12.

Line 5. ἀγ[ωνίζεσθαι. Cf. **114**, line 23, the restoration of which is supported by the sentiment of this text. Lines 6–7. The "salvation of the other Greeks" indicates a connection with the activities of Antigonos and Demetrios; cf. *IG* II², 466, lines 9–10, 498 (*SEG* XXI, 338), lines 15–18, and **122**, lines 10–13. But the employment of the phrase in the posthumous honors proposed by Stratokles (see **110**) for the statesman Lykourgos (if correctly restored in *IG* II², 457, line 15) suggests that it had become something of a catchword. On σωτηρία as a sentiment much in vogue without association with "the other Greeks" see *IG* II², 456b (*SEG* XXI, 328), lines 3–4, 470b, lines 7–8, 479, line 8, 492, line 14, 498, lines 19–20.

Line 8. The restoration of the secretary responsible for the inscription and erection of the stele introduces the γραμματεὺς τοῦ δήμου for the first time in an Agora decree. His first appearance is, as it appears, in the decree mentioned above, proposed by Stratokles in honor of Lykourgos, as quoted by Plutarch. Epigraphically he is found in *IG* II², 496 + 507 (Osborne, *Naturalization* I, pp. 137–139, D 61) of this very year, and restored (or barely discernible) in *IG* II², 576 and 696, dated by Osborne (*Naturalization* I, pp. 133–135, D 57, 58) to "*ca.* 307–303/2". He was restored by Schweigert in **115**, *q.v.* At the other end of the chronology, he appears sporadically to the end of the 2nd century B.C. (cf. *IG* II², 1008, line 87, 1011, line 62).

His identity is not discussed by P. J. Rhodes (*Athenian Boule*, pp. 136–141), although p. 136, note 3 implies an identification with the γραμματεὺς τῆς βουλῆς καὶ τοῦ δήμου, for whom see **114**, commentary on line 25. It seems more likely, as was urged by W. S. Ferguson (*Athenian Secretaries*, pp. 63–66) and M. Brillant (*Les secrétaires athéniens*, 1911, pp. 37–49, with full references to earlier literature) that this is yet another designation for the official better known as the γραμματεὺς ὁ κατὰ πρυτανείαν, also referred to as the γραμματεὺς τῆς βουλῆς (cf. **73**, commentary on lines 23–24); this was the view adopted by Pritchett in his edition of **121**, where the same secretary is to be restored. There remains the third possibility, that this was a functionary separate from those previously mentioned, with duties otherwise unclear. Among such a multiplicity of γραμματεῖς and ὑπογραμματεῖς this option cannot be lightly discarded. The modern enthusiasm for the "streamlining" of administration may well, in the Athenian context and particularly in the matter of these various secretaries, be a misleading criterion.

Line 11. If the ταμίας τοῦ δήμου is correctly restored here (and his presence in the comparable text **121** is undoubted), the year 302/1 is necessarily the *terminus ante quem* of this document. Cf. Henry, *Chiron* 14, 1984, pp. 51–52. Lines 11–13. The stele was evidently smaller than **121** or inferior in some other respect. It is less usual to express the numeral in full: cf. *IG* II², 212 (*SEG* XXXIV, 66, with earlier references, XXXVI, 148), 237 (*SEG* XXXIII, 86, with earlier references), 240 (*SEG* XXXI, 77), 276, 290, 299, 511 (Osborne, *Naturalization* I, pp. 130–131, D 55), 526 (= 555), and 589. Osborne observed that, if the disbursing officer be restored as ὁ ἐπὶ τῆι διοικήσει, other possibilities, showing ΔΔ or ΔΔΔ, are available; but this is a far less likely alternative. For the source of the funds see Henry, *Chiron* 12, 1982, p. 111, **45**, and **66**. A sum as small as twenty drachmas, though rare after *ca.* 332 (cf. **83**), is nevertheless a reasonable supposition at this period. Cf. **112**, commentary on lines 5–7.

A GRANT OF ATHENIAN CITIZENSHIP

121. A fragment of a stele of Pentelic marble (I 5036), with part of the original back and right side preserved, discovered on November 8, 1937, in a wall of a modern house west of the Panathenaic Way (R 19).

H. 0.155 m.; W. 0.19 m.; Th. 0.128 m.

LH. 0.005–0.007 m.

Στοιχ. (almost square and slightly irregular) Hor. *ca.* 0.012 m.; Vert. *ca.* 0.0118 m.

Ed. W. K. Pritchett, *Hesperia* 10, 1941, pp. 270–273, no. 70, with photograph; M. J. Osborne, *Naturalization* I, pp. 141–142, D 64, *Naturalization* II, p. 138.

a. 303/2–302/1 *a.*   ΣΤΟΙΧ. 32

```
         [----------------------------]
         [.................28.................· ε]ἴγ[α]
         [ι δ'αὐτοὺς Ἀθηναίους καὶ τοὺς ἐκ]γόνους
         [αὐτῶν, καὶ γράφασθαι φυλῆς] καὶ δήμου κα
         [ὶ φρατρίας ἧς ἂν βούλωντα]ι κατὰ τὸν νόμ
    5    [ον· ἀναγράψαι δὲ τόδε τὸ ψή]φισμα τὸν γρα
         [μματέα τοῦ δήμου ἐν στήλ]ει λιθίνει καὶ
```

[στῆσαι ἐν ἀκροπόλει· εἰς] δὲ τὴν ἀναγραφ
[ὴν τῆς στήλης δοῦναι τὸν] ταμίαν τοῦ δήμ
[ου ᵛ ΔΔΔ ᵛ δραχμὰς ἐκ τῶν εἰ]ς τὰ κατὰ ψηφί
10   [σματα ἀναλισκομένων τῶι δ]ήμωι· τοὺς δὲ
[πρυτάνεις τοὺς πρυτανεύον]τας εἰς τὴν
[πρώτην ἐκκλησίαν δοῦναι περὶ α]ὐ[τῶν] τὴ
[ν ψῆφον, καὶ τὴν δοκιμασίαν αὐτοῖς το]ὺς
[θεσμοθέτας εἰσαγαγεῖν(?) .....¹² .....]
[— —]

The text is that of Pritchett. The damaged edges of the inscribed surface may or may not betray traces of additional letters, especially where the break appears to run along a chiseled stroke. Thus Osborne's text added readings at four points as follows: Line 1.] ε̣ί̣γ̣[α]. Line 2. τοὺς ἐ[κ]γόνους. Line 10.] δήμωι. Line 12. περὶ] αὐ̣[τῶν].

The character of the enactment, the formulas employed, and the hand of the craftsman are all comparable with those of **120**, and the criteria for dating are similar; for all these matters see the commentary there. The section of the decree that survives here occurs slightly earlier in the expression of the grant, but the same ground is also partly covered. It may nevertheless be noted that, despite the overall comparability, there are differences of formulation, both in the order of the items and in minor particulars (e.g., ἐν στήλει λιθίνει for εἰστήλην λιθίνην). This tends to reinforce the conclusion that, even in documents closely contemporary and of identical intent, consistency was not regarded as a virtue among the drafters of Athenian decrees.

Line 9. The cost of the stele, as restored by Pritchett, was 30 drachmas. But the stone is thick and may have been sizable, and : ΔΔΔΔ : in five letter spaces is also a possible restoration. Cf. **83** (also στοιχ. 32). Osborne printed five letter spaces (. . . . .), remarking that "Pritchett's supplement is not the only possibility."

Lines 13–14. Osborne justly drew attention to the contorted wording of the scrutiny clause here proposed; but the clause naturally follows that prescribing the second vote (lines 10–13), and for its delay he compared *IG* II², 646 (Osborne, *Naturalization* I, pp. 145–148, D 68), of 295/4.

DECREE IN HONOR OF ADEIMANTOS OF LAMPSAKOS

122. Seven joined fragments of a stele of Pentelic marble, of which six, collectively fragment *a* (I 5709), were discovered on March 10, 1939, in the cellar wall of a modern house between the North Slope of the Akropolis and the Areopagos (S 23) and were at once joined together. They preserve part of the original rough-picked back but otherwise are broken all around. The seventh fragment (*b*, I 5444), was discovered on May 19, 1938, in a wall of a Byzantine building south of the Altar of the Twelve Gods (K 6). On its left it joins fragment *a* between lines 3 and 8 of the text, and it preserves the smooth-dressed right side of the monument, although it is broken elsewhere.

Measurements as joined: H. 0.43 m.; W. *ca.* 0.285 m.; Th. 0.11 m.
LH. 0.006 m.
Στοιχ. Hor. 0.115 m.; Vert. 0.012 m.

Ed. *a* only: E. Schweigert, *Hesperia* 9, 1940, pp. 348–351, no. 45, with photograph. See *SEG* XIV, 58 (improved text, with references to A. Wilhelm, *RhMus* 90, 1941, pp. 22–23; G. de Sanctis, *RivFil* n.s. 19, 1941, pp. 194–197; L. Robert, *Hellenica* II, 1946, pp. 15–33; W. S. Ferguson, *Hesperia* 17, 1948, pp. 127–128, note 40 (on lines 7–17); I. Calabi, *Athenaeum* n.s. 28, 1950, pp. 55–66; G. Daux, Ἀρχ. Ἐφ., 1953–1954 [εἰς μνήμην Γ. Π. Οἰκονόμου, I], pp. 245–254); *SEG* XXV, 80 (L. Moretti, *Iscrizioni storiche ellenistiche* I, pp. 17–21, no. 9, with text, Italian translation, bibliography, and commentary). See also H. H. Schmitt, *Die Staatsverträge des Altertums* III, 1969, pp. 75–76, quoting lines 6–8 and 11–17 as testimonia for the machinery and functioning of the Hellenic League, together with bibliographical references. *b* only (with corrections to *a* at lines 3–8): M. B. Walbank, *Hesperia* 58, 1989, pp. 89–90, no. 17, with photograph pl. 22. See also *SEG* XXXIX, 106.

The text below is that of *SEG* XIV, 58, with minor improvements, combined with fragment *b* and adjusted to take account of the requirements imposed by it. In the original publication, the location of fragment *a* in respect of the width of the monument was not known and was arbitrarily determined. Now that it is established, the text of the old version has been moved to the right by nine letter spaces.

a. 302 *a.*   ΣΤΟΙΧ. 35

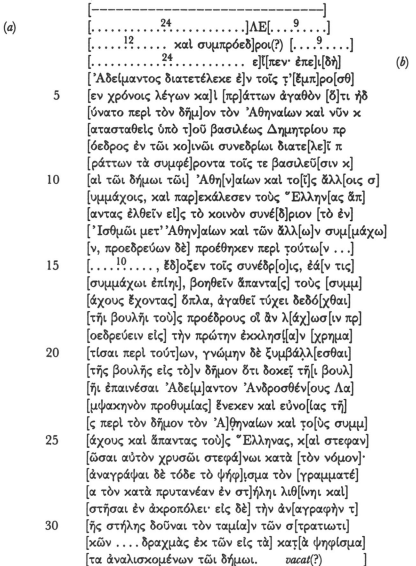

(a)

```
[----------------------------]
[...........24.........]ΛΕ[....9....]
[......12..... καὶ συμπρόεδ]ροι(?) [...9....]
[.............24............ ε]ἴ[πεν· ἐπε]ι[δὴ]                    (b)
['Αδείμαντος διατετέλεχε ἐ]ν τοῖς τ'[ἔμπ]ρο[σθ]
```
5
```
[εν χρόνοις λέγων κα]ὶ [πρ]άττων ἀγαθὸν [ὅ]τι ἠδ
[ύνατο περὶ τὸν δῆμ]ον τὸν 'Αθηναίων καὶ νῦν κ
[αταασταθεὶς ὑπὸ τ]οῦ βασιλέως Δημητρίου πρ
[όεδρος ἐν τῶι χο]ινῶι συνεδρίωι διατε[λε]ῖ π
[ράττων τὰ συμφέ]ροντα τοῖς τε βασιλεῦ[σιν χ]
```
10
```
[αὶ τῶι δήμωι τῶι] 'Αθη[ν]αίων καὶ το[ῖ]ς ἄλλ[οις σ]
[υμμάχοις, καὶ παρ]εχάλεσεν τοὺς Ἕλλην[ας ἅπ]
[αντας ἐλθεῖν εἰ]ς τὸ χοινὸν συνέ[δ]ριον [τὸ ἐν]
['Ισθμῶι μετ' 'Αθην]αίων καὶ τῶν ἄλλ[ω]ν συμ[μάχω]
[ν, προεδρεύων δὲ] προέθηκεν περὶ τούτω[ν ...]
```
15
```
[....10...., ἔδ]οξεν τοῖς συνέδρ[ο]ις, ἐά[ν τις]
[συμμάχωι ἐπίηι], βοηθεῖν ἅπαντα[ς] τοὺς [συμμ]
[άχους ἔχοντας] ὅπλα, ἀγαθεῖ τύχει δεδό[χθαι]
[τῆι βουλῆι τοὺ]ς προέδρους οἳ ἂν λ[άχ]ωσ[ιν πρ]
[οεδρεύειν εἰς] τὴν πρώτην ἐκκλησί[α]ν [χρημα]
```
20
```
[τίσαι περὶ τούτ]ων, γνώμην δὲ ξυμβάλλ[εσθαι]
[τῆς βουλῆς εἰς τὸ]ν δῆμον ὅτι δοκεῖ τῆ[ι βουλ]
[ῆι ἐπαινέσαι 'Αδείμ]αντον 'Ανδροσθέν[ους Λα]
[μψαχηνὸν προθυμίας] ἕνεχεν καὶ εὐνο[ίας τῆ]
[ς περὶ τὸν δῆμον τὸν 'Α]θηναίων καὶ το[ὺς συμμ]
```
25
```
[άχους καὶ ἅπαντας τοὺ]ς Ἕλληνας, κ[αὶ στεφαν]
[ῶσαι αὐτὸν χρυσῶι στεφά]νωι κατὰ [τὸν νόμον]·
[ἀναγράψαι δὲ τόδε τὸ ψήφ]ισμα τὸν [γραμματέ]
[α τὸν κατὰ πρυτανέαν ἐν στ]ήλῃ λιθ[ίνηι καὶ]
[στῆσαι ἐν ἀκροπόλει· εἰς δὲ] τὴν ἀν[αγραφὴν τ]
```
30
```
[ῆς στήλης δοῦναι τὸν ταμία]ν τῶν σ[τρατιωτι]
[κῶν .... δραχμὰς ἐκ τῶν εἰς τὰ] κατ[ὰ ψηφίσμα]
[τα ἀναλισκομένων τῶι δήμωι.     vacat(?)        ]
```

Line 2. καὶ συμπρόεδ]ροι(?) Schweigert; [———]ροι[———] Moretti. The preamble may indeed have come to an end before line 3: cf. Daux, *op. cit.*, p. 247. Line 4. Before the discovery of fragment *b*, Schweigert's reading and restoration ἐ]ν τοῖς ἔ[μπροσθεν χρόνοις] was generally adopted; but it is to be noted that Daux regarded the epsilon as impossible and with some hesitation proposed ἐ]ν τοῖ[ς] τρ[ῦ ...⁷... χρόνοις]. The upright of this letter alone survives and (if it is to be regarded as epsilon) is out of its true position in the stoichos. The reading of fragment *b* makes Schweigert's restoration invalid and suggests that Daux's interpretation was the correct one. This allows the more regular spelling of ἔμπροσθεν; and although elided τε is a rarity, it is not without parallel, especially in the later 4th and early 3rd centuries. Cf. L. Threatte, *Grammar*, p. 422.

Lines 10–11. συνέδροις Schweigert; συμμάχοις Wilhelm, Ferguson, *SEG* XIV, Moretti. Lines 11–12. συνα-γείρεσθαι(?) Schweigert; παραγίγνεσθαι Wilhelm, Schmitt; ἅπαντας ἐλθεῖν Ferguson, *SEG* XIV, Moretti. Lines 12–13. τὸ ἐν 'Ισθμῶι μετ' Schweigert, Ferguson, *SEG* XIV, Moretti; ἐν 'Ισθμίοις μετ' Robert, Calabi, Schmitt. Lines 12–14. [τῶν δὲ συνέδρων 'Αθην]αίων καὶ τῶν ἄλλ[ω]ν συμ[μάχων συγκαθημένων] προέθηκεν χτλ. E. Badian and T. R. Martin, *ZPE* 61, 1985, pp. 167–172 (cf. *SEG* XXXV, 78). Line 14. προεδρεύων δέ Schweigert, *ceteri* (except Calabi, who restored καὶ τὸ ψήφισμα). Lines 14–15. περὶ τούτω[ν ὧν ....¹¹.... ἔδο]ξεν Schweigert; περὶ τούτω[ν ......¹³...... ἔδο]ξεν *SEG* XIV; περὶ τοῦ τῶ[ν ......¹³...... ἔδο]ξεν De Sanctis, Moretti; περὶ τούτω[ν, ἐφ'οἷς καὶ πᾶσιν ἔδο]ξεν Wilhelm; περὶ τούτω[ν τὸ ψήφισμα ὃ καὶ ἔδο]ξεν Ferguson: περὶ τουτω[......¹⁴...... ἔδο]ξεν Schmitt.

Lines 15–16. ἐά[ν τις ἴηι ἐπὶ πολέμωι] Schweigert, Wilhelm, Schmitt (with mark of hesitation); ἐά[ν τις συμμάχωι ἐπίηι] Ferguson, *SEG* XIV, Moretti; ἐὰ[ν ἴωσι ἐπ''Ελάτειαν (or ἐπὶ τὰς Πύλας) or ἐά[ν τις ἴηι ἐπ''Ελάτειαν De Sanctis.

Lines 24–25. συμμάχους Calabi, *SEG* XIV, Moretti; συνέδρους Schweigert. Badian and Martin (*loc. cit.*) make three further suggestions, *exempli gratia*. See *ibid.*, p. 169, for a survey of earlier restorations.

Schweigert observed that the letter forms of this inscription are "very typical of the last decade of the fourth century B.C." Better executed than that of **115** and resembling (though in some respects differing from) that of **114** and **118**, the writing is generally untidy, and in the shaping of individual letters few angles are accurately formed. Kappa varies greatly in the position of its two arms; the "narrowing" of eta, mu, and nu is again noticeable, but sigma is also affected by being wide and vertically somewhat compressed. Cf. **151**.

Lines 3–4. Adeimantos of Lampsakos is well known in the literary sources, both as one of the most notable sons of his city (Strabo 13.1.19) and as a friend of the philosopher Theophrastos (Diogenes Laertius 5.57). One tradition saw him as a fawning courtier (κόλαξ) of Demetrios, on whom the Athenians heaped extravagant and unworthy honors (Athenaios 6.253a and 255c). On the other hand, that he was an important, influential, and evidently efficient member of Demetrios' staff is shown by the terms of this decree and by the decree of Eretria (*IG* XII, ix, 198) whereby he was accorded Eretrian citizenship and the honor of a statue. To the epigraphical evidence may perhaps be added the letter found at Delphi from an Adeimantos to a king Demetrios (*SEG* XIV, 411, with references).

Line 8. The "Common Council" is that of the new Hellenic League, and it is evident that this decree must be dated soon after the League's inauguration in early 302, although it remains uncertain whether it should fall in the archon year of Leostratos (303/2) or in that of Nikokles (302/1). For a summary of the evidence concerning the League see Schmitt, *op. cit.*, pp. 63–80, no. 446. It is generally accepted that, at its inception, Adeimantos served as one of the five proedroi (cf. line 14) on the nomination of Demetrios. When the war was over, the intended normal practice was to be that the proedroi should be chosen by lot from among the members of the Council (*IG* IV², i, 68, III, lines 76–78). Calabi preferred to regard Adeimantos as acting in his capacity as Demetrios' general, to whom a special responsibility had been assigned for supervising the initial work of the new organization, rather than to consider him an official of the organization itself.

Lines 14–16. The difficult lacunae have been variously interpreted; see the textual commentary above. The motion sponsored by Adeimantos was clearly fundamental to the League's *raison d'être* and concerned the implementation of an agreement for collective security, even though its precise terms cannot be established. Lines 17–21. The decree was probouleumatic. See P. J. Rhodes, *Athenian Boule*, p. 251. For the enactment formula see **89**, commentary on lines 2–9 (under "Line 1").

Line 23. προθυμίας] ἕνεχεν καὶ εὐνο[ίας. A. S. Henry (*Honours*, pp. 9–11) notes that "the range of phraseology in these ἕνεχα expressions is considerable" and lists a number of examples, among which προθυμία happens not to figure. The virtue is more familiar adjectivally as part of the clause explanatory of the original decision to sponsor the decree. Cf. (e.g.) *IG* II², 373 (*SEG* XXIV, 105, with other references), of 322/1, where Euenor of Akarnania is described in the early section of the document as πρόθυμος περὶ τὸν δῆμον τὸν 'Αθηναίων but is accorded a crown of olive φιλοτιμίας ἕνεκα καὶ ἐπιμελείας.

Line 26. The precise cost of the stephanos is no longer specified, the record being replaced by the phrase κατὰ τὸν νόμον. For the dating of this change of practice and formula see Henry, *Honours*, pp. 25–28 and **112**, commentary on lines 5–7. Line 27. κατὰ πρυτανέαν. For the spelling see **95**, commentary on line 5. Lines 29–32. The officer responsible for disbursing the required expenditure is now the Treasurer of the Military Fund, who appeared in **114** (*q.v.*, with commentary, p. 182, on line 17 concerning the fund's origin) as the paymaster for the special expense of the annual celebrations there provided for. This year (302/1) marks the last appearance of the ταμίας τοῦ δήμου as the disbursing officer. Cf. Henry (*Chiron* 14, 1984, pp. 51–60), who quotes these lines (p. 53). On the origins of the "analiskomena fund" see **45** and Henry, *Chiron* 12, 1982, p. 111. After 302/1 it was used only sporadically as a quoted source of payment for inscribed stelai: see Henry, *Chiron* 14, 1984, pp. 60–63.

On the relationship between the Athenians, together with the "other allies", and the revived League of Corinth, see further Badian and Martin, *op. cit.*, pp. 167–172.

THE ARCHONSHIP OF NIKOKLES, 302/1 B.C.

123, **124**, and **125** represent three of fourteen decrees attributable to Nikokles' year, although the attribution of **125** may be open to doubt. The preceding archonship had ended in a flurry of legislative activity, and its successor seems to have maintained the momentum, although the evidence is more widely spaced through the twelve prytanies. Of the eleven enactments other than those set out below, the fragment from the North Slope of the Akropolis published in *Hesperia* 1, 1932, p. 46, no. IV (with photograph p. 45, fig. 3), belongs to the second prytany, and another fragment from the same area, as yet unpublished but now in the Epigraphical Museum (E.M. 13321), belongs to the fifth, as does *SEG* XVIII, 16. *IG* II², 499 is of pryt. VII, 500, 501, and 562 (*Hesperia* 9, 1940, p. 342), of pryt. VIII, 502 (*SEG* XXV, 81), of pryt. X, 503, of pryt. XI, and, finally, 504 (*SEG* XXI, 339) and 505 (*SEG* XXIV, 113, XXXIII, 97, and cf. XXXIV, 259, XXXVII, 87), of pryt. XII.

Scholars have been in agreement that the year was ordinary. As such, it fits correctly into Meton's calendar (see B. D. Meritt, *TAPA* 95, 1964, p. 236) as the seventeenth year of the seventh cycle. On the nature of the year see J. Kirchner, *IG* II², 499, comm.; W. B. Dinsmoor, *Archons of Athens*, p. 386, *Athenian Archon List*, p. 20, *Hesperia* 23, 1954, p. 313; Meritt, *Hesperia* 4, 1935, pp. 545–547; W. K. Pritchett and Meritt, *Chronology*, p. xvi; Pritchett and O. Neugebauer, *Calendars*, p. 80; Meritt, *Athenian Year*, p. 232. Pritchett briefly considered the calendric data of *IG* II², 504 and 505 in *Ancient Athenian Calendars on Stone*, pp. 351–352. The year as a whole, with all the epigraphical evidence brought together, was fully reviewed by Meritt in *Hesperia* 33, 1964, pp. 10–11. His pattern for it, based on that evidence, shows an alternation of hollow and full months in the lunar (festival) calendar, with a total of 354 days. **124** indicates that two days had been intercalated into it later than Maimakterion 12, the date of E.M. 13221, and before Posideon 29. The effect of this intercalation continued into the month Gamelion, as is shown by *IG* II², 499, but compensation had been made for it before *IG* II², 500 was passed late in Anthesterion.

The pattern of prytanies was rather more complex. On Meritt's analysis, prytanies of 29 and 30 days alternated in accord with the festival months until the end of the sixth prytany. Thereafter, prytanies VII, XI, and XII consisted each of 30 days, VIII, IX, and X of 29. Phylai known to have been in prytany are II Aigeis, IV Akamantis, V Kekropis, VII Antigonis, VIII Oineis, X Leontis, XI Antiochis, XII Aiantis.

THE TAXIARCHOI OF 302/1 HONORED

123. A pedimental stele of Pentelic marble (I 5228), largely intact but broken away at the bottom and with the pediment and edges much battered and chipped, discovered on February 14, 1938, in the east face of the Post-Herulian Wall, south of the Eleusinion (T 22). At the time of the discovery the inscribed face was covered with mortar.

H. 0.63 m.; W. 0.43 m.; Th. 0.095 m.
LH. 0.007 m. (omicron *ca.* 0.005 m.).
Στοιχ. Hor. (slightly irregular) 0.014–0.016 m.; Vert. 0.014 m.

Ed. W. K. Pritchett, *Hesperia* 9, 1940, pp. 104–111, no. 20, with photograph. The calendric data of lines 3–7 are cited by Pritchett and O. Neugebauer, *Calendars*, p. 80. Lines 26–27 are quoted in *Agora* III, p. 82, no. 225, among the testimonia for the Eleusinion. See also U. Kahrstedt, *Hermes* 75, 1940, pp. 332–334.

a. 302/1 a., pryt. IV   ΣΤΟΙΧ. 27

```
          [Θ]      ε      o      ι.
          ᾿Επὶ Νικοκλέους ἄρχοντος ἐπὶ τῆς
          ᾿Ακαμαντίδος τετάρτης πρυτανεί
          ας ἧι Νίκων Θεοδώρου Πλωθεὺς ἐγρ
     5    αμμάτευεν, Πυανοψιῶνος ἕκτει μ[ε]
          τ᾿εἰκάδας, πέμπτει καὶ εἰκοστῆι τ
          ῆς πρυτανείας· ἐκκλησία· τῶν προ[έ]
          δρων ἐπεψήφιζεν Εὐθύδικος Κηφ[ι]
          σοδώρου ᾿Αναγυράσιος καὶ συμπρό
    10    εδροι· ἔδοξεν τῶι δήμωι· ᵛᵛ Μέμνων
          Μέδοντος ᾿Αφιδναῖος εἶπεν· ἐπειδ
          ἡ οἱ ταξίαρχοι οἱ ἐπὶ Νικοκλέους
          ἄρχοντος καλῶς καὶ φιλοτίμως ἐπ
          εμελήθησαν τῆς εὐκ[ο]σμίας τῆς ἐν
    15    τοῖς ἱεροῖς τῆς Δήμητρος καὶ ἐστ
```

εφάνωσαν αὐτοὺς οἱ ἐπὶ ταῦτα αἱ[ρ]
εθέντες ἐκ τῶν δήμων, ἀγαθῆι τύ[χη]
ι δεδόχθαι τῶι δήμωι ἐπαινέσαι [τ]
οὺς ταξιάρχους καὶ στεφανῶσαι ἕ
20 καστον αὐτῶν θαλλοῦ στεφάνωι ὑ[π]
ἐρ ὧν τὰς εὐθύνας δεδώκασιν, ὅπω[ς]
ἀν ὑπόμνημα εἶ τῆς ἐπιμελείας α[ὐ]
τῶν· ἀναγράψαι δὲ τόδε τὸ ψήφισμ[α]
καὶ τὰ ὀνόματα αὐτῶν πατρόθεν κ[α]
25 ὶ τοῦ δήμου ἐν στήληι λιθίνηι καὶ
[στῆ]σαι πρὸς τῶι ᾿Ελευσινίωι ἐν ἄ[σ]
[τει· εἰς δὲ] τὴν ἀναγραφὴν τῆς στήλ
[ης δοῦναι τὸν] ταμίαν τοῦ δήμου : Δ
[ΔΔ : δραχμὰς ἐκ τῶ]ν εἰς τὰ κατὰ ψηφ
30 [ίσματα ἀναλισκομένων τῶι] δήμωι.
[vacat   ]
[—————————————————————]

The horizontal cornice of the pediment, consisting of a taenia and an ovolo molding beneath it, is particularly heavy. Line 1 of the inscription is written on the taenia. The writing is tidy, plain, and of average quality for its period; letters are in general correctly articulated though not always "squared off". The circular letters vary in diameter but are throughout slightly smaller than the rest; sigma varies considerably in width. "Free ends" of strokes are not emphasized except in upsilon (see **120**). Although the decree is complete on what survives of the stone, the names of the taxiarchoi honored by it were to be inscribed below it (lines 23–25), and more of the stele has been lost than might casually appear.

The decree was passed in the fourth prytany of the year, which suggested to Pritchett a connection between the reference to the ἱερά of Demeter (line 15) and the Eleusinian Mysteries held a month previously in Boedromion. The latter may, he urged, have been the occasion for demonstrations against Demetrios Poliorketes, whose initiation into the Mysteries in Mounichion 303/2 had been irregular (Plutarch, *Demetrios* 26; Diodorus Siculus 20.110.1; cf. A. G. Woodhead, *Hesperia* 58, 1989, pp. 297–301), and the taxiarchoi as responsible for the maintenance of law and order would in that case have earned the special gratitude of Stratokles and those who supported his pro-Demetrian policy. For the duties of the taxiarchoi with regard to sacred processions see Busolt-Swoboda, II, pp. 1126–1127. Despite the sarcasm of Demosthenes (4.26), these duties represented a reasonable element of their overall responsibility, under the στρατηγοί, for the peace and security of Athens and Attika. Another element is represented in this same year by *IG* II², 500, proposed four months later than this decree by the same Memnon, son of Medon, of Aphidna, in honor of the taxiarchoi of an earlier year (305/4) for their maintenance of the city's defenses and for their general work of inspection. The defenses were currently of maximum public interest (see **109**). Other decrees in honor of taxiarchoi have been discovered in the Agora excavations, and for these see **182**, **185**, and **187**; see also *IG* II², 685. **295** honors a single taxiarchos by himself, as does *SEG* III, 116.

Line 4. Nikon, son of Theodoros, of Plotheia (*PA* 11117), the secretary of this year, was presumably the grandfather of the prytanis who bore the same name and was commended, together with his colleagues, in *Agora* XV, 85, at line 64 (there dated to 256/5). The Theodoros, son of Apollonios, of the same deme, who was commemorated by the grave monument *IG* II², 7238, of the 2nd century B.C., may well also belong to the same family. Lines 4–5. For Pyanopsion 25 as a meeting day for the Athenian assembly see J. D. Mikalson, *Sacred and Civil Calendar*, p. 77, who quotes lines 2–7 of this text.

Line 7. ᾿Εκκλησία. See **97**, line 7. Lines 8–9. Euthydikos, son of Kephisodoros, of Anagyrous, in all probability belonged to the well-known family of that deme in which the names Kephisodoros and Meidias were prominent, and his place in it is accepted by J. K. Davies, *Athenian Propertied Families*, p. 387, where he concludes the stemma there drawn up; see also *PA* 9719, with stemma. As the son of Kephisodoros (II) he will have been the grandson of the Meidias familiar in the pages of Demosthenes. Line 10. The decree was nonprobouleumatic; cf. P. J. Rhodes, *Athenian Boule*, p. 264. For the two vacant letter spaces, which serve to give emphasis to the name of the proposer, see A. S. Henry, *Prescripts*, p. 64 with note 60.

Lines 10–11. Memnon, son of Medon, of Aphidna, may well have been an ancestor of the Spoudias, son of Memnon, of that deme, who put **224** to the vote. Pritchett connected him with the prytanis Μελίτων Μέδοντος ᾿Αφιδναῖος of *Agora* XV, 275, line 10 (middle of the 1st century B.C.).

Lines 16–17. The taxiarchoi had already been given stephanoi by "those chosen from the demes for these purposes." Pritchett referred ἐπὶ ταῦτα to the εὐκοσμία and considered οἱ ἐπὶ ταῦτα αἱρεθέντες as the equivalent of οἱ λαχόντες ἐπιμεληταὶ τῆς εὐκοσμίας of *IG* II², 354 (*SEG* XXIII, 56, with earlier references), lines 15–19. O. Broneer pointed out in *Hesperia* 11, 1942, pp. 272–273, note 85 that this interpretation paid insufficient regard to ἐκ τῶν δήμων. The ἐπιμεληταί of *IG* II², 354 were concerned with εὐκοσμία περὶ τὸ θέατρον and were elected by the βουλή. It is to be presumed that the taxiarchoi had already been the subject of a decree or decrees passed by some body or bodies other than the Athenian assembly and that a committee formed by fellow demesmen of each taxiarchos was in charge of the ceremony at which the stephanoi were bestowed.

It may be noted that, whereas the award of a gold stephanos was, during the latter part of the 4th century, made subject to the successful passing of his *euthynai* by the recipient, this "saving clause" does not occur with grants of stephanoi of olive: see Henry, *Honours*, pp. 28 and 51, note 52. In the present case the taxiarchoi had in fact already passed their *euthynai*.

Line 17. Ἀγαθῆι Τύχηι had by this time become a regular formulaic element at this point of the prescript. Cf. **72**, commentary on lines 7–8.

Lines 21–23. The "hortatory intention" is of interest. Cf. **86**, commentary on lines 21–24. Line 23. Τὸν γραμματέα τοῦ δήμου, the presumed subject of the infinitive ἀναγράψαι, is here omitted, a rare phenomenon but not without its parallels. See **79**, line 19 and commentary.

Line 26. The stone did not move far from its original location in being built into the Post-Herulian Wall and provided additional evidence for the Eleusinion (see above). The site was doubtless chosen because of the special connection of the honors with the festival of Demeter. Line 28. The ταμίας τοῦ δήμου appears in this year for the last time as responsible for defraying the cost of stelai recording decrees. Cf. **120**, commentary on line 11. Lines 28–29. For the cost of the stele and the source of the funds see **120**, commentary on lines 11–13.

FRAGMENTS OF A DECREE

124. Three fragments of a flat-topped stele of Pentelic marble, with the upper moldings of the monument preserved on fragment *a* and its left side preserved on fragment *c*. Fragments *a* (I 219) and *b* (I 860) make a diagonal join on the left of the former and the right of the latter; fragment *c* (I 3619) may be exactly aligned with *a* + *b* on their left but does not quite make a direct join with them. Dates and places of discovery are as follows: fragment *a* on April 18, 1932, in a cistern in a mixed Greek-Byzantine context in the southwest corner of the Market Square (G 11); fragment *b* on May 23, 1933, in a Late Roman context east of the Tholos (H 11); fragment *c* on February 26, 1936, in a mediaeval storage pit on Kolonos Agoraios, south of the Hephaisteion (E 9).

Measurements of fragments *a* + *b*, as joined: H. 0.15 m.; W. 0.17 m.; Th. (inscribed face) 0.035 m.

c: H. 0.28 m.; W. 0.13 m.; Th. 0.047 m.

LH. 0.007 m. (omicron 0.0055 m.).

Στοιχ. Hor. 0.015 m.; Vert. 0.0163 m.

Ed. *a* only: B. D. Meritt, *Hesperia* 3, 1934, pp. 6–7, no. 7, with photograph. All fragments: Meritt, *Hesperia* 5, 1936, pp. 414–416, no. 12, with photograph. The calendric data are cited by W. K. Pritchett and O. Neugebauer, *Calendars*, p. 80; Meritt, *Hesperia* 33, 1964, p. 10.

a. 302/1 *a., pryt.* VII   ΣΤΟΙΧ. 26

                    [Θ]   ε   ο   [ι].
           [Ἐπὶ Νικοχ]λέους ἄρχον[τος ἐπὶ τῆ]
           ς Ἀν[τιγον]ίδος ἑβδόμη[ς πρυτανε]
           ίας ἧι Ν[ί]κων Θεοδώρου [Πλωθεὺς ἐ]
    5   γραμμά[τ]ευεν· Ποσιδεῶ[νος δευτέ]
           ραι μετ'[ε]ἰκάδας, [πρ]ώτ[ηι τῆς πρυτ]
           ανεία[ς· ᵛ ἐκκλησία ἐμ Πειραιεῖ τ]
           ῶν προ[έδρων ἐπεψήφιζεν ..⁶...]
           [.]ος Ἀν[......¹²..... καὶ συμπρό]
    10   [εδ]ροι· [————————————]
           [————————————]

The inscribed face is surmounted by an ovolo molding and taenia above it (on the latter of which line 1 is inscribed), similar in design to that illustrated by L. T. Shoe, *Profiles of Greek Mouldings*, 1936, pl. XXIV, no. 22. The horizontal striations of a toothed chisel are conspicuous on the taenia. The lettering is of good quality for its period, with some emphasis on the "free ends" of strokes and a genuine attempt (not always successful) at exactitude in the formation of individual letters. Alpha and lambda are noticeably "wide" in line 2 but less so elsewhere.

Line 6. [εἰ]κάδας Meritt: sufficient of the surface of the stone remains on the left to ensure the reading of iota, and the line of fracture seems to have followed the cut of the letter. Line 7. ἐν Διονύσου Meritt, M. H. Hansen (see below); ἐμ Πειραιεῖ W. A. McDonald, *Political Meeting Places*, p. 51, note 59 (see further below). Line 10. [εδρ]ο[ι ---] Meritt.

Line 4. On Nikon of Plotheia see **123**, line 4 and commentary. Lines 5–6. For Posideon 29 as a meeting day for the assembly see J. D. Mikalson, *Sacred and Civil Calendar*, pp. 95–96. If the restoration ἐμ Πειραιεῖ be accepted, this is the earliest instance of a meeting of the assembly so designated among the decrees discovered in the Agora excavations. For such meetings see McDonald, *Political Meeting Places*, pp. 51–56. Hansen (*GRBS* 20, 1979, pp. 149–156, esp. pp. 153–154 [= *Athenian Ecclesia*, pp. 73–80, esp. pp. 77–78]) contends that any *psephisma* dated to the first four days of a prytany must have been passed in an ἐκκλησία σύγκλητος (an emergency meeting summoned at short notice), and he cites this text as an example.

FRAGMENT OF A DECREE

125. A fragment of a stele of Pentelic marble (I 707), with part of the right side and the original back preserved, discovered on April 12, 1933, in a Late Roman context in the big drain at the northwest corner of the Library of Pantainos (Q 13).

H. 0.135 m.; W. 0.11 m.; Th. 0.064 m., decreasing to 0.05 m. at right edge.

LH. 0.006 m. (omicron 0.005 m., omega 0.004 m.).

Στοιχ. (square, with slight irregularities) 0.013 m.

Ed. J. H. Oliver, *Hesperia* 4, 1935, pp. 37–38, no. 6, with photograph, who adds that the restorations and commentary were provided by B. D. Meritt. W. K. Pritchett and O. Neugebauer (*Calendars*, pp. 83–84) quote this text but revise certain readings and offer a new text of lines 1–2, dissociating it from any necessary connection with the year of Nikokles.

a. 302/1 a., pryt. X(?)   ΣΤΟΙΧ. 27

```
        [――――――――――――――――――]
        [.........21.........]ΤΕ[....]
        [......13...... τῆς πρυτ]ανεία[ς· ἐ]
        [κκλησία κυρία· τῶν προέδ]ρων ἐπ[εψ]
        [ήφιζεν ........14.....]ου ᵛ ’Ικα[ρ]
    5   [ιεὺς καὶ συμπρόεδροι· ἔδ]οξεν τῶι
        [δήμωι· ........14..... ’Α]ναγυράσ
        [ιος εἶπεν· .....15........]Κ[...]
        [.........21.........]ΡΟΥ[...]
        [.........21.........]ΟΝ[....]
    10  [――――――――――――――――――]
```

Line 1. ΑΤΕ Oliver; ΣΤΕ Pritchett and Neugebauer, who identified the bottom oblique stroke of the sigma on the squeeze. Study of the stone suggests that no reading should be hazarded at this point. Lines 1–2 were read and restored by Meritt *apud* Oliver, with renumbering of the lines as follows, it being noted that the circumstances exactly suit the calendric requirements of 302/1 and that the restorations are based on the hypothesis that the inscription may be attributed to that year:

```
        [’Επὶ Νικοκλέους ἄρχοντος ἐπὶ τῆς]
        [Λεωντίδος δεκάτης πρυτανείας ἧ]
        [ι Νίκων Θεοδώρου Πλωθεὺς ἐγραμμ]
        [άτευεν· Μουνιχιῶνος δεκ]άτε[ι ἱστ]
    5   [αμένου, δεκάτει τῆς πρυτ]ανεία[ς·
```

Pritchett and Neugebauer, observing that the exact year could not be identified with assurance, proposed for lines 1–2 [.....11..... μετ’εἰκάδα]ς, τε[τάρτ|ει καὶ εἰκοστεῖ τῆς πρυτ]ανεία[ς· κτλ.]. Line 4. ΡΥ ᵛ Oliver, who supposed that ΠΟΥ had been intended by the mason; one space was left uninscribed to accommodate a correction which he at once noted as necessary but never in fact made. The first preserved letter, however, seems on the stone to be omicron, placed high within its stoichos, and it so appeared to Pritchett and Neugebauer on the squeeze. Line 8. ΑΟ[. . . .] Oliver.

The writing is moderate to poor, the letters being inconsistently formed (nu is a good example) but generally tidy. There is an inclination to use long horizontal strokes (gamma and epsilon). The abbreviated form of omega is also noteworthy.

Lines 4–5. Mounichion 10 is attested as a meeting-day of the assembly only in the restored portions of two inscriptions, of which this is one. See J. D. Mikalson, *Sacred and Civil Calendar*, p. 141.

Lines 5–6. The decree was nonprobouleumatic: cf. P. J. Rhodes, *Athenian Boule*, p. 264 (and corrigenda). Ἐκκλησία κυρία. See **101**, commentary on lines 7–8. Lines 9–10. Meritt suggested that the name might be Φυλαξίας Φανίου Ἀ]ναγυράσ[ιος (*PA* 15038), the proedros who put *IG* II², 483 to the vote in 304/3 and who is listed among the councillors of that year in *Agora* XV, 61, at line 178. He is further attested as the (former) owner of Glykera the wool worker in *SEG* XVIII, 36, side B, col. II, lines 240–241, part of *IG* II², 1554 and 1557/1558, to be dated between 330 and 310 B.C.: cf. *Agora* XV, index p. 465.

FRAGMENTS OF A DECREE (OR DECREES)

126. Two fragments of bluish Pentelic marble, which do not join and may not belong to the same document. Fragment *a* (I 4960) was discovered on June 11, 1937, in the original filling of the Post-Herulian Wall, over the paved court below Klepsydra (T 26–27): it preserves the left side of the stele to which it belongs but is otherwise broken all around. Fragment *b* (I 3918) was discovered on March 30, 1936, in a marble dump from the area of the eastern end of the Hephaisteion (F 7) and is broken all around.

a: H. 0.11 m.; W. 0.115 m.; Th. 0.077 m.

b: H. 0.084 m.; W. 0.185 m.; Th. 0.076 m.

LH. 0.005 m.

Στοιχ. (square) 0.01 m.

Ed. M. B. Walbank, *Hesperia* 58, 1989, pp. 91–92, no. 19, with photographs pl. 24. See also *SEG* XXXIX, 107.

ca. a. 302/1 *a.* ΣΤΟΙΧ.

(a)
```
   [------------------------------------]
   ι[-----------------------------------]
   τω[----------------------------------]
   νη[----------------------------------]
   ω[-----------------------------------]
5  δη[----------------------------------]
   αθ[----------------------------------]
   ι[-----------------------------------]
   τη[----------------------------------]
   ιε[----------------------------------]
10 [------------------------------------]
```

(b)
```
   [--------------------------------------]
   [--------------]ι[----------------------]
   [----------] τῶι δ[ήμωι(?) ------------]
   [---------]πᾶσι κα[--------------------]
   [--------]αν καὶ τὴν [-----------------]
5  [---------]ρονον βα[-------------------]
   [--------]εμος ἵνα [-------------------]
   [--------]ε[. ]ρ[---------------------]
   [--------------------------------------]
```

Walbank associated these two pieces by reason of the similarity of the marble employed, of the lettering, and of the stoichedon measurements and drew attention to their affinity in these respects with *IG* II², 503, of 302/1 (see also **193**). He also regarded *IG* II², 528, which has no secure date, as attributable to the same craftsman. The two fragments, however, were discovered in widely differing locations in the Agora, which does not lend credence to their likely association; and the resemblances, as often in such cases, may be ascribed to an overall similarity of style, taste, and practice among contemporary stonecutters, or to the character of an atelier, rather than to the activity of a single pair of hands. The dating nevertheless must be in the region of that of *IG* II², 503.

The meager remains offer no clue as to the contents, but the suggestion that they represent fragments of a decree or of two decrees is not unreasonable.

A BOARD OF OFFICIALS HONORED

127. A fragment of a stele of Pentelic marble (I 5824), with part of the right side and the original back preserved, discovered on May 9, 1939, in a context of the late 2nd–3rd century A.D. in a brick drain and shaft south of the Eleusinion (U 22:1).

H. 0.255 m.; W. 0.222 m.; Th. 0.155 m.
LH. *ca.* 0.008 m.
Στοιχ. (square, with slight irregularities) 0.016 m.

Ed. B. D. Meritt, *Hesperia* 13, 1944, pp. 243–246, no. 8, with photograph.

paullo ante a. 302/1 *a.*   ΣΤΟΙΧ. 31

```
        [--------------------------------]
        [ἐπειδὴ ------οἱ ἐπὶ -----ἄρχοντ]ο[ς ἦρξ]
        [αν τὴν ἀρχὴν καλῶς καὶ δικαί]ως, καὶ [περ]
        [ὶ πάντων ὧν ἐπεμελοῦντο τ]ὰς εὐθύνα[ς δ]
        [εδώκασιν, ἐπαινέσαι αὐ]τοὺς ἀρετῆς ἕ[ν]
   5    [εκα καὶ δικαιοσύνης τῆ]ς εἰς τὸν δῆμον
        [τὸν Ἀθηναίων καὶ στεφ]ανῶσαι ἕκαστον
        [αὐτῶν χρυσῶι στεφάνω]ι ἀπὸ : Χ : δραχμῶν Ε
        [----------------K]ηφισιέα, Νίκωνα
        [---------------, Δ]ιόφαντον Διονυ
   10   [--------------, --]νόστρατον Εὐφρ
        [--------------, ----]ν Εὐφήρου Αὐρί[δ]
        [ην, ---------------]τους Ἀφιδναῖ[ο]
        [ν· στεφανῶσαι δὲ καὶ αὐτῶ]ν τὸν κληρ[ωτὸ]
        [ν γραμματέα ------------]
   15   [--------------------------]
```

The well-formed and precise lettering of this text was justly compared by Meritt with that of *IG* II², 169 + 472 (*SEG* XXI, 335), of 306/5 B.C., which could well be the work of the same craftsman. The letters give the appearance of unusual width in proportion to height. "Free ends" of strokes are frequently enlarged and depressed, most notably in nu and upsilon, although hardly at all in tau. Junctions of strokes are generally made with care. The crossbar of alpha is twice omitted (lines 6 and 7).

The date of the inscription, conditioned in general terms by the lettering, is given a *terminus ante quem* by the provision in line 7 for the golden stephanoi, for which a specific cost is prescribed. This formula was abandoned by, or at latest in the course of, the year 302/1: see A. S. Henry, *Honours*, pp. 25–28, and **112**, commentary on lines 5–7.

The board of officials commended in the decree may well have been that of the sitophylakes (see **194**), concerning whose numbers and duties see Aristotle, *Athenaion Politeia* 51.3; Meritt, *op. cit.*, pp. 244–245; W. B. Dinsmoor, *Hesperia* 23, 1954, pp. 305–306; Busolt-Swoboda, II, pp. 1119–1120; J. J. Keaney, *Historia* 19, 1970, pp. 331–332; R. S. Stroud, *Hesperia* 43, 1974, p. 180, with notes 90, 91. They were selected by lot (Lysias 22.16; Aristotle, *loc. cit.*). At this stage in their history, during the period of the twelve phylai, there were probably twelve members of the board, six for the city and six for Peiraieus, each section having its own secretary. The six for whose names this text provides space probably constituted the half-board concerned with the city, and they are cited in the official order of phylai (Kephisia, Erechtheis III; Auridai, Hippothontis X; Aphidna, Aiantis XI). Aristotle refers to a total board of thirty-five (twenty for the city and fifteen for Peiraieus) as obtaining in his own time; but it appears that this was probably no more than a temporary enlargement from an original board constituted of one member per phyle, perhaps to deal with the shortages of the 320's and their aftermath. If that is so, Aristotle's information, the basis of lexicographical and other treatments of this board, is not be taken as a statement of regular practice.

Lines 7–13. The formulation whereby a list of the honorands is included in direct sequence from the cost provision for their stephanoi is unusual. Henry (*Honours*, p. 47, note 7[v]) properly draws attention to it and adduces *IG* II², 488 (*SEG* XXIII, 62, XXXIV, 75), of 303/2, and 896 (on which cf. S. V. Tracy, *Hesperia* 47, 1978, pp. 255–257), of 186/5, as comparanda. The officials named cannot otherwise be identified. Διόφαντος Διονυσοδώρου Φηγούσιος was secretary of the boule in 303/2 (see **116**), but Phegous was a deme of the phyle Erechtheis, which already possesses its member of this board in E– – – – of Kephisia, and the name of Diophantos Diony– – – here must be differently interpreted.

Lines 13–14. On the κληρωτὸς γραμματεύς see **194**, lines 7–8 and 22–23; *IG* II², 1711, lines 6–7; M. Crosby, *Hesperia* 6, 1937, pp. 446 and 460, no. 8, lines 8–9.

FRAGMENT OF A DECREE

128. Two nonjoining fragments of a stele of Hymettian marble, of which one (fragment *a*, I 3687) has the left side preserved but is broken elsewhere and the other (fragment *b*, I 2701) is broken all around. Fragment *a* was discovered on March 3, 1936, in the southern part of Kolonos Agoraios, in an unknown context; fragment *b* was discovered on April 6, 1935, in a wall of a modern house about twenty meters southwest of the Tholos (F 13).

a: H. 0.061 m.; W. 0.085 m.; Th. 0.017 m.

b: H. 0.105 m.; W. 0.085 m.; Th. 0.031 m.

LH. 0.005 m.

Στοιχ. (almost square) Hor. 0.007 m.; Vert. 0.0075 m.

Ed. E. Schweigert, *Hesperia* 8, 1939, pp. 44–45, no. 12, with photograph, and an additional note, *Hesperia* 9, 1940, p. 351.

ca. a. 300 *a.*   ΣΤΟΙΧ. 26

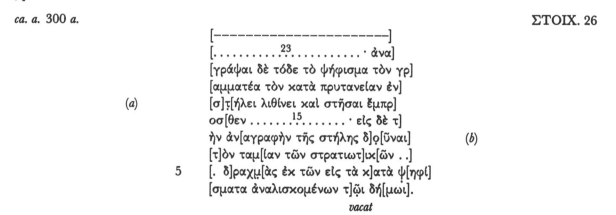

The lettering of this decree was originally included by Schweigert among the epigraphical considerations which necessitated "a date about the beginning of the last quarter of the third century B.C." This coincided with what he believed to be the requirements with regard to payment for the stele. Reconsideration of the letter forms and of the role of the Treasurer of the Military Fund in the payment for **114** and **122** prompted him to the revised hypothesis that this inscription, together with *IG* II², 806 and 809 (which contain the same formulas and comparable lettering), deserved an earlier date. For *IG* II², 806 see further M. J. Osborne, *Naturalization* I, pp. 119–121, D 48, *Naturalization* II, p. 127. The strict stoichedon order, the generous spacing, and the shapes of the letters, especially of mu, nu, and sigma, reinforce this conclusion in detail. Despite this general precision, the crossbar of alpha is regularly omitted, and the writing (deceptively, for dating purposes) is scratchy and second rate. "Free ends" of strokes are not emphasized.

Line 3. The verb of payment is δοῦναι, not μερίσαι: the former is in regular use to the end of the 4th century, while μερίσαι, first attested in 302/1, becomes more familiar in the 3rd century. See **139**; T. Eide, *Symbolae Osloenses* 59, 1984, pp. 21–28; A. S. Henry, *ZPE* 78, 1989, pp. 267–273.

Line 4. The ταμίας τῶν στρατιωτικῶν, for whom cf. **114**, commentary, appears as the officer paying for that monument, without any definition of the source of the funds on which he is to draw, and as paying for **122** and for *IG* II², 806 and 809, as here, from the "analiskomena fund". When Schweigert published his *editio princeps*, the responsibility of the Military Treasurer for expenditure on stelai had not been thought to antedate 229 B.C., a *terminus post quem* he was able to revise in the light of **122**. The source of funds named is a further indication of the date of the decree, since this formula is little attested after the early 3rd century. Cf. Henry, *Chiron* 14, 1984, p. 63, confirming the view long ago of W. Larfeld, *Handbuch der griechischen Epigraphik*, II, *Die attischen Inschriften*, 1902, p. 722.

It may be added that this present text, **122**, and *IG* II², 806 and 809 are not necessarily to be closely linked in date, even though Schweigert appeared to treat them as a quartet. Osborne (*Naturalization* II, p. 127) wrote of them as all clearly attributable to the year of **122** (defined by him as "*ca.*" 302): but they are not so attributable. *IG* II², 806 contains phraseology, present as well as reasonably restored, that should place it not earlier than the mid-280's. *IG* II², 809, like the present text, could be assigned to any year from 302 onwards into the early 3rd century, in which the Military Treasurer might be responsible for disbursement (i.e., excluding the known period when the exetastes and the trittyarchoi demonstrably hold this responsibility; see **129**). **122** on the other hand seems to be firmly (and not merely approximately) located in 302; see the commentary *ad loc.* Henry (*ZPE, loc. cit.*) follows Osborne, although with some justified reserve.

Thus the text under consideration must be reckoned to have a *terminus post quem* of 302 and could without injustice be assigned to any part of the periods 302–299/8 or 295–290. Of the alternatives, the former is perhaps to be preferred.

MILITARY COMMANDERS AND TROOPS HONORED

129 (Pl. 14). A fragment of a stele of Hymettian marble (I 5439), with part of the smoothly finished right side preserved but otherwise broken all around, discovered on May 12, 1938, in a late wall northeast of the Odeion, west of the north end of the Stoa of Attalos (N 8).

H. 0.24 m.; W. 0.194 m.; Th. 0.094 m.
LH. 0.006 m. (omicron 0.005 m.).
Στοιχ. (square, but with slight irregularities) 0.012–0.0125 m.

Ed. B. D. Meritt, *Hesperia* 11, 1942, pp. 278–280, no. 53, with photograph. See also *SEG* XXIX, 92.

a. 301/300–298/7 *a.*   ΣΤΟΙΧ. 30

```
                [-------------------------]
                [......13......  εὐνοίας ἕν]εκα [καὶ φι]
                [λοτιμίας τῆς εἰς τὴν βο]υλὴν καὶ τὸν [δ]
                [ῆμον τὸν Ἀθηναίων· ἐπαι]νέσαι δὲ καὶ Ὑ
                [........17........ Ἀ]μεινίαν Ξυπετ
        5       [αιόνα ....11.....]ἔα κ[α]ὶ τὰς ὑπηρεσ
                [ίας καὶ τοὺς στρατι]ώτας τοὺς μετ'αὐτ
                [ῶν οἱ .....12.....]σαν τὴν ἐν Τορνέα
                [ι, καὶ στεφανῶσαι θα]λλοῦ στεφάνωι· ἀν
                [αγράψαι δὲ τόδε τὸ ψή]φισμα τὸν γραμμ
        10      [ατέα τὸν κατὰ πρυταν]είαν ἐν στή[λει λ]
                [ιθίνει καὶ στῆσαι ἐν τ]εῖ αὐλεῖ [..5...]
                [....10.... · εἰς δὲ τὴ]ν ἀναγραφ[ὴν τῆς]
                [στήλης δοῦναι τὸν ἐξ]εταστὴν κα[ὶ τοὺ]
                [ς τριττυάρχους ....δραχμ]άς. vacat
```

The shallow, rather slapdash lettering of this text is characteristic of the period; cf. M. J. Osborne, *ZPE* 19, 1975, pp. 169–170, note 15, and for the cruciform phi see **102**. The awkward rendering of rho and of the circular letters is noteworthy, as are the long chisel strokes used in most occurrences of sigma.

The dating of this text, which Meritt in the *editio princeps* placed in 301/300, depends upon two principal factors: (1) the presence of the exetastes and trittyarchoi as the officials responsible for the payment for the inscription of the decree, and (2) the career of Ameinias of Xypete, the honorand named in lines 4–5, of whom something is known from literary sources. These factors require some consideration in detail.

(1) The period during which the exetastes and trittyarchoi served as disbursing officers in the matter of payment for stelai was brief, and the surviving texts that refer to them are few. For the evidence see most usefully C. Habicht, *Untersuchungen*, pp. 7–8 with note 30; A. S. Henry, *Chiron* 14, 1984, pp. 63–68 (on this text esp. pp. 64–65) and *ZPE* 78, 1989, pp. 267–270. As Henry has reemphasized, they were essentially military officials, "the exetastes being the paymaster of the mercenary soldiers and the trittyarchs officials concerned with military and naval finance." The earliest date to which they can be confidently assigned in their present capacity is the second prytany of 299/8,

the year of *IG* II², 641, a text for the inscribing costs of which they were responsible. **162**, however, the precise date of which has been the subject of controversy, may provide evidence that they were fulfilling this function earlier in 299, in the ninth prytany of the year 300/299. Because of the paucity of the evidence, no firm date can be given for any other stele for which they were responsible; but it may be reasonably assumed that that responsibility did not outlast the regime of the "tyrant" Lachares; see **162–166**. They appear for the last time in the ninth prytany of 295/4, but as paying for the erection of statues voted in the decrees in question, not as responsible for the inscribing of them: see *IG* II², 646 and 648, the latter without a clear date in its surviving section but surely of a date compatible with the former. On these texts see further Osborne, *Naturalization* I, pp. 144–150, D 68, 69, *Naturalization* II, pp. 144–153 (on the arrangements for payment esp. pp. 152–153).

Although, as noted above, the exetastes was an official (evidently elected) whose ordinary concern was with the mercenary troops (cf. *IG* II², 1270), his presence here has no connection with the fact that στρατιῶται are specifically mentioned, as M. Launey apparently thought (*Recherches sur les armées hellénistiques* II, 1950, p. 651, note 4). On the trittyarchoi see Busolt-Swoboda, II, pp. 972–973. On both exetastes and trittyarchoi see also W. S. Ferguson, *CP* 24, 1929, pp. 16–17, and references there.

(2) The defeat of Antigonos and Demetrios at Ipsos in summer 301 led in Athens to the overthrow of the democracy that had so fawned upon Demetrios. Stratokles, its most notable protagonist, was responsible for a decree in Metageitnion 301/300 (*IG* II², 640), but thereafter there was a reaction, of the circumstances of which nothing is known, resulting in what Ferguson (*Hellenistic Athens*, pp. 124–135) described as "the rule of the moderates". In effect this seems to have been a junta headed by the στρατηγοί, and their history was to some extent clarified by the publication of *P. Oxy.* 2082. Fragments 1 and 2 of this chronicle, in conjunction with the material of *P. Oxy.* 1235, lines 105–112, enabled a more explicit account of the rise to power of Lachares to be suggested. Ferguson (*CP* 24, 1929, pp. 1–31) provided an analysis that was for a number of years generally accepted but which was drastically revised by Habicht (*Untersuchungen*, pp. 16–21; for the present text see esp. pp. 20–21). Fragment 2 of the chronicle names Ameinias as having been put to death on a popular vote instigated by Lachares. This condemnation followed a sequence of events in which a quarrel within the junta had caused Charias, the στρατηγὸς ἐπὶ τῶν ὅπλων, to seize the Akropolis, in association, presumably, with Lysandros and Peithias as well as Ameinias, for all were condemned by a single decree. Habicht points out that the three latter cannot be assumed to have been στρατηγοί at the time, and the first two of them may not have held that office at any time, although the present text clearly implies that, on the occasion for which he was honored, Ameinias will have done so. Lachares, whom the papyrus names as commander of the mercenary forces, had the resources and the popular support to dislodge them and to establish himself as an effective autocrat, with a rule initially perhaps akin to that of Demetrios of Phaleron in the decennium 317–307 (cf. Pausanias 1.25.7) but later of increasing harshness. Cf. also Osborne, *Naturalization* II, pp. 144–153, esp. pp. 148–149, and on Lachares' tyranny in general, H. Berve, *Die Tyrannis bei den Griechen*, 1967, pp. 386–389 and 707–708.

Ferguson believed, on his interpretation of the evidence, the date of Lachares' seizure of power to be "about the time of the Dionysiac festival in 300 B.C." Since the present decree must antedate Ameinias' execution, its date of necessity was 301/300, and more precisely between Metageitnion and Elaphebolion of that year; and this, adopting Ferguson's analysis of events, was the date noted above as assigned by Meritt when the inscription first came to light. The victory mentioned in the text was reasonably to be connected with a στρατία referred to in fragment 1 of the papyrus; and this connection may stand, even if the date and occasion of the military operations be regarded as other than those identified by Ferguson.

Habicht's study has shown, on the other hand, that the stasis between Charias (together with his colleagues) and Lachares, while on the evidence of fragment 3 of the papyrus antedating the death of the Macedonian king Kassandros in 298/7, need not have antedated it by much. If, as he also believes, the data of fragments 1 and 2 of *P. Oxy.* 2082 belong closely together in time, and if (as Ferguson and Meritt held) the expedition for which Ameinias is here honored is indeed that of the papyrus, the present text is likely to belong to an earlier stage of the year 298/7, with decree, stasis, and the death of Kassandros occurring rapidly in succession. But the expedition and the decree could stand at a greater interval from the stasis and be attributable to 300/299 or 299/8: and it could be that the conflict at Tornea (the location of which is in any case unknown) referred to in lines 7–8 bears no relation to that mentioned in the papyrus. See also on these matters N. G. L. Hammond and F. W. Walbank, *A History of Macedonia* III, 1988, pp. 204–207.

It emerges, therefore, that 301/300–298/7, as shown here at the head of the text, represents the maximum span within which the present decree is to be dated. But the exetastes and trittyarchoi may not have received their responsibilities for the payment for stelai immediately upon the assumption of effective power by the junta, and it may be unwise so to press matters as to make this text potentially a criterion of the earliest evidence for them. A modified dating, in consequence, of 300/299–298/7 would confine it within a span that can be clearly asserted, and to that extent it is to be associated with the texts of that period that appear below at **162–164**.

Lines 1–2. εὐνοίας καὶ φιλοτιμίας τῆς εἰς κτλ. One of the most frequent formulations of merit. See A. S. Henry, *Honours*, p. 42.

Line 4. An Ameinias of the same deme (*PA* 682), whose son put *IG* II², 796 to the vote in 305/4 (for the date see Meritt, *Hesperia* 5, 1936, p. 303, with references), may have been a family connection. Lines 5–6. On ὑπηρεσία see **62**, commentary on lines 4–5. Line 8. This appears to be a comprehensive grant of stephanoi of olive, in a category not among those listed *exempli gratia* by Henry (*Honours*, p. 39) but worthy of note.

Lines 11–12. Meritt suggested τ]εῖ αὐλεῖ [τοῦ βο|υλευτηρίου but preferred τ]εῖ αὐλεῖ [τοῦ να|οῦ τοῦ Ἄρεως as more appropriate to the activities for which the honorands received the city's acclaim. However, the 5th-century Temple of Ares rediscovered in the Agora is now considered to have been systematically dismantled at its original site, perhaps at Acharnai, during the Early Roman period and reerected in the city. See *Agora* XIV, pp. 162–165; *Agora Guide* ³, pp. 106–109; J. M. Camp, *Athenian Agora*, pp. 184–186. A sanctuary of the god must be presumed to have existed somewhere in the Classical city center, and this stele might indeed have been erected in its precinct or antechamber. These lines are nevertheless cited among testimonia on the Bouleuterion in *Agora* III, p. 136, no. 430.

Line 14. [ς τριττυάρχους ᵛΔΔᵛ δραχμ]άς Meritt: but the vagaries in the recording of numerals in these decrees make it unwise to offer a restoration with any assurance.

FRAGMENT OF A DECREE OF A SOCIETY OF ORGEONES

130. A fragment of a pedimental stele of Hymettian marble (I 2161), with the left side preserved but otherwise broken all around, discovered on December 13, 1934, in a wall of a modern house over the southeastern part of the Odeion (M 11). A wide molding and part of the field of the pediment survive above the inscription.

H. 0.218 m.; W. 0.156 m.; Th. 0.054 m.
LH. *ca.* 0.007 m.

Ed. B. D. Meritt, *Hesperia* 10, 1941, pp. 56–57, no. 20, with photograph.

ca. a. 300 *a.*(?)   NON-ΣΤΟΙΧ. *ca.* 31

```
        Μνησιγείτων εἶπεν· [ἔδοξεν τοῖς ὀργεῶσι]·
        ἐπειδὴ Μνήσαρχος [ἀνὴρ ἀγαθός ἐστι πε]
        ρὶ τὸν δῆμον τὸ[ν Ἀθηναίων καὶ ἀποδεί]
        χνυται εὔνο[υς ὢν καὶ ἀεὶ φιλοτιμού]
   5    μενος τ[ῶι τε δήμωι καὶ τῶι κοινῶι τῶι ὀ]
        ργέων, δε[δόχθαι τοῖς ὀργεῶσι ἐπαινέσαι]
        [Μ]νήσαρ[χον – – – – – – – – – – – – – – – – –]
        [– – – – – – – – – – – – – – – – – – – – – – – –]
```

The writing is thin, disjointed, and amateurish, although Meritt observed that it is at least no worse than that of *IG* II², 378 (of at latest 294/3; see p. 146 above). The wide omega is reminiscent of the 4th century rather than the 3rd, and other letters, despite poor workmanship, show "standard" late 4th-century characteristics. There is a sporadic effort to accentuate "free ends" of letters.

This text represents one of only five decrees found in the Agora to 1968 that certainly or almost certainly emanate from a group of orgeones; for the others see **161**, **235**, **245**, and **329**. For other decrees of orgeones see *IG* II², 1249, 1252, and 1253 (*SEG* XIV, 82, XXVI, 135), 1255, 1256, 1259, 1283 (*SEG* XXIX, 136, with earlier references), 1284, 1294, 1301, 1314–1316, 1324, 1327, 1328 (*SEG* XXV, 159), 1329, 1334, and 1337. Groups which referred to themselves as thiasotai or by the name of a god (e.g., Dionysiastai) were of the same general character (cf. T. J. Cadoux, *OCD* ², *s.v.* Orgeones, with bibliography) and are well represented by other texts. See in particular the long discussion by W. S. Ferguson and A. D. Nock in *HarvThRev* 37, 1944, pp. 61–174, under the title "The Attic Orgeones and the Cult of Heroes" (on this inscription esp. pp. 82–83).

Lines 1–2. Mnesigeiton and Mnesarchos are not otherwise known. They may have been related; see Ferguson and Nock, *op. cit.*, p. 82; *Hesperia*, Index to vols. 1–10, p. 108.

Lines 5–6. ὀ|ργεών⟨ων⟩ Meritt, supposing a scribal error. A genitive form ὀργέων is quoted from Lysias (fr. 112 Sauppe), as Meritt noted, but rejected as a *lectio falsa* by LSJ, *s.v.* ὀργεών. Ferguson observed that the same genitive should properly be read in Aristotle, *Ethika Eudemia* 1241b25, and argued its correctness here. The supposed nominative of this genitive, ὀργεύς, is accepted in the *Supplement* (1968) to LSJ, p. 110. It is probable that the datives in lines 1 and 6 should, in consequence, be restored as ὀργεῦσι in preference to Meritt's ὀργεῶσι.

FRAGMENT OF A PROXENY DECREE

131. A fragment of a stele of Pentelic marble (I 5773), with part of the left side and original back preserved though much worn, but the stone elsewhere very battered and broken, discovered on April 13, 1939, in the wall of a late pithos north of Klepsydra (T 26).

H. 0.13 m.; W. 0.144 m.; Th. 0.05 m.
LH. 0.008 m.
Στοιχ. (square) *ca.* 0.016 m.: a measurement of five letters gives 0.079 m. horizontally and 0.077 m. vertically.

Ed. W. K. Pritchett, *Hesperia* 15, 1946, pp. 159–160, no. 16, with photograph. See *SEG* XXIV, 114, with additional reference to J. Pečírka, *Formula*, p. 133.

saec. IV *a., p. post.*   ΣΤΟΙΧ. 22

```
       [------------------]
       [..........18.......... και ε]
       [ἵνα]ι πρ[όξενον και εὐεργέτ]
       [ην] Ἀθηνα[ίων και αὐτὸν και ἐ]
       [κ]γόνους· [εἶναι δ'αὐτοῖς γῆς]
       και οἰκία[ς ἔγκτησιν κατὰ τ]
   5   οὺς νόμους, [ὅπως ἂν εἰδῶσιν]
       πάντες [ὅτι .....13......]
       [------------------]
```

The well-formed and generously spaced lettering is in general "standard" of the later 4th century. "Free ends" of letters are frequently emphasized, especially in upsilon (see commentary on **120**). Mu is unusually straight sided; the angled strokes of the alpha in line 6 are crossed at the top in a manner anticipating later apex writing.

Lines 1–3. For the formulation, that most usually employed when *proxenia* and *euergesia* are extended not only to the immediate recipient but also to his descendants, cf. A. S. Henry, *Honours*, p. 137. Lines 3–5. For the award of γῆς και οἰκίας ἔγκτησις see Pečírka, *Formula*. Pritchett dated this fragment to the end of the 4th century on the supposition that the inclusion of the words κατὰ τοὺς νόμους with the formula required it. Pečírka, however, demonstrated (*Formula*, pp. 140–142) that the evidence for the inclusion of κατὰ τὸν νόμον (or κατὰ τοὺς νόμους) is spread between 325/4 and the first half of the 2nd century B.C. No *terminus post quem*, unless in the vaguest terms *ca.* 350, can be suggested, since the inclusion of the phrase is somewhat irregular; see Henry, *Honours*, p. 214. The date assigned to the inscription by Pečírka in his table on pp. 156–157 is here adopted (cf. *SEG* XXIV, *loc. cit.*), but a dating in the fourth quarter of the century rather than the third is on balance more likely.

Lines 5–6. Or, with the placing of a colon after νόμους, [ὅπως δ'ἂν εἰδῶσι]| πάντες followed, in all probability, by the provision that the stele be inscribed. For the "hortatory intention" see **86**, commentary on lines 21–24.

FRAGMENT OF A DECREE(?)

132. A fragment of a stele of Pentelic marble (I 5792), broken all around including the back, discovered on April 28, 1939, in the wall of a modern house west of the Panathenaic Way and southwest of the Eleusinion (R 21).

H. 0.107 m.; W. 0.092 m.; Th. 0.036 m.
LH. 0.007–0.008 m.
Στοιχ. (square) 0.0158 m.

Ed. M. B. Walbank, *Hesperia* 58, 1989, pp. 84–85, no. 10, with photograph pl. 20.

saec. IV *a., p. post.*   ΣΤΟΙΧ.

```
       [------------------]
       [--------]ωνε[--------]
       [--------]ἐπιχ[--------]
       [-------] Θεογ[-------]
       [------] Ἀθην[α------]
   5   [--------]ιαι[--------]
       [------------------]
```

Walbank observed that this text may be the work of the craftsman responsible for **92**, of the archonship of Hegesias (324/3 B.C.), and in consequence he gave it a date in the same period. In so far as fourteen clearly surviving letters can be sufficiently indicative, identity of stonecutter (if acknowledged) and comparability of style (if admitted) impose no more than a proximity of date, within a decade perhaps, in either direction. The date, in the latter part of the 4th century, might be more closely expressed in terms such as those of **98**.

Interpreting the fragment as part of the upper section of a decree, he suggested that τῶν προέδρ]ων ἐ[πεψήφιζεν be restored in line 1, with ᾿Επιχ[ηφίσιος in line 2 the demotic of the proedros named. Θεογ–––– in line 3 would thus represent the patronymic of the proposer. See, however, *SEG* XXXIX, 92, where the text is noted as "too fragmentary to classify with confidence as a decree."

FRAGMENT OF A DECREE(?)

133. A fragment of a stele of Hymettian marble (I 2777), broken on all sides, discovered on April 18, 1935, in a context of Late Roman date over the auditorium of the Odeion (M 10).

H. 0.085 m.; W. 0.12 m.; Th. 0.037 m.
LH. 0.007 m.
Στοιχ. (square) *ca.* 0.012 m.

Ed. B. D. Meritt, *Hesperia* 29, 1960, p. 51, no. 64, with photograph pl. 13. See also *SEG* XIX, 62. *SEG* XXI, 347 (A. N. Oikonomides, *The Two Agoras in Ancient Athens*, 1964, pp. 98–99, no. 94, with fuller restoration of the text). See also *SEG* XLII, 93.

saec. IV *a., p. post.*   ΣΤΟΙΧ.

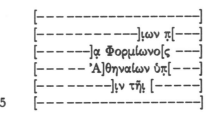

Line 1. So Meritt; but the first surviving letter might be tau and the last surviving letter gamma. Line 3. ὑσ–––– Meritt, followed by Oikonomides (see below). The stone has Υᷛ. A parallel-sided sigma is perhaps unlikely at so early a date.

The text of Oikonomides assumed allusions to Pasion and Phormion (*PA* 11672 and 14951; see for fuller detail J. K. Davies, *Athenian Propertied Families*, pp. 427–437), the famous bankers of 4th-century Athens. He claimed that in lines 3–4 there is a reference to the proving of Pasion's will in the Stoa Poikile described in Demosthenes 45.17–18, and he restored [–––– Πασ]ίων Π[ασικλέους(?) ᾿Αχαρνεὺς | –––– παρ]ὰ Φορμίωνο[ς ––– | διαιτητῶν δ' ᾿Α]θηναίων ὕσ[τερον –––|–––– διαθήκ]ην τὴν [Πασίωνος ––––].

The inscription seems to belong to the later 4th century but might be as late as the early 3rd. In appearance neat, the writing varies in detail of individual letters, especially mu and omega. Eta in line 3 is distinctive. "Free ends" are in places slightly deepened but not enlarged.

Line 3. Unless Oikonomides' hypothesis be accepted, Phormion is not otherwise identifiable. It was not an uncommon name.

A CITIZEN OF THESSALIAN LARISA HONORED(?)

134 (Pl. 15). A fragment of a stele of Pentelic marble (I 5256), with part of the flat top and (apparently) the original back preserved, discovered on February 24, 1938, among debris under the modern floor of the sanctuary in the Church of the Hypapanti (T 21).

The surface of the stone has been sheared away at the top and to the left, with the result that the total dimensions of the fragment, both horizontally and vertically, are considerably greater than those of the surviving inscribed area. There was a vertical space above the first (*vacat*) line noted, equal to five inscribed lines.

H. 0.36 m.; W. 0.20 m.; Th. 0.166 m.
LH. 0.006–0.007 m.
Στοιχ. (square) 0.015 m.

Unpublished.

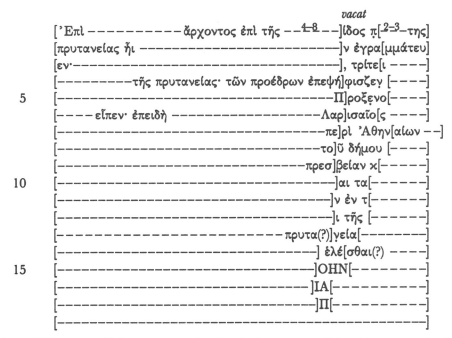

The lettering of this text, which suggests a date in the latter part of the 4th century (and possibly as late as the early 3rd), appears neater and more precise than it proves to be on closer inspection. It has a hesitant quality, and the strokes are not firmly made. The central horizontal of epsilon is short, and at times very short; the circular letters are smaller than the rest, and theta (line 7, probably also line 15) lacks a central dot. In xi (line 5) a dot replaces the central horizontal, and there is no upright stroke. There is a feeble attempt to enlarge some "free ends" of strokes.

Line 4. ἐπεψή]φισζεν. For the spelling see **102**, commentary on lines 7–8 and references there. Line 5. In this position, Π]ρόξενο[ς or Π]ροξένο[υ, the name or patronymic of the proposer. Line 15. Presumably Ἀ]θην[αι— —.

Substantial though this fragment appears to be, it admirably succeeds in denying to the inquirer that essential information by which its date and contents might be more accurately assessed. Even one or two more letters preserved at the point of fracture on either side might have served to resolve many obscurities. The length of line may be determined from lines 3–4, where (unless a reference to the type of assembly intervened, which seems unlikely) a minimum of ten and a maximum of thirteen letters are to be presumed in the lacuna. The prytany date will have been the 13th, 23rd, or (if the date be earlier than 307/6) 33rd of the month. Assemblies are not to be expected in the first four days of a prytany, a general rule to which exceptions are few: see M. H. Hansen, *GRBS* 20, 1979, pp. 153–154 and 23, 1982, pp. 335–336 (= *Athenian Ecclesia*, pp. 77–78, 81, 87–88), and *Athenian Assembly*, p. 31. Hansen explains all such exceptions as ἐκκλησίαι σύγκλητοι, regular assemblies specially summoned.

Two further factors condition any attempt at restoration of the text: (1) the prytany was the first or the fifth of the year (line 1); the last surviving letter is almost certainly pi and can only be epsilon (for ἕ[κτης, ἑ[βδομῆς, ἐ[νάτης, or ἑ[νδεκάτης) if the mason omitted the central horizontal stroke of that letter; (2) the demotic of the γραμματεύς ended in nu (line 2).

During the period to which the text may be assigned, three years only are known to fulfill this latter requirement: (1) 323/2, archon Kephisodoros, γραμματεύς Archias, son of Pythodoros, of Alopeke, (2) 305/4, archon Euxenippos, γραμματεύς Autolykos, son of Lykos, of Alopeke, (3) 299/8, archon Euktemon, γραμματεύς Theophilos, son of Xenophon, of Kephale. All these years were ordinary in the festival calendar. Aside from the decennium of the government of Demetrios of Phaleron, for which see p. 161 above, and to which this inscription is unlikely to belong, there are many archon years in which the demotic of the γραμματεύς is quite unknown, and six such years may well enter into consideration here: those of Lykiskos (344/3), Pythodelos (336/5), Aristophanes (331/30), Chremes (326/5), Mnesidemos (298/7), and Antiphates (297/6). The present text might belong to any of these years.

The remains of the decree below the prescript suggest that the honorand is a citizen of Larisa in Thessaly (line 6), who has shown himself especially deserving of reward in his relationship with the Athenians (line 7), and that there have been dealings with the demos (line 8) in respect of an embassy (line 9) from his city to Athens or *vice versa*. It may also be that within the present or subsequent prytany (line 13) the demos will select a delegation (line 14) to carry these pourparlers further.

It is remarkable that any attempt, on the basis of one of the three years identified above, at a restoration of the prescript seems to encounter anomalies, or at least calls for a combination of unusual features that individually can be paralleled and accepted, with the result that its total acceptability might be called into question. The possible dates in the festival calendar prove to be insufficient to fill line 3, while at the same time the prytany date in lines 3–4 is liable to overfill the space available. As mentioned above, it appears necessary to omit any mention of the type of the assembly (ἐκκλησία, ἐκκλησία κυρία, etc.), for which see A. S. Henry, *Prescripts*, pp. 38–39: but the omission is not unusual in this period. More surprising is the evident impossibility of accommodating an enactment formula ἔδοξεν (τῆι βουλῆι καὶ) τῶι δήμωι. Yet this omission also is not uncommon; for the examples at this period see Henry, *Prescripts*, pp. 44–45, 61.

The calendar for 323/2 is relatively well known; see p. 139 above. The phyle Hippothontis held the first prytany, Pandionis the fifth. The former might produce equations Hekatombaion 13 = pryt. I, 13, Hekatombaion 23 = pryt. I, 23, Metageitnion 3 = pryt. I, 33, the latter Posideon 7 = pryt. V, 13, Posideon 17 = pryt. V, 23, Posideon 27 = pryt. V, 33. None of these, however, proves satisfactory. More hopeful is an attribution to 305/4, in the period of twelve phylai, for the calendar of which see B. D. Meritt, *Hesperia* 33, 1964, pp. 9–10. The identities of the phylai in the relevant prytanies are not known, but they were not Erechtheis or Demetrias (see *IG* II², 796, 797). A text may be worked out *exempli gratia* for the fifth prytany, to which Hippothontis may be assigned, as follows:

a. 305/4 a., *pryt.* V   ΣΤΟΙΧ. 46

[Ἐπὶ Εὐξενίππου ἄρχοντος ἐπὶ τῆς Ἱπποθωντ]ίδος π[έμπτης]
[πρυτανείας ἧι Αὐτόλυκος Λύκου Ἀλωπεκῆθε]ν ἐγρα[μμάτευ]
[εν· ᵛ Μαιμακτηριῶνος ἑβδόμει μετ'εἰκάδας, ᵛ] τρίτε[ι καὶ εἰκ]
[οστεῖ τῆς πρυτανείας· τῶν προέδρων ἐπεψή]φισζεν [..⁶...]
5   [................¹⁹............ καὶ συμπρόεδροι· Π]ρόξενο[ς ..⁵..]
[————————εἶπεν· ἐπειδὴ ————————Λαρ]ισαῖο[ς ..⁵..]
κτλ.

Here Maimakterion 23 = pryt. V, 23 = 141st day: but even this is at the cost of introducing two vacant spaces in line 3, either to set off the festival date (cf. Henry, *Prescripts*, p. 63) or as "casual blank spaces", for which see **165**, commentary on line 1 and references there. Moreover, it is necessary to suppose the crowding of two letters into the space of one at some point in the expression of the prytany date. Twenty-six letters must be divided between the patronymic and demotic of the proposer and the patronymic of the honorand, an allowance not overly generous; but it is not unusual for the honorand's patronymic to be omitted at this point of an honorary decree and to appear at the repetition of his name when the main motion formula begins. To suppose that this was so in this context allows the remaining three names to be of "standard" length. Finally, this calendric equation requires a minor adjustment (by one day) in Meritt's tentative reconstruction of the prytany pattern of the year; but he particularly noted the uncertainty of this, and the adjustment is a simple one.

The extra length of the name of the γραμματεύς of 299/8 increases the difficulties in a comparable exercise for that year. In support of a possible dating in 305/4 it is worth remarking that the Athenians are known to have cultivated relations with Larisa in that period. Medeios of that city was honored in 303/2 (*IG* II², 498; *SEG* XXI, 338), and his nephew Oxythemis received Athenian citizenship at about the same time (*IG* II², 558; M. J. Osborne, *Naturalization* I, pp. 118–119, D 47, *Naturalization* II, pp. 124–126). Honors for another Larisaean might not be inappropriate two years earlier.

FRAGMENT OF A DECREE(?)

135. A fragment of a stele of bluish Pentelic marble (I 3367), broken all around including the back, discovered on February 10, 1936, in a modern context on the North Slope of the Akropolis, outside the Market Square to the southeast (T 17).

H. 0.03 m.; W. 0.062 m.; Th. 0.079 m.
LH. 0.006 m.
Στοιχ. (square) 0.0105 m.

Ed. M. B. Walbank, *Hesperia* 54, 1985, pp. 313–314, no. 3, with photograph pl. 87. See also *SEG* XXXV, 76.

saec. IV *a., p. post.* ΣTOIX.

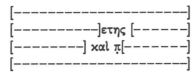

[––––––––––––––––––––]
[––––––––––]ετης [–––––]
[––––––––––] καὶ π[––––––]
[––––––––––––––––––––]

Line 2. Perhaps Ẹ or Γ̣. The letters show signs of slight enlargement at the "free ends" of strokes. Walbank regarded the style as identical with that of the small fragment E.M. 12736, which appeared to O. Broneer, who published it (*Hesperia* 2, 1933, pp. 397–398, no. 17), to be part of a treaty between the Athenians and the people of Lokris (not the Aitolians, as Walbank's commentary erroneously stated), perhaps to be associated with the outbreak of the Lamian War in 323/2. As Broneer remarked, the forms of the letters agree with such a date. But both fragments are too small to serve as a basis for decisive argument, and Walbank rightly saw that no closer association is to be attempted.

Walbank compared *IG* II², 400 (one of the numerous decrees proposed by the politician Demades), lines 11–12, in offering for line 1 the restoration [– – – πρόξενος ὢν καὶ εὐργ]έτης [τοῦ δήμου τοῦ Ἀθηναίων – – –].

A SUCCESSFUL CHOREGOS HONORED BY THE FELLOW MEMBERS OF HIS PHYLE

136. A fragment of a stele of Pentelic(?) marble (I 536), white with blue streaks, broken all around, discovered on March 2, 1933, built into a modern bothros over the northwestern part of the Library of Pantainos (Q 13).

H. 0.165 m.; W. 0.265 m.; Th. 0.145 m.
LH. 0.014 m. (circular letters 0.009 m.)

Ed. J. H. Oliver, *Hesperia* 4, 1935, pp. 41–42, no. 9, with photograph.

saec. IV *a., p. post.* NON-ΣTOIX.

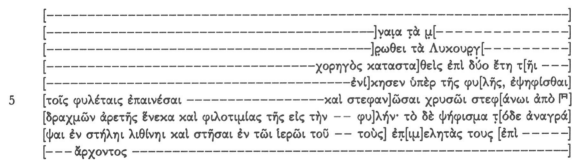

```
    [--------------------------------------------------------------]
    [-----------------------------------------------]γαια τὰ μ[-------------]
    [------------------------------------------]ρωθει τὰ Λυκουργ[--------]
    [----------------------------------χορηγὸς καταστα]θεὶς ἐπὶ δύο ἔτη τ[ῆι ---]
    [------------------------------------------ἐνί]κησεν ὑπὲρ τῆς φυ[λῆς, ἐψηφίσθαι]
5   [τοῖς φυλέταις ἐπαινέσαι ------------------καὶ στεφαν]ῶσαι χρυσῶι στεφ[άνωι ἀπὸ Ⴀ]
    [δραχμῶν ἀρετῆς ἕνεκα καὶ φιλοτιμίας τῆς εἰς τὴν -- φυ]λήν· τὸ δὲ ψήφισμα τ̣[όδε ἀναγρά]
    [ψαι ἐν στήληι λιθίνηι καὶ στῆσαι ἐν τῶι ἱερῶι τοῦ -- τοὺς] ἐπ[ιμ]ελητὰς τους [ἐπὶ -----]
    [---ἄρχοντος ------------------------------------------------]
```

The plain, large lettering lacks adornment of any kind and has been inexpertly done, with many strokes showing traces of repeated chisel blows. In general character it seems best attributed to the later 4th century. The upper and lower strokes of sigma, however, show slight curvature in some cases, while the lower curve of omega is drawn well in, and the form of this letter in line 5, with horizontal strokes set high, is uncommon in Attic epigraphy (cf. P. M. Fraser and T. Rönne, *Boeotian and West Greek Tombstones*, 1957, p. 83, note 6). These features are more appropriate to the 3rd century than to the 4th.

Oliver identified the contents as similar to that of *IG* II², 1157 of 326/5 B.C., and his restorations, shown here, follow that model. They require a minimum line length of 73 letters, and the thickness of the stele suggests that the monument was indeed substantial.

Line 1. ΑΙΛΙΛΙ Oliver. Τὰ Παναθή]ναια τὰ μ[εγάλα (or τὰ μ[ικρά) would be compatible with the surviving indications. Line 2. [– – – –]ωθει τὰ Λυκούργ[ια Oliver, who tentatively, though without further definition, supposed a reference to a festival. The Athenians seem unlikely to have honored in this way the legendary Thracian king, or the semilegendary Spartan lawgiver, or the very real Athenian statesman, and there is no supporting evidence in the literature. In the case of the last named, the posthumous decree in his honor sponsored by Stratokles (*IG* II², 457; cf. **110**) is insufficiently preserved to indicate the detail of the proposals. Traces of rho before omega in this line suggest some such phraseology as – – – ὅταν κυ]ρωθῆι τὰ Λυκούργ[ου νόμιμα. If lines 1 and 2 may be taken together, there is a possible connection with the Lykourgan reform of the Panathenaia reflected in **75** or with the provisions of the text from the North Slope of the Akropolis edited by E. Schweigert, *Hesperia* 7, 1938, pp. 294–296, no. 20 (now E.M. 12896). On Lykourgos' program see F. W. Mitchel, *Greece and Rome*, ser. 2, 12, 1965, p. 196, and *Lykourgan Athens, 338–322* (*Lectures in Memory of Louise Taft Semple*, second series), 1970, pp. 35–36.

Line 5. The restoration requires the cost of the stephanos to be specified. In public decrees this precision of cost in the award of stephanoi is a regular feature until the final years of the 4th century; see **127**. Smaller components of the body politic, such as phylai and demes, may not necessarily be judged according to the same formulaic evidence, but in any case the date of this text is unaffected by that particular consideration. Line 7. On the epimeletai of the phyle see **80** and the references there cited. Stelai concerned with the affairs of a phyle were customarily set up in the sanctuary of its eponymous hero: see **80**, commentary on lines 14–16.

FRAGMENT OF THE CONCLUSION OF A DECREE

137. A fragment of a stele of Pentelic marble (I 2609), broken on all sides, discovered on March 14, 1935, in a modern context east of the Odeion near the Panathenaic Way (O 11).

H. 0.19 m.; W. 0.10 m.; Th. 0.096 m.
LH. 0.007 m.
Στοιχ. (square) 0.013 m.

Ed. B. D. Meritt, *Hesperia* 21, 1952, p. 371, no. 17, with photograph pl. 94. See also *SEG* XII, 92.

ex. saec. IV *a.*　　　　　　　　　　　　　　　　　　　　　　　　　　ΣΤΟΙΧ. 28

```
            [------------------------]
            [..5..· τὸν δὲ γρα]μ[ματέα τὸν κατὰ πρ]
            [υτανείαν ἀναγρ]άψα[ι τόδε τὸ ψήφισ]
            [μα εἰς στήλην λ]ιθίν[ην καὶ στῆσαι ἐ]
            [ν ἀκροπόλει· εἰ]ς δὲ τ[ὴν ἀναγραφὴν τ]
      5     [ῆς στήλης δοῦν]αι τὸν [ταμίαν τοῦ δή]
            [μου ᵛ ΔΔ ᵛ δραχμ]ὰς ἐκ τ[ῶν εἰς τὰ κατὰ]
            [ψηφίσματα ἀνα]λισκο[μένων τῶι δήμ]
            [ωι.    vacat    ]
                        corona
```

Remains of an inscribed stephanos survive below the last line of the text. The writing is plain, rather thin and shallow, and reasonably neat, with slight enlargement of some "free ends" of strokes, and is characteristic of the later 4th century. The long lower angled stroke of kappa is distinctive.

The restorations depend on the familiar formulas for the erection and expense of the stele and the naming of the officers responsible. The presumed mention of the ταμίας τοῦ δήμου as the disbursing officer requires a date for the decree not later than 302/1: see **120**, commentary on line 11. The source of payment (the "analiskomena fund") further suggests 302/1 as the *terminus ante quem*: see **122**, commentary on lines 29–32. The final words τῶι δήμωι are not necessarily to be restored: see **79**, commentary on line 24 and **83**, commentary on line 4.

M. B. Walbank has suggested (*per ep.*) that this fragment may form part of the honorary decree *IG* II², 540 (dated by Kirchner "ante 303/2"), also στοιχ. 28, fragment *b* of which contains the honorand's name within a stephanos; both of these fragments were found on the Akropolis. See *BSA* 85, 1990, pp. 440–441, no. 9; *SEG* XL, 68.

FRAGMENT OF THE CONCLUSION OF A DECREE

138. A fragment of a stele of Hymettian marble (I 4906), with a part of the right side (below the inscribed surface) and the original rough-picked back preserved, discovered on May 22, 1937, in a late context on the North Slope of the Akropolis, west of the Post-Herulian Wall (T 23–24). The text is complete below but not in any other direction; the inscribed surface retains the almost vertical striations made by a toothed chisel.

H. 0.137 m.; W. 0.192 m.; Th. 0.072 m.
LH. 0.005 m. (alpha, lambda, omicron)–0.008 m. (sigma, tau).
Στοιχ. (square) 0.0116 m.

Ed. B. D. Meritt, *Hesperia* 26, 1957, pp. 208–209, no. 56, with photograph pl. 53. See also *SEG* XVII, 28.

ex. saec. IV *a.*   ΣΤΟΙΧ. 30

```
                 [––––––––––––––––––––––]
                 [.......15........]γω[... · καὶ ἀναγράψ]
                 [αι τὸ ψήφισμα τὸν γρ]αμ[ματέα τὸν κατὰ]
                 [πρυτανείαν ἐν στήλ]ει λι[θίνει καὶ στ]
                 [ῆσαι ἐν ἀκροπόλει]· εἰς δὲ τ[ὴν ἀναγραφ]
           5     [ὴν τῆς στήλης δοῦ]ναι τὸν ταμί[αν τοῦ δ]
                 [ήμου : ΔΔ : δραχμὰς] ἐκ τῶν εἰς τὰ κατ[ὰ ψη]
                 [φίσματ'ἀναλισκο]μένων τῶι δήμω[ι. ᵛᵛᵛ]
                                 vacat
```

The plain lettering, though not inaccurate, is indifferently executed. The work was evidently not well prepared, as the horizontal line of writing slopes downwards to the right. Alpha, delta, and lambda are comparatively small, and the stonecutter was inconsistent in the selection of his tools. For example, the length of the upright of tau and of the horizontals of epsilon vary markedly in different instances of the letters concerned. Omega, with two perfunctory angled cross-strokes at the end of the curve in place of the regular horizontals, is particularly distinctive.

The restorations are those of Meritt. Although most of the text may be restored in accordance with the familiar concluding formulas for publication of and payment for the decree, the surviving letters in line 1, which evidently occur almost at the end of their clause, present difficulties best resolved by the supposition that τόδε was omitted from the usual phrase τόδε τὸ ψήφισμα. *IG* II², 344 (*SEG* XXI, 279, XXXII, 92), lines 18–19, 368 (*SEG* XXI, 280, 296, XXXII, 92), lines 13–14, and 448 (*SEG* XXXI, 79, with earlier references, XXXII, 90), line 26 offer a parallel. In the light of this, Meritt suggested for the preceding phrase Παναθηναίων (or Διονυσίων) – – – τῶι ἀ]γῶ[νι ᵛ, with reference to *IG* II², 555, line 6.

Line 3. στήλ]ει λι[θίνει. For EI present and restored in the dative feminine singular, regular at this period, in place of HI, see **89**, commentary on line 2. Lines 5–7. The necessarily assumed appearance of the ταμίας τοῦ δήμου as the disbursing officer requires a date for the inscription not later than 302/1 B.C., and the source of funding confirms the indication. Cf. **137**. Line 7. The elision of the final alpha of ψηφίσματα which must here be introduced is attested through the second half of the 4th century, beginning with *IG* II², 264, line 14. Several examples concentrate around the end of the century and by that concentration may serve as a dating confirmation for this fragment. Cf. *IG* II², 479, line 29, 522, line 6, 534, line 4, and perhaps 531, line 4. The elision is restored in *IG* II², 196, line 9 and 573, line 18. See also **139** and **164**, and A. S. Henry, *ZPE* 78, 1989, p. 257, note 53, for a list of instances.

FRAGMENT OF THE CONCLUSION OF A DECREE

139. A fragment of a stele of Pentelic marble (I 5251), broken on all sides, discovered on February 22, 1938, in a sandy fill of early Byzantine context, west of the Post-Herulian Wall (S 19).

H. 0.109 m.; W. 0.06 m.; Th. 0.042 m.
LH. 0.006 m.
Στοιχ. Hor. 0.013 m.; Vert. 0.0142 m.

Ed. A. G. Woodhead, *Hesperia* 29, 1960, pp. 80–81, no. 156, with photograph pl. 26. See also *SEG* XVIII, 17.

ex. saec. IV *a.*   ΣΤΟΙΧ. 27

```
                 [––––––––––––––––––––––]
                 [...8....]ΕΣ[..5... · εἰς δὲ τὴν ἀναγ]
                 [ραφὴν τῆ]ς στ[ήλης δοῦναι τὸν ταμί]
                 [αν τοῦ δή]μου ᵛ [ΔΔΔ ᵛ δραχμὰς ἐκ τῶν]
                 [εἰς τὰ κα]τὰ ψη[φίσματ'ἀναλισκομέ]
           5     [νων τῶι δ]ήμωι. [      vacat        ]
                                 vacat
```

The lettering of this text is "standard" in character, with slight depression of the "free ends" of the strokes of upsilon and some diversity in the formation of sigma. The narrow omega, shaped like a horseshoe resting on a continuous horizontal, is noteworthy.

The division of the lines is arbitrary, since the fragment cannot be precisely located within the total width of the monument. The date depends upon the same criteria as those operative in the case of **138**, and reference may be made to the commentary there. The restorations follow those proposed in the footnote to *SEG* XVIII, 17, subsequently endorsed by T. Eide, *Symbolae Osloenses* 59, 1984, pp. 23–24 (cf. *SEG* XXXIV, 77), and by A. S. Henry, *ZPE* 78, 1989, p. 262, note 73. The assumption of the use of μερίσαι rather than δοῦναι, though supported by *IG* II², 500 (of 302/1, but with ὁ ἐπὶ τῆι διοικήσει as the disbursing officer), probably by 520, and possibly by 301 (with payment formulas as in the present text), is best avoided at this date.

Line 1. The instructions to the γραμματεύς to have the stele inscribed and set up (customarily on the Akropolis) normally precede the payment formula; but the preserved letters do not admit of the restoration of the στῆσαι ἐν ἀκροπόλει phraseology or any attested variant of it. It is possible, though unlikely, that the regular instructions were here omitted. More probably (unless some hitherto unsuspected location for the stele be supposed) another kind of intervening phrase must be presumed, either a ὅπως ἄν clause giving a "hortatory intention" (see **86**) as a reason for publication or some shorter form of words (as in *IG* II², 391, where δ......¹⁴...... separates εἰς ἀκρόπολιν from εἰς δὲ τὴν ἀναγραφήν).

Line 4. For the elision of the alpha of ψηφίσματα see **138**, commentary on line 7.

M. B. Walbank has suggested (*per ep.*) that the craftsman at work on this monument was also responsible for *IG* II², 1195 (*SEG* XXV, 145) and 1266. J. Kirchner dated the former of these "s. IV a. p. post." and the latter (with a mark of hesitation) "fin. s. IV a." But in a subsequent article (*BSA* 84, 1989, pp. 395–399), in which he attributed a larger number of inscriptions to the same hand, dating the craftsman's activity to the period 330–318 b.c., Walbank did not pursue this particular association, and a date closer to the end of the century seems in any case to be preferable for this text.

FRAGMENT OF THE CONCLUSION OF A DECREE

140. A fragment of a stele of Pentelic marble (I 6921), with the roughly dressed right edge preserved, though weathered, but otherwise broken all around, discovered on June 12, 1959, in the area of the Eleusinion (T 21).

H. 0.11 m.; W. 0.10 m.; Th. 0.07 m.
LH. 0.005 m.
Στοιχ. (almost square) Hor. 0.012 m.; Vert. 0.011 m.

Ed. B. D. Meritt, *Hesperia* 32, 1963, pp. 2–3, no. 3, with photograph pl. 1. See also *SEG* XXI, 344. The discovery of the stone was briefly reported by H. A. Thompson, *Hesperia* 29, 1960, p. 338.

ex. saec. IV *a.*   ΣΤΟΙΧ. 33

```
          [--------------------------------]
          [....¹⁰...., τὴν δὲ ἐν τῶι Ἐλευσι]νίωι ἐν ἅ
          [στει· εἰς δὲ τὴν ἀναγραφὴν τῶν στη]λῶν δοῦ
          [ναι τὸν ταμίαν τοῦ δήμου ΔΔΔ δραχ]μὰς ἐκ τ
          [ῶν κατὰ ψηφίσματα ἀναλισκομένων] τῶι δή
     5    [μωι· .............²⁷.............]ι[..]
          [---------------------------(?)]
```

The lettering is careless and inconsistent (note particularly the variations in the rendering of omega). Its characteristics are reminiscent rather of the 3rd century than of the 4th, but if the ταμίας τοῦ δήμου is to be restored as the disbursing officer in line 3, as appears inescapable, the text must be dated not later than 302/1 b.c.; and the source of payment provides a more general confirmatory indication. See **137**.

Lines 1–2. There were two stelai (at least, but presumably not more). The site of the discovery of this fragment, with its reference to the City Eleusinion, contributed to the establishment of the location of that sanctuary, for which see *Agora* III, pp. 74–85. Cf. also **123**. Line 3. Thirty drachmas sufficed to pay for two stelai of, apparently, standard dimensions. Cf. **73**, of 337/6, where twenty drachmas paid for two stelai, one of which at least carried relief sculpture of reasonable quality. Where two stelai are concerned, a separate allocation is sometimes made for each (e.g., *IG* II², 338 = *SEG* XXXIV, 68, with earlier references, of 333/2). Cf. A. S. Henry, *ZPE* 78, 1989, p. 263, note 75. Meritt inserted two-dot punctuation before and after the numeral, but the stoichedon arrangement leaves no room for this as part of the pattern. If they were included, they were added *extra ordinem* between normally spaced letters; and there was indeed room for this.

Line 5. The text could be complete with the letters μωι, but there seems to have been a further clause. Meritt marked vacant spaces before and after the surviving iota, which might suggest that that stroke was inscribed by mere error below a similar stroke in the line above. But the stone is damaged at this point, and lettering before and after iota is by no means precluded.

M. B. Walbank has expressed the opinion (*per ep.*) that the mason responsible for this text may also have inscribed *IG* II², 506, which he notes as having the same length of line.

FRAGMENT OF AN HONORARY DECREE

141. A fragment of a stele of Pentelic marble (I 5488), with part of the much-battered right side as well as the original rough-picked back preserved but otherwise broken all around, discovered on May 30, 1938, in the wall of a late cistern on the North Slope of the Akropolis (T 24).

H. 0.154 m.; W. 0.12 m.; Th. 0.091 m.
LH. 0.005 (omicron)–0.006 m.
Στοιχ. (square) 0.012 m.

Ed. B. D. Meritt, *Hesperia* 30, 1961, p. 210, no. 4, with photograph pl. 35. See also *SEG* XXI, 342.

ex. saec. IV *a.* (*ca. a.* 304/3 *a.*?)   ΣΤΟΙΧ. 35(?)

```
      [------------------------------]
      [-----------------------]ΣΙΠΕΡ[..]
      [----------------------]ι ἐν τῶι [..]
      [-----------------------]νεις ἀνει[.]
      [----------------------]Ο ἐν τῶ[ι ...]
  5   [-------------------ἐπαι]νέσαι Ο[..]
      [------------------------]ιονα Μενοι
      [.......17?.......καὶ στεφανῶ]σαι χρυσ[ῶ]
      [ι στεφάνωι ἑκάτερον αὐτῶν ἀπὸ Χ [δ]ραχμῶν κατὰ τ[ὸν]]
      [[νόμον·] ἀναγράψαι δὲ τόδε τὸ ψήφισμα εἰς σ]τήλην λ[ι
 10   [θίνην καὶ στῆσαι ἐν ἀκροπόλει· εἰς δὲ] τὴν ἀ[ν
      [αγραφὴν κτλ. ------------------------]
```

The battered state of the stone may cause the lettering to appear poorer than it is; but it is undeniably poor. The reworked line 8 is no worse than the rest in the slipshod rendering of nu and the perfunctory omega: sigma is inconsistently formed. Nevertheless, the junctions of strokes are for the most part accurately made. There is no attempt at the adornment of emphasized "free ends".

Too little of the inscription remains to permit more than the identification of its general character as honoring (presumably) two benefactors and the establishment of its probable width with reference to the formula for the erection of the stele. The restorations are those of Meritt, with some adjustment to the readings on the difficult right edge. In lines 1–7 and 9–10 Meritt supposed one letter less on the right than the stone seems to permit.

Line 1. ΣΙΚΕ Meritt. Perhaps σι περ, forming part of the phrase ἐπειδὴ – – –ἄνδρες ἀγαθοί εἰ]σι περ[ι ᵛ | τὸν δῆμον τὸν Ἀθηναίων καὶ νῦν κα]ὶ ἐν τῶι [πρ|όσθεν χρόνωι. Line 4. ΟΕΝΤ Meritt.

Lines 6–7. Probably Μενοι[τίου or Μενοι[τιάδου, leaving thirteen or eleven letters for the *ethnicum*. Line 8. The surviving letters are written *in rasura*, and the erasure may well have extended as far back as ἀπό. Meritt restored ἀπὸ χιλίων δ]ραχμῶν κατὰ τ[ὸ]ν, producing a line of 46 letters. In line 9, restoring εἰσ]τήλην, he envisaged a line of 38 letters. This assumes greater crowding than in fact exists. Had the stonecutter written ἀπὸ :Χ: δραχμῶν· ἀναγράψαι δὲ τόδε τὸ ψήφισμα εἰς στήλην he would have preserved the regularity of the inscription.

The surviving part of line 8 shows that thirteen letters were reinscribed in the place of eight. If the single numeral Χ (with punctuation, if any, *extra ordinem*) be retained in place of Meritt's fuller χιλίων, fourteen letters in the space of nine produce a line of 40 letters in conformity with that spatial pattern. Line 9, with five letters initially in the space of three (and retaining εἰς στήλην), contains 40 letters also.

Why did the stonecutter make this emergency erasure and revision? It may well be that alteration of the formula for the expression of the cost of a gold stephanos overtook him *media in opera*. It was noted above (see **112**, commentary on lines 5–7) that the specification of cost is last clearly attested in 306/5 B.C. and that certainly from 303/2 onwards that phraseology is replaced by the statement that the crowning is to be arranged "in accordance with the statute." Here the two are, extraordinarily, combined in a text clearly revised from the original draft. This seems to imply that the decree was inscribed at the very time that a decision to make the change was taken and carried into effect, and the craftsman made the best of both formulas, a suggestion endorsed by R. S. Stroud (*Hesperia* 40, 1971, p. 179, note 31) and by A. S. Henry (*Honours*, pp. 27 and 50–51, note 43). If so, the more precise date for this text of "*ca.* 304/3" is not unreasonable.

Lines 9–10. Mention of the γραμματεύς responsible for the inscription and erection of the stele is omitted. Cf., e.g., *IG* II², 493 + 518, 508 (M. J. Osborne, *Naturalization* I, pp. 128–129, D 53, *Naturalization* II, p. 132), and 517 (= 183: see *SEG* XXII, 99). These texts are all to be dated in the last few years of the century.

FRAGMENT OF A DECREE CONFERRING CITIZENSHIP

142. A fragment of a stele of Pentelic marble (I 5174), broken on all sides, discovered on February 3, 1938, in a modern context west of the Panathenaic Way and west of the Eleusinion (R 18).

H. 0.104 m.; W. 0.101 m.; Th. 0.041 m.
LH. 0.009 m.
Στοιχ. (square) 0.0167 m.

Ed. B. D. Meritt, *Hesperia* 30, 1961, pp. 210–211, no. 5, with photograph pl. 35. See also *SEG* XXI, 343. Further discussion by M. J. Osborne, *Naturalization* III/IV, pp. 134–135, X 31; cf. *SEG* XXXIII, 102.

ex. saec. IV a.   ΣΤΟΙΧ. 37

```
        [――――――――――――――――――――――γράψασθαι]
        [φυλῆς καὶ δήμου καὶ φρατρίας ἧς] ἂν β[ούλωνται]
        [κατὰ τὸν νόμον· εἶναι δὲ αὐτοῖς] καὶ πρ[οεδρίαν]
        [ἐν πᾶσι τοῖς ἀγῶσιν οὓς ἂν ἡ πόλι]ς τιθε[ῖ· τὸν δὲ]
        [ἀρχιτέκτονα τόπον εἰς θεὰν κατ]ανέμ[ειν οὗ ἂν]
   5    [καὶ τοῖς στρατηγοῖς κατανέμητα]ι· [....⁹....]
        [――――――――――――――――――――――――――――――]
```

The writing is on the large side for the later 4th century, clear, precise, and accurate save for slight failure in the correct junction of strokes in beta and epsilon. There is no attempt to emphasize "free ends". It is worth remark that a text so inscribed should be regarded as a near contemporary of **141**.

Meritt restored the fragment as the surviving portion of a decree conferring citizenship, as concerned with one benefactor only, with a stoichedon line of 44 letters, as follows:

```
        [――――――――――――――――――――――γράψασθαι φυλῆς καὶ δή]
        [μου καὶ φρατρίας ἧς] ἂν β[ούληται πλὴν ὧν οἱ νόμοι ἀπαγο]
        [ρεύουσιν· εἶναι δὲ] καὶ πρ[οεδρίαν αὐτῶι ἐν ἅπασιν τοῖς]
        [ἀγῶσιν οὓς ἂν ἡ πόλι]ς τιθε[ῖ· καὶ τὸν ἀρχιτέκτονα τὸν ἀε]
        [ὶ καθιστάμενον κατ]ανέμ[ειν αὐτῶι τὴν θεὰν οὗ ἂν ――――――]
   5    [―――――――――――――]Ι[――――――――――――――――]
```

On the other hand, Osborne (*loc. cit.*) rejected this document as a citizenship decree, on the grounds that too little text survives and that the granting formula, as restored by Meritt, would be anomalous. Nevertheless, the suggestion may stand, with the shorter line here preferred. The preference is based partly on considerations of economy (lines of between 27 and 40 letters being most commonly encountered in this type of document) and partly because the formulas adopted in the longer-line restorations are indeed, as Osborne observed, not of the regular kind. (For the rare πλὴν ὧν οἱ νόμοι ἀπαγορεύουσιν see **96** and A. S. Henry, *Honours*, p. 72, where this text is cited. Κατὰ τὸν νόμον is the regular formula at this epoch; cf. Henry, *op. cit.*, p. 73.)

Lines 1–2. If the restoration be accepted, the grant of citizenship appears to follow Osborne's "Formulation A" (*Naturalization* I, p. 16) well enough. Cf. also Henry, *Honours*, pp. 64–80. Lines 2–3. *Proedria*, or preferential seating at festivals, begins to be mentioned in a phraseology resembling that included here in 314/13 (*IG* II², 450 = Osborne, *Naturalization* I, pp. 109–112, D 42, *Naturalization* II, pp. 113–115). Closer parallels belong to the end of the century.

Lines 3–5. For the restorations compare *IG* II², 500, of 302/1, and 512 (*SEG* XXXI, 83, XXXIII, 100), of "fin. s. IV a." The present text is closer to the norm; cf. Henry, *Honours*, pp. 291–292. But Henry also had grounds for feeling "not uncomfortable" with the formulation in the *editio princeps*. However, the extended statement concerning the architect (τὸν ἀρχιτέκτονα τὸν ἀεὶ καθιστάμενον) does not otherwise occur in this form before 271/70 (**188**, lines 41–44), and the other examples cited are of later date; Henry's remark that Meritt's restoration offers the fuller phraseology more commonly used (*Honours*, p. 294) therefore demands modification in the present context.

FRAGMENT OF AN HONORARY DECREE

143. A fragment of a stele of bluish Pentelic marble (I 4914), with the right edge preserved but otherwise broken all around, discovered on May 25, 1937, in a Late Roman context, in a well outside the Market Square to the southwest (E 15:5). This part of the monument was at some time refashioned into the form of a basin, and the surviving inscribed surface represents the flat margin of a large part of the right side of the bowl, the diameter of which may be assessed at *ca.* 0.20 m.

H. 0.147 m.; W. 0.092 m.; Th. 0.068 m.
LH. 0.005–0.006 m.
Στοιχ. (almost square) Hor. 0.0091 m.; Vert. 0.0093 m.

Ed. M. B. Walbank, *Hesperia* 54, 1985, pp. 314–317, no. 4, with photograph pl. 87. See also *SEG* XXXV, 79.

ex. saec. IV *a.* ΣΤΟΙΧ.

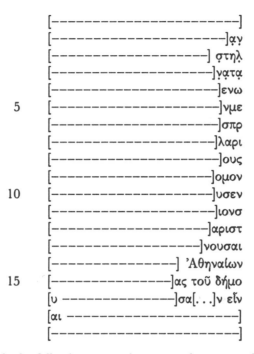

```
      [----------------------]
      [-------------------]αγ
      [-----------------] στηλ
      [------------------]γατα
      [--------------------]ενω
  5   [-------------------]νμε
      [-------------------]σπρ
      [-----------------]λαρι
      [-----------------]ους
      [-----------------]ομον
 10   [-----------------]υσεν
      [----------------]ιονσ
      [---------------]αριστ
      [--------------]νουσαι
      [-------------] Ἀθηναίων
 15   [------------]ας τοῦ δήμο
      [υ -----------]σα[...]ν εἶν
      [αι -----------------]
      [----------------------]
```

In his edition Walbank made the following suggestions towards a restored text: Lines 2–3. ἐν] στήλ|[ηι λιθίνηι. Lines 4–5. ἐν ὧ||[ι or ενω||ν (e.g., προξ]ένω||[ν. Lines 5–6. τὸ]ν μὲ|[ν. Lines 6–7. τού]ς πρ|[υτάνεις(?). Line 9. κατὰ τὸν ν]όμον. Line 10. – – –ε]υς ἐν. Lines 12–13. ἄριστ|[ον(?) or a *nomen proprium* Ἀριστ– –. At the end of line 13 the reading may be θῦσαι. Walbank also conjectured a line length of 41 letters, restoring lines 15–17 as

[εἶναι δὲ αὐτοὺς προξένους καὶ εὐεργέτ]ας τοῦ δήμο
[υ τοῦ Ἀθηναίων αὐτοὺς καὶ τοὺς ἐκγόνου]ς α[ὐτῶ]ν· εἶν
[αι δὲ καὶ ....³⁴...............]

and entering into the remainder of his text the number of dots in each line conforming to this pattern. (For the repeated αὐτούς ... αὐτῶν in this formulation cf. **79** and A. S. Henry, *Honours*, pp. 138 and 160, note 147.)

The lettering is poorly done. Walbank correctly described it as spidery, untidy, and hard to date. But its characteristics, as he noted, are those of **93**, equally hard to date but now established as of 324/3 B.C.; and Walbank attributed to the same hand *IG* II², 361 (*SEG* XVIII, 15) and 362 (*SEG* XXI, 291), of 325/4 and 324/3 respectively, with the possible additions of *IG* II², 533, 543, and 545 (*SEG* XXIV, 106). But work of this dismal quality is unlikely to have been the prerogative of a single individual. The date may still be closer to the end of the century or even into its successor, and here, as in Walbank's edition, no precise date is advanced.

If in lines 7–8 the honorand(s) may be described as of Larisa in Thessaly, the comparison with *IG* II², 545 (of 321/20?) may be additionally apposite. See **134**. But any further suggestions as to the nature of the privileges here bestowed or the order in which they are set out (e.g., that in lines 8–9 there was a grant of γῆς καὶ οἰκίας ἔγκτησις κατὰ τὸν νόμον) must remain matters of speculation.

HONORS FOR A FRIEND OF DEMETRIOS POLIORKETES(?)

144. A fragment of a stele of Pentelic marble (I 2173), with the top part of the left side preserved, as well as the original rough-picked back, but broken elsewhere and with the inscribed surface so abraded that only a few letters remain legible, discovered in December 1934 in a marble pile in the area of the southwestern corner of the Odeion, near the Civic Offices (H–K 11–14). The upper part of the fragment bears traces of a crowning molding and projecting fascia, both now trimmed off, and of a rectangular, centrally placed panel of relief sculpture above these. The surface has split from the stone diagonally from the upper left to the lower right.

H. 0.38 m.; W. 0.23 m.; Th. 0.122 m. (in the inscribed area, 0.115 m.).

LH. 0.007 m.

Στοιχ. (almost square) Hor. 0.0148 m.; Vert. 0.0146 m.

Ed. M. B. Walbank, *Hesperia* 54, 1985, pp. 317–319, no. 5, with photograph pl. 87. See also *SEG* XXXV, 80.

ex. saec. IV *a.* (*a.* 304/2 *a.?*)　　　　　　　　　　　　　　　　　　　　　　　ΣΤΟΙΧ.

```
        [------versus tres non legendi-------]
        [---------------· τῶν προέδρων ἐ]
   5    [πεψ]ήφ[ιζεν ---------------τῶ]
        [ι] δήμ[ωι· --------------------]
        [.]αν[--------------------------]
        [.]κλητ[------------------------]
        [.]νειτ[....]Λ[-----------------]
  10    [τ]οῦ βασιλέως [-----------------]
        [.]Λ[. ]ΠΑΚΑΙΥΠ[. ]Λ[-----------]
        [..]με[. ]ν[. .]Λ[. ]Λ[---------]
        [..]ενοι[. ]ποδ[----------------]
        [..]συμπ[. ]η[. ]ι[-------------]
  15    [..] αὐτῶι καὶ ἐ[κγόνοις(?) ------]
        [.]γκεω[. .]ι[-------------ὅπως]
        [ἂν] εἰδ[ῶσι] πάν[τες -------τὸν δῆ]
        [μο]ν τὸν Ἀθηνα[ί]ων [-----------]
        [..] εὐερ[γ]ετ[-----------------]
  20    [------------------------------]
```

Difficult though it is to evaluate clearly the characteristics of the lettering, by reason of the damaged state of the inscribed surface, Walbank regarded them as identical with those of **107**, where the letter height and spacing are also the same. The writing appears to be plain and carefully executed and is consistent with a date towards the end of the 4th century.

Walbank further suggested a line length of 49 letters, which he based upon his restoration of the "hortatory intention" (cf. **86**) of lines 16–19, which he presented as follows:

```
        -----------------------------ὅπως]
        [ἂν] εἰδ[ῶσι] πάν[τες ὅσοι ἂν εὔνοι ὄντες φιλοτιμῶνται ἐς τὸν δῆ]
        [μο]ν τὸν Ἀθηνα[ί]ων [ὅτι ὁ δῆμος ἀποδίδωσιν χάριτας καταξίας τ]
        [ῶν] εὐερ[γ]ετ[ημάτων .................34.................]
```

Ἐς for εἰς (line 17) at so late a date must be regarded as dubious; cf. L. Threatte, *Grammar*, p. 189. Walbank's text incorporated an arrangement of lines 1–4 conforming to this length of line and, with the attribution to the same craftsman of **107** in mind, conjectured for lines 1–2

```
        [Ἐπὶ Ἀναξικράτους ἄρχοντος, ἐπὶ τῆς.........20.........]
        [πρυτανείας ἧι Λυσίας Νοθίππου Διομειεὺς ἐγραμμάτευεν, ..]
```

thus setting the decree in the year 307/6.

Line 10. Walbank noted "The King is, presumably, Demetrios." If so, the above restoration for lines 1–2 presumably falls to the ground, for 306 B.C. seems to have been well advanced when Antigonos Monopthalmos assumed the royal title and conferred it upon his son (Diodorus Siculus 20.53). Furthermore, the honors so largely bestowed on Demetrios' friends, chiefly under the sponsorship of the politician Stratokles (cf. **117**), appear to be concentrated between 304 and 302, roughly speaking in the period of the successes celebrated in **114** and the institution of the Hellenic League. *IG* II², 466 (*SEG* XXIV, 110), of 307/6 (see p. 169 above), does not (*pace* M. J. Osborne, *Naturalization* II, p. 138) refer in its surviving section to Antigonos and Demetrios as βασιλεῖς. Nothing, however, would preclude the writer of **107** being still active a few years later than the date of that text, if indeed this inscription is attributable to him.

FRAGMENT OF AN HONORARY DECREE

145. A fragment of a stele of Pentelic marble (I 5645), broken on all sides except for the original rough-picked back, discovered on February 23, 1939, in a modern wall over the Panathenaic Way south of the Eleusinion (S 21). The piece is oblong in overall shape but offers a diagonal section of the inscribed surface, running from upper right to lower left. The surface of the lower half is sheared away, and the lower section of the upper half has been worn smooth. Thus in proportion to the size of the fragment comparatively little of the inscription has survived.

H. 0.28 m.; W. 0.23 m.; Th. 0.106 m.
LH. 0.008 m.
Στοιχ. (square) *ca.* 0.0155 m.

Ed. B. D. Meritt, *Hesperia* 30, 1961, p. 257, no. 58, with photograph pl. 47. See also *SEG* XXI, 348.

ex. saec. IV a.   ΣΤΟΙΧ.

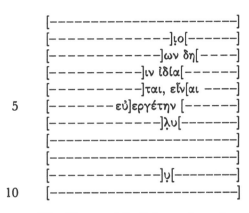

The lettering is plain and neat. The "free ends" of the strokes of upsilon (see commentary on **120**) and of the upright of tau are slightly depressed. In general character the writing resembles that of **88**, **89**, and **94**, and on that score a more precise dating for this inscription of *ca.* 325–320 might be hazarded.

M. B. Walbank (*per ep.*) has suggested a closer parallel with **127** and *IG* II², 169 + 472 (*SEG* XXI, 335), the latter being dated to 306/5, and he would attribute this fragment to the same craftsman. That seems less likely, however; but despite the inevitable element of subjectivity in drawing parallels on stylistic grounds, the attribution of this text to the last quarter of the 4th century appears reasonably assured.

Apart from the clue provided by line 5 as to the nature of this document, the fragment despite its size remains totally uninformative.

FRAGMENT OF A DECREE(?)

146. A fragment from the upper left corner of a pedimental stele of Pentelic marble (I 3392), with the left side of the monument preserved below the inscribed surface. The fragment is otherwise broken all around (including the back). It was discovered on February 10, 1936, in a context of the 4th century B.C. in a cistern south of the Hephaisteion (D 8–9). Line 1 is inscribed on the fascia below the pediment.

H. 0.17 m.; W. 0.1155 m.; Th. 0.092 m.
LH. 0.005 m. (line 1, 0.006 m.).
Στοιχ. (square) 0.0124 m.

Ed. M. B. Walbank, *Hesperia* 58, 1989, pp. 92–93, no. 20, with photograph pl. 23. See also *SEG* XXXIX, 113.

ex. saec. IV *a.*   ΣΤΟΙΧ.

```
           ['Α] γ α θ [ἦ ι  τ ύ χ η ι ·   vacat(?)]
           [....9....]ΥΣΕΤΑΙΟ[--------]
           [....10.....]του δι[----------]
           [....11.......]γαστ[----------]
        5  [....13........]ολ[----------]
           [---------------------]
```

The crossbar of alpha is consistently omitted: in other respects the lettering appears to be unremarkable.

Walbank's *editio princeps*, the readings of which are followed above, interpreted this fragment as part of an honorary decree, and the character of the monument, together with the remains of line 1, uncertain though they are, seems to bear this out. But what then follows bears little relation to a normal prescript, and this may be the enactment of a *collegium* or other section of the citizen body, of the kind in which nothing more than the proposer's name precedes the detail. Hence Walbank's [....9....]υσεταιο[ς εἶπεν in line 2, although no suggestion is made regarding the name lurking here except to exclude the *demoticum* Ξυπεταιών.

Speculation beyond this point is inappropriate. That the writer was the craftsman responsible for **152** is a further suggestion in the *editio princeps*, where it is, however, made clear that this fragment has no closer connection with that.

FRAGMENT OF A DECREE

147. The upper left corner of a stele of Pentelic marble (I 329), with top, left side, and original back preserved. The fragment, broken below and on the right, was discovered late in 1932 in a modern house wall immediately east of the Stoa of Zeus (I 6). Above the text of the decree is an ovolo molding surmounted by a flat taenia, on which line 1 is inscribed. This in turn is surmounted by a sculptured low relief depicting a tripod, with a blank space to the right so far as preserved. The upper edge of the stele was finished in a pattern of shallow scalloped curves.

H. 0.37 m.; W. 0.26 m.; Th. 0.11 m.

LH. (line 1) 0.013 m., (line 2) 0.008 m.

Ed. B. D. Meritt, *Hesperia* 3, 1934, pp. 1–2, no. 2, with photograph.

saec. IV *a.*

```
        Θ        ε        [ο        ι].
       ["Ε]δοξεν τ[-------------]
       [----------------------]
```

If line 1 was symmetrically spaced, the stele was *ca.* 0.434 m. wide on the taenia and *ca.* 0.41 m. wide at the first line of the main text. The surviving letters of ἔδοξεν are not evenly set out, but on the same allowance of space for succeeding groups of five letters the text contained *ca.* 30 letters per line. The characteristics of the plain, tidy lettering suggest a 4th-century date, perhaps in the generation between 350 and 320 B.C.

FRAGMENT OF A DECREE

148 (Pl. 16). A fragment of a stele of Pentelic marble (I 181), broken on all sides, discovered on March 7, 1932, at the south end of the porch of the Metroon, at a Late Roman level (H 10).

H. 0.10 m.; W. 0.06 m.; Th. 0.10 m.

LH. 0.007 m.

Στοιχ. Hor. 0.016 m.; Vert. 0.014 m.

Ed. B. D. Meritt, *Hesperia* 3, 1934, p. 3, no. 4, with photograph but no text given.

saec. IV *a.*   ΣΤΟΙΧ.

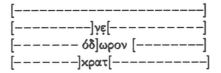

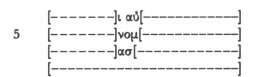

Meritt observed that "the letters are well cut and belong apparently to the fourth century B.C." In fact they so closely resemble those of **42** that the two texts seem certainly to fall within the same general period and might even be attributable to the same hand. Even so (to underscore the uncertainty of this criterion), apart from the open form of omega this text would stand comparison with good work of several decades later. And other considerations affect the issue, as the following commentary illustrates.

Line 5. It is tempting to elaborate these remains into the phrase κατὰ τὸν] νόμ[ον, and this would suggest for lines 4–5 καὶ εἶνα]ι αὐ[τῶι (or αὐ[τοῖς) γῆς καὶ οἰκίας ἔγκτησιν κατὰ τὸν] νόμ[ον – – –], requiring a stoichedon line of 33 or 34 letters. κατὰ τὸν νόμον, however, as a formula in connection with the grant of enktesis or other privileges seems not to antedate the last quarter of the 4th century; cf. A. S. Henry, *Honours*, p. 214. The possibility of its appearance before *ca.* 325 is not to be peremptorily excluded: see J. Pečírka, *Formula*, pp. 140–142 and table pp. 154–155; F. W. Mitchel, *Lykourgan Athens, 338–322* (*Lectures in Memory of Louise Taft Semple*, second series), 1970, pp. 32–33, note 123. If this text ought, on the grounds of the style of its lettering, to be placed earlier than the mid-century, this suggested supplement should on balance be discarded; but, if it may stand, it could support and be supported by an early dating of *IG* II², 425, which contains the same formula and which D. M. Lewis (quoted by Pečírka, *Formula*, p. 77) was prepared to envisage as of the second quarter of the century: cf. Henry, *Honours*, p. 230, note 48.

To complicate the issue further, M. B. Walbank, so far from accepting the resemblance noted above, has discerned (*per ep.*) the same hand at work here as on **205**, surely attributable to the 3rd century. This seems considerably less likely but is illustrative of the uncertainties attendant upon lettering and style as criteria of date. In the case of so small a fragment it is probably the wisest course, unless or until better evidence comes to hand, not to advance beyond Meritt's original observation.

FRAGMENT OF AN HONORARY(?) DECREE

149. A fragment (no more than a splinter) of a stele of Pentelic marble (I 2898), broken all around, discovered on April 16, 1935, in a context of the 3rd or 4th century A.D., east of the central part of the Stoa of Zeus (I 6).

H. 0.042 m.; W. 0.107 m.; Th. 0.024 m.
LH. 0.007–0.008 m.
Στοιχ. Hor. 0.011 m.; Vert. 0.015 m.

Ed. B. D. Meritt, *Hesperia* 29, 1960, p. 6, no. 6, with photograph pl. 5. See also *SEG* XIX, 65.

saec. IV/III *a.* ΣΤΟΙΧ.

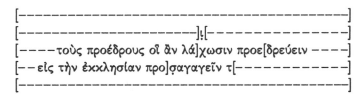

Lines 2–3. ἐν τῶι δήμωι may or may not have intervened between προεδρεύειν and εἰς τήν, and πρώτην (or ἐπιοῦσαν if the text is of a date not earlier than 299/8) will have stood between τήν and ἐκκλησίαν. On πρώτην/ἐπιοῦσαν cf. W. B. Dinsmoor, *Athenian Archon List*, pp. 18–19, and **162**. For the formula see **89**, commentary on lines 2–9 (under "Line 1").

The rather shallow lettering is adorned with pronounced serifs made by the chisel corner. It suggests the 3rd century rather than the 4th, but the latter is not to be excluded. M. B. Walbank has drawn attention (*per ep.*) to a resemblance between the style of this text and that of *IG* II², 722 (*SEG* XXIV, 120), dated between 298/7 and 295/4 (*SEG* XXIX, 93).

FRAGMENT OF AN HONORARY DECREE

150. A fragment of a stele of Hymettian marble (I 2895), broken on all sides, discovered on May 17, 1935, built into a modern wall over the eastern end of the Middle Stoa (O 13).

H. 0.14 m.; W. 0.09 m.; Th. 0.076 m.
LH. 0.005 m. (omicron and omega 0.006 m.).

Ed. B. D. Meritt, *Hesperia* 29, 1960, p. 52, no. 68, with photograph pl. 14. See also *SEG* XIX, 66.

saec. IV/III *a.*   NON-ΣΤΟΙΧ.

```
[------------------------------------]
[------------------]ο[.]ν[---------]
[-----------] ἅπερ καὶ [----------]
[-------το]ὺς ἠγωνισμέ[νους --------]
[-------]ς αὐτοὺς γε[-----------]
5   [-----πλεί]ω χρόνον καὶ [----------]
[----------]αν δὲ καὶ ἐγ [--------]
[---------]υτων ἐθυ[-----------]
[-----------]αι ἐποιη[----------]
[-----------] ἐντὸς [-----------]
10  [---------ὑ]π⟨ὸ⟩ πο[-----------]
[----------------------------]
```

Line 10. [---]ς ὅπω[ς ---] Meritt. The remains are uncertain, but while the circular letter undoubtedly carries a central dot, theta can hardly be accommodated to its surroundings.

The small and crowded lettering is plain and without special characteristics. The comparatively deep cutting in proportion to size causes it to appear stubby and thickset. The circular letters tend to be pendent from the upper lettering line; the "free ends" of the strokes of upsilon are emphasized (cf. **120**), but other letters are not so treated.

The fragment seems likely to belong to an honorary decree of uncertain application.

Lines 3 and 7 might be indicative of epimeletai for some festival. For line 5 Meritt compared the Delian text *IG* XI, iv, 759 (*Syll.*[3], 576), line 6, of a century later, ἐνδημήσας πλείω χρόνον, which would suppose a foreigner resident in Athens for a considerable period.

But it is not beyond the bounds of possibility that the reference to ἀγῶνες and perhaps to some celebratory sacrifice after the conclusion of perils that had lasted some time may have a connection with the circumstances of **114** and **120**; and it is also possible that the text published by A. P. Matthaiou in *Horos* 4, 1986, pp. 19–23 (see also *SEG* XXXVI, 165), is to be set in the same context (cf. A. G. Woodhead, *Hesperia* 58, 1989, pp. 297–301). If so, the date of the present inscription might be referred to the year 304/3 (*vel paullo post*), and the events concerned might be accorded an importance in the tradition hitherto unrecognized.

FRAGMENT OF A DECREE

151. A fragment of a stele of blue Hymettian marble (I 6314), with part of the left side (worked with a toothed chisel) and original rough-picked back preserved but otherwise broken all around, discovered on June 13, 1950, in the curbing of a Turkish well north of the Odeion (M 8). The inscribed surface is sheared off to the right, but evidently the greater part of the width of the stele is preserved either on or below the surface. The vertical striations of the toothed chisel remain clear on the inscribed surface.

H. 0.19 m.; W. 0.237 m.; Th. 0.048 m.
LH. 0.005 m.
Στοιχ. (square) 0.012 m.

Ed. B. D. Meritt, *Hesperia* 30, 1961, pp. 257–258, no. 60, with photograph pl. 47. See also *SEG* XXI, 529.

saec. IV/III *a.*   ΣΤΟΙΧ. 20

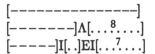

```
[---------------]
[-------]Λ[...8....]
[-----]Ι[..]ΕΙ[...7...]
```

```
           [...8....]πλιας [...7....]
           [...7....]ειδαι[...8....]
    5      [.]νέων· ἀναγράψ[αι δὲ τόδε]
           [τ]ὸ ψήφισμα ἐ[ν στήλαις λι]
           [θ]ίναις τρι[σὶν καὶ στῆσα]
           [ι] τὴν μὲν ἐ[ν ....11......]
           [....]γ, τὴν [δὲ ...10......]
    10     [..6...]ωι ἐγ[....9...]
           [...8....]ι ποσ[...8....]
           [....9....]τρε[...8...]
           [....11....]Ι[...8...]
           [....11....]Γ[...8...]
    15     [----------------]
```

Line 1. So Meritt, but "*reliquiae incertae*" might be a preferable description.   Line 2. [————]ει Meritt. Line 3. [....9....]σιας Meritt.   Line 4. ΕΙΔΑΙΜ[...7....] Meritt, but the mu must be regarded as doubtful. Line 9. [————]ι τὴν Meritt, perhaps rightly. Line 10. Or ἐχ.

The thin, rather scratchy writing is tolerably well formed. It looks forward to the 3rd century rather than back to the 4th in its overall appearance. The narrow omega, with horizontals almost as angled serifs, is distinctive. M. B. Walbank in an extensive study (*BSA* 84, 1989, pp. 399–405; cf. *SEG* XXXIX, 329) has included this inscription with thirty-three others (to which six further possibilities are added) that he considers to be the work of a single craftsman, whom he names the "Mason of *IG* II² 497". **114, 115, 118, 120, 122, 129,** and **155** are among those he attributes to this hand, the securely dated evidence for which lies between 307/6 and *ca.* 299/8; but the career of this same man, if all the material be taken into account, may extend from the late 320's to *ca.* 280. For the cruciform shape of phi (line 6), itself indicative for dating purposes, see **102.** J. Kirchner regarded the archonship of Isaios (284/3) as its lower chronological limit.

Lines 5–8. These lines alone offer the possibility of connected sense in this fragment and delimit its lateral dimension. The provision that three stone stelai be erected is unusual: cf. *IG* II², 125 (M. N. Tod, *GHI* II, pp. 161–163, no. 154; *SEG* XXXIV, 67), lines 17–19. Meritt took this clause as an indication that the decree probably emanated not from the Athenian boule and demos but from a society or a religious group or even from a phyle or deme.

FRAGMENT OF AN HONORARY DECREE

152. A fragment of a stele of Pentelic marble (I 2767), with part of the left edge preserved but otherwise broken all around, discovered on April 13, 1935, in a context of Early Byzantine date southwest of the Stoa of Attalos (P 13–14).

H. 0.235 m.; W. 0.09 m.; Th. 0.105 m.
LH. 0.005 m.
Στοιχ. (square, with slight irregularities) 0.0125 m.

Ed. B. D. Meritt, *Hesperia* 29, 1960, p. 5, no. 4, with photograph pl. 1. See also *SEG* XIX, 63, where suggested readings by A. M. Woodward for lines 4, 6, and 8 are recorded.

saec. IV/III *a.*   ΣΤΟΙΧ.

```
        [--------------------------]
        [..5..]π[------------------]
        [....]στα[-----------------]
        [....]ιαι[-----------------]
        [...]ιτω[------------------]
    5   [..]αι 'Αθ[-----------------]
        [.]ανιας [-------------εὐε]
        ργέτη[ν -----------τῶι δήμω]
        ι τῶι 'Αθ[ηναίων -----------]
        ἐπιμε[ληθῆναι(?) -----------]
    10  νου χα[--------------------]
```

[.]ι εἰ[ς --------------------]
[. .]τη[--------------------]
[--------------------------]

Line 3. ιδι Meritt. Line 4. ιτω Woodward, correctly; ιτο Meritt. Line 5. [. .]διδο[----] Meritt; ἀπ' Ἀθ[ην---] is also possible. Line 6. So Meritt, correctly; Woodward's [.]ληι ἀσ[---] (βο|υ]λῆι[?]) is not supported by the stone. A name such as Λυ|σ]ανίας or Παυ|σ]ανίας is possible. Line 8. ι τῶι λο[--] Meritt; ι τῶι Ἀθ[-----] Woodward, which seems to find confirmation on the stone. Lines 9–10. ἐπιμε[ληθῆναι ----τῆς ποιήσεως τοῦ στεφά]||νου χα[ὶ τῆς ἀναγορεύσεως ----] Meritt.

The rather pusillanimous writing is reminiscent of **140** in the inconsistency of its lettering (especially epsilon and omega), but the letters are more carefully set out, with generous spacing. The "triangular letters" (alpha, delta, and lambda) are widely spread. The cross-stroke of alpha is in places omitted and gives rise to confusion with delta elsewhere. Meritt assigned the inscription on the grounds of its lettering to the 4th century, without further definition. It may perhaps be more closely associated with the end of the century, with the possibility that it may belong after rather than before 300 B.C. M. B. Walbank (*per ep.*) has made comparisons with *IG* II², 579, for which J. Kirchner accepted U. Koehler's date of "fin. s. IV a.", and with 461 (= 726), where in the former entry the inscription is set in 307/6, the year of Anaxikrates (see p. 169 above), and in the latter the date is given as "init. s. III". If these comparisons are valid, they would reinforce the dating for the fragment here proposed.

Line 7 suggests that the text is that of an honorary decree; but beyond that the fragmentary remains offer no assistance.

THE WIFE AND SON OF OLYMPIODOROS OF GARGETTOS HONORED

153. A stele of Pentelic marble (I 6968) remade from an orthostate block and much damaged and discolored, removed during 1959 from a tower of the Post-Herulian Wall opposite the Church of the Holy Apostles (Q–R 16) but not recognized as bearing an inscription until June, 1962. The orthostate block showed anathyrosis on its right side and a cutting for a hook clamp in its top surface on the right. It also carried a molding 0.08 m. in height across the top of its front face. To fit it for reuse as a stele designed for an inscriptional record, the block was roughly trimmed down on the left side, and the molding was cut away. An area of the front face was additionally smoothed down to receive the inscription, which is thus written in a slightly depressed panel. At a later stage, the inscription was deliberately but inefficiently erased, with the result that some of the text is still reasonably legible, although for the most part it can be deciphered only with difficulty, if at all.

H. 0.796 m.; W. 0.32 m.; Th. 0.145 m. (at top)–0.17 m. (at bottom).
LH. 0.006 m.

Ed. B. D. Meritt, *Hesperia* 36, 1967, pp. 58–59, no. 4, with photographs pls. 19, 20. See also *SEG* XXIV, 116.

saec. IV/III *a.*   NON-ΣΤΟΙΧ. *ca.* 35

[----------------------------](?)
[....ᶜᵃ·¹¹....]ΝΙΔΙ[. .]ΙΑΛΗ[...ᶜᵃ·⁸... ἔθυ]
[σεν τὰ] ἱερὰ τ[ὰ χ]αίρια τεῖ Ἀθην[ᾶι χ]αὶ τοῖς
[ἄλλοι]ς θεοῖς, χαὶ στεφανῶσαι αὐτὴν θαλ[λοῦ]
[στεφά]νωι· ἐπαινέσαι δὲ χαὶ τὸν ὑὸν αὐτῆς
5 [.ᶜᵃ·⁵. χ]λέα Ὀλυ[μ]πιο[δ]ώρου Γαργήττιον χαὶ στ[ε]
[φανῶσ]αι αὐτὸν θαλλοῦ στεφάνωι ὅτι ἐπιμε[μέ]
[ληται] πισ[τ]ῷ[ς ²⁻³] τοῦ παρασιτίου χαὶ [³⁻⁴.]
[......ᶜᵃ·¹⁴.....χ]αὶ τ[οῦ] οἰκοδομήματος [. .]ΓΟ
[---------]ι[ς πρ]υταν[εί]α αὐτοὺς [------]
10 [³⁻⁴.] ἄλλων Τ[...]ΝΓΑ[.ᶜᵃ·⁶..]Ν[..ᶜᵃ·⁷... ἀναγρά]
[ψαι δ]ὲ τόδε τὸ ψήφισμα τοὺς ἄρχοντας του[. .]
[.ᶜᵃ·⁵.]ηνος ἐν τῶι ἱερ[ῶι] ἐν στήληι λιθίνηι. *vacat*
vacat

Meritt assessed the date of this inscription as "probably near the end of the fourth century", largely on the basis of the cruciform phi best visible in lines 3 and 6, for which see **102** and **114**. The difficulties of reading the semiobliterated text are compounded by the execrable script in which it was inscribed. Even though the damage which the stone has suffered may permit less than justice to be done to it, the lettering is undeniably poor in quality, irregular in arrangement, and incompetent in execution. Individual letters are wide in proportion to their height, and the strokes are badly articulated. Especially noteworthy, as well as the phi already mentioned, are epsilon with three long horizontal strokes of equal length, sigma with external strokes parallel, and a perfunctory omega very open at the base and with vestigial side strokes.

The *editio princeps* offered a provisional text, especially in lines 7, 8, and 10, in the hope that more might eventually be won by more prolonged study of the stone, the squeezes, and the photographs. A very little has emerged from this process, and further study faces the law of diminishing returns. If Meritt's reading of line 9, retained in the above text, is indeed correct (see below), the enactment mentions one of the phylai during its period in prytany and thus involves the Athenian demos as a whole. But the poverty of the workmanship argues against the recognition of this document as a decree of the boule and demos, and in other respects also it need be no more than the enactment of a religious organization or comparable group. The formula instructing that the stele be inscribed and erected (lines 10–12) also suggests as much in its departure from the recognized phraseology and reference to the usual officials. Line 9 should therefore, perhaps, be reconsidered in this light, and the archons in line 11 are likely to be officers of the organization concerned. If the inscription was confined to the "depressed panel", described above, it seems to have consisted of no more than twelve lines, but the material in lines 2–3 can hardly be reckoned to come so early in the total enactment.

Line 1. Before nu, possibly a circular letter. Line 5. No other Olympiodoros of Gargettos or of its phyle Aigeis (after 307/6, Antigonis) is attested. Line 7. [λῆται –]ΓΙΣ. ΣΩ. ΤΟΥ. Κ[–––]ΣΙΤΙΟΥΚΑΙ[–––] Meritt. Line 9. Meritt's reading is shown in the text: but the traces also seem to offer [–––]ΚΕΝ[.³⁻⁴.]ΥΤΑΝ[...] αὐτούς. Meritt's alpha before αὐτούς is doubtful. Line 10. [–––––]ΑΛΙΩΝΤ...ΝΓΑ..Ω[–––ἀναγρά] Meritt. Line 11. [–––––]Ε[..$^{ca.}$ 8...]ΛΙΟ. ΟΝΟΑΡΜΗΜΑΤΟΣ...ΓΟ Meritt.

Lines 3–5. For the award of an olive stephanos to Athenian citizens cf. **123**, line 20 and A. S. Henry, *Honours*, pp. 39–40. Strictly speaking, neither Olympiodoros' wife nor his son (if under age) was a citizen, but both could be (and clearly were) subsumed under the same general formula.

FRAGMENT OF AN HONORARY DECREE

154. A narrow fragment of a stele of bluish Pentelic marble (I 200), broken all around (including the back), discovered on March 17, 1932, in a marble pile in the west part of the Market Square (H–K 8–11). The face of the fragment is much rubbed, and in the eleven surviving lines of the text no more than twenty-two letters can be clearly read.

H. 0.17 m.; W. 0.088 m.; Th. 0.021 m.

LH. 0.007 m.

Στοιχ. Hor. 0.012 m.; Vert. 0.0146 m.

Ed. M. B. Walbank, *Hesperia* 54, 1985, pp. 319–321, no. 6, with photograph pl. 88. See also *SEG* XXXV, 82.

saec. IV/III *a.*   ΣΤΟΙΧ.

```
      [————————————————]
      [——————————]Θ[——————]
      [———————]ΥΦΑ[——————]
      [————————]ιδεχ[——————]
      [———————]νθεομ[——————]
  5   [——————]προβ[————————]
      [——————]ευθ[————————]
      [—————]ροξε[————————]
      [——————]Φ[——————————]
      [————————————————]
 10   [——————]Ε[——————————]
      [——————]Ο[——————————]
      [————————————————]
```

The readings are those of the *editio princeps*. Walbank further noted that in lines 8 and 9 the traces suggest

```
      [———————]ΕΦΑ[———————]
      [————————]Ξ[————————].
```

The lettering appears to be plain and without marked characteristics.

Believing that line 2 contains the name of the γραμματεύς of the year (end of the patronymic and the beginning of the demotic) as part of the prescript of a decree, Walbank was prepared to attribute the inscription to 295/4 B.C., when the γραμματεύς is known to have been Δωρόθεος Ἀριστο[..]νου Φαληρεύς. If this is indeed the *initium decreti*, and if the three letters in question are to be so interpreted, it should be noted that the details of the γραμματεύς of 306/5, who might have come from Phaleron, are not known and that the phyle Aiantis may have provided the equally unknown γραμματεύς of 311/10, a year unlikely on other grounds for the attribution of a text such as this (see p. 161 above).

Walbank continued with the suggestion that line 3 contains the remains of the prytany day, and he offered a reconstruction of lines 1–6 (shown below, but omitted in *SEG, loc. cit.*) in which, as he noted, it is necessary to presume the lack of the name of the month (in this case Posideon) as well as of the phrase ἐκκλησία (or a variant of it). For the omission of the name of the month cf., for example, *IG* II², 348, 354, 356, 357, and 360. The omission of the ἐκκλησία formula is not uncommon, and this too occurs predominantly in the last decades of the 4th century.

On Walbank's calculation, the date proves to be either Posideon 13 = pryt. VI, 16 = 161st day or Posideon 16 = pryt. VI, 19 = 164th day. The latter date is perhaps attested as a meeting day of the assembly on two occasions in the 4th century: see J. D. Mikalson, *Sacred and Civil Calendar*, pp. 91–92. Walbank's restored text is thus as follows:

ΣΤΟΙΧ. 42

[Ἐπὶ Νικοστράτου ἄρχοντος ἐπὶ τῆς Ἐρεχ]θ[εῖδος ἕκτη]
[ς πρυτανείας, ἧι Δωρόθεος Ἀριστο..νο]υ Φα[ληρεὺς ἐγ]
[ραμμάτευεν, ..5–6.. ἐπὶ δέκα, ..5–6.. κα]ὶ δεκ[άτει τῆς π]
[ρυτανείας· τῶν προέδρων ἐπεψήφιζε]ν Θεομ[...8....]
5   [.. καὶ συμπρόεδροι· ἔδοξεν τῶι δήμω]ι· Πρόβ[ουλος(?) ...]
[–––––––––εἶπεν· κτλ.]

Walbank doubted that line 7, on his interpretation, contained any reference to *proxenia*.

Much of the foregoing consists of accumulated hypotheses, and a general date, with a text showing no reconstruction (as in the original presentation of it), has been preferred here.

MEMBERS OF AN EMBASSY HONORED

155. A fragment of a stele of Pentelic marble (I 5836), with the left edge and original back preserved, but otherwise broken, discovered on May 16, 1939, on the North Slope between the Akropolis and the Areopagos (R 23).

H. 0.11 m.; W. 0.09 m.; Th. 0.04 m.
LH. 0.006 m.
Στοιχ. (square) *ca.* 0.01 m.

Ed. B. D. Meritt, *Hesperia* 30, 1961, pp. 258–259, no. 62, with photograph pl. 47. See also *SEG* XXI, 361.

init. saec. III *a.*   ΣΤΟΙΧ. 30

[––––––––––––––––––––]
[....]ε[..............25..............]
[.]ου Παι[...........24...........]
ἐκ Φωκέω[ν........22...........]
ν τὰ συμφ[έροντα τῶι δήμωι τῶι Ἀθηναί]
5   ων, ἀγαθῆ[ι τύχηι δεδόχθαι τῶι δήμωι ἐ]
παινέσ[αι αὐτοὺς καὶ στεφανῶσαι ἕκα]
στον αὐ[τῶν χρυσῶι στεφάνωι κατὰ τὸν]
νόμον [..............25..............]
[.]⌐[––––––––––––––––]
10   [––––––––––––––––––]

The writing is characteristic of the early 3rd century, with some "disjointing" and lack of precision but at the same time a general tidiness of appearance. Its most notable features are the cruciform phi, for which see **102**, and the narrow omega with angled "horizontals", for which see **114** and **118**; nu is variable in shape. There is some emphasis on the "free ends" of strokes. M. B. Walbank has included this inscription among those attributed to his "Mason of *IG* II² 497": see **151**.

A *terminus post quem* for the enactment is provided by the partly restored reference to a stephanos awarded κατὰ τὸν νόμον (lines 6–8), phraseology which postdates 302 B.C. Cf. **112**, commentary on lines 5–7 and **122**, commentary on line 26, with references there.

Lines 2–3. The surviving letters of the second line suggest a patronymic and Attic demotic. Lack of space prevents their interpretation as part of the name of the proposer of the decree, with honors being voted to an embassy from Phokis, and it is more likely, as Meritt suggested, that Athenian ambassadors returning from Phokis were here honored. As an example of honors decreed for a successful delegation Meritt compared **182**. Lines 3–4. Perhaps ἐκ Φωκέω[ν ἀφικόμενοι, ἀεὶ πράττουσι]|ν or ἐκ Φωκέω[ν ἀεὶ πράττοντες διετέλεσα]|ν.

Line 5 begins the motion formula. For ἀγαθῆι τύχηι cf. **72**, commentary on lines 7–8. The decree was apparently nonprobouleumatic; cf. P. J. Rhodes, *Athenian Boule*, p. 264.

FRAGMENT OF AN HONORARY DECREE

156. A small fragment of a stele of Pentelic marble (I 5526), with the right side preserved but broken elsewhere, discovered on June 8, 1938, in a marble pile in the area west of the Stoa of Attalos (N–P 7–12).

H. 0.082 m.; W. 0.059 m.; Th. 0.038 m.
LH. 0.006 m.
Στοιχ. (square) 0.0103 m.

Ed. M. B. Walbank, *Hesperia* 58, 1989, pp. 93–94, no. 21, with photograph pl. 24. See also *SEG* XXXIX, 117.

init. saec. III *a.*   ΣΤΟΙΧ.

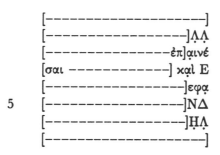

Walbank believed the similarity of style and lettering of this fragment with those of the text immediately preceding, **155**, to be such that it might have been a part of that inscription, from a point a little higher on the original stele.

Line 4. Alpha (if alpha it is) lacks a crossbar, as do other alphas on the fragment. The *editio princeps* suggested στ]εφα||[νῶσαι in lines 4–5.

ARISTOMENES OF PAIANIA HONORED

157. A small fragment of a stele of Hymettian marble (I 4848), with the right side preserved and with damage to the center of the inscribed surface, discovered on May 15, 1937, among the Late Roman destruction debris of a large monument at the fork of the Great Drain east of the Tholos (I 12). The fragment was identified as part of the same monument as *IG* II², 691, now in the Epigraphical Museum (E.M. 7330), which was discovered in 1851 on the opposite side of the site of the agora, between the Church of Christ and the Hypapanti. The new fragment (*a*) belongs to a section of the text higher up the stele.

H. 0.09 m.; W. 0.075 m.; Th. 0.043 m.
LH. 0.007 m.
Στοιχ. (square) 0.02 m.

Ed. E. Schweigert, *Hesperia* 8, 1939, pp. 42–44, no. 11, with photograph. Schweigert also gave a text of *IG* II², 691 (hereafter fragment *b*), and this is, for convenience, repeated below.

init. saec. III *a.*   ΣΤΟΙΧ. 20

(a)
```
            [—————————————]
            [........19........]α
            [....8...., ἀγαθεῖ τύ]χει δ
            [εδόχθαι τεῖ βουλεῖ] ἐπαι
            [νέσαι ᾿Αριστομένην] ᾿Α[ρ]ισ
   5        [τ..5... Παιανιέα ἀρ]ε[τ]ῆς
            [ἕνεκα καὶ δικαιοσύν]ης ἣ
            [ν ἔχων διετέλεσεν περὶ] τ
            [ὴν βουλὴν καὶ τὸν δῆμον]
                        lacuna
```
(b)
```
            [....10.... εἰς τὴν πρώτ]
   10       [ην] ἐκκλησ[ίαν χρηματίσα]
            ι περὶ τούτ[ων, γνώμην δὲ ξ]
            υμβάλλεσθα[ι τῆς βουλῆς]
            εἰς τὸν δῆμον ὅ[τι δοκεῖ τ]
            εῖ βουλεῖ ἐπα[ινέσαι ᾿Αρι]
   15       στομένην ᾿Αρ[ι]στ[..5... Πα]
            ιανιέα ἀρετῆς ἕ[νεκα καὶ]
            δικαιοσύνης [ἣ]ν [ἔχων διε]
            τέλεσεν περὶ τὴ[ν βουλὴν]
            καὶ τὸν δῆμο[ν, καὶ στεφαν]
   20       ῶσαι αὐτὸν [χρυσῶι στεφά]
            νωι κατ[ὰ τὸν νόμον· ὅπως δ’]
            ἂν ε[........16.......τ]
            ῆς πόλε[ως .....12......]
            ἔχειν [......15.......]
   25       ς νομ[......16.......]
            ον[........18.........]
            τ[.........19........]
            [——————————————]
```

The letters are relatively large and widely spaced. An early 3rd-century date, as indicated by Schweigert, appears to suit them well. The incision betrays some hesitancy, not dissimilar from that in **182**, but the lettering is not careless or "disjointed". With no more than 20 letters per line, the text is unusually narrow for the period. The restorations of fragment *a* were modeled by Schweigert on the text of fragment *b*.

Line 2. ἀγαθεῖ τύχει. See **72**, commentary on lines 7–8. Fragment *a* provides part of the *probouleuma*, which appears as a ratified enactment of the boule and demos in the context of fragment *b*. Cf. P. J. Rhodes (*Athenian Boule*, pp. 251 and 272), who overlooked the connection between the two fragments. The relationship in its complete form is illustrated by *IG* II², 330, lines 29–65; see Schweigert's commentary.

Line 4. Aristomenes (*PA* 2003) is otherwise unknown.

Lines 5–8 and 16–19. Schweigert argued on the basis of the phraseology that Aristomenes had been a religious or secular official of the state. This "more elaborate formulation of the honorand's virtues", with the abstract noun qualified by a relative clause, occurs here at an earlier date than the earliest examples (especially with the nouns in evidence in this context) admitted by A. S. Henry, *Honours*, p. 43. Lines 9–18. For the full probouleumatic enactment formula see **52** and Rhodes, *Athenian Boule*, p. 65.

Line 21. That the stephanos is to be awarded κατὰ τὸν νόμον indicates that the enactment is to be dated later than 302 B.C., and this is the dating formula for *IG* II², 691, shown by J. Kirchner; see **155** and references there. This line appears to mark the beginning of a statement of "hortatory intention": see **86**, commentary on lines 21–24.

FRAGMENT OF AN HONORARY DECREE

158. A fragment of a stele of Pentelic marble (I 3632), with the original smooth-finished back and rough-picked bottom preserved, discovered on February 29, 1936, in a modern wall northeast of the Odeion (N 7).

H. 0.34 m.; W. 0.165 m.; Th. 0.171 m.

LH. 0.003 (omega in line 17)–0.007 m. (sigma).

Στοιχ. (square) Hor. 0.0096 m.; Vert. 0.0095 m.

Ed. B. D. Meritt, *Hesperia* 29, 1960, p. 52, no. 69, with photograph pl. 15. See also *SEG* XIX, 68 (with additional suggestions for lines 9, 11, and 19 by A. M. Woodward).

init. saec. III *a.*   ΣΤΟΙΧ.

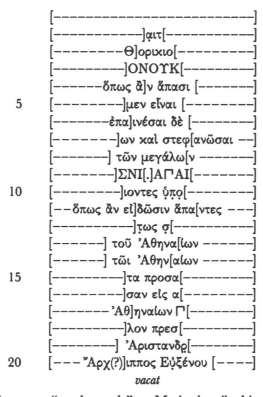

```
          [----------------------]
          [-----------]αιτ[-----------]
          [---------Θ]ορικιο[----------]
          [----------]ΟΝΟΥΚ[----------]
          [------ὅπως ἃ]ν ἅπασι [-------]
    5     [---------]μεν εἶναι [--------]
          [--------ἐπα]ινέσαι δὲ [--------]
          [-------]ων καὶ στεφ[ανῶσαι --]
          [--------] τῶν μεγάλω[ν -------]
          [-------]ΣΝΙ[.]ΑΓΑΙ[-------]
   10     [---------]ιοντες ὑπο[--------]
          [--ὅπως ἂν εἰ]δῶσιν ἅπα[ντες ---]
          [------------]τως σ[----------]
          [-------] τοῦ Ἀθηνα[ίων ------]
          [-------] τῶι Ἀθην[αίων ------]
   15     [---------]τα προσα[----------]
          [---------]σαν εἰς α[--------]
          [------- Ἀθ]ηναίων Γ[--------]
          [---------]λον πρεσ[--------]
          [---------] Ἀριστανδρ[--------]
   20     [--- Ἄρχ(?)]ιππος Εὐξένου [----]
                    vacat
```

The lettering is of the 3rd-century "careless style", as Meritt described it, generally puny and untidy. Omega is conspicuously small and flat; sigma and epsilon on the other hand are clumsy. The "circular letters" vary considerably in size and shape. The cruciform phi suggests that the text should be considered as antedating *ca.* 280 B.C.; see **102** and **151**. M. B. Walbank regarded the hand as close to that of *SEG* XXXII, 107 (*Hesperia* 51, 1982, pp. 52–53, no. 9; see **255B**), dated by him "*post a.* 286/5 *a.*" and in *SEG* as between 286/5 and 262.

The text is that of Meritt, with minor adjustments of reading. Line 4. ὅπως] ἂν Meritt. Line 9. So Meritt; ἀναγορεύ]σηι ὁ ἀγων[οθέτης --] Woodward, from the photograph. The difficult remains on the stone suggest ΣΝ (or Μ or Η) ▧ΟΑΓΩΙ. Line 10. ΥΠΟ is added to the letters discerned by Meritt. Line 11. δῶσιν ἂν Meritt; [-- εἰ]δῶσιν ἅπ[αντες Woodward. ΠΑ are visible on the stone. Line 12. Σ[.]ΟΣ Meritt. Line 13. τοῦ Ἀθη[ναίων Meritt. Line 18. Possibly πρεσ[βεῖς. Line 19. ἄριστα Ν[--] Meritt; Ἀριστανδ[ρο---] Woodward, from the photograph. The delta and the upright of rho are visible on the stone. The concluding list of names seems likely to represent a committee or board of delegates selected by the demos in the light of the content of the decree.

Line 20. [--]ιππος Εὔξενος Meritt. The reading is however Εὐξένου rather than Εὔξενος. The preceding name may be Ἄρχ]ιππος if, as is tempting, the connection may be made with a family of Eiresidai of which there are certainly two, perhaps three, pertinent testimonia. Εὔξενος Εἰρεσίδης was father of an ἔφηβος of 306/5 (*IG* II², 478, col. III, line 72) and might be identical with the Euxenos named here. An [---]ιππος Εὐξένου (*PA* 5889), designated only as Ἀθηναῖος, won the pankration at the Panathenaia at the end of the 3rd century (*IG* II², 2313, line 40). Finally, a Εὔξενος Ἀρχίππου Εἰρεσίδης was praised as ἐπιμελητὴς τῆς πομπῆς in 186/5 (*IG* II², 896, line 44): see *PA* 5892.

Lines 11 and perhaps 4 appear to introduce "hortatory intentions" of some kind; see **86**. But just too little survives on the fragment for coherent sense.

FRAGMENT OF AN HONORARY DECREE

159. A fragment of a stele of Pentelic marble (I 4496), with the right side and original rough-picked back preserved but very battered and pitted elsewhere, discovered on February 9, 1937, in a wall of a modern house east of the Post-Herulian Wall, southeast of the Market Square (U 22).

H. 0.18 m.; W. 0.17 m.; Th. 0.089 m.
LH. 0.008 m.

Ed. B. D. Meritt, *Hesperia* 29, 1960, p. 7, no. 8, with photograph pl. 2. See also *SEG* XIX, 70 (where the title "Honores generis eiusdem" should be corrected to "Honores cuiusdam").

init. saec. III *a.*   NON-ΣΤΟΙΧ. *ca.* 57

```
[------------------------------------------------------------]
[-------------------------------------------------]σ[----]
[----------------------------------δεδόχθ]αι τεῖ βουλεῖ τοὺ[ς]
[πρυτάνεις οἳ ἂν λάχωσι προεδρεύειν ἐν τῶι δήμωι χρη]ματί[σα]ι περὶ το[ύ]
[των, γνώμην δὲ ξυμβάλλεσθαι τῆς βουλῆς εἰς τὸν δ]ῆμον ὅτι δοκ[εῖ τεῖ βου]
[λεῖ ἐπαινέσαι . . . . . . . . . . ca. 21 . . . . . . . . . καὶ στεφ]ανῶσαι αὐτὸν χ[ρ]υ
[σῶι στεφάνωι κατὰ τὸν νόμον ἀρετῆς ἕνεκα καὶ φι]λοτιμίας τῆ[ς εἰς . . .]
[---------------------------------------]εν[. ca. 5 .]ν[------]
[------------------------------------------------------------]
```
5 (marks line 5)

The plain lettering is a little untidy but not slapdash and may be regarded as characteristic of its period. If χατὰ τὸν νόμον is correctly restored in line 6, the inscription must postdate 302 B.C.; see **155** and references there.

The text is that of Meritt, with slight adjustments of readings in lines 2–3 and 6–7. The decree was probouleumatic; cf. P. J. Rhodes, *Athenian Boule*, p. 253.

Lines 2–5. For the phraseology of the enactment formula, which omits the usual εἰς τὴν πρώτην (or ἐπιοῦσαν) ἐκκλησίαν, Meritt compared *IG* II², 676, lines 15–20. See, for the formula in general, **157**, commentary on lines 9–18 and references there. Line 6. On the virtues of the honorand cf. A. S. Henry, *Honours*, p. 42.

DECREE OF THE DEMESMEN OF PEIRAIEUS

160. Two joining fragments of the upper left section of a stele of Hymettian marble (I 217), with the flat top, left side, and original back preserved but with the upper left corner broken away, discovered on April 15, 1932, in the wall of a well in a modern pit at the north foot of the Areopagos (H 17). The inscribed surface shows the striations of a toothed chisel mostly in a diagonal direction from upper right to lower left.

Measurements of combined fragments: H. 0.475 m.; W. 0.385 m.; Th. 0.11 m.
LH. 0.005 (omicron)–0.009 m.
Στοιχ. (square) 0.016 m.

Ed. B. D. Meritt, *Hesperia* 3, 1934, pp. 44–46, no. 33, with photograph. See also P. Roussel, *BCH* 58, 1934, p. 91, note 1.

init. saec. III *a.*   ΣΤΟΙΧ.

```
        [. . . . .10. . . . .]ς Φιλιστίδου εἶπ[εν· -------------------]
        [. . . .8. . . .]ιου Πείρωνος τοῦ Α[-------------------]
        [. . .7. . .]ν ὑπὲρ ὑγιείας καὶ [-------------------]
        [. . .7. . .] δήμωι κτημάτων ε[-------------------]
    5   [. .5. . Π]ειραέων τῶι Ο[.]Ω[-------------------]
        [. . .]σον ἂν ἕκαστος βού[ληται -------------------]
        [. .] ἐπέδοσαν λίθους ὅπ[ως ἂν -------------χαὶ τὰ λ]
        [ο]ιπὰ φραχθεῖ, ἐψηφίσ[θαι Πειραεῦσιν -------------π]
        άντας Πειραέας κοιν[-------------------τὴ]
   10   ν οἰκοδομίαν ⋮ ΗΗ δρα[χμὰς -------------------]
        αὐ⟨τ⟩ῶν καὶ γυναικῶ[ν -------------------]
```

κοινῆι ⟨τ⟩ε φιλοτιμ[--------------------------------οἱ ἄλ]
λοι δημόται μετὰ τ[ῶν ----------------------------------]
[ἐ]παρχὴν εἶναι τῶι [--------------------------------Βο]

15 ηδρομιῶνι καὶ Πυα[νοψιῶνι ----------------------------]
ν· ἀναγράψαι δὲ τόδ[ε τὸ ψήφισμα --------εἰς στήλην λιθί]
νην καὶ στῆσαι πρὸ[ς---------------------------ἐπὶ τοῦ τ]
οίχου πρὸς τὴν εἴσ[οδον----------------------τὰς δὲ ἐπι]
δόσεις ἐπιδόντω[ν---------------------------------ἐ]

20 πάρξωνται τῶι [------------------------------ἔχ]
αστος ἐπήρξατ[ο--------------------------τὴν οἰκοδ]
ομίαν καὶ την [-----------------------------------]
ηται τὰ χρή[ματα---------------------------------]
ι δὲ καὶ τ[---]

25 ἐπαρχε[--]
ημη[--]
[---]

The lettering of this text, well characteristic of its period, is of a tidy and regular appearance with thin strokes; but, while not positively of the "careless style", it is inaccurate in detail, with overlapping or "disjointing" of elements of letters. Many letters are inconsistently written, kappa and omega being notable among them; the oval of phi is pointed at its ends; the shapes of upsilon and chi are especially distinctive. There is some emphasis on the "free ends" of strokes.

Line 1. As commonly with decrees of phylai, demes, etc., the decree is introduced only by the name of the proposer, without other preamble. Line 2. Πείρωνος. Clear on the stone, this is apparently a proper name (patronymic after [– – – –]ιου ?), unique in Attic prosopography. Roussel hesitated over it ("le nom propre . . . me parait suspect"). τοῦ Α[– – – – –]. Meritt's commentary envisaged that both names were preceded by the definite article and compared the preambles of early-3rd-century decrees during the second period of the *anagrapheis*, in which the patronymic of the *anagrapheus* is so qualified. These instances are very much *sui generis*, but a problem does arise when both name and patronymic are in the genitive case, and it is possible that Α– – – – is here a papponymic, differentiated from the patronymic preceding it by the article in order to avoid three immediately succeeding personal names in the genitive. Cf. the article used before the siglum for the patronymic, as in *IG* II², 4513, line 4. Alternatively, τοῦ Α[– – –] may begin a phrase of a different character, on some such lines as ἐπὶ – – – –]ίου Πείρωνος τοῦ ᾿Α[σκληπιοῦ ἱερέως or τοῦ ᾿Α[σκληπιείου ἐπιμελομένου. For the Asklepieion in Peiraieus see Schol. Aristophanes, *Plutus*, line 621.

Line 3. Cf. *IG* II², 1215, line 18. Line 5. A. M. Woodward (*per ep.*) suggested θ[ε]ῶ[ι, and this may well be correct. On the other hand, examination of the stone suggests that the penultimate surviving letter might be nu, eta, or even rho, with epsilon a less likely candidate: thus τῶι ὀρω[ι – –] might be possible. The issue remains open.

Line 6. ὅ]σον G. A. Stamires, in a personal note. Line 9. κοιν[ῆι Stamires. Line 11. *Lapis* ΑΥΓΩΝ. Line 12. *Lapis* ΓΕ. Line 14. [ἀ]παρχὴν Meritt; [ἐ]παρχὴν Roussel. Cf. lines 19–21 and 25 and *IG* II², 1215, lines 12–19.

The decree appears to be concerned with contributions by the members of the deme to some public construction or works of importance to the community as a whole, whether religious (e.g., the Asklepieion, on which cf. line 2) or secular (as, for instance, the theater, on which see **93**). For another decree of the demesmen of Peiraieus, of this period, see *IG* II², 1214.

This text is no. 88 among the deme decrees of Peiraieus (nos. 83–90) listed by D. Whitehead (*The Demes of Athens, 508/7–ca. 250 B.C.*, 1986, pp. 385–386), who regards demes which we know to have put up public inscriptions in the 3rd century as always, for one reason or another, special cases, and Peiraieus as always an anomaly. Among details of this inscription, he treats lines 11 (pp. 79–80, note 54) and 12 (pp. 244–245): for the proposer see p. 445, no. 307. See also R. Garland, *The Piraeus from the Fifth to the First Century B.C.*, 1987, p. 227, no. 5.

A DECREE OF THE COMBINED ORGEONES OF THE HERO ECHELOS AND OF THE HEROINES

161. The damaged upper section of a stele of Hymettian marble (I 1906); both sides, the original back, and the projection of the crowning molding are preserved, but the stele is broken below and at both upper corners. It was discovered on April 28, 1934, in a Byzantine pithos on the North Slope of the Areopagos (I 19).

H. 0.293 m.; W. 0.315 m.; Th. 0.082 m.
LH. 0.008 m. (omicron 0.006 m., omega 0.005 m.). Ten lines occupy 0.10 m.

Ed. B. D. Meritt, *Hesperia* 11, 1942, pp. 282–287, no. 55, with photograph. Further discussion: J. and L. Robert, *REG* 57, 1944, pp. 197–198, no. 67; W. S. Ferguson, *HarvThRev* 37, 1944, pp. 73–79 and 94–95; S. Dow, *HarvThRev* 37, 1944, pp. 135–136 (on the spacing of the letters); Ferguson, *Hesperia*, Supplement VIII, 1949, pp. 130–131 (on lines 16–23, with revised text by Meritt); F. Sokolowski, *Lois sacrées, Supplément*, pp. 54–56, no. 20 (text with some revised restorations and a brief commentary on details). See also *SEG* XXI, 530. Since the original edition, a small chip of the stone has been lost at the beginnings of lines 5 and 6.

init. saec. III *a.*   NON-ΣΤΟΙΧ.

```
        [Λυσίας Περι]άνδρου Πλωθεὺς εἶ[πεν· ἀγαθεῖ τύχει]
        [δεδόχθαι] τοῖς ὀ[ρ]γεῶσιν· ὅπως ἂν δι[ατηρῆται τῶν]
        [θυσιῶν ἡ κοινω]νία εἰς τὸν ἅπαντα χρό[νον τῶι κοι]
        [ν]ῶι τῶι πρὸς τοῖς Καλλιφάνους καὶ τῶ[ι τοῦ ἥρωος Ἐ]
   5    χέλου, ἀναγράψαντας τοὺς ὀφείλοντά[ς τι εἰς τὴν κοι]
        νωνίαν ἐν στήλει λιθίνει στῆσαι παρὰ τ[ὸν βωμὸν]
        ἐν τῶι ἱερῶι τά τε κεφάλαια καὶ τὸν τόκο[ν ὁπόσου]
        ἂν ἔχει ἕκαστος· ἀναγράψαι δὲ καὶ τὰ ψη[φίσματα]
        τὰ ἀρχαῖα εἰς τὴν στήλην· ἐπιμεληθῆναι δ[ὲ . . .ca. 8. . .]
  10    να τῆς ἀναγραφῆς καὶ τῆς στάσεως τῆς στήλης χ[αὶ λο]
        γίσ[α]σθαι ὅ τι ἂν εἰς ταῦτα ἀναλώσει τῶι κοινῶι.

        Ἔδοξεν τοῖς ὀργεῶσιν· τὸν ἑστιάτορα θύειν τὴν [θυσί]
        αν μηνὸς Ἑκατονβαιῶνος ἑβδόμει καὶ ὀγδόει ἐπ[ὶ] δ
        ἑκα· θύειν δὲ τεῖ πρώτει ταῖς ἡρωίναις χοῖρον, τῶι δὲ [ἥ]
  15    [ρ]ωι ἱερεῖον τέλεον καὶ τράπεζαν παρατιθέναι, τεῖ δ[ὲ]
        [ὑστερ]αίαι τῶι ἥρωι ἱερεῖον τέλεον· λογίζεσθαι δὲ ὅ τι ἂν
        [ἀναλ]ώσει· ἀναλίσκειν δὲ μὴ πλέον τῆς προσόδου· [ν]
        [εμέτω] δὲ τὰ κρέα τοῖς {οις} ὀργεῶσι τοῖς παροῦσι καὶ τοῖ[ς]
        [ὑοῖς τὴν] εἰς ἡμίσεαν καὶ ταῖς γυναιξὶ ταῖς τῶν ὀργεώ[ν]
  20    [ων, διδ]οὺς ταῖς ἐλευθέραις τὴν ἰσαίαν καὶ ταῖς θυγα[α]
        [τράσι τὴν εἰς ἡμί]σεαν καὶ ἀκολούθωι μιᾶι τὴν εἰς ἡμ[ί]
        [σεαν· παραδιδότω δὲ τ]ῶι ἀνδρὶ τῆς γυναικὸς τὴν με
        [ρίδα.          vacat          ]          vacat

        [Ἔδοξεν τοῖς ὀργεῶσιν· τὸν ἑστιά]τορα τῶν ἐπιγενομέ
  25    [νων —————————————————————————————]
        [—————————————————————————————————]
```

The lettering is plain, rather crowded, and generally inelegant, with each letter stroke the evident product of repeated action with the chisel. The forms of the letters are not inaccurate, but there is considerable variety among the different instances of the same letter, most particularly in sigma and omega. Mu is exceptionally wide, but conversely iota is crowded in. This makes it the more difficult to assess space available in lacunae; see Dow, *loc. cit.* The inscribed surface is covered with short horizontal striations made by a toothed chisel.

Line 1. The proposer is restored, conformably with the available space, as Lysias, son of Periandros, of Plotheia and was identified by Meritt with the father of the prytanis Periandros, son of Lysias, who served on the boule perhaps in the 250's (*PA* 9380 and 11799). If this is correct, it reinforces the indications of the style of the lettering that the inscription is to be dated in the early part of the 3rd century, a generation before 256/5.

Lines 3–5. There were two organizations (κοινά) of orgeones, acting in concert (κοινωνία) and forming a united institution (κοινόν). See Meritt, *op. cit.*, p. 283, with bibliography, Ferguson, *HarvThRev*, *vol. cit.*, p. 76. One κοινόν is identified by the site of its meeting place (near the property of Kalliphanes) and the other by the hero whose cult it fostered. In the first of the ἀρχαῖα ψηφίσματα this hero is referred to as "the hero" and no more; in lines 4–5 he is identified as Echelos, eponymous of the district Echelidai near Neon Phaleron. See *IG* II², 4546 (*SEG* XII, 163, XXXVI, 268) and A. Milchhöfer, *RE* V, ii, *s.v.* Echelidai. The headquarters of his κοινόν was probably in the same district. Thus, since the present text was found in the area of the agora in the city, it more likely emanated from the precinct "of the heroines" belonging to the other κοινόν, near Kalliphanes' property. See Meritt, *op. cit.*, pp. 284–286.

Lines 8–9. Of the "old decrees", the first, preserved almost entire, runs from line 12 through line 23. Of a second, only a fragment of the first line survives in line 24. In both, the fact of the decision is alone recorded, and the names of the proposers have not been transmitted.

Lines 9–10. δ[ὲ τὸν μνῆμο]||να Sokolowski, who adds further bibliography on the title. Cf. *IG* II², 1247, lines 19–20; Aristotle, *Politics* 1321b39; R. Martin, *BCH* 64/65, 1940/1941, p. 188. Line 12. On the ἑστιάτωρ see L. Robert, *RevPhil*, 3rd ser. 13, 1939, p. 124 and note 2; Sokolowski, *loc. cit.* The office of "host" was apparently a *liturgy* among the orgeones, which was filled by rotation. See Ferguson, *HarvThRev, vol. cit.*, pp. 94–95.

Lines 17–18. [ν|έμειν] Sokolowski, following Meritt's first text and the suggestion of J. Bousquet; [ν|εμέτω] Meritt, in revision. See on line 20 below. Lines 18–19. τοῖ[ς | υοῖς τὴν] Meritt; τοῖ[ς | παισὶ τὴν] Sokolowski, but this is less likely for reasons of space unless pi be removed to the end of line 18, where there may be room in the lacuna for it. Line 20. [ων μετ'αὐτ]οὺς Meritt, in the *editio princeps*; [ων, ἂν ἦι β]οὺς Ferguson, *HarvThRev, loc. cit.* Both suggestions were abandoned in favor of the text shown by Meritt and Ferguson, *Hesperia*, Supplement VIII, *loc. cit.* [ων ἐκ γέν]ους Sokolowski, tentatively, but although this would come within the limits of space set by Dow, *loc. cit.*, it is probably too long for the space available. Διδούς in line 20 requires νεμέτω and probably παραδιδότω in lines 17–18 and 22, but a *constructio ad sensum* retaining the infinitives with the nominative participle would not be impossible; cf. Meisterhans-Schwyzer³, p. 204, no. 4. Ταῖς ἐλευθέραις. "The grown women, both wives and non-wives, as distinguished from minors and servants" (Meritt). Cf. Ferguson, *Hesperia*, Supplement VIII, p. 131 and note 2.

Line 22. παραδιδότω Meritt, in revision; παραδοῦναι Sokolowski, following the *editio princeps*.

For other decrees of orgeones, found both in the Agora excavations and elsewhere, see **130**.

CITIZENSHIP BESTOWED UPON ARISTOLAS AND SOSTRATOS

162 (Pl. 16). A fragment of a stele of Hymettian marble (I 4812), broken on all sides, discovered on May 6, 1937, near the surface under what was formerly Akropolis Street, east of the Post-Herulian Wall (T 24–25). E. Schweigert noted that it formed the upper section (fragment *a*) of the stele *IG* II², 643 (thenceforward fragment *b*), there being no join between the stones. The inscribed surface of both pieces is marked by the striations of a toothed chisel, mostly in a diagonal direction from upper left to lower right.

a: H. 0.095 m.; W. 0.15 m.; Th. 0.075 m.

b: H. 0.53 m.; W. 0.48 m.; Th. 0.10 m.

LH. 0.006 m. (omicron 0.004–0.005 m.).
Στοιχ. (square, with slight irregularities) ca. 0.013 m.

Ed. B. D. Meritt, *Hesperia* 9, 1940, pp. 80–83, no. 13, with photographs of both fragments. The decree was there assigned to the year 298/7; for subsequent discussion as to the date and restoration of fragment *a* see the commentary below. An amended text of lines 4–6 by Meritt was offered in *Hesperia* 38, 1969, p. 108; see also *SEG* XXV, 85, with references to the discussion of the calendric date up to 1971.

inter annos 300/299 *et* 295/4 *a.*   ΣΤΟΙΧ. 29

    (*a*)   ['Επὶ.....................²⁶.................]
            [....¹⁰.... ἐνάτης] πρ[υτανείας ἧι .]
            [.........¹⁵.......]νους Φ[...⁷... ἐγ]
            [ραμμάτευεν· 'Ελαφη]βολιῶν[ο]ς ἐνά[τει]
    5   [μετ'εἰκάδας, τρίτει] καὶ εἰκοστε[ῖ τῆ]
           [ς πρυτανείας· ἐκκλη]σία κυρία· τῶ[ν πρ]
           [οέδρων ἐπεψήφιζεν 'Α]ντίμαχος Α[...]
           [....¹¹..... καὶ συμπρ]όεδροι· [ἔδοξ]
           [εν τῶι δήμωι· .....¹².....]Υ[..⁶..]
    10   [– – – εἶπεν· ἐπειδὴ – – – – – – – – – – – –]

                  lacuna
    (*b*)   [........¹⁷........ · δοῦναι δὲ τοὺς]
            [πρυτά]νει[ς] τ[ῆς ...⁹.... περὶ τῆς π]
            ολιτείας αὐτ[ῶν τὴν ψῆφον τῶι δήμωι]
            εἰς τ[ὴ]ν ἐπιοῦσαν ἐκ[κλησίαν· ἀναγρά]
    15   ψαι δ[ὲ] τόδε τὸ ψήφισμ[α τὸν γραμματέ]

α τὸν [κα]τὰ πρυτανείαν ἐν [στήλει λιθ]
[ί]νει καὶ στῆσαι τὴν στήλην [ἐν ἀκροπ]
[ό]λε[ι] παρὰ τὴν ἑτέραν στήλη[ν ἐν ἧι οἱ]
[πρ]ότ[ε]ρον τὴν πολιτείαν λα[βόντες .]
20   [..⁵..]ίων ἀναγεγραμμένοι [εἰσίν· εἰ]
[ς δ]ὲ τ[ὴ]ν ἀναγραφὴν τηστήλης δ[οῦναι τ]
[ὸν ἐ]ξε[τ]αστὴν καὶ τοὺς τριττ[υάρχου]
[ς ᵛ ΔΔ]Δ ᵛ δραχμάς.
             (in corona)   (in corona)
             ῾Ο δῆμος   ῾Ο δῆμος
25   ᾿Αριστόλαν   Σώστρατον

The writing is "standard" for the period, tidily done but with inconsistencies and slight inaccuracies in the composition of the letters, especially of nu. There is also, for example, considerable variation in the size of omicron and in the appearance of omega. Sigma appears large and clumsy: the narrow "oval" of phi is particularly noteworthy. In line 21 the letters ΑΦΗ are inscribed in the space of two letters, after some recutting by the stonemason. There is an uninscribed space of one line between line 23 and the top of the corona.

That the two fragments here associated belong to the same stele was urged by Schweigert soon after the discovery of the Agora fragment, and the *editio princeps* provided a text of both. The identity of the stoichedon order and the character of the lettering (by the same hand as **163** but perhaps more precisely executed) prompted the association. It is additionally confirmed by the surface treatment of the now broken monument, again not, as it appears, comparably reproduced on **163**. The association is therefore maintained here, to the exclusion of **163**, despite the remark of M. B. Walbank (*ZPE* 69, 1987, p. 265) that "*S.E.G.*, XXV, 85a could just as well be linked with *S.E.G.*, XXI, 362 as with *S.E.G.*, XXV, 85b," and even though the similarities between all these fragments, to which he draws attention, are undoubted.

The general dating for the text is prescribed by the appearance in lines 20–24 of the exetastes and trittyarchs as responsible for defraying the cost of the stele. These officials, and the span of years within which they are seen to have operated, are discussed under **129** (pp. 202–203). Efforts to achieve a more precise dating have, on examination, failed to carry conviction but require statement in this context.

Meritt's edition of 1940 presented fragment *a*, lines 1–8, in the following form:

a. 298/7 *a*.   ΣΤΟΙΧ. 29

['Επὶ Μνησιδήμου ἄρχοντος ἐπὶ τῆς ..]
[. ντίδος ἐνάτης] πρ[υτανείας ἧι ....]
[.....¹².....]νους Φ[υλάσιος ἐγραμ]
[μάτευεν· 'Ελαφη]βολιῶν[ο]ς ἐνά[τει μετ']
5   [εἰκάδας, τρίτει] καὶ εἰκοστε[ῖ τῆς πρ]
[υτανείας· ἐκκλη]σία κυρία· τῶ[ν προέδ]
[ρων ἐπεψήφιζεν 'Α]ντίμαχος 'Α[..⁶...]
[...⁸... καὶ συμπρ]όεδροι· κτλ.

Closer examination of the Metonic cycle, however, caused Meritt to allow, in his 1969 revision of the calendric equation, that the year 298/7 should have been intercalary rather than ordinary and that the restoration of lines 4–5 as for an ordinary year could not stand. More than that, the unavoidable restoration of the demotic of the γραμματεύς, required in order to conform to the secretary cycle, involved the supposition that the deme Phyle, hitherto held to have been transferred in 307/6 to the new phyle Demetrias, had been in fact divided between that phyle and its original phyle Oineis. J. S. Traill, who drew attention to this latter point, incorporated Meritt's revision in presenting a fresh version of both fragments in *Political Organization*, pp. 129–131, while moving the date to the next intercalary year of the cycle, 295/4. His text of the same lines 1–8 ran as follows:

a. 295/4 *a*.   ΣΤΟΙΧ. 29

['Επὶ Νικοστράτου ἄρχοντος ἐπὶ τῆς Δ]
[ημητριάδος ἐνάτης] πρ[υτανείας ἧι Δ]
[ωρόθεος 'Αριστο..]νους Φ[αληρεὺς ἐγ]

[ραμμάτευεν· Ἐλαφη]βολιῶν[ο]ς ἐνά[τει]

5   [ἱσταμένου, πέμπτει] καὶ εἰκοστε[ῖ τῆ]

[ς πρυτανείας· ἐκκλη]σία κυρία· τῶ[ν πρ]

[οέδρων ἐπεψήφιζεν Ἀ]ντίμαχος Ἀ[ντί]

[νου Ἀχαρνεὺς καὶ συμπρ]όεδροι· κτλ.

The decree will thus have been passed on the same day as *IG* II², 646 (*SEG* XXV, 86; M. J. Osborne, *Naturalization* I, pp. 145–148, D 68, *Naturalization* II, pp. 144–153) and 647. These conclusions were accepted by C. Habicht, *Untersuchungen*, pp. 1–2 and 4, with note 18.

There can be no doubt that if, without supposing any variation of the stoichedon order, eight letters precisely are available for the demotic in line 3, Φ[αληρεύς is the only possibility, with 295/4 the only available year if the secretary cycle is to be accommodated. In that case, the alarming discrepancy between the festival and prytany calendars is already and exactly evidenced in *IG* II², 646 and 647 (see Meritt, *Hesperia* 38, 1969, p. 108) and does not have to be postulated for another neighboring year as Meritt had earlier thought necessary.

Attractive as Traill's proposition was, objections to it were raised by Osborne and A. S. Henry, principally on the grounds that it had repercussions which affected the lower part of the text. Osborne indeed preferred a more conservative version of the decree (*Naturalization* I, pp. 144–145, D 67, *Naturalization* II, pp. 138–144), objecting to Traill's proposal chiefly on the grounds that the two citizenship decrees (this decree and *IG* II², 646), allegedly passed at the same meeting of the assembly, are remarkably different in their formulation and that in the latter it is the Single Officer of Administration, ὁ ἐπὶ τῇ διοικήσει, who is responsible for payment. In these objections he was supported by Henry (*Honours*, p. 100, note 96 and *Chiron* 14, 1984, pp. 65–67; cf. *SEG* XXXIII, 105, XXXIV, 79). Osborne printed a "minimalist" text of fragment *a*, avoiding restorations, and his example has been followed in the version printed above; but he also ventured a possible attribution to the year 300/299, on which see further below. This was a year ordinary in the festival calendar and thus allowed Meritt's original calendric equation to be retained. The proposal required that the fragment be located a little further to the left on the stele than is shown in the text above and presented the following version (*Naturalization* II, p. 142):

a. 300/299 *a*.   ΣΤΟΙΧ. 29

['Επὶ Ἡγεμάχου ἄρχοντος ἐπὶ τῆς . . . ν]

[τίδος ἐνάτης] πρυ[τανείας ἧι .. ⁶ ..]

[. . . . ¹⁰ . . . .]νους Φ[ρεάρριος ἐγραμμ]

[άτευε· Ἐλαφη]βολιῶν[ο]ς ἐνά[τει μετ'εἰ]

5   [κάδας, τρίτει] καὶ εἰκοστε[ῖ τῆς πρυτ]

[ανείας· ἐκκλη]σία κυρία· τῶ[ν προέδρω]

[ν ἐπεψήφιζεν Ἀ]ντίμαχος Ἀ[. . . ⁸ . . . .]

[. . ⁶ . . . καὶ συμπρ]όεδροι· κτλ.

Phrearrhioi belonged to the phyle Leontis and thus fulfills the requirement of the secretary cycle for this year.

Walbank, *ZPE* 69, 1987, pp. 261–265, attempted a text which incorporated **163** between fragments *a* and *b* of the present document, but after discussion his verdict was a *non liquet*. His composite draft followed Osborne's proposals for fragment *a* but included Traill's suggestion for the name of the chairman of the proedroi in lines 7–8, which was relevant only to the context in which Traill had set it. See *SEG* XXXVII, 90, *SEG* XXXIX, 112, XL, 86.

The conclusion must be that, in the present state of knowledge, no date can prudently be assigned to this decree, as it stands, more exact than that provided in general terms by the exetastes and trittyarchs, a view to which Osborne, Henry, and Walbank have all, in the end, subscribed. But a little more may yet usefully be said: (1) Despite the objections raised against his overall text, Traill's solution for lines 1–5 remains undeniably attractive. The coincidences between this prescript and that of *IG* II², 646 may be judged too remarkable to be discarded. (2) That being so, there may be good grounds for obviating the objections (which all involve fragment *b*) by dissociation of the two fragments. Yet the physical similarities and Schweigert's firm judgment about them as soon as fragment *a* was discovered cannot be denied, and no observer has yet refuted them. One may justly hesitate over so radical a solution to the problem; Osborne described it as "far from easy to accept". But it may be the right one. (3) Meritt's original restoration of the calendric equation accounts for all the data on the basis of an ordinary and regular festival year, with the prytany and festival dates running in close accord. Elaphebolion was to be a full month, and there may have been two full months in succession earlier in the year. Calendric regularity should ordinarily be assumed unless the contrary is clearly demonstrable, and the year of this decree ought *prima facie*, on these grounds, to be regarded as ordinary. (4) Of the four ordinary years available, however, 299/8 and 296/5 may be eliminated, the former because its γραμματεύς was clearly not the person appearing in lines 2–3, and the latter because, by the time of Elaphebolion, a set of truncated prytanies was in process of being instituted (see p. 237 below) with which the indications of the text cannot agree. 300/299 and 297/6 alone remain, as Osborne, in the course of a thorough analysis of the situation (*Naturalization* II, pp. 141–143), correctly saw. The formula of line 14 (see below) might suggest the later date, but the necessary restoration of Φλυεύς as the only available demotic for the γραμματεύς, leaving two letter spaces unaccounted for, militates against it. 300/299 is thus left for consideration, and Osborne constructed for it the text shown above. But this solution too is not without its difficulty, for here it proves necessary, in line 3, to omit the ephelkystic nu of the expected ἐγραμμάτευεν. No example of this omission before a following vowel is attested in the period between 323 and 175 B.C., and its omission before a vowel even in the case of other verbs is a rarity. It should not perhaps be postulated in this context. Cf. Henry, *CQ* n.s. 17, 1967, pp. 277–282.

That Elaphebolion 22 was a day on which meetings of the assembly were evidently held is confirmed by J. D. Mikalson, *Sacred and Civil Calendars*, pp. 133–134.

Line 6. ἐκκλησία κυρία. See **101**, commentary on lines 7–8. Lines 8–9. The decree was presumably non-probouleumatic but was not listed by P. J. Rhodes, *Athenian Boule*, p. 264.

Lines 11–14. The citizenship formula stands by itself, as regards procedure, as category IX in Osborne's "Formulation A" (*Naturalization* I, p. 20). It omits the "scrutiny clause". Line 12. το[ὺς Δημητριάδος Traill, and indeed the battered edge of the fragment suggests an omicron on the squeeze; but doubt remains, the more so since τῆς is surely to be expected. Cf. Osborne, *Naturalization* II, p. 140; Henry, *Chiron* 14, 1984, p. 66; Walbank, *ZPE* 69, 1987, pp. 261–265. The version shown in the text at the outset is what is to be expected, and if that is so, the phyle to be restored (here and in lines 1–2) must be Leontis or Aiantis.

Line 14. *IG* II², 646 retains πρώτην in this formula. This is the first clearly attested instance of the replacement of πρώτην by ἐπιοῦσαν, a usage later regular but not again met with until 283/2 (*IG* II², 659). Cf. Henry in *"Owls to Athens": Essays on Classical Subjects Presented to Sir Kenneth Dover*, E. M. Craik, ed., 1990, pp. 183–184 and 187. But it occurs in *IG* II², 806, a document which has been attributed to 303/2 by Osborne (*Naturalization* I, pp. 119–121, D 48) and Henry (*ZPE* 78, 1989, p. 268, following *Chiron* 14, 1984, pp. 53–54). Its presence there may however be an argument against that exact dating, which was originally proposed by Schweigert (*Hesperia* 9, 1940, p. 351) because of an alleged association with *IG* II², 809, **122** and **128** (see **128**, commentary on line 4). The lettering may suggest an early-3rd-century date, in any period in which the Military Treasurer defrayed the cost of stelai (cf. Henry, *Chiron* 14, 1984, p. 71).

Line 20. Schweigert suggested [ὧν] Μηλίων, but the traces on the stone do not confirm it. The same must be said of other proposals envisaging Rhodians (for whom see Habicht, *Untersuchungen*, pp. 4–8), Tenians, Tyrians, and Samians (these last favored by Osborne, *Naturalization* II, p. 143).

FRAGMENT OF AN HONORARY DECREE

163. A fragment of a stele of Hymettian marble (I 6844), with part of the left side (below the inscribed surface) and the original rough-picked back preserved, discovered on April 7, 1959, east of the Eleusinion (U 19). The stone is much more bulky than reference solely to the remains of the inscription would indicate and is patchily discolored.

H. 0.30 m.; W. 0.27 m.; Th. 0.10 m.
LH. 0.0045 (omicron, omega)–0.007 m.
Στοιχ. Hor. 0.0135 m.; Vert. 0.012 m.

Ed. B. D. Meritt, *Hesperia* 32, 1963, p. 5, no. 5, with photograph pl. 1. See also *SEG* XXI, 362. Further discussion by M. B. Walbank, *ZPE* 69, 1987, pp. 261–265; see also *SEG* XXXVII, 90.

inter annos 300/299 *et* 295/4 *a.*(?)   ΣΤΟΙΧ. 29

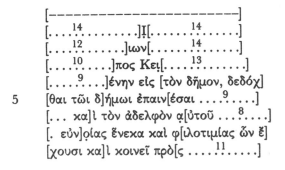

<pre>
        [.....⁹....] καὶ ἰδίαι [εἰς τὸν δῆμον, κ]
   10   [αἱ στεφανῶσα]ι χρυσ[ῶι στεφάνωι ἑκά]
        [τερον αὐτῶν κα]τὰ τὸ[ν νόμον· ...⁷...]
        [.....¹³.....]ιστ[....¹³.......]
        [.....¹⁴......]ν[....¹⁴......]
        [————————————————————]
</pre>

The lettering is thinly cut, precise, and of good quality, with some clumsiness only in sigma. The narrow phi, with pointed ends to the "oval", and the small omega, with long horizontal strokes meeting in the middle, are especially distinctive. There is, in some places, a slight emphasis on the "free ends" of strokes. The hand is so close to that of **162** that the same craftsman must be considered responsible for both texts. Despite this identity, and despite the identical stoichedon pattern of 29 letters, it remains debatable whether this fragment is in fact part of that stele: but see further below.

The text is that of Meritt, with the addition of the traces of a letter (iota or tau) in a new line 1. The award of a stephanos κατὰ τὸν νόμον (lines 9–11) requires that 302 b.c. be regarded as the *terminus post quem* of the enactment: see **112**, commentary on lines 5–7, and cf. **141**. In any case the date must be comparable with that of **162**.

Line 8. Κοινεῖ καὶ ἰδίαι. Cf. **49**, line 5. πρὸ[ς ἅπαντας τοὺς(?) Meritt, Walbank.

Walbank, *loc. cit.*, attempted a reconciliation of this fragment with **162**, supposing a brief lacuna between fragment *a* of that text and the beginning of the text under present discussion and producing a connected text for this fragment and **162**, fragment *b*. This read as follows (lines 4–18 of Walbank's restoration):

<pre>
        [....⁹....]ένην εἰς [τὸν δῆμον· δεδόχ]
    5   [θαι τῶι δ]ήμωι· ἐπαιν[έσαι μὲν Ἀριστό]
        [λαν κ]αὶ τὸν ἀδελφὸν α[ὐτοῦ Σώστρατο]
        [ν εὐνο]ίας ἕνεκα καὶ φ[ιλοτιμίας ὧν ἔ]
        [χουσι κα]ὶ κοινεῖ πρὸ[ς ἅπαντας τοὺς]
        [....⁹....] καὶ ἰδίαι [εἰς τὸν δῆμον, κ]
   10   [αἱ στεφανῶσ]αι χρυσ[ῶι στεφάνωι ἑκά]
        [τερον αὐτῶν κα]τὰ τὸ[ν νόμον ἀνδραγα]
        [θίας(?) ἕνεκα τῆς ε]ἰς τ[ὸν δῆμον τὸν Ἀθη]
        [ναίων· εἶναι δ'Ἀθη]ν[αίους αὐτοὺς καὶ]
        [ἐκγόνους αὐτῶν, καὶ γράψασθαι φυλῆ]
   15   [ς καὶ δήμου καὶ φρατρίας ἧς ἂν βούλω]
        [νται κατὰ τὸν νόμον· καὶ δοῦναι τοὺς]
        [πρυτά]νεις τ[ῆς ... ντίδος περὶ τῆς π]
        ολιτείας αὐτῶν [τὴν ψῆφον τῶι δήμωι]
        κτλ.
</pre>

But this text presents difficulties of formulation, especially in lines 4–5 and 10–12, as well as in the fragmentary lines that precede the restorations. In the end they persuaded Walbank that what are involved here are, in all probability, "at least two inscriptions of approximately the same date, engraved by the same mason, and with the same line length" (*loc. cit.*, p. 264). It may be additionally noted that **164** also has a line length of 29 letters and that this pattern may, at the time, not have been uncommon.

MIKALION OF ALEXANDRIA HONORED

164. A fragment from the lower left section of a stele of Hymettian marble (I 5772), broken above, below (after the completion of the inscribed text), and to the right, but with the left side and original back preserved, discovered on April 5, 1939, in a late accumulation below the Akropolis cliffs, east of Klepsydra (U 26). Much of the left edge of the inscribed surface is broken away towards the top of the fragment.

H. 0.372 m.; W. 0.275 m.; Th. *ca.* 0.085 m.

LH. 0.005 m.

Στοιχ. (square) 0.01 m.

Ed. B. D. Meritt, *Hesperia* 13, 1944, pp. 242–243, no. 7, with photograph. See also *SEG* XXIV, 119, with reference to further discussion by J. Pečírka (*Formula*, pp. 132–133), who reproduces Meritt's text. On the date and context see also *SEG* XXIX, 93.

inter annos 300/299 *et* 295/4 *a.*　　　　　　　　　　　　　　ΣΤΟΙΧ. 29

```
        [――――――――――――――――――]
        [.]η[.............27.............]
        [..] δημο[. το. Ἀθηναίων.....11.....]
        [.]ον ἑαυτ[ὸν παρεχ......15.......]
        [.]ναι ὅτου ἂν ἕκ[αστος δέηται· ἀγαθεῖ]
    5   [τ]ύχει δεδόχθαι τῶι δή[μωι ἐπαινέσα]
        ι Μικαλίωνα Φίλωνος Ἀλεξ[ανδρέια κ]
        [α]ὶ στεφανῶσαι αὐτὸν χρυσῶι [στεφάν]
        [ω]ι κατὰ τὸν νόμον ἀρετῆς ἕνε[κα καὶ ε]
        [ὐ]νοίας τῆς πρὸς τὸν δῆμον τ[ὸν Ἀθηνα]
   10   [ί]ων· εἶναι δὲ Μικαλίωνα καὶ [τοὺς ἐκγ]
        [ό]νους αὐτοῦ προξένους καὶ [εὐεργέτ]
        [α]ς τοῦ δήμου τοῦ Ἀθηναίων, κ[αὶ γῆς κα]
        [ὶ] οἰκίας ἔνκτησιν εἶναι α[ὐτοῖς κατ]
        ὰ τὸν νόμον, ὅπως ἂν εἰδῶσι[ν καὶ οἱ ἄλ]
   15   λοι πάντες ὅτι ὁ δῆμος τιμ[ᾶι τοὺς ἐν]
        δεικνυμένους αὐτῶι τὴν ε[ὔνοιαν κα]
        τὰ τὴν ἀξίαν ἑκάστους· ἀνα[γράψαι δὲ]
        τόδε τὸ ψήφισμα ἐν στήλει [λιθίνει τ]
        ὸν γραμματέα τοῦ δήμου κα[ὶ στῆσαι ἐ]
   20   ν ἀκροπόλει· εἰς δὲ τὴν ἀνα[γραφὴν τῆ]
        ς στήλης δοῦναι τοὺς τριττ[υάρχους]
        καὶ τὸν ἐξεταστὴν ᵛ ΔΔΔ : δ[ραχμὰς ἐκ]
        τῶν εἰς τὰ κατὰ ψηφίσματ' ἀ[ναλισκομ]
        ένων τῶι δήμωι.        vacat
                        vacat
```

The small size of the lettering is achieved at the cost of accuracy in detail, but although the style is careless, the overall appearance is tidy. The letters are plain, being too small for convenient elaboration, and are in general standard for the period. Meritt justly compared in particular *IG* II², 557, of the close of the 4th century. Xi lacks the upright stroke; phi is in that cruciform shape indicative of the period, for which see **102** and **151**.

The date of the decree may be derived from the reference to the exetastes and trittyarchoi as the officials charged with defraying the cost of the stele (lines 20–24). It may be confirmed, though with less precision, by the terms of the award of the stephanos (post-302; see **163** and commentary there) and by the appearance in line 19 of the γραμματεὺς τοῦ δήμου (post-307/6; see **120**, commentary on line 8).

The text is that of Meritt, who in addition restored lines 2–4 as follows:

> [..] δῆμο[ν τὸν Ἀθηναίων καὶ ἀεὶ πρόθυ]
> [μ]ον ἑαυτ[ὸν παρέχει πᾶσιν ἰδίαι διδ]
> [ό]ναι ὅτου ἂν κτλ.

This gives an acceptable indication of the general sense. In lines 2–3 χρήσιμον would at this date and in such a context be more likely than πρόθυμον, and in line 3 ἰδίαι would in normal usage be balanced by a corresponding κοινῆι: hence it may be better to supply ἐκ τῶν ἰδίων in place of πᾶσιν ἰδίαι. Cf. *IG* II², 479 (SEG XXXIII, 93), line 2, 480, line 18, 505 (*SEG* XIX, 61, XXIV, 113, XXXIII, 97, XXXIV, 259, XXXVII, 87), lines 38–39, and 649 (*SEG* XXXIII, 107, XXXV, 85), line 14, all of comparable date.

Lines 4–5. This was a nonprobouleumatic decree: cf. P. J. Rhodes, *Athenian Boule*, p. 264. Line 6. Mikalion is not otherwise known. Cf. H. Pope, *Foreigners in Attic Inscriptions*, 1947, p. 16. At the end of the line Meritt assumed an engraver's error in his restoration of Ἀλεξ[ανδρ{ε}έα, in which he was followed by Pečírka. The extant text is, however, free from such errors, and it is preferable to assume the intrusion of iota, as commonly in this period in words ending in -εύς, e.g., Ἀχαρνεία, Φαληρεία. For these and other instances (e.g., νέιος) see L. Threatte, *Grammar*, pp. 147–153 (esp. p. 152) and **66**, commentary on line 14. See also the tombstone *IG* II², 8008, of "*s.* I *a./*I *p.*", line 3 (Ἀλεξανδρέως). Line 8. Κατὰ τὸν νόμον. See above, on the dating of the text.

Lines 12–13. Γῆς καὶ οἰκίας ἔγκτησις. See Pečírka, *loc. cit.* and **131**. Line 14. Ὅπως ἄν. For the "hortatory intention" see **86**, commentary on lines 21–24.

Lines 21–22. The exetastes and the trittyarchs, in their function as responsible for defraying the cost of the stele, are briefly discussed under **129**. Line 23. For the elision of the final alpha in ψηφίσματα see **138**, line 7. For the "analiskomena fund" see **120**, commentary on lines 11–13, and for its more sporadic appearance in the 3rd century and later cf. A. S. Henry, *Chiron* 14, 1984, p. 63, with note 64.

THE ARCHONSHIP OF NIKIAS, 296/5 B.C.

Nikias is epigraphically attested as archon in **165** and in *IG* II², 644 (*SEG* XXXV, 84, XXXVI, 167) and 645. In the two last named he is described as ἄρχων ὕστερος, and a similar phrase is supplied in line 1 of **165**. This is to be explained with reference to the restoration of democratic government in Athens after the fall of Lachares, the dating of which was established on a new footing with collation of the literary and epigraphical data by W. S. Ferguson in *CP* 24, 1929, pp. 1–20. His interpretation was followed by W. B. Dinsmoor, *Archons of Athens*, pp. 389–390 and 510, and is here adopted.

But it was not uncontested at the time and was more recently challenged by C. Habicht, *Untersuchungen*, pp. 1–21 (esp. pp. 2–13), who regarded the change of designation of the archon, by the addition of ὕστερος to his name, and the fresh start given to the "conciliar" or prytany year, as indicative not of the restoration of democracy after Lachares' fall but of the tyrant's accession to power. Habicht's contentions were, however, sufficiently answered by M. J. Osborne, *Naturalization* II, pp. 144–153, esp. pp. 147–152 (cf. A. S. Henry, *Chiron* 14, 1984, p. 68, with note 94), and the essentials of the argument were presented afresh by Osborne in *ZPE* 58, 1985, pp. 275–282 (cf. *SEG* XXXV, 84).

On the course of Lachares' tyranny see H. Berve, *Die Tyrannis bei den Griechen*, 1967, pp. 387–389, and cf. **129**. Earlier dispute concerning the connection between the epigraphical description of Nikias and the development of events with regard to Lachares produced also the suggestion that Nikias was the second archon in a year in which there were two eponymoi. It is however now generally agreed that, whatever the interpretation of the circumstances of change of regime responsible for his designation, Nikias held office without interruption for the entire year (cf. *IG* II², 644, comm.). That Nikias ὕστερος was not the Nikias of 296/5 but his homonym of 282/1 was proposed by P. Gauthier, *REG* 92, 1979, pp. 381–399 (*SEG* XXIX, 101). This argument also was controverted by Osborne, *locc. citt.*

It is uncertain what "constitutional" arrangements had been operative under the rule of Lachares or how his "council" (if any) was subdivided. It was presumably replaced at his departure, as were other officials (Plutarch, *Demetrios* 34; cf. Ferguson, *op. cit.*, pp. 9–10). The democracy was reestablished immediately after the Dionysiac festival, and to mark the new departure what remained of the year was divided between twelve prytanies, so that each held office for eight or nine days. The first day of prytany I fell on, or very nearly on, Elaphebolion 14 (cf. Dinsmoor, *loc. cit.* and B. D. Meritt, *Athenian Year*, p. 179). Aigeis apparently held office as prytany II during part of Elaphebolion (**165**), and Akamantis served as prytany IV during part of Mounichion (*IG* II², 644 and 645). No other phyle in prytany is attested for this year.

That the year was ordinary in the Athenian calendar has not been in doubt (see Dinsmoor, *op. cit.*, pp. 30 and 390; W. K. Pritchett and Meritt, *Chronology*, p. xvi; Pritchett and O. Neugebauer, *Calendars*, p. 80; Meritt, *Athenian Year*, p. 232). This was the fourth year of the eighth Metonic cycle and as such was determined as ordinary in character (Meritt, *TAPA* 95, 1964, p. 236).

FRAGMENT OF A DECREE

165 (Pl. 16). A small fragment of the upper left corner of a stele of Pentelic marble (I 5886), with the left side preserved and the spring of a molding at the top but otherwise broken all around and much battered at the edges, discovered on October 17, 1939, on the North Slope of the Akropolis, in a modern wall just below Akropolis Street.

H. 0.20 m.; W. 0.10 m.; Th. 0.13 m.

LH. 0.01 m.

Στοιχ. (square) *ca.* 0.02 m.

Ed. B. D. Meritt, *Hesperia* 11, 1942, p. 281, no. 54, with photograph. This text has been regularly cited when the chronology and events of its year have been discussed; for these references see the general introduction (p. 237 above) on the year of Nikias' archonship. See also *SEG* XXIX, 101.

a. 296/5 a., pryt. II *of the "democratic restoration"*   ΣΤΟΙΧ. 33

vacat

'Επὶ Ν[ικίου ἄρχοντος τοῦ ὑστέρου ἐπὶ τῆς]
Αἰγε[ῖδος δευτέρας πρυτανείας ἧι 'Αντικ]
ράτη[ς Κρατίνου . . . . ίδης ἐγραμμάτευεν]·
'Ελαφ[ηβολιῶνος . . .⁷. . . μετ'εἰκάδας· τῶν]
5   προέδ[ρων ἐπεψήφιζεν . . . . . . .¹⁵. . . . . . .]
ος [.] ^[. . . . . .²⁹. . . . .]
[————————————————————]

The lettering is clear, unadorned, well spaced, and wide in proportion to its height. The center stroke of epsilon appears as very short in relation to the width of the letter. *IG* II², 649 (*SEG* XXXIII, 107, XXXV, 85), 650 (*SEG* XXVIII, 55, XXIX, 98), and 651 (*SEG* XXIV, 122) show comparable characteristics. For generosity of spacing between letters at this period cf. *IG* II², 654 (M. J. Osborne, *Naturalization* I, pp. 163–167, D 76), of 285/4.

Line 1. In *IG* II², 644 and 645 the phrase is ἐπὶ Νικίου ἄρχοντος ὑστέρου, without the definite article. Cf. C. Habicht, *Untersuchungen*, p. 2, note 9. The addition of τοῦ may therefore be an unwelcome hypothesis; but it may fairly be said that these were astonishing and unparalleled circumstances for which no formulaic "standard" may necessarily be supposed. By the fourth prytany, Antikrates, as γραμματεύς, may have achieved one; and this, on balance, remains the preferable proposition.

However, if the intrusive τοῦ seems nevertheless unpalatable, there is another possibility. J. S. Traill, who with S. V. Tracy reexamined the stone, has suggested (*per ep.*) the assumption of a stoichedon line of 31 letters in place of 33 and has proposed for lines 1–4

'Επὶ Ν[ικίου ἄρχοντος ὑστέρου ᵛ ἐπὶ τῆς]
Αἰγε[ῖδος πρώτης πρυτανείας ἧι 'Αντικ]
ράτη[ς Κρατίνου Αὐρίδης ἐγραμμάτευε]·
'Ελαφ[ηβολιῶνος δεκάτηι προτέραι· τῶν]
5   κτλ.

(For the restored demotic in line 3 see below.) For "irrational vacant spaces" such as that proposed for line 1 cf. S. Dow, *HSCP* 67, 1963, pp. 63–66; M. J. Osborne, *ZPE* 10, 1973, pp. 264–265; A. G. Woodhead, *Hesperia* 58, 1989, p. 299. The restored calendric data are acceptable: the first prytany is likely to have run from *ca.* Elaphebolion 14 at least to Elaphebolion 22 and would certainly include δεκάτη προτέρα, the 20th of the month. The one objection, which is considerable and possibly decisive, concerns the omission of ephelkystic nu at the end of line 3, for which see the commentary on **162**.

Another alternative to the assumption that τοῦ was included here is to suppose that the stonemason made an error similar perhaps to that dittography in the word ἄρχοντος in line 2 of *Agora* XV, 71. Assignment of the decree to another year, in order to avoid the difficulty, is precluded by the requirement in line 3 of the name of the γραμματεύς as well as by the fourth letter of line 1 (which might be gamma or pi). The year of Nikias Otryneus (266/5), for whom the γραμματεύς was 'Ισοκράτης 'Ισοκράτου 'Αλωπεκῆθεν, cannot be reconciled with the space available and seems late for the style of the text. The archonships of Gorgias (280/79), Glaukippos (273/2), and Pytharatos (271/70) are even more clearly to be eliminated.

Line 2. The available space requires δευτέρας (in a 33-letter line) or πρώτης (in a 31-letter line), as does the necessity of the date within the month Elaphebolion. In *IG* II², 644, Mounichion 16 = pryt. IV, 7, and so the festival date of the present text, if seventeen letter spaces are available for it, must have fallen within the last third of the month. With fifteen letters available, there is no alternative to the date proposed by Traill and Tracy, unless a further casual blank space be supposed. Line 3. The patronymic of Antikrates is supplied by *IG* II², 644. That his deme was Azenia, fitting the apparent requirements of the stone and of the secretary cycle, was suggested by W. S. Ferguson (*Athenian Secretaries*, p. 50); see *PA* 1078. However, a revision of that text by Osborne (*ZPE* 58, 1985, pp. 281–282; cf. *SEG* XXXV, 84 and 240) produced a new reading for the demotic in question, [. . . .]ίδης, for which he suggested Κρωπίδης or Συβρίδης, and this has been introduced into the present restoration. But the suggested demotics would involve a reassessment of Ferguson's proposed secretary cycle as applicable to this year. Traill, noting that Osborne had also proposed the demotic Ἰωνίδης (although he had found it less acceptable), suggested Αὐρίδης (*Demos and Trittys: Epigraphical and Topographical Studies in the Organization of Attica*, 1986, pp. 16–17, note 9; cf. *SEG* XXXVI, 167), a deme belonging to the same phyle (Hippothontis) as Azenia. This restoration in the 33-letter line avoids calling the secretary cycle into question but necessitates one blank space in line 3 of the text, perhaps a single uninscribed space at the end of the line of the same "casual" character already discussed.

Line 6. ος [ʽΡ]α[μνούσιος καὶ συμπρόεδροι ...⁷...] Meritt. Of the fourth letter only an upper angle appears to survive and that very doubtfully: preceding it, enough of the surface of the stone remains to make restored rho (as well as a number of other possibilities) unlikely. [Φ]α[ληρεύς may be more appropriate to the conditions, unless indeed the third letter space was in fact uninscribed, a suggestion endorsed by Tracy and Traill in their reexamination (see above), who were prepared to see in it another casual blank space supporting their contention concerning line 1.

A FOREIGNER HONORED FOR SERVICES TO THE ARTISTIC LIFE OF ATHENS

166. A fragment of a stele of Hymettian marble (I 6987), with the left side and original rough-picked back preserved, discovered in August 1964 in a disturbed area below the Church of St. Dionysios the Areopagite (N 23). Very little of the inscribed surface remains, the stone being worn away above and to the right. What remains is corroded and discolored.

H. 0.23 m.; W. 0.175 m.; Th. 0.08 m.
LH. 0.006 m.
Στοιχ. (square) 0.012 m.

Ed. B. D. Meritt, *Hesperia* 37, 1968, pp. 268–269, no. 4, with photograph pl. 77. See also *SEG* XXV, 84.

a. 295/4 *a. vel paullo post*   ΣΤΟΙΧ. 22

$$
\begin{array}{ll}
& [\text{---------------------}] \\
& [\ldots\ldots\ldots^{15}\ldots\ldots \text{ στεφανῶ}] \\
& \text{σαι κ}[\text{ιττοῦ στεφάνωι· εἶναι}] \\
& [\text{δ}]\text{ὲ αὐ}[\text{τῶι καὶ ἐκγόνοις γῆς ἔ}] \\
& \text{νκτη}[\text{σ}]\text{ι}[\text{ν καὶ οἰκίας οἰκοῦσ}] \\
5 & [\text{ι Ἀ}]\text{θ}[\text{ήνησιν· ἀναγράψαι δὲ τό}] \\
& \text{δε τὸ ψή}[\text{φισμα τὸν γραμματέ}] \\
& \text{α ἐν στή}[\text{ληι λιθίνηι καὶ στῆ}] \\
& \text{σαι ἐν ἀ}[\text{κροπόλει· εἰς δὲ τὴν}] \\
& \text{ἀναγρα}[\text{φὴν τηστήλης δοῦναι}] \\
10 & \text{τὸν ἐπὶ }[\text{τῆι διοικήσει. } \textit{vvvv}] \\
& \textit{vacat}
\end{array}
$$

The lettering is slightly "disjointed", with the junctions of two meeting strokes inaccurately made, but it is not markedly careless. There is some enlargement of "free ends" of strokes and some variation in the formation of sigma.

Line 2. Meritt observed, with *IG* II², 347 (*SEG* XIV, 55; C. J. Schwenk, *Athens in the Age of Alexander*, pp. 192–195, no. 38) and 551 (*SEG* XXIV, 109) as parallels, that ivy crowns were honors particularly associated with participants in or benefactors of dramatic performances. See further A. S. Henry, *Honours*, pp. 40–41 and (on this text) 60, note 127.

Lines 2–5. The restorations are those of Meritt's edition. It was claimed by J. Pečírka (*Formula*, pp. 139–140) that the limiting formula οἰκοῦσι Ἀθήνησιν occurs only in the highly exceptional cases (*IG* II², 237 and possibly 545) of foreign exiles accorded temporary refuge in Athens. Meritt while acknowledging this (*op. cit.*, p. 269, note 16) urged that the restoration is made necessary here by the certain theta in line 5. It may however be noted that this letter falls in an area where the surface of the stone is badly pitted, and the supposed dot of the theta could be a fortuitous indentation of this kind. If that is so, Pečírka's objections can be met and the customary (though not obligatory) formula of accordance with the statute may be included by supposing more than one honorand and inserting the privilege of ἰσοτέλεια. This privilege, as Meritt observed, was indeed probably granted by this decree, and the two privileges in combination are not infrequently met with; cf. Henry, *Honours*, pp. 246–247. Lines 3–5 might then appear, on the model of *IG* II², 551, as

$$
\begin{array}{ll}
& [\text{δ}]\text{ὲ αὐ}[\text{τοῖς ἰσοτέλειαν καὶ ἔ}] \\
& \text{νκτη}[\text{σ}]\text{ι}[\text{ν γῆς καὶ οἰκίας κατ}] \\
5 & [\text{ὰ τ}]\text{ὸ}[\text{ν νόμον· ἀναγράψαι δὲ κτλ.}].
\end{array}
$$

Lines 6–7. The γραμματεύς is not more closely defined, whether as ὁ κατὰ πρυτανείαν or as τοῦ δήμου. This lack of precision is infrequently met with, but examples occur from time to time: see, e.g., *IG* II², 456 (*SEG* XXI, 328), of 307/6, 519 and 567 (*SEG* XXX, 73), both of the late 4th century, and cf. **214**, where (as in *IG* II², 567) it is a necessary restoration. Neither in this context nor in that of **214** did Meritt's publication remark on the point. There are of course examples also of the formula whereby the accusative noun is omitted altogether: in all such cases the subject of the infinitive is presumed to be the familiar official, under whatever designation (see **120**, commentary on line 8).

Line 9. The line, even with the restoration τηστήλης, requires 23 letters, and the final iota may have been crowded in. For the assumed haplography cf. L. Threatte, *Grammar*, p. 578. Line 10. The paymaster is the Single Officer of Administration (ὁ ἐπὶ τῇ διοικήσει), who here makes his first appearance in this capacity among the decrees discovered in the Agora excavations. For the origin and functions of this official see **77**, commentary on lines 8–9, and in particular Henry, *Chiron* 14, 1984, p. 52, note 13. The Single Officer first appears as responsible for the cost of stelai in 303/2 (*IG* II², 496 + 507, of the twelfth prytany); cf. Henry, *op. cit.*, p. 55. The present decree must be dated outside the limits of the period within which the responsibility was given to the exetastes and trittyarchs, more probably after it rather than in the brief two years before it in which ὁ ἐπὶ τῇ διοικήσει appears in the record. This is evidently also the view of Henry, *op. cit.*, p. 69, and *ZPE* 78, 1989, pp. 271–272.

Lines 10–11. Meritt's reading here was confirmed by P. R. Wilson (*per ep.*). Henry (*ZPE, loc. cit.*), judging from the photograph, suggested that the stone might be broken at this point, so that the text might have continued and provided some or all of the usual information: but this is not the case. For the truncated ending, with the omission of the cost of the stele and the source of funding, cf. *IG* II², 646 (M. J. Osborne, *Naturalization* I, pp. 145–148, D 68).

THE SECOND ARCHONSHIP OF OLYMPIODOROS, 293/2 B.C.

The archon of 294/3 retained his position in the following year, and in *IG* II², 389 (*SEG* XXI, 354) the phrase ἄρχοντος δεύτε[ρον ἔτος is included in the preamble. **167** omits this detail, as does *IG* II², 649 (*SEG* XXXIII, 107, XXXV, 85), for which see W. B. Dinsmoor, *Archons of Athens*, pp. 3–12: but both of these were passed on the same day as *IG* II², 389 and suggest that distinction between Olympiodoros' two years was immaterial. These three texts alone provide evidence for the official year, and no inscription certainly survives from Olympiodoros' first year. The three decrees were passed on the first day of the eleventh prytany (that of Pandionis), which was the last day of Mounichion in the festival calendar, thereby constituting evidence for this day as a meeting day for the assembly (cf. J. D. Mikalson, *Sacred and Civil Calendar*, pp. 149–150).

This single correspondence suffices to indicate that 293/2 was an ordinary year, and as such it agreed with Meton's arrangement for the seventh year of his cycle (cf. B. D. Meritt, *TAPA* 95, 1964, p. 236). Dinsmoor (*loc. cit.*) identified the character of the year and analyzed the detail of *IG* II², 389 and 649. **167**, when discovered, served to confirm his interpretation. See also W. K. Pritchett and Meritt, *Chronology*, p. xvii; Pritchett and O. Neugebauer, *Calendars*, p. 80; Meritt, *Athenian Year*, p. 232, *Historia* 26, 1977, p. 172.

Olympiodoros was, it is generally agreed, the well-known and popular general whose successes against Macedon at various times inspired the Athenians (*PA* 11388; J. Kirchner, *RE* XVIII, i, col. 199, *s.v.* Olympiodoros; Dinsmoor, *op. cit.*, pp. 12–13; S. Dow, *HSCP* 67, 1963, pp. 40–41; C. Habicht, *Pausanias' Guide to Ancient Greece*, 1985, pp. 92–94; for his family see J. K. Davies, *Athenian Propertied Families*, pp. 164–165).

For discussion of these years and the character of Athenian government at the time see especially C. Mossé, *Athens in Decline, 404–86 B.C.*, 1973, pp. 122–123; T. L. Shear, *Kallias*, pp. 53–55; M. J. Osborne, *Naturalization* II, p. 151, note 653; Habicht, *Untersuchungen*, pp. 22–33. The "liberation" of Athens by Demetrios Poliorketes in the spring of 294 from the "tyranny" of Lachares seemed *prima facie* to involve the restoration of the democracy (cf. W. S. Ferguson, *Hellenistic Athens*, pp. 136–138), and democratic adherents of Demetrios, such as Stratokles and indeed Olympiodoros himself, were active in the years that followed. Plutarch (*Demetrios* 34) wrote specifically of the competition among demagogoi in Demetrios' support. But there were others, among them Demochares of Leukonoe and Kallias of Sphettos, to whom these years of alleged liberation appeared as oligarchic rather than democratic, and the period was in later times so described (cf. Plutarch, *Moralia* 851F; *SEG* XXVIII, 60, line 81).

There was good reason for this opinion. Many of the forms of the democracy were indeed once again in evident operation. The assembly met, decrees were voted upon, and the familiar machinery of government was visibly at work. But Demetrios apparently nominated the chief officials, taking care to select men acceptable to the demos (cf. Plutarch, *Demetrios* 34), and Olympiodoros' appointment as eponymous archon, with his prolongation in office into a second year, is evidence of it. Habicht (*Untersuchungen*, p. 27, note 38) has remarked the unlikelihood of the lot having so conveniently fallen upon the most popular of the Athenians. Indicative also of the flavor of the regime is the replacement of γραμματεῖς by ἀναγραφεῖς, on the model of the arrangements that existed between 321 and 318 (see **97**, p. 147 above; Dow, *HSCP* 67, 1963, p. 51; R. M. Errington, *Hermes* 105, 1977, pp. 488–491). Moreover, the presence of the Macedonian garrisons on the Mouseion hill and in the Peiraieus was a constant reminder that, in the last resort, power did not reside with the boule and demos.

Although by 291/90 the lot was, as far as can be judged, again in use in the selection of archons, and although the reinstituted *anagrapheis* lasted for no more than three years, the government may have become perceptibly more oligarchic in the process of time. The return of the exiled oligarchs in 292/1 will have contributed to such a perception. It is of note that few decrees are recognizably to be dated to the period between 294 and 286, and this may reflect the inactivity of the assembly as much as the accident of survival. Cf. Shear, *Kallias*, p. 64; Habicht, *Untersuchungen*, p. 51.

FRAGMENT OF A DECREE

167. A fragment of the upper left section of a pedimental stele of Pentelic marble (I 4317); part of the left side (below the inscribed surface) and of the pediment is preserved but the fragment is otherwise broken all around and most of its epistyle molding is roughly hacked away. It was discovered on October 27, 1936, in the wall of a modern house on the North Slope of the Areopagos (M–N 18).

H. 0.281 m.; W. 0.19 m.; Th. 0.088 m.
LH. 0.005 m.
Στοιχ. (square) *ca.* 0.0125 m.

Ed. B. D. Meritt, *Hesperia* 7, 1938, pp. 97–100, no. 17, with photograph. For the citation of lines 3–6 in connection with the calendar of the year see above.

a. 293/2 *a., pryt.* XI   ΣΤΟΙΧ. 27

```
        ['Επ]ὶ 'Ολυμπιοδ[ώρου ἄρχοντος, ἀναγ]
        [ρα]φέως δὲ 'Επι[χούρου τοῦ 'Επιτέλο]
        [υς] 'Ραμνουσί[ου, ἐπὶ τῆς Πανδιονίδ]
        [ος ἐ]νδεχάτη[ς πρυτανείας, Μουνιχ]
     5  [ιῶν]ος ἕνε[ι καὶ νέαι, πρώτηι τῆς πρ]
        [υτα]νείας· [ἐκκλησία κυρία ἐν τῶι θ]
        [εάτρωι· τ]ῷ[ν προέδρων ἐπεψήφιζεν]
        [Νικόβουλος Νικίου Φρεάρριος ..]
        [——————————————————]
```

The writing so closely resembles that of *IG* II², 389 ("litterae neglegenter incisae") that the two inscriptions may well be the work of the same stonemason. The height and spacing of the letters are the same in both texts. There is the same carelessness (bad jointing of strokes, omitted central bar in epsilon), the same rendering of small omicron and omega, and the same tendency to write sigma with horizontal top and bottom strokes.

Lines 1–3. On the "second period of *anagrapheis*", which lasted for three years (294/3–292/1), see S. Dow, *HSCP* 67, 1963, pp. 51–53 and A. S. Henry, *Prescripts*, pp. 50–57; and cf. the commentary on **97**. Epikouros, son of Epiteles, listed among known Rhamnousians by J. Pouilloux (*Forteresse*, p. 173), is otherwise unknown. It is probably his brother who was commemorated in death by *SEG* XXX, 225 and who proposed *SEG* XXIV, 154. *IG* II², 389 was formerly dated in 319/18, in the earlier period of the *anagrapheis*, and at that time Epikouros was identified with the man of that name who figures among the accusers of Phokion named by Plutarch (*Phokion* 38.1). The name, although familiar by reason of the famous philosopher (from Gargettos) who bore it, is rare in Attic prosopography. The phraseology of the prescript represents Henry's Type II, a, among those of the two *anagrapheis* periods.

Lines 6–7. 'Εν τῶι θεάτρωι. The designation of the assembly's place of meeting is restored from *IG* II², 389, which was enacted on the same day. It is not given in *IG* II², 649, also a product of the same meeting, which is content with the designation ἐκκλησία alone. The statement that the assembly was held in the theater, no longer admitted in **85**, thus appears for the first time here among the decrees discovered in the Agora. See W. A. McDonald, *Political*

Meeting Places, pp. 56–61, with note 74. Line 8. Nikoboulos, son of Nikias, of Phrearrhioi is not otherwise attested, but the family to which he belonged may perhaps be identified. A Nikias son of Nik––– (probably Nikoboulos), of the same deme, is recorded as diaitetes in *IG* II², 1924 + 2409, of 330/29; cf. *SEG* XXX, 115 (with earlier references), XXXVII, 124, and *PA* 10826.

TWO FRAGMENTS OF A DECREE

168. Two fragments, which do not join, of a stele of Pentelic marble, both discovered during the summer of 1935 in a marble pile at the southwest corner of the Market Square (G 14). Fragment *a* (I 3233) is broken on all sides and at the back; fragment *b* (I 3234) is similarly broken, save that the right side of the stele is preserved on it.

a: H. 0.132 m.; W. 0.092 m.; Th. 0.056 m.

b: H. 0.116 m.; W. 0.11 m.; Th. 0.054 m.

LH. 0.006 m.
Στοιχ. (square) 0.012 m.

Ed. M. B. Walbank, *Hesperia* 58, 1989, pp. 94–95, no. 22, with photographs pl. 23. See also *SEG* XXXIX, 115.

init. saec. III *a.* (*a.* 292/1?) ΣΤΟΙΧ.

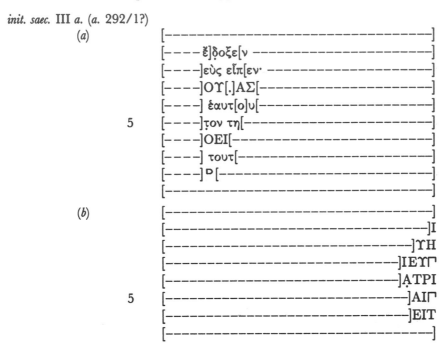

The readings are those of the *editio princeps*, which however in fragment *a* supposes only one letter missing at the left end of the lines. Walbank also inserted into his text a number of restorations, as follows:

a: Line 6. [.]ποεῖ? (*sic*), followed by [ὅτι δύναται ἀγαθόν? – – – – –].

b: Lines 3–4. διατελε]ῖ εὖ π|[οίων (*sic*) – – –]. Lines 4–5. τὴν π]ατρι||[κὴν εὔνοιαν – –].

The style of the lettering on these fragments seems to set them in the context of the early 3rd century. Small as they are, Walbank was prepared to associate them with *IG* II², 385a (*SEG* XXI, 355), a text with a stoichedon line of 34 letters, now held to belong to 292/1 B.C.: and he went on to suggest an interpretation based on that association. Though tempted to see here a possible grant of *proxenia*, he noted that none of the formulas customary in such grants can be restored in the present state of the evidence.

THE ARCHONSHIP OF CHARINOS, 291/90 B.C.

Beyond the archonship of Philippos, a basis of annalistic literary evidence for the succession of the Athenian eponymous archons is lacking (cf. W. B. Dinsmoor, *Archons of Athens*, p. 35), and the assignment of subsequent archons to their years has been the subject of long scholarly research and controversy. Correction and recorrection of carefully argued sequences, in the light of new discoveries which have produced new data and disrupted theories concerning the old, have been and will no doubt continue to be a regular feature of the study of Hellenistic Athens. From this point onwards, the years which have been assigned to the texts in this volume datable by the name of the archon are those generally acceptable and accepted at the time of writing, although in some cases alternative interpretations to which the same evidence lends itself will be given due weight. Future discoveries may well cause some readjustment in detail; but there is no longer the ample room for maneuver that once there was. The efforts of earlier scholars have produced the result that the overall sequence, at any rate as far as the mid-260's, may be regarded as established. It is in the years of, and following, the Chremonidean War that the real difficulties begin, and it is on these that controversy has concentrated in more recent times.

In this situation a wide variety of evidence from disparate sources has been laid under contribution in a succession of complex and ingenious studies. Much has depended on the supposed regularity of the "tribal cycle" observed and analyzed by W. S. Ferguson, whereby the γραμματεῖς were chosen annually from a different phyle, in the "official" order of the latter. Interpretation of this by B. D. Meritt, in a series of studies, led him to preserve the validity of the cycle to the fullest extent he could. But even he had to allow that there were times at which the cycle was demonstrably not in operation, and scholars following up his work have been prepared to place less weight upon the preservation of it than he did.

To these indications may be added a comparable cycle derived from the annual priests of Asklepios among documents connected with the cult of that god which bear cross-references to the eponymous archon. Yet the importance of this too may have been overemphasized. The conclusion of S. B. Aleshire (*The Athenian Asklepieion*, 1989, pp. 75–81) is that the priestly cycle "cannot be used as the basis of an archon list or other chronological scheme for the third or second century." Nevertheless, all this material may make its contribution within its limits, and it may be reinforced by study of the calendric data and the order of intercalary and ordinary years. Occasional literary testimony that names an eponymous archon, or sometimes more than one of them, may serve at the least to suggest the relative order in office of those so named.

Compared with the problems of the archon list later in the century, the identification of Charinos' year evolved in a less controversial fashion and is a simpler matter: but a brief account of it may provide an example of such evolution. In the absence of the direct epigraphical contribution that later became available, Dinsmoor (*Archons of Athens*, pp. 67–68 and *Athenian Archon List*, pp. 50 and 54) used literary evidence (that Charinos' archonship was earlier than that of Diokles) and the secretary cycle as then evaluated to place Charinos, tentatively, in 289/8. This assessment was partly based on the belief, derived from A. C. Johnson, that his name was to be restored in *IG* II², 697, which gave him a γραμματεύς from the phyle Demetrias, second in order. Earlier assessments by K. J. Beloch and W. Kolbe had also set him there, but other reconstructions had variously assigned him to 293/2, 291/90, and 290/89. Dinsmoor later (*Hesperia* 23, 1954, p. 313) placed him a year earlier, in 290/89, following the example of W. K. Pritchett and Meritt, *Chronology*, p. xvii.

The hesitation was to some extent conditioned by the uncertainty as to how long the substitution of ἀναγραφεῖς for γραμματεῖς may have continued beyond the second year of Olympiodoros (see p. 241 above) and to what degree and in what manner this substitution had affected the secretary cycle. The discovery of **169** finally established that in Charinos' year there was a γραμματεύς, not an ἀναγραφεύς, and that he belonged to Aiantis, the phyle eleventh in order. This was the point at which the cycle had been interrupted after 295/4, and it became clear that there was no question of beginning a fresh cycle after the interruption and of assigning to this year the archon Aristonymos, whose γραμματεύς was a member of the phyle Antigonis (I), a solution attractive to many earlier commentators. Charinos was thus most suitably set in the year immediately following that of Philippos, and this now firmly established dating has been followed here. Cf. Meritt, *Athenian Year*, p. 232 and *Historia* 26, 1977, p. 172.

169 and **170** represent the entire epigraphical evidence concerning Charinos' year, and *IG* II², 697 (see above) is no longer to be assigned to it. As the ninth year of the Metonic cycle it may be presumed to have been ordinary in the festival calendar, with that of Philippos before it intercalary, and restorations for **170** have been proposed on that assumption, following Meritt's indications. The phyle Antiochis held the fourth prytany, and in **170** the suggestion of a dating in the twelfth prytany of the year would involve a choice, according to the possibilities of restoration, between Aigeis, Oineis, or Hippothontis as the phyle then in office.

FRAGMENT OF A DECREE

169. A pedimental stele of gray marble (I 6703), broken below and with a deep crack to the left but otherwise complete except for the apex and right akroterion of the pediment, discovered on February 18, 1955, in the third shop from the southern end of the Stoa of Attalos, where it had been reused as a doorstep (R 12). This reuse no doubt accounts for the fact that the inscribed surface is almost entirely worn away, leaving lines 1–3 alone to some extent decipherable.

H. 0.76 m.; W. 0.41 m.; Th. 0.15 m.
LH. 0.005 m.
Στοιχ. (square) 0.01–0.011 m.

Ed. B. D. Meritt, *Hesperia* 26, 1957, pp. 53–54, no. 10, with photograph pl. 9. See also *SEG* XVI, 61.

a. 291/90 *a., pryt.* IV　　　　　　　　　　　　　　　　　　　　　　　　　　ΣΤΟΙΧ. 40

['Επὶ Χ]αρίνου ἄρχοντος ἐπὶ τῆς 'Αντιοχίδος τετάρτ
[ης πρ]υτανείας ἧι Θεότιμος [.]α[. . .]λ[. . .]ς Τρ[ι]χορύσ-
[ιος ἐ]γραμμάτευ[εν ————————————————]
[——————————*versus fere liii non legendi*——————————]

What survives of the lettering reveals it as comparable in height and spacing, character, and quality with **166** and **167**. Omicron is small, and the top and bottom strokes of sigma almost parallel. The loop of rho is angular in form.

The significance of the surviving text has been noted above, in connection with the date of Charinos' archonship. The γραμματεύς (lines 2–3) is otherwise unknown: his name, ordinary enough, had not been earlier attested among members of this deme. The reading of the demotic is difficult and crucial, but the spatial requirements and the surviving traces correspond with the deme Trikorynthos and with no other deme in Attica.

FRAGMENT OF A DECREE, POSSIBLY HONORING A BOARD OR COMMISSION

170. A fragment of a stele of Pentelic marble (I 5923), with the left side and original back preserved, discovered on July 17, 1947, in a modern house wall above the Civic Offices. The inscribed face is much abraded: little of the lettering remains, and of the decipherable letters many are, and perhaps more should be, underdotted.

H. 0.26 m.; W. 0.18 m.; Th. 0.155 m.
LH. 0.005–0.006 m.

The text is nonstoichedon: the vertical interval between the lines is 0.011 m.

Ed. M. B. Walbank, *Hesperia* 54, 1985, pp. 321–323, no. 7, with photograph pl. 88. See also *SEG* XXXV, 86.

a. 291/90 *a.*　　　　　　　　　　　　　　　　　　　　　　NON-ΣΤΟΙΧ. *ca.* 67–71

['Επὶ Χ]αρίνο[υ] ἄρ[χοντος ἐπὶ τῆς . . . . .17–21. . . . . πρυτανείας ἧι Θεότιμος . α. . . λ]
[. . . ς Τρ]ιχο[ρύσιος ἐγραμμάτευεν· . . . . .30–34. . . . . τῆς πρυταν]
[είας· ἐκ]κλ[ησία· τῶν προέδρων ἐπεψήφιζεν . . . . .19–23. . . . . καὶ συμπρόεδροι· ἔ]
[δοξε]ν τε[ῖ β]ου[λ]ε[ῖ καὶ τῶι δήμωι· ——————————εἶπεν· ἐπειδὴ ——————————]
5　[²⁻³]ΕΛ[——————————————————————————————————]
　　[. .⁶⁻⁷. .]Ο[——————————————————————————————————]
　　[——————————————————————————————————————]
　　[.⁴⁻⁵.]ΙΝ[——————————————————————————————————]
　　[. . . .¹¹⁻¹². . . .]Ο[—————————————————————————————]
10　[. .⁶⁻⁷. .]ΝΙΟΣ[²⁻³]Δ[²⁻³]Ο[————————————————————————]
　　[.⁴⁻⁵. ι]ππος Σωπ[———————————————————————————————]
　　[. . .⁸⁻⁹. . . Χο]λα[ρ]γεύ[ς, ——————————————————————————]
　　[.⁵⁻⁶.] Καλλίου [—————————————————————————————————]
　　[. .⁶⁻⁷. .]άτης [————————————————————————————————]
15　[. . .⁷⁻⁸. . .]ς Λα[———————————————————————————————]
　　[. . .⁷⁻⁸. . .]Ι[.]Ν[————————————————————————————————]
　　[———————————————————————————————————————]

The above text is that of the *editio princeps*. On the basis of lines 10–15, where a number of names, patronymics, and demotics evidently appear, and on the analogy of *IG* II², 676 (where such a list is recorded after eleven lines of a decree) and of **186**, both of the late 270's, Walbank suggested that honors for a board or college of some kind were likely to be the subject of this decree.

If that is so, on the same analogy the date of the enactment probably fell in the final month and prytany of Charinos' year. Δωδεχάτης and Σχιροφοριῶνος could thus be supplied in lines 1 and 2. This being an ordinary year, Walbank additionally noted that the further restoration of phyle and day (Αἰγεῖδος or Οἰνεῖδος in line 1, with ἐνδεχάτει, ἐνδεχάτει in line 2, or ᾽Ιπποθωντίδος with ἕνει χαὶ νέαι, τριαχοστεῖ) may also be accommodated.

THE ARCHONSHIP OF DIOKLES, 286/5 B.C.

It is a matter of controversy whether the uprising of the Athenians against the garrison installed by Demetrios Poliorketes on the Mouseion hill, and the subsequent liberation of the *asty*, took place in spring 287 or spring 286. The latter date was strongly advocated by T. L. Shear (*Kallias*, pp. 61–73). The former has been equally strongly propounded by C. Habicht, *Untersuchungen*, pp. 48–62, with support from M. J. Osborne (*ZPE* 35, 1979, pp. 181–194 and *Naturalization* II, p. 155: cf. *SEG* XXIX, 102) and N. G. L. Hammond and F. W. Walbank (*A History of Macedonia* III, 1988, p. 230). It is, however, abundantly clear, and has long been agreed, that in the archonship of Diokles the democracy was fully restored and in operation; it is in this year that the evidence of inscriptions once again becomes more extensive, not indeed, so far as surviving texts suggest, with the intensity of legislation that followed the democratic restoration of 307/6 but sufficient to point a contrast with the preceding period down to the end of 287/6.

The name of Diokles as archon is preserved in three inscriptions: *IG* II², 650, 651 (sufficiently to leave no room for doubt), and **172** (cf. *IG* II², 663). *IG* II², 650 (*SEG* XXVIII, 55, XXIX, 98) and 651 (*SEG* XXIV, 122) between them provide the full name of the γραμματεύς, Xenophon of Halai, whose phyle (Aigeis IV) limits the possibilities for dating the archonship. Enough is preserved of **171** to make the identification of the year certain. Diokles' name appears also in *IG* II², 652 (*SEG* XXIII, 65; Osborne, *Naturalization* I, pp. 161–163, D 75), in a backward reference to his year. For literary references (*Papyri Herculanenses* 176 and Plutarch, *Moralia* 851E–F) cf. W. K. Pritchett and B. D. Meritt, *Chronology*, p. xvii.

These literary references, together with the historical allusions in *IG* II², 650 and **172**, made the period of Diokles' archonship evident. For earlier attempts at a precise dating, ranging from 290/89 to 287/6, see W. B. Dinsmoor, *Archons of Athens*, pp. 54 and 68. Much depended on how the secretary cycle was restarted after the break during the period of the *anagrapheis*. Reconsideration of the point of resumption resulting from new data on the archonship of Charinos (see p. 243 above) placed the dating of Diokles in 286/5, already urged by Dinsmoor in *Hesperia* 23, 1954, p. 314, upon a surer footing. Cf. Meritt, *Athenian Year*, p. 233, *Historia* 26, 1977, p. 172.

The year was the fourteenth in the eighth Metonic cycle. As such it should have been ordinary in the festival calendar; and the evidence provided by the inscriptions shows that the twelve months and the twelve prytanies coincided. Cf. Pritchett and O. Neugebauer, *Calendars*, p. 80 (where Diokles' date is still shown as 288/7). The year presumably began with a full Hekatombaion. Phylai whose months in prytany may be identified are I Antigonis, or Pandionis, or Akamantis, VIII Leontis, and IX Kekropis.

FRAGMENT OF A DECREE

171. A small fragment of the upper left corner of a stele of Pentelic marble (I 2841), with the left side preserved but otherwise broken all around, discovered on May 2, 1935, in an Early Byzantine context over the northeast corner of the East Building (O 13). There is a wide margin (0.025 m.) above the first line of text.

H. 0.11 m.; W. 0.055 m.; Th. 0.11 m.
LH. 0.006 m.
Στοιχ. (square) 0.015 m.

Ed. E. Schweigert, *Hesperia* 8, 1939, p. 42, no. 10, with photograph.

a. 286/5 *a., pryt.* VIII   ΣΤΟΙΧ. 28

'Επὶ [Διοκλέους ἄρχοντος ἐπὶ τῆς Λε]
ων[τίδος ὀγδόης πρυτανείας ἧι Ξεν]
οφ[ῶν Νικέου 'Αλαιεὺς ἐγραμμάτευε]
ν· 'Α[νθεστηριῶνος ἐνάτηι ἐπὶ δέκα, ἐ]
5   ν[άτηι καὶ δεκάτηι τῆς πρυτανείας]·
[— — — — — — — — — — — — — — — — —]

Although no more than ten letters survive on this small piece, it can be accurately restored on the analogy of *IG* II², 651 (*SEG* XXIV, 122), in a manner consistent with having been passed on the same day at the same assembly. The general form of the lettering is the same in both texts, but *IG* II², 651 is a much better piece of work. The letters of the present inscription are shallow and hesitant, in the style of **176**. The circular letters in particular are formed by a number of very small strokes, with a tremulous effect.

The text itself requires no further commentary than is contained in the discussion above on the archonship of Diokles. For Anthesterion 19 as a day on which the assembly might meet see J. D. Mikalson, *Sacred and Civil Calendar*, p. 116.

HONORS AND CITIZENSHIP CONFERRED UPON ARTEMIDOROS OF PERINTHOS, A FRIEND OF LYSIMACHOS, KING OF THRACE

172. The upper left corner of a flat-topped stele of Hymettian marble (I 6560), with the remains of a molding on the front and left side which has been roughly hacked away, but otherwise broken all around, discovered in February 1933 during demolition of a modern house near the southwest corner of the Market Square (I–J 15). It was identified as a part (hereafter fragment *a*) of the stele of which the upper right section survives as *IG* II², 662 (hereafter fragment *b*); another small fragment (hereafter fragment *c*) also apparently survives as *IG* II², 760.

a: H. 0.175 m.; W. 0.28 m.; Th. 0.13 m.

b: H. 0.29 m.; W. 0.173 m.; Th. 0.17 m.

c: H. 0.088 m.; W. 0.067 m.; Th. 0.081 m.

LH. 0.005–0.006 m.

Στοιχ. Hor. 0.009 m.; Vert. 0.0144 m.

Ed. *b* only: *IG* II², 662, with references to earlier literature; A. Wilhelm, *AthMitt* 39, 1914, pp. 293–295, no. 2 (= *IG* II², addenda, p. 663), on lines 6–12. *c* only: *IG* II², 760, from the notes of Wilhelm. *a* + *b*: G. A. Stamires, *Hesperia* 26, 1957, pp. 29–30, no. 2, with photograph of fragment *a* pl. 5; see also *SEG* XVI, 62; M. J. Osborne, *Naturalization* I, pp. 157–159, D 74 (Copy "A"), *Naturalization* II, pp. 155–158. The text of *SEG* XVI, 62 quoted by T. L. Shear, *Kallias*, p. 96, no. 12. Fragment *c* identified from a squeeze and added, with revised text of lines 11–15: S. V. Tracy, *Hesperia* 57, 1988, p. 308; measurements reviewed on the stone by P. R. Wilson (*per ep.*). See also *SEG* XXXVIII, 71.

a. 286/5 *a., pryt.* IX   ΣΤΟΙΧ. 43
    (a)   *(b)*

'Επὶ Διοκλέους ἄρχον[τος ἐπὶ τῆς Κεκ]ροπίδος ἐνάτης π
ρυτανείας· 'Ελαφηβολ[ιῶνος ἔνει καὶ] νέαι, τριακοστεῖ
τῆς πρυτανε[ίας· ἐ]κκλ[ησία κυρία· ᵛ τῶ]ν προέδρων ἐπεψή
[φ]ιζεν   *vacat*   [*vacat*   ]   *vacat*   ἔδοξεν τῆ
5   [ι βο]υλῆι καὶ τῶι δήμωι· [.....¹².....]τος 'Αφιδναῖος ᵛ
[εἶπεν]· ἐπειδὴ [ᵛ 'Αρ]τ[εμίδωρος ἐμ πίστ]ει καὶ φιλίαι ὢν τ
[οῦ βασιλέως Λυσιμάχου καὶ ἀποστελλ]όμενος ὑπὸ τοῦ β
[ασιλέως πλεονάκις εἰς τὴν 'Ελλάδα κα]τὰ τὰς πρεσβεία
[ς ταύτας χρήσιμος ἦν τῶι τε βασιλεῖ Λ]υσιμάχωι καὶ τῶ
10   [ι δήμωι τῶι 'Αθηναίων, καὶ ἀνελθὼν πρὸ]ς τὸν βασιλέα ἐμ
  (c)   [παντὶ καιρῶι δια]τε[λεῖ καὶ λέγων(?) ὑπ]ὲρ τοῦ δήμου ἀγαθ
[ὸν ὅ τι ἂν δύνητ]αι ᵛ κ[αὶ ταῖς πρεσβεία]ις ταῖς ἀποστελ

[λομέναις πρ]ὸς τὸμ β[ασιλέα συναγωνί]ζεται εἰς ὅ τι ἄ[ν]
[αὐτὸν παραχ]αλῶσιν, [ᵛ τύχηι ἀγαθῆι δεδόχθαι] τῆι βου[λ]
15 [ῆι τοὺς προέδ]ρους ο[ἵτινες ἂν προεδρεύωσιν χτλ. -----]
[--]

Osborne (*Naturalization* I, p. 157) gives a usefully detailed description of fragments *a* and *b*. The craftsman was subsequently identified by Tracy as the "Cutter of Agora I 3238 and I 4169", and this stele proves to be his earliest extant work. For his characteristics (his hand, Tracy noted, "is very distinctive and easy to recognize") see Tracy, *GRBS* 14, 1973, pp. 190–192, with pl. 4, where he is listed as "Mason 4", and *Hesperia* 57, 1988, pp. 304–311, with pl. 85:a. Seven other Agora decrees ascribed by Tracy to this mason (whose activity appears to have spanned four decades, from this year to 245/4) are **184**, **185**, **192**, **194**, **195**, **199**, and **203**. Osborne noted that the last letters of lines 1–4 of this text appear to have been engraved *in rasura*.

The mason evidently left an occasional vacant letter space to mark a break in the sense (lines 3, 12, 14) and possibly to emphasize a name (lines 5, 6), for he apparently did not aim to avoid an awkward division of a word at the end of a line (cf. lines 1, 6, 7, 9). The uninscribed space of line 6 was originally restored in front of ἐπειδή, its natural place. The discovery of the Agora fragment corrected this, but its position may still be the result of *incuria* rather than of a wish to make the name of Artemidoros more prominent, as Stamires supposed. But it is not always necessary to explain every instance of such a blank space on rational grounds. For "irrational" vacant spaces cf. S. Dow, *HSCP* 67, 1963, pp. 62–66; Osborne, *ZPE* 10, 1973, pp. 264–265; A. G. Woodhead, *Hesperia* 58, 1989, p. 299. With this modification, the restorations in lines 6–12 are those of Wilhelm; on variant restorations see further below.

It has long been recognized that *IG* II², 663 reproduces this same enactment, reconsidered by Osborne (*Naturalization* I, pp. 159–161), under the rubric of the present text as Copy "B"; cf. Shear, *Kallias*, pp. 96–97, no. 13. It begins recognizably at line 7 of the present text but with a shorter stoichedon line of 30 letters and continues beyond it to the end of the decree. It is curious that the instructions to the γραμματεύς in the concluding formulation with regard to the erection and inscription of the stele refer only to one single stele (i.e., that one). It is equally curious that the stele is to be erected in the sanctuary of Aglauros. This location for an inscribed copy of a public decree is without parallel save for *SEG* XXXIII, 115, which was appropriately placed there since it recorded honors for a priestess of that cult. The Aglaureion was formerly thought to have been located on the North Slope of the Akropolis, near the Cave of Pan and closely beneath the Akropolis itself. Cf. W. Judeich, *Topographie*, pp. 303–304; *Agora* XIV, p. 46. But more recent investigations have identified it at the east end of the Akropolis: see G. S. Dontas, *Hesperia* 52, 1983, pp. 57–63, with references to earlier literature. *IG* II², 662 was found on the Akropolis (as indeed was 663), but doubtless the γραμματεύς was instructed to erect it there in the usual manner.

Why and in what circumstances a second copy for the Sanctuary of Aglauros was provided, independently of the first, can only be a matter of speculation: but since provision had evidently not been made for two stelai under a single enactment, it would require fresh instructions from the assembly to the γραμματεύς and to οἱ ἐπὶ τῇ διοικήσει as to provision and expenditure. This may have required restatement of the whole decree, in much the same terms; but it cannot be guaranteed that this took place at the same assembly as that which enacted *IG* II², 662, or that the repeated decree was identical in all textual respects with the original. There are, not infrequently, variations in detail between two published copies of the same decree; cf., e.g., **322**, *IG* II², 479 and 480, 666 and 667, and see G. Klaffenbach, *Bermerkungen zum griechischen Urkundenwesen* (= *SbAkadBerlin* 1960, 6), p. 34 and B. D. Meritt, *Hesperia* 32, 1963, p. 30. While it is tempting to restore the present text on the evidence (not always clear) of *IG* II², 663, the complete identity of the two versions cannot be assured.

Line 3. ἐ]χχλησ[ία Osborne. Line 5. β]ουλῆι Osborne. Lines 8–9. [ασιλέως Λυσιμάχου πρὸς τὸν δῆμον χα]τὰ τὰς πρεσβεία|[ς ταύτας εὔνοιαν ἐνδείχνυται τῶι βασιλεῖ χτλ.] Osborne, following A. C. Johnson, on the basis of *IG* II², 663. Line 10. ἐπανιὼν πρ]ὸς Osborne: cf. *IG* II², 663, lines 7–8. Line 11. διατελεῖ χαὶ λέγων(?) Osborne, following the indications of *IG* II², 663, a supplement confirmed by the identification of fragment *c*. Wilhelm had preferred the standard phrase παντὶ χαιρῶι ᵛ λέγει χαὶ πράττει.

Line 2. The formula recording the name of the γραμματεύς is here omitted. The omission is unusual but not without parallels: see W. K. Pritchett and O. Neugebauer, *Calendars*, p. 39; Stamires, *op. cit.*, p. 36 with note 17; A. S. Henry, *Prescripts*, pp. 71–72 with note 31. There may be no significance in it beyond oversight, incompetence in drafting, or lack of hard-and-fast procedural rules. For the last day of Elaphebolion as a meeting day of the assembly see J. D. Mikalson, *Sacred and Civil Calendar*, pp. 136–137 (where "G. A. Stamires" is to be read for "M. Lethen" in the citation of the present text).

Line 3. Ἐχχλησία χυρία. Cf. **101**, commentary on lines 7–8. Ἐχχλησίαι χυρίαι tended to be held late in the prytany; this one was very late. Cf. M. H. Hansen, *GRBS* 23, 1982, pp. 337–338 (= *Athenian Ecclesia*, pp. 89–90).
Line 4. Space was left for the name of the chairman of the proedroi, missing (it appears) in the working copy given to the mason, with or without the phrase χαὶ συμπρόεδροι. If the latter were included, as customarily, this would leave

sixteen spaces for the chairman's *tria nomina*, sufficient only if all the elements were short or the demotic abbreviated. The omission and the reasons for it have caused much speculation. See Osborne, *Naturalization* I, pp. 158–159; Henry, *Prescripts*, p. 72, with references to comparable examples. Lines 4–5. The enactment was probouleumatic. Cf. P. J. Rhodes, *Athenian Boule*, p. 252.

Accounts by earlier scholars of these years (e.g., W. S. Ferguson, *Hellenistic Athens*, pp. 146–147 and 150; M. Chambers, *AJP* 75, 1954, pp. 385–394) have been to some extent put out of court by reason of the dating, now accepted as incorrect, that they gave to the archonship of Diokles. The discovery of *SEG* XXVIII, 60 also provided new evidence which altered and enhanced the picture considerably. Much depends on the date at which the "liberation" of Athens took place, whether in 287 or 286, and for references to the controversy over this see the discussion above on Diokles' archonship. From this stems further controversy on the nature of Lysimachos' involvement in the Athenian settlement with Demetrios and the occasions and duration of Artemidoros' missions. Shear (*Kallias*, esp. pp. 76–77, 81–82) saw Artemidoros as Lysimachos' representative at a peace conference involving the "four kings" (Ptolemy, Lysimachos, Seleukos, and Pyrrhos) and effecting a general accord with Demetrios. C. Habicht on the other hand (*Untersuchungen*, pp. 64–65) has denied that the decree honoring Artemidoros provides any evidence that Lysimachos was concerned in the peace with Demetrios, or that Shear's proposal of a general settlement has any substance. That Artemidoros was a citizen of Perinthos was deduced by Habicht (*Chiron* 2, 1972, pp. 107–109; cf. *SEG* XXVIII, 56) from an inscription from Ephesos (British Museum Inscriptions, no. 464); cf. Shear, *Kallias*, p. 76, note 210. The terms of the grant of Athenian citizenship are preserved on *IG* II², 663 and are fully discussed by Osborne, *Naturalization* II, *loc. cit.*

Other benefactors of Athens during these stirring and crowded times also received their rewards sooner or later. Cf. **173**, *IG* II², 653–655, 657, 666, and 667. Zenon, naval commander of the Egyptian fleet, had already received his in the first month of Diokles' year (*IG* II², 650). It is possible that the fragmentary *IG* II², 743 records honors that form part of this series.

GRANT OF ATHENIAN CITIZENSHIP TO PHILOKLES, KING OF SIDON

173 (Pl. 17). Fragment of a stele of Hymettian marble (I 5039), broken on all sides, discovered on November 11, 1937, in the wall of a modern house west of the Panathenaic Way (R 19). The stone is discolored almost horizontally into lighter and darker zones.

H. 0.23 m.; W. 0.265 m.; Th. 0.075 m.
LH. 0.0045 m. (omicron)–0.0075 m.
Στοιχ. (square) 0.0135 m.

Ed. E. Schweigert, *Hesperia* 9, 1940, pp. 352–354, no. 48, with photograph; M. J. Osborne, *Naturalization* I, pp. 166–167, D 77, *Naturalization* II, pp. 161–163.

a. 286/5 a. vel paullo post   ΣΤΟΙΧ. 40

```
     [----------------------------------]
     [........18.........]Ι[....]Σ[.......16.......]
     [.......16........ · δ]πως ἂν οὔ[ν φαίνηται ἅπασιν ὁ]
     [δῆμος τιμῶν τοὺς εὐε]ργετοῦν[τας αὐτόν, ἀγαθῆι τύχ]
     [ηι δεδόχθαι τῆι βουλ]ῆι τοὺς [προέδρους οἵτινες ἂ]
 5   [ν λάχωσιν προεδρεύ]ειν εἰς τ[ὴν πρώτην ἐκκλησίαν]
     [χρηματίσαι πε]ρὶ τούτων, γν[ώμην δὲ ξυμβάλλεσθαι]
     [τῆς βουλῆς εἰ]ς τὸν δῆμον ὅτ[ι δοκεῖ τῆι βουλῆι ἐπα]
     [ινέσαι Φιλο]κλέα τὸν Σιδο[νίων βασιλέα καὶ στεφα]
     [νῶσαι χρυσ]ῶι στεφάνωι κ[ατὰ τὸν νόμον εὐνοίας ἕν]
10   [εκα ἧς ἔχων] διατελεῖ πρ[ὸς τὸν δῆμον· εἶναι δ᾽ Ἀθηνα]
     [ῖον αὐτὸν κα]ὶ ἐκγόνους· [γράψασθαι δὲ φρατρίας κα]
     [ὶ δήμου καὶ φυ]λῆς ἧς ἂν [βούληται· δοῦναι δὲ τὴν ψῆφ]
     [ον τοὺς πρυτά]νεις τῆ[ς ----δος πρυτανείας -----]
     [----------------------------------]
```

In line 3 it is evident that ΡΓΕΤΟ was written in the space of four letters. Osborne detected a very shallow *rasura* at this point, evidence that the mason corrected an original error. The lettering is characteristic of the period, well spaced and clear but clumsy in details, especially in the rendering of omicron (pendent from the upper line of the lettering), phi, and omega. "Free ends" of strokes are in some cases enlarged. The loop of rho is squared, a form that became a feature of the period from 285 to 230 and of which this is the earliest appearance among the Agora *psephismata*. Cf. **169**, where it begins to approach this shape.

Lines 10–11. So Schweigert; εἶναι δ'αὐτὸν | 'Αθηναῖον Osborne: but the formulation shown seems more appropriate here and is equally acceptable. Cf. A. S. Henry, *Honours*, pp. 68, 91, note 27, 93, note 40. Lines 12–13. Osborne, while allowing the possibility of various reconstructions, considers that the phrase περὶ αὐτοῦ ought to be included in the formulation and proposes καὶ δοῦναι περὶ α|ὐτοῦ τὴν ψῆφον] εἰς τὴ[ν πρώτην ἐκκλησίαν τοὺς πρυ|τάνεις -----].

The decree was probouleumatic. Cf. P. J. Rhodes, *Athenian Boule*, p. 252, who follows Schweigert in dating the text to the decennium 287–278 B.C. Most of the surviving text is composed of the formulas standard to the enactment of grants of citizenship at this period; but see below on lines 11–12.

Line 2. ὅπως ἂν οὖν. For the "hortatory intention" cf. **86**, commentary on lines 21–24: on the order of words, and parallel phraseology, see Henry, *CQ* n.s. 16, 1966, pp. 293–297. Line 5. πρώτην is to be restored, since ἐπιοῦσαν cannot be: and it is to be expected if the decree is of the date suggested. See **162**, commentary on line 14, p. 234 above.

Line 8. Σιδο[νίων, not Σιδω[νίων. For the spelling see *IG* II², 3425, *SEG* I, 363, line 7, *Syll.*³, 390, line 2, and Schweigert, *op. cit.*, p. 354, note 21. Lines 8–9. For the gold stephanos κατὰ τὸν νόμον see **122**, commentary on line 26.

Lines 11–12. The sequence phratry–deme–phyle is unusual: cf. Henry, *Honours*, pp. 69 and 95, note 52. The formula of the grant follows Osborne's "Formulation A" and lies within his category XIII (*Naturalization* I, p. 21). The phrase κατὰ τὸν νόμον which sometimes follows the enrolment clause is here evidently omitted.

The date of the decree is provided principally by the historical circumstances. The activities of Philokles, commander of the Ptolemaic navy in the Aegean at the time of the liberation of Athens, have formed an element of the discussions referred to under **172** and the general statement on Diokles' archonship. As nauarch, Philokles was of superior rank to Zenon, honored early in 286/5 for his help in overcoming the problem of the food supply. The revolt of Athens had created severe difficulties in this respect, both in the harvesting of local grain and in the import of foreign supplies, since the Macedonian forces still held the Peiraieus. W. S. Ferguson (*Hellenistic Athens*, p. 151, note 5) assigned to this episode, which he dated in 288/7, the erection of a statue in honor of Philokles (*IG* II², 3425, *SEG* XXV, 209), and in this he was followed by Osborne (*Naturalization* II, p. 163). The Athenians evidently felt themselves greatly indebted to Philokles, and the suggestion of T. L. Shear (*Kallias*, p. 34, note 79) that a different occasion should be sought, possibly in 281/80, when the institution of the Ptolemaia in honor of Ptolemy I Soter was being undertaken, seems less commendable.

Philokles remained in command of the Egyptian fleet until 278/7 (W. W. Tarn, *JHS* 53, 1933, p. 67), and so this decree should be assigned to a date earlier than that, even though the king lived some seventeen years longer (*RE* IIA, ii, col. 2224, *s.v.* Sidon). Schweigert, as noted, gave it a general dating to the decennium 287–278; but it is on balance likely that it should fall within the two years 286/5–285/4, even though the long-held interpretation that, after 284, Egyptian support for Athens waned has been controverted by C. Habicht (*Untersuchungen*, pp. 80–81).

On the career of Philokles in general see also L. Moretti, *Iscrizioni ellenistiche greche* I, pp. 36–37, no. 17; W. Peremans and E. van 't Dack, *Prosopographia Ptolemaica* VI, 1968 (= *Studia Hellenistica* 17), pp. 95–97, no. 15085; I. L. Merker, *Historia* 19, 1970, pp. 143–150 (where the present text is assigned positively to 286/5); and the earlier references assembled by Schweigert, *loc. cit.*

AN ARCHON AND HIS PAREDROI HONORED

174. A fragment of a stele of Pentelic marble (I 749), broken on all sides, discovered on April 29, 1933, in a late context east of the Great Drain opposite the south wing of the Stoa of Zeus Eleutherios (J 7). A beveled edge on the left, held to determine the left side of the inscription, runs at an angle to the vertical stoichos and probably originates in a reuse of the stone, which on a lower plane extends to the left beyond it. The text below is nevertheless set out for convenience as in the *editio princeps*, the width of line being assured by lines 7–8.

H. 0.169 m.; W. 0.20 m.; Th. 0.057 m.
LH. 0.005 m. (omicron)–0.006 m.; 0.008 m. (phi).
Στοιχ. (with syllabic division) Hor. 0.0113 m.; Vert. 0.0125 m.

Ed. B. D. Meritt, *Hesperia* 5, 1936, pp. 416–417, no. 13, with photograph. Lines 7–8 quoted in *Agora* III, pp. 28–29, no. 38, among the literary and epigraphical evidence for the Stoa of Zeus Eleutherios.

a. 286–262 a. (sed vix post a. 270 a.?) ΣΤΟΙΧ. 39

[----------------------------------]
[το]ὺς ἐπὶ [τῆ]ι [διοικήσει . . . . .²⁰. . . . .]
[.]όμενον ἐκ τοῦ νόμ[ο]υ· [ᵛ ἐπαινέσαι δὲ καὶ τοὺς παᵛ]
[ρ]έδρους αὐτοῦ ᵛ Θρα[. . . . . .²³. . . . .]
Κτησιφῶντα Κτησι[. . . . . . . .¹⁸. . . . ., καὶ στε]
5 φανῶσαι ἑκάτερο[ν αὐτῶν κατὰ τὸν νόμον· ἀναγράᵛ]
ψαι δὲ τόδε τὸ ψή[φισμα τὸν γραμματέα τὸν κατὰ ᵛᵛ]
πρυτανείαν ἐν [στήληι λιθίνηι καὶ στῆσαι ἔμπρο]
[σ]θεν τῆς τοῦ Δ[ιὸς στοᾶς· εἰς δὲ τὴν ἀναγραφὴν τῆς]
[σ]τήλης μερ[ίσαι τοὺς ἐπὶ τῆι διοικήσει . . . δραχ]
10 [μάς]. *vacat*

The plain and clear writing is of good quality and without careless features. The small omicron is pendent from the upper line of the lettering: the upright of phi is unusually long (cf. **100**). There is no emphasis on "free ends" of strokes except in upsilon (cf. **120**). Meritt noted the style as "eminently suitable for the first half of the third century B.C."

The date of the decree is however further determined by the officials responsible for the payment for its record on stone (line 9). What their function may be in line 1 is far from clear. The *dioikesis* is now in the care of a board of officials (the Plural Board) and not of the Single Officer (ὁ ἐπὶ τῇ διοικήσει), although the possibility cannot be discounted entirely that the Single Officer might be restored here and the text dated between 295 and 286; cf. **175**. In that case, the remains in line 1 must be otherwise interpreted. However, on the assumption that the restoration as shown may stand, it has long been appreciated that the appearance of the Plural Board involved Athenian freedom from Macedonian domination and conversely that the Single Officer betokens a period in which Athens was subservient to Macedonian interests and direction. See W. B. Dinsmoor, *Archons of Athens*, pp. 64–66; C. Habicht, *Untersuchungen*, pp. 70–71 with note 11; and in particular A. S. Henry, *Chiron* 14, 1984, pp. 71–74 and *ZPE* 72, 1988, pp. 132–133. The discovery of *SEG* XXXIII, 115 has made the picture less clear cut than formerly, since this decree, for which the Plural Board was responsible, is to be dated to the period 247–245. But it remains a general truth that, otherwise, datable references to the Board concentrate in the quarter-century between the departure from Attica of Demetrios Poliorketes and the Chremonidean War. The text is therefore dated within that general range; but see further below, on lines 8–10.

Line 2. On the paredroi see Aristotle (*Athenaion Politeia* 48.4 and 56.1), who states that the ten euthynoi and the three principal archons each had two of them. Cf. Busolt-Swoboda, II, pp. 1059–1060. A decree of this kind is likely to have referred to one of the archons (cf. **181**). Since the stone was discovered in the near neighborhood of the Stoa of Zeus Eleutherios, the honorand was surely the archon eponymous. This assertion was open to doubt when the Stoa Basileios and the Stoa of Zeus Eleutherios were held to be one and the same (see Meritt's note *ad loc., Agora* III, pp. 30–31; I. T. Hill, *The Ancient City of Athens*, 1953, pp. 43–45: the fundamental arguments were those of H. A. Thompson, *Hesperia* 6, 1937, pp. 64–76 and 225–226). However, the discovery in 1970 of the Royal Stoa resolved the long-debated issue: cf. *Agora* XIV, pp. 96–103; *Agora Guide*³, pp. 79–82; J. M. Camp, *Athenian Agora*, pp. 105–107.

Line 4. The paredros Ktesiphon cannot be further identified. Line 5. Κατὰ τὸν νόμον. See **112**, commentary on lines 5–7 and **141**, commentary on lines 8–9. Lines 7–8. For stelai erected in front of the Stoa of Zeus (Eleutherios) see *Agora* XIV, p. 102 with note 106.

Lines 8–10. It may be noted that, as always with the Plural Board, the verb is μερίσαι: see **175** and Henry, *Chiron* 14, 1984, p. 70, note 103, *ZPE* 78, 1989, p. 276. In lines 9–10 Meritt proposed διοικήσει ᵛ Δ ᵛ δραχ||μάς, but the figure should remain unrestored in view of the uncertainty concerning the arrangement of the present text on the stone and of numerals in general within the space available for them. Cf. **129**, line 14. Since **187** offers the latest certain instance of the statement of cost of a stele, this text should perhaps be assigned a date not later than 270. Cf. **175**.

FRAGMENT OF AN HONORARY DECREE

175. A fragment of the lower left section of a stele of Hymettian marble (I 1832), with the left edge preserved but otherwise broken, discovered on April 17, 1934, in a context of the 4th century A.D., in a well east of the Southwest Fountain House (I 15:1), in the area of the Rectangular Peribolos in its southeastern part. There is a generous margin on the left (0.02 m. between the edge of the stone and the first stoichos) and a long uninscribed space (0.078 m.) below the last line of text. Striations on the surface run from upper right to lower left, slightly off the vertical line.

H. 0.15 m.; W. 0.085 m.; Th. 0.12 m.
LH. 0.007 m. (iota 0.008 m.).
Στοιχ. Hor. *ca.* 0.013 m.; Vert. 0.012 m.

Ed. B. D. Meritt, *Hesperia* 7, 1938, p. 109, no. 19, with photograph.

probabiliter a. 286–262 *a.* (*sed vix post a.* 270 *a.?*)   ΣΤΟΙΧ. 45

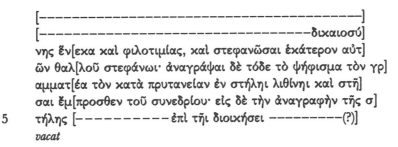

```
     [----------------------------------------]
     [---------------------------------δικαιοσύ]
     νης ἔν[εκα καὶ φιλοτιμίας, καὶ στεφανῶσαι ἑκάτερον αὐτ]
     ῶν θαλ[λοῦ στεφάνωι· ἀναγράψαι δὲ τόδε τὸ ψήφισμα τὸν γρ]
     αμματ[έα τὸν κατὰ πρυτανείαν ἐν στήληι λιθίνηι καὶ στῆ]
     σαι ἔμ[προσθεν τοῦ συνεδρίου· εἰς δὲ τὴν ἀναγραφὴν τῆς σ]
5    τήλης [----------ἐπὶ τῆι διοικήσει----------(?)]
     vacat
```

The lettering, in thin, unadorned strokes, is clumsy work, especially in the rendering of mu and omega. Its general character is that of the first half of the 3rd century. Meritt hesitantly read a circular letter in the line above the epsilon of line 1. The length of line is conditioned by the formula of lines 2–4. The other restorations (which are those of Meritt) are based on the suggestion that the paredroi of an archon are here honored, and they follow the phraseology of **181**; see also **174**. But the paredroi in **181** are awarded stephanoi of gold (in **174** the quality of the stephanoi is not recorded). That the stephanoi here are no more than of olive is therefore perhaps to be remarked.

Line 1. This combination is paralleled in *IG* II², 488 (*SEG* XXIII, 62, XXXIV, 75), of 304/3 or 303/2 B.C., and in **181** and **194**. The qualification κατὰ τὸν νόμον (cf. **174**) is here omitted. Line 2. For the stephanos of olive, frequently bestowed upon citizens who have performed official or semiofficial duties well, see A. S. Henry, *Honours*, pp. 39–40 and 123.

Lines 3–4. The stele is to be erected in front of the "Synedrion" (as in **181**), if the restoration be accepted—and it is reasonable enough. The space does not suffice for the Stoa of Zeus, as in **174**, or for the Bouleuterion. For the Synedrion see *Agora* III, pp. 126–128 (cf. R. E. Wycherley, *JHS* 75, 1955, pp. 118–121), where the references, including this inscription, are collected, and J. M. Camp, *Athenian Agora*, p. 100. While evidently used for a variety of buildings, the term may here refer to the Thesmotheteion (for the site of which see *Agora* III, p. 179); see further on **194**. P. J. Rhodes (*Athenian Boule*, pp. 31–32, note 6) argues that the Bouleuterion is in fact intended.

Lines 4–5. Unless the text ended with διοικήσει, the cost must have been defined. The phrase τὸ γενόμενον ἀνάλωμα would have carried over into the next line. Since this latter method of expressing cost predominates after 270 (cf. Henry, *ZPE* 78, 1989, pp. 273–280), 271/70 showing the last clearly dated example of the amount expressed in drachmas (see **187**), this should suggest a reasonable *terminus ante quem* for the present text. It remains an open question whether the payment is to be made by the Single Officer of Administration or the Plural Board and whether the verb of disbursement should be δοῦναι or μερίσαι. Meritt, whose restoration of the line included the specified sum and read [μερίσαι τοὺς(?) ἐπὶ τῆι διοικήσει --- δραχμάς], tentatively included the Plural Board and therefore μερίσαι (see **174**, commentary on line 8). But a date between 295 and 286, although less likely, remains a possibility. The Single Officer might be paired with δοῦναι or μερίσαι and the sum to be expended might not have been expressed at all; cf. Henry, *op. cit.*, pp. 270–273 and **166**, commentary on lines 10–11.

FRAGMENT OF A DECREE

176. A fragment of a stele of Pentelic marble (I 5723), with the original rough-picked back preserved but broken on all sides, discovered on March 14, 1939, in a context of mid- to Late Roman date on the North Slope of the Akropolis. More than half of the inscribed surface has "layered" off the stone, which has evidently suffered by fire and is much larger than the meager surviving text would by itself suggest. A dark diagonal stripe disfigures the inscribed surface that remains.

H. 0.21 m.; W. 0.185 m.; Th. 0.095 m.
LH. 0.006–0.007 m.
Στοιχ. (square) *ca.* 0.012 m.

Ed. B. D. Meritt, *Hesperia* 30, 1961, pp. 211–212, no. 6, with photograph pl. 35. See also *SEG* XXI, 358.

a. 286–262 *a.*(?)   ΣΤΟΙΧ.

```
[----------------------------]
[------------]επι[------------]
[----------]ωι λαμ[----------]
[----------]το τῶι [----------]
[--------]εμει[. . .]ιο[--------]
5  [------] τὸν Πει[ρ]αιᾶ α[------]
[----κ]ομίσηται ὁ δῆ[μος -----]
[---- τ]αύτας τὰς εὐε[ργεσίας --]
[----ἐ]ποήσατο ὁ δῆ[μος -----]
[----------------------------]
```

The script is a good representative of the style to be associated with the first half of the 3rd century. Junctions between contiguous strokes are inclined to be inaccurate, especially in epsilon (in one instance of which the bottom stroke is curved). Sigma varies in size, the mason having been inconsistent in the length of the chisel adopted to cut it. "Horizontals" in alpha and delta slope, usually from left to right. Line 2. The doubtful central letter may equally, perhaps better, be read as delta. Line 4. Meritt read MO as the last surviving letters. The appearance of the supposed mu is deceptive on stone and squeeze: there is a central *hasta* in this space, and the letter is iota or tau, followed by omicron or theta. Some form of (δια)πολεμεῖν may underlie the remains earlier in this line.

Meritt connected such clues as the few identifiable words offer with the effort of the Athenians to recover the Peiraieus, which had remained in Macedonian hands despite the liberation of the *asty* from Demetrios' forces. This was in the forefront of their political endeavors, and their vital interests dictated its recapture at the earliest possible moment. Philippides the comic poet urged Lysimachos of Thrace to assist them to this end; see *IG* II², 657, lines 33–36, of 283/2 (*SEG* XXXII, 109, with earlier references, XXXV, 87), and **172**: and in 285/4 Audoleon, king of the Paionians, promised his help for the same purpose (*IG* II², 654, lines 30–35; cf. M. J. Osborne, *Naturalization* I, pp. 163–166, D 76, *Naturalization* II, pp. 160–161). Lines 5–6 of the present text reflect the phraseology of the passages cited and suggest a dating for the inscription coincidental with them: but since the recovery of the Peiraieus remained a constant concern of the Athenians throughout the period from the "liberation" to the Chremonidean War, of which it was the major Athenian cause, the decree could find a date anywhere within that general period.

Whether the Peiraieus was ever recovered at any rate once, perhaps even twice, and then lost again between 286/5 and the Chremonidean War (more precisely, during the 270's) has been a long-running and celebrated matter of dispute. W. W. Tarn (*Antigonos Gonatas*, 1913, pp. 118 and 125) urged that the capture of Mounychia and the Peiraieus mentioned by Pausanias (1.26.3) as among the exploits of Olympiodoros (see pp. 240–241 above) belongs to this juncture, and that Antigonos recovered the seaport soon afterwards. Cf. J. Papastavrou, *RE, Suppl.* X, 1965, col. 83, *s.v.* Athenai; Meritt, *Hesperia* 7, 1938, p. 103. W. S. Ferguson (*Hellenistic Athens*, p. 162) considered that the Macedonians never lost the Peiraieus in this period, the view preferred by A. Momigliano (*Terzo contributo alla storia degli studi classici e del mondo antico* I, 1966, pp. 30–31, with note 19 containing further bibliography). See further on **181**. Twenty years later, Ferguson (*Athenian Tribal Cycles*, p. 72) had come to accept that the Athenians held the Peiraieus between 280/79 and 275/4. But continuing developments in the study of the archon list, on the basis of fresh epigraphical evidence, began to invalidate much earlier argumentation; e.g., Meritt's arguments in *Hesperia* 4, 1935, pp. 576–578 (see *Hesperia* 7, 1938, p. 103) ceased to apply by reason of fundamental changes in the dating of the relevant archons since that time; and the same is true of the article by Tarn in *JHS* 54, 1934, pp. 31–36, with bibliography, note 36.

It has now become clear that the Peiraieus was indeed in Macedonian hands continuously throughout the period from 287/6 to the Chremonidean War. C. Habicht (*Untersuchungen*, pp. 95–107), in demonstrating as much, examined the theories of his predecessors and gave a critical review of the evidence, among it (p. 100 with note 32) lines 5–7 of the present text. The most that this fragment can suggest, as Meritt appreciated, is that at the time (whenever that was) it appears to speak, in Habicht's words, "von dem Bemühen der Athener den Hafen zurückzugewinnen" and to show that someone deserved recognition for valued assistance towards that evidently unachieved end. In respect of the controversy described above its role could in any case have been no more than neutral, even though it was in fact published too late for serious involvement in it.

On the character of the writing of this text see further *SEG* XXXIX, 118 and 329.

FRAGMENT OF A DECREE

177. A small fragment of a stele of Pentelic marble (I 4181), with the left side (below the inscribed surface) and original back preserved, discovered on May 22, 1936, among marbles from a modern wall in the southeastern part of the Market Square (N–O 15). There is a long uninscribed space (0.108 m.) below the last line of text.

H. 0.295 m.; W. 0.135 m.; Th. 0.105 m.
LH. 0.004 m. (omicron)–0.005 m.
Στοιχ. Hor. *ca.* 0.013 m.; Vert. 0.0145 m.

Ed. E. Schweigert, *Hesperia* 9, 1940, p. 352, no. 47, with photograph.

a. 286–262 *a.*   ΣΤΟΙΧ. 37

$$
\begin{array}{l}
\text{[------------------------------]} \\
[..\overset{5}{..}]\text{νο}[.............\overset{29}{.............} \cdot \text{ά}] \\
[\text{ναγρ}]\text{άψαι [δὲ τόδε τὸ ψήφισμα τὸν γραμματέα τὸ]} \\
[\text{ν κατ}]\text{ὰ πρυ[τανείαν ἐν στήληι λιθίνηι καὶ στῆσ]} \\
[\text{αι ἐ}]\text{ν τῶι τ[εμένει} .....\overset{12}{.....} \cdot \text{εἰς δὲ τὴν ἀνα]} \\
\text{[γρ]αφὴν τῆ[ς στήλης μερίσαι τοὺς ἐπὶ τῆι διοικ]} \\
\text{[ή]σει τὸ γε[νόμενον ἀνάλωμα].}
\end{array}
$$

The length of line is determined by the formula of lines 2–3. This in turn necessitates the restoration of the Plural Board of officials in line 5, from which the date of the inscription is to be derived (see **174**).

The writing is small and pusillanimous but not imprecise. The small omicron is pendent from the upper line of the lettering. Omega is open and looped; cf. **175** and *IG* II², 710 (*SEG* XXXIV, 81, with earlier references) for not dissimilar examples. For their size the letters are widely spaced.

At the beginning of the fragment Schweigert restored [στεφανῶσαι – – – – ἀρετῆς ἕνεχεν | χαὶ εὐ]νο[ίας τῆς πρὸς τὸν δῆμον τὸν Ἀθηναίων· ἀ|ναγρ]άψαι [δὲ χτλ., perhaps correctly but, with no more than two letters on which to base his restoration, perhaps also adventurously. Line 4. Schweigert suggested τ[εμένει τοῦ Ἀσχληπιοῦ· εἰς δὲ χτλ.]. Apollo would have been equally suitable; for his precinct as a *temenos* cf. *IG* I³, 138, lines 15–16. The sanctuary of Asklepios, which was at a distance from the Agora, on the south side of the Akropolis, is in other such instances always referred to as a *hieron*.

Line 6. For the phrase τὸ γενόμενον ἀνάλωμα see **175**, commentary on lines 4–5. It is not clearly attested before the archonship of Nikias of Otryne in 266/5; cf. A. S. Henry, *ZPE* 78, 1989, pp. 273–277 and the summary of evidence in table 3 there. At an earlier stage, in place of the specified sum of drachmas, a variety of phraseology was tried. Henry believes it possible that τὸ γενόμενον ἀνάλωμα as a formula is to be detected as early as 286/5 (in *IG* II², 663; see **172**): but in the light of visible present evidence it may be reasonable to add at least "*vix ante a.* 270 *a.*" to the date given at the head of the text. See also Henry's table 22.2 in *"Owls to Athens": Essays on Classical Subjects Presented to Sir Kenneth Dover*, E. M. Craik, ed., 1990, p. 188.

ATHENIAN CITIZENSHIP CONFERRED UPON A SIKYONIAN

178. A considerable fragment of an unusually wide stele of Hymettian marble (I 5657), broken on all sides, discovered on February 20, 1939, among marbles removed during the demolition of modern houses at the north foot of the Areopagos.

H. 0.20 m.; W. 0.35 m.; Th. 0.17 m.
LH. 0.005 m.
Στοιχ. Hor. 0.01 m.; Vert. 0.0116 m.

Ed. B. D. Meritt, *Hesperia* 30, 1961, pp. 212–213, no. 7, with photograph pl. 36; see also *SEG* XXI, 359: M. J. Osborne, *Naturalization* I, pp. 174–178, D 82, *Naturalization* II, pp. 168–169.

a. 286–262 *a.*(?)   ΣΤΟΙΧ. 107(?)

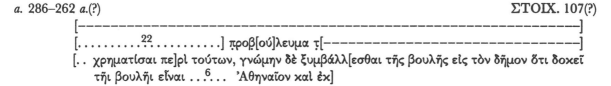

$$
\begin{array}{l}
\text{[--]} \\
[.........\overset{22}{.........}] \text{ προβ[ού]λευμα τ[-----------------------------]} \\
[.. \text{ χρηματίσαι πε]ρὶ τούτων, γνώμην δὲ ξυμβάλλ[εσθαι τῆς βουλῆς εἰς τὸν δῆμον ὅτι δοκεῖ} \\
\text{τῆι βουλῆι εἶναι} ...\overset{6}{...} \text{ Ἀθηναῖον χαὶ ἐκ]}
\end{array}
$$

[γόνους αὐτοῦ, χα]ὶ γράψασθ[αι] φυλῆς [χ]αὶ δήμου χα[ὶ φρατρίας ἧς ἂν βούληται κατὰ
τὸν νόμον ——]

[.......¹³.......]ΑΙ[..⁵..]ΣΙ[..⁶... π]ρυτανε[————————————————————————————————————]

5   [..........²¹..........]ς [ἐν τῶι ψη]φίσματι αι[——————· τοὺς δὲ θεσμοθέτας εἰσαγαγ]

[εῖν] αὐτῶι τὴ[ν] δ[ο]χιμ[ασί]αν [τῆς δωρε]ᾶς κατὰ τοy [νόμον ————————————————————]

[..⁵..]μου δωρεᾶς· ᵛ τὸν γραμματέ[α τ]ο[ῦ] δ[ήμ]ου ἀν[αγράψαι τόδε τὸ ψήφισμα ἐν στήληι
λιθίνηι χαὶ στῆσαι ἐν ἀχροπόλει· τὸ δὲ γενόμενον ἀν]

[άλωμα] εἰς τὴν στήλην χαὶ τὴν ἀναγ[ρα]φὴν μερί[σαι τοὺς ἐπὶ τῆι διοιχήσει. ————————
εἶπεν· ——]

[....]ισθένου Σιχυώνιος αἰτεῖ, [——]

10   [....]ον τοῦ τε πάππου χαὶ τοῦ π[ατ]ρὸς ΗΜΩ[————————————————————————————]

[..⁵..]α τῶν αἱρουμένων ᵛ [...]ππ[——]

[....⁸....]αντας ὁμοίως τοῖς τ[——]

[.....¹².....]ΚΑΙΑ[.]ΝΕΙ[———]

[——]

The stone is very battered and chipped at the edges and has horizontal scratches and gouges across the inscribed surface. A dowel hole cuts into lines 4–5. The writing is scratchy and hesitant, almost quavery, in character, but it is reasonably precise and in form "standard" for the period. Omega is wide.

Because the fragment is broken all around, the positioning of the text in relation to the supposed edges of the monument is arbitrary. Its unusual width seems to be imposed by the formula for the grant of citizenship incorporated in lines 2–3 and by the formulas for the inscribing and erection of the stele and the source of payment for it in lines 7–8. When less than half survives of a text with lines more than fifty letters in width, attempts at restoration are generally unwise. Here the minimum requirements suggest a line of some 107 letters, whereas in the most productive line (8) no more than twenty-nine letters are visible. This does not deter speculation, but supplements beyond plausible formulas for lines 2–3 and 7–8 (even so, to be treated with some reserve) have been excluded from the text.

The date of the inscription depends in general upon the style of the writing, regarded by Meritt as appropriate to the early 3rd century, and in particular upon line 8, where the verb μερίσαι suggests the period of the Plural Board of Administration, for whom it represents the invariable instruction (cf. **174**, commentary on lines 8–10). If the instruction is to the Single Officer, the date would be in all probability post-262 rather than ante-286, for in the period before 286 surviving inscriptions are comparatively few (see p. 241) and the use of μερίσαι is not well established (see **175**, commentary on lines 4–5).

Line 1. After προβ[ού]λευμα Osborne continues [ᵛ δεδόχθαι τῆι βουλῆι τοὺς προέδρους οἳ ἂν λάχωσιν προεδρεύειν εἰς τὴν ἐπιοῦσαν ἐχχλησί|αν χρηματίσαι πε]ρὶ τούτων χτλ. For the restored ἐπιοῦσαν cf. **162**, commentary on line 14, and for the "irrational" blank space (here and elsewhere in the text) cf. **172** and references there. Following alpha, however, is the clear trace of a central upright stroke (iota or tau), and the tempting restoration must therefore be placed in some doubt. Lines 2–3. Ἀθηναῖον εἶναι ...^{ca. 10}... ισθέν|ου Σιχυώνιον χα]ὶ Meritt. The above text shows Osborne's proposal, which correctly takes account of the formulaic need to include the honorand's descendants. It also meets the objections of A. S. Henry (*Honours*, pp. 65 and 91, note 19), who drew attention to the rarity of a formula containing name, patronymic, and ethnic: "There is nothing except the unusually wide stele to justify the restoration." The *tria nomina* nevertheless appear in full in lines 8–9, at the start of what is evidently an amendment or rider to the enactment. Osborne also added χατὰ τὸν νόμον after βούληται and continued in lines 3–4 with ᵛ δοῦναι δὲ χαὶ τὴν ψῆφον περὶ αὐτοῦ τῶι δήμω|ι εἰς τὴν ἐπιοῦσ]αν [ἐχχλ]ησί[αν τοὺς π]ρυτάνε[ι]ς τ[οὺς ————].

Line 5. ἐ[ν Osborne. Line 6. Meritt compared *IG* II², 654, lines 53–54. Osborne listed various formulaic possibilities for the long lacuna. Lines 8–9. εἶπεν· περὶ μὲν τῆς δωρεᾶς ἧς ...⁶... |....]ισθένου Σιχυώνιος αἰτεῖ, [δεδόχθαι τῶι δήμωι πάντα τὰ ἄλλα πράττειν ————] Meritt. His restoration was based on the analogy of *IG* II², 682, lines 93–96, the validity of which was doubted by Osborne. On the basis of the restoration (and presumably of line 1 also), P. J. Rhodes judged the decree to have been probouleumatic (*Athenian Boule*, p. 251).

For the naturalization procedure of the period, under his "Formulation A", see Osborne, *Naturalization* I, p. 16, and for this text, under subdivision XIII, p. 22. The γραμματεύς is here (line 7) named as τοῦ δήμου rather than ὁ χατὰ πρυτανείαν. See **120**, commentary on line 8.

For Athenian relations with Sikyon and such account as may be given of Sikyonian history in the first half of the 3rd century see C. H. Skalet, *Ancient Sikyon*, 1928, p. 82 and **115**. The present text implies some continuing relationship of goodwill between Athens and at least one prominent Sikyonian family (cf. line 10) but offers no wider historical perspectives.

THE ARCHONSHIP OF DIOTIMOS, 285/4 B.C.

The name of Diotimos as archon survives on four inscriptions: *IG* II², 653 (*SEG* XXVIII, 57, XXXII, 108, XXXIII, 111) and 654 (M. J. Osborne, *Naturalization* I, pp. 163–166, D 74, *Naturalization* II, pp. 160–161), **179**, and **180**. In addition, it is plausibly to be restored in *IG* II², 655, which refers to the same circumstances as 654 and was passed, apparently, at the same assembly. In the first three of these texts, the name of the γραμματεύς of the year is sufficiently preserved for the whole of it to be assured, and it is partly preserved also in the fourth. His deme, Paiania, belonged to the phyle Pandionis, fifth in official order. The historical content of *IG* II², 653–655 requires Diotimos' close association with Athenian efforts to be rid of the Macedonian forces of occupation still in Attic territory; while the honors for Spartokos III, king of Bosporos (*IG* II², 653), must antedate that monarch's death in 284/3 (Diodorus Siculus 20.100.7, where his accession is narrated under the year 304/3 and it is noted that he reigned for twenty years). The requirements of the cycle of secretaries also imply that Diotimos, with a γραμματεύς from Pandionis V, is best placed in the year immediately following that of Diokles with a γραμματεύς from Aigeis IV. This association and order have been adopted by all modern commentators, and the year assigned to Diotimos in their various reconstructions of the archon list has varied *pari passu* with their assignment of the year of Diokles. Cf. B. D. Meritt, *Athenian Year*, p. 233, *Historia* 26, 1977, p. 173; C. Habicht, *Untersuchungen*, p. 98, note 23.

The evidence reveals the year as clearly ordinary in the festival calendar, and as the fifteenth in the Metonic cycle it coincided with the generally regular correspondence between that cycle and that calendar. Full and hollow months were thus more or less concurrent with prytanies of 30 and 29 days. Known phylai in prytany were III Kekropis, VI Demetrias or Akamantis, VII Antigonis, and XII Pandionis.

FRAGMENT OF A DECREE

179. The upper left corner of a pedimental stele of Hymettian marble (I 3460), with the left side and the left section of the pediment preserved, first noted in February 1936, when it was brought into the excavation headquarters of the Agora, although it had for some years been lying in the Stoa of Attalos. A generous upper margin (0.03 m.) separates the simple horizontal molding from the first line of the text.

H. 0.23 m.; W. 0.146 m.; Th. 0.095 m.
LH. 0.006 m.
Στοιχ. (almost square) Hor. 0.0136 m.; Vert. 0.013 m.

Ed. B. D. Meritt, *Hesperia* 9, 1940, p. 83, no. 14, with photograph.

a. 285/4 *a., pryt.* III   ΣΤΟΙΧ. 23

'Επὶ Διοτίμ[ου ἄρχοντος ἐπὶ τ]
ῆς Κεκροπί[δος τρίτης πρυτα]
νείας ἧι Λυσ[ίστρατος 'Αριστομ]
άχου Παιαν[ιεὺς ἐγραμμάτευ]
5   ε[ν· Β]οηδρομ[ιῶνος ἐνάτηι ἱστ]
[αμένο]υ, ἐν[άτηι τῆς πρυτανεί]
[ας]· ἐκ[κ]λησ[ία κυρία· τῶν προέδ]
[ρων ἐπε]ψή[φιζεν . . . . ¹⁰ . . . . .]
[——————————————]

In line 3 the stonemason evidently cut ΗΙΛΥΣΤΡΑΤΟΣ, which he managed to correct as far as the preserved portion of the stone is concerned by inserting a fresh iota at the midpoint between the stoichoi of eta and its neighbor on the right, converting the former iota in that neighboring space into lambda, and by writing ΥΣΙ in the former space of ΛΥ. This was a matter of adaptation, for the original letters can be clearly seen: there was no erasure. Meritt read a dotted iota after the last surviving sigma, which may perhaps be represented by the line of break. Apart from this error, the plain writing, "standard" for its period although with an unusual mu, is reasonably precise. It shows however some variation in the detail of epsilon and sigma and in the size of omicron. Line 7. ἐκκ]λησ[ία Meritt.

Beyond its relevance to the calendar of the year, for which see the commentary above on the year of Diotimos, the text calls for little discussion. Line 2. The restoration τρίτης is conditioned by the name of the month preserved in line 5. Lines 3–4. Nothing further is known of the γραμματεύς of the year, Lysistratos of Paiania (*PA* 9623), nor have any members of his family been identified. Line 5. It was noted by W. K. Pritchett (*Hesperia* 15, 1946, p. 157, note 44) that ὀγδόηι could be restored as the numeral here. This introduces a variation of one day between prytany and festival calendar which may be judged less likely at this early stage of the year.

Lines 5–6. For Boedromion 9 as a meeting day of the assembly see J. D. Mikalson, *Sacred and Civil Calendar*, pp. 51–52. Line 7. This is early in the prytany for an ἐκκλησία κυρία. Cf. **172**, commentary on line 3.

FRAGMENT OF A DECREE

180. A fragment of the upper part of a pedimental stele of Hymettian marble (I 1524), with the left edge (at the base of the pediment) and the original rough-picked back preserved, discovered on March 5, 1934, in the wall of the Church of SS. Elias and Charalampes, north of the Southwest Fountain House (H–I 14). The pediment has been roughly hacked away, but a transitional taenia and fillet survive between it and the inscribed surface.

H. 0.29 m.; W. 0.49 m.; Th. 0.165 m.

LH. 0.006 m.

Στοιχ. Hor. (not well plotted by the mason) 0.0146 m. at left diminishing to 0.013 m. on the right; Vert. 0.014 m.

Ed. W. K. Pritchett, *Hesperia* 15, 1946, pp. 156–158, no. 14, with photograph.

a. 285/4 *a., pryt.* VI   ΣΤΟΙΧ. 40

```
        ['Ἐπ]ὶ Διοτίμου ἄρχοντος ἐπ[ὶ τῆς . . . 8 . . . . δος ἕκτη]
        [ς π]ρυτανείας ἧι Λυσίσ[τρατος 'Αριστομάχου Παιαν]
        [ιεὺ]ς ἐγραμμάτευε[ν· Ποσιδεῶνος δευτέραι μετ'εἰκ]
        [άδα]ς, τριακοστε[ῖ τῆς πρυτανείας· ἐκκλησία· τῶν πρ]
   5    [οέδ]ρων ἐπεψ[ήφιζεν . . . . . . . . . . . 24 . . . . . . . . . . . .]
        [. . κ]αὶ συ[μπρόεδροι· . . . . . . . . . . . 24 . . . . . . . . . . .]
        [----------------------------------------------]
```

Pritchett observed, correctly, that the writing is very similar to that of *IG* II², 657, the decree of 283/2 in honor of the comic poet Philippides. Small omicron, awkward omega, rho with a high loop, and upsilon with slightly curved angle strokes are characteristic. The straight-sided mu with short, high "v" and the peculiar alpha in line 3 also deserve remark and are similarly to be paralleled in *IG* II², 657.

Lines 1 and 3 were left unrestored by Pritchett, who produced alternative suggestions to meet the requirement of either forward or backward count in the date μετ'εἰκάδας, at that time believed to be possible in the reckoning of the final third of the festival month; cf. B. D. Meritt, *Athenian Year*, pp. 38–59 (esp. pp. 57–59). But it has long since been recognized that such count is always backward, as was proposed by Pritchett (with O. Neugebauer, *Calendars*, p. 26; see also Pritchett, *CP* 54, 1959, pp. 155–157, *Ancient Athenian Calendars on Stone*, 1963, pp. 349–354) and acknowledged by Meritt (*TAPA* 95, 1964, pp. 225 and 256, note 200): see also D. M. Lewis, *JHS* 83, 1963, p. 195; A. G. Woodhead, *Study of Greek Inscriptions*, pp. 120–122. Pritchett's restoration δευτέραι μετ'εἰκάδας, and the corresponding name of the month and ordinal numeral of the prytany that this entails, may be entered into the definitive text. Thus Posideon 29 = pryt. VI, 30. The variation of one day in the numeration, within the context of an ordinary year during the period of twelve phylai, and at a comparatively advanced point in the year, is without significance. For the penultimate day of Posideon as a meeting day of the assembly see J. D. Mikalson, *Sacred and Civil Calendar*, pp. 95–96. This text does not form part of the evidence there cited.

Line 1. The phyle in prytany was Demetrias or Akamantis. Antigonis and Pandionis, which also would fit the space available, are already pre-empted by the evidence for the seventh and twelfth prytanies.

THE ARCHONSHIPS OF EUTHIOS AND NIKIAS, 283/2 AND 282/1 B.C.

181 shows the archon Euthios (who held the eponymous archonship, for *IG* II², 657 [*SEG* XXXII, 109, with earlier references, XXXV, 87], 658, and 659 [*SEG* XXV, 88] are dated with reference to him) as honored in the archonship of Nikias. This establishes the order of these two archonships but need not imply that Nikias followed immediately upon Euthios. However, the γραμματεύς of Nikias' year, Theophilos, son of Theodotos, of Acharnai belonged to the phyle Oineis, eighth in order, while the γραμματεύς of Euthios' year, Nausimenes, son of Nausikydes, of Cholargos belonged to the phyle Akamantis, seventh in order. Nikias was thus Euthios' successor, and the historical content of *IG* II², 657, taken with the indications afforded by **181**, assigns both archons to this period of hopes and efforts to dislodge the Macedonian forces still in occupation of the Peiraieus. The secretary cycle also establishes their position relative to the years of Diokles and Diotimos discussed above (pp. 245 and 255). Nikias' archonship was unsuspected until the discovery of **181**, there being no other evidence for him (see below for another possible epigraphical reference), with the result that commentaries on the archon list and on the historical developments written earlier than 1938 take no account of him.

It had already been universally acknowledged, on the evidence already cited, that Euthios was to be assigned to a date in the 280's. This had varied from 287/6 to 284/3, the year 285/4 being the most popular choice and the date preferred by, among others, W. B. Dinsmoor (*Archons of Athens*, pp. 30, 60–61, 69). A date as late as 283/2 had not then been contemplated. Soon after its publication, the new evidence of **181** was examined by Dinsmoor (*Athenian Archon List*, esp. pp. 40–41), who established the succession Diokles–Diotimos–Isaios (cf. *IG* II², 657, line 39)–Euthios–Nikias which has since then remained unchallenged. To this group may be added Ourias, the γραμματεύς of whose year was from the phyle Kekropis (IX) and who on other evidence belongs in this period (see p. 260 below). The final evaluation of the dates of Diokles and Diotimos (*qq.v.*) affected the other archons linked with them, the result being to place Euthios in 283/2 and Nikias in 282/1, the dating here followed. See Dinsmoor, *Hesperia* 23, 1954, p. 314; B. D. Meritt, *Athenian Year*, p. 233, *Historia* 26, 1977, p. 173; C. Habicht, *Untersuchungen*, p. 99, note 24; M. J. Osborne, *ZPE* 58, 1985, p. 275.

IG II², 1273, lines 1–27, a decree of the thiasotai of the Mother of the Gods, honors one Soterichos of Troizen for his services to the group in the archonship of Nikias and was passed [ἐπὶ – – – –]ου ἄρχοντος in the month Anthesterion. It seemed not unlikely that the archon was the Nikias of 282/1 and that the decree was dated with reference either to Nikias himself or to his successor Ourias (cf. Meritt, *Hesperia* 7, 1938, p. 108). This interpretation was, however, doubted by Dinsmoor (*Athenian Archon List*, pp. 45–46) and was put into additional doubt by A. N. Oikonomides (*ZPE* 32, 1978, pp. 85–86; see also *SEG* XXVIII, 108), who proposed to read [ἐπὶ Εὐξεί]νου ἄρχοντος and to date the inscription to 222/1, thus setting the Nikias of that text in 223/2. A date there or thereabouts for *IG* II², 1273 was accepted also by Habicht (*ZPE* 39, 1980, pp. 1–5; see also *SEG* XXX, 96), although without discussion of the Nikias involved.

However, the alleged nu was not in fact read by Dinsmoor, as was claimed by Oikonomides in citing him (*loc. cit.*, note 6); and S. V. Tracy (*Attic Letter-Cutters*, p. 259) has confirmed that the decree should be placed in the first half of the century. Dinsmoor was confident that the name of the archon should be no longer than Meritt had postulated. The archon of 265/4, whether this be Peithidemos, Phanomachos, or another, could well be a preferable candidate, with the Nikias of the preceding year being Nikias of Otryne (although in this instance the mention of him will have lacked the demotic which distinguishes him in the epigraphical record from his two predecessors of the same name).

The Nikias of 282/1 did however prove to be the archon in whose year Phaidros of Sphettos served as agonothetes (*IG* II², 682, lines 53–54; cf. T. L. Shear, *Kallias*, pp. 66, 87–89, 100), a matter which had, before 1938, given rise to much controversy. For the suggestion that this Nikias should be identified with the Nikias ὕστερος of *IG* II², 644 and 645, and of **165**, and for its refutation see p. 237 above.

The dating by the festival and prytany calendars provided by the inscriptional evidence indicates that the year of Euthios was ordinary and that of Nikias intercalary. **181** shows that the latter year was proceeding with complete regularity in both calendars. The two years were the seventeenth and eighteenth in the (eighth) Metonic cycle, which the cycle required should be ordinary and intercalary respectively (cf. Meritt, *TAPA* 95, 1964, p. 236). The cycle and the arrangement of the festival years in Athens were thus fully in concord, and if this concordance be accepted as the general rule of the Athenian calendar (cf. Meritt, 'Αρχ. 'Εφ., 1968, pp. 92–105), the dating of the two archons receives additional confirmation. The only known phyle in prytany in the year of Nikias was VII Oineis. The hipparchs and phylarchs of the year are honored and listed in *SEG* XXI, 525 (XXV, 147).

EUTHIOS OF TEITHRAS HONORED, AS EX-ARCHON, TOGETHER WITH HIS PAREDROI

181 (Pl. 18). A complete pedimental stele of Hymettian marble (I 4266), slightly tapered towards the top, discovered on July 7, 1936, in use as a cover slab over a Late Roman drain in the north room of the Metroon (H 8–9). The stone is discolored on the left to a depth of 4–5 stoichoi and on the right to a depth of up to 13 stoichoi.

H. 1.31 m.; W. (inscribed face) 0.418 m. at top, 0.517 m. at foot; Th. 0.10 m. at top, 0.13 m. at foot.
LH. 0.007 m.
Στοιχ. (almost square) Hor. 0.013 m.; Vert. 0.0125 m.

Ed. B. D. Meritt, *Hesperia* 7, 1938, pp. 100–109, no. 18, with photograph. See *SEG* XXV, 89, with reference also to the text, with commentary and translation into Italian, of L. Moretti, *Iscrizioni storiche ellenistiche* I, pp. 28–31, no. 14. The discovery of the stele was mentioned by H. A. Thompson, *Hesperia* 6, 1937, p. 197, note 1: see also *Agora Guide*[3], p. 286.

a. 282/1 *a.*, *pryt.* VII   ΣΤΟΙΧ. 31

Θ   ε   ο   ι.

Ἐπὶ Νικίου ἄρχοντος ἐπὶ τῆς Οἰνηίδος
ἑβδόμης πρυτανείας ἧι Θεόφιλος Θεοδ
ότου Ἀχαρνεὺς ἐγραμμάτευεν· Γαμηλιῶ
5   νος ἐνάτηι ἱσταμένου, τρίτηι καὶ εἰκο
στεῖ τῆς πρυτανείας· ἐκκλησία· τῶν προ
έδρων ἐπεψήφιζεν Οἰνοκράτης Οἰνοβί
ου Ἐλε[υ]σίνιος καὶ συνπρόεδροι· *vv* ἔδο
ξεν τῶι δήμωι· Ἀγύρριος Καλλιμέδοντο
10 ς Κολλυτεὺς εἶπεν· ἐπειδὴ Εὔθιος ἄρχω
ν γενόμενος τάς τε θυσίας ἔθυσεν τοῖς
θεοῖς κατὰ τὰ πάτρια καὶ τῆς πομπῆς τῶ
ι Διονύσωι ἐπεμελήθη φιλοτίμως καὶ τ
ἄλλα πάντα ἔπραξεν τὰ περὶ τὴν ἀρχὴν δ
15 ικαίως πειθόμενος τοῖς τε νόμοις καὶ
τοῖς ψηφίσμασιν τῆς βουλῆς καὶ τοῦ δή
μου, καὶ διὰ ταῦτα αὐτὸν καὶ πρότερον ὁ
δῆμος ἐπήινεσεν καὶ ἐστεφάνωσεν ἐν τ
ῆι ἐκκλησίαι τῆι ἐν Διονύσου, ὅπως ἂν ο
20 ὖν πᾶσιν φανερὸν ἦι ὅτι ὁ δῆμος καὶ νῦν
καὶ εἰς τὸν λοιπὸν χρόνον τιμήσει τοῦ
ς δικαίως ἄρχοντας τὰς ἀρχὰς καὶ κατὰ
τοὺς νόμους, ἀγαθεῖ τύχει δεδόχθαι τῶ
ι δήμωι ἐπαινέσαι Εὔθιον Ἀντιφῶντος
25 Τειθράσιον φιλοτιμίας ἕνεκα καὶ εὐν
οίας ἣν ἔχων διατελεῖ πρὸς τὸν δῆμον, κ
αὶ στεφανῶσαι αὐτὸν χρυσῶι στεφάνωι
κατὰ {τα} τὸν νόμον· εἶναι δὲ αὐτῶι καὶ ἄλ
λο ἀγαθὸν εὑρέσθαι παρὰ τοῦ δήμου ὅτο
30 υ ἂν δοκεῖ ἄξιος εἶναι ὅταν ὁ Πειραιεὺ
ς καὶ τὸ ἄστυ ἐν τῶι αὐτῶι γένηται· ἐπαι
[ν]έσαι δὲ καὶ τοὺς παρέδρους αὐτοῦ Μει
δογένην Μείδωνος Ἀθμονέα, Σωκράτην Σ
ωδάμου Παιανιέα, δικαιοσύνης ἕνεκα κ
35 αὶ φιλοτι(μ)ίας, καὶ στεφανῶσαι ἑκάτερο
ν αὐτῶν χρυσῶι στεφάνωι κατὰ τὸν νόμο
ν· ἀναγράψαι δὲ τόδε τὸ ψήφισμα τὸν γρα
μματέα τὸν κατὰ πρυτανείαν ἐν στήληι

λιθίνει καὶ στῆσαι ἔμπροσθε τοῦ συνε
40 δρίου· εἰς δὲ τὴν ἀναγραφὴν τῆς στήλης
μερίσαι τοὺς ἐπὶ τῆι διοικήσει ᵛ Δ ᵛ δρ
αχμάς.   *vacat*
(*in corona*)
ʽΟ δῆμος
(*in corona*)   (*in corona*)
ʽΟ δῆμος   Οἱ φυλέται
45 ὁ Σαλαμινίων

The writing is clear and generally regular, with small circular letters pendent from the upper line of the lettering. The execution of omega is variable. The mason frequently omitted the horizontal stroke of alpha, and in line 35 he omitted the central "v" of mu. In the same line, thirty-two letters have been inscribed instead of the thirty-one of the regular pattern, ΙΣΤ in καὶ στεφανῶσαι occupying two letter spaces. In line 45 Σαλαμίνιοι was first written, and the last two letters were corrected subsequently. The three citations are written within carefully engraved stephanoi below the text of the decree.

Lines 3 and 7. Neither Theophilos nor Oinokrates is otherwise known. Indeed the latter name appears to be unattested elsewhere in Attic epigraphy. Lines 4–5. For Gamelion 9 as a meeting day of the assembly cf. J. D. Mikalson, *Sacred and Civil Calendar*, pp. 100–101: this text is in fact the sole evidence for it.

Lines 5–6 and 38–39. The "mixed" spelling of the feminine dative endings may be noted, HI and EI being used apparently at will in this text. For examples of decrees with both endings in more or less equal frequency cf. L. Threatte, *Grammar*, p. 378, and for the phenomenon in general see **101**, commentary on lines 5–7. Line 6. ἐκκλησία. See **97**, commentary on line 7. Line 8. The two vacant letter spaces are evidently designed to emphasize the enactment formula. See A. S. Henry, *Prescripts*, pp. 64–65 and 68 (where this text is cited). Lines 8–9. This was a nonprobouleumatic decree; see P. J. Rhodes, *Athenian Boule*, p. 264. Line 9. Agyrrhios (*PA* 180) was a member of the family from Kollytos of which his great-grandfather of the same name (*PA* 179) is the best-known representative; see J. K. Davies, *Athenian Propertied Families*, pp. 277–282 (esp. p. 279), with stemma (p. 281). He has left a record elsewhere in the tradition, in that he was the proposer of a decree (*IG* II², 653) in honor of Spartokos III, king of Bosporos (see p. 255 above). Davies remarked that that decree and this are both "markedly nationalist in tone." He is also mentioned by Athenaios (8.340e) as having been the butt of the witticisms of the poet Philemon in the Μετίων.

Lines 12–13. The eponymous archon, according to Aristotle (*Athenaion Politeia* 56.4), with the assistance of his paredroi (*IG* II², 668, line 14), and with a board of epimeletai sharing the responsibility (Aristotle, *loc. cit.*; *IG* II², 668, lines 14–15), had charge of the procession in honor of the god at the Great Dionysia. Cf. L. Deubner, *Attische Feste*, pp. 138–142. Lines 18–19. Ἐκκλησία ἡ ἐν Διονύσου. Cf. **79**, commentary on lines 1–7. Lines 19–20. ὅπως ἂν οὖν. See **173**, commentary on line 2.

Line 23. ἀγαθεῖ τύχει. Cf. **72**, commentary on lines 7–8. Lines 25–26. For the expression of the virtues of the honorand see Henry, *Honours*, pp. 42–44 (this phraseology listed on p. 43). Lines 27–28 and 36–37. On the gold stephanoi κατὰ τὸν νόμον cf. **112**, commentary on lines 5–7 and **141**. Lines 28–30. εἶναι δὲ αὐτῶι κτλ. For the additional unspecified benefits introduced in the form of an "open clause" see Henry, *Honours*, pp. 311–315 (this text cited on pp. 311 and 315); cf. also Rhodes, *Athenian Boule*, pp. 281–283.

Lines 30–31. On the evidence of these lines the Peiraieus was firmly in Macedonian hands; cf. C. Habicht, *Untersuchungen*, p. 99. Moretti (*op. cit.*, p. 30) made the interesting deduction from the wording that the Macedonians had recaptured the *asty* itself ("l'iscrizione mostra che nel Febbraio 281 l'ἄστυ non era in mano degli Ateniesi"). The sense of the inscription is, however, clearly otherwise. The Athenians look forward to the time when the Peiraieus has been recovered and reunited with the *asty*, of which they had been in possession for the past five years or so; when this has taken place, Euthios, they promise, will receive other honors he will have merited. That Moretti was in error here was apparent also to T. L. Shear (*Kallias*, p. 28, note 58; cf. *SEG* XXVIII, 59) and to P. Gauthier (*REG* 92, 1979, pp. 349–399; cf. *SEG* XXIX, 100), although the latter believed that the Peiraieus was indeed recovered in 281 and that this clause shows the imminent expectation of that. Thus this inscription takes its place in the controversy concerning the recovery or nonrecovery of Athens' seaport between 286 and 262, for which see p. 252 above.

Lines 31–34. On the paredroi see **174**, commentary on line 2. Neither Meidogenes nor Sokrates is otherwise known, save that the latter may well be the father of that Moschine, "daughter of Sokrates of Paiania", who made the dedication to Asklepios on record in *IG* II², 1534A, lines 47–48 (= S. B. Aleshire, *The Athenian Asklepieion*, 1989, pp. 177–248, inventory IV, lines 70–71; see esp. p. 233). Lines 34–35. See on lines 25–26. This particular form of words is quoted by Henry from *IG* II², 488 (of 303/2), where, however, it is followed by the fuller explanation τῆς εἰς κτλ., which is not present here. Cf. **175**, commentary on line 1.

Lines 39–40. ἔμπροσθε τοῦ συνεδρίου. See **175**, commentary on lines 3–4 and **194**, commentary on line 12, with references there given. Line 41. οἱ ἐπὶ τῆι διοικήσει. See on **174**. This text lies firmly within the period of their responsibility. Ten drachmas seem a modest cost for so considerable a record, but towards the end of the period during which costs were specified the amount allocated seems to have diminished. Compare tables 2 and 3 in Henry, *ZPE* 78, 1989, pp. 268 and 273.

THE ARCHONSHIP OF OURIAS, 281/80 B.C.

The connection between the assessment of the date of Ourias and that of the archons preceding him has been mentioned above (p. 257), and the establishment of his year largely depends on the considerations that prompted the determination of theirs. See B. D. Meritt, *Athenian Year*, p. 233, *Historia* 26, 1977, p. 173. The γραμματεύς of his archonship, Euxenos of Aixone (Kekropis IX), is placed by the secretary cycle in the year following that of Nikias. Ourias has left other epigraphical legacies besides **182**. A poletai record (*Hesperia* 4, 1935, pp. 565–572, no. 41; *Agora* XIX, P52) links him (in an uncertain temporal relationship) with the earlier archons Telokles and – – – –ppos (probably Philippos; see Meritt, *Hesperia* 7, 1938, p. 107 and W. K. Pritchett and Meritt, *Chronology*, pp. 88–91). Honors were accorded to the island of Tenos in the eleventh prytany of his year (*IG* II², 660, lines 25–46) and reflect the continuing need of the Athenians to maintain their Aegean communications. A list of members of the boule best ascribed to the same year survives in great part (*Agora* XV, 72; *SEG* XXXVI, 217, with earlier references; J. S. Traill, *Hesperia* 38, 1969, pp. 459–494). Meritt (*Hesperia* 7, 1938, p. 108) also restored his name as archon in *IG* II², 1273, line 1. This text has recently been relocated to a date later in the century and with a different restoration (see p. 257 above), but it surely belongs to this period, and Meritt's suggestion remains acceptable.

This year was the last in the current Metonic cycle, and the concluding year of Meton's nineteen-year series was designed as ordinary. The inscriptions show that the festival calendar agreed with this arrangement, and it may be assumed that the prytanies and the lunar months were exactly concurrent, the year beginning with a full month. Phylai identified in prytany are II Aiantis and XI Demetrias.

HONORS FOR THE TAXIARCHOI SENT AS DELEGATES TO BOIOTIA

182. A pedimental stele of Hymettian marble (I 863), slightly tapering towards the top, completely preserved with the exception of the apex of the pediment and the left akroterion with the left end of the epistyle molding, discovered on May 25, 1933, in the wall of a Byzantine well east of the Tholos (H 11:1). There is some pitting of the inscribed surface, especially on the right.

H. 0.93 m.; W. 0.473 m. (at pediment), 0.414 m. (at top of inscribed surface), 0.449 m. (at foot of stele); Th. 0.085 m.
LH. *ca.* 0.006 m.
Στοιχ. (almost square, increasing by one letter at lines 25 and 30) Hor. 0.0116 m.; Vert. 0.012 m.

Ed. B. D. Meritt, *Hesperia* 4, 1935, pp. 562–565, no. 40, with photograph. See *SEG* XXV, 90, with reference also to the text, with commentary and translation into Italian, of L. Moretti, *Iscrizioni storiche ellenistiche* I, pp. 31–33, no. 15. W. B. Dinsmoor (*Hesperia* 23, 1954, pp. 291–296) discussed decrees concerned with taxiarchoi, and the present inscription specifically on pp. 292–293. Line 30 was quoted in *Agora* III, p. 176, no. 581, among evidence for the location of the Strategion.

a. 281/80 a., *pryt.* II   ΣTOIX. 32 (lines 1–24)
                                                                          33 (lines 25–29)
                                                                          34 (lines 30–31)

    Ἄρχων Οὐρίας· ἐπὶ τῆς Αἰαντίδο[ς δ]ευ[τ]έρ
    ας πρυτανείας ἧι Εὔξενος Καλλί[ου] Αἰξω
    νεὺς ἐγραμμάτευεν· Μεταγειτνιῶνος δε
    υτέραι μετ'εἰκάδας, ὀγδόει καὶ ε[ἰκο]στε
 5   ῖ τῆς πρυτανείας· ἐκκλησία· τῶν προέδρω
    ν ἐπεψήφιζεν Διοκλῆς Ἰσχυρίου Πτελεά
    σιος καὶ συμπρόεδροι· ἔδοξεν τε[ῖ β]ουλε
    ῖ καὶ τῶι δήμωι· Λέων Κιχησίου Αἰξωνεὺς

εἶπεν· περὶ ὧν λέγουσιν οἱ ἀποσταλέντε

10 ς τ⟨ῶ⟩ν ταξιάρχων εἰς τὰ Βασίλεια ὑπὲρ τῆ
ς θυσίας ἧς ἔθυσαν, ἀγαθεῖ τύχει δεδόχθ
αι τεῖ βουλεῖ τοὺς προέδρους οἳ ἂν λάχω
σιν προεδρεύειν ἐν τῶι δήμωι εἰς τὴν πρ
ώτην ἐκκλησίαν π[ρ]οσαγαγεῖν αὐτοὺς χα

15 ὶ χρηματίσαι, γνώμην δὲ ξυμβάλλε[σ]θαι τ
ῆς βουλῆς εἰς τὸν δῆμον ὅτι δοκεῖ [τεῖ] βο
υλεῖ τὰ μὲν ἀγαθὰ δέχεσθαι ἃ [φ]α̣σ̣[ιν] γ̣ε̣γ̣ο̣
νέναι ἐν τοῖς ἱεροῖς ἐφ'ὑγιείαι καὶ σωτ
ηρίαι τῆς βουλῆς καὶ τοῦ δήμου, ἐπαινέσ

20 αι δὲ τοὺς ταξιάρχους τοὺς ἀποσταλέντ
ας εἰς [Β]οιωτοὺς Δεινόστρατον Δεινίδ *v*
ου Χολλείδην, Εὐκλείδην Λυσιστράτου Π
ειραιέα, Αὐτί[αν] Αὐτοκλέους Ἀχαρνέα, *vv*
Ἄβρωνα Ἐπιγένου Ἀλαιέα, *v* Ἀριστόδη[μο]ν

25 Ἀριστοφῶντος Στειριέα, Θεόφαντον Νι[κ]ο
στράτου Γαργήττιον φιλοτιμίας ἕνεκα *v*
τῆς πρὸς τὴν βουλὴν καὶ τὸν δῆμον· ἀναγρά
ψαι δὲ [τόδε] τόδε τὸ ψήφισμα τὸν γραμματέ
α τὸν κατὰ πρυτανείαν ἐν στήληι λιθίνει

30 καὶ στῆσαι πρὸς τῶι στρατηγίωι· εἰς δὲ τὴν
ἀναγραφὴν τῆς στήλης μερίσαι τοὺς ἐπὶ *vv*
τῆι διοικήσει Δ δραχμάς. *vacat*

The writing is regular and without marked idiosyncrasies save for a slight curve in some straight strokes, the omission of the upright in xi, and variation in the articulation of epsilon and sigma. A few lines (23, 24, 26, 31) have blank spaces at points where account is taken of the broadening of the stele, displaying some care to avoid awkward word division; but the same concern is not in evidence elsewhere (e.g., 10, 14, 15).

Line 1. The expression here of the archon's name in the nominative rather than in the usual genitival formula has only one parallel, *IG* II², 658, line 2, of 283/2. See A. S. Henry, *Prescripts*, pp. 55 and 71. Meritt's restoration of another example in *IG* II², 697 (see *SEG* XXI, 356) proved to be unnecessary. The meager evidence suggests that it may be a phenomenon restricted to this period and perhaps an experimental formulation that did not "catch on". Line 2. Euxenos of Aixone, the γραμματεύς (*PA* 5891), is not known beyond his tenure of this office, but his father was identified by J. Kirchner (*PA* 7848) with the priest of the Herakleidai (*IG* II², 1199, lines 23–24) attested in 325/4. If this is correct, and if the priesthood was still in the same hereditary hands, Euxenos had as an ancestor Plato's Lysis. See Plato, *Lysis* 205c–d and J. K. Davies, *Athenian Propertied Families*, pp. 359–361. Lines 3–4. For the penultimate day of Metageitnion as a meeting day of the assembly see J. D. Mikalson, *Sacred and Civil Calendar*, p. 45. It is attested also in 302/1 and in the archonship of Ergochares in 226/5 (**224**). Line 5. ἐκκλησία. See **97**, commentary on line 7.

Line 6. For the reading of the patronymic see A. E. Raubitschek, *Hesperia* 11, 1942, p. 305, note 14, a correction to the original text overlooked by Moretti, *loc. cit.* The mention of Diokles dates to this year the bouleutic list *Agora* XV, 72 (see above), in which he appears at line 117. See J. S. Traill, *Hesperia* 38, 1969, pp. 472 and 488. It is likely that the Diokles Pteleasios who was a member of the boule in 360/59 (*PA* 4051) was his ancestor, perhaps his grandfather (*Agora* XV, 17, line 10). Lines 7–8. This was probouleumatic enactment; see P. J. Rhodes, *Athenian Boule*, p. 252, where the inscription is dated in error to 283/2. Line 8. That Leon, son of Kichesias, had (like Memnon, son of Medon, of Aphidna in the preceding generation; cf. **123**) shown a special concern for the taxiarchoi was observed by Dinsmoor, *op. cit.*, p. 291. See **185**. The family may be traced through six generations (the detail in Dinsmoor's note 18, to which may be added *SEG* XXI, 435, line 14; on this see C. Habicht, *AthMitt* 76, 1961, pp. 130–131).

Line 10. The stone has ΣΤΟΝ at the beginning of the line. The Basileia, in honor of Zeus Basileios, were held at Lebadeia and had been established in commemoration of the battle of Leuktra (Diodorus Siculus 15.53). Meritt drew attention to *RE* III, col. 82, *s.v.* Basileus (2), and Moretti to his *Iscrizioni agonistiche greche*, 1953, pp. 105–107. See also particularly M. Feyel, *Contribution à l'épigraphie béotienne*, 1942, pp. 67–87.

That the Athenians saw fit to send half (as it may be assumed; cf. Dinsmoor, *op. cit.*, p. 292) of the body of taxiarchoi as a special delegation to the festival on this occasion suggests that the political and military soundings for which the national gathering would provide an opportunity were of some significance. The festival had evidently taken place not long before the decree was passed, for, as Meritt noted, the taxiarchoi are not described as those of a preceding year. The delegates were personally men of note (see below). The mission ought probably to be put into some relation with the battle of Koroupedion and its consequences, since that battle may be dated to February/March 281; see references in T. L. Shear, *Kallias*, pp. 31–32 with note 71; E. Will in *CAH* VII, 2nd ed., i, 1984, p. 113 with note 43. Seleukos Nikator was still alive at this time; but the Greeks might expect some effect on the position of Antigonos Gonatas and wish to make provision for it. There was perhaps some hope of detaching Boiotia from Antigonos at this juncture, although in the event the Boiotians did not shake themselves free of Macedonian rule until the naval defeat of Antigonos by Ptolemy Keraunos in spring 280. The mission therefore preceded what Shear called "the turmoil of that autumn", and whatever its intention the rapid turns of events overtook it.

Line 11. ἀγαθεῖ τύχει. See **72**, commentary on lines 7–8.

Lines 20–26. Name lists of this kind are uncommon: cf. Henry, *Honours*, pp. 46–47, note 7(v), where this text is cited. All the taxiarchoi have been identified on other evidence, with a greater or lesser degree of probability, as members of known families. For the details see Dinsmoor, *op. cit.*, pp. 292–293. The alleged tombstone of Deinostratos (*IG* II², 7795) may from its style be that of his grandson. Autias was also honored by the Oropians at this time (*IG* VII, 4266; see A. E. Raubitschek, *Hesperia* 11, 1942, p. 305). Whether Dinsmoor's correlations are acceptable or not, there is sufficient evidence to suggest that this was a "high-powered" delegation, and considerable importance seems to have been attached to it. On the duties of the taxiarchoi see commentary on **123**.

Line 26. For the expression of the virtues of the honorands cf. **181**, commentary on lines 25–26. Henry (*Honours*, p. 43) quotes two comparable examples from later in the century, including **188**. Line 28. τόδε was written twice. The mason erased the first τόδε but insufficiently to prevent every letter being still visible.

Line 30. The stele was to be set up in the neighborhood of the office of the strategoi. See *Agora* III, pp. 174–177. The place of discovery of this and other inscriptions reinforces the evidence of Aischines (2.85) that this office stood in the Agora. See further *Agora* XIV, pp. 73–74 and J. M. Camp, *Athenian Agora*, pp. 116–118, as well as Dinsmoor, *op. cit.*, pp. 295–296. Lines 30–32. Like the larger **181**, this stele cost no more than ten drachmas; and here again the cost seems small for so considerable a monument. Cf. also **187**. Finally it is perhaps noteworthy that, unlike the taxiarchoi honored in **185** and **187**, these delegates are not credited with any display of ἀρετή. The phraseology of the honorands' virtues was standard, but the virtues themselves varied and must have been nicely chosen for their appropriateness. A good deal must lie behind the list of variations compiled by Henry (*Honours*, pp. 42–44).

FRAGMENT OF A DECREE

183. A thin fragment of a stele of bluish Hymettian marble (I 1273), with the left edge preserved but otherwise broken all around, discovered on February 3, 1934, in a Late Roman context under the floor of a Byzantine building north of the Temple of Ares (K 6).

H. 0.12 m.; W. 0.093 m.; Th. 0.03 m.

LH. 0.006 m.

Στοιχ. (almost square) Hor. *ca.* 0.015 m.; Vert. 0.0145 m.

Ed. B. D. Meritt, *Hesperia* 10, 1941, pp. 57–58, no. 21, with photograph.

ca. a. 280–270 *a.*   ΣΤΟΙΧ. 34(?)

```
[----------------------------------]
[ἐ]x[κλησία κυρία· ᵛ τῶν προέδρων ἐπεψήφιζε]
ν Νικο[.........²²......... καὶ συμπ]
ρόεδρ[οι· ᵛ ἔδοξεν τῆι βουλῆι καὶ τῶι δήμωι]·
Μνησίε[ργος Μνησίου Ἀθμονεὺς εἶπεν· περὶ]
ὧν ἀπαν[γέλλουσιν οἱ θεωροί(?) οἱ ἀποσταλέν]
τες εἰς [....¹⁰..... περὶ τῶν θυσιῶν ὧν ἔθυ]
ον τῶι [....⁹.... καὶ τοῖς ἄλλοις θεοῖς οἷ]
ς πάτ[ριον ἦν ὅσας αὐτοῖς οἵ τε νόμοι προσέ]
ταττ[τον καὶ τὰ ψηφίσματα τοῦ δήμου, ἀγαθῆι]
[τύχηι δεδόχθαι τῆι βουλῆι κτλ. --------]
[----------------------------------]
```

The restorations are those of Meritt, undoubtedly extensive in comparison with what survives on the stone but reasonably acceptable once the stoichedon pattern has been established by the phraseology of lines 3 and 7–9. He regarded the text as that of a decree in honor of a delegation of theoroi and suggested that they had been sent to the festival of the Herakleia at Thebes, with τὰ Ἡράχλεια and τε Ἡραχλεῖ as suitable supplements in lines 6 and 7.

The writing was said in the *editio princeps* to resemble that of *IG* II², 657, of 283/2 (cf. **180**). It has perhaps greater affinities with *IG* II², 689, of 272/1, especially in the variety of nu, sigma, and omega. The inscribing of the last-named letter and the size of omicron are quite other than in *IG* II², 657. If on these grounds the decree proves more attuned to the later 270's, the prosopographical considerations of line 4 may be additionally helpful. On the other hand, a delegation to Boiotia may conveniently be brought into connection with **182**, as Meritt himself observed, and assigned to a historical context consonant with the diplomatic effort evidenced there. Thus a date within the decennium suggested may appear more acceptably precise than Meritt's original "early third century" dating.

Line 1. ἐχχλησία χυρία, in restoration. Cf. **101**, commentary on lines 7–8. Line 3. As restored, this was a probouleumatic enactment; cf. P. J. Rhodes, *Athenian Boule*, p. 252 (where Meritt's dating is reproduced). Line 4. The name Mnesiergides appears only once in Attic prosopography: in the prytany list *Agora* XV, 58, at line 59. Otherwise, the only name beginning Mnesie– – – is Mnesiergos, and the restoration of this name here, acceptable on grounds of frequency, is reinforced by the evidence of *IG* II², 704, also of 272/1, of which the proposer was Mnesiergos, son of Mnesias, of Athmonon. The name fits the apparent requirements of line 4 remarkably well. At the time of the *editio princeps*, *IG* II², 657 was dated to 285/4 and 704 to 262/1. The gap of twenty-three years created difficulties for the orator in the latter and in the present text; but the reconsideration of the dates of both has eliminated these. If Mnesiergos is correctly identified, he is doubtless to be connected with the Mnesiergos of Athmonon who was secretary of the board of ταμίαι τῶν ἱερῶν χρημάτων in 398/7 (*PA* 10275; *IG* II², 1388, lines 7–8). See also J. Sundwall, *Nachträge zur prosopographia Attica*, 1910, p. 130.

It may be added that Boiotia was within this period independent of the Macedonians, and there is no historical objection to the supposition of a theoric delegation to the Theban festival. Cf. W. W. Tarn, *Antigonos Gonatas*, 1913, pp. 207–208.

THE ARCHONSHIP OF OLBIOS, 275/4 B.C.

The name of Olbios as archon survives on **185**, on which it is accompanied by the completely preserved name of the γραμματεύς of his year, Kydias, son of Timonides, of Euonymon (Erechtheis III). Sufficient of this name appears in **184** to dictate the attribution of that text also to Olbios' archonship. Before the discovery of these Agora texts, Olbios was known only from a decree of the Mesogeioi (*IG* II², 1245), who honored their own archon Polyeuktos of Bate, on the motion of Amynomachos, son of Philokrates, of the same deme, an heir of the philosopher Epikouros (Diogenes Laertius 10.16). This connection seemed to place Olbios in the appropriate generation, and the identity of the proposer of **185** and **182** made a close association between the years of Olbios and Ourias clearly desirable, the secretary cycle imposing at the minimum a five-year interval between the two.

A previously accepted date for Olbios, after many variants (one as late as 247/6) in earlier studies, was 277/6 (B. D. Meritt, *Hesperia* 7, 1938, p. 133; W. K. Pritchett and Meritt, *Chronology*, p. xviii; Pritchett and O. Neugebauer, *Calendars*, p. 81). W. B. Dinsmoor (*Hesperia* 23, 1954, p. 314) lowered this date by two years, and 275/4 has remained the accepted year (cf. Meritt, *Athenian Year*, p. 233, *Historia* 26, 1977, p. 173). The sole dissentient was C. Pelekides (*REG* 69, 1956, p. 192, note 1), who, without regard to the identity of the proposer in **185** and **182**, claimed that the year 251/50 was equally possible. Meritt (*Hesperia* 4, 1935, p. 564) proposed the restoration of Olbios' name as that of the archon in *IG* II², 792, line 5, where its last four letters survive: this is a decree in honor of the sitonai of that archon's year and is thus likely to be datable to the following year, 274/3. He subsequently abandoned the suggestion; but the case for it was cogently (and independently) revived both by S. V. Tracy (*Hesperia* 57, 1988, pp. 309–310) and M. J. Osborne (*ZPE* 78, 1989, pp. 221–222, note 65).

The year 275/4 was the sixth of the ninth Metonic cycle, and as such was an ordinary year (cf. Meritt, *TAPA* 95, 1964, p. 236). The inscriptions show that the festival year was indeed ordinary. In **184** the month Elaphebolion may be restored to coincide with the ninth prytany, so that Elaphebolion 9 = pryt. IX, 10; and in **185**, passed on the last day of the year, Skirophorion 29 or 30 = pryt. XII, 29. The numerical concordance between the festival and lunar calendars was thus exact or within one day of being so. Known phylai in prytany are IX Erechtheis and XII Leontis.

FRAGMENT OF A DECREE

184. The upper right corner of a stele of Hymettian marble (I 6533), with part of the right side and the original back preserved, discovered on May 5, 1952, in the foundation packing of a Late Roman well at the north end of the terrace of the Stoa of Attalos (Q 7). The inscribed surface is complete at the top, above which a part of the broken crowning molding survives. Marks of a toothed chisel, running both horizontally and vertically, are very evident on the inscribed face.

H. 0.16 m.; W. 0.024 m.; Th. 0.11 m.
LH. 0.006 m.
Στοιχ. Hor. 0.011 m.; Vert. 0.015 m.

Ed. B. D. Meritt, *Hesperia* 33, 1964, pp. 170–171, no. 25, with photograph pl. 29. See also *SEG* XXI, 367.

a. 275/4 a., pryt. IX   ΣΤΟΙΧ. 38

```
        ['Επὶ 'Ολβίου ἄρχοντος ἐπὶ τῆ]ς 'Ερεχθεῖδος ἐνάτη
        [ς πρυτανείας ἧι Κυδίας Τιμω]γίδου Εὐωνυμεὺς ἐ
        [γραμμάτευεν· 'Ελαφηβολιῶνος] ἐνάτει ἱσταμένο
        [υ, δεκάτει τῆς πρυτανείας· ἐκκλησί]α· τῶν προέδρ
   5    [ων ἐπεψήφιζεν . . . . . . . . . . . . .²⁶. . . . . . . . . . . . .]
        [––––––––––––––––––––––––––––––]
```

The stele is ascribed by S. V. Tracy (*Hesperia* 57, 1988, p. 306) to the craftsman he has designated the "Cutter of Agora I 3238 and I 4169". See **172**, his earliest known work, and **185**, also his product.

Line 2. Kydias of Euonymon is not otherwise known. Lines 3–4. Elaphebolion 9 is well attested as a meeting day of the assembly: see J. D. Mikalson, *Sacred and Civil Calendar*, pp. 124–126. Line 4. ἐκκλησία. See **97**, commentary on line 7.

THE TAXIARCHOI OF 275/4 HONORED

185. Two joining fragments of a flat-topped stele of sand-colored Pentelic marble. On the upper fragment (*a*, I 96) the original back and the whole width of the stele are preserved, although at the right edge the inscribed surface has been destroyed. The lower fragment (*b*, I 15) has the left side and original back preserved but is broken elsewhere. The crowning molding is broken at both ends; it has the character of an Ionic epistyle crown, similar in type to L. T. Shoe, *Profiles of Greek Mouldings*, 1936, pl. XXVII, no. 27, but with greater emphasis on the lower element of the cyma reversa.

Both fragments were among the earliest in this volume to have been recovered from the Agora excavations. Fragment *a* was recognized in the western part of the Market Square during the process of clearing up at the end of the 1931 season; no precise date is recorded. Fragment *b* was discovered on June 6, 1931, in a late wall east of the south end of the Metroon (H–I 10).

Measurements as joined: H. 0.475 m.; W. 0.43 m.; Th. 0.13 m.
LH. 0.006 m.
Στοιχ. Hor. 0.01 m.; Vert. 0.013 m.

Ed. B. D. Meritt, *Hesperia* 2, 1933, pp. 156–158, no. 5, with photograph. See also *SEG* XV, 101, with references also to W. B. Dinsmoor, *Hesperia* 23, 1954, p. 290, on lines 12–13 and C. Pelekides, *REG* 69, 1956, pp. 192–194, on lines 7–16. On Pelekides' text see Meritt, *Hesperia* 26, 1957, p. 55, note 6. The data of the opening lines have been frequently adduced in studies of the archon list and the calendar, for references to which see above (p. 263). The restoration in lines 28–29 is listed in *Agora* III, p. 176; see **182**. Lines 1–4 are reproduced by J. D. Mikalson, *Sacred and Civil Calendar*, p. 179.

a. 275/4 a., pryt. XII   ΣΤΟΙΧ. 43

```
     (a)
            'Επὶ 'Ολβίου ἄρχοντος ἐπὶ τῆς Λεωντίδος δωδεκάτ[ης πρ]
            υτανείας ἧι Κυδίας Τιμωνίδου Εὐωνυμεὺς ἐγρα[μμάτε]
            υεν, Σκιροφοριῶνος ἔνει καὶ νέαι, ἐνάτει καὶ εἰ[κοστε]
            ῖ τῆς πρυτανείας· ἐκκλησία· τῶν προέδρων ἐπεψή[φιζεν]
    5       Αἰσχίνης 'Αντικράτου Φαληρεὺς καὶ συμπρόεδρ[οι· ἔδο]
            ξεν τεῖ βουλεῖ καὶ τῶι δήμωι· Λέων Κιχησίου Αἰ[ξωνεὺς]
            εἶπεν· ἐπειδὴ οἱ ταξίαρχοι οἱ ἐπὶ 'Ολβίου ἄρχο[ντος ἦρ]
```

(b)

[ξα]ν τὴν ἀρχὴν χαλῶς χ[αὶ] κατὰ το[ὺς νόμου]ς [καὶ τάς τε θυ]
σίας ὅσας ἔδει αὐτοὺς θῦσ[αι μετὰ τῶν στρατηγῶν ἁπάσ]

10   ας ἐκ τῶν ἰδίων τεθύκασιν [καθάπερ ἐτάχθησαν ὑπὸ(?) τοῦ]
δήμου, ἐπεμελήθησαν δὲ καὶ [.........²¹..........]
τῆς τάξεως τῆς ἑαυτοῦ ἕκασ[τος ὅπως ἂν ὡς ἄριστα κατε]
σκευασμένοι τοῖς ὅπλοις ε[ἴς τε τοὺς ἐξετασμοὺς καὶ]
τὰς φυλακὰς πορεύωνται, δι[ετέλεσαν δὲ καὶ ἐν τοῖς ἄλ]

15   λοις πᾶσιν πειθαρχοῦντες [τοῖς στρατηγοῖς ἀκολούθ]
ως τοῖς νόμοις, ὅπως ἂν οὖν ἐ[φάμιλλον ἦι τοῖς ἄρξουσι]
ν τὴν ἀρχὴν ταύτην φιλοτίμ[ως καὶ δικαίως ἄρχειν, ἀγα]
θεῖ τύχει δεδόχθαι τεῖ βου[λεῖ τοὺς προέδρους οἵτιν]
ες ἂν λάχωσιν προεδρεύειν ἐ[ν τῶι δήμωι εἰς τὴν ἐπιοῦ]

20   σαν ἐκκλησίαν χρηματίσαι π[ερὶ τούτων, γνώμην δὲ ξυμ]
βάλλεσθαι τῆς βουλῆς εἰς [τὸν δῆμον ὅτι δοκεῖ τεῖ βου]
λεῖ ἐπαινέσαι τοὺς τα[ξιάρχους τοὺς ἐπὶ 'Ολβίου ἄρχο]
ντος καὶ στεφανῶ[σαι αὐτοὺς χρυσῶι στεφάνωι κατὰ τὸ]
ν νόμον ἀρε[τῆς ἕνεκα καὶ ἀνδραγαθίας τῆς εἰς τὴν βου]

25   λὴν καὶ τὸ[ν δῆμον τὸν 'Αθηναίων· εἶναι δὲ αὐτοῖς καὶ πρ]
οεδρία[ν ἐν ἅπασιν τοῖς ἀγῶσιν οὓς ἂν ἡ πόλις τιθεῖ· ἀν]
αγρά[ψαι δὲ τόδε τὸ ψήφισμα τὸν γραμματέα τὸν κατὰ πρ]
υ[τανείαν ἐν στήλει λιθίνει καὶ στῆσαι ἔμπροσθεν το]
[ῦ στρατηγίου· –––––––––––––––––––––––]

30   [–––––––––––––––––––––––––––––]

S. V. Tracy (*Hesperia* 57, 1988, p. 305) claimed this inscription as part of the very substantial oeuvre of the craftsman whom he at first named "Cutter 4" and later the "Cutter of Agora I 3238 and I 4169". The present text falls well within the long span of his career between 286/5 and 245/4. For the references to Tracy's description and illustrations of his characteristics see **172** (also the work of the same man). Earlier in this year he had already worked on **184**.

Lines 1–8 and 15–29 are shown as restored by Meritt. They consist in the main of standard formulas based on the phraseology of *IG* II², 500. Lines 9–10. So Pelekides. θῦσ[αι καλῶς καὶ φιλοτίμως πάσ]||ας Meritt. Lines 10–11. So Meritt. Pelekides restored τεθύκασιν [ὑπέρ τε τῆς βουλῆς καὶ τοῦ], which is too short for the line by one letter. Line 11. καὶ [ὡς κάλλιστα τῆς εὐοπλίας] Meritt. Pelekides left the line unrestored but noted as possibilities [τῶν ὅπλων τῶν στρατιωτῶν], [τῶν ὅπλων καὶ τῶν ἀσπίδων], [ἐκτενῶς καὶ μεγαλομερῶς]. Lines 12–15. So Pelekides. Meritt's text ran ἕκασ[τος ὅπως ἂν πάντες εὖ παρε]||σκευασμένοι τοῖς ὅπλοις ἐ[κτενεῖς καὶ πρόθυμοι εἰς]|| τὰς φυλακὰς πορεύωνται, δι[ετέλεσαν δ'ἐν τοῖς ἐξετασ]||μοῖς πᾶσιν πειθαρχοῦντες κτλ., but the first letter of line 15 is undoubtedly lambda. Dinsmoor (*loc. cit.*) preferred κατε||σκευασμένοι on the basis of **187**, lines 14–15.

Line 2. Kydias of Euonymon. See **184**, commentary on line 2. Line 3. The last day of the year, Skirophorion 29 or 30, is well attested as a meeting day of the assembly. See Mikalson, *op. cit.*, pp. 177–181 and **116**. Line 4. ἐκκλησία. See **97**, commentary on line 7. Line 5. Aischines' tombstone was discovered in 1959 at Kallithea and may be dated to the second quarter of the century. See *SEG* XXI, 930 (E. Mastrokostas, 'Αρχ. 'Εφ., 1961, Χρονικά, p. 16, no. 56). Another monument of this family and of the same period is that mentioned in *SEG* XVIII, 110.

Lines 5–6. The enactment was probouleumatic; cf. P. J. Rhodes, *Athenian Boule*, p. 252. Line 6. Leon, son of Kichesias. See **182**, commentary on line 8. Line 7. On the taxiarchoi and their duties see the lemma to **182** and references there and the commentary on **123**.

Lines 16–17. The "hortatory intention" (see **86**, commentary on lines 21–24) is here expressed in terms of hoped-for rivalry between officials in the quality of their execution of their duties; for comparable sentiments cf., e.g., *IG* II², 667, of 266/5, lines 10–12 and 663, of 286/5, effectively the continuation of **172**, lines 30–33. Lines 17–18. ἀγαθεῖ τύχει. Cf. **72**, commentary on lines 7–8. Lines 19–20. ἐπιοῦσαν, not πρώτην, by contrast with **182**. See **162**, commentary on line 14 and Dinsmoor, *Athenian Archon List*, pp. 18–19 and 41, *Hesperia* 23, 1954, pp. 290 and 303. Dinsmoor also commented (p. 290) on the ephelkystic nu in λάχωσιν. Cf. A. S. Henry, *CQ* n.s. 17, 1967, pp. 277–284; L. Threatte, *Grammar*, pp. 640–643 (esp. p. 641).

Lines 23–24. On the stephanos κατὰ τὸν νόμον see **112**, commentary on lines 5–7 and **141**, commentary on lines 8–9. Lines 24–25. For the expression of the particular virtues of the taxiarchoi, here described, see Henry,

Honours, p. 42, where two 4th-century instances are cited (one of them *IG* II², 500, the model for the restoration of this text, as noted above).

Lines 25–26. οὓς ἂν ἡ πόλις τιθεῖ. The first "standard" formulation of a general *proedria* occurs at the end of the 4th century (*IG* II², 555), as was noted by Henry (*Honours*, p. 291), who deals with this privilege on pp. 291–292; in citing its award to taxiarchoi he listed *IG* II², 500 and **187** but omitted the present example. The usual phraseology runs οἷς ἡ πόλις τίθησι. The use here of the subjunctive with ἂν and with οὓς rather than οἷς is rarely encountered: Dinsmoor (*Hesperia* 23, 1954, p. 290) quotes only *IG* II², 500 to set beside this example, but **142** may be added to the total (*q.v.*, commentary on lines 2–3, for the early formulation, and the nature, of grants of *proedria*). Lines 28–29. On the Strategion see **182**, commentary on line 30.

THE ARCHONSHIP OF LYSITHEIDES, 272/1 B.C.

The final determination of the year of Lysitheides is of considerable historical interest for students of the unfolding development of the archon list of the 3rd century and well demonstrates the progressive results of new discovery and continuing analysis. A useful account of it was given by W. B. Dinsmoor, *Hesperia* 23, 1954, pp. 284–287. Before the discovery of **187** and **188**, Lysitheides was known only from *IG* II², 1316 and 1317 (*SEG* III, 127), decrees of the orgeones of the Mother of the Gods(?) and of the thiasotai of Bendis; for dating purposes these could offer nothing beyond the evidence of the lettering and some slight prosopographical indications. J. Kirchner set both inscriptions at the end of the 3rd century and included Lysitheides among the "archontes saeculi III quorum tempora accuratius definiri nequeunt" (*IG* II², iv, 1, pp. 16–17).

More precise estimates of Lysitheides' year varied, according to different reconstructions, between 274/3 and 229/8. Dinsmoor himself had come to prefer the year 253/2 (*Athenian Archon List*, p. 146). For W. S. Ferguson (*Athenian Tribal Cycles*, pp. 24, 26, 81, note 1) and B. D. Meritt (*Hesperia* 7, 1938, p. 136) Lysitheides conveniently filled a gap in 245/4. In *Chronology*, p. xxii, W. K. Pritchett and Meritt advanced him by a year to 246/5, but this date was again revised (Meritt, *Hesperia* 17, 1948, p. 13) when Philoneos was assigned to that year, and Lysitheides was removed to 242/1, at that time left vacant in the reconstructed list.

The discovery of **187** and **188** ended Lysitheides' usefulness as a conveniently movable element in the problem of evolving a satisfactory list. Somewhat surprisingly, since opinion had come to favor the decade 250–240 as most suitable for him, the newly found texts showed his year as preceding, and doubtless immediately preceding, that of Pytharatos. Pytharatos (see p. 268 below) is one of the four archons of this century firmly dated in the literary tradition with reference to an Olympiad, and his year (271/70) has formed a fixed point in any arrangement of the chronological order of the archons. His γραμματεύς, previously unknown, proved to belong to Akamantis (VII), and the succession of archons had to be attuned to his date in a manner compatible with the secretary cycle. For Dinsmoor's solution to this, see *Hesperia* 23, 1954, p. 314. Dinsmoor further attributed to Lysitheides' year *IG* II², 704 (*SEG* XXI, 368), in which the γραμματεύς had the appropriate demotic Σουνιεύς (Leontis VI); see *SEG* XVI, 65.

That Lysitheides belonged in the year 272/1 was confirmed by the discovery of **186**, where the name of the γραμματεύς of his year, Semonides, son of Timesios, of Sounion is completely preserved and served to justify Dinsmoor's hypothesis. See Meritt, *Athenian Year*, p. 233, *Historia* 26, 1977, p. 173. The archonship has now become a fixed and accepted element of the chronology of Athens before the Chremonidean War. Meritt proceeded to ascribe to the same archonship also *IG* II², 689 and 816 (*SEG* XVI, 64 and 66). Thus four decrees of the boule and demos have proved to belong to this year, in addition to the two long-known decrees of the orgeones and thiasotai, the data of which must be accommodated to a period much earlier than originally thought. Finally, that Lysitheides' year preceded that of Peithidemos was additionally confirmed by the discovery of *SEG* XXIV, 154.

All the "public" decrees except *IG* II², 816 contain, or require the restoration of, dates by the festival and prytany calendars which show that the year was ordinary and that the two calendars were exactly in concord. The year was the ninth of the ninth Metonic cycle and as such was ordinary in Meton's arrangement, with which the lunar or festival calendar at Athens continued to be in general agreement. Phylai attested in prytany are VI Leontis or Aiantis and XII Kekropis. For prytany IX (*IG* II², 704) Akamantis, Antigonis, Demetrias, and Pandionis are all possible candidates.

HONORS FOR THE EPIMELETAI OF THE FESTIVAL OF ZEUS SOTER

186. The upper part of a pedimental stele of Hymettian marble (I 6696), broken below but intact elsewhere, discovered on February 12, 1955, in loose earth west of the Great Drain and some eleven meters south of the north end of the Metroon, just below the level of the preserved tops of the monument bases (I 9). Line 1 is inscribed on the epistyle, above a plain, rather angular ovolo molding.

H. 0.42 m.; W. (at base of pediment) 0.37 m., (inscribed surface) 0.33 m.; Th. 0.10 m.
LH. 0.006 m.
Στοιχ. (with adjustment at the end of lines, to preserve syllabic division) Hor. 0.012 m.; Vert. 0.013 m.

Ed. B. D. Meritt, *Hesperia* 26, 1957, pp. 54–55, no. 11, with photograph pl. 9: see also *SEG* XVI, 63.

a. 272/1 a., pryt. XII   ΣΤΟΙΧ. ca. 27

<pre>
                  Θ   ε   ο   ι.
              'Επὶ Λυσιθείδου ἄρχοντος ἐπὶ τῆς
              Κεκροπίδος δωδεκάτης πρυτανεί
              ας εἷ Σημωνίδης Τιμησίου Σουνιε(ὺς)
       5   ἐγραμμάτευε. Σκιροφοριῶνος ἐν
              δεκάτει, ἐνδεκάτει τῆς πρυτανεί
              [α]ς· ἐκκλησία· τῶν προέδρων ἐπεψήφι
              [ζ]εν 'Αντιδώτης Σπουδίου Πλωθεὺς
              καὶ συμπρόεδροι· ἔδοξεν τῶι δήμωι·
      10   Προμένης Προμένου Κεφαλῆθεν εἷ
              πεν· ἐπειδὴ οἱ κεχειροτονημένοι
              ὑπὸ τοῦ δήμου ἐπὶ τὴν ἐπιμέλειαν
              τῆς θυσίας καλῶς καὶ φιλοτίμως ἔ
              [θυ]σαν μετὰ τοῦ ἱερέως τῶι τε Διὶ τῶι
      15   [Σωτῆρι κ]αὶ τεῖ 'Αθηνᾶι τεῖ Σωτείραι,
              [ἐπεμελήθησα]ν δὲ καὶ τῆς πομπῆς
              [καὶ τῆς στρώσεως τ]ῆς κ⟨λ⟩ίνης καὶ
              [τῆς ἐπικοσμήσεως τῆ]ς τραπέ[ζης]
              [————————————————————]
</pre>

The lettering of the inscription is regular and of respectable quality although "thin" in appearance. There is some emphasis on the "free ends" of strokes. The execution of omega, a difficult letter for the mason, is variable, and the strokes of epsilon are not always well joined. The style is comparable with, but rather better than, that of **187**. In line 17 the stone reads ḤΣΚΑΙΝΗΣ.

Line 4. Semonides, son of Timesios, of Sounion was probably the son of that Timesios, son of Semonides, of Sounion who appears in an inscription from the Amphiaraion at Oropos as a lochagos among the ephebes of 324/3 at line 5 and col. II, line 27. See B. Leonardos, 'Αρχ. 'Εφ., 1918, pp. 73–100, nos. 95–97; O. W. Reinmuth, *The Ephebic Inscriptions of the Fourth Century B.C.*, 1971, pp. 58–82, no. 15, esp. p. 61 (where read "Semonides" for "Simonides", as also in the index, p. 165). Semonides of Sounion, owner of certain ἐδάφη in the poletai record of ca. 342/1, *Agora* XIX, P26, line 328 (cf. M. Crosby, *Hesperia* 19, 1950, p. 250), is probably the grandfather of the γραμματεύς. Line 5. ἐγραμμάτευε. The lack of ephelkystic nu before the consonant is surprising at this date. A. S. Henry (*CQ* n.s. 17, 1967, p. 278) lists only a single example (perhaps this one) for the period 274–250 in his table of frequencies; cf. also L. Threatte, *Grammar*, p. 641.

Lines 5–6. For Skirophorion 11 as a meeting day of the assembly see J. D. Mikalson, *Sacred and Civil Calendar*, pp. 169–170. This is the only positive evidence for it, but it has figured in restored texts. Line 7. ἐκκλησία. See **97**, commentary on line 7. Line 8. The family of Antidotes, son of Spoudias, of Plotheia is not otherwise known. The name Antidotes appears unique in Attic prosopography. Line 9. This was a nonprobouleumatic enactment: see P. J. Rhodes, *Athenian Boule*, p. 264. Line 10. The family of Promenes, son of Promenes, of Kephale is also not otherwise known. Six months earlier Promenes had been the proposer of *IG* II², 689 (*SEG* XVI, 64), which praises the priest of Zeus Soter for his performance of the same sacrifices mentioned in lines 13–14 of the present text. He evidently had some special interest in the matter which brought about, after an interval, recognition of the services of the epimeletai also.

Lines 13–14. On these ceremonies and the part played in them by the epimeletai see L. Deubner, *Attische Feste*, pp. 174–176 and *IG* II², 676, which belongs to 273/2 and of which the phraseology is echoed in the present decree as restored at lines 16–18.

IG II², 689 was erected near the Stoa of Zeus Eleutherios (alias Zeus Soter); see *Agora* III, p. 29, no. 43; *Agora* XIV, p. 101. As Meritt noted, it is reasonable to assume, and to confirm from the place of discovery, that this monument was set up in the same locality.

THE ARCHONSHIP OF PYTHARATOS, 271/70 B.C.

The date of Pytharatos' archonship is one of the four in this century fixed by reference to an Olympiad in the literary evidence, and it has never been open to doubt or called into question. Diogenes Laertius (10.15) quotes Apollodoros (frag. 42) to the effect that the philosopher Epikouros died in the second year of the 127th Olympiad, in the archonship of Pytharatos. For other literary references see *PA* 12339; W. K. Pritchett and B. D. Meritt, *Chronology*, p. xix; W. B. Dinsmoor, *Hesperia* 23, 1954, p. 285. The well-known choregic monument of Thrasykles, beside the chapel of the Panagia Spiliotissa high up above the Theater of Dionysos, is dated by the same archonship (*IG* II², 3083).

Until the discovery of **187** and **188**, to which **189** and *Agora* XV, 80 were subsequently added, no decree had been found which was dated to Pytharatos' archonship. Thus the name of the γραμματεύς of his year remained unknown, and the lack of it deprived the secretary cycle of what would have been a firm point of reference. Cf. Meritt, *Hesperia* 7, 1938, p. 131; Dinsmoor, *Athenian Archon List*, p. 37, *Hesperia* 23, 1954, p. 284. Different reconstructions therefore assigned Pytharatos' known year to various points in the cycle (Dinsmoor, *op. cit.*, p. 286, note 14). In the event, the γραμματεύς was found to belong to Akamantis VII (rather than to Kekropis IX, as Pritchett and Meritt, *Chronology*, had most recently postulated), and the issue was thenceforward settled. Cf. Meritt, *Athenian Year*, p. 233, *Historia* 26, 1977, p. 174.

This year was the tenth in the ninth Metonic cycle and scheduled there to be intercalary. The calendric detail of the texts showed that it was indeed intercalary in the Athenian festival year. Dinsmoor's study of it (*Hesperia* 23, 1954, pp. 309–312) was superseded by the discovery of **189** and of *Agora* XV, 80. In **187**, Metageitnion 9 = pryt. II, 7; in **188**, the fourth intercalated Elaphebolion 9 = pryt. IX, 27; in **189**, Skirophorion 21 is equated with pryt. XII, 23; and in *Agora* XV, 80, Skirophorion 29 = pryt. XII, 31. The second of these equations was characterized by Meritt (*Athenian Year*, p. 151) as "the classic example of retardation of the festival calendar by extra days" and came on top of four days already evidently intercalated. The first month was thus of 30 days and the first prytany of 32 days, which produced an equation in **187** normal for an intercalary year. The dating of **189** and of *Agora* XV, 80 shows the intercalary year as functioning normally at the year's end. Skirophorion was planned as a hollow month (see Meritt, *Athenian Year*, pp. 46 and 195), but towards the end of the month it was found necessary to make it full (see on the archonship of Pherekles, 304/3 B.C., on p. 180 above, and the references there). The year was brought to 384 days, and the days intercalated in Elaphebolion were apparently compensated for at an earlier stage, certainly before the last part of Skirophorion and probably before the end of Elaphebolion itself. The discrepancy of one day which remained in Skirophorion *praeter exspectationem* required the insertion of one day before the last.

The prytany calendar seems to have been regular for an intercalary year, each prytany lasting 32 days (Meritt, *Athenian Year*, p. 150). The arrangement of the year was probably similar to that shown for 303/2 (see p. 187 above) in *Hesperia* 33, 1964, p. 5, except that Pytharatos' year began with a full Hekatombaion (see above) and that the pattern was upset by the intercalations in (and perhaps before) Elaphebolion already noted. Elaphebolion was particularly susceptible to dislocation, by reason of decisions by the administration to postpone (for whatever cause) the City Dionysia. See Meritt, *Athenian Year*, pp. 161–166.

Phylai attested in prytany are II Antigonis, IX Leontis, and XII Oineis.

THE TAXIARCHOI OF 272/1 HONORED

187. The upper section (representing the major part) of a flat-topped, slightly tapering stele of Pentelic marble (I 6664), broken below but complete elsewhere save for the left end of the crowning molding, discovered on April 22, 1954, in a wall of a Roman house west of the west end of the Middle Stoa (H 13). The bottom of the stele is broken off diagonally downwards towards the right. Line 1 is written on the crowning taenia above the simple, rather angular ovolo molding.

H. 0.765 m.; W. 0.375 m. (at line 1), 0.332 m. (at line 2), 0.352 m. (at line 36), 0.355 m. (at lowest measurable point); Th. (inscribed surface) 0.10 m.

LH. 0.004–0.007 m.

Non-στοιχηδόν. Syllabic divisions are preferred, and the number of letters per line varies from 31 (line 32) to 40 (line 11).

Ed. W. B. Dinsmoor, *Hesperia* 23, 1954, pp. 287–296, no. 182, with photograph pl. 63. See also *SEG* XIV, 64, XXV, 94 (with reference to the text, with short commentary and translation into Italian, of L. Moretti, *Iscrizioni storiche ellenistiche* I, pp. 37–40, no. 18). A small correction (already included in *SEG* XIV, 64) was made to Dinsmoor's text in line 26 by C. Pelekides, *REG* 69, 1956, p. 193, note 1; cf. B. D. Meritt, *Hesperia* 26, 1957, p. 55, note 6. See also Meritt, *Inscriptions from the Athenian Agora* (A.P.B., no. 10, 1966), no. 18, with photograph.

a. 271/70 a., pryt. II   NON-ΣTOIX.

```
                      [Θ]      ε      ο      ι.
               Ἐπὶ Πυθαράτου ἄρχοντος ἐπὶ τῆς Ἀντιγονί
               δος δευτέρας πρυτανείας ἧι Ἰσήγορος Ἰσοκρά
               του Κεφαλῆθεν ἐγραμμάτευεν· Μεταγειτνιῶ
        5      νος ἐνάτει ἱσταμένου, ἑβδόμει τῆς πρυτανεί
               ας· ἐκκλησία κυρία· τῶν προέδρων ἐπεψήφιζεν Αἰ
               [σ]χίνης Νικομάχου Ἀναφλύστιος καὶ συμπρόε
               [δρ]οι· ἔδοξεν τεῖ βουλεῖ καὶ τῶι δήμωι· Εὔβουλος
               [Λυσ]ιδήμου Μελιτεὺς εἶπεν· ἐπειδὴ οἱ ταξίαρχοι
       10      [οἱ ἐ]πὶ Λυσιθείδου ἄρχοντος τάς τε θυσίας ὅσας
               [ἔδε]ι αὐτοὺς θῦσαι μετὰ τῶν στρατηγῶν τεθύκασιν
               ἀπάσας ἐκ τῶν ἰδίων ὑπὲρ τῆς βουλῆς καὶ τοῦ δή
               μου, ἐπεμελήθησαν δὲ καὶ τῆς φυλῆς τῆς ἑαυτοῦ
               ἕκαστος ὅπως ἂν ὡς βέλτιστα τοῖς ὅπλοις κατε
       15      σκευασμένοι εἴς τε τὰς φυλακὰς καὶ τὰς ἐφε
               δρείας καὶ τοὺς ἐξετασμοὺς πορεύωνται, διε
               τέλεσαν δὲ καὶ ἐν τοῖς ἄλλοις ἅπασιν πειθαρ
               χοῦντες τοῖς στρατηγοῖς ἀκολούθως τοῖς νό
               μοις, ὅπως ἂν οὖν καὶ ἡ βουλὴ καὶ ὁ δῆμος φαίνη
       20      ται τιμῶν τοὺς χρείας αὑτῶι παρεχομένους,
               τύχει ἀγαθεῖ δεδόχθαι τεῖ βουλεῖ τοὺς προέ
               δρους οἵτινες ἂν λάχωσι προεδρεύειν ἐν τῶι
               δήμωι εἰς τὴν ἐπιοῦσαν ἐκκλησίαν χρηματί
               σαι περὶ τούτων, γ⟨ν⟩ώμην δὲ ξυμβάλλεσθαι
       25      [τ]ῆς βουλῆς εἰς τὸν δῆμον ὅτι δοκεῖ τεῖ βουλεῖ
               [ἐ]παινέσαι τοὺς ταξιάρχους τοὺς ἐπὶ Λυσιθεί
               [δ]ου ἄρχοντος καὶ στεφανῶσαι ἕκαστον αὐ
               τῶν χρυσῶι στεφάνωι κατὰ τὸν νόμον ἀρετῆς
               ἕνεκα καὶ φιλοτιμίας τῆς εἰς τὴν βουλὴν καὶ
       30      τὸν δῆμον τὸν Ἀθηναίων· εἶναι δὲ αὐτοῖς καὶ προ
               ⟨ε⟩δρίαν ἐμ πᾶσι τοῖς ἀγῶσιν οἷς ἡ πόλις τίθησιν·
               ἀναγράψαι δὲ τόδε τὸ ψήφισμα τὸν γραμ
               ματέα τὸν κατὰ πρυτανείαν ἐν στήλει λιθίνει
               καὶ τὰ ὀνόματα τῶν ταξιάρχων, καὶ στῆσαι ἐμ
       35      προσθεν τοῦ στρατηγίου· εἰς δὲ τὴν ἀναγρα
               φὴν μερίσαι τοὺς ἐπὶ τεῖ διοικήσει :Δ: δραχμάς.
                         [[Ἀντιγονίδος]]
               Λυσικράτης Ναυσιφάνου Κυθήρριο⟨ς⟩
                         Ἐρεχθεῖδος
```

[Φ]ιλίσκος Μοσχίωνος Θημακεύς
          Πανδιονίδος
Δημόστρατος Ἀριστοφάνου Παιανιεύ(ς)
          Λεωντίδος
[Φι]λόθεος Διοδότου Σουνιεύς
45   Ἀκαμαντίδος
[. ᶜᵃ· ⁶ .] Χαρισάνδρου Κικυννεύς
          [Ο]ἰνεῖδος
[...ᶜᵃ· ⁸...]ος Κόνωνος Ὀῆθεν
          [Κεκροπ]ίδος
50 [....ᶜᵃ·¹¹.... χ]λέους Φλυεύς
          ['Ιπποθωντί]δος
[......ᶜᵃ· ¹⁵......]του Ἐλευσίνιος
          [Αἰαντίδος]
[.........ᶜᵃ· ¹⁸......... Ἀ]φιδναῖος
55   ['Αντιοχίδος]
[..........ᶜᵃ· ²⁰........ Ἀλ]ωπεκ(ῆθεν).
          vacat

The character of the writing, both in the aspect of the individual letters and in the standard of exactitude shown in the inscribing, is average for the period. Most letters show variation in size to a slight degree (more particularly omicron, upsilon, and omega) or in appearance (for example, the loop of rho varies in size, the lower stroke of kappa is variously angled, sigma is jointed and angled in many different ways, and so forth). Epsilon, nu, and tau in particular suffer from poor articulation. The vertical stroke of xi is omitted. See also **186**.

In line 24 the stone has ΓΜΩΜΗΝ, and in line 31 HΔPIAN. Line 37. Ἀντιγονίδος was erased after the *damnatio memoriae* of the "Macedonian" phylai in 201/200 B.C. This stele therefore stood in the Agora at least for more than seventy years. For the circumstances of these erasures, which were not consistently carried out on every monument, see Livy 31.44; W. K. Pritchett, *TAPA* 85, 1954, pp. 162–164. The demotic Κυθήρριος ensures that Ἀντιγονίδος, not Δημητριάδος, is to be supplied. See Pritchett, *The Five Attic Tribes after Kleisthenes*, 1943, pp. 5 and 7 (= *AJP* 61, 1940, pp. 186 and 188) and Dinsmoor, *op. cit.*, p. 294.

Line 3. Isegoros, son of Isokrates, of Kephale is not otherwise known, but the name Isegoros, not frequently encountered, occurs earlier in that deme in the grave monument *IG* II², 5607, of the first half of the 4th century. The Isegoros whose son – – – – des participated in a dedication attributable to 267/6 is probably to be identified with the γραμματεύς. See Meritt, *Hesperia* 30, 1961, pp. 250–251, no. 49; *SEG* XXI, 671. Lines 4–5. For Metageitnion 9 as a day on which the assembly might meet see J. D. Mikalson, *Sacred and Civil Calendar*, p. 37, where lines 1–5 of this text are quoted. This evidence is confirmed by two other instances, and the same date has been restored in two other inscriptions.

Line 6. ἐκκλησία κυρία. See **101**, commentary on lines 7–8, and for such an assembly so early in the prytany (which was not usual) cf. **179** and **172**, commentary on line 3. Lines 6–7. Aischines, son of Nikomachos, of Anaphlystos was connected by Dinsmoor, perhaps hazardously, with the Aischines who was the father of Xenokrates of Anaphlystos commemorated on *IG* II², 5675, a grave monument of the 4th century. Line 8. The decree is listed among probouleumatic decrees, and its character is noted, by P. J. Rhodes, *Athenian Boule*, p. 252; see also *ibid.*, p. 43, note 6. Lines 8–9. Euboulos of Melite, who appears also as the proposer of **188**, is otherwise unknown; cf. Dinsmoor, *op. cit.*, p. 291.

Lines 10–19. For the phraseology cf. **185**, lines 8–16. There is some variation between the two, both in order and in choice of words; e.g., ὑπὲρ τῆς βουλῆς καὶ τοῦ δήμου is too short for **185**, and βέλτιστα too long. Line 19. ὅπως ἂν οὖν. The "hortatory intention" (see **86**, commentary on lines 21–24) here looks less to the encouragement of emulation between officials in carrying out their duties, as in **185**, and emphasizes instead an administrative concern to be seen to do the right thing. Boule and demos (together "the administration") are counted as a singular collective noun in the formulation.

Line 21. τύχει ἀγαθεῖ unusually in the reverse order. Line 22. λάχωσι lacks the ephelkystic nu; contrast **185**, line 19 (where see the commentary) and **188**, line 33. Line 23. εἰς τὴν ἐπιοῦσαν ἐκκλησίαν. See **185**, commentary on lines 19–20. Line 28. On the stephanos κατὰ τὸν νόμον see **112**, commentary on lines 5–7 and **141**, commentary on lines 8–9.

Lines 30–31. For the grant of a general *proedria* see **185**, commentary on lines 25–26. The formulation here, οἷς ἡ πόλις τίθησιν, is the normal one. Lines 34–35. On the Strategion see **182**, commentary on line 30. *Agora* III, p. 177, refers to this text and quotes these two lines. Line 36. The stele, which was substantial, cost no more than ten drachmas, as did **181** and **182**; see **181**, commentary on line 41. This enactment is the latest, so far identified, for which the expenditure is specified as a sum of money. See A. S. Henry, *ZPE* 78, 1989, table 3 on p. 273.

Lines 37–56. On the taxiarchoi and their duties see the lemma to **182** and references there and the commentary on **123**. Ten taxiarchoi are listed, even though there were at this period twelve phylai and therefore, presumably, twelve phyletic contingents. Representatives of Demetrias and Aigeis are missing here. This matter was briefly discussed by Moretti (*op. cit.*, pp. 39–40), whose suggestion, developing a hint from Dinsmoor, that the number of contingents had remained at ten does not commend itself. Nor is an error in drafting acceptable as a hypothesis. It is possible, for instance, that two of the taxiarchoi had died by the time that the decree was passed. But on the evidence the problem of their number can only be noted, not resolved.

The ten are named in the "official" order of the phylai. For prosopographical details and possible family connections see Dinsmoor, *op. cit.*, p. 294 (and cf. **182**, commentary on lines 20–26). *IG* II², 6209 is presumably the grave monument of Philiskos, son of Moschion, of Themakos (line 40); cf. *PA* 14424. Demostratos (line 42) may be the grandson of that Demostratos of Paiania (*PA* 3627) whose son (the name is lost) dedicated a silver phiale *ca.* 330 B.C., in *IG* II², 1566, line 27 (see also *Agora* XV, 47, line 12). The Philotheos and Philokles of Sounion who figure in the ephebic dedication of 333/2 published by Meritt in *Hesperia* 9, 1940 (pp. 59–66, no. 8; see *SEG* XXI, 513 and O. Reinmuth, *The Ephebic Inscriptions of the Fourth Century B.C.*, 1971, pp. 25–33, no. 9) were probably, according to Dinsmoor, great-grandfather and grandfather respectively of the Philotheos of Sounion listed here (line 44).

The virtues for which the taxiarchoi are commended (lines 28–29) differ slightly from those in **185**, where the space demands a characteristic more lengthy than φιλοτιμία. This is the sole example of this particular formulation quoted by Henry (*Honours*, p. 42); but cf. *IG* II², 277 + 428, of *ca.* 303/2 (M. B. Walbank, *Classical Views* n.s. 6, 1987, pp. 229–233), and 652, of *ca.* 285/4. The taxiarchoi of 281/80 (**182**) evidently lacked the opportunity to display that ἀρετή with which their successors of 275/4 and 272/1 were specifically credited.

THE SITONAI OF 272/1 HONORED

188. The upper section (representing the major part) of a slightly tapering pedimental stele of Pentelic marble (I 6096), broken below (diagonally downwards towards the right) and with the apex of the pediment missing but the stele otherwise complete, discovered on April 7, 1948, in the northwest corner of the Southwest Fountain House, where it had been reused face down as cover slab for a drain (H 15). The result of this reuse is that the lettering at the top and bottom, where the stele rested on the side walls of the drain, is fairly well preserved, but the middle portion of the text has been badly worn away by the action of the water.

> H. 1.02 m.; W. 0.465 m. (at base of pediment), 0.423 m. (at line 1), 0.457 m. (at line 45); Th. (inscribed surface) 0.12 m. at top increasing to 0.13 m. at bottom.
> LH. 0.005–0.006 m.
> Στοιχ. (modified by the taper of the stele, syllabic division, and occasional crowding of letters) Hor. *ca.* 0.012 m.; Vert. 0.012 m. at top increasing to 0.013 m. at bottom.

Ed. W. B. Dinsmoor, *Hesperia* 23, 1954, pp. 296–309, no. 183, with photographs pls. 63 and 64. See also *SEG* XIV, 65. Lines 1–5 are quoted by B. D. Meritt, *Athenian Year*, p. 151.

a. 271/70 a., *pryt.* IX　　　　　　　　　　　　　　　　　　　　ΣΤΟΙΧ. 34–38

'Επὶ Πυθαράτου ἄρχοντος ἐπὶ τῆς Λεωντίδο[ς]
[ἐ]νάτης πρυτανείας ἧι 'Ισήγορος 'Ισοκράτο[υ]
[Κ]εφαλῆθεν ἐγραμμάτευεν· 'Ελαφηβολιῶνο[ς]
[ἐ]νάτει ἱσταμένου τετάρτει ἐμβολίμωι, ἐβδ[ό]
5　[μ]ει καὶ εἰκοστεῖ τῆς πρυτ[α]νείας· ἐκκλησί[α]·
[τῶν] προέ[δ]ρω[ν ἐ]πεψήφιζεν Πειθίας Θεοφίλο[υ]
['Α]θ[μο]ν[εὺς καὶ συμπρ]ό[εδρ]οι· ἔδοξεν τεῖ βο[υ]
[λ]ε[ῖ κ]α[ὶ τῶι δήμωι· Εὔβουλος Λ]υ[σ]ιδήμου Με[λι]
τε[ὺς εἶπεν· ᵛ ἐπειδὴ οἱ πρότεροι] σιτῶναι ο[ἱ]

10 [ἐ]πὶ Λ[υσιθείδου ἄρχοντος φιλοτιμ]ούμενο[ι]

[.]ρηστονο[.....¹³..... τὸν ἐνι]α[υ]τὸν τὸν

[μ]ετ[ὰ Λυσιθείδην ἄρχοντα ----------]οι

[.]ο[----------------------] καὶ [τὰ]

[σ]υμφ[έρ]ο[ντα τῶι δήμωι τῶι Ἀθηναίων...]λο[.]

15 [.]ιω[--------------------------]τ[....]

[.]η[--------------------------------]

[.]ατ[--------------------------------]

[..]οι[----------------------------]η[.]

[.]γ[.]ε[.]ιαδιοτελ[.]γα[------------]δ[.]

20 [.]αγ[...]ιοτ[----------------------]ξ[.]

[..]ι[------------------------------]ι[..]

[....⁶....]γχοπο[--------------------]

[.]άντων ἐπὶ του[----------------]ησυ[.]

βουλῆς κατουσεδ[--------------------]

25 [.]ιντω[----------------------------]

[....]υ[.]ις[--------------------]ο[.]

[..⁶..]τ[--------------------------]

[..⁵..]λσ[--------------------------]

[..⁵..]η[----------------------------]

30 [--------------------------]θ[....]

[--------------------------------]

[....⁹...., ἀγαθεῖ τύχει δεδόχθαι τ]εῖ [βουλεῖ]

[τοὺς προέδρο]υ[ς οἳ ἂν λάχωσιν προεδ]ρεύε[ιν]

ἐ[ν τῶι δήμωι εἰς τὴν ἐπιοῦσαν ἐκκλησίαν χρη]

35 [μα]τ[ίσαι περὶ αὐτῶν, γνώμην δὲ ξυμβάλλεσθαι]

τῆς βουλ[ῆς εἰς τὸν δῆμον ὅτι δοκεῖ τ]ε[ῖ β]ουλ[εῖ]

ἐπαινέσαι μὲν του[ὺς σιτώνας] τ[οὺς σι]των[ησ]αμ[έ]

[ν]ους ἐπὶ Λυσιθείδου [ἄρχο]ν[τος καὶ στε]φανῶ

σαι αὐτῶν ἕκαστ⟨ο⟩ν χρυσῶι στεφάνωι κατὰ τον

40 [νόμ]ον φιλοτιμίας ἕνεκα τῆς πρὸς τὸν δῆμον·

[ε]ἶναι δὲ αὐτοῖς καὶ προεδρίαν ἐν πᾶσι τοῖς ἀγ[ῶ]

σιν οἷς ἡ πόλις τίθησιν, καὶ [τ]ὸ[ν] ἀρχιτέκτον[α]

[τ]ὸν ἀεὶ καθιστάμενον κατανέ[μ]ειν αὐτοῖς τὴ[ν]

[θέα]ν· ἐπαινέσαι δὲ καὶ τὸν [γ]ραμματέα ⟨α⟩ὐτ[ῶ]ν χ[αὶ]

45 [στεφ]ανῶσαι θαλλοῦ στεφ[ά]νωι· ἀναγράψα[ι] δὲ [τό]

[δε τὸ] ψήφισμα καὶ τὰ ὀνόμ[α]τα τῶν σιτωνῶ[ν καὶ]

[τοῦ γραμ]ματέως αὐτῶν ἐν στήληι λιθίνη[ι τὸν]

[γραμματέ]α τὸν κατὰ πρυτανείαν, καὶ στῆσ[αι ἐν]

[τῆι ἀγορᾶι· τὸ] δὲ ἀνάλωμα τὸ γενόμενον ε[ἰς τὴν]

50 [ποίησιν τῆς στή]λης καὶ τὴν ἀν[αγρ]α[φὴν] μερί[σαι]

[τὸν ταμίαν.   *vacat*]   *vacat*

[................¹⁶.........]τρά[τ]ου Γα[ρ]γήττ[ιο]ς

[....................¹⁸.......... Ξυ]πεται[ώ]ν

[................¹⁶........ Εὐωνυ]μεύς

55 [......................²³..........]ΟΓ[---]

[....................²².......... Πα]ιαν[ιεύς]

[......................²⁴.......... Σ]ουγ[ιεύς]

[....................²².......... Κεφα]λ[ῆ]θ[εν]

[(Oineis)--------------------]

60   [(Kekropis) ––––––––––––––––––]
      [(Hippothontis)–––––––––––––––]
      [(Aiantis)–––––––––––––––––––]
      [(Antiochis)–––––––––––––––––]
      [γραμματεύς ––––––––––––––––––]

The above text is for the most part that of Dinsmoor, and for discussion of the readings of this difficult stone see his commentary, *op. cit.*, pp. 301–305. In lines 2, 4, and 6 the pairs of letters ΙΙ, ΙΕ, and ΕΙ in ἧι ᾿Ισήγορος, τετάρτει ἐμβολίμωι, and Πειθίας are written in single letter spaces. Line 5. εἰχ[οσ]τεῖ Dinsmoor. Line 10. ...⁷....]ουμενο[ι] Dinsmoor. The restoration shown was proposed to him by G. A. Stamires and A. E. Raubitschek. Lines 37–38. σι]τωγ[ήσαν|τ]⟨α⟩ς Dinsmoor, who rejected the reading shown in the text (also proposed by Stamires and Raubitschek) on the score that it could not be accommodated into *IG* II², 792, a decree (which he then believed to belong to 253/2) in which a board of sitonai is similarly honored. But that decree may now be seen to refer to the year 275/4, where the name of the archon in fact permits the restoration. M. J. Osborne (*ZPE* 78, 1989, pp. 221–222, note 65; see *SEG* XXXIX, 120) discussed this matter and reverted to the solution of Stamires and Raubitschek, which also avoids the supposition of an error on the part of the mason. But other errors on his part soon follow. Line 39. *Lapis* ΕΚΑΣΤΩΝ. Line 44. *Lapis* ΡΑΜΜΑΤΕΑΥΤ.

The characteristics of the writing of so worn a text are not easy to discern. In general the lettering resembles that of **187**, with perhaps less accurate joining of contiguous strokes.

Line 2. Isegoros of Kephale. See **187**, commentary on line 3. Lines 3–4. This remarkable date for a meeting of the assembly was not discussed by J. D. Mikalson, *Sacred and Civil Calendar*. It was noted by Meritt (᾿Αρχ. ᾿Εφ., 1968, p. 109 with note 8) that the γραμματεύς evidently felt under no obligation to explain the "cumbersome terminology", as did his counterpart in 307/6 (see p. 168 above, and on **85**, lines 3–4). Cf. A. S. Henry, *Prescripts*, pp. 60–61 with note 44.

Line 6. Peithias, son of Theophilos, of Athmonon is not otherwise known. Dinsmoor connected him with the Theophilos of Athmonon who dedicated a silver phiale *ca.* 330 B.C. (*IG* II², 1575B, lines 36–37). The identification of the deme in the present text is however based on the reading of no more than two uncertain letters. Lines 7–8. This was a probouleumatic enactment. Cf. P. J. Rhodes, *Athenian Boule*, p. 252, and p. 43, where its general character is briefly discussed. Line 8. Euboulos of Melite. See **187**, commentary on lines 8–9. Line 9. On the functions and number of the sitonai see *RE* IIIA, i, cols. 396–397 (and under σιτωνία, *ibid.*, cols. 397–398); Busolt-Swoboda I, p. 433, II, pp. 1067 and 1121. The office was, as it appears, an extraordinary one, and a board (here of one member from each phyle) was elected to control the food supply at a time of shortage. It is not mentioned by Aristotle, *Athenaion Politeia* 51, at the point where he discusses the sitophylakes (see **127**).

Line 32. ἀγαθεῖ τύχει. Cf. **72**, commentary on lines 7–8. Line 33. λάχωσιν here evidently has the ephelkystic nu; see **187**, commentary on line 22. The phraseology that follows is based on *IG* II², 792 (see above). Line 34. ἐπιοῦσαν. See **185**, commentary on lines 19–20.

Lines 39–40. On the stephanos κατὰ τὸν νόμον see **112**, commentary on lines 5–7 and **141**, commentary on lines 8–9. On the particular virtue attributed to those honored cf. Henry, *Honours*, p. 43.

Lines 41–42. For the "general" grant of *proedria* and for the formula οἷς ἡ πόλις τίθησιν see **185**, commentary on lines 26–27 and **187**, commentary on lines 30–31. Lines 42–44. For the function of the ἀρχιτέκτων in the allocation of seating at the festivals, and the phraseology by which he and his function are described, see Henry, *Honours*, pp. 293–294, where this text is repeatedly cited in the discussion, and **142**, commentary on lines 3–5. No instructions to him were set down in the grants bestowed in **185** and **187**, but if preferred seating was guaranteed he presumably had some hand in it. Line 45. The stephanos is of olive, the not-infrequent reward for Athenian officials or semiofficials who had carried out their duties particularly well. See **175**, commentary on line 2.

Line 48. The space available for restoration does not permit the location for the stele to be more precisely described than by the general term "in the agora". Cf. *IG* II², 792, which according to the restoration there given was set up "in the agora where the statue of Zeus stands" (lines 13–14): but it is a restoration open to doubt (cf. *Agora* III, p. 29, no. 44). Line 49. The formulation of expense has not yet dropped into the standard τὸ γενόμενον ἀνάλωμα (not clearly attested before 266/5) and may mark a brief transitional period of uncertainty. Cf. **175**, commentary on lines 4–5 and **177**, commentary on line 6.

Line 51. The identity of the official meeting the cost of the stele is not disclosed, but the space does not permit a normal reference either to the Plural Board or to the Treasurer of the Military Fund. But the latter is no doubt intended, as Dinsmoor suggested (*op. cit.*, p. 304); cf. Henry, *Chiron* 14, 1984, pp. 73–74. Lines 52–63. The sitonai were listed in the "official" order of the phylai, and there seems to have been one sitones per phyle to constitute a board of twelve. See above, commentary on line 9.

FRAGMENT OF A DECREE

189. A fragment of a stele of Hymettian marble (I 6731), with the original rough-picked back preserved; it is otherwise broken all around save that above line 1 of the text the trace line of a molding (itself entirely lost) is visible. It was discovered on April 19, 1955, among marbles collected in the southeastern area of the Market Square.

H. 0.235 m.; W. 0.19 m.; Th. 0.08 m.
LH. 0.004–0.007 m.

Ed. B. D. Meritt, *Athenian Year*, pp. 194–195, no. 2, with photograph fig. 4. See also *SEG* XXI, 370. Meritt made a small correction to the reading of line 3, Ἀρχ. Ἐφ., 1968, p. 77, note 1 (see *SEG* XXV, 95), and provided a revised text in Ἀρχ. Ἐφ., 1973, p. 241. A new reading in line 5 by C. N. Edmonson and continuing discussion of the legibility of the archon's name in line 2, for both of which see the commentary below, prompted Meritt to a fresh and final exposition in *AAA* 9, 1977, pp. 193–197, with photograph fig. 1. See *SEG* XXVI, 93.

a. 271/70 a., pryt. XII   NON-ΣΤΟΙΧ. ca. 32–34

```
        [Θ]              ε           [ο            ι].
        ['Επὶ Πυθ]αράτου ἄρχοντος ἐ[πὶ τῆς Οἰνεῖδος]
        [δωδεκ]άτης πρυτανεία[ς· Σκιροφοριῶνος]
        [δεκάτ]ει ὑστέραι, τρίτ[ει καὶ εἰκοστεῖ τῆς]
  5     [πρυτανε]ίας· [-------------------]
        [---------------------------]
```

On this very battered fragment the letters (especially alpha and nu) appear wide in proportion to their height. Omicron is notably smaller than the other letters; the central bar of epsilon is short and ill attached to the upright stroke.

Taken with *Agora* XV, 80, the date of the passage of this decree shown in lines 3–5 helped to demonstrate that δεκάτη ὑστέρα, the 21st day of the month, was not the day omitted in a hollow month but rather that the omitted day was ἐνάτη φθίνοντος (or ἐνάτη μετ'εἰκάδας). Cf. Meritt, *Athenian Year*, pp. 46–47, *Mnemosyne* ser. 4, 30, 1977, pp. 217–242. W. K. Pritchett (*BCH* 88, 1964, pp. 464–465) argued that in both decrees too much was restored to permit the deduction. Meritt in reply (Ἀρχ. Ἐφ., 1968, pp. 77–80) reiterated that ἕνη καὶ νέα προτέρα (cf. Pritchett, *Ancient Athenian Calendars*, pp. 361–363) was here inserted as an extra day into a month expected to be hollow and that if the day omitted in a hollow month was δευτέρα μετ'εἰκάδας, its name would have been available for use in order to make the hollow month full just before its end; see also *Mnemosyne*, ser. 4, 30, 1977, pp. 227–229, and for a comparable instance the year of Pherekles (304/3), p. 180 above.

In *CSCA* 3, 1970, pp. 209–211, Pritchett put forward four further proposals for the restoration of the calendar equations of these lines in order to show that Meritt's conclusions were not imposed on him by the evidence. These were controverted *seriatim* by Meritt, Ἀρχ. Ἐφ., 1973, pp. 240–245; but Pritchett persevered in his contention that Meritt's thesis concerning the omitted day was erroneous and dealt further with this text in *ZPE* 20, 1976, pp. 185–192 and 30, 1978, pp. 281–285. Nevertheless, the accumulated evidence compels the acceptance of Meritt's interpretation. See J. A. Walsh, *ZPE* 41, 1981, pp. 107–124 (cf. *SEG* XXXI, 274); A. G. Woodhead, *Study of Greek Inscriptions*, pp. 120–122 and 140–141, notes 17–28.

Line 2. Pritchett (*locc. citt.*) also contested the reading of the name of the archon, denying that any trace of the initial alpha was to be seen and suggesting a possible restoration [ἐπὶ – – – – – τ]ράτου. For Meritt's final discussion see *AAA* 9, 1977, pp. 193–197, and his evaluation is adopted here. Resolution of the issue depends upon (a) the position of the left margin of the stele, which governs the number of letters that may be restored. This is additionally determined by (b) the spacing in line 1 and the restorations that suit the requirements of lines 3–5. Further (c), the text, like **187** and **188**, appears to recognize syllabic division between lines, and in fact all the surviving lines are to be reckoned as ending with complete words. Finally (d) the survey by Meritt of the names of the known archons of the period made it clear that none save that of Pytharatos could be accommodated to the requirements already stated as well as to the likely dating of the inscription on more general grounds of style.

Line 3. The "secretary formula" ἧι Ἰσήγορος Ἰσοχράτου Κεφαλῆθεν ἐγραμμάτευεν is here omitted. See A. S. Henry, *Prescripts*, p. 71. This omission is unusual but not a rarity; see **172**, commentary on line 2. Lines 3–4. For the date cf. J. D. Mikalson, *Sacred and Civil Calendar*, pp. 173–174. It is well attested as a meeting day of the assembly. Line 5. The reading, accepted by Meritt, is that of Edmonson *apud* Pritchett, *ZPE* 20, 1976, p. 190.

THE ARCHONSHIP OF PEITHIDEMOS, 268/7 OR 265/4 B.C.

With this archonship, of which neither the name nor the phyle of the γραμματεύς is known, is involved the complex problem of the chronology of the Chremonidean War, which hinges upon it. The decree of Chremonides establishing the alliance between Athens and Sparta, to act in concert with Ptolemy II Philadelphos against the domination of Antigonos Gonatas in southern Greece, was passed in the second prytany of Peithidemos' year (*IG* II², 686 + 687; see addenda, pp. 664–665). **190** is dated to the third prytany. In both cases the name of the γραμματεύς is entirely omitted; space was left for it on both stelai but was never filled, which may be a matter of some significance. *SEG* XXIV, 154 is a record of honors voted by the Rhamnousians for Epichares, strategos in the same year, the terms of which make it clear that important warlike activity took place in the course of it. Other chronological indications depend principally upon the literary tradition.

The history of the determination of Peithidemos' year was well and fully set out by H. Heinen, *Untersuchungen zur hellenistischen Geschichte des 3. Jahrhunderts v.Chr.* (*Historia*, Einzelschriften 20), 1972, pp. 102–110. Earlier studies of the archon list of the first half of the 260's had set Peithidemos as early as 270/69 (W. B. Dinsmoor, *Athenian Archon List*, pp. 58–59) or as late as 265/4 (B. D. Meritt, *Hesperia* 26, 1957, p. 97). The uncertainty was reflected in more general accounts of the period, e.g., C. Mossé, *Athens in Decline, 404–86 B.C.*, 1973, pp. 126–129; see also H. H. Schmitt, *Staatsverträge* III, 1969, pp. 129–133, no. 476.

However, 267/6 was the most favored attribution until it became clear that Menekles and Nikias Otryneus had to be placed in 267/6 and 266/5 respectively (Dinsmoor, *Hesperia* 23, 1954, p. 287). This effectively reduced the choice to 268/7 or 265/4. The first of these, in the light of other indications, seemed to extend the Chremonidean War beyond the limits implied by the literary evidence, while the latter seemed to compress the sequence of events unduly, the more so since Pausanias (3.6.4–7) emphasized that Athens held out under siege by Antigonos for a very long time.

Heinen himself (*op. cit.*, pp. 110–117; cf. p. 213, where he gave a chronological table of the course of events as he saw them) expressed a preference for the earlier date, prompted in no small part by the evidence of hostilities in Attica in the years of Menekles and of Nikias of Otryne (*IG* II², 665 and 668, as also *SEG* XXIV, 154 mentioned above, for which see Heinen, *op. cit.*, pp. 152–159; cf. also *IG* II², 666 and 667 and M. J. Osborne, *Naturalization* I, pp. 167–170, D 78, *Naturalization* II, pp. 164–167). This dating was adopted with enthusiasm by C. Habicht (*Untersuchungen*, pp. 116–117, note 11) and by Osborne (*Naturalization* II, pp. 165–167); cf. *SEG* XXXI, 91. The latter reemphasized his view in *ZPE* 78, 1989, p. 229, note 93, regarding the warfare mentioned in 267/5 as "clearly the Chremonidean War."

Meritt, on the other hand, responded to these opinions with a restatement of his own (*Hesperia* 50, 1981, pp. 78–79), emphasizing the problems created in the secretary cycle in consequence of the removal of Diogeiton from 268/7 in favor of Peithidemos and stressing the role of Peithidemos as (so he urged) the initiator of a new cycle in 265/4. The former argument will not hold for those who deny any compelling force to the cycle after 266/5. The latter argument was based on the understanding that the beginning of a fresh cycle is visible in *IG* II², 1534B, with a new cycle of priests of Asklepios associated with the archon, whose name (Pe–––) occurs at line 145. S. B. Aleshire, for whom this reference is inventory V, line 5, has made it clear that in her judgment Pe–––is a priest and not an archon (*The Athenian Asklepieion*, 1989, pp. 250, 293–298) and has emphasized that the priestly cycle "cannot be used as a basis of an archon-list or other chronological scheme for the third or second century" (p. 81).

Nevertheless, 265/4 remains a reasonable possibility on other grounds. The arguments of J. J. Gabbert (*CJ* 82, 1987, pp. 230–235), though dismissed out of hand by Osborne (*ZPE* 78, 1989, p. 229, note 93), demonstrated anew the difficulties in the interpretation of events recorded in the literary tradition if the war began as early as 268/7, even though that date had been adopted more widely (e.g., by F. W. Walbank in *CAH* VII, 2nd ed., 1984, pp. 236–237) and a reconstruction of the war essayed on that basis by Heinen (*op. cit.*, pp. 159–202, esp. 197–202).

It may also be suggested that, although Chremonides gave his name to the war in the historical tradition, hostilities between Macedon and Athens of an intermittent nature could well have preceded the grand alliance to which his decree bears witness. Confrontations do sometimes develop only slowly into a wider conflict, and the "war" need not have borne Chremonides' name until after he had shaped its final character. Wars are not infrequently named following their conclusion, with reference to their duration

("The Seven Years War"), or to what proved to be their principal theater ("The Peninsular War"), or to some significant event that may have followed and crowned earlier hostilities ("The War of the Spanish Armada"). Thus Peithidemos and Chremonides may indeed be associated with the escalation rather than with the initiation of warfare, and the literary evidence may be interpreted as Gabbert interpreted it without violence to the epigraphical data of 267/5. On a strict analysis, to assume that these data, indicating as they do some kind of hostilities, require that Chremonides' alliance was already in existence goes beyond the evidence at present available: such war as there was need not (yet) have been "The War of Chremonides".

The phyle of Peithidemos' γραμματεύς would be Antigonis (I) if his year was 265/4. In the circumstances of that time he might have felt some reticence about the inclusion of his name and deme in the drafts of the decrees for which he was responsible as an unwelcome allusion to the Macedonian enemy. Dinsmoor (*Hesperia* 23, 1954, p. 314) and Meritt at one time (*Athenian Year*, p. 223) envisaged a break at this point in the secretary cycle, omitting *pro hac vice* the two "Macedonian" phylai: but the break comes at a later date. If the date be 268/7, the phyle of the γραμματεύς would be Hippothontis (X), and for this no such explanation of the omission would serve. The suggestion of A. S. Henry (*Prescripts*, pp. 71–72) that "even by the fourteenth day of the third prytany the secretary of this year was still not known" by reason of a vacancy unfilled through sudden death may be more plausible; but in view of the lapse of time between the two existing enactments this too strains credulity: see the commentary on **190**. The omission of the details cannot have been a repeated oversight, nor can there have been doubt as to the existence of an official to whom express instructions were given in *IG* II², 686 + 687 (lines 64–65) for the erection of the stele and to whom similar instructions were doubtless given in **190**.

The years 268/7 and 265/4 were respectively the thirteenth and the sixteenth in the Metonic cycle and as such were scheduled on Meton's system to be intercalary. The calendric data of **190**, in the improved reading published by Meritt in *Hesperia* 38, 1969, bear this out, indicating that the first two months of the festival calendar were of 30 days each and the first two prytanies of 32 days. This equation is however in conflict with *IG* II², 686 + 687, which was passed on Metageitnion 9 (= pryt. II, 9), a correlation exactly suited to an ordinary year. The former reading of **190** had made Boedromion 18 the equivalent of pryt. III, 17, also indicative of an ordinary year, with the result that the year of Peithidemos was considered as surely ordinary in every study of the subject antedating 1969. In explanation of the dilemma posed by his new reading, Meritt supposed that two days were intercalated into Hekatombaion late in the month, to postpone the Panathenaia, and that they were not eliminated until after Metageitnion 9. In the agitated circumstances of the time, such an intercalation might be the more readily understandable. Thus a Hekatombaion of 30 + 2 days would coincide with a first prytany, regular for an intercalary year, of 32 days, and the numeration of the second month and the second prytany would run in parallel until the correction was made. This hypothesis preserves the continuing correlation of the Metonic system and the Athenian festival calendar, which have up to this point coincided without interruption. It should however be observed both that line 4 of **190** presents great difficulties of reading and that in Peithidemos' year, for reasons of crisis, some adjustment to normal calendric practice, rectified as soon as possible thereafter, might have been made. The evidence in any case requires assumptions of some kind to be made, and a satisfactory solution may have to await some fortunate increase in it.

Known phylai in prytany are II Erechtheis and III Akamantis.

FRAGMENT OF A DECREE

190 (Pl. 19). A large pedimental stele of Hymettian marble (I 1051), almost completely preserved, discovered on July 8, 1933, laid face upwards on a threshold block in a Byzantine building in the northwestern part of the Market Square (J 6). Its reuse caused the inscribed surface to become so worn and battered that, except for parts of lines 1–4 and 6, it is entirely illegible.

H. 1.4 m.; W. 0.53 m. (at base of pediment), 0.46 m. (at top of inscribed face), 0.53 m. (at bottom); Th. 0.155 m.
LH. 0.005 m.
Στοιχ. (nearly square, with syllabic division) Hor. 0.011 m.; Vert. 0.0105 m.

Ed. B. D. Meritt, *Hesperia* 5, 1936, pp. 418–419, no. 14, with photograph; *Hesperia* 38, 1969, pp. 110–112. See *SEG* XXV, 98.

a. 268/7 a. vel 265/4 a., pryt. III   ΣΤΟΙΧ. 43

```
[Θ]              ε              [ο              ι].
Ἐπὶ Πειθιδή[μ]ο̅υ̣ ἄρχ[ον]τος ἐπὶ τῆ[ς Ἀ]χαμαντίδος τρ[ὶ ᵛᵛ]
[της πρυταν]ε̣ί[ας]        vacat
[Βοηδρομῶνος] ὀ[γ]δόει [ἐπ]ὶ̣ δέχα, τ̣[ετάρτε]ι̣ χαὶ δεχ[άτει]
[τῆς πρυτανείας· ἐχχλησία· τῶν προέδρων ἐπεψήφιζεν ᵛ]
[...............²⁶............. χαὶ συμπ]ρόεδ[ροι· ᵛᵛᵛ]
[―――――――――――――――――――――――――――――]
```

The lettering, in so far as it is visible, is plain and "standard" in character, with no special peculiarity.

Line 3. As in **189** (see commentary on line 3), the "secretary formula" has been omitted. These omissions are in themselves not infrequent; but here space has been deliberately left for the later insertion of the detail. The same phenomenon is to be found in the other known text of Peithidemos' year, *IG* II², 687 (*SEG* XXXI, 91, with earlier references). A. S. Henry (*Prescripts*, pp. 71–72) hazarded the "only feasible explanation" that even by this date (pryt. III, 14) the identity of the γραμματεύς was not known, perhaps because the original nominee had died early in his tenure and a successor had not been appointed. Even so, a delay in so important a nomination from pryt. II, 9 (*IG* II², 687) to pryt. III, 14 and possibly longer (by extension at either end) remains remarkable: and in *IG* II², 687, the γραμματεύς is specifically instructed to attend to the inscribing of the stone, which was presumably the case in this text also. The formula was of course standard and could be interpreted as referring to the office without implying the presence or absence of the office holder of the time. No breakdown in the secretary cycle is in question, for on any interpretation this did not occur until the end of the Chremonidean War. *IG* II², 1270 (*SEG* XXV, 151, XXVIII, 106) probably belongs to this year (cf. C. Habicht, *Untersuchungen*, p. 8, note 30, pp. 78–79, note 17) but is of no assistance for this purpose.

Line 4. Boedromion 18 is five times in the record as a day on which the assembly met. See J. D. Mikalson, *Sacred and Civil Calendar*, pp. 57–58. Line 5. ἐχχλησία. This restoration *tout simple* is required by the need for sufficient space in line 6 for the *tria nomina* of the chairman of the proedroi. Three of the assemblies attested for this day, however, were in fact ἐχχλησίαι χυρίαι, and with briefer names in line 6 such an assembly could be accommodated here. See **97**, commentary on line 7 and **101**, commentary on lines 7–8.

HONORS FOR A SPARTAN(?)

191 (Pl. 19). Two joining fragments of a stele of Pentelic marble (I 242), broken on all sides but with their original rough-picked back preserved, discovered in 1932 during the clearing of bedrock on Kolonos Agoraios behind the Stoa of Zeus Eleutherios (F–G 5–6).

Measurements as joined: H. 0.33 m.; W. 0.18 m.; Th. 0.13 m.
LH. 0.007 m.
Στοιχ. (almost square) Hor. 0.014 m.; Vert. 0.0145 m.

Ed. B. D. Meritt, *Hesperia* 3, 1934, pp. 7–8, no. 9, with drawing.

a. 267/2 a.(?)   ΣΤΟΙΧ.

```
[―――――――――――――――――――――――――――]
[――――――] reliquiae incertae [―――――――]
[―――――――] Ἱππο[ν]ι̣[χ]ο̣[―――――――]
[――――――το]ὺς προ[έ]δ[ρ]ο[υς ―――――]
[―――――――]μα[―――――――――]
[――――――――έ]δωχεν [――――――――]
[――――――]ς ὑπὲρ τ[ο]ῦ [――――――]
[―――――――]ν Λαχεδα[ι]μ[ονι――――――]
[―――――――]ν τῶι δήμωι τ[――――――]
[――――――]δον τοῦ δή[μου ―――――]
[――――――]οις τοῖς μετὰ [――――――]
[――――χ]αὶ εἰς τὴν [ο]ἰχο[δομίαν ―――――]
[――――――]χοντα τάλαντα [――――――]
[――――――τῆ]ς [π]όλεως [..]αφε[――――――]
```

```
        [――――τῶι δήμωι] τῶι ᾿Αθηναίων [――――]
  15    [――――εἰς τὰς ν]αῦς ἐπ[έ]δωκε[ν ――――]
        [――――――――]κλιον [. . . .]ν[――――――]
        [―――――Λακεδαι]μονίων στρ[ατ――――――]
        [――――――――]τευων ἐψηφι[――――――――]
        [―――――δυοῖν] λίθοιν· παραχ[αλ――――――]
  20    [――――――――――]Α[. . .]ΣΛ[――――――――]
        [―――――――――――――――――――――]
```

The stone was reused in the Roman period for an inscription set at right angles to the earlier text, of which two final letters [――――――]ΗΣ, 0.02 m. in height, overlie the surviving beginnings of lines 16–19. The surface of the inscribed face is badly weathered, and over much of it the letters are difficult to read and their traces deceptive. Revision of the stone has gleaned a few more letters than appear in the *editio princeps*, and has prompted a different opinion about some of the earlier readings, but has yielded nothing sufficient to establish any connected sense or to give some indication of the dimensions of the text. The writing shows the general characteristics of the middle of the 3rd century B.C. Omega is widespread; the crossbar of alpha is omitted at least once.

Meritt suggested that the text is that of a decree honoring a Lakedaimonian who had been generous in gifts to the Athenians (lines 10, 11, and 14) and that it may well belong to the period of the Chremonidean War. Both hypotheses appear reasonable, and there is nothing to add to them.

THE ARCHONSHIP OF DIOGNETOS, 264/3 B.C.

Diognetos was eponymous archon at Athens at the time when the chronicle known as the Marmor Parium was committed to stone-cut record (*IG* XII, v, 444; F. Jacoby, *FGrHist*, no. 239). The chronological indications of the chronicle are given as backward references from this archonship as a fixed terminal date, and 264/3 is thus one of the most secure points in the archon list: cf. W. B. Dinsmoor, *Archons of Athens*, pp. 46, 54, 86, *Athenian Archon List*, pp. 37, 64.

Question concerning the chronographer's use of inclusive or exclusive reckoning in determining his intervals had caused some scholars to place Diognetos in 263/2 (for details see Dinsmoor, *Archons of Athens*, p. 46), and Dinsmoor himself opted for 265/4 in his 1954 revision of the archon list (*Hesperia* 23, p. 314); but 264/3 has been generally agreed and is currently accepted as most satisfactorily meeting the indications of the Marmor Parium and the exigencies of the succession of archons. See B. D. Meritt, *Athenian Year*, p. 233, *Hesperia* 38, 1969, p. 112, *Historia* 26, 1977, p. 174, *Hesperia* 50, 1981, pp. 79 and 94; also W. K. Pritchett and Meritt, *Chronology*, p. xx; C. Habicht, *Untersuchungen*, pp. 113–114; M. J. Osborne, *ZPE* 78, 1989, p. 241.

No data concerning the calendar or the nature of the year survive in the epigraphical record. The fragmentary *IG* II², 688 preserves the archon's name and part of a prescript of a decree, but the section recording the date is lost beyond the initial letter of the month Skirophorion. It is nevertheless clear that no space was left for the name of the γραμματεύς. The secretary cycle requires this official to belong to Demetrias, the second of the "Macedonian" phylai, and in the circumstances of the Chremonidean War the omission may be judged deliberate: but see **189**, commentary on line 3. The situation was assuredly not that of **190**. The year may be postulated as ordinary in the festival calendar, following an intercalary 265/4, which is demonstrable if that year saw the the archonship of Peithidemos and presumable if the archon was other than he; see p. 276 above. As the seventeenth year in Meton's cycle it was scheduled as ordinary in that system (cf. Meritt, *TAPA* 95, 1964, p. 236), and the cycle and the pattern of the Athenian festival years would thus remain in accord. Antiochis held the twelfth prytany (*IG* II², 688). No other prytanies are known.

FRAGMENT OF THE DECREE OF A DEME

192. A fragment of a stele of Pentelic marble (I 2455), with the left edge preserved, discovered on February 18, 1935, in a wall of the Turkish period east of the Odeion (N 10).

H. 0.23 m.; W. 0.13 m.; Th. 0.05 m.
LH. 0.005 m.

Ed. B. D. Meritt, *Hesperia* 23, 1954, pp. 242–243, no. 15, with photograph pl. 51. See also *SEG* XIV, 81.

a. 264/3 *a.*   NON-ΣΤΟΙΧ. *ca.* 50

```
      [--------------------------------------------]
      ΓΩΝΕ[------------------------------------------]
      λους [------------------------------------------]
      χασιν ε[---------------------· εἰς δὲ τὴν ἀναγραφὴν τῆς]
      στήλης μερ[ίσαι τὸν δήμαρχον :ΔΔ: δραχμὰς καὶ λογίσασθαι τ]
   5  οῖς δημόταις.
             in corona                          [in corona]
          οἱ δημ[όται]
          ἐπὶ Διογ⟨ν⟩ήτ[ου]
```

In line 7 the stone reads ΔΙΟΓΗΤ. This text is one of those attributed by S. V. Tracy to the long and evidently prolific career of his "Cutter of Agora I 3238 and I 4169" (formerly designated by him "Cutter 4"); see *Hesperia* 57, 1988, p. 305. For fuller references, and for details of his characteristics, see **172**, the earliest work ascribed to him.

Lines 3–5. See *IG* II², 1206 (*SEG* XXXVI, 191), lines 16–19. The assumed cost of twenty drachmas (a figure treated with reserve by D. Whitehead, *The Demes of Attica, 508/7–ca. 250 B.C.*, 1986, p. 162, note 86) is double that of the substantial stelai **181**, **182**, and **187**. The sum may have been expressed in full as δέκα: cf. *IG* II², 555, line 37, 1148, line 16. Lines 6–7. The engraved stephanos is of the "radiate" type, resembling a schematic sunflower. On stephanoi for honorands in deme decrees see Whitehead, *op. cit.*, pp. 162–163.

This decree is no. 137 among the decrees listed by Whitehead; see *op. cit.*, esp. p. 392. He considers demes that we know to have put up public inscriptions in the 3rd century as special cases, and this must be considered one such case. See **160** and Whitehead, *op. cit.*, p. 361.

FRAGMENT OF A DECREE

193. A fragment of a stele of bluish Pentelic marble (I 3828), preserving the left side of the monument, discovered on March 21, 1936, in a Late Roman context over the foundations of the terrace wall of the Stoa of Attalos, opposite Shop XVIII (P 8).

H. 0.129 m.; W. 0.071 m.; Th. 0.027 m.
LH. 0.006 m.
Στοιχ. (square) 0.01 m.

Ed. M. B. Walbank, *Hesperia* 58, 1989, pp. 95–96, no. 23, with photograph pl. 25. See also *SEG* XXXIX, 119.

paullo post a. 262 *a.*(?)   ΣΤΟΙΧ.

```
      [----------------------------------------]
      [. . .] reliquiae [-------------------------]
      ἐπαινέ[σαι ----------------------------]
      [x]αι(?) τ[------------------------------]
      [.]ΗΣ [---------------------------------]
         reliquiae trium versuum
   8  ΛΗΣ[----------------------τὸ γενό]
      μενον [ἀνάλωμα.          vacat        ]
      vacat
```

The surface of the stone is so badly damaged that few letters can be read at all, and scarcely any with certainty. Walbank in his commentary admitted that different readings seemed to offer themselves at different times, but he was prepared to go further than the conservative text preferred above and presented his *editio princeps* in the following form, with a suggested line of 34 letters:

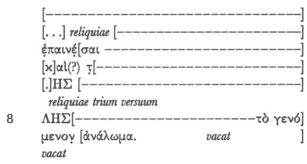

```
      [. . .]σα [. . . . . . . . . . . .29. . . . . . . . . . . .]
      ἐπαινέ[σαι . . . . . . . . . . .25. . . . . . . . . .]
      [x]αι τ[. . . . . . . . . . . . .30. . . . . . . . . . .]
      [.]ης π[. . . . . . . . . . . . .30. . . . . . . . . . .]
   5  [.]ΑΣΤΟ [. . . . . . .17. . . . . . . . τὸν γραμματέα]
```

[τ]ὸν χα[τὰ πρυτανείαν εἰς στήλην καὶ στῆσα]
ι ἐν ἀ[κροπόλει· εἰς δὲ τὴν ἀναγραφὴν τηστή]
λης δ[οῦναι τοὺς ἐπὶ τεῖ διοικήσει τὸ γενό]
μενον [ἀνάλωμα.   *vacat*   ]
vacat

The uncertainties of reading in lines 5 and 6 however allowed him to prefer for these lines ἀναγρά[ψαι δὲ τόδε τὸ ψήφισμα τὸν γραμμα|τ]έα τοῦ δ[ήμου ἐν στήληι λιθίνηι καὶ στῆσα]|ι and to suggest a parallel with *IG* II², 660, of 281/80 B.C. (especially, for the title of the γραμματεύς, lines 43–46; on the title see **120**, commentary on line 8).

The agreed reading of line 2 indicates that this fragment formed part of an honorary decree of some kind. As to its date, Walbank held that the hand appears to be the same as that of *IG* II², 503, of 302/1, but this is in sharp conflict not only with the parallel already quoted but also with other indications within the text as read or restored. In particular, the concluding phrase τὸ γενόμενον ἀνάλωμα, if correctly identified, makes its first certain appearance no earlier than 266/5 (for possible but doubtful earlier instances see A. S. Henry, *ZPE* 78, 1989, pp. 272–273). This indeed falls within the period during which the Plural Board, rather than the Single Officer, of Administration was responsible for defraying the cost of stelai: but on the other hand the verb of payment should by 281/80 be μερίσαι rather than δοῦναι. See **174**, commentary on line 8. The alleged delta of line 8 is, however, more than doubtful, and a reading of μ[ερίσαι paired with the Single Officer cannot be excluded, maintaining the same length of line. The decree would in that case either antedate 286/5, and be closer to Walbank's parallel for the hand, or postdate the Chremonidean War, after which the Single Officer resumed his pre-286 function, replacing the Plural Board. The former alternative would add to the problematical earlier instances of this combination with τὸ γενόμενον ἀνάλωμα, examined by Henry; the condition of this inscription is such that these complications cannot and ought not to be resolved by it. The attribution to the later period of the Single Officer, on the other hand, offers no such difficulty, for by then the formula τὸ γενόμενον ἀνάλωμα had become standard. There remains the possible criterion of the hand of the craftsman, but the evidence is in any case thin and is the more unreliable on so damaged a stone. The surviving lettering gives every appearance of being compatible, in general terms, with the date here preferred.

Lines 7–8. For the assumed haplography in Walbank's text cf. **166**, line 9, with commentary.

THE ARCHONSHIP OF ATHENODOROS, 256/5 OR 254/3 B.C.

With the surrender of Athens to the forces of Antigonos Gonatas and the inauguration, under the watchful eyes of the Macedonian garrison on the Mouseion hill, of a phase of Athenian democracy which, while retaining its familiar aspect, paid proper regard to Macedonian interests, there begins the period of some thirty years of the greatest uncertainty and controversy among scholars concerning the order in office of the eponymous archons and the years in which we are to believe that they held that office. The names of nearly all of them are known, although the same is less true of the γραμματεῖς οἱ κατὰ πρυτανείαν who served contemporaneously with them. W. S. Ferguson recognized them as a group deserving of special attention (*The Priests of Asklepios*, 2nd ed., 1907, p. 155), and throughout the continuing study of the period new evidence, as it appeared, seemed only to increase the well-recognized uncertainties rather than to resolve them.

The "secretary cycle", whereby the γραμματεῖς succeeded one another, year by year, in the "official" order of their phylai (for the beginning of this system see p. 107 above, on the Archonship of Themistokles, 347/6), appeared to scholars earlier in the 20th century to offer the best foundation for a reconstruction of the archon list. In the latest pronouncement of his long career on the subject, B. D. Meritt insisted upon its continuing validity (*Hesperia* 50, 1981, pp. 79, 93–94). It had indeed long been recognized that there was during the period at any rate one break in the smooth operation of the cycle, but the hypothesis of further breaks in order to accommodate other evidence was as far as practicable generally avoided.

A later generation has tended to reverse this principle and to go so far as to rely entirely on the claims of evidence other than the cycle, denying any validity to the latter save perhaps by accident or coincidence. Thus the archon list proposed by M. J. Osborne (*ZPE* 78, 1989, p. 241) places a break in the cycle after 262/1 and excludes any conclusive argument from it until its resumption in 229/8 save for two brief and uncertain sequences from 249/8 to 245/4 and from 237/6 to 234/3.

The interruption in the cycle during the (second) period of the *anagrapheis* from 294/3 to 292/1, during the early years of the regime instituted by Demetrios Poliorketes (p. 241 above), does indeed suggest that the capitulation to Antigonos in 262/1 could have produced a similar result. But there is evidence that on the earlier occasion certain individuals who were known to support the regime were named to important office, initially at least, including the archonship; and even so the cycle was speedily resumed. The archons of 261/60 and later are not necessarily to be viewed as direct appointees of Antigonos Gonatas, for we know too little about any of them (cf., however, A. S. Henry, *Chiron* 18, 1988, p. 223): but even if they, or some of them, were of political consequence in the democracy of the time, the system of selection of the γραμματεῖς by rotation of phylai was politically innocuous. Their role was, for example, not of the potential importance of that of the official(s) in charge of the *dioikesis*, as is clearly demonstrated by the change from the Plural Board back to the Single Officer after 262/1, and there was no evident reason for the Macedonian authorities to interfere with it.

The instinct of Meritt, and of his predecessors, to preserve the cycle as far as possible must therefore be respected; more modern iconoclasm, though the understandable reaction of a fresh generation in face of the undoubted difficulties presented by the evidence, may be too drastic. Until new information becomes available, uncertainty must prevail. Osborne justly remarked (*ZPE* 78, 1989, p. 240) that "no chronological scheme proposed to date has survived entirely intact from the discovery of a new document bearing an archon or secretary date." One may cite the respectful dedication to the archon Kydenor by W. B. Dinsmoor of his book *Athenian Archon List*. Readjustments of the archon list, however closely and plausibly argued, must remain in essence speculative—an enjoyable intellectual exercise for the scholars engaged in argument and counterargument but, at the end of the day, without real consequence until more missing pieces of the puzzle come to light.

The first archons of this difficult period among the Agora decrees are Athenodoros, archon in the year preceding the enactment of **194**, and Philinos, in office at the time of the passage of **195**. It has indeed become a matter of dispute which one of them held office before the other, and Athenodoros' arrival in this general location is in itself a development of the 1980's. For J. Kirchner (*IG* II^2, iv, 1, p. 14) his year was 240/39, and this was the dating that prevailed through the 20th-century literature until the list drawn up by Meritt in 1977 (*Historia* 26, p. 176), the exceptions being A. C. Johnson in 1914 (241/40), cited by Dinsmoor, whose 1931 study (*Archons of Athens*, pp. 169, 177) set him at 243/2. But Dinsmoor revoked this opinion in his study of 1939 (see above) and returned to 240/39 (*Athenian Archon List*, p. 154).

C. Habicht (*Untersuchungen*, pp. 137–141) devoted particular attention to Athenodoros and concluded that 240/39 must on the evidence be regarded as too late for him. His reasoning convinced Meritt (*Hesperia* 50, 1981, pp. 79, 82–83), who relocated the archon in 256/5, in accord with the secretary cycle (cf. *ibid.*, p. 94). This "evidence of the cycles" was seen as "manipulation" by Osborne (*ZPE* 78, 1989, pp. 212–213), in whose arrangement Athenodoros is placed in 254/3 (on his reckoning, the year after that of Philinos). This would envisage the passage of **194** in the archonship either of Philostratos or of Kleomachos, according to the variant schemes presented. For Meritt, Athenodoros' successor was the unknown archon of *Agora* XV, 84 (who might possibly be Lykeas or Alkibiades).

Factors which may (or may not) be relevant to the establishment of Athenodoros' year are the following: (1) The γραμματεύς was Ἄρχετος Ἀρχίου Ἁμαξαντεύς (Hippothontis X). (2) *IG* II^2, 784 (*SEG* XXIX, 110), passed in his year, shows that the year was ordinary in the festival calendar. In the Metonic cycle, 256/5 should have been ordinary, 254/3 intercalary. (3) The same inscription honors athlothetai, and this fact has, for some, compelled the conclusion that it was passed in a year of the celebration of the Greater Panathenaia. 254/3 was such a year (cf. Habicht, *Untersuchungen*, p. 140); 256/5 was not.

THE SITOPHYLAKES OF 256/5(?) OR 254/3(?) HONORED

194 (Pl. 20). Two nonjoining fragments of a stele of Hymettian marble, of which fragment *a* (I 3238) is broken all around save for the original rough-picked back and fragment *b* (I 4169) has part of the right edge preserved but is broken elsewhere. Fragment *a* was discovered on September 24, 1935, in the wall of a built drain of Late Roman date over the north end of the East Building (O 13); fragment *b* was discovered on May 19, 1936, in a late level north of the Odeion and east of the Altar of Ares (M 7).

   a: H. 0.16 m.; W. 0.292 m.; Th. 0.106 m.

   b: H. 0.11 m.; W. 0.111 m.; Th. 0.037 m.

LH. 0.005 m.
Στοιχ. Hor. 0.007 m.; Vert. 0.0092 m.

Ed. M. Crosby, *Hesperia* 6, 1937, pp. 444–448, no. 2, with photographs. See also *SEG* XXXIII, 117.

a. 255/4 a.(?) *vel* 253/2 a.(?)   ΣΤΟΙΧ. 50

```
           [------------------------------------------------]
(a)        [.....¹².....]υ δικαίως ἄρχει[ν τὴν ἀρχὴν κατὰ ψηφίσματα τῆς]
           [βουλῆς καὶ τ]ο[ῦ] δήμου, ᵛ τοὺς λαχό[ντας προέδρους εἰς τὴν ἐπιοῦ]
           [σαν ἐκκλη]σίαν χρηματίσαι περὶ τ[ούτων, γνώμην δὲ ξυμβάλλεσθ]
           [αι τῆς βο]υλῆς εἰς τὸν δῆμον ὅτι δοκ[εῖ τῆι βουλῆι ᵛ ἐπαινέσαι τ]
5          [οὺς σιτο]φύλακας τοὺς ἐπὶ Ἀθηνοδώρ[ου ἄρχοντος ...⁸....ιον]
           [Ἐρχιέα], ᵛ Ἀρχῖνον Ἀχαρνέα, ᵛ Ἀγάθαρχο[ν Λαμπτρέα, ᵛ Δημ..⁵.. Ἀν]
           [αφλύ]στιον, ᵛ Εὐθύδημον Μελιτέα, ᵛ καὶ τ[ὸν κληρωτὸν γραμματέα]
           [Ἐργο]κλῆν Κρωπίδην, καὶ στεφανῶσαι αὐτ[οὺς χρυσῶι στεφάνωι κ]
           [ατὰ] τὸν νόμον φιλοτιμίας ἕνεκα καὶ δικα[ιοσύνης τῆς εἰς τὴν β]
10         [ουλ]ὴν καὶ τὸν δῆμον τὸν Ἀθηναίων· ᵛᵛ ἀναγρ[άψαι δὲ τόδε τὸ ψήφι]
           [σμ]α τὸν γραμματέα τὸν κατὰ πρυτανείαν ἐν στ[ήληι λιθίνηι καὶ]
           [σ]τῆσαι πρὸς τῶι συνεδρίωι· ᵛ εἰς δὲ τὴν ἀναγραφ[ὴν τῆς στήλης μ]
           [ε]ρίσαι τὸν ταμίαν τῶν στρατιωτικῶν τὸ γενόμε[νον ἀνάλωμα. ᵛᵛ]
                        vacat

                        lacuna
(b)        [.......................⁴⁰............... το]ῦ δήμ[ου ..]
15         [.......................³⁹..............] τῶι ἀγωνοθ[έτ]
           [ηι .................³⁶..............., χ]ρησίμους δ[ὲ .]
           [...................³²............· ὅπως ἂν ο]ὖν ἐφάμιλλο[ν]
           [ἦι τὸ φιλοτιμεῖσθαι προθύμως καὶ δικαίως ἄρχ]ειν τὴν ἀρχήν [ᵛ]
           [ἀγαθῆι τύχηι ᵛᵛ δεδόχθαι τῶι δήμωι ᵛ ἐπαινέσ]αι τοὺς σιτοφύλ
20         [ακας τοὺς ἐπὶ Ἀθηνοδώρου ἄρχοντος ...⁸....]ιον Ἐρ[χ]ιέα, ᵛ Ἀρχ
           [ῖ]νον Ἀχαρνέα, ᵛ Εὐθύδημον Μελιτέα, ᵛ Ἀγάθαρχον] Λαμπτρέα, ᵛ Δημ
           [..⁵.. Ἀ]ναφλύστιον, ᵛ καὶ τὸν κληρωτὸν γραμματ]έα Ἐργοκλῆν Κρ
           [ωπίδην ᵛ φιλοτιμίας ἕνεκα καὶ δικαιοσύνης τῆς ε]ἰ̣ς τὴν βουλὴ
           [ν καὶ τὸν δῆμον τὸν Ἀθηναίων καὶ τὸν βασιλέα Ἀντίγον]ον· ἐπα[ιν]
25         [έσαι δὲ καὶ -----------------------------------------]
           [------------------------------------------------]
```

The text shown above is that of Crosby with minor corrections of a few readings, at points of break in the stones, not worth the distinction of an *apparatus criticus*. This inscription is the "name piece" of the craftsman identified by S. V. Tracy as responsible for some sixty-seven texts inscribed between 286/5 and 245/4; see *Hesperia* 57, 1988, pp. 304–311, with plate 85:a (a detail of lines 3–6 of the present text), and **172**. It may nevertheless remain advisable to think in terms of a style or an *atelier* and to be guarded in the assignment of so substantial a number of texts, covering so wide a span of years, to one single individual. Cf. A. G. Woodhead, *AJA* 81, 1977, p. 251.

In line 15 omega is superimposed on an erroneous alpha that the mason did not trouble to erase. Single and sometimes double letter spaces are left vacant at appropriate places to separate names or to distinguish clauses. Cf. A. S. Henry, *Prescripts*, pp. 67–70 and the commentary on **172**.

Lines 4, 11, 19. Crosby restored EI in the feminine datives in these lines except in the word ἀγαθῆι (line 19). This is in fact the preponderant usage in the mid-3rd century, but HI is well attested: cf. Henry, *CQ* n.s. 14, 1964, pp. 240–245. Either usage may therefore be supposed here, or even inconsistency of use. Lines 4–5. On the number and duties of the sitophylakes see **127** and references there, most notably B. D. Meritt, *Hesperia* 13, 1944, pp. 244–245 and R. S. Stroud, *Hesperia* 43, 1974, p. 180, with notes 90 and 91. The stele records two enactments, or one enactment enlarged and restated, thanking and bestowing honors upon the same grain commissioners. The second enactment appears to add to the number of recipients of the honors and gratitude and to associate the Macedonian king with the Athenians in the expression of them. On the relationship between the two enactments or sections see further below. Believing that the archonship of Athenodoros was to be dated to 240/39, Crosby restored in line 24 the name of Demetrios (II), son and successor of Antigonos Gonatas. The revised dating requires the substitution of the name of Antigonos himself, if her supplement is acceptable (she did not comment upon it).

There were originally ten sitophylakes, five for the city and five for the Peiraieus. Five officials, that is, a complete half-board, are named here, a reduction by one from the number commended in **127**. Aristotle's evidence suggests that the number was subject to variation, and it is possible that, in the interval of some forty-five years between **127** and the present text, the γραμματεὺς κληρωτός (whose phyle here differs from those of the other five honorands) became included in, rather than excluded from, the count of one official per phyle. There was a γραμματεὺς εἰς ἄστυ (cf. Crosby, *op. cit.*, pp. 460–461, no. 8, line 8), and therefore a corresponding γραμματεὺς εἰς Πειραιᾶ may be postulated to make up the total of twelve officials selected by lot. The sitophylakes are not, as in **127**, named in the "official order" of their phylai. Crosby assumed, no doubt correctly, that they had held office in the year preceding that in which they were honored, and the date at the head of the text reflects this.

Lines 5–8 and 20–23. The men honored are not otherwise identifiable. Crosby suggested that Agatharchos of Lamptrai may well have been the son of Pyrgion of that deme (*PA* 12487), whose father was named Agatharchos (*PA* 31) and who as proedros put *IG* II², 672 to the vote in 277/6. Line 7. For the "allotted secretary" see **127**, commentary on lines 13–14. He was still κληρωτός in the middle of the 2nd century, whether or not the sitophylakes themselves then continued to be so appointed (Crosby, *op. cit.*, p. 460 with note 1). Lines 8–9. θάλλου στεφάνωι Crosby: but the formula κατὰ τὸν νόμον indicates that the stephanos must have been of gold, for it is not attached to stephanoi of any other kind. Cf. Henry, *Honours*, p. 59, note 116, where the restoration is attributed to Meritt. Lines 9 and 23. For the expression of the honorands' virtues, used in this form also in **175** and **181**, see **175**, commentary on line 1.

Line 12. Πρὸς τῶι συνεδρίωι. See **175**, commentary on lines 3–4, and cf. **181**, lines 37–40. The identity of the συνέδριον was discussed by Crosby, *op. cit.*, pp. 446–448, and by R. E. Wycherley, in *Agora* III, pp. 126–128, where the references (including this inscription) are collected. H. A. Thompson once thought that, if not otherwise qualified, the word was likely to refer to the Bouleuterion (*Hesperia* 6, 1937, p. 215, note 4), and this view was endorsed by P. J. Rhodes (*Athenian Boule*, 1972, pp. 31–32, note 6), who regarded Wycherley (*loc. cit.*) as too willing to apply to a building uses of a word which probably refer to a meeting. But Wycherley was right to suggest that it had flexibility in use and described various buildings. It should probably be understood to refer to the place of meeting of the officials concerned in the given context. Here the place of discovery of the stone may well suggest that the office of the sitophylakes was located in that area of the Agora.

Line 13. Payment for the stele is in this case the province of the ταμίας τῶν στρατιωτικῶν, on whose responsibilities in this direction earlier than 229 B.C. see Henry, *Chiron* 14, 1984, pp. 53–54, 73–74, 80–81, and cf. W. K. Pritchett and Meritt, *Chronology*, p. 43, note 41, where this inscription is cited. Henry observed (*op. cit.*, p. 80, note 162) that the Military Treasurer is several times associated in the mid 3rd century with stelai honoring officials connected with the grain supply; cf. **188**. Phraseology with μερίσαι and τὸ γενόμενον ἀνάλωμα is now standard; cf. Henry, *ZPE* 78, 1989, p. 277 and **175**, commentary on lines 4–5.

Lines 17–18. Ὅπως ἂν οὖν. For the "hortatory intention" cf. **86**, commentary on line 21–24. Here the emphasis is not on publicity for the Athenians' propensity to reward virtues where they see them, as in **173**, **181**, and **187**, but on the encouragement of emulation among officials in their standard of efficiency, as in **185** (where see the commentary on lines 16–17). Line 19. Ἀγαθῆι τύχηι. See **72**, commentary on lines 7–8.

Line 24. The name of King Antigonos, and the further commendations apparently introduced by a new clause where the stone breaks off, are additions to the original *probouleuma*, in which the relevant clause ended with Ἀθηναίων (line 10). They appear nevertheless in the substantive decree, not in an amendment "from the floor of the ekklesia". In effect, therefore, the text appears to incorporate a *probouleuma*, set out as a probouleumatic decree (cf. Rhodes, *Athenian Boule*, p. 253), and the ultimate, revised decree of the demos classed by Rhodes (p. 265) among the nonprobouleumatic decrees (as indicated by the formula restored in line 19). The introduction of new material is only partly relevant, for the pattern may be paralleled in, e.g., *Agora* XV, 115. Since the final decree incorporates the substance of the *probouleuma* it could equally well be regarded as probouleumatic; cf. *IG* II², 330, lines 47–65. The difference for classification purposes is one of form rather than of nature; the procedural differentiation, which must have been significant and appears complex, remains obscure despite the comparative abundance of material. It is not unlikely that fragment *a* of the present text was at some point preceded by a full formula including the phrase ἔδοξεν τῆι βουλῆι καὶ τῶι δήμωι.

[A further fragment of this monument, discovered in the Third Ephorate of the Greek Archaeological Service, may or may not make a significant contribution to the text and to the resolution of the date of the archon Athenodoros. Information of it, received after the delivery of the manuscript of this work, does not extend beyond the fact of its existence.]

THE ARCHONSHIP OF PHILINOS, 252/1 (OR 255/4) B.C.

Philinos has been one of the nomads among Athenian archons of the 3rd century. For the history of earlier attempts to determine his date see the full account of B. D. Meritt in *Hesperia* 30, 1961, pp. 213–214 (see **195**) and 38, 1969, pp. 432–433. Known only from a reference in *IG* II², 1304b (addenda, p. 672; cf. *SEG* XXII, 126), he was placed by J. Kirchner (*IG* II², iv, 1, p. 16) among the "archontes saeculi III quorum tempora accuratius definiri nequeunt", and assigned more specifically "ultimis annis s. III". W. B. Dinsmoor and A. C. Johnson found 212/11 a year for Philinos that appeared to harmonize with other considerations; other scholars had tried "*ca.* 218/17" (for details see Dinsmoor, *Archons of Athens*, pp. 55 and 213, *Athenian Archon List*, pp. 164–165). W. K. Pritchett and Meritt (*Chronology*, p. xxv) found him a hesitant place in 210/09, and this dating was adopted by Dinsmoor in 1954 (*Hesperia* 23, p. 316).

This picture was radically altered by the edition of **195** below. As the result of it, Philinos was transferred to the middle part of the century, where a place was found for him in 269/8, regarded as close to the date of the inscriptions with lettering comparable with that of the new text. See *SEG* XXI, 371; Meritt, *Athenian Year*, p. 233; Y. Garlan, *BCH* 89, 1965, pp. 339–344 (*SEG* XXII, 125). But this assignment too failed to stand the test of new and better evidence. *Agora* XV, 89, discovered in 1968, at last provided a complete prescript of Philinos' year, which showed that its γραμματεύς was Theotimos, son of Stratokles, of Thorai (Demetrias II). On Meritt's view, this compelled his removal to a position compatible with the secretary cycle, and the year 254/3, where he dispossessed Philostratos previously placed there, fitted the requirements; cf. *Hesperia* 38, 1969, pp. 432–433 and *Historia* 26, 1977, p. 175. The prosopographical data of the new prytany text reinforced the advisability of such a dating, which remained in accord with the character of the lettering of **195** and with what is now seen to be the career of the "Cutter of Agora I 3238 and I 4169" (see **172**) to whose skill it has more recently been attributed.

Relying on the apparent requirements of the career of Thoukritos of Myrrhinous, identified by Garlan (*loc. cit.*) as hipparch in Philinos' year (*IG* II², 1279 [as revised in *SEG* XXII, 125] and 2856), C. Habicht concluded that Philinos should be assigned to a date rather earlier than 254/3 and hardly later than the mid-250's (*Untersuchungen*, pp. 126–128, 145). Meritt's response (*Hesperia* 50, 1981, pp. 85–87) emphasized a weakness in the argument from Thoukritos, which depends on the order in which the entries of his various generalships recorded on *IG* II², 2856 are to be read. He also corrected his own previous dating, which had postulated a break in the secretary cycle after 260/59, in the light of the new dating of Athenodoros (p. 281 above). It was in any case his consistent and firm belief that "the paramount claim of the secretary-cycle must be honored" (*ibid.*, p. 79) and that the cycle beginning in 253/2 continued until the year of Diomedon (pp. 300–301 below), at which point "the known irregularities" begin. Meritt's revised date for Philinos was, in consequence, 252/1.

In *ZPE* 58, 1985, pp. 290–294, M. J. Osborne maintained Habicht's interpretation of Thoukritos' career and added to it criticism of Meritt's prosopographical argument (although both depend on the supposed archonship of Euboulos II, on which doubt has been cast: see A. S. Henry, *Chiron* 18, 1988, pp. 215–224); but he suggested no firm date for Philinos. He followed this study, however, with a longer discussion in *ZPE* 78, 1989, pp. 209–242 (on Philinos especially pp. 230–233, on Euboulos II p. 228, note 90), in the course of which he assigned Philinos' archonship to 255/4. In view of the large degree of uncertainty surrounding this whole matter, much depends on the weight given by individual judgments to the conflicting factors.

And there is one further factor to be considered: that of the Athenians' propensity (many times referred to in earlier contexts) for maintaining a close degree of coordination between their festival calendar and the Metonic cycle. There being no calendric data for Philinos' year, his assignment had not been conditioned by the character of it in relation to its potential neighbors. *Agora* XV, 89 was passed on Hekatombaion 11 (= pryt. I, 11), and this conveys no information concerning the year's character. But the name of the γραμματεύς, now known, enabled Meritt to restore and to date in Philinos' year *IG* II², 697 (*SEG* XXI, 356); see *Hesperia* 38, 1969, pp. 433–434. This, as there restored, shows Skirophorion 21 as the equivalent of pryt. XII, 24; the year was thus intercalary, with Skirophorion a hollow month at its end. In the tenth Metonic cycle the year 255/4 (the seventh year of the cycle) will have been ordinary, 252/1 (like 254/3) intercalary.

Phylai identifiable in their prytanies in the year of Philinos are I Aigeis and XII Antigonis, Demetrias, Pandionis, or Akamantis.

FRAGMENT OF AN HONORARY DECREE

195. A fragment of the upper left section of a pedimental(?) stele of Pentelic marble (I 5592), with heavy moldings above the inscribed face consisting of a concave superposed on a convex member, from which it is divided by a channel, combined with a wide taenia below descending in an apophyge to an uninscribed space of 0.02 m. immediately above the text. The fragment, battered and broken elsewhere, was discovered on October 17, 1938, in the wall of a modern house southeast of the Market Square (S 21).

H. 0.156 m.; W. 0.19 m.; Th. 0.10 m.
LH. 0.005 m. (phi 0.009 m.)

Ed. B. D. Meritt, *Hesperia* 30, 1961, pp. 213–214, no. 8, with photograph pl. 36. See also *SEG* XXI, 371.

a. 252/1 *a.*(?) NON-ΣΤΟΙΧ.

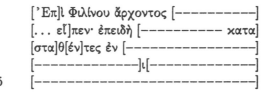

```
['Ἐπ]ὶ Φιλίνου ἄρχοντος [----------]
[... εἶ]πεν· ἐπειδὴ [---------- κατα]
[στα]θ[έν]τες ἐν [----------------]
[-------------]ι[------------]
5  [--------------------------]
```

Before the discovery of *Agora* XV, 89, with its evidence of the γραμματεύς of the year of Philinos (see above), the lettering of this text was determinative in the assignment of the archon to a mid-century date; more recent analysis has made a dating in the middle to later 250's relatively secure. Indeed the stele has proved to be yet another identifiable element in the *oeuvre* of the "Cutter of Agora I 3238 and I 4169" distinguished by S. V. Tracy; for the references see **172** and **194**. The fragment was associated by M. B. Walbank (*Hesperia* 51, 1982, p. 51) with the text he published there (I 7312; see **255G**), but that fragment was not included by Tracy in his list of the cutter's output (*Hesperia* 57, 1988, pp. 304–306).

It is impossible to estimate the width of the stele, but there can have been no room for the full preamble of a regular decree of the boule and demos. The truncated prescript of an enactment of a religious organization or of some subunit of the body politic is better adapted to the space likely to have been available here. Cf., for example, *IG* II², 1262, 1270, 1301, and particularly 1287. This view was accepted by A. S. Henry, *Prescripts*, p. 75.

FRAGMENT OF A DECREE

196. [The fragment originally placed at this point as an independent inscription (see *SEG* XXXV, 90) has been shown by S. V. Tracy (*Attic Letter-Cutters*, p. 159) to provide the ends of lines 33–35 of *Agora* XV, 240 (*SEG* XXI, 464). The text and commentary, thus rendered otiose, have been withdrawn. Cf. *SEG* XL, 116.]

FRAGMENT OF A DECREE

197. A fragment of a stele of Hymettian marble (I 5653), with the flat top preserved, dressed with a toothed chisel and without a crowning molding, but otherwise broken all around, discovered on February 20, 1939, among marbles from the demolition of modern houses at the north foot of the Areopagos. The inscribed surface shows deep gashes and is generally worn and battered.

H. 0.20 m.; W. 0.26 m.; Th. 0.105 m.
LH. *ca.* 0.006 m.

Ed. B. D. Meritt, *Hesperia* 30, 1961, pp. 214–215, no. 9, with photograph pl. 37. See also *SEG* XXI, 380; L. Moretti, *Iscrizioni storiche ellenistiche* I, 1967, p. 50, note 9.

ca. med. saec. III *a.* NON-ΣΤΟΙΧ.

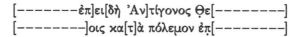

```
[-------ἐπ]ει[δὴ 'Αν]τίγονος Θε[--------]
[-------]οις κα[τ]ὰ πόλεμον ἐπ[--------]
```

```
     [————————] Ἑλλήνω[ν] ἐλευθερία[————————]
     [—————————]ιναι εἰς [χ]ρημάτω[ν —————————]
  5  [———————————————] εὐεργ[ε——————————————]
     [—————————————] πρὸς οὐθ[ὲν] σε[——————————]
     [——————————————] τοῦ [δ]ήμου [——————————]
     [——————————————τῶ]ι τε ἀγῶν[ι ——————————]
     [————————————————]ΙΣΜ[————————————————]
  10 [——————————————————]Ο[————————————————]
     [——————————————————————————————————————]
```

The writing on this fragment is shallow and variable in execution, especially in the inscribing of sigma and omega. Meritt correctly observed that the latter, with horizontals set now high, now low, or obliquely ("winged" omega) is very much of mid-3rd-century character; cf. P. M. Fraser and T. Rönne, *Boeotian and West Greek Tombstones*, 1957, p. 83, note 6. Line 1. [————— 'Αν]τίγονος [.]ε[—————] Meritt. Line 4. [——————]αι κτλ. Meritt. Line 8. [—————]ΤΕΑΓΩΜ[—————] Meritt.

Meritt assumed that the Antigonos named in line 1 is Antigonos Gonatas (the indications of the script being too early, presumably, for Doson) and suggested that this is a fragment of a decree in his honor, to be associated with his war against Alexander, son of Krateros, his former commander in southern Greece, who had set up an independent monarchy in Corinth and Euboia. In this war the Athenians and Argives (the latter under their tyrant Aristomachos) supported the Macedonian king. Aristomachos is praised by the Athenians in *IG* II², 774 (*SEG* XXV, 103, XXIX, 108, XXXI, 95, XLI, 53), a decree then thought to be datable to 253/2 (cf. Meritt, *Hesperia* 38, 1969, p. 436), in which "freedom" and a sum of money (fifty talents) are also involved (lines 12–13 and 19–20; cf. lines 3–4 of the present text). Meritt placed this inscription therefore in 253/2, to suit the apparent requirement of the events. However, the redating of *IG* II², 774 in the 240's, perhaps as late as 243/2 (see M. J. Osborne, *ZPE* 78, 1989, pp. 223–225), makes such a connection unlikely.

In any case it is to be doubted whether the name Antigonos must necessarily be associated with the king, or the reference to freedom with that particular occasion. The top edge of the stele is complete, and its treatment suggests that it did not form part of a larger monument, even though it is not finished off with a crowning molding. If, therefore, line 1 represents the beginning of the decree, either the stele was exceptionally wide, so that the regular prescript of a decree could somehow be accommodated in it before the body of the enactment was reached, or the prescript was truncated, perhaps to a simple reference to the proposer, in a manner compatible with the enactment of a deme, religious organization, or other community subgroup. Such a group may indeed have honored the Macedonian king, but it is more likely to have left this to the national assembly and to have had more parochial interests at heart in honoring a benefactor of lesser stature. If the letters at the end of the first line are correctly assessed, this Antigonos was perhaps a son of The———, and thence without any discernible relationship to the Macedonian royal house. Nevertheless, in general terms, and as the lettering indicates, the decree may be associated with this mid-century period, even if its precise reference remains obscure.

FRAGMENT OF A DECREE

198. A fragment of a stele of Hymettian marble (I 2986), broken on all sides, discovered on June 3, 1935, in a disturbed Byzantine context over the east end of the Middle Stoa (O 13). The stone is badly discolored.

H. 0.109 m.; W. 0.085 m.; Th. 0.026 m.
LH. 0.005 m.
Στοιχ. Hor. 0.0105 m.; Vert. 0.0125 m.

Ed. B. D. Meritt, *Hesperia* 37, 1968, pp. 269–270, no. 5, with photograph pl. 77. See also *SEG* XXV, 101.

ca. med. saec. III a.   ΣΤΟΙΧ. 38

```
     [——————————————————————————————————]
     [....8.... ἀ]γαθεῖ [τύχει δεδόχθαι τεῖ βουλεῖ το]
     [ὑς λαχόντ]ας προέδ[ρους εἰς τὴν ἐπιοῦσαν ἐκκλη]
     [σίαν χρημ]ατίσαι π[ερὶ τούτων ἐν ἱεροῖς, γνώμην]
     [δὲ ξυμβάλλε]σθαι τ[ῆς βουλῆς εἰς τὸν δῆμον ὅτι δ]
  5  [οκεῖ τεῖ βου]λεῖ ἐπ[αινέσαι ........17........]
     [——————————————————————————————————]
```

The lettering is plain and "standard" for the period and offers the principal guide to the date of the fragment. The bottom stroke of epsilon has a propensity to slope downwards; the loop of rho would be of significance in any attempt to match another fragment to this text. There is no clue to the position of the piece on the stele, and the line divisions shown, those of the *editio princeps*, are wholly arbitrary. All that remains is a section of a regular referral or probouleumatic formula, for which see **52**, commentary on lines 16–19 and references there.

Line 2. The stoichedon pattern calls for the restoration of ἐπιοῦσαν in this formula, which at least reinforces the conclusion that the inscription is to be dated no earlier than the second quarter of the century. See **185**, commentary on lines 19–20. Line 3. The addition of ἐν ἱεροῖς in the restoration, if acceptable, provides further aid for dating purposes in virtue of its rarity. As Meritt observed, this formula is exactly paralleled in *IG* II², 772, of the archonship of Diogeiton in the 260's or 250's. But it is the sole instance of it in *IG* II². The length of line is, however, assured by the other elements of the formula, and ἐν ἱεροῖς precisely meets the evident spatial requirements.

FRAGMENT OF AN HONORARY DECREE

199. A fragment of a stele of Pentelic marble (I 3048), broken on all sides but with the original rough-picked back preserved, discovered on June 19, 1935, in a late context over the northeast corner of the Middle Stoa (P 12). The surviving stone is much larger than is indicated by the present area of the inscribed surface, most of which has been broken away.

H. 0.14 m.; W. 0.162 m.; Th. 0.11 m.
LH. 0.005 m. (phi 0.008 m.).
Στοιχ. Hor. 0.00875 m.; Vert. 0.013 m.

Ed. B. D. Meritt, *Hesperia* 37, 1968, p. 270, no. 6, with photograph pl. 77. See also *SEG* XXV, 102.

ca. med. saec. III a.   ΣΤΟΙΧ. 44(?)

```
[-------------------------------------------]
[....9...., πέ]γπ[τει κ]αὶ δ[εκάτει τῆς πρυτανείας· ἐκκλη]
[σία· τῶν προέδρ]ων ἐπεψήφι[ζεν .........20.........]
[. καὶ συμπρόεδ]ροι· ᵛ ἔδοξε[ν τῶι δήμωι· ......14......]
[....9.... Εἱρ]εσίδης εἶπ[εν· ἐπειδὴ ......15.......]
5  [....9.... ἀν]ὴρ εὔνους ὢ[ν πρὸς τὸν δῆμον τὸν Ἀθηναίων]
[χρήσιμον παρε]ίχετ[ο ἑαυτὸν -----------------------]
[-------------------------------------------]
```

The mason at work here was, once again, S. V. Tracy's "Cutter of Agora I 3238 and I 4169", for whose career and characteristics see **172** and **194**, with references there. The last datable inscription assigned to him by Tracy belongs to the archonship of Diomedon (see p. 300 below), which ought therefore to be regarded as the *terminus ante quem* for this text.

It is impossible to know the position of this fragment on the stele, and the line divisions are arbitrary. Meritt, whose text is shown above, claimed that the length of line was fixed by the restoration of lines 1–2. Restoration with a line of 50 letters is, however, equally practicable and has two possible recommendations. (1) The introduction of ἀνήρ (customarily paired with ἀγαθός) in this position in honorary decrees scarcely survived the 4th century (cf. J. Kirchner, *IG* II², iv, 1, p. 41); (2) the reflexive ἑαυτόν more frequently intervenes before the verb in the phrase χρήσιμον ἑαυτὸν παρέχειν or παρέχεσθαι. *IG* II², 649 offers a parallel for the preliminary introduction of a mention of the services of the honorand's father. The text might therefore run

```
[.......15......., πέ]γπ[τει κ]αὶ δ[εκάτει τῆς πρυτανείας· ἐκκλη]
[σία κυρία· ᵛ τῶν προέδρ]ων ἐπεψήφι[ζεν .........20.........]
[...7... καὶ συμπρόεδ]ροι· ᵛ ἔδοξε[ν τεῖ βουλεῖ καὶ τῶι δήμωι· ..]
[.......15....... Εἱρ]εσίδης εἶπ[εν· ἐπειδὴ πρότερόν τε ..5..]
5  [... ὁ .....10.... πατ]ὴρ εὔνους ὢ[ν πρὸς τὸν δῆμον τὸν Ἀθηναίων]
[χρήσιμον ἑαυτὸν παρε]ίχετ[ο -----------------------].
```

Line 3. In view of the vacant letter space before ἔδοξεν, A. S. Henry (*Prescripts*, p. 68; cf. pp. 63–67) listed this text among examples of emphasis given to this formula in the 3rd century. It is a regular feature of the work of the "Cutter of Agora I 3238 and I 4169", who appears in Henry's list as the most prominent exponent of this form of emphasis in his generation. Despite the restoration of the formula in Meritt's text, it is clear from the alternative suggested above that it must remain uncertain whether the decree was probouleumatic or nonprobouleumatic.

FRAGMENT OF THE CONCLUSION OF A DECREE

200. A small fragment of a stele of Pentelic(?) marble (I 5460), badly burned and discolored and broken all around, discovered on May 24, 1938, in a Byzantine context in a drain shaft south of the Eleusinion (U 22:1).

H. 0.13 m.; W. 0.07 m.; Th. 0.076 m.
LH. 0.006 m.
Ed. B. D. Meritt, *Hesperia* 30, 1961, p. 259, no. 64, with photograph pl. 48. See also *SEG* XXI, 388.

ca. med. saec. III *a.*   NON-ΣΤΟΙΧ. *ca.* 34–37

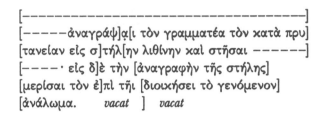

```
        [------------------------------------]
        [-----ἀναγράψ]α[ι τὸν γραμματέα τὸν κατὰ πρυ]
        [τανείαν εἰς σ]τήλ[ην λιθίνην καὶ στῆσαι ------]
        [----· εἰς δ]ὲ τὴν [ἀναγραφὴν τῆς στήλης]
        [μερίσαι τὸν ἐ]πὶ τῆι [διοικήσει τὸ γενόμενον]
   5    [ἀνάλωμα.    vacat  ]   vacat
```

The writing is plain and without special characteristic. The letter surviving in line 1 was not read by Meritt, and the lines have been renumbered from the *editio princeps*. Payment for the stele may have been met either by the Plural Board or by the Single Officer ἐπὶ τῇ διοικήσει. If the latter, the decree is to be dated later than 262/1: see the commentary on **174**. The style of the writing renders this more probable. It is impossible to determine to what place on the latitude of the stele this fragment belongs, and the line divisions are therefore arbitrary. The restorations employ phraseology customary at the time, but minor variants of formula are of course possible.

FRAGMENT OF THE CONCLUSION OF A DECREE

201. A fragment of a stele of Pentelic marble (I 5495), with the right side preserved, discovered on June 2, 1938, in filling behind the parapet wall of Klepsydra (T 27:1) in a context of the mid 1st century B.C. (on which see A. W. Parsons, *Hesperia* 12, 1943, pp. 240–241). On the right side of the stone a smooth band is left along the forward edge, which otherwise is chisel dressed.

H. 0.078 m.; W. 0.058 m.; Th. 0.041 m.
LH. 0.005–0.006 m.
Στοιχ. Hor. 0.008 m.; Vert. 0.011 m.
Ed. B. D. Meritt, *Hesperia* 30, 1961, pp. 215–216, no. 10, with photograph pl. 37. See also *SEG* XXI, 389.

ca. med. saec. III *a.*   ΣΤΟΙΧ. 40(?)

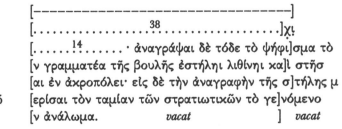

```
        [--------------------------------]
        [.........................38.........................]χι
        [......14...... · ἀναγράψαι δὲ τόδε τὸ ψήφι]σμα τὸ
        [ν γραμματέα τῆς βουλῆς ἐστήληι λιθίνηι κα]ὶ στῆσ
        [αι ἐν ἀκροπόλει· εἰς δὲ τὴν ἀναγραφὴν τῆς σ]τήλης μ
   5    [ερίσαι τὸν ταμίαν τῶν στρατιωτικῶν τὸ γε]νόμενο
        [ν ἀνάλωμα.         vacat          ]   vacat
```

Apart from some clumsiness in the shaping of nu and sigma, the lettering is capably done in a plain style without idiosyncrasies. That the text is stoichedon implies a date earlier than *ca.* 225 B.C. (cf. the commentary on **202**), and with this the character of the writing is in agreement. The first line here shown was not read by Meritt, and the lines are renumbered from the *editio princeps*.

Lines 2–6. The restorations are those of Meritt, who supposed from the place of discovery that the stone came from the Akropolis. They follow recognized formulas for the inscribing and setting up of a stele and for the provision for payment. However, Meritt noted, but discounted, two difficulties: (1) that the γραμματεύς ὁ κατὰ πρυτανείαν, normally responsible for the inscription of the enactment, could not be restored in the text without violation of the stoichedon order and (2) that the stele would have to be paid for, unusually, by the ταμίας τῶν στρατιωτικῶν. He restored a variant designation of the γραμματεύς, for which see **120**, commentary on line 8. He also observed that, contrary to earlier opinion, the Military Treasurer did indeed meet the cost of certain stelai earlier in the century than 229 B.C.; on this matter, which has been the subject of further study since Meritt's edition, see **194**, commentary on line 13.

The γραμματεύς ὁ κατὰ πρυτανείαν may nevertheless occupy his normal place if a line of 34 letters be adopted and alternative formulaic elements employed. In particular it may be supposed that the stele was set up in the Agora and that it need not have come down from the Akropolis, and the official responsible for meeting the expense of it may be the Single Officer ἐπὶ τῇ διοικήσει, as regularly; this will imply a date for the decree not earlier than 262/1 (see **174**). The following text may thus be suggested:

2 [...⁸.... · ἀναγράψαι δὲ τόδε τὸ ψήφι]σμα τὸ
[ν γραμματέα τὸν κατὰ πρυτανείαν κα]ὶ στῆσ
[αι ἐν ἀγορᾶι· εἰς δὲ τὴν ποίησιν τησ]τήλης μ
5 [ερίσαι τὸν ἐπὶ τῆι διοικήσει τὸ γε]νόμενο
[ν ἀνάλωμα].

(Omission of a reference to the στήλη λιθίνη is unusual but by no means without parallel: cf., e.g., *IG* II², 652, lines 33–35, 721, lines 21–23).

FRAGMENT OF A DECREE OF A RELIGIOUS GROUP(?)

202. A fragment of a stele of Pentelic marble (I 3241), with the left edge and original rough-picked back preserved, discovered on January 29, 1936, in a modern context over the northwest corner of the Palace of the Giants (L 9).

H. 0.115 m.; W. 0.123 m.; Th. 0.037 m.
LH. 0.005 m. (omicron 0.004 m., psi 0.008 m.).
Στοιχ. Hor. 0.0095 m.; Vert. 0.011 m.

Ed. M. Crosby, *Hesperia* 6, 1937, pp. 453–454, no. 4, with photograph.

ca. med. saec. III *a.*   ΣΤΟΙΧ.

[————————————————]
[.. ἐπιμ]ελητα[————————————]
[.] ἐγραμμάτευ[εν —————————]
ιον ἢ εἰς τὴν [—————————————]
ων εἶπει ἢ γρά[ψει ——————————]
5 ΝΙΣΤΑΣ ὀφειλ[—————τεῖ Ἀφ]
ροδίτει καὶ [——————————————]
ΜΑΤΩΝ ἐχοντ[————————————]
δὲ τόδε τὸ ψή[φισμα ——————]
[ἀναγρά]ψαι δ[έ ———————————]
10 [————————————————]

The inscription is written in the stoichedon style, which implies a date earlier than *ca.* 225 B.C. (see A. G. Woodhead, *Study of Greek Inscriptions*, p. 31); but the writing is poor and slapdash in character. The rectangular oval of phi and loop of rho, however, and indeed the execution of some of the other letters, are reminiscent of the style of the "Cutter of Agora I 3238 and I 4169", for whom see **172**. The present text looks like the work of a less competent follower or member of the same *atelier* but deserves to be dated within the same general range as that of the master. Omega here has rudimentary "wings"; sigma is very varied in execution.

Line 1. [– – –τοὺς ἐπιμ]ελητὰ[ς οἷς – – – –] Crosby.   Line 5. ΝΙΣ τὰς ὀφειλ[ούσας – – –] or [ἐρα]νιστὰς ὀφειλ[οντας – – –] Crosby.   Line 7. ΜΑ τῶν ἐχόντ[ων – – – –] Crosby.

Line 4. For the phrase cf. *IG* II², 1275, line 14, where εἶπει ἢ πράξει prompts the suggestion that the mason may not have completed the pi in the present text and that εἶπει ἢ ⟨π⟩ρά[ξει might be a preferable reading. For decrees of eranistai see *IG* II², 1265 and 1291, and on the ἔρανος and its place as a Greek social institution see J. Vondeling, *Eranos*, 1961.

The text shown above avoids restorations beyond the self-evident. With a line of 37 letters, which is likely to be the minimum width or close to it, it is possible to suggest some consecutive sense:

$$-----\grave{\epsilon}\grave{\alpha}\nu\ \delta\acute{\epsilon}\ \tau\iota\varsigma\ \tau\tilde{\omega}\nu\ \grave{\epsilon}\rho\alpha\nu\iota\sigma]$$
$$\tilde{\omega}\nu\ \epsilon\tilde{\iota}\pi\epsilon\iota\ \mathring{\eta}\ \gamma\rho\acute{\alpha}[\psi\epsilon\iota\ \pi\alpha\rho\grave{\alpha}\ \tau\grave{\partial}\nu\ \nu\acute{\partial}\mu\partial\nu\ \pi\epsilon\rho\grave{\iota}\ \tau\partial\grave{\upsilon}\varsigma\ \grave{\epsilon}\rho\alpha]$$

5    $\nu\iota\sigma\tau\grave{\alpha}\varsigma\ \dot{\partial}\phi\epsilon\iota\lambda[\acute{\epsilon}\tau\omega\ ..^{6}...\ \delta\rho\alpha\chi\mu\grave{\alpha}\varsigma\ \iota\epsilon\rho\grave{\alpha}\varsigma\ \tau\epsilon\tilde{\iota}\ \text{'}A\phi]$

$\rho\partial\delta\acute{\iota}\tau\epsilon\iota\ \varkappa\alpha\grave{\iota}\ [........^{21}.........\ \tau\tilde{\omega}\nu\ \chi\rho\eta]$

$\mu\acute{\alpha}\tau\omega\nu\ \grave{\epsilon}\chi\partial\nu\tau[.......^{18}.......\ \cdot\ \grave{\alpha}\nu\alpha\gamma\rho\acute{\alpha}\psi\alpha\iota]$

$\delta\grave{\epsilon}\ \tau\acute{\partial}\delta\epsilon\ \tau\grave{\partial}\ \psi\acute{\eta}[\phi\iota\sigma\mu\alpha\ \tau\partial\grave{\upsilon}\varsigma\ \grave{\epsilon}\pi\iota\mu\epsilon\lambda\eta\tau\grave{\alpha}\varsigma\ \grave{\epsilon}\nu\ \sigma\tau\acute{\eta}\lambda\epsilon\iota]\cdot$

$[\grave{\alpha}\nu\alpha\gamma\rho\acute{\alpha}]\psi\alpha\iota\ \delta[\grave{\epsilon}\ \varkappa\alpha\grave{\iota}\ (\text{e.g.})\ \tau\grave{\alpha}\ \grave{\partial}\nu\acute{\partial}\mu\alpha\tau\alpha\ --------]$

Line 5. For such fines among *sodalicii* cf. *IG* II², 1273 (*SEG* XXVIII, 108, XXX, 96), lines 22–24, 1292, lines 16–17. Line 9. Cf. *IG* II², 1301, line 15. For epimeletai as prominent officials of such organizations cf. *IG* II², 1277, 1290, 1291 (*SEG* XXXIII, 1570), 1301, 1324, etc.

A VICTOR IN THE ANTHIPPASIA AT THE OLYMPIC GAMES HONORED BY HIS PHYLE

203. A fragment of a stele of Pentelic marble (I 5326), with the right side and original rough-picked back preserved, discovered on March 17, 1938, in a Byzantine context south of the Eleusinion (U 21). The inscribed surface has been badly damaged at the lower center and lower right.

H. 0.128 m.; W. 0.272 m.; Th. 0.084 m.
LH. 0.006 m.
Στοιχ. (almost square, with slight irregularities) Hor. 0.0105 m.; Vert. 0.0115 m.

Ed. W. K. Pritchett, *Hesperia* 9, 1940, pp. 111–112, no. 21, with photograph.

ca. med. saec. III *a.*   ΣΤΟΙΧ. 26

$$[------------------------]$$
$$[........^{17}........\ \tau\grave{\partial}]\nu\ \grave{\alpha}\gamma\tilde{\omega}\nu[\alpha\ \tau]$$
$$[\mathring{\eta}\varsigma\ \grave{\alpha}\nu\theta\iota]\pi\pi\alpha\sigma\acute{\iota}\alpha\varsigma\ [\tau\partial\tilde{\iota}]\varsigma\ \text{'}O\lambda\upsilon\mu\pi\iota\epsilon\iota\partial$$
$$[\iota\varsigma\ \nu]\iota\varkappa\acute{\eta}\sigma\alpha\varsigma\ \varkappa\alpha\grave{\iota}\ \lambda\alpha\beta\grave{\omega}\nu\ \tau\grave{\partial}\nu\ \tau\rho\acute{\iota}\pi\partial\delta$$
$$[\alpha\ \grave{\epsilon}]\sigma\tau\epsilon\phi\acute{\alpha}\nu\omega\sigma\epsilon\nu\ \tau\grave{\eta}\nu\ \phi\upsilon\lambda\acute{\eta}\nu,\ \grave{\alpha}\pi\partial\delta\epsilon\iota$$
5    $[\varkappa\nu\acute{\upsilon}]\mu\epsilon\nu\partial\varsigma\ \tau\grave{\eta}\nu\ \epsilon\tilde{\upsilon}\nu\partial\iota\alpha\nu\ \tau\grave{\eta}\nu\ \grave{\epsilon}\alpha\upsilon\tau\partial$
$$[\tilde{\upsilon}\ \varkappa\alpha]\grave{\iota}\ \phi\iota\lambda\partial\tau[\iota]\mu\acute{\iota}\alpha\nu\ \mathring{\eta}\nu\ \grave{\epsilon}\chi\omega\nu\ \delta\iota\alpha\tau\epsilon\lambda$$
$$[\epsilon\tilde{\iota}\ \pi\rho]\acute{\partial}\varsigma\ \tau\epsilon\ \tau\grave{\partial}[\nu\ \delta]\mathring{\eta}\mu\partial\nu\ \tau\grave{\partial}\nu\ \text{'}A[\theta]\eta\nu\alpha\acute{\iota}\omega$$
$$[\nu\ \varkappa\alpha\grave{\iota}]\ \pi\rho\grave{\partial}\varsigma\ \tau\partial\grave{\upsilon}\varsigma\ \grave{\epsilon}\alpha\upsilon\tau\partial\tilde{\upsilon}\ \phi[\upsilon\lambda\acute{\epsilon}\tau]\alpha\varsigma\cdot\ \ddot{\partial}$$
$$[\pi\omega\varsigma]\ \mathring{\alpha}\nu\ \partial\tilde{\upsilon}\nu\ \grave{\epsilon}\mu\phi\alpha\nu[.....^{13}......]$$
10   $[------------------------]$

In the *editio princeps* this inscription was dated to the early 3rd century. But it has been identified by S. V. Tracy (*GRBS* 14, 1973, pp. 190–192 and *Hesperia* 57, 1988, pp. 304–311, esp. p. 306) as the work of the "Cutter of Agora I 3238 and I 4168", on whose character and activity see **172** and **194**. This text is the last in series among the Agora decrees attributed to him: among datable inscriptions, *IG* II², 1534B (= S. B. Aleshire, *The Athenian Asklepieion*, 1989, pp. 249–267, inventory V), of the archonship of Diomedon (p. 301 below) marks his latest identifiable work.

Lines 1–2. τὸ]ν ἀγῶνα [τ|ῆι ἀνθι]ππασία[ι κτλ.] Pritchett, but the traces of the dotted alpha are not discernible beyond doubt in line 1, and in line 2 the bottom stroke of sigma is visible. Line 4. ἐσ]τεφ. Pritchett. Lines 9–10. ἐ[μ]-φαν[ῆ ἦι τὰ ἐψηφισμέ||να Pritchett. The verb ἐμφανίζειν may however have been used.

Line 1. On the *anthippasia* at the Olympic and Panathenaic Games, at which a phylarch with his cavalry squadron might compete, cf. *IG* II², 379, of the later 4th century, 3079 (cf. *SEG* XXVII, 11), of 266/5 and so near to the date of this decree, E. Vanderpool, *Hesperia* 43, 1974, pp. 311–313, nos. 1 and 2, both of the later 4th or earlier 3rd century, *IG* II², 3130 (*SEG* XXXII, 250, with earlier references), and the data in Pritchett's commentary. A tripod was evidently the prize (lines 3–4), and representations in relief of three of these are carved on *IG* II², 3130. See also *Syll.*³, note 2 on no. 1074; L. Moretti, *Iscrizioni agonistiche greche*, 1953, pp. 66–68, no. 28, with further bibliography. As a cavalry maneuver, the *anthippasia* is mentioned *en passant* by Xenophon, *Hipparchikos* 1.20, and described more fully as executed ceremonially, *ibid.*, 3.11–14; but this is unconnected with the contest at the Games. Cf. Pritchett, *op. cit.*, p. 112, note 48; Vanderpool, *Hesperia* 43, 1974, p. 311.

Lines 3–4. Being presumably the phylarch, the honorand had the victory proclaimed as of his phyle, not, evidently, as of his city alone, which was the usual practice. The proclamation was evidence of patriotic sentiment and valued as such. Cf. L. Robert, *RevPhil* ser. 3, 41, 1967, p. 22: "Le rapport intime entre 'la couronne' du vainqueur et la patrie de celui-ci est illustré par un très grand nombre de textes." In some instances the crown was transferred to a city of which the victor was not a citizen. Cf. the case of Athenodoros, an *isoteles* resident in Ephesos *ca.* 300 B.C. (J. Keil and G. Maresch, *ÖJh* 45, 1960, Beiblatt, cols. 77–80, no. 5), and others assembled by Robert, *op. cit.*, pp. 18–27.

HONORS FOR A BOARD OF OFFICIALS(?)

204. A slim fragment of the upper section of a stele of Pentelic marble (I 23), broken all around but with the top of the inscribed surface preserved below the remains of a crowning molding, discovered on June 9, 1931, at a Late Roman level east of the central part of the Metroon (I 9). The marble is of particularly good quality and very honey-colored.

H. 0.20 m.; W. 0.07 m.; Th. 0.078 m.
LH. 0.006 m.

Ed. B. D. Meritt, *Hesperia* 3, 1934, p. 9, no. 11, with photograph; further comment on and restoration of lines 6–8 by Meritt, *Hesperia* 13, 1944, p. 248. See also *SEG* XXXVIII, 88.

ca. med. saec. III *a.*   quasi-ΣTOIX. *ca.* 54

```
     ['Επὶ ------ ἄρχοντος ἐπὶ τῆς ------------πρυταν]εί[ας ἧι --]
     [------------------ ἐγραμμάτευεν· ------ ὦνο]ς δ[------]
     [------------------ τῆς πρυτανείας· ἐκκλ]ησ[ία κυρία· τῶν πρ]
     [οέδρων ἐπεψήφιζεν ------------------]ς χα[ὶ συμπρόεδροι]·
  5  [     vacat      ἔδοξεν ------------]     vacat
     [-------------εἶπεν· ἐπειδὴ οἱ ------]ι οἱ χ[ειροτονηθέντ]
     [ες εἰς τὸν ἐπὶ ------- ἄρχοντος ἐνιαυτὸν τ]ὴν πᾶσ[αν ἐπιμέλειαν]
     [ἐποιήσαντο ὅπως ------------------χ]αὶ ε[---------]
     [----------------------------------------]
```

In his edition of **209**, Meritt noted that its style of writing was so comparable with that of this fragment that the two texts were at one time thought to belong together. The observation was well made. More than forty years later, S. V. Tracy developed a study of the lettering of these and comparable texts into the identification of them as the work of an individual craftsman, whom he named the "Cutter of *IG* II² 788" and to whom he attributed a total of some fifty inscriptions, spread through a career of some twenty-seven years, from *ca.* 262 to 235/4 B.C. Ten decrees from the Agora, the present text among them, make a considerable contribution to this number; the other nine are **208–213** and **216–218**. See *Hesperia* 57, 1988, pp. 311–322 (for this text, esp. p. 321), with a photograph of part of the name piece pl. 86, *Hesperia* 59, 1990, pp. 543–547. For the characteristics of this mason's workmanship, both in general style and in individual letters, see *Hesperia* 57, 1988, pp. 311–312. On the attribution to a single craftsman or to a workshop following a common general pattern cf. the commentary to **194**.

The interlinear distances vary, and there is a double space between lines 4 and 6 which surely betrays the existence of the "perfect design" isolating the enactment formula ἔδοξεν κτλ. from the rest of the prescript into a separate line. On this see S. Dow, *AJA* 40, 1936, pp. 64–66 and A. S. Henry, *Prescripts*, pp. 67–69. Henry noted *IG* II², 778 and 781 (both, as it has proved, works of this mason), of the archonship of Thersilochos (see p. 294 below), as the earliest datable examples of this attractive arrangement. Tracy, who also noted the likelihood of the "perfect design" in line 5, though envisaging a slightly different arrangement of the text than that shown above, regards the evidence as suggesting that "rather than being a style of the time, as Dow thought, it was a mannerism of this particular cutter" (*Hesperia* 57, 1988, p. 321). But it is to be found in texts of the period of the cutter's activity which are not from his hand: **205**, for example.

Lines 6–8 are restored in accordance with conventional formulas. Cf. *IG* II², 779, 1227, 1286; *SEG* XXI, 526. Χειροτονηθείς, like αἱρεθείς, presumably lays more emphasis on the fact of election to the office in question than the equally formulaic κατασταθείς or γενόμενος, but in practice the phraseology may have been too stereotyped to allow significance to these nuances.

AN ATHENIAN COUNCILLOR HONORED FOR SPECIAL SERVICES

205. A fragment of a stele of honey-colored Pentelic marble (I 5760), with the right side and original rough-picked back preserved, discovered on April 5, 1939, in a modern wall west of the Panathenaic Way and southwest of the Eleusinion (S 22). The inscribed surface is sheared off to the right of the fragment and does not extend to the preserved right edge.

H. 0.27 m.; W. 0.19 m.; Th. 0.135 m.
LH. 0.006 m.
Στοιχ. (square) *ca.* 0.015 m.

Ed. B. D. Meritt, *Hesperia* 30, 1961, p. 258, no. 61, with photograph pl. 47. See also *SEG* XXI, 360.

saec. III *a., p. prior*   ΣΤΟΙΧ. 28

```
        [------------------------]
        [.........17.........· τ]ῶν [προέδρων]
        [ἐπεψήφιζεν ...7...]ίας Κ[...7...]
        [.....12..... καὶ σ]υμπρόε[δροι· ℣]
        [℣℣℣℣ ἔδοξεν τεῖ βο]υλεῖ· ℣℣℣[℣℣℣℣]
   5    [.......15.......]ου Πιθεὺς ε[ἶπεν]·
        [ἐπειδὴ ...8.... β]ουλεύειν λ[αχὼν]
        [ἐπὶ ...7... ἄρχο]ντος καλῶς [καὶ δι]
        [καίως διατετέλεχ]ε τὸν ἐνια[υτὸν ε]
        [ὔνους καὶ φιλοτιμ]ούμενος ἀ[εὶ περ]
  10    [ὶ τὴν πρὸς τοὺς θεο]ὺς εὐσέβε[ιαν κα]
        [ὶ τὸ τῆς πόλεως συμ]φέρον, καὶ [πρεσβ]
        [εύων ἐν ταῖς πρεσβ]είαις αἴ[τιος ἐγ]
        [ένετο ....11.....]ιδι[....9....]
        [........16.......]νο[....10....]
  15    [------------------------]
```

The clear, well-spaced, and generally well-formed and accurate lettering, with some occasional enlargement of the "free ends" of the strokes, seems better attributed to the early part of the 3rd century B.C., and the text was indeed dated "*init. saec.* III *a.*" by Meritt. A good parallel might be found in *IG* II², 716 + 1226 (M. J. Osborne, *Naturalization* I, pp. 182–185, D 86, *Naturalization* II, pp. 170–171).

There are however other indications of date which appear to be in some disagreement with this criterion:

(1) *IG* II², 716 seemed to J. Kirchner, on the basis of its lettering, to belong to the 4th century. *IG* II², 697 (*SEG* XXI, 356), which also appears to offer a stylistic parallel, while once thought to belong early in the 3rd century, is now associated with the archonship of Philinos, for whose date see p. 284 above. Cf. Meritt, *Hesperia* 38, 1969, pp. 432–434.

(2) The formula in lines 6–7 is not otherwise attested before the mid 250's (*IG* II², 678; *SEG* XXI, 377; *Agora* XV, 85).

(3) The arrangement in lines 3–5, by which the formula of enactment ἔδοξεν τεῖ βουλεῖ is isolated and centered in a separate line, is an example of the "perfect design", which S. Dow particularly associated with the middle of the 3rd century and of which there is no datable evidence earlier than the archonship of Thersilochos in the early 240's. See on **204**, and A. S. Henry, *Prescripts*, p. 65, where lines 1–5 of the text are quoted.

(4) The possibilities for the name of the archon in line 7, if the first half of the century be surveyed, are four only: Charinos (291/90), Kimon (288/7), Gorgias (280/79), and Philinos (252/1?).

It seems preferable therefore to attribute this text to a date later than that given in the *editio princeps*, despite a certain conservatism of style, and to suggest more specifically the year following the archonship of Philinos, thus 251/50(?) or on other reckoning 254/3(?). If it belongs to the 291–279 period, its avant-garde arrangement must be allowed to precede by a quarter of a century other examples of the same character.

The restorations are those of Meritt. There are slight changes from the reading of the *editio princeps* in lines 1, 6, 13, and 14.

A BOARD OF EPIMELETAI(?) HONORED

206 (Pl. 17). Two joining fragments of Hymettian marble (I 220), with the left edge and original back preserved but with the inscribed surface badly worn, discovered on April 18, 1932, among repair slabs over the Great Drain east of the Metroon (I 9). Other fragments of the same stele were found in the same area, on which the lettering had been entirely worn away.

Measurements as joined: H. 0.41 m.; W. 0.28 m.; Th. 0.075 m.
LH. 0.008 m.
Στοιχ. (almost square, and with syllabic division perhaps not regularly applied) Hor. *ca.* 0.012 m.; Vert. 0.0125 m.

Ed. B. D. Meritt, *Hesperia* 3, 1934, p. 7, no. 8; a better text by Meritt after restudy in *Hesperia* 15, 1946, pp. 189–190, no. 36.

saec. III *a.*, *p. prior*   ΣΤΟΙΧ. 29

```
        [---------------------]
        [.]τυχ[..........25..........]
        [.]εσο[..........25..........]
        [.]ιδο[..........25..........]
        ἐπιμελ[ητα.........20.........]
  5     'Αντιπ[ατρο(?)........20........]
        στρα[...........25..........]
        ευ[-------------------]
        [.....16.....]ΙΟΝ[....10....]
        [......15......]ηθηντ[...9....]
 10     [......15...... Θ]ουδόσι[ον..5..]
        [......15.......]ιέα εὐσεβ[είας ἒ ᵛ]
        [νεχα τῆς πρὸς τοὺς] θεοὺς χαὶ [φιλοτι]
        [μίας τῆς εἰς τὴν β]ουλὴν χαὶ τ[ὸν δῆ ᵛᵛ]
        [μον χαὶ στεφανῶσ]αι ἕχαστον [αὐτῶν ᵛ]
 15     [χρυσῶι στεφάνωι]· ἐπαινέσαι [δὲ χαὶ ᵛ]
        [......15...... 'Α]χαρνέα· ἀ[ναγρά ᵛ]
        [ψαι δὲ τόδε τὸ ψήφισ]μα χαὶ τὰ [..6...]
        [...7... τὸν γραμ]ματέα τὸν χ[ατὰ πρυ]
        [τανείαν ἐν στήλει] λιθίνει χ[αὶ στῆ ᵛ]
 20     [σαι.....12.....]ιωι· [--------]
        [---------------------]
```

The lettering is plain and regular without any notable characteristic. Omicron varies in size; sigma is unusually consistent in form. The strokes of epsilon and kappa in particular, however, are not well articulated. Restudy of the stone indicates that one more stoichos exists to the left on the upper fragment than was previously thought, and a few more letters have been discerned without adding significantly to the clarification of the contents.

The decree evidently bestowed honors on a board of officials, perhaps epimeletai (line 4), whose names seem to have been inscribed between lines 5 and 11.

Lines 11–14. For the virtues of the honorands see A. S. Henry, *Honours*, p. 10: the parallels in this form there quoted belong to the middle third of the century (one of them assuredly to 267/6). Line 15. The qualification χατὰ τὸν νόμον usually accompanying the grant of the stephanos is here omitted. Cf. Henry, *Honours*, p. 27.

Lines 17–18. τὰ [ἄλλα ψηφίσματα(?) Meritt; τὰ [προεψηφισμένα A. Wilhelm, in a letter to Meritt of August 21, 1947. Perhaps τὰ [τούτων ὀνόματα. Line 20. [ἐν τῶι 'Ελευσιν]ίωι Meritt, as consistent with the available space and naming a well-known locale for stelai. There are however reasons against the assumption that the *honorati* were epimeletai of the Mysteries; see Meritt, *Hesperia* 15, 1946, p. 190. The stone is broken at the relevant place, and while what is shown is a possible interpretation of the surviving traces, no more is visible than the upper curve of a circular letter flanked by two upright strokes.

FRAGMENT OF AN HONORARY DECREE

207. A fragment of a stele of Pentelic marble (I 4606), broken on all sides except for part of the rough-picked back, discovered on March 12, 1937, at the surface on the North Slope of the Akropolis, in the area of the Post-Herulian Wall (T 24–25).

H. 0.278 m.; W. 0.215 m.; Th. 0.111 m.
LH. 0.007–0.009 m.

Ed. B. D. Meritt, *Hesperia* 23, 1954, p. 233, no. 1, with photograph pl. 49. See also *SEG* XIV, 59; J. and L. Robert, *REG* 68, 1955, p. 207, no. 68.

saec. III *a., p. prior*

(*in corona*)
Ἡ β ουλὴ
Φιλισ τίδην.

The writing is rough, and although Meritt gave it a dating "*saec.* IV/III *a.*" in the *editio princeps*, it is tempting to refer the inscription more definitely to the 3rd century. It is however not as late in date as **237**, where Meritt discussed but rejected a possible association of the Phil—— there honored with the Philistides of this text. The two stones are not part of the same inscription: see Meritt, *Hesperia* 29, 1960, p. 11. That text too is now to be dated some forty or more years later than the date attributed to it when it was first published.

The two lines of text represent a citation from an honorary decree in the course of which a stephanos was awarded to the otherwise unknown Philistides and are written within a corona of leaves and berries, in a complex design, engraved in outline. They are bisected vertically by a lancelike shaft, notched, and pointed at the base, which J. and L. Robert describe more vaguely as "une sorte de bandelette". At the upper left of the fragment, uncertain remains of another "relief", similarly engraved in outline, are visible. Traces of the working of a toothed chisel form a diagonal pattern (from upper right to lower left) on the inscribed face.

THE ARCHONSHIP OF THERSILOCHOS, 248/7 OR 247/6 B.C.

The γραμματεύς of Thersilochos' year, Diodotos, son of Diognetos, of Phrearrhioi belonged to Leontis, the phyle sixth in the "official" order (cf. *IG* II², 780B, 781, and 782, the other decrees of the Athenian people attributable to Thersilochos' archonship). That the year preceded that of Polyeuktos was established by the ephebic decree *Hesperia* 7, 1938, pp. 121–123, no. 24, in which the ephebes and their instructors of Thersilochos' year were honored in that of Polyeuktos. Before that connection was known, Thersilochos, placed by *IG* II², 780B and 2856 (for which see p. 284 above) in the neighborhood of Kleomachos and Kallimedes, was most generally assigned to 244/3; but dates for him as far apart as 288/7 and 233/2 had been proposed, and W. B. Dinsmoor in 1931 saw reason to decide for 235/4 (*Archons of Athens*, pp. 55, 181–182).

Apart from a further connection, via prosopographical evidence, with the archonship of Hieron (*IG* II², 1317b, addenda, p. 673), nothing beyond the lettering of *IG* II², 778/9, 780B, and 781/2, the historical allusions of 778 (of which nothing certainly was known but much surmised), and the position of the archonship in the secretary cycle were available as criteria. A decree of a thiasos from Salamis (*SEG* II, 9) had, however, established Polyeuktos, Hieron, and Diomedon as a group of consecutive archons, and Thersilochos' attachment to the beginning of it caused him to be placed in 249/8 by Dinsmoor, after a long analysis of the evidence for Polyeuktos and Diomedon (*Athenian Archon List*, p. 152, following pp. 65–140). This was amended to 250/49 by W. K. Pritchett and B. D. Meritt (*Chronology*, p. xxi), who moved the whole group back by one year in order to accommodate Lysitheides in 246/5. Dinsmoor retained this dating even after it was found that Lysitheides belonged to 272/1 (see p. 266 above), and the mutually interdependent framework seemed for some time thereafter to keep Thersilochos in that year. Cf. Meritt, *Athenian Year*, p. 234, *Historia* 26, 1977, p. 175.

The background to all this was discussed at some length by C. Habicht, *Untersuchungen*, pp. 116–133, 142–146. Part of his conclusion was to move Thersilochos to 247/6, a date already proposed by G. Nachtergael in 1976 (*Historia* 25, p. 77), the issue in essence hinging upon the date of Polyeuktos and the founding at Delphi of the festival of the Soteria, accepted at Athens in his archonship (*IG* II², 680). In the light of these studies (while believing that Nachtergael's dating was a year too late), Meritt revised his previous opinions and placed Thersilochos accordingly in 248/7 (*Hesperia* 50, 1981, pp. 80–82, 95): this continued to accord with his interpretation of a secretary cycle regular until the archonship of Diomedon. M. J. Osborne's abandonment of that criterion did not of course affect the grouping of archons of which Thersilochos stands at the head, nor the issue of the Delphic Soteria. On this latter he supported Nachtergael and Habicht and saw further reason from **208** to reinforce the conclusion that 247/6 was Thersilochos' year (*ZPE* 78, 1989, pp. 218–219, 241).

The year of Thersilochos was demonstrably ordinary in the festival calendar of Athens, and if the general correspondence between that calendar and the Metonic cycle was still being adhered to (see p. 284 above), this fact would support either year under scrutiny; for 248/7 and 247/6 were the fourteenth and fifteenth years of the tenth cycle, and both were scheduled in it as ordinary years (cf. Meritt, *TAPA* 95, 1964, p. 236, with note 122). The data in **208** show an exact correspondence between the festival and prytany calendars in the second prytany. *IG* II², 780B and 781 show the prytany calendar in advance by three days in the month Elaphebolion, which (with the adjustment of one day) would be the result of a delay in the preponderance of 30-day prytanies until late in the year: cf. Meritt, *Athenian Year*, pp. 136–137. *IG* II², 781 was passed on the same day as 780B and offers no additional evidence. Calendric data are not preserved on *IG* II², 782, do not exist on 779 (which represents the implementation of **208**), and do not assist on *SEG* II, 10, a thiasotic decree of this year.

The only prytany in which a phyle is identifiable is the second, recorded in **208**, and this was held by either Aiantis or Leontis.

THE CITY OF LAMIA HONORED FOR ARBITRATION IN A DISPUTE BETWEEN ATHENS AND BOIOTIA

208 (Pl. 21). A fragment of a stele of Pentelic marble (I 4622), with the left edge and the original back preserved, broken elsewhere and very battered especially at the top and on the left, discovered on March 10, 1937, in a marble pile on the North Slope of the Areopagos. Its top edge was found to make a join with the bottom of *IG* II², 778 (henceforward fragment *a*), and the striations of a toothed chisel are noticeable on the inscribed surface of both fragments.

Measurements as joined: H. 0.445 m.; W. 0.146 m.; Th. 0.093 m.
LH. 0.005 m. (phi and psi 0.007 m.).
Στοιχ. (almost square) Hor. 0.01 m.; Vert. 0.012 m.

Ed. both fragments: B. D. Meritt, *Hesperia* 7, 1938, pp. 118–121, no. 23, with photograph. See also H. H. Schmitt, *Staatsverträge* III, 1969, p. 159, no. 487. Text reprinted, with a lemma noting discussion of matter derived from the text, *SEG* XXXII, 117.

a. 248/7 *a. vel* 247/6 *a., pryt.* II   ΣΤΟΙΧ. 33

(a)
        Ἐπὶ Θερσιλόχου ἄρχοντος ἐ[πὶ τῆς ... ντὶ]
        [δ]ος δευτέρας πρυτανείας ᵛ ἧ[ι Διόδοτος Δ]
        ιογνήτου Φρεάρριος ἐγραμμ[άτευεν· Μετα]
        γειτνιῶνος δωδεκάτηι, δωδε[κάτηι τῆς πρ]
5   υτανείας· ᵛ ἐκκλησία κυρία· τ[ῶν προέδρων]
        ἐπεψήφιζεν ᵛ Πυθογένης Γλαυ[κίππου Ἁλω]
        πεκῆθεν καὶ συμπρόεδροι·   *vacat*
        ᵛᵛᵛ ἔδοξεν τῆι βουλῆι καὶ τῶ[ι δήμωι· ᵛᵛᵛᵛ]
        Καλάτδης Καλάτδου Ξυπεταιὼν [εἶπεν· ἐπε]
10   ιδὴ τοῦ δήμου τοῦ Ἀθηναίων καὶ [τοῦ κοινο]
        ῦ τοῦ Βοιωτῶν σύμβολον ποιησαμ[ένων πρὸ]
        ς ἀλλήλους καὶ ἑλομένων ἔκκλητ[ον τὴν Λα]
        μιέων πόλιν, ἀνεδέξατο καθιεῖν [τὸ δικασ]
        τήριον καὶ νῦν οἱ ἀποσταλέντε[ς ὑπὸ τῶν Λ]
15   [αμιέων] ἐπὶ [τὰς] δ[ί]κας ἀποφα[ίνουσιν ....]
        [––––––––––––––––––––––––––––––]

(b)
        [. .]Ε[––––––––––––––––––––––––––]
        [.]ΚΝ[.....¹²....., δεδόχθαι τῆι βουλῆι τ]

οὓς λαχ[όντας προέδρους εἰς τὴν ἐπιοῦσα]
20   ν ἐκκλησί[αν χρηματίσαι περὶ τούτων, γνώ]
μην δὲ ξυμβ[άλλεσθαι τῆς βουλῆς εἰς τὸν δ]
ῆμον ὅτι δο[κεῖ τῆι βουλῆι ᵛ ἐπαινέσαι τὴ]
ν πόλιν τῶν Λ[αμιέων καὶ στεφανῶσαι αὐτὴ]
ν χρυσῶι στε[φάνωι κατὰ τὸν νόμον εὐνοία]
25   ς ἕνεκα ἣν ἔχ[ουσα διατελεῖ περὶ τὸν δῆμο]
ν τὸν Ἀθηναίω[ν, ᵛ καὶ ἀναγορεῦσαι τὸν στέ]
φανον Διονυσ[ίων τῶν μεγάλων καινοῖς τρ]
αγωιδοῖς καὶ [Παναθηναίων τῶν μεγάλων τ]
ῶι γυμνικῶι ἀ[γῶνι· ᵛ τῆς δὲ ποιήσεως τοῦ σ]
30   τεφάνου κα[ὶ τῆς ἀναγορεύσεως ἐπιμεληθ]
ῆναι [τὸν ἐπὶ τῆι διοικήσει· . . . .¹¹. . . . .]
[————————————————————]

This text, which Kirchner described as exhibiting "litterae bonae", is a product of the personal skill, or at least of the workshop, of the "Cutter of *IG* II² 788", as identified by S. V. Tracy: for details and references see the commentary on **204**. Line 8 provides an example of this craftsman's penchant for the "perfect design", discussed in the same context.

Line 2. Diodotos, son of Diognetos, of Phrearrhioi (*PA* 3907) is not known other than in virtue of his office in this year. Lines 3–4. For Metageitnion 12 as a meeting day of the assembly see J. D. Mikalson, *Sacred and Civil Calendar*, pp. 38–39. This text constitutes the sole evidence for it.

Line 6. Pythogenes, son of Glaukippos, of Alopeke. See *PA* 12374. A century earlier, a likely ancestor Glaukippos, son of Glaukon, was a member of a board of officials who dedicated *IG* II², 2826. Line 8. The decree was probouleumatic: cf. P. J. Rhodes, *Athenian Boule*, p. 253. Line 9. Kalaides, son of Kalaides, of Xypete (*PA* 7747) also proposed *IG* II², 779, which appears to put into effect part of this present decree. The name is extremely rare. A Kalaides, son of Lytides, dedicated *IG* II², 4610 to Bona Fortuna and has been restored as a councillor of 304/3 in *Agora* XV, 61, line 1, in which year he also proposed *SEG* XXXVI, 165. In the 3rd century another Kalaides (or indeed perhaps the proposer of the present decree himself) was subjected along with others to a curse (*IG* III, iii, 23, line 6).

Line 12. Ἔκκλητος πόλις. The city called upon to be arbiter. See M. N. Tod, *GHI* II, pp. 131–132, *International Arbitration amongst the Greeks*, 1913, p. 61.

Line 18. Meritt restored EI in τῆι βουλῆι and is followed in *SEG* XXXII, 117: but HI is used or restored in the dative feminine singular elsewhere in this text.

Line 24. On the gold stephanos κατὰ τὸν νόμον cf. **112**, commentary on lines 5–7 and **141**. For the "more elaborate formulation" of the virtues ascribed to the Lamians cf. A. S. Henry, *Honours*, pp. 43–44.

Lines 26–29. The announcement of the honors is to be made at the Greater Dionysia and the Greater Panathenaia. A celebration of the Lesser Panathenaia had only just taken place (Hekatombaion 28), the decree being enacted a mere two weeks later. There was a celebration of the Greater Panathenaia in 246/5, and M. J. Osborne (*ZPE* 78, 1989, pp. 218–219; cf. *SEG* XXXIX, 130) regarded this as a conclusive argument for the dating of Thersilochos' archonship. Were that date to be the year 248/7, the Lamians would have had to wait two years all but fourteen days for their announcement. It may be noted that, when the decree was thought to date to 244/3, also two years before a celebration of the festival, Meritt found the delay worthy of remark. He used it to argue that such a reference did not necessarily imply (as had already been contended) that the decree containing it must be dated in the year immediately preceding a Greater Panathenaia: with Thersilochos' year later held to be 250/49, an even greater delay was not regarded as of consequence. The argument for 247/6 is indeed not necessarily decisive on that score. The holding back of the announcement (already made at a celebration of the Greater Dionysia and so not without its publicity) to the more important festival suggested the greater honor and would repeat, after an interval, a public reminder of the Lamians' services. For the announcement of honors at these and similar festivals, using the less common formula with ἀναγορεῦσαι rather than with ἀνειπεῖν, cf. Henry, *Honours*, pp. 33 and 55, note 82. *IG* II², 682 (the honorary decree for Phaidros of Sphettos, of 255/4?), lines 75–78, offers an almost exact parallel to the phraseology of the present example. Lines 29–31. The Single Officer ἐπὶ τῇ διοικήσει is likely to have had the responsibility for the stephanos and its proclamation, as in *IG* II², 682, lines 78–80. This was not inevitable, especially perhaps where foreigners were concerned; cf. *IG* II², 693. But that the Single Officer did indeed act in these cases also is shown by *IG* II², 708.

The circumstances which called forth Lamian arbitration are not known. When Thersilochos' archonship was dated later than 245, the inscription was used as evidence that the Boiotians' freedom of action had not been wholly extinguished by their defeat by the Aitolians at Chaironeia and that an Aitolian city, Lamia, could arbitrate from an independent position: cf. W. W. Tarn, *Antigonos Gonatas*, 1913, pp. 384–385, *CAH* VII, 1928, pp. 732–733. On the events of, and leading to, that battle see Plutarch, *Aratus* 16, and cf. J. A. O. Larsen, *Greek Federal States*, 1968, pp. 206 and 306; F. W. Walbank, *Aratus of Sicyon*, 1933, pp. 42–43. The arbitration, as now clearly appears, preceded the battle of Chaironeia by two or three years and cannot be brought into connection with it, so that its evidential value for the history of the period remains obscure. The general tenor of the decree seems to accord with the existence of a Boiotia enjoying the greater independence of the years before its crushing defeat at Aitolian hands. Probably the most that can be said is briefly stated in a short paragraph by C. Habicht, *Studien*, p. 25.

REPLY TO AN EMBASSY FROM SMYRNA

209. A fragment of a stele of Pentelic marble (I 672), broken on all sides, discovered on April 5, 1933, in a late context in the north porch of the Library of Pantainos (Q 13).

H. 0.165 m.; W. 0.147 m.; Th. 0.06 m.
LH. 0.005 m.
Στοιχ. Hor. 0.0094 m.; Vert. 0.014 m.

Ed. B. D. Meritt, *Hesperia* 13, 1944, pp. 246–249, no. 9, with photograph of a squeeze. See also J. and L. Robert, *REG* 57, 1944, p. 192, no. 59.

a. 246 a.(?)   ΣΤΟΙΧ.

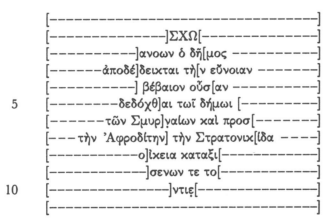

S. V. Tracy has attributed this text also to the professional activity of the craftsman he named the "Cutter of *IG* II² 788": for details and references see the commentary on **204**.

Lines 1–6. For Meritt's text see below. Line 2. δι]ανοῶν J. and L. Robert. Line 8. ο]ἰκεῖα κατάξι[α(?) Meritt. Line 10. Perhaps ντιπ.

The reference in line 7 allows the decree to be connected with the recognition by Seleukos II of the right of *asylia* at the precinct of Aphrodite Stratonikis in Smyrna (cf. line 6) and with his request to the Hellenic world in general to grant the same recognition. His letter on the subject to Delphi, reinforced by the presence of two ambassadors from the Smyrnaians, evoked the response set out in *OGIS* 228. The circumstances and details are more fully recorded in the lengthy treaty of *sympoliteia* between Smyrna and Magnesia-ad-Sipylum: see *OGIS* 229; H. H. Schmitt, *Staatsverträge* III, pp. 163–173, no. 492; *Die Inschriften von Magnesia am Sipylos* (T. Ihnken, ed.), no. 1 (cf. *SEG* XXVIII, 909); *Die Inschriften von Smyrna* (G. Petzl, ed.), no. 573 (these last two being *Inschriften griechischer Städte aus Kleinasien* 8 and 24, i, respectively). Meritt used phraseology from lines 8–9 of the Delphic reply as a restoration for the first line of the present text and restored lines 1–6 with a stoichedon pattern of 49 letters as follows:

[--καὶ τήν τε ὑπάρ]
[χουσαν αὐτοῖ]ς χώ[ραν βεβαιοῖ καὶ τὴν πάτριον ἐπαγγέλλεται]
[ἀποδώσειν]· ἃ νοῶν ὁ δῆ[μος ὁ Σμυρναίων πρεσβευτὰς ἀπέσταλκε]
[καὶ ἀποδέ]δεικται τὴ[ν εὔνοιαν τοῦ βασιλέως Σελεύκου εἱλικ]

[ρινῆ καὶ] βέβαιον οὖσ[αν πρὸς τὴν πόλιν αὐτῶν καὶ πρὸς τὸ ἱερό]

5   [ν· δεδόχθ]αι τῶι δήμωι [ἐπαινέσαι τοὺς ἥχοντας πρεσβευτὰς πα]

[ρὰ Σμυρν]αίων κτλ.

(In line 1 πάτριον is a correction by J. and L. Robert for Meritt's original πατρίδα.)

The Delphians gave their answer to Smyrna in a year in which the Pythian games were celebrated. With Seleukos II Kallinikos already on the throne of Syria, this must be 246 or 242. Meritt preferred 246 on the supposition that the Smyrnaians accepted the Aitolian Soteria earlier rather than later, perhaps by the agency of the same two ambassadors who approached the Athenians (*Fouilles de Delphes* III, i, pp. 296–297, no. 483; cf. *SEG* XXXIV, 381). Thus a comparable date may be set for the present text, with which C. Habicht also agreed in a brief allusion to it (*Studien*, p. 25 with note 61). For earlier bibliography see W. B. Dinsmoor, *Athenian Archon List*, pp. 117–118, to which add T. J. Cadoux, *Ancient Smyrna*, 1938, pp. 116–118; Cadoux was among those preferring the year 242 for these events; Schmitt (*loc. cit.*) gave the date as "kurz nach 243(?)". 246 has however been strongly advocated by Ihnken (*loc. cit.*) and is the preferable choice: cf. A. G. Woodhead, *JHS* 102, 1982, p. 295. S. Elwyn (*JHS* 110, 1990, pp. 177–180) argues for 243 as the date of the Delphic response to Smyrna.

For this as the first instance of an increasingly claimed and granted right of asylum cf. W. W. Tarn and G. T. Griffith, *Hellenistic Civilisation*, 3rd ed., 1952, pp. 82–84; F. W. Walbank, *The Hellenistic World*, 1981, pp. 145–151.

TWO FRAGMENTS OF A DECREE

210. Two fragments of a stele of gray marble (I 1497), both of which preserve the smooth left side of the monument but are broken elsewhere, discovered on March 10, 1934, in a late fill north of the Tholos (G 11).

a: H. 0.135 m.; W. 0.04 m.; Th. 0.082 m.

b: H. 0.121 m.; W. 0.04 m.; Th. 0.038 m.

LH. 0.005 m.

Ed. S. V. Tracy, *Hesperia* 57, 1988, pp. 315–316, no. 3, with photographs pl. 87. See also *SEG* XXXVIII, 93.

ca. a. 245 a.   ΣΤΟΙΧ.

```
(a)   [————————————————————]
      E[———————————————————]
      ΝΣΟ[—————————————————]
      ΡΧΟ[—————————————————]
      ΙΔ[——————————————————]
  5   ΙΠ[——————————————————]
      ΙΤ[——————————————————]
      ΚΑ[——————————————————]
      [.]Ε[—————————————————]
      Χ[———————————————————]
 10   Ι[———————————————————]
      [————————————————————]
                lacuna
      [————————————————————]
(b)   ΥΠ[——————————————————]
      ΜΑΤ[—————————————————]
      ΣΑ[——————————————————]
                vacat
```

Sufficient lettering is preserved on these small fragments for Tracy to have been able to ascribe them to the "Cutter of *IG* II² 788", for whose characteristics see the commentary on **204**. The dating proposed is an arbitrary attribution to the middle part of his known datable career. Examination of the left margins of the two pieces suggests that the stele tapered towards the top. A careful erasure in line 8 of fragment *a* was interpreted in the *editio princeps* as evidence of an original reference to Antigonos Monophthalmos, Demetrios Poliorketes, or both.

Fragment *b*: Tracy advanced a possible restoration to provide a line of 43 letters as follows:

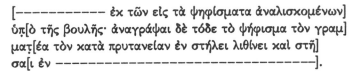

[––––––––––– ἐκ τῶν εἰς τὰ ψηφίσματα ἀναλισκομένων]
ὑπ[ὸ τῆς βουλῆς· ἀναγράψαι δὲ τόδε τὸ ψήφισμα τὸν γραμ]
ματ[έα τὸν κατὰ πρυτανείαν ἐν στήλει λιθίνει καὶ στῆ]
σα[ι ἐν ––––––––––––––––––––––––––––––––].

Although the *editio princeps* did not quote it, this phraseology may be paralleled by *Agora* XV, 78 (of 273/2 B.C.), lines 20–23, suggesting that the words πόρον δὲ ὑπάρχειν could precede the above restoration and that τῶι πρυτανικῶι could well follow it: cf. *Agora* XV, 77, lines 30–34. If that is so, this text should be classified as a prytany decree and as such will more properly belong in that collection as an addendum to *Agora* XV. These parallels are however too early for the *floruit* of the craftsman of this text, and the formula is not in evidence in the surviving prytany texts of his period. It seems out of place in decrees of the normal character, for which the people's expense account, rather than that of the Council, had met the cost. For the Council's expense account cf. P. J. Rhodes, *Athenian Boule*, pp. 103–104.

FRAGMENT OF A DECREE

211. A small fragment of a stele of gray marble (I 3870), broken on all sides and at the back, discovered on March 28, 1936, in a marble pile in the western part of the Odeion.

H. 0.055 m.; W. 0.11 m.; Th. 0.055 m.
LH. 0.005–0.006 m.

Ed. S. V. Tracy, *Hesperia* 57, 1988, pp. 316–317, no. 4, with photograph pl. 87. See also *SEG* XXXVIII, 92.

ca. a. 245 *a.*   ΣΤΟΙΧ.

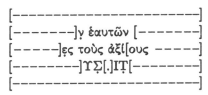

[––––––––––––––––––––]
[–––––––]ν ἑαυτῶν [–––––––]
[–––––]ες τοὺς ἀξί[ους –––––]
[–––––––––]ΥΣ[.]ΙΤ[––––––––]
[––––––––––––––––––––]

Line 2. [––––τιμῶντ]ες(?) τοὺς ἀξί[ους τῶν –––––] Tracy, who compared (e.g.) *IG* II², 1028, line 94.

The style of a dozen clearly seen letters was sufficiently characteristic for this fragment to be listed among the works of the "Cutter of *IG* II² 788", for whom see the commentary on **204**. As in the case of **210** and **212**, the date shown is for convenience set at the midpoint of the craftsman's attested career.

A CITIZEN OF THE DEME ALOPEKE HONORED

212. A fragment of a stele of Hymettian marble (I 4526), with the right side and original back preserved, discovered on February 16, 1937, in a modern wall on the North Slope of the Areopagos (M 18). The stone is very "craggy", and the inscribed surface is in places badly pitted.

H. 0.11 m.; W. 0.175 m.; Th. 0.068 m.
LH. 0.005 m.
Στοιχ. Hor. 0.095 m.; Vert. 0.011 m.

Ed. B. D. Meritt, *Hesperia* 29, 1960, pp. 7–8, no. 9, with photograph pl. 2. See also *SEG* XIX, 72.

ca. a. 245 *a.*(?)   ΣΤΟΙΧ. 54(?)

[––––––––––––––––––––––––––––––––––––––]
[–––––––––––––––––––––––––––––––––] ἐπαινέσ[αι ..]
[–––––––––––––––––––––––––––] ᾿Αλωπ]εκῆθεν καὶ στεφα[νῶ]
[σαι –––––––––––––––––––––––––ἀ]ρετῆς ἕνεκα καὶ εὐ ^{v}
[νοίας ἣν ἔχων διατελεῖ εἰς τὴν βουλὴν καὶ τὸν δ]ῆμον καὶ τὸ ναυτι ^{vv}
5   [κὸν –––––––––––––––––––––– · ἀναγ]ράψαι δὲ τόδε τὸ ψή ^{v}
[φισμα –––––––––––––––––––]ς τῶν τριηρ[άρχων ^{vv}]
[–––––––––––––––––––––––––]ΙΝΚΑ[......^{12}......]
[–––––––––––––––––––––––––]ΤΥΑ[......^{13}......]
[––––––––––––––––––––––––––––––]

This text, like **204**, **208–211**, **213**, and **216–218**, has been attributed by S. V. Tracy to the workshop of the "Cutter of *IG* II² 788". Lacking other indications of date, it is for convenience assigned here (as in the case of **210** and **211**) to the middle point of the datable span of that identified style for which evidence exists (*ca.* 255–235/4). See the commentary on **204** for details and references. This ascription revises by half a century the original dating offered in the *editio princeps* and accepted by commentators since then, which had its basis in Meritt's interpretation of line 8 (see below). The characteristics of the script were not seen by him as inconsistent with a date in the early 3rd century; in any event, if this stone does provide an example of the work of the "Cutter of *IG* II² 788", it is not one of his better pieces, with elements of the "careless style" of an earlier time. If it is the work of a less competent follower, however, it will presumably be attributable to the same general period as that of the master.

Lines 1–7. The restorations are those of Meritt, who based his proposed length of line on the formulas of lines 3–4 and 7–8. But it must be recognized that this appears to require a name and patronymic in lines 1–2 comprising thirty-six letters (or, if ἐπαινέσ[αι δὲ | καὶ – – –] be read, thirty-one letters), and more than one person may therefore have been named as in receipt of public honors. The services of the honorand(s) seem to have been connected with the navy: see the unusual formulation of line 4 and the apparent reference to trierarchs in line 6. It may be speculated what kind of navy the Athenians maintained at, or just after, the middle of the 3rd century. When the text was dated to the century's opening years, A. S. Henry (*Chiron* 14, 1984, p. 68, note 93) was prepared to suggest a connection between this decree and the ὑπηρεσίαι of **129**, lines 5–6.

The phraseology of lines 5–6, to which Meritt did not draw attention, evidently diverges from the normal pattern of instructions to the γραμματεύς, and the involvement of the trierarchs at this stage of the business remains unclear.

What most particularly dictated Meritt's attribution of this decree to the early 3rd century (and specifically to the period from 301/300 to 295/4), as well as reinforcing his opinion on the length of line in the text, was his interpretation of lines 7–9 as

[– – – – – – – – – – – – – – – – – – – –· εἰς δὲ τὴν ἀνάθεσ]ιν κα[ὶ τὴν ποίησιν ᵛ]
[τῆς στήλης δοῦναι τὸν ἐξεταστὴν καὶ τοὺς τριτ]τυά[ρχους τὸ γενόμε]
[νον ἀνάλωμα.   *vacat*   ]

SEG XIX, 72 reversed the order of the nouns in line 7 to the attested and more logical τὴν ποίησ]ιν κα[ὶ τὴν ἀνάθεσιν], thus also avoiding the vacant letter space at the end of the line: but the parallel is of considerably later date (*SEG* XXVIII, 75, lines 31–35). Cf. Henry, *Chiron* 14, 1984, pp. 67–68, *ZPE* 78, 1989, p. 270. For the exetastes and trittyarchs as the officers responsible for defraying the costs of stelai, see **129** and **162**. Their restoration here, on the basis of one clear and two fragmentary letters, even though Meritt claimed that the traces required it, was justly described by C. Habicht (*Untersuchungen*, p. 8, note 50) as "ganz zweifelhaft" and by Henry as flimsy. The revision of the date by Tracy invalidates the restoration altogether. Although line 5 seems to suggest that the conclusion of the text is near at hand, it is impossible to judge what additional measures may have been introduced into the lines immediately following or how much further the text may have extended. That the concluding formula τὸ γενόμενον ἀνάλωμα proposed by Meritt is unlikely in view of his dating (not attested before 266/5: see **177**, commentary on line 6) is no longer a relevant problem: in any event, a more satisfactory formulation could easily have been substituted. Cf. Henry, *Chiron* 14, 1984, p. 68.

THE ARCHONSHIP OF DIOMEDON, 245/4 OR 244/3 B.C.

Since the publication of *SEG* II, 9 it has been generally agreed that the archonship of Diomedon concluded a direct sequence of three archons (Polyeuktos, Hieron, Diomedon), to the beginning of which Thersilochos was also clearly to be attached. Thus the arguments that placed Thersilochos in 248/7 or 247/6 (see pp. 294–295 above) will place Diomedon in 245/4 or 244/3. For the revaluations of the evidence that have produced this result see the references to the work of G. Nachtergael, C. Habicht, B. D. Meritt, and M. J. Osborne there discussed. Whichever the absolute date advocated (differing only by a single year), the order and relationship of the archons concerned remain identical: see, e.g., Habicht, *Untersuchungen*, p. 143; Meritt, *Hesperia* 50, 1981, p. 95.

Diomedon's also proved to be a key archonship in that this close connection compelled the recognition of a break in the secretary cycle when he took office and introduced the subsequently developed argument that, if there was one break in this period, why should there not have been more than one? Or, further, why should the cycle be accorded any primary recognition in mid-3rd-century Athens? The γραμματεύς in the year of Hieron, who preceded Diomedon, was Phainylos, son of Pamphilos, of Oe (Oineis VIII); the phyle affiliation of Diomedon's γραμματεύς Phoryskides, son of Aristomenes, hinged on the interpretation of the initial letter, which alone survives, of his demotic in line 4 of **213**. For a summary of earlier discussions of this see W. B. Dinsmoor, *Archons of Athens*, pp. 96–99; J. Kirchner, *Athenian Studies Presented to W. S. Ferguson* (*HSCP* Supplement 1), 1940, pp. 503–507.

The earlier reconstructions, ignorant of *SEG* II, 9, accepting that Phoryskides was of Leukonoion (Leontis VI), had set Diomedon in a suitable context in the 230's or 220's within a regularly revolving cycle; but it had thereafter to be allowed that at this point there was an interruption of the pattern and that on this occasion Oineis VIII was succeeded by Leontis VI. The date that Dinsmoor advocated in his 1931 discussion of Diomedon's year, 247/6, was lowered by him to 246/5 in his 1939 reconsideration (*Athenian Archon List*, pp. 65–108). In the interim, Meritt in proposing Phoryskides' demotic as Δ[αιδαλίδης (Kekropis IX) had tried to preserve the secretary cycle without interruption, placing Diomedon in 253/2 (*Hesperia* 4, 1935, p. 585). Later, he lowered this date by a complete cycle and brought the archonship down to 241/40 (*Hesperia* 7, 1938, p. 136).

But the alpha of the demotic is not open to reasonable doubt, as was acknowledged by W. K. Pritchett and Meritt in *Chronology*, pp. 28–29, when they adopted Dinsmoor's 1939 estimate (*ibid.*, p. xxii), raising it by one year in order to insert Lysitheides (see p. 266), and thereby restored Diomedon to 247/6. The reading then adopted for the demotic of Phoryskides, 'Α[ναγυράσιος (Erechtheis III), must be replaced by 'Α[λωπεκῆθεν (Antiochis XII): see J. H. Kroll, *Hesperia* 46, 1977, pp. 121–122, no. 54; Meritt, *Historia* 26, 1977, pp. 163–164. The year 247/6 continued, from 1940 onwards, to be the accepted date for Diomedon (cf. Dinsmoor, *Hesperia* 23, 1954, p. 315; Meritt, *Athenian Year*, p. 234, *Historia* 26, 1977, p. 176) until the reopening of the discussion by Nachtergael caused the revisions already noted.

Diomedon's year was also, as it happened, the year in which an ἐξετασμός was made of the dedications in the sanctuary of Asklepios. His name appears in the record of this (*IG* II², 1534B) at line 162 and is restored in line 141 in the prescript of the decree authorizing the inventory. Pritchett and Meritt (*Chronology*, pp. 60–73), building on the "long and patient study" of their predecessors, argued that this survey covered two secretary cycles (in total, twenty years), beginning with the archonship of Peithidemos and ending with that of Hieron, and that a close relationship existed between that cycle and the cycle of the priests of Asklepios named in the inventory. The priestly cycles were further discussed by Habicht (*Studien*, pp. 64–78), where he agreed the relationship between them and the secretary cycles while (as noted above) redating the archons concerned. More recently, however, S. B. Aleshire (*The Athenian Asklepieion*, 1989, pp. 293–297), who designated *IG* II², 1534B "inventory V", with the references to Diomedon at lines 1 and 22, denied the contention that the inventory covers either two secretary cycles or two priestly cycles and argued that no conclusions may be drawn from it with regard to archon dates. That the survey was decreed in Diomedon's archonship thus had no bearing on the dating of the latter, which she accepted as 244/3. See pp. 275–276 above, on the archonship of Peithidemos.

213 offers, for additional dating control, historical and prosopographical considerations with which all the proposals mentioned above were required to harmonize; but these can be of limited effect in a span reduced to a choice between two successive years.

A decree of the thiasotai of Artemis of this year (*IG* II², 1298) was passed in the month Skirophorion but gives no further details of date. "Inventory V", line 1, shows Antigonis in office during the sixth prytany, but nothing more of the dating content of the prescript is preserved. Thus **213** alone illustrates the character of the year, which was clearly ordinary. See Pritchett and O. Neugebauer, *Calendars*, p. 82; Meritt, *Athenian Year*, pp. 137–138; Pritchett, *Ancient Athenian Calendars on Stone*, p. 341. The first six prytanies were of 29 days each, and the remainder of 30 days. In the festival calendar the months evidently alternated from a hollow Hekatombaion until Elaphebolion, when the month, scheduled as hollow, was made full (cf. the discussion of the year of Pytharatos, p. 268 above). Alternation will have proceeded regularly thereafter.

The years 245/4 and 244/3 were the seventeenth and eighteenth in the tenth Metonic cycle and in that cycle will have been ordinary and intercalary respectively. This would be an argument in support of the former date for Diomedon's archonship if the cycle and the Athenian festival calendar had preserved that concord which hitherto had generally obtained between them. But Meritt had himself been prepared to admit a lapse in the correspondence at this point (*Athenian Year*, p. 234 and *Historia* 26, 1977, pp. 163–164), even though he restored the proper sequence in his final version of the pattern of these years (*Hesperia* 50, 1981, p. 95): thus no argument can be derived from Meton's calendar. The nature of the years of Philoneos and Lysiades, both of whom have been urged for the year following that of Diomedon, is not known. That of Hieron, who preceded him, was certainly intercalary.

The phyle Antigonis held the sixth prytany (see above). The erased name of the phyle holding the tenth prytany in **213** must therefore be that of the other "Macedonian" phyle, Demetrias, as Dinsmoor appreciated long since: see the commentary on **213**, line 3.

DECREE CALLING FOR VOLUNTARY CONTRIBUTIONS TO A DEFENSE FUND

213. Two fragments of a slightly tapering stele of Hymettian marble, designated as *e* (I 4536 a) and *f* (I 4536 b), which were recognized to form part of *IG* II², 791, itself composed of four fragments of which three, *a–c*, join to form the upper left section (with pediment) of the stele. Fragment *e*, with the right side partly preserved but otherwise broken all around and with the inscribed surface badly worn, was discovered on February 24, 1937, in a late wall west of the Odeion (K 10). Fragment *f* has part of the left edge preserved but is otherwise broken all around; it was discovered on February 25, 1938, in a modern wall over the Post-Herulian Wall southeast of the Market Square (S 18). Fragments *a–d* had been discovered in the ruins of the Hypapanti church, in the same locality as fragment *f* but higher up the North Slope of the Akropolis.

The left side of fragment *e* makes a direct join with the right side of the united fragments *b + c*, giving the right sections of lines 13–29 of the decree and of the heading to the three columns of the names of the contributors (lines 30–32), as well as the first nine lines of the third column of names. A lacuna of uncertain length separates fragments *c + e* from fragment *d*. The top of fragment *f* makes a direct join with the bottom of fragment *d*, adding four more names to the foot of Column I and augmenting the remains of a fifth (lines 76–81), as well as adding one name to Column II and augmenting a second (lines 80–81). The long uninscribed space below the lowest names confirms that this is the end of the text.

Measurements of the Agora fragments only:
e: H. 0.336 m.; W. 0.155 m.; Th. 0.077 m.

f: H. 0.236 m.; W. 0.201 m.; Th. 0.065 m.

LH. 0.004 m. (lines 30–33 0.006 m.).

Στοιχ. (lines 13–29) Hor. 0.008 m.; Vert. 0.0098 m. The list of names is non-Στοιχ.

Ed. B. D. Meritt, *Hesperia* 11, 1942, pp. 287–292, no. 56, with complete text of all fragments and with photographs. Complete text also in *SEG* XXXII, 118, with references to material in *SEG* XXVI, 94 and XXIX, 113. Lines 5–6 quoted by Meritt, *Athenian Year*, p. 137; cf. W. K. Pritchett and O. Neugebauer, *Calendars*, p. 82. Lines 9–12, 16–17, 27–29 quoted by P. J. Rhodes, *Athenian Boule*, pp. 98, 231.

a. 245/4 *vel* 244/3 *a., pryt.* X   ΣΤΟΙΧ. 48 (lines 3–29)

```
          Ταμίας στρατιω[τικῶν]
          Εὐρυκλείδης Μικίωνος [Κηφισιεύς]
          ['Ε]πὶ Διομέδοντος ἄρχοντος ἐπὶ τῆς [[Δημητριάδος]] δεκάτης πρ]
          υτανείας ἧι Φορυσκίδης 'Αριστομένου 'Α[λωπεκῆθεν ἐγραμμά]
    5     [τε]υεν· ᵛ 'Ελαφηβολιῶνος ἕνει καὶ νέαι ἐμ[βολίμωι, δευτέραι τ]
          [ῆς] πρυτανείας· ἐκκλησία· τῶν προέδρων ἐ[πεψήφισζεν Καλλίσ]
          [τρ]ατος Τελεσίνου 'Ερχιε[ὺς κ]αὶ συμ[πρόεδροι]·
                    ἔδοξεν τῶι δήμωι·
          [Θε]όφημος Τιμοκλέους Μαραθώνιος εἴπε[ν·ᵛ ὅπως ἂν χρημάτων]
   10     [π]ορισθέντων ἔχει ὁ ταμίας μερίζειν τὰ [δεόμενα, ἵνα κατὰ τὸ]
          [ν κ]ατάλοιπον χρόνον τοῦ ἐνιαυτοῦ συνκ[ομισθῶσιν οἱ ἐκ γῆς]
          [κ]αρποὶ μετ'ἀσφαλείας, ᵛ ἀγαθεῖ τύχει δε[δόχθαι τῆι βουλεῖ ᵛ]
          [τ]οὺς λαχόντας προέδρους εἰς τὴν ἐπιοῦ[σ]αν ἐκκλησίαν χρημ
          [α]τίσαι περὶ τούτων, γνώμην δὲ ξυμβάλλε[σ]θαι τῆς βουλῆς, ὅτι
   15     δοκεῖ τῆι βουλεῖ ᵛ τοὺς βουλομένους τῶ[ν] πολιτῶν καὶ τῶν ἄλ
          λων τῶν οἰκούντων ἐν τῆι πόλει ἐπιδιδό[να]ι εἰς τὴν σωτηρία
          ν τῆς πόλεως καὶ τὴν φυλακὴν τῆς χώρας ἐ[ν] τῶι δήμωι ἢ ἐν τῆι β
          ουλεῖ ἢ πρὸς τοὺς στρατηγοὺς ἀπογραψα[μ]ένους μέχρι τοῦ Μο
```

υνιχιῶνος· ^υ μὴ ἐξέστω δὲ μηθενὶ ἐπιδο̱ῦνα[ι] πλέον ΗΗ^υ δραχμῶν

20 μηδ'ἔλαττον ^υ Ϝ·^υ εἶναι δὲ τοῖς ἐπιδοῦσι[ν κ]αὶ κοινεῖ καὶ ἰδία
ι ἐπαινεθῆναι καὶ τιμηθῆναι ὑπὸ τοῦ δήμου καθότι ἂν εἴ ἄξι
ος ἕκαστος αὐτῶν· ^υ τὸν δὲ γραμματέα τοῦ δ[ή]μου ἀναγράψαι τό
[δ]ε τὸ ψήφι[σμα] καὶ τὰ ὀνόματα τῶν ἐπιδόντ[ω]ν ἐν στήλει λιθίν
ει κ[α]ὶ στῆσαι ἐν τῆι ἀγορᾶι, ὅπως ἂν φανερ[ὰ] ἦι ἅπασιν ἡ φιλοτ

25 ιμία τῶν βουλομένων εὐεργετεῖν τ[ὸν] δῆμ[ο]ν· ^υ τὸ δὲ ἀνάλωμα τ
ὸ γενόμενον εἴς τε τὴν στήλην καὶ τὴν ἀ[ναγ]ραφὴν τῶν ὀνομάτ
ων μερίσαι τὸν ἐπὶ τῆι διοικήσει· τὸ δὲ ψή[φ]ισμα τόδε, ἐπειδὴ
περὶ πόρου χρημάτων ἐστὶν στρατιωτικῶ[ν, ἅπαν] εἶναι εἰς φυ
λακὴν τῆς χώρας.   *vacat*

30 Ο ἴ δ ε ἐ π έ δ ω κ α ν ε ἰ ς τ ὴ ν σ ω [τ] η ρ ί α ν τ ῆ ς π [ό]
λ ε ω ς κ α ὶ τ ὴ ν φ υ λ α κ ὴ ν τ ῆ ς [χ] ώ ρ α ς κ α τ ὰ τ [ὸ]
ψ ή φ ι σ μ α τ ο ῦ δ ή μ ο υ.   *vacat*

Ἀντιφῶν Ἐρχι	ΗΗ	Δρακοντίδης Ἐρχι	ΗΗ	[---]κλῆ[ς Σ]φήτ [---]	
Εὐρυκλείδης Κηφισ	ΗΗ	Ἀριστοφῶν Ἐρχι	ΗΗ	[....]όμαχος Ὄηθ [---]	
35 Μικίων Κηφισι	ΗΗ	Ἱεροκλῆς Σουνιε	ΗΗ	[....]δοτος Ἀχαρ [---]	
[Δ]ρομέας Ἐρχιε	ΗΗ	Μικίων Θριάσι	ΗΗ	[...⁷...]δης Πρ[-----]	
[Διο]κλῆς ['Ε]ρχιε	ΗΗ	Σπουδίας Τειθρά	ΗΗ	ὑπὲρ αὑτοῦ καὶ [τοῦ ὑοῦ]	
[-----------------]		[....]ορος Θημαχ	ΗΗ	[...]ΙΩ[.]ΙΔΩ[-------]	
[-----------------]		[..⁶...]ρας Ἀφιδ	ΗΗ	[...]κλῆς Ἀζ[ην] [----]	
40 [-----------------]		[-------] Εἰρεσ	ΗΗ	Ἀ[ντ]ιφάτης [-------]	
[-----------------]		[-----ἐκ Κ]οιλ	Η[Η]	[..⁵..]ωπος [--------]	
		lacuna			
[-----------------]		[...]ωνίδης Κολων		[-----------------]	
[-----------------]		ὑπὲρ αὑτοῦ καὶ τοῦ ὑοῦ	ΗΗ	Ὑ[-----------------]	
45 [----------]υ	ΗΗ	Σῶσος Ἁλαιεύς	ΗΗ	Λυ[----------------]	
[---------ἐξ] Οἴου	ΗΗ	Ζήνων Ἁλαιεύς	ΗΗ	Θε[----------------]	
[-------------]αθο	ΗΗ	Νικαγόρας Ἐρχι	ΗΗ	Κα[----------------]	
[..⁶..]ης Μαχε	ΗΗ	Λυσίας Κηφισιε	ΗΗ	Φιλ[---------------]	
[..⁵..]ων Ἀφιδναῖ	Η	Στράτιος Σφήττ	ΗΗ	Αἰ[----------------]	
50 [..⁵..]γνωτος Ἀλωπ	Η	Παυσίμαχος ἐκ Κολ	ΗΗ	Κτ[----------------]	
Εὔμαχος Σωκράτου		Παυσίας Παιανι	ΗΗ	Δ[-----------------]	
Εὐπυρίδης	ΗΗ	Σωσίβιος ἰσοτε	Ϝ	Ἱερ[---------------]	
Φιλίσκος Παμβω	ΗΗ	καὶ ὑπὲρ τοῦ ὑοῦ		Ἱερ[---------------]	
Ἀριστόλας Ἐρχι	ΗΗ	Διο[ν]υσίου		Τιμ[---------------]	
55 Θουμόριος Εὔων	ΗΗ	Ξέν[ω]ν Ἀσκληπιάδου		Τι[μ---------------]	
Ἀρισταγόρας ἐκ Κολ	ΗΗ	Φυλάσιος	[Η]Η	Αἰ[----------------]	
[Ξ]ενοκλῆς Σφήττ	ΗΗ	Ἀσκληπιάδη[ς Ξ]ένω		Ἀλκ[---------------]	
[Ξ]άνθιππος Ἐρχι	ΗΗ	νος Φυλ[ά]σιος	ΗΗ	Δημ[---------------]	
[Ζ]ώπυρος Συραχ	ΗΗ	Εὐαγίδης Φιλαΐ	ΗΗ	Φυστ[--------------]	
60 [.]ίμων Ὄηθεν	ΗΗ	Κηφισοφ[ῶν Ἀθ]μον	ΗΗ	[Κηφι[σ-----------]]	
[Δ]ημόφιλος ἐξ Οἴ	ΗΗ	Ἄρχανδρος Ἐλευσίν	ΗΗ	Φειδ[--------------]	
Ἐρώτος Μελιτ	ΗΗ	Χαιρεφῶν Εἰτεαῖ	Η	Διογ[--------------]	
Νικοκλῆς Φλυε	ΗΗ	Ἀρίστων Παιανι	ΗΗ	Φιλι[--------------]	
Νικοσθένης Φλυ	ΗΗ	Ἀντίπατρος Παιαν	ΗΗ	Πυθο[--------------]	
65 Φι[λ]οκλῆς Κορίν	ΗΗ	[Ἀγ]νοκ[ράτ]ης Ἁλαι	ΗΗ	Ἀμοι[-------------]	
Διοπείθης Φυλά	ΗΗ	Φυρόμ[α]χος Στε⟨ι⟩ρι	ΗΗ	Ἀριστ[------------]	
Τίμων Σφήττι	ΗΗ	Αἴσχρων Παιανι	ΗΗ	Θεα[ί]τ[ητος--------]	
Ἀπολλόδωρος Σωγέν		Ἀπολλοφάνης Ἀλωπ	ΗΗ	Ἐπι[φ]ά[νης ---------]	
ου Ὀτρυνεύς	ΗΗ	Σωσιγένης Παιαν	Η	Πραξιτ[έλης Τιμάρχου]	
70 Καλλίμαχος	ΗΗ	Θυμοχάρης Σφήττι	ΗΗ	Εἰρεσ[ίδης ---------]	

	Λύκων φιλόσο	HH	Θεόπομπος Λαμπτρ	HH	Θούκρ[ιτος ─────────]
	Ἄλε[ξ]ι[ς] Φυλάσι	HH	Αὐτίας Ἀχαρνε	HH	[Δωρίων][───────────]
	Ἑκαταῖος Μεσημβρι	HH	Θεόπομπος Αἰγιλ	HH	Λαχάρ[ης ──────────]
	Νικήτης Περγασῆ	H	Λυσιθείδης Ἐρχι	HH	Σιμίας Δ[──────────]
75	[Νικ]οκρά[τη]ς Μελ	HH	Φιλόθεος Φρεάρρι	HH	Θ[ε]μ[ι]στο[─────────]
	[──────────] Σφήτ	HH	Δημόφιλος Φρεάρρι	H	[Ν]ικόμα[χος ───────]
	[...]ροθ[ένη]ς Σφήτ	HH	Σώφιλος Κολλυτ	HH	*vacat*
	Νικήρατος Φλυε	[──]	Ἀριστίων Θημαχ	H	
	[Θρά]συλλος Ἐλευσ	HH	[──────]ος Φλυεύ	HH	
80	[Λ]υσιάδης ἐξ Οἴου	HH	Κ[.]λ[─── Εἰ]ρεσί	H	
	[Λ]υσίμαχος Οἰναῖ	HH	Ἰπ[πό]λ[ο]χο[ς ──]	ḤΗ	
	vacat		*vacat*		

Line 3. The stone breaks off after four letters of the *rasura*, but of these four letters nothing is now to be seen. The name of the phyle erased (doubtless at the time of the abolition of the "Macedonian" phylai in 201/200) was that of Demetrias rather than of Antigonis: see p. 302 above on the archonship of Diomedon. For the restoration, over-looked in Meritt's text and in *SEG* XXXII, see W. B. Dinsmoor, *Archons of Athens*, p. 96 with note 1. It was more recently reiterated by S. B. Aleshire (*ZPE* 64, 1986, p. 82); cf. *SEG* XXXVI, 170. It is incorrect to print [Δημη[τριάδος]], for this would indicate the legibility of ΔΗΜΗ. The fact of the erasure demonstrates that the stele remained *in situ* for at least forty-four years. Lines 6–7. ἐ[πεψήφιζεν ^v Καλλίσ|τρ]ατος or ἐ[πεψήφιζε(ν) ...^{7–8}... |. .]ατος C. Pelekides, Μελέτες ἀρχαίας ἱστορίας, 1979, pp. 40–60 (where the text is reprinted); cf. *SEG* XXIX, 113.

Line 10. [δέοντα ^v, or [ἀναγκαῖα Pelekides. Lines 10–12. On the restoration of these lines see C. Habicht, *Studien*, p. 27, note 76. Line 23. ἐν στίλει Meritt, followed by *SEG* XXXII. Surely a *lapsus calami*; eta is clearly on the stone.

Col. I: Line 50. [Τηλέ]γνωτος Habicht, *Studien*, p. 32, note 92; cf. *Agora* XV, 62, line 309. Line 60. So *IG* II², Meritt, and *SEG* XXXII; ["Ι]δμων S. V. Tracy, *Hesperia* 57, 1988, p. 319; cf. *SEG* XXXVIII, 99. Col. II: Line 66. Lapis ΣΤΕΡΙ.

This text is one of the many to be attributed to the "Cutter of *IG* II² 788", according to Tracy, *Hesperia* 57, 1988, pp. 311–322. For details of his career and characteristics see **204**. Two letters are inscribed in a single space in lines 19 and 20, and three letters in the space of two also in line 19. Lines 1–2 and 30–32 are inscribed in larger lettering. Vacant letter spaces are left at certain appropriate places to separate numerals and to indicate breaks between clauses. Cf. A. S. Henry, *Prescripts*, pp. 67, 70. The arrangement of line 8 illustrates the "perfect design", for which this mason seems to have had a particular liking: cf. Henry, *op. cit.*, p. 68, and the commentary on **204**.

Habicht, who discussed in detail the contents of this enactment and the circumstances that prompted it (*Studien*, pp. 26–33), with good reason described it, alongside *IG* II², 774 and 1534B, as without doubt the most important document of the period that survives to us (p. 26). Assessment of the threat that provoked this call for personal contributions to the defense of Attica, totaling on estimate between 4 and 6 talents, depends upon the year in which Diomedon is regarded as having held office (pp. 301–302 above). If that year was 244/3, as Habicht accepted, the occasion was in his view the likelihood of an invasion of Attica by Aratos of Sikyon, an attack which in the event did not take place until 242, for in 243 Aratos turned the Achaian League's attention to Corinth, with the capture of which he "reversed the balance of power in southern Greece" (F. W. Walbank, *CAH* VII, 2nd ed., i, 1984, p. 247). If Diomedon held office in 245/4, the apprehensions of the Athenians had arisen from the consequences of the battle of Chaironeia in 245, in which the Boiotians had suffered a crushing defeat at the hands of the Aitolians, resulting in a general instability in Central Greece in the face of Aitolian expansionism. Earlier assessments (e.g., that of W. S. Ferguson, *Hellenistic Athens*, p. 196, note 1) are invalidated by more recent study of the archon list and the redating of this text in consequence of it.

Lines 1–2. The emphasis on the Military Treasurer (cf. Rhodes, *Athenian Boule*, p. 100; Henry, *Prescripts*, p. 70) reflects the centrality of his interest in the passage of the measure and doubtless his promotion of it. He himself gave 200 drachmas towards the fund (Col. I, line 34), as did his brother Mikion (line 35). On these two, who played important roles in Athenian politics during the last third of the century, see *PA* 5966 and 10188 and Habicht, *Studien*, pp. 118–127 and 179–182 (and cf. *SEG* XXXII, 119). For the general background to Athenian politics in the years during which the brothers were prominent in them see also Ferguson, *Hellenistic Athens*, pp. 205–257 and C. Mossé, *Athens in Decline, 404–86 B.C.*, 1973, pp. 132–137. Eurykleides' political career may now be seen from the dating of Diomedon's archonship to have been somewhat longer than was at one time believed (cf. Ferguson, *Hellenistic Athens*, p. 205 and *RE* VI, i, 1907, cols. 1328–1329, *s.v.* Eurykleides [J. Kirchner]). Line 4. For the reading of the *demoticum* of the γραμματεύς and its bearing on the reconstruction of the archon list see p. 301 above.

Line 5. On the calendar equation (Elaphebolion 30 = pryt. X, 2 = 266th day) see Pritchett and Neugebauer, *Calendars*, p. 82; Meritt, *Athenian Year*, pp. 137–138; Pritchett, *Ancient Athenian Calendars on Stone*, p. 341. This meeting of the assembly is not among the evidence collected by J. D. Mikalson, *Sacred and Civil Calendar*, pp. 136–137. Line 6. ἐπεψήφιοζεν (as restored). See **102**, commentary on lines 7–8 and references there. Lines 6–7. Kallistratos, son of Telesinos, of Erchia. For him and his family, see *PA* 8165; S. Dow, *Prytaneis*, p. 51; J. K. Davies, *Athenian Propertied Families*, pp. 361–363 (*s.v.* Λύσις Ἐρχιεύς); *Agora* XV, 85, line 27 and p. 414. He was also the proposer of **217**. Line 8. ἔδοξεν τῶι δήμωι. But lines 12–15 show clearly that the decree was probouleumatic. On the apparent anomaly (not without parallels) see Rhodes, *Athenian Boule*, pp. 77–78, 253. Line 9. Theophemos, son of Timokles, of Marathon (*PA* 7098) is not otherwise known, unless he be the archon whose year of office has latterly been variously assessed as 243/2, 242/1, or 241/40.

Lines 10–12. On the timing (cf. lines 18–19) see Ferguson, *Hellenistic Athens*, pp. 203–204 and Habicht, *Studien*, pp. 27–28. Line 12. ἀγαθεῖ τύχει. See **72**, commentary on lines 7–8.

Lines 16–17. The note of urgency and impending danger is very clear. On the φυλακὴ τῆς χώρας (also in lines 28–31) see Rhodes, *Athenian Boule*, pp. 231–235.

Lines 20–21. κοινεῖ καὶ ἰδίαι. Cf. **237**, lines 5–6. Line 22. The γραμματεύς responsible for the inscribing of the decree and of the list of names is designated τοῦ δήμου rather than κατὰ πρυτανείαν: cf. **120**, commentary on line 8. It is probable, but not entirely demonstrable, that the two designations refer in fact to the same official. Line 24. ἐν τῆι ἀγορᾶι. Cf. **224**, line 47. The position of the monument is not more closely defined. Lines 24–25. The "hortatory intention" is here attached to the publication of the decree and list as a permanent and visible record of the patriotism and generosity of the contributors, rather than to the more usual aim of encouraging future emulation or publicising the gratitude of the demos, and it is well tailored to the particular circumstances. See **239**, commentary on line 7.

Lines 25–27. The cost of the stele and its inscription is to be met, as regularly in this period, by the Single Officer. Cf. the commentary on **174**, as well as Henry, *Chiron* 14, 1984, pp. 74–81, *ZPE* 72, 1988, pp. 133–134, *ZPE* 78, 1989, pp. 277–280. It would have been possible, and perhaps in the circumstances to be expected, that the expense might be met from the funds of the Military Treasurer, for at this time he did on occasion act as disbursing officer for the costs of stelai. See **194**, commentary on line 13 and references there.

Lines 33–81. More than half of the Athenian citizens appearing in this list are known from other sources, and it is beyond the present intention to embark upon the prosopographical details of each contributor who can be certainly or plausibly identified. The importance of this text for the study of mid-3rd-century Athenian society is nevertheless considerable, as Habicht briefly emphasized (*Studien*, pp. 31–33). Seven contributors seem to have held office as eponymous archon: a number are attested or appear to be identifiable as ἱππεῖς among the lead tablets of the Athenian cavalry published by K. Braun (*AthMitt* 85, 1970, pp. 198–269) and J. H. Kroll (*Hesperia* 46, 1977, pp. 83–140). Some belonged to old families known as wealthy in earlier generations and discussed by Davies, *Athenian Propertied Families* (for cross-references see Habicht, *Studien*, p. 33, note 96). Those recorded in *IG* II², 791 were treated in Kirchner's *Prosopographia Attica*. A few particular details may however be usefully noted.

Col. I: Line 36. Dromeas of Erchia. See Habicht, *Studien*, pp. 183–185, building upon the earlier work of *PA* 4559 and 4023; S. Dow, *HSCP* 48, 1937, pp. 106–108; Davies, *Athenian Propertied Families*, *s.v.* Ἁγνίας Ἐρχιεύς. The Diokles of the following line was his brother. Line 79. Cf. the statue base *SEG* XXI, 754. Line 80. Lysiades, son of Astynomos, of Oion. Probably to be identified with the archon variously assigned to the years 253/2 or 243/2 or to an uncertain year at any rate earlier than that of Thersilochos (see pp. 294–295 above). See further Habicht, *Studien*, p. 33 with notes 97 and 99 and *SEG* XXXII, 559.

Col. II: Line 78. It was noted by Habicht (*Studien*, p. 32, note 95) that Aristion of Themakos is not to be identified with the ἱππεύς Aristion (Kroll, *Hesperia* 46, 1977, pp. 130, 132–133, nos. 75, 81–82): the phyle of the latter was Leontis, whereas Themakos was a deme of Erechtheis. But he may be the archon of 238/7: cf. Meritt, *Historia* 26, 1977, p. 176; *SEG* XXXII, 149.

Col. III: Line 40. Habicht (*Studien*, p. 32, note 92) suggested that this might be the Ἀντιφάτης Κικυννεύς of *Agora* XV, 102, line 2 but warned that the name was not uncommon in Attic prosopography and is found with other *demotica*.

THE ARCHONSHIP OF PHILONEOS, BETWEEN 244 AND 241 B.C.

When Philoneos' archonship was known only by a fragment giving no more than his name as archon (*IG* II², 765) and a decree in commendation of the ephebes of his year (*IG* II², 766, later augmented as *SEG* XXI, 392), no criteria beyond prosopographical indications derived from the latter text (especially concerning the career of the paidotribes, Hermodoros of Acharnai) and the style of writing of both were available to suggest its date. J. Kirchner proposed "ca. a. 260" (*IG* II², iv, 1, pp. 16–17) or "paullo post a. 260" (*IG* II², 765, comm.) as suitable for it. Other guesses had concentrated about 271/70 (cf. W. B. Dinsmoor, *Archons of Athens*, pp. 54, 169). Dinsmoor's own reassessment, especially of the chronology of Hermodoros, caused him to prefer a date in 256/5 (*op. cit.*, pp. 167–171). W. S. Ferguson, on similar grounds, opted hesitantly for 241/40 (*Athenian Tribal Cycles*, pp. 25, 102–107). The "archon list" provided by *SEG* II, 9 did not help, as Philoneos' name does not appear on it. However, the discovery of **217**, by which Philoneos was linked to Kydenor (in whose archonship *SEG* II, 9 was voted), suggested that an entry concerning Philoneos' archonship was lost in a lacuna of that thiasotic decree and that Philoneos should precede Kydenor either directly or at an interval of one or at most two years. Cf. M. J. Osborne, *ZPE* 78, 1989, p. 215. Dinsmoor wryly observed that **217** contradicted "all hypotheses erected in the sixteen years since the publication of . . . *S.E.G.*, II, 9" (*Athenian Archon List*, p. 71), and he dedicated his book to Kydenor in recognition of his achievement in twice (*via SEG* II, 9 and **217**) invalidating the best efforts of scholars in the field of Athenian chronology of the Hellenistic period. In particular he had invalidated B. D. Meritt's hesitant acceptance (*Hesperia* 4, 1935, p. 585) of Ferguson's 241/40 for Philoneos, as well as his later suggestions (*Hesperia* 7, 1938, p. 135, at a time when *Agora* XV, 87 was conjectured to belong to Philoneos' year) of 250/49.

Dinsmoor in 1939 had prepublication knowledge of **214**, with its indication of the demotic of the γραμματεύς of Philoneos' archonship, of which the initial letter partly survived (upsilon or chi). On the reading of this doubtful letter and the interpretation of possible traces of the letter following depended the major arguments thereafter. His revised date of 244/3 (*Athenian Archon List*, pp. 152–153) accommodated all the evidence by then accumulated and was followed by W. K. Pritchett and Meritt in their *editio princeps* of **214**. The demotic ῾Υ[βάδης for Philoneos' γραμματεύς (Leontis VI) was able to concord with the Εἰρεσί]δης (Akamantis VII) written into **217** for the year of Kydenor regarded as immediately following and thus preserved the secretary cycle as then established.

The discovery of more evidence for Kydenor's year in 1947 caused that archon to disrupt for the third time all previous conclusions. The name of his γραμματεύς was fully preserved in the new text (**216**) and showed that the demotic ending – – – – δης was Εὐπυρίδης (Leontis VI), of the same phyle as the deme of Philoneos' γραμματεύς. A new fragment assigned to *IG* II², 766 (see *SEG* XXI, 392) provided part of the prescript of that decree and confirmed the close connection between Kydenor and Philoneos by making it clear that the ephebes of Philoneos' year were commended during that of Kydenor. See Meritt, *Hesperia* 17, 1948, pp. 3–13. Some conflict between the implications of *IG* II², 766 and of *SEG* II, 9 left doubt whether Philoneos' archonship should immediately precede that of Kydenor or whether that of Theophemos should intervene between them. Meritt opted for the latter arrangement (especially as the year of Theophemos was known to be ordinary and that of Kydenor was thought to be intercalary), and the terms of *SEG* II, 9 do in fact make this more likely. The order Diomedon–Philoneos–Theophemos–Kydenor has been accepted since that time; see the references in C. Habicht, *Untersuchungen*, p. 133, note 96, to which may be added Meritt, *Hesperia* 50, 1981, p. 95. Habicht also observed that an additional archonship might intervene between Diomedon and Theophemos, and Osborne (*ZPE* 78, 1989, pp. 219–222) found reason to place Lysiades there.

Meritt's tentative reading of the demotic of Philoneos' γραμματεύς as ῾Υπ[ωρειεύς surmounted the problem of the secretary cycle, for it enabled him to suggest that Hyporeia belonged to Aigeis (IV), thus in correct sequence with the cycle which, he then believed, had begun afresh with Erechtheis (III) in Diomedon's archonship and which, two years later, would reach Kydenor with a γραμματεύς from Leontis (VI). Philoneos' archonship was therefore set by him in 246/5, a decision unaffected by a subsequent change of view concerning the calendric character of Kydenor's year (*Athenian Year*, pp. 146–148, 234).

Objections to ῾Υπωρειεύς were stressed by C. Pelekides (*BCH* 85, 1961, pp. 56–67; cf. also J. and L. Robert, *REG* 62, 1949, p. 106, no. 45). Retention of ῾Υβάδης made it necessary to discount the secretary cycle altogether at this juncture, augmenting the confusion already admitted by the acknowledged break before Diomedon's archonship. Pelekides went on to urge that the cycle was not resumed until the "liberation" of 229 B.C. (Μελέτες ἀρχαίας ἱστορίας, 1979, pp. 33–60), and Habicht's study of the same year as well as subsequent discussions have tended to accept a comparable conclusion. The effect at the time was to give to Philoneos the year 244/3 in the revised list of the archons of that decade.

Meritt's reply (*The Classical Tradition: Literary and Historical Studies in Honor of Harry Caplan*, 1966, pp. 31–42), besides revising the text of **214** (see below), sought to reaffirm the validity of the secretary cycle from the year of Diomedon onwards; and he argued more fully for ῾Υπωρειεύς as the demotic in dispute. But strong objections to the admission of Hyporeia as a deme, at any rate in this period, and to its association with Aigeis in any case, were voiced by J. S. Traill, *Political Organization*, pp. 87–88 with note 54, and Meritt acknowledged that the contention, which he described as a "heroic but misguided effort", could not be maintained (*Historia* 26, 1977, p. 164). Nevertheless, Philoneos' relative position with regard to the archons around him remains firm and as the result of progressive discoveries has become more evident.

Thus Habicht's dating of Thersilochos in 247/6 had as its consequence the dating of Philoneos in 243/2 (*Untersuchungen*, p. 143), and equally for Meritt (*Hesperia* 50, 1981, p. 95) the same interval between the two placed Philoneos in 244/3. He had hoped (*Historia* 26, 1977, p. 176) that the secretary cycle could begin again with Theophemos in 245/4, at a time when he still dated Philoneos in 246/5, but in his last study he was prepared to postpone its reintroduction to the archonship of Lysias (see pp. 312–313 below). Osborne's introduction of Lysiades between Diomedon and Philoneos (see his table, *ZPE* 78, 1989, p. 241) delayed the latter's entry upon office by one further year. According therefore to the interpretation of the scholar concerned and of those who study their respective findings, **214** and **215** may be assigned to 244/3, 243/2, or 242/1. Future discoveries may be able to confirm any one of these—or to invalidate them all.

The character of Philoneos' year cannot be determined. The year of Theophemos, now universally agreed to have succeeded it, was certainly ordinary. If it was preceded by that of Diomedon, which also was certainly ordinary, it must be presumed to have been intercalary. On Meritt's dating this would accord with its position as the eighteenth year of the (tenth) Metonic cycle. If Theophemos be placed in 242/1, Philoneos' year should be ordinary also. Akamantis held the twelfth prytany, if Meritt's restoration of **214** be accepted; but the eleventh prytany is an equal possibility.

FRAGMENT OF AN HONORARY DECREE

214. The upper left section of a flat-topped stele of Hymettian marble (I 5559), with the smooth left side, smooth top, and traces of a crowning molding as well as the original rough-picked back preserved, discovered on September 12, 1938, in a wall of a modern house southeast of the Market Square and west of the Panathenaic Way (Q 21). The inscribed surface is very badly worn, and the readings are difficult and uncertain in many places.

H. 0.46 m.; W. 0.29 m.; Th. 0.095 m.

LH. 0.006 m.

Στοιχ. Hor. 0.009 m.; Vert. *ca.* 0.014 m.

Ed. W. K. Pritchett and B. D. Meritt, *Chronology*, pp. 22–23, with photographs (a stoichedon text of 43 letters per line); revised text (Στοιχ. 48) by Meritt, *Hesperia* 17, 1948, pp. 7–13; further revision by Meritt, *The Classical Tradition: Literary and Historical Studies in Honor of Harry Caplan*, 1966, pp. 31–42 (Στοιχ. 55), with photograph, which is the text shown in *SEG* XXIII, 67, where the bibliography to that date is assembled. The text below, with additional but unimportant readings in lines 11 and 17, has been revised for a stoichedon line of 52 letters.

inter annos 244 et 241 a., pryt. XI *vel* XII   ΣΤΟΙΧ. 52

```
      ['Ε]πὶ Φιλόνεω ἄρχ[οντος] ἐπὶ τῆς 'Ακα[μαντίδος .. δεκάτης πρυτανεί]
      [ας ἧι .........17........]δήμου ῾Υ[βάδης ἐγραμμάτευεν· ἐκκλησία]·
      [τῶν προέδρων] ἐπ[εψ]ή[φ]ι[ζεν Δ]ιονυσόδ[ωρος .........19.........]
      [καὶ συμπρόεδροι· vvvvvv ἔδ]ο[ξ]εν τ[ῆι βουλῆι καὶ τῶι δήμωι· vvvvv]
  5   [.........21.........εἶπεν]· ὑπ[ὲρ ὧν ἀπαγγέλλει ....10.....]
      [.........26.........]χη[.........24.........]
                    Vss. 7–10 non legendi videntur
 11   [.........16.....εὐ]σεβῶς [.]επ[.........26.........]
      [.........19.........]ων[.........31.........]
      [.]ε[.........50.........]
      μενα[.........48.........]
 15   [....] καὶ [.........45.........]
      ετ[...]κρο[.........44.........]
```

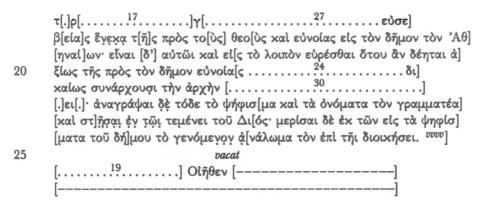

τ[.]ρ[.........¹⁷.........]γ[...................²⁷.............εὖσε]
β[εία]ς ἔνεχα τ[ῆ]ς πρὸς το[ὺς] θεο[ὺς καὶ εὐνοίας εἰς τὸν δῆμον τὸν Ἀθ]
[ηναί]ων· εἶναι [δ'] αὐτῶι καὶ εἰ[ς τὸ λοιπὸν εὑρέσθαι ὅτου ἂν δέηται ἀ]
20　ξίως τῆς πρὸς τὸν δῆμον εὐνοία[ς.........²⁴.........δι]
καλῶς συνάρχουσι τὴν ἀρχὴν [...............³⁰...............]
[.]ει[.]· ἀναγράψαι δὲ τόδε τὸ ψήφισ[μα καὶ τὰ ὀνόματα τὸν γραμματέα]
[καὶ στ]ῆσαι ἐν τῶι τεμένει τοῦ Δι[ός· μερίσαι δὲ ἐκ τῶν εἰς τὰ ψηφίσ]
[ματα τοῦ δή]μου τὸ γενόμενον ἀ[νάλωμα τὸν ἐπὶ τῆι διοικήσει. ᵛᵛᵛᵛ]
25　　　　　　　　　　　　　*vacat*
[.........¹⁹.........] Οἰῆθεν [––––––––––––––––––]
[–––]

The lettering of this text has something in common with the work of the "Cutter of *IG* II² 788" (see **204**) but has not been attributed to him. It may be said to represent a reasonably "standard" mid-century script. The prescript is set out in a form intermediate to the "perfect design", with the enactment formula isolated but not quite centered nor given a line wholly to itself. A. S. Henry referred to it as the "economy design" (*Prescripts*, p. 68); cf. **216**. On the "perfect design" see **204** and references there.

The restorations follow the general pattern of those in Meritt's text of 1966. In line 2, however, his hypothesis of 55 letters required that the name of the γραμματεύς, together with his patronymic, should occupy twenty-five letter spaces, well above average for Athenian nomenclature though not beyond possibility. A slightly modified line, in itself more economical, alleviates the difficulty. The date by prytany and festival calendars is omitted: cf. Henry, *Prescripts*, p. 72.

Line 2. Ἐκκλησία. See **97**, commentary on line 7. Line 4. It may be inferred from the spacing and arrangement that the decree was probouleumatic. Cf. P. J. Rhodes, *Athenian Boule*, p. 253.

Line 22. τὸ ψήφισ[μα τὸν γραμματέα ἐν στήλει λιθίνει] Meritt. For the inclusion here of καὶ τὰ ὀνόματα cf. (e.g.) **187**, line 34 and **188**, line 46. The restoration requires that the more precise designation of the γραμματεύς (as ὁ κατὰ πρυτανείαν or τοῦ δήμου) be omitted. See **166**, commentary on lines 6–7. Line 23. This passage is quoted in *Agora* III, p. 29, no. 40, among the evidence for the stoa and sanctuary of Zeus Eleutherios in the Agora. Cf. **174**, commentary on lines 7–8. Lines 23–24. The first three surviving letters in line 24 make it clear that the formula for the disbursement of the cost of the stele was unusual. In the first place, the phrase εἰς τὴν ἀναγραφὴν τῆς στήλης (*vel sim.*) was evidently omitted. As for what follows, in his 1948 edition, with a shorter line (48 letters), Meritt proposed μερίσαι δὲ ἐκ τῶν κατὰ ψη|φίσματα δή]μου κτλ. His later text (55 letters) offered ἐκ δὲ τῶν ἀναλισκομένων χρημάτω|ν ὑπὸ τοῦ δή]μου, with μερίσαι placed after ἀ[νάλωμα. For this unusual phraseology, found in connection with the expense account of the boule rather than of the demos, see the commentary on **210**. It was rightly discounted by Henry, who summarized and discussed the problem and its proposed solutions in *Chiron* 14, 1984, pp. 78–80 (*SEG* XXXIV, 89), himself suggesting (though allowing that it is nowhere paralleled in this form) μερίσαι δ'ἐκ τῶν εἰς τὰ κατὰ ψηφίσ|ματα τοῦ δή]μου and retaining thereby Meritt's length of line. For the elided epsilon (an unusual feature in this position) cf. line 19 and see L. Threatte, *Grammar*, p. 422. The omission of ἀναλισκομένων, which might be regarded as an essential element in the formula, is surprising but appears necessary. Κατά, a more otiose element, is here dispensed with, in conformity with the shorter line. In any event, a reference to the "analiskomena fund" at this date is a matter of remark: cf. Henry, *op. cit.*, pp. 62–63 with note 64. *IG* II², 707, probably to be dated between 260 and 250, seems to offer the most recent example and has few immediate predecessors: among the Agora decrees there is (apart from the present text) no instance later than **164**. It may be that the very unfamiliarity of an express call on the fund had caused the old, precise formula to be misremembered by those concerned with the drafting of the decree.

Line 26. After a blank line it seems that a series of names may well have followed, and line 22 is restored to take account of this. Despite line 19, which seems to give special honors to one of them, there were probably several honorands (cf. line 21). On the form of the surviving demotic see S. Dow, *AJP* 84, 1963, pp. 166–181.

FRAGMENT OF A DECREE

215. A fragment from the top of a flat-topped stele of Hymettian marble (I 7029), on which the upper ovolo molding (with traces of painted egg-and-dart decoration) and taenia above it (on which line 1 is inscribed) are preserved but which is otherwise broken all around, discovered on May 12, 1967, in a cut between the first and second columns (from the east) of South Stoa II (O 15:1).

H. 0.055 m.; W. 0.127 m.; Th. 0.02 m.
LH. *ca.* 0.006 m.

Ed. B. D. Meritt, *Hesperia* 37, 1968, p. 271, no. 8, with photograph pl. 78. See also *SEG* XXV, 104.

inter annos 244 *et* 241 *a.*

```
[Θ]        ε        [ο        ι].
['Επὶ Φιλ]όνεω ἄ[ρχοντος -----]
[----------------------]
```

The six surviving letters allow little comment. Omega has its horizontal strokes set high: cf. **197** and the reference there quoted. The strokes of epsilon are not well joined. If the lettering in both lines was regularly spaced, the decree was inscribed with *ca.* 33 letters to the line.

THE ARCHONSHIP OF KYDENOR, BETWEEN 242 AND 239 B.C.

Kydenor and his archonship were unknown before the discovery of *SEG* II, 9, the decree of the thiasotai from Salamis that associated him satisfactorily with other archons of the middle of the 3rd century. W. B. Dinsmoor (*Archons of Athens*, p. 55) placed him in 245/4; although inscriptions dated by his archonship have more than once thrown scholarship into confusion, and although dates differing by as much as eighteen years have tentatively been assigned to him, the years finally attributed to him have moved little from the point at which Dinsmoor originally set him. For the developing analysis of his dating and the dating of the archons with whom the evidence connects him, see the commentary above on the archonship of Philoneos (pp. 305–307).

The discovery of **216** provided the full name of the γραμματεύς of Kydenor's year and made it evident that he belonged not to the deme Eiresidai (Akamantis VII), as had been supposed on the basis of **217** (see W. K. Pritchett and B. D. Meritt, *Chronology*, pp. 23–26), but to Eupyridai (Leontis VI). In consequence, the archonship was moved from 243/2 (where Dinsmoor had later put it) to 244/3 (Meritt, *Hesperia* 17, 1948, pp. 7, 13; Dinsmoor, *Hesperia* 23, 1954, p. 315), and that dating was generally accepted throughout the next thirty years; cf. Meritt, *Historia* 26, 1977, p. 176.

But it was not without challenge. In his reconsideration of the archons of this period, which depended on the rejection of the validity of the secretary cycle (see pp. 300–301 above), C. Pelekides wished to move Kydenor to 242/1 (*BCH* 85, 1961, pp. 60–67). But the suggestion received no further support at the time and was answered, with a reaffirmation of the evidence of the cycle, by Meritt in *The Classical Tradition: Literary and Historical Studies in Honor of Harry Caplan*, 1966, pp. 31–42. However, the archon list as revised by G. Nachtergael in his study of the Aitolian Soteria (*Historia* 25, 1976, p. 77), followed by the reconsideration of the whole series from Polyeuktos to Lysias by C. Habicht (*Untersuchungen*, pp. 133–146), which placed Philoneos in 243/2, had as their necessary consequence the dating of Kydenor, next-but-one to Philoneos, in 241/40. Similarly, Meritt's reconsidered list (*Hesperia* 50, 1981, p. 95) dated him in 242/1, while M. J. Osborne, having inserted an extra archon (Lysiades) before Philoneos, set Kydenor in 240/39 (*ZPE* 78, 1989, pp. 215, 219, 241). The alternatives remain, until fresh evidence is found to confirm one of them or to disprove them all.

In addition to **216**, **217**, and *SEG* XXI, 392, the first decree of *IG* II², 775 + 803 (*SEG* XVIII, 19, XXXV, 91) has been attributed to the archonship of Kydenor. It provides no data concerning the calendar or circumstances of the year, and even if correctly attributed is not helpful in any discussion of its problems. On the basis of **217** the year was tentatively, but without evidence beyond the character of assumed neighboring years, set down as ordinary. **216**, and **217** itself when restored in correspondence with the new text, revealed it as intercalary (Elaphebolion 9 = pryt. IX, 17). It was, however, necessary to suppose that one of the earlier prytanies had contained 33 days instead of the 32 regular in an intercalary year or that three successive festival months had been hollow. *SEG* XXI, 392, in which the calendric data are lost, could be restored in conformity with this hypothesis as passed on Mounichion 12 (= pryt. X, 19). Nevertheless, the year could be interpreted as ordinary on the supposition that six days had been intercalated into the festival calendar, perhaps (as Meritt suggested, *Athenian Year*, pp. 146–148) in order to retard the celebration of the City Dionysia in this same month Elaphebolion (cf. p. 268 above, on the archonship of Pytharatos). In this case, *SEG* XXI, 392, is possibly to be restored as of Posideon 12 = pryt. VI, 4. Either interpretation calls for some irregularity in the year. Since the date of the archonship remains a matter of controversy, and the former general correspondence of the Metonic cycle with the Athenian festival calendar is in this period no longer to be depended upon, it is necessary to accept, with whatever reluctance, one of the unusual features described above as an inescapable postulate.

Known phylai in prytany during the year are VI or X(?) Antigonis or Demetrias, IX Erechtheis. The γραμματεύς Polyktemon, son of Euktimenos, of the deme Eupyridai is not otherwise known. The Euktimenos, son of Euktimenos, who was an ephebos in 324/3(?) presumably belonged to an earlier generation in this same family; see B. Leonardos, Ἀρχ. Ἐφ., 1918, pp. 73–100, nos. 95–97; O. W. Reinmuth, *The Ephebic Inscriptions of the Fourth Century B.C.*, 1971, pp. 58–82, no. 15, col. III, line 11.

COMMENDATION OF THE SITONAI OF THE YEAR OF DIOMEDON

216. The upper part of a pedimental stele of Hymettian marble (I 6064), broken below and with the apex of the pediment missing but otherwise intact, discovered on August 1, 1947, built into the north wall of the Civic Offices (I 12).

H. 0.30 m.; W. (foot of pediment) 0.49 m., (top of inscribed surface) 0.438 m.; Th. (inscribed surface) 0.10 m.
LH. 0.006 m.
Στοιχ. Hor. 0.0095 m.; Vert. 0.012 m.

Ed. B. D. Meritt, *Hesperia* 17, 1948, pp. 3–13, no. 3, with photograph pl. 4. Cf. J. and L. Robert, *REG* 62, 1949, pp. 105–106, no. 45.

a. 242/1 *vel* 241/40 *vel* 240/39 a., *pryt.* IX   ΣΤΟΙΧ. *ca.* 44

```
                    Θ          ε         ο          ι.
              Ἐπὶ Κυδήνορος ἄρχοντος ἐπὶ τῆς Ἐρεχθεῖδος ἐνάτης πρυ
              τανείας ἧι Πολυκτήμων Εὐκτιμένου Εὐπυρίδης ἔγραμ
              μάτευεν· ᵛ Ἐλαφηβολιῶνος ἐνάτηι ἱσταμένου, ἑβδόμηι καὶ
       5      δεκάτηι τῆς πρυτανείας· ἐκκλ[η]σία κ[υ]ρία· τῶν προέδρων
              ἐπεψήφιζεν Ἀντικλῆς Ἐξηκέστου Αἰξωνεὺς καὶ συμπρό
              εδροι· ᵛᵛᵛᵛ ἔδοξεν τεῖ βουλεῖ καὶ τῶι δήμωι· ᵛᵛᵛᵛᵛᵛᵛ
              Μολοττὸς Αἰσχίνου Οἰναῖος εἶπεν· ᵛ ἐπειδὴ οἱ σιτῶναι
              οἱ χειροτονηθέντες εἰς τὸν ἐνιαυτὸν τὸν ἐπὶ Διομέδον
      10      τος ἄρχοντος ἐποιήσαντο τὴν πᾶσαν ἐπιμέλειαν ὅπως ἂν
              [ὡς κά]λλιστος καὶ ε[ὐωνότ]ατος σῖτος ἀγορασθῆι τῶι δή
              [μωι ...]Γ[.........²¹.........]ΣΗΤΕΤΟΝ παρεκαλέσα[ν]
              [το ............³¹.............]οι τὰς χρεί[ας]
              [————————————————————————————]
```

Below the horizontal cornice of the pediment, the transition to the face of the inscribed surface is effected by a molding consisting of an ovolo with cavetto crown, in general resembling the mid-3rd-century Pergamene altar crown L. T. Shoe, *Profiles of Greek Mouldings*, 1936, pl. XXIII, no. 25. Line 1 of the text is inscribed on the cavetto.

This stele provides a further sample of the work of the "Cutter of *IG* II² 788" or his workshop: see the commentary on **204**. In this text his layout emphasizes the enactment formula but, by including a few letters at the beginning of line 7, does not achieve the "perfect design". This is referred to by A. S. Henry (*Prescripts*, p. 68) as the "economy design" and is there listed by him among the examples of it. The stoichedon pattern breaks down towards the ends of the lines, to permit syllabic division or whole-word endings. In lines 4 and 8 a vacant letter space marks a break between clauses; cf. Henry, *op. cit.*, p. 67. In line 12 Meritt read Γ[.........²².........]υ[.]τον κτλ.

The text provided essential data for Kydenor's year; see especially Meritt, *Athenian Year*, p. 147. Its prescript formed the basis for the restoration of that of **217**, which proved to have been enacted at the same meeting of the assembly.

Line 4. For Elaphebolion 9 as a day on which the assembly might meet see J. D. Mikalson, *Sacred and Civil Calendar*, pp. 124–126, where lines 1–4 of this text are quoted. It is a well-attested date and has been restored in a considerable number of texts. Line 5. ἐκκλησία κυρία. See **101**, commentary on lines 7–8. Line 6. Antikles, son of Exekestos, of Aixone. An Exekestos of this deme was epistates at Brauron in an earlier generation (*PA* 4728). Line 7. The decree was probouleumatic; cf. P. J. Rhodes, *Athenian Boule*, p. 253. The formula shows EI in the dative feminine singular, whereas HI appears elsewhere in this text. Line 8. Molottos, son of Aischines, of Oinoe is not otherwise known, nor does either name recur among identified Οἰναῖοι.

For the commendation of officials during these years cf. C. Habicht, *Studien*, p. 22. On the sitonai and their duties see **188**, commentary on line 9. The members of the board in office during the archonship of Diomedon had to wait nearly three, or perhaps nearly four, years from the end of their term before their merits were acknowledged; cf. **217** and *SEG* XXI, 392. There was clearly some extraordinary delay in the completion of routine public business during the middle and later 240's, for reasons not now clearly to be discerned but surely connected in some way with the generally unsettled state of Hellas and the dangers reflected in **213**. But such delays were not unique to this period. Cf. most notably *IG* II², 500, which shows that the taxiarchoi of 305/4 were not commended until 302/1. See Meritt, Χαριστήριον εἰς ᾿Αναστάσιον Κ. ᾿Ορλάνδον I, 1964, pp. 195–196.

COMMENDATION OF THE AGORANOMOI OF THE YEAR OF PHILONEOS

217. A fragment of a stele of Pentelic marble (I 5191), with parts of the left side and original rough-picked back preserved, and with the spring of a crowning molding just perceptible at the top of the inscribed face, but broken elsewhere and with the inscribed surface damaged all around except at the top, discovered on January 24, 1938, in a wall of a modern house in the area south of the Church of the Holy Apostles (Q 19).

H. 0.278 m.; W. 0.175 m.; Th. 0.068 m.
LH. 0.005 m.
Στοιχ. (almost square) Hor. *ca.* 0.0094 m.; Vert. *ca.* 0.0098 m.; syllabic division at the ends of the lines.

Ed. W. K. Pritchett and B. D. Meritt, *Chronology*, pp. 23–27, with photograph. Cf. W. B. Dinsmoor, *Athenian Archon List*, p. 70. Improved text of lines 1–4 by Meritt in *Hesperia* 17, 1948, p. 4.

a. 242/1 *vel* 241/40 *vel* 240/39 a., pryt. IX   ΣΤΟΙΧ. 38

```
       [᾿Επὶ Κυ]δήνορ[ος ἄρχοντος ἐπὶ τῆς ᾿Ερεχθεῖδος ἐ ᵛ]
       [νάτης] πρυταν[είας ἧι Πολυκτήμων Εὐκτιμένου ᵛ]
       [Εὐπυρί]δης ἐγρ[αμμάτευεν· ᾿Ελαφηβολιῶνος ἐνά ᵛ]
       [τηι ἱσ]ταμένου, [ἑβδόμηι καὶ δεκάτηι τῆς πρυτα ᵛ]
    5  [νεία]ς· ἐκκλησία [κυρία· τῶν προέδρων ἐπεψήφι ᵛᵛ]
       [σζε]ν ᾿Αντικλῆς ᾿Ε[ξηκέστου Αἰξωνεὺς καὶ συμπρό]
       [εδρ]οι· ᵛᵛ ἔδοξεν τ[ῆι βουλῆι καὶ τῶι δήμωι· ᵛᵛᵛᵛᵛ]
       [Κα]λλίστρατος Τε[λεσίνου ᾿Ερχιεὺς εἶπεν· ᵛ ἐπεὶ]
       [δὴ] οἱ ἀγορανόμοι [οἱ ἐπὶ Φιλόνεω ἄρχοντος ἦρ ᵛᵛ]
   10  [ξα]ν τὴν ἀρχὴν κατά [τε τοὺς νόμους καὶ τὰ ψηφίσ ᵛ]
       [μα]τα τῆς βουλῆς κα[ὶ τοῦ δήμου, ᵛ ἐπεμελήθησαν ᵛ]
       [δὲ] καὶ τῶν κατὰ τὴν [ἀγορὰν καλῶς καὶ δικαίως ᵛᵛ]
       [κ]αὶ ὑπὲρ τούτων δε[δώκασιν τὰς εὐθύνας, ᵛ ὅπως ᵛ]
       [ἂν] οὖν ἐφάμιλλον [ἧι ἅπασιν τοῖς ἄρξουσιν τὴν ᵛ]
   15  [ἀρ]χὴν ταύτην ἄρχε[ιν κατὰ τοὺς νόμους, ᵛ ἀγαθῆι]
       [τύχ]ηι δεδόχθαι τῆ[ι βουλῆι τοὺς προέδρους οἳ ᵛ]
       [ἂν λ]άχωσιν προεδρ[εύειν εἰς τὴν ἐπιοῦσαν ἐκ ᵛᵛ]
       [κλ]ησίαν χρηματίσ[αι περὶ τούτων, γνώμην δὲ ξυμ]
       [βά]λλεσθαι τῆς βου[λῆς εἰς τὸν δῆμον ὅτι δοκεῖ ᵛ]
   20  [τῆι] βουλῆι ᵛ ἐπαιν[έσαι τοὺς ἀγορανόμους τοὺς]
       [ἐπὶ] Φιλ[ό]νεω ἄρχ[οντος . . . . . . . .²⁰. . . . . . . . . .],
       [Τελεσ]ῖνον ᾿Ερχ[ιέα, . . . . . . . .²³. . . . . . . .]
       [. . .⁵. . .]ένην Βο[υτάδην . . . . . . . . . . . .²¹. . . . . . . . .]
       [————————————————————————————]
```

This decree was enacted at the same meeting of the assembly at which **216** was also passed, a detail established when that inscription was discovered, nine and a half years later than this present text. The commission for the inscribing of both was entrusted to the same workshop, that of the "Cutter of *IG* II² 788": see the commentary on **204** for the relevant details and references. In this example the requirement of vacant spaces at the ends of the lines, to permit syllabic division or whole-word endings, is very marked. Vacant letter spaces between clauses, visible only in lines 7 and 20, are to be supposed also in lines 8, 11, 13, and 15. Line 7 offers a further instance of the "economy design", for which see **214** and **216**.

Lines 1–7. For the details of the preamble see **216**, on which the restorations here depend. This decree also was probouleumatic; cf. P. J. Rhodes, *Athenian Boule*, p. 253 for contemporary examples. This text is not there listed, presumably on the grounds that the formula is restored and might have been ἔδοξεν τῶι δήμωι (i.e., nonprobouleumatic), despite the terms of lines 15–20; cf. **213**. But those instructions, together with the parallels of **216** and of *SEG* XXI, 392, suggest otherwise, and the briefer formula would upset the balance of the "economy design" by which the craftsman evidently set much store.

Lines 5–6. ἐπεψήφισζεν. For the spelling see **102**, commentary on lines 7–8 and **213**, line 6. Line 8. Kallistratos, son of Telesinos, of Aphidna. See **213**, commentary on lines 6–7. Telesinos himself was one of the agoranomoi honored, and Kallistratos thus had a particularly personal interest in making his proposal (line 22). Line 9. For the number and functions of the agoranomoi see Aristotle, *Athenaion Politeia* 51.1; Busolt-Swoboda, II, p. 118; U. Kahrstedt, *Untersuchungen zur Magistratur in Athen*, 1936, pp. 213–214 *et alibi*. Boards of officials of this kind and graduating classes of epheboi were usually commended in the year following that of their office or final year of service. See for example **187** and **188**. This originally created the presupposition that Kydenor's year followed immediately upon that of Philoneos; but *SEG* II, 9 provided the counter-indication, as described above and universally accepted, that the archonship of Theophemos intervened between the two. For the delay, reflecting no doubt the disturbed circumstances of the time which interfered with routine business, see the commentary on **216**. These agoranomoi were considerably better off than the sitonai there commended and had to wait less than two years for their reward.

Line 13. Ὅπως ἂν οὖν. For the "hortatory intention" see **86**, commentary on lines 21–24 and **173**, commentary on line 2. For the expression in terms of hoped-for emulation among officials see **185**, commentary on lines 16–17 and **194**, commentary on lines 17–18. If the restoration here is acceptable, the emphasis is not in this case on honor and fair dealing but on action conformable with the laws. Line 15. ἀγαθῆι τύχηι. Cf. **72**, commentary on lines 7–8.

Lines 16–17. Οἳ ἂν λάχωσιν. The older turn of phrase is retained here, in preference to the now more customary τοὺς λαχόντας προέδρους: cf., e.g., **194** (the earliest instance of the latter among the Agora decrees of this collection), **208**, and **213**. It remained in use at least until the archonship of Diokles (215/14); see *IG* II², 847 and 889: and it is restored in **261** (196/5). The ephelkystic nu is regular in this formula; see **185**, commentary on lines 19–20 and references there.

THE ARCHONSHIP OF LYSIAS, 239/8 OR 238/7 B.C.

Before the discovery of **218**, Lysias' archonship was known only from the two decrees in honor of the strategos Aristophanes of Leukonoion, voted by the Athenian and mercenary troops stationed in Eleusis, Panakton, and Phyle and by the Eleusinians, inscribed together on a single stele (*IG* II², 1299). Aristophanes' military career is there expressly associated with the archonships of Lysias and Kimon, and that of Lysias is further described as the archonship ἐν ᾧ ὁ πόλεμος ἐνέστη (line 57). In the same decree the services of Aristophanes to King Demetrios and his children are mentioned, the name having escaped the erasures that obscured the names of the king and of his queen in lines 10–11.

Earlier scholars, identifying Kimon with the archon of that name known at the beginning of the century and now firmly dated in 288/7, believed that the Demetrios referred to was Poliorketes. Hence Lysias was given a date as early as 293/2, and the "war" was that of Athens' liberation from Macedonian control at that period. But after the demonstration by W. Kolbe that the Demetrios was of necessity Demetrios II, Lysias' date has on all interpretations varied only through the quadrennium 241/40 to 237/6, depending upon the varied assessments of the outbreak and course of the "Demetrian War". Two different Aristophanes were in consequence confused in *PA* 2092. For fuller discussion of the development of the problem see W. B. Dinsmoor (*Archons of Athens*, pp. 55, 101–103, 180), whose own analysis set Lysias in 241/40, and on the outbreak of the Demetrian War, C. Habicht, *Untersuchungen*, pp. 134–135, note 99.

On the basis of the historical considerations, P. Treves (*Athenaeum* n.s. 12, 1934, pp. 400–401) assigned Lysias to 239/8, and this appeared at the time to coincide with the requirements of the secretary cycle: cf. B. D. Meritt, *Hesperia* 4, 1935, p. 585. Meritt's views of Lysias' relationship with his predecessors underwent repeated revision between 1935 and his final discussion of the matter (*Hesperia* 50, 1981, pp. 82, 96), by which time he had come to recognize that at that juncture the secretary cycle could not be envisaged as in regular operation; but the same dating of Lysias had been accepted by Dinsmoor (*Athenian Archon*

List, pp. 82–83, 155) and in all subsequent reconsiderations of the archon list from W. K. Pritchett and Meritt (*Chronology*, pp. xxii–xxiii) to Habicht (*Untersuchungen*, p. 143). The insertion by M. J. Osborne of an extra archon between Diomedon and Philoneos, mentioned above in the context of those archonships, pp. 305–306, depressed the dates of Philoneos and his successors by one year and placed Lysias in 238/7, which can still be reckoned a reasonable dating for the outbreak of the Demetrian War (considered by some to have begun as late as 237/6): see *ZPE* 78, 1989, pp. 224–226 with note 79, p. 241. Lysias was a man of means, if as seems highly likely he is to be identified with the Lysias of Kephisia who contributed the maximum permitted sum to the *epidosis* of the year of Diomedon (**213**, col. II, line 48); cf. Habicht, *Studien*, p. 33.

That the year of Lysias was an intercalary year was made apparent by **218**, in which sufficient of the prescript survives to require an equation between the festival and prytany months giving the latter a length of 32 days regular in such a year. As restored, Elaphebolion 22 = pryt. IX, 32 = 288th day. The year was the fourth in the (eleventh) Metonic cycle, in which it was scheduled as ordinary, or the fifth, in which case it should indeed have been intercalary (cf. Meritt, *TAPA* 95, 1964, p. 236). But the former general regularity of correspondence between Meton's arrangement and the Athenian festival calendar, already neglected during the tenth cycle, had ceased to be a matter of regard and offers no guidance towards an absolute date. Nothing is known of the phylai in prytany. If **218** is correctly restored, the ninth prytany was held by Antigonis, Demetrias, Pandionis, or Akamantis.

The γραμματεύς of the year probably came from Aphidna (Aiantis XI) but might have come from Oinoe (see the commentary on **218**, line 3). Oinoe gave its name to two demes, one in the phyle Hippothontis (X) and the other in Aiantis (XI): but the Oinoe of Hippothontis may have been transferred to the phyle Demetrias (II) on the latter's creation in 307/6. See J. S. Traill, *Political Organization*, p. 27; Habicht, *Untersuchungen*, pp. 142–143, note 147; Osborne, *ZPE* 78, 1989, p. 220, note 58. At an earlier period of studies of the archon list these variant possibilities would have been of considerable significance in determining Lysias' year in relation to the secretary cycle; for those who regard the cycle as inoperative in his time, they are without real consequence, but it was Meritt's ultimate contention that the cycle began again, with Aiantis XI, in this very year (*Hesperia* 50, 1981, p. 96).

COMMENDATION FOR THE ARCHITECT WORKING ON THE SHRINE OF BASILE

218. A diagonally broken fragment of the upper part of a stele of bluish white Pentelic marble (I 4138), with part of the upper ovolo molding and pedimental top preserved, as well as the original rough-picked back, but broken elsewhere, discovered on May 8, 1936, in a late context above South Stoa II (M 15).

H. 0.38 m.; W. 0.30 m.; Th. 0.115 m.
LH. 0.006 m.
Στοιχ. Hor. 0.01 m.; Vert. 0.015 m.

Ed. B. D. Meritt, *Hesperia* 7, 1938, pp. 123–126, no. 25, with photograph. See *SEG* XIX, 78, with a change in the phraseology restored in lines 14–16 suggested by M. N. Tod, and with reference to R. E. Wycherley (*BSA* 55, 1960, p. 63), who drew upon lines 9–16 in a discussion of the precinct of Basile.

a. 239/8 *vel* 238/7 a., *pryt.* IX   ΣΤΟΙΧ. 34

ΈπΙ Λυσίου ἄρχ[οντος ἐπὶ τῆς . . . .⁸. . . . δος]
[ἐνά]της πρυτανε[ίας ἧι . . . . . . .¹⁶. . . . . . .]
['Αφιδ]ναῖος ἐγρ[αμμάτευεν· 'Ελαφηβολιῶνος]
[ὀγδόη]ι μετ'εἰκ[άδας, δευτέραι καὶ τριακοσ]
5   [τῆι τῆς] πρυταν[είας· ἐκκλησία· τῶν προέδρω]
[ν ἐπεψή]φιζεν Σ[. . . . . .²². . . . .]
[καὶ συμπ]ρόεδρ[οι.   vacat   ]
[ᵛᵛᵛᵛ ἔδο]ξεν τῆ[ι βουλῆι καὶ τῶι δήμωι· ᵛᵛᵛ]
[. . .⁸. . . .] Πρωτογ[. . . . .¹¹. . . . . εἶπεν· ἐπεὶ]
10   [δὴ ἡ ἱέρεια] τῆς Βασιλ[ης . . . . . .¹⁵. . . . . . .]

[καὶ οἱ ἱεροπ]οιοὶ οἱ χειρο[τονηθέντες ἐπὶ]
[....¹⁰.... ἐπ]αινοῦσιν τὸν ἀ[ρχιτέκτονα]
[καὶ κελεύουσιν] πέμψαι εἰς τὴ[ν πομπὴν τῶν]
[Παναθηναίων τὴν] αὐτοῦ θυγατέ[ρα, ὅτι τὴν ἐ]
15   [πιμέλειαν τοῦ ναο]ῦ καλῶς καὶ φ[ιλοτίμως ἐ]
[ποιήσατο, δεδόχθαι τ]ῆι βο[υ]λεῖ [τοὺς λαχόν]
[τας προέδρους εἰς τὴν] ἐπιοῦσαν [ἐκκλησίαν]
[χρηματίσαι περὶ τούτω]ν, γνώ[μην δὲ ξυμβάλ]
[λεσθαι τῆς βουλῆς εἰς τὸν δῆμον ὅτι δοκεῖ]
20   [κτλ. —————————————————————]

This inscription offers the latest in date of the ten decrees from the Agora assembled here which have been attributed by S. V. Tracy to the "Cutter of *IG* II² 788", although texts several years later than the archonship of Lysias have been judged to be works of his establishment, the name piece itself and *IG* II², 790 (*Agora* XV, 115), both of 235/4, being the latest to which a date may be assigned. For the details see Tracy, *Hesperia* 57, 1988, pp. 311–322 and the commentary on **204**. The mason maintains his penchant for the "perfect design" (discussed above under **204**), even at the cost of leaving line 7 less than half filled. Cf. A. S. Henry, *Prescripts*, p. 68. On the other hand, he has paid less regard to the leaving of vacant letter spaces between clauses or significant elements and has apparently not cared to end lines with similar blank spaces in order to achieve syllabic division or whole-word endings, a consideration that may have bearing on the restorations of lines 2–3 and 11–12.

Line 3. ['Αφιδ]ναῖος rather than [.. Οἰ]ναῖος, if it is judged preferable to end line 2 and begin line 3 with complete words: but the latter remains a possibility. Line 4. [ἐνάτη]ι Meritt, with the assumption that the month was full. But if Elaphebolion 22 is to fall on the 288th day of the year, in complete concordance with the prytany date, either Anthesterion was also full or there had been two successive full months earlier in the year. However, [ὀγδόη]ι is an equally possible restoration and has been adopted in the above text. This makes Elaphebolion a hollow month, but the date in modern terms (Elaphebolion 22 = 288th day) remains the same, ἐνάτη μετ'εἰκάδας being the day omitted in such a month (cf. A. G. Woodhead, *Study of Greek Inscriptions*, p. 121; J. A. Walsh, *ZPE* 41, 1981, pp. 107–124). If the year began with full Hekatombaion, the months will have succeeded each other throughout in a regular alternation of 30 and 29 days, to produce a year of 384 days. Both ἐνάτη and ὀγδόη μετ'εἰκάδας in Elaphebolion were days in which the assembly is otherwise attested as having met: see J. D. Mikalson, *Sacred and Civil Calendar*, pp. 133–134 (under Elaphebolion 22 and 23, since for convenience every month there studied is treated as full; cf. pp. 8–9).

Line 8. The decree was probouleumatic: cf. P. J. Rhodes, *Athenian Boule*, p. 253. Lines 10–11. On the precinct of Basile, united with those of Neleus and Kodros and located on the right bank of the Ilissos in the southeastern suburbs of Athens, see Wycherley, *op. cit.*, pp. 60–66; W. Judeich, *Topographie*, pp. 387–388; J. Travlos, *A Pictorial Dictionary of Ancient Athens*, 1971, p. 322, with bibliography. The site has been identified as lying between Syngrou Boulevard and Makriyianni Street and was extensive (Travlos, *op. cit.*, p. 333, fig. 435). *SEG* XXIV, 58, of the 5th century, is a boundary marker delimiting its area. Lines 11–12. ἐπὶ | 'Αθηνοδώρου Meritt, a restoration made at a time when he believed Athenodoros to have held office in the year immediately preceding that of Lysias. But Athenodoros has been relocated to the mid 250's, and the restoration cannot stand. Of the archons of the years that may be considered relevant, only Thersilochos will fit the space in the same way, but it may be hard to suppose the hieropoioi in office for almost a decade. Disregard of syllabic division would allow ἐπ'Ε|ὐρυκλείδου, Eurykleides being generally accepted as having held office in the year immediately or at most next-but-one before Lysias. However, the lacuna may have contained a formula different from that originally conjectured.

Lines 14–16. τῆς ἐ||πιμελείας and ἐ|πεμελήθη Meritt. Line 16. τῆι, but βουλεῖ: cf. Henry, *CQ* n.s. 14, 1964, pp. 240–241 and L. Threatte, *Grammar*, p. 378. Lines 16–17. τοὺς λαχόντας προέδρους. The developed formula: compare **217**. There are 35 letters in line 17, for which Meritt suggested the crowding in of an extra letter in violation of the stoichedon order. The phraseology of the regular formula indeed imposes the supposition.

THE ARCHONSHIP OF PHEIDOSTRATOS, BEFORE 229/8 B.C.

The discovery of **219** did nothing to resolve the problem of the date of Pheidostratos' year in office beyond demonstrating that the year, whenever it was, was ordinary in the Athenian festival calendar. The evidence for it already known depended wholly on two dedications, *IG* II², 2854 and 2855. Of these the latter is uninformative, save that its dedicator, Deinias, son of Kephisodotos, of the deme Boutadai, was surely a descendant of that Kephisodotos, son of Deinias, of the same deme who was a councillor in 303/2

(*SEG* XXIV, 161, line 123 = *Agora* XV, 62, line 186). If the councillor was a young man at that time, and Pheidostratos held office in the early 240's, as some suppose (see below), the dedicator could be the councillor's son in middle age. B. D. Meritt, dating Pheidostratos in 231/30 (see below), was prepared to accept the same relationship, with the son then "a man of mature years". If the councillor in 303/2 was already into middle age, with an infant grandson born at the time or soon after, the dedicator could be his great-grandson, and for this relationship the later dating of Pheidostratos would be eminently suitable.

But it is around *IG* II², 2854 that discussion has centered. This records a dedication by Kallisthenes of Prospalta, στρατηγὸς ἐπὶ τὴν παραλίαν, discovered at Rhamnous, on which see J. Pouilloux, *Forteresse*, pp. 121–122, no. 9 and L. Moretti, *Iscrizioni storiche ellenistiche* I, pp. 56–58, no. 26, with *SEG* XXV, 205, XXXI, 156, XXXII, 243. It states that the donor was phylarch in the archonship of Philostratos, hipparch in that of Antimachos, and general in those of Phanostratos and Pheidostratos, with the consequence that these four archonships are to be interpreted as going closely or reasonably closely together within the span of one man's experienced military career: and they were placed by J. Kirchner in the mid-250's (*IG* II², iv, 1, p. 14). Other scholars felt able to place them fifty years later or to separate one or two of the four archonships from the others. See W. B. Dinsmoor (*Archons of Athens*, pp. 54–55 and 171–173), who himself gave them the four consecutive years 254/3 to 251/50, with Pheidostratos in 252/1.

The same order of connection of the four archons was retained by W. S. Ferguson (*Athenian Tribal Cycles*, pp. 24–25), with the dates 260/59 to 257/6, and followed by Meritt (*Hesperia* 4, 1935, pp. 584–585), save that the latter moved Philostratos to 261/60 and introduced the archonship of Euboulos between his and that of Phanostratos. A subsequent readjustment (*Hesperia* 7, 1938, p. 135) carried further the supposition that the group was not necessarily immediately consecutive and set the four between 258/7 and 254/3, with Pheidostratos in the last-named year and Kleomachos intervening in 256/5 between Antimachos and Phanostratos. But the group's fragmentation was taken to extreme limits by Dinsmoor's 1939 revision (*Athenian Archon List*, pp. 21–22, 150–151, 156–158), in which he spread Kallisthenes' military activity through twenty-one years, from Philostratos in 254/3 to Phanostratos in 234/3, with Pheidostratos tentatively in 238/7.

In reaching his conclusion, Dinsmoor had knowledge of **219** in advance of its publication, and his interpretation of the demotic of the γραμματεύς in line 3 of that text as Βη]σ[αιεύς, which set him in the phyle Antiochis (XII), accorded with the secretary cycle. W. K. Pritchett and Meritt, in their *editio princeps* (see **219**), read ʼẸ[ρχιεύς as the demotic and in consequence interchanged Phanostratos and Pheidostratos in Dinsmoor's arrangement, retaining the same dates 238/7 and 234/3 (*Chronology*, pp. xxii–xxiii). 234/3 became thereafter the generally accepted date for Pheidostratos, adopted by Pritchett and O. Neugebauer, *Calendars*, p. 83; Pouilloux, *Forteresse*; Moretti, *Iscrizione storiche ellenistiche* I, pp. 56–58, no. 26; and Dinsmoor, *Hesperia* 23, 1954, p. 315; and repeated by Meritt, *Athenian Year*, p. 234.

The identification by E. Vanderpool of a hitherto unknown archon Aristion, whom on epigraphical and historical grounds he found it advisable to assign to 238/7 (*SEG* XXIV, 156, XXV, 205), displaced Phanostratos from that accepted position. Vanderpool tentatively set him and Pheidostratos in the successive years 234/3 and 233/2, and advised that the epsilon of the controlling demotic ʼẸ[ρχιεύς was not to be seen on the stone, thus freeing Pheidostratos from the assumed requirements of the secretary cycle. Meritt's reassignment of Philinos to 254/3 as the result of the discovery of *Agora* XV, 89 (see p. 284 above) also dispossessed Philostratos, who had been the earliest in accepted date of the group of four. Meritt reexamined the whole question in the light of these two pieces of newly acquired evidence (*Hesperia* 38, 1969, pp. 434–435) and restored Kallisthenes' career as a military commander to the economical compactness of four consecutive years in the reign of Demetrios II from 234/3 to 231/0 (Philostratos to Pheidostratos). But there is uncertainty also about the year of Jason, Pheidostratos' putative successor, who may intervene between Phanostratos and Pheidostratos rather than succeed the latter, and alternative dates had therefore to be given for Pheidostratos' archonship. Cf. Meritt, *Historia* 26, 1977, p. 177.

Meritt's conclusions formed the starting-point for a further analysis of the problem by C. Habicht (*Untersuchungen*, pp. 128–133), under the title "Antimachos und seine Gruppe", justly so described, for it is the evidence regarding Antimachos that conditions the rest. This led him to the belief that the four-archon group should be set in the latter half of the 250's, reverting thus to the period favored in earlier analyses. But none of the elements of this evidence, whether taken separately or together, can be regarded as conclusive.

Meritt, who continued to accept the validity of the secretary cycle for the period advocated by Habicht as well as for the period after the archonship of Lysias (239/8), and thus to accept the significance of the detail that the phyle of the γραμματεύς of Antimachos' year was Pandionis (V), reiterated his preferred dating (*Hesperia* 59, 1981, pp. 92–93, 96).

M. J. Osborne, for whom the secretary cycle was inoperative between 261/60 and 229/8 (except by possible coincidence between 250 and 245), found a place for the group in his reconstruction of the archon list between Athenodoros and Polyeuktos, allowing three possible variants (*ZPE* 78, 1989, pp. 237, 241). From this, Pheidostratos' year emerges as 249/8 or 248/7, the lowest limit envisaged for it by Habicht.

With scholarly opinion so divided, yet equally based on interpretation of the same limited evidence and resulting in a difference of nearly twenty years between the dates assigned to Pheidostratos' year of office, the prudent conclusion must be to avoid speculation and await some helpful new discovery. The date prefacing **219** reflects that impasse.

The obvious restorations introduced into **219** on the basis of the sufficient indications of the surviving text showed that Pheidostratos' year was ordinary, as mentioned earlier, with festival and prytany dates in harmony. Cf. Pritchett and Neugebauer, *Calendars*, p. 83. Pandionis held the last prytany of the year, of which no other details are known.

FRAGMENT OF A DECREE

219. A fragment of the upper part of a stele of Pentelic marble (I 5796), with the original rough-picked back and part of a heavy molding above the inscribed surface preserved, discovered on April 28, 1939, in a modern wall at the north foot of the Areopagos. The stone is worn, and much battered at the edges.

H. 0.19 m.; W. 0.195 m.; Th. 0.095 m.
LH. 0.005 m.

Ed. W. K. Pritchett and B. D. Meritt, *Chronology*, pp. 100–101, with photograph. See also *SEG* XXXII, 126 (the text of the *editio princeps*, with additional references to E. Vanderpool, Δελτ. 23, Α', 1968, p. 5 and note 14, and to Meritt, *Hesperia* 38, 1969, p. 435 with note 25, for readings in line 3). The same text, but with new readings in line 3, by M. J. Osborne, *ZPE* 78, 1989, p. 240 with note 136; cf. *SEG* XXXIX, 126.

anni incerti (*sed ante a.* 229/8 *a.*), *pryt.* XII   NON-ΣΤΟΙΧ. *ca.* 30–33

```
        ['Επὶ] Φειδοστράτου [ἄρ]χο[ντος ἐπὶ τῆς Π]
        [ανδ]ιονίδος δωδε[κάτ]ης [πρυτανείας ἧι]
        [...]οχάρης Κτησι[.³⁻⁴.]⁻[. ᶜᵃ·⁶.. ἐγραμμ]
        [άτευ]εν· Σκιροφορ[ιῶ]νος π[έμπτηι μετ'εἰκ]
   5    [άδας, ἕκτηι καὶ] εἰκο[σ]τῆι [τῆς πρυτανείας]·
        [ἐκκλησία] κυ[ρ]ία· [--------------]
        [------------------------]
```

The writing is plain and regular, with no peculiarities, and offers no help in the general problem of the date to which the decree is to be assigned. The chief interest and difficulty of the text concentrate in the patronymic and demotic of the γραμματεύς in line 3. The demotic is of consequence if, as Meritt believed, the secretary cycle had been revived in the archonship of Lysias, which he dated in 239/8; the demotic should therefore refer to Akamantis (VII) or Oineis (VIII) in order to uphold his proposed dates for Pheidostratos of 231/30 or 230/29. But nothing of it can effectively be read, and no conclusion may be drawn beyond the observation that it was evidently short (no more than five letters, on the reading of Osborne, *ZPE* 78, 1989, p. 240). In that case 'Οῆθεν would suit the second of Meritt's suggested years. On the earlier dating for Pheidostratos described above, evidence for the secretary cycle is irrelevant and the reading is of no consequence beyond the satisfaction of scholarly precision. Analysis has developed as follows: E. Schweigert reported epsilon or sigma as the fifth letter after iota, and the *editio princeps* "inclined to the belief that a vertical stroke of pi occurs in the patronymic." Hence the Κτησίπ[που] 'Ε[ρχιεύς of the first publication and the implied rejection of Κτήσ[ωνος Βη]σ[αιεύς of W. B. Dinsmoor, who had prepublication knowledge of the fragment (*Athenian Archon List*, p. 157). Vanderpool noted that no cross-stroke for the supposed pi was visible, and he did not believe in the existence of the epsilon, judgments accepted by Meritt (*Hesperia* 38, 1969, p. 435). Osborne described the results of his close examination of the stone as showing a likely kappa where previously the pi had been discerned, with OY in the fourth and fifth spaces thereafter, hence Κτησιχ[ράτ]ου [. . . . . χτλ.]. Perceptions may vary in so difficult a context. The upright of the pi or kappa is assured, as is an angled stroke in the fifth space thereafter: Κτησιχ[λέου]ς followed by a short demotic may be possible.

Lines 4–5. For Skirophorion 26 (as here restored) as a meeting day of the assembly see J. D. Mikalson, *Sacred and Civil Calendar*, pp. 176–177. While conjectured in this and one other text, there is no clear independent evidence about it. Line 6. ἐκκλησία κυρία. See **101**, commentary on lines 7–8.

FRAGMENT OF AN HONORARY DECREE

220 (Pl. 22). A fragment of a stele of Hymettian marble (I 5791), with the right side and original rough-picked back preserved, discovered on April 25, 1939, among marbles from the area south of the Eleusinion.

H. 0.31 m.; W. 0.27 m.; Th. 0.14 m.
LH. 0.005 m.

Ed. W. K. Pritchett, *Hesperia* 15, 1946, pp. 149–150, no. 9, with photograph. Lines 3–4 quoted in *Agora* III, p. 82, no. 227, among the testimonia for the Eleusinion.

a. 245–229 *a.*(?)   NON-ΣΤΟΙΧ. *ca.* 36

```
     [----------------------------------]
     [------------------------------· ἀνα]
     [γράψαι δὲ τόδε τὸ ψήφισμα τ]ὸγ [γραμματέα τὸν κα]
     [τὰ πρυτανείαν ἐν στήλ]ηι λιθίνηι κ[αὶ στῆσαι ἐν]
     [τῶι Ἐλευσινίωι τῶι ἐν] ἄσ[τ]ει· εἰς δὲ τὴν ἀνα[γραφὴν]
     [τῆς στήλης μερίσαι] τὸν ἐπὶ τεῖ διοικήσ[ει τὸ γ]
5    [ενόμενον ἀνάλωμα].
                            vacat 0.10 m.
     [ἡ βουλή]          ἡ βουλή        ἡ βουλή
     [ὁ δῆμος]          ὁ δῆμος        ὁ δῆμος.
                        vacat
```

The lettering of this inscription displays in an extreme form that affection for the "squaring off" of loops and of circular letters that was a feature of the style of the "Cutter of Agora I 3238 and I 4169", whom S. V. Tracy identified as active during the forty years from 286/5 to 245/4: see *Hesperia* 57, 1988, pp. 304–311 and the commentary on **172**. But this text is of inferior quality (Pritchett described it as "degenerate"), as if undertaken by a less competent imitator or member of the workshop.

That the decree is to be dated earlier than 229 and later than 261 is made clear by the reference to the Single Officer of Administration as responsible for payment for the stele: cf. **174** and A. S. Henry, *Chiron* 14, 1984, pp. 74–81, *ZPE* 72, 1988, pp. 133–134, *ZPE* 78, 1989, pp. 277–278. That it is not inscribed stoichedon may suggest that it should be dated later rather than earlier in that general period; but the conclusion is not obligatory (cf., e.g., **195** and **197**).

Lines 6–7. Three persons (at least) were apparently honored, but their names were not shown in the citations. For the phenomenon, which is unusual, Pritchett compared *IG* II², 312, 314, and 573, to which may be added 1155 and perhaps 907, 1002, and 1233. The location decreed for the stele implies that they had a particular connection with the cult of the Eleusinian deities; cf. **239**.

FRAGMENT OF THE CONCLUSION OF AN HONORARY DECREE

221. A small fragment of a stele of Pentelic marble (I 1048), broken on all sides, discovered on July 5, 1933, in a stratum of black earth above the Classical level in front of the central part of the Stoa of Zeus Eleutherios (I 6).

H. 0.092 m.; W. 0.059 m.; Th. 0.025 m.
LH. 0.006 m.
Στοιχ. Hor. 0.011 m.; Vert. 0.013 m.

Ed. B. D. Meritt, *Hesperia* 16, 1947, p. 159, no. 54, with photograph pl. XXVIII. Indexed in *Agora* III, pp. 244–245, but not cited in the context indicated.

ante a. 229 *a.*   ΣTOIX. 47

[————————————————————————————————]
[————————χαὶ στεφανῶσ]αι θαλλ[οῦ στεφάνωι·ᵛ ἀναγράψαι δὲ]
[τόδε τὸ ψήφισμα τὸν γραμ]ματέα [τὸν κατὰ πρυτανείαν ἐν στή]
[λει λιθίνει χαὶ στῆσαι π]αρὰ τὸ [Μητρῶιον· εἰς δὲ τὴν ἀναγρα]
[φὴν μερίσαι τὸν ἐπὶ τεῖ δι]οιχή[σει τὸ γενόμενον ἀνάλωμα. ᵛᵛᵛ]
vacat

The writing is nondescript and generally indicative of a date in the third quarter of the 3rd century. The sole idiosyncrasy occurs in the inscribing of tau, in which the horizontal stroke rises from left to right, and the upright stroke is off-center to the right. The restorations conform to standard phraseology: line divisions are arbitrary, as there are no means of assessing the situation of the fragment in relation to the total width of the stele.

Meritt's publication dated the text "*ca.* 240" but did not discuss that date's comparative precision. If, as is consonant with the stoichedon order, the Single Officer of Administration is correctly restored in line 4, the decree will antedate 229 and postdate 261 B.C. Cf. **220** and references there.

Line 1. The stephanos is of olive: its recipient may well have been an Athenian official, if the restoration in line 3 is acceptable. See A. S. Henry, *Honours*, pp. 38–40. Line 3. παρὰ τὸ Μητρῶιον. The restoration was suggested by the space made available by the stoichedon pattern and by the place of discovery. But as a location for the erection of stelai it is rarely attested; cf. *Agora* III, p. 151.

FRAGMENT OF A DECREE

222 (Pl. 22). A fragment of a stele of Pentelic marble (I 5090), with the right side and original rough-picked back preserved, discovered on December 15, 1937, in a wall of a modern house south of the Market Square (N 19). The inscribed surface is worn away before extending to the right edge.

H. 0.182 m.; W. 0.161 m.; Th. 0.09 m.
LH. 0.005 m.

Ed. A. G. Woodhead, *Studies Presented to Sterling Dow on His Eightieth Birthday*, 1984, pp. 315–318, with photograph pl. 22. See also *SEG* XXXIV, 91. Brief prepublication reference by S. Dow, *Hesperia* 32, 1963, p. 337, in a study of lists of proedroi by name in the prescripts of Athenian decrees.

a. 229/8–225/4 *a.*   NON-ΣTOIX. *ca.* 33

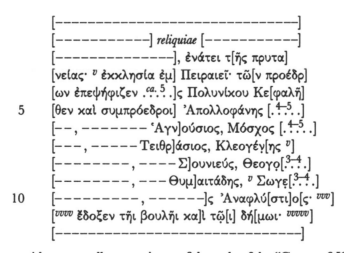

This inscription provides an excellent specimen of the style of the "Cutter of *IG* II² 1706", so designated by S. V. Tracy (*Hesperia* 47, 1978, pp. 247–255, *Attic Letter-Cutters*, pp. 44–54, with photograph of part of the name piece, fig. 2; the present text is listed on p. 48). Tracy regards this man's career as spanning the last thirty years of the 3rd century, identifying more than eighty inscriptions as from his hand. His work is "plain and rather sloppy" and gives the impression of haste in execution. Eight other public decrees in this present collection have been assigned to him: **224**, **225**, and **227–232**; see also **255J**. The style is distinctive and was first recognized by A. Wilhelm in seven different texts, a number expanded to over thirty by Dow (*AJA* 40, 1936, pp. 58–60; cf. *HSCP* 48, 1937, pp. 105–106), who referred to it as "the disjointed style", with a studied carelessness amounting almost to mannerism. All known texts in it are nonstoichedon.

Dow observed and Tracy confirmed that the style does not antedate 229/8 in dated examples, nor does it outlast the end of the century. 229/8 must therefore be regarded as a *terminus post quem* for the present text. The number of proedroi as listed (eleven, omitting a representative of the phyle in prytany) shows that the decree belongs to the period of twelve phylai, i.e., before the establishment of the phyle Ptolemais in 224/3. This sets 225/4 as the *terminus ante quem* and confines the date of the enactment to a span of five years.

Dow also studied (*Hesperia* 32, 1963, pp. 335–365) the decrees in which all the proedroi were listed by name. The present text, together with *IG* II², 852, constituted the last in date. These same two also share the virtue of being set out in the "perfect design", discussed in the context of **204**, and quite evidently, despite its calligraphic shortcomings, the present text has been carefully planned.

The proedroi are listed in the "official order" of the phylai. By deduction it may be asserted that Oineis or Kekropis was the phyle in prytany at the time, since the chairman was of Akamantis (VII), and one name only occupies the space between the proedroi of the demes Sounion (Leontis VI) and Thymaitadai (Hippothontis X). None of the proedroi listed can be further identified.

Line 3. The assembly took place in the Peiraieus, and this appears to be the earliest instance of its being convened in that location. Such an assembly was an impossibility until the withdrawal of the Macedonian garrison in 230/29 and the recovery by the Athenians of the full control of their port.

THE ARCHONSHIP OF THEOPHILOS, 227/6 B.C.

The first part of the fragment of the inscribed list of archons, *IG* II², 1706, on which see the fundamental study of S. Dow, *Hesperia* 2, 1933, pp. 418–446, provides a consecutive series of eponymous archons [Heliodoros]–Leochares–Theophilos–Ergochares–Niketes–Antiphilos, who can therefore only be assigned or reassigned as a group to a six-year period in the archon list. The γραμματεῖς of the first four are known and follow the official order of phylai from Kekropis (IX) to Antiochis (XII). The six years were identified by J. Kirchner (*IG* II², iv, 1, pp. 14–15), following W. S. Ferguson, as 229/8 to 224/3, with Theophilos therefore in 227/6. This arrangement was generally accepted and still stands; but it did not pass completely unquestioned. W. B. Dinsmoor (*Archons of Athens*, pp. 191–203) reexamined the evidence, especially in relation to the date of the creation of the phyle Ptolemais, which came into being during the period covered by the fragment of the archon list, and he concluded that the succession of the six archons ran from 232/1 to 227/6, with Theophilos in 230/29. By 1939, however, he had thought better of his unorthodoxy (*Athenian Archon List*, pp. 159–161).

The year 227/6, then, remaining unchallenged as the date agreed for Theophilos' year of office since that time, is shown as such in the following tables of archons: W. K. Pritchett and B. D. Meritt, *Chronology*, p. xxiii; Dinsmoor, *Hesperia* 23, 1954, p. 315; Meritt, *Athenian Year*, p. 234 and *Historia* 26, 1977, p. 177. See also Pritchett and O. Neugebauer, *Calendars*, p. 83. That the γραμματεῖς of this group conform to the official order of the phylai in their sequence demonstrates that the secretary cycle had been effectively resumed by 229/8. The γραμματεύς of Theophilos' year was Philippos, son of Kephisodoros, of Aphidna (Aiantis XI); see *IG* II², 837.

IG II², 837 also showed that the year was ordinary in the festival calendar, and a revision of its text (Meritt, *Athenian Year*, p. 143; *SEG* XXI, 399) eliminated a discrepancy of two days between the festival and prytany dates which had been the consequence of the *IG* text. Cf. Pritchett and Neugebauer, *Calendars*, p. 83. The year began with full Hekatombaion. **223** adds nothing to the calendric data for the year. It was the sixteenth year of the (eleventh) Metonic cycle. Had the Athenian festival year still kept some accord with Meton's system the year would have been intercalary at Athens, but it seems that there was now no correspondence between them save by coincidence. From *IG* II², 837 it also appears that the third prytany was held by Kekropis; nothing further is known of the prytany year.

DECREE OF A THIASOS IN HONOR OF GNATHIS(?) AND HIS SONS(?)

223. The upper left corner of a flat-topped stele of Hymettian marble (I 5887), with the rough-picked top, original back, and left side preserved but with the crowning molding roughly chiseled away, discovered on November 8, 1939, outside the area of the Market Square near the Church of St. Demetrios on the saddle between the hills of the Pnyx and Philopappos. The inscribed surface is battered and worn, especially in its lower section.

H. 0.37 m.; W. 0.155 m.; Th. 0.08 m.
LH. *ca.* 0.006 m.

Ed. B. D. Meritt, *Hesperia* 30, 1961, pp. 227–228, no. 26, with photograph pl. 41. See also *SEG* XXI, 532.

a. 227/6 a.   *tantum non* ΣΤΟΙΧ. *ca.* 32

```
          ['Ε]πὶ Θεοφίλου ἄρ[χοντος· ἀγορᾶι κυρίαι· ᵛ]
          [Ν]ικόμαχος Νίκω[νος . . ᶜᵃ˙⁷ . . εἶπεν· δεδό]
          [χ]θαι τῶι κοινῶι [τῶν θιασωτῶν· ἐπειδὴ Γν(?)]
          [ἄ]θις διατετέλε[κεν τῶι κοινῶι αὐτὸς με]
   5      [γ]άλας χρείας πα[ρέχων καὶ οἱ παῖδες αὐτοῦ(?)]
          [ε]ὔνους ἦσαν τῶ[ι κοινῶι κατὰ τὸ δυνατόν],
          καὶ γραμματε[ὺς αὐτὸς κατασταθεὶς δικαί]
          [ω]ς ἐξήγαγεν τὴ[ν λειτουργίαν ἐπιδιδοὺς]
          [πλ]ειονάκις, ᵛ ὁ[μοίως δὲ καὶ ὅσων χρεία ἦν]
  10      [ἐφ]ρόντισεν πά[ντων ὅπως ἂν καὶ ἄλλοι βο]
          [ηθ]οῦντες συνερ[γῶσι εἰς πᾶν τὸ συμφέρον],
          [καὶ] διὰ ταῦτα στ[εφανωθεὶς ––––––––––]
          [. . . ᶜᵃ˙⁹ . . .]τε[––––––––––––––––––––]
          [.³⁻⁴.]ευε[–––––––––––––––––––––––]
  15      [²⁻³]ω[. . . ᶜᵃ˙⁸ . . .]ον[––––––––––––––––]
          [. .]ι καὶ [.ᶜᵃ˙⁵.]υτ[–––––––––––––––––]
          [.ᶜᵃ˙⁶. . .]εχ[.ᶜᵃ˙⁴.]ια[–––––––––––––––]
          [.ᶜᵃ˙⁴. τ]οῖς ἄ[λ]λοι[ς ––––––––––––––]
          [.ᶜᵃ˙⁵.]αι ευθυ[ν –––––––––––––––––]
  20      [.ᶜᵃ˙⁵.] ταμίας [–––––––––––––––––]
          [.ᶜᵃ˙⁴.]π[.³⁻⁴.]το τῶν [––––––––––––––]
          [––––––––––––––––––––––––––––––]
```

The writing is competent but undistinguished. S. V. Tracy (*Attic Letter-Cutters*, pp. 31, 254) saw it as "rather ordinary" and was unable to assign it to an identified craftsman, although the style has in his view some general affinity with that of the "Cutter of *IG* II² 788", for whom see **204**. The early lines preserve reasonable stoichedon order, but this is less accurately followed after line 10, and in line 5 ΣΧΡ occupies the space of two letters. Omega is wide, with horizontal strokes set relatively high. Mu and sigma have in some instances parallel external strokes, and there is one example (line 5) of pi with both upright strokes equal in length, the earliest among the Agora public decrees. Xi lacks its vertical stroke.

The brevity of the prescript and the text of line 3 combine to indicate that the decree emanates not from the Athenian body politic but from an association of some kind. Meritt restored it as the enactment of a thiasos, and his restorations are followed in lines 1–12 of the above text, based in line 1 upon *IG* II², 1283, and in line 3 upon *IG* II², 1298. For line 8 cf. *IG* II², 1304, lines 4 and 14. The presence of the plural verb in line 6 suggested that others besides –––this himself were involved in the honors. Readings of the lower part of the stone have been improved without adding to the intelligibility of that section of the text.

Line 2. The proposer cannot be further identified. Lines 3–4. Κρᾶ]θις is also possible. Cf. *SEG* X, 424, stele III, line 7 (not now to be considered part of *SEG* X, 424; see *SEG* XXI, 131). Line 6. For εὔνους as nominative plural see Meisterhans-Schwyzer³, p. 149, §6, with note 1287.

THE ARCHONSHIP OF ERGOCHARES, 226/5 B.C.

The fragment of the archon list mentioned at an earlier stage, *IG* II², 1706, shows the year of Ergochares as the immediate successor of that of Theophilos; for the details of the dates of the connected series of archons of which they form part, and references to expositions of them, see p. 319 above.

If the archon year requires little comment, the same cannot be said of the Athenian calendar during Ergochares' term of office. In **224**, Metageitnion 29 = pryt. III, 27, an indication that a second Hekatombaion had been intercalated. *Agora* XV, 121 as originally restored shows Anthesterion 8 = pryt. VIII, 22, and *IG* II², 838 (*SEG* XXXII, 120) provides the interesting correspondence Metageitnion 22 intercalated the second time (Metag. 22³) = pryt. III, 20: cf. W. K. Pritchett, *Ancient Athenian Calendars on Stone*, p. 341. The last-mentioned decree was presumably passed on the 84th day of the month, after two prytanies each of 32 days, as regularly in an intercalary year. Metageitnion 22³ was thus actually the 24th day of the month and must as it seems have followed two Hekatombaions each of 30 days, unless some additional adjustment to the calendar at an earlier stage be envisaged (see below). For Metageitnion also was a full month, the date of *IG* II², 838, ἐνάτη μετ'εἰκάδας, being possible only in a month of 30 days (cf. **218**, commentary on line 4). Pritchett and O. Neugebauer, *Calendars*, pp. 73–74, assumed the three consecutive full months (the third of them with the two extra days added to give a month of 32 days), followed by four months of 29 days each and one of 30, to give the correct equation (246th day) for *Agora* XV, 121.

This extreme irregularity in the festival calendar was irreconcilable with the principle advocated by B. D. Meritt (*Athenian Year*, pp. 33–36) that full and hollow months alternated with as much regularity as possible. Meritt therefore (*op. cit.*, pp. 152–154) preferred to postulate that Hekatombaion I was full and Hekatombaion II hollow, with three days added to full Metageitnion, one of them before the 22nd and the other two, attested in *IG* II², 838, as 22² and 22³. The calendar in Ergochares' year was thus irregular on any interpretation, and if the regular alternation of months was followed after Metageitnion, a discrepancy of two days between the festival and the prytany calendars still existed at the time of the passage of *Agora* XV, 121. This is not eliminated even by the alternative restoration of the date in that text (Pyanopsion 8 = pryt. IV, 32 = 128th day; cf. Pritchett, *AJP* 63, 1942, p. 422 = *The Five Attic Tribes after Kleisthenes*, 1943, p. 22, note 34), unless only one of the intercalated days had by then been compensated for. That such compensation was made progressively in the months following Metageitnion is intrinsically more likely than that it was delayed to the later part of the year. It was not made as early as Meritt at one time thought possible; his suggestion for *Agora* XV, 121, of Boedromion 8 = pryt. IV, 2 = 98th day (*op. cit.*, p. 154; cf. *SEG* XXI, 400, note) cannot be maintained and is not repeated in *Agora* XV.

Hippothontis held the third prytany, Aiantis the fourth or eighth. No other details of separate prytanies are known.

PRYTANIS OF KARYSTOS, THE PHILOSOPHER, HONORED

224 (Pl. 23). A pedimental stele of Pentelic marble (I 918), complete save for the akroteria, the raking cornice on the right, and the right end of the horizontal cornice of the pediment, discovered on June 3, 1933, in the floor of a Roman house of the 1st–2nd century A.D. over the Civic Offices (I 12). The left side has been reworked. Below the pediment, the transition to the face of the inscribed surface is effected by an ovolo molding with cavetto crown resembling that of **216**.

H. 1.135 m.; W. 0.39 m. (at base of pediment), 0.357 m. (at line 1), 0.382 m. (at line 50); Th. 0.125 m.
LH. 0.005 m. (lines 51–53, 0.008 m.).

Ed. B. D. Meritt, *Hesperia* 4, 1935, pp. 525–561, no. 39, with photograph. See also *SEG* XXV, 106, with references to L. Robert, *BCH* 59, 1935, pp. 436–437 (on line 21); P. Roussel, *BCH* 59, 1935, pp. 520–521 (on lines 12–13 and 23–24); L. Moretti, *Iscrizioni storiche ellenistiche* I, pp. 60–63, no. 28 (full text, Italian translation, and commentary). The text is also reproduced in *IG* XII, Supplement, pp. 200–201, no. 2. On the historical circumstances and the erasures in line 16 and 19 see S. Dow and C. F. Edson, *HSCP* 48, 1937, pp. 168–172.

a. 226/5 *a.*, *pryt.* III   NON-ΣTOIX. *ca.* 36

Θ   ε   ο   ι.

'Επὶ 'Εργοχάρου ἄρχοντος ἐπὶ τῆς 'Ιπποθων
τίδος τρίτης πρυτανείας ἧι Ζωίλος Διφί
λου 'Αλωπεκῆθεν ἐγραμμάτευεν· Μεταγειτνι
5   ῶνος δευτέραι μετ'εἰκάδας, ἑβδόμει καὶ εἰ
κοστεῖ τῆς πρυτανείας· ἐκκλησία ἐν τῶι θεά
τρωι· τῶν προέδρων ἐπεψήφιζεν Σπουδίας Μέ
μνωνος 'Αφιδναῖος καὶ συμπρόεδροι·   *vacat*
ἔδοξεν τεῖ βουλεῖ καὶ τῶι δήμωι·

10   Θούκριτος Ἀλκιμάχου Μυρρινούσιος εἶπεν· ἐ
      πειδὴ Πρύτανις εὔνους ὢν τῶι δήμωι καὶ πολ
      λάκις τὴν ἀπόδειξιν αὐτοῦ καὶ πρότερον πεπο
      ημέν⟨η⟩ν ἀποφηναμένων τῶν στρατηγῶν, παρα
      κληθεὶς ὑπὸ τοῦ δήμου καὶ δοὺς ἑαυτὸν ἀπροφ[α]
15   σίστως εἰς τὴν κοινὴν χρείαν τῆς πόλεως ἀπ[ε]
      δήμησεν [. . . . .^{ca. 22}. . . . .] οὔτε πό
      νον οὔτε κίνδυνον ὑπολογισάμενος οὐθένα
      τῶν ἐσομένων οὔτε δαπάνης οὐδεμίας φροντί
      σας, καὶ παραγενόμενος [. . .^{ca. 9}. . .] κα[ὶ] διαλε
20   χθεὶς ὑπὲρ τῶν κοινεῖ ^v χρησίμων μετ[ὰ] παρ⟨ρ⟩η
      σίας ὡς ἂν ὑπὲρ ἰδία⟨ς πατρ⟩ιδο[[ς τὴν πᾶσαν σπου]]
      δὴν ποι⟨ο⟩ύμενος ἀπήγγελκεν τῶι δήμωι περ[ὶ] τού
      των ἐν οὐθενὶ καιρῶι προθυμίας οὐθὲν ἐν[λ]ελοι
      π⟨ὼς π⟩οτ᾽οὐδὲ τῶν καθηκόντων εἰς τὴν τοῦ δήμου
25   χρείαν παραλείπων, ὅπως ἂν οὖν ὁ δῆμος ἐμ παν
      τὶ καιρῶι μεμνημένος φαίνηται τῶν ἐκτενῶς
      τὰς χρείας αὐτῶι παρεσχημένων, ^{vv} ἀγαθεῖ τύ
      χει δεδόχθαι τῆι βουλῆι τοὺς λαχόντας προ
      έδρους εἰς τὴν ἐπιοῦσαν ἐκκλησίαν χρηματί
30   σαι περὶ τούτων, γνώμην δὲ ξυμβάλλεσθαι τῆς
      βουλῆς εἰς τὸν δῆμον ὅτι δοκεῖ τῆι βουλῆι ^{vv}
      ἐπαινέσαι Πρύτανιν Ἀστυλείδου Καρύστιον
      καὶ στεφανῶσαι αὐτὸν χρυσῶι στεφάνωι κατὰ
      τὸν νόμον εὐνοίας ἕνεκα καὶ φιλοτιμίας ἣν ἔ
35   χων διατελεῖ περὶ τὴν βουλὴν καὶ τὸν δῆμον
      τὸν Ἀθηναίων, καὶ ἀνειπεῖν τὸν στέφανον τοῦ
      τον Διονυσίων τῶν ἐν ἄστει τραγωιδοῖ[ς] τῶι
      καινῶι ἀγῶνι καὶ Παναθηναίων τῶι γυμνικῶι·
      τῆς δὲ ποήσεως τοῦ στεφάνου καὶ τῆς ἀναγο^{vv}
40   ρεύσεως ἐπιμεληθῆναι τοὺ[ς] στρατηγοὺς καὶ
      [[ι]] τὸν ταμίαν τῶν στρατιωτικῶν· εἶναι δὲ αὐτῶι
      διατηροῦντι τὴν αἵρεσιν εὑρέσθαι παρὰ τοῦ
      δήμου καὶ ἄλλο ἀγαθὸν ὅτου ἂν δοκῆι ἄξιος εἶναι·
      καλέσαι δὲ αὐτὸν καὶ ἐπὶ δεῖπνον εἰς τὸ πρυτα
45   νεῖον εἰς αὔριον· ἀναγράψαι δὲ τόδε τὸ ψήφισ
      μα τὸν γραμματέα τὸν κατὰ πρυτανείαν ἐν στή
      ληι λιθίνηι καὶ στῆσαι ἐν ἀγορᾶι· τὸ δὲ ἀνάλω
      μα τὸ γενόμενον εἰς τὴν ἀνάθεσιν καὶ τὴν ἀνα
      γραφὴν τῆς στήλης μερίσαι τὸν ταμί[[------]]
50   αν τῶν στρατιωτικῶν.   vacat

                              (in corona)
                              Ἡ βουλή
                              ὁ δῆμος
                              Πρύτανιν.

      The text is that of *SEG* XXV, 106, with some additional but minor adjustments in the underdotting of certain
letters and in the readings of lines 21 and 48. Lines 12–13. *Lapis* πεποημένων, as also Meritt *in editione principe*;
πεποημέν⟨η⟩ν Roussel. Line 16. The *rasura* (as in line 19) was presumably the result of the *damnatio memoriae* of
201/200, on which see **187**. Meritt suggested [πρὸς τὸν βασιλέα Ἀντίγονον] as the erased reference to the
Macedonian king Antigonos III Doson. Line 19. [τῶι βασιλεῖ] or [Ἀντιγόνωι] Meritt. The former seems preferable.
Line 20. *Lapis* ΠΑΡΗ. Line 21. *Lapis* ΙΔΙΑΙΔΟΣ (not ΙΔΙΑΓΔΟΣ as in the *editio princeps*). ὑπὲρ ἰδιαγδος Meritt;
ὑπὲρ ἰδία⟨ς⟩ π[α]τ[ρ]ίδος Robert. The last part of the line was written *in rasura*. Meritt observed, "The form ἰδιαγδος

is corrupt; a pi once stood where the second delta is now cut, and a tau once stood where the sigma is now cut." It ought further to be remarked, but has not hitherto been noticed, that sigma once stood where the third iota is now cut (it is the top stroke of this letter which has created the false impression of gamma), that alpha underlies omicron, and that beyond the tau with sigma superimposed rho, iota, delta, and omicron may still be discerned beneath τήν, with the rho and iota apparently converted into tau and rho, before the *rasura* becomes more thoroughgoing. The mason has therefore originally written ἰδίας πατριδο at least, before he set about a partial and then a more radical correction of it. Since this is the phrase which it is now believed he should have written, and to which the accepted text has been amended, it is difficult to guess what confusion of mind prompted the mason's "corrections" at this point. Line 22. *Lapis* ΠΟΙΥΜΕΝΟΣ. Lines 23–24. *Lapis* ΕΝ[.]ΕΛΟΙ|ΠΟΤΟΥ. ἐν[δ]ηλου | ποτ'οὐδέ Meritt; ἐν[λ]ελοι|π⟨ώς π⟩οτ'οὐδέ Roussel, assuming haplography on the part of the already errant mason. Line 41. The otiose iota was erased but remains visible on the stone. Line 48. ἀνάθε[σ]ι[ν] Meritt; the whole word is however discernible. Line 49. The last part of the line was erased, but the correct text was set on the next line rather than rewritten in the *rasura*.

The writing and general "construction" of the inscription are of a quality as reasonable as this period has to offer in the inscribing of long texts, but it must be admitted that between lines 20 and 24, and in line 49, the mason's facility, such as it was, for whatever cause temporarily deserted him. The mason in question has been shown by S. V. Tracy to have been the "Cutter of *IG* II² 1706" (*Attic Letter-Cutters*, pp. 44–54), for whose characteristics and prolific output see **222**. The judgment there cited, that his work gives "the overall impression of haste," is well exemplified by this text and not least by the citation at the end (lines 51–53), which Tracy illustrates (*op. cit.*, pl. 5). The mason has left a vacant space at the end of line 8 in order to achieve the "perfect design" (see **204** and A. S. Henry, *Prescripts*, p. 69), at the end of line 31 perhaps to emphasize the operative verb and the honorand's name as a unit in the line following, and at the end of line 39 for no clearly identifiable reason.

The benefactor honored in this decree, Prytanis, the philosopher of the Peripatetic School (which was pro-Macedonian in sentiment), is known from the literary sources as commissioned by Antigonos Doson to frame a new constitution for Megalopolis in Arkadia (Polybios 5.93.8) and as the teacher of Euphorion (Athenaios 11.477e). He was evidently well suited to be an intermediary between Athens and Doson. See K. Ziegler, *RE* XXIII A, 1957, col. 1158, *s.v.* Prytanis (5); Dow and Edson, *HSCP* 48, 1937, pp. 168–172; Dow, *HSCP* 48, 1937, pp. 124–126; P. Treves, *Euforione e la storia ellenistica*, 1955, pp. 23–25; R. Kassel, *ZPE* 60, 1985, pp. 23–24. On the political situation which made the cultivation of good relations with Doson part of current Athenian policy, cf. F. W. Walbank, *Aratos of Sicyon*, 1933, pp. 89–93; J. V. A. Fine, *AJP* 61, 1940, pp. 130–150; C. Habicht, *Studien*, pp. 93–105 (esp. pp. 102–103); Walbank, *CAH* VII, 2nd ed., i, 1984, pp. 454–455; see also É. Will, *Histoire politique du monde hellénistique* I, 1966, pp. 332–351 (on Prytanis, p. 334).

Lines 3–4. Zoilos, son of Diphilos, of Alopeke, the γραμματεύς of Ergochares' year (*PA* 6236), was probably the grandson of the Zoilos with the same patronymic and demotic whose gravestone (*IG* II², 5557) is dated at the end of the 4th century. Lines 4–5. The penultimate day of Metageitnion is well attested as a day on which the assembly might meet. See J. D. Mikalson, *Sacred and Civil Calendar*, p. 45, who quotes lines 1–6 of this text.

Lines 6–7. Ἐκκλησία ἐν τῶι θεάτρωι. See **167**, commentary on lines 6–7. Line 7. The decree was probouleumatic; see P. J. Rhodes, *Athenian Boule*, p. 254. Lines 7–8. Spoudias, son of Memnon, of Aphidna was probably a descendant of the Spoudias of Aphidna whose statue stood beside that of his wife Kleokrateia of Teithra on the base *SEG* XVII, 83. On this family see Meritt, *Hesperia* 26, 1957, p. 203 and **213**, col. II, line 37 with commentary, where the name Spoudias is also in the deme Teithra.

Line 10. Thoukritos, son of Alkimachos, of Myrrhinous (*PA* 7261). The honors paid to him by reason of his earlier military career as hipparch and general (*IG* II², 2856, on which see J. Pouilloux, *Forteresse*, pp. 126–127, no. 12; 1279, on which see *SEG* XXII, 125; 1286, on which see Pouilloux, *op. cit.*, pp. 124–126, no. 11; and on all these see further *SEG* XXXV, 105, with earlier references) have played a part in the dating problems surrounding the archonships of the middle of the 3rd century. See above on the archonship of Philinos (p. 284), and cf. also Moretti, *Iscrizioni storiche ellenistiche* I, p. 62 and *SEG* XXIX, 289. For further prosopographical references see J. S. Traill, *Hesperia* 38, 1969, p. 431, note on line 88 of the prytany text later appearing as *Agora* XV, 130, which shows Thoukritos as a councillor towards what must have been the close of long and active public service. Line 12. τὴν ἀπόδειξιν αὐτοῦ. See Roussel, *loc. cit.*

Lines 20–21. μετὰ παρρησίας. Robert compared the decree of Kallatis *SGDI* 3089 (*SEG* XXIV, 1024), lines 3–4. Line 21. ὑπὲρ ἰδίας πατρίδος. See also Robert, *Anatolian Studies Presented to William Hepburn Buckler*, 1939, p. 236 (= *Opera minora selecta* I, 1969, p. 620), note 4.

Line 25. ὅπως ἂν οὖν. For the "hortatory intention" see **86**, commentary on lines 21–24, and for the phraseology cf. **173**, commentary on line 2. Lines 27–28. ἀγαθεῖ τύχει. Cf. **72**, commentary on lines 7–8.

Lines 33–34. On the golden stephanos κατὰ τὸν νόμον see **112**, commentary on lines 5–7 and **141**, commentary on lines 8–9. Lines 34–36. Prytanis is honored for his continuing εὔνοια and φιλοτιμία, two of the most regularly praised virtues in decrees of this kind: cf. Henry, *Honours*, p. 43, where this passage is cited. Lines 36–38. The announcement of the stephanos was to be made at the City Dionysia and the Panathenaia, the latter not the great Panathenaia, which had taken place in the previous year. The Ptolemaia, which became the additional occasion of announcements of this kind, had not yet been instituted. For the provisions regarding announcement, and its formulation, see Henry, *Honours*, pp. 28–36 (esp. p. 33, where this passage is cited). The formula here contains the more commonly used verb ἀνειπεῖν but is otherwise comparable with that of **208**, lines 26–29. Lines 39–41. The generals were understandably responsible for the proclamation in the case of a foreigner; cf. *IG* II², 693. But contrast **208**, lines 29–31 with commentary. The involvement here of the Military Treasurer reflects his new position as disbursing officer (see below), in replacement of the Single Officer who was functioning at the time of the enactment of **208**. On the responsibility for the making and proclamation of stephanoi see further Henry, *Honours*, pp. 34–36.

Lines 41–43. For the phraseology cf. **214**, lines 19–20, *IG* II², 856 (M. J. Osborne, *Naturalization* I, pp. 205–206, D 97), lines 8–11, 862 (*SEG* XXIV, 132, XXXIII, 124), lines 8–9, 908 (*SEG* XXIX, 118), lines 15–17. Lines 44–45. The formula of invitation to hospitality in the Prytaneion, well known from the earliest decrees of the 5th-century democracy onwards, was examined by W. A. McDonald, *AJA* 59, 1955, pp. 151–155. Moretti referred to M. Burzachechi, *RendAccArchNapoli* 36, 1961, pp. 103–104; and see also *Agora* III, with a reference to this text. The study of these invitations was taken further by Osborne (*ZPE* 41, 1981, pp. 153–170) and by Henry (*Honours*, pp. 262–290, following a briefer contribution in *Antichthon* 15, 1981, pp. 100–110). McDonald noted that the custom "reached its peak in the early Hellenistic era." It is comparatively little met with after the date of this text. *IG* II², 1024, at the end of the 2nd century, may be the last example in this form. It was usual to invite foreign honorands ἐπὶ ξένια rather than ἐπὶ δεῖπνον, but a number of exceptions occur, of which this would seem to be one. It drew particular attention from Osborne (*ZPE, op. cit.*, pp. 154–155), with the present text adduced as an excellent example, where he claimed that ἐπὶ δεῖπνον might indeed be used with persons who had acted or were acting on Athens' behalf in some official capacity, that is, *vice* an Athenian citizen. Henry (*Antichthon* 15, 1981, pp. 101–103) agreed this possibility in the case of Prytanis, although not in other cases brought by Osborne into this category, and for present purposes this reason for the apparent anomaly may be accepted. In his later treatment of the "confusion between δεῖπνον and ξένια" (*Honours*, pp. 271–275), Henry cited this text (p. 272) in the same sense; but his general conclusion was that "no hard and fast rule was rigidly applied." Rhodes, *ZPE* 57, 1984, pp. 193–197 (see also *SEG* XXXIV, 268), considered these anomalies as possibly the result of simple error in formulation.

Line 47. ἐν ἀγορᾶι. The location is not more exactly defined. Cf. **213**, line 24. Lines 48–49. ἀνάθεσις is illogically referred to before ἀναγραφή, although the latter process actually came first, as in *Agora* XV, 137 (*IG* II², 913), lines 10–11 (where, however, ποίη]σιν could be read in place of ἀνάθε]σιν in the nonstoichedon text) and in *SEG* XXVI, 96, lines 11–13. Cf. *Agora* XV, 163, line 3 and Meritt, *Hesperia* 36, 1967, p. 232. Lines 49–50. Payment for the ἀναγραφή and ἀνάθεσις is the responsibility of the ταμίας τῶν στρατιωτικῶν, the Military Treasurer, who had at an earlier period been involved in expenditure of this kind: see **194**, commentary on line 13 and references there. After 230/29, while not displacing the now-revived Plural Board of Administration in this duty and sometimes acting in cooperation with that Board, the Military Treasurer is seen to be the official predominantly concerned, being on occasion referred to *tout simple* as ὁ ταμίας. For a full discussion, including the prytany decrees (which from this time onwards appear to be a separate issue), see Henry, *Chiron* 14, 1984, pp. 81–90 (the present text cited on p. 83); and cf. also Osborne, *ZPE* 11, 1973, p. 159.

Lines 51–53. The engraved stephanos is of the "radiate" type, its leaves stiff, straight, and overlapping, and it closely resembles that of **192**. *IG* II², 443, which carries the same text as these lines, within a stephanos of identical character, was written by the same mason. Cf. Tracy, *Attic Letter-Cutters*, pp. 52–53, with photograph pl. 6. The γραμματεύς had no instructions to provide more than a single copy of the present text (lines 45–47). It cannot therefore be assumed that *IG* II², 443 is a fragment of a second copy of the decree here recorded. Prytanis may have been voted other honors concurrently with these or have been separately honored for other services at roughly this period. It is instructive for the fallibility of the criterion of letter forms in Greek Epigraphy that *IG* II², 443 was formerly classed among decrees of the 336/5–319/18 period.

AN EMBASSY FROM THE CITY OF EPHESOS HONORED

225. The central section of a stele of Hymettian marble (I 2361), broken above and below but with the original rough-picked back and both edges preserved (that on the left with some damage), discovered in August 1934 in a Late Roman context east of the Tholos, over the fork in the Great Drain (I 12). The marble is of a sugary, crumbly texture, and the inscribed surface is cracked and discolored. The striations of a toothed chisel are especially noticeable diagonally on the lower left and vertically on the right.

H. 0.65 m.; W. 0.445 m.; Th. 0.10–0.105 m.
LH. 0.006–0.007 m.

Ed. M. Crosby, *Hesperia* 6, 1937, pp. 448–453, no. 3, with photograph. Discussed by L. Robert, *Études épigraphiques et philologiques*, 1938, pp. 62–69, no. 10, with quotation of lines 1–23 and particular consideration of lines 1–11. The same lines reconsidered and a new text presented by B. D. Meritt, *Hesperia* 13, 1944, pp. 251–253, in the light of **238**. See further *SEG* XXV, 108, with reference also to L. Moretti, *Iscrizioni storiche ellenistiche* I, pp. 66–69, no. 30 (text, Italian translation, and commentary).

a. 224/3–222/1 *a.*   NON-ΣΤΟΙΧ. *ca.* 50

[---]·
[τ]οὺς δὲ ἥκο[ντας πρεσβευτὰς παρ' Ἐφεσίων παρελθόντας ἀναγορεύ]
[ε]ιν, ἐπειδὰν ὁ γυμν[ικὸς ἀγὼν γένηται, ὅτι ὁ δῆμος ὁ Ἐφεσίων στε]
φανοῖ χρυσῶι στεφάνωι [τὸν δῆμον τὸν Ἀθηναίων κατὰ τὸν νόμον εὐσε]
[β]είας ἕνεκα τῆς πρὸς τοὺς [θεοὺς καὶ εὐνοίας τῆς εἰς τὴν βουλὴν]
5 [κ]αὶ τὸν δῆμον τὸν Ἐφεσίων· [τούτοις δὲ τὸν δῆμον χειροτονῆσαι]
[θ]εωροδόκὸν ἐξ Ἀθηναίων ἁπάντ[ων· ἐπαινέσαι δὲ τὸν δῆμον τὸν]
['Ἐφ]εσίων καὶ στεφαν[ῶ]σαι χρυσῶι στεφάνωι [κατὰ τὸν νόμον εὐσεβεί]
[α]ς ἕνεκα τῆς πρὸς τοὺς θεοὺς καὶ εὐνοίας τῆς εἰς τ[ὸν δῆμον τὸν Ἀθη]
ναίων καὶ τὸν βασιλέα Πτολεμαῖον, καὶ ἀνειπεῖν τὸν [στέφανον]
10 τοῦτον Διονυσίων τῶν ἐν ἄστει καινοῖς τραγωιδοῖς καὶ Πανα[θη]
ναί[ω]ν καὶ Ἐλευσινίων καὶ Πτολεμαίων τοῖς γυμνικοῖς ἀγῶσιν·
[τῆς δὲ] ποιήσεως τοῦ στεφάνου καὶ τῆς ἀναγορεύσεως ἐπιμελ[η]
[θῆναι] τοὺς στρατηγοὺς κα[ὶ τὸ]ν ταμίαν τῶν στρατιωτικῶν· *vvv*
[ἐπαιν]έσαι δὲ καὶ τοὺς παραγεγονότας πρεσβευτὰς παρ' Ἐφεσίων
15 [καὶ στ]εφανῶσαι ἕκαστον αὐτῶν θαλλοῦ στεφάνωι Δ(ι)ον⟨υ⟩σικλῆν
[Διονυ]σικλέους, *v* Νικοφῶντα Χαριδήμου, *v* [Πάν]ταινον Τεισιδήμου·
[καλ]έσαι δὲ αὐτοὺς καὶ ἐπὶ δεῖπνον εἰς τὸ πρυτανεῖον εἰς αὔριον·
[ἀνα]γράψαι δὲ τόδε τὸ ψήφισμα τὸν γραμματέα τὸν κατὰ πρυτανεί
[αν] ἐν στήλει λιθίνει καὶ στῆσαι ἐν ἀγορᾶι παρὰ τὸμ βωμὸν τῆς Ἀρτέμι
20 [δ]ος τῆς Βουλαίας· εἰς δὲ τὴν ἀναγραφὴν καὶ τὴν ἀνάθεσιν τῆς στή *v*
λης μερίσαι τὸν ταμίαν τῶν στρατιωτικῶν καὶ τοὺς ἐπὶ τεῖ διοική
σει τὸ γενόμενον ἀνάλωμα.   *vacat*
                              vacat
Θεωροδόκος κεχειροτόνηται Πρ[α]ξι[τέ]λης Τιμάρχου Εἰρεσίδης.

                         (*in corona*)
                         Ἡ βουλὴ
25   ὁ δῆμος
                         [τὸν δ]ῆμον τὸν
                         [Ἐφε]σίων

[Ἡ βουλὴ]   [Ἡ βουλὴ]   [Ἡ β]ουλὴ
[ὁ δῆμος]   [ὁ δῆμος]   [ὁ] δῆμος
30 [Διονυσικλῆν]   [Νικοφῶντα]   Πάνταιν[ον]
[Διονυσικλέους] 35 [Χαριδήμου]   Τ[ει]σιδή[μου].

The text is that of *SEG* XXV, 108, which follows that of Meritt with a correction in line 20 and some minor and unimportant revisions of readings in lines 4–5, 17–19, and 38–39. The inscription offers a further example of the work of the "Cutter of *IG* II² 1706", ascribed to him by S. V. Tracy, and it belongs to the earlier part of his career. For the details see Tracy, *Attic Letter-Cutters*, pp. 44–54 and **222**.

The fragment begins after the lost preamble, motivation, resolution, and some part of the provisions of the decree. On the subject matter see below.

Lines 1–7. Crosby's and Robert's texts for these lines, reprinted here for the completeness of the record, are as follows:

(Crosby)

[. .]ΟΥΣΔΕΙΚΟ[-------------------------------]
[. .]ΙΝ ἐπειδὰν ὁ γυμνα[σίαρχος ὁ πανηγύρεως γυμνασιαρχήσας(?) στε]
φανοῖ χρυσῶι στεφάνωι [.................²⁶⁻³⁰............. εὔσε]
βείας ἕνεχα τῆς πρὸς τοὺς [θεοὺς καὶ εὐνοίας τῆς εἰς τὴν βουλὴν]
5   καὶ τὸν δῆμον τὸν Ἐφεσίων· [ἑλέσθαι δὲ τὸν δῆμον τὸν Ἀθηναίων]
[θ]εωροδόχον ἐξ Ἀθηναίων ἁπάντ[ων· ἐπαινέσαι δὲ τὸν δῆμον τὸν]
[Ἐφ]εσίων κτλ.

(Robert)

[. .]ΟΥΣΔΕΙΚΟ[--------τὸν ἀγωνοθέτην (vel ἱεροκήρυκα) ἀναγορε]
[ύε]ιν, ἐπειδὰν ὁ γυμν[ικὸς ἀγὼν συντελεσθῆι, ὅτι ὁ δῆμος στε]
φανοῖ χρυσῶι στεφάνωι [κατὰ τὸν νόμον τὸν δῆμον τὸν Ἀθηναίων εὔσε]
βείας ἕνεχα τῆς πρὸς τοὺς [θεοὺς καὶ εὐνοίας τῆς εἰς τὴν βουλὴν]
5   καὶ τὸν δῆμον τὸν Ἐφεσίων· [δεδόχθαι τῶι δήμωι ἑλέσθαι μὲν]
[θ]εωροδόχον ἐξ Ἀθηναίων ἁπάντ[ων· ἐπαινέσαι δὲ τὸν δῆμον τὸν]
[Ἐφ]εσίων κτλ.

Line 14. καὶ omitted by Crosby and Robert. Line 15. *Lapis* ΔΥΟΝΙΣΙΚΛΗΝ (retained by Crosby and restored by her in lines 30–31); corr. Robert. Line 20. τῆς omitted by Crosby, Robert, Meritt.

Lines 5–6. The decision left by the *probouleuma* to the free choice of the assembly is recorded in line 23. It is thus clear that this was a probouleumatic decree, although not listed as such by P. J. Rhodes in *Athenian Boule*. Line 7. On the golden stephanos κατὰ τὸν νόμον see **112**, commentary on lines 5–7 and **141**, commentary on lines 8–9. Lines 7–9. For the virtues of the citizens of Ephesos here signalized and honored, identical with those of the Athenians themselves reciprocally recognized by the Ephesians (lines 3–5), see A. S. Henry, *Honours*, pp. 42–44. The present pairing is not among the examples there represented. Line 9. Βασιλεὺς Πτολεμαῖος. That is, Ptolemy III Euergetes I (246–221 b.c.), in whose honor the Ptolemaic Games and the phyle Ptolemais had recently been established. Ephesos had long been a center of Egyptian power in Ionia; for references see *RE* V, ii, 1905, col. 2794, *s.v.* Ephesos (L. Bürchner). At a time when the Athenians had been able to resume friendly relations with Egypt, the cordial diplomatic contacts between Athens and Ephesos, and the reference to the king in that context, were particularly apposite. On the *rapprochement* with Ptolemy, the institution of the new festival and phyle, and the historical developments in general, see especially C. Habicht, *Studien*, pp. 105–117 (on the present decree and its date, esp. p. 109, note 138). Robert (*op. cit.*, p. 69) justly preferred a date in the late 220's for this text to the alternative possibility of *ca.* 200 (cf. Crosby, *op. cit.*, pp. 452–453), and subsequent commentators have concurred. Moretti (*loc. cit.*) advocated the years immediately following the honors accorded to the Egyptian king, and that dating (shown above) was adopted also by Habicht.

Lines 9–11. The stephanoi are to be announced at no fewer than four separate festivals. Contrast **224**, lines 36–38, where the Eleusinia were not included and the decree in any case antedates the institution of the Ptolemaia. The present example is cited in the "representative list of variables" in the provisions for proclamation (where ἀνειπεῖν is the operative verb) assembled by Henry (*Honours*, pp. 32–33; cf. also pp. 28–32). The penteteric Ptolemaia are here included for the first time among Agora *psephismata*.

Lines 12–13. On the officials responsible for the quadruple announcement see **224**, commentary on lines 39–41. Lines 15–16. The Ephesian ambassadors, listed by H. Pope (*Foreigners in Attic Inscriptions*, 1947, p. 50), are not otherwise known. Line 17. On the invitation to hospitality in the Prytaneion see **224**, commentary on lines 44–45. Here as there, the foreign honorands are invited ἐπὶ δεῖπνον rather than ἐπὶ ξένια. In discussing this apparent anomaly, M. J. Osborne (*ZPE* 41, 1981, pp. 153–156) was inclined to regard an example such as this as indicative of a growing breakdown in terminology towards the end of the 3rd century. Henry (*Antichthon* 15, 1981, pp. 100–110), while not citing this particular instance of the "confusion", concluded that the Athenians exercised "discretion in either direction", and he did not accept the supposed breakdown in terminology. This judgment was repeated in *Honours*, pp. 274–275 and 286, note 57: in the latter context Henry was prepared to allow Osborne's tentative suggestion (*op. cit.*, p. 155, note 6) that at this period the Ephesians enjoyed *isopoliteia* with the Athenians and would thus be entitled to treatment as citizens. If that was not the case, it was, he judged, evidence of no more than "arbitrary preferential treatment." Lines 19–20. The stele is to be erected ἐν ἀγορᾶι (cf. **188**, commentary on line 48 and **224**, commentary on line 47); but the location is here more exactly prescribed. For the altar of Artemis Boulaia see *Agora* III, p. 55, no. 118, where these lines are quoted. The cult of Artemis Boulaia was particularly associated with the prytaneis. See *Agora* XV, index III; *Agora* III, pp. 56–57; and *Agora* XIV, p. 45.

Lines 21–22. The ταμίας τῶν στρατιωτικῶν is here named jointly with the Plural Board ἐπὶ τῇ διοικήσει as responsible for defraying the cost of the stele and work on it. See **224**, commentary on lines 49–50 and references there (esp. Henry, *Chiron* 14, 1984, pp. 82–83, where the present text is cited). Line 23. Praxiteles, son of Timarchos, of the deme Eiresidai (*PA* 12169) was priest of Asklepios in 250/49 (*IG* II², 1534B, line 268 = S. B. Aleshire, *The Athenian Asklepieion*, 1989, inventory V, line 143); he was also a contributor to the fund-raising appeal of 245/4 (**213**, Col. III, lines 69–70); cf. Habicht, *Studien*, pp. 70 and 33, note 96, and see also *IG* II², 4440. In the later 220's he was evidently a wealthy senior citizen eminently suited to fulfill the obligations imposed on him by the assembly. For his family see J. K. Davies, *Athenian Propertied Families*, pp. 286–290.

Lines 24–27. The engraved stephanos is of the "radiate" type, more perfunctory in style than that of **224**. No engraved stephanoi accompany the citations for the ambassadors, and references to these should be deleted from the texts given by Moretti and in *SEG* XXV. If the stephanoi were inserted in paint, it must be allowed that there was little room for them. But they were crowns of olive rather than of gold and to that extent did not merit the treatment given to the stephanos bestowed upon the Ephesian people as a whole. Ambassadors formed a well-attested category of recipient of such stephanoi: see Henry (*Honours*, p. 38), who notes particularly that when this occurs the city from which the delegation was sent "frequently and not unexpectedly" received a stephanos of gold.

THE ARCHONSHIP OF CHAIREPHON, 219/18 B.C.

When W. B. Dinsmoor published *The Archons of Athens in the Hellenistic Age* in 1931, Chairephon's archonship was known only from *IG* II², 1304 (*SEG* XV, 110), a decree of Athenian citizens and others on garrison duty at Eleusis and the border forts in honor of the general Demainetos, son of Hermokles, of Athmonon (*PA* 3269). In this text, usefully discussed by C. Habicht (*Studien*, pp. 134–135; cf. *SEG* XXXII, 155), three archons are mentioned during whose tenures of office Demainetos served at Eleusis: Chairephon, Diokles, and Aischron; and references to the penteteric Great Eleusinia held in each of their years dictate a four-year interval between them. Favorable reference to Philip V of Macedon also required that at least the last of the three should have held office between 221 and 201.

On the basis of this evidence, opinion had come to prefer a date for Chairephon's archonship between 219 and 216 (see Dinsmoor, *Archons of Athens*, pp. 55 and 209–212). Dinsmoor himself argued for 215/14. Two other elements intervened as conditioning factors. The first is the assurance that Thrasyphon was archon in 221/20, with a γραμματεύς from Upper or Lower Paiania (Antigonis I or Pandionis V), for which see Dinsmoor, *op. cit.*, p. 45. The other factor is provided by the archon list *IG* II², 1706 (see p. 319 above, on the archonship of Theophilos), the latter part of which gives a connected series of four eponymous archons, of whom Diokles is the second, following a lacuna of uncertain length. The discovery of **227**, soon after the appearance of Dinsmoor's work, revealed that the γραμματεύς of Chairephon's archonship belonged to the deme Kydantidai (Ptolemais VII) and confirmed Chairephon's date as 219/18 or 215/14, according to the place of Thrasyphon in the secretary cycle.

S. Dow's restudy of *IG* II², 1706 (*Hesperia* 2, 1933, pp. 418–446, cf. *Hesperia* 3, 1934, p. 177) established 219/18 as the preferable choice by the identification of part of Chairephon's name (see esp. p. 437), confirming what W. S. Ferguson had already discerned (*Athenian Tribal Cycles*, p. 27) as the more suitable arrangement. This was followed by B. D. Meritt (*Hesperia* 7, 1938, p. 138) and accepted by Dinsmoor (*Athenian Archon List*, pp. 162–163). It has remained the agreed dating: see W. K. Pritchett and Meritt, *Chronology*, pp. xxiv and 44; Pritchett and O. Neugebauer, *Calendars*, p. 91; Dinsmoor, *Hesperia* 23, 1954, p. 316; Meritt, *Athenian Year*, p. 235, and *Historia* 26, 1977, p. 178; Habicht, *Studien*, p. 176.

That the year was ordinary in character was established by **227**, where it appears that Boedromion 11 or 12 = pryt. III, 15 = 70th or 71st day, with the first two prytanies (of what was now a thirteen-prytany year) consisting of 28 and 27 (or 27 and 28) days, or each of 28 days. Cf. Pritchett and Neugebauer, *Calendars*, p. 91 and Meritt, *Athenian Year*, pp. 168–169. It was the fifth year of the (twelfth) Metonic cycle, but it did not coincide with the provisions of that cycle, in which year 5 was intercalary. For the sequence of the twelfth cycle see Meritt, *Hesperia* 38, 1969, pp. 436–441. There is no information concerning the phylai in prytany during this year.

FRAGMENT OF A DECREE

226. A part of the upper section of a pedimental stele of Pentelic marble (I 5458), with the original back and a series of moldings above the inscribed face preserved, together with part of the pediment, but broken elsewhere, discovered on May 16, 1938, in the wall of a modern house south of the Market Square (O–P 18). The stone is sheared off to the right and is much more bulky than the meager remains of the text would by themselves suggest. The molding consists of an ovolo with a strongly concave cavetto crown and with a wide taenia and apophyge as a transition to the inscribed surface.

H. 0.35 m.; W. 0.25 m.; Th. 0.19 m.
LH. 0.008 m. (omicron and omega 0.005 m.)

Ed. B. D. Meritt, *Hesperia* 29, 1960, p. 76, no. 153, with photograph pl. 25. See also *SEG* XIX, 81.

a. 219/18 a., pryt. II vel IV   NON-ΣTOIX. ca. 36–38

```
        ['Επὶ Χαι]ρεφῶντος ἀρχ[οντος ἐπὶ τῆς ...8–9....]
        [δευτέρα]ς πρυτανείας [ἧι Φ.......15–16.... Κυ]
        [δαντίδης ἐγραμμ]άτευ[εν· Μεταγειτνιῶνος ὀγδό]
        [ει ἐπὶ δέκα, εἰκοστεῖ] τῆς [πρυτανείας· ἐκκλησία]·
   5    [τῶν προέδρων ἐπεψήφ]ιζ[εν ......ca. 16.....]
        [...ca. 8... καὶ συμπρό]εδρ[οι· .....ca. 16......]
        [---------------]Υ[---------------]
        [------------------------------]
```

The above text is that of Meritt, slightly augmented with readings in lines 4–7. The restoration in line 2 is valid for the second prytany. The prytany numeral may however be [τετάρτη]ς no less than [δευτέρα]ς, and calendric data could be devised to supply lines 3–4 on that supposition, e.g., [Βοηδρομιῶνος δευτέραι μετ'εἰκάδας, ἕκτηι] τῆς [πρυτανείας = 88th day.

S. V. Tracy's studies of the lettering of the inscribed texts of this period led him to attribute this inscription to the "Cutter of Agora I 7181" (*Attic Letter-Cutters*, pp. 61–67, with a photograph of part of the name piece, fig. 4). Texts ascribed to him that may be dated on other grounds span the years 224/3–188/7, and this therefore comes comparatively early in his thirty-five-year career. Of twenty-six inscriptions for which he has been considered responsible, three are counted among the Agora decrees of this collection: the present text and the very fragmentary **246** and **247**. This mason appears as one of the earliest exponents of apex- or serif-writing, though on a modest scale. To Tracy's detail of his characteristics (pp. 61–62) it may be added that the appearance of his sigmas is very variable and that in this text at least the oval of phi is pointed.

Lines 2–3. The name of the γραμματεύς is restored from **227**. Lines 3–4. For Metageitnion 18 as a day on which the assembly might meet see J. D. Mikalson, *Sacred and Civil Calendar*, p. 41 (cf. p. 46). There is no positive evidence to attest it, and this is the sole instance of its restoration. For the alternative possibility suggested above, see Mikalson, *op. cit.*, p. 64: for this too no positive evidence exists, but it has been proposed in three restored texts.

FRAGMENT OF A DECREE

227 (Pl. 24). A fragment of the upper left section of a pedimental stele of Pentelic marble (I 79), broken below and to the right, but with the original back and part of the pediment with the left akroterion preserved, discovered on July 21, 1931, east of the altar of Zeus Agoraios at a Late Roman level (J 10). The transition from the base of the pediment to the inscribed face is effected by a molding similar to that of **216**.

H. 0.196 m.; W. 0.252 m.; Th. 0.127 m. (pediment), 0.085 m. (inscribed surface).
LH. 0.005–0.007 m.

Ed. B. D. Meritt, *Hesperia* 2, 1933, pp. 160–161, no. 7, with drawing fig. 7. A better text also by Meritt, *Hesperia* 11, 1942, pp. 298–299, no. 59; lines 1–5 repeated by him, *Athenian Year*, p. 169.

a. 219/18 a., pryt. III   NON-ΣTOIX. ca. 32–37

```
        ['Ε]πὶ Χαιρεφῶντος ἄρχοντ[ος ἐπὶ τῆς ...8–9...]
        [τ]ρίτης πρυτανείας ἧι Φ[.....15–16......]
        [Κυ]δαντίδης ἐγραμμάτ[ευεν· Βοηδρομιῶνος]
```

        [ἐν]δεκάτει, πέμπτηι κ[αὶ δεκάτηι τῆς πρυ]
5   [ταν]είας· ἐκκλησία· τ[ῶν προέδρων ἐπεψήφι]
        [ζεν Θε]όδοτος Νίκων[ος ––––––––––––]
        [––––––––] reliquiae incertae [––––––––]
        [––––––––––––––––––––––––––––––]

This text is to be considered a further example of the handiwork of the "Cutter of *IG* II² 1706", originally attributed to that mason, then unnamed, by S. Dow. See **222**.

Lines 3–5. For the restored calendric data see above (p. 327) on the archonship of Chairephon. Boedromion 11 is known from 4th-century evidence as a possible meeting day of the assembly and has been restored in one other text besides this. See J. D. Mikalson, *Sacred and Civil Calendar*, p. 53. Line 4. The rendering of the dative of the ordinal numeral is notably inconsistent.

Line 6. Or Δι]όδοτος. The chairman of the proedroi cannot be further identified.

THE EPIMELETAI OF THE MYSTERIES(?) HONORED

228. A fragment of a stele of grayish Pentelic marble (I 4541), broken on all sides, discovered on February 24, 1937, in a modern context on the North Slope of the Akropolis, under what was formerly Akropolis Street and west of the Post-Herulian Wall (R 25).

H. 0.11 m.; W. 0.116 m.; Th. 0.04 m.

LH. 0.005 m.

Ed. B. D. Meritt, *Hesperia* 26, 1957, pp. 57–58, no. 12, with photograph pl. 10. See also *SEG* XVI, 72.

ca. a. 215 *a.*   NON-ΣΤΟΙΧ. *ca.* 33–37

        [––––––––––––––––––––––––––––––]
        [–– ἐπαινέσαι αὐτοὺ]ς εὐ[σ]εβ[είας ἕνεκα τῆς πρὸς]
        [τοὺς θεοὺς καὶ φιλο]τιμίας τ[ῆς εἰς τὴν βουλὴν]
        [καὶ τὸν δῆμον καὶ] στεφανῶ[σαι ......¹²⁻¹⁶......]
        [.ᶜᵃ·⁵. ἑκάτερον α]ὐτῶν μ[υρρίνης στεφάνωι]·
5   [ἀναγράψαι δὲ τόδε] τὸ ψή[φισμα τὸν γραμμα]
        [τέα τὸν κατὰ πρυταν]είαν ἐ[ν στήληι λιθίνηι]
        [καὶ στῆσαι πρὸς τῶι Ἐλε]υσι[νίωι· ....⁷⁻¹¹....]
        [––––––––––––––––––––––––––––––]

This inscription, like **222, 224, 225, 227,** and **229–232,** has been assigned by S. V. Tracy to the craftsmanship of the "Cutter of *IG* II² 1706": for the references to his career and characteristics see **222**. The four texts dealt with earlier may be dated by means other than solely an assessment of the style of the lettering, and they and other datable work of this mason show that he was active between 229/8 and the end of the century. This present fragment and the four inscriptions next following are to be dated only with reference to the craftsman and his style and may therefore be attributable to any point within his known floruit. For convenience, the group has been placed at that career's approximate midpoint, which indeed follows Tracy's practice (see note appended to **232**).

Meritt, whose assessment of the date as "*ante fin. saec.* III *a.*" has been confirmed by these considerations, suggested that the decree voted honors to the two epimeletai of the Mysteries, comparing *IG* II², 847, of 215/14, on lines 45–48 of which the restoration of lines 1–4 was based. There also the stephanos was of myrtle and represents the earliest known example (to date) of the award: cf. A. S. Henry, *Honours*, p. 41. For a decree possibly of a similar kind see **300**.

Lines 1–3. For the virtues for which the honorands are praised see Henry, *Honours*, pp. 42–44, with parallels for this formulation cited on p. 43. Lines 3–4. καθὼς πάτριόν | ἐστιν] Meritt, who compared the honors accorded to the demarch of the Eleusinians in 165/4, the award to whom of a myrtle stephanos was qualified by a similar phrase (*IG* II², 949, lines 18–19). The restoration was rejected by Henry (*Honours*, p. 41; cf. *SEG* XXXIII, 126), on the grounds that it lacked a parallel and intervened awkwardly between verb and object. His criticism that it was "rather far" from Meritt's comparison carried less conviction, and his proposed substitution of a dittography {καὶ στεφα||νῶσαι} in the restoration, the rest of the visible text being free from blemish, might be adjudged desperate. It is wiser on present evidence to leave the lacuna unrestored.

Line 7. πρὸς τῶι Ἐλε]υσι[νίωι. Cf. **239**, line 13 and commentary. The restoration conforms to the traces on the stone as well as to the place at which the fragment was found and thus reinforces the hypothesis that the decree was concerned with the epimeletai of the Mysteries of Eleusis. R. E. Wycherley (*Agora* III, p. 81, no. 223) quoted this context among other evidence for the erection of stelai in this location.

FRAGMENT OF AN HONORARY(?) DECREE

229. A small fragment of a stele of grayish white marble (I 5446), broken on all sides, discovered on May 20, 1938, in a wall of a Byzantine building south of the Altar of the Twelve Gods (K 6).

H. 0.108 m.; W. 0.085 m.; Th. 0.02 m.
LH. 0.006 m.

Ed. S. V. Tracy, *Hesperia* 47, 1978, pp. 252–253, no. 4, with photograph pl. 65:b. See also *SEG* XXVIII, 68.

ca. a. 215 *a.*   NON-ΣTOIX.

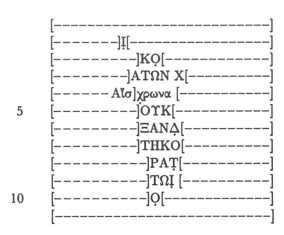

The readings are those of the *editio princeps*, where in line 6 Tracy suggested the presence of the name Alexandros.

For the "Cutter of *IG* II² 1706", to whom this fragment has been attributed, see **222**, and for the dating here given see commentary on **228**.

A THIASOS HONORS ITS TREASURER

230. A fragment of a stele of Hymettian marble (I 524), with the original rough-picked right side preserved but otherwise broken all around, discovered on March 3, 1933, in a modern wall over the terrace of the Middle Stoa near its western end (J 12).

H. 0.195 m.; W. 0.19 m.; Th. 0.063 m.
LH. 0.005 m.

Ed. B. D. Meritt, *Hesperia* 15, 1946, pp. 214–215, no. 43, with photograph of a squeeze.

ca. a. 215 *a.*   NON-ΣTOIX.

[Οἱ θιασ]ῶται
τὸν ταμίαν
Φιλιστίωνα.

For the "Cutter of *IG* II² 1706", to whom S. V. Tracy has attributed the lettering of this fragment, see **222**, and for the dating, which as it happens was also that of the *editio princeps*, see the commentary on **228**.

The text is the citation from the foot of an honorary decree passed, apparently, by a thiasos in recognition of the services of its treasurer. Its position on the stone in relation to the right side suggests that the decree may also have honored another benefactor of the same organization, perhaps the secretary; cf. the arrangement of *IG* II², 1298. For other decrees in honor of the treasurer of a thiasos or of a comparable body see **231** and *IG* II², 1291, 1317, 1318(?), 1323, 1325, 1327, 1329, etc.

Line 1. The three lines are symmetrically arranged, and this suggests the restoration given rather than something longer, e.g., [Οἱ στρατι]ῶται.

A THIASOS HONORS ITS TREASURER

231. A fragment of a stele of Hymettian marble (I 5691), broken on all sides, discovered on February 27, 1939, in a wall of a modern house at the north foot of the Areopagos (O 22). The stone is very battered.

H. 0.21 m.; W. 0.185 m.; Th. 0.06 m.
LH. 0.005 m.

Ed. W. K. Pritchett, *Hesperia* 15, 1946, p. 156, no. 13, with photograph. Improved text by B. D. Meritt, *Hesperia* 30, 1961, p. 228, no. 27. See also *SEG* XXI, 533.

ca. a. 215 *a.*   NON-ΣTOIX.

[Οἱ]
θι[ασῶται]
τὸν τα[μίαν]
Εὐάγγελο[ν]
5   Σουνιέα.

For the craftsman to whom this text has been attributed (the "Cutter of *IG* II² 1706") and the date here given, see **228** and references there. The dating in *SEG* (*loc. cit.*, "ex. s. III*ᵃ*.") was not wide of the mark, but the inscription may belong to any point within the last three decades of the century.

Lines 4–5. Euangelos of Sounion is otherwise unknown. It is perhaps worth recording that a Euangelos of this deme was the father of two epheboi, Dionysippos and Thallippos, who figure at col. II, lines 29 and 32, in the ephebic list of 324/3 from the Amphiaraion at Oropos published by B. Leonardos, Ἀρχ. Ἐφ., 1918, pp. 73–100, nos. 95–97, and republished with commentary by O. W. Reinmuth, *The Ephebic Inscriptions of the Fourth Century B.C.*, 1971, pp. 58–82, no. 15, with photographs pls. XVII, XVIII. Cf. **186**, commentary on line 4. Reinmuth, however, considered (p. 64) that the two epheboi were not to be regarded as brothers.

FRAGMENT OF AN HONORARY DECREE

232. A fragment of a stele of Pentelic marble (I 5617), broken on all sides (although a small part of the original back may indeed survive), discovered on November 1, 1938, in a wall of a modern house at the north foot of the Areopagos (L 20).

H. 0.10 m.; W. 0.13 m.; Th. 0.082 m.
LH. 0.006 m.

Ed. B. D. Meritt, *Hesperia* 30, 1961, p. 259, no. 65, with photograph pl. 48. See also *SEG* XXI, 416.

ca. a. 215 *a.*   NON-ΣTOIX.

(*in corona*)
Εἰ[. .]ΛΛ[– – –]
Ἐργοχάρο[υς]
Σφήττιον.

The execution of this inscription has been attributed by S. V. Tracy to the "Cutter of *IG* II² 1706": see **228** and references there, where the dating here shown is also explained. The prosopographical indications (see below) would suggest that this text is likely to belong later rather than earlier in this mason's career. The inscribed stephanos is of the "radiate" type; see **192**.

Ergochares of Sphettos was eponymous archon in 226/5 B.C. (see pp. 320–321 above). It is likely that this is his son who is here the recipient of the honors voted in the lost main section of the stele, and these would in all probability have been accorded not earlier than the last fifteen or twenty years of the century. The other known name in this family is Theoros (*PA* 7230; *IG* II², 2411, line 18, 7518). This does not accord with the traces in line 1, which seem to suggest Ἐπ[ίμ]αχ[ος] *vel aliquid simile*.

Note. Tracy (*Attic Letter-Cutters*, pp. 50–51, nos. 1–4, with photographs pls. 1–4) published (and dated *ca. a.* 215 *a.*) four small fragments, I 1731, I 5597, I 5929, and I 6090 respectively. All are attributable, in his view, to the "Cutter of *IG* II² 1706", but none yields clear or continuous text save no. 4, where lines 5–8 read

NON-ΣTOIX.

Θησέ
α ᾿Αρμα
τίδου
Τ[ηι]ον.

This text is aligned with the remains of a name to the left, similarly disposed but in larger lettering. This may represent part of an honorary decree and as such calls for notice in this context. See *SEG* XL, 96. The character of the other three texts cannot be determined.

The same may be said of the small fragment I 6979 (Tracy, *Hesperia* 47, 1978, p. 253, no. 5, with photograph pl. 66:a; *SEG* XXVIII, 362), of no more than eight letters and two lines.

A TAXIARCHOS HONORED BY HIS PHYLE

233. A fragment of a stele of Pentelic marble (I 6827), with the right side and original back preserved, discovered on January 14, 1959, in a wall of a modern house east of the Church of the Holy Apostles (R 16). A substantial part of the inscribed surface has broken away at the upper and center right of the surviving stone.

H. 0.20 m.; W. 0.145 m.; Th. 0.06 m.
LH. 0.006 m.

Ed. B. D. Meritt, *Hesperia* 32, 1963, pp. 14–15, no. 13, with photograph pl. 4. See also *SEG* XXI, 522.

ca. a. 212/11 *a.*   NON-ΣTOIX. *ca.* 38

```
[------------------------------------]
[------------------------τ]ὴν ἀρχὴν [.ᶜᵃ·⁵.]
[--------------------τὴ]ν φυλὴν ἐστεφ[ανῶᵛᵛ]
[σθαι καὶ ἁπάντων τῶν ἐν τῆ]ι τάξει ἐπιμε[μελῆᵛᵛ]
[σθαι καλῶς καὶ φιλοτίμως, δ]εδόχθαι τοῖ[ς φυλέᵛ]
5   [ταις ἐπαινέσαι Δημοκλῆν Φιλ]ιστίωνος ᾿Αφιδ[ναῖον]
[καὶ στεφανῶσαι αὐτὸν θαλλο]ῦ στεφάνωι ἀ[ρετῆς]
[ἕνεκεν καὶ εὐνοίας τῆς εἰς το]ὺς φυλέτας, ὅπ[ως ἀν]
[καὶ ἄλλοι ἀποφαίνοντες τὰ] προπονούμενα [ὑπὲρ]
[τῆς Πτολεμαιδος φυλῆς εἰ]δῶσιν ὅτι χάρ[ιτας ᵛ]
10  [ἀπολήψονται καταξίας, καὶ ἀ]ναθεῖναι αὐτοῦ τό[ν]
[τε στέφανον καὶ εἰκόνα χαλκ]ῆν οὗ ἀν δοκεῖ τοῖς
[ἐπιμεληταῖς· ἑλέσθαι δὲ πέ]ντε ἄνδρας οἵτινε[ς]
[ἐπιμελήσονται τῆς ποιήσεω]ς καὶ τῆς ἀναθέσ[εως]
[τῆς εἰκόνος· ἀναγράψαι δὲ τό]δε τὸ ψήφισμα [ἐν στή]
15  [ληι λιθίνηι καὶ στῆσαι ἐν τῶι Ε]ὐρυσακε[ίωι].
[------------------------------](?)
```

S. V. Tracy (*Attic Letter-Cutters*, pp. 68–70) attributed three inscriptions, of which this is one, to a mason whom he designated the "Cutter of *IG* II² 1318", with a photograph of the name piece, fig. 5. Of the three, the only text datable on grounds other than those of the lettering style is *IG* II², 848 (*Agora* XV, 129), of the archonship of Archelaos. The year of Archelaos was for a long time held to have been 222/1 B.C. (see Meritt, *Historia* 26, 1977, p. 177, with earlier references): but a reassessment on the basis of fresh evidence led C. Habicht (*Studien*, pp. 160–161) to revert to the date earlier advocated by W. S. Ferguson, *Athenian Tribal Cycles*, p. 27 (cf. Meritt, *Hesperia* 4, 1935, p. 557, *Hesperia* 7, 1938, p. 138). The length of this mason's career cannot be assessed, and the date shown above is therefore based on the one fact known of it. The restoration in line 9, if acceptable, would set 224/3 as a *terminus post quem*. The lettering is plain; generous interlinear spacing contrasts not inartistically with comparatively close juxtaposition of the letters. The restorations are those of Meritt.

Honors paid by the Council and People of Athens to the whole body of taxiarchoi are recorded in **123, 182, 185,** and **187.** In this decree a single taxiarchos (cf. line 3) is honored by his phyle. Aphidna was a deme of the phyle Aiantis until the new phyle Ptolemais was created, at which time it was transferred to the new unit. See W. K. Pritchett, *AJP* 63, 1942, pp. 413–432 = *The Five Attic Tribes after Kleisthenes*, 1943, pp. 12–22; J. S. Traill,

Political Organization, pp. 29–30 with table XIII. The space for the phyle name in line 9 better accords with the longer Πτολεμαιδος than with the shorter Αιαντιδος.

Line 5. The name of the honorand is reasonably restored as that of Demokles, son of Philistion, of Aphidna, who belonged to a well-known family that could claim descent from the tyrannicides Harmodios and Aristogeiton. On the family see J. K. Davies, *Athenian Propertied Families*, pp. 472–479 (on the Demokles of this text, esp. p. 476). Another Demokles (*PA* 3495) was trierarch in the later 4th century (*IG* II², 1632, col. b, line 152) and appears as a κλητήρ in the poletai record of 342/1(?), *Agora* XIX, P26, at line 512. His son was in all probability the proposer of **86**. A Philistion, son of Demokles, was an ephebos in 117/16 (*PA* 14457; *IG* II², 1009, col. II, line 83). Lines 6–7. The award of the stephanos of olive on the part of the phyletai, and the expression of the virtues of the taxiarchos thus honored, closely follow the practice and formulation used by the Athenian state at large. See A. S. Henry, *Honours*, pp. 38–40, and 42. Lines 7–10. On the "hortatory intention" see **86**, commentary on lines 21–24. Line 8. προπονεῖν seems to have been a verb particularly favored by Xenophon.

Lines 11–12. Statues for distinguished citizens (or foreigners) were sparingly awarded, and the deserts of this taxiarchos are likely to have been exceptional. For the formulation of the honor see Henry, *Honours*, pp. 294–298, who however did not include in his survey divisions of the Athenian body politic (as here). Line 12. The epimeletai are those of the phyle, three in number (one for each trittys). See **80**, with references there cited, and cf. **136**, line 7.

Line 15. The Eurysakeion was particularly associated with the phyle Aiantis, and this connection was evidently maintained by those demes transferred to newly created phylai and thence, perhaps, by the new phyle as a whole. For the location of stelai there, and for evidence of the situation of the shrine, see *Agora* III, pp. 90–93, nos. 246–255, and cf. **86** and N. F. Jones, *Hesperia* 64, 1995, p. 509. There is no indication that the decree ended with line 15. The source of the funds for the stephanos and eikon has not yet been designated (cf., e.g., *IG* II², 1148), although this may not be necessary (cf., e.g., *IG* II², 1157, on which however see C. J. Schwenk, *Athens in the Age of Alexander*, pp. 316–319, no. 65).

THE ARCHONSHIP OF KALLISTRATOS, 208/7 B.C.

IG II², 849 associates the archon Kallistratos with the γραμματεύς Hagnonides, son of Apatourios, whose *demoticum* is unfortunately lost in a lacuna. The name Hagnonides is unusual (cf. W. B. Dinsmoor, *Archons of Athens*, p. 217), but his phyle affiliation may not be argued on the basis of restriction to the phylai of other known bearers of the name. However, the literary evidence concerning the death of the philosopher Lakydes, "in the archonship of Kallistratos," though far from unambiguous, was generally agreed to place Kallistratos in 206/5, and all discussions of the archon list until 1976 regarded this as an acceptably fixed point. Cf., for instance, J. Kirchner, *IG* II², 849, in comm.; Dinsmoor, *op. cit.*, pp. 48–50, 217, *Athenian Archon List*, pp. 167–168 (with a little hesitation), *Hesperia* 23, 1954, p. 316; W. K. Pritchett and B. D. Meritt, *Chronology*, p. xxv; Meritt, *Athenian Year*, p. 235. On the literary evidence (Apollodoros, fr. 47 [Jacoby], quoting Philodemos) see F. Jacoby, *FGrHist*, IIB, 1930, pp. 739–740; *PA* 8137; *RE* XIIA, 1924, cols. 530–531, *s.v.* Lakydes (W. Capelle).

However, in his republication of the ephebic text I 7181 (first published by O. W. Reinmuth, *Hesperia* 43, 1974, pp. 246–259), J. S. Traill made it clear that that decree, passed in the archonship of Apollodoros (204/3), praised the ephebes of the preceding year which was specifically that of the archon Diodotos, previously assigned with some reservations to 202/1. See Traill, *Hesperia* 45, 1976, pp. 296–303 and *SEG* XXVI, 98, XXXII, 125. It was recognized from the literary tradition that Kallistratos' year was followed by that of Pantiades, who was displaced from the previously accepted 205/4 in consequence of this new evidence. Traill, and after him Meritt (*Historia* 26, 1977, p. 179), moved Pantiades back to 206/5 and Kallistratos to 207/6 (a "vacant" year for which no name had been satisfactorily proposed).

Further study by C. Habicht, *Studien*, pp. 163–165, determined that 206/5 should belong to the archon Isokrates, until then considered to have held office in 201/200. This renewed displacement of Pantiades was readily accommodated by a further backward move; Kallistratos may be assigned to 208/7, which earlier, by reason of other readjustments (cf. Meritt, *Historia* 26, 1977, pp. 178–179), had become another "vacant" year. See Habicht, *Studien*, p. 177. This does no violence to the testimonia concerning the death of Lakydes.

234 is attributable to the Kallistratos here under discussion rather than to the year 156/5, when the eponymous archon had the same name, solely on the basis of the style of the lettering. Apart from *IG* II², 849 already mentioned, there is no further evidence for Kallistratos' year. His name was thought to appear in *IG* II², 1309, but this is better referred to Kallimedes in the middle of the 3rd century; see J. Pouilloux, *BCH* 70, 1946, p. 493, notes 2 and 7.

FRAGMENT OF A DECREE

234. A fragment of the upper left corner of a pedimental stele of Hymettian marble (I 6989), discovered in August 1964 on the surface north of the Archbishop's Palace (N 23). Very little of the inscribed surface remains, attached to a large section of the pediment from which the left akroterion has been lost. The transition from the base of the pediment to the inscribed surface is effected by a simple quarter-round ovolo molding, below which a flat taenia carries line 1 of the text, with a shallow apophyge leading to line 2.

    H. 0.16 m.; W. 0.30 m.; Th. 0.13 m.
    LH. 0.005–0.006 m.
    Ed. B. D. Meritt, *Hesperia* 37, 1968, p. 271, no. 9, with photograph pl. 78. See also *SEG* XXV, 109.

    a. 208/7 *a.*   NON-ΣΤΟΙΧ.

```
          Θ          ε          [ο          ι].
       Ἐπὶ Καλλισ[τράτου ἄρχοντος ------]
       [--------------------------------]
```

    What survives of the plain lettering suggests the attribution of this fragment to the Kallistratos of 208/7 rather than to his homonym of half a century later (see above). S. V. Tracy (*Attic Letter-Cutters*, p. 34) was unable to assign the meager remains to any identifiable mason, the surviving letters being too few for meaningful evaluation. The extensive remains of the pediment, as well as the measurement of line 1, indicate the original width of the inscribed surface as *ca.* 0.42 m., with approximately fifty letters to the line in the body of the text.

THE ARCHONSHIP OF EUANDROS, BETWEEN 202/1 AND 197/6 (BUT NOT 199/8) B.C.

The first in date of the two inscriptions on the small altar *IG* II², 4441 (*SEG* III, 148, XII, 162) is a dedication to Amphiaraos and Hygieia made by Timokles of Halai, "priest in the archonship of Euandros". Before its discovery, Euandros' tenure of office was not known, and he did not figure in considerations of the Athenian archons and their dates until J. Kirchner was able to list him, on the basis of the as yet unpublished text, among the "archontes saeculi III quorum tempora accuratius definiri nequeunt" (*IG* II², iv, 1, pp. 16–17). Kirchner postulated a lost first line of the dedication [Ἀσκληπιῶι], following J. Sundwall (*Nachträge zur Prosopographia Attica*, 1910, p. 160), who had attributed the inscription to the Euandros who was archon in 382/1. W. B. Dinsmoor (*Archons of Athens*, pp. 55, 164, 214) accommodated this indication to the cycle of priests of Asklepios and determined 208/7 as Euandros' date. He further suggested Euandros' name as that of the archon in *IG* II², 845B, where the restoration by Kirchner of the γραμματεύς as a man belonging to Acharnai (Oineis IX) implied to W. S. Ferguson (*Athenian Tribal Cycles*, pp. 27, 101–102) that Euandros' year should follow next-but-one after Chairephon, i.e., in 217/16. So also S. Dow, *Hesperia* 2, 1933, p. 437; A. Wilhelm, Πραγματεῖαι τῆς Ἀκαδημίας Ἀθηνῶν IV, i, 1936, pp. 27–28; B. D. Meritt, *Hesperia* 7, 1938, p. 138.

    Reconsideration of the priestly cycles caused Dinsmoor in 1939 (*Athenian Archon List*, pp. 103, 106, 168) to defer Euandros' year to the next cycle and place him in 205/4. However, W. K. Pritchett and Meritt (*Chronology*, pp. 103–108) recognized that *IG* II², 845B did not belong to Euandros' year and that the γραμματεύς named there was not the man of Acharnai as had been believed. Thus the cycle of the priests of Asklepios, unaided by the secretary cycle, remained alone as a guide to the dating of Euandros, and their restudy of this caused Pritchett and Meritt to assign his archonship to 212/11.

    D. D. Feaver's demonstration that [Ἀσκληπιῶι] was not after all to be restored in *IG* II², 4441 (see *SEG* XII, 162) made even this piece of evidential assistance invalid. Dinsmoor thus reverted in 1954 to the date 217/16 (*Hesperia* 23, p. 316), accepted by Meritt in the *editio princeps* of **235**; but in the absence of evidence any more substantial than the lettering of **235, 236**, and *IG* II², 4441 to offer any guidance, any year in this general period not preempted by another archon appeared to suffice. In *The Athenian Year* (p. 235), Meritt again included Euandros at 212/11, leaving 217/16 blank in his table, a blank later filled by a newly identified archon Hoplon; cf. Meritt, *Historia* 26, 1977, p. 178, where Euandros remains in place at 212/11.

C. Habicht's reconsideration of the archonships of these years (*Studien*, pp. 159–163, 177) required that 212/11 be assigned to Archelaos, displaced by new evidence from 222/1 (see **233**); but, as he observed (pp. 162–163), there is space for Euandros in one of the so far unassigned, "vacant" years from 202/1 to 200/199 and again in 198/7 or 197/6. Among these there is some slight indication that 200/199 may be the most preferable. S. V. Tracy (*Attic Letter-Cutters*, pp. 71–79, esp. p. 74) assigned *IG* II², 4441, lines 1–7 to the "Cutter of *IG* II² 913", whose otherwise datable career lies between 210/09 (slightly too late for the date previously accepted for Euandros) and 174/3: see **248**. Thus **235** and **236** should in any case fall within these limits.

A PRIESTESS OF MAGNA MATER HONORED BY A GROUP OF ORGEONES(?)

235. A fragment of a stele of Hymettian marble (I 4991), with the original back and right side preserved: broken elsewhere and with the inscribed surface broken all around, it was discovered on July 2, 1937, in a modern retaining wall east of the Post-Herulian Wall on the North Slope of the Akropolis (S 23 or thereabouts). The piece is so jagged that the measurements of its dimensions given below are no more than approximate.

H. *ca.* 0.27 m.; W. *ca.* 0.245 m.; Th. *ca.* 0.12 m.
LH. 0.008 m.

Ed. B. D. Meritt, *Hesperia* 26, 1957, pp. 209–210, no. 57, with photograph pl. 53. Lines 1–4 discussed with new restorations by G. Klaffenbach, *Varia epigraphica* (= *AbhAkadBerlin*, 1958, 2), pp. 25–26, no. IX; cf. A. G. Woodhead, *CR*, n.s. 10, 1960, p. 176. See also *SEG* XVII, 36.

a. 202/1 *a., vel paullo post*   NON-ΣΤΟΙΧ. 33–37

```
         [---------------------------]
         [--------εἶπεν]· ἐπ⟨ε⟩ιδὴ Ἱερο[---------]
         [------------]ΙΓΕΝΕΙ[.]ΟΥΛΑΜ[..5̄-6̄..]
         [..ca.7.. τὸν ἐνιαυτὸν] τὸν ἐπὶ Εὐάνδ[ρου 2̄-3̄]
         [....ca.13.... εὐσ]εβῶς τὴν ἱερω[σύνην]
    5    [ἐξήγαγεν καὶ τὰς θυσ]ίας τὰς καθηκού[σας ἔ]
         [θυσεν καὶ τὰ λοιπ]ὰ ἐφιλοτιμήθ[η ἐ]π[-----]
         [--------------· ἐπεμ]ελήθη δὲ τῆς στ[ρώ]
         [σεως τῆς κλίνης τῶν θε]ῶν μετὰ πάσης [σπου]
         [δῆς καὶ προθυμίας· ἐπεμελήθ]η δὲ καὶ τῶν ὀργ[εών]
   10    [ων -----------· διεν]έμησε δὲ κα[ὶ 3̄-4̄.]
         [-----------· ἐπεμελήθ]η δὲ καὶ ε[..6̄-7̄...]
         [---------------------------]
```

The lettering is large, shallow, and moderately competent, with variable spacing between the letters. The style is plain, and the junctions of strokes reasonably accurate. The external strokes of mu and sigma are parallel or nearly so; pi in line 1 has its two vertical strokes of equal length. There has been a very clumsy erasure in line 6. At the ends of lines 9–11 more letters have been lost than are shown in the *editio princeps*. S. V. Tracy (*Attic Letter-Cutters*, p. 253) was not able to attribute this text to an identifiable mason.

Line 1. *Lapis* ΕΠΙΔΗ. Lines 1–4 were restored by Meritt and Klaffenbach as follows:

Meritt

```
         [----------εἶπεν]· ἐπ⟨ε⟩ιδὴ Ἱερο[------]
         [ἱέρεια λαχοῦσα -----]ΙΓΕΝΕΙ[.]ΟΥΛΑΜ[ca.5̄-6̄.]
         [.... εἰς τὸν ἐνιαυτὸ]ν τὸν ἐπὶ Εὐάνδ[ρου ἄρ]
         [χοντος καλῶς καὶ εὐσ]εβῶς κτλ.
```

Klaffenbach

```
         [-----------εἶπεν]· ἐπ⟨ε⟩ιδὴ Ἱερό[κλεια(?)]
         [..ca.8..., γυνὴ δὲ Ἀντ]ιγενεί[δ]ου Λαμ[πτρέως]
         [ἱέρεια εἰς(?) τὸν ἐνιαυτὸ]ν τὸν ἐπὶ Εὐάνδ[ρου λα]
         [χοῦσα καλῶς καὶ εὐσ]εβῶς κτλ.
```

Meritt based his restorations on the varied phraseology of *IG* II², 1314 and 1315, decrees of the same group of orgeones dated to 213/12 and 211/10. In neither case is the priestess identified by the name of father and husband. Klaffenbach referred also to the decree of the boule and demos *IG* II², 788. Lines 6–7. So Meritt. Perhaps ἐ]πα[κολ|ουθῶς τοῖς νόμοις· ἐπεμ]ελήθη κτλ. Lines 9–10. ὀργ[εώ||νων Meritt. Line 10. κ[αὶ ..] Meritt, who supposed only five letters after the final epsilon of line 11.

Line 10. διεν]έμησε. The weak aorist is quoted from Didymos by LSJ. The future of νέμω, classically νεμῶ, developed to the form νεμήσω both in the simple verb and in compounds. An aorist on the same principle may have replaced ἔνειμα in ordinary parlance (which a decree of a body of orgeones might reflect more readily than a state enactment) more effectively than the literary evidence indicates. The reading on the stone is not in doubt.

FRAGMENT OF A DECREE

236. The upper left corner of a pedimental stele of Pentelic marble (I 260), broken below and to the right and with part of the left akroterion sheared off but complete elsewhere, discovered in October 1932 in a wall of a modern house over the eastern part of the Tholos (H 11–12). An ovolo molding, with a taenia and apophyge below it, effects the transition from the horizontal cornice of the pediment to the inscribed face. Line 1 is partly inscribed within the curve of the apophyge.

H. 0.18 m.; W. 0.195 m.; Th. 0.10 m.
LH. 0.006 m.

Ed. B. D. Meritt, *Hesperia* 3, 1934, p. 11, no. 14, with photograph. Brief references by W. B. Dinsmoor, *Athenian Archon List*, p. 168; W. K. Pritchett and Meritt, *Chronology*, p. 104; A. Wilhelm, Πραγματεῖαι τῆς ᾽Ακαδημίας ᾽Αθηνῶν IV, i, 1936, pp. 27–28.

a. 202/1 *a., vel paullo post*　　　　　　　　　　　　　　　NON-ΣΤΟΙΧ.

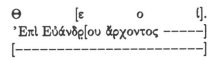

```
        Θ        [ε        ο         ι].
     ᾽Επὶ Εὐάνδρ[ου ἄρχοντος —————]
     [————————————————————]
```

The lettering is careful and plain, with slight apices on epsilon and nu, and with pi in the form Γ. S. V. Tracy (*Attic Letter-Cutters*, p. 250) regarded the evidence as too slight to permit attribution to a known "hand", but he detected some general similarity to the style of the "Cutter of *IG* II² 913", on whom see **248**.

FRAGMENT OF AN HONORARY DECREE

237. A fragment of a stele (I 4605) of a marble which is bluish gray but not of the kind conventionally termed Hymettian, broken all around except on the right below the level of the inscribed surface, discovered on March 11, 1937, near the surface under what was formerly Akropolis Street, west of the Post-Herulian Wall (S 25).

H. 0.108 m.; W. 0.073 m.; Th. 0.025 m.
LH. 0.006–0.007 m. (omicron 0.004 m.).

Ed. B. D. Meritt, *Hesperia* 29, 1960, pp. 10–11, no. 13, with photograph pl. 3. See also *SEG* XIX, 75.

ex. saec. III *a.*　　　　　　　　　　　　　　　　　NON-ΣΤΟΙΧ. *ca.* 33–37

```
       [————————————————————————]
       [————————————————————Καλ]λίστρα
       [τος ..........14–18.......... εἶπεν· ἐπει]δὴ Φιλι[.]
       [..4–5.. διατελεῖ τὴν πατρικὴν εὔνοι]αν ἀποδ[ει]
       [κνύμενος τῶι δήμωι τῶι ᾽Αθηναίων κ]αὶ τοῖς ἀ[φι]
   5   [κνουμένοις αὐτῶν εἰς ...4–8...]ην καὶ κοιν[ῆι]
       [καὶ ἰδίαι ἐμ παντὶ καιρῶι παρέχ]ων ἑαυτὸν
       [χρήσιμον τῶι δήμωι τῶι ᾽Αθηναίων, ἀ]γαθεῖ τύ
       [χει δεδόχθαι τεῖ βουλεῖ τοὺς προ]έδρου[ς]
       [οἵτινες ἂν λάχωσιν προεδρεύειν ἐν] τῶ[ι δή]
  10   [μωι ————————————————————]
       [————————————————————————]
```

In the *editio princeps* of this text, for which he rightly sought a 3rd-century date, Meritt suggested that the proposer of the decree (lines 1–2) might be identified with the orator Kallistratos, son of Glaukon, of Kropidai: see *IG* II², 661 (*SEG* XVI, 67), datable by the archon Menekles to 267/6. He was also tempted to connect the honorand with the Philistides of **207**, a stone found close by, and on the day after, the discovery of the present piece. As a result, he gave a date "*ca. a. 267/6 a.*" to this text on publication.

However, neither association can stand. In the latter case the character of the two stones differs, and they cannot belong to the same monument, as Meritt himself acknowledged. The connection with the Kallistratos of 267/6 was invalidated by S. V. Tracy's study of the lettering of this fragment. In *GRBS* 11, 1970 (pp. 328–330, with photographs pls. 25 and 26), Tracy included it among his attributions to the craftsman he then designated "Mason 1", whose activities appeared at that time to span the last quarter of the 3rd century and the first two decades of the 2nd. Further investigation produced a total of thirty-two inscriptions that may be assigned to him, five of them being Agora *psephismata* (**238, 239, 241**, and **242** in addition to the present text), and he has been redesignated the "Cutter of *IG* II² 912". See Tracy, *Attic Letter-Cutters*, pp. 55–60, with photograph of part of the name piece, fig. 3. The earliest datable work attributed to this mason belongs to the archonship of Ergochares (226/5); the latest is now set at "*ca. a. 190 a.*". Thus the present text, like the other four already referred to, must be dated within these limits. Tracy's brief description of the mason's characteristics as graceful, simple, and economic may perhaps overvalue his aesthetic appeal. There is much in his work that is slipshod and at times (e.g., in his name piece) pusillanimous.

Lines 1–2. Neither the proposer nor the honorand can be further identified (see above). Lines 5–6. κοινῆι καὶ ἰδίαι. See the commentary on **49**.

Lines 7–8. ἀγαθεῖ τύχει. See **72**, commentary on lines 7–8. Lines 8–10. The formula shows that the decree was probouleumatic, and it was so listed by P. J. Rhodes, *Athenian Boule*, p. 252 (with Meritt's original dating). Line 9. The use of the "earlier" formula in place of τοὺς λαχόντας προέδρους (see **217**, commentary on lines 16–17), which the apparent structure of the decree seems to require, may suggest that it belongs earlier rather than later in this craftsman's career.

The technique of the inscribing of this document was discussed by C. G. Higgins and W. K. Pritchett, *AJA* 69, 1965, p. 370 (cf. pp. 367–371), with photographs pl. 98:B–E. See also *SEG* XXII, 204.

HONORS FOR THE CITY OF EPHESOS

238. A fragment of a stele of Hymettian marble (I 5589), with the right side and original rough-picked back preserved, discovered on October 17, 1938, in a wall of a modern house southeast of the Market Square and west of the Panathenaic Way (R 21).

H. 0.16 m.; W. 0.223 m.; Th. 0.128 m.
LH. 0.008 m.

Ed. B. D. Meritt, *Hesperia* 13, 1944, pp. 249–251, no. 10, with photograph.

ex. saec. III *a.*   NON-ΣΤΟΙΧ. *ca.* 50

```
[----------------------------------------]
[-------------------------]α[. . .]ες θεω[ρ]οὶ τὴν
[ἐπιδημίαν Ἀθήνησιν κατὰ τὰ Πτολεμαῖα(?) ἐ]πεδήμησαν καλῶς κ[αὶ]
[καταξίως τοῦ δήμου τοῦ Ἐφεσίων, δεδό]χθαι τεῖ βουλεῖ τοὺς λ[α]
[χόντας προέδρους εἰς τὴν ἐπιοῦσαν ἐκ]κλησίαν χρηματίσαι περ[ὶ]
5  [τούτων, γνώμην δὲ ξυμβάλλεσθαι τῆς β]ουλῆς εἰς τὸν δῆμον ὅτι δ[ο]
[κεῖ τεῖ βουλεῖ ἐπαινέσαι τὸν δῆμον τ]⟨ὸ⟩ν Ἐφεσίων καὶ στεφανῶσα[ι]
[χρυσῶι στεφάνωι κατὰ τὸν νόμον εὐνοία]ς ἕνεκα καὶ φιλοτιμίας τῆς
[εἰς τὸν δῆμον τὸν Ἀθηναίων, καὶ ἀνειπε]ῖν τὸν στέφανον τοῦτον Δι
[ονυσίων τῶν ἐν ἄστει τραγωιδῶν τῶι καιν]ῶι ἀγῶνι· τῆς δὲ ποιήσεως
10 [τοῦ στεφάνου καὶ τῆς ἀναγορεύσεως ἐπιμεληθῆ]ναι τοὺς στρατηγοὺ[ς]
[καὶ τὸν ταμίαν τῶν στρατιωτικῶν· τὰ δὲ ψηφίσματα] τὰ ἀποστα
[λέντα ----------------------------------------]
[----------------------------------------]
```

The restorations, which follow recognized formulas, are those of Meritt, with the exception of line 1, in which his ἀποστα]λ[έντ]ες is not assured by the traces on the stone. These appear to offer – – –]α[. . .]ες or possibly – – –]αγ[. .]ες. Line 6. *Lapis* ΩΝ.

This inscription, like **237**, was attributed by S. V. Tracy to his "Mason 1", whom later he redesignated the "Cutter of *IG* II² 912". For this craftsman's floruit and characteristics see the commentary on **237**. Historical considerations (see below) suggest that this text does not, at the least, belong at the very end of his career. Meritt's date of "*ca. a.* 200 *a.*" is certainly acceptable.

For relations between Athens and Ephesos at this period see **225**. The present decree should antedate 197/6, when Antiochos III's forces took possession of the Ionian coast and the Egyptian connection, important to the Athenians, was broken; but nothing further can be deduced concerning its immediate occasion, nor to what degree it is separated in time from the circumstances of **225**. The decree is probouleumatic and is cited as such by P. J. Rhodes, *Athenian Boule*, p. 254.

Lines 3–4. τοὺς λαχόντας προέδρους. Contrast **237**, lines 8–10, where see the commentary. Lines 6–7. On the golden stephanos κατὰ τὸν νόμον see **112**, commentary on lines 5–7 and **141**, commentary on lines 8–9. For the virtues commended in the Ephesian demos cf. **224**, commentary on lines 34–36. Lines 8–9. The stephanos was to be announced only at the Dionysia: the Panathenaia, Eleusinia, and Ptolemaia are not designated as further occasions on which to repeat the honor. The single announcement retains the simpler form of earlier practice. This is not the only version of the formula that might be accommodated here: cf. A. S. Henry, *Honours*, pp. 32–33.

Lines 10–11. The generals, and the Military Treasurer (in the restoration), are to be responsible for the announcement. Cf. **224**, commentary on lines 39–41 and references there. But responsibility might rest with the generals alone, as it frequently did, and in that case line 11 will be open to other possibilities of restoration.

GRANTS OF ATHENIAN CITIZENSHIP

239 (Pl. 25). Two nonjoining fragments of a stele of Hymettian marble, of which that on the left, fragment *a* (I 4260), preserves the left side of the monument but is broken elsewhere: it was discovered on June 8, 1936, in a late fill to the west of the East Building (N 15).

Fragment *b* (I 5322) preserves the right edge of the stele but is otherwise broken all around, and the inscribed surface is badly abraded save on the extreme right: it was discovered on March 14, 1938, in the east wall of the Church of the Hypapanti (T 21).

a: H. 0.115 m.; W. 0.141 m.; Th. 0.073 m.

b: H. 0.14 m.; W. 0.30 m.; Th. 0.133 m.

LH. 0.005–0.006 m. (omicron 0.004 m.).

Ed. *a* only: B. D. Meritt, *Hesperia* 26, 1957, pp. 58–59, no. 13, with photograph pl. 10. See also *SEG* XVI, 73. Fragment *b* unpublished; its connection with fragment *a* was observed by A. G. Woodhead and the information made available to S. V. Tracy (see *GRBS* 14, 1973, p. 189) and to A. S. Henry (see *Antichthon* 15, 1981, p. 102, *Honours*, p. 115, note 203). A draft text of the combined fragments was also made available to M. J. Osborne, who added his own observations and incorporated a prepublication text into *Naturalization* I, pp. 236–237, D 119, *Naturalization* II, pp. 196–198.

ex. saec. III *a.*   NON-ΣΤΟΙΧ. *ca.* 54–57

```
      [--------------------------------------------------]
      [------ca. 19------]ΛΟ[3–4.]Ε[ca. 4.]Δ[--------ca. 25--------]          (b)
      [------ca. 19------]Α[2–3.]Τ[.5–6..]ΕΠ[--------ca. 25--------]
      [------ca. 19------]ΛΟ[..]ΝΗΝ[--ca. 9--]ΙΑΣ[----ca. 18------]
      [καὶ στεφανῶσαι ἕκαστ]ον αὐτῷ[ν μυρρίν]ης σ[τε]φάνωι [----ca. 14----]
  5   [------ca. 19------] γράψ[ασ]θα[ι φυλῆς καὶ δήμου καὶ φρατρ[ίας ἧς]
      [ἂν αὐτοὶ βούλωνται· καλέσαι δὲ αὐτοὺς καὶ] ἐπὶ ξένια εἰς τὸ πρυτανεῖον
      [εἰς αὔριον· ὅπως δ'ἂν οὖν καὶ ὁ δῆμος ἀεὶ μεμ]νημένος φαίνηται τῶν [ἐν]
(a)   τοῖς πρότερον χρόγ[οις εὐεργετηθ]έ[ντων ε]ἰ̣ς αὐτὸν καὶ τὰς ἀξίας ἑκά[σ]
      [{σ}]τοις ἀποδιδοὺς χά[ριτας, εἶναι τοῖς] υἱοῖς [αὐτῶν παρὰ] τοῦ δήμου πολ[ι]
 10   τείαν, καὶ εἶναι αὐτο[ῖς δοκιμασθεῖσ]ι γ[ρ]άφασθαι φυλῆς καὶ δήμου κ[αὶ]
      φρατρίας ἧς ἂν ἕκα[στος αὐτῶν βούλ]η[τα]ι· [ἀν]αγράψαι δὲ τόδε τὸ ψήφισ[μα]
      τὸν γραμματέα τὸν κ[ατὰ πρυτανείαν εἰς σ]τήλην λιθίνην καὶ στ[ῆσαι]
      πρὸς τῶι Ἐλευσινίωι· [εἰς δὲ τὴν ἀναγραφὴν καὶ τὴν ἀνάθεσιν τῆς στήλης]
      [μ]ερίσαι τὸ γενόμενον [ἀνάλωμα τὸν ταμίαν τῶν στρατιωτικῶν. vacat    ]
              vacat
```

Line 9 *init.* In this spoiled area there appear to be the remains of a superfluous but not successfully deleted sigma. Osborne's text is defined as "*ca.* 51–54", but lines 10–13 show that the figure must be increased by a few letters.

Lines 1–4. There is little certainty in the reading of these lines, which, as in some other lines of the abraded area, for the most part require the eye of faith. Readings by Osborne that differ notably from the above text are as follows: Line 4. μ[υρ]ρίνης σ[τ]εφάνωι. Line 6 *init.* [ἂν βούλωνται· καλέσαι δὲ αὐτ]ρο[ὺ]ς κ[αὶ] κτλ. Lines 7–8. ἐ[ν]| τοῖς πρότερον χρόν[οις ––––––]Σ[–––– εἰ]ς αὐτόν κτλ. Line 9. χά[ριτας ––––]ιϰ[–––]ΙΟΙ[–––––] τοῦ δήμου (where there may indeed be space for his suggestion εἶναι καὶ τοῖς υἱοῖς τὴν παρὰ τοῦ δήμου). However, whether or not this or that letter is really to be discerned, the essentials of the enactment are undoubted.

This is a further inscription attributed by Tracy to the "Cutter of *IG* II² 912": see **237** and references there. The implication of this must be that the decree should be dated between 226/5 and the end of the first decade of the 2nd century. That it should be set in the later stages of the mason's datable career may emerge from other considerations (see below).

The formulation of enactments conferring Athenian citizenship on deserving foreigners changed radically after the reestablishment of freedom from Macedonian control in 229. For the essentials of the new formula and its variants see Osborne, *Naturalization* I, pp. 16–17, 192–196 and Henry, *Honours*, pp. 80–88. Osborne named the new practice "Formulation B" and subdivided it into three or perhaps four types, of which the third is the best attested. The present text appears to belong to Type III and if so is an early, perhaps the earliest, example of it. But it is peculiar in that the enrollment clause is repeated (lines 5–6, 10–11), a feature probably to be explained by the extension of the grant to a further group, perhaps the sons of the first-named recipients of the honor. Osborne considered that, in the case of the first group, the decree provided for the reaffirmation of an existing grant or other honor (lines 7–8) rather than an initial award, especially as the usual instructions to the thesmothetai to provide for a scrutiny seem to have been omitted. Osborne's chronological scheme suggests that, omitting consideration of this text, the change from Type I to Types II and III is to be set at *ca.* 202: if that is so, this inscription may perhaps be dated more narrowly to the turn of the century.

Line 4. For the stephanos of myrtle see **228**. Line 6. The honorands are invited ἐπὶ ξένια even though, as potential or newly enrolled citizens, they would more properly be summoned ἐπὶ δεῖπνον. For the apparent anomaly see **224**, commentary on lines 44–45 and **225**, commentary on line 17, both instances being the reverse of this. Osborne (*ZPE* 41, 1981, p. 155, note 7) noted that a "citizen" could be invited ἐπὶ ξένια at a period before what he regarded as the breakdown in the terminology. Henry (*Antichthon* 15, 1981, p. 109, note 25) saw the present instance as displaying "a degree of discretion" on the part of the Athenians and (p. 102) pointed out that the circumstances of the benefactions here rewarded are unknown, not necessarily qualifying in the terms suggested for **224** (cf. also Osborne, *Naturalization* II, pp. 197–198). Nevertheless, procedural muddle or insouciance may yet underlie the discrepancy.

Line 7. The expression of the "hortatory intention" (see **86**, commentary on lines 21–24 and **173**, commentary on line 2) is open to a wide variety of phraseology, to suit the sentiments deemed appropriate to the particular occasion. In place of encouraging emulation in other prospective honorands (e.g., **185**, **240**) or action by them conformable with the laws (**217**), the emphasis here is on the demos itself and its anxiety to be seen to be grateful to those who have done it good service, as in **173** and **224**. Cf. *IG* II², 891, lines 8–10, 966, lines 12–14.

Line 13. πρὸς τῶι Ἐλευσινίωι. Cf. **228**, line 7. This context was quoted by R. E. Wycherley (*Agora* III, p. 81, no. 221) among evidence for the erection of stelai in this location. Surviving instances suggest that those concerned had a particular connection with the Eleusinian cult, and this connection should in all probability be assumed in the case of the present honorands. Line 14. The Military Treasurer is surely to be restored as the official providing for the relevant costs: see **224**, commentary on lines 45–50. The alternative of the Plural Board of Administration, while theoretically possible, is to be discounted. See Henry, *Chiron* 14, 1984, pp. 81–82 with note 169. The vacant space below line 14 makes it clear that shared responsibility is not an option.

A CERTAIN THERSON HONORED

240. A fragment of a stele of Hymettian marble (I 2373), with the right side and original rough-picked back preserved and with the inscribed surface dressed roughly away on the left for more than half the total preserved width, down a more or less vertical line; discovered on February 7, 1935, in a wall of a modern house west of the Odeion (K 10). The almost vertical striations of a toothed chisel are visible towards the right edge.

H. 0.24 m.; W. 0.15 m.; Th. 0.14 m.
LH. 0.006 m.

Ed. B. D. Meritt, *Hesperia* 29, 1960, pp. 12–13, no. 15, with photograph pl. 3. See also *SEG* XIX, 90.

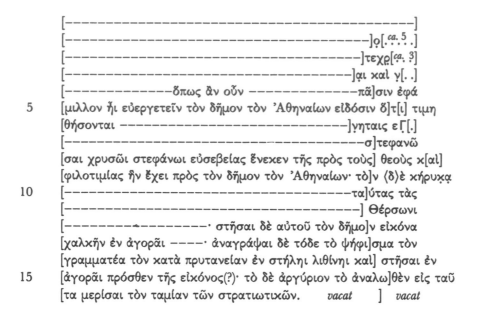

The writing of this text is not well done, and the letters are variably spaced. Alpha is "disjointed", in the manner of the "Cutter of *IG* II² 1706" (see **222**), but the other criteria of that style are absent. Nu tends to be widely spread; the angles of epsilon are haphazard. Especially notable is the form of phi, in which the left end of the oval remains open (Φ). Cf., e.g., *IG* II², 876. S. V. Tracy (*Attic Letter-Cutters*, p. 252) was not able to assign the piece to an identifiable mason, classing the lettering as rather ordinary and "unfamiliar" (cf. p. 238). Noting that it is perhaps to be dated before 229, he nevertheless saw some affinity with the style of the "Cutter of *IG* II² 1318", whose only dated work belongs to 212/11; see **233**. A generalized date towards the end of the 3rd century is probably the preferable conclusion.

The restorations shown follow those of the *editio princeps* except in lines 9 and 16. The length of the lines is controlled by the standard formula contained in lines 13–14 and to some extent confirmed also by line 8.

Lines 4–5. The "hortatory intention" is here addressed to the competitive instincts of other potential honorands. See **239**, commentary on line 7 and (for the phraseology here) *IG* II², 721 (M.J. Osborne, *Naturalization* I, pp. 153–155, D 71, *Naturalization* II, p. 154), lines 2–5.

Line 6 *ad fin.* ιητας ε Γ[.] Meritt. An iota seems, however, to intervene between alpha and sigma. Suitable word division recommends ἐπ[ι] at the conclusion of the line. Line 8. χρυσῶι στεφάνωι. So Meritt: but the available space does not permit the inclusion of the usual qualifying formula κατὰ τὸν νόμον. A stephanos of olive (θαλλοῦ στεφάνωι) would be an acceptable alternative. It is, however, fair to point out, as has been observed by A. S. Henry (*Honours*, p. 27) that with gold stephanoi this qualification is indeed omitted at times; and if the suggestion below for lines 12–13 has any plausibility, the stephanos here must certainly be of gold. Lines 9–10. *Lapis* NAEK. ἱ]να(?) ἐκηρύκ[ευ||εν Meritt. For the phraseology restored in the earlier part of line 9 see Henry, *Honours*, pp. 42–43; but other formulations are equally possible. Meritt's text read [φιλοτιμίας τῆς εἰς τὸν δῆμον τὸν Ἀθηναίων – – – – ἱ]να κτλ., which left a difficult lacuna: the insertion into the formula of τὴν βουλὴν καί would add too greatly to the proposed length of the line.

Line 11. Therson is not identifiable: cf. Meritt, *op. cit.*, p. 13. Lines 12–13. An εἰκὼν χαλκῆ was a very notable honor: see **233**, commentary on lines 11–12 and Henry, *Honours*, pp. 295–296, where this text is listed. The εἰκών was usually set up in the Agora; hence the present supplement. But Meritt's text leaves a lacuna the brevity of which is unhelpful in regard to the limitation (or grant of choice) of the precise site that may be added to the regular formula. It is possible to insert here [χαλκῆν ἐφ'ἵππου ἐν τῆι ἀγορᾶι· ἀναγράψαι δὲ κτλ.], a formulation that has its parallels (cf. Henry, *loc. cit.*): but this postulates a very extraordinary honor, shared on the evidence only by kings and princes at this epoch.

Line 16. Meritt did not include in his text a restoration of the official(s) responsible for payment; but the Military Treasurer was almost certainly the officer concerned. The blank space at the end of the line precludes his association here with the Plural Board of Administration. See **224**, commentary on lines 49–50.

FRAGMENT OF AN HONORARY DECREE

241. A fragment of a stele of Hymettian marble (I 1036), broken on all sides, discovered on June 27, 1933, in a Byzantine context east of the Stoa of Zeus (I 6).

H. 0.185 m.; W. 0.135 m.; Th. 0.04 m.
LH. 0.008 m.

Ed. S. V. Tracy, *Hesperia* 39, 1970, p. 308, no. 1, with photograph pl. 76.

ex. saec. III *a.*   NON-ΣΤΟΙΧ.

Ὁ δῆμος
Σώστρατον
Χολαργέα.
vacat

This fragment preserves a citation from the foot of a decree whereby Sostratos of Cholargos was a recipient (perhaps among others) of honors at the hands of the Athenian people. The honorand is surely to be identified with the Σώστρατος Νικοστράτου Χολα(ργεύς) who was among the ephebes of the archonship of (coincidentally) Sostratos in 210/09 praised in *SEG* XIX, 77 + XXII, 101, at line 23 (for the line numeration see Tracy, *Hesperia* 47, 1978, pp. 259–260 and *SEG* XXVIII, 200). He was ταμίας of the Council later in his career, as evidenced by *Agora* XV, 204 (lines 11–12) and 205 (lines 12–13), both of which are dated between 176/5 and 170/69: by that time Sostratos will have been a man in his later fifties.

Brief as it is, this text provided Tracy with sufficient evidence for its assignment in the *editio princeps* to the mason he later came to describe as the "Cutter of *IG* II² 912": see **237** for the details of, and references to, his *oeuvre* and career. This inscription must have been a work of his later years: it is unlikely that an ephebe of 210/09 would receive public honors much before the turn of the century.

FRAGMENT OF A DECREE

242 (Pl. 26). A fragment of a stele of white marble (I 6267), broken on all sides, discovered in January 1950 in a Late Roman wall east of the Panathenaic Way (N–P 7–12): the inscribed surface is badly abraded, and very little is legible.

H. 0.30 m.; W. 0.143 m.; Th. 0.127 m.
LH. 0.007 m.

Ed. S. V. Tracy, *Attic Letter-Cutters*, pp. 59–60, no. 2, with photograph pl. 8. See also *SEG* XL, 98.

ex. saec. III *a.*   NON-ΣΤΟΙΧ.

```
   [--------------------------------------------]
   [-------------- πρυ]τανεία[ς ------------------]
   [-------------- Με]νεκράτου[-------------------]
   [-------------- -]ν Φίλωνο[ς ------------------]
   [---------------]σιαδος Π[------------------]
5  [-------------- -]ν υπαρχ[--------------------]
   [-------------- -]Ο[. . .]Ι[------------------]
   [-------------- -]ΗΣΑΠΕΡ[-------------------]
   [------------------ -]ΕΔ[--------------------]
   [------------------ -]Ο[--------------------]
10 [-------------- -]Ε[--------------------------]
   [-------------- -]Τ[------------------------]
   [-------------- -]Ε[------------------------]
   [--------------------------------------------]
```

In the upper section of this fragment sufficient is visible for Tracy to have been able to ascribe the workmanship to the "Cutter of *IG* II² 912": see **237**. Below line 12 he noted "illegible traces of at least eight more lines."

Lines 1–3. Evidently the remains of part of the prescript to the decree. Tracy suggested (with a line of *ca.* 56 letters):

[----------------τῆς πρυ]τανεία[ς· ἐκκλησία ἐν τῶι θεάτρωι· τῶν]
[προέδρων ἐπεψήφιζεν ---- Με]νεκράτου[---- καὶ συμπρόεδροι]·
[ἔδοξεν τῆι βουλῆι καὶ τῶι δήμωι· ---]ν Φίλωνο[ς ---εἶπεν· ἐπειδὴ]
[κτλ.]

However, the disposition and formulation of line 3, together with the need for adequate space for the nomen and *demoticum* there and in line 2, imply that τῶν in line 1 would be better positioned at the beginning of the second line, with the line length extended to *ca.* 61. For the ἐκκλησία ἐν τῶι θεάτρωι see **167**, commentary on lines 6–7.

Line 5. Perhaps [---- εὔνους τῶι δήμωι τῶι ᾿Αθηναίω]ν ὑπάρχ[ει -----] Tracy, who compared *IG* II², 1330, line 70.

FRAGMENT OF A DECREE

243. A fragment of a stele of Pentelic marble (I 4185), with part of the left side preserved but broken elsewhere and very worn and battered, discovered on May 28, 1936, in disturbed earth west of the Post-Herulian Wall (S 17).

H. 0.128 m.; W. 0.088 m.; Th. 0.054 m.
LH. 0.005–0.006 m.

Ed. B. D. Meritt, *Hesperia* 29, 1960, p. 10, no. 12, with photograph pl. 2. See also *SEG* XIX, 83.

ante fin. saec. III *a.*   NON-ΣTOIX. *ca.* 40

['Επὶ ------ ἄρχοντος ἐπὶ τῆς -----------]
πρυταν[είας ἧι ------------------------ ἐ]
γραμμά[τευεν· ------------------------]
εἰκοστ[εῖ τῆς πρυτανείας· ἐκκλησία ἐν τῶι θεάτρωι]·
5   [τῶ]ν πρ[οέδρων ἐπεψήφιζεν ----------------]
[...]εὐ[ς καὶ συμπρόεδροι· ἔδοξεν τῆι βουλῆι καὶ τῶι]
[δή]μωι· [----------------------------]
[...]TH[----------------------------]
[....]O[----------------------------]
10   [----------------------------]

The lettering is plain and not helpful in the attribution of a date to the inscription save in the most general terms, although it is the sole criterion available beyond the standard formula of the prescript. Pi has both verticals of equal length; omega is spread rather in the 4th-century manner. The external strokes of mu and sigma are not parallel. The overall aspect is indicative of the later 3rd century, and it may be noted that the text is not in the stoichedon style. However, it was not treated by S. V. Tracy among the works of Attic letter cutters *post* 229 B.C.

While the detail of the prescript cannot be elucidated, enough of the text survives to determine the approximate length of line, and this seems to require in line 4 that the location of the ἐκκλησία be identified, with ἐν Διονύσου or ἐμ Πειραιεῖ (cf. **222**) perhaps insufficient for the available space. For the assembly in the theater (so expressed), cf. **242** and the reference there.

Spatial requirements also make it tolerably certain that the decree was probouleumatic; but it is not among those listed as such by P. J. Rhodes, *Athenian Boule*, pp. 246–258.

AN UNCERTAIN FRAGMENT

244. A small fragment of a stele of Hymettian marble (I 2446), broken all around, discovered on February 19, 1935, in a late context southwest of the Tholos (G 12).

H. 0.106 m.; W. 0.044 m.; Th. 0.036 m.
LH. 0.006–0.008 m. (lines 1–3), 0.007 m. (lines 5–7).

Ed. B. D. Meritt, *Hesperia* 21, 1952, pp. 378–379, no. 36, with photograph pl. 98. See also *SEG* XII, 93.

saec. III *a.*   NON-ΣTOIX.

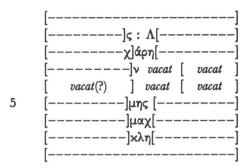

Two hands are in evidence on this fragment. The lettering of lines 5–7 is wider and more flattened in character, with greater interlinear spacing and some use of enlargement in the "free ends" of strokes. It appears to belong relatively early in the century, yet it is not written in the stoichedon style, and this in the case of a public decree would be unusual.

Though identified at the time of publication as a *psephisma*, the piece is included here with considerable reservations. Meritt interpreted it as appearing to contain the end of one decree, which had terminated in a list of names, and the opening lines of a second, with preamble much abbreviated, which he restored with a line of *ca.* 30 letters as follows: ['Επὶ τῆς –––––– ἐβδό]μης [πρυτα|νείας ἧι –––––]μάχ[ου –––––– |–––– ἐγραμμάτευεν· ἐx]xλη[σία· ––––]. There is however no reason why the whole fragment should not be construed as a *catalogus nominum* of some kind, with a name such as Χρέ]μης in line 5 and any number of familiar possibilities in lines 6 and 7. It may have formed a part of a monument to which additions were from time to time made in a variety of hands, as in the *didascaliae* (*IG* II², 2318 *et sqq.*). The use of two-dot punctuation without any apparent association with a numeral is also indicative of a text that is not a public decree, but it occurs in that section of the inscription which Meritt in any case acknowledged as a list of names.

A FRAGMENT OF A DECREE OF THE ORGEONES OF BENDIS(?)

245. A fragment of a stele of Hymettian marble (I 5664), with the original flat top and rough-picked back preserved. Broken elsewhere and generally much battered, it was discovered on February 21, 1939, during the demolition of houses on the North Slope between the Akropolis and the Areopagos.

H. 0.20 m.; W. 0.23 m.; Th. 0.09 m.

LH. 0.009 m. (line 1), 0.006 m. (lines 2–5).

Ed. B. D. Meritt, *Hesperia* 30, 1961, p. 227, no. 25, with photograph pl. 40. See also *SEG* XXI, 531.

saec. III *a.*   NON-ΣTOIX. *ca.* 45

```
      [Θ              ε]           ο              [ι].
      [........ ca. 17 .......] Μαραθώνιος εἶπεν· δε[δόχθαι τῶι κοινῶι]
      [τῶν ὀργεώνων· ἐπειδὴ] οἱ ἱερο[πο]ιοὶ οἱ α[ἱρεθέντες ἐπὶ ca. 3]
      [. ca. 6 . ἄρχοντος χα]λῶς χαὶ [φ]ιλοτίμως [ἐπεμελήθησαν τῶν]
5     [τε χοινῶν ἁπάντω]ν [ὧν π]ρ[οσῆχεν α]ὐ[τοῖς –––––––––––]
      [–––––––––––––––––––]Ο[–––––––––––––––––]
      [–––––––––––––––––––––––––––––––––––]
```

The characteristics of the tolerably regular lettering are indeterminate but in general point to a 3rd-century date. The nonstoichedon text is somewhat crowded. Omega is very open; the outer strokes of sigma are almost parallel.

Meritt proposed a line length of *ca.* 40 letters, but the spacing of line 1 seems to require a slightly longer line to which, with additional readings in lines 5 and 6, his text has been accommodated. He identified the probable nature of the enactment on the analogy of *IG* II², 1255, a decree of the 4th century in honor of the hieropoioi of this cult association. That the text begins at once with the name of the proposer and without the preamble customary in decrees of the boule and demos indicates, in any event, that it emanates from a subgroup, religious or secular, of the body politic.

Lines 2–3. Cf. *IG* II², 1334, line 14. Lines 4–5. Cf. *IG* II², 1261, lines 4–5.

FRAGMENT OF AN HONORARY DECREE

246 (Pl. 26). A fragment of a stele of gray marble (I 1330), broken on all sides, discovered on February 12, 1934, beneath the floor of a Byzantine building east of the Stoa of Zeus (J 6).

H. 0.075 m.; W. 0.10 m.; Th. 0.042 m.
LH. 0.005 m.

Ed. S. V. Tracy, *Attic Letter-Cutters*, p. 64, no. 1, with photograph pl. 9. See also *SEG* XL, 99.

saec. III/II *a.* NON-ΣΤΟΙΧ.

(*in corona*)

[– – – – –]

[– – – – –]ν Ξε

[ναιο]υ Σφήτ

τιον.

Lines 1–2. Ξέ‖[νων]α Tracy. But in this position a patronymic in the genitive case is to be expected (cf. **232**), and the first visible remains in line 2 indicate upsilon rather than alpha. For the name restored here cf. *PA* 11177. It is unusual and featured in a family from Sphettos known from other evidence. Philippe, daughter of a Xenaios, is commemorated in a funerary inscription (*IG* II², 7530) dated to the 2nd century, and she could well have been the sister of the present honorand. Xenaios, son of Epainetos, served as bouleutes among the quota of Σφήττιοι in 303/2 and could have been the honorand's great-grandfather. It is possible that the honorand was himself named Epainetos, but the name could probably not have been wholly contained in line 1. Tracy noted that two lines, and not merely one, might stand above the first preserved line and thus some such arrangement as ['Επαί‖νετο]ν might be envisaged, with or without [ὁ δῆμος] (*vel aliquid simile*) in a preceding line.

The stephanos is a stiff and clumsy piece of work, with diamond-shaped leaves hardly, if at all, attached to the circle round the citation.

Tracy ascribed the workmanship of this fragment to the "Cutter of Agora I 7181": for the details of his activity (which spanned the period from 224/3 to 188/7) and characteristics see **226**, a text from his workshop that can be precisely dated. Tracy's dating of the present text ("*ca. a.* 205 *a.*") sets it for convenience at the middle point of the mason's career.

FRAGMENT OF A DECREE(?)

247 (Pl. 27). A fragment of a stele of gray marble (I 4615), which preserves the right side of the monument but is broken elsewhere, discovered on March 10, 1937, in the filling of a road of Late Roman date west of the southern part of the Stoa of Attalos (P 11).

H. 0.089 m.; W. 0.09 m.; Th. 0.06 m.
LH. 0.005 m.

Ed. S. V. Tracy, *Attic Letter-Cutters*, pp. 64–65, no. 2, with photograph pl. 10. See also *SEG* XL, 100.

saec. III/II *a.* NON-ΣΤΟΙΧ.

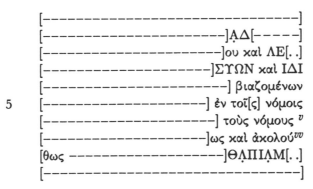

This stele, like **246**, was ascribed by Tracy to the "Cutter of Agora I 7181" and similarly dated by him at the middle point of that mason's career. Lines 5 and 6, in referring to the *nomoi*, suggest that this may be a public enactment of some kind; but no more is to be said of it beyond that.

A DECREE CONFERRING ATHENIAN CITIZENSHIP

248. Three fragments of a stele of Hymettian marble, of which two, fragments *a* (E.M. 7493) and *b* (E.M. 7510), have long been known and the third, fragment *c* (I 5871), has more recently been associated with them. Fragment *a*, which preserves the original rough-picked back but is otherwise broken all around, was discovered on the Akropolis and first published as *IG* II, 402; it is now in the Epigraphical Museum. Fragment *b*, broken on all sides save that, as first observed by M. J. Osborne (see below), part of the left side of the monument is preserved below the inscribed surface, was also discovered on the Akropolis (at an earlier date than fragment *a*); it too is now in the Epigraphical Museum. Fragment *c*, broken all around, was discovered on June 7, 1939, in a wall of a modern cesspool west of the Panathenaic Way and southwest of the Eleusinion (Q 21). Fragments *a* and *b* were remeasured by Osborne.

a: H. 0.277 m.; W. 0.16 m.; Th. 0.135 m.

b: H. 0.16 m.; W. 0.164 m.; Th. 0.094 m.

c: H. 0.13 m.; W. 0.18 m.; Th. 0.12 m.

LH. 0.006–0.007 m. (omicron 0.005 m.).

Ed. *a* + *b*: *IG* II², 851, with earlier references, and addenda, p. 668; their relationship adjusted by M. J. Osborne, after his observation concerning the left edge of fragment *b*, with revised text, *ZPE* 11, 1973, pp. 157–159; see also *SEG* XXVI, 97. *c* only: B. D. Meritt, *Hesperia* 30, 1961, pp. 219–220, no. 16, with photograph pl. 46; see also *SEG* XXI, 414.

Fragment *c* noted as making a join with *a*, with consolidated and improved text of lines 18–25, S. V. Tracy, *Hesperia* 47, 1978, pp. 258–259, with photograph of fragments *a* + *c*, as joined, pl. 68:b; see also *SEG* XXVIII, 71.

Combined fragments: Osborne, *Naturalization* I, pp. 198–199, D 91, *Naturalization* II, pp. 181–182.

saec. III/II *a.*   NON-ΣΤΟΙΧ. *ca.* 38–42

```
[------------------------------------]
[-------------------]Ι[.³̣⁻⁴.]ΥΘΙ[..⁷̣⁻⁸..]                    (a)
[------ ca. 20-25 ------χ]αὶ τῶν ἑαυτὸν [.⁵̣⁻⁶..]
[------ ca. 20-25 ------]ς τοῖς ἐνδόξοι[ς ³̣⁻⁴.]
[------ ca. 20-25 ------ε]ὐχαριστίαι τεῖ ε[ἰς ²̣⁻³ ]
 5  [--- ca. 13-17 ---, ἀγαθεῖ τύχ]ει δεδόχθαι τεῖ β[ουλεῖ]
    [τοὺς λαχόντας προέδρους εἰς τ]ὴν ἐπιοῦσαν ἐχ⟨χ⟩λ[ησίαν]
    [χρηματίσαι περὶ τούτων, γν]ώμην δὲ ξυμβάλλ[εσθαι]
    [τῆς βουλῆς εἰς τὸν δῆμον ὅτι δ]οκεῖ τεῖ βουλεῖ ἐ[παινέ]
    [σαι ---------------]ν καὶ στεφανῶσα[ι χρυ]
10  [σῶι στεφάνωι ἀρετῆς ἕνεκα καὶ εὐν]οίας ἣν ἔχων διατ[ε]
    [λεῖ πρὸς τὴν βουλὴν καὶ τὸν δῆμον τὸν] Ἀθηναίων, καὶ ἀνε[ι]
    [πεῖν τὸν στέφανον Διονυσίων τε] τῶν ἐν ἄστε⟨ι⟩ καιγ[ο]
    [ῖς τραγωιδοῖς καὶ Παναθηναίων καὶ Ἐ]λευσιν[ίω]ν τοῖς [γυ]
    [μνικοῖς ἀγῶσι· δεδόσθαι δὲ αὐτῶι καὶ] πολιτείαν καὶ [γρά]
15  [ψασθαι φυλῆς καὶ δήμου καὶ φρατρία]ς ἧς ἂν θέλει· το[ὺς]
    [δὲ θεσμοθέτας, ὅταν πληρῶσι δικαστήρι]α εἰς ἕνα καὶ πε[ν]
    [τακοσίους δικαστάς, εἰσαγαγεῖν αὐτῶι τ]ὴν δοκιμασίαν [ᵛ]
    [τῆς δωρεᾶς· εἶναι δὲ αὐτῶι χ]αὶ εἰς [τὸ λο]ιπὸν [[ἐπα]]ύξον[τι]
(b) [τὴν π]ρὸς Ἀθ[ηναίους εὔ]νοιαν καθότι ἂν [εἴ δ]υνατὸς καὶ ἄλ      (c)
20  [λα]ις μείζοσ[ι τιμ⟨αῖς τιμ⟩ηθῆ]ναι καταξίως το[ῦ δήμου· τῆς δὲ] π̣ο[ιήσε]
    ως τοῦ στεφ[άνου χ]αὶ τῆς ἀναγορεύσ[εως ἐπιμεληθῆναι]
    τοὺς στρατη[γούς· ἀ]ναγράψαι δὲ τόδε τ[ὸ ψήφισμα ἐν στή]
    λει λιθίνηι τ[ὸν γραμ]ματέα τὸν κατὰ πρ[υτανείαν καὶ στή]
    [σ]αι ἐν ἀκροπ[όλει· τὸ δὲ] γενόμενον [ἀνάλωμα εἰς αὐτὴν με]
25  [ρ]ίσαι τὸν τ[αμίαν τῶν στρατιωτικῶν.     vacat    ]
              vacat
```

The above text follows that of Osborne (*Naturalization* I, *loc. cit.*). Line 1. Osborne (*ZPE* 11, 1973) envisaged --- τ]ην [ἐλε]υθε[ρίαν ---]. Line 6 *ad fin. Lapis* ΕΚΛ. Line 12. *Lapis* ΑΣΤΕΚΑΙΝ. Line 18 *ad fin.* The mason apparently began to repeat ΛΟΙΠΟΝ: cf. Tracy, *loc. cit.*, who noted the remains of ΛΟΙ in the erasure. Line 20. The text required by the placing of fragments *b* and *c* is too long for the line. Tracy supposed crowding by the mason at the beginning of the line, but sufficient of the text remains for this not to be apparent. Osborne postulated an error in the inscribing, as shown. Since errors occur elsewhere in the extant text, this supposition is reasonable.

The formulation of this grant of citizenship conforms to Type I of Formulation B as defined by Osborne, a type that in his opinion did not outlast the 3rd century. See **239** and references there.

The inscribing of the stele was attributed by Tracy (*op. cit.*, pp. 255–261) to the "Cutter of *IG* II² 913", with photographs of specimen letters and parts of the name piece, pls. 67 and 68:a. See also *Attic Letter-Cutters*, pp. 71–79, with fig. 6, where the mason's characteristics are again described and further attributions made. Described by Tracy as one of the major letter cutters working in Athens around 190 B.C., he is credited with some sixty-five extant texts, of which seven are Agora *psephismata* included in this collection (**249–253** and **281**, in addition to the present decree). The latest datable inscription attributed to him belongs to the archonship of Antigenes (171/70), the earliest to the year of Sostratos (210/09). This decree, if the typology of the formulation of the citizenship grant be also taken into account, should be set early in his career, just before or at latest just after the turn of the century: but, on the dating, see further below. His style is careful and elegant, with a neatness and sense of space that could be thought old fashioned for its time.

The decree was probouleumatic: see P. J. Rhodes, *Athenian Boule*, p. 254.

Lines 9–10. For the golden stephanos without the qualification κατὰ τὸν νόμον see **240**, commentary on line 8. Line 10. The honorand's virtues, legible and restored, are among those more regularly invoked in contexts of this kind: cf. A. S. Henry, *Honours*, p. 42.

Lines 12–14. The honors are to be announced at three festivals. That the Ptolemaia are here omitted led previous editors to date the decree earlier than the institution of that celebration in 224 (or to the middle of the 2nd century, when the Ptolemaia had lost something of their prominence). See Osborne (*Naturalization* II, pp. 181–182), who argued there as on earlier occasions for a date before 224. The floruit of the mason, however, if correctly assessed can hardly be extended so long, as Osborne also reluctantly allowed. Nor is an error of omission on the part of the mason an acceptable refuge.

It seems however that the number of, and occasions for, announcements of this character lacked consistency. Cf. **238**, where honors for the people of Ephesos, a city closely connected with the Egyptian kingdom, were announced only at the Dionysia (by contrast with **225**), and **224**, where the Dionysia and Panathenaia, but not the Eleusinia, were involved. The Ptolemaia are also omitted in **249**. See Henry, *Honours*, pp. 32–33, for a selection of possibilities. Thus the absence of the Ptolemaia cannot be considered a firm argument for the dating of this decree.

Lines 14–18. See also Henry, *Honours*, pp. 81–83, where this text is cited. Henry also observed (p. 97, note 67) that the use of θέλει for βούληται is, on present evidence, unique. Lines 18–20. For the promise of future benefits see Henry, *op. cit.*, pp. 315–318, with this passage quoted p. 317, and cf. Rhodes, *Athenian Boule*, pp. 281–283. The qualification of the participial formula by an additional clause is a further *unicum*, as Henry also pointed out (*op. cit.*, p. 322, note 31).

Lines 21–22. The generals are responsible for the proclamation, here unsupported by the Military Treasurer. Cf. **224**, commentary on lines 39–41 and Henry, *Honours*, p. 35. Lines 22–23. στή]λει, but λιθίνηι. This is the only instance of HI in the dative feminine singular in this text; EI is otherwise used throughout. Lines 24–25. The Military Treasurer is, as regularly, the official charged with disbursing the costs of the implementation of the decree. The available space does not permit that duty to be shared with the Plural Board of Administration. See **224**, commentary on lines 49–50 and references there; and cf. **240**, line 16.

FRAGMENT OF AN HONORARY DECREE

249. A fragment of a stele of Hymettian marble (I 1966), battered and broken on all sides and with a piece gouged out of the center of the inscribed surface, discovered on May 7, 1934, in earth disturbed from a previous excavation north of the Southwest Fountain House (I 15). The blueness and smoothness of the inscribed surface are noteworthy.

H. 0.095 m.; W. 0.18 m.; Th. 0.095 m.
LH. 0.005 m.

Ed. B. D. Meritt, *Hesperia* 10, 1941, pp. 58–59, no. 22, with photograph.

saec. III/II *a.*   NON-ΣTOIX. *ca.* 46

[——]
[– – – ἕνεκα κ]αὶ φιλο[τ]ι[μίας ἣν ἔχων διατελεῖ πρὸς τὸν δῆμον]
[τὸν] Ἀθηναίων καὶ ἀναγ[ορεῦσαι τὸν στέφανον τοῦτον Διονυ]
[σίω]ν τῶν ἐν ἄστει τρα[γωιδῶν τῶι καινῶι ἀγῶνι καὶ Παναθη]

[ναί]ων καὶ ᾽Ε[λε]υσινίων [τῶι γυμνικῶι ἀγῶνι· τῆς δὲ ποιήσε]
5 [ως το]ῦ [σ]τ[εφ]άνου κα[ὶ τῆς ἀναγορεύσεως ἐπιμεληθῆναι]
[τοὺς σ]τρ[ατηγ]οὺς καὶ [τὸν ταμίαν τῶν στρατιωτικῶν· εἶναι]
[δὲ αὐτ]ῷ[ι –]
[–]

When first discovered, this fragment was thought to be part of *IG* II², 702, now *Agora* XV, 87, although in the event the contents of the two could not be reconciled. The resemblance between them was so clear, however, that the same hand might have been at work on a piece of the same consignment of quarried stone, an observation which might yet be correct. At the time, and for many years thereafter, *Agora* XV, 87 was held to belong to the middle of the 3rd century. The criterion of the style of the lettering appeared suited to such a date, and one or two minor considerations in the present text (see below) might have pointed in the same direction. In the *editio princeps* of this fragment, nevertheless, Meritt opted for a dating "*ca. a.* 225 *a.*(?)", citing resemblances to the style of *IG* II², 837, of 227/6, which is indeed similar but less apposite.

S. V. Tracy, however, attributed both *Agora* XV, 87 and this text to the "Cutter of *IG* II² 913" (*Hesperia* 47, 1978, pp. 256–259, *Attic Letter-Cutters*, pp. 73–74), which necessitated their redating within the attested limits of his career; see **248**. The conservative character of this mason's work, which made an earlier dating plausible, is of significance. The rearrangement has given rise to certain problems concerning *Agora* XV, 87 which do not call for discussion here. In the present case, the generalized date given above is prudent and the most that the evidence permits.

Line 1. φιλο[τ]ιμ[ίας] Meritt. The supplements that follow reflect the recognized formulations of the period: cf. **224** and **248**. Lines 2–4. That the Ptolemaia are not included as a festival at which the stephanos is to be announced might have argued for a dating earlier than 224 B.C. and did in fact influence Meritt's decision about it. But see **248**, commentary on lines 12–14. The operative verb is ἀναγορεῦσαι, in place of the more usual ἀνειπεῖν. This also might indicate the practice of an earlier period; see **208**, commentary on lines 26–29. But the usage is found also in the 2nd century; cf. A. S. Henry, *Honours*, p. 33.

Lines 4–6. The καί of line 6 makes it clear that the generals and the Military Treasurer are jointly to be responsible for the arrangements concerning the manufacture and proclamation of the stephanos. See **224**, commentary on lines 39–41 and references there.

A CITIZEN OF THE DEME MELITE HONORED

250. A fragment of a stele of Hymettian marble (I 2527), with the smooth left side preserved, discovered on February 27, 1935, in a modern wall over the southern part of the Odeion (M 12). The marble has what B. D. Meritt (see below) described as a "curiously mottled appearance", comparing that of **261**. The striations of a toothed chisel in both diagonal directions are clearly to be seen.

H. 0.14 m.; W. 0.16 m.; Th. 0.065 m.
LH. 0.006–0.007 m.

Ed. B. D. Meritt, *Hesperia* 10, 1941, pp. 59–60, no. 23, with photograph.

saec. III/II *a.*   NON-ΣΤΟΙΧ. *ca.* 54

[–]
[– – – – – – – – – – – – – – –ὅπως ἂν οὖν ὁ δῆμος φανερὸς ἦι ἀποδιδοὺς τοῖς]
[φιλοτιμ]ουμένο[ις χάριτας καταξίας τῶν εὐεργετημάτων, ἀγαθεῖ τύχει]
δεδόχθαι τεῖ βο[υλεῖ τοὺς λαχόντας προέδρους εἰς τὴν ἐπιοῦσαν ἐκ]
κλησίαν χρηματί[σαι περὶ τούτων, γνώμην δὲ ξυμβάλλεσθαι τῆς βου]
5 λῆς εἰς τὸν δῆμο[ν ὅτι δοκεῖ τεῖ βουλεῖ ἐπαινέσαι – – – – – – – – –]
Μελιτέα καὶ στε[φανῶσαι αὐτὸν θαλλοῦ στεφάνωι εὐσεβείας ἕνεκα]
τῆς πρὸς τοὺς θ[εοὺς καὶ φιλοτιμίας τῆς εἰς τὸν δῆμον τὸν ᾽Αθηναίων]·
ἀναγράψαι δὲ τ[όδε τὸ ψήφισμα τὸν γραμματέα τὸν κατὰ πρυτανείαν]
ἐν στήληι λι[θίνηι καὶ στῆσαι – – – – – – – – – – – – – – – – · εἰς δὲ τὴν]
10 ἀναγραφ[ὴν καὶ τὴν ἀνάθεσιν τῆς στήλης μερίσαι τὸν ταμίαν τῶν στρα]
[τι]ωτικ[ῶν τὸ γενόμενον ἀνάλωμα.   *vacat*   ]
     vacat

This inscription was attributed to the "Cutter of *IG* II² 913" by S. V. Tracy, *Hesperia* 47, 1978, p. 257 (cf. also *Attic Letter-Cutters*, p. 74) and is therefore to be dated within the limits of the mason's attested career. See **248**. Meritt's date in the *editio princeps* (*ca. a.* 200 *a.*) was well judged.

What survives of the text provides the basis for formulations standard at the time, in respect of instructions to the proedroi, the award of a stephanos and its motivation, and the provisions for the erection and cost of the stele. The decree was probouleumatic: see P. J. Rhodes, *Athenian Boule*, p. 254.

Lines 1–2. For the "hortatory intention" see **86**, commentary on lines 21–24, and for the formula restored here cf. *IG* II², 717 (M. J. Osborne, *Naturalization* I, pp. 178–180, D 83, *Naturalization* II, p. 169), lines 5–7; but there are other possibilities. In the *editio princeps* Meritt restored ὅπως ἂν οὖν ἡ βουλὴ καὶ ὁ δῆμος φαίνωνται εἰδότες τοῖς | φιλοτιμ]ουμένο[ις κτλ.]. In either case the emphasis here is on the demos itself and its wish to be recognized as suitably grateful and generous to those who have served it well. See **239**, commentary on line 7. Line 2. ἀγαθεῖ τύχει. See **72**, commentary on lines 7–8. Line 3. τεῖ, but στήληι in line 9. Cf. **248**, lines 22–23.

Line 6. The stephanos of olive restored here was frequently bestowed on citizens who had acquitted themselves well in some official or semiofficial capacity, as may have been the present case. See A. S. Henry, *Honours*, pp. 38–39. Lines 6–7. Εὐσέβεια towards the gods and φιλοτιμία towards the Athenian people represent a regular pair of virtues praised in a context of this kind. Cf. Henry, *Honours*, p. 43 and **240**, lines 8–9 (as restored). Lines 7–8. Since the original discovery and transcription of the text, a small fragment has been lost from the right edge of the fragment carrying the last two recorded letters of these lines.

Lines 10–11. The meager remains of line 11 make it clear that the Military Treasurer was to provide for the cost of the stele: but there would be room for the addition of the Plural Board of Administration with whom the Treasurer sometimes shared the responsibility. See Henry, *Chiron* 14, 1984, pp. 81–86 and **224**, commentary on lines 49–50.

FRAGMENT OF A DECREE OF THE DEMESMEN OF MELITE(?)

251. A fragment from the upper right section of a pedimental stele of Hymettian marble (I 3142), with part of the right side (below the inscribed surface) and of the raking cornice of the pediment preserved, discovered on December 13, 1935, in a wall of a modern house over the east end of South Stoa II (N 15). The back of the fragment is broken. The horizontal cornice and the moldings below it have been hacked away but seem to have been substantial. The remains represent a bulky piece of what was evidently a considerable monument, but disappointingly little survives of the inscribed surface.

H. 0.346 m.; W. 0.277 m.; Th. 0.225 m.
LH. 0.007 m.

Ed. B. D. Meritt, *Hesperia* 37, 1968, p. 270, no. 7, with photograph pl. 78. See also *SEG* XXV, 110.

saec. III/II *a.*   NON-ΣΤΟΙΧ.

```
       [--------εἶπεν· ἐπειδὴ ----]τος ὁ ἱερεὺς ἐμφ[ανίζει]
       [----------------------] τοῦ δήμου τ[οῦ Μελι]
       [τέων ---------------------, δ]εδόχθαι Μ[ελιτεῦ]
       [σιν ----------------------]ν τὰ ψηφ[ίσματα]
  5    [-----------------------------] vacat [------]
       [-------------------------------------]
```

The workmanship of this inscription was identified by S. V. Tracy as that of the "Cutter of *IG* II² 913", and it offers a further example of his workshop's considerable output: see **248**. His somewhat old-fashioned style, already alluded to, makes Meritt's general dating to the 3rd century, in the *editio princeps*, an understandable estimate: but the date must accord with the span of the mason's career, i.e., between *ca.* 210/09 and 171/70 on the available evidence. Here he was evidently working not for the Athenian body politic but for a subdivision of it, as the abridged form of the prescript makes apparent. Cf. **245**.

The dimensions of the pediment and the overall size of the block imply that the inscription was of some length. The vacant space of line 5 does not signal more than the conclusion of an opening statement. Possibly a short initial measure required the inscribing below of other enactments, at the original instance of the ἱερεύς. Cf. *IG* II², 1155, 1261, 1284, 1299, 1328, etc. The text is restored as a decree of the deme Melite. Cf. **277**.

Line 1. [-----]εος Meritt, but the break makes the squeeze and photograph deceptive. The upright is too far to the right for a convincing epsilon. Lines 2–3. τοῦ δήμου τ[οῦ Ἀθη^ν|ναίων ----] Meritt. Line 3. δ]εδόχθαι μ[ὲν *ca.* 4.] Meritt. Line 4. ---κα]ὶ τὰ ψηφ[ίσματα] Meritt; the diagonal stroke of nu survives at the edge of the break.

FRAGMENT OF THE CONCLUSION OF A DECREE

252 (Pl. 27). A fragment of a stele of gray marble (I 3954), broken on all sides, discovered on April 2, 1936, in a context of Turkish date west of the northern part of the Stoa of Attalos (P 8).

H. 0.068 m.; W. 0.133 m.; Th. 0.081 m.
LH. 0.006–0.007 m.

Ed. S. V. Tracy, *Attic Letter-Cutters*, pp. 75–76, no. 1, with photograph pl. 12. See also *SEG* XL, 103.

saec. III/II *a.*   NON-ΣΤΟΙΧ.

```
[----------------------------------------]
[----------] τοῖς φιλο[τιμουμένοις ----------]
[-----· εἰς δὲ τὴν ἀν]αγραφὴν τῆς σ[τήλης --------]
[----------ἐκ] τῶν εἰς τὰ κατ[ὰ ψηφίσματα -----]
[------------------]   vacat  [   vacat   ]
                    vacat
```

Tracy's attribution of this fragment to the hand of the "Cutter of *IG* II² 913" requires a date for it, as for **248–251** and **253**, within the last decade of the 3rd century or the first three decades of the 2nd. The dating in the *editio princeps* ("*ca. a.* 190 *a.*") is set for convenience at the middle point of the mason's attested span.

For the sentiment in line 1 Tracy compared *IG* II², 808 (M. J. Osborne, *Naturalization* I, pp. 185–187, D 87, *Naturalization* II, pp. 172–177), lines 21–22 and 891, line 9. For the concluding clause he proposed, *exempli gratia*:

```
                                            --------εἰς]
[δὲ τὴν ἀν]αγραφὴν τῆς σ[τήλης μερίσαι τὸν ταμίαν τῶν στρα]
[τιωτικῶν ἐκ] τῶν εἰς τὰ κατ[ὰ ψηφίσματα ἀναλισκομένων τὸ]
[ἀνάλωμα].
```

The introduction of the "analiskomena fund" as the source of payment is surprising at so late a date and after so long an interval. See A. S. Henry, *Chiron* 14, 1984, p. 63, with note 64, where the sporadic appearance of this fund in the 3rd and 2nd centuries is briefly discussed, and *ZPE* 78, 1989, pp. 284–285. Among the *psephismata* in this collection it was last in evidence in **164**, of the early years of the 3rd century. Apart from the unusual cases of the so-called Salaminian decree of the late 2nd century (*IG* II², 1008, III, line 88 and 1011, III, line 63) this formulation fell into apparent disuse after 283/2 B.C. Cf. Henry, *ZPE* 78, 1989, p. 274, table 3. The present text appears to provide evidence that its existence and availability could be called upon throughout the period.

FRAGMENT OF A DECREE

253 (Pl. 27). A fragment of a stele of Hymettian marble (I 5224), broken on all sides, discovered on February 15, 1938, in a Byzantine context west of the Panathenaic Way and west of the Eleusinion (S 19).

H. 0.073 m.; W. 0.125 m.; Th. 0.057 m.
LH. 0.006 m.

Unpublished.

saec. III/II *a.*   NON-ΣΤΟΙΧ. *ca.* 41–45

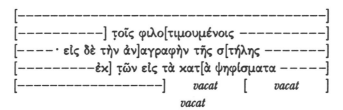

```
   [-------------------------------------------]
   [----------]ΑΙΕ[-----------------------------]
   [....ca. 9....το]ῦ δήμ[ου· ἀναγράψαι δὲ τὸ ψήφισμα τόδε τὸν]
   [γραμματέα] τὸν κατ[ὰ πρυτανείαν ἐν στήληι λιθίνηι καὶ]
   [στῆσαι ἐν] ἀκροπό[λει· τὸ δὲ γενόμενον εἰς αὐτὴν ἀνάλωμα]
5  [μερίσαι] τὸν τ[αμίαν τῶν στρατιωτικῶν. ....ca. 11–14....]
   [.ca. 6..]ριεα [--------------------------------]
   [-----------------------------------------(?)]
```

The attribution of this inscription to the hand of the "Cutter of *IG* II² 913" by S. V. Tracy (*Attic Letter-Cutters*, p. 74, following *Hesperia* 47, 1978, p. 257) sets its date within the period of that mason's activity: see **248**. The instructions for the inscribing and erection of the stele, and for the payment of its cost by the Military Treasurer, correspond to the normal phraseology of the period.

Lines 1–2. The clause may be interpreted as concerned with additional benefits to be accorded to the honorand if he perseveres in his acknowledged good works, e.g., εἶναι δὲ αὐτῶι ––––χ]αὶ ε[ὑρέσθαι ἄλλο ἀγαθὸν οὗ ἂν δοχῆι ἄξιος | εἶναι παρὰ το]ῦ δήμ[ου, on the lines of *IG* II², 861, 891, 892, 893, etc., or εἶναι δὲ αὐτῶι χ]αὶ ε[ἰς τὸ λοιπὸν χρείας παρεχομένωι τι|μᾶσθαι ὑπὸ το]ῦ δήμ[ου, for which see *IG* II², 844, lines 27–28. Cf. A. S. Henry, *Honours*, pp. 315–318. Lines 4–5. For the form of words cf. *IG* II², 922, lines 15–16. The letters of line 5 are spaced more widely than those in the other lines.

Lines 5–6. The instructions for payment usually conclude the enactment. Where a new decree or a stephanos is recorded lower on the stele, a blank space is customarily left between it and the preceding text. Here the inscription runs on with additional matter without any apparent break. Cf., e.g., **301**, *IG* II², 868, *SEG* XXI, 436. An invitation to hospitality might form such an addendum, e.g., *IG* II², 238, 282, 288, etc.: so here, χαλέσαι δὲ –––––– ᾿Ερετ]ριέα [χαὶ ἐπὶ ξένια χτλ. (For contemporary honors conferred on a citizen of Eretria cf. *IG* II², 893, M. J. Osborne, *Naturalization* I, pp. 206–208, D 98.) But a new subject may equally have been introduced at this point.

FRAGMENT OF A DECREE

254. The upper left corner of a pedimental stele of Hymettian marble (I 84), broken below and to the right, discovered on July 28, 1931, in the annex of the Stoa of Zeus Eleutherios, at a Late Roman level (H 6). The transition between the floor of the pediment and the inscribed surface is effected by an ovolo molding with shallow cavetto crown, a wide taenia below descending in an apophyge to a vacant space on the inscribed surface preceding the only surviving line of text. The total effect is heavy and suggests that the stele may have been sizable even though, to judge from the angle at which the raking cornice ascends, not especially wide.

H. 0.135 m.; W. 0.127 m.; Th. 0.082 m.
LH. 0.005 m.

Ed. B. D. Meritt, *Hesperia* 3, 1934, p. 10, no. 12, with photograph.

saec. III/II *a.* NON-ΣTOIX.

$$\text{᾿Επὶ [.]ι[––––ἄρχοντος ἐπὶ τῆς –––––––––––––]}$$
$$\text{[––––––––––––––––––––––––––––––––]}$$

The text is adjudged nonstoichedon on the evidence of the irregular spacing of the surviving letters. On the basis of this and of the precisely written pi with unequal upright strokes, Meritt dated the inscription between 250 and 150 B.C. S. V. Tracy (*Attic Letter-Cutters*, p. 22) noted the surviving letters as too few for the formation of any judgment concerning the style. Within Meritt's hundred-year range, some eighteen archons held office whose names contained iota as second letter, and speculation as to the identity of the man named here is pointless.

The Pergamene-type ovolo (cf. L. T. Shoe, *Profiles of Greek Mouldings* I, 1936, p. 22) below a graceful cavetto indicates a date in the 3rd rather than the 2nd century. The style resembles that of **216** and **224**, but the taller, more gently curving cavetto might suggest that this example is not the latest of the three.

FRAGMENT OF A DECREE CONFERRING CITIZENSHIP

255. A fragment of a stele of Pentelic marble (I 4608), with part of the right side preserved but broken elsewhere, discovered on March 12, 1937, in a late context under what was formerly Akropolis Street, west of the Post-Herulian Wall (S 24–25 to T 24). The vertical striations of a toothed chisel are very evident on the inscribed surface.

H. 0.094 m.; W. 0.07 m.; Th. 0.031 m.
LH. 0.005–0.006 m.

Ed. B. D. Meritt, *Hesperia* 30, 1961, p. 259, no. 66, with photograph pl. 48; see also *SEG* XXI, 417: M. J. Osborne, *Naturalization* I, pp. 201–202, D 94, *Naturalization* II, p. 183.

saec. III/II *a.* NON-ΣTOIX. *ca.* 31

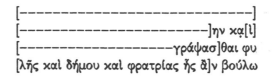

[–––––––––––––––––––––––––––––––]
[––––––––––––––––––––––––]ην χα[ὶ]
[–––––––––––––––––––γράψασ]θαι φυ
[λῆς χαὶ δήμου χαὶ φρατρίας ἧς ἂ]ν βούλω

[νται ------------------] περὶ αὐ
5   [τῶν ----------------τοὺς] θεσμ[ο]
[θέτας --------------------]ιτ[. .]
[------------------------------]

Line 1. So Osborne: INK[. .] Meritt. Lines 2–6. The text follows the *editio princeps*.

Meritt gave this inscription a date of "*init. saec.* II *a*.", without comment. Enough of the formula of the grant survives for Osborne to have concluded that it belongs to Type I of his Formulation B, which was in his view current during the last quarter of the 3rd century, a period to which he also judged the style of the lettering to belong. On the typology see **239** and references there. S. V. Tracy (*Attic Letter-Cutters*, p. 253) found the lettering too worn to permit its assignment to an identifiable mason. While observing that "Osborne's date seems a good one," he nevertheless saw stylistic affinities with the work of the "Cutter of *IG* II² 783", whose datable activity concentrates between 173/2 and 161/60 (*op. cit.*, pp. 143–145). In view of these conflicting signals and of the fragmentary state of the text, it is prudent to venture no further than the generalized dating shown above.

That more than one honorand was involved is shown by line 3. Osborne provided "an attempt to illustrate the general sense of the original document," as follows:

[--------------------]ην· χα[ὶ]
[δεδόσθαι αὐτοῖς πολιτείαν· καὶ γράψα]σθαι φυ
[λῆς καὶ δήμου καὶ φρατρίας ἧς ἂ]ν βούλω
[νται· τοὺς δὲ θεσμοθέτας δοῦναι] περὶ αὐ
5   [τῶν τὴν ψῆφον· καὶ εἰσαγαγεῖν τοὺς] θεσμ[ο]
[θέτας καὶ τὴν δοκιμασίαν τῆς πολ]ιτ[ογ]
[ραφίας ὅταν πληρῶσιν δικαστήρια εἰς ἕνα]
[καὶ πεντακοσίους δικαστάς -----].

APPENDIX: MATERIAL DISCOVERED SINCE 1967

255A. Honors for a friend of Demetrios Poliorketes (I 7070). Discovered on September 29, 1969; see **117**.

255B. Fragment of the concluding section of an honorary decree (I 7137), between 286/5 and 262/1 *a*. The left edge of this stele of Pentelic marble is preserved, but it is broken elsewhere. It was discovered on June 10, 1970, in a Byzantine wall (N 6). The date is determined by the necessity (imposed by the stoichedon order) to restore the Plural Board of Administration as responsible for defraying the cost of the monument, which is to be met by the "analiskomena fund" and restored in the figure of 20 drachmas. For the appearance of this fund in the 3rd and 2nd centuries see the commentary on **252**.

The text was edited by M. B. Walbank (*Hesperia* 51, 1982, pp. 52–53, no. 9, with photograph pl. 21), who regarded the lettering style as close to that of **158**. See also *SEG* XXXII, 107.

255C. Decree in honor of the priest of Amphiaraos (I 7163), dated by the name of the archon (Glaukippos) to 273/2 *a*. This is the upper section of a pedimental stele of Hymettian marble, broken below but with top, both sides, and rough-picked back preserved, discovered on July 29, 1970, at O 16 on the Agora grid. Edited by M. B. Walbank, *Hesperia* 51, 1982, pp. 53–54, no. 10, with photograph pl. 21. See also *SEG* XXXII, 110.

The fully preserved calendar equation shows Mounichion 21 = pryt. X, 29 (the 316th or 317th day, for there is a one-day discrepancy between the two, rectified by the time of the enactment of *IG* II², 676 in Skirophorion). This evidence amends the entry concerning this date as a meeting day of the assembly in J. D. Mikalson, *Sacred and Civil Calendar*, p. 147. The year was intercalary, as was already well recognized: cf. B. D. Meritt, *Historia* 26, 1977, p. 173.

255D. Decree in honor of Kallias of Sphettos (I 7295), dated by the name of the archon (Sosistratos) to 270/69 *a*. The completely preserved stele of Pentelic marble was discovered on May 20, 1971, reused as a cover slab in a late repair of the Great Drain (J 5). It was edited by T. L. Shear Jr. and published as a separate monograph (*Hesperia*, Supplement XVII, 1978) under the title "Kallias of Sphettos and the Revolt of Athens in 286 B.C.": the text also in *SEG* XXVIII, 60.

This important document, which is referred to on numerous occasions in earlier pages of this section, where it impinges on relevant matters under consideration, gave rise to much discussion: for subsequent references see *SEG* XXIX, 102, XXXV, 88, XXXVII, 91, and XLII, 98. The controversy in the early stages centered largely upon the sequence of events and the precise date of the revolution. There is no epigraphical problem.

255E. Two(?) decrees from a monument perhaps set up by a *sodalitas* (I 7093), possibly to be dated to 266/5 *a.* A fragment of a block of blue-gray Hymettian marble, apparently from a constructed monument, with inscriptions (by different hands) on two adjoining faces, discovered on September 10, 1969, in the wall of the Athens–Peiraieus railway (J 3). Edited by M. B. Walbank, *Hesperia* 51, 1982, pp. 54–56, no. 11, with photographs pl. 22. See also *SEG* XXXII, 113, where it is erroneously stated that the monument is opisthographic.

On face A are preserved the first few letters of seven lines of text, on face B the last few letters of five lines of text. The lettering style is of the second to third quarter of the 3rd century; the suggested closer dating is derived from what may be the name of an archon Nikias in face A, line 3, whom Walbank considered to be Nikias of Otryne (see p. 275 above).

255F. Enactment of a phratry (I 7500), perhaps to be identified with the Therrikleidai, dated by the editor "*ante med. saec.* III *a.*". A fragment of a stele of Pentelic marble, with the left side preserved but otherwise broken all around including the back, discovered in May 1975 beneath a step leading to the Gate of Athena (V 13). Edited by M. B. Walbank, *Hesperia* 51, 1982, pp. 48–50, no. 7, with photograph pl. 20. See also *SEG* XXXII, 150, which includes a reference to notes and textual suggestions by C. W. Hedrick Jr., *Hesperia* 52, 1983, pp. 299–302 (to whom is also due the proposal that the phratry is that of the Therrikleidai), and expresses the dating as "*ca.* 300–250 B.C."

255G. Fragment of a decree (I 7312), dated by the editor "*ante med. saec.* III *a.*". A fragment of a stele of Pentelic marble, broken on all sides (although the back may possibly be original), discovered on June 4, 1971, in a modern wall (S 13). Edited by M. B. Walbank, *Hesperia* 51, 1982, pp. 50–51, no. 8, with photograph pl. 21. See also *SEG* XXXII, 114. Walbank suggested, on the basis of the meager remains of the text, that the enactment honored a board of officials such as the agoranomoi.

255H. Fragment of a decree conferring citizenship (I 7254), of *ca.* 225 *a.* A fragment of a stele of gray marble, with the left side preserved, discovered on March 31, 1971, in a modern wall (Q 21). Edited by S. V. Tracy, *Hesperia* 45, 1976, pp. 283–285, no. 1, with photograph pl. 66. Tracy's text was reproduced as *SEG* XXVI, 96. Tracy later (*Attic Letter-Cutters*, p. 63) identified the workmanship as that of the "Cutter of Agora I 7181", for whose date and characteristics see **226**.

The text was republished by M. J. Osborne, *Naturalization* I, pp. 199–200, D 92, with commentary in *Naturalization* II, pp. 182–183, in which he identified the formula of grant as Type I of Formulation B: see **239** and references there.

A. S. Henry (*Chiron* 14, 1984, pp. 81–82 and *ZPE* 72, 1988, pp. 134–135) drew attention to the point that, in the provisions for payment of the cost of the stele (lines 11–13), the Plural Board of Administration alone has the responsibility and that this is unique among decrees dated later than 229: otherwise the Board is always associated with the Military Treasurer (see **224**, commentary on lines 49–50 and **225**, commentary on lines 21–22). The decree may perhaps be datable to a year very soon after 229, before the procedures instituted when the Athenians recovered their freedom from Macedonian control became fully regularized. See also *SEG* XXXIV, 90.

255J. Decree conferring Athenian citizenship on the people of Chrysaorean Antioch (Alabanda) in Karia, dated by the historical circumstances *ca.* 203 *a.* This is inscribed on two joining fragments of a stele of Hymettian marble (I 7182), which together preserve the sides of the monument as well as the original back but are broken above and below. The larger fragment was discovered on August 10, 1970, at a Byzantine level above the Royal Stoa (K 5), and the smaller in a marble pile during autumn 1975. Edited by R. L. Pounder, *Hesperia* 47, 1978, pp. 49–57, with photograph pl. 8. Pounder's text, with one correction made by him, was repeated in *SEG* XXVIII, 75.

M. J. Osborne discussed and amended the original version of lines 19–21 in *ZPE* 38, 1980, pp. 99–101 (cf. *SEG* XXX, 77) and subsequently printed his version of the text in *Naturalization* I, pp. 202–204, as D 95, with commentary in *Naturalization* II, pp. 183–185. The date of the text is relevant to, and confirmed by, evidence from Delphi: see *SEG* XXVIII, 488, XXXVII, 393.

S. V. Tracy (*Attic Letter-Cutters*, p. 49) identified this text from its lettering as one item in the considerable output of the "Cutter of *IG* II² 1706", for whom see **222**, and it represents a very late, perhaps the latest recognizable, product of his long career.

Payment for the stele is to be made by ὁ ταμίας, that is, the Military Treasurer, in conjunction with the Plural Board. For this designation of the Treasurer see **224**, commentary on lines 49–50.

SECTION 4

ATHENS AND THE ROMAN REPUBLIC
FROM CONCORD TO CONQUEST
200–86 B.C.
(**256–332**)

SECTION 4

ATHENS AND THE ROMAN REPUBLIC
FROM CONCORD TO CONQUEST
200–86 B.C.: **256–332**

Writing of the prescripts to the decrees of this period, A. S. Henry (*Prescripts*, p. 84; cf. **331**) remarked upon "the dwindling significance of, and lack of care and interest in, the resolutions of the Athenian body politic." This is certainly reflected in the number of decrees of the 2nd century B.C. discovered during the Agora excavations, for the eighty-three items in Section 4 (inclusive of the appendix) amount to little more than half of the total considered in Section 3. The Athenians at this juncture were looking inward upon themselves; where the evidence is clear, honors for citizens exceeded in number honorary decrees (including citizenship) for foreigners, while the honoring of prytaneis (109 texts in *Agora* XV) and of graduating classes of epheboi came to dominate the inscribed record of public business.

The concerns and relationships to which the previous centuries had testified in the documents treated earlier gradually died away. There are no texts in this section that may be classed under the head of "foreign affairs", no grants of *proxenia*, a form of reward which endured elsewhere rather longer than at Athens (cf. C. Marek, *Die Proxenie*, 1984, pp. 387–391), no *nomoi*, and few "miscellaneous" items of public importance (**305**, **322**, and a sanctuary repair recorded in **296** being the only texts in this category, though clearly of some consequence in themselves). Religious groups provide seven decrees, while one (**277**) represents the last surviving decree of a deme.

Analysis of this kind is, however, seriously impeded by the remarkable fact that more than one third (thirty-four) of the eighty-three texts considered here are so fragmentary that they give no clue to the character of the enactments recorded. Of the remaining forty-nine, thirty-seven attest the award of honors (sixteen for citizens, eleven for noncitizens, including three for monarchs or their close associates, and ten inconclusive). Where such honorary decrees are well preserved, there is a tendency towards comparative prolixity and extravagance of expression. There is a similar tendency in the now highly formalized prytany texts of the period; and the decrees honoring epheboi, which increase in number during the same century, are lengthy and carefully detailed.

Finally, one interesting feature to emerge in this time of shifting balance in the official output of inscribed public business is a concern for absolute calendric accuracy in the dates shown in the prescripts to the decrees. Very great care was taken to record the true date "according to god" at times when, for whatever reasons, the authorities had seen fit to retard the onward progress of the festival calendar. This is largely matched by the general detail provided for archival purposes or for the determination of responsibility among officials required to take action in the publication of enactments or fulfillment of their terms. This had assumed a standard and elaborate form in the previous century and was carefully maintained in this one.

FRAGMENT OF AN HONORARY DECREE

256. A fragment of a stele of Hymettian marble (I 4597), with the smooth right side and perhaps the original rough-picked back preserved, discovered on March 8, 1937, in a modern context north of Kolonos Agoraios, near the tracks of the railroad (E 4).

H. 0.167 m.; W. 0.13 m.; Th. 0.075 m.
LH. 0.006 m.

Ed. B. D. Meritt, *Hesperia* 37, 1968, pp. 271–272, no. 10, with photograph pl. 78. See also *SEG* XXV, 111.

ca. a. 200 a., vel paullo post   NON-ΣΤΟΙΧ.

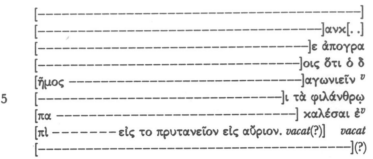

```
[————————————————————————————————]
[————————————————————————————]ανχ[. .]
[——————————————————————————]ε ἀπογρα
[——————————————————————————]οις ὅτι ὁ δ
[ἦμος ———————————————————————]αγωνιεῖν ⱽ
[——————————————————————————]ι τὰ φιλάνθρω
[πα ——————————————————————] καλέσαι ἐⱽ
[πὶ ——————— εἰς το πρυτανεῖον εἰς αὔριον. vacat(?)]   vacat
[————————————————————————————————](?)
```

The writing is very distinctive, with letters widely spaced, wide in proportion to their height, and decorated with serifs. The external strokes of sigma are parallel or nearly so. The horizontals of omega are angled upwards ("winged" omega). On alpha the crossbar is curved (cf. J. Kirchner, *IIA²*, 1948, p. 23 and pl. 39, no. 98; P. M. Fraser and T. Rönne, *Boeotian and West Greek Tombstones*, 1957, pp. 83–84, with notes 6 and 7), the first occurrence of this form among the Agora *psephismata*. Syllabic division is disregarded. All these features appeared to point to, or at least not to contradict, a date for the inscription in the first part of the 2nd century, and Meritt very reasonably gave it a dating in the *editio princeps* of "*init. saec.* II a."

S. V. Tracy, however, associated it with four other texts, including **257**, and ascribed the group to the "Cutter of *IG* II² 1131" (*Attic Letter-Cutters*, pp. 89–91, with a photograph of the name piece, fig. 9). While allowing that all five inscriptions had been dated "to the mid-second century or later" (although this was not so in the present case), he set this text and its fellows at *ca.* 200 by reason of the wide interlinear spacing, a mannerism which he saw as looking back to that date or even earlier. Cf. perhaps the "Cutter of *IG* II² 1318" (**233**). Nevertheless, this may be interpreted as a personal idiosyncrasy independent of precise chronology, and pending better evidence an early 2nd-century dating remains the more attractive option. None of the five texts in the group may be firmly dated on other grounds.

The decree evidently concerned the appropriate recognition by the demos of benefits received, with a concluding invitation to hospitality in the Prytaneion (for which see **224**, commentary on lines 44–45). If, as Meritt suggested, the uninscribed space in line 7 marks the end of the inscription, the instructions for the erection of the stele and defrayment of the costs were unusually lacking or out of place.

Meritt hazarded that lines 3–4 may have expressed some such sentiments as ὅπως ἂν ἦι φανερὸν πᾶσιν τοῖς ἐπιγινομέν]οις ὅτι ὁ δ‖[ῆμος ἐπίσταται τιμᾶν τοὺς ἀγαθοὺς τῶν ἀνδρῶν τοὺς μέλλοντας συν]αγωνιεῖν κτλ. Ἀγωνιεῖν as the future infinitive of an active ἀγωνίζειν is a noteworthy phenomenon. The verb, whether simple or in compound, is normally middle (ἀγωνίζεσθαι), with a contracted future (ἀγωνιεῖσθαι). The active aorist participle ἀγωνίσας is epigraphically attested at Sikyon in *IG* IV, 429.

Lines 5–6. On the basis of *IG* II², 844, of 193/2, lines 59–60, Meritt suggested ἐμ παντὶ καιρῶ]ι τὰ φιλάνθρω[πα πράττηται.

AN ENACTMENT OF UNCERTAIN CHARACTER IN THE DORIC DIALECT

257. Two joining fragments of a stele of Pentelic marble (I 6234), which (as joined) preserve the left side and original back of the monument but are broken elsewhere, discovered on October 21 and November 5, 1949, packed behind the blocks of the middle tower of the Post-Herulian Wall in the central part of the Stoa of Attalos (Q 10).

Measurements as joined: H. 0.40 m.; W. 0.46 m.; Th. 0.18 m.
LH. 0.006 m. (omicron and omega 0.004–0.005 m.).

Ed. B. D. Meritt, *Hesperia* 30, 1961, pp. 222–223, no. 19, with photograph pl. 38. See also *SEG* XXI, 484 (with additional reference to J. and L. Robert, *REG* 75, 1962, pp. 144–145, no. 107), S. V. Tracy, *Attic Letter-Cutters*, p. 91, and *SEG* XXXIX, 154.

ca. a. 200 a., vel paullo post   NON-ΣΤΟΙΧ.

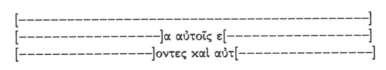

```
[————————————————————————————]
[———————————————]α αὐτοῖς ε[———————————]
[———————————————]οντες χαὶ αὐτ[——————————]
```

```
        [---------------]ασσων τὰν φιλία[ν ------------]
        [--------]ε λαμι[----- τ]αῖς πόλεσιν συντε[λ --------]
    5   [----]ι περὶ τοῦ κυριεύ[ει]ν τᾶς ἰδίας πατρίδος ἀπ[άσας ---]
        [----] νόμοι νομίζων ἅπ[ασ]ιν ἀνθρώποις συμφέρε[ιν -----]
        [----]θα[ι· π]ερὶ δὲ τῶν χρημάτων ὧν ἀξιοῦντι ΒΟ[-----ἀ]
        [ν]ηλοῦν ἅπαντα ποτὶ τοὺς φίλους πραγμα[-------------]
        [μ]εγάλας, νόμους ἐθήκατο περὶ τῶν πρ[---------------]
   10   [.]ασων δὲ πάντα γεν[έ]σθαι εὐβ[-----------------]
        αν καὶ καθάπερ ἐν τὰν ἰδίαν α[-----------------]
        [σ]θαι καὶ τιμὰς τούτοις ε[-------------------]
        σι τοῖς τὰ χρήματα σ[---------------------]
        ησάσθων παραχρ[-----------------------]
   15   αν ἦ δανε[ίζειν ---------------------------]
        [.]ομε[-------------------------------]
        [----------------------------------]
```

Line 3. ΑΣΕΩΝ Meritt; – – – Μυλ]ασέων(?) J. and L. Robert; ΑΣΣΩΝ Tracy. Line 7. Perhaps Βο[λοέντιοι – – – J. and L. Robert.

Meritt's dating for this text was a simple recognition that it belonged to the 2nd century B.C. The suggestion by J. and L. Robert (with reference to *IG* II², 1135 [*SEG* XXXIII, 134], a treaty between the Cretan cities of Olous and Lyttos, dated to 111/10 by the appearance of the Athenian archon Sosikrates in its prescript) that the people of Olous were also involved here, in some way concerned with the recognition of the services of foreign arbiters, implied no necessary attribution to the end of the century despite their cross-reference. Tracy's finding concerning the craftsmanship of the inscription, that it was the work of the "Cutter of *IG* II² 1131" (see **256**), has set it more precisely in the early years of the century. It is of interest that *IG* II², 1131 is itself in the Doric dialect and was regarded by J. Kirchner as part of a Rhodian decree. The content of the present enactment remains obscure.

There are few documents in the Attic corpus that emanate from other Greek states; see *IG* II², 1126–1137. The majority of these concern Delphi and the Amphiktyons, but *IG* II², 1130 is also in dialect and refers to Crete. It was found in the same area as *IG* II², 1131, and U. Koehler suggested that it belonged to the same monument, although it is not written by the same hand. Tracy (*op. cit.*, p. 242) dated it to the beginning of the 2nd century.

FRAGMENT OF A DECREE

258. A fragment of the upper part of a stele of Hymettian marble (I 3365), broken on all sides, discovered on February 10, 1936, in a modern context outside the Market Square to the southeast (T 17). The spring of a crowning molding survives at a distance of 0.055 m. above the first line of text. Within this space is a roughly abraded area running across the fragment and narrowing from left to right, which does not seem to be a *rasura* connected with the inscription.

H. 0.105 m.; W. 0.08 m.; Th. 0.065 m.
LH. 0.006 m.

Ed. B. D. Meritt, *Hesperia* 26, 1957, p. 61, no. 15, with photograph pl. 10. See also *SEG* XVI, 85.

init. saec. II a.   NON-ΣΤΟΙΧ.

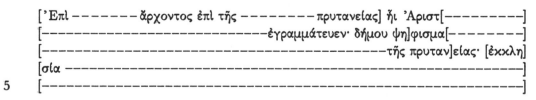

```
    ['Επὶ ------- ἄρχοντος ἐπὶ τῆς -------- πρυτανείας] ἧι 'Αριστ[---------]
    [------------------------- ἐγραμμ]άτευεν· δήμου ψη]φισμα[-------]
    [----------------------------------τῆς πρυταν]είας· [ἐκκλη]
    [σία ---------------------------------------------]
 5  [----------------------------------------------]
```

The plain writing is well spaced and generally neat. The external strokes of mu and sigma are angled; the crossbar of alpha is curved (see **256**). A date early in the 2nd century seems to accord with these meager indications, as Meritt himself noted in the *editio princeps*. S. V. Tracy (*Attic Letter-Cutters*, p. 84) saw some affinity between the style of this lettering and that of the "Cutter of Agora I 656 + 6355", for whose details and date see **260**. This observation also suggests that the early decades of the 2nd century offer an appropriate dating for this text.

The remains of the name of the γραμματεύς are doubtfully helpful. There were γραμματεῖς in the years 218/17, 215/14, and 214/13 whose names began thus: see Meritt, *Historia* 26, 1977, p. 178 and C. Habicht, *Studien*, p. 176. That this text belongs as early as these years may be possible, but on balance it seems less likely than an association with the γραμματεύς Arist――― of an unknown year between *ca.* 182 and *ca.* 150, attested in *Agora* XV, 218 (*SEG* XVI, 87), especially if the latter belongs to a year earlier rather than later within the span to which it has been assigned. Nevertheless, there remain a few years early in the 2nd century for which the name of the γραμματεύς has yet to be discovered.

Line 2. δήμου ψήφισμα(τα). The inclusion of this phrase in the prescript requires on the evidence a date later than 229/8; for the archonship of Heliodoros seems to provide its earliest datable appearance (*IG* II², 832). Cf. A. S. Henry (*Prescripts*, pp. 72–73, 88–89), who refers to it as a "minute-heading" and notes that texts in which these "headings" appear occur sporadically to the end of the 1st century B.C. This is its first occurrence among the Agora *psephismata* of this collection. It possibly represents an additional index of material, for classification purposes, for the convenience of the archivists in the Metroon.

THE ARCHONSHIP OF . . . IPPOS, 199/8 B.C.

That the eponymous archonship was held by one . . . ippos with a γραμματεύς who was the son of Demokles (as distinct from the . . . ippos of 177/6, whose γραμματεύς was the son of Hegetor, and for whom see p. 392 below) was first made known by the discovery of **259**, and this . . . ippos does not therefore figure in discussions of the list of archons earlier than 1957. B. D. Meritt placed him in 199/8 B.C. (*Hesperia* 26, 1957, pp. 62–63 and 94), a date which he maintained thereafter (*Athenian Year*, p. 235, *Historia* 26, 1977, p. 179).

The fuller restoration of the name of the γραμματεύς relies upon his presumed identity with the dedicator of the round base *SEG* XVI, 179, made after he had served as polemarch, where the name is [Δ]ημοσθένης and the demotic survives as ―――ίδης. The dissolution of the "Macedonian" phylai in 201/200 caused a break in the secretary cycle, which Meritt believed to have begun again with Ptolemais (now fifth in the official order). The attribution of Demosthenes the γραμματεύς to the deme Kothokidai (Oineis VII) thus agreed with 199/8 for his tenure of office which the then-current composition of the archon list had left vacant. The sole alternatives, Ptolemais V and Kekropis VIII, were less well to be accommodated to the list.

Meritt regarded Isokrates as the archon of 201/200, with the γραμματεύς from Ptolemais (V), and Nikophon as his successor in 200/199, with a γραμματεύς from Akamantis (VI). In 196/5 (see p. 362 below) the archon Charikles certainly had a γραμματεύς from Aiantis (X). But it is to be doubted if the break in the cycle came between 202/1 and 201/200: it is more plausibly to be set two years later, to begin therefore with Oineis, although this makes no difference to the hypothesis concerning 199/8. More significantly, C. Habicht's study of the archons of these years (*Studien*, pp. 159–177) displaced Isokrates and Nikophon from the years to which Meritt had assigned them (*Studien*, pp. 163–165, 171). But his analysis of the year of . . . ippos (p. 170) agreed with Meritt's reasons for regarding his term of office as 199/8, albeit with a slight hesitation expressed also by a query mark against his entry on the final list (p. 177).

Meritt's restored dating of **260** (see below) would make . . . ippos' year ordinary in the Athenian festival calendar, with the festival dates running in parallel with those of the prytany year, now back to its pre-224 pattern of twelve prytanies after the subtraction of Antigonis and Demetrias and the addition of Attalis. But while Meritt showed it thus in 1961, his 1977 list, without explanation or proposed textual revision of **260**, showed it as intercalary. In the Metonic cycle it will have been ordinary, this being the sixth year of the thirteenth cycle. Meritt also judged, by reason of the spacing in line 2 of **260**, that Erechtheis was the phyle in office in the twelfth prytany; but there is no real guarantee of this. No other prytany is known.

FRAGMENT OF A DECREE

259. A fragment of the central section of the upper part of a pedimental stele of Hymettian marble (I 6100), broken all around but with the moldings and part of the pediment preserved above the inscribed face, discovered on April 5, 1948, among marbles from the area immediately outside the Market Square to the southwest. The molding is a Pergamene-style ovolo (see **216**), which apparently comes immediately below the horizontal cornice of the pediment. A broad taenia beneath the ovolo descends with a sharp apophyge into the first line of text. B. D. Meritt noted a similarity of the molding and quality of the marble with those of **261**.

H. 0.16 m.; W. 0.15 m.; Th. *ca.* 0.10 m.
LH. 0.007 m.

Ed. B. D. Meritt, *Hesperia* 26, 1957, pp. 61–62, no. 16, with photograph pl. 10. See also *SEG* XVI, 74.

a. 199/8 *a., pryt.* XII   NON-ΣΤΟΙΧ. *ca.* 54

```
        ['Επὶ ϲα̣ ³ἰ]ππου ἄρχοντος ἐπὶ [τῆς . . . ᶜᵃ˙ ¹⁰ . . . δωδεκάτης πρυτανείας]
        [ἧι Δημοσ]θένης Δημοκλέου[ς Κοθωκίδης ἐγραμμάτευεν· δήμου ψηφίσ]
        [ματα· Σκιροφ]οριῶνος [------------------------ τῆς πρυτα]
        [νείας· ἐκκλησ]ία ἐμ Π[ειραιεῖ· τῶν προέδρων ἐπεψήφιζεν --------]
   5    [-----------------------------------------------------------------]
```

S. V. Tracy identified this text as the work of the "Cutter of *IG* II² 1326", and indeed as his earliest datable
piece, *Attic Letter-Cutters*, pp. 92–95 (cf. also pp. 231–232), with photograph of part of the name piece, fig. 10. This
mason's career cannot be traced beyond 176/5 B.C. His work, close in style to that of the "Cutter of *IG* II² 897"
(for whom see **270**), is generally plain; its carelessness and variety in detail do not make for any overall impression
of untidiness. Tracy assigned nine other inscriptions to his hand: **267** and two more texts may be his but cannot with
assurance be so listed.

Line 1. The number of the prytany is deduced from the name of the month in line 3. Meritt supplied 'Ερεχθεῖδος
on the basis of the evidence and spacing in line 2 of **260**. Line 2. Demosthenes, son of Demokles, of Kothokidai. See
p. 360 above for the dedication attributed to him. A Demosthenes of the same deme appears as the husband of
Aristandra on the tombstone of the latter, *IG* II², 6027 of the 1st century A.D., and could well be a descendant.
Lines 2–3. δήμου ψηφίσματα. Restored here to account for the available space. See **258**, commentary on line 2.

Line 4. ἐκκλησία ἐμ Πειραιεῖ. See **222**, commentary on line 3. W. A. McDonald (*Political Meeting Places*,
pp. 51–56), who listed examples then known through the 2nd century to 137/6, observed that on the evidence these
Peiraieus meetings always fell within the last third of the month, perhaps representing the fourth and last of the
obligatory meetings of each prytany (Aristotle, *Athenaion Politeia* 43.3). If this is correct, and if Meritt's calendar
date of **260** be accepted, the present decree must have been passed a few days later than the adoption of that measure
by the boule.

FRAGMENT OF A DECREE

260. A small fragment of a stele of Pentelic marble (I 1886), broken all around but with the smooth top preserved,
discovered on April 28, 1934, in a late context west of the Tholos (F 11).

H. 0.10 m.; W. 0.048 m.; Th. 0.025 m.
LH. 0.008 m.

Ed. B. D. Meritt, *Hesperia* 9, 1940, pp. 85–86, no. 16, with photograph (actual size). A revised text also by Meritt,
Hesperia 26, 1957, pp. 62–63. See *SEG* XVI, 75.

a. 199/8 *a.*   NON-ΣΤΟΙΧ. *ca.* 39

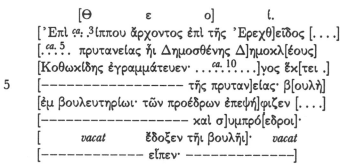

```
        [Θ        ε        ο]        ι̣.
        ['Επὶ ϲα̣ ³ἰ]ππου ἄρχοντος ἐπὶ τῆς 'Ερεχθ]εῖδος [. . . .]
        [. ᶜᵃ˙ ⁵. πρυτανείας ἧι Δημοσθένης Δ]ημοκλ[έους]
        [Κοθωκίδης ἐγραμμάτευεν· . . . ᶜᵃ˙ ¹⁰ . . .]γος ἔχ[τει .]
   5    [------------------ τῆς πρυταν]είας· β[ουλὴ]
        [ἐμ βουλευτηρίωι· τῶν προέδρων ἐπεψή]φιζεν [. . . .]
        [------------------ καὶ σ]υμπρό[εδροι]·
        [      vacat      ἔδοξεν τῆι βουλῆι]·      vacat
        [------------ εἶπεν· ------------]
```

At the time of its first publication, before its association with **259** suggested a closer dating, Meritt assigned
this text to a date *ca.* 200 B.C. on the style of its writing alone. That writing was subsequently recognized by S. V.
Tracy as the work of the craftsman he named the "Cutter of Agora I 656 + 6355"; **258** was perhaps another of
his productions. See *Attic Letter-Cutters*, pp. 82–88, with photograph of the name piece, fig. 8, and (on his relationship
to the "Cutter of Agora I 6006", for whom see **296**) p. 232. This mason's style was regular and competent, the
letters not always exactly articulated but of a standard higher than in most nonmonumental work of the period.

Lines 2–3. The alternative possible phylai are Aigeis and Oineis, both of which appear to be too short for the presumed requirements of space derived from lines 5–6. Meritt restored δωδεκάτης and, in line 4, Σχιροφοριῶνος, regarding this prescript and that of **259** as giving each other mutual support; but of this there can be no certainty. Lines 4–5. ἔχ[τει ἐ||πὶ δέχα, ἔχτει χαὶ δεχάτει τῆς πρυταν]είας Meritt, on the assumption that this was an ordinary year: but see p. 360 above, on the archonship of . . . ippos.

Lines 5–6. βουλὴ ἐμ βουλευτηρίωι. The first instance of this descriptive addition among the Agora *psephismata* of the present collection, although it appears as early as 336/5 (*IG* II², 330, lines 30–31). See A. S. Henry, *Prescripts*, p. 39. For decrees of the boule without the demos see P. J. Rhodes, *Athenian Boule*, pp. 82–87 and 271–275 (this text listed on p. 273). After the middle of the 3rd century, these are mostly decrees honoring the officers of the prytaneis (the so-called second decree of prytany texts), for which see *Agora* XV, pp. 5–6, 9–10. Line 8. The surviving blank space prompted Meritt to assume the "perfect design", with a corresponding blank space on the left. See **204**.

THE ARCHONSHIP OF CHARIKLES, 196/5 B.C.

Charikles' year of office was first attested by *IG* II², 785, a nonstoichedon text of an intercalary year in a period of twelve rather than thirteen phylai, in which honors were voted to Aristokreon, nephew of the philosopher Chrysippos who became head of the Stoic school in 231/30. A year corresponding to these indications and to the prosopography of the inscription, together with the important *datum* that Charikles' γραμματεύς came from the deme Rhamnous (Aiantis XI), seemed best available in the 3rd century before the creation of the phyle Ptolemais. J. Kirchner (*IG* II², iv, 1, pp. 14–15) preferred 239/8, the year now recognized as that of Lysias (see pp. 312–313 above). This period was adopted by W. B. Dinsmoor (*Archons of Athens*, pp. 179–180), who also assigned *IG* II², 798 to Charikles, restoring in that text the name Ἀ[θηνοδώρου] in lines 10–11 where the preceding archon year appears to be mentioned. Dinsmoor himself placed Charikles in 242/1, a year he regarded as certain (*op. cit.*, p. 187). Other earlier assessments had set this archonship in the same general region.

The discovery of **261** immediately and radically altered this situation. B. D. Meritt assigned Charikles to 196/5, in the restored period of twelve phylai and after the institution of the Ptolemaia which are mentioned in the text, at a point where the secretary cycle evidently required a representative of Aiantis (now X). This accorded with the activities of Kephisodoros, placed in their context by the references to earlier archonships in the inscription and by the information supplied by Pausanias (1.36.5–6), which called for a date later than Athens' conflict with Philip V of Macedon and preferably later than the final defeat of the king by the Roman forces under Quinctius Flamininus. Aristokreon's honors awarded in *IG* II², 785 were thus earned some forty years later than had previously been believed, while *IG* II², 798 could no longer be dealt with as Dinsmoor had suggested. See Meritt, *Hesperia* 5, 1936, pp. 427–428 and *Hesperia* 7, 1938, p. 139.

The new dating was accepted by Dinsmoor, *Athenian Archon List*, p. 184, and became a fixed point in subsequent studies (W. K. Pritchett and Meritt, *Chronology*, pp. xxvi and 111; Pritchett and O. Neugebauer, *Calendars*, pp. 15–16, 75; Dinsmoor, *Hesperia* 23, 1954, p. 316; Meritt, *Athenian Year*, p. 235, *Hesperia* 37, 1968, pp. 235–236, *Historia* 26, 1977, p. 180): see also C. Habicht, *Studien*, pp. 163–164, 177.

The suggestion of C. A. P. Ruck (*IG II² 2323: The List of the Victors in Comedies at the Dionysia*, 1967, pp. 25–28; cf. *SEG* XXV, 194) that Charikles be placed in 184/3 won no support at the time; but it was revived when a new fragment of that text was published which is to be inserted between those relating to the archon group Symmachos–Theoxenos–Zopyros and the connected pair Hermogenes–Timesianax (cf. pp. 373 and 381 below). See A. P. Matthaiou, Ὅρος 6, 1988, pp. 13–18. A reference to what is clearly the archonship of Eupolemos, assured as of the year 185/4, is immediately followed by an entry dated [ἐπὶ ^{ca.4}.]λέους (restored by Matthaiou as [ἐπὶ – – – x]λέους). D. M. Lewis, Ὅρος 6, 1988, pp. 19–20, claimed Charikles as the best candidate. Cf. *SEG* XXXVIII, 162. But this is to go beyond the evidence: names ending in -αχλῆς, -εχλῆς, -υχλῆς, -οχλῆς, and -υχλῆς, of the required length, are very numerous, and the possibilities in consequence make acceptance of the hypothesis inadvisable unless and until more certain evidence becomes available. The logic of the historical circumstances detailed above and in the commentary to **261**, which have a strength of their own not easily to be denied or circumvented, continues to compel the retention of 196/5 as Charikles' year. The redating of Charikles to 184/3 was accepted also by J. S. Traill (*ZPE* 103, 1994, pp. 111–112), who proposed that Pleistainos, formerly placed in 184/3, be transferred to 196/5 in his stead. *SEG* XVI, 162, a private commemoration of an official of Charikles' year, does not affect the issue.

To the two inscriptions of the year of Charikles already mentioned must be added a third, *Agora* XV, 166. The data they together provide concerning the character of the year are as follows: (1) *IG* II², 785 was passed on Posideon II 11 = pryt. VI, 29; (2) **261** was passed on Elaphebolion 13 (correctly 18) = pryt. IX, 28 (on the date see the commentary on the text itself); (3) *Agora* XV, 166 was passed on Thargelion 23 = pryt. [XI, 28]. The year was thus intercalary, with two successive months of 30 days at an early stage in it but thereafter a regular alternation of months of 29 and 30 days; there were 32 days in each prytany, as regularly in intercalary years during the periods of twelve phylai. Cf. Pritchett and Neugebauer, *Calendars*, p. 75 and Meritt, *Hesperia* 37, 1968, pp. 235–236. In the Metonic cycle, in which it stood ninth, the year should have been ordinary; see Meritt, *TAPA* 95, 1964, p. 240, an error which he corrected in *Hesperia, loc. cit.*

Phylai known in prytany are VI Erechtheis and IX Aigeis. The name of the prytanizing phyle in *Agora* XV, 166, passed in the eleventh prytany (see above), is lost in a lacuna.

DECREE IN HONOR OF KEPHISODOROS OF XYPETE

261 (Pl. 28 [*a* and *c* + *d*]). The upper and major section of a pedimental stele of Hymettian marble (fragment *a*, I 605), broken below but complete elsewhere (including the akroteria), and three small pieces of the same stele (fragments *b*, *c*, *d*: I 605 c, I 834, I 909), two of which (*c* and *d*) join, but none of which makes a join with fragment *a*. Fragment *a* was discovered on March 24, 1933, in a Late Roman context west of the Temple of Ares (J 7), fragment *b* on May 9, 1933, from exploration inside the porch of the Metroon, probably in the upper (Byzantine) level (H 9), fragment *c* on May 18, 1933, in a Late Roman context in the south wing of the Stoa of Zeus Eleutherios (H 7), and fragment *d* on May 29, 1933, in a context similar to that of fragment *c*. The stone is very mottled in appearance, and its color varies, exactly as B. D. Meritt described it, "irregularly from milky white to bluish gray." Cf. **259**. Besides the similarity of the marble, Meritt also noted a similarity between the molding of **259**, so far as preserved, and the molding of this stele. This point is however less well to be substantiated. The ovolo of **259** has a more sharply turning curved profile, and the taenia below it is broader, with a more abrupt apophyge to the inscribed face. The graceful cavetto of **261** above the ovolo may not have existed on **259**, on which the damaged molding surmounting the ovolo seems to represent the horizontal cornice of the pediment.

a: H. 0.85 m.; W. (at base of pediment) 0.526 m., (at line 1 of the text) 0.468 m., (at line 29 of the text) 0.479 m.; Th. 0.15 m. (max.), (at dressed edges) 0.075 m.

b: H. 0.132 m.; W. 0.091 m.; Th. 0.032 m.

c + *d*: H. 0.12 m.; W. 0.171 m.; Th. 0.035 m.

LH. *ca.* 0.006 m.

Ed. B. D. Meritt, *Hesperia* 5, 1936, pp. 419–428, no. 15, with photographs of all fragments, after a preliminary reference concerning the date in *Hesperia* 4, 1935, p. 556 with note 1. See also *SEG* XXV, 112; L. Moretti, *Iscrizioni storiche ellenistiche* I, pp. 74–79, no. 33 (text, commentary, and Italian translation). For the use of the data of lines 1–4 in discussions of the calendar of the year see the references under the account of the archonship of Charikles above.

a. 196/5 a., *pryt.* IX   NON-ΣTOIX. *ca.* 48–56

```
       Ἐπὶ Χαρικλέους ἄρχοντος ἐπὶ τῆς Αἰγεῖδος ἐνάτης πρυτανείας ἧι ᵛᵛ
       Αἰσχρίων Εὐαινέτου Ῥαμνούσιος ἐγραμμάτευεν· δήμου ψηφίσματα·
       Ἐλαφηβολιῶνος τρίτει ἐπὶ δέκα, {κατὰ θεὸν δὲ} ὀγδόει καὶ εἰκοστεῖ
       τῆς πρυτανείας· ἐκκλησία κυρία ἐμ Πειραιεῖ· τῶν προέδρων ἐπεψή
  5    φιζεν Ἀντίπατρος Ποτάμωνος Λαμπτρεὺς καὶ συμπρόεδροι· ᵛᵛᵛ
              ἔδοξεν τεῖ βουλεῖ καὶ τῶι δήμωι·
       Σώδαμος Τιμασιθέου ἐξ Οἴου εἶπεν· ᵛ ἐπειδὴ Κηφισόδωρος ἐκτενὴν
       προσενηνεγμένος τὴν πρὸς τὸν δῆμον εὔνοιαν ἐμ παντὶ καιρῶι
       καὶ πεπολιτευμένος μὲν πρὸς τὰ τριάκοντα ἔτη καθαρῶς καὶ ἀδωρο
 10    δοκήτως, οὐθένα δὲ οὔτε πόνον οὔτε κίνδυνον ἐκκεχλικὼς ἕνεκεν
       τοῦ κοινοῦ συμφέροντος, ᵛ καὶ τάς τε ἄλλας λειτουργίας ὑπομεμενη
       κὼς πάσας ἐφ'ἃς αὐτὸν κατέστησεν ὁ δῆμος, ᵛ γεγονὼς δὲ καὶ ταμίας
```

στρατιωτικῶν καλῶς καὶ φιλοδόξως καὶ τὴν τῶν σιτωνικῶν *vvv*
ταμιείαν συνδιεξηχὼς τρίτος ἔν τε τῶι ἐπὶ Ἀπολλοδώρου καὶ

15 Προξενίδου ἐνιαυτῶι, *v* τεθηκὼς δὲ καὶ νόμους συμφέροντας
ἐφ᾽ὁμονοίαι πάντων Ἀθηναίων, *v* καὶ πόρους χρημάτων ἴσους καὶ
δικαίους συμβεβουλευκώς, *v* εἰσηγημένος δὲ καὶ δι᾽οὗ τρόπου *vv*
τούς τε ὄντας φίλους ὁ δῆμος διατηρήσει βεβαίους ἐν τεῖ πίστε[ι]
μένοντας καὶ ἑτέρους προσκτήσεται, *v* καὶ τὰς γινομένας ἐπιβου

20 λὰς ὑπὸ τῶν ἔξωθεν προεωραμένος καὶ ἀντιστῆνα[ι] πρ[οσ]τεταγ
μένος, *v* καὶ συμμαχίας συμβεβουλευκὼς καλὰς καὶ [συν]ενηνο
χείας τῶι δήμωι, *v* καὶ πρεσβείας πεπρεσβευκὼς ὑπὲρ [τῶν] μεγί
στων εἰς σωτηρίαν ταῖς πόλεσιν καὶ τῆι χώραι, *v* καὶ χρήματα ἠχὼς
καὶ σῖτον καὶ ἄλλας δωρεὰς οὐκ ὀλίγας, *v* εἰσενηνοχὼς δὲ καὶ ψη

25 φίσματα πολλὰ καὶ χρήσιμα καὶ δόξαν ἔχοντα καὶ πρᾶξιν καὶ εὐ
σχημοσύνην τῶι δήμωι, *v* καὶ διαμεμενηκὼς ἐπὶ τῆς αὐτῆς
αἱρέσεως ἅπαντα τὸν χρόνον μισοπονήρως, *vv* καὶ διὰ τὴν συνέ
χειαν τῶν πραττομένων καὶ ἐπινοουμένων μάλιστα αἴτιος γεγο
νὼς μετὰ τῆς τῶν θεῶν εὐμενείας τοῦ διατηρῆσαι τὸν δῆμον

30 [τ]ὴν αὐτονομίαν, *v* οὐκ ὀλίγοις δὲ καὶ τῶν ἄλλων Ἑλλήνων περιπε
[ποηκέ]ναι τὰ μέγιστα τῶν ἀγαθῶν, *vv* καὶ διὰ ταῦτα πάντα δίκαι
[ον ἀποφαί]νων ἑαυτὸν τυχεῖν τιμῆς κατὰ τὸν νόμον, *vv* αἰτεῖ*vv*
[ται νῦν δοῦν]αι ἑαυτοῦ τὸν δῆμον εἰκόνα χαλκῆν ἐν ἀγορᾶι καὶ
[ἄλλην ἐμ Πειραιε]ῖ ἐν τῶι ἐμπορίωι καὶ σίτησιν ἑαυτῶι ἐν πρυ

35 [τανείωι καὶ ἐγγόνων ἀ]εὶ τῶι πρεσβυτάτωι καὶ προεδρίαν ἐν πᾶσι
[τοῖς ἀγῶσιν οἷς ἡ πόλις τί]θησιν, *vv* καὶ τὴν αἴτησιν δέδωκεν πρὸς
[τὴν βουλὴν καὶ τὸν δῆμον] κατὰ μέρος τῶν πεπραγμένων, *vvvvvv*
[ὅπως ἂν οὖν ὁ δῆμος φαίνη]ται τιμῶν τοὺς ἀγαθοὺς ἄνδρας καὶ
[ὅπως ἂν εἰδῶσιν καὶ οἱ ἄλλοι ζη]λωταὶ τῆς τοιαύτης αἱρέσεως ὅτι

40 [ἀεὶ παρὰ τοῦ δήμου τοῦ Ἀθηναί]ων τῆς προσηκούσης τυγχάνου
[σιν τιμῆς, *vvvvvv* ἀγαθεῖ τύχει δε]δόχθαι τεῖ βουλεῖ τοὺς προέ*v*
[δρους οἵτινες ἂν λάχωσιν προεδρεύειν εἰς τ]ὴν κυρίαν ἐκκλ[ησίαν]
[τὴν ἐπὶ τῆς Αἰγεῖδος πρυτανείας χρηματίσαι π]ερὶ τού[των κα]
[τὰ τὸν νόμον, γνώμην δὲ ξ]υμ[βάλλεσθαι τῆς βουλῆς εἰς τὸν δῆμον ὅτι]

45 [δοκεῖ τεῖ βουλεῖ] ἐπαινέσ[αι Κηφισόδωρον ——————————]
[καὶ στεφανῶσα]ι χρυσῶι [στεφάνωι κατὰ τὸν νόμον ἀρετῆς ἕνεκεν]
[καὶ εὐνοίας ἣν ἔχω]ν διατελ[εῖ πρὸς τὸν δῆμον τ]ὸ[ν Ἀθηναίων· *v* ἀνειπεῖν]
[δὲ τὸν στέφανο]ν τοῦτον [Διονυσίων τε τῶν ἐν] ἄσ[τει καινοῖς τραγωι]
[δοῖς καὶ Παναθ]ηναίων χ[αὶ Ἐλευσινίων κα]ὶ Πτολ[εμαίων τοῖς γυμνι]

50 [κοῖς ἀγῶσιν· *v*]*vv* τῆς δὲ [ποιήσεως τοῦ] στεφάνο[υ καὶ τῆς ἀναγο]
[ρεύσεως ἐπιμελ]ηθῆναι τοὺς [στρατηγοὺ]ς καὶ τὸν τα[μίαν τῶν στρα]
[τιωτικῶν· *vvv*] στῆσαι δὲ [αὐτοῦ κα]ὶ εἰκόνα χαλκῆ[ν ἐν ἀγορᾶι καὶ]
[ἄλλην ἐμ Πειραι]εῖ ἐν τῶ[ι ἐμπορίω]ι· *vv* εἶναι δὲ αὐτῶ[ι καὶ σίτησιν]
[ἐν πρυτανείωι κα]ὶ ἐγ[γόνων ἀ]εὶ τῶι πρεσβυτάτωι [καὶ προεδρίαν]

55 [ἐν πᾶσι τοῖς ἀγῶσιν οἷς ἡ πόλις] τίθησιν· *vv* τοὺς [δ]ὲ θεσ[μοθέτας εἰσα]
[γαγεῖν τὴν δοκιμασίαν αὐτῶι ὅ]ταν ἐξέλθωσιν [αἱ] ἐκ τ[οῦ νόμου ἡμέραι]
[τῆς αἰτήσεως ——————————————————————]

The text is that of Meritt, except for the beginning of line 34, where the reading and restoration were suggested by G. Daux (*per ep.*), early in 1939, in substitution for the [εἰκόνα χαλκῆ]ν of the *editio princeps* (retained also by Moretti). For the proposed restoration of στῆσα]ι (for νῦν δοῦν]αι) in line 33 and of λιθίνη]ν (for ἐμ Πειραιε]ῖ) in line 34 see *SEG* XLI, 59.

The lettering of this long inscription is regular and in general tidy, and the ensemble of the work has claims to artistic merit. S. V. Tracy identified it as the handiwork of the craftsman named by him the "Cutter of Agora I 656 + 6355", to whom he attributed fifteen texts, ranging in date (where this may be independently determined) from

203/2 to 164/3; see **260**. Especially characteristic of this mason and well in evidence here are a curve to the crossbar of alpha, a narrow kappa, and a small omega which lacks horizontal attachments: there is some enlargement of the "free ends" of strokes. Apart from **260**, other texts in the present collection attributed to the same craftsman are **265** and **268**. The prescript (see especially lines 5–6) is set out in the "perfect design", for which see **204** and **205**.

Line 2. Aischrion, son of Euainetos, of Rhamnous. His complete name was first made known by this text: *IG* II², 785 preserves only the patronymic and demotic. Cf. J. Pouilloux, *Forteresse*, p. 169 (and for Euainetos, p. 173). A Euainetos was demarch of Rhamnous in the middle of the 5th century (*IG* I³, 248, line 27). Δήμου ψηφίσματα. See **258**, commentary on line 2. There it remained doubtful whether the expression was singular or plural, but here it is assuredly plural, which A. S. Henry (*Prescripts*, p. 89 with note 75) regarded as probably the commoner form.

Line 3. If there was an adjustment in the calendar, it was in all probability connected with the celebration of the City Dionysia; see Meritt, *Athenian Year*, pp. 164–165. However, as it stands the text is nonsensical, since κατὰ θεὸν δέ can only introduce a true date in the festival calendar when the latter has undergone some temporary alteration κατ'ἄρχοντα; it has no relevance to the prytany calendar, a manmade system that owed nothing to the deity. Meritt originally postulated what remains the most economical explanation, a haplography on the part of the mason for κατὰ θεὸν δὲ ὀγδόει (ἐπὶ δέκα, ὀγδόει) καὶ εἰκοστεῖ τῆς πρυτανείας. Cf. W. K. Pritchett and O. Neugebauer, *Calendars*, pp. 15–16 and 75. On the expression of κατὰ θεόν and κατ'ἄρχοντα dates, the so-called triple dating, of which this is the earliest instance, see further Pritchett, *Ancient Athenian Calendars on Stone*, pp. 330–354; Meritt, *TAPA* 95, 1964, pp. 228–260, 'Αρχ. 'Εφ., 1968, pp. 92–105; Henry, *Prescripts*, pp. 78–80. Meritt later sought to tie the κατὰ θεόν dating to the Metonic cycle, but since 196/5 was ordinary in the cycle while intercalary at Athens (see p. 363 above), he urged ('Αρχ. 'Εφ., 1968, p. 105) that κατὰ θεόν here could never have introduced a Metonic date and must therefore be regarded as an error of draftsmanship (perhaps induced by the unfamiliarity of the recorded expression). Hence the phrase earns the braces shown in the text.

It may however be open to question whether the calendric thinking behind the error was quite so sophisticated. Although the alternation of months of 29 and 30 days, on the Metonic pattern, was (*pace* contentions to the contrary) the regular element in the Athenian reckoning of their calendar, consistent connection with the succession of intercalary and ordinary years as prescribed by Meton had disappeared long since. An attempt here to write a κατὰ θεόν date, bungled in execution as it was, was surely related to a tampering κατ'ἄρχοντα with the festival calendar as it then stood, irrespective of the true Metonic cycle. Meritt's earliest explanation of the passage thus remains preferable; the year should stand as intercalary on the table in *TAPA* 95, 1964, p. 237, with the discussion on p. 238 cancelled.

Lines 3–4. For Elaphebolion 13 as a day on which the assembly might meet see J. D. Mikalson (*Sacred and Civil Calendar*, pp. 128–129), who quoted lines 1–4 of this text (the sole evidence for an assembly on this date) and observed that the error in line 3 may be "only a symptom of deeper confusion." Line 4. 'Εκκλησία κυρία ἐμ Πειραιεῖ. See **259**, commentary on line 4. This is one of only two examples of an ἐκκλησία κυρία at the Peiraieus (see W. A. McDonald, *Political Meeting Places*, p. 56 and **296**, where it is restored), and it is interesting that this important assembly (Aristotle, *Athenaion Politeia* 43.4) should be the last in the prytany. Line 5. Antipatros, son of Potamon, of Lamptrai. Although several holders of the name Antipatros are known as members of this deme, this is the only instance of a Potamon Λαμπτρεύς. Antipatros may have been the husband of the Dionysia of Herakleia commemorated by the gravestone *SEG* XIX, 279. He may well also be the ancestor of the 'Αντίπατρος Λαμπτρεύς whose son was ephebe in 123/2 (see *IG* II², 1006, line 108). Line 7. Sodamos, son of Timasitheos, of Oion. Neither name is otherwise attested from Oion.

Kephisodoros, the honorand of the decree, was a considerable political figure at Athens over a long period. For the literary references to him, most notably Pausanias (1.36.5–6), see *PA* 8353, and for narrative based on them, W. S. Ferguson, *Hellenistic Athens*, pp. 269–270, 279 and C. Mossé, *Athens in Decline 404–86 B.C.*, 1973, pp. 138–140. On Pausanias' evidence see further C. Habicht (*Pausanias' Guide to Ancient Greece*, 1985, pp. 92–94), who also provided a photograph of the present text, fig. 30. The inscriptional evidence added a fresh dimension to the history of his career, but it remains unique, and for a statesman of such evident importance the paucity of available material is remarkable. Habicht suggested that Pausanias saw a number of decrees concerning Kephisodoros near his monument, which he was content simply to summarize.

His political career is generally agreed to have begun at the time of the restoration of Athenian independence from Macedon in 229/8. His patronymic and demotic are not preserved in the present text. They would, however, complete line 45 very exactly if he is to be identified with that Kephisodoros, son of Aristodemos, of Xypete (*PA* 8380) who, in 229/8, proposed *IG* II², 832, a decree the provisions of which appear so strikingly to establish the νόμος under which he made his present application for honors (lines 32–37) that M. J. Osborne (*ZPE* 41, 1981, p. 161) regarded the identification as to be "embraced with confidence." It was accepted by Habicht (*Pausanias' Guide to Ancient Greece*; so also *Studien*, pp. 124–127, 156) and is accepted here. The more so, indeed, since in 196/5 the statement (line 9) that he had been politically active for "upwards of thirty years" with an unimpeachable record will accommodate such a span. The intentional vagueness of the phraseology adds to the conviction. The exact precision called for by Meritt and by Moretti, who is hesitant about the identification (*op. cit.*, p. 79, note 11: "nel 229/8 siamo fuori del trentennio di vita politica del nostro Kephisodoros [226–196]"), is pedantic and not in point. However, if the archonship of Charikles and the date of this text are to be transferred to 184/3 (see above), the identification could hardly be maintained: cf. D. M. Lewis, Ὅρος 6, 1988, pp. 19–20, with the comment that after all "Kephisodoros is not an uncommon name."

After the deaths of Eurykleides and Mikion (between 211 and 207), Kephisodoros was evidently regarded as the leading Athenian diplomat and advisor on policy and finance. On his diplomacy in connection with Rome's Second Macedonian War, and for an evaluation of lines 7–31 of the text, see especially A. H. McDonald, *JRS* 27, 1937, pp. 198–203; cf. also F. W. Walbank, *Philip V of Macedon*, 1940, pp. 130–132, 312–313; R. M. Errington, *CAH* VIII, 2nd ed., 1989, pp. 257–258.

If, as Osborne suggested, the rewards Kephisodoros claimed required at the minimum a thirty-year career of good service (see below), and since the confrontation between Athens and Philip V had ended, thanks to the Romans, so recently and so successfully, signalized by Flamininus' proclamation of liberty for the Greeks (alluded to, as Meritt observed, in lines 27–31), the year 196/5 emerges even more markedly as preeminently the juncture when Kephisodoros might with every justification and prospect of success claim and receive the honors recorded here.

Lines 14–15. The archonships of Apollodoros and Proxenides belong to 204/3 and 203/2 (cf. Pritchett and Meritt, *Chronology*, pp. xxv–xxvi and 104–108; Meritt, *Athenian Year*, p. 235, *TAPA* 95, 1964, p. 240, *Historia* 26, 1977, p. 179; Habicht, *Studien*, pp. 161 and 177. The latter coincided with the pressure exerted upon maritime communications through the Hellespont by Philip V in the early months of 202. See Walbank, *op. cit.*, pp. 114–115 and F. M. Heichelheim, *Aegyptus* 17, 1937, pp. 61–64. As ταμίας τῶν σιτωνικῶν, Kephisodoros had two colleagues. These three officials evidently coexisted and cooperated with the σιτῶναι, on whom see **188**, commentary on line 9. From *IG* II², 1272 and 1708 it would appear that in 267/6 and again in the early 2nd century a single treasurer sufficed; and indeed the emphasis in this context upon a triple sharing of the office may suggest that the arrangement was unusual and made to meet a particular emergency.

Line 23. ταῖς πόλεσιν. I.e., Athens and the Peiraieus. Cf. *IG* II², 903, line 9 (revised in *SEG* XXXII, 132, with further references). Lines 27–31. The reference to the successful outcome of the Second Macedonian War and to Flamininus' proclamation of Greek liberty more than nine months previously remains implicit rather than explicit, since these desirable consequences were more dependent upon Roman generosity than attributable to Kephisodoros' statecraft.

Lines 32–37. The initiative had come from Kephisodoros himself. Osborne (*ZPE* 41, 1981, pp. 160–162) maintained that he was entitled to claim the honors described as being eligible κατὰ τὸν νόμον under the terms expressed in *IG* II², 832, the decree he had himself proposed thirty-three years previously (see above), in his case line 16 of that text. Osborne further suggested that thirty years was a required or at least generally accepted minimum of good service, and that in consequence a politician eligible to make the claim would be at least sixty years of age. Line 33. The honor of a statue was rarely bestowed. The fact that the request was granted and that not merely one but two statues were to be erected (an even greater rarity) reflects the merit of Kephisodoros' claims. Osborne (*op. cit.*, pp. 167–168) saw it not only as a novelty but also as a legal concomitant to the grant of σίτησις (see below) claimed κατὰ τὸν νόμον. See Henry, *Honours*, pp. 294–296, 307–308, notes 36–37, **233**, commentary on lines 11–12, **240**, and **310**, commentary on lines 45–48.

Lines 34–35. For the grant of σίτησις see Henry, *Honours*, pp. 275–278 and Osborne, *ZPE* 41, 1981, pp. 158–170; and cf. **310**, lines 49–50. The categories of persons so privileged were very restricted. "To be made one of this company was to receive Athens' most practical and most ornamental honor" (S. Dow, *HSCP* 67, 1963, p. 83). For an earlier period see *IG* I³, 131 (*SEG* XXXI, 11, with references to earlier volumes, XXXII, 4), where the list of those privileged consists of (1) the priests of the Eleusinian goddesses, (2) the closest lineal descendants of the tyrannicides Harmodios and Aristogeiton, (3) according to different interpretations, either those designated by Apollo as expounders of the sacred and ancestral law, or the manteis (or a mantis) of Apollo himself, (4) victors in the γυμνικοὶ ἀγῶνες of the four great Panhellenic games, and (5) victors in the horse races at the same games. For eligibility at the time of the present decree cf. *IG* II², 832 already quoted, which appears to add to rather than emend these categories, or at least to define more closely a general category of "public benefactors" with a claim to the privilege, referring particularly to military success, to the defense of freedom, to the contribution of personal wealth for the common good, and to the provision of good advice and general good works to Athens' benefit. Individual grants of this kind known from epigraphical evidence range from the late 4th century to the late 2nd, but they are few in number. See S. Dow, *HSCP* 67, 1963, pp. 82–83, 85–86; *Agora* III, p. 172, no. 567 and pp. 173–174; *Agora* XIV, p. 47 with note 132; Osborne, *ZPE* 41, 1981, pp. 158–160; Henry, *Honours*, pp. 275–276; cf. also **310**, lines 49–50.

Lines 35–36. *Proedria* was also, apparently, a recognized concomitant of σίτησις κατὰ τὸν νόμον: cf. M. Maass, *Die Prohedrie des Dionysostheaters in Athen* (*Vestigia* 15), 1972, p. 86. But it did not accompany the grant in **310**. On the phraseology of the award cf. **185**, lines 25–26 with commentary and **187**, lines 30–31. Lines 38–41. The "hortatory intention" is unusually doubled, which again perhaps is an index of the honorand's perceived merits. On the "intention" cf. **173**, commentary on line 2 and references there. For ζηλωταί Meritt compared the Oropian text *IG* VII, 411 (*SEG* XXV, 493), lines 27–28; and see further **292**, commentary on lines 14–16. In the present case the motives represent both the wish of the assembly to be seen to reward good service and the aim of encouraging emulation in others who will be assured, from this demonstration of it, that suitable reward will follow. For the former cf., e.g., **224**, lines 25–27, and for the latter, e.g., **285**, lines 5–8.

Line 41. Ἀγαθεῖ τύχει. See **72**, commentary on lines 7–8. Lines 41–42. The older phraseology οἵτινες ἂν λάχωσιν is retained (cf. **217**, commentary on lines 16–17). The ἐκκλησία is defined as that κυρία in the prytany of the phyle then in office, not merely as ἐπιοῦσα. For this as a probouleumatic decree cf. P. J. Rhodes, *Athenian Boule*, p. 254. The business is being passed quickly through all its stages; cf. **291**. Although the ἐκκλησία κυρία might well be any of the regular meetings of the prytany, it is probable that it was usually the second or third (cf. M. H. Hansen, *The Athenian Assembly*, 1987, p. 31, in reference to 4th-century practice). On this occasion it was fortunate that it had not already been held before so late a stage of the prytany, since business of this character, like decrees conferring citizenship, was surely required to come before it. That it cannot have been an assembly specially so designated, extra to the normal ἐκκλησία κυρία if that had already been held in this prytany, is precluded by the phraseology of line 42 and its restored continuation in line 43.

Lines 47–50. The designated games represent the full quota of four embodied in such provisions after 224 B.C. See **225**, commentary on lines 9–11.

Lines 50–52. The generals and the Military Treasurer are made responsible for the provision and proclamaion of the stephanos. The official(s) so charged varied according to the occasion; cf. **208**, lines 26–31, **248**, lines 20–22. See Henry (*Honours*, pp. 34–36), who notes this particular combination of generals and Treasurer only in the case of ephebic texts: but it is found also in **224**, lines 39–41, **225**, lines 12–13, and **249**, lines 4–6. Lines 55–56. For the functions of the thesmothetai in this connection see Busolt-Swoboda, II, 1926, pp. 1072–1073. *Dokimasia* in this and other particular cases, e.g., grants of citizenship (for which see Osborne, *Naturalization* III–IV, pp. 164–167), was their special province.

THE ARCHONSHIP OF PHANARCHIDES, 193/2 B.C.

The continuing analysis that finally brought Phanarchides, with his γραμματεύς [Μενέ]μαχος Μενεστράτου Λαμπτρεύς (Erechtheis I), into conjunction with 193/2 has provoked a more than ordinary series of revisions of opinion. The fact that Phanarchides, whose name is unique in Attic prosopography, had held the archonship had long been known from *IG* II², 844C, line 49 (lines 49–70 constituting the third of three decrees on this stele) and 916, line 8 (= *Agora* XV, 187, line 32, where the dating is to be corrected; see below and J. S. Traill, *Hesperia* 47, 1978, p. 327), in which the archon year is identified as that succeeding his (cf. *PA* 14000). He was listed by J. Kirchner (*IG* II², iv, 1, pp. 16–17) among the "archontes saeculi III quorum tempora accuratius definiri nequeunt" and by W. S. Ferguson (*Athenian Tribal Cycles*, p. 34) as "before or after 200".

W. B. Dinsmoor (*Archons of Athens*, pp. 252–254) set Phanarchides in 196/5 on the basis of the same two pieces of evidence, but by 1939 he had been compelled to revise this attribution (see p. 362 above on the archonship of Charikles). Moreover, the discovery of a new fragment of *IG* II², 864 (*Agora* XV, 186, where also the dating is to be corrected) provided the name of Phanarchides as archon in association for the first time with the γραμματεύς of his year, who proved to be a man from Lamptrai. This official had already been known from *IG* II², 886, in which the archon's name had not been preserved. Dinsmoor therefore moved Phanarchides to the year 193/2, in conformity with Ferguson's evaluation of the secretary cycle which he had then come to accept: see *Athenian Archon List*, pp. 184–185. And there he remained for a quarter of a century: see W. K. Pritchett and B. D. Meritt, *Chronology*, p. xxvi; Pritchett and O. Neugebauer, *Calendars*, p. 84; Meritt, *Hesperia* 26, 1957, p. 94, *Athenian Year*, p. 235 (cf. pp. 198–199).

The discovery of **262** confirmed the demotic of the γραμματεύς (and added four letters to his name); and it showed, by a calendar equation of the 25th of an unknown full month with the 25th of an unknown prytany, that the festival calendar was ordinary in Phanarchides' year. (As the twelfth year in the thirteenth Metonic cycle this in fact agreed with Meton's arrangement.) *IG* II², 844C had revealed no more than that the third prytany coincided with the month Boedromion, which as an indication was useful though insufficient: but *IG* II², 886 showed Gamelion 11 = pryt. VII, 11, and *Agora* XV, 186 showed Hekatombaion 25[9] = pryt. II, 3 (see Pritchett and Meritt, *Chronology*, pp. 112–113, corrected by Meritt, *Hesperia* 32, 1963, pp. 16–17, no. 15). Thus the year had already been recognizable as ordinary on the evidence available in 1939 and had been so indicated by Dinsmoor and others in the studies cited above.

Meritt's belief that **263** belonged to 191/90 as an ordinary year led him to the conclusion that 193/2 should have been intercalary, and in consequence he exchanged the archonship of Hippias, whose year was indeed intercalary and whose γραμματεύς was also of Erechtheis (I), for that of Phanarchides, who was thus removed to 181/80. See *TAPA* 95, 1964, pp. 238–239. Phanarchides appears as of this date in *Agora* XV, 186 (cf. 187) and in A. E. Samuel, *Greek and Roman Chronology*, 1972, p. 217. H. B. Mattingly found some additional indications in support of it (*Historia* 20, 1971, pp. 26–28). But this revision took place under two false assumptions, one that dates κατὰ θεόν were "specifically Metonic dates", and the other concerning the restoration of **263** as necessarily indicating an ordinary year. Meritt later withdrew it (*Historia* 26, 1977, pp. 161–162 and 180; cf. J. S. Traill, *Hesperia* 45, 1976, pp. 302–303, note 13), and the one decree of Phanarchides' year that the Agora has so far yielded (apart from the prytany text already referred to) is thus restored to 193/2, the date subsequently accepted for this archon: cf. C. Habicht, *Studien*, pp. 167, 177.

At the beginning of the year at least eight extra days were inserted into Hekatombaion, but these were doubtless compensated for shortly afterwards. By Gamelion the festival and prytany calendars were in accord, as they were also in **262**, the month of which should be full in the festival calendar (see above). Meetings of the assembly on the 25th of the month are attested for six of the Athenian months: see J. D. Mikalson, *Sacred and Civil Calendar*, p. 195. Among the first six prytanies there will have been three of 30 days and three of 29. Phylai identified in their respective prytanies are II Aiantis or Leontis (*Agora* XV, 186), III Pandionis (*IG* II², 844C), and VII Hippothontis (*IG* II², 886).

FRAGMENT OF A DECREE

262. The upper left corner of a pedimental stele of Pentelic marble (I 6156), broken below, at the back, and to the right, and with the left akroterion also partly broken away, discovered on April 18, 1949, in the Late Roman wall that runs east of the Panathenaic Way, at the central part of the Stoa of Attalos (O 9). The inscribed surface is considerably worn, and a coating of hard cement still clings to part of it. The wide horizontal cornice of the pediment surmounts an ovolo molding rather heavy in style, below which a narrow taenia descends to the surface of the inscribed face with an abrupt apophyge. A vacant space of 0.01 m. intervenes between this and the first line of text.

H. 0.21 m.; W. 0.195 m.; Th. 0.055 m.
LH. 0.005 m.

Ed. G. A. Stamires, *Hesperia* 26, 1957, pp. 31–32, no. 4, with photograph pl. 5. See also *SEG* XVI, 77.

a. 193/2 *a.*   NON-ΣTOIX. *ca.* 51–55

> ᾽Επὶ Φαναρχίδου ἄρχον[τος ἐπὶ τῆς . ⁴⁻⁵ . ίδος . . ⁵⁻⁶ . . ς πρυτανείας ἧι Μενέ]
> μαχος Μενεστράτου Λαμπτ[ρεὺς ἐγραμμάτευεν . . . *ca. 9* . . . ιῶνος]
> ἕκτει μετ᾽εἰκάδας, πέμπτ[ει καὶ εἰκοστεῖ τῆς πρυτανείας· ἐκκλησία]
> ἐν τῶι θεάτρωι· τῶν προ[έδρων ἐπεψήφιζεν . . . . *ca. 19* . . . .]
> 5 [Συπ]αλήττιος καὶ συμ[πρόεδροι· ἔδοξεν τεῖ βουλεῖ καὶ τῶι δήμωι]·
> [. *ca. 5* .]ίων Σ[. .]Ο[. .]Ε[– – –εἶπεν· –]
> [– –]

The restorations shown are those of Stamires. In lines 1–2 the possibility of Νικό]μαχος was raised by Stamires (see *SEG*, *loc. cit.*, in comm.), citing evidence collected by A. E. Raubitschek, *Hesperia* 11, 1942, p. 310. Line 6. So Stamires: [. *ca. 5* .]ίων Σευθ[ου] Σ[ουνιεὺς εἶπεν is a very possible interpretation of what may be discerned, in which case the proposer might be the father of the Σεύθης Σουνιεύς who was a βουλευτής in 173/2 (*Agora* XV, 206, line 71).

The writing on this fragment is thin, scratchy, and awkward but despite lack of exactitude shows no marked idiosyncrasy. The external strokes of mu and sigma are well angled. The stone proved too worn for S. V. Tracy to assign the lettering to an identifiable craftsman or school: see *Attic Letter-Cutters*, p. 31.

Lines 1–2. The name of (Mene)machos, son of Menestratos, of Lamptrai here slightly fills out previous knowledge which, from the composite evidence of Agora I 5573 (*Agora* XV, 186, fragment *a*) and *IG* II², 886, had been restricted to [– – – – –]ς Μενεστράτου Λαμ[πτρεύς]. He seems to have been a βουλευτής early in the 2nd century; cf. J. S. Traill, *Hesperia* 40, 1971, pp. 311–313, no. 10, line 24 (especially p. 313, note on line 24). Apart from the possible identification of his son (*PA* 273; *IG* II², 6640), nothing more is known of the family. Lines 3–4. For the location of the assembly see **167**, commentary on lines 6–7.

Line 5. The decree may be presumed to have been proboulematic; cf. P. J. Rhodes, *Athenian Boule*, p. 254.

THE ARCHONSHIP OF TIMOUCHOS(?), 191/90 B.C.

As a name in the table of Athenian archons Timouchos makes no appearance until the publication of B. D. Meritt's list of 1977 (*Historia* 26, p. 180), for his existence had remained unknown until the first edition in 1964 of the prytany list that subsequently became *Agora* XV, 163; see *SEG* XXI, 421. Even there it is not preserved in full and required a query mark where it appears in line 9. But, having been discovered, Timouchos appears to suit **263**; and his name has been introduced into *Agora* XV, 207, the date of which, there assigned to 173/2, is now to be amended (see Meritt, *op. cit.*, p. 163 and *SEG* XXVI, 105). Nevertheless the association remains somewhat tentative and awaits final proof or disproof.

The year 191/90 has emerged as a problem year in the evolution of the archon list. Its position within the secretary cycle requires a γραμματεύς from the phyle Pandionis (III), to which the deme Prasiai belonged (**263**, line 3). Originally attributed to 179/8, the next year available in the cycle, **263** was relocated in 191/90 when it became clear that Menedemos, the archon of 179/8, was to be associated with a γραμματεύς from Angele (see **278**). At an earlier stage of the study of the archon list, 191/90 had remained unassigned, except that W. B. Dinsmoor (*Archons of Athens*, p. 255; cf. p. 222) had placed *IG* II², 889 there, postulating a γραμματεύς from Leontis (IV); and the archon of the year would, in the state of knowledge at that time, have been the [. . . . .]ς surviving on that stone.

The identification of the archonship of Hippias, to which *IG* II², 889 proved to belong, invalidated this hypothesis, for Dinsmoor placed Hippias in 190/89; but he replaced it with the hesitant attribution to this year of *IG* II², 978 (*Athenian Archon List*, p. 186), in which the archon's name was nine letters in length and the γραμματεύς was Kephalos, whose *demoticum*, preserved as – – – – es, was restored as Κονθυλίδ]ης (Pandionis III). Subsequently, however, 191/90 was attributed to Hippias after all (see p. 384 below), for E. Schweigert observed (see **275**) that the evidence required Hippias' year to be intercalary. This led W. K. Pritchett and Meritt to date it, following his suggestion (*Hesperia* 9, 1940, p. 355), one year earlier than Dinsmoor had done, for in 191/90 it would fit more exactly into the series of intercalary and ordinary years as Dinsmoor and they had assessed it (*Chronology*, pp. xxvi and 116–117). The matter so remained until 1961, and in the meantime, when its γραμματεύς was more completely known on other evidence, *IG* II², 978 could be more definitely assigned to the archon Euthykritos (*SEG* XVI, 82). When Hippias was moved ten years on, to 181/80, this again left 191/90 untenanted (Meritt, *Athenian Year*, p. 235) until, as described above, it became by elimination the best year available for **263**. No attribution was made to it by A. E. Samuel (*Greek and Roman Chronology*, 1972, p. 217).

The name of the γραμματεύς of the year is not preserved in **263** or in *Agora* XV, 207 and was not considered by Meritt in his reedition of the former. But in *Agora* XV, 163, line 10 the letters Σωκ– – – appear to provide the beginning of his name, which, from the space available in the other two texts, must be short. C. Habicht (*Studien*, pp. 172–173), who accepted Timouchos(?) as the archon of this year (p. 177), regarded it as certain that the name must be Sokles. The name of Sokles' father must have been comparably short.

The year was the fourteenth in the thirteenth Metonic cycle. As such it was ordinary in the cycle, and **263** was at first restored to make it ordinary also in the Athenian festival calendar. However, the theory of the one is at this stage no necessary index of the practice of the other. Meritt at one time held that dates expressed κατὰ θεόν, as in **263**, indicated that the festival calendar was expressly following the arrangements of the Metonic cycle and interpreted the year of Timouchos in this light (*TAPA* 95, 1964, p. 238; cf. *Hesperia* 37, 1968, p. 236). But, although the festival calendar and Meton's calendar were in general accord in the 4th and early 3rd centuries, the connection cannot be rigidly applied thereafter; indeed, from the tenth cycle onward it demonstrably breaks down. See *Agora* XV, pp. 23–24. In earlier reconstructions (Dinsmoor, *Athenian Archon List*, p. 23; Meritt, *Athenian Year*, p. 235) 191/90 had appeared as intercalary, and **263** proved open to restoration on such a hypothesis.

Agora XV, 207 (see above) does indeed belong to an intercalary year and if correctly assigned indicates that Hippothontis held the eleventh prytany. Beyond this there is no calendric evidence; the prytanies evidently ran in a straight sequence of 32 days each. This pattern would be unaffected by the fact that in Thargelion the festival calendar had been interfered with by the archon, who had interpolated seven days into it, with the result that Thargelion 11 according to him was Thargelion 18 "according to god". Forty-one days remained in the year, and it is likely that the readjustment was made before the end of the same month.

FRAGMENT OF A DECREE

263. A fragment of a stele of Pentelic marble (I 1318), with the right edge preserved but broken and much battered elsewhere, discovered on February 10, 1934, in a wall of a cellar of a modern house south of the central part of the Middle Stoa (M 14). Above the inscribed face are the remains of a heavy crowning molding, the characteristics of which have been obliterated by the damage to the stone.

H. 0.15 m.; W. 0.074 m.; Th. 0.097 m.
LH. 0.005–0.006 m.

Ed. B. D. Meritt, *Hesperia* 5, 1936, pp. 428–429, no. 16, with photograph. Further discussion by Meritt, *Hesperia* 34, 1965, p. 89 (revision of the date; see also *SEG* XXII, 102 and *TAPA* 95, 1964, p. 238), and Ἀρχ. Ἐφ., 1968, p. 96 (with a revised text; see also *SEG* XXV, 113). Further revision, with restorations as for an intercalary year, by Meritt, *Historia* 26, 1977, p. 162: see also *SEG* XXVI, 106. The date κατὰ θεόν in line 5 discussed or cited also by W. K. Pritchett and O. Neugebauer, *Calendars*, pp. 15, 19, 85; Pritchett, *Ancient Athenian Calendars on Stone*, p. 337.

a. 191/90 a.(?), pryt. IX   NON-ΣΤΟΙΧ. 22–26

```
      ['Επὶ Τιμούχου(?) ἄρχοντ]ος ἐπ[ὶ]
      [τῆς ...ca. 10... ἐνάτης π]ρυτα
      [νείας ἧι Σωκλῆς .ca. 5.] Πρα[σ]ιεὺς
      [ἐγραμμάτευεν· Ἀνθεστ]ηριῶνος
   5  [ἕνηι καὶ νέαι κατὰ θε]όν, ἐνά[τηι]
      [τῆς πρυτανείας· ἐκκλησ]ία κυ[ρία]·
      [τῶν προέδρων ἐπεψήφιζ]εν Ε[.3-4.]
      [————————————————————]
```

The restorations, except for the name of the γραμματεύς (see above), are those of Meritt, *Historia, loc. cit.* He had previously restored ὀγδόης in line 2 and ἐνάτηι ἱσταμένου κατὰ θε]όν in line 5. That line 1, as restored, contains no more than 22 letters, while the other lines are required to contain 24, 25, or 26, without demonstrable variations in size or spacing, may offer reason for doubt concerning the archon but does not rule the name out of court. A name with ten or eleven letters in the genitive case might perhaps be preferable.

S. V. Tracy's examination of the lettering of this text concluded that it was in the style of, but not with assurance to be ascribed to, the "Cutter of Agora I 656 + 6355", whose datable career spanned the four decades from 203/2 to 164/3 (*Attic Letter-Cutters*, p. 84). For details see **260**, and cf. also **258**. This general indication accords with the dating already discussed.

Lines 4–5. The last day of Anthesterion is twice clearly attested (in the 3rd century) as a day on which the assembly met, and this serves to corroborate the restoration here. See J. D. Mikalson, *Sacred and Civil Calendar*, pp. 119–120. The festival date is given κατὰ θεόν, without a corresponding date κατ'ἄρχοντα. Contrast *Agora* XV, 207, where both are given. This detail formed part of the evidence used by Pritchett and Neugebauer to advance the hypothesis that all dates not specified are to be interpreted as dates κατ'ἄρχοντα rather than κατὰ θεόν (*op. cit.*, pp. 17 and 19). The κατὰ θεόν date represented the "normal" date in the Athenian festival calendar, generally in accord with the astronomical calendar of full and hollow months. See also Pritchett, *Ancient Athenian Calendars on Stone*, pp. 339–340; Meritt, *TAPA* 95, 1964, pp. 230–235, Ἀρχ. Ἐφ., 1968, pp. 96–97, 105. It may originally have been envisaged as identical with the calendar of Meton (see above) but had long ceased to be so in practice and simply followed a pattern determined in advance in relation to the lunar cycle. Accepting that dates without specification are to be regarded as κατ'ἄρχοντα dates, Meritt argued that, in this instance, the inclusion of the phrase κατὰ θεόν shows that the civil date could at times be the κατὰ θεόν date even if not so specified. It is to be observed that all dating quoted κατὰ θεόν and κατ'ἄρχοντα falls, on the evidence, within the period 195/4 to 95/4, which may suggest a new consciousness at this time that the Athenian calendar had not, in recent decades, been managed (or at least recorded) with sufficiently explicit care. It may further be suggested that unspecified dates are generally to be regarded as dates both κατὰ θεόν and κατ'ἄρχοντα, since the government would ordinarily agree with god's time unless it had good reason to juggle with it. In the present case, the omission of a date κατ'ἄρχοντα may plausibly be seen as the result of the mason's oversight or as an indication (as Meritt envisaged) that where tampering had taken place the γραμματεύς did not feel obliged to record the revised date in preference to, or as well as, the "normal" one.

Line 6. ἐκκλησία κυρία. See **101**, commentary on lines 7–8.

THE ARCHONSHIP OF ACHAIOS, 190/89 B.C.

IG II², 946 and 947 contain in their prescripts the name of Achaios as archon together with parts of the name of the γραμματεύς of his year, Herakleon, son of Nannakos, of Eupyridai (Leontis IV), parts that were mutually complementary and enabled the whole to be established. A small portion of Herakleon's name survives in *IG* II², 948, enough to make it clear that that text also belongs to Achaios' year. Once these associations had been made, the position of Achaios in the archon list appeared relatively assured. The secretary cycle called for 166/5 as his year, and this was generally agreed (see J. Kirchner, *IG* II², iv, 1, pp. 18–19; W. S. Ferguson, *Athenian Tribal Cycles*, p. 29; B. D. Meritt, *Hesperia* 3, 1934, p. 23; S. Dow, *Prytaneis*, pp. 135–136).

But the more recent relocation of Achaios in 190/89 (see below) was in fact no more than a reassertion, on new and better grounds, of an old proposal. For earlier views had been divergent, and there had been an inclination to set Achaios early in the 2nd century: on these theories, which need not be detailed here, see W. B. Dinsmoor, *Archons of Athens*, pp. 222 and 258–259: and Kirchner for a while preferred the very date now adopted, 190/89, which is the only possible alternative to 166/5 both available and permitted by the secretary cycle (see *IG* II², 946, commentary). Dinsmoor's own date of 167/6, conditioned by his one-year deviation from Ferguson's cycle, was abandoned in 1939; see *Athenian Archon List*, pp. 171 and 189, where Achaios was returned to 166/5. From this location he was not disturbed for the next generation; see W. K. Pritchett and Meritt, *Chronology*, pp. xxix and 127; Pritchett and O. Neugebauer, *Calendars*, p. 85; Meritt, *Hesperia* 26, 1957, p. 95, *Athenian Year*, pp. 175–176, 183–184, 236, *TAPA* 95, 1964, pp. 237, 242–247, 'Αρχ. 'Εφ., 1968, pp. 94–96, *Historia* 26, 1977, p. 182; A. E. Samuel, *Greek and Roman Chronology*, 1972, p. 218. In *Ancient Athenian Calendars on Stone*, pp. 332–334 *et alibi*, Pritchett avoided a mention of the year in terms of the Christian eras.

This well-accepted attribution was, however, challenged by S. V. Tracy's examination of the stylistic criteria provided by the craftsmen who cut the inscriptions concerned. He was able to determine that *Agora* XV, 216, a prytany text discovered in 1932 (see Meritt, *Hesperia* 3, 1934, pp. 21–27; Dow, *Prytaneis*, pp. 135–136), was inscribed by the "Cutter of *IG* II² 912", whose datable output is confined within the period 226/5 to *ca.* 190: see **237** for details of his style and work. It is indeed *Agora* XV, 216, with its clear statement of the names of both archon and γραμματεύς, which offers his latest datable evidence, and to extend his career as far as 166/5 is obviously impossible. See Tracy, *AJAH* 9, 1984, pp. 43–47 and *Attic Letter-Cutters*, p. 57. Since the sole alternative for Achaios remained 190/89, which the craftsman's career could certainly accommodate (*Agora* XV, 187 = *IG* II², 916, of 192/1, is also his work), this redating called for a more general revision of archon attributions (for example, of the archon Demetrios, displaced from this year) and occasioned wider historical consequences: see C. Habicht, *Hesperia* 57, 1988, p. 245 and *Hesperia* 59, 1990, pp. 564–567. Arguments for the retention of the archonship of Achaios in 166/5 were nevertheless reemphasized by J. S. Traill, *ZPE* 103, 1994, pp. 112–113.

It is however the vicissitudes of the Athenian festival calendar rather than the identity of the archon that constitute the great problem of the year, and these, though not taken into account or affecting the transfer to 190/89, were much discussed in the context of 166/5. Meritt wrote of Achaios' year as he saw it that "with [it] we are confronted with one of the most serious anomalies in the festival calendar" (*Athenian Year*, p. 183). The three decrees *IG* II², 946–948, together with *Agora* XV, 216 and **264**, present calendric data as follows (in chronological order, to the extent that the evidence permits):

Agora XV, 216:	Maimakterion 5 = pryt. VI, 5 or 6, as restored
IG II², 946:	Anthesterion 29 κατ'ἄρχοντα = Elaphebolion 27 κατὰ θεόν = pryt. IX, 27
IG II², 947:	Mounichion 12 κατ'ἄρχοντα = Thargelion 12 κατὰ θεόν = pryt. XI, 12
IG II², 948:	? 13? = pryt. ?, 13
264:	? 14 = pryt. ?, 14.

The year was demonstrably ordinary, but the two clear pieces of evidence show that the festival and prytany calendars were consistently and precisely a month apart. A further decree, **276**, may belong to Achaios' year, but in any case it provides no data helpful in the present context and may be left out of account. The date of *Agora* XV, 216, the nature of which is not specified, must be a κατ'ἄρχοντα date, supporting Pritchett's contention that all unspecified dates in the festival calendar were to be reckoned as such (*Calendars*, p. 19). In *IG* II², 948, **264**, and also **276** if it belongs in this year, it may similarly be supposed that the festival dates are those κατ'ἄρχοντα, again running precisely one month at variance with the calendar κατὰ θεόν.

In 'Αρχ. 'Εφ., 1968, pp. 93–96 and *Historia* 26, 1977, pp. 164–165, Meritt found reason to argue that the year 167/6, planned as an ordinary year, was altered so as to contain thirteen months, causing an overrun into what he regarded as Achaios' year, with the result that Achaios did not take office κατ'ἄρχοντα until a month of "his" natural year had elapsed. This, Meritt urged, also had an effect on the year of Pelops (165/4), which became a thirteen-month year beginning with the Skirophorion properly belonging to Achaios. But with the relocation of Achaios in 190/89 this contention can no longer stand. There is nothing in the years of Timouchos(?) (see pp. 369–370 above) or of Euthykritos (189/8) to suggest any calendric difficulty save for a very minor problem in the latter (see Meritt, *Athenian Year*, pp. 149–150). Both years were intercalary, and the data show no irregularity. What caused the extraordinary deviations of Achaios' year remains unknown, but the discrepancy of one complete month between the festival and prytany calendars for so much of the year (all of it, indeed, for which evidence exists), compounded by further minor discrepancy in Anthesterion/Elaphebolion, is without parallel in Athenian calendric history. On the "triple dating" see also A. S. Henry, *Prescripts*, pp. 78–80.

Of phylai holding office in what were twelve regular prytanies, no single name is preserved despite the comparative extent of the calendric details surviving in the prescripts of the five decrees concerned.

FRAGMENT OF A DECREE

264. Four major and several minor fragments of a pedimental stele of Hymettian marble (I 4241), so joined as to preserve the entire width of the pediment, with all three akroteria, and the entire width also of the inscribed face but with the surface so extensively sheared away that only a small portion of the upper left part of the inscription survives, from the preserved left edge almost to the median vertical line of the stele as determined by the central akroterion. The original fragment (that on the extreme left, preserving the left corner of the text with the left angle of the pediment and the akroterion) was discovered on June 1, 1936, in an Early Roman context over a wall of the Square Peristyle (lawcourt complex) west of the north end of the Stoa of Attalos (P 8). The subsequent fragments were discovered on July 30, 1953, in a context running from the 4th century B.C. to the middle of the Roman period, in foundation packing of the monopteros west of the north end of the Stoa of Attalos (P 8). The vertical striations of a toothed chisel are visible on the inscribed surface.

H. 0.42 m.; W. 0.47 m.; Th. 0.09 m.

LH. 0.006 m. (omicron in three of four occurrences 0.004 m.).

Ed. original fragment only: W. K. Pritchett and B. D. Meritt, *Chronology*, pp. 127–128, with photograph. All fragments: Meritt, *Hesperia* 23, 1954, p. 240, no. 10, with photograph pl. 51. See also *SEG* XIV, 75.

a. 190/89 *a.*   NON-ΣTOIX. *ca.* 49

'Επὶ 'Αχαιοῦ ἄρχοντος ἐπὶ τῆ[ς . . . .^{ca. 17} . . . . πρυτανείας ἧι]
'Ηρακλέων ⟨Ν⟩αννάκου Εὐπυ[ρίδης ἐγραμμάτευεν· . . .^{ca. 8} . . . ῶνος]
τετρ[άδι ἐπὶ] δέκα, τετά[ρτει καὶ δεκάτει τῆς πρυτανείας· ἐκκλη]
σία κ[υρία ἐν τῶι θεάτ[ρωι· τῶν προέδρων ἐπεψήφιζεν . .^{ca. 8} . . .]
5   Νικ[--]
[--]

The text is that of *SEG* XIV, 75 save that in line 2 it had been previously overlooked that the mason was guilty of haplography and wrote ΗΡΑΚΛΕΩΝΑΝΝΑΚΟΥ, a point observed also by S. V. Tracy, *Attic Letter-Cutters*, p. 108.

Tracy ascribed this text, together with sixty-six others, to the craftsman whom he designated the "Cutter of Agora I 247" (*op. cit.*, pp. 99–109, with photograph of part of the name piece, fig. 12). This style is economical to the point of being tachygraphic, notable for the frequency, amounting to regularity, with which the crossbar of alpha, central horizontal of epsilon, and central dot of theta are omitted. Circular or curved letters are perfunctorily cut, sometimes as a series of straight strokes. This mason's datable career covered some forty-five years, from 194/3 to 148/7, which serves to account for the evidently abundant output of his workshop. The present text, an early work of his, is the first of ten *psephismata* in this collection assigned to him: see also **276, 279, 280, 283–288,** and **332E.**

W. B. Dinsmoor learned of the original fragment in time to refer to it (as of the archonship of A–––––) in *Athenian Archon List,* p. 167, note 237, and assigned it to the archonship of Antiphilos (224/3), believing it to have been written in the "disjointed style" current at that time. Pritchett and Meritt demonstrated that this was a false estimate; and in any case enough was preserved of the name of the γραμματεύς to assure the attribution, confirmed by the evidence of the subsequent discovery.

Line 2. The name Nannakos is otherwise unknown to Athenian prosopography. Other members of the deme Eupyridai named Herakleon are attested as councillors and epheboi in the imperial period (*PA* 6511); see *Agora* XV, pp. 402–403. Lines 3–4. For the location of the assembly see **167,** commentary on lines 6–7, and for the designation as κυρία, **101,** commentary on lines 7–8. The assembly took place on the fourteenth day of an unknown month. J. D. Mikalson's analysis showed that this is an attested meeting day of the assembly in only three months out of the twelve, Boedromion, Elaphebolion, and Thargelion (*Sacred and Civil Calendar,* calendar I on p. 184). It is a reasonable hypothesis that the name of the month to be supplied here is likely to be one of these three.

THE ARCHONSHIP OF SYMMACHOS, 188/7 B.C.

In the didascalic list *IG* II², 2323, the archonships of Symmachos, Theoxenos, and Zopyros appear in sequence (see *SEG* XXV, 194, lines 236–238; W. B. Dinsmoor, *Archons of Athens,* pp. 464–470). Symmachos' archonship is well attested epigraphically, and **265** no more than adds to the cumulative evidence, long known, that the γραμματεύς of his year belonged to the phyle Akamantis (VI). In accordance with the then newly evaluated secretary cycle, he was placed in 188/7 by W. S. Ferguson (*Athenian Secretaries,* p. 55) and was retained there by J. Kirchner (*IG* II², iv, 1, pp. 18–19). Dinsmoor's application of the cycle differed by a year from that of Ferguson at this point, and his date was therefore 189/8 (*op. cit.,* p. 255; cf. p. 222), but the principle of evaluation remained the same. Ferguson repeated his original estimate (*Athenian Tribal Cycles,* p. 28), and Dinsmoor revised his opinion (*Athenian Archon List,* p. 171, 187; cf. p. 23), accepting Symmachos as of 188/7, in which year he has remained ever since: see W. K. Pritchett and B. D. Meritt, *Chronology,* p. xxvii; Pritchett and O. Neugebauer, *Calendars,* pp. 29–30; Meritt, *AJP* 78, 1957, pp. 375–381, *Hesperia* 26, 1957, pp. 65–66, 94, *Athenian Year,* pp. 154–158, 236, *TAPA* 95, 1964, p. 240, *Klio* 52, 1970, pp. 277–282 (where all the material of this year is assembled), *Historia* 26, 1977, p. 180; C. Habicht, *Studien,* p. 177. E. Manni (*Athenaeum* 33, 1955, pp. 259, note 2, and 265) did indeed revive the suggestion of 189/8, but that this was not a viable proposition was briefly and sufficiently demonstrated by Habicht, *AthMitt* 76, 1961, p. 130, note 6.

It is the calendric character of 188/7 rather than its attribution to a named archon that has provided its major cause of difficulty. Symmachos' year was regarded as certainly intercalary by Kirchner (*loc. cit.,* and *IG* II², 892, commentary) and by earlier commentators, and this supposition formed the basis of the restorations shown in *IG* II², 890–893 and in the *editio princeps* of **265.** As such, it followed two ordinary years in Dinsmoor's revised (1939) table and in that of Pritchett and Meritt, *Chronology,* p. xxvii. Pritchett and Neugebauer, however, reconsidered the calendric data of the five texts of the year and concluded that the evidence was best served by regarding the year as ordinary, even though this involved discrepancies between the festival and prytany calendars in *IG* II², 891 (*SEG* XVI, 83, XXI, 430) and in **265** (*Calendars,* pp. 84–85). This conclusion was accepted by Meritt, *AJP* 78, 1957, pp. 375–381, whose revised study of *IG* II², 891 and 893 (*SEG* XVI, 84, XXI, 434) pointed in that direction and in fact lessened the disturbance in the calendar that had of necessity been postulated. It was the more to be recommended since Meritt also discovered, on the basis of the newly supplemented prytany text *Agora* XV, 173 (*SEG* XVI, 81, XXVI, 107), that 189/8, the year of Euthykritos, must be considered intercalary, and the hypothesis of two intercalary years in succession was unacceptable (*Hesperia* 26, 1957, pp. 65–66). He reviewed all the evidence in *Athenian Year,* pp. 154–158 (see *SEG* XXI, 430–434), and was able to devise a satisfactory arrangement of months and prytanies, with alternation of 29 and 30 days among the former (save that both Metageitnion and Boedromion were to be regarded as full), and in the latter one prytany of 30 days followed by six of 29 and five more of 30.

But to maintain regularity in the calendric equation of *IG* II², 892 (*SEG* XXI, 433) required forward count with the date μετ'εἰκάδας, and Meritt's subsequent conviction was that all such dates involved backward count ('Ἀρχ. 'Ἐφ., 1968, pp. 77–91; cf. Pritchett, *Ancient Athenian Calendars on Stone*, pp. 349–353). Hence he returned to a study of this year in *Klio* 52, 1970, pp. 277–282, where he added *IG* II², 954 and 955 to the five pieces of evidence already recognized, these two being in his view attributable to the same day as *IG* II², 892 (Mounichion 29 = pryt. X, 29). *IG* II², 954 is however in all probability to be dissociated from the other texts; see **276**. Meritt's evaluation of the year (of 355 days) was revised to a pattern (in the festival calendar) of alternation of months of 30 and 29 days, with the exception that full Pyanopsion followed full Boedromion, and a prytany calendar of five prytanies of 30 days followed by four of 29, two of 30, and one more of 29. For the irregularity of the calendar in **265**, as already noted, see the commentary *ad loc*.

The year was seventeenth in the Metonic cycle, and that that year was ordinary in the Athenian festival calendar coincided, as it happened, with the arrangement of Meton's system. Of the prytanizing phylai, Aigeis is attested for the ninth prytany, Leontis for the tenth, and Antiochis for the twelfth. For *IG* II², 890, of the sixth prytany but with phyle unknown, see *Agora* XV, 174; *IG* II², 891, with phyle equally unknown, probably belongs to the fifth prytany.

FRAGMENT OF A DECREE

265. A fragment from the upper left corner of a pedimental stele of Hymettian marble (I 4144), with the left side and original rough-picked back preserved, as well as a very battered section of crowning molding and pediment, but broken elsewhere, discovered on May 14, 1936, in a late wall west of the Odeion (J 11).

H. 0.27 m.; W. 0.38 m.; Th. 0.13 m.

LH. 0.005 m.

Ed. W. K. Pritchett, *Hesperia* 15, 1946, pp. 144–146, no. 6, with photograph. See also Pritchett and O. Neugebauer, *Calendars*, pp. 29 and 84. Revised text of lines 1–4 by B. D. Meritt, *Athenian Year*, p. 156; see also *SEG* XXI, 432, for complete text. Lines 1–4 again revised by Meritt, *Klio* 52, 1970, p. 281.

a. 188/7 *a., pryt.* IX   NON-ΣΤΟΙΧ. *ca.* 58

```
        Ἐπὶ Συμμάχου ἄρχοντος ἐπ[ὶ τῆς Αἰγεῖδος ἐνάτης πρυτανείας ἧι Ἀρχι]
        [κ]λῆς Θεοδώρου Θορίκιος ἐ[γραμμάτευεν· δήμου ψήφισμα· Ἐλαφηβολιῶνος]
        ὀγ[δ]όει ἐπὶ δέκα, μιᾶι κα[ὶ εἰκοστεῖ τῆς πρυτανείας· ἐκκλησία κυρία ἐν τῶι]
        θε[ά]τρωι· τῶν πρ[οέδρων ἐπεψήφιζεν ————————————————καὶ συμ]
    5   [πρ]όεδροι· ᵛ ἔ[δοξεν τῶι δήμωι· ————————————————εἶπεν· ἐπειδὴ]
        [. . ⁵ . .]κρατ[————————————————————————————————————————]
        [. . ⁵ . .]θυ[—————————————————————————————————————————]
        [————————————————————————————————————————————————————]
```

The above text is based on Meritt's final evaluation of the calendric data. Line 1. The name of the phyle was left unrestored by Meritt, *Klio, loc. cit.*; Αἰγεῖδος J. Labarbe, on the basis of *Agora* XV, 176, see *SEG* XXVIII, 78; ἐπ[ὶ τῆς Ἀντιοχίδος δωδεκάτης πρυτανείας Pritchett; ἐπ[ὶ τῆς ———————ὀγδόης πρυτανείας Meritt (1961). Line 2 *ad fin.* Σκιροφοριῶνος Pritchett; Ἀνθεστηριῶνος Meritt (1961). Line 3. τῆς πρυτανείας· ᵛᵛ ἐκκλησία ἐν τῶι] Pritchett.

This inscription is the third of four among the Agora *psephismata* in this collection attributed by S. V. Tracy to the "Cutter of Agora I 656 + 6355", and it falls almost at the middle point of his datable career: for this and other details see **260**. Besides **261** and **268**, also assigned to him, **258** and **263** are in his general style, on Tracy's assessment, even if not assuredly by his hand.

Lines 1–2. Archikles, son of Theodoros, of Thorikos (*PA* 2499) is not known beyond his tenure as γραμματεύς in this year. He was presumably a relative (nephew?) of the Ἀρχικλῆς Θορίκιος (*PA* 2498) who was θεσμοθέτης in the archonship of Diokles (215/14): see *IG* II², 1706, line 105. Line 2. δήμου ψήφισμα. So Pritchett, but ψηφίσματα could be accommodated. See **258**, commentary on line 2. Lines 2–3. Elaphebolion 18 is equated with pryt. IX, 21. The date of the month indicates the 255th day of the year; on reckoning by prytanies it is the 258th day. It is to be supposed that three extra days had been inserted into the calendar as ἐμβόλιμοι and that the irregularity had not yet been eliminated by a compensating omission. Such an insertion occurred most usually in Elaphebolion, in connection with the festival of the Dionysia, and the irregularity led Meritt to prefer this month in his proposed restoration. There is no evidence of such insertion and compensation in the last month of the year, Skirophorion.

See Meritt, *Klio* 52, 1970, p. 281 and the discussion of the archonship of Pytharatos, p. 268 above. For meetings of the assembly on Elaphebolion 18 see J. D. Mikalson, *Sacred and Civil Calendar*, p. 130. His references to the date of the assembly in this text (pp. 116 and 173) are to restorations already discarded.

Lines 3–4. On the location and character of the assembly see **264**, commentary on lines 3–4 and references there. Line 5. The restoration, which must allow for the proposer's name, patronymic, and demotic, indicates this as a nonprobouleumatic decree: cf. P. J. Rhodes, *Athenian Boule*, pp. 64–68, 265.

THE ARCHONSHIP OF THEOXENOS, 187/6 B.C.

That the year of Theoxenos succeeded that of Symmachos and preceded that of Zopyros has long been recognized on the evidence of the didascalic list *IG* II², 2323 (*SEG* XXV, 194), lines 236–238; see p. 373 above on the year of Symmachos. His date has therefore remained, throughout all discussions, in a constant relationship to that of Symmachos, the absolute date assigned to him differing only in the minor variations already noted in the dating of the latter, to the above account of which it is sufficient to refer.

Theoxenos is mentioned as archon in *IG* II², 1329, in which the orgeones of the cult of the Magna Mater honored, in the year of Sonikos (175/4), Chaireas of Athmonon, who had been their treasurer since this year (lines 4–6). The cavalry of Symmachos' year honored their hipparchoi in the year following, *SEG* XXI, 435 and 436 being dated by Theoxenos' archonship (on the date see C. Habicht, *AthMitt* 76, 1961, p. 130, note 6). These, with the reference in the didascalic list and with **266**, comprise the total of the epigraphical evidence.

It was clear from the secretary cycle that the γραμματεύς of Theoxenos' year must belong to the phyle Oineis (VII); but his identity was unknown in earlier discussions (cf. *IG* II², iv, 1, pp. 18–19; W. B. Dinsmoor, *Archons of Athens*, p. 255; W. S. Ferguson, *Athenian Tribal Cycles*, p. 28). The discovery of **266** supplied the lack, even though the archon's name is in fact missing from it. The fragment came to light in time to be taken into account by Dinsmoor in *Athenian Archon List*, p. 187; he suggested its attribution to Theoxenos' year and restored the fragmentary demotic Π---- as Π[εριθοίδης, Perithoidai being conveniently a deme of Oineis and Bioteles being an unusual name attested, to Dinsmoor's knowledge, from there alone (*PA* 2853; but for a Bioteles from Rhamnous see J. Sundwall, *Nachträge zur Prosopographia Attica*, 1910, p. 42). This attribution was adopted in the *editio princeps* of the text and was generally accepted thereafter.

The year was the eighteenth in the thirteenth Metonic cycle, but although it was intercalary in the cycle (cf. B. D. Meritt, *TAPA* 95, 1964, p. 236), it was ordinary in the Athenian festival calendar. This is demonstrable from **266** but had been postulated by Dinsmoor (*Archons of Athens*, p. 32) and by Ferguson (*loc. cit.*) on the basis that the year of Zopyros after it was intercalary and that of Symmachos before it was at that time believed to have been so. By the tenth prytany, during which Erechtheis was the phyle in prytany, the prytany and festival calendars appear to have become out of phase by two days: cf. W. K. Pritchett and O. Neugebauer, *Calendars*, p. 85. But Meritt showed (*Athenian Year*, p. 138) that this calendar equation was compatible with a festival calendar of regularly alternating full and hollow months, coordinated with an arrangement of prytanies whereby six prytanies each of 29 days were followed by six of 30 days. This would result in the enactment of **266** on the 277th day of the year, on the reckoning of both calendars, without any implication of irregularity in either of them.

DECREE IN HONOR OF A FRIEND OF SELEUKOS IV

266. A fragment of the upper section of a stele of Hymettian marble (I 2155), with part of the left edge and the original rough-picked back preserved and with the spring of a crowning molding above the inscribed face, discovered on December 8, 1934, in a wall of a modern house east of the southern part of the Odeion (N–O 11). Documentary evidence of this text also survives, of which Eugene Vanderpool has written as follows (letter of March 22, 1972):

> The inscription was found where the house of L. F. S. Fauvel, French consul in Athens from 1807 to 1813, had stood in the early nineteenth century, and many marbles known to have belonged to Fauvel have been found in the area. Until recently, however, there had been no direct evidence that I 2155 had ever been in Fauvel's possession.
>
> In the summer of 1970 the Gennadius Library acquired at auction in London a sketch book containing a collection of some seventy-five drawings executed in Athens between the years 1810 and 1813 for the Honourable Frederic North, later the fifth Lord Guilford. On page 25 of the sketch book there is a partial copy of this inscription with the notation that it belonged to Fauvel (ἐκ τῶν τοῦ Φαυβέλου)—a piece of information which coincides nicely with the place of finding of the inscription.

What we have in the sketch book is not a simple transcription of the text but rather a sort of partial squeeze or rubbing made by moistening the paper and applying it to the face of the stone with a little pressure over a small area so as to obtain an impression of the letters. The letters were then pencilled in. Because the book was already bound when this was done, only a small area could be 'squeezed' at any one time, and as a result we have eight short snippets of text from different parts of the stone.

The first two lines of the squeeze give the first line of the stone. At the beginning the *chi* of [ἄρ]χοντος is visible as an impression on the paper, but it was not pencilled in. At the end of the line we read Ἐρεχθε[ῖδος], of which the third *epsilon* is visible as an impression on the paper but was not pencilled in. Since the stone shows only the letters EPE, we see that a fragment three letters wide at this point has been broken away at the right since the early nineteenth century.

The letters ΛΟΥ ΔΟ in the third line of the squeeze do not appear on the stone as it now exists. They are unevenly spaced and perhaps therefore not consecutive.

The fourth line of the squeeze preserves part of the phrase ὑπὸ τοῦ βασιλέως to be found in line 10 on the stone. The occurrence of the phrase clinches the identity of copy and stone.

The letters ΓΝΗΤΟΣ of line 5 of the squeeze should go with ΔΙΟΓ of line 6 of the stone, and give the name of the chairman of the proedroi as Διόγνητος. We see that at this point five letters have been lost at the right since the early nineteenth century.

Of the remaining lines of the squeeze, the letters TON are to be found in line 12 of the stone, ΔΗΜΩΙ in line 11 or perhaps the missing part of line 8, and NKOIN in line 11.

Letters derived from this copy and not now extant are underlined in the text below.

H. 0.24 m.; W. 0.285 m.; Th. 0.115 m.
LH. 0.007 m. (omicron varies between 0.004 and 0.007 m.).

Ed. W. K. Pritchett and B. D. Meritt, *Chronology*, pp. 117–118, with photograph.

a. 187/6 a., pryt. X   NON-ΣΤΟΙΧ. *ca.* 41–52

```
        [Θ          ε]          o          [ι.
   ['Επὶ Θεοξένου ἄρ]χοντος ἐπὶ τῆς Ἐρεχθε[ῖδος δεκάτης]
   [πρυτ]ανείας ἧι Βιοτέλης Λευκίου Π[εριθοίδης ἐγραμμά]
   [τε]υεν· Μουνυχιῶνος ἑνδεκάτηι, τ[ρίτηι καὶ δεκάτηι]
5  [τῆ]ς πρυτανείας· ἐκκλησία κυρία [ἐν τῶι θεάτρωι]·
   [τ]ῶν προέδρων ἐπεψήφιζεν Διόγνητος [------]
   Χολαργεὺς καὶ συμπρόεδροι·        vacat
             ἔδοξεν τεῖ βουλεῖ καὶ [τ]ῶι δ[ήμωι]·
   Κτήσων Καλλικλέους Κολλυτεὺς εἶπεν· ἐπειδὴ -----τιμώ]
10 [μεν]ος ὑπὸ τοῦ βασιλέως Σελεύκου καὶ ὧν ἐμ [προαγωγῆι μεγάληι εὔ]
   [νους] ἐστὶν κοινεῖ τε [τ]ῶι δήμωι καὶ ἰδίαι το[ῖς τῶν πολιτῶν ἀφι]
   [κνο]υμένοις πρὸς τὸν βασιλέα [Σελ]ε[υκ]ον [--------------]
   [--------------------------------------------]
```

The letters of this text are well but irregularly spaced (hence the considerable variation in the number of them per line), and there is wide interlinear space. The lettering gives an appearance of neatness, but on closer inspection some of the letters are not well or consistently executed. S. V. Tracy found that *IG* II², 892 and 925 (for which see below) shared the same characteristics, and these three texts form the complete identifiable *oeuvre* of the mason he named the "Cutter of *IG* II² 892": see *Attic Letter-Cutters*, pp. 117–120, with photograph of fragment a of the name piece, fig. 15. This limits the mason's known and datable career to just two years, 188–186 B.C. *IG* II², 925 contains no indication of date and was given by J. Kirchner the general dating "c. init. s. II": in his republication of it, M. J. Osborne (*Naturalization* I, pp. 217–218, D 104, *Naturalization* II, p. 191) dated it "*ca.* 190–166/5". In lines 7–8 the prescript exemplifies the "perfect design", for which see **204** and references there.

Tracy went on to urge (*op. cit.*, pp. 119–120) that *IG* II², 925 is in fact to be regarded as "almost certainly" part of the same inscription as the present fragment. If so, it reveals that King Seleukos' envoy received Athenian citizenship and a stephanos as the result of this decree. *IG* II², 925 is a small fragment preserving part of the left edge of the stele, and Osborne's text of it is for convenience reproduced here:

```
   [----------------------------------------]
   [...] τὸν δῆμ[ον τὸν Ἀθηναίων καὶ ἀνειπεῖν τὸν στέφανον]
   τοῦτον Δ[ιονυσίων τῶν ἐν ἄστει τραγωιδῶν τῶι καινῶι ἀγῶ]
```

νι· τῆς δὲ ἀ[ναγορεύσεως ἐπιμεληθῆναι τοὺς στρατηγούς]·
δεδόσθα[ι δὲ αὐτῶι καὶ πολιτείαν δοκιμασθέντι ἐν τῶι δι]
5 καστηρ[ίωι· τοὺς δὲ θεσμοθέτας, ὅταν πληρῶσι δικαστήρια]
εἰς ἕν[α καὶ πεντακοσίους δικαστάς, εἰσαγαγεῖν τὴν δοκι]
μασ[ίαν τῆς πολιτογραφίας· γράψασθαι δὲ αὐτὸν φυλῆς καὶ δή]
μου [καὶ φρατρίας ἧς ἂν βούληται· ―――――――――]
[――――――――――――――――――――――――――――――]

Line 3. Βιοτέλης Λευκίου Περιθοίδης was probably the father of Παυσανίας Βιοτέλου Περιθοίδης, the γραμματεύς of the year of Sonikos (175/4), and thus to be identified with *PA* 2853. Cf. *PA* 11723; *Agora* XV, 199 and 200 (lines 1–2 in each case). That the name Λεύκιος belonged to this family in the preceding generation might appear to suggest the early stages of Italian influence and Roman interest in Greece. But the name is Greek enough: cf. *IG* II², 417, line 16, 1180, lines 4–5, etc., and *Syll.*³, 913, note 1. Line 4. Mounichion 11 is three times attested (apart from this instance) as a meeting day of the assembly and has been restored in several other texts: see J. D. Mikalson (*Sacred and Civil Calendar*, pp. 141–142), who quotes lines 1–4 of this inscription. The spelling Μουνυχιῶνος for Μουνιχιῶνος is rarely encountered. See L. Threatte, *Grammar*, pp. 264–265.

Line 5. For the nature and location of the assembly see **264**, commentary on lines 3–4 and references there. Lines 6–7. Diognetos of Cholargos. The name appears to be otherwise unattested in that deme. Line 9. Kteson, son of Kallikles, of Kollytos, the proposer of the decree, is not otherwise known. The restoration of lines 9–12, proposed by Pritchett and Meritt, is based on *IG* II², 897, lines 9–12, a text of the year 185/4.

Lines 10 and 12. Seleukos IV Philopator, second son of Antiochos III, "the Great", became coregent with his father in 189 and sole monarch on Antiochos' death in July 187. The date of his accession necessarily conditions the dating of the archon Theoxenos (cf. C. Habicht, *AthMitt* 76, 1961, p. 130, note 6), who on this account cannot be placed earlier than the year to which he is now assigned. The present decree suggests that despite the restrictions imposed on him by the Treaty of Apamea (188 B.C.) he was ready to foster good relations in the west with the Athenians as with the Achaian League (Polybios 22.1.6) and Macedonia (Livy 42.12.3). The present honorand was probably an ambassador to Athens in this cause. Line 10. On προαγωγὴ μεγάλη see L. Robert, *BCH* 54, 1930, p. 342 with note 3 (= *Opera minora selecta* I, 1969, p. 161) and Ἀρχ. Ἐφ., 1969, p. 5, note 3; M. Holleaux, *Études d'épigraphie et d'histoire grecques* II, 1938, p. 89, III, 1943, pp. 221–222; C. B. Welles, *Royal Correspondence in the Hellenistic Period*, 1934, p. 356.

Line 11. κοινεῖ καὶ ἰδίαι. See the commentary on **49**.

FRAGMENT OF A DECREE CONFERRING CITIZENSHIP

267. A fragment of a stele of Pentelic marble (I 5651), with the right side and original rough-picked back preserved, discovered on February 25, 1939, in a wall of a modern house west of the Panathenaic Way and southwest of the Eleusinion (S 21). Below the last line of the inscription, the inscribed surface is blank in a vertical measurement of 0.15 m. The striations of a toothed chisel are visible, varying in direction from the vertical to the diagonal (upper right to lower left).

H. 0.285 m.; W. 0.17 m.; Th. 0.085 m.
LH. 0.005–0.006 m.

Ed. B. D. Meritt, *Hesperia* 30, 1961, pp. 217–218, no. 13, with photograph pl. 38 (see also *SEG* XXI, 407); M. J. Osborne, *Naturalization* I, p. 226, D 110, *Naturalization* II, p. 194.

ca. a. 187/6 *a.* (*inter a.* 199/8 *et* 176/5 *a.*)   NON-ΣΤΟΙΧ. 38–46

[――――――――――――――――――――――――――――]
[..⁵⁻⁷... · δεδόσθαι δὲ αὐτῶι καὶ πολιτείαν δοκιμα]σ[θέν]
[τι ἐν τῶι δικαστηρίωι κατὰ τὸν νόμον· τοὺς δὲ] θεσμο[θέ]
[τας, ὅταν πληρῶσι δικαστήρια εἰς ἕνα κα]ὶ πεντακοσίο[υς]
[δικαστάς, εἰσαγαγεῖν αὐτῶι τὴν δοκιμα]σίαν καὶ γράψα
5 [σθαι αὐτὸν φυλῆς καὶ δήμου καὶ φρατρίας] ἧς ἂν βούληται· ἀ
[ναγράψαι δὲ τόδε τὸ ψήφισμα τὸν γρ]αμματέα τὸν

[κατὰ πρυτανείαν ἐν στήληι λιθίνηι καὶ σ]τῆσαι ἐν ἀκροπό
[λει· εἰς δὲ τὴν ἀναγραφὴν καὶ τὴν ἀνάθεσι]ν τῆς στήλης με
[ρίσαι τὸν ταμίαν τῶν στρατιωτικῶν τὸ γ]ενόμενον ἀνάλωμα.
vacat

The above text is that of Osborne, *loc. cit.* Line 1. Osborne observed far-from-clear remains of sigma in this line and added it, with the accompanying restoration of the clause; the lines have in consequence been renumbered from the *editio princeps*. Line 2. δὲ θεσ]μο[θέ Meritt. Line 4. εἰσάγειν Meritt. Line 5. Osborne added αὐτόν, not present in the *editio princeps*: but line 6 shows that the addition *spatii complendi causa* may be unnecessary. See, however, A. S. Henry, *Honours*, p. 87. *Ad fin.*, ἧ]ς Meritt. Line 6. "Possibly . . . a dittography early in the line" Osborne.

Meritt dated this inscription "*fin. saec.* III *a.*" without giving his reasons, which were probably compounded from his judgment of the style of the lettering and the fact that he based his reconstructed text on *IG* II², 855, so dated by J. Kirchner. The citizenship formula employed is however that of Type III of Formulation B, in Osborne's categorization, a type which on his analysis does not antedate *ca.* 202 B.C.: see the commentary on **239** and references there. Hence Osborne lowered Meritt's date to the early part of the 2nd century.

S. V. Tracy's study of the lettering led him to the conclusion that this text, if not the actual work of the "Cutter of *IG* II² 1326" (for whom see **259**), was certainly in his general style and susceptible therefore of a comparable dating: see *Attic Letter-Cutters*, p. 94. That mason's datable career ran from 199/8 to 176/5, and this decree has therefore been placed for convenience at the central point of his span. It may also be noted that Tracy's date for *IG* II², 855, which he regarded as the work of the "Cutter of *IG* II² 913" (see **248**), is very comparable.

Line 9. The Military Treasurer (without the cooperation of the Plural Board of Administration) is clearly required by the space available as the officer responsible for defraying the outlay of the stele.

FRAGMENT OF AN HONORARY DECREE

268. A fragment of a stele of Pentelic marble (I 3028), with part of the left side preserved but otherwise broken all around, discovered on June 19, 1935, in a context of the 3rd and 4th centuries A.D. overlying the foundation of the interior north wall of the Odeion (L 10). The stone is mottled in appearance.

H. 0.135 m.; W. 0.067 m.; Th. 0.032 m.
LH. 0.006 m.

Ed. B. D. Meritt, *Hesperia* 29, 1960, p. 54, no. 75, with photograph pl. 16. See also *SEG* XIX, 107.

ca. a. 185 *a.* (*inter* 203/2 et 164/3 *a.*)   NON-ΣΤΟΙΧ.

[------------------------------]
[. ⁴⁻⁵ .]Ι[.]ΙL[----------------------]
[τῶ]ι δήμω[ι ----------------------]
ἐτιμήθη [-------------------------]
παρὰ τῶι [------------------------]
5   ὅτι ἂν δύ[νηται -----------------]
τρεπετ[--------------------------]
λειν κα[-------------------------]
διατε[λ(?)----------------------]
ὑπὲρ [--------------------------]
10 [------------------------------]

Meritt's hesitant and generalized attribution of this uncommunicative fragment to the 2nd century ("*saec.* II *a.* [?]") was presumably based on his appreciation of the lettering. On this point S. V. Tracy's comparative analysis was able to achieve a greater measure of precision and to see in these meager remains the characteristics of the mason Tracy named the "Cutter of Agora I 656 + 6355", active according to securely datable evidence between 203/2 and 164/3 B.C. See *Attic-Letter Cutters*, p. 84, and for further detail see **260**. Lacking other means of dating, this text has been placed for convenience at the acme of the craftsman's known career.

Of the contents little can be said. Lines 3, 5, and 8–9 suggest that a benefactor (or possibly more than one) was honored in the decree for services rendered. It appears that he had received previous recognition by the Athenians but that continuing good works (line 8) had earned him this further tribute. The surviving letters of line 8 could, nevertheless, be divided as διά τε [----------].

FRAGMENT OF A DECREE HONORING A BOARD OF OFFICIALS (?)

269. A very small fragment of a stele of Pentelic marble (I 4003), broken on all sides, discovered on April 8, 1936, in a late context west of the north end of the Stoa of Attalos (P 8).

H. 0.082 m.; W. 0.089 m.; Th. 0.048 m.
LH. 0.007–0.008 m. (omicron 0.005 m.)

Ed. B. D. Meritt, *Hesperia* 23, 1954, p. 239, no. 8, with photograph pl. 50. See also *SEG* XIV, 69.

a. 184/3 *a.*   NON-ΣΤΟΙΧ.

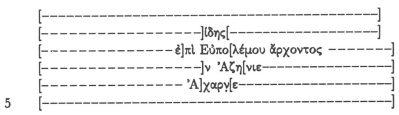

No more than seventeen letters clearly survive on this fragment, but they sufficed to permit S. V. Tracy to identify the general style, if not with assurance the hand, of the mason whom he designated the "Cutter of *IG* II² 913": see *Attic Letter-Cutters*, p. 75 and **248**.

The occurrence of demotics in lines 3 and 4 suggests a succession of names, probably related to a board of officials whether secular or religious, whose period of duty is referred to in line 2. Eupolemos' archonship is to be dated in 185/4, and it is a reasonable supposition that a decree possibly in their honor was passed in the year following; cf. **217**, commentary on line 9.

TWO HIPPARCHOI HONORED

270. A fragment of a stele of Hymettian marble (I 5143), with the left side, original back, and part of the crowning molding above the inscribed face preserved. Otherwise broken all around, generally battered, and especially worn on the left, it was discovered on November 30, 1937, in a wall of a modern house southeast of the Market Square (O 18).

H. 0.18 m.; W. 0.215 m.; Th. 0.096 m.
LH. 0.005 m.

Ed. A. G. Woodhead, *Hesperia* 29, 1960, pp. 78–80, no. 155, with photograph pl. 26: cf. *SEG* XVIII, 31. Revised text (also with *ca.* 65 letters to the line), C. Habicht (*AthMitt* 76, 1961, pp. 141–143), who saw it as a decree of the ἱππεῖς and so restored it. See also J. and L. Robert, *REG* 77, 1964, pp. 154–155, no. 132. For this text cf. *SEG* XXI, 526, where also appears the text of J. Threpsiades and E. Vanderpool, Δελτ. 18, Α΄, 1963, pp. 106–107 (cf. p. 99, note), whose more economical length of line (*ca.* 48 letters), with some improved readings, is to be preferred and is repeated here.

ca. a. 184/3 *a.* (*inter* 189/8 *et* 178/7 *a.*)   NON-ΣΤΟΙΧ. *ca.* 48

Νικογένης Νί[κω]νος Φιλ[αίδης εἶπεν· ἐπειδὴ οἱ χειροτονηθέν]
τες ἱππάρχο[ι] εἰς τὸν ἐ[νιαυτὸν τὸν ἐπὶ . . .*ca.* 9. . . ἄρχοντος]
Τιμιάδης Γαργήττιο[ς καὶ . . . . . .*ca.* 14. . . . . ἔθυσαν τὰ ἱερὰ τὰ]
εἰσιτητήρια καλῶς κ[αὶ εὐσεβῶς τῶι τε Δήμωι καὶ ταῖς Χάρι]
σιν καὶ τῶι Ποσειδῶνι [τῶι Ἱππίωι κατὰ τὰ πάτρια, καὶ ἀρχό]
μενοι ἀπὸ τῶν θεῶν διε[τέλεσαν πράττοντες ἀκολούθως τοῖς]
[τ]ε νόμοις καὶ τοῖς ψηφ[ίσμασιν τοῦ δήμου, σπουδῆς καὶ φιλο]
τιμίας οὐθὲν [ἐλλείποντες ————————————————]
[————————————————————————————]

The date of the text was set in the *editio princeps* at *ca.* 160 B.C., on the basis both of the style of the lettering and of the known career of Nikogenes, son of Nikon, of the deme Philaidai (*PA* 10850), on whom see further below. That it is now given a date some quarter of a century earlier stems from the analysis of the lettering by S. V. Tracy (*Attic Letter-Cutters*, pp. 113–116), who assigned both this inscription and **271** to the hand or atelier of the "Cutter of *IG* II² 897" (photograph of the name piece, fig. 14) among the fourteen he attributed to him. Three of these texts belong to the year 185/4: the earliest that can be dated (*Agora* XV, 173) is of 189/8, the latest (see **332D**) is of 178/7. The present text has been treated at the center point between these two extremes, but it is likely to belong to the later rather than the earlier part of the mason's span of activity. The lettering at least in the above example appears more scrappy than the plain, ordinary, but slightly inconsistent style of Tracy's description: the central horizontals of alpha and epsilon are regularly omitted.

Line 1. Nikogenes appears twice in the victor lists of the Theseia, as hipparchos in *IG* II², 957, col. I, line 39 and as agonothetes in *IG* II², 956, lines 2, 29, 40. For the dates of these lists (157/6 and 161/60 respectively) see B. D. Meritt, *Historia* 26, 1977, p. 183 and Habicht, *Hesperia* 57, 1988, pp. 239–241. The same Nikogenes contributed to the building fund of the theater in the Peiraieus in his own name and in those of his sons Nikogenes and Lyandros (*IG* II², 2334, lines 4–5; on the Peiraieus theaters see **93**). For his appearance as a magistrate on the silver coinage of the new style see M. Thompson, *The New Style Silver Coinage of Athens*, 1961, pp. 576–577. His daughter Apollonia is apparently commemorated on the grave monument *IG* II², 7646. For a *stemma* of the family see *PA* II, p. 134, and cf. J. Sundwall, *Nachträge zur Prosopographia Attica*, 1910, p. 134.

Line 3. Timiades is a name unique in Attic prosopography. Threpsiades and Vanderpool regarded Simiades as a possibility or envisaged a longer name carried over from the previous line: but these alternatives seem less likely. Lines 4–5. On the cult of the Δῆμος and Χάριτες, see *Agora* III, pp. 59–61; A. E. Raubitschek, *Hesperia* 31, 1962, pp. 240–241 and in *Akte des IV. Internationalen Kongresses für griechische und lateinische Epigraphik, 1962*, 1964, pp. 335–336; Habicht, *Studien*, pp. 85–93. This sanctuary lay on the north slope of Kolonos Agoraios and close therefore to the Stoa of the Herms and an intervening area particularly associated with monuments of the ἱππεῖς: see *Agora* III, pp. 102–108; Threpsiades and Vanderpool, Δελτ. 18, A′, 1963, pp. 99–114; J. Travlos, *Pictorial Dictionary of Ancient Athens*, 1971, pp. 79–82; and cf. *Agora* XIV, pp. 159–160. The Hipparcheion (*IG* II², 895, line 6; *Agora* III, p. 177) was in all probability in this same neighborhood.

Line 5. On the cult of Poseidon Hippios and his connection with the ἱππεῖς see W. Judeich, *Topographie*, pp. 45 and 414, and cf. Aristophanes, *Equites* 551, *IG* II², 4691 and Travlos, *op. cit.*, p. 42.

DECREE OF THE GENOS OF THE KERYKES

271. Three fragments, two of which join, of a stele of Hymettian marble. Fragment *a* (I 5424 a), which preserves part of a projecting molding above the inscribed face and the original rough-picked back, but which is otherwise broken all around, was discovered on May 7, 1938, in the original filling of the Post-Herulian Wall (T 21). Fragment *b* (I 3087) joins fragment *a* on the right; it preserves the right edge (though chipped and battered) and original back but is broken elsewhere and was discovered on December 13, 1935, in a wall of a modern house west of the north end of the Stoa of Attalos (O 8). Fragment *c* (I 5424 b) is broken all around save that the original back survives; it was discovered in the same place and on the same day as fragment *a*. The striations of a toothed chisel are visible on all three fragments, vertically on fragment *a*, diagonally on fragment *c* from upper right to lower left, and in both these directions on fragment *b*.

a + *b*: H. 0.213 m.; W. 0.10 m.; Th. 0.077 m.

c: H. 0.17 m.; W. 0.063 m.; Th. 0.077 m.

LH. 0.006 m. (omicron variable).

Ed. *a* and *c*: B. D. Meritt, *Hesperia* 29, 1960, pp. 17–18, no. 23, with photographs pl. 5. See also *SEG* XIX, 123. *b*: B. D. Meritt, *Hesperia* 29, 1960, p. 54, no. 73, with photograph pl. 15. See also *SEG* XIX, 94.

ca. a. 184/3 a. (*inter* 189/8 *et* 178/7 a.)   NON-ΣTOIX. ca. 38

(a)
```
       [. . . . . . . . . . . . ca. 27 . . . . . . . . . . εἶ]πεν· ἐπειδὴ
       [. ca. 6 . . ἱερεὺς γενόμενος εἰς τὸ]ν ἐνιαυτὸν τὸ[ν]
       [ἐπὶ — — — — — — — — ἄρχοντος τάς τε] θυσίας τ[ὰ]ς        (b)
       [καθηκούσας ἐν τῶι ἐνιαυτῶι τέθυ]χε τοῖς θεοῖς
5      [καλῶς καὶ ἱεροπρεπῶς ὑπὲρ τοῦ γέ]νους τοῦ Κηρύ
       [κων καὶ εὐσεβῶς ἐξήγαγεν τὴν ἀρ]χὴν τὴ[ν] ἐν τῶ[ι]
       [ἐνιαυτῶι(?) οὐθὲν φιλοτιμίας ἐλ]λιπὼν(?) κατὰ τὴν
       [ἱερεωσύνην — — — — — — — — — — —]ι[.] ἐπιμελει
       [— — — — — — — — — — — — — — — —] τὰ πάντα
10     [— — — — — — — — — — — — — — —]ων οὐκ ὀλι
       [— — — — — — — — — — — — — — —]ωι λυσ[. . .]
```

```
          [------------------------------------]ηχ[. ᶜᵃ· ⁶..]
          [------------------------------------]
 (c)      [------------------------------------]
          [---------------] αν[---------------]
          [-----------]αι ταμι[---------------]
          [-----------δι]χαίως [---------------]
          [-----------] χαὶ ἐτ[---------------]
  5       [--------------]ωντ[---------------]
          [--------------]εβο[---------------]
          [------------------------------------]
```

Below the inscribed surface of fragment *c* the stone projects too far to permit any close association between this fragment and fragments *a* + *b*. The honorand perhaps served as Treasurer (*c*, line 2) as well as in the office of priest(?), and his further record in this second function seems to have been set out lower down the stele.

The mason at work on this inscription was identified by S. V. Tracy as the "Cutter of *IG* II² 897": see *Attic Letter-Cutters*, p. 115, and for details of his style, date, and career, **270**. As in that context, here also the inscription has been placed at the midpoint of the craftsman's known span of activity. When Meritt dated these fragments separately in the *editiones principes*, he set them in the correct general area ("*init. saec.* II a.").

The truncated prescript on fragment *a* indicates, as Meritt recognized, that this is not a decree of the boule and demos, and he reasoned that it was a vote taken by some religious organization. The connection with fragment *b* and the improved reading at the end of line 5 confirm the correctness of his argument and show that this is a decree of the genos of the Kerykes. See **77** for another decree of this same genos, with further material in the commentary on line 2 of that text.

Lines 1–7. Cf. *IG* II², 1314 and 1315 for the phraseology. Line 5 *ad fin*. In publishing fragment *b* separately, Meritt read ΚΡΥ. Line 7. ἐλλείπων or ἐνλελοιπώς would be usual, but the right-hand stroke of lambda is clear before iota. Line 10. ΟΝ Meritt.

THE ARCHONSHIP OF HERMOGENES, 183/2 B.C.

The didascalic list *IG* II², 2323, which established the triplet of successive archons Symmachos–Theoxenos–Zopyros (see p. 373 above), also established that Hermogenes and Timesianax were archons in consecutive years at a slightly later date (see *SEG* XXV, 194, lines 269–270). The first of the two decrees of the orgeones of the cult of the Magna Mater inscribed on the stele *IG* II², 1328 was dated to Hermogenes' archonship (the second being of the year of Sonikos with a reference to that of Hippakos, for which see pp. 393–394 below). The subscription list *IG* II², 2332 is attributed to the year of Hermogenes (line 1; cf. col. I, line 119), and **306** also contains a passing reference to him (line 7). None of this evidence provides the further detail that could determine his year more closely than "*ca.* 180" (cf. *PA* 5121) were it not that W. S. Ferguson's evaluation of the secretary cycles showed that Timesianax, with a γραμματεύς from Attalis (XII), could be assigned to 182/1. This placed Hermogenes in 183/2, from which he was removed only by W. B. Dinsmoor, who soon repented of it (*Archons of Athens*, pp. 255–256 *et alibi*, *Athenian Archon List*, p. 187). All other studies have retained Ferguson's original date: so J. Kirchner, *IG* II², iv, 1, pp. 18–19; W. K. Pritchett and B. D. Meritt, *Chronology*, p. xxvii, who also attributed to this year, though not without hesitation, the prytany text I 4187 (*Agora* XV, 182), *ibid.*, p. 119, showing a γραμματεύς with the appropriate demotic Παλληνεύς (Antiochis XI); Meritt, *Hesperia* 26, 1957, p. 94, *Athenian Year*, p. 236, *TAPA* 95, 1964, p. 239, *Historia* 26, 1977, p. 181; C. Habicht, *Studien*, p. 177. **272** added nothing of value to the available material.

Without direct evidence concerning the calendric character of the festival year, scholars assigned it in accord with the general schemes for the period that commended themselves. Kirchner left the issue open. Ferguson (*Athenian Tribal Cycles*, p. 29) saw the year as probably ordinary after a probably intercalary 185/4 and an ordinary 186/5. Dinsmoor in 1939 proposed it as intercalary after two ordinary years and in this was followed by Pritchett and Meritt, *Chronology*, and again by Meritt in *Hesperia* 26, 1957, *loc. cit*. However, Meritt's subsequent preference for making 184/3 intercalary caused him to regard 183/2 as ordinary (*Athenian Year*, pp. 182 and 236), a preference he maintained (cf. *TAPA* 95, 1964 and *Historia* 26, 1977, *locc. citt.*). The matter remains in doubt. There is no evidence for the succession of phylai in prytany or for the arrangement of the prytany calendar.

FRAGMENT OF A DECREE

272. The upper left corner of a pedimental stele of Hymettian marble (I 6771), broken on all sides save for a little of the original left edge, discovered on April 2, 1957, in a wall of a modern cellar southeast of the Church of the Holy Apostles (R 17). The inscription was surmounted by a heavy ovolo molding below the horizontal cornice of the pediment, now much battered; beneath the ovolo a narrow taenia effects the transition to the inscribed face by means of an abrupt apophyge.

H. 0.13 m.; W. 0.12 m.; Th. 0.55 m.
LH. 0.006 m.

Ed. B. D. Meritt, *Hesperia* 32, 1963, p. 17, no. 16, with photograph pl. 5. See also *SEG* XXI, 439.

a. 183/2 a.   NON-ΣTOIX. *ca.* 40–44

```
᾿Επὶ ῾Ερμο[γένου ἄρχοντος ἐπὶ τῆς ----------]
[. ης] πρυτ[ανείας ἧι ......ca.15...... ς Παλληνεὺς]
[ἐγραμμάτευεν· --------------------------]
[--------------------------------------]
```

Small as it is, the fragment provided sufficient data for S. V. Tracy to be able to attribute the execution of the inscription to the craftsman named by him the "Cutter of *IG* II² 886": see *Attic Letter-Cutters*, pp. 96–98, with photograph of the name piece, fig. 11. No more than five texts (including this one) and part of a sixth are claimed as his, but the dates to be derived from them indicate the mason's floruit as the seventeen-year period 194/3–178/7. His style, though comparatively plain, shows variety in individual letters. The angular loop of rho seen in this text is particularly characteristic.

Line 2. The demotic of the γραμματεύς and the last letter of his patronymic are restored from *Agora* XV, 182, which the secretary cycle requires to be placed in Hermogenes' year, although an alternative date for it of 159/8, the year of Aristaichmos, is also possible.

THE ARCHONSHIP OF TIMESIANAX, 182/1 B.C.

Timesianax' year is closely tied to that of Hermogenes by the didascalic list *IG* II², 2323; see the commentary on the archonship of the latter, p. 381 above. *IG* II², 902 (*Agora* XV, 183) was passed in his term of office, and a second prytany decree belonging to the same archonship, *SEG* XVI, 86 (*Agora* XV, 184), was discovered in the Agora. *IG* II², 902 established that the γραμματεύς of the year came from Probalinthos (Attalis XII) and provided his patronymic. That his own name was Philo . . . s was revealed by *Agora* XV, 184 (though apparently not accepted by C. Habicht, *Studien*, p. 177). The demotic, long known, was the factor that had enabled the positions of Hermogenes and Timesianax in the archon list to be promptly confirmed in the light of "Ferguson's Law" (W. S. Ferguson, *Athenian Secretaries*, p. 55). The discovery of **273** added no data of significance.

The year was the fourth in the fourteenth Metonic cycle, in which it would have been ordinary (*TAPA* 95, 1964, p. 236), and its character in the Athenian festival calendar was until recently agreed by all commentators to have been ordinary also (although without direct evidence) according to their various assessments of the characters of Hermogenes' year (*q.v.*) and of the year following Timesianax' archonship. On none of the three surviving decrees already mentioned is the dating of their enactment by month and prytany preserved. Ferguson (*Athenian Tribal Cycles*, p. 29) regarded the year as ordinary in the belief that 181/80 was certainly intercalary; W. B. Dinsmoor (*Athenian Archon List*, p. 23) also held it to be ordinary following an intercalary 183/2, a view followed by W. K. Pritchett and B. D. Meritt, *Chronology*, p. xxvii, and by Meritt in *Hesperia* 26, 1957, p. 94. Meritt retained it as ordinary in *Athenian Year*, p. 236, although he had by then decided that 183/2 was ordinary, since 181/80, to which he at that time, as later, assigned the archon Hippias (see p. 384 below), was to be regarded as certainly intercalary. The temporary removal of Hippias to 193/2 and his replacement in 181/80 by Phanarchides, whose year was certainly ordinary, resulted in the hypothesis, for the first time, that Timesianax was archon in an intercalary year (Meritt, *TAPA* 95, 1964, pp. 238–239); but Meritt reversed this judgment (*Historia* 26, 1977, pp. 161–162 and 181; cf. J. S. Traill, *Hesperia* 45, 1976, pp. 302–303, note 13), and Timesianax' year was once again listed as ordinary. **275** and *Agora* XV, 167 confirm this since they show the following year, that of Hippias, to be intercalary.

There is no information concerning the succession either of months in the festival calendar or of the prytanies in the prytany calendar. Attalis and Akamantis were the prytanizing phylai in *Agora* XV, 183 and 184, but the ordinal numeral describing the prytany is not preserved in either text.

The name Timesianax is unusual in Attic prosopography, only three other examples being known, one from Koile and two from Epieikidai (*Agora* XV, 205, line 35, and *PA* 13647, the latter registering a father and son of the same name). All the instances date from the 2nd century B.C., and the Timesianax of *Agora* XV, 205 could be identified with the archon.

FRAGMENT OF A DECREE

273. Part of the upper left corner of a stele of Hymettian marble (I 4267), with the left side and original back preserved and with much of the inscribed surface sheared away to the left of a surface crack running almost vertically down the center of the stone, discovered on July 7, 1936, in a Late Roman foundation in the north room of the Hellenistic Metroon (G–H 8–9). Part of a crowning molding similar to that of **272** is preserved above the first line of the text.

H. 0.11 m.; W. 0.05 m.; Th. 0.093 m.
LH. 0.007–0.008 m. (omicron 0.005 m.).

Ed. B. D. Meritt, *Hesperia* 29, 1960, pp. 15–16, no. 20, with photograph pl. 5. See also *SEG* XIX, 98.

a. 182/1 *a.*   NON-ΣΤΟΙΧ. *ca.* 45

Θ   [ε   ο   ι].
['Ἐπὶ] Τι[μησιάναχτος ἄρχοντος ἐπὶ τῆς ———————]
[. ης] πρ[υτανείας ἧι Φιλο . . . ς Ἀριστομάχου Προβαλίσιος]
[ἐγ]ραμ[μάτευεν· δήμου ψηφίσματα· ———————— ἱσταμέ]
5   νου, τε[τάρτει τῆς πρυτανείας· ἐκκλησία κυρία ἐν τῶι θεά]
[τρω]ι· τ[ῶν προέδρων ἐπεψήφιζεν ————————————]
[————————————————————————————————]

The writing in its general aspect represents plain, competent work of the period, but the mason adopted the elements of what W. K. Pritchett described as the "tachygraphic style" (*Hesperia* 16, 1947, p. 188), and the result is a text very much in the character of the "Cutter of Agora I 247", for whom see **264**, as S. V. Tracy's analysis showed (*Attic Letter-Cutters*, p. 104). Tracy was, however, rightly hesitant to make this inscription a definite attribution to that craftsman; but it could well be a product of his workshop, of a pupil, or of a deliberate imitator.

Line 3. The name of the γραμματεύς is restored from the united evidence of *Agora* XV, 183 and 184. Nothing further is known of him or of his family. Line 4. δήμου ψηφίσματα. See **258**, commentary on line 2: ψήφισμα is of course equally possible as a restoration. Lines 5–6. On the location and character of the assembly see **264**, commentary on lines 3–4 and references there.

THE ARCHONSHIP OF HIPPIAS, 181/80 B.C.

In addition to **274** and **275**, the Agora has yielded a prytany text of Hippias' year, *Agora* XV, 167 (cf. *SEG* XXI, 440), and a further decree, *SEG* XXXIV, 94 (see **332C**). To these inscriptions must be added the evidence concerning the year recognized as provided by *IG* II², 920 (*Agora* XV, 168; *SEG* XXI, 442) and 889 (*SEG* XXI, 443), which C. Karapa (Δελτ. 29, Α', 1974 [1977], pp. 163–164, no. 3) joined with *IG* II², 904 (see *SEG* XXVI, 108). See also E. Schweigert, *Hesperia* 9, 1940, pp. 355–356, no. 50. Despite this impressive total of inscriptional texts, the evidence came to light only in comparatively recent years. The archonship of Hippias was unknown to scholarship before the discovery of **275**, which was notified to W. B. Dinsmoor in time for inclusion in *Athenian Archon List* in 1939; see pp. 7 and 186. The association with *IG* II², 889 was immediately recognized, but the demotic of the γραμματεύς Theodosios was not preserved in either text, and in consequence Hippias' year could not at that stage be precisely located in relation to the secretary cycle.

On the prosopographical grounds provided by the two texts Dinsmoor tentatively assigned Hippias to 190/89 (cf. *op. cit.*, p. 23). This date was varied by one year, to 191/90, by W. K. Pritchett and B. D. Meritt, *Chronology*, pp. xxvi and 116–117; see p. 369 above, on the archonship of Timouchos. 191/90 was retained by Pritchett and O. Neugebauer (*Calendars*, p. 75) and by Meritt (*Hesperia* 26, 1957, p. 94) and was regarded as acceptable until the discovery of *Agora* XV, 167. That such continuing discoveries entailed recurrent revision of accepted texts and ideas says much for the vitality of the study of Attic epigraphy and the readiness of those engaged in it to rethink their conclusions. *Pace* Pritchett, *Ancient Athenian Calendars on Stone*, p. 379, it reflects no discredit on those who have advocated with conviction what must thereupon be abandoned.

The secretary cycle required for 181/80 a γραμματεύς from Erechtheis (I). J. Kirchner (*IG* II², iv, 1, pp. 18–19) showed this correctly in his list but had no names to attach to it, and the year is thus a blank in his table. The same was true of Dinsmoor's table in *Archons of Athens*, p. 32; at that time he postulated that the γραμματεύς should belong to Aigeis (II), although he later reverted to W. S. Ferguson's arrangement of the secretary cycle. He had, however (*op. cit.*, p. 256), attributed to 182/1 a prytany decree, *IG* II², 917, in which the archon's name was lost but where the demotic of the γραμματεύς survived as ἐκ] Κηδῶν (Erechtheis I). Ferguson's arrangement (*Athenian Tribal Cycles*, p. 29) placed this γραμματεύς in 181/80 and showed the year as surely intercalary. But this decree, which later became *Agora* XV, 128, was shown by S. Dow (*Hesperia* 2, 1933, pp. 436–438; *AJA* 40, 1936, pp. 57–60) to belong to 223/2 and was thereby removed from the discussion. Thus 181/80 again appeared as a blank in Dinsmoor's 1939 table (*Athenian Archon List*, p. 23), as in that of Pritchett and Meritt in 1940 (*Chronology*, p. xxvii). The hesitant attribution to this conveniently vacant year of the archon Apolexis in the *editio princeps* of **284** lasted only until the correct name, Alexis, was established and a firm date for him assured. See Meritt, *Hesperia* 16, 1947, p. 163; G. A. Stamires, *Hesperia* 26, 1957, p. 37 and note 23.

In 1957 Meritt suggested that the archonship of Aphrodisios might be placed in 181/80, shorn as it now was of the false Apolexis (*Hesperia* 26, 1957, p. 38, note 28), and he adopted the suggestion in his revised list of archons (*ibid.*, p. 94). But the proposal was short-lived. The discovery, by means of *Agora* XV, 167, that the γραμματεύς of the year of the recently found archon Hippias belonged to Erechtheis (I) caused Hippias to be assigned to what was an obviously suitable and available date (Meritt, *Athenian Year*, pp. 195–200, 236). The other texts of the year were reassessed in conformity with the new data (cf. *SEG* XXI, 441–444).

But there was another possible date for Hippias: 193/2 B.C., then as now occupied in the reckoning by Phanarchides; see pp. 367–368 above. Meritt saw reason to believe that the calendric evidence was better suited if Hippias were assigned to 193/2 and Phanarchides relocated in 181/80 (*TAPA* 95, 1964, pp. 238–239). This dating appears in *Agora* XV at the relevant entries. Yet this revision too proved unsound: Meritt later withdrew it (*Historia* 26, 1977, pp. 161–162 and 181; cf. J. S. Traill, *Hesperia* 45, 1976, pp. 302–303, note 13).

Thus 181/80 once again became the acceptable and accepted year for Hippias' tenure of the archonship: cf. C. Habicht, *Studien*, p. 177. Ironically, all these discussions and revisions would have been avoided if only the decree *SEG* XXXIV, 94 had been discovered at an earlier stage of the Agora excavations. For the functionaries there honored, in a text clearly dated to Hippias' year, had performed their duties ἐπὶ Τιμησιάναχτος ἄρχοντος: and such honors were customarily voted in the year immediately succeeding that in which they had been earned; cf. **187** and **188**. The year of Timesianax as 182/1 has never been seriously in doubt (see p. 382 above). The discovery and editing of this text (S. V. Tracy, *Hesperia* 53, 1984, pp. 370–374, no. 3), although not in time to prevent so much scholarly labor and dispute, settled the issue for good.

The year 181/80 was the fifth in Meton's cycle, in which it would therefore be intercalary. That Hippias' year in Athens was indeed intercalary was placed beyond all doubt by the data of **275**, in which Gamelion, the seventh month in an ordinary year, coincides with the eighth prytany. The character of the year was made more explicit still by *Agora* XV, 167, passed in Posideon II on the 232nd day of the year and suggesting that in the festival calendar one of the earlier months had been full where in regular succession a hollow month was to be expected. Phylai known to have been in prytany are VI Leontis, VIII Pandionis, and XI Attalis. *IG* II², 889 + 904 and *SEG* XXXIV, 94 were passed in the month Skirophorion, but the name of the twelfth phyle in prytany is not preserved in either of them. It should however be a short name (Aigeis or Oineis).

FRAGMENT OF A DECREE

274. A small fragment of the upper right corner of a pedimental stele of Hymettian marble (I 5400), with the right side and part of the pediment preserved (the latter much battered), discovered on April 15, 1938, in a modern context south of the eastern part of the Market Square (P 20). Below the pediment a broad taenia stands above an apophyge descending to the inscribed face of the stele, where there is an uninscribed space of *ca.* 0.012 m. before the first line of text.

H. 0.118 m.; W. 0.115 m.; Th. 0.04 m.
LH. 0.006 m. (omicron 0.003 m.).

Ed. E. Schweigert, *Hesperia* 9, 1940, p. 355, no. 49, with photograph. Fuller restorations in the light of *Agora* XV, 167 by B. D. Meritt, *Athenian Year*, p. 198. See *SEG* XXI, 444.

a. 181/80 *a.*, *pryt.* VI(?)   NON-ΣTOIX.

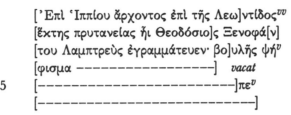

$$
\begin{array}{l}
[\text{'Επὶ 'Ιππίου ἄρχοντος ἐπὶ τῆς Λεω}]ντίδος^{vv} \\
[\text{ἕκτης πρυτανείας ἧι Θεοδόσιο}]ς \text{ Ξενοφά}[ν] \\
[\text{του Λαμπτρεὺς ἐγραμμάτευεν· βο}]υλῆς \psi ή^{v} \\
[\text{φισμα} \text{-----------------}] \quad vacat \\
[\text{------------------------}]πε^{v} \\
[\text{------------------------}]
\end{array}
$$

(line number 5 at left)

Too little of this piece survives for much to be said of its characteristics, but the writing is clumsily executed (especially sigma, phi, and psi). Omicron is small and pendent from the upper line of the lettering. The outer strokes of sigma are parallel, a feature which suggested to S. V. Tracy (*Attic Letter-Cutters*, p. 253) a date for the text later than the mid-century, were it not that the remains of the prescript make it clear that the decree belongs to the year of Hippias. Tracy found the lettering without any parallel he could determine but saw it as owing something to the style of the "Cutter of *IG* II² 1324", a mason to whom he attributed four texts (none of them an Agora *psephisma*) and who seems to have flourished *ca.* 190 B.C. (*Attic Letter-Cutters*, pp. 110–112). Some of his sigmas do indeed show their outer strokes parallel, and as a criterion of post-150 date the feature evidently requires to be treated with some caution.

Line 1. That Leontis held the sixth prytany was derived from *Agora* XV, 167. Since this is a nonstoichedon text, it remains possible to accommodate Αἰα]ντίδος with a different ordinal numeral, e.g., τρίτης, as taking up little additional space. Line 2. Nothing more is known of Theodosios, son of Xenophantos, of Lamptrai beyond his tenure of office in Hippias' year.

Line 3. βουλῆς ψήφισμα (or ψηφίσματα). With **275**, where it is part of the restoration, this is the earliest occurrence of this element of the prescript among the Agora *psephismata* in this collection, although it is to be found already in the 3rd century in *IG* II², 847, of 215/14 B.C. Cf. **260**, commentary on lines 5–6; P. J. Rhodes, *Athenian Boule*, pp. 64 and (for the prescript of this decree) 273; A. S. Henry, *Prescripts*, p. 89. As a "minute-heading" it is analogous to the δήμου ψηφίσμα(τα) discussed earlier and was doubtless introduced for comparable reasons: see **258**, commentary on line 2.

DECREE IN HONOR OF AN AD HOC COMMITTEE OF INSPECTION OF THE SKIAS

275. The lower left section of a large stele of Pentelic marble (I 5344), broken above and to the right but with the original rough-picked back and left side preserved, together with the bottom edge complete with tenon for insertion into a supporting foundation or cutting, discovered on February 15, 1938, in a Late Roman level in the Tholos precinct, immediately southeast of the building itself (G 12). The inscribed face has suffered from weathering and maltreatment.

H. 0.75 m.; W. 0.505 m.; Th. 0.135 m.
LH. 0.006 m. (omicron 0.005 m.).

Ed. E. Schweigert *apud* H. A. Thompson, *The Tholos of Athens and Its Predecessors* (*Hesperia*, Supplement IV), 1940, pp. 144–147, with photograph fig. 105. Cf. J. and L. Robert, *REG* 57, 1944, p. 202, no. 81. Corrected text of lines 10–11 by B. D. Meritt, *Athenian Year*, p. 197; see also *SEG* XXI, 441. Lines 5 and 13–14 quoted among evidence for the Tholos by R. E. Wycherley (*Agora* III, p. 184, no. 608, with reference to line 17 concerning the Metroon, p. 160).

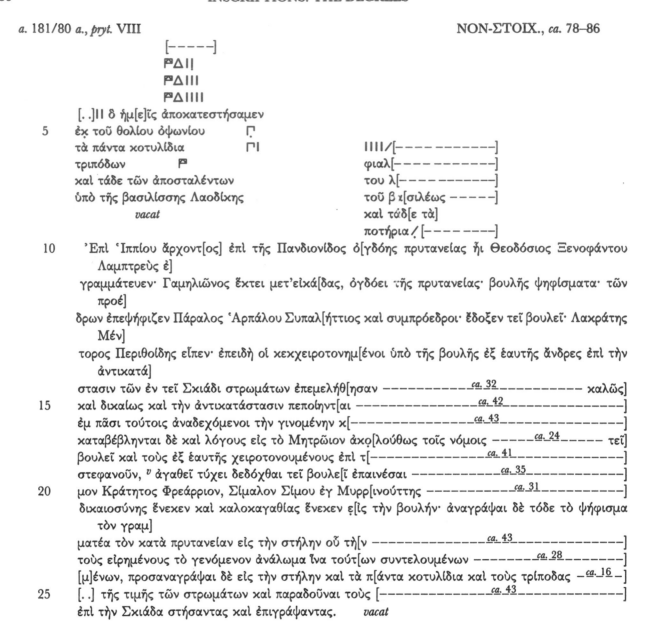

a. 181/80 *a., pryt.* VIII NON-ΣΤΟΙΧ., *ca.* 78–86

```
                    [------]
                    ☰Δ‖
                    ☰Δ‖‖
                    ☰Δ‖‖‖
      [..]‖‖ δ ἡμ[ε]ῖς ἀποκατεστήσαμεν
  5   ἐκ τοῦ θολίου ὀψωνίου          ☰
      τὰ πάντα κοτυλίδια             ☰Ι           ‖‖‖/[------------]
      τριπόδων            ☰                       φιαλ[------------]
      καὶ τάδε τῶν ἀποσταλέντων                   του λ[------------]
      ὑπὸ τῆς βασιλίσσης Λαοδίκης                 τοῦ β ι[σιλέως -----]
                vacat                             καὶ τάδ[ε τὰ]
                                                  ποτήρια/[--------]
```

10   Ἐπὶ Ἱππίου ἄρχοντ[ος] ἐπὶ τῆς Πανδιονίδος ὀ[γδόης πρυτανείας ἧι Θεοδόσιος Ξενοφάντου Λαμπτρεὺς ἐ]
γραμμάτευεν· Γαμηλιῶνος ἕκτει μετ'εἰκά[δας, ὀγδόει τῆς πρυτανείας· βουλῆς ψηφίσματα· τῶν προέ]
δρων ἐπεψήφιζεν Πάραλος Ἁρπάλου Συπαλ[ήττιος καὶ συμπρόεδροι· ἔδοξεν τεῖ βουλεῖ· Λακράτης Μέν]
τορος Περιθοίδης εἶπεν· ἐπειδὴ οἱ κεχειροτονημ[ένοι ὑπὸ τῆς βουλῆς ἐξ ἑαυτῆς ἄνδρες ἐπὶ τὴν ἀντικατά]
στασιν τῶν ἐν τεῖ Σκιάδι στρωμάτων ἐπεμελήθ[ησαν ————————*ca. 32*———————— καλῶς]
15   καὶ δικαίως καὶ τὴν ἀντικατάστασιν πεποίηντ[αι ——————————*ca. 42*——————————]
ἐμ πᾶσι τούτοις ἀναδεχόμενοι τὴν γινομένην κ[——————————*ca. 43*——————————]
καταβέβληνται δὲ καὶ λόγους εἰς τὸ Μητρῷον ἀκο[λούθως τοῖς νόμοις —————*ca. 24*————— τεῖ]
βουλεῖ καὶ τοὺς ἐξ ἑαυτῆς χειροτονουμένους ἐπὶ τ[——————————*ca. 41*——————————]
στεφανοῦν, ᵛ ἀγαθεῖ τύχει δεδόχθαι τεῖ βουλε[ῖ ἐπαινέσαι ————————*ca. 35*————————]
20   μον Κράτητος Φρεάρριον, Σίμαλον Σίμου ἐγ Μυρρ[ινούττης ————————*ca. 31*————————]
δικαιοσύνης ἕνεκεν καὶ καλοκαγαθίας ἕνεκεν ε[ἰς τὴν βουλήν· ἀναγράψαι δὲ τόδε τὸ ψήφισμα τὸν γραμ]
ματέα τὸν κατὰ πρυτανείαν εἰς τὴν στήλην οὗ τὴ[ν ——————————*ca. 43*——————————]
τοὺς εἰρημένους τὸ γενόμενον ἀνάλωμα ἵνα τούτ[ων συντελουμένων ————————*ca. 28*————————]
[μ]ένων, προσαναγράψαι δὲ εἰς τὴν στήλην καὶ τὰ π[άντα κοτυλίδια καὶ τοὺς τρίποδας —*ca. 16*—]
25   [..] τῆς τιμῆς τῶν στρωμάτων καὶ παραδοῦναι τοὺς [——————————*ca. 43*——————————]
ἐπὶ τὴν Σκιάδα στήσαντας καὶ ἐπιγράψαντας.   *vacat*

The size of the fragment and its state of preservation give to a poorly executed text the appearance of being a worse piece of work than it is. Schweigert noted the letters as small, but they are in fact of regular size, that of **274**, for example, of the same year (where omicron is indeed smaller). But the writing is careless, with variations of form among examples of the same individual letter, and the articulation of strokes is haphazard, especially in epsilon, kappa, and sigma: omicron is sometimes, but not always, smaller and is pendent from the upper line of the lettering.

S. V. Tracy (*Attic Letter-Cutters*, pp. 121–124) added this text to four others and ascribed them to the "Cutter of Agora I 6765", with photograph of the name piece (= *Agora* XV, 167), fig. 16. His description of the writing as having "a crowded and busy look about it" is both reasonable and charitable. He pointed out the interesting detail that of the five inscriptions attributed to this mason four are of Hippias' year (the fifth being of the year of Symmachos, 188/7 B.C.). Moreover, the proposer of this decree also proposed two others of the four (*Agora* XV, 167 and 168) and, as it happens, was chairman of the proedroi on the day in Symmachos' year when the enactment inscribed by this same mason (*IG* II², 891) was put to the vote. See further p. 387 below.

Schweigert's estimates of the number of letters to be supposed in many of the lines of the text were arbitrary and, in one case at least, very wide of the mark. Lines which may be completely restored have a length of from 78 (line 11) to 84 (line 13) letters. All Schweigert's estimates fall below that range save in lines 14 and 23, and in lines 22 and 25 his proposals were for 67 and 70 letters respectively. Yet the spacing of the letters, though stylistically unhappy, remains constant in character throughout the text. The line numeration is that of the *editio princeps*.

Line 4. [τ]ῶν ἡμ[ε]ῖς Schweigert. Lines 10–11. – – – ευς]| ἐγραμμάτευεν Schweigert. The epsilon is not on the stone and, unless it was omitted *per incuriam*, must have been written at the end of line 10. Line 12. ἔδοξεν τεῖ βουλεῖ A. S. Henry, *Prescripts*, p. 89; cf. *SEG* XXVI, 109; βουλὴ ἐμ βουλευτηρίωι Schweigert. Line 16 *init.* ἐμ πᾶσι is clear on the stone: [.]ς ἅπασι Schweigert. γινομένην: γιν[ο]μένην Schweigert. *Ad fin.* κ[ακοπαθίαν J. and L. Robert. Line 17 *fin.* ἀκ[ολούθως Schweigert. Line 19. βουλ[εῖ] Schweigert. Line 21. ἔνεκεν [εἰς Schweigert. The restorations except in lines 10–12 follow those of Schweigert.

The Skias, the inventory of the contents of which was the prime duty of the committee here honored, is more familiar as the Tholos, the round building at the southern end of the west side of the Agora which was the headquarters of the prytaneis during their period of office. One third of the prytaneis regularly slept there (hence the στρώματα of lines 14 and 25, which required replacement). The precinct was apparently the area known as the Prytanikon. For details see Thompson, *Tholos* (*Hesperia*, Supplement IV), 1940; *Agora* III, pp. 179–184; I. T. Hill, *The Ancient City of Athens*, 1953, pp. 55–61 and 228–229; J. Travlos, *Pictorial Dictionary of Ancient Athens*, 1971, pp. 553–561; *Agora* XIV, pp. 41–46 (the present text is cited on p. 44); *Agora Guide*[3], pp. 54–57; J. M. Camp, *Athenian Agora*, pp. 94–97.

Line 9. Evidently Laodike III, daughter of Mithridates II of Pontic Cappadocia and wife of Antiochos III, "the Great", of Syria, whom she married in 221/20. See F. Stähelin, *RE* XII, i, 1924, cols. 706–707, *s.v.* Laodike (17). Schweigert's comment in this connection appears to confuse her with her daughter Laodike IV (*RE* XII, i, col. 707, *s.v.* Laodike [18]), who in 196/5 married the crown prince and coregent Antiochos in a brother-sister alliance and who after his death may have married a younger brother, later Antiochos IV Epiphanes; cf. J. and L. Robert, *REG* 57, 1944, p. 203, no. 81, with erroneous reference to *RE*. Line 10. The full name of the γραμματεύς of the year, unknown to Schweigert, is derived from *Agora* XV, 167: cf. **274**.

Line 11. On the calendar equation see Meritt, *loc. cit.* For Gamelion 25 (in a full month) or 24 (in a hollow month) as a meeting day see J. D. Mikalson, *Sacred and Civil Calendar*, pp. 105–106 and [Plutarch], *Vitae X oratorum* 850A. βουλῆς ψηφίσματα. See **274**, commentary on line 3. Line 12. Paralos, son of Harpalos, of Sypalettos is not otherwise known. The name is unusual. Cf. the son of the 5th-century statesman Perikles and Πάραλος Λ– – – – in *IG* II², 1959, line 6. Lines 12–13. Lakrates, son of Mentor, of the deme Perithoidai, the proposer of this decree and of others in this year (see p. 386 above), was the sponsor (again in Hippias' year) also of the citizenship decree *IG* II², 889 + 904 (M. J. Osborne, *Naturalization* I, pp. 208–209, D 99, *Naturalization* II, p. 186). He was evidently a βουλευτής in both 188/7 and 181/80: see P. J. Rhodes, *ZPE* 41, 1981, pp. 101–102.

Line 17. On the Metroon and its function see *Agora* III, pp. 150–160; *Agora* XIV, pp. 35–38; Camp, *Athenian Agora*, pp. 91–94; and cf. **221**, commentary on line 3. Line 19. ἀγαθεῖ τύχει. See **72**, commentary on lines 7–8.

Lines 19–20. Schweigert stated that the committee was composed of three members, but the available space would accommodate four. – – – mos, son of Krates, of Phrearrhioi is not otherwise known. Simalos, son of Simos, of Myrrhinoutta, who served as an official of the boule in this period (*Agora* XV, 159), is probably a member of a well-known family of that deme in which the name Simos is prominent; see *PA* 12674–12676. He may indeed be the son of that Simos (*PA* 12675) who appears among those making dedications to Asklepios catalogued in 245/4 or 244/3 (*IG* II², 1534B, line 235 = S. B. Aleshire, *The Athenian Asklepieion*, 1989, inventory V, line 110). Simos, son of Anthesterios, epimeletes later in the century (*IG* II², 1939, line 8), perhaps belongs to a collateral branch (*PA* 12676).

Lines 21–22. The γραμματεύς responsible for the inscribing of the honors is to add them, with the inventory, to an already existing stele. Other officials (line 26) apparently maintain other records relevant to the equipment in the Skias.

DECREE GRANTING ATHENIAN CITIZENSHIP TO PAUSIMACHOS, SON OF PHILOSTRATOS

276. A fragment of a pedimental stele of Hymettian marble (I 2105), with moldings preserved above the inscribed face but otherwise much chipped and battered, discovered on November 29, 1934, in a wall of a modern house east of the southern part of the Odeion (O 11–12). The principal molding consists of a straight-sided ovolo and below it a narrow band with abrupt apophyge to the inscribed surface. Above the ovolo is a taenia which appears to represent the horizontal cornice of a pediment.

It was demonstrated by S. V. Tracy (see below) that the fragment forms the upper left section of *IG* II², 954, its position being directly to the left of fragment a of that inscription. The two fragments appear to make contact below the inscribed surface, although at that surface they are separated by the distance of three letters in lines 1 and 2. The Agora fragment may be designated fragment *a*, with fragments a and b of *IG* II², 954 becoming *b* and *c* respectively.

a: W. 0.149 m.; W. 0.143 m.; Th. 0.111 m.
Width of fragments *a* + *b* at line 1 *ca.* 0.288 m.
LH. 0.006 m.

(For the measurements and details of fragments *b* and *c* see M. J. Osborne, *loc. cit.* below.)

Ed. *a* only: B. D. Meritt, *Hesperia* 37, 1968, pp. 272–273, no. 11, with photograph pl. 79; see also *SEG* XXV, 124. *a* + *b*: S. V. Tracy, *Hesperia* 41, 1972, pp. 46–49, no. II. *b* + *c*: *IG* II², 954. *a–c*: M. J. Osborne, *Naturalization* I, pp. 209–211, D 100, *Naturalization* II, pp. 187–188. Lines 1–5 quoted by A. S. Henry, *Prescripts*, pp. 89–90 (cf. pp. 84–85).

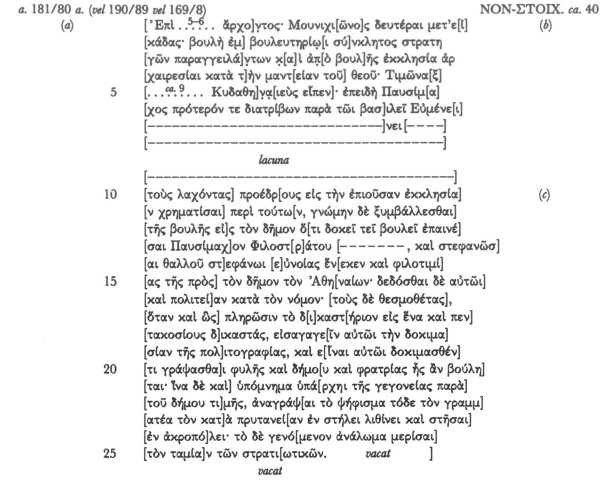

a. 181/80 a. (*vel* 190/89 *vel* 169/8)   NON-ΣΤΟΙΧ. *ca.* 40

(a)

['Επὶ ..⁵⁻⁶.. ἄρχο]ντος· Μουνιχι[ῶνο]ς δευτέραι μετ'ε[ἰ]
[κάδας· βουλὴ ἐμ] βουλευτηρίω[ι σύ]νκλητος στρατη
[γῶν παραγγειλά]ντων χ[α]ὶ ἀπ[ὸ βουλ]ῆς ἐκκλησία ἀρ
[χαιρεσίαι κατὰ τ]ὴν μαντ[είαν τοῦ] θεοῦ· Τιμῶνα[ξ]

5   [...*ca.* 9... Κυδαθη]να[ιεὺς εἶπεν]· ἐπειδὴ Παυσίμ[α]
[χος πρότερόν τε διατρίβων παρὰ τῶι βασ]ιλεῖ Εὐμένε[ι]
[————————————————]νει[————]
[————————————————————]

lacuna

[————————————————————]

10   [τοὺς λαχόντας] προέδρ[ους εἰς τὴν ἐπιοῦσαν ἐκκλησία]
[ν χρηματίσαι] περὶ τούτω[ν, γνώμην δὲ ξυμβάλλεσθαι]
[τῆς βουλῆς εἰ]ς τὸν δῆμον ὅ[τι δοκεῖ τεῖ βουλεῖ ἐπαινέ]
[σαι Παυσίμαχ]ον Φιλοστ[ρ]άτου [——————, καὶ στεφανῶσ]
[αι θαλλοῦ στ]εφάνωι [ε]ὐνοίας ἕν[εκεν καὶ φιλοτιμί]

15   [ας τῆς πρὸς] τὸν δῆμον τὸν 'Αθη[ναίων· δεδόσθαι δὲ αὐτῶι]
[καὶ πολιτεί]αν κατὰ τὸν νόμον· [τοὺς δὲ θεσμοθέτας],
[ὅταν καὶ ὡς] πληρῶσιν τὸ δ[ι]καστ[ήριον εἰς ἕνα καὶ πεν]
[τακοσίους δ]ικαστάς, εἰσαγαγε[ῖν αὐτῶι τὴν δοκιμα]
[σίαν τῆς πολ]ιτογραφίας, καὶ ε[ἶναι αὐτῶι δοκιμασθέν]

20   [τι γράψασθα]ι φυλῆς καὶ δήμο[υ καὶ φρατρίας ἧς ἂν βούλη]
[ται· ἵνα δὲ καὶ] ὑπόμνημα ὑπά[ρχηι τῆς γεγονείας παρὰ]
[τοῦ δήμου τι]μῆς, ἀναγράψ[αι τὸ ψήφισμα τόδε τὸν γραμμ]
[ατέα τὸν κατ]ὰ πρυτανεί[αν ἐν στήλει λιθίνει καὶ στῆσαι]
[ἐν ἀκροπό]λει· τὸ δὲ γενό[μενον ἀνάλωμα μερίσαι]

25   [τὸν ταμία]ν τῶν στρατι[ωτικῶν.   *vacat*   ]

vacat

(b)

(c)

Lines 1–3. So Tracy, followed by Osborne, who however read εἰ *ad fin.* Line 4. Τιμῶνα[ξ] J. Kirchner. Tracy doubted the name and preferred Τίμων Α[. ||––] advocated by A. Wilhelm (*IG* II², Addendum, p. 669). Τίμων Α|| [––––] Osborne, in whose opinion alpha "surely ended the line." The name Timonax is, however, perfectly acceptable and avoids a division of the patronymic awkward on Wilhelm's interpretation and even more so on that of Osborne; even this mason might have shunned it, for the rest of his line endings are respectable enough. Line 5. [.....*ca.* 15......]ΝΔ[... εἶπεν] Tracy, in his text; but he noted (p. 49) the most probable restoration as that adopted here (and endorsed by Osborne), adding that 'Αμφιτρο]πα[ιεύς and 'Ιπποτο]μά[δης were "less likely but at least possible."

Line 6. So Kirchner, followed by Tracy: Osborne eschewed a restoration after the name of the honorand and continued ———]π[αρὰ τῶι βασι]λεῖ Εὐμένε[ι ²⁻³.]. Line 7. ———εὔ]νους [..*ca.* 8...] Osborne.

In fragment *c* Osborne introduced a line above line 10 as follows: [....*ca.* 13.....] ἀ[γαθῆι τύχηι δεδόχθαι τῆι βουλῆι] (where ΕΙ should no doubt be substituted for ΗΙ in the datives to conform to current practice); in the rest of the text he was able to discern remains of letters which had eluded earlier editors, none of them affecting the essentials of the passages concerned: line 13, Παυσίμα]χον, line 15, 'Αθηγ[αίων, line 16, τ[οὺς, line 17, δικαστ[ήριον, line 24, γενόμ[ενον, line 25, στρατιω[τικῶν.

Tracy identified this inscription as the work of the "Cutter of Agora I 247" (*Attic Letter-Cutters*, p. 101; see **264**). Any of the three dates proposed could be accommodated by his long career, although the earliest of them represents the earliest date at which, in consequence of Tracy's redating of the year of Achaios (see p. 371 above), he is otherwise attested. Meritt in his independent edition of fragment *a* gave it a date "*ante med. saec.* II *a.*"; *IG* II², 954 was given a date "*ante* 159".

The prescript is extraordinarily truncated, with the name of the γραμματεύς, the phyle in prytany, the prytany date, and the usual reference to the proedroi entirely omitted. Henry (*loc. cit.*; cf. pp. 84–85) added two further examples. There is no convincing explanation for any of them, unless in the present case it be that the long and unusual formula of lines 2–4 was the focus of attention and so consumptive of space that economies elsewhere were considered appropriate.

This formula of the βουλὴ σύγκλητος as it appears here, as far as ἀπὸ βουλῆς ἐκκλησία, has its parallels in *IG* II², 897 (185/4) and *Agora* XV, 167 (181/80). For assemblies held for an election κατὰ μαντείαν τοῦ θεοῦ, without references to a preceding βουλὴ σύγκλητος, see *IG* II², 892 (188/7) and 955 (162/1 or 159/8; see C. Habicht, *Hesperia* 59, 1990, pp. 567–568 and 576–577). Meritt (*Klio* 52, 1970, pp. 277–282) sought to concentrate the last-named text and the decree under present discussion along with *IG* II², 892 into 188/7, the year of Symmachos (see pp. 373–374 above), and indeed into a single meeting of the assembly, that of Mounichion 29. At that time *IG* II², 954 had not been associated with the Agora fragment I 2105, and Meritt's proposal involved the restoration in line 1, as it then stood, of ['Επὶ Συμμάχου ἄρχοντος]. When he made the association, Tracy pointed out that the archon's name thus restored would be too long for the lacuna as reassessed (although it might not be beyond the capacity of this mason to have written ΕΠΙΣΥΜΜΑΡΧΟΝΤΟΣ). Cf. Henry, *Prescripts*, p. 86, note 61. During the period now recognized as compatible with the contents and the craftsman, few archon names are short enough for consideration. At the time of Tracy's first analysis, Hippias' archonship was thought to belong to 193/2, which he rejected on historical grounds, assigning the decree to the year of Achaios, the apparently sole alternative, then agreed as 166/5. The relocation of Hippias to 181/80 and of Achaios to 190/89 allowed both archons to be considered; cf. Henry, *op. cit.*, pp. 86–87. Tracy's continuing preference for Achaios was accepted by Habicht, *op. cit.*, p. 567. 169/8, the year of Eunikos, is a further possibility (*pace* Osborne, *Naturalization* I, p. 210) if the iota of ἐπί be elided before Εὐνίκου: good relations between Athens and Eumenes II, with a specially summoned assembly involved, are attested at that time also. See Habicht, *loc. cit.* and **291**.

The ֺvere disruption of the calendar during the year of Achaios is a factor that must be taken into account; see pp. 371–372 above. It was particularly acute in this very month, Mounichion κατ'ἄρχοντα being equated with Thargelion κατὰ θεόν. This phenomenon and the careful inscriptional expression of it there evidenced is in no way reflected in the present context, and it may be suggested in consequence that 190/89 is after all less attractive as the year to which this decree is to be assigned. On balance, therefore, the year of Hippias has been preferred here; but the possibility that it is to be placed nine years earlier or a dozen years later cannot be excluded and awaits the discovery of fresh evidence.

Line 1. For the date of the assembly see J. D. Mikalson, *Sacred and Civil Calendar*, p. 149. Line 2. βουλὴ ἐμ βουλευτηρίωι. See **260**, commentary on lines 5–6. σύγκλητος. The meaning and implications of this description of the session of the boule have been much discussed. M. H. Hansen (*GRBS* 20, 1979, pp. 149–156 = *Athenian Ecclesia*, pp. 73–81) collected the epigraphical evidence for its use in connection with both the βουλή (as here) and the ἐκκλησία (pp. 151–152 = pp. 75–76), urging that (1) when the βουλή is so described the ἐκκλησία that followed must also have been σύγκλητος and that (2) these meetings were not additional to the regular meetings but were meetings of the regular kind called at short notice. He reemphasized this view in *GRBS* 28, 1987, pp. 48–50 (= *Athenian Ecclesia* II, pp. 190–192), chiefly against the criticisms of E. M. Harris, *CQ* n.s. 36, 1986, pp. 374–377, who asserted the traditional interpretation that these were extra meetings for sudden additional business. Cf. also Hansen, *The Athenian Assembly*, 1987, pp. 28–30, and see S. V. Tracy (*ZPE* 75, 1988, pp. 186–188), who also assembled the evidence and discussed the formulas employed (cf. **289**). Hansen's view was followed by Habicht, *Hesperia* 59, 1990, p. 570 with note 45.

Lines 2–3. στρατηγῶν παραγγειλάντων. For meetings of the βουλή and ἐκκλησία recorded as summoned at the instance of the στρατηγοί see also *IG* II², 897 and 911, *Agora* XV, 167, and *ID* 1507, in addition to **289**: and cf. P. J. Rhodes, *Athenian Boule*, p. 46 and Hansen, *The Athenian Assembly*, 1987, p. 25. Lines 3–4. It seems probable that a sudden declaration of a favorable μαντεία, perhaps after some delay in obtaining it, created the need for the next ἐκκλησία in prospect to be summoned at short notice. The business of the present decree is not urgent and was taken at the same meeting, a fact which supported Hansen's argument concerning the nature of σύγκλητοι assemblies (*GRBS* 20, 1979, p. 155 = *Athenian Ecclesia*, p. 79).

Line 5. On Pausimachos, who as the honorand of this decree was to receive full Athenian citizenship, see *PA* 11737; Wilhelm, *Beiträge zur griechischen Inschriftenkunde*, 1909, p. 81, no. 66. Wilhelm urged that he was the father of Philtera mentioned in a metrical inscription on the statue base *IG* II², 3474 (*SEG* XXXI, 166, XXXIII, 182), dated to the middle of the 2nd century; see *PA* 11738. The verses there record that he was five times ταγὸς στρατιᾶς and that his φρατρία was that of the Eteoboutadai. But Osborne regarded the connection as very improbable (*Naturalization* II, pp. 187–188). Line 6. For relations between the Athenians and the Pergamene kingdom in the reign of Eumenes II see Habicht, *Hesperia* 59, 1990, pp. 563–573 (on Pausimachos, p. 567).

Line 10. The decree was from its nature probouleumatic, and the proedroi acted without delay on their instructions as soon as the boule had risen. See Rhodes, *Athenian Boule*, p. 255. Lines 13–14. The stephanos awarded to Pausimachos was of olive, and the award is evidenced in a number of citizenship decrees: see Henry, *Honours*,

p. 39. The virtues for which Pausimachos is praised are two of those most regularly cited in decrees of this kind; see **224**, commentary on lines 34–36.

Lines 15–21. The formulas employed show this grant of citizenship as an example of Type III of Osborne's classification of citizenship decrees, a type which accounts for almost all such inscribed grants in the 2nd century; see Osborne, *Naturalization* I, pp. 16–17, 23, 194–196, and **239**. Lines 15–16. δεδόσθαι δὲ αὐτῶι | καὶ πολιτεί]αν. Osborne retained the δεδόσθαι δὲ αὐ|τῶι πολιτεί]αν of *IG* II², 954. Henry however pointed out (*Honours*, p. 109, note 159) that in Type III grants καί is regular in this position and suggested its inclusion here. The result does not make line 15 excessively long; cf., e.g., lines 17 and 20.

Lines 21–22. This variant of the "hortatory intention" is to be noted and is introduced here (as restored) by ἵνα rather than ὅπως. The use of ἵνα in such clauses is particularly attested in the first quarter of the 2nd century: see Henry, *CQ* n.s. 16, 1966, p. 292. Lines 24–25. The Military Treasurer is, as usual in this period, responsible for the expenditure. In the formula used here the phrase τὸ γενόμενον ἀνάλωμα is moved to the front of the clause. Cf. Henry, *ZPE* 78, 1989, pp. 285–290, and contrast **267**. Examples of this formulaic inversion occur as early as the 220's; see *IG* II², 844, of 229/8, and cf. also **224**.

THE DEMESMEN OF MELITE HONOR THE PRIESTESS SATYRA

277. The upper central and right section of a pedimental stele of Hymettian marble (I 5165), broken below and to the left, and with the right akroterion sheared away, but with the right side, the greater part of the pediment, and the original back preserved, discovered on January 24, 1938, in a modern wall west of the Panathenaic Way and west of the Eleusinion (R 19). The marble has a very pronounced diagonal grain, from upper right to lower left. The striations of a toothed chisel are faintly discernible, chiefly in a vertical or nearly vertical direction, over most of the inscribed surface. The inscription is complete below and is followed by a blank area over the remainder of the surviving surface.

H. 0.528 m.; W. 0.36 m.; Th. 0.117 m.

LH. 0.006 m. (omicron 0.004 m., phi 0.01 m.).

Ed. O. Broneer, *Hesperia* 11, 1942, pp. 265–274, no. 51, with photograph fig. 1. See also J. and L. Robert, *REG* 57, 1944, p. 200, no. 78. Broneer's text is reprinted in *SEG* XLII, 116, where further bibliography is added.

ca. a. 180 *a.*   NON-ΣΤΟΙΧ. 52–56

```
        [.........ca. 18.......x]λέους εἶπεν· ἐπειδὴ ἡ ἱέρεια τῶν Θεσμοφό
        [ρων προχεχριμένη ὑπὸ τῶν] δημοτῶν, Σατύρα, Κρατέου Μελιτέως γυν[ή],
        [ἔθυσεν ὑπὲρ τῶν δημοτῶν καλῶ]ς καὶ εὐσεβῶς πάσας τὰς καθηκούσας
        [θυσίας ἃς οἱ νόμοι προσέταττ]ον, ἐπεσκεύαχεν δὲ καὶ τοὺς ναοὺς πά[ν]
5       [τας τοὺς ἐν τῶι Ἐλευσινίωι, ἐπε]σκεύαχεν δὲ καὶ πά[ν]τα ἐν τῶι τοῦ Πλ[ού]
        [τωνος ἱερῶι, προσανήλωχεν δὲ καὶ] ἐκ τῶν ἰδίων ὑπὲρ τὰς ἑκατὸν δρα
        [χμὰς εἰς τὰς θυσίας τὰς γιγνομένα]ς κατ'ἐνιαυτόν, ἀγαθεῖ τύχει δεδό
        [χθαι τοῖς Μελιτεῦσι, ἐπαινέσαι τὴν ἱ]έρειαν τῶν Θ[ε]σμοφόρων Σατύρα⟨ν⟩
        [Κρατέου Μελιτέως γυναῖκα καὶ στε]φ[α]νῶσαι αὐτὴν μυρρίνης στεφά
10      [νωι εὐνοίας ἕνεκα καὶ εὐσεβείας τῆς εἰς τὰ]ς θεὰς καὶ τὸν δῆμον τὸν
        [Μελιτέων, δοῦναι δὲ αὐτῆι καὶ εἰκόνος ἀ]νάθεσιν ἐν πίνακι, καθάπε⟨ρ⟩
        [δέδοται καὶ ἄλλαις ἱερείαις ἐν τῶι ναῶι] τῆς Δήμητρος καὶ τῆς Κόρη[ς].
        [ἀναγράψαι δὲ τόδε τὸ ψήφισμα τὸν ταμίαν] τῶν δημοτῶν ἐν στήλει λ[ι]
        [θίνει καὶ στῆσαι πρὸς τῶι Ἐλευσινίωι· τὸ δὲ] ἀνάλωμα εἰς ταῦτα με[ρί]
15      [σαι ἐκ τῆς κοινῆς διοικήσεως].
```

The writing is slapdash and uncouth but not untypical of a good deal of the work of this period. Broneer compared the lettering of the prytany texts which now appear as *Agora* XV, 181 and 213; that of *IG* II², 895 is also comparable. The letters are badly articulated and often crowded. Epsilon, pi, and sigma are all particularly ill done. The outer strokes of sigma are sometimes parallel; the center stroke of alpha and epsilon is frequently omitted; the uprights of pi are, or seem intended to be, of equal length. The "oval" of phi is reduced to a narrow rectangle (line 9) almost indistinguishable from a simple line (line 8); the upright of the same letter projects considerably above and below the lines of writing. S. V. Tracy found himself unable to ascribe this text to an identifiable and "named" craftsman, but he regarded it as in the general style of the "Cutter of Agora I 247"; see *Attic Letter-Cutters*, p. 253, and **264**. Broneer, whose restorations are here followed (with one variation in line 5), gave to the inscription the generalized dating "Early Second Century B.C.": Tracy's proposed "*ca. a.* 180 *a.*" seems to fit the available criteria with slightly greater precision and is adopted here.

Line 1. On the truncated prescript see **245** and **251**. Line 2. For the restoration Broneer referred to Isaios 8.19–20. Krateas of Melite, whose wife the priestess Satyra was, is almost certainly to be equated with the Krateas of that deme, son of Nikolaos, whose tombstone survives as *IG* II², 6860. There is no other example of the name in Attic prosopography. Line 5. ἐπε]σκεύακεν J. and L. Robert; παρε]σκεύακεν Broneer. But cf. the restorations of *IG* II², 1219 and 1221.

Lines 5–6. The reading and restoration of Πλούτωνος ἱερόν (rather than, e.g., Π⟨α⟩νὸς ἱερόν) are prompted not only by the available space but also by the association of Plouton with the cult of the Eleusinian goddesses. Lines 6–7. Broneer cited the parallel of *IG* II², 956, lines 18–19. Line 7. ἀγαθεῖ τύχει. See **72**, commentary on lines 7–8. Line 8 *ad fin. Lapis* ΣΑΤΥΡΑᵛ. Line 9. For the stephanos of myrtle in honors bestowed upon cult officials see **228**, commentary; and see also A. S. Henry, *Honours*, pp. 41–42.

Line 11. Cf. *IG* II², 1327, lines 24–25, where the phrase is ἀναθεῖναι εἰκόνα ἐμ πίνακι, and the πίναξ is expressly paid for ἐκ τοῦ κοινοῦ. Broneer thought that the present turn of phrase offered no more than permission for a personal dedication by Satyra at her (or her husband's) own expense and that εἰς ταῦτα in line 14 refers only to ἀναγράψαι and στῆσαι in lines 13 and 14; but this is not a necessary deduction. At the end of the line, the stone shows ΚΑΘΑΠΕᵛ. Line 14. Πρὸς τῶι 'Ελευσινίωι. Cf. **228**, line 7 and **239**, line 13, with commentaries. On the restoration of the Eleusinion, at this point and in line 5, and its relationship with the Thesmophorion (usually held to have been located near the Pnyx) see Broneer, *op. cit.*, pp. 250–264 and 273–274; *Agora* III, pp. 81–82, no. 224, with further references; *Agora* XIV, p. 152 with note 178, where this piece of evidence is discussed.

D. Whitehead (*The Demes of Attica, 508/7–ca. 250 B.C.*, 1986) listed this decree on p. 384 as no. 80 and noted (p. 362) that it is the latest deme decree so far known. For Satyra herself, see p. 443, no. 293. Whether Melite should be restored as the deme concerned was doubted by K. Clinton; see *SEG* XLII, 116.

THE ARCHONSHIP OF MENEDEMOS, 179/8 B.C.

A Menedemos known as archon on papyrological evidence and assigned to the early 2nd century (*Papyrus Herculanensis* 1780; cf. W. Crönert, *Kolotes und Menedemos*, 1906, pp. 83 and 87) was identified by W. B. Dinsmoor (*Archons of Athens*, pp. 289–290) with the Menedemos latterly assigned to the year 92/1 B.C. (cf. B. D. Meritt, *Athenian Year*, p. 238, *Historia* 26, 1977, p. 188) and listed by J. Kirchner (*IG* II², iv, 1, pp. 22–23) among the "archontes saeculi II quorum tempora accuratius definiri nequeunt." The discovery of the prytany text Agora I 1025 (see S. Dow, *Prytaneis*, pp. 120–124, no. 64), later to become *Agora* XV, 194, gave the assurance that the archonship of Philon, securely dated to 178/7 on other grounds (see Dinsmoor, *op. cit.*, pp. 256–257) was the immediate successor to that of Menedemos; and the year of Menedemos, for which a γραμματεύς from Pandionis (III) was therefore to be expected, was at once fixed as 179/8, a year until then blank in all assessments (Dinsmoor, *op. cit.*, p. 222).

Dinsmoor registered these conclusions in *Athenian Archon List*, p. 188, where he further attributed to this year **263**, for in that text the demotic of the γραμματεύς, Πρασιεύς, belonged to Pandionis, with the added assurance that "the allowance of about ten letters for the archon's name would approximately fit that of Menedemos." This was the correspondence listed by W. K. Pritchett and Meritt in *Chronology*, p. xxvii, and (on the basis of **263**) the year was shown as certainly ordinary in character. Cf. Pritchett and O. Neugebauer, *Calendars*, p. 85. The same arrangement was retained by Meritt in *Hesperia* 26, 1957, p. 94 and in *Athenian Year*, p. 236.

The publication of **278** made it clear that Menedemos was to be associated with a γραμματεύς from the deme Angele rather than from Prasiai, and **263** was therefore dissociated from his archonship. But the date of Menedemos' year remained unaffected; see Meritt, *Historia* 26, 1977, p. 181 and C. Habicht, *Studien*, pp. 168, 177.

Although **278** provided no calendric evidence, Meritt regarded it as likely that the year was intercalary rather than ordinary (*TAPA* 95, 1964, p. 239), with two surely ordinary years preceding it and another immediately following it. The earlier of the two preceding years, 181/80, had however to be accepted as intercalary when Hippias was finally located there (see Meritt, *Historia* 26, 1977, p. 181 and p. 384 above): but 180/79 must remain ordinary in the reckoning. In the arrangement of Meton, 179/8 would have been ordinary, as the seventh year in the fourteenth cycle. There is no information regarding the prytany calendar or the succession of phylai in prytany.

FRAGMENT OF A DECREE

278. The upper left corner of a pedimental stele of Hymettian marble (I 6986), with part of the left side and part of the pediment preserved but with the left akroterion missing, discovered in August 1964 in a disturbed area below the Church of St. Dionysios (N 23). A heavy ovolo molding, considerably battered, intervenes between the narrow horizontal cornice of the pediment and an equally narrow taenia, below which a rough apophyge descends to the inscribed surface.

H. 0.14 m.; W. 0.09 m.; Th. 0.075 m.
LH. 0.005 m.

Ed. B. D. Meritt, *Hesperia* 34, 1965, p. 89, no. 1, with photograph pl. 25. See also *SEG* XXII, 104.

a. 179/8 a.   NON-ΣTOIX. *ca.* 59(?)

```
        Ἐπὶ Μενεδήμο[υ ἄρχοντος ἐπὶ τῆς –––––––––––––πρυτανείας ἧι –––––]
        Δημητρίου Ἀγγ[ελῆθεν ἐγραμμάτευεν· –––––––––––––––––––––– τῆς]
        [π]ρυτανείας· ἐ[κκλησία κυρία ἐν τῶι θεάτρωι· τῶν προέδρων ἐπεψήφιζεν –––]
        [. .]ς Φαινίππ[ου ––––––––––––––––––––––––––––––––––––––––––––––]
5       [––––––––––––––––––––––––––––––––––––––––––––––––––––––––––––]
```

The lettering of this fragment gives an appearance of lateral crowding but is neither untidy nor inaccurate. There is some attempt at the addition of serifs or at least of some deeper emphasis to the "free ends" of some of the strokes. These and other characteristics led S. V. Tracy to identify the inscription as the work, in fact the earliest datable work, of the craftsman he named the "Cutter of *IG* II² 903": see *Attic Letter-Cutters*, pp. 132–136, with photograph of the name piece, fig. 19. **290** and **292** are also to be attributed to this mason, whose output can be traced as far as 161/60 (*IG* II², 956).

Lines 1–2. The family of the γραμματεύς cannot be further identified. Line 3. For the character and location of the assembly, restored here to suit the evident requirements of the length of line, see **167**, commentary on lines 6–7 and **101**, commentary on lines 7–8.

THE ARCHONSHIP OF – – – – IPPOS, 177/6 B.C.

The archons Hippakos and Sonikos, the latter of whom had in his year a γραμματεύς from the deme Perithoidai (Oineis VII), are known from the second decree on the stele *IG* II², 1328 (see p. 393 below) to have held office in successive years; and the operation of the secretary cycle combined with other indications to define those years as 176/5 and 175/4. With Philon surely attributed to 178/7, the intervening year 177/6 lacked identification with a known archon in the estimates of W. S. Ferguson, J. Kirchner (*IG* II², iv, 1, pp. 18–19), and others. W. B. Dinsmoor's interpretation of the cycle, varying at this point by one year from that of Ferguson, assigned 177/6 to Hippakos and 176/5 to Sonikos (*Archons of Athens*, pp. 222, 256–257); but Ferguson again left the year blank in his restated arrangement (*Athenian Tribal Cycles*, p. 29). The discovery of the prytany fragment I 1057 (see S. Dow, *Prytaneis*, p. 125, no. 65), later republished as *Agora* XV, 228, provided evidence of an archon Speusippos, with a γραμματεύς from Phlya (Ptolemais V); and the style of the inscription suggested that the year 177/6, which did indeed require a γραμματεύς from Ptolemais, was admirably suited for attribution to the new archon. Dow's proposal was welcomed by Dinsmoor (*Athenian Archon List*, p. 188) and was followed by W. K. Pritchett and B. D. Meritt, *Chronology*, p. xxviii.

The publication of **279**, showing a γραμματεύς from Oinoe who, as the son of Hegetor, was identifiable on prosopographical grounds (see below) as a member of the phyle Ptolemais, subsequently displaced Speusippos from this year to a date in the later 150's; see Meritt, *Historia* 26, 1977, p. 183 and C. Habicht, *Hesperia* 57, 1988, pp. 241, 246: but the archon in whose year Hegetor's son held office remained unidentified.

The publication of *SEG* XXI, 447 (*Agora* XV, 197) again provided the patronymic and demotic of the same γραμματεύς but not his own name. This time, however, the last part at least of the archon's name did survive, sufficiently to show that it ended as – – – –ippos. See Meritt, *Athenian Year*, pp. 201 and 236, correcting his entry in *Hesperia* 26, 1957, p. 94 (cf. *ibid.*, p. 38, note 28), which had preceded the publication of the evidence. Until some further discovery enlarges the evidential material, the year remains as additionally defined by Meritt in *TAPA* 95, 1964, p. 239 and *Historia* 26, 1977, p. 181. Cf. A. E. Samuel, *Greek and Roman Chronology*, 1972, p. 218.

The year of Sonikos (175/4) is known to have been intercalary in the Athenian festival calendar, and that of Philon (178/7) was certainly ordinary. Meritt's earlier view had been that 177/6 was intercalary (*Athenian Year*, p. 236); cf. Dinsmoor, *Athenian Archon List*, p. 23; Pritchett and Meritt, *Chronology*, p. xxviii; Meritt, *Hesperia* 26, 1957, p. 94. This was, however, revised in the light of the changes in the preceding years introduced by Meritt in *TAPA* 95, 1964, p. 239, and he was prepared to see the year as ordinary (cf. *Historia* 26, p. 181). It was indeed ordinary in the Metonic calendar, in which it was the ninth year of the fourteenth cycle.

There is no evidence, in either of the two surviving texts of the year of – – – – ippos, for the festival or prytany calendars. **279** shows the phyle Akamantis in office in a prytany thought by Pritchett to have been possibly the fourth but shown by Meritt to be unidentifiable.

FRAGMENT OF A DECREE

279. A fragment of the upper right corner of a pedimental stele of Hymettian marble (I 4900), considerably worn, with the right side and part of the pediment preserved, discovered on May 20, 1937, in a Byzantine context on the North Slope of the Akropolis, east of the Post-Herulian Wall (T 23–24). The architecture of the stele is perfunctory. The pediment is raised in low relief against a larger background. It has no horizontal cornice, but a taenia, 0.01 m. in vertical measurement, is set back directly below it, descending with a very sharp apophyge to the inscribed face.

H. 0.125 m.; W. 0.14 m.; Th. 0.07 m.

LH. 0.005 m. (omicron 0.003 m.).

Ed. W. K. Pritchett, *Hesperia* 16, 1947, pp. 188–191, no. 94, with photograph pl. XXXIX. A correction to lines 1–2 by B. D. Meritt, *Athenian Year*, p. 201, note 17. Cf. also *SEG* XXI, 447, *in lemmate*.

a. 177/6 a.   NON-ΣTOIX. *ca.* 36–38

[’Επι – – – – ἱππου ἄρχοντος ἐπὶ τῆς ’Α]καμαντίδος
[– – – – – πρυτανείας ἧι – – – – –]ης ‘Ηγήτορος Οἰ
[ναῖος ἐγραμμάτευεν· – – – – ῶν]ος τ[ετ]ράδι [. . .]
[—————————————————————]

The writing of this text, characterized by Pritchett as "tachygraphic", proved to be the work of the craftsman identified by S. V. Tracy as the "Cutter of Agora I 247", for whose career and characteristics, as well as a list of his remarkable output, see **264** and references there. On this small fragment the attenuated omicron and the two strokes forming the loop of rho are very typical.

Lines 2–3. Hegetor of Oinoe, son of Aristoboulos and father of the γραμματεύς of this year, was himself ταμίας of the boule *ca.* 190 (*Agora* XV, 170, lines 10–11 and 103–104) and ταμίας of the prytaneis of Ptolemais in 192/1 (*Agora* XV, 187). The Οἰναῖοι Aristoboulos, Aristoteles, and Theodoros, commemorated in *SEG* XVIII, 106, of the early 3rd century, could well be members of this family in an earlier generation.

THE ARCHONSHIP OF HIPPAKOS, 176/5 B.C.

The second of the decrees of the orgeones of the cult of the Magna Mater inscribed on *IG* II², 1328, dated by the archon Sonikos, honors the zakoros Metrodora whose duties began in the archonship of Hippakos (*PA* 7587), evidently the year preceding that of Sonikos. The demotic of the γραμματεύς of Sonikos' year (Perithoides, from Oineis [VII]) gave his archonship a firm place on the original reckoning of W. S. Ferguson (*Athenian Secretaries*, p. 55) at 175/4, with the year of Hippakos designated in consequence as 176/5. These attributions have remained constant throughout subsequent studies of the archon list, save for the modification, soon discarded, by which W. B. Dinsmoor sought to set them one year earlier (*Archons of Athens*, pp. 256–257, retracted in *Athenian Archon List*, pp. 170–171, 188–189). See J. Kirchner, *IG* II², iv, 1, pp. 18–19; Ferguson, *Athenian Tribal Cycles*, p. 29; W. K. Pritchett and B. D. Meritt, *Chronology*, p. xxviii; Pritcheett and O. Neugebauer, *Calendars*, p. 75; Meritt, *Hesperia* 26, 1957, p. 95, *Athenian Year*, pp. 144–145 and 236, *TAPA* 95, 1964, p. 239, *Historia* 26, 1977, p. 181; A. E. Samuel, *Greek and Roman Chronology*, 1972, p. 218. The attribution of Hippakos received additional confirmation from the discovery of **280**, in which the archon's name and the demotic of the γραμματεύς, who belonged to the deme Iphistiadai (Akamantis VI), are alike preserved.

Besides *IG* II², 1328, Hippakos as archon was referred to in *IG* II², 903 (*SEG* XXXII, 132), at line 6; and *IG* II², 904 offered a fragment of a prescript with his name preserved only as far as its third letter but regarded by Kirchner, S. Dow (*Prytaneis*, p. 125), Dinsmoor (*Athenian Archon List*, p. 189), and Pritchett and Meritt (*Chronology*, p. 117) as better attributed to this year than to that of Hippias. But *IG* II², 904 had subsequently to be removed from consideration, since it was shown (by C. Karapa, Δελτ. 29, A', 1974 [1977], pp. 163–164; cf. *SEG* XXVI, 108) to form part of *IG* II², 889, so that, in consequence, it demonstrably belongs to Hippias' year; see p. 383 above. *IG* II², 1326, a decree of the society of the Dionysiastai, is also dated by the archonship of Hippakos. Meritt ascribed to this same year the fragment E.M. 454, published by Pritchett in *Hesperia* 16, 1947 (p. 187, no. 93), and identified the γραμματεύς more fully (*Hesperia* 26, 1957, pp. 69–71; *SEG* XVI, 88; see below in the commentary to **280**).

The name Hippakos, it may be added, is extremely unusual in Attic prosopography, and only one other holder of it has been positively identified (for *PA* 7588 see also J. Sundwall, *Nachträge zur Prosopographia Attica*, 1910, p. 101). A third Hippakos is perhaps to be restored in *IG* II², 2064, an ephebic text of the 2nd century A.D., at line 24.

Before the publication of **280**, none of the evidence offered confirmation of the calendric character of the year; but the year of Sonikos was certainly intercalary, and that of Hippakos was therefore inferred to have been ordinary. So Ferguson, *Athenian Tribal Cycles*, p. 29; Dinsmoor, *Athenian Archon List*, p. 23, following *Archons of Athens*, p. 32. The evidence of **280** was equivocal, since, as restored, it appeared to equate the 31st day of a prytany with a date early in a lunar month. Pritchett and Meritt retained the year as notionally ordinary (*Chronology*, p. xxviii); but Pritchett and Neugebauer (*Calendars*, p. 76), stating that "a 31-day prytany is not possible in an ordinary year of twelve phylae," were compelled to suspend judgment on both 176/5 and 175/4 in order to escape the potential conclusion that both years might have been intercalary. *SEG* XVI, 88 could not help in a solution to the problem, to which Meritt returned briefly in *Athenian Year*, pp. 144–145, where he opposed the claim of Pritchett and Neugebauer concerning 31-day prytanies. He continued to regard the year as ordinary (cf. *Historia* 26, 1977, p. 181) and in ultimately accepting the unacceptability of a 31-day prytany in it he revised the restoration of **280** to eliminate such a proposition, *GRBS* 17, 1976, pp. 150–151. In the Metonic calendar the year would have been intercalary, as the tenth of the fourteenth period.

There is no evidence, beyond the anomalies of **280**, for either the prytany or the festival calendar, nor yet for the phylai in office during the prytany year.

FRAGMENT OF A DECREE

280. The upper left corner of a pedimental stele of Hymettian marble (I 4250), with a small part of the left side, the original back, and more than half of the pediment preserved but the fragment otherwise broken, discovered on June 12, 1936, in a marble pile in the area of the western part of the Odeion. The horizontal cornice of the pediment surmounts an ovolo molding, taenia, and apophyge very similar in character to the moldings of **272** and **273**.

H. 0.277 m.; W. 0.25 m.; Th. 0.098 m.

LH. 0.005 m. (omicron 0.003 m.).

Ed. W. K. Pritchett and B. D. Meritt, *Chronology*, pp. 119–121, with photograph. See also Meritt, *Hesperia* 26, 1957, p. 70; A. S. Henry, *Prescripts*, pp. 91–92.

a. 176/5 a.   NON-ΣΤΟΙΧ. *ca.* 52

> 'Επὶ 'Ιππάκου ἄρχοντος ἐπὶ [τῆς ————————πρυτανείας ἧι ——————]
> [..]κράτου 'Ιφιστιάδης ἐγ[ραμμάτευεν· μηνὸς . . . . ᶜᵃ·¹⁸. . . . .]
> [. . .] ἐσιόντος, μιᾶι καὶ [εἰκοστεῖ τῆς πρυτανείας· ἐκκλησία κυρία]·
> [τῶ]ν προέδρων ἐπε[ψήφιζεν . . . . . ᶜᵃ·¹⁵. . . . . . καὶ συμπρόεδροι· ἔδοξεν]
> 5   [τεῖ βουλεῖ] καὶ τῶι [δήμωι· ————————————————————]
> [————————] *reliquiae incertae* [————————————————]
> [——————————————————————————————————]

Like the immediately preceding text, **279**, this inscription was identified by S. V. Tracy as one of the many productions of the "Cutter of Agora I 247"; see **264** and references there. In this example the omicrons and the loops of rho are expressed in a more circular form than in some of his more extreme "tachygraphic" work.

Lines 2–3. μηνὸς Ἐλαφηβολιῶνος ἐνά|τει] ἐσιόντος, μιᾶι καὶ [εἰκοστεῖ Meritt, *GRBS* 17, 1976, pp. 150–151; whence the prytany to be restored in line 1 would be the ninth. The festival calendar must be supposed to have been retarded by the addition of ten extra days. This is a reasonable but not the only possible solution. The *editio princeps* showed μιᾶι καὶ [τριακοστεῖ in line 3, without restorations elsewhere beyond those adopted in the present text.

The apex of the pediment is preserved, and from it the median vertical line of the stele may be determined. This in turn conditions the extent of the lacuna for which restorations may be offered. Since the name of the γραμματεύς must be the final element in line 1, this would make it impossible for an ordinal numeral to accompany the name of the phyle in prytany, which should appear earlier in the line, were that γραμματεύς to be the Charinos whose name, patronymic, and demotic are partly preserved and partly restored in *SEG* XVI, 88. Cf. Meritt, *Hesperia, loc. cit.*, where the citation of a parallel from **295** is inexact, Meritt having himself corrected his original text and included an ordinal numeral in it. See the lemma *ad loc.* A text of the present inscription shown by Henry, *loc. cit.*, which incorporates the full name of the γραμματεύς derived from *SEG* XVI, 88, omits to observe that the first two letters of line 2 are subject to restoration and must be viewed with skepticism. In the absence of satisfactory documentation it seems preferable to reject the proposition that the γραμματεύς of *SEG* XVI, 88, Χαρῖνος Σωκρ[– – – –], is to be identified with the [– – – – – – – –]κράτου Ἰφιστιάδης of this text. A short name of five letters at the end of line 1 would leave *ca.* fourteen letters for the name of the phyle and the ordinal numeral, sufficient (for example) for Αἰγεῖδος ἐνάτης. Meritt (*loc. cit.*) produced strong arguments against the possible alternative attribution of Charinos to 195/4, where the γραμματεύς was at the time thought to be [. . . . .*ca.*14. . . . .]κράτου Σημαχί[δης]. It is a more likely hypothesis that he was γραμματεύς in a year such as 180/79, for which firm evidence has not as yet been forthcoming.

The expression of the festival date (lines 2–3) is remarkable. Pritchett and Meritt urged as a parallel the [μηνὸς Ποσιδεῶνος] πέμπτει ἀπιόντος of *IG* II², 951, lines 1–2, a text of 167/6: its validity for the present example is rejected by Henry (*Prescripts*, pp. 91–92), who further noted (p. 91, note 89) that ἐσ[– –] for εἰσ[– – –] is a strange occurrence in a text of this date. The present document remains in this respect, as Henry concluded, "unique and unexplained."

Line 3. ἐκκλησία κυρία. See **101**, commentary on lines 6–7. This phrase, without further designation of the venue of the assembly, is last clearly attested in **263**. It is unlikely that the lettering towards the end of the line became sufficiently crowded to permit ἐκκλησία ἐμ Πειραιεῖ. See **282**. Lines 4–5. The enactment was evidently probouleumatic; but it was not listed by P. J. Rhodes, *Athenian Boule*.

THE ARCHONSHIP OF ALEXANDROS, 174/3 B.C.

283, on its discovery, provided the first epigraphical testimony of the archon Alexandros, although he appears in a fragment of Apollodoros (F. Jacoby, *FGrHist*, no. 244, fr. 47), who quoted Philodemos to the effect that, in his archonship, the death took place of the philosopher Euboulos of Erythrai. The range of dates to be derived from this context lies between 185/4 and 168/7. This led W. Kolbe and J. Kirchner to a date "paullo ante 168/7" for the archonship (see Jacoby *in comm., IG* II², iv, 1, pp. 22–23; *PA* 484 add.) and W. B. Dinsmoor to a more exact but still tentative attribution to 173/2 (*Archons of Athens*, pp. 256–258; cf. p. 222). W. S. Ferguson (*Athenian Tribal Cycles*, p. 34) was content with a more general estimate of 174/3–170/69, which Dinsmoor later took as adequate confirmation of his tentative proposal, repeated as it was in *Athenian Archon List*, p. 189. The attribution, with a question mark, was adopted by W. K. Pritchett and B. D. Meritt, *Chronology*, p. xxviii.

The publication of **283**, while giving inscriptional evidence for Alexandros as archon, could do nothing for his date in terms more precise than the general character of the writing could indicate. Nor was the second text of his year that came to light, **282**, any more helpful, although it did provide the first five letters (Αὐτοχ– –) of the name of the γραμματεύς. It was not until the publication of a third text by Meritt in 1957 (*Hesperia* 26, pp. 71–72, no. 21; *SEG* XVI, 90; *Agora* XV, 202) that the full name of the γραμματεύς was established. This showed him as of the deme Pithos (Kekropis VIII), for which the secretary cycle indicated 174/3 as the necessary dating. Alexandros was therefore listed as of this date in Meritt's revised table of archons (*Hesperia* 26, 1957, p. 95) and has so remained in subsequent accounts (Meritt, *Athenian Year*, p. 236, *TAPA* 95, 1964, p. 239, *Historia* 26, 1977, p. 181; cf. A. E. Samuel, *Greek and Roman Chronology*, 1972, p. 218).

Before its ultimate attribution to Alexandros, 174/3 had stood as a blank in the lists drawn up by Kirchner, Ferguson, and Dinsmoor. But Pritchett and Meritt placed here that archon Demetrios, with a γραμματεύς allegedly from Halai, whose varying assignments have provided so much difficulty in the developing study of the archon list (see p. 405 below). This determination made the year certainly ordinary in the festival calendar. That it was ordinary had been a reasonable hypothesis, since the year of Sonikos before it had been certainly intercalary, and it had been so indicated by both Ferguson and Dinsmoor. As such it formed part of the study of ordinary years in the period of twelve phylai by Pritchett and O. Neugebauer, *Calendars*, p. 85. The discovery of *Agora* XV, 202 invalidated the hypothesis concerning Demetrios' archonship, but neither it nor any other of the texts of the year contained data sufficient to establish its calendric character. That it was ordinary remained nevertheless the obvious supposition, and it was so shown by Meritt in *Hesperia* 26, 1957, p. 95, and in his later publications (see above). The year was the twelfth in the fourteenth Metonic cycle and was, as it happened, ordinary in the cycle as well as (by hypothesis) in the Athenian festival calendar. Of the phylai in prytany, evidence exists only for IV Leontis and perhaps V Attalis.

FRAGMENT OF A DECREE

281. A fragment from the upper central section of a pedimental stele of Hymettian marble (I 6589), broken on all sides but with the crowning moldings and part of the pediment, much battered, preserved above the inscribed surface, discovered on March 23, 1953, in a late wall over the northwest corner of the Rectangular Peribolos (I 14). The molding, more elaborate than those of **272**, **273**, and **278**, consists principally of an ovolo with cavetto crown, more in the style of **254** though with a more sharply curved cavetto. Beneath the ovolo, a taenia 0.009 m. in height surmounts a sharp apophyge descending to the inscribed surface. The marble is somewhat "milky" in appearance, and on the inscribed face the striations of a toothed chisel are visible, running diagonally from upper right to lower left.

H. 0.185 m.; W. 0.20 m.; Th. 0.08 m. (horizontal cornice of pediment), 0.035 m. (inscribed surface).
LH. 0.006 m.

Ed. B. D. Meritt, *Hesperia* 32, 1963, p. 20, no. 19, with photograph pl. 5. See also *SEG* XXI, 449.

a. 174/3 a., pryt. V(?)   NON-ΣΤΟΙΧ. ca. 47

```
        [Θ]              ε              ο              [ι].
        ['Επὶ 'Αλεξάνδρου ἄ]ρχοντος ἐπὶ τῆς 'Αττ[αλίδος πέμπτης πρυτα]
        [νείας ἧι Αὐτοκρ]άτης Α[ὐτοκράτου Πιθεὺς ἐγραμμάτευεν]·
        [Μαιμακτηριῶ]νο[ς ------------------------]
    5   [------------------------------------]
```

If the spacing of line 1 was reasonably symmetrical, there will have been room for ἐπί at the beginning of line 2, in place of Meritt's ἐπ'. Line 3 seems to be slightly more generously spaced than line 2, and there is no need to suppose, as Meritt did, two vacant spaces at the end of it.

The firm and clean lettering of this fragment revealed it, on the reckoning of S. V. Tracy (*Hesperia* 47, 1978, p. 257, *Attic Letter-Cutters*, p. 75), as the work of the "Cutter of *IG* II² 913". It is one of the latest pieces in a long career that began some forty years earlier and is not known to have outlasted the archonship of Antigenes (171/70). See **248**.

Lines 2 and 4. The restoration of πέμπτης and Μαιμακτηριῶνος, conforming to the supposition that this was an ordinary year, provides the best combination to take account both of the calendar and of the disposable space. But in default of corroborative evidence it remains no more than a hypothesis. Line 3. Autokrates, son of Autokrates, of Pithos is restored on the basis of *Agora* XV, 202, line 2. Neither he nor his family can be further identified.

FRAGMENT OF A DECREE

282. The upper left corner of a pedimental stele of Hymettian marble (I 3804 b), with parts of the left side, left akroterion, pediment, and original back preserved, discovered on October 21, 1937, in a wall of a modern house outside the Market Square to the southeast (P 21). The ovolo molding directly beneath the wide horizontal cornice and set above a narrow taenia with sharp apophyge to the inscribed surface of the stele is comparable with that of **272**.

H. 0.16 m.; W. 0.155 m.; Th. 0.156 m.
LH. 0.006 m.

Ed. W. K. Pritchett, *Hesperia* 16, 1947, p. 191, no. 95, with photograph pl. XXXIX. A passing reference by J. and L. Robert, *REG* 61, 1948, p. 147, no. 44.

a. 174/3 *a.*   NON-ΣTOIX. *ca.* 55

'Επὶ 'Αλεξάν[δρου ἄρχοντος ἐπὶ τῆς ....^{ca. 21}......... πρυτανε]
[ία]ς ἧι Αὐτοχ[ράτης Αὐτοχράτου Πιθεὺς ἐγραμμάτευεν· ...^{ca. 8}... ῶνος]
[ἔνηι καὶ] νέα[ι, τριαχοστεῖ τῆς πρυτανείας· ἐκκλησία ἐμ Πειραιεῖ· τῶν]
[προέδρ]ων [ἐπεψήφιζεν —————————————————————————]
5   [—————————————————————————————————————]

The lettering is elegant and well constructed, with the letters precisely articulated, very different in style and character from its contemporary **283**. The "free ends" of strokes are decorated with well-cut serifs. The two upright strokes of pi are of equal length; xi retains its vertical stroke. The crossbar of alpha is curved or broken, the latter being in any case a novelty in Attic epigraphy at this time: S. V. Tracy's "Cutter of *IG* II² 1329" and "Cutter of Agora I 6512" (*Attic Letter-Cutters*, pp. 125–131), whose earliest works are of 183/2 and *ca.* 180 respectively, seem to have been its first exponents. Omicron is full and well rounded. The vertical strokes throughout lean slightly forward, and the writing runs "downhill" in relation to the cornice above. The left margin of the text is unusually well set in from the edge of the stele. Tracy found nothing to provide a convincing parallel with this style and classed it as unique of its kind (*op. cit.*, p. 252).

Pritchett assessed the length of line at *ca.* 50–53 letters. Line 3 is here restored with the greatest possible economy to show a prytany of 30 days and an ordinary assembly in the Peiraieus; and this produced a line of 55 letters. The hypothesis of a prytany of 29 days (for a hollow month), or an assembly in the theater, would require more letters to the line: furthermore, it would tend to produce difficulties for the name of the month in line 2 as well as for the name of the phyle and for the ordinal numeral in line 1, where twenty-one letters would in fact account for the maximum possible entry, 'Ιπποθωντίδος ἐνδεχάτης or δωδεχάτης. But the lettering in line 1 may be slightly more generously spaced than that in the lines below it. The designation of the assembly as ἐκκλησία or as ἐκκλησία χυρία *tout simple* cannot be assumed at this period. **263** gives the last firm example of the latter among the Agora *psephismata* of this collection, although it has been restored in **278**; and **227** shows the last example of the former. Meetings in the Peiraieus tended to take place in the last third of the month; see **259**, commentary on line 4. For the γραμματεύς see **281**, commentary on line 3.

FRAGMENT OF A DECREE

283. The upper left corner of a pedimental stele of Hymettian marble (I 2115), with the left side and more than half of the pediment (including the left and part of the central akroterion) as well as part of the original back preserved, discovered on October 1, 1934, in a wall of a modern house over the northern part of the Odeion (L 10). The moldings between the floor of the pediment and the inscribed face are closely similar to those of **282**.

H. 0.255 m.; W. 0.24 m.; Th. 0.12 m. (horizontal cornice of pediment), 0.075 m. (inscribed surface).
LH. 0.006 m. (omicron 0.004 m.)

Ed. W. K. Pritchett, *Hesperia* 10, 1941, pp. 279–280, no. 75, with photograph.

a. 174/3 *a.*   NON-ΣTOIX. *ca.* 38–42

'Επὶ 'Αλεξάνδρου [ἄρχοντος ἐπὶ τῆς .....^{13–14}.....]
πρυτανείας ε[ἶ Αὐτοχράτης Αὐτοχράτου Πιθεὺς ἐ]
γραμμάτευεν· [..........^{ca. 26}.........., πέμ]
πτει καὶ εἰκ[οστεῖ τῆς πρυτανείας· ἐκκλησία ἐμ Πει]
5   ραιεῖ· τῶ[ν προέδρων ἐπεψήφιζεν .....^{ca. 14}.....]
[Θυ]μαι[τάδης(?) καὶ συμπρόεδροι· ἔδοξεν τεῖ βουλεῖ καὶ]
[τῶι δ]ή[μωι· ——————————————————]
[—————————————————————————————]

The lettering of this fragment presents a striking contrast with the quality of that of its contemporary **282**. On analysis it proved to be one more work by the slapdash "Cutter of Agora I 247" and exhibits the regular, far from commendable characteristics of that mason. See S. V. Tracy, *Attic Letter-Cutters*, p. 102 and **264**.

At the time of the *editio princeps* the identity of the γραμματεύς of the year of Alexandros was as yet unknown, but the existence of the apex of the pediment provided the median vertical line of the monument, and the length of the lines of writing was assured as of *ca.* 40 letters. Lines 4 and 6, as restored by Pritchett, showed 41 and 42 letters respectively; line 2, with the inclusion of the name of the γραμματεύς, produced a length of 38 letters. The name of the phyle in prytany and the ordinal numeral together in line 1 will account for not more than 13–14 letters, and the date in line 3 *ca.* 26 letters. A combination of Αἰγεῖδος (or Οἰνεῖδος) ἕκτης in line 1 with Ποσιδεῶνος ἕκτης or πέμπτης μετ'εἰκάδας in line 3 (of which the former is more acceptable; cf. J. D. Mikalson, *Sacred and Civil Calendar*, pp. 94–95) would correspond most conveniently to the requirements.

Line 2. εἴ for ἧι in the dative singular of the relative pronoun is a rarity at any time, especially in this formula and particularly at this period. See A. S. Henry, *CQ* n.s. 14, 1964, pp. 244–245 and L. Threatte, *Grammar*, p. 378. For the γραμματεύς see **281**, commentary on line 3. Line 4. ἐκκλησία ἐμ Πειραιεῖ. See **259**, commentary on line 4. Here too the assembly in the Peiraieus was held in the last third of the prytany.

Lines 6–7. The decree may be interpreted as probouleumatic, if the remains in line 7 are accurately assessed, and was so accepted by P. J. Rhodes, *Athenian Boule*, p. 255.

THE ARCHONSHIP OF ALEXIS, 173/2 B.C.

The year 173/2 B.C., for which no firm evidence existed either in the literary or in the epigraphical record, remained a blank in the reconstruction of the archon list after the evaluation of the secretary cycle had showed that its γραμματεύς must have belonged to the phyle Hippothontis (IX). See W. S. Ferguson, *Athenian Secretaries*, p. 55; J. Kirchner, *IG* II², iv, 1, pp. 18–19; W. B. Dinsmoor, *Archons of Athens*, p. 222. Dinsmoor himself (*ibid.*, pp. 256–258) sought to place Alexandros in this year (see p. 395 above), and although it was passed over by Ferguson in *Athenian Tribal Cycles* (pp. 29 and 34), he repeated this tentative attribution in 1939 (*Athenian Archon List*, p. 189), after which it was adopted by W. K. Pritchett and B. D. Meritt, *Chronology*, p. xxviii.

The discovery in 1954 of Agora I 6671, published by G. A. Stamires in *Hesperia* 26, 1957 (pp. 33–47, no. 6; see *SEG* XVI, 91) and later appearing as *Agora* XV, 206, gave a date by a new and complete archon Alexis, although without any mention of the γραμματεύς. Stamires was able to demonstrate that combined prosopographical and calendric requirements (the year was shown by an intercalated Metageitnion to have been intercalary) conspired to make 173/2 a justifiable year in which to place the newly found archon (*loc. cit.*, pp. 37–38). He further attributed **284** to this year and added *IG* II², 996 as a third document of Alexis' archonship. See *SEG* XVI, 92 and 93. It is of interest that none of these texts leaves room for mention of the γραμματεύς: see **284**, commentary on line 2. Since Stamires' publication, the attribution of 173/2 to Alexis has not been disputed. See Meritt, *Hesperia* 26, 1957, p. 95, *Athenian Year*, pp. 159, 165, 236, *TAPA* 95, 1964, p. 239, *Historia* 26, 1977, p. 182; C. Habicht, *Studien*, p. 173, note 76. It was hesitantly accepted by A. E. Samuel, *Greek and Roman Chronology*, 1972, p. 218.

Meritt at one time attributed to this year the prytany text *SEG* XXI, 422 (see also XXV, 115), which became *Agora* XV, 207: but his revised determination was that this decree is preferably to be located in the year of Timouchos(?), 191/90 B.C. See p. 369 above, and cf. A. S. Henry (*Prescripts*, p. 80), who wished to place it later rather than earlier in the century but at any rate appreciated that it did not belong to Alexis' archonship.

One feature of the three texts of Alexis' year, thus assembled, is that two of them, as restored, specify a dating in the festival calendar κατὰ θεόν: cf. Henry, *Prescripts*, pp. 78–79. For the discussion concerning the date κατὰ θεόν without corresponding qualification "according to the archon" see **263**, commentary on lines 4–5 and the commentary below on **284**. Further, two of the three (**284** and *IG* II², 996) were interpreted by Stamires as having been enacted on the same day, Mounichion 11 κατὰ θεόν = pryt. X, 18 = 306th day of the year. The implication is that the date κατ'ἄρχοντα was not the same. If the festival calendar followed the regular pattern of generally alternating full and hollow months on the Metonic principle, Mounichion 11 does indeed prove to be the 306th day of the year (see the table for the thirteenth year of a Metonic cycle given by Meritt, ᾿Αρχ. ᾿Εφ., 1968, p. 98, fig. 1). The two equations in *Agora* XV, 206, however, show dates of Metageitnion 21 = pryt. II, 19 = 51st day and Metageitnion II 8 =

pryt. III, 4 = 68th day. Thus Hekatombaion was given 30 days instead of 29 and was followed (correctly) by a full Metageitnion. Both unspecified dates are therefore, as regularly, dates κατ'ἄρχοντα: κατὰ θεόν they would have been Metageitnion 22 and Metageitnion II 9, and it may be assumed that the irregularity was compensated for at a later stage of the year. But the dating in **284** specified as κατὰ θεόν suggests that this compensation had been delayed as far as Mounichion, so that κατ'ἄρχοντα the date of that decree may be judged to have been Mounichion 10.

Each prytany during the year contained 32 days, as was regular in an intercalary year. Meritt's hypothesis of the lengths of the festival months and his supposition of a day added to and subtracted from Mounichion, as shown in *The Athenian Year*, p. 159, were withdrawn by him in the light of further study of the Metonic arrangement ('Αρχ. 'Εφ., 1968, pp. 96–98 and 102–103, with note 4 on p. 97). Since adjustments to the calendar κατ'ἄρχοντα were always, so far as is known, rectified before Skirophorion, the arrangement of the calendar κατὰ θεόν should now be shown as 29+1 30 29 30 29 30 30 29 30 29 30 29−1 30. Κατ'ἄρχοντα, therefore, the number of days in each month emerges as 30 30 29 30 29 30 30 29 30 29 30 28 30. The year was intercalary alike in the Metonic cycle as in the Athenian festival calendar. The epigraphical evidence suggests that while the Athenian officials were perfectly clear about what they were doing with the festival calendar, they did not always find it necessary to be explicit about it on stone, or, insofar as they *were* explicit, the γραμματεύς might choose to express himself in a variety of ways, not always as fully specific as might now be wished.

Phylai identifiable in office in their respective prytanies are II Attalis, III Pandionis, and X Ptolemais.

THE EPIMELETAI OF THE ELEUSINIAN MYSTERIES HONORED

284 (Pl. 29). A fragment of a stele of Hymettian marble (I 5761), with the left side preserved but otherwise broken all around, discovered on April 6, 1939, in a modern wall west of the Panathenaic Way and west of the Eleusinion (S 21). The inscribed surface is rough and scratched, but the text remains legible.

H. 0.24 m.; W. 0.235 m.; Th. 0.065 m.
LH. 0.006 m. (omicron 0.004 m.).

Ed. B. D. Meritt, *Hesperia* 16, 1947, p. 163, no. 61, with photograph pl. XXX. See J. and L. Robert, *REG* 61, 1948, p. 146, no. 43 (rejecting the tentative restoration in line 9). Lines 1–4 expanded and renumbered by G. A. Stamires (*Hesperia* 26, 1957, p. 39) in the light of Agora I 6671 (= *Agora* XV, 206). See *SEG* XVI, 92. Lines 8–10, as renumbered, revised, and improved by R. Hubbe, *Hesperia* 29, 1960, p. 417. See *SEG* XIX, 100. The restoration of line 3 defended by Meritt (*Athenian Year*, p. 159) against the criticism of being "surely incorrect" made by W. K. Pritchett, *BCH* 81, 1957, p. 279, note 5. See *SEG* XXI, 450a. The same further criticized by Pritchett (*Ancient Athenian Calendars on Stone*, p. 336, note 9) and again defended by Meritt, 'Αρχ. 'Εφ., 1968, pp. 96–97, where lines 1–5 of the text are reprinted. See *SEG* XXV, 114a.

a. 173/2 a., pryt. X   NON-ΣΤΟΙΧ. ca. 40–45

```
        ['Επὶ 'Αλέξιδος ἄρχοντος ἐπὶ τῆς Πτολεμαῖδος δεκάτης]
        [π]ρυ[τανείας· δήμου ψηφίσματα· Μουνιχιῶνος ἔνδε]
        κάτε[ι κατὰ θεόν, ὀγδόει καὶ δεκάτει τῆς πρυτανείας· ἐκ]
        κλησία κ[υρία ἐν τῶι θεάτρωι· τῶν προέδρων ἐπεψήφιζεν Φι]
   5    λήσιος Διογ[υσοδ..ου .ᶜᵃ·⁵. καὶ συμπρόεδροι· ἔδοξεν]
        τεῖ βουλεῖ κα[ὶ τῶι δήμωι· .........ᶜᵃ·²³.........]
        εἶπεν· ἐπειδὴ [οἱ ἐπιμεληταὶ τῶν Μυστηρίων οἱ ἐπὶ 'Αλε]
        ξίδος ἄρχοντος [ἔθυσαν τὰς θυσίας τῶν μεγάλων Μυστη]
        ρίων καὶ τῶν πρὸ[ς Ἄγραν Μυστηρίων ἐν τοῖς καθήκουσι]
   10   χρόνοις μεθ'ὧν πάτρ[ιον ἦν .......ᶜᵃ·²⁰....... κα]
        λῶς καὶ φιλοτίμως· ἔθυ[σαν δὲ καὶ τεῖ τε Δήμητρι καὶ τεῖ Κό]
        ρει καὶ τοῖς ἄλλοις θεο[ῖς οἷς πάτριον ἦν· προθύμως δὲ ἅπαν]
        τα πεπράχασιν ἐφ' ὑγιεί[αι καὶ σωτηρίαι τῆς τε βουλῆς]
        [καὶ] τοῦ δήμου τοῦ 'Αθηναί[ων καὶ παίδων καὶ γυναικῶν καὶ]
   15   [τῶν συμ]μάχων, καὶ ἀπήνγε[ιλαν ————————————]
```

[..ᶜᵃ˙⁶.. σωτ]ηρίαι· παρεσχ[εύασαν δὲ καὶ τὸ ζεῦγος ------]
[...ᶜᵃ˙¹¹....]ς τὸν βουλό[μενον --------------------]
[.....ᶜᵃ˙¹³.....] εὐσ[εβ-------------------------]
[---]

This text, like **283** of the previous year, was the work of S. V. Tracy's "Cutter of Agora I 247": for his career and style see **264** and references there.

Line 2. The name of the γραμματεύς was evidently not recorded. A. S. Henry (*Prescripts*, pp. 83–84) observed that of nine known instances of this remarkable omission four occur in this year. On the "minute-heading" δήμου ψηφίσματα restored in this line see **258**, commentary on line 2.

Line 3. The restoration is that of Stamires, defended and adopted by Meritt. Pritchett's objection was that it is improper to restore a κατὰ θεόν date without a corresponding date κατ'ἄρχοντα, and his table (*Ancient Athenian Calendars on Stone*, p. 337, table 11) seeks to show that prytany dates regularly correspond with dates κατὰ θεόν, being out of step, where these occur, with dates κατ'ἄρχοντα. In the above text the restoration takes this general rule into account. Mounichion 11 κατ'ἄρχοντα would be the nineteenth, not the eighteenth, day of the prytany. The day is the 306th of the year. It is, however, clear from **263** (see the commentary on line 5) that a date κατὰ θεόν may indeed be expressed by itself, and no general rule may be enunciated as to how these dates should or should not be framed. Much was evidently left to individual initiative. The γραμματεύς did not feel obliged to record the "adjusted" date in place of or in addition to the "normal" one. In ordinary circumstances the "normal" date was also the official date. Where adjustments had taken place, and no special mention is made of god or archon, the date recorded (as in *Agora* XV, 206) is, as Pritchett argued, that κατ'ἄρχοντα. On dates κατὰ θεόν and κατ'ἄρχοντα see also on the archonship of Achaios (p. 372 above) and Henry, *Prescripts*, pp. 78–80. For meetings of the assembly on Mounichion 11 see J. D. Mikalson, *Sacred and Civil Calendar*, pp. 141–142.

Lines 3–4. For the character and location of the assembly see **101**, commentary on lines 7–8 and **167**, commentary on lines 6–7. Lines 4–5. The name of the chairman of the proedroi is confirmed and amplified by *IG* II², 996, as corrected by Hubbe, *Hesperia* 28, 1959, pp. 181–182. Nothing further is known of him or his family.

Lines 5–6. The decree was probouleumatic; cf. P. J. Rhodes, *Athenian Boule*, p. 255. Line 7. An earlier board of epimeletai of the Mysteries is honored in **228**, a later in **300**; **206** is a doubtful case. See also *IG* II², 847, of 215/14, the text of which offers a close parallel to the phraseology above. Line 9. On the Mysteries πρὸς Ἄγραν see L. Deubner, *Attische Feste*, p. 70; M. Nilsson, *Geschichte der griechischen Religion* I, 3rd ed., 1967, pp. 668–669; G. Daux, *BCH* 87, 1963, pp. 624–625; M. H. Jameson, *BCH* 89, 1965, pp. 159–162; J. D. Mikalson, *Athenian Popular Religion*, 1983, p. 85.

Line 10. μεθ'ὦν πατέ[ρες(?) Meritt, *in editione principe*. Revision of the squeeze by Hubbe (see *SEG* XIX, 100) confirmed the suggestion of J. and L. Robert, *REG* 61, 1948, that the last surviving letter was rho rather than epsilon. Line 16. For the ζεῦγος cf. *IG* II², 847, line 17. Line 18. Traces before and after upsilon are of doubtful interpretation. Meritt read ---]συ[---.

FRAGMENT OF AN HONORARY DECREE

285. A fragment of a stele of Hymettian marble (I 6843), with the right side and original rough-picked back preserved, discovered on April 6, 1959, in a wall of a modern house east of the Eleusinion (U 19). The inscribed surface is broken away before reaching the edge of the stele. The striations of a toothed chisel are clearly visible, vertical near the right edge of the fragment and diagonal (from upper right to lower left) on the left section.

H. 0.18 m.; W. 0.18 m.; Th. 0.085 m.
LH. 0.006 m. (omicron 0.004 m.).

Ed. B. D. Meritt, *Hesperia* 32, 1963, pp. 15–16, no. 14, with photograph pl. 4. See also *SEG* XXI, 419.

ca. a. 170 *a.* NON-ΣΤΟΙΧ. *ca.* 36

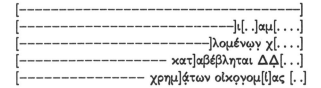

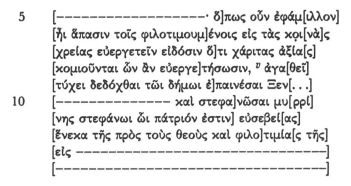

5 [— — — — — — — — — — — — — — — · ὅ]πως οὖν ἐφάμ[ιλλον]
[ᾖ ἅπασιν τοῖς φιλοτιμουμ]ένοις εἰς τὰς κρι[νὰ]ς
[χρείας εὐεργετεῖν εἰδόσιν ὅ]τι χάριτας ἀξία[ς]
[κομιοῦνται ὧν ἂν εὐεργε]τήσωσιν, ᵛ ἀγα[θεῖ]
[τύχει δεδόχθαι τῶι δήμωι ἐ]παινέσαι Ξεν[. . .]
10 [— — — — — — — — — καὶ στεφα]νῶσαι μυ[ρρί]
[νης στεφάνωι ὧι πάτριόν ἐστιν] εὐσεβεί[ας]
[ἕνεκα τῆς πρὸς τοὺς θεοὺς καὶ φιλο]τιμία[ς τῆς]
[εἰς —]
[— —]

This text is among those included by S. V. Tracy among the very considerable output of the "Cutter of Agora I 247"; see *Attic Letter-Cutters*, pp. 99–109 and **264**. Earlier examples in this collection of the work of this mason have been susceptible of dating with reference to the name of the archon in whose year the enactment concerned was voted and inscribed, and it has been possible to arrange them in chronological order: see **264, 276, 279, 280, 283**, and **284**. The above text and the three that follow it (**286–288**) cannot be dated otherwise than by the style of their lettering and therefore by the very fact of their attribution to this craftsman. As a result, they have been grouped together at the midpoint of his datable career (which seems to have spanned some forty-five years), it being understood that this is a matter of convenience and that any of them may have been inscribed at any point within four-and-a-half decades. Meritt's dating of the present text ("*init. saec.* II *a.*") was in the right region but, as it has proved, a little early; possibly, if his instinct is to be followed, this is an earlier rather than a later work of this prolific writer on stone.

In line 6 the stone appears to read ΚΩΙ: but the "omega" is on the lower line of writing and apparently has horizontal strokes in the usual place, unlike the other omegas in the texts. ΚΟΙ was evidently intended, and the peculiarity is perhaps more attributable to the inattention of the mason while cutting so small and awkward a letter than to his positive error. Lines 6–7 incorporate suggestions of A. S. Henry (*per ep.*): τοῖς ἑαυτοὺς φιλοτιμουμ]ένοις and χρείας παρέχεσθαι Meritt.

Xen– – – had deserved particularly well of the state by reason of a financial contribution (lines 2–3), which adds significance to the more routine formula of "hortatory intention" in lines 5–8. For these Meritt compared *Syll.*³, 333, a Samian decree of the late 4th century, *IG* II², 847 (see above on **228**), and 1329, lines 19–22. In the clause of hortatory intention itself, for which see **86**, commentary on lines 21–24, the omission of ἄν is without parallel before 250 B.C. but gradually became more frequent, until in the 1st century it was the "regular" turn of phrase. See A. S. Henry, *CQ* n.s. 16, 1966, pp. 291–293. The emphasis here is on encouragement to others to rival Xen– – – in generosity to the state when need arises. On the sentiment see **240**, commentary on lines 4–5. Lines 8–9. ἀγαθεῖ τύχει. See **72**, commentary on lines 7–8.

Lines 10–11. A stephanos of myrtle is a rare award, not attested before 215/14: see Henry, *Honours*, pp. 40–41 and **228** and **300**, where such stephanoi are awarded to epimeletai of the Mysteries. See also *IG* II², 1045 (*SEG* III, 104), in which a hierophantes(?) is so honored. For the phrase ὧι πάτριόν ἐστιν Meritt compared *IG* II², 949, lines 18–19 (cf. **228**, commentary on lines 4–5), in which the demarch of the Eleusinians received a myrtle stephanos similarly described. The total formulation here restored can be accepted with confidence, according to Henry, who quoted it (*op. cit.*, p. 41). On the evidence the implication may be that Xen– – – is likely to have been an Athenian citizen rather than an alien. Lines 11–12. On the virtues for which Xen– – – is commended see Henry, *op. cit.*, pp. 42–44, with parallels for the formulation on p. 43.

A CITIZEN OF MILETOS HONORED

286. Two joining fragments of a stele of Pentelic marble (I 3777), with the original back preserved; the stele is otherwise broken all around, although the first line of the inscription is included in the surviving text. The fragments were discovered on March 18 and 19, 1936, near the Church of Christ southeast of the Market Square (T 17). The center and lower parts of the inscribed surface are much worn, and the text there is open to doubt.

H. 0.24 m.; W. 0.21 m.; Th. 0.20 m.
LH. 0.005 m.

Ed. B. D. Meritt, *Hesperia* 29, 1960, pp. 18–19, no. 24, with photograph pl. 4. See *SEG* XIX, 103, with reference also to J. and L. Robert, *REG* 74, 1961, p. 155, no. 264.

ca. a. 170 *a.*   NON-ΣΤΟΙΧ. *ca.* 50

```
        ['Επὶ ...ca. 11.... ἄρχοντο]ς ἐπὶ [τῆς ..ca. 7.. ίδος ἕκτης πρυτα]
        [νείας ἧι ...ca. 8... 'Α]γαθοδώρου [....ca. 12.... ἐγραμμάτευεν]·
        [δήμου ψηφίσματα· Π]οσιδεῶνος ὀ[γδόηι ─────────────]
        [───────τῆς πρυταν]είας· ἐκκλησί[α κυρία ἐν τῶι θεάτρωι· τῶν προ]
   5    [έδρων ἐπεψήφιζε]ν Δημήτριος [─────────────καὶ συμπρόεδροι·
        (ἔδοξεν τεῖ βουλεῖ καὶ τῶι δήμωι· ........ca. 20....... εἶπεν·)
        [ἐπειδὴ .ca. 6..]ς Ζηνοθέμιδ[ος Μιλήσιος ─────────────]
        [...] Μιλησίων [δ]ιὰ τὴν οἰκειό[τητα ────────────── τὴν]
        [τῶν] προγόνων [φι]λίαν οὐ μόνο[ν ─────────────]
  10    [....]ει τε πᾶσιν 'Αθηναίοις πάγ[τα ─────────────]
        [καὶ νῦ]ν διατελεῖ πράττων ἀγα[θὸν ─────────────]
        [.. ψη]φισθέντων ἀλλὰ καὶ ὅσα ἄλ[λα ─────────────]
        [..ca. 7..]εται[..ca. 7..]νας κα[─────────────────]
        [.. μ]ήτε δαπάνης μήτε κινδύ[νου ─────────────]
  15    [..5..] τινος μελ[....]Γ\ [─────────────────]
        [..6...]ΛΙΟ[..]Ν[..]ΝΣ[─────────────────]
        [..6...]ΜΙ[.]ΩΝ καθότι [α]ὐτοι[─────────────]
        [────] reliquiae incertae [─────────────────]
        [..5..]ενοι τῶν πρ[ὸς] τὸν δ[ῆμον ─────────────]
  20    [..ca. 7..] 'Αθ[ηναῖ]ον [─────────────────]
        [────] reliquiae incertae [─────────────────]
        [────] reliquiae incertae [─────────────────]
        [─────────────────────────────────]
```

For the dating of this text and the attribution of the inscribing of it see **285**. Of the forty-five years of the mason's long activity, the names (or at least the patronymics) of the γραμματεῖς in some twenty-five are sufficiently known to exclude them from consideration as responsible for the setting-up of this stele. The remainder are evenly divided pre- and post-170, but there is a marked concentration of "unknowns" towards the end of the mason's career, and there is some chance that Agathodoros' son was in office during the decennium 159/8–149/8. The thickness of the stele appears to indicate that the monument was a substantial one.

It has evidently escaped earlier commentators on this text, and may well have escaped the notice of those who approved and paid for the original monument, that no mention is made of the proposer of the decree and that the enactment formula is totally lacking. The latter is occasionally omitted in this period; see A. S. Henry, *Prescripts*, pp. 88–89. The name of the orator is however *de rigueur*. The omissions show all the signs of a lapse on the part of the mason, unnoticed at the time and since, and the record and characteristics of this particular craftsman make the supposition even more credible.

The missing elements would in fact have comfortably made up a complete line following line 5, and this has therefore been inserted into the text. The error may be the more readily accounted for by the recurrence of epsilon at the beginning of three consecutive lines. The mason's eye might well have deceived him into overlooking the middle epsilon of the three and thereby failing to include the entire line that it introduced.

Line 1. The ordinal numeral of the prytany is restored (on the assumption of an ordinary year) from the month in line 3. Line 2. Meritt drew attention to the name as not otherwise attested in Attic prosopography before the 1st century B.C.; see *IG* II², 1961 (*SEG* XXXIV, 153), line 7. It is in any case a rarity. It appears neither in *PA* nor in *Agora* XV, but see *SEG* XXVIII, 174, lines 16–17 (a prytany text of the 2nd century A.D.). Line 3. δήμου ψηφίσματα. See **258**, commentary on line 2. For the character and location of the assembly see **101**, commentary on lines 7–8 and **167**, commentary on lines 6–7.

Lines 7–10. Meritt's restoration of these lines, for a criticism of which see J. and L. Robert, *loc. cit.*, was as follows:

```
        [ἐπειδὴ ───────]ς Ζηνοθέμιδ[ος Μιλήσιος προαγόμενος μάλιστα]
        [τῶν] Μιλησίων [δ]ιὰ τὴν οἰκειό[τητα τὴν πρὸς τὸν δῆμον καὶ τὴν]
        [τῶν] προγόνων [φι]λίαν οὐ μόνο[ν κατὰ τὸ δυνατὸν πρότερον ἀεὶ ἐ]
        [βοήθ]ει τε πᾶσιν 'Αθηναίοις πάγ[τα ὅσα ἠιτοῦντο παρεχόμενος]
        κτλ.
```

Lines 15–20. A few more letters have been discerned than Meritt's original text showed, but no additional sense can be won. The ἐπειδή clause seems to have been lengthy, since there is no recognizable trace of any such formula as ἀγαθῆι τύχηι δεδόχθαι τῆι βουλῆι καὶ τῶι δήμωι to indicate its termination.

For honors paid to other citizens of Miletos at this period see *IG* II², 982 (M. J. Osborne, *Naturalization* I, pp. 229–230, D 113, *Naturalization* II, p. 195) and 985. Theoroi from Miletos are also honored in *IG* II², 992. The connections between Athens and Miletos evidently grew closer in this century, and what came to be a substantial metic population of Milesians at Athens is attested by the numerous gravestones of Μιλήσιοι (*IG* II², 9358–9965 and *Agora* XVII, 549–631, with addenda in *SEG passim*), a long series which begins in the 2nd century B.C. For the possible use of Μιλήσιοι as a generic term to indicate foreigners in ephebic catalogues see O. W. Reinmuth, *The Foreigners in the Attic Ephebia*, 1929, pp. 40–41, 45–46 and C. Pelekides, *Histoire de l'éphébie attique*, 1962, pp. 190–195, with references.

FRAGMENT OF A DECREE (IN HONOR OF A PRIEST AND HIS WIFE?)

287 (Pl. 29). A fragment of a stele of gray marble (I 896), broken all around, discovered on June 2, 1933, in a marble pile east of the Metroon.

H. 0.09 m.; W. 0.065 m.; Th. 0.035 m.
LH. 0.006 m.

Ed. S. V. Tracy, *Attic Letter-Cutters*, p. 104, no. 1, with photograph pl. 15. See also *SEG* XL, 108.

ca. a. 170 *a.* NON-ΣTOIX.

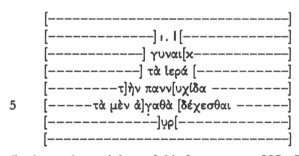

For the dating and attribution to its workshop of this fragment see **285**. In connection with the *pannychis* of line 4 Tracy referred to *IG* II², 334, 704, 775+803, 974–976, and 1199; the majority of these texts emphasize it as a particular feature of the cult of Asklepios.

FRAGMENT OF A DECREE

288. A fragment of the upper part of a stele of white marble (I 4886), broken all around but preserving above the inscription a rough ovolo molding (below the floor of a pediment?), beneath which a narrow band and a sharp apophyge effect the transition to the inscribed surface, similar in general character to **272**, **273**, and **280**; discovered on May 22, 1937, in a Late Roman context in the Classical floor of the Tholos (G 12).

H. 0.10 m.; W. 0.13 m.; Th. 0.065 m.
LH. 0.006 m.

Ed. S. V. Tracy, *Attic Letter-Cutters*, p. 107, no. 5, with photograph pl. 19. See also *SEG* XL, 109.

ca. a. 170 *a.* NON-ΣTOIX.

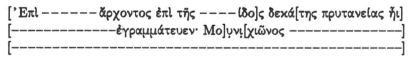

For the dating and attribution to its workshop of this fragment see **285**. The text is likely to have been not less than *ca.* 50 letters in width.

Note. In the same context S. V. Tracy published (*op. cit.*, pp. 104–106, nos. 2–4, with photographs pls. 16–18), and gave the same dating to, three further fragments, Agora I 968, I 2768, and I 4503. All are in his view attributable to the "Cutter of Agora I 247". Of these, no. 2 preserves only fourteen letters in whole or in part and no. 4 no more than eleven. Both these fragments, unusually, show incised guidelines, for the rarity of which in Attic epigraphy cf. A. G. Woodhead, *Study of Greek Inscriptions*, pp. 129–130, note 17: but they do not, apparently, belong to the same monument. No. 3 (*SEG* XL, 123), a long, narrow fragment preserving twenty lines of text not more than eight letters wide, seems to contain the elements of a *lex sacra* of some kind, and Tracy adduced *IG* II², 1243, lines 5–9 and *SEG* XXVIII, 103, lines 36–41 as *comparanda* for the sentiments apparently expressed.

FRAGMENT OF A DECREE

289. A fragment from the upper right section of a pedimental stele of Hymettian marble (I 6103), broken below, to right, and to left, but with the original back and part of the pediment preserved, discovered on April 12, 1948, in a context of Turkish date southwest of the Market Square and west of the Great Drain. Below the horizontal cornice of the pediment is a heavy quarter-round molding, beneath which a flat, narrow band (0.01 m.) leads into an apophyge descending to the inscribed surface. An uninscribed space of one line then precedes the first line of text.

H. 0.20 m.; W. 0.22 m.; Th. 0.14 m.
LH. 0.006 m.

Ed. B. D. Meritt, *Hesperia* 36, 1967, p. 64, no. 9, with photograph pl. 19. See also *SEG* XXIV, 134.

ca. a. 170 *a.*   NON-ΣΤΟΙΧ. *ca.* 57

['Επι – – – – ἄρχοντος ἐπὶ τῆς – – – – δ]ος πέμπ[της πρυτανείας ἧι . ca. 6 . .]
[. . . . . ca. 22 . . . . ἐγραμμά]τευεν· [Μαιμακτηριῶνος ἔνει καὶ νέαι],
[τριακοστεῖ τῆς πρυτανείας· ἐκκλησ]ία σύ[γκλητος ἐμ Πειραιεῖ στρατη]
[γῶν παραγγειλάντων· τῶν προέδρων ἐπ]εψή[φιζεν . . . . ca. 23 . . . .]
5   [καὶ συμπρόεδροι· ἔδοξεν τεῖ βουλεῖ κα]ὶ [τῶι δήμωι· – – – – – – – – – – – – – – –]
[– –]

S. V. Tracy (*Attic Letter-Cutters*, p. 135) saw the style of the lettering on this fragment as resembling the work of the "Cutter of *IG* II² 903", for whom see **278** (and cf. **290** and **292**); but he hesitated to make a definite attribution. Meritt's dating in the *editio princeps*, followed by *SEG* XXIV, was a more generalized "*init. saec.* II *a.*" It is perhaps appropriate to set the text at the midpoint of the known career of the craftsman whose style it reflects, there being no more precise guide to a date for it.

Line 2. The name of the month is restored from the number of the prytany. This leaves limited space for the day of the month and prytany, and what is restored here (though there are other possibilities) fulfills the conditions, especially if taken into consideration with the restoration of line 3 suggested below. For the date cf. also **282** and J. D. Mikalson, *Sacred and Civil Calendar*, pp. 85–86.

Lines 3–4. The surviving letters in each line, few as they are, call for a long qualifying formula to accompany what is clearly an ἐκκλησία σύγκλητος. For discussion of such assemblies, for the phraseology here introduced, and for the summoning of an assembly at the instance of the στρατηγοί, see **276** and references there. Meritt restored ἀπὸ βουλῆς after σύγκλητος: but Tracy (*ZPE* 75, 1988, p. 187; cf. *SEG* XXXVIII, 104) pointed out that this phrase is attested only when a meeting of the boule is expressly coupled with a meeting of the demos (as in **276**), that it then precedes the word ἐκκλησία, and that the words then following, where preserved, always indicate the location of the assembly. He himself suggested ἐν τῶι θεάτρωι(?) for this passage. This is perhaps too long for the space available: ἐμ Πειραιεῖ (cf. **291**, and to be restored, as Tracy urged, in *IG* II², 911, lines 5–7) is more suitable and is consonant with the dates proposed in lines 2–3. For meetings in the Peiraieus in the final third of a prytany see **259**, commentary on line 4.

Line 5. If the remains have been correctly assessed, the decree was probouleumatic; but there can be no certainty, and P. J. Rhodes (*Athenian Boule*) did not include this text in his survey.

THE ARCHONSHIP OF DEMETRIOS, 170/69 B.C.

The association of Demetrios with the year 170/69 has not been proposed hitherto, and the convergence of the two may best be appreciated if earlier proposals concerning them are considered separately.

I. *170/69 B.C.* W. S. Ferguson's initial investigations into the archon list made no assignment for this year, and it long remained untenanted: see W. B. Dinsmoor, *Archons of Athens*, p. 222; *IG* II², iv, 1, p. 18. The first attempt to attach a name to it was made by Dinsmoor, who placed Eunikos here (*op. cit.*, pp. 32, 258, *et alibi*): but by 1939 he had appreciated that the system of secretary cycles that he had previously advocated was in error by one year. Under his revised scheme Eunikos was returned to 169/8 (see p. 407 below), and 170/69 was once more left unassigned (*Athenian Archon List*, pp. 170–171, 189).

It remained so in the table drawn up by W. K. Pritchett and B. D. Meritt, *Chronology*, p. xxviii. However, the discovery of **296** produced (in line 42 as then published) the name, as it appeared, of a previously unknown archon Aphrodisios, whom Meritt, in editing the text, assigned to this year (*Hesperia* 16, 1947, p. 168 and 26, 1957, p. 38, note 28). The attribution, generally accepted, was repeated by Meritt in *Athenian Year*, pp. 181–182, 198–199, 236, and *Historia* 26, 1977, p. 182, and was agreed by C. Habicht, *Studien*, p. 173.

The publication of fragment *i* of **296** (see the commentary *ad loc.* on line 45) made it clear that Aphrodisios in that context was the name not of an archon but of the dedicator of one of the items inventoried, and since this was the sole evidence for the supposed archonship the assignment could not stand: cf. Habicht, *Hesperia* 59, 1990, p. 576, note 85. 170/69 thus became a "vacant" year once more and has so remained.

II. *Demetrios*. An archon of this name has long been known as the immediate predecessor of Nikodemos (see p. 449 below) from *IG* II², 1006, line 6, and as the immediate successor of Nikias and Isigenes from 1713, line 8: he has in consequence been firmly attributed to 123/2; see Dinsmoor, *Archons of Athens*, p. 223 and Meritt, *Historia* 26, 1977, p. 186. When the prytany text that later became *Agora* XV, 172 was discovered, Dinsmoor (*Athenian Archon List*, p. 199) thought that the fragmentary name (Δι---) of the γραμματεύς there associated with an archon Demetrios belonged with this Demetrios of 123/2. But the further discovery of *Agora* XV, 171 clearly revealed that there was a hitherto unknown Demetrios as archon, and the original editors of that text (Pritchett and Meritt, *Chronology*, pp. 121–127) assigned it and him to 174/3. To this year they also ascribed *Agora* XV, 172. From this material the γραμματεύς could be evaluated as Δη[μήτριος Δημάδου(?)] Ἀλ[αιεύς (cf. *IG* II², 1027, lines 15–16, also assigned to the same year).

It later emerged that 174/3 must be given to the archon Alexandros (see pp. 395–396 above), and Meritt's reconsideration of the problem led to the placing of Demetrios in 159/8 (*Hesperia* 26, 1957, pp. 71–72). Unless there was some irregularity in the secretary cycle, this required that the demotic of the γραμματεύς be read as Π]αλ[ληνεύς (Antiochis XI). C. Pelekides (*BCH* 81, 1957, pp. 478–482) independently assigned Demetrios to 159/8 and in an addendum (pp. 483–484) was able to take account of **290**, which he wished to ascribe to the same year. This involved the dissociation of *IG* II², 1027 from *Agora* XV, 171 and 172, and he saw this as belonging to the last third of the century (p. 481). See *SEG* XVII, 30 and 32 and J. and L. Robert, *REG* 72, 1959, pp. 182–183, no. 135, where Pelekides' conclusion in this respect is not adequately represented.

By 1961 Meritt had come to recognize that 159/8 was not acceptable for Demetrios, and like Pelekides he dissociated *IG* II², 1027 from the other texts (see *SEG* XVI, 98 and XXI, 457). The reason was that, *pari passu* with these developments, the publication of **290** had induced him to postulate an earlier Demetrios, since it coupled an archon of that name with an apparently different γραμματεύς, and the style of its lettering seemed to point to an early 2nd-century date. The year 198/7 was assigned to it, and for a brief period it seemed that the available texts must be distributed between Demetrios I and Demetrios II: but Meritt's treatment of the matter in *Athenian Year* (pp. 184–187), where he dealt with it *in extenso*, showed that it was more economical, as Pelekides had realized, to associate *Agora* XV, 171 and 172 with **290**. The name of the γραμματεύς could be built up as Δι[οx]λῆς Νομ[ίου Δειρ]αδ[ιώτης. See also *TAPA* 95, 1964, p. 240. *Agora* XV, 172 also required that the year be ordinary, and for this purpose 190/89, where Leontis (IV) was the phyle of the deme Deiradiotai, was appropriate. It was therefore to be concluded that there was only one archon Demetrios in this period, and 159/8 was finally abandoned. See also *Historia* 26, 1977, p. 180 and Habicht, *Studien*, pp. 170 and 177.

The removal to 190/89 of the archon Achaios by S. V. Tracy (see p. 371 above) necessarily disrupted this conclusion, as far as the attribution of Demetrios to that year was concerned, and the latter became unassigned yet again. Habicht (*Hesperia* 57, 1988, pp. 245–246) noted that consideration of the craftsmen who inscribed the known texts of his year required that he be dated no later than 161/60 (see on **290** and, for *Agora* XV, 171 and 172, Tracy, *Attic Letter-Cutters*, pp. 102 and 134). The mason who worked on *Agora* XV, 171 (see **264**) had a longer career than his counterpart who inscribed the other two texts, and Tracy placed the archonship of Demetrios at the center point of the latter's known span of activity, as "*ca.* 170 B.C.". In the course of his study on Achaios he had doubted the reading of the demotic of the γραμματεύς in *Agora* XV, 172, line 2 (see on **290**, lines 1–2): all that is claimed for the traces in question (if their existence is acknowledged) is that they offer the apices of two triangular letters, and the possibilities are more extensive than Tracy's note on the subject envisaged.

Habicht (*Hesperia* 57, 1988, pp. 245–246) was considering in that context archons of a date later than 160 and was concerned to note that Demetrios could not be included among them. The limitations imposed by the craftsman's career confine the possibilities, in fact, to the two decades 180–160, concerning which Habicht had earlier noted (*Studien*, p. 173) that only 180/79 and 170/69 remained open. The former year he claimed for the archon he named Philon I (*ibid.*, pp. 168–170). 170/69 is left, in consequence, as the only possible and available year for Demetrios, who may there at last find his place of rest.

This leaves the problem of the γραμματεύς, whom the secretary cycle requires to be a member of the phyle Attalis. The requirement is answered, and the traces on *Agora* XV, 172, if they exist, fully catered for, by the supposition that his demotic was Προβ]αλ[ίσιος: see on **290**. The requirement that the year be ordinary is also met, since it follows the undoubted intercalary year 171/70 and was itself followed by two years respectively (and equally without doubt) ordinary and intercalary.

From the two prytany texts of the year it appears that Antiochis held the ninth prytany and Ptolemais the eleventh. There was some interference with the festival calendar by the archon during Elaphebolion, presumably in connection with the City Dionysia; but by Thargelion this had been set right, and the festival and prytany calendars were by then in evident correspondence.

FRAGMENT OF A DECREE

290. A fragment of a stele of Hymettian marble (I 6081), with part of the left side and the spring of a molding above the inscribed face preserved, but which is broken elsewhere, discovered on March 17, 1948, in the wall of a modern cesspool south of the southwest corner of the Middle Stoa (H 14).

H. 0.098 m.; W. 0.095 m.; Th. 0.035 m.
LH. 0.006–0.007 m.

Ed. G. A. Stamires, *Hesperia* 26, 1957, pp. 30–31, no. 3, with photograph pl. 5. See also *SEG* XVI, 76. Discussion by C. Pelekides, *BCH* 81, 1957, pp. 483–484 (see *SEG* XVII, 30), and by B. D. Meritt, *Athenian Year*, pp. 185–187 (see *SEG* XXI, 427).

a. 170/69 a., *pryt.* IV   NON-ΣTOIX. *ca.* 50–60

```
        ['Επὶ Δ]ημητ[ρίου ἄρχοντος ἐπὶ τῆς ----- τετάρτης πρυτανείας ἧι Διο]
        [κ]λῆς Νομ[ίου Προβαλίσιος ἐγραμμάτευεν· δήμου ψηφίσματα· Πυα]
        νοψιῶνος [-------------------- τῆς πρυτανείας· ἐκκλησία]
        ἐμ Πειρ[αιεῖ· τῶν προέδρων ἐπεψήφιζεν -------------------------]
   5    [-----------------------------------------------------------]
```

Lines 1–2. Διοκ]λῆς Νομ[ίου(?) Παλληνεύς Pelekides, who dated the text to 159/8; ---κ]λῆς Νομ[--- Αἰξωνεύς(?) Stamires; Διοκ]λῆς Νομ[ίου Δειραδιώτης Meritt, the demotic derived from *Agora* XV, 172, line 2; cf. *Athenian Year*, pp. 184–186. S. V. Tracy (*AJAH* 9, 1984, pp. 46–47, note 15) doubted both the patronymic and the reading of the demotic in the *Agora* XV text. Line 2 as restored contains 50 letters, but it appears to be more generously spaced than line 3. With the restoration of a phyle with the shortest name (Aigeis or Oineis), line 1 will contain 57 letters, and as the spacing of line 1 is almost that of line 2 such a restoration is probably desirable.

The character of the lettering led Tracy to identify it as the work of the mason named by him the "Cutter of *IG* II² 903" (*Attic Letter-Cutters*, p. 134). For this craftsman's career and style see **278**, for which (with **292**) he is also considered responsible.

Lines 1–2. Diokles, son of Nomios(?), of the deme Probalinthos is, as γραμματεύς of the year, the product of argumentation surveyed earlier (p. 405 above), and uncertainty must of necessity still cling to him. A Diokles Probalisios is listed (at line 26) among the στρατιῶται who subscribed to the dedication *IG* II², 1958, dated towards the end of the 3rd century; cf. *PA* 4049 and C. Habicht, *Studien*, pp. 161–162; he could have been the grandfather of the Diokles named here.

Line 2. Δήμου ψηφίσματα. See **258**, commentary on line 2. The phrase is restored, as Stamires frankly admitted, because there is space to be filled at this point; but the inclusion is appropriate and well attested. The location given in line 4 requires a meeting of the assembly. On that location see **259**, commentary on line 4. The date of the meeting, not preserved in line 3, may well have fallen in the final third of the prytany.

THE ARCHONSHIP OF EUNIKOS, 169/8 B.C.

IG II², 910 (*Agora* XV, 212) long ago provided the essential information linking Eunikos (*PA* 5848) as archon with the γραμματεύς Hieronymos, son of Boethos, of Kephisia, whose deme belonged to the phyle Erechtheis (I). *IG* II², 911, with part of the name of the γραμματεύς surviving, could be restored in conformity with it, and both texts provided evidence that Eunikos' year was ordinary in the festival calendar. W. S. Ferguson placed Eunikos in 169/8 in his original list (*Athenian Secretaries*, p. 55), where he has remained undisturbed, save for the brief interlude during which W. B. Dinsmoor moved the secretary cycle in this period earlier by one year than Ferguson had had it, thereby putting Eunikos in 170/69 (*Archons of Athens*, pp. 222 and 258). For the "normal" dating see Ferguson, *Athenian Tribal Cycles*, p. 29 (cf. pp. 11–12, note 1); B. D. Meritt, in the *editio princeps* of **291**; S. Dow, *Prytaneis*, pp. 129–133, no. 71; Dinsmoor, *Athenian Archon List*, pp. 23 and 189; W. K. Pritchett and Meritt, *Chronology*, p. xxviii; Pritchett and O. Neugebauer, *Calendars*, p. 85; Meritt, *Hesperia* 26, 1957, p. 95, *Athenian Year*, pp. 143–144 and 236, *TAPA* 95, 1964, p. 239, *Historia* 26, 1977, p. 182; and cf. C. Habicht, *Hesperia* 59, 1990, p. 570.

The didascalic list *IG* II², 2323 (see *SEG* XXV, 194) shows that Eunikos' archonship immediately preceded that of Xenokles, whose term of office was associated by Apollodoros (F. Jacoby, *FGrHist*, no. 224, fr. 47) with the aftermath of the capture by the Romans of Perseus, king of Macedon. The battle of Pydna (see below), which had resulted in Perseus' defeat and flight, was fought in Eunikos' archonship. This therefore had not ended on June 22, 168, the day after the eclipse of the moon recorded by Livy (44.37.5–9) and Plutarch (*Aemilius Paullus* 17.3–5), and it continued for the remainder of the lunar month: see **291**.

For the character of the year, recognized throughout all discussions of the subject, see especially Pritchett and Neugebauer, *loc. cit.*, and Meritt, *Athenian Year*, pp. 143–144. *Agora* XV, 212 shows the equation Gamelion 25 = pryt. VII, 22. The apparent discrepancy of three days between festival and prytany calendars may be resolved by the assumption that the first six prytanies were all 30 days in length and that in the festival calendar the months alternated regularly after full Hekatombaion and hollow Metageitnion. This therefore was the 202nd day of the year. *IG* II², 911 gives the last day of Skirophorion as the equivalent of pryt. XII, 29. This is the same date as that on which **291** was enacted, and both decrees may have been concerned with the same business. The year had come correctly to its conclusion with a hollow month and a 29-day prytany, the last of six prytanies of the same length. The year was the seventeenth in the fourteenth Metonic cycle and ordinary also in Meton's arrangement.

Of the phylai in office during the various prytanies, only VII Oineis and XII Attalis are known.

DECREE IN HONOR OF KALLIPHANES, WHO BROUGHT THE NEWS OF THE BATTLE OF PYDNA

291. A complete stele of Pentelic marble (I 164), with pediment and akroteria preserved, discovered on February 11, 1932, in position as a cover slab of the Great Drain, east of the Metroon (I 9). Because of its reuse in the drain with inscribed face downwards, the front surface has become badly corroded, and the inscription is in large part almost or totally illegible.

H. 1.72 m.; W. (at top of inscribed surface) 0.40 m., (at bottom of stele) 0.46 m.; Th. (at top) 0.076 m., (at bottom) 0.083 m.

LH. 0.008 m.

Ed. B. D. Meritt, *Hesperia* 3, 1934, pp. 18–21, no. 18, with photograph. Revision also by Meritt, in the light of his own further study and of readings and suggestions by A. M. Woodward, *Hesperia* 5, 1936, pp. 429–430, no. 17. See *SEG* XXV, 118, full text and bibliography, with reference also to L. Moretti, *Iscrizioni storiche ellenistiche* I, pp. 81–83, no. 35 (text, Italian translation, and brief commentary).

a. 169/8 a., *pryt*. XII   NON-ΣΤΟΙΧ. *ca.* 30

Θ   ε   ο   ι.

'Επὶ Εὐνίκου ἄρχοντος ἐπὶ τῆς 'Ατταλί

δος δωδεκάτης πρυτανείας ἧι 'Ιερώνυ

μος Βοήθου Κηφισιεὺς ἐγραμμάτευεν,

5   Σκιροφοριῶνος ἔνει καὶ νέαι, ἐνάτει

καὶ εἰκοστεῖ τῆς πρυτανείας· ἐκκλη
σία ἐμ Πειραιεῖ· τῶν προέδρων ἐπεψήφι
ζεν   *vacat*
         vacat
10   *vacat*
    ἔδοξεν τεῖ βουλεῖ καὶ τῶι δήμωι·
Σάτυρος Σατύρου ἐκ Κολ[ων]οῦ εἶπεν· ἐπει
δὴ Καλλιφάνης Φυλάσιος στρατευόμε
νος μετὰ ʽΡωμαί[ων] καὶ τῶν [τ]οῦ βασιλέ
15 ως Ε[ὐ]μένους ἀδελφῶν ᾽Αττάλου καὶ
᾽Αθηναίου καὶ χρήσιμον ἑαυτὸν παρα
σκευάζειν βουλόμενος τῆι πατρίδι
συμπ[αρ]ῆν τ[ῆ]ι γενομέ[νη]ι [ν]ίκηι ʽΡωμαίοις
ἐμ Μα[κ]εδ[ο]νίαι, καὶ φιλοτιμούμενος ὢν [α]ὐ
20 τὸς ἀπαγγεῖλαι τοῖς πολίτ[α]ις τὰ γ[εγο]ν[ό]
τα [––––––––––––––––––––––]
    versus quinque non legendi
[––––––––––]ων, ᵛ ἀγαθεῖ τύχει δ[ε]δό
[χθαι τεῖ βουλεῖ τ]ο[ὺ]ς [λ]αχόντ[ας] προέ
[δρους εἰς τὴν ἐπι]ο[ῦ]σαν ἐκκλησίαν
30 [χρημα]τίσαι περὶ [τού]των, γνώμην δὲ
[ξυμβάλλε]σθαι τῆς βουλῆς εἰς τὸν
[δῆ]μ[ον] ὅτι δοκε[ῖ] τεῖ βουλεῖ ἐπαινέσα[ι]
[Κα]λλ[ιφ]άνην Καλλιφάνου Φυλάσιο[ν]
[καὶ στεφανῶσαι αὐτὸν θαλλοῦ] στε[φάνωι εὐ]
35 [νοίας ἔνεκεν κ]αὶ φιλοτιμίας [–––––––]
[–––––––––––––––––––––––––––]
[–––––––––––––––––––––––––––]
[––––––––––––––––––]· ἀναγρ[ά]
[ψαι] δὲ τ[όδ]ε τὸ ψήφισμα τὸν γραμματέ[α]
40 [τὸ]ν [κατὰ] πρυτανε[ίαν] ἐν στήλει λιθίνει
[καὶ στῆσ]αι ἐν ἀγορᾶι παρὰ τὴν εἰκόνα
[––––––––]· τὸ δὲ γενόμενον ἀνάλωμα
[εἰς τὴν γραφὴ]ν καὶ τὴν ἀνάθεσιν τῆς
[στ]ήλης μερίσαι τὸν ταμίαν τῶν στρ[α]
45 [τιωτικ]ῶν.   *vacat*
    (*in corona*)
    ʽΗ βουλὴ
    ὁ δῆμος
    Καλλιφάνην
    Καλλιφάνου
50   Φυλ[άσιο]ν.

So far as may be judged, the lettering of this text was competent, regular, and without decoration. There is some emphasis on the "free ends" of strokes, especially in upsilon. The external strokes of mu and sigma are well angled; omicron is small; the right vertical stroke of pi is almost equal to that on the left. S. V. Tracy (*Attic Letter-Cutters*, pp. 235 and 249) found the stone too worn for any attribution of it to an identifiable craftsman to be possible; but he saw some affinity with the style of the "Cutter of Agora I 247" (for whom see **264**). The general impression, however, is of a quality rather better than that mason's overall standard. More can be made of the text from the photographs than from either the squeeze or the stone itself.

The prescript was set out in the "perfect design", for which see **204** and **205**. The stone was inscribed without waiting for the information concerning the identity of the chairman of the proedroi, which was presumably painted into the available space, if indeed any trouble at all was subsequently undertaken to fill the lacuna. The name may be supplied from *IG* II², 911, which was enacted on the same day, as N[– – – – – – – –]. For the omission cf. A. S. Henry, *Prescripts*, p. 88 (see also p. 72).

Lines 3–4. For Hieronymos, son of Boethos, of Kephisia see *PA* 7565. Neither he nor his family is known other than through the evidence for his function as γραμματεύς in this year. Lines 5–6. The date is that of the first new moon after the eclipse that occurred on the eve of the battle of Pydna (8:07 p.m. on June 21, 168 B.C.), news of which had just arrived. Kalliphanes, who had doubtless made the best speed he could in order to be the first messenger of it, was presumably honored with the maximum promptitude, in immediate recognition of his services. Combination of this text with *IG* II², 911, where the assembly is specifically designated σύγλκητος, shows that the assembly was held in the Peiraieus and that it had been summoned at the instance of the generals immediately following a session of the boule. The circumstances of this decree therefore militate against the conclusions of M. H. Hansen (see **276**) concerning the nature of an ἐκκλησία σύγκλητος, that an assembly so described was a regular assembly (i.e., one of those statutorily required to be held during each prytany) called at short notice. The assembly on this occasion was held on the last day of the prytany (as happened not infrequently) and indeed on the last day of the year: cf. J. D. Mikalson, *Sacred and Civil Calendar*, pp. 177–181 (for the last day of Skirophorion) and the table on p. 195 and (e.g.) **116** and **185**. Such an assembly could not be postponed, and the holding of it must therefore have been envisaged well beforehand, so that the four days notice procedurally required will have been given by the prytaneis in regular form. It was not susceptible of a sudden convoking; no intervention of the generals was needed for it. The present situation was unexpected and exciting; the generals had received the news and called the people together *extra ordinem*. The final, regular assembly of the prytany had, it must be concluded, already taken place. This text was not among the inscriptions discussed by E. M. Harris (*CQ* n.s. 36, 1986, pp. 374–377) in his refutation of Hansen's arguments, but its data support his contentions. It also follows that, since without *IG* II², 911 the contents of the prescript would not have revealed the true nature of this assembly, there may be many other cases of ἐκκλησίαι σύγκλητοι of which, on present evidence, history remains unaware. On the prescript see also *SEG* XXXVIII, 106.

No time, evidently, was lost on receipt of the news of the Roman victory, and the location of the assembly (though customary for a meeting in the third part of the prytany; see **259**) suggests that Kalliphanes had arrived by sea and that the people went as it were to meet him rather than that he went up to the *asty* to meet the people. His journey thus took slightly less than two weeks. The end of the Athenian year fell at July 7–8, 168. Earlier historiography gave variant dates for the battle of Pydna. That given by Livy and Plutarch (see commentary on the archonship of Eunikos) in relation to the eclipse was always the most generally accepted; but Livy elsewhere places the battle after the summer solstice (44.36.1), and Beloch argued that the close connection with the eclipse was no more than a legend which gained popular currency (cf. F. Jacoby, *FGrHist*, no. 260, [Porphyrion von Tyros], commentary, p. 855). The alternative date in September favored by Beloch and Jacoby was adopted also by W. Kolbe and J. Kirchner. But the discovery of this stele confirmed the June date beyond all doubt: cf. Meritt, *in editione principe*; P. S. Derow, *CAH* VIII, 2nd ed., 1989, p. 316. For earlier theories and their resolution see W. B. Dinsmoor, *Archons of Athens*, pp. 199–200 and 509 and *Athenian Archon List*, pp. 170–171.

Lines 8 (after ζεν), 9, and 10 are blank on the stone. Line 12. Satyros, son of Satyros, of Kolonos, the proposer of the decree, is not otherwise known. Line 13. Kalliphanes, son of Kalliphanes, of Phyle, honored in this decree, was the father of Dexiphon, victor in the Theseia in the archonships of Anthesterios (157/6) and Aristophantos (146/5?; see C. Habicht, *Hesperia* 57, 1988, pp. 243–244, 246), on the first occasion as a παῖς in the lampadedromia and on the second in a horse race. See *IG* II², 957, lines 46–48, and 958, lines 89–90; *PA* 3240 and 8218. Nothing further is known of him beyond his participation in the battle of Pydna and his bringing of the news of it to Athens. Lines 14–16. That Prince Attalos (later King Attalos II) led a Pergamene contingent to the army of Aemilius Paullus stood in Livy's record (44.36.8). This text adds his brother Athenaios as his colleague. Athenaios subsequently remained with Paullus during the latter's tour of Greece in 167; cf. Livy 45.27.6. See further P. Meloni, *Perseo e la fine della monarchia Macedone*, 1953, pp. 371–397; P. B. MacShane, *The Foreign Policy of the Attalids of Pergamon*, 1964, pp. 180–182; E. V. Hansen, *The Attalids of Pergamum*, 2nd ed., 1971, p. 119, with notes 155–157.

Line 21. C. Habicht (*Hesperia* 59, 1990, p. 465) proposed the restoration [ἀγαθά· – – –]. See *SEG* XL, 110.

Line 27. Ἀγαθεῖ τύχει. See **72**, commentary on lines 7–8. Lines 27–32. The instruct. ns to the proedroi were immediately acted upon (see above), and the assembly was at once summoned. The resultant decree was probouleumatic; see P. J. Rhodes, *Athenian Boule*, p. 255.

Line 33. The honorand's name is in a line by itself and reflects the care taken to provide the "perfect design" in line 11. Line 34. The stephanos is restored as of olive, probably correctly both for the surviving text (which does not permit it to be of gold, unless the condition κατὰ τὸν νόμον was dispensed with; cf. **310**, lines 43–44) and for the recipient as a citizen performing a "semiofficial" function. See Henry, *Honours*, pp. 39–40. Lines 34–35. The virtues of Kalliphanes are those more regularly in evidence as ascribed to honorands; see Henry, *Honours*, p. 43; but ἀρετή might be an alternative here for εὔνοια.

Lines 41–42. The statue remains unidentified, but seven or eight letters must have sufficed to describe it. For the phraseology cf. *IG* II², 682, lines 80–81, 88–89 and **310**, lines 50–52. Lines 42–45. The use of γραφή for ἀναγραφή is unusual. For the word order of this clause see **276**, commentary on lines 24–25.

Lines 46–50. The citation is set within a well-cut and elegantly designed olive wreath in low relief, which confirms the restoration of line 34.

DECREE IN HONOR OF ARRHIDAïOS, AN AIDE OF KING ANTIOCHOS IV OF SYRIA

292. A fragment of a stele of Hymettian marble (I 6367), with the right edge preserved, discovered on June 2, 1951, east of the south end of the base of the statues of the Eponymous Heroes (I 11). The stone is mottled and discolored.

H. 0.20 m.; W. 0.295 m.; Th. *ca.* 0.089 m.
LH. 0.006–0.007 m.

Ed. G. A. Stamires, *Hesperia* 26, 1957, pp. 47–51, no. 7, with photograph pl. 8. See *SEG* XVI, 94. This edition sharply attacked by J. and L. Robert, *REG* 71, 1958, p. 229, no. 178, and at greater length by L. Robert (*Hellenica* XI/XII, 1960, pp. 92–111, with photograph of squeeze pl. XVII), who produced a new text with shorter lines. Cf. J. and L. Robert, *REG* 74, 1961, p. 162, no. 281, where the revised text is commended. See *SEG* XXI, 452 and XXV, 116 (the latter in reference to L. Moretti, *Iscrizioni storiche ellenistiche* I, pp. 80–81, no. 34, who gives Robert's text, Italian translation, and brief commentary). The discovery of the inscription was reported by H. A. Thompson, *Hesperia* 21, 1952, p. 113, *ArchAnz* (*JdI* 67) 1952, p. 168; see also *AJA* 56, 1952, p. 123; *BCH* 76, 1952, p. 214.

a. 169/8 a.(?), *pryt.* V(?)   NON-ΣTOIX. *ca.* 32–37

```
        ['Επι ..6–7.. ἀρχ]οντ[ο]ς ἐπ[ὶ τῆς ....8–13....]
        [..5–6.. πρυτα]νείας, Μαιμακτηρι[ῶνος .ca.6..]
        [..ca.7.. · ἐκκ]λησία ἐμ Πειραιεῖ· Μ[..ca.9...]
        [..ca.9....ε]ὺς εἶπεν· ἐπειδὴ 'Αρρι[δαῖος τι]
   5    [μώμενος ὑπὸ] τοῦ βασιλέως 'Αντιόχο[υ ἔν τε]
        [ταῖς στρ]ατείαις τὴμ μεγίστην ἔχ[ων τῶν]
        [πίστεων, τε]ταγμένος ἐπὶ τῆς τοῦ στρατο[πέ]
        [δου .4–5.. κα]ὶ εὐταξίας, καὶ ἐν τῶι λοιπ[ῶι χρό]
        [νωι περὶ τὸ σ]ῶμα τοῦ βασιλέως ἀναστρ[εφόμε]
   10   [νος, πᾶσι μὲν τ]οῖς παραγινομένοις 'Αθη[ναίων]
        [πρεσβευταῖς κ]αὶ σπονδοφόροις καὶ ἐπιτ[ca.4.]
        [..ca.7... ὁμοίω]ς δὲ καὶ τοῖς καθ'ἰδίαν εὐχρ[ησ]
        [τός ἐστι, καὶ περ]ὶ τούτων ἀπαμεμαρτύρηται
        [αὐτῶι, καθήκει δὲ τι]μᾶν τοὺς τοιούτους, ὅπως
   15   [καὶ ἄλλοι ζηλῶσι φιλο]δοξεῖν, εἰδό(τ)ες ὅτι κο
        [μιοῦνται τὰς καταξίας χάρι]τας, ἀγαθεῖ τύχει
        [δεδόχθαι τεῖ βουλεῖ τοὺς λαχόντας πρ]οέδρους
        [– – – – – – – – – – – – – – – – – – – – – – – – –]
```

The lettering is generously spaced and almost gives the superficial appearance of a stoichedon text. S. V. Tracy identified it as the work of the "Cutter of *IG* II² 903", whose datable activity spans roughly two decades, from 179/8 to 161/60 B.C. On his output and characteristics see Tracy, *Attic Letter-Cutters*, pp. 133–136 and **278**: **290** is also attributed to him. Unusually in an Attic inscription, guidelines to demarcate the upper and lower limits within which the letters were to be written were incised on the stone. Cf. M. Guarducci, *Epigrafia greca* I, 1967, pp. 458–459 *et alibi*; A. G. Woodhead, *Study of Greek Inscriptions*, pp. 129–130, note 17 (where this text is cited); Tracy, *op. cit.*, pp. 105 and 135–136 (where it is specifically under discussion). See also *IG* II², 945, *Agora* XV, 209, and *SEG* XXV, 196, all of this period. For an example a century earlier in date see *Agora* XV, 72 (J. S. Traill, *Hesperia* 38, 1969, pp. 459–494), a bouleutic list of 281/80 (on the guidelines see p. 465, par. 6). In line 15 of the above text the stone reads ΕΙΔΟΙΕΣ.

The text shown is that of L. Robert (*SEG* XXI, 452), whose restorations are throughout plausible if not assured; but there has been reassessment and minor adjustment of the space available in the lacunae at the beginning of the first three lines. The version of G. A. Stamires (*SEG* XVI, 94) is given below, for convenience of reference.

NON-ΣΤΟΙΧ. *ca.* 34–39

```
        ['Επὶ ..ᶜᵃ·⁸.. ἄρχ]οντ[ο]ς ἐπ[ὶ τῆς 'Ιπποθωντίδος ᵛᵛ]
        [πέμπτης πρυτα]νείας· Μαιμακτηρι[ῶνος .ᶜᵃ·⁶..]
        [...ᶜᵃ·⁹.... · ἐκκ]λησία ἐμ Πειραιεῖ· Μ[...ᶜᵃ·⁹...]
        [...ᶜᵃ·¹¹.....ε]ὺς εἶπεν· ἐπειδὴ 'Αρρι[δαῖος φα ᵛ]
   5    [νερός ἐστι παρὰ] τοῦ βασιλέως 'Αντιόχο[υ ἐν ἀπά]
        [σαις ταῖς στρ]ατείαις τὴμ μεγίστην ἔχ[ων προ]
        [αγωγήν, τε]ταγμένος ἐπὶ τῆς τοῦ στρατο[πέ ᵛ]
        [δου φυλακῆς κα]ὶ εὐταξίας, καὶ ἐν τῶι λοιπ[ῶι χρό]
        [νωι κατὰ τὸ ἀξί]ωμα τοῦ βασιλέως ἀναστρ[έφε ᵛ]
  10    [ται φιλοτίμως τ]οῖς παραγινομένοις 'Αθη[ναί ᵛ]
        [ων πρεσβευταῖς κ]αὶ σπονδοφόροις καὶ ἐπιπ[εμπο]
        [μένοις, παρέσχηκ]ε δὲ καὶ τοῖς καθ'ἰδίαν εὐχ[ρη]
        [στον ἑαυτὸν καὶ περ]ὶ τούτων ἀπομεμαρτύρηται
        [αὐτῶι πλεονάκις τι]μᾶν τοὺς τοιούτους· ὅπως
  15    [οὖν καὶ ἄλλοι ζηλῶσι φιλο]δοξεῖν, εἰδότες ὅτι κο
        [μιοῦνται τὰς καταξίας χάρι]τας· ἀγαθεῖ τύχει
        [δεδόχθαι τεῖ βουλεῖ τοὺς λαχόντας πρ]οέδρους
        [εἰς τὴν ἐπιοῦσαν ἐκκλησίαν ------------]
        [---------------------------------]
```

If the slightly narrower length of line preferred by Robert is correct, and if the text should be dated within the limits 173/2–168/7 found advisable by Stamires, the archonship of Eunikos alone will satisfy the requirements of line 1, and the text is therefore dated tentatively to his year. This would suit the indications of Polybios 28.16–17, with which Stamires sought to associate Arrhidaios' services to Athens. Robert (*Hellenica* XI/XII, 1960, p. 93, note 5) saw no reason why the decree should not belong to the later years of the reign of Antiochos IV, and if a later date be admitted, 165/4 (the archonship of Pelops) would be a possible year. It too was ordinary in the festival calendar. For the beginning of line 2, in consequence, Stamires' πέμπτης seems the most likely restoration. Stamires noted that the name of the γραμματεύς was omitted from the prescript, and since this omission occurs also in three texts (one with two decrees) from the year 173/2 (see pp. 398–399 above on the archonship of Alexis), he was encouraged to suggest that year as the occasion of this decree also. A. S. Henry (*Prescripts*, p. 84) sought an explanation in the possibility that the inscription was undertaken at private expense or that the omission reflects a growing carelessness of expression as the significance of Athenian decrees declined. Cf. also Tracy, *Attic Letter-Cutters*, p. 136.

Line 3. For the location of the assembly see **259**, commentary on line 4. It may suggest that the decree was enacted in the final third of the month. Line 4. Arrhidaios, honored in this decree as high in the confidence of Antiochos Epiphanes and as benefactor of visiting Athenian officials, is otherwise unknown to history. Evidently of Macedonian descent, he was associated by Stamires with the Diodoros honored in *IG* II², 945 (of 168/7) by the common link of the dedication *OGIS* 301, a dedication by Diodoros, son of Arrhidaios, to Zeus Soter, Athena Nikephoros, and Apollo Pythios in the name of King Eumenes II of Pergamon and his wife and brothers, found at Panion in Thrace. This hypothesis was brusquely discounted by Robert (*Hellenica* XI/XII, 1960, pp. 99–101) as of "la plus haute témérité". Cf. Moretti, *op. cit.*, p. 81.

Lines 6–7. On πίστις see Robert, *Hellenica* XI/XII, 1960, pp. 105–107, with abundant bibliography, and *Hellenica* XIII, 1965, p. 42, note 2. Lines 7–8. στρατο[ῦ φυλακῆς κα]ὶ εὐταξίας, proposed by J. and L. Robert (*REG* 74, 1961, p. 162), was adopted by Moretti but seems too short for the lacuna. On εὐταξία see L. Robert *apud* N. Fıratlı, *Les stèles funéraires de Byzance greco-romaine*, 1964, pp. 160–162 and *RevPhil*, ser. 3, 1, 1927, p. 121, no. 5 (= *Opera minora selecta* II, 1969, p. 1076); L. and J. Robert, *La Carie* II, 1954, p. 289, with note 1. The term was most generally associated with military virtue, as here; see also Thucydides 2.89, 6.72, etc. For personal or political self-discipline cf. the use of εὐτακτεῖν in Thucydides 8.1.4. Lines 9–10. See Robert, *Hellenica* XI/XII, 1960, pp. 104–105.

Line 11. On the σπονδοφόροι, the Athenian ambassadors who announced the Panathenaic and Eleusinian festivals and the Mysteries, Robert gave substantial commentary, *loc. cit.*, pp. 108–111. Cf. *IG* II², 785, of 196/5 (for the date, the correction to which was overlooked by Robert, see p. 362 above), 1235, 1236, etc. Lines 12–14. Cf. *IG* II², 945, lines 12–16. Lines 14–16. An unusual variant of the "hortatory intention" in an Attic context. For φιλοδοξεῖν cf. *IG* II², 1227, lines 20–22, 1304, line 40; on ζηλοῦν (or ζηλωτὴς γενέσθαι) see Robert, *loc. cit.*, p. 98, note 1. Near to home, and of the middle of the century, is the Oropian text *IG* VII, 411 (*SEG* XXV, 493),

lines 25–29. Customary Attic phraseology, as frequently evidenced in the texts of this volume, revolved around
φιλοτιμία—φιλοτιμεῖσθαι. Line 16. ἀγαθεῖ τύχει. See **72**, commentary on lines 7–8.

FRAGMENT OF AN HONORARY DECREE

293. A fragment of a stele of Hymettian marble (I 3755), which preserves the left side of the monument but is broken
elsewhere, discovered on March 14, 1936, in a Late Roman context north of the Odeion (M 8).

H. 0.086 m.; W. 0.084 m.; Th. 0.027 m.
LH. 0.006 m.

Ed. M. B. Walbank, *Hesperia* 54, 1985, pp. 324–325, no. 9, with photograph pl. 88. See also *SEG* XXXV, 97.

ca. a. 167/6 *a.*   NON-ΣTOIX.

```
              [----------------------------]
              O[---------------------------]
              δύγατ[αι-----------------------]
              προξενο ι [--------------------]
              σάντων τὴγ [-------------------]
          5   θεωροὺς του[-------------------]
              ΡΙΩΝΕΠΡ[---------------------]
              [¹⁻²]απυρ[----------------------]
              [³⁻⁴]σα[-----------------------]
              [----------------------------]
```

Line 3. προξένοι[ς(?) Walbank: perhaps πρόξενον or προξένου[ς. Line 5. τοὺ[ς Walbank. Line 6. ρίων
ἐπρυ[τάνευεν Walbank; but the upsilon is to be doubted: possibly πε]|ρὶ ὧν ἐπρ[– – –]. Line 7. [Λ]άπυρι[– – –]
Walbank.

Walbank gave to this fragment the date "*fin. s.* III *a.*": but S. V. Tracy (*Attic Letter-Cutters*, pp. 143–145) regarded it
as in the style of, although probably not to be directly attributed to, the "Cutter of *IG* II² 783". Inscriptions by
this mason datable on other grounds span the years 173/2 to 161/60, *IG* II², 996 and 952 representing the outer
limits. This does not necessarily confine the dating of the present text, but since no other criteria exist it is placed here
at the midpoint of the known career of the craftsman whose manner it reflects.

The contents appear to indicate the material of an honorary enactment of some kind. Walbank interpreted
line 7 as a proper name and made the connection between Lapyris in this text and his homonym of an earlier time,
son of Kallias of Kleonai, honored in 323/2, for whom see *IG* II², 365 (*SEG* XXX, 66, XXXII, 89, XXXVI, 157).

THE ARCHONSHIP OF EUERGETES, 164/3 B.C.

It was not until 1957, when B. D. Meritt (*Hesperia* 26, pp. 72–74) published the prytany text which later
became *Agora* XV, 219, that Euergetes and his archonship were clearly known to students of Athenian
history. In the didascalic list *IG* II², 2323 (*SEG* XXV, 194), which has at earlier stages provided important
information for the reconstruction of the archon list (see also W. B. Dinsmoor, *Archons of Athens*, pp. 464–470),
lines 433–436 mention the archons Erastos, Poseidonios, and (after a *rasura* of one line) Aristolas. In the
line before Erastos appear the letters [. . .] Εὐερ[– – –], expanded in *IG* II² into [ὑπὸ] Εὐερ[γ– – ἐνίκα].
Dinsmoor (*op. cit.*, pp. 259–260 and 466; cf. p. 222) accepted the supposition that Euerg– – – was an actor,
not an archon, although his archonship had been admitted by W. S. Ferguson in his original publication
(*Athenian Secretaries*, p. 55) and placed in 164/3. In his 1932 publication (*Athenian Tribal Cycles*, p. 29) Ferguson
abandoned this hypothesis and hesitantly attributed Epainetos to this year; but Epainetos was displaced,
and Euerg– – – apparently confirmed as a fiction, by the discovery of **295** (see Meritt, *Hesperia* 3, 1934,
p. 31), where in the year of Erastos a taxiarchos is honored for services performed (as it was presumed)
in the preceding year. That year appeared to be described as of an archon Charias, who thus figures as
the archon of 164/3 in Dinsmoor's revised study (*Athenian Archon List*, pp. 23 and 190). So also in W. K.
Pritchett and Meritt, *Chronology*, p. xxix.

Agora XV, 219, when discovered in 1954, not only gave the correct archon's name in full but also
proved the complete name of the γραμματεύς of the year, whose deme Kephale, belonging to the phyle

Akamantis (VI), confirmed Euergetes' place in the archon series by means of the secretary cycle. The didascalic list could thus be correctly restored, and two other prytany texts (S. Dow, *Prytaneis*, pp. 142–147, nos. 79 and 80; *Agora* XV, 220 and 221) could be attributed to this year. See *SEG* XVI, 95–96, 141. Since that time, Euergetes' year has not been in dispute. See Meritt, *Hesperia* 26, 1957, p. 95; A. G. Woodhead, *Hesperia* 28, 1959, pp. 273–274; Meritt, *Athenian Year*, pp. 164–165, 236, *TAPA* 95, 1964 p. 237, *Historia* 26, p. 182; C. Habicht, *Hesperia* 57, 1988, p. 237.

In the festival calendar the year was ordinary, but there was an official readjustment in the latter part of it which interrupted the regularity of its course. The calendar equations in *Agora* XV, 220 show, with restorations, that Gamelion 21 = pryt. VII, 21 and that Anthesterion 4 = pryt. VIII, 4. Neither *Agora* XV, 221 nor **294** provides any evidence for the calendar. But in *Agora* XV, 219, Elaphebolion 19 is equated with Elaphebolion 21 κατὰ θεόν and with pryt. IX, 22. The calendar in Elaphebolion had been retarded by two days, for which compensation was presumably made before the end of Thargelion and probably before the end of Elaphebolion itself (see p. 268 above). The adjustment no doubt concerned the City Dionysia, as in 196/5 and 170/69. The detail was discussed by Meritt in *Athenian Year*, pp. 164–165, and in ᾿Αρχ. ᾿Εφ., 1968, pp. 103–104, with citation of the relevant texts. See also Pritchett, *Ancient Athenian Calendars on Stone*, p. 337 and A. S. Henry, *Prescripts*, p. 79. This is the only occasion so far evidenced on which the prytany calendar appears to be out of complete accord with the calendar κατὰ θεόν, but there was evidently, in this year, no exact correspondence between "natural" months and prytanies, and in view of the data concerning the seventh and eighth prytanies it seems that, while Anthesterion was a full month, the eighth prytany contained only 29 days. See Meritt's table in ᾿Αρχ. ᾿Εφ., 1968, p. 104. The year was the third in the fifteenth Metonic cycle and was also ordinary in Meton's calendar, with 355 days.

Phylai to be identified with known prytanies are VII Erechtheis, VIII Leontis, and IX Hippothontis.

FRAGMENT OF A DECREE

294. Part of the upper left corner of a pedimental stele of Pentelic marble (I 5032), with the original rough-picked back and part of the pediment with moldings and raking cornice preserved, discovered on October 21, 1937, in a wall of a modern house southeast of the Market Square (R 18). The horizontal cornice of the pediment is represented by a wide fascia, and below it a well-rounded ovolo molding surmounts a flat band, from the ill-defined lower edge of which an apophyge descends in a gentle curve to the inscribed face. A space of 0.009 m. intervenes before the first line of text.

H. 0.18 m.; W. 0.132 m.; Th. 0.12 m.
LH. 0.007 m.

Ed. A. G. Woodhead, *Hesperia* 28, 1959, pp. 273–274, no. 1, with photograph pl. 55. See also *SEG* XVIII, 23.

a. 164/3 a., *pryt.* IX(?)   NON-ΣΤΟΙΧ. *ca.* 34

[᾿Επὶ Εὐ]εργέτου [ἄρχοντος ἐπὶ τῆς ῾Ιπποθωντί(?)]
[δος ἐνά]της π[ρυτανείας ἧι Διονυσόδωρος]
[Φιλίππου Κεφαλῆθεν ἐγραμμάτευεν· – – –]
[– –]

Like **293**, this fragment was adjudged by S. V. Tracy to be in the style of, but not assuredly from the hand of, the "Cutter of *IG* II² 783": see *Attic Letter-Cutters*, pp. 143–145. The letters are inscribed with reasonable accuracy, and no omission of strokes occurs. The loop of rho is very full; the external strokes of sigma are well angled and make the letter appear tall.

For the reconstruction of lines 1–2 see the *editio princeps*, where it was argued that the fragment was not likely to be the lost upper section of *IG* II², 972 (*Agora* XV, 221), which is in the "tachygraphic style" and was later confirmed by Tracy (*Attic Letter-Cutters*, p. 101) as a work of the "Cutter of Agora I 247" (see **264**).

Lines 2–3. The name of the γραμματεύς is restored from *Agora* XV, 219. No other Dionysodoros of this deme is known in Attic prosopography, and only one other Philippos (of the 4th century B.C.; see J. Sundwall, *Nachträge zur Prosopographia Attica*, 1910, p. 163). For a dedication to Eilytheia made, in all probability, by the parents of the γραμματεύς on behalf of his sister, see *SEG* XVIII, 88.

THE ARCHONSHIP OF ERASTOS, 163/2 B.C.

The appearance of Erastos as archon in the didascalic list *IG* II², 2323 (see pp. 412–413 above on the archonship of Euergetes) long ago assured his relationship with the archons who followed him and ultimately with the archon who preceded him. Placed in 163/2 by W. S. Ferguson in his original study (*Athenian Secretaries*, p. 56), he has remained undisturbed in that position ever since, except for W. B. Dinsmoor's short-lived divagation from Ferguson's arrangement which temporarily set him in 164/3 (*Archons of Athens*, pp. 222 and 259–260, retracted in *Athenian Archon List*, pp. 23, 170, 190). The discovery of **295**, providing the remains of the name and patronymic of the γραμματεύς of the year, together with his demotic in full, Ἐπικηφίσιος (Oineis VII), confirmed Erastos' place in relation to the secretary cycle as drawn up by Ferguson. In the light of it, B. D. Meritt (*Hesperia* 3, 1934, pp. 29–31) was able to assign *IG* II², 783 also to this year (cf. Dinsmoor, *Archons of Athens*, p. 206). For Erastos and his place in the archonship series see also Ferguson, *Athenian Tribal Cycles*, p. 29; W. K. Pritchett and Meritt, *Chronology*, p. xxix; Pritchett and O. Neugebauer, *Calendars*, p. 86; Meritt, *Hesperia* 26, 1957, p. 95, *Athenian Year*, p. 236, *Historia* 26, 1977, p. 183; C. Habicht, *Hesperia* 57, 1988, p. 237.

The year was the fourth in the fifteenth Metonic cycle and was ordinary in the cycle as it was also in the Athenian festival calendar. It is without calendric problems. The details of date in **295** show an exact correspondence between the festival and prytany calendars, where Anthesterion 18 = pryt. VIII, 18. Similarly in *IG* II², 783, [Skirophori]on 23 = pryt. XII, 23. Cf. Pritchett and Neugebauer, *Calendars*, p. 86. Of phylai in office during known prytanies, the evidence extends only to VIII Leontis and XII Aiantis.

A TAXIARCHOS HONORED

295. A pedimental stele of Pentelic marble (I 73), completely preserved save for the left akroterion and parts of the other two akroteria, discovered on July 20, 1931, built with inscribed face downwards as a cover slab into the Great Drain east of the Metroon (I 9). Because of its reuse in this context, the inscribed surface has become seriously corroded, and the inscription is almost totally illegible with the exception of parts of a few lines at the top of the stele and three or four points elsewhere. Cf. **291**, which formed an adjacent slab covering the same drain. A sculptured urn stands at the center of the pedimental field. The molding below the horizontal cornice consists of a graceful ovolo with cavetto crown and a flat band with apophyge to the inscribed face beneath it.

H. 1.72 m.; W. (top of inscribed surface) 0.602 m., (foot of stele) 0.665 m.; Th. (top of inscribed surface) 0.16 m., (foot of stele) 0.19 m.

LH. 0.01 m.

Ed. B. D. Meritt, *Hesperia* 3, 1934, pp. 27–31, no. 20, with photograph. Text of lines 2–3 corrected by Meritt in *Hesperia* 13, 1944, p. 266, no. 20, and the archon's name at the end of line 9 also amended by him in *Hesperia* 26, 1957, p. 73. See *SEG* XVI, 97 and XXI, 455 (reference to Meritt, *Athenian Year*, p. 236, note 36, where the same correction to line 9 is mentioned), and XXXVIII, 108 (full text).

a. 163/2 a., *pryt.* VIII   NON-ΣΤΟΙΧ. *ca.* 50

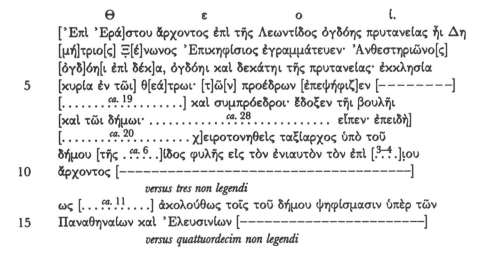

```
                   Θ            ε           o           ι.
        ['Επὶ 'Ερά]στου ἄρχοντος ἐπὶ τῆς Λεωντίδος ὀγδόης πρυτανείας ἧι Δη
        [μή]τριο[ς] Ξ[έ]νωνος 'Επικηφίσιος ἐγραμμάτευεν· 'Ανθεστηριῶνο[ς]
        [ὀγδ]όη[ι ἐπὶ δέκ]α, ὀγδόηι καὶ δεκάτηι τῆς πρυτανείας· ἐκκλησία
5       [κυρία ἐν τῶι] θ[εά]τρωι· [τ]ῶ[ν] προέδρων [ἐπεψήφιζ]εν [‒‒‒‒‒‒‒]
        [.........ca. 19.........] καὶ συμπρόεδροι· ἔδοξεν τῆι βουλῆι
        [καὶ τῶι δήμωι·.............ca. 28............. εἶπεν· ἐπειδὴ]
        [.........ca. 20.........χ]ειροτονηθεὶς ταξίαρχος ὑπὸ τοῦ
        δήμου [τῆς .ca. 6.]ίδος φυλῆς εἰς τὸν ἐνιαυτὸν τὸν ἐπὶ [.3-4.]ιου
10      ἄρχοντος [‒‒‒‒‒‒‒‒‒‒‒‒‒‒‒‒‒‒‒‒‒‒‒‒‒‒‒‒‒‒]
                        versus tres non legendi
        ως [...ca. 11....] ἀκολούθως τοῖς τοῦ δήμου ψηφίσμασιν ὑπὲρ τῶν
15      Παναθηναίων καὶ 'Ελευσινίων [‒‒‒‒‒‒‒‒‒‒‒‒‒‒‒‒]
                        versus quattuordecim non legendi
```

30 ποίησιν τῆς στήλης καὶ τὴν ἀναγραφὴν μερίσαι τὸν ταμίαν τῶν στρατιω
  τικῶν τὸ γενόμενον ἀνάλωμα. *vacat*

(in corona)

versus quattuor vel quinque non legendi

Ἐπὶ Ἐράστου ἄρχοντος [------------------------]

versus tredecim non legendi

vacat

S. V. Tracy (*Attic Letter-Cutters*, p. 249) found the state of preservation of the lettering of this inscription too poor to permit its attribution to any mason he had identified, although he believed that what he could see of it bore some similarity to the style of the "Cutter of *IG* II² 903", for whom see **278**. As in the case of **291**, the text is more legible in a good photograph than on the stone itself or from a squeeze. Little can be said of the lettering save that it is unusually large: there appears to be no decoration in the form of serifs or apices.

The text, except for the end of line 9, is that of Meritt, which the difficulties of reading make it hard either to confirm or to deny. It is possible to be overskeptical or overcredulous. The chief problem is presented by the name of the archon in whose year of office the honorand served as taxiarchos. In his original edition Meritt read ἐπὶ Χαρίου at this point, on the supposition that, as usually, the official concerned was honored in the year immediately following that in which he had held office. The archon Charias was a new discovery and was assigned in consequence to 164/3, the year before the well-recognized year of Erastos: see W. K. Pritchett and Meritt, *Chronology*, p. xxix.

New evidence however made it clear that the archon of 164/3 was Euergetes (see pp. 412–413 above), and Charias had to be dismissed as fiction. Euergetes could not be accommodated to the text as it stood; but it sometimes happened that a year or more might elapse between a man's tenure of office and the decree honoring his record in it, as may be seen in, e.g., **216** and **217**; see the commentary on **216**. Meritt therefore substituted for the name of Charias that of Achaios, then thought to be the archon of 166/5; but this suggestion, made in 1957, was invalidated nearly a generation later by the removal of that archon to 190/89 (see p. 371 above), unless the removal itself be called into question by these uncertain traces. For, if Meritt's reading is reasonably acceptable, not only Euergetes but other archons also of the years preceding Erastos fail to fit the requirements, including Epainetos, whom C. Habicht (*Hesperia* 57, 1988, p. 245) assigned to 166/5 in Achaios' place. In view of the second decree on the same stone, it might be suggested that the first decree constitutes in essentials a restatement of honors for a function performed twenty-seven years previously; but this is hard to credit. The issue remains unresolved.

Honors for taxiarchoi are recorded also in **123**, **182**, **185**, and **187**. In this example it is a single taxiarchos from among the twelve who has evidently merited individual honors for his personal services. Cf. *SEG* III, 116, which is not however an enactment of the boule and demos. For the duties of the taxiarchoi see the commentary on **123**.

Lines 2–3. Demetrios, son of Xenon, of Epikephisia. Neither he nor his family is otherwise identifiable. A Demetrios of this deme, who could be the grandfather of the γραμματεύς, appears in a list of prytaneis of Oineis dated *ca.* 225 B.C. (*Agora* XV, 124 = *SEG* XXI, 401). Lines 3–4. For Anthesterion 18 as a day on which meetings of the assembly might be held see J. D. Mikalson, *Sacred and Civil Calendar*, pp. 115–116, where lines 2–5 of this text are quoted. Cf. **265**, where the same date was contemplated by Meritt for a time but later rejected in favor of the month following. Lines 4–5. On the character and location of the assembly see **101**, lines 7–8 and **167**, lines 6–7.

Lines 30–31. Sufficient of the text is visible at this point to confirm that the Military Treasurer was required to perform his normal function in defraying the cost of the monument and its inscription. Below line 32 an olive stephanos in well-executed relief encloses an illegible citation of four or five lines.

THE ARCHONSHIP OF ARISTOLAS, 161/60 B.C.

Aristolas is the third of the triplet of archons associated in lines 433–436 of the didascalic list *IG* II², 2323 (*SEG* XXV, 194), on which see the commentary on the archonship of Euergetes (p. 412 above). His association with a γραμματεύς whose deme was Eleusis (Hippothontis IX) was assured by the textual requirements of *IG* II², 952 (*Agora* XV, 222), and his place with reference to the secretary cycle and in relation to the archons preceding him was thereby conditioned and confirmed. See W. S. Ferguson, *Athenian Secretaries*, p. 56; W. B. Dinsmoor, *Archons of Athens*, pp. 222 and 259–260 (where Dinsmoor's brief divergence from Ferguson's arrangement attributed him to 162/1). Dinsmoor returned him to 161/60 in *Athenian Archon List*, pp. 23 and 190. On his date see also J. Kirchner, *IG* II², iv, 1, pp. 18–19; Ferguson, *Athenian Tribal Cycles*, p. 29; S. Dow, *Prytaneis*, pp. 136–137, no. 75; W. K. Pritchett and B. D. Meritt, *Chronology*, p. xxix; Pritchett and O. Neugebauer, *Calendars*, p. 86; Meritt, *Hesperia* 26, 1957, p. 95, *Athenian Year*, p. 236, *TAPA* 95, 1964, p. 237, *Historia* 26, 1977, p. 183; C. Habicht, *Hesperia* 57, 1988, p. 237. The victor list of the Theseia, *IG* II², 956, is also dated by Aristolas' archonship; and Poseidonios and Aristolas, in that order, are named in the inventory *ID* 1408, A, col. II, lines 44–47. Cf. **296**, lines 10 and 16.

The year was the sixth in the fifteenth Metonic cycle, in which it was scheduled as ordinary with 355 days. It was ordinary also in the Athenian festival calendar, as had long since been deduced from the data of *IG* II², 952, in which Skirophorion 4 = pryt. XII, 4. **296** revealed on its discovery that in the earlier stages of the year Aristolas had intervened to adjust the calendar. The κατ'ἄρχοντα date is lost in the lacuna of line 2. Κατὰ θεόν the festival calendar ran as regularly *pari passu* with the prytany calendar, and Boedromion 16 = pryt. III, 16. Cf. Pritchett and Neugebauer, *loc. cit.*; Pritchett, *Ancient Athenian Calendars on Stone*, p. 337; Meritt, ᾿Αρχ. ᾿Εφ., 1968, p. 105; A. S. Henry, *Prescripts*, p. 79.

For the phylai in prytany during the year the evidence extends only to XII Hippothontis.

DECREE CONCERNING THE REPAIR AND RESTORATION OF A SANCTUARY (OF DIONYSOS?)

296. Nine fragments of an opisthographic stele of Hymettian marble (I 984: *a–g*; I 6700: *h*; I 7492: *i*), with the text on the reverse side so badly worn that nothing of it can be discerned beyond a few letters here and there.

The dates and places of discovery of the fragments, and details of their physical state, are as follows:

a. A fragment from the top of the stele, with the left side and rough-picked top preserved, but broken elsewhere, discovered on December 11, 1934, in a wall of a modern house over the East Building (O 14). The back and side retain traces of a molding which has been hacked away (see fragment *b*). The front face has been used as a step, and its upper part has been worn smooth. It makes a join on its right with fragment *b* and below with fragment *c*.

b. A fragment with both obverse and reverse faces preserved, as well as the original top, but broken elsewhere, discovered on June 14, 1933, in a wall of a modern house over the Panathenaic Way, west of the Library of Pantainos (Q 14–15). A crowning molding 0.09 m. high, which has been roughly hacked away, has left traces on both faces. On its left the fragment joins the right side of fragment *a*.

c. A fragment preserving both faces and the left side of the stele but otherwise broken, discovered on December 11, 1934, with fragment *a*. It joins the bottom of fragment *a*, and the small fragment *d* attaches to its right side. Below, it makes a join with fragment *e* below the inscribed surface.

d. A very small piece, broken all around (including the back), which joins the right side of fragment *c*, discovered on February 22, 1935, in a late context west of the East Building (N–O 14).

e. A fragment on which both faces and the left side of the stele are preserved, although broken elsewhere, discovered on December 11, 1934, with fragment *a*. It makes a join at the top with fragment *c* below the surface but not in the way in which it appeared in the *editio princeps*, the line numeration of which is amended in consequence.

f + *g*. These two fragments join and were closely associated from the time of their discovery, being found together on December 11, 1934, with fragment *a*. As joined they are broken all around, save that the reverse face is preserved. They may be aligned to the right of fragment *e* and join fragment *i* at the bottom left of the latter.

h. A large fragment preserving both faces and the left side, discovered in 1954 among stones from the demolition of the modern western addition of the Church of the Holy Apostles. Its place is below all the other fragments, and it makes no join with any of them.

i. A narrow fragment with smooth back, otherwise broken all around, discovered on August 13, 1974, in a modern wall near the south end of the Stoa of Attalos (R 13). At the top it joins the bottom of fragment *b*, and at its lower left it joins the upper right of fragment *f*.

> *a*: H. 0.35 m.; W. 0.295 m.; Th. 0.125 m.
> *b*: H. 0.38 m.; W. 0.265 m.; Th. 0.15 m.
> *c*: H. 0.305 m.; W. 0.16 m.; Th. 0.125 m.
> *d*: H. 0.035 m.; W. 0.034 m.; Th. 0.076 m.
> *e*: H. 0.35 m.; W. 0.241 m.; Th. 0.129 m.
> *f*+*g*: H. 0.405 m.; W. 0.228 m.; Th. 0.13 m.
> *h*: H. 0.63 m.; W. 0.43 m.; Th. 0.135 m.
> *i*: H. 0.355 m.; W. 0.17 m.; Th. 0.13 m.
>
> LH. 0.006–0.007 m.

S. V. Tracy (see below) assessed the height of the eight joined fragments as 0.988 m. and their width as 0.557 m.

Ed. *a–g*: B. D. Meritt, *Hesperia* 16, 1947, pp. 164–168, no. 64, with photographs pls. XXX, XXXI. *h*: Meritt, *Hesperia* 32, 1963, pp. 33–36, no. 32, with photograph pl. 9; see also *SEG* XXI, 456. *i*, with revision of the relevant sections of *c–f*: S. V. Tracy, *Hesperia* 53, 1984, pp. 374–377, no. 4, with photographs of the eight joined fragments, pl. 72 and of fragment *i* separately, pl. 70; see also *SEG* XXXIV, 95, where a complete text of the whole inscription is provided. On fragments *a–g*, see J. and L. Robert, *REG* 61, 1948, p. 146, no. 43, who mentioned fragment *h* also, *REG* 77, 1964, p. 150, no. 117.

a. 161/60 *a., pryt.* III   NON-ΣΤΟΙΧ. *ca.* 86–90

(a)
['Επὶ 'Αριστόλα ἄρχοντος ἐπὶ τῆς . .⁴⁻⁵.]ιδος τρίτης πρυτανείας ⟨ἧι⟩ Βαχ[χύλος Φιλωνίδου
    'Ελευσίνιος ἐγραμμάτευεν]·
                                                                                                          (b)
[Βοηδρομιῶνος . . . . . ᶜᵃ·¹⁴ . . . . , κατὰ θ]εὸν δὲ ἔκτει ἐπὶ δέκα, ἔκτει κα[ὶ δεχάτει τῆς
    πρυτανείας· ἐκκλησία κυρία]
[ἐμ Πειραιεῖ· τῶν προέδρων ἐπεψήφιζεν] Σῶσος Ἴωνος Φαληρεὺς καὶ σ[υμπρόεδροι· ἔδοξεν τεῖ
    βουλεῖ καὶ τῶι δήμωι]·
[. . . . . ᶜᵃ· ²⁹ . . . .]ος εἶπεν· ἀγαθεῖ τύχει δεδόχθ[αι τεῖ βουλεῖ τοὺς λαχόντας
    προέδρους εἰς]

5 [τὴν κυρίαν ἐκκλησίαν χρηματίσαι περὶ το]ύτων, γνώμην δὲ ξυμβάλλεσθα[ι τῆς βουλῆς εἰς τὸν
    δῆμον ὅτι δοκεῖ τεῖ]
[βουλεῖ ἑλέσθαι τὸν δῆμον πέντε ἄνδρ]ας ἐξ 'Αθηναίων ἁπάντων οἵτινες μ[ετά τε τοῦ ἱερέως καὶ
    τοῦ στρατηγοῦ]
[τοῦ ἐπὶ τὴν παρασκευὴν καὶ τοῦ ἀρχι]τέκτονος τοῦ ἐπὶ τὰ ἱερὰ ἐπισκ[――――――――――]
[. . . . . ᶜᵃ· ²⁷ . . . . , ὁμ]οίως δὲ καὶ τὰ λοιπὰ τῶν ἐν τῶι ἱε[ρῶι ――――――――]
[. . . . . ᶜᵃ· ¹⁹ . . . . ὅπου ἂν ἄλλο]θεν εὑρίσκωσιν τῶν τῆς πόλε[ως ――――――――]

10 [. . . . . ᶜᵃ· ¹⁴ . . . . . καὶ τὰ] χρυσᾶ τὰ ὑπ[άρ]χοντα τοῖς θεοῖς μέχρι Ποσειδ[ωνίου ἄρχοντος ――――]
[ᶜᵃ· ⁴.]ΑΕΙΣΑΕΙΝΑΝ εἰ μὴ προσδεόμενα [κ]ατασκευῆς ὁλοσχεροῦς θειασ[――――――――]
[. . . . . ᶜᵃ· ²⁷ . . . . τῶι ἱ]ερῶι ποιήσουσιν ἃ ἂν αὐτοῖς φ[αίνηται ――――――――]
[. . . . ᶜᵃ· ¹² . . . .]Τ[. .]Ι[.⁴⁻⁵.]μένα [τὰ ἐλ]αφρὰ τῶμ ποτηρίων ἢ τῶν ἄλλ[ων ――――――――]
[. . . . ᶜᵃ· ¹² . . . .]ΧΑ[.]μενοι πρὸς [τὰς τῶν] συνόδων χρείας καὶ ὅταν σ[――――――――]

15 [. . ᶜᵃ· ⁹ . .] ἐναντίον τῆ[ς βουλῆς, παρ]αλαβεῖν δὲ αὐτοὺς καὶ τὰ [――――――――――]
[. . ᶜᵃ· ¹⁰ . .]ωι· ὁμοίως [δὲ καὶ τὸ νόμισ]μα τὸ ἀνακείμενον μέχρι Π[οσειδωνίου ἄρχοντος ――]
[. . ᶜᵃ· ¹⁰ . .]ΗΗΗ⊢ΔΔ[. . . . ᶜᵃ· ¹² . . . .]σι γεγονότα ἐχλογισμό[ν ―――――――――]
[. . ᶜᵃ· ¹⁰ . .] ὑπο[. . . . ᶜᵃ· ¹⁰ . . . τῶν ἀν]ατεθηκότων ὅσοι μὴ ε[――――――――]

(c)
[. . ᶜᵃ· ⁷ . .]σιος [. . . ᶜᵃ· ⁹ . . · τὸ δὲ γενόμεν]ον ἀνάλωμα εἴς τε τ[ὴν ἀναγραφὴν καὶ τὴν ἀνάθεσιν
    τῆς στήλης μερίσαι]

20 [τὸν γεν]ησόμε[νον ταμίαν(?) καὶ τοὺς στρατη]γοὺς ἀπ[ὸ] νε[――――――――――――]
[ψή]φισμα εἰς στή[λην λιθίνην . . . . ᶜᵃ· ¹² . . . .]ΕΝΑΛ[―――――――――――――
    ――――――]
                                                                                                          (i)
μενει ὅσαι ἡμέρα[ι . . . . ᶜᵃ· ²¹ . . . .]ΕΣ[. ⁵⁻⁶ .]ΤΟ[――――――――――]
τες τὸν ναὸν το[. . . . . ᶜᵃ· ²² . . . .]ΠΡΑΞ[ᶜᵃ· ⁴]ΚΑΤ[―――――――――]
Ξενοκλῆς ἐκ Κερ[αμέων ᵛᵛ . . . ᶜᵃ· ⁸ . . . Τριχ]ορύσιος ᵛᵛ Δημοσ[―――――――――]
25   *vacat* 0.01 m.

'Επὶ 'Αριστόλα ἄρχο[ντος . . . . . . ᶜᵃ· ¹⁵ . . . . .]ε]ι ἱσταμένου, κατὰ θ[εὸν δὲ ――――――――]
Εὐπυρίδου συμπα[ρόντων . . ᶜᵃ· ⁶ . . τοῦ στρατ]ηγοῦ ἐπὶ τὴμ παρ[ασκευήν ――――――――]
νος 'Ολυμπίωνος [. . . . . ᶜᵃ· ²⁰ . . . .]ιου Ζω[π]ύρου χρυ[σᾶ(?) ―――――――――χρυ]
(d)
σοῖ πέντε ὀβολοὶ τρ[εῖ]ς [. . . . . . ᶜᵃ· ¹⁴ . . . . . στ]εφάνου οὗ εἶχεν ἡ [――――――――ἑβδο]
30 μήχοντα δύο καὶ ἀ[στ]ρα[γαλίσκους(?) . ᶜᵃ· ⁶ . · ὁλ]κή χρυσοῖ πέντε ἀ[νετεθήχει ――――――]
τα δέκα ἓξ καὶ ἐλαίας ἐννέα . . . ᶜᵃ· ¹¹ . . . ὀβο]λοὶ πέντε ἀνετεθή[κει ――――――――]
καὶ ἐλαίας ἑπτά· ὁλκή [. . . . . . . ᶜᵃ· ¹⁹ . . . . . . ο]ι ἀνετεθήκει Ξεν[――――――――]
χρυσοῦς ὀβολός· ἡμιω[βέλιον(?) . . . . . ᶜᵃ· ¹⁵ . . . . .]ΙΟ[ᶜᵃ· ³]εσιος ΑΛΑ[―――――――τέτ]
ταρες ἀνετεθήκει Αισ[. . . . . ᶜᵃ· ¹⁸ . . . . στέ]φαν[ον] τρία φύλ[λα ――――――― 'Αρι]
35 στομήδης 'Ραμνούσι[ος . . . . ᶜᵃ· ²⁰ . . . .]ον δέκα ὀκτώ· ὀλ[κή· ――――――――]
κη ἡμίχρυσον ἀνετεθ[ήκει . . . . ᶜᵃ· ¹⁶ . . . . ἀμφ]ορίσκων· ὁλκή· ὀβ[ολοί ――――――ἀνετε]
θήκε[ι 'Ηρακλείδης Αλ[. . . . . . . ᶜᵃ· ²² . . . .] στεφάνιον μικρὸ[ν ――――――ἀνετεθή]
κει Διότιμος 'Αλωπε[κῆθεν . . . . ᶜᵃ· ¹⁶ . . . . · ὁ]λκή· χρυσοῦς ἀνε[τεθήκει ――――――χο]
ρύμβους δύο· ὁλκή· [. . . . . ᶜᵃ· ²³ . . . .]φων Φυλάσιος σ[――――――――Κυζι]
40 κηνὸς στεφάνιο[ν . . . . ᶜᵃ· ²⁴ . . . . χ]ρυσὸν ὀβολοὶ πέν[τε ――――――――]
[―――――――――――――――――]λιον ἀνετεθήκε[ι ――――――――――]

(e)

(f + g)

[.. *ca.* 12 ..... ὁλκ]ή· ὀβολ[οὶ .... *ca.* 18 .....]λα λεπτά· ὁλκή· ὀβολο[ὶ ――――――――――]

[..... *ca.* 15 ....]ΤΟΕ[.... *ca.* 13 ....]ΡΔ[.] δύ[ο Ἀφρ]οδισίου Ἀραφην[ίου ――――――――]

[... *ca.* 9 ... Ποσιδ]εῶνος Ε[.. 6–7 .. μετ'εἰκά]δας, κατὰ θ[ε]ὸν δὲ ἑβδόμει μ[ετ'εἰκάδας ――――――]

45   [.. δύ]ο ὀβολοὶ τρεῖς· ^v κατεσκ[.. *ca.* 10 .... Ἀφ]ροδισίου Ἀρ[α]φηνίου ἃ ἔχου[σι ――――――――]

[δισ]χίλους ἑβδομήκοντα τε[.... *ca.* 12 ....] δὲ εἴκοσι τέτταρας· ὁλκή· [――――――――――――]

[ρ]ες Ἀφροδίτης καὶ τροχίσκο[ι *ca.* 10 .....]ς κιττόφυλλ[α τ]ὰ ΕΝΤΗΚΟ[――――――――――χρυ]

σοῖ δέκα πέντε ἡμίχρυσον ὀβο[λοὶ *ca.* 6 .]· κεφάλαιον χρυσῶ]ν τρία [――――――――――]

σαν χρυσοῖ ἒξ ἡμίχρυσον [―――――]   *vacat*

50   καὶ τάδε ἀργυρᾶ· καυλοὺς τ[ετταράκοντα] δύο καὶ ἐλαίας δέκα [――――――――――ἐπὶ Ζωπύ]

ρου· ὁλκή· ΗΡΓΗΗ· κανοῦν ἐν[.... *ca.* 11 ....]ην ἐπὶ Διονυσίου· ὁλ[κή· ――――――――――]

ὁλκή· ΔΔΗΙΙΙ· φοίνικα· ὁλκή [.... *ca.* 13 ....]ημην μικρά· κατοπ[τρ――――――――]

ἣν Δίων Σκαμβωνίδης· [ὁλκή· *ca.* 5 . ἄλ]λην λείαν ἣν Ξ[ε]νοκ[ράτης ――――――]

ἄλλην ἣν Ξενοκράτης [... *ca.* 10 ... ὁ]λκή· ΔΔΔΔΓΗ· [ἄ]λλην [ἣν ――――――――]

55   [ὁ]λκή· ΡΓΙΙΙ· ἄλλο δ Θεόφιλο[ς .. *ca.* 8 ...]ιος· ὁλκή· ΡΗ· ἄ[λλ]ο δ Δ[――――――――]

ἔχον δ Σάμος Ἐρχιεύς· [ὁλκή· . . ἄλλο δ] Εὐθυκρ[ά]της 'Ρα[μ]νο[ύσιος ――――――――· ἄλ]

λ(ην) ἐπὶ Ζωπύρου· ὁλ[κή· .. *ca.* 7 . · ἄ]λ]ο δ Ἀσκληπιάδης Δι[ομειεύς· ὁλκή· ――――――ἐπὶ]

Νικοσθένου· ὁλκή· ΡΗΗ· [ἄλλο δ . *ca.* 6 .]ν Σαλαμίνιος· ὁλκή· ΔΔ[――――――――――]

Χολλείδης· ὁλκή· ΔΔΔΔ[... · ἄλλο δ Μύ]ννιον· ὁλκή· ΔΔΔΔΓΗ· ἄ[λλο δ ――――――]

60   'Ραμνούσιος· ὁλκή· Ρ· ^v ἄ[λ]ο δ .. *ca.* 7 ..]κλῆς 'Ραμνούσιος· ὁλκή· [――――――――]

κλεια· ὁλκή· ΔΓΗΗΗΙΙΙ· σφ[... *ca.* 11 ....]ένης· ὁλκή· ΔΔΓΗΗ· φιάλ[ην ――――――――]

[δ] Ἀσκληπιάδης· ὁλκή· [... · ἄλλο δ Δημή]τριο[ς]· ὁλκή· ΡΓ· Κλεων[――――――――――]

[κλ]εια· ὁλκή· ΔΓΗΗ· [.... *ca.* 13 ....]η· ὁλκή· ΔΓΗΗΗ· ἄλλο δ Συρί[σκος ――――――]

[...] κύαθον δν Ε[..... *ca.* 15 .....]· ἄλλον δν Συρίσκος· ὁλκ[ή· ――――――――――]

65   [......... *ca.* 26 ......]ζης· ὁλκή· ΔΔΗΗ· ἄλλον δ[ν ――――――――――]

[......... *ca.* 26 ......]ιον δ Νικοβούλη· ὁ[λκή· ――――――――――]

vacat

vacat

vacat

70   [Ἐπὶ ――――――ἄρχοντο]ς, ἱερέως [δ]ὲ [―――――――――――――]

[......... *ca.* 20 .... Κ]ικυννέ[ως ――――――――――――]

[――――――――――――――――――――]

lacuna

(h)   *vss. 73–77: reliquiae litterarum vix discernendae*

vss. 78–86 vacant

Col. I	Col. II	Col. III
τάδε ἀργυρᾶ	*usque ad vs. 116*	*omnino*
[τ]ράπεζα ἐντελής	*non legenda*	*deperdita*

[τρί]πους ἀνεπίγρα[φο]ς α[―――――]

90   [κρατ]ὴρ δν ἀνέθηκ[εν] 'Ηρα[―――]

[.. 5 ...]ος οὗ ὁλκὴ κατὰ τ[ὴν ἐπιγραφήν]

[*vacat*]ΧΧΧ·

   [θ]υμιατήρια

[θυμια]τήριον τεῖ κατασκευ[εῖ ἀνῆκον]

95   [καὶ β]ωμί[σκ]ος δν ἀνέθηκεν [――――――]

[――――] ἐπὶ Σωστράτου ἄ[ρχ]οντο[ς]

[οὗ ὁλκὴ κ]ατὰ τὴν ἐπιγρ[αφήν ―― · ἄλλο]

[καὶ βωμί]σκοι δύο ἃ ἀνέθ[ηκεν ―――――]

[―――――――]ανου ὧν ὁλ[κὴ κατὰ τὰς]

100 [ἐπιγραφὰ]ς ΗΗΡΔΔΓ[..]·

[ἄλλα Δ]ΔΓ ἀνάκειται ἐν [τ]ῶι [――――――]

[ὑπάρ]γυρα δεξιᾶς πρὸς τῶι τοί[χωι]·

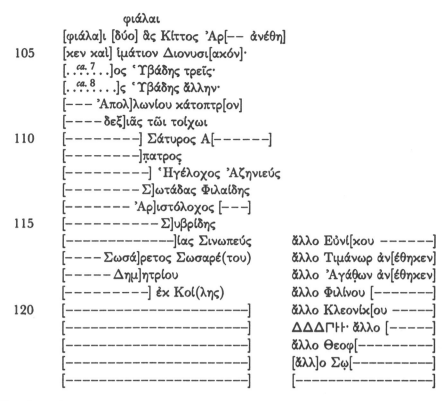

```
                    φιάλαι
        [φιάλα]ι [δύο] ἇς Κίττος Ἀρ[-- ἀνέθη]
105     [κεν καὶ] ἱμάτιον Διονυσι[ακόν]·
        [..ᶜᵃ·⁷..]ος Ὑβάδης τρεῖς·
        [..ᶜᵃ·⁸...]ς Ὑβάδης ἄλλην·
        [--- Ἀπολ]λωνίου κάτοπτρ[ον]
        [----δεξ]ιᾶς τῶι τοίχωι
110     [--------] Σάτυρος Α[------]
        [--------]πατρος
        [---------] Ἡγέλοχος Ἀζηνιεύς
        [-------- Σ]ωτάδας Φιλαίδης
        [------- Ἀρ]ιστόλοχος [---]
115     [----------- Σ]υβρίδης
        [------------]ίας Σινωπεύς          ἄλλο Εὐνί[κου ------]
        [---- Σωσά]ρετος Σωσαρέ(του)         ἄλλο Τιμάνωρ ἀν[έθηκεν]
        [----- Δημ]ητρίου                   ἄλλο Ἀγάθων ἀν[έθηκεν]
        [---------] ἐκ Κοί(λης)             ἄλλο Φιλίνου [-------]
120     [----------------------]            ἄλλο Κλεονίκ[ου -----]
        [----------------------]            ΔΔΔΓΗΗ· ἄλλο [-----]
        [----------------------]            ἄλλο Θεοφ[---------]
        [----------------------]            [ἄλλ]ο Σω[----------]
        [----------------------]            [---------------]
```

The lines from 39 onwards have been renumbered (see above), a requirement noted also by Tracy. Tracy also observed that line 118, in Column II, as shown above was omitted by Meritt and in *SEG* XXI, 456. Many of the readings are difficult, and a few improvements have been made here and there, especially between lines 21 and 48 by Tracy in the course of his insertion of fragment *i*.

The lettering is plain and fairly regular, despite the size of the monument and the complexity of the material and its arrangement. Tracy ascribed it to the "Cutter of Agora I 6006", a prolific craftsman who seems to have been associated with, and was perhaps trained by, the "Cutter of Agora I 656 + 6355" (for whom see **260**): see *Attic Letter-Cutters*, pp. 146–162, with photograph of part of the name piece, fig. 22. Works ascribed to this mason that can be independently dated span the years 169/8 to 135/4: Tracy's count of his output amounts to 76 identifiable texts. Among the Agora *psephismata* of the present collection this inscription is the earliest in date of those that may be assigned to him; for the others see **298, 299, 305, 306**, and **309**. (See also **332G**).

The first twenty-four lines of the inscription record a public decree authorizing the appointment of five commissioners who, with the cooperation of the priest(s), the general ἐπὶ τὴν παρασκευήν, and the clerk of works, are evidently to check and inventory the dedications, cash (line 16), and utensils in a certain sanctuary, and to assess the value of the items (line 17). Of the chosen commissioners the remains of three names and their patronymics survive (line 24). Line 26 begins their inventory, prefaced by another date. Their work was apparently protracted beyond the year of Aristolas, for one of the priests named in line 71 appears to differ from his counterpart in lines 26–27, and the name of Tychandros as archon (160/59) could well supply the lacuna at the beginning of line 70. At that stage it had become desirable to continue the inventory in an arrangement of three parallel columns, two of which partially survive (fragment *h*). For the appointment of a similar commission of oversight and inspection see **275**.

The apparent reference in line 105 to a Dionysiac robe led Meritt to suggest that the sanctuary which the commission was to investigate was one shared by Dionysos with certain other gods (line 10). Such a sanctuary was noted by Pausanias (1.2.4–5) at the northwest approach to the Agora; cf. *Agora* III, pp. 20–21, no. 2. However, Tracy's reading of the line (see below), if accepted, would cast some doubt on the suggestion.

In the Roman period there were two priests of Dionysos Melpomenos; cf. *IG* II², 5056 and 5060. One was of the family of the Euneidai, and the other belonged to the guild of Dionysiac technitai. That being so, it is not unlikely that both would be regarded as equally eponymous during their tenure, and Meritt suggested that the restoration of lines 26–27, where the lacuna to be filled is a long one, should take account of it. Cf. lines 70–71. In line 6 it is in consequence probable that τῶν ἱερέων should be restored in preference to Meritt's τοῦ ἱερέως shown above.

Line 1. ΙΗ is on the stone. For the patronymic and the demotic of the γραμματεύς see *Agora* XV, 222, line 2. The letters Βαχ—-- added to that context permit no more than Βαχ[..⁵..], and for this the name Βαχχύλος offers the most likely solution. Βάχχιος is possible but may be judged too short. In neither case can any further identification of the family of the γραμματεύς be made. Line 2. κατὰ] θεόν Meritt. For the intervention by the archon in the adjustment of the festival calendar, which line 26 now reveals as prolonged beyond Boedromion, see p. 416 above on the archonship of Aristolas. Lines 2–3. For the ἐκκλησία κυρία in the Peiraieus, held customarily in the last third of the month (though not so in the present instance), see **259**, commentary on line 4. Line 3. Ion of Phaleron, doubtless the father of the chairman, was a βουλευτής representing Aiantis *ca.* 190/89 (*Agora* XV, 170, line 85). Lines 3–5. The decree was probouleumatic; cf. P. J. Rhodes, *Athenian Boule*, p. 255. Line 4. ἀγαθεῖ τύχει. See **72**, commentary on lines 7–8.

Lines 6–7. For the general ἐπὶ τὴν παρασκευήν see Busolt-Swoboda, II, p. 1123, with references in note 1: and cf. in particular *IG* II², 682, lines 22–23, 839, lines 27–30 (which provided the model for the restorations offered here), 840, lines 12–13, 841, lines 13–15, 842 *init.* Line 10. x]αὶ τὰ χρυσᾶ Meritt. Lines 10 and 16. I.e., 162/1 B.C., the preceding year; cf. p. 412 above.

Line 11. θείας(?) Meritt. In a letter of December 11, 1947, A. M. Woodward raised the possibility of reading θε⟨ι⟩ασ[άμενοι. At the beginning of the line Meritt read no more than πρ[ο]σδεόμενα. Line 15. Rhodes (*Athenian Boule*, p. 126) quoted this line in a discussion of the boule's responsibility for public works and claimed this text as the latest example of "the old kind of bouleutic control." Line 20. The cost of the stele is to be met from an unusual source, which included, apparently, the funds of the generals, and clearly falls outside the regular arrangements for such expenditure.

Line 24. Xenokles of Kerameis was reasonably regarded by Meritt as the son of that Ἴσαρχος Ξενοκλέους ἐκ Κεραμέων who was an ephebe in the archonship of Philoneos (between 244 and 241; see p. 306 above); cf. *IG* II², 766, line 26. Isarchos would have been seventy years old *ca.* 190, and his son is likely to have been about that age in 161/60. The commissioners were thus, as it seems, men of good family and considerable seniority, carefully chosen for a complex and responsible duty.

Line 28. The name Olympion is less frequent in Attic prosopography than might be assumed. Only four other holders of it are so far known (*PA* 11434, 11435; *Agora* XV, 240, line 109, 293, line 52). Line 29. οὗ εἶχεν ἡ [θεός(?) –––––––] Tracy. Line 30. α[. .]ρα[––– Meritt, Tracy; ἀ[στ]ρα[γαλίσκους Woodward.

Lines 34–35. On Aristomedes of Rhamnous cf. J. Pouilloux, *Forteresse*, p. 170, and see also *SEG* XIII, 129. Line 38. Diotimos of Alopeke is not otherwise known, and no other possessor of that name has yet occurred in that deme. Lines 38–39. ––––]|τύμβους Meritt, Tracy; –––κο]|ρύμβους Woodward; ––––| x]ύμβους or –– κο|ρ]ύμβους J. and L. Robert.

Line 45. ἐπὶ Ἀφ]ροδισίου ἄρ[χοντος ––––] Meritt: this was the sole evidence for such an archonship, assigned by Meritt to 170/69 (cf. *Historia* 26, 1977, p. 182), an assignment regarded as well founded by C. Habicht, *Studien*, p. 173. But the discovery of fragment *i* revealed that the restoration could not stand and that therefore Aphrodisios and his archonship were illusory. Cf. Habicht, *Hesperia* 59, 1990, p. 576, note 85. Nothing is known of the newly discovered Aphrodisios of Araphen.

Line 47 *ad fin.* J. Tréheux has suggested τ]ὰ ἐν τῇ κο[ίτηι ––– (or κο[ιτίδι –––)]; see *SEG* XXXIX, 139. If the subscript iota be admitted, κο[ίτη should perhaps be substituted.

Line 50. τ[ετταράκοντ]α Meritt. Lines 50–51 and 57. I.e., 186/5 B.C.; see p. 373 above. Line 51. The date of the archonship of Dionysios remains uncertain. Meritt believed that there were two archons of that name within a few years of each other (202/1 and 194/3); see *Historia* 26, 1977, pp. 179–180; Habicht, in a special study of the matter (*Studien*, pp. 165–168, 177), concluded that there was only one such archonship, and he retained it in 194/3.

Line 52 *ad fin.* κατοι[–– Meritt: κατοπ[τρ–– Woodward; cf. line 108. Line 53. Dion Σκαμβωνίδης cannot be further identified, and the name appears to be unique in his deme. Line 55 *ad fin.* δ [–––– Meritt. Line 56. Σάμος. So Meritt; but it migh be Σᾶμος, a name met with in Crete in the Hellenistic period (see *SEG* XXXII, 894, XXXV, 989, line 5; O. Masson, *BCH* 109, 1985, p. 194). In Attica there are examples of Samios and Samias, but Samos appears to be without parallel. For Euthykrates of Rhamnous see Pouilloux, *Forteresse*, p. 173; the name is unique in his deme. Line 57. *Lapis* ΛΗΗ. Asklepiades of Diomeia. Apart from the Flavius Asklepiades who was archon in the 3rd century A.D. (*IG* II², 2239, lines 4–5, 2773, lines 4 and 17, 3705, lines 3–4; *SEG* XXXIII, 188, with further references), no other Asklepiades of this deme is recorded. Lines 57–58. I.e., 167/6 B.C.; see Meritt, *Historia* 26, 1977, p. 182; Habicht, *Studien*, p. 167, note 46 and *Hesperia* 57, 1988, p. 245. Line 59. Μύ]ννιον was Woodward's suggestion; cf. *PA* 10473. Line 60. ΗΡ Meritt; Tracy noted that the supposed Η is in fact the final letter of ὁλκή.

Line 64. [. . . x]ύαθον Meritt. Line 66. δ Νικοβούλη, as Tracy also observed, rather than Meritt's ὃν Νικοβούλη.

Line 96. The archonship of Sostratos was unknown before the discovery of this fragment. In the light of the knowledge of the archon list as it stood at the time of the *editio princeps* of fragment *h*, Meritt was inclined to assign it to one of the years early in the 2nd century for which no positive attribution had then been made: 197/6, 195/4, or 194/3. But the publication soon afterwards of an ephebic text belonging to Sostratos' year (*SEG* XXII, 101) led to a firmer dating in the late 3rd century, 210/09, and this has remained the accepted and acceptable date. See Tracy, *Hesperia* 41, 1972, pp. 43–46; Meritt, *Historia* 26, 1977, p. 178; Habicht, *Studien*, pp. 160 and 167, note 46, and cf. **248**.

Line 104. Perhaps Ἀρ[αφήνιος. But neither Kittos nor his family is in any case otherwise identifiable. Line 105. So Meritt: but Tracy (*Hesperia* 53, 1984, p. 376) claimed [Προσ]πα⟨λ⟩τίου ᵛ Διονυσι[– – – –] as the correct reading and by eliminating the Dionysiac reference suggested that the sanctuary with which this document was concerned was that of Aphrodite, either Hegemone or Ourania; cf. line 47. But the first surviving letter is surely iota, the stroke being too long for the upright *hasta* of pi; the alpha is undoubted; and the final letter is certainly not upsilon. Nor is it nu; it seems to be a clear gamma, inscribed *per errorem* or as a false assimilation. The text should perhaps be shown as ἱμάτιο⟨ν⟩, and the possible reference to Dionysos may be allowed to stand.

Line 112. Hegelochos of Azenia is in all probability to be identified with the ὑπογραμματεύς of *Agora* XV, 213, lines 14–15 and 214, line 11, texts of *ca.* 168 B.C. Line 113. Sotadas was probably the father, or more likely the grandfather, of that Σωτάδας Σωτάδου Φιλαΐδης who was an ephebe in 128/7 (*SEG* XV, 104, line 158). Line 117 (Col. I). The name Sosaretos is otherwise unattested in Attic prosopography.

THE ARCHONSHIP OF MNESITHEOS, 155/4 B.C.

The didascalic list *IG* II², 2323 (*SEG* XXV, 194, XXXVIII, 162), which has provided valuable evidence, as noted in previous contexts, for earlier sections of the archon list, shows at lines 483–485 a triplet of successive archons Anthesterios, Kallistratos, and Mnesitheos. W. S. Ferguson (*The Athenian Archons of the Third and Second Centuries before Christ*, 1899, p. 67; cf. *Athenian Secretaries*, p. 56) argued from the detail of *IG* II², 956, lines 71–72 and 957, line 35 that Anthesterios followed Aristolas (see pp. 415–416 above) by not more than four years; he placed him in 158/7, with Mnesitheos therefore in 156/5. In this he was followed by J. Kirchner (*PA* 10285; *IG* II², iv, 1, pp. 18–19); but a date one year later was urged by W. B. Dinsmoor and adopted independently by W. Kolbe and P. Roussel (see Dinsmoor, *Archons of Athens*, pp. 222, 262, 467–470). The proposal also convinced Ferguson (*Athenian Tribal Cycles*, p. 30). To that time, no information concerning the γραμματεῖς of any of these three years had come to light, by means of which the correctness or otherwise of the attributions made could be separately assessed with a reference to the secretary cycle. But the publication of the long prytany text of Mnesitheos' year found in the Agora in 1933 (B. D. Meritt, *Hesperia* 3, 1934, pp. 31–35, no. 21, republished with four additional fragments by S. Dow, *Prytaneis*, pp. 148–153, no. 84; see *Agora* XV, 225) gave the full name of the γραμματεύς, Philiskos, son of Krates, of Paiania (Pandionis III). On this evidence *IG* II², 979 (*SEG* XXXIII, 130), on which had stood the meager remains of the name of a γραμματεύς Φιλ[– – – – – –]νιεύς, could also be assigned to Mnesitheos' archonship and fully restored.

Thus Mnesitheos' date, agreed on other arguments, finally received separate confirmation from the cycle, as Dinsmoor was happy to observe (*Athenian Archon List*, pp. 191–192). 155/4 as Mnesitheos' year has since that time remained the accepted attribution. See W. K. Pritchett and Meritt, *Chronology*, p. xxx; Meritt, *Hesperia* 10, 1941, p. 61; Pritchett and O. Neugebauer, *Calendars*, pp. 15 and 86; Meritt, *Hesperia* 26, 1957, p. 95, *Athenian Year*, p. 237, *TAPA* 95, 1964, p. 237, *Historia* 26, 1977, p. 183; C. Habicht, *Hesperia* 57, 1988, pp. 239–241, 246.

The year was the twelfth in the fifteenth Metonic cycle and thus scheduled as ordinary in that cycle. It was also ordinary in the Athenian festival calendar. The calendric details of the second of the two decrees constituting *Agora* XV, 225, which are fully preserved at lines 43–44, show Metageitnion 4 = pryt. II, 4, a date reproduced in the restoration of lines 2–3. *IG* II², 979 however shows that at some later stage in the year Mnesitheos had occasion to retard the official calendar by at least three days, for the text of it requires the inclusion of a date κατὰ θεόν, and the whole date (in an unknown month and prytany) may be rendered (Meritt, *Hesperia* 3, 1934, p. 34) as the 21st ⟨κατ'ἄρχοντα⟩ = 24th κατὰ θεόν = the 24th day of the prytany. As regularly, the prytany and κατὰ θεόν dates coincide; see p. 400 above. In **297** the lacuna at lines 3–4 is so extensive that a similar arrangement for the expression of the date must be postulated there also, where the spatial requirements imply a retardation by two days in an unknown month and prytany: the 4th ⟨κατ'ἄρχοντα⟩ = 6th κατὰ θεόν = the 6th day of the prytany. See Pritchett and Neugebauer, *loc. cit.*; Pritchett, *Ancient Athenian Calendars on Stone*, p. 337; A. S. Henry, *Prescripts*, p. 79.

Knowledge of the phylai in prytany during the year is confined to the first two out of the twelve: I Pandionis and II Hippothontis.

FRAGMENT OF A DECREE

297 (Pl. 29). A fragment from the upper part of a pedimental stele of Hymettian marble (I 2211), with the original back, part of the pediment (including its apex and left raking cornice), and a small piece of the inscribed face preserved, discovered on November 23, 1934, in a wall of a modern house west of the northern part of the Odeion (K 10). The pediment is low, lower in height than the total of the moldings that intervene between its horizontal cornice and the inscription. These are composed of a somewhat clumsy ovolo with cavetto crown, the latter larger than the former and with a shallow curve. Beneath the ovolo, a flat band and apophyge complete the transition to the inscribed face. The jagged, battered, and weathered stone is more substantial than the slight remains of the text would, *prima facie*, lead one to suppose.

H. 0.29 m.; W. 0.31 m.; Th. 0.10 m.
LH. 0.005 m.

The existence of the apex of the pediment enables the median vertical line of the stele to be calculated and the total original width to be assessed as *ca.* 0.45 m.

Ed. B. D. Meritt, *Hesperia* 10, 1941, pp. 60–61, no. 25, with photograph.

a. 155/4 *a.*   NON-ΣTOIX. *ca.* 48

['Επὶ Μ]νησιθέου ἄρ[χοντος ἐπὶ τῆς .... *ca.* 21 ....]
[πρυταν]είας ἧι Φ[ιλίσκος Κράτητος Παιανιεὺς ἐγραμμάτευεν]·
[...⁸....]ος τε[τράδι ἱσταμένου, κατὰ θεὸν δὲ ἕκτηι ἱσταμένου],
[ἕκτηι τῆς π]ρυτ[ανείας· —————————————————]
5   [————————————————————————————————]

A little more may be discerned on the stone than is suggested in the *editio princeps*, the text of which is otherwise reproduced above, save for the correction of the name of the γραμματεύς in line 2. Meritt noted that the fragment cannot form part of *Agora* XV, 225.

Of the lettering little may be said. S. V. Tracy (*Attic Letter-Cutters*, p. 26) found it too worn and obscure for any attribution to an identifiable craftsman to be practicable. In general it displays a scratchiness characteristic of the period, and the outer strokes of sigma are well angled.

Line 2. The γραμματεύς Philiskos, son of Krates, of Paiania is restored from *Agora* XV, 225. Neither name is otherwise attested in that deme, and the family cannot be further identified. Lines 3–4. On the date see the commentary above on the archonship of Mnesitheos.

FRAGMENT OF A DECREE

298 (Pl. 30). A fragment of a stele of white marble (I 2016), broken all around, discovered in November 1934 in a marble pile in the area of the Tholos (F–H 11–12).

H. 0.08 m.; W. 0.034 m.; Th. 0.023 m.
LH. 0.006 m.

Ed. S. V. Tracy, *Attic Letter-Cutters*, pp. 151–152, no. 1, with photograph pl. 22. See also *SEG* XL, 114.

ca. a. 150 *a.*   NON-ΣTOIX.

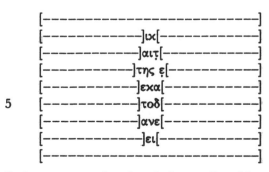

Tracy recognized this small piece as part of an inscription attributable to the "Cutter of Agora I 6006", on whose career, characteristics, and prolific output see **296**. Lacking any other criterion of date, the text is placed here for convenience at the midpoint of the mason's datable activity.

Line 2. The last visible letter could be zeta. Tracy regarded the fragment as in all probability containing elements of the concluding section of an honorary decree, and *exempli gratia* suggested a text for lines 4–7 as follows (with lines of 36–39 letters):

[καὶ στεφανῶσαι] ἕκα[στον αὐτῶν θαλλοῦ στεφάνωι]·
[ἀναγράψαι δὲ] τόδ[ε τὸ ψήφισμα τὸν γραμματέα]
[τὸν κατὰ πρυτ]ανε[ίαν εἰς στήλην λιθίνην καὶ στῆ]
[σαι ἐν ἀκροπόλ]ει· [τὸ δὲ γενόμενον ἀνάλωμα κτλ.]

FRAGMENT OF A DECREE(?)

299. A fragment of a stele of Hymettian marble (I 4234), broken on all sides, discovered on June 3, 1936, in a pit of Byzantine date east of the altar of Ares (M 7).

H. 0.163 m.; W. 0.103 m.; Th. 0.087 m.
LH. 0.007 m.

Ed. S. V. Tracy, *Hesperia* 47, 1978, pp. 264–265, no. 8, with photograph pl. 70:d. See also *SEG* XXVIII, 80.

ca. a. 150 *a.*   NON-ΣΤΟΙΧ.

```
   [----------------------]
   [----------]ΛΕΙ[----------]
   [----------]του Π[----------]
   [--------] ὅσαι ΣΥ[--------]
   [--------]Κ καινὸν [--------]
 5 [-------]ΑΤΑΣΤΑΘΕ[-------]
   [-------] πάντα κατα[------]
   [------ἡ(?)]γούμενοι Π[-------]
   [--------]οι δὲ καὶ ΑΡ[-------]
   [-------]ς τοῖς θεοῖ[ς -------]
10 [---------]ιας καὶ [---------]
   [--------χ]αὶ τῶν [---------]
   [---------]ΑΝΤΑ[---------]
   [---------]ΤΕΣΔ[---------]
   [----------]ΣΥΣ[----------]
15 [----------------------]
```

Like **296** (*q.v.*) and **298**, this text was regarded by Tracy as the work of the "Cutter of Agora I 6006", and it has been placed at the midpoint of his dated career, there being no other means of giving a date to it: cf. *Attic Letter-Cutters*, p. 150. It seems to present part of a decree of an unidentifiable character: suggestions for its restoration are too speculative for record and may be judged inadvisable.

Note. Also to be assigned to the "Cutter of Agora I 6006" and given a similar dating is a fragment (I 3791) preserving nine lines of text, of which the longest extends only to seven letters, published by Tracy in *Hesperia* 47, 1978, p. 264, no. 7, with photograph pl. 70:c: see also *Attic Letter-Cutters*, p. 150. That it is to be classed as a decree seems doubtful: cf. its republication as *SEG* XXVIII, 363, where it is shown as a "fragmentum incertum".

THE EPIMELETAI OF THE MYSTERIES(?) HONORED

300. A fragment of a stele of Pentelic marble (I 1299), broken all around and much battered and worn but with part of the left side preserved below the inscribed surface, discovered on February 9, 1934, in a modern context on the southeast slope of Kolonos Agoraios (E 12).

H. 0.18 m.; W. 0.19 m.; Th. 0.056 m.
LH. 0.007 m.

Ed. B. D. Meritt, *Hesperia* 16, 1947, p. 160, no. 56, with photograph pl. XXIX.

saec. II a., p. prior						NON-ΣΤΟΙΧ.

```
[----------------------------------------------]
[....ca. 12....]Ο[------------------------------]
[.ca. 6..]σεν[....]οι[-------------------------]
[.ca. 6..]τ[....]λ[...]τω[--------------------]
[.ἀγ]γ[ελ]λομ[έ]νοις ὑπὸ [--------------------]
[....]' τοῖς μ[υσ]τικοῖς ἱε[ροῖς ---------------]
[...ca. 9...]ον αὐτοῖς π[---------------------]
[..]ι καὶ περὶ πάντων [-------------- ὅπως ἂν]
[οὖν] ἐφάμιλλο[ν ἦι τοῖς φιλοτιμουμένοις -------]
[.ca. 6..]ειν δ[----------------------------]
[..ca. 8...]οε[-----------------------------]
[----------------------------------------------]
```

The writing is regular and without special characteristics. S. V. Tracy (*Attic Letter-Cutters*, p. 251) found the hand unfamiliar but saw in it some influence of the "Cutter of *IG* II² 897", whose datable career covered the dozen years 189/8–178/7: see **270**. Tracy's preferred date ("probably the first half of the second century") is more widely drawn than that of the *editio princeps* ("*ca.* 200 B.C.") and as being less precise is more acceptable. The letters are not well articulated, but there is nothing of the "tachygraphic style" about them. Sigma is indeed unusually precise, with open-angled external strokes and short center strokes; the circular letters are of generous dimensions.

Meritt interpreted the document, on the basis of clues in lines 8 and 5, as a decree in honor of the epimeletai of the Eleusinian Mysteries (cf. **228** and **284**), and in lines 7 and 8 he inserted restorations on the model of *IG* II², 847, of 215/14, in which these officials are honored. The remains of line 9 do not fit well with any standard form of words based on line 8 but suggest that the stele is likely to have been wide if anything resembling familiar phraseology is to be accommodated.

Line 3. ι[...]λ Meritt. Line 7. The first letter is iota, tau, or upsilon. Meritt showed a dotted upsilon in his text, and after περὶ πάντων restored [τὰς εὐθύνας δεδώκασιν ---]. Lines 8–9. The "hortatory intention" evidently stressed the competitive element to be encouraged among the epimeletai no less than among other public officers and benefactors. For the turn of phrase cf. **240**. It is, however, doubtful whether at this date ἂν should be included in the formula, although Meritt did so include it: see **285**, commentary on lines 5–8. Line 9. δ[εδόχθαι τεῖ βουλεῖ Meritt.

FRAGMENT OF A DECREE CONFERRING CITIZENSHIP

301. A fragment of a stele of Hymettian marble (I 6372), with part of the right side and the original back preserved, but which is otherwise broken all around, discovered on May 24, 1951, among marbles collected southwest of the Odeion.

H. 0.012 m.; W. 0.013 m.; Th. 0.07 m.
LH. 0.005–0.007 m.

Ed. B. D. Meritt, *Hesperia* 30, 1961, pp. 221–222, no. 18, with photograph pl. 37 (see also *SEG* XXI, 418); M. J. Osborne, *Naturalization* I, pp. 226–227, D 111, *Naturalization* II, p. 194.

saec. II a., p. prior						NON-ΣΤΟΙΧ. 56–64

```
[--------------------------------------------------------]
[-----------------------------------------------]· τ[οὺς]
[δὲ θεσμοθέτας, ὅταν πληρῶσιν δικαστήριον εἰς ἕνα καὶ πεντακοσίου]ς δικαστά
[ς, εἰσαγαγεῖν αὐτοῖς τὴν δοκιμασίαν τῆς πολιτογραφίας· εἶναι δ]ὲ αὐτοῖς δοκιμ
[ασθεῖσι γράψασθαι φυλῆς καὶ δήμου καὶ φρατρίας ἧς ἂν βού]λ⟨ω⟩νται· ἀναγράψα
[ι δὲ τὸ ψήφισμα τόδε τὸν γραμματέα τὸν κατὰ πρυτανείαν] εἰς στήλην λιθίνην
[καὶ στῆσαι ἐν ἀκροπόλει(?) παρὰ τὰς --------------]υ εἰκόνας· τὸ δὲ γεν
[όμενον εἰς τὴν ἀναγραφὴν τῆς στήλης καὶ τὴν ἀνάθεσι]ν ἀνάλωμα μερίσ
[αι τὸν ταμίαν τῶν στρατιωτικῶν· --------------]φη τόδε τὸ ⟨ψ⟩ήφ
[ισμα -----------------------------------------]ήμου προνο
[θέντων -----------------------------------------]ΦΤΑΝΕΙΧ
```

[------------------------------ἐπὶ ---------------------εἰς τὸ πρυτανεῖον] εἰς αὖρ
[ιον· --προ]νοηθ[έ]
[ντων(?) --]

This ill-written piece is a poor example of the mason's craft and contains a variety of errors. S. V. Tracy (*Attic Letter-Cutters*, p. 254) was unable to identify its perpetrator. The letters are heavy, crowded, and badly articulated. The cross-stroke of alpha and the central dot of theta are occasionally omitted; epsilon, nu, and sigma are all particularly clumsy. Phi (line 8) has a rectangular "oval" (not closed off in the second example at the end of the line); the apparent "regular" phi is in fact an error for psi, which is correctly engraved in line 4. Rather better lettering of the same general type in the work of the "Cutter of Agora I 6006" (see **296**), indicative of the middle third of the century, offers some slight guidance. The present fragment may indeed be suitably dated "ca. med. s. II a.", but its inadequacies may provide a deceptive index. Meritt's date was "*init. saec.* II *a.*", but this seems too early. Osborne's decision to set it more widely into the first half of the 2nd century is a reasonable compromise and is followed here.

Line 3. τὴν δοκιμασίαν κατὰ τὸν νόμον]· εἶναι δέ Meritt: but (1) this was an erroneous reading, for the break in the stone occurs as shown in the text; and (2) Osborne noted that κατὰ τὸν νόμον does not usually qualify this clause, whereas τῆς πολιτογραφίας is a regular qualification in this period. Cf. (e.g.) **276**, lines 18–19. Line 4. *Lapis* ΛΛΝΤΑΙ. Line 8 *ad fin. Lapis* ΦΗ‡. Line 10. The chi (if chi it is) seems especially ungainly, and the break of the stone may give a false impression of it. Line 12. ΙΟΗ^c Osborne. The number of letters per line of the text was underestimated in Osborne's edition.

The grant of citizenship (to more than one person; cf. line 3) follows the pattern of Type III of Formulation B in Osborne's categorization, the type usual after the beginning of the 2nd century. See **239** and references there.

Line 8. The restoration of the Military Treasurer as the official charged with defraying the cost of the stele follows the general practice of the period. The formula is expressed in an exceptionally awkward manner. Lines 8–13. The decree continues after the formula for payment which is usually the concluding item. Cf. **253**. Osborne's text omitted restorations here and was printed in majuscule. He objected also to Meritt's inclusion of the invitation formula in lines 11–12, on the score of its rarity after the end of the 4th century. But it does occur, and what survives here strongly suggests its presence in this context. Cf. **224**, commentary on lines 44–45. However, it says nothing of the character of the services rewarded by the grant of citizenship: cf. Osborne, *ZPE* 41, 1981, p. 157 and the response of A. S. Henry, *Antichthon* 15, 1981, pp. 102–103. Whatever the nature of the supplements proposed, there is evidently much new material added to the main decree, the character of which is unclear. Line 10. Meritt suspected that some form of the word πρυτανείας underlay this garbled assortment of letters.

FRAGMENT OF AN HONORARY DECREE

302. A fragment of a stele of Pentelic marble (I 5310), broken on all sides, discovered on March 10, 1938, in a wall of a modern house outside the Market Square south of the Church of the Holy Apostles (O 19). Although the fragment is large, the surviving text is situated only in the upper part of it on the right, within a well-executed olive stephanos in relief. The remains of a similar stephanos on the left correspond with this, but the citation within it is not preserved. The remainder of the front surface of the stele as preserved is uninscribed and undecorated.

H. 0.23 m.; W. 0.25 m.; Th. 0.085 m.
LH. 0.007 m.

Ed. B. D. Meritt, *Hesperia* 29, 1960, p. 54, no. 74, with photograph pl. 15. See also *SEG* XIX, 106.

saec. II *a., p. prior* (?)

(*in corona*)
Θεογέν[ην]
Φώχου [Κη]
φι[σ]ιέ[α].

The writing is a little haphazard in the construction of epsilon and kappa but not of markedly inferior quality. The small "feet" to omega resemble those in **292**. There is some slight emphasis on the "free ends" of strokes. The characteristics indicate a 2nd-century date, perhaps in the first rather than in the second half. S. V. Tracy (*Attic Letter-Cutters*, p. 30) regarded the fragment as too worn for any attribution to an identifiable craftsman to be practicable.

Meritt suggested that Myrrhine, daughter of Phokos of Kephisia, whose tombstone survives as *IG* II², 6432, was probably the sister of Theogenes. *IG* II², 6432 was dated in the 1st century B.C. by J. Kirchner, but Meritt claimed that it may belong to the second, and its general character supports this. The external strokes of mu and sigma are not parallel; the horizontal bar of alpha is curved, and omega is notably "open". But if the present text belongs relatively early in the century, Myrrhine may have been of the generation of Theogenes' grandchildren rather than his contemporary.

The two citations are presumed to have concluded an honorary decree now lost, which (to judge from the proportions of the surviving fragment) may have been of no inconsiderable length.

FRAGMENT OF A DECREE

303 (Pl. 30). A fragment of a stele of Pentelic marble characterized by streaks of green (I 319), with the right edge and original back preserved, but which is broken elsewhere, discovered late in 1932 in a wall of a modern house east of the Temple of Apollo Patroos (I 8).

H. 0.18 m.; W. 0.11 m.; Th. 0.095 m.
LH. 0.006 m. (omicron 0.004 m.).

Ed. B. D. Meritt, *Hesperia* 3, 1934, p. 11, no. 15, with drawing.

saec. II *a., p. prior*NON-ΣΤΟΙΧ.

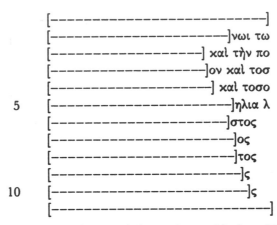

The lettering of this difficult fragment has much in common with that of **300**, not well articulated, as Meritt's drawing conveyed, but not markedly "tachygraphic": here also sigma is notably precise. As in the case of **300**, S. V. Tracy (*Attic Letter-Cutters*, p. 250) found the style unfamiliar and made no direct attribution, but he saw some influence of the "Cutter of *IG* II² 897", for whose date and characteristics see **270**. The date for the text given in the *editio princeps* ("the late third century B.C.") is clearly too early. The first half of the 2nd century, a dating favored also by Tracy, better suits the available criteria.

Meritt regarded the fragment as apparently forming part of a decree. From line 6 onwards the lines end irregularly, and this, together with the repetitive character of the line endings, may suggest that a list of some kind occupies this part of the stone. Too little of the upper section is preserved to make the nature of its contents clear.

FRAGMENT OF AN HONORARY DECREE

304. A fragment of a stele of Pentelic marble (I 6529), with much of the inscribed surface lost, broken all around except that part of the left side is preserved below the level of the front face, discovered on May 22, 1952, in a wall of a Late Roman building south of the Altar of the Twelve Gods (K 6).

H. 0.215 m.; W. 0.34 m.; Th. 0.17 m.
LH. 0.007 m.

Ed. B. D. Meritt, *Hesperia* 32, 1963, pp. 20–21, no. 20, with photograph pl. 5. See also *SEG* XXI, 458, with reference also to J. and L. Robert, *REG* 77, 1964, p. 149, no. 117, who report the edition without the text but with the comment "à reprendre".

ante med. saec. II *a.*NON-ΣΤΟΙΧ.

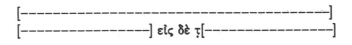

```
[----------------]ς ὑπολαμ[----------------]
[--------------τ]ούτων ΕΛΛ[--------------]
[----------- ’Αθη]ναίων προπολ[-----------]
5    [-------------]ίας· ἔτι δὲ καὶ τόδε τὸ [ψήφισμα ----]
[----------ε]ἰς τὰ ’Ελευθέρια κατ[-----------]
[---------- ’Αθη]ναίων γεγενημένα [--- καὶ στῆσαι]
[ἔμπροσθεν τῆς τοῦ Διὸς] στοᾶς· δοῦναι δὲ [--------]
[----------κατασκε]υὰς τῶν στηλῶν [---------]
10   [-------------ἀ]νάθεσιν τῶν [--------------]
[------------------] ᴧ [----------------]
[--------------------------------------]
```

This is a craggy piece, with untidy and "thick" lettering. S. V. Tracy (*Attic Letter-Cutters*, p. 254) classed it as "unfamiliar" and was unable to assign it to any of his identified craftsmen. There is poor articulation of strokes, especially at the apex of triangular letters, and horizontal strokes in alpha and epsilon are omitted; omega also lacks its horizontal attachments. The external strokes of mu and sigma are angled, but the latter is inconsistently treated. The loop of rho remains "open". The thickness of the fragment, which, though 0.17 m., is not preserved in its entirety, suggests that it belongs to a stele of considerable dimensions.

The only clues to the subject matter of the document indicate that it was of a significance to be recorded on more than one copy (line 9) and that it referred to the Eleutheria, the festival vowed after the battle of Plataia in 479 on the motion of Aristeides "the Just" and still celebrated in the imperial period (Plutarch, *Aristeides* 21; see E. Kirsten, *RE* XX, ii, 1950, cols. 2326–2328, *s.v.* Plataiai; L. Robert, *REA* 31, 1929, p. 15 [= *Opera minora selecta* II, 1969, p. 760], note 1). For a mention of the festival roughly contemporaneous with the present document see *IG* II², 3149a (part of the same monument as *IG* II², 3147 and 3150). It may be possible to see further allusions to the famous battle and its legacy in lines 3 (‘Ελλ[ην---] or ‘Ελλ[α----]), 4 (προπολ[εμουντ---]), and 5 (--- ἐλευθερ]ίας[?]). The connection with the Eleutheria implies that the Agora stele will have been appropriately erected near the Stoa of Zeus Eleutherios (lines 7–8), and Meritt so restored the text. Cf. *Agora* III, pp. 28–29, no. 38. The place of discovery serves to confirm the hypothesis. It may be suggested, in conclusion, that the decree bestowed honors on the Plataians in particular relation to their role as guardians of this piece of the Panhellenic heritage (cf. Plutarch, *loc. cit.*). For the Hellenistic connections between Plataia and Athens, and references to the evidence, see Kirsten, *loc. cit.*, col. 2310, and N. Robertson, *Hesperia* 55, 1986, pp. 88–102 (on this inscription, p. 101, note 45, where he suggests that the decree honored an orator who spoke for the Athenians in the διάλογος between Athenian and Spartan representatives which preceded the festival).

Line 3. ἐλλ[ειπ---] Meritt. Line 4. πρὸ πολ[----] Meritt. Line 7. γεγενημένω[ν -- Meritt.

THE ARCHONSHIP OF LYSIADES, 148/7 B.C.

A decree from Delos (*ID* 1505), in which the Athenian cleruchs in the island honored the agoranomoi of the year of Archon, gives a backward reference to Lysiades' archonship, which is also the dating reference of the list of Athenian hieropoioi *IG* II², 1938, whereby the year is shown to be one in which the Ptolemaia were celebrated, thus the first year of an Olympiad (see W. B. Dinsmoor, *Athenian Archon List*, p. 193). Lysiades thus postdated the Athenian occupation of Delos (and W. S. Ferguson originally assigned him to 166/5, the first year of that occupation, *The Athenian Archons of the Third and Second Centuries before Christ*, 1899, pp. 62–64), while he also antedated the archonship of Archon, assigned at first to 151/50 but later evaluated as 147/6. Continuing discussion, for which see J. Kirchner, *IG* II², iv, 1, pp. 20–21 and II², 1938, in comm., as well as P. Roussel, *ID* 1505, caused a date of *ca.* 150, or more precisely 152/1, to be proposed for Lysiades, to which Ferguson assented. Dinsmoor, however, in *Archons of Athens*, pp. 261–262, doubted the validity of the arguments advanced, and on grounds of the prosopography of the list of hieropoioi urged 159/8 as more acceptable. But his proposal found no adherents. Ferguson, with some hesitation, opted for 148/7, the year immediately preceding that determined for Archon (*Athenian Tribal Cycles*, p. 30), and Dinsmoor ultimately agreed with him (*Athenian Archon List*, *loc. cit.*), having assigned the possible alternative 152/1 to Phaidrias.

This dating was maintained by W. K. Pritchett and B. D. Meritt, *Chronology*, p. xxx. The publication soon afterwards of **306** added no new testimony to resolve the issue but did reveal Lysiades' year as one in which the calendar was temporarily adjusted by the archon (cf. Pritchett and O. Neugebauer, *Calendars*, pp. 14–21, esp. p. 19). Meritt subsequently used the evidence of coinage as grounds for preferring 152/1 for Lysiades, moving Phaidrias two years earlier (*Athenian Year*, pp. 187–188, 237), and this was the archon's position in "Scheme A" for the archons of 155/4–145/4 published in *Hesperia* 33, 1964, p. 207. In "Scheme B" (*ibid.*) Meritt assigned Lysiades to Ferguson's 148/7, and this was, in the end, his preferred dating; see *TAPA* 95, 1964, p. 237, table 3 and *Historia* 26, 1977, p. 184. The top fragment of **305**, when published, gave the name of the γραμματεύς of Lysiades' year but not his demotic and was not additionally helpful in determining its accurate date.

There matters stood until 1988, when C. Habicht, in a general restudy of the archons of the period 159/8 to 141/40 B.C. (*Hesperia* 57, 1988, pp. 237–247; cf. *SEG* XXXVIII, 274), preferred to begin the Delian list of Athenian gymnasiarchs (*ID* 2589) in 167/6 rather than 166/5, claiming the former dating (that of P. Roussel, followed by Kirchner and Kolbe) as orthodox, whereas the latter had formed the basis (*inter alia*) for the reconstructions offered by Ferguson, Dinsmoor, and their successors, accepted, for example, by Pritchett, *Hesperia* 9, 1940, pp. 130–131. The gymnasiarch Gorgias, twentieth in sequence, is known to have held his office in the year of the Athenian archon Archon, already mentioned as 147/6. This reversion to Roussel's dates for the gymnasiarchs had the effect of assigning Archon to 148/7 and Lysiades, in consequence, to a probable 149/8 (Habicht, *loc. cit.*, p. 246). But, unless or until evidence more concrete than an interpretational assumption comes to hand, there is no convincing reason to jettison the accepted sequence, and good reason especially in connection with the celebration of the Ptolemaia to retain it; cf. H. B. Mattingly, *Historia* 20, 1971, p. 46. The date for Lysiades as earlier agreed is therefore maintained here. See also the commentary on **307**.

There is no indication of the character of the year. It was the last in Meton's fifteenth cycle, and in his system was scheduled as ordinary. On the intervention by the archon referred to above, see the commentary on **305**.

A DECREE CONCERNED WITH ALLOCATIONS

305. Three joining fragments from the left side of a stele of Pentelic marble (I 6977: *a*; I 6980: *b*; I 6978: *c*), with a battered crowning molding which also returns along the left side and with part of the original back preserved on the uppermost fragment, but the stele broken below and to the right. Fragments *a* and *c* were discovered on January 28, 1964, in a Late Roman wall over the southeast corner of the Middle Stoa (O 13); fragment *b* was discovered on May 12, 1964, in a late wall in the same location.

Measurements as joined: H. 0.49 m.; W. 0.17 m.; Th. (fragment *a*) 0.17 m.
LH. 0.006–0.007 m.

Ed. *a* only: B. D. Meritt, *Hesperia* 34, 1965, pp. 89–90, no. 2, with photograph pl. 25; see also *SEG* XXII, 107. All fragments: S. V. Tracy, *Attic Letter-Cutters*, pp. 152–154, no. 2, with photograph pl. 23. See also *SEG* XL, 115.

a. 148/7 *a., pryt.* IV(?) NON-ΣTOIX. *ca.* 52

(*a*)
'Επὶ Λυσιά[δου ἄρχοντος ἐπὶ τῆς ....16–18........ πρυτανείας]
ἧι Διόδω[ρος ------------- ἐγραμμάτευεν· -------------]
ῶνος ὀγ[δόει -------------------- κατ'ἄρχοντα, κατὰ θεὸν δὲ]
ἐνάτ[ει -------------, ------------- τῆς πρυτανείας· ἐκκλη]
5 σία [κυρία ἐν τῶι θεάτρωι· τῶν προέδρων ἐπεψήφιζεν ...*ca.*11....]

(*b*)
[...]ΥΟ[-------- καὶ συμπρόεδροι· *vacat*]
vacat [ἔδοξεν τεῖ βουλεῖ καὶ τῶι δήμωι· *vacat*]
['Αφθ]όνητο[ς --------------εῖπεν· ἐπειδὴ ----------------]
[.....]ρας το[--------------------------------]
10 [.....] κληρω[σ --------------------------------]
[.3–4.] ὑπαρ[χο --------------------------------]
[...]ν ἀναγε[γραμμέν-------------------------------]
ὁλοσχερῶ[ς -----------------------------------γε]
γονείας ἀρχ[--------------------------------]
15 ὑπαρχουσα[--------------------------------]
πολλοὺς το[--------------------------------]
διὰ τὸ μετ[--------------------------------]
ἑτέρας κατ[--------------------------------]

κληρώσεως [--]

20 [.]εν τοιουτ[--]

[.]η καὶ ἡ κλήρω[σις . ^{ca. 6}.., ἀγαθεῖ τύχει δεδόχθαι τεῖ βουλεῖ τοὺς]

λαχόντας π[ροέδρους εἰς τὴν ἐπιοῦσαν ἐκκλησίαν χρηματίσαι πε]

ρὶ τούτων, γν[ώμην δὲ ξυμβάλλεσθαι τῆς βουλῆς εἰς τὸν δῆμον ὅτι]

δοκεῖ τεῖ βου[λεῖ --]

25 τόδε τὸ ψήφισ[μα --]

reliquiae incertae [--]

(c)   *reliquiae incertae* [--]

σονται τὴν ἀγ[αγραφὴν --]

στήλας λιθίν[ας --]

30 γεγραμμένα[--τεῖ β]

[ο]υλεῖ τὰς ἐπι[--]

Φιλώταν Θριά[σιον ------------------------------ εἰς]

στήλας λ[ι]θ[ίνας δύο καὶ στῆσαι τὴμ μὲν ἐν ἀγορᾶι ἔμπροσθεν]

τῆς στοᾶς τ[------------------, τὴν δὲ ------------------]

35 ται τὴν ἀναγρ[αφὴν τῶν στηλῶν ------------------ τῶν ἐν]

νέ'ἀρχόντων π[--]

ἐξετάζειν ^ν τόδ[ε τὸ --]

τῶν στηλῶν Λ[--]

[--]

The above text, worked out earlier than and independently of that of Tracy, is almost entirely confirmed by his publication; but it underdots faint or partially preserved letters about which his version shows greater certainty. The restoration of the name of the proposer (line 8) is entirely his: he commented that it is the only Attic nomen suiting the evident requirements. He did not offer restorations in lines 3, 5 (*init.*), or 33–34. Divergences elsewhere, all minor, are as follows: Line 9. ΙΑΣ Tracy; but rho is certain. Line 12. [τ]ῶν ἀναγε[γραμμένων Tracy; omega is far from assured, and two letters rather than one precede it. Line 17. μετα[--- Tracy; the alpha is probable, but what remains is too faint for assured recording. Line 28. The initial sigma, not underdotted by Tracy, is unsure and may be chi. Line 34. τῆς στοᾶς τῆ[ς--- Tracy.

Tracy identified this text as the work of the most prolific mason of the age, the "Cutter of Agora I 6006"; it is a work of his middle period and displays all the features of his plain and generally well ordered style as Tracy describes them. The pi of line 16 shows both uprights of equal length; the diameter of omicron is variable. For this craftsman, responsible also for **296, 298, 299, 306,** and **309,** see **296.**

Tracy labeled the line length of his text as "*ca.* 49"; but Meritt established the length of the lines in fragment *a* as of *ca.* 52 letters, and this is confirmed by the formulaic phraseology of lines 22–23 (which contain 52 and 51 letters respectively). It served also to confirm his hypothesis, not included in the text of *SEG* XXII, 107 but recorded in the commentary, that the date, like that of **306,** must have been given both κατ'ἄρχοντα and κατὰ θεόν. **306** establishes that the discrepancy existed in the month of Pyanopsion. It could have been continued into Maimakterion or carried over from Boedromion but as a measure of economy Meritt restored the opening lines of this text as also giving a date in Pyanopsion, as follows:

Ἐπὶ Λυσιά[δου ἄρχοντος ἐπὶ τῆς ..^{4–6}.. ίδος τετάρτης πρυτανείας]

ἧι Διόδω[ρος .... ^{ca. 23} .... ἐγραμμάτευεν· Πυανοψι]

ῶνος ὀγ[δόει ἱσταμένου τρίτει ἐμβολίμωι κατ'ἄρχοντα, κατὰ θεὸν δὲ]

ἐνάτ[ει μετ'εἰκάδας, δευτέραι καὶ εἰκοστεῖ τῆς πρυτανείας· ἐκκλη]

5 σία [------ κτλ.

For dates κατ'ἄρχοντα and κατὰ θεόν (the so-called triple dating) see **261,** commentary on line 3 and the literature there cited. The examples are listed by W. K. Pritchett (*Ancient Athenian Calendars on Stone,* p. 337), by Meritt (*TAPA* 95, 1964, p. 237), and by A. S. Henry (*Prescripts,* pp. 78–80, where the present text is no. 14).

In **306,** Pyanopsion 5 κατ'ἄρχοντα = 16 κατὰ θεόν, with no prytany date given by reason of the nature of the enactment. In the present case Meritt supposed that Pyanopsion 8 had been repeated three times, thus making this decree six days later in date than **306,** on the 22nd κατὰ θεόν, which in turn would be the twenty-second day of the fourth prytany. Pyanopsion will have been a full month, and this will be the 110th day of the year. The prytany date, as Pritchett showed (see p. 400 above), is regularly in concord with the date κατὰ θεόν. The length of the line requires that the expression of date was of this order of magnitude, whether or not this particular hypothesis be found acceptable: but Tracy's text did not include it. For Pyanopsion 22 as a day on which the assembly might meet see J. D. Mikalson, *Sacred and Civil Calendar*, p. 76. The retardation of the calendar by the archon, if confined to Pyanopsion, may have been connected with the celebration of the Apatouria, which took place in that month at an uncertain date (cf. Mikalson, *op. cit.*, p. 79).

Despite the substantial remains of the text, its content and reference remain uncertain. Some allotment (of territory?) is evidently the concern, and the outcome was of sufficient importance to warrant record on more than one stele and apparently to involve the whole board of archons (line 36).

Lines 4–5. For the suggested location of the assembly see **167**, commentary on lines 6–7. Line 7. It has to be supposed that the enactment formula was set out in the "perfect design": see **204** and references there. If the restoration is correct, this is a late example of the arrangement: cf. **266**, of 187/6. Lines 13–14. γε]|γονείας. This spelling of original γεγονυίας is normal in the Hellenistic period. Cf. L. Threatte, *Grammar*, pp. 314, 343; Henry, *CQ* n.s. 17, 1967, p. 260, and the restoration in **276**, line 21.

Line 32. Philotas of Thria. The tombstone *IG* II², 6268, dated to the 3rd century B.C., presumably records one of his forebears (cf. Tracy, *Attic Letter-Cutters*), unless its style and character may after all permit its attribution to the man himself named here. Lines 33–34. The stoa in question is probably that now referred to as the Middle Stoa, if the place of discovery of the three fragments offers a reliable indication. For stelai erected in front of the Stoa of Zeus cf. **174** and **186**. On the Middle Stoa see *Agora* XIV, pp. 66–68; *Agora Guide*³, pp. 164–166; J. M. Camp, *Athenian Agora*, pp. 175–177.

THE GENOS OF THE EUMOLPIDAI HONORS A HIEROPHANT

306. Three fragments of a stele of Hymettian marble, two of which (*a* and *c*) were found to join and received the same inventory number (I 4389). Fragment *a* was discovered on January 18, 1937, in a wall of a modern house over the southwestern part of the Eleusinion (S–T 20), fragment *b* (I 5556) on September 12, 1938, in a wall of a modern house southeast of the Market Square and west of the Panathenaic Way (Q–R 20), and fragment *c* on March 3, 1937, among marbles from the Eleusinion area. Fragments *a* and *c*, as joined, preserve the upper left corner and central section of the stele, with the left edge, upper molding, and original back. They are broken away below and to the right, and much of the inscribed surface is lost at the junction of the two pieces. Fragment *b* joins them on the right, below the inscribed surface. It is complete above, including (less well preserved) remains of the crowning molding, but is broken elsewhere. The molding, resembling that of **305**, consists of a wide upper taenia below which a quarter-round molding descends to a narrower flat band, with brisk apophyge to the inscribed surface. It may, again as in **305**, have been carried around the left side of the stele. Traces of red coloring matter are discernible in some letters of the text.

Measurements as joined: *a + c*: H. 0.42 m.; W. 0.315 m.; Th. 0.19 m. (inscribed surface, 0.162 m.).

b: H. 0.20 m.; W. 0.175 m.; Th. 0.112 m.

a–c: W. (at molding) 0.40 m., (inscribed surface) 0.387 m.

LH. 0.006–0.007 m.

Ed. B. D. Meritt, *Hesperia* 11, 1942, pp. 293–298, no. 58, with photographs. Improved readings of lines 13–23 by R. Hubbe, *Hesperia* 29, 1960, p. 417, where the text for lines 21–23 proposed by J. and L. Robert (*REG* 57, 1944, p. 197, no. 66) was shown to be unacceptable. Full text incorporating revisions, *SEG* XIX, 124. Further edition, with certain new readings and restorations, K. Clinton, *The Sacred Officials of the Eleusinian Mysteries* (*TAPS*, n.s. 64, part 3), 1974, pp. 24–27, under no. 11 ('Αριστοκλῆς Περιθοίδης), with photograph fig. 2.

a. 148/7 a. NON-ΣΤΟΙΧ. *ca.* 38–43

(a) (b)

'Επὶ Λυσιάδου ἄρχοντος, Π[υανοψ]ιῶνος ἕκ[τει ἐπὶ]
δέκα κατὰ θεόν, κατὰ δὲ ἄρ[χοντ]α πέμπτει [ἰστα]
μένου· ἀγορᾶι κυρίαι ἐν [. *ca.*6 .]νδίωι· 'Αμυν[όμαχος]
Εὐκλέους 'Αλαιεὺς ε[ἶπεν· ἐπε]ιδὴ ὁ ἱεροφά[ντης]
5 'Αριστοκλῆς Περιθοίδ[ης εὔνου]ς τε ὢν διατ[ελεῖ]
κατ'ἰδίαν ἑκάστωι κα[ὶ κοινῆι π]ᾶσιν Εὐμολπ[ίδαις],
κατασταθεὶς δὲ ἱερο[φάντης ἐπ]ὶ 'Ερμογέν[ου ἄρχοντος]
ἀνενεώσατό τε τὴ[ν ἀναγραφὴ]ν τὴν τοῦ [...⁷⁻¹⁰....]
ἐκ τῶν ἀρχαίων γρα[μματε]ίων [τῶ]ν ἐν τ[ῶι 'Ελευσινι] (c)
10 ωι καθ'ἣν ἔδει τὸν [ἀεὶ ἱερ]οφαντ[οῦ]ντ[α ...*ca.*10....]

συνέγραψαν Εὐμ[ολπ]ίδαι ἐπιδι[δόναι(?), καὶ κατὰ τὸ]
ψήφισμα Φιλον[αύ]του καὶ κατὰ τ[ὰ ἄλλα ψηφίσματα]
τοῦ δήμου τὰ ε[ἰσα]γώγεια καλῶς π[ράττει ὅσα ἐτά]
[χ]θη μετασχόντ[ω]ν καὶ Εὐμολπιδῶν [μετὰ πάσης παρα]
15 [σκ]ευῆς καὶ φιλοτιμίας, ψήφισμά τε ε[ἰσήνεγκεν ἵ]
[να ἀ]ναγρα[φῆι] ἡ εἰσαγωγὴ ἐν στήλη[ι λιθίνηι ἐν]
[τῶι ᾿Ε]λευσ[ιν]ίωι, ἐκλελειμμένων [δὲ πολλῶν θυσιῶν]
[δι᾿ἐτ]ῶν [π]λειόνων διὰ τοὺς καιρ[οὺς ἐν ἑκάστωι]
[τῶι ἐνια]υτῶι ἔθυσέν τε αὐτός, [καὶ νῦν(?) πρόσοδον]
20 [ποιησ]άμενος πρὸς τὴν βουλὴν χ[.⁴⁻⁵. ἐνεφάνισεν]
[περ]ὶ αὐτῶν καὶ ψήφισμα ἐπεκύρ[ωσεν ἵνα προσόδων]
[πολ]λῶν γινομένων εἰς [τὰ ἱερὰ αἱ θυσίαι συντελῶνται]
[τοῖ]ς θεοῖς κατὰ τὰ [πάτρια —————————————]
[πα]τρίου ἀγῶγ[ος ————————————————]
25 [. . .]⌃NK[————————————————————]
[——————————————————————————]

    This text, like **305**, was attributed by S. V. Tracy to the "Cutter of Agora I 6006": see *Attic Letter-Cutters*, p. 150, and **296**. The decree is an enactment of the genos of the Eumolpidai, who are concerned in **57** but have left no other record among the Agora *psephismata* in this collection, although their *confrères* the Kerykes, with whom they were closely associated in the Eleusinian cult organization, are twice represented (**77** and **271**). For other decrees of the Eumolpidai, with or without the Kerykes, see *IG* II², 1231 (*SEG* XXX, 98), 1235 (*SEG* XXIX, 134), and 1236.

    Lines 1–4. A fuller statement of the date by archon and festival month, and of the nature of the assembly, became a feature of enactments of *collegia* during the Hellenistic period, but the precision of the date as expressed here is noteworthy, as is the addition of the location of the agora. For the double date and the retardation of the calendar by the archon see **305**. The date as prescribed by the archon, Pyanopsion 5, was that of the festival Proerosia: cf. L. Deubner, *Attische Feste*, pp. 68–69; W. K. Pritchett and O. Neugebauer, *Calendars*, p. 19; *IG* II², 1363 (*SEG* XXIII, 80, with bibliography). J. D. Mikalson (*Sacred and Civil Calendar*, pp. 66–67) noted (in quoting this text and *IG* II², 1263 as showing that private associations held meetings on this day) that it did not entail a "festival day" either in Athens or in Eleusis.

    Line 3. What survived on the stone cannot be identified with a known locale. If the delta may be regarded as an error, ἐν [᾿Ελευσι]ν{δ}ίωι would answer the spatial requirements: but when the Eleusinion is named, the definite article is apparently always used (as elsewhere in the present text), save perhaps in *IG* II², 2317, line 48, of *ca.* 160 B.C. (*Agora* III, pp. 80–81, no. 216). If *IG* II², 1045 is another copy of this decree (see below), it is to be noted that one of the three stelai there prescribed was to be set up in the Eleusinion, where the fragments of the present text were discovered.

    Lines 3–4. Amynomachos of Halai (*PA* 739) was himself hierophantes at a later date; cf. Clinton, *op. cit.*, p. 27, no. 12 and *IG* II², 3469 as read by Meritt, *Hesperia* 11, 1942, p. 297. He was evidently a much younger brother or half-brother of the Aristokles of Perithoidai (*PA* 1881) honored in this decree and had been adopted by Eukles of Halai. On Aristokles' age and the precise relationship with Amynomachos see the discussion by Clinton *ad loc.* Aristokles' contributions to the fund catalogued in *IG* II², 2332, lines 49–52 coincided with the year of his appointment to his priestly office. That office he had by now held for thirty-five years, and it was perhaps his retirement (in favor of his brother or half-brother?) that occasioned the vote of honors. It was once proposed (by E. Vanderpool) that *IG* II², 1045 (now in Leningrad/St. Petersburg), of which Clinton provided a text and photograph (*op. cit.*, pp. 119–120, with fig. 15), with its references to ἱερ]οφάντης ᾿Αρισ[——— in line 5 and to ᾿Αριστοκλέους in line 9, might form part of this decree, but this proposition cannot be maintained: but it may be another copy of the same decree, inscribed by the same hand. See further Tracy (*Attic Letter-Cutters*, pp. 155–156), who identified Aristokles with the [῾Ιεροφάν]της Νουφράδου Περιθοίδης of *IG* II², 1934, line 6, a text redated by him and included among the output of the "Cutter of Agora I 6006". The same man, in his youth, appears among the ephebes of *SEG* XXII, 101 at line 25 (= *SEG* XXVIII, 200, line 28), a list belonging to the archonship of Sostratos (210/09 or 209/8); by the date of this decree he will, in consequence, have been some eighty years of age. For the year of Hermogenes (line 7), when he took office, see p. 381 above. Cf. also C. Habicht, *Untersuchungen*, p. 152, note 10.

    Line 8. So Clinton: διαγραφ]ὴν and (*ad fin.*) [ἱεροφάντου] Meritt. Line 10. ἱεροφάντ[η] τ[. . . . .] Meritt. Line 11. ΕΠΙΔΙ[..⁵.. καὶ κτλ.] Clinton. Lines 11–12. Unless by chance Philonautes' decree is represented by *IG* I³, 6, it is not otherwise identifiable. Lines 13–14. ἔ[πραττεν ὅσα ἐτάχ]θη Meritt, Hubbe. The last letter visible in line 13 is not epsilon, as Clinton observed: Clinton took it as kappa, restoring κ[αταγράφει ὅσα ἐπράχθ]η, but this may be judged too lengthy for the space available. Line 19. νῦν was criticized by J. and L. Robert, *loc. cit.*, but was retained by Hubbe though omitted by Clinton. Considerations of space seem to recommend it. For the extended form of the phraseology in lines 19–20 as evidenced at this period cf. *IG* II², 971 (M. J. Osborne, *Naturalization* I, pp. 213–216, D 102, *Naturalization* II, pp. 189–191), lines 11–13, of 140/39 B.C. Other examples are of later date. The earliest dated example, *IG* II², 950 (*SEG* XVIII, 22), lines 6–7, of 165/4, uses ἀπαγγέλλειν rather than ἐμφανίζειν. Meritt, and later Hubbe, read [γνώμην ἐνεφάνισεν (or γνώμας)]: this was rejected by J. and L. Robert as without parallel, although enactments of *collegia*, while generally imitative of those of the body politic, did not always adhere precisely to the formulaic rules. Clinton's proposed χα[ὶ comes awkwardly here and may be too short for the lacuna; but a substitute for it is not readily come by.

Line 21. So Clinton. ἐπεχήρ[υξεν Meritt, Hubbe, criticized by J. and L. Robert. For the reading see Clinton's commentary. Line 22. [πολ]λῶν Meritt (*Hesperia* 29, 1960, p. 417). Line 24. Clinton's reading and restoration replace the [. . . .]ΟΥΑΓΩ [– – – of the *editio princeps*.

AN OFFICIAL OF A GENOS OR SIMILAR ORGANIZATION HONORED

307. The upper right section of a stele of Pentelic marble (I 2165), with the right side and original rough-picked back preserved, but which is broken elsewhere, discovered on December 17, 1934, in a wall of a modern house east of the southern part of the Odeion (N–O 11). The stele is surmounted by a molding consisting of a broad upper taenia with an ovolo beneath it descending with a sharply turning profile and straight lower section to a narrower flat band. The molding returns around the right side of the stele. Below it, a small apophyge effects the transition to the inscribed surface, with an uninscribed space of 0.024 m. intervening before the first line of the decree. Line 1 of the text is inscribed on the upper taenia, which serves also as the floor for relief sculpture set between antas. The representation is of a draped figure, possibly the honorand himself, half-turned leftwards to an altar in the center of the composition (cf. lines 5–6 of the decree).

H. 0.263 m.; W. 0.262 m.; Th. 0.128 m.
LH. (line 1) 0.013 m., (lines 2–6) 0.009 m. (sigma 0.011 m.).

Ed. B. D. Meritt, *Hesperia* 37, 1968, p. 273, no. 12, with photograph pl. 79. See also *SEG* XXV, 126.

a. 145/4 *a., vel paullo post*NON-ΣΤΟΙΧ. *ca.* 35–40

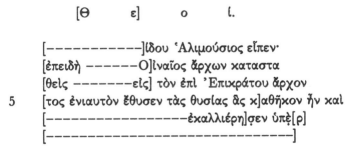

The writing is undistinguished and somewhat clumsy, with multiple chisel blows discernible in certain strokes, e.g., in the delta and mu of line 2. Apices or slight widening may be seen on a few "free ends" of strokes. Sigma is clumsily large and wide angled; the crossbar of alpha is straight, tending to slope downwards from left to right. The circular letters and especially the loop of rho are awkwardly executed, and the strokes are in many instances badly placed or joined. The spacing of the lettering is very variable. S. V. Tracy (*Attic Letter-Cutters*, p. 251) classed it as "unfamiliar" and made no attribution of it to an identifiable craftsman: but he saw it as in some respects derivative of the style of the " Cutter of *IG* II² 783", for whom see **293.**

Meritt interpreted the text as probably bestowing public honors upon an Athenian who had been archon in one of the overseas dependencies such as Imbros or Skyros. The truncated prescript however indicates that this may well be an enactment not of the boule and demos but of some subdivision, whether religious or secular, of the body politic. Apart from its use for the nine chief officers of the Athenian state and for governors or representatives abroad (as the "archons in the cities" in the period of the Athenian Empire of the 5th century), the title of archon is found in Attic cult organizations (cf. **324** and **325** with references there) and is also attested for the γένη of the Eumolpidai and Kerykes (*IG* II², 1235, line 24, 1236, line 19), for the Mesogeioi (*IG* II², 1244, line 6, 1247, lines 28–29, 1248, line 2), and for the Eikadeis (*IG* II², 1258, line 22). The structure of the decree doubtless resembled that of *IG* II², 1235. It may be tentatively concluded that the honorand had fulfilled his year of office at the head of an organization largely if not wholly concerned with cult or ritual and that the relief sculpture emphasized that aspect of his duties. The honors will have been paid to him in the year following his tenure, but a slight postponement cannot be discounted. On the prescript see also the brief mention by A. S. Henry, *Prescripts*, p. 92.

Line 4. The archon Epikrates is named in the Delian decree *ID* 1505 discussed above (p. 427) in connection with the year of Lysiades. There it is shown to have followed directly upon the year of Archon, generally dated to 147/6 on the basis of *ID* 1952 and 2589, line 25. His γραμματεύς, Xen——— of Sypalettos, gave some clue to, and at the same time has posed serious problems concerning, the secretary cycle at an otherwise obscure period. Although he and Archon had at first been placed in the biennium 151–149 (*IG* II², iv, 1, p. 20), their assignment to 147–145 has not until comparatively recently been in doubt. See W. B. Dinsmoor, *Archons of Athens*, pp. 239 and 265 (cf. also 233); W. S. Ferguson, *Athenian Tribal Cycles*, p. 30; Dinsmoor, *Athenian Archon List*, p. 193; W. K. Pritchett and Meritt, *Chronology*, p. xxx; Pritchett and O. Neugebauer, *Calendars*, p. 86; Meritt, *Hesperia* 26, 1957, p. 96, *Athenian Year*, pp. 228 and 237, *TAPA* 95, 1964, pp. 254–255, *Hesperia* 33, 1964, p. 207; A. E. Samuel, *Greek and Roman Chronology*, 1972, p. 219; Meritt, *Historia* 26, 1977, p. 184. The secretary cycle was evidently broken at this point, for the notion of a divided deme, with Sypalettos B belonging to Attalis (XII) and so preserving the regularity of the cycle, cannot be maintained despite what H. B. Mattingly called "heroic efforts" in its advocacy. See Mattingly, *Historia* 20, 1971, p. 32; J. S. Traill, *Political Organization*, pp. 10–11, 85, 121; Meritt, *Historia* 26, 1977, pp. 165–166.

C. Habicht has proposed to move both archons back by one year, to 148/7 and 147/6 respectively, to accord with his interpretation of the data of *ID* 2589 (*Hesperia* 57, 1988, pp. 238, 242, 246); see p. 428 above, on the archonship of Lysiades. The case is not compelling, and, as in the year of Lysiades, the generally accepted dating has been retained here.

Line 6. ———]σεν ὑπὸ Meritt. For the reading cf., e.g., *IG* II², 1030, line 17.

THE ARCHONSHIP OF DIOKLES, 139/8 B.C.

That Diokles was archon in the year 139/8 was established by G. Daux (*Hesperia* 16, 1947, pp. 55–57) in the light of a decree of a group of orgeones concerned with the cult of Aphrodite (N. Kyparissis and W. Peek, *AthMitt* 66, 1941, pp. 228–232, no. 4), praising in the archonship of Timarchos the good services of one Serapion, son of Poseidonios, who had served as the group's epimeletes in Diokles' year. Diokles' association with Timarchos, himself firmly dated to 138/7 (see W. K. Pritchett and B. D. Meritt, *Chronology*, p. xxxi; Meritt, *Historia* 26, 1977, p. 184) was in apparent contradiction to the indication of *ID* 1580, in which the epheboi of Diokles' year honored Prince Nikomedes of Bithynia, with the inclusion of other prosopographical detail whereby any year between 167/6 and 112/11 seemed to be excluded. Daux demonstrated that this restriction was unreal and that 139/8 was in fact a suitable date for the Delian text.

Timarchos' year had a γραμματεύς from the phyle Kekropis (VIII); see *IG* II², 974. The secretary cycle thus required his predecessor in Diokles' term of office to be of Oineis (VII), and Daux tentatively suggested that *IG* II², 978 could be restored with the name of Diokles as archon and a γραμματεύς Kephalos, son of Kephalos, whose demotic could be suitably [Περιθοίδ]ης: but this hypothesis was destroyed by the discovery of *Agora* XV, 173 and the confirmation that Kephalos was γραμματεύς in the archonship of Euthykritos (189/8 B.C.). **308** gives evidence of a γραμματεύς from Thria, also part of Oineis, at some time in the middle to later part of the 2nd century. Considerations of space, as well as evidence of other γραμματεῖς from Oineis during the period concerned, suggested the name either of Zaleukos, who is likely to have served as archon in 151/50, or of Diokles as suited to the lacuna in the first line. There are good reasons for the adoption of either alternative, but of these two possibilities the year of Diokles is preferable, and it may indeed be desirable to find for **308** a date even later in the century; see the commentary *ad loc.*

For 139/8 as the year of Diokles see also Meritt, *Hesperia* 26, 1957, p. 96, *The Athenian Year*, p. 237, *Historia* 26, 1977, p. 184; C. Habicht, *Hesperia* 57, 1988, p. 237. Earlier attributions of Diokles to 104/3 (W. B. Dinsmoor, *Athenian Archon List*, pp. 201–203; Pritchett and Meritt, *Chronology*, p. xxxv) or to 95/4 (Dinsmoor, *Archons of Athens*, pp. 280, 289; W. S. Ferguson, *Athenian Tribal Cycles*, p. 32) are of historical interest.

If **308** does belong to this year, Hippothontis is known to have held the ninth prytany in it. It was the ninth year in Meton's sixteenth cycle, and the calendar equation of **308** suggests that it was an ordinary year, as the cycle prescribed (cf. Meritt, *TAPA* 95, 1964, p. 236).

KLEOMACHIDES OF LARISA HONORED

308. The upper right corner of a flat-topped stele of Pentelic marble (I 5469), broken below and to the left but with the original back preserved, discovered on May 25, 1938, in the 19th-century repair of the Post-Herulian Wall opposite Klepsydra (T 27). The inscribed surface is flaked off before reaching the preserved right edge. The battered crowning molding consists of an ovolo surmounting a narrow taenia, with a gentle apophyge to the inscribed face, below which there is an uninscribed space of 0.018 m. before the first line of the text.

This fragment (hereafter fragment *a*) was subsequently identified by C. Habicht as the upper part of the monument of which a small piece is preserved as *IG* II², 933 (hereafter fragment *b*). The latter is in the Epigraphical Museum (E.M. 2658); its date and place of discovery are not on record. The two fragments do not join.

a: H. 0.226 m.; W. 0.26 m.; Th. 0.07 m.

b: H. 0.33 m.; W. 0.20 m.; Th. 0.07 m.

LH. *ca.* 0.007 m.

Ed. *a*: B. D. Meritt, *Hesperia* 29, 1960, pp. 76–77, no. 154, with photograph pl. 23. See also *SEG* XIX, 102, with further reference to J. and L. Robert, *REG* 74, 1961, p. 157, no. 264. *b*: *IG* II², 933. *a* and *b*: C. Habicht, *ZPE* 20, 1976, pp. 193–199; see *SEG* XXVI, 112. On the dating see further remarks by Habicht (*Hesperia* 57, 1988, p. 246) and S. V. Tracy (*Attic Letter-Cutters*, p. 167, note 1).

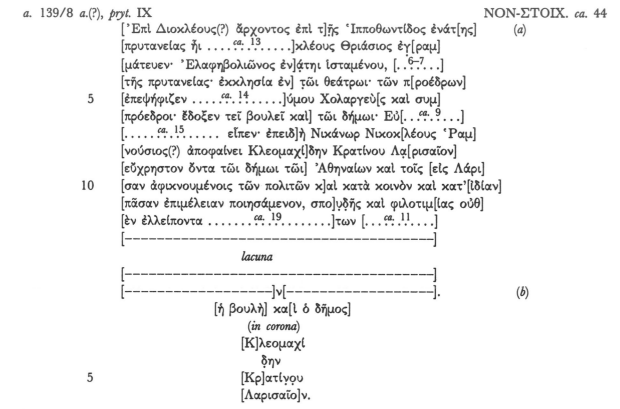

a. 139/8 a.(?), pryt. IX   NON-ΣTOIX. ca. 44

```
        ['Επὶ Διοκλέους(?) ἄρχοντος ἐπὶ τ]ῆς 'Ιπποθωντίδος ἐνάτ[ης]      (a)
        [πρυτανείας ἧι .....ᶜᵃ·¹³.....]χλέους Θριάσιος ἐγ[ραμ]
        [μάτευεν· 'Ελαφηβολιῶνος ἐν]άτηι ἱσταμένου, [..ᶜ·⁶⁻⁷...]
        [τῆς πρυτανείας· ἐκκλησία ἐν] τῶι θεάτρωι· τῶν π[ροέδρων]
    5   [ἐπεψήφιζεν .....ᶜᵃ·¹⁴.....]ύμου Χολαργεὺ[ς καὶ συμ]
        [πρόεδροι· ἔδοξεν τεῖ βουλεῖ καὶ] τῶι δήμωι· Εὐ[..ᶜᵃ·⁹...]
        [.....ᶜᵃ·¹⁵..... εἶπεν· ἐπειδ]ὴ Νικάνωρ Νικοχ[λέους 'Ραμ]
        [νούσιος(?) ἀποφαίνει Κλεομαχί]δην Κρατίνου Λα[ρισαῖον]
        [εὔχρηστον ὄντα τῶι δήμωι τῶι] 'Αθηναίων καὶ τοῖς [εἰς Λάρι]
   10   [σαν ἀφικνουμένοις τῶν πολιτῶν κ]αὶ κατὰ κοινὸν καὶ κατ'[ἰδίαν]
        [πᾶσαν ἐπιμέλειαν ποιησάμενον, σπο]υδῆς καὶ φιλοτιμ[ίας οὔθ]
        [ἐν ἐλλείποντα .......ᶜᵃ·¹⁹.......]των [...ᶜᵃ·¹¹....]
        [––––––––––––––––––––––––––––––––––––]
                              lacuna
        [––––––––––––––––––––––––––––––––––––]
        [–––––––––––––––]ν[–––––––––––––––––].              (b)
                [ἡ βουλὴ] κα[ὶ ὁ δῆμος]
                      (in corona)
                      [Κ]λεομαχί
                         δην
    5                 [Κρ]ατίνου
                      [Λαρισαῖο]ν.
```

Fragment *a*: In lines 1–6 the text is that of the *editio princeps*, with new readings of no material consequence in lines 3 and 4; in lines 7–12 the restorations are those of Habicht, *ZPE* 20, 1976, pp. 193–199, with a consequential supplement in fragment *b*, line 6. Lines 8–9. Λα[μπτρέα Meritt; J. and L. Robert proposed an ethnicum such as Λα[μψακη]νόν. Line 11. σπο]υδῆς J. and L. Robert; βο]υλῆς Meritt. *Ad fin.* φιλοτιμ[ίας τῆς] Meritt; φιλοτιμ[ίας οὐδὲν] Habicht, for which the available space is insufficient. The association of the two fragments established the name of the honorand in line 8 of fragment *a* and, as a result, the approximate extent of the lacuna before the verb. Fragment *b*: Tracy (*Attic Letter-Cutters*, p. 169) noted that whereas line 1 evidently concludes the decree, line 2 (read as – – – KA – – – by Kirchner) is written in larger letters, of the same size as those within the stephanos.

The writing is plain and rather scrappy in character and in places somewhat crowded. Omega is particularly awkward in execution. It is of relevance to the dating of the text that alpha has a broken crossbar, theta a central stroke in replacement of the dot, and that the external strokes of sigma are parallel, those of mu almost so. Moreover, the two upright strokes of pi are of equal length.

Meritt's attribution of the decree to 139/8 is retained here but for convenience rather than from firm conviction. The dating depends upon the coordination of five distinct criteria that cannot be completely resolved either individually or in combination. They may be considered separately as follows (nos. 1–4 in the order of their appearance in the text):

1. The archon's name. In the genitive case it requires from 7 to 9 letters. This will accommodate Diokles, most archons of the later 150's and early 140's (depending upon the validity or otherwise of the secretary cycle during that period), and one later possibility discussed below.

2. The nature of the year. It is likely that the year was ordinary, for line 3 allows little latitude for the alternative. The date restored there represents the 236th day of an ordinary year. If the year were intercalary, the festival date Elaphebolion 9 would represent the 274th or 275th day, i.e., the eighteenth or nineteenth of the ninth prytany, for the expression of which there is insufficient space. (For assemblies on Elaphebolion 9 see J. D. Mikalson, *Sacred and Civil Calendar*, pp. 124–126.) Among the years considered in the next paragraph (other than 139/8), 103/2 is known to have been ordinary and 127/6 intercalary. If the cycles operated normally, 154/3, 151/50, 149/8, and 147/6 would have been intercalary, 115/14 and other years between 153/2 and 148/7 ordinary.

3. The γραμματεύς. Within the latter part of the 2nd century, a γραμματεύς from Oineis (VII) is to be looked for in 151/50, 139/8, 127/6, 115/14, and 103/2. The γραμματεῖς of 127/6 and 103/2 are known and differ from the evidence of the present text. It is also known that there was a break in the cycle in 146/5 (see Meritt, *Historia* 26, 1977, pp. 166 and 184 and **307**). This provides the opportunity to discount the operation of the cycle over a longer period, if to do so assists in the resolution of the problem; cf. Habicht, *Hesperia* 57, 1988, p. 246.

4. The prosopography. The name in line 7 does not help. Meritt suggested that the Nikanor at whose instance the honors here decreed had been initiated was Nikanor, son of – – –okles, whose funerary monument survives as *IG* II², 7845, noting that Kirchner's date there recorded of "post fin. s. IV a." did not exclude a date in the 2nd century. Indeed the lettering of that text certainly suggests that a 2nd-century dating is appropriate for it, and Kirchner himself tentatively so dated it under *PA* 10698. If *IG* II², 7845 was to any degree symmetrically disposed, it should read [N]ιϰ[ά]νωρ | [Νιϰ]οϰλέου | [....]ευς, and there is therefore no connection to be found in it with the family of the better-known Νιϰάνωρ Νιϰάνορος Λευϰονοεύς of the next generation. Habicht (*ZPE* 20, 1976, pp. 193–199) was able to define more precisely the space available for the demotic in lines 7–8 and preferred an association with the Νιϰάνωρ Νιϰοϰλέους ʽΡαμνούσιος of *IG* II², 7361 (*saec.* I *p.*), whose demotic exactly fits it (as indeed would Λευϰονοεύς).

Of greater significance is the identity of the honorand himself, shown by Habicht to have been Kleomachides, son of Kratinos, of Larisa in Thessaly. His was a prominent family, members of which are attested in various contexts in the earlier part of the century: see J. Pouilloux, *BCH* 79, 1955, pp. 456–457 (cf. *SEG* XV, 370, *c*, lines 38–42) and Habicht, *op. cit.*, pp. 193–194. In view of the likely stemma of Kleomachides and his connections, Habicht (p. 197) decided that an earlier rather than a later date which accorded with the requirements of criterion 3 above would be suitable: thus 151/50, when it was thought that the archon was Epainetos. Later, having removed Epainetos to 166/5, he substituted Zaleukos as the archon of 151/50, an attribution already made by Meritt (*Historia, loc. cit.*): with either archon a γραμματεύς from Oineis (VII) remains appropriate. However, since the archon Epikrates, whom he assigned to 147/6, had a γραμματεύς from Kekropis (VIII), Habicht further suggested that the archon Archon's γραμματεύς in the preceding year may have belonged to Oineis and that the present text could in consequence be assigned to 148/7. Cf. *SEG* XXXVIII, 109. Tracy (*op. cit.*, p. 168), referring to a stemma of Kleomachides' family provided by H. Kramolisch (*Die Strategen des Thessalischen Bundes vom Jahr 196 v. Chr. bis zum Ausgang der römischen Republik* [*Demetrias* II], 1978, p. 29), noted that the names Kleomachides and Kratinos alternated in that branch of the family and that the person honored here might therefore belong to a later generation that that envisaged by Habicht.

5. The style of the lettering. The idiosyncratic style of the mason who inscribed this text stands almost in a class by itself. Tracy (*loc. cit.*) made this inscription the name piece of the "Cutter of Agora I 5469" and provided a photograph of it (fig. 25). He gave the date of the mason's floruit as 151/50, guided by the indications of dating adopted by Habicht in 1976. But he also observed the elements of comparative lateness in the letter forms already described and urged with justice that these "suggest, but do not absolutely demand, a date nearer 100 B.C." To this may be added that *IG* II², 1037, an ephebic text, which is the only other inscription Tracy attributed to this craftsman, was dated by Kirchner "in. s. I a."

It may well be that the year of Diokles best answers the various and discordant demands of these five criteria. On the other hand, it may be useful to consider the claim of the archon Nausias, who held office nearer to the end of the century, in 115/14; see Meritt, *Historia* 26, 1977, p. 186. Attribution to this date satisfies the criterion of inscriptional style. The year will have been ordinary (criterion 2), and his γραμματεύς will have been a member of the phyle Oineis (criterion 3). The family history of the honorand can probably be accommodated to such a date (criterion 4); and the space available in the prescript does not preclude Nausias' name in the genitive case (criterion 1). For the evidence concerning Nausias' year see W. B. Dinsmoor, *Athenian Archon List*, p. 199.

Line 4. For the location of the assembly see **167**, commentary on lines 6–7. Lines 7–8. For the phraseology Meritt compared *IG* II², 896, 971, and 978 (the two latter using ἐμφανίζειν rather than ἀποφαίνειν). It is regular in the case of honors paid to prytaneis, for which see *Agora* XV, *passim*.

THE ARCHONSHIP OF DIONYSIOS "WHO SUCCEEDED TIMARCHIDES", 135/4 B.C.

The discovery of the upper section of I 2145, a prytany decree later reedited as *Agora* XV, 243 (cf. *SEG* XII, 101), gave the full title of this archon, a formula of distinction which the frequency of the name Dionysios made advisable (cf. the archons of 128/7 and 112/11 and S. Dow, *Hesperia* 4, 1935, p. 78). Its effect was described by W. K. Pritchett, *Hesperia* 9, 1940, pp. 129–132. With the prytany text he associated *IG* II², 887; and **309**, when published, provided a third decree attributable to Dionysios' year. Cf. *ID* 2566, in which P. Roussel (*REA* 34, 1932, p. 201) had indeed already suggested the restoration of Dionysios' name in its full form and had posited the connection with *IG* II², 887, hesitantly adding *ID* 1750 also. W. B. Dinsmoor, who had information of the new fragment of I 2145 in advance of its publication (*Athenian Archon List*, pp. 195–196), observed that the new discovery served to confirm Roussel's hypothesis and to show that Theolytos, the γραμματεύς of Dionysios' year, whose personal name but not demotic is preserved in *IG* II², 887, came from Amphitrope (Antiochis XI), thus assuring 135/4 as his date by reference to the secretary cycle. Timarchides' date had already been assured by his association with the Delian gymnasiarch Satyrion (*ID* 1922), traceable in the sequence of gymnasiarchs provided by *ID* 2589. Cf. Dinsmoor, *Archons of Athens*, pp. 229–233. Dionysios' date has been a secure point in the reconstructed archon list since 1940. See Pritchett and B. D. Meritt, *Chronology*, pp. xxxi–xxxii; Pritchett and O. Neugebauer, *Calendars*, p. 75; Meritt, *Hesperia* 26, 1957, p. 96, *Athenian Year*, p. 237; H. B. Mattingly, *Historia* 20, 1971, pp. 44–46; Meritt, *Historia* 26, 1977, p. 185.

Earlier assessments of this archon, based solely upon *IG* II², 887, had placed him variously between 194 and 189 (Dinsmoor, *Archons of Athens*, p. 254), "before or after 200" (W. S. Ferguson, *Athenian Tribal Cycles*, p. 34), or in the early 2nd century (*IG* II², iv, 1, pp. 22–23 and *IG* II², 887, in comm.). In publishing the first-discovered section of *Agora* XV, 243, in which the first lines showed no more than the first four letters of Dionysios' name, Dow regarded the lettering as of the early 2nd century, and this appeared to accord with the dating then favored; see Dow, *Prytaneis*, pp. 112–113, no. 56.

Agora XV, 243 demonstrated that Dionysios' year was intercalary in the Athenian festival calendar, offering two dates, Gamelion 29 = pryt. VIII, 11 and Gamelion 22 = pryt. VIII, 4. Cf. Pritchett and Neugebauer, *loc. cit.*. No adequate dates are preserved in *IG* II², 887 or in **309**, and no date at all in *Agora* XV, 244. That 135/4 was intercalary accorded with the pattern of Meton's arrangement, in which the year was the thirteenth in the sixteenth cycle. Cf. Meritt, *Historia* 26, 1977, p. 166. Of phylai in prytany only VIII Ptolemais is known. The ninth prytany saw in office a phyle with *ca.* 9 letters in its name, and Leontis therefore (*IG* II², 887) held some prytany other than the eighth or ninth.

FRAGMENT OF A DECREE

309. Three small joining fragments of a stele of Hymettian marble (I 6003), broken on all sides, discovered together on June 11, 1947, among destruction debris on the floor of the Civic Offices (I 12). The striations of a toothed chisel are visible on the largest fragment, running in both diagonal directions.

Measurements as joined: H. 0.06 m.; W. 0.15 m.; Th. 0.026 m.
LH. 0.006 m.

Ed. B. D. Meritt, *Hesperia* 17, 1948, pp. 22–23, no. 10, with photograph pl. 7.

['Επι Διονυ]σίου ἄρχοντος [τοῦ μετὰ Τιμαρχίδην ἐπὶ τῆς ..$^{ca.\ 8}$..]
[δος ἐνάτ]ης πρυ[τανε]ίας [ἧι Θεόλυτος Θεοδότου 'Αμφιτροπῆθεν ἐγραμ]
[μάτευεν]· 'Ελαφ[ηβολι]ῶ[νος ――――――――――――――――――――]
[――――――――]⁻⁻[――――――――――――――――――――――]
5   [――――――――――――――――――――――――――――――――]

This stele was, in the judgment of S. V. Tracy (*Attic Letter-Cutters*, p. 150), the work of the "Cutter of Agora I 6006" and is the last example in this collection of his very considerable output. Indeed this is the latest year to which a text attributable to him can be firmly dated. For his career and characteristics see **296**.

The attribution to 135/4 and the restorations showing the officials of that year, based on *Agora* XV, 243, are those of the *editio princeps*. It would be equally possible to ascribe the text to 128/7, with the readings [τοῦ μετὰ Λυκίσκον κτλ.] in line 1 and [ἧι ――――――― νος Κεφαλῆθεν ἐγραμ] in line 2, reducing the length of line to *ca.* 50 letters. However, even before Tracy's studies set the matter on a more secure footing, Meritt had observed that the lettering so closely resembled that of *Agora* XV, 243 that the same mason was probably responsible for both texts. The "Cutter of Agora I 6006" had already, by 135/4, enjoyed a long career, and to presume its extension as far as 128/7, while of course possible, might be injudicious.

Line 2. Theolytos' funerary monument is preserved as *IG* II², 5611, there dated "s. II/I a.". The name is not otherwise met with in Attic prosopography but is to be found elsewhere (e.g., Thucydides 2.102).

DECREE IN HONOR OF MENODOROS (OR ZENODOROS), SON OF EUMENES, OF TRINEMEA

310. Eighteen fragments of a stele of Pentelic marble, one of them now lost and another known only from a squeeze, ten of which combine to produce a united section preserving the full width of the monument, much of either edge, and part of the foot, including a tenon for insertion into a separate base or foundation. A nineteenth fragment, attributed to the stele in the *editio princeps* (where it is designated fragment *a*), does not belong to this decree and was subsequently reedited separately as *Agora* XV, 245. In this edition the fragments are therefore redesignated, and a line omitted in the *editio princeps* has been included, with consequentially revised line numeration from line 28 onward. Details of the separate fragments, some composed of reunited pieces found together, are as follows:

a. Three joined fragments (I 4798 c), together preserving the left side and original rough-picked back but broken elsewhere, discovered on May 20, 1938, in the original filling of the Post-Herulian Wall, south of the Eleusinion (T 21).

b. A fragment (E.M. 2404) identified by E. Schweigert among material in the Epigraphical Museum at Athens, joining fragment *a* above and fragment *c* below. The left edge and original back of the stele are preserved on it, but it is broken elsewhere.

c. Also attributed to this monument by Schweigert, this small fragment (I 4522) makes a join at its top edge with fragment *b*; it preserves the left edge of the stele but is broken elsewhere. Discovered on February 16, 1937, at a Roman level south of the Stoa of Attalos (P 12).

d. Three joined fragments (I 4798 d), together preserving the right edge and original back of the stele, discovered on May 20 and 21, 1938, in the same context as fragment *a*. At the left the configuration of this combined piece comes roughly to a point, and on the upper side of this point it makes a join with the lower right of fragment *a*.

e. A fragment composed of four joining pieces (I 4920), identified by Schweigert as part of this monument, discovered on May 24, 1937, in the fill of the Post-Herulian Wall, south of the Eleusinion (T 20). It preserves part of the left side of the stele but is otherwise broken. Its bottom edge makes a join with fragment *f*.

f. A small triangular fragment (E.M. 2402), preserving part of the left side but otherwise broken, which was identified in the Epigraphical Museum by Schweigert and found by him to join at its upper edge the lower part of fragment *e*.

g. A large fragment mended from two pieces (I 4798), preserving the lower right corner of the stele and the original back. The inscribed surface is broken away in its upper right quarter, but this fragmented piece survived independently to be recorded as *IG* II², 937 (fragment *h* below). Discovered on April 28, 1937, in the same context as fragment *a*.

h. *IG* II², 937, now lost, copied by K. S. Pittakys and stated by J. Kirchner to be, or to have been, in the Hypapanti Church.

j. A fragment preserving the original back (I 4798 b), reaching to the last line of the text, though not to the bottom of the stele, but broken elsewhere, discovered on May 19, 1938, in the same context as fragment *a*.

k. A fragment known only from a squeeze in the collection of the Institute for Advanced Study, Princeton, N.J., identified by S. V. Tracy and referred to by him as *IG* II², 937, fragment *x*. It evidently makes a join with fragment *g* at the upper right of the latter and with fragment *d* at that fragment's lowest point, and it extends to the right edge of the stele.

a, as joined: H. 0.415 m.; W. 0.20 m.; Th. 0.145 m.

b: H. 0.125 m.; W. 0.105 m.; Th. *ca.* 0.15 m.

c: H. 0.096 m.; W. 0.077 m.; Th. 0.047 m.

d, as joined: H. 0.34 m.; W. 0.31 m.; Th. 0.15 m.

e, as joined: H. 0.195 m.; W. 0.135 m.; Th. 0.05 m.

f: H. 0.123 m.; W. *ca.* 0.07 m.; Th. *ca.* 0.05 m.

g, as joined: H. 0.58 m.; W. 0.25 m.; Th. 0.155 m.

h: No detail.

j: H. 0.25 m.; W. 0.24 m.; Th. *ca.* 0.15 m.

k: No detail.

LH. 0.011 m.

Ed. B. D. Meritt, *Hesperia* 36, 1967, pp. 59–63, no. 6, with photograph pl. 21. See *SEG* XXIV, 135 and J. and L. Robert, *REG* 81, 1968, p. 446, no. 190. The study promised in this last context by L. Robert subsequently appeared in Ἀρχ. Ἐφ., 1969, pp. 1–6, no. I. Revised text, inclusive of fragment *k* and of Meritt's omitted line, S. V. Tracy, *GRBS* 29, 1988, pp. 383–388, with photograph of the squeeze of fragment *k*, pl. 1. See also *SEG* XXXVIII, 112.

ca. a. 135 *a.*   NON-ΣΤΟΙΧ. *ca.* 38–44

```
     [----------------------------------]
     [-------------------------------- · ἔδο]
(a)  [ξ]εν [τῶι δήμωι· .........ca. 22......... εἶπεν]·
     [ἐ]πειδ[ὴ καὶ πρότερον Εὐμένης ὁ πατὴρ .ηνοδώρου]
     τροφεὺς κ[αὶ τιθηνὸς τοῦ βασιλέως ...ca. 11....]
 5   [ἐ]πιδημήσα[ς ἐν τεῖ πόλει ἡμῶν ἀνεστράφη καλῶς]
     καὶ εὐσχημ[όνως καὶ κοινῆι τῶι δήμωι καὶ ἰδίαι τῶν]
     πολιτῶν ἀεὶ [τοῖς ἀφικνουμένοις εἰς Ἀντιοχείαν],
     ἀνθ'ὧν ὁ δῆμ[ος βουλόμενος ἀξίως τιμᾶν τοὺς ἀγαθοὺς]
     ἄνδρας ἐστε[φάνωσεν αὐτὸν χρυσῶι στεφάνωι καὶ]
10   πολίτην ἐποί[ησεν· καὶ νῦν .ηνόδωρος παραλαβὼν]
     τὴν πατρώιαν [εὔνοιαν χρήσιμον ἑαυτὸν παρέχει]
     καὶ πρὸς τὸν δῆ[μον καὶ πρὸς ἰδίους ὥστε τιμηθῆ]
     ναι ὑπ'αὐ[το]ῦ· ΑΛ[.....ca. 15..... τῆς φιλοστορ]
     γίας καὶ τῆς π[ρὸς τὸν δῆμον εὐνοίας πολλὰς καὶ]
15   μεγάλας ἀποδ[είξεις ἐμ παντὶ καιρῶι ἐποιήσατο καὶ]
     παρέσχετο χρεί[ας --------------------]
     νημένος, καὶ παρεχ[--------------------]
     τε αὐτῶι τάξιν ἔχειν [.......ca. 18.......]αν προ[σ]         (d)
(b)  άγων τά τε κοινεῖ χρή[σιμα ...ca. 10...]ν πράττειν
20   εὐνούστατα διακείμε[νος πρὸς αὐτ]όν, vv νυνί τε ἀ
     ποσταλεὶς ὑπὸ τοῦ βασιλ[έως πρεσβευ]τὴς [π]ροθύμω[ς]
     ἑαυτὸν εἰς τὴν πρεσβεί[αν ἐπέδ]ωκεν ἕνεκεν τοῦ χ[α]
     ρίζεσθαι τῶ[ι δ]ήμωι διὰ τὸ ἐκ τῆς πρεσβείας μεγάλα χ[αὶ]
     χρήσιμα π[ορίζ]εσθαι κοινῆι τε πᾶσιν καὶ ἰδίαι τῶν π[ο]
25   λιτῶν ἐκ[άστωι καὶ π]αρελθὼν εἰς τὴν ἐκκ[λησί]αν προ
(c)  ηνέγκατ[ο λόγους(?) ὑ]πὲρ ὧν οἱ πρόγονοι τ[οῦ βασι]λέω[ς]
     [ἔ]δωκα[ν τῶι δήμωι δωρ]εῶν καὶ ὧν περιε[ποίη]σαν φ[ι]
     [λ]αν[θρώπων ...ca. 9...]σοντως τὰ πρὸς [α]ὐτὸν Ι[.]
```

```
                          [........ca. 20........]οντες ἔκ τε τῶν ἄλλων
          30         [.....ca. 13.... εὐεργετη]μάτων εὐχαριστοῦν ἀ
(e)                  ξίω[ς ...ca. 9....· ἀπελογίσ]ατο δὲ καὶ περὶ τῆς το[ῦ]
                     βασ[ιλέως εὐνοίας(?) ....ca. 12....]ι ἐπανορθῶσαι ᵛ
                     τὸν δῆ[μ]ον Ι[.....ca. 16.....]ήσατο κατὰ τὴν πό          (g, k)
                     λιν συνανασ[τρεφ...ca. 10...] ἐμ πᾶσιν ἀξίως ἀνε
          35         στράφη τῆς τ[....ca. 12.... κ]ρίσεως· [ἐ]ξηγήσατο
                     δὲ καὶ περὶ ἧς [.....ca. 14.....]ς εἰσ[ὶ τ]εῖ πόλε[ι χ]ρή
                     σιμα ἐκτεν[ῶς ...ca. 11....]· ὅπως [ἂν οὖν] [καὶ ὁ] δῆμ[ος]
(f)                  φαίνηται τι[μῶν τοὺς ἀγαθοὺς] ἄνδρας, ᵛ ἀγ[αθ]εῖ τύ[χει δε]
                     δόχθαι τεῖ [βουλεῖ τοὺς λαχ]όντας προέδρους εἰς [τὴν ἐ]   (h)
          40         πιοῦσ[α]ν ἐ[κκλησίαν χρημ]ατίσαι περὶ τούτων, γνώ
                     μην δ[ὲ ξυμβάλλεσθαι τῆς] βουλῆς εἰς τὸν δῆμον ὅτ[ι]
                     δοκε[ῖ τεῖ βουλεῖ ἐπαινέσαι .η]νόδωρον Εὐμένου Τρινε
(j)                  με[έα ἐπὶ τεῖ πρ]οαιρ[έσει καὶ στ]εφανῶσα[ι [χρυ]σῶι στεφάνω[ι]
                     [ἀρετῆς ἔνεκ]εν καὶ εὐ[νοίας ἧ]ν ἔχων [διατελ]εῖ πρὸς τὸν
          45         [δῆμον τὸν Ἀθη]ναίων· ᵛ σ[τῆσαι δ]ὲ αὐ[τοῦ καὶ εἰκ]όνα χαλκῆ[ν]
                     [ἐν ἀγορᾶι πα]ρὰ τὴν εἰκόν[α τοῦ βασιλέως Ἀντ]ιόχο[υ· ἐπι]
                     [μεληθῆναι δὲ τ]οὺς στρ[ατηγοὺς ³⁻⁴.] ἵνα ἀναγορευθῆι ὁ στ[έ]
                     [φανος καὶ ἡ ε]ἰκὼν ἐν τ[οῖς ἀγῶσ]ι πᾶσιν οἷς τίθησιν ἡ πόλις·
                     [εἶναι δὲ αὐτ]ῶι καὶ σίτησ[ιν ἐμ πρ]υτανείωι αἰτησαμένωι κ[α]
          50         [τὰ τοὺς νό]μους· τὸ δὲ ψήφισ[μ]α τόδε ἀναγράψαι τὸν γραμ
                     [ματέα τὸν] κατὰ πρυτανείαν [εἰ]ς στήλην λιθίνην καὶ ἀνα
                     [θεῖναι παρὰ] τὴν εἰκόνα· τὸ δὲ γ[εν]όμενον ἀνάλωμα δοῦνα[ι]
                     [εἰς αὐτὸ τὸν τα]μίαν τῶν στ[ρ[ατ]ιωτικ]ῶν.     vacat
                                                        vacat
```

Meritt, for historical reasons, set the date of this decree as *ca.* 170 B.C.: but the character of the lettering undoubtedly suggests a later date, and it was in the process of investigating this that Tracy was able to add fragment *k* to the text. In the event, he identified nine inscriptions as the work of the mason who produced the stele under discussion (**312–315** being among them) and entitled him the "Cutter of *IG* II² 937" on the basis of this text. See *Attic Letter-Cutters*, pp. 173–180, with photograph of fragment *g* as representative of the name piece, fig. 27. The only text attributable to this craftsman that may be firmly dated belongs to 131/30 B.C. Tracy defined his floruit as "*ca.* 135–123/2" and justly described his work as unusually precise and elegant. Alpha has a broken crossbar; the two uprights of mu and the two outer strokes of sigma are parallel. Serifs or apices are used neatly and with exactitude.

The above text, with I 4758 omitted and the lines renumbered, accords for the most part with that of Tracy; the readings are in general those of the *editio princeps*, with some minor revisions and with account taken of the proposals of L. Robert. Meritt introduced no restorations into lines 1–15, where the supplements shown were proposed by Tracy, *adiuvante* C. Habicht; they surely reflect the likely tenor of the decree, even if word-for-word exactitude cannot be guaranteed. The remainder, except in the section augmented by fragment *k*, repeats for the most part the restorations suggested by Robert; more significant variations are indicated below. The complete, partial, or nonvisible state of letters at the edge of a fragment is viewed differently by different observers, but the identity of the letters in question, in almost all cases, is in no doubt.

The dating required by the stylistic considerations excludes the attribution of the decree to the context of the reign of Antiochos IV Epiphanes (175–163 B.C.) as proposed by Meritt, and Tracy argued for an association with Antiochos VII Euergetes, nicknamed Sidetes, whose reign (139–129 B.C.) more accurately coincided with the craftsman's career. But the restorations of the first ten lines assume an allusion to an earlier generation, and lines 26–37 evidently look back in particular to the munificence of Antiochos IV towards Athens among the benefactions of the Seleucids which Meno/Zenodoros detailed to his Athenian audience. Meritt assumed that the statue referred to in line 46 was that of Epiphanes, a view adopted also by H. A. Thompson and R. E. Wycherley in *Agora* XIV, p. 159, note 218; cf. *Agora* III, p. 208. This may be correct: but Sidetes could have been so honored if he had been taking trouble to renew close ties with Athens, and his statue would be the natural companion for that of his ambassador.

Meritt proposed the name of the honorand (lines 3 and 4) as Menodoros and identified him with the Menodoros of *OGIS* 315, an envoy of the priest of Pessinos to King Attalos II of Pergamon. Robert discounted this identification, Menodoros being no uncommon name, and observed also that the name could be Zenodoros no less than that suggested, a point remaining valid even though Meritt's identification is to be rejected.

Line 4. τροφεὺς κ[αὶ τιθηνός. The intial tau is visible, despite the [τ]ροφεύς of Meritt and Robert, and Tracy correctly showed it so. The supplement is that of Robert, who developed a discussion of the titles, Ἀρχ. Ἐφ., 1969, pp. 5–6, with notes. Line 11. By reason of the grant to his father, the present honorand appears in lines 42–43 with his Athenian demotic: if the restorations are acceptable, it may not be just, or strictly accurate, to refer to him as "naturalized" and to categorize him as a foreigner; see A. S. Henry, *Honours*, p. 289, note 76.

Line 11. See Robert, *op. cit.*, pp. 4–5, with discussion of the meaning of πατρῷος. Lines 13–14. Robert (*op. cit.*, p. 6, note 4) proposed τῆς τε πρὸς τὸν βασιλέα φιλοστορ]γίας, which would leave insufficient room for the completion of satisfactory sense in the preceding phrase. On φιλοστοργία see Robert, *Hellenica* XIII, 1965, pp. 38–42. Line 15. ἀπο[--- Meritt, Robert, but the delta is clear; ἀποδ[είξεις Tracy; ἀποδ[όσεις is also a possibility. Lines 18–19. So Meritt. Robert suggested προάγων, adopted also by Tracy (for προαγωγή cf. **266**, line 10); but there is space for a final letter in line 18, and the preceding letters were so engineered as to provide for it (contrast line 25). Line 19. κοινεῖ here, but κοινῆι in line 24.

Line 22. ἐπέδ]ωκεν Robert, Ἀρχ. Ἐφ., 1969, p. 2, note 2, followed by Tracy; παρέδ]ωκεν Meritt. Line 24. π[ράττ]εσθαι Meritt, a supplement Robert affected not to understand, regarding the sense as requiring π[εριγεν]έσθαι. But this is too long for the lacuna, and Robert's less-favored suggestion π[ορίζ]εσθαι is preferred here; it was also adopted by Tracy. Lines 25–26. λόγους Tracy; προ[σ]ηνέγκατ[ο ὑπόμνημα ὑ]πὲρ ὧν Meritt. There seems no room for the sigma at the end of line 25, although Tracy retained it. Robert (*op. cit.*, p. 3, note 3) again did not understand Meritt's supplement (there misquoted). Some statement before the people is evidently being described. Lines 27–28. So Robert, *op. cit.*, p. 3. Meritt restored φ[ιλί]αν [---- and left line 27 otherwise without restoration.

Lines 30–31. ---]μάτων εὐχαριστοῦνα[ι ει[--- Meritt *in editione principe*. Εὐχάριστος was a title of Ptolemy V Epiphanes, king of Egypt, and Meritt subsequently thought that this might be a reference to him: see *SEG* XXIV, *loc. cit.* Robert was content to characterize εὐχαριστοῦναι as enigmatic. Alpha however concludes line 30, and the first three letters of line 31 are more correctly read as ΞΙΩ. Εὐχαριστοῦν therefore may represent a form in -οω of the verb εὐχαριστεῖν. For variant stems in contracted verbs see E. Schwyzer, *Griechische Grammatik* I, 1939, pp. 727–729, with references there. The note on this passage by L. Threatte, *Grammar*, p. 269, cannot now stand. For the active infinitive after ἄξιος cf. Thucydides 1.138.3. ἀπελογίσ]ατο Robert, Tracy; ---]ατο Meritt.

Line 35. κ]ρίσεως Meritt; --]ρίσεως Tracy. Line 36. That two letters towards the end of the line were engraved *in rasura* was noticed by Tracy (so also the *rasurae* of line 37 and 53). A *rasura* supposed by him in line 49, accommodating the second and third letters visible there, is less sure. Line 37. The "hortatory intention" here reflects the wish of the demos not only to reward benefactors but also to be seen to be doing so (in order to encourage emulation). See **173**, commentary on line 2 and references there. The same sentiment is more fully expressed in **261**, lines 38–41. Line 38. ἀγαθεῖ τύχει. See **72**, commentary on lines 7–8.

Lines 42–43. Meno/Zenodoros and his family are not known beyond the evidence of this text. Line 43. ἐπὶ τεῖ προαιρέσει. For the phraseology see Henry, *Honours*, p. 11. The anomaly pointed out in Henry's note (p. 20, note 59) is remedied by the revised dating of the text. The phrase κατὰ τὸν νόμον accompanying the reference to the golden stephanos is now lacking in the formula: for the omission see Henry, *Honours*, pp. 27–28. Line 44. ἀρετή and εὔνοια are among the stock virtues for which honorands are commended. For the form of words here cf. *IG* II², 682, lines 73–75, **261**, lines 46–47, and Henry, *Honours*, p. 43.

Lines 45–48. The honor of a statue was a great rarity; see Henry, *Honours*, pp. 294–296 and **233**, commentary on lines 11–12, as well as **240**. What, as it seems, is unique here is that the generals are made responsible for the proclamation of both the stephanos and the statue (without, it may be added, the cooperation of the Military Treasurer) at all the festivals organized by the city; see Henry, *Honours*, p. 299, where the relevant lines are quoted, and pp. 29 (on the proclamation of the stephanos) and 56, note 88. The *agones* are not specified, which also differs from normal practice: cf., e.g., **208**, lines 26–29, **249**, lines 2–6, **261**, lines 47–50. For the responsibility of the generals in this connection see **224**, lines 39–41, **261**, lines 50–52. Lines 46–47. ἐπιμελεῖσθαι Meritt: but the aorist, as restored here, represents the customary usage, as was noted by Henry (*Honours*, p. 56, note 88) and adopted by Tracy. Line 47. στρ[ατηγοὺ]ς καὶ ἵνα Tracy.

Lines 49–50. To the considerable honors already accorded to Meno/Zenodoros is added the remarkable privilege of dining in the Prytaneion if he requests it κατὰ τοὺς νόμους. See Henry (*Honours*, pp. 275–278), who observed (p. 277) that this decree constitutes the latest example of the grant (later, indeed, than was thought at that time), and that it was not accompanied as formerly by a grant of *proedria* at the festivals or the extension of the privilege to the honorand's descendants via the eldest in line. Contrast **261**, lines 53–55; and on σίτησις in general see the commentary there. M. J. Osborne (*ZPE* 41, 1981, pp. 168–169), who noted the same anomalies, suggested that a line might have been omitted in the inscribing of the text between lines 48 and 49, reading (e.g.) ⟨καὶ εἶναι αὐτῶι προεδρίαν ἐν τοῖς ἀγῶσι οἷς τίθησιν ἡ πόλις⟩: the omission would readily be accounted for by the similarity of the line endings. But the omission of the descendants yet remains, and Osborne's preferred interpretation was that Meno/Zenodoros was eligible for σίτησις (and would be granted it) only if he made the proper request. Henry (*loc. cit.*) raised convincing objections to the first of these proposals, and as to the second, eligibility is not in question. The requirement of αἴτησις is always part of the formula where citizens are concerned, and the grant as such is already enshrined in the decree. By the later 2nd century, as Henry surmised, "sitesis grants may have been made without an accompanying grant of *proedria* and perhaps only for the enjoyment of the original recipient."

Line 52. Unusually, the verb is δοῦναι rather than μερίσαι: cf. Henry, *ZPE* 78, 1989, p. 289. Line 53. αὐτῶι Meritt; εἰς αὐτό Tracy, which better suits the spatial requirement. The insertion of either at this point in the formula is worth remark: cf. Henry, *op. cit.*, pp. 289, 291.

THE ARCHONSHIP OF XENON, 133/2 B.C.

ID 1949 and 2594, the one a dedication and the other a list of epheboi, associate Xenon as archon with the Delian gymnasiarch Dion, son of Damon, whose position in the list of gymnasiarchs in series, *ID* 2589, guarantees his date. See *IG* II², iv, 1, pp. 20–21; W. B. Dinsmoor, *Archons of Athens*, pp. 232, 266, 270, *Athenian Archon List*, p. 196; W. S. Ferguson, *Athenian Tribal Cycles*, p. 31; W. K. Pritchett and B. D. Meritt, *Chronology*, p. xxxii; Meritt, *Hesperia* 26, 1957, p. 96, *Athenian Year*, p. 237, *Historia* 26, 1977, p. 185; H. B. Mattingly, *Historia* 20, 1971, p. 44. Before this definite indication, earlier scholarship had effectively placed Xenon in the correct quinquennium. See Ferguson, *The Athenian Archons of the Third and Second Centuries before Christ*, 1899, p. 73, and *PA* 11323. The secretary cycle required that the γραμματεύς of his year be of the phyle Erechtheis (I); see below on **311**.

Except for **311**, if correctly attributed, no Athenian documents of Xenon's year are preserved, and there is no direct information concerning the year's character. 135/4 was certainly intercalary (Meritt, *Athenian Year*, p. 190). That 134/3 was also intercalary is highly unlikely (see Mattingly, *op. cit.*, pp. 39–40); whether it was or was not, the probability must be that the festival year 133/2 was ordinary. It was the fifteenth year in the (sixteenth) Metonic cycle, and as such was scheduled as ordinary in the cycle. Cf. Mattingly (*op. cit.*, p. 46), who noted the correspondence between Metonic theory and Athenian practice in this period as "very remarkable". See also Meritt, *Historia* 26, 1977, p. 166.

FRAGMENT OF A DECREE

311. A fragment of a pedimental stele of Pentelic marble (I 6275), broken all around but with the original rough-picked back preserved (although much worn) as well as the upper molding above the inscribed surface and part of the pediment, discovered on April 28, 1950, in the wall of a pithos in the area north of the Odeion (M 8). The molding follows the regular pattern of a broad taenia (which forms the floor of the pediment), with the ovolo beneath it descending to a lower narrow flat band with gentle apophyge to the inscribed surface. The inscribed area is badly battered, and nothing can be read with assurance below the third line of text.

H. 0.255 m.; W. 0.155 m.; Th. 0.08 m.
LH. 0.006 m.

Ed. B. D. Meritt, *Hesperia* 30, 1961, p. 223, no. 20, with photograph pl. 39. See also *SEG* XXI, 475.

a. 133/2 *a.*   NON-ΣΤΟΙΧ. *ca.* 53

    [Ἐπὶ Ξένω]νος ἄρχον[τος ἐπὶ τῆς ––––––––––––––––––πρυτανείας ἧι]
    [Ἀσωποκλ]ῆς Ἀσωποχ[λέους Ἀγρυλῆθεν ἐγραμμάτευεν· ––––ῶνος ὀγ]
    [δόηι ἱσταμ]ένου, [–––––––––––– τῆς πρυτανείας· –––––––––––]
       versus octo non legendi

S. V. Tracy (*Attic Letter-Cutters*, p. 32) found the evidence insufficient for any attribution of this fragment to an identifiable craftsman. For the style Meritt compared J. Kirchner, *IIA²*, pp. 24–25, nos. 106 and 111 (*IG* II², 971 and 1029). Among the more clearly visible letters, alpha with exaggeratedly broken crossbar and pi with elongated horizontal stroke are notable; the external strokes of sigma are well angled. Other letters seem to be plain and without special characteristics.

On the basis of the lettering and of his recognition that the γραμματεύς belonged to the phyle Erechtheis (I), Meritt regarded the date as a choice between the archonships of Xenon (133/2) and Phokion (121/20), preferring the latter as a slightly longer name better answering to the apparent requirements of line 1. This decision overlooked the evidence that the γραμματεύς of Phokion's year was Euandros (*IG* II², 1015), so that the decree must after all be assigned to the archonship of Xenon, whose γραμματεύς may thus be more securely identified. Meritt later acknowledged this; cf. *Historia* 26, 1977, p. 185. If Meritt's argument concerning the γραμματεύς and his phyle be not accepted, there is no other year with an archon whose name ends conformably with this text and whose γραμματεύς is unknown in the same general period of thirty years. Kriton (93/2?) may however not be too late, nor Mikion (150/49?, 142/1?) too early, for consideration.

Line 2. The name Asopokles is a rarity in Attic prosopography, although not, in the light of accumulating material, so rare as appeared in *PA* where the sole example (2673), identified by Meritt with the γραμματεύς of this text, is nevertheless still the best attested holder of it. His family was evidently wealthy. His father, Asopokles, had been honored with a statue dedication by his sister (*IG* II², 3870) and had contributed to a patriotic fund in 164/3 (*SEG* XXIV, 194, line 26). The younger Asopokles appears as an epimeletes in the list *IG* II², 1939 (line 18), of a date unlikely to be later than *ca.* 135. His brother Pyrikles (*PA* 12492) figures in a *catalogus hominum nobilium* of uncertain date in the latter part of the century (*IG* II², 2452, line 52). It is highly probable that one of the two brothers in this distinguished family from Agryle could have served as γραμματεύς when the turn of Erechtheis came round. The name Πυρικλ]ῆς could equally well have stood in line 2, perhaps (in order the better to accommodate line 3) with the transference of ἦι from the end of line 1 to the beginning of line 2: but Meritt's proposal has been retained in the text.

FRAGMENT OF A DECREE

312. A fragment of a stele of Pentelic marble (I 3668), with the left side preserved but otherwise broken all around, discovered on March 7, 1936, in a Late Roman context north of the Civic Offices (I 11). The stone is much discolored.

H. 0.118 m.; W. 0.078 m.; Th. 0.043 m.
LH. 0.008 m.

Ed. B. D. Meritt, *Hesperia* 23, 1954, p. 242, no. 14, with photograph pl. 50. See also *SEG* XIV, 76.

ca. a. 130 *a.*   NON-ΣΤΟΙΧ. *ca.* 42

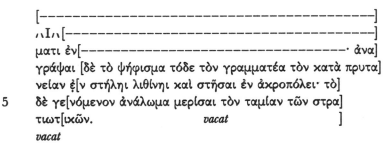

```
     [-----------------------------------------------]
     ‚ΛΙ‚[----------------------------------------------]
     ματι ἐν[------------------------------· ἀνα]
     γράψαι [δὲ τὸ ψήφισμα τόδε τὸν γραμματέα τὸν κατὰ πρυτα]
     νείαν ἐ[ν στήληι λιθίνηι καὶ στῆσαι ἐν ἀκροπόλει· τὸ]
5    δὲ γε[νόμενον ἀνάλωμα μερίσαι τὸν ταμίαν τῶν στρα]
     τιωτ[ικῶν.              vacat              ]
     vacat
```

This text, and the three next in sequence, were identified by S. V. Tracy as the work of the mason he named the "Cutter of *IG* II² 937": see *Attic Letter-Cutters*, pp. 173–180. *IG* II², 937 forms part of **310**, where the characteristics of this craftsman's style and the dates within which he seems to have been active are more fully considered. His activity appears to have been limited to a dozen years or so, from about 135 to 123/2, and, since there are no other means of dating this fragment and **313–315**, they have been given the date *ca.* 130 *a.* as a matter of convenience.

The fragment forms part of the conclusion of a decree, and the regular formulas for the inscribing and erection of the stele, and the payment for it, determine the length of the lines.

FRAGMENT OF A DECREE

313. A fragment of a stele of Pentelic marble (I 4811), broken on all sides, discovered on April 29, 1937, in a well of Early Byzantine date on the North Slope of the Akropolis (S 27:6).

H. 0.068 m.; W. 0.077 m.; Th. 0.046 m.
LH. 0.006–0.007 m.

Ed. B. D. Meritt, *Hesperia* 33, 1964, pp. 195–196, no. 46, with photograph pl. 33. See also *SEG* XXI, 490.

ca. a. 130 a.   NON-ΣTOIX. *ca.* 50(?)

['Eπὶ ————————ἄρχοντος ἐπὶ τ]ῆς [————————πρυτανείας ἧι]
[————————————ἐγρ]αμμάτε[υεν· ————————————]
[————· ἐκκλησία ἐν τῶι θεάτ]ρωι· ⱽ ἔδοξε[ν τῶι δήμωι· ————]
[————————————εἶπεν· ὑπὲρ] ὧν ἀπαγ[γέλλ————————————]
5 [————————————————]ρμε[————————————————]
[————————————————————————————————]

For the style of the lettering of this inscription, the craftsman to whom it has been attributed, and the date here assigned to it, see **312**.

The phrase in line 4 ὑπὲρ (or περὶ)] ὧν ἀπαγ[γέλλει (or ἀπαγ[γέλλουσιν) is familiar in the formulaic introductions to prytany decrees (e.g., of comparable date, *Agora* XV, 246, lines 6–7) and found in ephebic texts (*IG* II², 1039 = *SEG* XXII, 110, XXIX, 124, of 79/8 or 65/4 B.C.): the latter require a meeting of the boule rather than (as here) of the demos, and the customary formulas of prytany decrees fail to accommodate the surviving traces of line 5. The "report formula" is however also used in other contexts, e.g., in decrees honoring priestly officials, for which see **319** as well as *IG* II², 976 (*SEG* XVIII, 28), or in the honors decreed to an ἀγωνοθέτης in the archonship of Kallimedes (middle of the 3rd century; see *IG* II², 780 = *SEG* XXI, 382), or in those for a demarch (*IG* II², 949, of 165/4).

Line 3. The restorations are those of Meritt. For the location of the assembly see **167**, commentary on lines 6–7. Meritt assumed the decree to have been nonprobouleumatic; but at this period the evidence for decrees of this kind is wholly confined to prytany texts and (in two cases) to honors for epheboi. Cf. P. J. Rhodes, *Athenian Boule*, p. 266. Since this text appears to fall into neither category, the supplement must be open to doubt.

Line 5. Meritt regarded the traces as part of the *nomen demoticum* of the "reporter", ῾E]ρμε[ιος (Tυ]ρμε[ίδης would also have been possible), but the reporter's name is likely to have followed more directly upon the main verb in line 4, and the alternative that the report concerns the proper carrying-out of sacrifices, e.g., ῾E]ρμε[ῖ, has more to recommend it. However, the matter does not really admit of more than speculation, and no supplement has been entered into the text.

FRAGMENT OF A DECREE (IN HONOR OF A PRIESTLY OFFICIAL?)

314 (Pl. 30). A fragment of a stele of white marble (I 750), broken on all sides, discovered on June 2, 1933, in a disturbed area east of the Civic Offices (J 12).

H. 0.162 m.; W. 0.095 m.; Th. 0.047 m.
LH. 0.008 m.

Ed. S. V. Tracy, *Attic Letter-Cutters*, p. 176, no. 1, with photograph pl. 25. See also *SEG* XL, 118.

ca. a. 130 a.   NON-ΣTOIX.

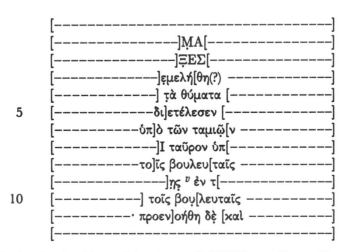

[————————————————————————————]
[————————————]ΜΑ[————————————]
[————————————]ΞΕΣ[————————————]
[————————————]εμελή[θη(?) ————————————]
[————————————] τὰ θύματα [————————————]
5 [————————————δι]ετέλεσεν [————————————]
[————————ὑπ]ὸ τῶν ταμιῶ[ν ————————————]
[————————————]Ι ταῦρον ὑπ[————————————]
[————————————το]ῖς βουλευ[ταῖς ————————————]
[————————————]ης ⱽ ἐν τ[————————————]
10 [————————————] τοῖς βου[λευταῖς ————————————]
[————————————· προεν]οήθη δὲ [καὶ ————————————]
[————————————————————————————]

Line 8. ἐν τῶι] βουλευ[τηρίωι Tracy. Line 9. ———]ΜΕΝΤ[——— Tracy. For the style of the lettering of this text, the craftsman whose work it is considered to have been, and the date assigned to it, see **312**. Lines 4 and

7 suggest that the honorand has carried out certain duties with regard to sacrifices, in which financial officials and the members of the boule (lines 6, 8, and 10) seem also to have been involved.

FRAGMENT OF A DECREE

315. A fragment of a stele of white marble (I 1912), which preserves the left side of the monument but is otherwise broken all around, discovered on May 4, 1934, in a late context south of the Tholos (G 12).

H. 0.13 m.; W. 0.064 m.; Th. 0.042 m.
LH. 0.008 m.

Ed. S. V. Tracy, *Attic Letter-Cutters*, p. 177, no. 2, with photograph pl. 26. See also *SEG* XL, 119.

ca. a. 130 *a.*   NON-ΣΤΟΙΧ.

```
      [----------------------------------]
      ΘΕ[--------------------------------]
      ΤΑΣ[-------------------------------]
      ΘΗΚ[------------------------- Πει]
      ραιεῖ [-------------------------- δ]
  5   δῆμος [--------------------------]
      τοῦ δή[μου --------------------]
      μα δι[---------------------------]
      ΝΕΕ[----------------------------]
      [----------------------------------]
```

Line 8. The third letter might be Γ or Π, but the upper horizontal extended to the left and, adorned with serifs, ought in that case to be visible: Tracy's suggestion of epsilon is the sole possibility.

For the style of the lettering, the craftsman to whom it has been attributed, and the date here assigned to the inscription, see **312**. Too little remains for any interpretation to be offered; but Tracy noted that the size of the lettering and of the vertical spacing are in accord with **314** and suggested that they might come from the same text.

CITIZENSHIP CONFERRED ON A MAN OF ALEXANDRIA

316. A fragment of a stele of white marble (I 3804 a), broken on all sides including, apparently, the back, discovered on March 17, 1936, at the surface north of the Odeion (M 8).

H. 0.09 m.; W. 0.14 m.; Th. 0.10 m.
LH. 0.007–0.008 m. (omicron 0.005 m.)

Ed. B. D. Meritt, *Hesperia* 23, 1954, pp. 241–242, no. 13, with photograph pl. 51; see also *SEG* XIV, 73: M. J. Osborne, *Naturalization* I, p. 239, D 121, *Naturalization* II, p. 198.

ca. a. 130 *a.*   NON-ΣΤΟΙΧ. *ca.* 46

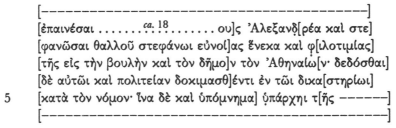

```
      [------------------------------------------------]
      [ἐπαινέσαι ....... ca. 18 ....... ου]ς Ἀλεξανδ[ρέα καὶ στε]
      [φανῶσαι θαλλοῦ στεφάνωι εὐνοί]ας ἕνεκα καὶ φ[ιλοτιμίας]
      [τῆς εἰς τὴν βουλὴν καὶ τὸν δῆμο]ν τὸν Ἀθηναίω[ν· δεδόσθαι]
      [δὲ αὐτῶι καὶ πολιτείαν δοκιμασθ]έντι ἐν τῶι δικα[στηρίωι]
  5   [κατὰ τὸν νόμον· ἵνα δὲ καὶ ὑπόμνημα] ὑπάρχηι τ[ῆς -------]
      [------------------------------------------------]
```

The position of the fragment in relation to the width of the stele is shown *exempli gratia* but allows the lines as restored to end, in nearly all instances, with a complete word. Osborne marked the text as "non-στοιχ. *ca.* 42–43"; but lines 2–4 contain, as restored, 46, 45, and 47 letters respectively, while line 5, inclusive of Osborne's suggestion for it (see below), will contain 44 letters. If ἐπαινέσαι be placed as shown, the names of the honorand and of his father will have been relatively long.

The lettering is distinguished both for its neatness and for its thoroughgoing use of apex or serif decoration, all "free ends" of strokes being so adorned. S. V. Tracy (*Attic Letter-Cutters*, p. 176) found that it resembled, but could not with assurance be claimed as, the work of the "Cutter of *IG* II² 973", for whom see **310**. It has been given here a date in keeping with that mason's period of activity, there being no other means of dating it. Meritt had originally expressed the date in more general terms: *"post med. saec. II a.".* Tracy studied the inscription briefly in *The Lettering of an Athenian Mason* (*Hesperia* Supplement XV), 1975, p. 10, with photograph pl. 3:a, rejecting it as part of the *oeuvre* of the "Cutter of *IG* II² 1028" (for whom see **326**), active during the last thirty years of the century: but the fact that the suggestion was made, even though dismissed, encouraged Osborne to a dating for the present text of "soon after 140 B.C.".

The restorations proposed by Meritt follow recognized phraseology and agree in suggesting an acceptable length of line. Sufficient of the decree remains to indicate honors for goodwill and services rendered (lines 2–3), with the formula for approval of a grant of citizenship in a severely truncated form (lines 3–5). Osborne pointed out that this is in fact the latest citizenship decree to have survived of a long series that began in the 5th century B.C., and its shortened form perhaps reflects the ultimate rarity of the procedure, replaced at this period by readier access to Athenian citizenship by way of the ephebate. He made it the sole example of Type IV of Formulation B in his categorization (*Naturalization* I, pp. 24, 195), containing the "statement clause" alone. See also A. S. Henry (*Honours*, pp. 88 and 115, notes 207–209), who drew attention to the break in the stele below line 5 and to the possibility that the missing text could have contained scrutiny and the enrollment provisions of the usual kind after the interruption of the "hortatory intention".

Line 2. The stephanos might have been of gold, since the qualifying phrase κατὰ τὸν νόμον was not necessarily to be expected at this period; see **310**, commentary on line 43. Henry (*Honours*, p. 59, note 111) observed that newly naturalized foreigners were normally offered gold crowns. But stephanoi of olive occur not infrequently in such contexts: see Henry, *op. cit.*, p. 39 and **276**, lines 13–14 with commentary. On the virtues for which the Alexandrian is commended see **224**, commentary on lines 34–36.

Line 5. Cf. **276**, lines 21–22; *IG* II², 891, line 17, 982, lines 15–16, 984, lines 21–22, etc. Lines 5–6. τῆ[ς πολιτο|γραφίας(?) ----] Osborne.

FRAGMENT OF AN HONORARY DECREE

317. A fragment of a stele of Hymettian marble (I 4609), with part of the original rough-picked back preserved, discovered on March 13, 1937, in a late context below what was formerly Akropolis Street, west of the Post-Herulian Wall (S 24–25 to T 24).

H. 0.125 m.; W. 0.127 m.; Th. 0.078 m.
LH. 0.007 m. (omicron and omega 0.004–0.006 m.).

Ed. B. D. Meritt, *Hesperia* 29, 1960, pp. 19–20, no. 25, with photograph pl. 6. See also *SEG* XIX, 104 and XXIV, 140, with further reference to J. Pečírka, *Formula*, pp. 133–134, where Meritt's text is reproduced.

ca. a. 130 *a.*   NON-ΣΤΟΙΧ. *ca.* 50

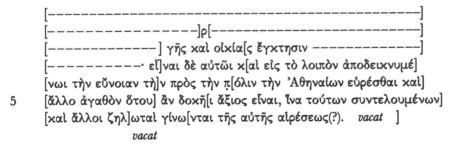

This is a battered and scrappy fragment, and the lettering on it is of the same general character and quality as that of **322**. The serifs are small and not heavily incised, nor are they universally applied. The writing is crowded and irregular. The crossbar of alpha is straight but sloping, the right *hasta* of pi short, the external strokes of sigma in one instance angled and in the other parallel. S. V. Tracy, *Attic Letter-Cutters*, p. 253, classed the hand as "unfamiliar" and gave it the date, here adopted, of *"ca. a.* 130 *a.".*

What survives of the text appears to represent the conclusion of an honorary decree granting to a foreign benefactor the privilege of ownership of land and property and the promise of further benefits in the future. For decrees awarding γῆς καὶ οἰκίας ἔγκτησις see Pečírka, *op. cit.* This text, if acceptably dated, is the latest in the series (*ibid.*, pp. 158–159). For other such decrees among the Agora *psephismata* of this collection see **131** and **164**.

Lines 2–3. Meritt restored

[– – – – – · εἶναι δὲ καὶ] γῆς καὶ οἰκία[ς ἔγκτησιν αὐτῶι αἰτησαμένωι]
[κατὰ τὸν νόμον· εἶ]ναι δὲ αὐτῶι κτλ.

which Pečírka regarded as hypothetical in the extreme. For the formula, see *IG* II², 907 (*SEG* XXIV, 138), lines 5–8, of the 2nd century B.C., in which that of lines 3–5 also appears, and Pečírka, *op. cit.*, p. 120. Lines 3–5. The phraseology conditions the estimated width of the stele. For its appearance in decrees of comparable date see *IG* II², 982, lines 13–15, 997, lines 3–4, 1006, line 96, 1028 (*SEG* XXI, 480, XXIV, 188), lines 102–103. Lines 5–6. For the phraseology of the formula of motivation cf. *IG* II², 1046, lines 30–32. On the expression ζηλωτὴς γενέσθαι see L. Robert, *Hellenica* XI/XII, 1960, p. 98, note 1 and **292**, commentary on lines 14–16.

THE ARCHONSHIP OF DIOTIMOS, 126/5 B.C.

The date of Diotimos' year of office is supported by three diverse but secure pieces of evidence, and since W. S. Ferguson's earliest study (*Athenian Secretaries*, pp. 46 and 57) there has been no doubt concerning its attribution. (1) *IG* II², 1713 is a fragment of an inscribed list of eponymous archons which was set out in five columns of names. The earliest name in the first column is that of Lykiskos, who is followed by Dionysios, Theodorides, and then Diotimos, with three further years below him before the column breaks off. Diotimos' place in sequence is thus assured. (2) *ID* 1923 (cf. 1923 *bis*) associates Diotimos as archon with the Delian gymnasiarch Theodosios, son of Jason, of Myrrhinoutta. Theodosios' place in the sequence of gymnasiarchs is assured by *ID* 2589, line 51. (3) Ferguson long ago observed (*op. cit.*, pp. 48–49) that the priests of Serapis on the island of Delos held office in rotation in the official order of the Athenian phylai to which they belonged and that this cycle corresponded with that of the γραμματεῖς at Athens. Cf. W. B. Dinsmoor, *Archons of Athens*, pp. 228–229. Thus a framework equal in significance to that of the secretary cycle may be constructed upon the basis of their inscribed list in series (*ID* 2610). Athenagoras of Melite (line 16 of the list; cf. *ID* 1047), of the phyle Kekropis (VIII), agrees with Diotimos' year in the secretary cycle, for Jason, Diotimos' successor in *IG* II², 1713, certainly had a γραμματεύς of the phyle Hippothontis (IX) and is securely dated on other grounds by a correspondence with the Roman consuls of 125, M. Plautius Hypsaeus and M. Fulvius Flaccus (B. D. Meritt, *TAPA* 95, 1964, p. 252; cf. H. B. Mattingly, *Historia* 20, 1971, p. 44).

See further *IG* II², iv, 1, pp. 20–21; *PA* 4375; Dinsmoor, *Archons of Athens*, pp. 223 and 273; Ferguson, *Athenian Tribal Cycles*, p. 31; Dinsmoor, *Athenian Archon List*, p. 198; W. K. Pritchett and Meritt, *Chronology*, p. xxxii; Meritt, *Hesperia* 26, 1957, p. 96, *Athenian Year*, p. 237, *TAPA* 95, 1964, p. 252; Mattingly, *loc. cit.*; Meritt, *Historia* 26, 1977, p. 185. Diotimos' name is probably to be restored in *IG* II², 1016, where line 1 reads ['Επι – – – –]μου ἄρχοντ[ος – – –]. If so, the name of the γραμματεύς of his year began Συ[– – – – – – – –], and that his deme may have been Aixone is suggested in the commentary to **319**.

The year 127/6 is known to have been intercalary, and it is therefore to be assumed that Diotimos' year was ordinary in the festival calendar. It was the third year in the seventeenth cycle of Meton, and in the Metonic arrangement year 3 was indeed scheduled as ordinary. There is however no direct information concerning either the festival or the prytany calendar of 126/5.

FRAGMENT OF A DECREE

318. A battered fragment of the upper part of a stele of Pentelic marble (I 6155), with the molding above the inscribed surface and part of the pediment preserved (although severely damaged), as well as the original rough-picked back, discovered on April 19, 1949, in the Late Roman wall that runs east of the Panathenaic Way, at the central part of the Stoa of Attalos (O 9). A wide taenia, equal in depth to the molding beneath it, forms the floor of the pediment. It is connected with the inscribed surface immediately above the first line of text by a sloping band, in replacement of or by a later reworking of the usual ovolo. There is no narrow band forming the lowest member of the molding.

H. 0.14 m.; W. 0.13 m.; Th. 0.08 m.
LH. *ca.* 0.008 m.

Ed. B. D. Meritt, *Hesperia* 33, 1964, p. 193, no. 42, with photograph pl. 32. See also *SEG* XXI, 471.

a. 126/5 *a.*   NON-ΣΤΟΙΧ.

[ʹΕπὶ Δ]ιοτίμου ἄρχον[τος ――――――――]
[―――――] *reliquiae incertae* [――――――――]
[――――――――――――――――――――――]

The letters are wide (especially mu, the external strokes of which are almost parallel), and "free ends" of strokes carry apices or serifs; alpha has a slightly curved crossbar; omicron and the loop of rho are well rounded. S. V. Tracy, *Attic Letter-Cutters*, p. 254, was not able to assign them to an identifiable mason, although he regarded what remains as in a general way comparable to the work (not represented in this collection) of the craftsman he named the "Cutter of *IG* II² 1009", active between 116/15 and 94/3 B.C. (*op. cit.*, pp. 197–200).

FRAGMENT OF A DECREE

319. A fragment from the upper central section of a flat-topped stele of Pentelic marble (I 3939), preserving the original back and top including the crowning moldings but broken elsewhere, discovered on March 30, 1936, in a Byzantine wall north of the Odeion (M 8). The inscribed surface has suffered random damage, most particularly between lines 9 and 13 of the text. The crowning molding consists of a broad taenia surmounting two ovolo moldings, the height of the upper molding being twice that of the lower.

H. 0.455 m.; W. 0.20 m.; Th. 0.185 m.
LH. 0.006 m.

Ed. B. D. Meritt, *Hesperia* 26, 1957, pp. 77–78, no. 23, with photograph pl. 15; see also *SEG* XVI, 102.

a. 126/5 *a.*(?)   NON-ΣΤΟΙΧ. *ca.* 45–53

```
     [ʹΕπὶ Διοτίμου(?) ἄρχοντος ἐπὶ τῆ]ς Πτολεμαιΐδος ε[. .⁶⁻⁷. . .]
     [πρυτανείας ἧι ――――――――]ς Αἰξωνεὺς ἐγραμμ[άτευεν· ²⁻³ ]
     [――――――――――――, τ]ετάρτηι καὶ εἰκοστ[ῆι τῆς πρυτα]
     [νείας· ἐκκλησία ἐν τῶι θεάτρωι ἡ μ]εταχθεῖσα ἐκ Πειρ[αιέως κατὰ τὸ]
  5  [ψήφισμα δ .ᶜᵃ·⁶.. εἶπεν· τῶν προέδ]ρων ἐπεψήφιζεν [. . . .ᶜᵃ·¹². . . .]
     [. . . . . . .ᶜᵃ·¹⁷. . . . . . . . καὶ συμπρόεδ]ροι·        vacat
     [    vacat   ἔδοξεν τεῖ βουλεῖ κ]αὶ τῶι δήμωι·        vacat
     [. . . . . . . . . . .ᶜᵃ·²⁷. . . . . . . . . . .] εἶπεν· ὑπὲρ ὧν [ἀπαγγέλλει ..]
     [. . . . . . . . . .ᶜᵃ·²⁷. . . . . . . . . . Λαμ]πτρέως θυγα[τ―――――]
 10  [――――――――――――――――]ιζο[.]ν[.]αν[―――――]
     [――――――――――――――――――――――]
     [――――――――――――――――]ων[―――――――]
     [――――――――――――――], ἀγαθεῖ τύ[χει δεδόχθαι τεῖ]
     [βουλεῖ τοὺς λαχόντας προέδρο]υς εἰς τὴ[ν ἐπιοῦσαν ἐκκλη]
 15  [σίαν χρηματίσαι περὶ τούτων, γν]ώμην [δὲ ξυμβάλλεσθαι]
     [τῆς βουλῆς εἰς τὸν δῆμον ὅτ]ι δοκε[ῖ τεῖ βουλεῖ ―――――]
     [――――――――――――]ενπ[――――――――]
     [――――――――――――]κα[――――――――]
     [――――――――――――――――――――――]
```

The battered state of the inscribed surface perhaps allows less than justice to be done to the character of the lettering, which appears poor but has a certain *panache*. Meritt regarded it as determining an approximate date within the second half of the 2nd century. Closer analysis allowed S. V. Tracy to include this inscription among those he attributed in *GRBS* 11, 1970, pp. 330–331, with photographs pls. 26–28, figs. 4–7, to the craftsman he then named "Mason 2", where he also assigned to him **320** as well as ten other texts; to this number he added one more in *GRBS* 14, 1973, p. 189. Four further additions accompanied Tracy's fuller review of the same mason's work in *Attic Letter-Cutters*, pp. 187–191, where he renamed him the "Cutter of Agora I 286" and included a photograph of the name piece, fig. 29, which does not repeat those from the same text in *GRBS* 11, *loc. cit.* The lettering is crowded, and serifs or apices are variously applied: the crossbar of alpha is curved in the text considered here, and the external strokes of mu and sigma are rarely parallel, their angles varying randomly. Delta is noticeably wide and clumsy in appearance. Inscriptions datable on external grounds indicate that this craftsman was active between 130/29 and 117/16 B.C.; for the possibility of prolonging his career at least to 114/13 see below.

The prescript is set out in the "perfect design", for which see **204** and **205**. The design is not represented among the Agora *psephismata* of this collection, except in this instance, after 148/7 (**305**); but the lack is coincidental, since it survives to the end of the century and beyond among prytany and ephebic texts: cf. A. S. Henry, *Prescripts*, p. 82.

The γραμματεύς of the year in which this decree was enacted belonged to the deme Aixone (Kekropis VIII), and this, on the present evidence concerning the career of the craftsman who inscribed it, permits consideration of no more than two archonships: that of Diotimos in 126/5 or that of the archon of 114/13, whose name in the genitive case was . . . . ratou (see *ID* 2208; Meritt, *Historia* 26, 1977, p. 186), if the lower date ascribed to the mason's activity be slightly extended. The archon's name in line 1 thus consisted of eight or nine letters, and this determines the position of the fragment relative to the total width of the stele, the latter being conditioned by the formulaic content of lines 3–5 and 13–16. The decree was probouleumatic (lines 7, 13–16); cf. P. J. Rhodes, *Athenian Boule*, p. 256.

Meritt suggested that the decree honored the daughter of an Athenian citizen of the deme Lamptrai who was serving as the priestess of an official cult, and on the analogy of *IG* II², 976 (*SEG* XVIII, 28), lines 2–3, he restored lines 8–10 as follows:

$$[\ldots\ldots\ldots\ldots\overset{ca.\ 27}{\ldots\ldots\ldots\ldots\ldots}] \ εἶπεν· \ ὑπὲρ \ ὧν \ [ἀπαγγέλλει \ ἡ]$$
$$[ἱέρεια \ τῆς \ \ldots\ldots\ldots\overset{ca.\ 18}{\ldots\ldots\ldots} \ Λαμ]πτρέως \ θυγά[τηρ \ ὑπὲρ \ τῶν \ ἱε]$$
$$10 \quad [ρῶν \ ὧν \ -------κτλ.]$$

The remains of line 9 do not however allow the parallel to be closely pressed, and the lacuna at the beginning of it is insufficient for the data it might be expected to contain. For the phraseology of line 8 cf. **313**, commentary on line 4.

Line 1. The length of line suggests ἑ[βδόμης or ἑ[νάτης rather than ἕ[κτης as the ordinal numeral of the prytany. Line 3. τ]ετάρτηι here, but ἀγαθεῖ in line 13. In lines 7, 13–14, and 16 Meritt restored τῆι βουλῆι, but the EI form was the more likely usage: cf. Henry, *CQ* n.s. 14, 1964, pp. 240–241. Lines 4–5. This is the third example of the removal of an assembly from the Peiraieus to the Theater of Dionysos on a motion put before it. For the others see *IG* II², 977 (*Agora* XV, 246), of 131/30, and *SEG* XVI, 88, which appears not to belong to 176/5 as previously thought (see **280**); cf. Henry, *Prescripts*, pp. 87–88, with note 67. For assemblies in the theater see **167**, commentary on lines 6–7. The assembly in the Peiraieus was, as regularly, held in this instance also in the final "third" of the prytany. See W. A. McDonald, *Political Meeting Places*, pp. 51–56 and **259**, commentary on line 4.

Line 13. ἀγαθεῖ τύχει. See **72**, commentary on lines 7–8.

FRAGMENT OF AN HONORARY DECREE (?)

320. A fragment of a stele of Pentelic marble (I 4547), broken on all sides, discovered on February 27, 1937, in a modern context west of the Post-Herulian Wall (R 25).

H. 0.112 m.; W. 0.091 m.; Th. 0.053 m.
LH. 0.009 m.

Ed. S. V. Tracy, *Hesperia* 39, 1970, p. 311, no. 4, with photograph pl. 76.

ca. a. 125 *a.*   NON-ΣTOIX.

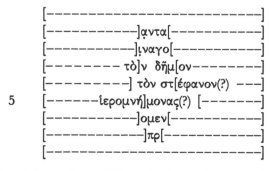

The suggestions in lines 4 and 5 are those of Tracy in the *editio princeps*. The meager remains of the text were sufficient for its attribution by him to the "Cutter of Agora I 286", for whose date, output, and characteristics see **319**.

THE ARCHONSHIP OF NIKODEMOS, 122/1 B.C.

Column I of *IG* II², 1713 (see p. 446 above on the archonship of Diotimos) ends with the name of the archon Demetrios (123/2 B.C.). The epheboi who completed their program in his archonship were honored in the customary way in the following year, and *IG* II², 1006 (*SEG* XIX, 108), recording the honors voted to them and their officials, was passed ἐπὶ Νικοδήμου ἄρχοντος. The name of the γραμματεύς of the year is Epigenes, son of Epigenes, of Oinoe, fully preserved in that same text, and his phyle (Attalis XII) confirms Nikodemos' year as 122/1 in respect of the secretary cycle. This may be further supported by the Delian list of priests of Serapis (*ID* 2610), where Diokles of the deme Tyrmeidai appears at line 20 in the position appropriate to Nikodemos' archonship. Nikodemos was thus firmly established in his year by W. S. Ferguson (*Athenian Secretaries*, pp. 46 and 57) and has not been in dispute since that time. See also *IG* II², iv, 1, pp. 20–21; *PA* 10858; W. B. Dinsmoor, *Archons of Athens*, pp. 223, 227–228, 232, 273; Ferguson, *Athenian Tribal Cycles*, p. 31; S. Dow, *Prytaneis*, p. 160, no. 93; Dinsmoor, *Athenian Archon List*, pp. 198–199; W. K. Pritchett and B. D. Meritt, *Chronology*, p. xxxiii; Pritchett and O. Neugebauer, *Calendars*, pp. 15 and 86; Meritt, *Hesperia* 26, 1957, p. 96, *Athenian Year*, p. 237, *TAPA* 95, 1964, p. 237; H. B. Mattingly, *Historia* 20, 1971, p. 44; Meritt, *Historia* 26, 1977, p. 186.

Other decrees of Nikodemos' year (apart from *IG* II², 1006 already mentioned) are represented by *IG* II², 1004 (*Agora* XV, 252) and 1005. The latter was enacted on the sixth day of an unknown month in an unidentified prytany. 1004 and 1006 were passed at the same assembly, held on Boedromion 8² κατ'ἄρχοντα = Boedromion 9 κατὰ θεόν = pryt. III, 9, the 68th day of the year. 122/1 was thus clearly a year ordinary in the festival calendar (cf. Pritchett and Neugebauer, *Calendars*, p. 86; Mattingly, *Historia* 20, 1971, p. 46), and it was scheduled as such in the Metonic calendar, in which it was the seventh year of the seventeenth cycle (cf. Meritt, *TAPA* 95, 1964, pp. 236–237). For the archon's intervention to retard the calendar see also Pritchett and Neugebauer, *Calendars*, p. 15; Pritchett, *Ancient Athenian Calendars on Stone*, p. 337; A. S. Henry, *Prescripts*, pp. 78–80 (the present text listed as no. 19 on p. 79). The retardation may have had some connection with the festival Boedromia, which took place on the 7th of the month (L. Deubner, *Attische Feste*, p. 202; J. D. Mikalson, *Sacred and Civil Calendar*, p. 51). **321** was passed in the month Maimakterion (line 3), and for reasons of space Meritt urged that there had been considerable interference with the calendar, producing a dual date with differing months. But this hypothesis must be considered doubtful (see below), and the variation κατ'ἄρχοντα, attested as of no more than a single day, is more economically to be postulated as (1) minimal in its dislocation and (2) rectified before the end of the month in which it occurred.

Of the succession of the phylai holding prytanizing office, Aigeis is certainly known as filling the third prytany, and in **321**, since as short a name as possible is likely to be required, V Oineis may be an appropriate suggestion.

FRAGMENT OF A DECREE

321. A fragment of the upper part of a pedimental stele of Pentelic marble (I 1594), with most of the left section of the pediment preserved, including the raking cornice and part of the central akroterion, but broken elsewhere, discovered on March 9, 1934, in a Hellenistic context in a cistern outside the Market Square to the southwest (F 15:2). Very little inscribed text is preserved in proportion to the bulk of the surviving stone. Beneath the taenia which forms the horizontal cornice of the pediment, a sharply turning ovolo descends to a narrower flat band, with abrupt apophyge to the inscribed surface.

H. 0.225 m.; W. 0.215 m.; Th. 0.115 m.

LH. 0.008–0.01 m.

Ed. B. D. Meritt, *Hesperia* 10, 1941, pp. 61–62, no. 26, with photograph. See also W. K. Pritchett and O. Neugebauer, *Calendars*, p. 87, with note 28 and (for a photograph) S. V. Tracy, *Attic Letter-Cutters*, p. 193, fig. 30.

a. 122/1 a., *pryt.* V.   NON-ΣΤΟΙΧ.

[’Επὶ Νικ]οδήμου ἄ[ρχοντος ἐπὶ τῆς ———————πέμπτης]
[πρυτανείας ἧι] ’Επιγένης ’Ε[πιγένου Οἰναῖος ἐγραμμάτευεν· ——————]
[...⁸⁻⁹... Μαιμα]κτηριῶ[νος ———————————————]
[—————————————————————————————]

The style of the lettering of this inscription, slight though the evidence is, is highly distinctive, as Tracy found when he made it the name piece of its mason, the "Cutter of Agora I 1594" (*op. cit.*, pp. 192–193). He identified only one other text (*Agora* XV, 262) as of the same workmanship, and since that is not independently to be dated the year of Nikodemos represents the sole means of describing the mason's floruit. In the present text, small serifs or apices are attached to the "free ends" of strokes; the external strokes of mu and sigma are parallel; the crossbar of alpha is apparently straight. There is slight curvature of the top horizontal stroke of epsilon and of the horizontals of gamma and pi; in the last-named letter the right *hasta* is equal in length to that on the left. Omega is full and well executed.

The central akroterion affords some guide to the likely position of the median vertical line of the stele. This appears to fall after the nu or tau of ἄ[ρχοντος in line 1, where the letters are widely spaced, and if the same generous spacing was maintained across the stele as on the surviving fragment, line 1 will have contained some 35–37 letters. In line 2, more crowded in composition, a line of *ca.* 53–55 letters may be proposed. Thus the suggestion of Pritchett and Neugebauer that the lines may have been shorter than envisaged in the *editio princeps* is not inapposite. Meritt's text gave 44 and 71 letters to lines 1 and 2, and read as follows:

['Επὶ Νικ]οδήμου ἄ[ρχοντος ἐπὶ τῆς . . . . *ca.* 11 . . . . πέμπτης]

[πρυτανείας ἧι 'Ε]πιγένης 'Ε[πιγένου Οἰναῖος ἐγραμμάτευεν· Πυανοψιῶνος . . . . *ca.* 13 . . . . .]

[κατὰ θεὸν δὲ Μαιμα]κτηριῶ[νος ———————————————————————————]

It is possible that in line 1 either the name or the ordinal numeral of the prytany was omitted: but surviving texts of this period show remarkable consistency in recording both name and numeral, and it is more probable that, in order to accommodate both, the lettering became more crowded in the second half of the line. Even so, the shortest available tribal name, Oineis, is to be preferred, and the resultant line of 41 letters is still, on the evidence of what survives in the first line, too long for comfort. Meritt's line 2 was, on the other hand, at least sixteen letters too long. It would perhaps be reasonable to suggest [ἐγραμμάτευεν· *vv* δήμου | ψηφίσματα· in lines 2–3, on the analogy of *IG* II², 978, and eliminate thereby the hypothesis of a double date even though intervention by the archon is evidenced for this year (see p. 449 above).

Line 2. The full name of the γραμματεύς is restored from *IG* II², 1006, line 2: see *PA* 4818. 'Επιγένης Οἰναῖος who was a βουλευτής from Attalis in 173/2 (*Agora* XV, 206, line 85; cf. *SEG* XVI, 91 and p. 398 above on the archonship of Alexis) may well have been the grandfather of the γραμματεύς.

FRAGMENT OF A DECREE CONCERNING WEIGHTS AND MEASURES

322 (Pl. 31). A fragment of a stele of bluish white marble (I 1250), broken on all sides (including, probably, the back), discovered on January 29, 1934, in a late wall northeast of the Tholos (H 11). The inscribed surface is much battered and pitted.

H. 0.192 m.; W. 0.21 m.; Th. 0.06 m.
LH. 0.005–0.006 m.

Ed. B. D. Meritt, *Hesperia* 7, 1938, pp. 127–131, no. 27, with photograph. See *SEG* XXIV, 147, with reference also to H. W. Pleket, *Epigraphica* I, 1964, pp. 22–27, no. 14. Cf. *Agora* III, p. 183, no. 605.

ca. a. 120 *a.*   NON-ΣΤΟΙΧ. *ca.* 60–73

[——]
[———————————καθισταμ]έ[νοις δημοσίοις μετ'ἀναγραφῆς πάντα τὰ μέτρα καὶ σταθμά· ἐὰν]
[δέ τι μὴ παραδῶσιν εἰσπ]ραττέσθωσα[ν ὑπὸ τῶν τεταγμένων ἐπ'αὐτοὺς κατὰ τὸ ψήφισμα, καὶ ἐάν]
[τινα ἀπολέσωσιν κατασκ]ευαζέσθωσαν ἀ[ντὶ τῶν ἀπολομένων ἕτερα τοιαῦτα· καταβαλλέ]
[σθωσαν δὲ καὶ χειρόγρ]αφον ἐν [τῶι] Μητρώωι [ὧν ἂν παραλάβωσι καὶ παραδῶσιν· ἐὰν δὲ τοῦ]
5 [το μὴ καταβάλλων]ται μὴ ἐ[ξέσ]τω αὐτοῖς ἐλ[ευθέραν λειτουργίαν θητωνεῖν· ἀνα]
[τιθέσθω δὲ καὶ εἰς ἀ]κ[ρ]ό[π]ολ[ιν ση]κώματα τοῦ [τε ἐμπορικοῦ ταλάντου καὶ δεκάμνου καὶ πεν]
[τάμνου καὶ δίμνου κ]αὶ μνᾶ[ς] καὶ ἡ[μι]μναίου καὶ ταρ[τημόρου καὶ χοὸς καὶ χοί]
[νικος· ἐὰν δέ τις ἁλί]σκη[ται κ]ακο[υρ]γῶν περὶ τὰ μέτ[ρα καὶ τὰ σταθμὰ τὰ κείμενα ἕν τε]
[τῆι Σκιάδι καὶ ἐν 'Ελ]ευσῖνι κ[α]ὶ ἐμ [Πε]ιραιεῖ καὶ ἐν ἀκ[ρ]ο[πόλει, ἐάν τε ἄρχων ἐάν τε ἰδιώ]
10 [της ἐάν τε δημόσιο]ς, ἔνοχος ἔστω τῶι νόμωι τῶι κειμ[ένωι περὶ τῆς τῶν κακούρ]
[γων ζημίας· ἐπιμελείσ[θω δὲ κ]αὶ ἡ βουλὴ ἡ ἐξ 'Αρήο[υ Πάγου καὶ τὸν κακουργοῦντά τι]
[περὶ ταῦτα κολαζέ]τω κατὰ τοὺς περὶ τῶν κακού[ργων κειμένους νόμους· *vvvv*]

[ἀναγράψαι δὲ τόδε τὸ] ψήφισμα εἰς στήλας λιθ[ίνας τὸν καθεσταμένον ἄνδρα]
[ἐπὶ τὴν κατασκευὴν τ]ῶν μέτρων καὶ σταθμ[ῶν, καὶ στῆσαι ἐν τοῖς οἴκοις ἐν οἷς]
15 [καὶ τὰ μέτρα καὶ τὰ σταθμ]ὰ κεῖται.   *vacat*
                                    vacat

This inscription is part of a copy of the decree represented in fuller form by *IG* II², 1013. Copies of the text were to be set up where the exemplars of the weights and measures were to be housed, *viz.*, on the Akropolis, in the Skias (Tholos), at the Peiraieus, and at Eleusis (lines 8–9; cf. *IG* II², 1013, lines 56–57, 60–62). *IG* II², 1013, copied by Fourmont and now lost, was evidently the copy erected on the Akropolis. The Agora fragment, which covers lines 49–62 of the *IG* text, does not form part of that monument, as the division of the lines differs from that recorded by Fourmont, and it presumably comes from the copy set up in the Tholos, near which it was discovered.

Meritt's dating for this text followed and confirmed that given to *IG* II², 1013 ("fin. s. II a.") and was expressed as "Late Second Century B.C." S. V. Tracy (*Attic Letter-Cutters*, p. 251) was not able to assign the lettering to an identifiable mason and classed it as "unfamiliar" but also as having some affinity with the style of the "Cutter of *IG* II² 1028", for whom see **326**. That craftsman's career appears to have spanned the last three decades of the century and suggests that on stylistic grounds Meritt's assessment was correct. Tracy's dating, for convenience adopted here, may imply greater precision than is warranted. As to the details of significant letters, the crossbar of alpha is straight but inclined to rise from left to right; the external strokes of mu and sigma are parallel; theta has a central dot, not a cross-stroke; and xi retains its central upright. Serifs or apices are attached to the "free ends" of strokes. In general the lettering appears variable and clumsy, but, with due allowance for its inadequacies, reflects the four-square monumentality which became characteristic of the style of the Roman period.

The text may be completed from *IG* II², 1013 (and conversely the latter may be checked from the Agora fragment; see Meritt, *loc. cit.*). In lines 61–62, *IG* II², 1013 has τῶν [μέτρων | καὶ τῶν στ]αθμῶν, which Meritt wished to correct from line 14 of the present text. But this need not be an error on the part of Fourmont. Inscribed copies of the same text frequently differed in points of detail. See Meritt, *Hesperia* 32, 1963, p. 30 with note 49, for further references, and cf. **172**. On *IG* II², 1013, see *SEG* XV, 106 and XXIV, 148; M. Rostovtzeff, *A Social and Economic History of the Hellenistic World*, 1941, pp. 1297, 1503; J. Day, *An Economic History of Athens under Roman Domination*, 1942, pp. 85–86; D. J. Geagan, *Athenian Constitution*, pp. 48–49. H. W. Pleket (*loc. cit.*) gives a full text revised in the light of the readings of the Agora copy, with further bibliographical references.

Line 4. For the note of what is received and deposited in the Metroon see *Agora* III, pp. 150–151 and 158, no. 503; for the deposition of such documents in the public archives see G. Klaffenbach, *Bemerkungen zum griechischen Urkundenwesen* (*SbAkadBerlin* 1960, 6).

FRAGMENT OF A DECREE

323. A fragment of a stele of Hymettian marble (I 2453), with the right side preserved; the stele is otherwise broken all around (unless the very roughly picked back be original). It was discovered on February 23, 1935, in a Byzantine context over the western part of the Odeion (L 10).

H. 0.11 m.; W. 0.123 m.; Th. 0.05 m.
LH. 0.006 m.

Ed. B. D. Meritt, *Hesperia* 37, 1968, pp. 273–274, no. 13, with photograph pl. 80. See also *SEG* XXV, 128.

ca. a. 120–110 *a.*   NON-ΣΤΟΙΧ. *ca.* 50

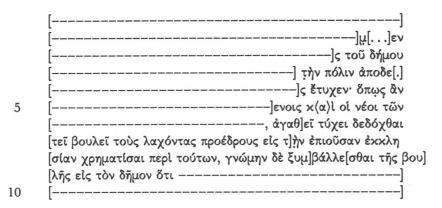

```
    [---------------------------------------------]
    [-------------------------------------]μ[...]εν
    [-------------------------------------]ς τοῦ δήμου
    [----------------------------------] τὴν πόλιν ἀποδε[.]
    [------------------------------------]ς ἔτυχεν· ὅπως ἂν
5   [-----------------------------------]ενοις κ⟨α⟩ὶ οἱ νέοι τῶν
    [------------------------------, ἀγαθ]εῖ τύχει δεδόχθαι
    [τεῖ βουλεῖ τοὺς λαχόντας προέδρους εἰς τ]ὴν ἐπιοῦσαν ἐκκλη
    [σίαν χρηματίσαι περὶ τούτων, γνώμην δὲ ξυμ]βάλλε[σθαι τῆς βου]
    [λῆς εἰς τὸν δῆμον ὅτι -----------------------------]
10  [-------------------------------------------]
```

The dating of this fragment depends entirely on its lettering, which is poor work, its strokes clumsily articulated and in places more scratched than engraved but dressed up with heavy serifs to give it some semblance of style. The crossbar of alpha is straight but is omitted altogether in line 5; the external strokes of mu are almost parallel, but those of sigma are well angled. The right *hasta* of pi is almost equal in length to that on the left (line 3), but in line 7 this letter appears to be represented by a gamma with an exaggerated serif. S. V. Tracy (*Attic Letter-Cutters*, p. 252) regarded this text as in a class by itself, labeling it "unique/school of [the Cutter of *IG* II²] 1028", by which he intended it to be understood that it showed marked idiosyncrasies but that the general style was reminiscent of the mason named (*op. cit.*, p. 238).

Meritt's dating ("*fin. saec.* II *a.*") is comfortably generalized but perhaps emphasizes too definitely the century's end: Tracy's "around 120 B.C." may imply overprecision (cf. **322**). The date given above, while a reasonable hypothesis, should be allowed latitude at the upper and especially the lower limit.

Line 4. Ὅπως ἄν suggests the formula of "hortatory intention" in an honorary decree, indicating the readiness of the demos to be demonstrably grateful for services rendered, in encouragement of other potential benefactors. Line 5.]ένοις Meritt: possibly ἐν οἷς. Line 6. ἀγαθεῖ τύχει. See **72**, lines 7–8. Lines 6–9. The decree was evidently probouleumatic: the restoration of the familiar phraseology provides the index to the approximate length of the lines of the text.

THE ARCHONSHIP OF DIONYSIOS "WHO SUCCEEDED PARAMONOS", 112/11 B.C.

The date of Dionysios' archonship, which is as certainly fixed as any in the entire archon list, is supported from a number of different directions. His year is equated in a text from Delphi with that of the Roman consuls of 112, M. Livius Drusus and L. Calpurnius Piso, in circumstances which require it to be 112/11 rather than 113/12 (*Fouilles de Delphes* III, ii, no. 70; *Syll.*³, 705; R. K. Sherk, *Roman Documents from the Greek East*, 1969, pp. 86–93, no. 15). Because he possessed a common name he is defined as ὁ μετὰ Παράμονον (*IG* II², 1012, lines 1–2; cf. **324** and p. 436 above). His γραμματεύς Lamios, son of Timouchos (*PA* 8986; cf. J. Pouilloux, *Forteresse*, p. 176), belonged to the deme Rhamnous (Aiantis X), and this places Dionysios in his correct position within the secretary cycle (*IG* II², 1012, lines 3–4). Finally, the cycle of the priests of Serapis on Delos, which runs parallel with that of the Athenian γραμματεῖς (see p. 446 above), shows Seleukos of Rhamnous (*PA* 12627; cf. Pouilloux, *op. cit.*, p. 179) as officiating in the appropriate year (*ID* 2610, line 33; cf. 2229, 2614, and commentary on 2060). This firm attribution has remained undisputed. See *IG* II², iv, 1, pp. 22–23; W. B. Dinsmoor, *Archons of Athens*, pp. 225, 228–229, 275–276; W. S. Ferguson, *Athenian Tribal Cycles*, p. 31; S. Dow, *Hesperia* 4, 1935, p. 78; Dinsmoor, *Athenian Archon List*, pp. 174–175, 200; W. K. Pritchett and B. D. Meritt, *Chronology*, p. xxxiv; Pritchett and O. Neugebauer, *Calendars*, p. 87; Meritt, *Athenian Year*, p. 238; H. B. Mattingly, *Historia* 20, 1971, pp. 44–45; Meritt, *Historia* 26, 1977, p. 186.

That the year was ordinary in the Athenian festival calendar is made clear by the calendric data of *IG* II², 1012, lines 4–6, where Gamelion 8 is the equivalent of pryt. VII, 8, and it figures as such in all discussions of the Athenian calendar. See especially Pritchett and Neugebauer, *Calendars*, p. 87. It was the seventeenth year of the seventeenth Metonic cycle, and thus was ordinary also in Meton's arrangement. Of the phylai in prytany, only VII Aiantis is known.

EUNIKOS HONORED BY THE CULT ORGANIZATION OF THE ΜΕΓΑΛΟΙ ΘΕΟΙ

324. A fragment of a stele of Pentelic marble (I 6282), with the left side and original rough-picked back preserved, as well as the spring of a molding above the inscribed surface, discovered on March 28, 1950, in a context of Late Roman date east of the Middle Stoa (P 12–13).

H. 0.145 m.; W. 0.185 m.; Th. 0.05 m.
LH. 0.006 m.

Ed. B. D. Meritt, *Hesperia* 30, 1961, p. 229, no. 28, with photograph pl. 41. See *SEG* XXI, 535, with reference also to J. and L. Robert, *REG* 75, 1962, p. 145, no. 107. The further study promised by L. Robert in the last-named context for *Hellenica* XIII appeared in Ἀρχ. Ἐφ., 1969, pp. 7–14, no. II (see also **325**).

a. 112/11 a.   NON-ΣΤΟΙΧ. ca. 39

[Ἀγαθῆι τύχηι· ἐπὶ] Διονυσίο[υ ἄρχοντος τοῦ μετὰ]
[Παράμονον], ἐ[ν] ὅ[ὲ] τῶι οἴκωι Ν[...ᶜᵃ·⁸... τοῦ Ἀπολ]
[λωνίου Ἀ]λεξανδρέως· Σκιρο[φοριῶνος εἰκάδι]·

[ἀγο]ρὰι κυρία ἐν τῶι οἴκωι· Ἀν[.....ᶜᵃ·¹³....· Ἀν]
5   τιοχεὺς εἶπεν· ἐπειδὴ Εὔνι[κος ......ᶜᵃ·¹⁵......]
[..]σιος νομοφυλακῶν ἐν τῶι ἐπ[ὶ Διονυσίου τοῦ μετὰ]
[Παρ]άμονον ἄρχοντος ἐνιαυτῶ[ι εὐσεβῶς καὶ φιλο]
[τίμ]ως διακείμενος τὰ πρὸς τοὺς [θεοὺς ..ᶜᵃ·⁸...]
[...] πάντας ἀνθρώπους φιλανθ[ρώπως ...ᶜᵃ·¹⁰...]
10   [..ᶜᵃ·⁶.]υ αὐτῶι τὴν ὑπά[ρχ]ουσα[ν ----------]
[..ᶜᵃ·⁹....]ης τὸ τῆς Η[----------------]
[..ᶜᵃ·¹¹.....]ΛΡ[----------------]
[------------------------]

The craftsman who inscribed this text evidently worked to the complete satisfaction of his clients, for he was entrusted in the next year with the execution of **325**. These two inscriptions, together with *SEG* XVIII, 27, constitute his whole surviving work as recognized by S. V. Tracy (*Attic Letter-Cutters*, pp. 201–203), who gave him a name drawn from **325** as the "Cutter of Agora I 6108", with a photograph of the name piece, fig. 33. His datable career is limited to the evidence of this text and **325**. His style is in general regular, and he uses serifs freely: his letters tend to be crowded laterally, though always clearly separated, with the result that the interlinear space, though narrow, is the more clearly emphasized. The above text is that of the *editio princeps*, with some additional under-dots to barely discernible letters at the edge of the stone.

This decree, like **325**, is the enactment of a cult association that describes its organization as an οἶκος and its presiding officer as the archon. In the latter case the simple title is unusual, although it was used by other groups, e.g., the γένη (see **307**), and the element ἀρχι-- generally appears in the designation of the chief official of such societies. See F. Poland, *Geschichte des griechischen Vereinswesens*, 1909, pp. 361–362; E. Ziebarth, *Das griechische Vereinswesen*, 1896, p. 149. From **325** (see commentary on lines 7–8) it is evident that the association was devoted to the worship of the Μεγάλοι Θεοί and, apparently, Aphrodite. Its assembly is described in the same terms as that of an Attic deme, as an agora, and this meeting of it is further identified as κυρία, a regular meeting prescribed by statute perhaps for certain obligatory business. The members of the group were evidently in whole or in part μέτοικοι. The archon, who held office in two consecutive years and is also the honorand of **325**, came from Alexandria, and the proposer of both decrees was a citizen of Antioch. For οἶκος as the designation of such an organization see Poland, *op. cit.*, p. 114; A. Wilhelm, *Beiträge zur griechischen Inschriftenkunde*, 1909, pp. 51–52; L. Robert, Ἀρχ. Ἐφ., pp. 8–9. As it happens, the other examples from other parts of the Greek world (all of imperial date) refer the organizations so designated to ναύκληροι, and it is very probable that in this Athenian instance also the association was one of merchants and shippers. The Μεγάλοι Θεοί and Aphrodite were especially concerned with sailors and the sea; see Robert, *op. cit.*, pp. 10–11 and **325**. For another example of an Athenian οἶκος see *IG* II², 2350 (Wilhelm, *loc. cit.*; L. Robert in *Collection Froehner*, 1936, pp. 5–6, no. 8), of the late 4th or early 3rd century; for οἶκοι τῶν ναυκλήρων cf. *SEG* XXXIII, 570, XXXV, 1717.

Line 1. Ἀγαθῆι τύχηι. See **72**, commentary on lines 7–8. Line 4. For the iota added to ἀγορά see *IG* II², 9181 and note; P. M. Fraser and T. Rönne, *Boeotian and West Greek Tombstones*, 1957, p. 170 and note 79; L. Threatte, *Grammar*, pp. 365–367. Line 6. νομοφυλακῶν. For the nomophylax as an official of such cult organizations see Poland, *op. cit.*, p. 404.

THE ARCHONSHIP OF SOSIKRATES, 111/10 B.C.

IG II², 1135, a treaty between the Cretan cities of Lyttos and Olous dated by the Athenian archon and recorded at Athens (cf. M. Guarducci, *Inscriptiones Creticae* I, pp. 187–189, no. 9; *SEG* XXXIII, 134, XXXVII, 93), links the archonship of Sosikrates (*PA* 13244) with a γραμματεύς from Krioa (Antiochis XI). This connection was not known to W. S. Ferguson at the time of his original study (*Athenian Secretaries*, p. 58), where Sosikrates was placed in 116/15 and 111/10 was left untenanted. But the secretary cycle, in demanding a year for a γραμματεύς from Antiochis, also left no other possible year unoccupied in the relevant period, and the attribution was immediately assured. Three ephebic dedications, *IG* II², 2983–2985, made in the archonships of Sosikrates, Agathokles, and Herakleides, all mention Neon of Aphidna as παιδοτρίβης, and this led Ferguson to date these archons in adjacent years. But subsequent evidence set the two latter archons in 106/5 and 104/3 respectively, and in any case Neon's function did not make consecutive years mandatory for the archons with whom he was associated (Ferguson, *Klio* 2, 1909, p. 324, note 5; W. B. Dinsmoor, *Archons of Athens*, p. 276, note 9). The Delian priest of Serapis this year was Demetrios of Anaphlystos (Antiochis XI), named in direct succession to the Seleukos of Rhamnous who functioned in the year of Dionysios (*ID* 2610, line 34; cf. 2070, 2125). **325** shows the same archon of the cult organization in office as in the year of Dionysios, and the same proposer also, and this helps to emphasize the close link between the two years.

Since the publication of *IG* II², 1135, Sosikrates' date has not been called into question, except by H. B. Mattingly, *Historia* 20, 1971, p. 45, where the query against the date is left unexplained. See *IG* II², iv, 1, pp. 22–23; Dinsmoor, *Archons of Athens*, pp. 223 and 276; Ferguson, *Athenian Tribal Cycles*, p. 31; Dinsmoor, *Athenian Archon List*, p. 200; W. K. Pritchett and B. D. Meritt, *Chronology*, p. xxxiv; Meritt, *Athenian Year*, p. 238, *Historia* 26, 1977, p. 186. No evidence exists concerning the character of the year in the Athenian festival calendar. On Meton's system it would have been intercalary, as the eighteenth year of the (seventeenth) cycle (*TAPA* 95, 1964, p. 236).

THE CULT ORGANIZATION OF THE ΜΕΓΑΛΟΙ ΘΕΟΙ HONORS ITS ARCHON

325. The upper left section of a pedimental stele of Pentelic marble (I 6108), broken below, to the right, and at the back but elsewhere intact, discovered on April 23, 1948, in a context of Late Roman date southwest of the Market Square (D 16). The pediment is preserved for almost half its total width. In its center is a sculptured rosette in relief, on either side of which two letters of line 1 were inscribed. The left and part of the central akroterion are preserved, raised in relief from a rougher background, the outer edge of which runs parallel with the raking cornice of the pediment. Below the horizontal cornice of the pediment is a plain fascia surmounting a straight-sided ovolo molding, which descends without interruption to the inscribed face of the stele.

H. 0.235 m.; W. 0.16 m.; Th. 0.054 m.
LH. 0.006 m. (line 1, 0.009 m.).

Ed. B. D. Meritt, *Hesperia* 30, 1961, pp. 229–230, no. 29, with photograph pl. 41; see *SEG* XXI, 536 and other references cited under **324**. A photograph also in S. V. Tracy, *Attic Letter-Cutters*, p. 202, fig. 33.

a. 111/10 *a.*   NON-ΣΤΟΙΧ. *ca.* 36–45

```
                          Θε      (rosa)      [οι].
               Ἐπὶ Σωσικράτου ἄρχοντος, ἐ[ν δὲ τῶι οἴκωι Ν. . ᶜᵃ·⁸. . . τοῦ]
               Ἀπολλωνίου Ἀλεξανδ[ρέως· Σκιροφοριῶνος εἱ]
               χάδι· ἀγορὰ χυρία ἐν τῶι οἴχ[ωι· Ἀν. . . . .ᶜᵃ·¹³. . . . . Ἀν]
          5    τιοχεὺς εἶπεν· ἐπειδὴ [Ν. . ᶜᵃ·⁸. . . Ἀπολλωνίου]
               Ἀλεξανδρεὺς εὐσεβῶς [διαχείμενος τὰ πρὸς τοὺς]
               θεοὺς ὑπομείνας ἱερεὺς [ἄρχειν ἐν τῶι οἴχωι(?) τῶν]
               Μεγάλων Θεῶν καὶ τῆς Ἀ[φροδίτης – – – – – – ἀνε]
               στράφη φιλοδόξως καὶ ἔθυ[σεν τὰς θυσίας ὑπέρ τε]
          10   [τῶ]ν καταχεχλειμένων ἐξ ο[– – – – – – – χαὶ – – – – – – – –]
               [.ᶜᵃ·⁶. .]ν[. . . ἀν]άγχηι συνε[– – – – – – – – – – – – – – – –]
               [. . .ᶜᵃ·¹⁰. . . .]ΟΓΟΥ[– – – – – – – – – – – – – – – – – – – – –]
               [– – – – – – – – – – – – – – – – – – – – – – – – – – – – – – –]
```

This inscription is the work of the mason who in the previous year had been engaged to inscribe **324**, and the characteristics of the lettering are identical: see Tracy, *op. cit.*, pp. 201–203. The text is that of Meritt, with a mark of hesitation added in line 7 (see below) and the name of the goddess supplied in line 8.

On the cult organization see the commentary on **324**. Lines 3–4. Meritt proposed the same date in both texts, as suited to the lacuna and, apparently, to a meeting fixed by the rules of the association. Here and elsewhere the material in the two texts serves to support restorations in each of them. Line 7. ὑπομείνας. For the phraseology see L. Robert (Ἀρχ. Ἐφ., 1969, p. 10), who also pointed out that it is unnecessary to supply an infinitive after it; he added that the other restorations in this line, as shown in the *editio princeps*, are also unnecessary and indeed unlikely. Line 8. For the Μεγάλοι Θεοί see B. Hemberg, *Die Kabiren*, 1950, and on their association with a goddess, especially pp. 288–290 and references there. The gods are to be identified with the twin gods of Samothrace, who were particularly the tutelary deities of seafarers. Robert (*op. cit.*, pp. 10–11) strongly urged that Aphrodite is the goddess to be associated with them. Cf. Hemberg, *op. cit.*, pp. 68–69, 85–86, 306. Line 9. φιλοδόξως. Cf. **292**, commentary on lines 14–16.

Line 10. Καταχεχλειμένων. From καταχλίνεσθαι, as argued by Robert (*op. cit.*, pp. 12–14), who discussed κατάχλισις, σύγχλινοι, and the officials κλίναρχοι and πρωτοκλίναρχοι in connection with cult organizations, adding abundant references and notes.

FRAGMENTS OF AN HONORARY DECREE (OR OF MORE THAN ONE DECREE)

326. Three fragments, two of which join, possibly but by no means certainly belonging to a single stele of Pentelic marble. Fragment *a* (I 3871 a), broken on all sides, was discovered on March 27, 1936, in a Late Roman context in a wall on Kolonos Agoraios (C 12). Fragment *b* (I 4026) preserves the right side of the stele but is broken elsewhere; it was discovered on April 18, 1936, in a Late Roman context west of the Stoa of Attalos (P 8). Fragment *c* (I 3871 b), which similarly preserves the right side of the stele but is broken elsewhere, joins the bottom of fragment *b* and was discovered on April 27, 1936, in the same area as, and in a context similar to, that fragment.

Measurements as joined: *a*: H. 0.165 m.; W. 0.125 m.; Th. 0.06 m.

b + *c*: H. 0.222 m.; W. 0.055 m.; Th. 0.07 m.

LH. 0.007 m.

Ed. S. V. Tracy, *Hesperia* 36, 1967, pp. 242–244, no. 51, with photographs pl. 61; see also *SEG* XXIV, 139 and J. and L. Robert, *REG* 81, 1968, p. 447, no. 192. Republished by Tracy as two separate decrees in *The Lettering of an Athenian Mason* (*Hesperia*, Supplement XV), 1975, pp. 70–71, nos. 10 and 11, with photographs pl. 31:c and d.

ex. saec. II *a.*   NON-ΣΤΟΙΧ.

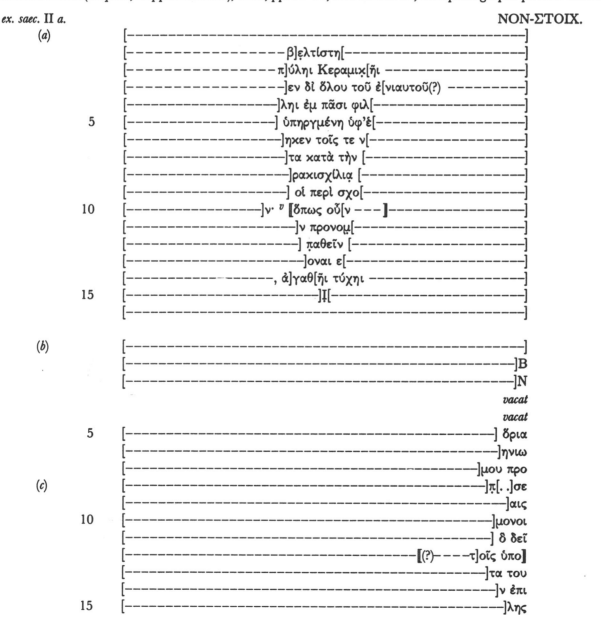

The lettering on these fragments is distinctive, and the work of the mason, a craftsman of evident verve and individuality, was identified by Tracy on a number of Attic inscriptions of the latter part of the 2nd century and the very beginning of the 1st, including parts of the great Pythais record *IG* II², 2336 (*SEG* XXXII, 218, with earlier references; see also p. 460 below) and of the Delphic record of the Pythais of 98/7 B.C. (Tracy, *The Lettering of an Athenian Mason*, pp. 48–68, no. 7). In this study, his list of inscriptions (nineteen, or, if **326** be two distinct texts, twenty) enlarged that originally observed by S. Dow, who was the first to discern the unity of the work of this mason among six different texts, including the Pythais record (*HarvThRev* 30, 1937, p. 209). For a full discussion see Tracy, *op. cit.*, where he is named the "Cutter of *IG* II² 1028"; cf. also *GRBS* 11, 1970, pp. 331–333, with photographs pls. 28, 29, figs. 8–10, where Tracy referred to him as "Mason 3", *GRBS* 14, 1973, pp. 189–190, and a later summation in *Attic Letter-Cutters*, pp. 181–186, with photograph of part of the name piece, fig. 28 (which does not repeat any illustration in *GRBS* 11). The range of dates of the texts attributed by Tracy to this one hand is considerable, from 131/30 (*IG* II², 1227, dated by the archon Epikles) to 98/7; but recognizable consistency of stylistic idiosyncrasy through thirty-four years is by no means an impossibility and has its evident parallels. Although both fragment *a* and the combined fragment *b* + *c* are the work of this mason, the nature of the marble does not compel the attribution of both sections to the same monument. On the other hand, it remains a possibility.

The present text differs from that of Tracy at no more than five points. *a*: line 2. So J. and L. Robert; −−]υληι κεραμιχ[−− Tracy. Elsewhere, Tracy read at line 7, −−−] τὰ κατὰ τὴν [−−−, line 8, −−−]ράκις χιλια [−−, line 11, −−]νᵛ πρὸ νομ[−−−. *c*: line 13. −−] τὰ τοῦ. Lines 10 and 14 of fragment *a* imply a decree in honor of some benefactor or official who has deserved well of the Athenians; cf. lines 3–4. But the text is too fragmentary for useful commentary.

a: line 10. For ὅπως οὖν without ἄν in the formula of "hortatory intention" see **285**, commentary on line 5. Line 14. The restoration assumes that this marks the beginning of the enactment formula; for the "Wunschformel" ἀγαθῆι τύχηι see **72**, commentary on lines 7–8.

FRAGMENT OF AN HONORARY DECREE

327. A fragment of a stele of Pentelic marble (I 6995), broken all around but with the original rough-picked back and part of the right side preserved, discovered on May 6, 1965, built into a pithos east of the Church of the Holy Apostles (S 16).

H. 0.19 m.; W. 0.16 m.; Th. 0.06 m.
LH. 0.004–0.005 m.

Ed. B. D. Meritt, *Hesperia* 36, 1967, pp. 64–65, no. 10, with photograph pl. 22. See also *SEG* XXIV, 137.

saec. II *a., p. post.*   NON-ΣΤΟΙΧ. *ca.* 50

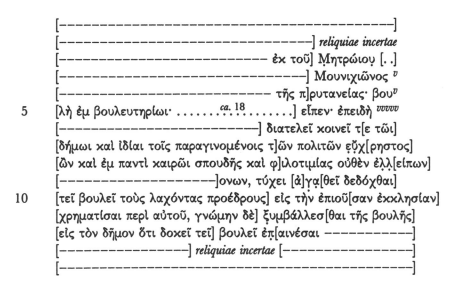

The dating depends upon the style of the writing. The lettering tends to be rather wide, with serifs, and the interlinear spacing is also wide, though irregularly so. Line 10 on the other hand has crowded lettering, and line 11 rises slightly to meet it. Alpha, delta, and lambda are "spread", with low serifs; the external strokes of mu and sigma are parallel. Beta, always difficult for a mason, is a clumsy and varied piece of work in all three occurrences of it. Rho is in the form Ρ, a feature which evidently influenced Meritt in his attribution of the fragment to the first half of the century, when parallels are to be found: but the general style is that of a later period, and S. V. Tracy (*Attic Letter-Cutters*, p. 255), while unable to assign it to an identifiable mason, with some justice regarded the end of the century as a more likely date. Moreover, he saw in it some affinity with the style of the craftsman he named the "Cutter of *IG* II² 1009", active as he judged between 116/15 and 94/3 (*op. cit.*, pp. 197–200). Nevertheless, a date for this text as early as *ca.* 140–130 is not precluded.

The restorations are those of the *editio princeps*, except that the lines are renumbered to take account of the uncertain traces at the top of the fragment, and line 9 has been deciphered to better effect.

Line 2. Ἐκ τοῦ] Μητρώιου. Meritt compared *IG* II², 1132, lines 2 and 40. Cf. *Agora* III, p. 158, nos. 504 and 507. On the Metroon see **221**, commentary on line 3 and **275**, commentary on line 17. Lines 4–5. βουλὴ ἐμ βουλευτηρίωι. See **260**, commentary on lines 5–6.

Lines 6–7. For the restoration Meritt compared *IG* II², 908 (*SEG* XVII, 31, XXIX, 118), line 2. See also **266**, lines 10–12. Line 7. εὔχ[ρηστος. Cf. **292**, lines 12–13. Line 8. The restoration was modeled by Meritt on *IG* II², 949, line 34. Line 9. – – –]ον ἐν τῶι Σ[.ᶜᵃˑ⁵. δεδόχθαι Meritt. τύχει ἀγαθεῖ. See **72**, commentary on lines 7–8. For the unusually reversed order of words cf. **187**, line 21. The formula reveals that this was a probouleumatic decree. Line 10. Meritt restored τῇ βουλῇ, but the unanimity of the EI form in the preserved part of the text indicates that it should be retained there also.

FRAGMENT OF A DECREE IN HONOR OF THARSYTAS OF APTERA IN CRETE AND OTHERS

328. A fragment of a stele of Pentelic marble (I 4377), with the left side and original rough-picked back preserved, discovered on December 18, 1936, in a wall of a modern house over the southern part of the Eleusinion (T–U 20).

H. 0.17 m.; W. 0.201 m.; Th. 0.14 m.

LH. (lines 1–3) 0.005 m., (lines 4–8) 0.007 m.

Ed. B. D. Meritt, *Hesperia* 29, 1960, p. 20, no. 26, with photograph pl. 6. See also *SEG* XIX, 105, with further reference to J. and L. Robert, *REG* 74, 1961, pp. 155–156, no. 264, especially concerning lines 6–8.

saec. II *a.*   NON-ΣΤΟΙΧ.

```
[--------------------------------]
[--------------------------καὶ στεφα]
[νῶ]σαι ἑκα[– – ον αὐτῶν ----------------]
[. .]ν τελεσθέντω[ν -----------------]
[. . .] τοὺς ἀγαθοὺς ἄνδρας.   vacat  [      vacat      ]
        (in corona oleaginea)
          Ἡ βουλή
5      ὁ δῆμος
         Θαρσύτ[αν]
     [Ὑπεράν[θους]]
       Ἀπτε[ραῖον].
```

The inscribed surface of the fragment is in major part taken up by the left section of a well-cut stephanos of olive leaves and berries in relief, delineated with some degree of naturalism. Line 3 of the text runs into, and is partly inscribed upon, the intertwined stems of the olive fronds. The lettering is plain but thin and scratchy in character. On one or two letters in the citation there is a hesitant attempt to add serifs to the "free ends" of the strokes. The upper angles of the triangular letters tend to be open: the external strokes of sigma are parallel in lines 1–3, oblique in line 6; those of mu are oblique in line 5; the right *hasta* of pi is short. On comparative grounds of the style of the writing it seems preferable to date the text to the earlier rather than the later part of the century. It is some corroboration of this preference that S. V. Tracy (*Attic Letter-Cutters*, p. 252), while unable to assign this piece of work to an identifiable mason, added the note that "the date *saec.* II *a.* is safe, but it might be earlier." But a date in the 3rd century does not seem likely.

Line 1. ἑκά[τερον Meritt. There is unlikely to have been room for more than two sculptured stephanoi, of the dimensions evident on this fragment, laterally on the stele. But there may have been a second row of them, and M. N. Tod (*SEG* XIX, 105) preferred to supply ἕκα[στον. Line 2. Meritt suggested that the honorands were connected with the Eleusinian Mysteries and the initiates of that cult. The location in which the fragment was found would support the suggestion. At the beginning of this line he therefore read [τῶ]ν τελεσθέντω[ν – – –. On the other hand, it is possible that συ]ντελεσθέντω[ν – – – is a variant for the customary συντελουμένων (cf. **317**), as part of the "hortatory intention", e.g., ἵνα τούτων| συ]ντελεσθέντω[ν ὁ δῆμος φαίνηται ἐν παντὶ καιρῶι τι|μῶν] τοὺς ἀγαθοὺς ἄνδρας: cf. *IG* II², 853 (*SEG* XXXIII, 132, with earlier references), lines 18–19.

Lines 6–8. Meritt preferred Θάρσυτ[ον] (*IG* II², 896, line 48) to Θαρσύτ[αν] (*IG* II², 6757) and restored the ethnic as Ἀπτε[ρέα]. J. and L. Robert pointed out that the honorand is, as Meritt observed, more likely to have come from Aptera in Crete than from the little-known town of the same name in Lykia, and that the ethnic of Cretan Aptera is regularly Ἀπτεραῖος. As a Cretan name, Θαρσύτας but not Θάρσυτος is to be expected; see M. Guarducci, *Inscriptiones Creticae* II, p. 7 and cf. *SEG* XXVIII, 750. The patronymic is written *in rasura*, perhaps as the result of an initial error on the part of the mason, the name being unfamiliar. For the name Hyperanthes see, e.g., *Inscriptiones Creticae* III, p. 71, no. 50, lines 2 (from Hierapytna), probably of the 2nd century B.C., and p. 153, no. 23, line 1 (from Praisos), of the 3rd century. It occurs also, though rarely, in Athens, e.g., *SEG* XXVIII, 148 (of 371/70 B.C.), line 24; cf. J. S. Traill, *Hesperia* 47, 1978, p. 92, with further references.

DECREE OF THE ORGEONES OF BENDIS

329. A fragment of a stele of Hymettian marble (I 4143), with the right side and original back preserved, discovered on May 14, 1936, in a Byzantine foundation wall in the northwest corner of the Market Square north of the railroad (G 4).

H. 0.12 m.; W. 0.24 m.; Th. 0.063 m.
LH. (lines 1–2) 0.007 (omicron)–0.009 m., (lines 3–6) 0.005 (omicron)–0.007 m.

Ed. B. D. Meritt, *Hesperia* 29, 1960, p. 21, no. 27, with photograph pl. 6; see also *SEG* XIX, 125. Cf. D. Behrend, *Attische Pachturkunden*, p. 99, no. 42 (a brief mention, without text); *Agora* XIX, L16.

saec. II/I a. NON-ΣΤΟΙΧ.

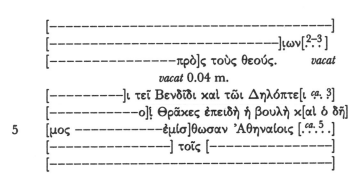

Both the upper and the lower sections of the text preserved on this fragment appear to have been inscribed by the same hand, but in lines 3–6 the letters are of smaller size and more closely packed. The writing is clumsy and second rate but makes every effort to be neat and stylish, with serifs attached to the "free ends" of most (though not all) strokes and an elegant curve given to the crossbar of alpha. Beta, upsilon, and omega are especially poor and variable in execution; the right *hasta* of pi is almost equal to that on the left; the external strokes of sigma are parallel (line 2) or almost so. The date depends upon the assessment of the lettering, which S. V. Tracy (*Attic Letter-Cutters*, p. 252) regarded as of *ca.* 100 B.C. Tracy was unable to assign the work to an identifiable mason but saw it as reflecting in its general style that of the "Cutter of *IG* II² 1028", for whom see **326**.

For an earlier decree from the Agora attributed to the orgeones of Bendis see **245**. On orgeones of this and other cults and their inscribed enactments see the commentary on **130** and especially the discussion by W. S. Ferguson, *HarvThRev* 37, 1944, pp. 61–140.

Line 1. Perhaps – – –]των. Line 3. Deloptes was a god particularly associated with Bendis; see *IG* II², 1324, lines 14–16 (a decree of these same orgeones perhaps of the early 2nd century B.C.; cf. Tracy, *Attic Letter-Cutters*, pp. 110–112); F. Cumont, *RE* IV, 1901, col. 2459, *s.v.* Deloptes; and Ferguson, *op. cit.*, pp. 96–107 (esp. p. 102).

DECREE OF A THIASOS OR SIMILAR ORGANIZATION

330 (Pl. 32). A fragment from the left side of a stele of Pentelic marble (I 456), with the left edge and original rough-picked back preserved, discovered on February 11, 1933, in a wall of a modern house south of the Library of Pantainos (Q–R 15).

H. 0.235 m.; W. 0.245 m.; Th. 0.10 m.
LH. 0.008 m.

Ed. B. D. Meritt, *Hesperia* 3, 1934, pp. 37–38, no. 25, with photograph. Discussion and tentative supplements for lines 6–9 and 11–12 by P. Roussel (*BCH* 58, 1934, pp. 93–96).

init. saec. I *a.*   NON-ΣΤΟΙΧ. *ca.* 51(?)

```
        [-----------------------------------------------]
        [.....ca. 12....]τω[-------------------------------]
        [..ca. 8...] αὑτοῦ καὶ [------------------------------]
        [..] εἰκόνα τε ἔνοπ[λον ---------------------- τοὺς]
        [θ]εοὺς καὶ ἐπίχυσιν [---------------- μηνὸς Ποσι]
  5     δεῶνος τῆι ἐνάτηι ἱ[σταμένου ---------------------]
        Φιλήμονος εὐεργετ[-----------------------------]
        [γ]ενομένης πᾶσιν [-----------------------------]
        καὶ προθυμότερος [-----------------------------]
        τῶν κοινῶν ἐπιμελε[---------------------- ἐνι]
  10    αυτοῦ(?) μετὰ τὴν τριετ[ίαν ---------------------]
        [ὑ]πομένοντος ταμίο[υ ----------------------------]
        [ἐ]νιαυτὸν καὶ [.3–4.]εα[------------------------]
        [τ]ὰ πάτρια· ᵛ συν[..4–5..]ν[--------------------]
        μηνὸς κατασ[ταθ(?)---------------------------]
  15    [.]αν ταμιευ[-----------------------------------]
        [...]την του[-----------------------------------]
        [-----------------------------------------------]
```

Line 3. Or εἰκόνα τε ἐν ὅπ[λωι –]. Lines 6–9 and 11–12. Roussel's suggestions, proposed *exempli gratia*, were as follows:

ἵνα ταύτης τῆς ἀναγγελίας]
[γ]ενομένης πᾶσιν [φανεροὶ ὦσιν οἱ θιασῶται χάριν ἀποδιδόντες]
καὶ προθυμότερος [αὐτὸς ἦι –––––––––––––––––––––––]
τῶν κοινῶν ἐπιμελε[ῖσθαι –––––––]

[ὑ]πομένοντος ταμίο[υ γενέσθαι εἰς τὸν ἐπὶ –––––– ἄρχοντος]
[ἐ]νιαυτόν κτλ.

The date of the inscription depends upon the style of the writing, which favors regular and laterally somewhat elongated letters with variable intervals between them. The inscribed surface has suffered wear, but the generally tidy effect of the lettering is preserved. Serifs are attached to some of but by no means all the "free ends" of strokes. Alpha has a broken crossbar; the external strokes of mu and sigma are parallel or almost so. S. V. Tracy (*Attic Letter-Cutters*, p. 250) was not able to recognize it as the work of an identifiable mason and listed it as "unfamiliar"; but he judged that it might postdate rather than antedate the capture of Athens by L. Cornelius Sulla in 86 B.C.

Meritt observed that the decree emanated from a club or religious organization and compared *IG* II², 1325, 1326, and 1338. Roussel's agreement is exemplified in his proposal for line 7 of the text. It seems likely that in this document a thiasos or similar group honored an official who had (*inter alia?*) held the office of treasurer. Cf. **230**, **231**, and *IG* II², 1278, 1292, 1317, 1323, 1327, 1329.

Line 3. εἰκὼν ἔνοπλος. On this phrase see G. Klaffenbach, *Philologus* 105, 1961, pp. 295–297 and *Philologus* 107, 1963, pp. 156–157; J. and L. Robert, *REG* 75, 1962, pp. 176–177, no. 203; *SEG* XXIV, 917, XXVIII, 1656. For such εἰχόνες in prytany and ephebic decrees see A. S. Henry, *Honours*, pp. 300–303. Line 4. Ἐπίχυσις was discussed by Roussel, *op. cit.*, pp. 94–95, with literary and epigraphical references. See also F. Sokolowski, *Lois sacrées*, pp. 230–233, no. 135, line 21 (*IG* XII, iii, 330). Lines 4–5. Posideon 9 was the day following the celebration of the Posidea (*IG* II², 1367, lines 16–20; L. Deubner, *Attische Feste*, pp. 214–215); but J. D. Mikalson (*Sacred and Civil Calendar*, p. 89) regarded this date as probable rather than certain.

Line 6. Philemon may be the benefactor himself, and if so, although the name is not unusual, he may perhaps be equated with *PA* 14269 or 14270. Lines 9–11. Cf. *IG* II², 1368, lines 146–147.

THE ARCHONSHIP OF PROKLES, 99/8 B.C.

Prokles' position in the list of archons relative to those in adjoining years has long been firmly established by the great record of the Athenian Pythais *IG* II², 2336, for which see S. V. Tracy, *I.G., II², 2336: Contributions of First Fruits for the Pythais* (*Beiträge zur Klassischen Philologie* 139), 1982, a publication that makes it unnecessary to assemble earlier references. What is proclaimed (line 2) as the first nine-year period of the new Athenian tribute to Delphic Apollo began in the archonship of Theokles (line 5). The archon in the sixth year of which details are given, Argeios, may be equated with the Roman consuls of 97 B.C., Cn. Cornelius Lentulus and P. Licinius Crassus, since the epimeletes of Delos in his year (*IG* II², 2336, lines 188–189, on Tracy's numeration) was the well-known Medeios, son of Medeios, of Peiraieus, whose term of office in the island is recorded in association with the consular date (*ID* 1745, 1757; cf. Tracy, *HSCP* 83, 1979, p. 223). Prokles as the archon of the fifth year in the Pythais record thus held office in 99/8 or 98/7, for the Roman consular year equated with his successor's tenure spread over the two archon years 98/7 and 97/6.

J. Kirchner believed that *IG* II², 1034 must belong to a Panathenaic year and was to be attributed to Prokles' archonship, thus placing him in 98/7 (*IG* II², iv, 1, p. 24, reflected in *IG* II², 1034 and 2336, as well as in *PA* 12211). But the secretary cycle requires that Prokles' year should have a γραμματεύς from Antiochis (XI), since the archonship of Medeios, in the third year of the Pythais record, is associated by *IG* II², 1028, lines 1–2 with a γραμματεύς from Eleusis (Hippothontis IX). In *IG* II², 1034, however, the demotic of the γραμματεύς is Κοθωκίδης (Oineis VII), and the archon's name in that context must therefore be supplied as Theokl]es rather than as Prokl]es. The coordination of these indications of the cycle with earlier years for which there is other evidence and for which the lists of the Delian gymnasiarchs and priests of Serapis provide additional confirmation of date places the beginning of the Pythais in 103/2, Medeios' archonship in 101/100, and Prokles' tenure of office therefore in 99/8. See Tracy, *I.G., II², 2336*, p. 129. W. B. Dinsmoor (*Archons of Athens*, pp. 240–244) demonstrated that it is unnecessary to attribute *IG* II², 1034 to a Panathenaic year and that no compelling argument can be based upon it.

Prokles' archonship was evaluated as of 99/8 by W. S. Ferguson in his earliest study (*Athenian Secretaries*, p. 58), and this dating has been accepted by all later commentators with the exception of Kirchner. See Dinsmoor, *op. cit.*, pp. 240–241, 280–281; *ID* 1711, in comm., 1619, 1886, 2570; Ferguson, *Athenian Tribal Cycles*, p. 32; Dinsmoor, *Athenian Archon List*, pp. 203–204; S. Dow, *HSCP* 51, 1940, pp. 121, 123; B. D. Meritt, *Athenian Year*, p. 238, *Historia* 26, 1977, p. 187.

No further details of the year of Prokles, or of Prokles himself, are known. **331** does not add to them.

FRAGMENT OF A DECREE

331. The upper left section of a pedimental stele of Pentelic marble (I 6885), broken below and to the right but with the major portion of the pediment preserved, including a round shield in relief in the center of the pedimental field, discovered on May 9, 1959, in a late context in the area of the Eleusinion (U 21). A broad taenia defines the raking and horizontal cornices of the pediment; below the horizontal cornice, a ponderous ovolo descends to a narrower flat band, with sharp apophyge to the inscribed surface. The inscribed surface itself has flaked off in thin layers, and despite the considerable superficial area which survives much of the inscription on it is in fact lost.

H. 0.31 m.; W. 0.30 m.; Th. 0.08 m.
LH. 0.008 m.

Ed. B. D. Meritt, *Hesperia* 32, 1963, pp. 23–24, no. 24, with photograph pl. 6; see also *SEG* XXI, 487. Text quoted by A. S. Henry, *Prescripts*, p. 90.

a. 99/8 a.   NON-ΣTOIX.

```
        [Θ]        ε         [o         ι].
      Ἀγαθῆ[ι τύ]χη[ι· ἐ]πὶ Πρ[οκλέους ἄρχοντος· ..6–7...]
      [.]ιῶνο[ς ὀ]γδό[ηι μ]ετ'ε[ἰκάδας· βουλὴ ἐν τῶι Ἐλευ]
      [σ]ινίωι· E[..]υ[.]ν[...]λα[------------------]
   5  [..]OI^‾[.]‾Σ[....]Σ[------------------]
      [------------------------------------]
```

The lettering (insofar as it is clearly to be seen) is plain but with enlargement of the "free ends" of strokes in some places. The crossbar of alpha is apparently broken; in pi the right *hasta* is short, and the horizontal stroke overlaps both *hastae*. The aspect of the monument and the style of writing alike suggest a date in the late 2nd or early 1st century B.C., and indeed S. V. Tracy was able to add it to eight other texts inscribed wholly or in part, as he judged, by the mason he named the "Cutter of *FD* [*Fouilles de Delphes*] III, 2, no. 5": see *Attic Letter-Cutters*, pp. 212–215, with further references and photograph of part of the name piece, fig. 37. Work attributed to him that may be independently dated shows him as active between 106/5 and 96/5, a decade into which the present text neatly fits: for Prokles is the only known archon of the period whose name can be accommodated to the remains of line 2, and the text may with little hesitation be assigned to his year.

Lines 2–4. The prescript is in an unusual form, and in the breakdown of hitherto regular formulas it may constitute an additional confirmation of date. Cf. Henry, *Prescripts*, p. 82. Ἀγαθῆι τύχηι in this position is to be found also ʼ ι *IC* II², 1011, lines 1, 31, 63, 73 (106/5 B.C.) and 1028, lines 1 and 66 (101/100 B.C.). There is no reference to ϑhe γραμματεύς or apparently to the phyle in prytany, the prytany date, or the chairman of the proedroi. This led Henry to suggest (*op. cit.*, pp. 84, 90) either that the inscription had been put up at private expense or (as envisaged above) that traditional forms were now being disregarded: "In other words, we may have a reflection of the dwindling significance of, and lack of care and interest in, the resolutions of the Athenian body politic."

Lines 2–3. Βοηδρο|μ|ιῶνο[ς Meritt, for whose further argument from the restoration see below. However, the spacing of the letters is too variable for other months to be excluded, and the position of iota in line 3 relative to the first alpha in the line above it makes it doubtful if so wide a letter as mu preceded it. It is therefore inadvisable to use it for evidential purposes.

Lines 3–4. Βουλὴ ἐν τῶι Ἐλευσινίωι. U. Koehler's restoration of the phrase in *IG* II², 794, line 4, dated to 216/15, adducing Andokides 1.111, was rejected by J. Kirchner but accepted by S. Dow (*HSCP* 48, 1937, p. 108). However, such acceptance involves "forward count" in the last third of the month, an evaluation of Athenian practice now rejected; the date would in fact fall on Boedromion 26 or 27, too late for association with the celebration of the Mysteries. The law of Solon quoted by Andokides prescribed a meeting of the boule in the Eleusinion on the day after this was concluded, i.e., on Boedromion 23. More relevant is the meeting of the boule transferred to the Eleusinion from the Bouleuterion as recorded in *IG* II², 848 (*Agora* XV, 129), lines 30–31 (212/11 B.C.?) and referred to by Henry, *Prescripts*, p. 85 (cf. Meritt, *Mnemosyne*, ser. 4, 30, 1977, pp. 237–238, *ZPE* 35, 1979, pp. 149–151); see also *Agora* III, p. 79, nos. 211 and 212. Meritt adduced this text as evidence of such a meeting on Boedromion 23, the date being expressed as ἑβδόμη μετ'εἰκάδας, and the month therefore being hollow. In the present inscription the same date was expressed as ὀγδόη μετ'εἰκάδας and the month was full; in *IG* II², 1072 the date was equally ὀγδόη μετ'εἰκάδας, but there it refers to the last day of the Mysteries, Boedromion 22, and in that case the month was hollow. Cf. *SEG* XXIX, 123. Taken together, this served to confirm that the day omitted in a hollow month was ἐνάτη μετ'εἰκάδας. The conclusion is undoubtedly correct; cf. A. G. Woodhead, *Study of Greek Inscriptions*, p. 121. It was disputed by W. K. Pritchett (*ZPE* 41, 1981, pp. 146–147; cf. *SEG* XXXI, 105), who was nevertheless justified in doubting the validity of the support Meritt had claimed from this fragmentary text (see on lines 2–3) even though Meritt's general thesis stands. On the dates of the Mysteries see G. E. Mylonas, *Eleusis*, 1961, pp. 252–279; J. D. Mikalson, *Sacred and Civil Calendar*, pp. 60–61, 65 (see Meritt, *ZPE* 35, 1979, p. 148).

FRAGMENT OF A DECREE IN HONOR OF A GYMNASIARCH(?)

332. A small fragment of a stele of Pentelic marble (I 4875), broken all around, discovered on May 19, 1937, in a Late Roman context in the Classical floor southeast of the Propylon (H 11).

H. 0.55 m.; W. 0.215 m.; Th. 0.065 m.
LH. 0.006 m.

Ed. B. D. Meritt, *Hesperia* 29, 1960, p. 15, no. 19, with photograph pl. 5. See also *SEG* XIX, 95.

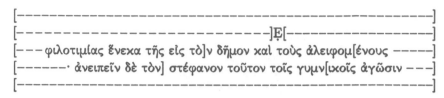

[---]
[--------------------------------]Ε[------------------]
[--- φιλοτιμίας ἕνεκα τῆς εἰς τὸ]ν δῆμον καὶ τοὺς ἀλειφομ[ένους -----]
[-------· ἀνειπεῖν δὲ τὸν] στέφανον τοῦτον τοῖς γυμν[ικοῖς ἀγῶσιν ---]
[---]

    The plain style of the lettering of this fragment doubtless induced Meritt to give it (without explanation) a date of "*init. saec.* II *a.*" in the *editio princeps*, even though as a guide to the restorations he cited two texts of the later part of the century. S. V. Tracy (*Attic Letter-Cutters*, pp. 220–221, 264) found that it was to be considered the work of an assistant to the master mason of the record of the Pythais of 98/7 inscribed on the wall of the Athenian Treasury at Delphi, for part of which he was responsible. In naming him the "Cutter of *FD* [*Fouilles de Delphes*] III, 2, no. 26, lines 1–24(I)" Tracy noted his resemblance to the "Cutter of *FD* III, 2, no. 5", for whom see **331**, and attributed to him one further text and part of another in addition to the Pythais record and the present fragment. The Pythais represents the sole means of dating his career. Of particular note in this fragment are the alpha with sharply broken crossbar and the phi in which the oval has become a figure eight on its side, or the mathematical symbol of infinity.
    What survives of the contents of the decree suggested to Meritt that the inscription recorded honors voted to a gymnasiarch, and he compared *IG* II², 1227, lines 4–7 and 29–32. The γυμνικοὶ ἀγῶνες are apparently not specified. It may perhaps be suggested that, like *IG* II², 1227, this is not a decree of the boule and demos, and that the δῆμος, the ἀλειφόμενοι, and the ἀγῶνες all have a more local reference. For a deme gymnasium (at Kephisia) cf. E. Vanderpool, Δελτ. 24, Α', 1969 [1971], pp. 6–7: for deme gymnasiarchs cf. D. Whitehead, *The Demes of Attica, 508/7–ca. 250 B.C.*, 1986, pp. 152, 224–225.

APPENDIX: MATERIAL DISCOVERED SINCE 1967

332A. Decree in honor of – – – stratos of Phlya, dated by the name of the archon (Eupolemos) to 185/4 B.C. Two joining fragments (I 7197 and I 7199) of a stele of Hymettian marble, which as joined preserve the width of the monument, were discovered on July 16, 1970, in a Late Roman context along the Panthenaic Way (J 6). They proved to form the main section of the decree of which *IG* II², 898 (which makes no direct join with them) contains part of the prescript. The whole text was edited by C. Habicht, *Hesperia* 56, 1987, pp. 63–71, with photograph of the Agora fragments, pl. 11. See also *SEG* XXXVII, 92, XXXVIII, 103. S. V. Tracy (*Attic Letter-Cutters*, p. 115) identified this inscription as the work of the "Cutter of *IG* II² 897", for whose style and career see **270**.

332B. Fragment of the prescript of a decree (I 7226), broken all around, discovered on March 29, 1971, in a marble pile in the area H–I 4–5. M. B. Walbank edited it, *Hesperia* 51, 1982, p. 56, no. 12, with photograph pl. 22 (see also *SEG* XXXII, 124) and dated it to the end of the 3rd century B.C. S. V. Tracy (*Attic Letter-Cutters*, p. 115) regarded it as another of the works of the "Cutter of *IG* II² 897" (see above), whose datable career spanned the decade 189/8–178/7, and he preferred a dating *ca.* 185 in keeping with this. The assembly mentioned in this fragment was held in the theater; the decree was probouleumatic, and it contained a "minute heading" (see **258**, commentary on line 2): but that is the limit of its information.

332C. Decree in honor of magistrates ἐπὶ τὰς προσόδους. A large fragment of a stele of gray marble (I 7496), preserving both sides and the original back of the monument, discovered in July 1975 in a modern wall in area R 13. It proved to be the main part of the text of which *IG* II², 1707, from lower down the stele, provides part of the list of names of the honorands. Both fragments were edited by S. V. Tracy, *Hesperia* 53, 1984, pp. 370–374, no. 3, with photograph of the Agora fragment, pl. 71. See also *SEG* XXXIV, 94, XXXIX, 137. The prescript dates the decree to the archonship of Hippias (181/80), on which see pp. 383–384 above. In *REG* 100, 1987, p. 256, P. Gauthier doubted the association of the fragments and suggested restorations. Tracy (*Attic Letter-Cutters*, p. 122) ascribed the stele to the "Cutter of Agora I 6765", for whose date and characteristics see **275**.

332D. Decree in honor of King Antiochos IV Epiphanes. The upper left corner of a pedimental stele of white marble (I 7453), preserving part of the pediment (with akroterion chipped away), the left side, and perhaps the original back of the monument, discovered on May 10, 1973, in a modern wall in area T 14. The date (178/7 B.C.) is provided by the name of the archon in the prescript, Philon "who succeeded Menedemos", for whom see B. D. Meritt, *Historia* 26, 1977, p. 181 and C. Habicht, *Studien*, pp. 168–170 and 177. The text was edited by S. V. Tracy, *Hesperia* 51, 1982, pp. 60–62, no. 3, with photograph pl. 24. See also *SEG* XXXII, 131. The decree was probouleumatic and was set out in the "perfect design". Tracy later (*Attic Letter-Cutters*, p. 115) identified this as yet another product of the workshop of the "Cutter of *IG* II² 897" (see **332B**), and it represents his latest datable work. For later suggestions concerning the text see D. Knoepfler, *Gnomon* 60, 1988, p. 266, citing J. and L. Robert (see *SEG* XXXVI, 173), and Habicht, *Chiron* 19, 1989, p. 13, note 33 (see *SEG* XXXIX, 138).

332E. Fragment of an honorary decree. A small fragment of a stele of gray marble (I 7235), broken all around, discovered on March 22, 1971, in a modern fill in area Q 21. It contains the remnants of twelve lines of text, the widest of these showing eleven letters: a stephanos is involved, and there may be mention of a πρεσβευτής. The text was edited by S. V. Tracy, *Hesperia* 51, 1982, p. 62, no. 4, with photograph pl. 23. See also *SEG* XXXII, 133. The date, which Tracy gave as "*ca. a.* 175 *a.*", is derived solely from the identification by him of the mason who inscribed the stele as the "Cutter of Agora I 247", for whose long career and prolific output see **264**.

332F. The repair and restoration of a sanctuary. For I 7492, discovered on August 13, 1974, see **296**, fragment *i*.

332G. Fragment of a decree granting citizenship. A long, narrow fragment of a stele of white marble (I 7421), broken all around save for the original rough-picked back, discovered in June 1972 in a marble pile in the general area designated BΓ. It preserves the remains of eighteen lines of text, none more than ten letters in width. The decree was probouleumatic; the honorand's name might be Dion, and his patronymic was certainly Peithagoras. Also surviving are elements of the "hortatory intention", the resolution to award a stephanos (presumably of olive), and the record of the honorand's virtues, together with the further provision for *dokimasia* and enrollment. The text was edited by S. V. Tracy, *Hesperia* 48, 1979, pp. 178–179, no. 2, with photograph pl. 60 (see also *SEG* XXIX, 121), and he identified it as the work of the "Cutter of Agora I 6006", active between 169/8 and 135/4, for whom see **296**. The date is shown in the *editio princeps* as *ca. a.* 140 *a.* but could fall anywhere within the span of the mason's career.

Tracy's text was republished by M. J. Osborne (*Naturalization* I, p. 225, D 109, *Naturalization* II, p. 194), who gave the date as "148/7–135/4" and made a correction in the restoration of line 13, the need for which was observed also by A. S. Henry, *Honours*, p. 113, note 189 (see also *SEG* XXXIII, 133). The decree belongs to Type III of Osborne's categorization of citizenship decrees of Formulation B (*Naturalization* I, p. 24; see **239** and references there).

SECTION 5

ATHENS IN THE ROMAN EMPIRE
86 B.C.–A.D. 203
(333–342)

SECTION 5

ATHENS IN THE ROMAN EMPIRE

86 B.C.–A.D. 203: **333–342**

The length of the final section of this volume speaks for itself. Ten decrees, whether of the boule and demos, the boule alone, or the Council of the Areopagos, span nearly three hundred years of Athenian history. (Agora I 6173, a decree of the boule, for which see B. D. Meritt, *Hesperia* 33, 1964, pp. 199–200, no. 31, with photograph pl. 33, and *SEG* XXI, 499 may offer an eleventh, but it is more likely to represent the introduction to a prytany decree than an honorary enactment of the old-fashioned type.)

In post-Sullan Athens the boule and demos retained certain areas of competence, for which see particularly D. J. Geagan, *Athenian Constitution*, pp. 62–91 (esp. pp. 83–90). But the inscriptional evidence for decrees of the character familiar in earlier centuries is thin. Prytany texts of a new kind, for which see *Agora* XV, pp. 16–17, and honors for epheboi which rapidly become *catalogi* erected by and for the epheboi themselves, form the major part of the epigraphical legacy of this period, and the Agora excavations have made a significant contribution to it. By contrast with the ten decrees treated here, the record of *Agora* XV comprises 191 texts of the same period.

Among the ten, one early *nomos* (**333**), dealing with a very particular set of circumstances, seems to be as it were a holdover from earlier times; and **335** shows a concern for Lemnos which has a long history. For the rest, the honoring of the imperial house or of a substantial benefactor alone seems to have called for old-style treatment, so old style, in one case, as to reemploy the stoichedon order for the inscribing of the text. But archaistic echoes of this kind sound a false note which serves perhaps only to emphasize that this was a new world in which traditional forms were no more than a veneer cloaking fundamental social and constitutional change. Moreover, the very quality and character of the lettering and workmanship of the imperial texts is a further reflection of a new age, as if art, and not meaningful business, were now the dominant consideration.

DECREE CONCERNED WITH CONSTITUTIONAL PROVISIONS

333. Three fragments of a stele of Pentelic marble, two of which join to make up fragment *a* (I 2351) and preserve part of the left side of the monument, although it is broken elsewhere: this united fragment was discovered on January 31, 1935, in a modern context west of the East Stoa (O 13). Fragment *b* (I 1619) is a small chip preserving no more than sixteen discernible letters and broken on all sides; it was discovered on March 19, 1934, in a late context over the south porch of the New Bouleuterion (F 10).

a: H. 0.37 m.; W. 0.25 m.; Th. 0.08 m.

b: H. 0.09 m.; W. 0.05 m.; Th. 0.08 m.

LH. *ca.* 0.01 m.

Ed. D. J. Geagan, *Hesperia* 40, 1971, pp. 101–108, no. 3, with photograph pl. 16. See also *SEG* XXVI, 120. Revised restorations of lines 7–24 and new readings in lines 13–14 by J. H. Oliver, *JHS* 100, 1980, pp. 199–201; see also *SEG* XXX, 80.

paullo ante, vel non multum post, a. 86 a.   NON-ΣΤΟΙΧ. *ca.* 46–50

   (a)   ['Αγαθῆι τύχηι τῆς βουλῆς καὶ τοῦ δήμου τοῦ 'Αθηναίων, ἐπὶ ———]
          [ἄρχ]οντ[ος ἐπὶ τῆς —————— πρυτανείας ἧι ————————— Δημη]
          [τρ]ίου 'Ανα[—————— ἐγραμμάτευεν· ————————————],
          [ἕ]κτηι καὶ εἰκ[οστῆι τῆς πρυτανείας· ἐκκλησία ἐν ———————]
  5   ἡ μεταχθεῖσα [ἐκ —————————· τῶν προέδρων ἐπεψήφιζεν]

Νέων Δωροθέο̣[υ ‒ ‒ ‒ ‒ ‒ ‒ ‒ ‒ ‒ καὶ συμπρόεδροι· ἔδοξεν τῶι δήμωι]·
Δημέας Δημέ[ου Ἀζηνιεὺς(?) εἶπεν· ἐπειδὴ ὁ δῆμος ὁ Ἀθηναίων]
ἐν δημοκρατίαι κ[ατὰ τοὺς παλαιοὺς νόμους καὶ τὰ ἐπιτάγματα]
τῶν κλήρωι καὶ χε[ιροτονίαι ἐκλεγομένων πολιτεύεσθαι βούλεται]
10 καὶ χάριν διδομεν[‒ ‒]
τὰς δὲ κληρωτὰς [. . .]ΙΣΗΕ[‒ ‒]
τινὲς δὲ διὰ κακοτ̣[ρό]πων πα̣[λαιοὶ νόμοι ‒ ‒ ‒ ‒ ‒ ‒ ‒ ‒ ‒ ‒ ‒ ‒ ‒ ‒]
τοὺς προαιρουμέν[ο]υς συνη[γόρους ‒ ‒ ‒ ‒ ‒ ‒ ‒ ‒ ‒ ‒ ‒ ‒ ‒ ‒ ‒ ‒]
ἐξ [ὧ]ν̣ συνβαίνει κ[ο]ινῆς καὶ̣ [μέσης πολιτείας αὐτοὺς τετυχέ]
15 να[ι ε]ὔνους κατὰ τ[ὸ ὃ]μοιον περὶ τ[‒ ‒ ‒ ‒ ‒ ‒ ‒ ‒ ‒ ‒ ‒ ‒ ‒ ‒ ἐσ]
τιν πᾶσιν Ἀθηναίοις ἤδη ποτὲ [ποιεῖσθαι τῶν ἐν τοῖς νόμοις γε]
γρ⟨α⟩μμένων π[ρ]όγοιαν, vvvv ἀ[γαθῆι τύχηι δεδόχθαι τῶι δήμωι]
[τὰ] μὲν προνενομοθετημέν[α σὺν Ἀθηνίωνι(?) ὑπὸ τῆς βουλῆς τῆς]
[ἐν Ἀ]ρείωι Πάγωι κύρια εἶναι· vv [ὑπαίτιον δὲ μὴ κληροῦσθαι]
20 [ἀλλ]ὰ̣ ἐξεῖναι το[ῖς] ἄλλοις Ἀ[θηναίοις λ΄ ἔτη γεγονόσιν με]
[τιέν]αι τὰς κληρ[ω]τὰς ἀρχά[ς· vacat εἶναι δὲ τὸν ἐπιχειροῦντα]
[ὃν δή] ποτε οὖν τρό[π]ον καταλ[ύειν τινὰ τῶν κληρωτῶν ἀρχῶν]
[ἄτιμο]ν̣ καὶ ἐπάρατον· v ὧ[ιτινι δὲ ‒ ‒ ‒ ‒ ‒ ‒ ‒ ‒ ‒ ‒ ‒ ‒ ‒ ‒]
[ἀρχή ἐσ]τι κληρωτή, τινα[‒ ‒ ‒ ‒ ‒ ‒ ‒ ‒ ‒ ‒ ‒ ‒ ‒ ‒ ‒ ‒ ‒ ‒ ‒]
25 [‒ ‒ ‒ ‒ ‒ ‒ ‒]ο̣τ̣[. . .]ι̣ηεν[‒ ‒ ‒ ‒ ‒ ‒ ‒ ‒ ‒ ‒ ‒ ‒ ‒ ‒ ‒ ‒ ‒ ‒ ‒]
[‒ ‒]

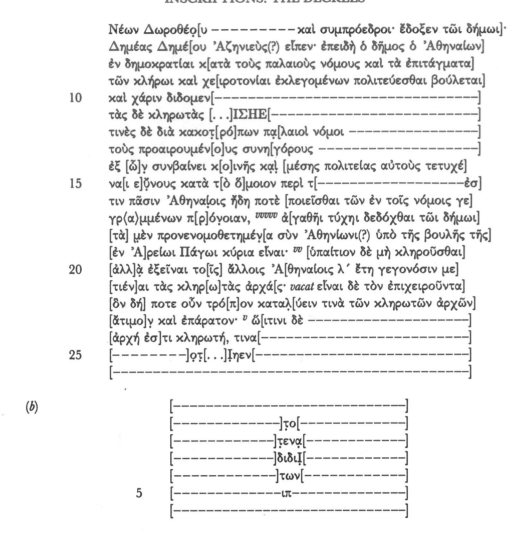

(b)
[‒ ‒]
[‒ ‒ ‒ ‒ ‒ ‒ ‒ ‒ ‒ ‒ ‒]τ̣ο[‒ ‒ ‒ ‒ ‒ ‒ ‒ ‒ ‒]
[‒ ‒ ‒ ‒ ‒ ‒ ‒ ‒ ‒ ‒]τενα̣[‒ ‒ ‒ ‒ ‒ ‒ ‒ ‒]
[‒ ‒ ‒ ‒ ‒ ‒ ‒ ‒ ‒ ‒]διδι̣[‒ ‒ ‒ ‒ ‒ ‒ ‒ ‒]
[‒ ‒ ‒ ‒ ‒ ‒ ‒ ‒ ‒ ‒]των[‒ ‒ ‒ ‒ ‒ ‒ ‒ ‒]
5 [‒ ‒ ‒ ‒ ‒ ‒ ‒ ‒ ‒ ‒ ‒ιπ‒ ‒ ‒ ‒ ‒ ‒ ‒ ‒ ‒]
[‒ ‒]

The first line of this text, wholly restored, was given no number in the *editio princeps*, and the same line numbering was followed by Oliver. The numeration here therefore differs throughout by one from its predecessors. The text of fragment *a*, lines 1–6 and 25, and of fragment *b* is that of Geagan, of fragment *a*, lines 7–24, that of Oliver. In line 13 Geagan read συνδ[ίκους and in line 14 ἐξ[ῆ]ς συνβαίνει κοινῆς καὶ ἐκ[‒ ‒ ‒ ‒. He estimated the width of the text as of *ca.* 46 letters; but line 1 requires 45 letters without the name of the archon, unless the words τῆς βουλῆς καί be omitted, and line 17, common to both Geagan and Oliver, requires 49; line 7 contains 46 letters without the blank space added by Oliver after εἶπεν, while his lines 16 and 18 call for 50 and 48 letters respectively. Line 11. *SEG* XXX, 80 includes in its text Oliver's suggestion (in his commentary) [ἐφ'α]ῖ̣ς ἡ ἐ[κκλησία‒ ‒ ‒. Line 17. *Lapis* ΓΡΜΜΕΝΩΝ.

The lettering shows a superficial neatness, but there are variations, especially in the size of the circular letters: serifs are abundant but often perfunctory. Alpha has a broken crossbar, theta a bar in place of a central dot, pi a short right *hasta*: while the outer strokes of sigma are parallel, those of mu are not. S. V. Tracy did not include this text in his survey of Attic letter cutters, which terminated at 86 B.C., but clearly there is no decisive evidence in the style of the lettering to confirm or disprove the dates sought on historical grounds. Geagan's estimate that the inscription might fall, on stylistic criteria, "anywhere from the early second century B.C. down to the time of Augustus" must be regarded as over-generous: "s. I a., pars prior" is a proposal that could be comfortably sustained.

The content of the decree is more helpful. Athens is enjoying "democracy", which at this date may not mean what it seems to imply. Nevertheless, the officials have been chosen by lot or direct election, and a constitution approved by or with the cooperation of the Areopagos is being ratified by the demos. It was Geagan's view that, despite the use of the word *demokratia*, this amounted to an oligarchic restoration, more precisely to that put in place after Sulla's capture of Athens. His suggested date of 84/3, when Sulla called at Athens on his way home from the East, took cognizance also of the secretary cycle, which in that year called for a γραμματεύς from Hippothontis (IX): but no confidence can be placed in the existence of the cycle at that date; cf. B. D. Meritt, *Historia* 26, 1977, pp. 188–189.

E. Badian (*AJAH* 1, 1976, pp. 116–117, 127, notes 55–58; cf. *SEG* XXVI, *loc. cit.*) urged that the "democracy" was that of Athenion, instituted in 88/7 in the interests of Mithridates VI, king of Pontos, and rapidly converted into a tyranny, a suggestion further developed by Oliver, *loc. cit.*, whose restoration of line 18 in particular took account of it. Oliver's view was that the constitutional revision was a "follow-up" to Athenion's provisions, perhaps in the archonship of Philanthes (87/6); but he did not preclude a "much later period of reconciliation".

Line 1. Geagan based his restoration of the missing first line on the formula of *Agora* XV, 266 and *IG* II², 1043: it occurs also in *IG* II², 1046. Cf. A. S. Henry, *Prescripts*, p. 96. All are of dates later in the century, and this may argue for a post-Sullan rather than a pre-Sullan dating. Line 3. Ἀνα[χαιεύς Geagan, on the supposition (see p. 468 above) that the secretary cycle may still have been in operation.

Lines 6–7. While nothing is known of Neon, son of Dorotheos, Geagan's restoration of the deme of Demeas relied upon an association with the Δημέας Ἀζηνιεύς who was a mint magistrate and perhaps epimeletes of the Peiraieus in the late 2nd century; cf. O. W. Reinmuth, *BCH* 90, 1966, pp. 96–97; *Agora* XV, 278, line 34. However, Tracy (*I.G. II² 2336: Contributors of First Fruits for the Pythais*, 1982, p. 37) retained the deme of the epimeletes as Ἁ[λαιεύς, and Ἁλαιεύς could be restored here. Cf. also *PA* 3315. Line 9. Oliver drew attention to Aristotle, *Politics* 1320b11–14, similarly in line 14 to *Politics* 1294a41–42, both of which would in his view echo the Peripatetic color of Athenion's constitution. For Athenian relations with Mithridates in the early 80's and the tyranny of Athenion and Aristion (who may or may not be one and same person) cf. C. Mossé, *Athens in Decline, 404–86 B.C.*, 1973, pp. 148–151; Badian, *AJAH* 1, 1976, pp. 104–128. The account by W. S. Ferguson, *Hellenistic Athens*, pp. 440–453, retains both its vigor and its utility.

FRAGMENT OF AN HONORARY DECREE

334. A fragment of a stele of Pentelic marble (I 5426), broken all around but with the original rough-picked back preserved, discovered on May 6, 1938, in the east boundary wall of the Roman road north of the Odeion (N 7–8). The inscribed face is damaged by a surface fracture on the left and abrasion at the right edge.

H. 0.295 m.; W. 0.30 m.; Th. 0.104 m.
LH. *ca.* 0.014 m.

Ed. B. D. Meritt, *Hesperia* 37, 1968, p. 277, no. 15, with photograph pl. 80. See also *SEG* XXV, 129.

ca. a. 80 *a.*(?)   NON-ΣΤΟΙΧ.

```
    [------------------------------------]
    [----------]ελεσθ[----------------]
    [------ τοῖς πρυ]τάνεσι π[-----------]
    [----------] βιοῦντος κα[------------]
    [---- ἐν τῷ ἐνι]αυτῷ πολλὰ [----------]
5   [------------]ν[..] τὴν ταμιείαν [-------]
    [-----------]ε[. α]ὐξήσει τῶν [---------]
    [-------- προ]γόνων ἀρετῆς χ[---------]
    [----------- τ]ὸ Οἰνοφίλου ψήφισ[μα ----]
    [----------]ο[.]του κατὰ τοὺς Διον[υσ---]
10  [----------- γ]ραπτῆς ἰχόνος ἀν[άθεσιν --]
    [-----------]σω προσήχει δε[------]
    [-----------]ιοις ὑπ'αὐτῶ[---------]
    [-----------]ι Διοχλῆν [---------]
    [-----------]ωω[---------]
15  [------------------------------------]
```

A general date in the 1st century B.C. for this text is provided by the lettering, and that this postdates 86 B.C. in the view of S. V. Tracy was implicit in its omission from consideration in his *Attic Letter-Cutters*. The letters are large and foursquare in the manner of the Roman period, although with thinly cut strokes. The crossbar of alpha is broken, the external strokes of mu and sigma are parallel, and the center strokes of the latter are drawn back to form an obtuse angle. The two upright strokes of pi are of equal length; xi lacks a central upright, and its center horizontal stroke is short; omega has decorative side strokes, but the other letters are without finials of any kind. Iota adscript is not written; cf. Meisterhans-Schwyzer³, pp. 67–68. The change of EI to I in ἰχόνος (line 10) is also to be noted as suggesting though not necessitating a date after 100 B.C. It is found as early as 175/4 (*IG* II², 1329, lines 27–28); cf. L. Threatte, *Grammar*, pp. 195–198.

Meritt derived a more precise dating from the biographical detail of Oinophilos (line 8), whom he identified with Οἰνόφιλος Συνδρόμου Στειριεύς, βουλευτής and treasurer of the prytaneis of Pandionis *ca.* 80 B.C. (*IG* II², 1050 = *Agora* XV, 264), to be distinguished from the Oinophilos, son of Syndromos, of Steiria (*PA* 11367; cf. **335**), who was perhaps his great-nephew. There were however other owners of the name Oinophilos attested in public office during the same general period, such as Οἰνόφιλος ᾿Αμφίου ᾿Αφιδναῖος (*PA* 11364, surely to be identified with the Οἰνόφιλος ᾿Αφιδναῖος of *Agora* XV, 257 = *SEG* XXI, 486, lines 14–18; cf. Meritt, *Hesperia* 33, 1964, p. 194) or the Oinophilos who was a βουλευτής of Ptolemais in 97/6 (*Agora* XV, 259, line 45, unless this be dated a century earlier, to the archonship of Phanarchides, as urged by H. B. Mattingly, *Historia* 20, 1971, pp. 26–28).

The detailed content of the decree can be no more than conjecture. Meritt suggested ἐπεμ]ελέσθ[η in line 1 and a reference to a gift of money to the prytaneis for a sacrifice in line 2. The recipient of the honors may have been the Diokles of line 13, who may have been treasurer (line 5) of some group or board and who was of distinguished ancestry (line 7), the former nobility of which he had perhaps enhanced (line 6). Lines 9 and 11 may contain references to the god Dionysos and his festival (κατὰ τοὺς Διον[υσιακούς – – – and – – – Διονύ]σῳ. Line 10 undoubtedly included a portrait statue or bust among the honors decreed; for the phraseology cf. A. S. Henry, *Honours*, p. 301.

DECREE CONCERNING ATHENIAN SETTLERS ON LEMNOS

335. A fragment (I 6691) from the lower part of the stele of Pentelic marble to which *IG* II², 1051 and 1058 also belong, with the left side (dressed with a toothed chisel) and original rough-picked back of the monument preserved, discovered on October 19, 1954, in the wall of the east apse of the Church of the Holy Apostles (P 16). It was first observed by D. M. Lewis that on its right it makes a direct join with fragment *d* of *IG* II², 1051 (E.M. 7615).

H. 0.26 m.; W. 0.29 m.; Th. 0.13 m.
LH. 0.01 m.

Ed. B. D. Meritt, *Hesperia* 36, 1967, pp. 66–68, no. 12, with photographs pl. 22 and 23. See also *SEG* XXIV, 141; J. and L. Robert, *REG* 81, 1968, pp. 446–447, no. 190. Meritt further noted the observation of Lewis and A. E. Raubitschek that *IG* II², 1058 (E.M. 5267) forms part of this text, joining fragment *a* of *IG* II², 1051 (E.M. 7618) at the upper right of the latter, and he published a revised text of lines 1–10 of the decree thus augmented, as well as of the conclusion, of which the Agora fragment forms part. For convenience, the entire text is reproduced here. *IG* II², 1058 is designated fragment *e*, and Agora I 6691 fragment *f*.

a. 31–21/20 a.(?)   NON-ΣTOIX. *ca.* 57

['Επι....*ca.* 11.... ἄρχοντος ἐπὶ τῆς.........*ca.* 20......... πρυτανήας]
[ἢ..........*ca.* 22......... ἐγρ]αμμάτε[υεν·.........*ca.* 20.........]   (*e*)
[......*ca.* 16...... τῆς πρυτα]νήας· ᵛ ἐκκλησ[ία κυρία ἐν τῶι θεάτρωι· τῶν]
[προέδρων ἐπεψήφιζεν..*ca.* 7... Δ]ωροθέου [...*ca.* 8... καὶ συμπρόεδροι·
5   [ἔδοξεν τῶι δήμωι· ²⁻³]ΟΣ[...*ca.* 8...]στου Πε[. *ca.* 6.. εἶπεν· οἴδε ἐκ τῆς πόλε]
(*a*)   [ως τεταγμένοι ἦσαν] ὑπὸ το[ῦ δήμο]υ γράψαι [καὶ ἀνακοινῶσαι τὸ ψήφισμα]
   [τόδε τοῖς ἐμ Μυρ]ίνῃ ὁ ἐπὶ τ[οὺς ὁπ]λίτας [στρατηγὸς.......*ca.* 17.......]
   [καὶ ὁ] κῆρυξ [τῆς] ἐξ ᾿Αρείου Πάγου βο[υλ]ῆς Πλ[....*ca.* 13..... καὶ ὁ κῆρυξ]
   [τῆς] βουλῆς καὶ τοῦ δήμου ᵛ Οἰνόφιλ[ος Στειριεύς· ἐπειδὴ οἱ πρέσβεις]
10 [ἐπελ]θόντες ἐμφανίζουσιν ψήφισμα [––––––––––––––––––––––––––]
   [...]ς ἐν Λήμνῳ ἀδέσποτοι καὶ δημό[σιοι ––––––––––––––––––––]
   [. ἐκ] Μυρίνης οὓς καὶ ἐπελθόντας ἐπὶ τ[––––––––––––––––––––]
   [...]εις αὐτοῖς καὶ ἀπαλλαγὴ γενηθ[––––––––––––––––––––––]
   [. τά] τε δημόσια τοῖς ἐμ Μυρίνῃ ὑ[π––––––––––––––––––––––]
15 [τοῖ]ς προγεγονόσιν ἐνγράφοις [––––––––––––––––––––––––]
   [τὸ ὄ]νομα μὴ ἐμπεριεχόμενον ε[–––––––––––––––––––––––]
   [..] πρὸ τῆς συνθέσεως πραγμ[α ––––––––––––––––––– ἀμφι]
   [σβ]ητούμενον ἢ ἐπίβασιν ἔχον [–––––––––––––––––––––––]
   καὶ συμπεπολιτευμένους περ[ι ––––––––––––––––––––––––]
20 τοῦ μηδεμίαν ἀφορμὴ[ν –––––––––––––––––––––– μη]
   δένα τρόπον· ᵛᵛ ἀγαθῇι τ[ύ]χ[ηι δεδόχθαι τῶι δήμωι –––––––––]
   πᾶσαν ἐν ταῖς ἀποφάσεσιν [––––––––––––––––––– εἰς]

Λῆμνον ἐπὶ τὸν ἐξετασμὸ[ν ―――――――――――――― ἐπὶ ―――――]

νέως ἄρχοντος Κυδα[――――――――――――――――――――――――]

25   [――――]ου αὐτοῖς [――――――――――――――――――――――――]

[――――――――――――――――――――――――――――――――――――]

lacuna

(b)   [――――――――――――――――――――――――――――――――――――]

[―――――――――――――――――――― ἐν τῶι ἐπὶ ―――― ἄρχοντος ἐνια]

[υ]τῷ κα[τα]πεπτω[κοτ(?) ―――――――――――――――――― ἐπὶ ῾Ηρ]

30   ῴδου στρατηγοῦντο[ς ἐπὶ τοὺς ὁπλίτας(?) ―――――――――― ἄ]

[ρ]χοντος ἐνιαυτῷ κα[―――――――――――――――――――――――]

ου Παλληνέως στρατ[ηγοῦντος ―――――――――――――――――]

ων δεδομένων κατα[―――――――――――― ἐν τῶι ἐπὶ ――――― ἄρ]

χοντος ἐνιαυτῷ κα[――――――――――――――――――――――]

35   [.] καὶ τὸ ψήφισμα π[――――――――――――――――――――――]

ν μηδενὸς ἔχοντο[ς ――――――――――――――――――――――]

ναι τοῦ δήμου μη[――――――――――――――――――――――――]

[λ]ε[ί]πεσθαι κατὰ χ[ώραν ――――――――――――――――――――]

[――――――――――――――――――――――――――――――――――――]

lacuna

40   [――――――――――――――――――――――――――――――――――――]

(c)   [――――――――] δεκατ[――――――――――――――――――――――]

[―――]α καθότι καὶ ἀπο[――――――――――――――――――――]

[εἰ]σαγωγαί, ὀφείλω[σι ―――――――――――――――――――――]

[.] συστάσεις αὐτῶν κα[―――――――――――――――――――――]

45   καὶ ἐν Λήμνῳ καὶ ἐν ᾿Αθή[ναις ――――――――――――――――]

τας ἐν τῶι ἐχομένω[ι ―――――――――――――――――――――]

μή τινες ἀγῶνες ἰδ[ιωτικοὶ ―――――――――――― ἐν τῶι ―――――]

[――] μηνὶ μὴ ἐξεῖναι κατα[――――――――――――――――――――]

[―――]ν ποιήσασθαι μήτε [――――――――――――――――――――]

50   [πα]ρὰ τὸν προγεγραμμέ[νον νόμον(?) ―――――――――――― χάρ]

[ι]ν δὲ τοῦ καὶ τὴν τοῦ δή[μου ―――――――――――――――――]

ναι καὶ φανεράν, ἣν εἰς τ[――――――――――――――――――――]

[ἐ]μφυσιωθῆν[αι τ]οὺς ἐμ Μ[υρίνῃ ――――――――――――― συ]

[ν]θέσεως ἐνκλημάτων α[――――――― ἀναγράψαι ―――――― τὸ ψή]

55   φισμα εἰς στήλην λιθίνη[ν καὶ στῆσαι ἐ]ν ἀκρ[οπόλει ――――――]

(d)   τὰ τῆς ἀποικίας πρὸς τῶ[ν ―――――――――]ας τῶν πο[λιτῶν ――――]

[.]ου[ς ἐ]μεσείτευσαν δ[ικαίως(?)]· ἐπαινέσαι δὲ καὶ τ[οὺς ――――――]

[πρέσβ]εις ᵛᵛᵛ Κριτίαν ᾿Αφιδ[ναῖο]ν, Κλέωνα ᾿Αλωπεκῆθε[ν, ――――――――]

[――――――]ριον, Λάμπ[ων]α Λαμ[πτρ]έα, Διογένην Εἰτεαῖον, Θεοδωρ[―――――]

60   [――――――]τον Φη[γ]ούσ[ιον, Τη]λεφάνην Οἰῆθεν, ῾Ηρόδωρον ᾿Αχαρ[νέα ――――]

[―――――――― ἐπὶ τῶι τετελ]εκέναι τὴν πρεσβήαν ὁμονοήσ[αντας συμφέρου]

[σαν ἀμφοτέροις τοῖς δήμ]οις, καὶ στεφανῶσαι θαλλοῦ σ[τεφάνωι· καλέ]

(f)   [σαι δὲ αὐτοὺς ἐπὶ τὴν κοινὴ]ν τῆς πόλεως ἑστίαν· πέμψαι δὲ [καὶ μετὰ τῶν]

[πρέσβεων ἐκ τῆ]ς πόλεως Δι[ο]νύσιον Πειραιέα, ᵛ ἵνα τούτω[ν συντελουμέ]

65   [νων ὁ δῆ]μος φαίνηται τὰ πρὸ[ς] τοὺς συγγενεῖς τηρῶν δίκα[ια. Τῶν ψήφων]

[αἱ] πλήρεις αἷς ἐδόκει τὴν ἐ[γφ]ερομένην γνώμην κυρίαν [εἶναι ...ᶜᵃ·⁷...]

[..]ΔΔΓ, αἱ δὲ τετρυπημέ[ναι α]ἷς οὐκ ἐδόκει οὐδεμία.   *vacat*

vacat

For earlier texts in the present collection of Agora *psephismata* concerned with Athenian settlers on Lemnos see **41, 68**, and **72**. Lemnos, like Delos, had been in Athenian hands since 166 B.C. See *IG* XII, viii, *praefatio de Lemno et Imbro*, pp. 4–5. Some dispute seems to have arisen concerning the occupation of land (lines 11–17). The difficulties were apparently considerable and are also reflected in *IG* II², 1052 and 1053 (*SEG* XXIV, 142, XXVIII, 93). The announcement of the present decree to the Lemnians was, perhaps significantly, entrusted to three of the highest officers of state (lines 5–9; cf. S. Dow, *Prytaneis*, p. 17), to whom one more was added (lines 63–65). Their selection is inserted as a statement of fact between the name of the proposer of the decree and the beginning of the decree proper, as if this were a matter that had been independently decided and is simply placed on record at this point. At an earlier period the practice had been to agree the number of delegates in the decree and to add at the very end of the text the names of those selected. Cf., e.g., *IG* II², 682, 793, and **225**. On this decree see also D. J. Geagan, *Athenian Constitution*, pp. 27, 50–51, 59, 106–107.

The lettering of the inscription has the "foursquare imperial" character associated with the Roman period, regular and well constructed, and with considerable artistic sensibility. This is not one of the better examples, but it possesses the characteristics of the style. "Free ends" of strokes carry serifs. The crossbar of alpha is straight, and theta carries a short cross-stroke in place of a central dot. The external strokes of mu and sigma are parallel; in pi the right *hasta* is short, and the horizontal stroke substantially overlaps both uprights. The vertical stroke of phi projects well above, though not below, the lines of the lettering; omega is in a spread, decorated form (cf. **334**). Iota adscript is sometimes but not always written. H replaces EI in πρυτανεία (lines 1 and 3) and πρεσβεία (line 61); see L. Threatte, *Grammar*, pp. 202–205. Early examples of the replacement are to be found in the later 3rd and the 2nd centuries B.C., but Threatte observed that "the phenomenon remains rare until about 50 B.C."

Line 3. For the character and location of the assembly see **101**, commentary on lines 7–8 and **167**, commentary on lines 6–7. Line 9. Oinophilos, (son of Syndromos), of Steiria. Cf. **334** and *PA* 11367. He appears as κῆρυξ τῆς βουλῆς in the prytany text *Agora* XV, 290 + 292b, lines 23–30, dated *ca.* 21/20 B.C.; cf. J. S. Traill, *Hesperia* 47, 1978, pp. 297–299, no. 22 and *SEG* XXVIII, 161. The identification encouraged J. H. Kroll (Δελτ. 27, Α', 1972 [1973], p. 103 with note 58) to regard the present text as "post-Actian"; cf. *SEG* XXXII, 136. In the *editio princeps* of the Agora fragment Meritt was content to note the date as later than 38 B.C., when the aristocracy was again in control in Athens. If Oinophilos' father was the Syndromos, son of Kallikratides, who was archon in 37/6 and honored by the boule and demos at this period (W. K. Pritchett, *Hesperia* 11, 1942, pp. 247–249, no. 50; *PA* 13039), he was perhaps great-nephew of the Oinophilos of **334**.

Lines 29–30. If the στρατηγὸς ἐπὶ τοὺς ὁπλίτας is indeed referred to here, he would be Herodes, son of Eukles, of Marathon, ancestor of the famous Herodes Atticus, who is considered to have held the office a little before 60 B.C. See *IG* II², 3595; T. C. Sarikakis, *The Hoplite General in Athens*, 1951, p. 61.

Lines 58–61. There is room for twelve names, but they are not listed in the "official" order of the phylai, nor is each a delegate from a different phyle. In *IG* II², the restoration καὶ τ[οὺς ἥκοντας ἐκ – – – –] presupposes, probably correctly, that these names were those of representatives of the Lemnian settlers who, as cleruchs, retained their Attic deme affiliations; but they may have been members of an earlier delegation from Athens to Lemnos that is here thanked and rewarded. There is a comparable list, with the addition of the patronymics of those listed, in *IG* II², 1053. Line 62. The award of stephanoi of olive, regular in this period for the officials named in prytany decrees and for the teachers of the ephebes honored in ephebic texts, remains standard also for Athenians who have acted in some other official capacity; cf. A. S. Henry (*Honours*, pp. 38–40), who cited the present text (p. 39). Line 64. Dionysios of Peiraieus (*PA* 4239) cannot be otherwise identified, but Meritt noted that his name is to be restored in *IG* II², 1053, lines 10–11.

Line 65. δικα[ίως Kirchner, Meritt; δίκ[αια J. and L. Robert. Lines 65–67. Cf. *IG* II², 1053, lines 11–12. The registration of the number of votes cast in a council or assembly, which begins to appear sporadically at various points in the Greek world in the Late Hellenistic or Early Roman period, is extremely unusual in Athens. For the phraseology cf. *IG* II², 1641, lines 30–33. See further A. Wilhelm, *Neue Beiträge* 6 (= *SbAkadWien* 183, 3), 1921, pp. 4–9, no. 2; L. Robert, *Études anatoliennes*, 1937, p. 451; J. H. Oliver, *The Sacred Gerusia* (*Hesperia*, Supplement VI), 1941, pp. 125–141, no. 31, lines 30–32 with commentary; *SEG* XXIII, 208; Geagan, *Athenian Constitution*, p. 89. The numbers voting "aye", written in full in *IG* II², 1053, are expressed in acrophonic numerals, the use of which evidently still survived, at least for official purposes. See M. N. Tod, *BSA* 18, 1911/1912, pp. 128–129; A. G. Woodhead, *Study of Greek Inscriptions*, pp. 108–110. The survival lasted longer than was suggested by M. Guarducci, *Epigrafia Greca* I, 1967, p. 419 (cf. pp. 417–422).

DECREE CONCERNING THE CELEBRATION OF THE BIRTHDAY OF THE EMPEROR AUGUSTUS

336. Two nonjoining fragments of a stele of Pentelic marble, of which *IG* II², 1071 (E.M. 5314, hereafter fragment *a*) also forms a part. The larger of the two, fragment *b* (I 2619), preserves the right side and original rough-picked back of the stele but is broken elsewhere, and a strip some 0.07 m. in width has, in a later adaptation to some other usage, been shaved off the inscribed surface on the right. It was discovered on March 15, 1935, in a late wall east of the East Building (P 14). The smaller fragment, fragment *c* (I 5334), broken all around, was discovered on

March 14, 1938, in a late context northeast of the Odeion (N 7). The association of the three fragments was first observed by A. E. Raubitschek.

b: H. 0.28 m.; W. 0.195 m.; Th. 0.09 m.

c: H. 0.10 m.; W. 0.066 m.; Th. 0.052 m.

LH. 0.009–0.011 m.
Στοιχ. Hor. 0.013 m.; Vert. 0.0166 m.

Ed. G. A. Stamires, *Hesperia* 26, 1957, pp. 260–265, no. 98, with photographs of all fragments pl. 63. See also *SEG* XVII, 34.

a. 22/1 a., *vel paullo ante* ΣΤΟΙΧ. 39

(a)
["Εδοξεν τῆι βουλῆι]· Αἰαντὶς ἐ[πρυτάνευε, ...⁶... ἐ]
[γραμμάτευε, ...]ιος ἐπεστάτ[ει, ...⁹.... ἦρχε]·
['Αντίπατρος ᵛᵛ] 'Αντιπάτρου ᵛᵛ Φ[λυεὺς ᵛᵛ εἶπε· ᵛᵛ]
[ὁπόσα μὲν πρ]ότερον ἐψηφίσατο ὁ δ[ῆμος Αὐτοκράτ]
5 [ορι Καίσα]ρι Σεβαστῶι πράττεσθα[ι ....¹¹.....]
[....⁹....]ων ταῖς ἔναις τιμαῖς Γ[.....¹².....]
[....⁹....]εται ᵛ τὴν μὲν δωδεκάτ[ην Βοηδρομιῶν]
[ος Καίσαρος] γενέθλιον ἑορτάζει[ν θυσίαις καθά]
[περ τῶι 'Από]λλωνι τὴν ἑβδόμην ἱερ[ὰν νομίζομεν]·
10 [....⁹....]ων εἰσὶ δημοτελεῖς Γ` [.....¹².....]
[...⁸..]Ι ᵛ παρόντων μὲν [.......¹⁸.......]
[...⁶... καθ]ιεροῦντε[ς ....²¹.........]
[....⁹....]τοντας [........²⁴.........]
[————————————————————]

lacuna

(b) 15 [————————————————————]
[.........³¹.........]Σ[..⁷...]
[.......²⁸.......]ΕΤΑΣΣΙ[..⁶...]
[........²⁹........] βωμὸν ∕[....]
[........²⁹........]νον ἀλλ[....]
20 [.........³⁰.........] διὰ κλ[....]
[.......²⁷.......]∖οντας ᵛ ὁ[πόσ.]
[.......²⁸.......] ἐξεταζε[....]
[........²⁹........]ν ᵛ ὁπόσ[....]
[.........²².........] ἀγῶνα ἰσο]πύθιο[ν(?) ...]
25 [.........²².........] ἐπιφανέσ]τατα ᵛ [....]
[........²⁹........]ος ᵛ ἔν τ[ε ...]
[.........³⁰.........]ΤΗΡΙΣ[....]
[..........³².........]ΠΟΙ[....]
[————————————————————]

lacuna

(c) 30 [————————————————————]
[.......¹⁷.......]ιος ηⱵ[.......¹⁷.......]
[.......¹⁷.......]ος παρ[.......¹⁷.......]
[.......¹⁷.......] τοὺς ε[.......¹⁷.......]
[.......¹⁷.......]ΗΣΦΑΣ[.......¹⁷.......]
35 [........¹⁹........]ΤΟ[.......¹⁸.......]
[————————————————————]

Line 17. Possibly rho rather than epsilon as the first preserved letter. Line 31. The last preserved letter may be eta or rho. The position of fragment *c* in relation to the width of the stele is uncertain, and the amount of space on either side of it shown above is inserted *exempli gratia* only.

This inscription is particularly remarkable in its reversion to the use of the stoichedon style, of which it is apparently the latest example in Attic epigraphy. See R. P. Austin, *The Stoichedon Style in Greek Inscriptions*, 1938, pp. 36 and 114, with pl. 14. With this exception, the last dated example among the Agora *psephismata* of this collection is **218**, of 239/8 or 238/7 B.C.; cf. also **221** and **223**. Among prytany texts see *Agora* XV, 116–119, all dated *ca.* 230 B.C. There is indeed an archaistic flavor to the text, which is characterized by plainness, simplicity, and excellent articulation of the components of each letter. The style of writing is nevertheless the "foursquare imperial", with the upright strokes of phi and psi projecting above and below the lines of the lettering and with the external strokes of sigma (though not of mu) parallel. The "free ends" of the strokes are enlarged into slight wedges reminiscent of the middle and later 4th century. The crossbar of alpha is straight, and the right *hasta* of pi short. Theta twice has a central dot, once a short cross-stroke; xi lacks a central upright, and its center horizontal stroke is short.

The archaism is carried further by the readoption of the simple form of prescript characteristic of the 5th and early 4th centuries, with all elements expressed by means of a succession of nominatives and main verbs. Cf. A. S. Henry (*Prescripts*, p. 95), who quoted lines 1–3. The decree however emanates from the boule alone, if line 1 be correctly restored, with independent legal force. See D. J. Geagan, *Athenian Constitution*, p. 73.

Reference to *IG* II², 1071, now augmented with these two scarcely helpful fragments, has been regularly introduced into studies of Augustan Athens, for which see P. Graindor, *Athènes sous Auguste*, 1927, pp. 25–32 and the bibliography given by Stamires, *op. cit.*, pp. 261–262. Cf. also J. and L. Robert, *REG* 71, 1958, pp. 229–230, no. 179, where it is noted that the new fragments add nothing of significance. The decree was concerned with the official celebration of Augustus' birthday, recognized as Boedromion 12. On the date and occasion of its passage see further Geagan, *AJP* 100, 1979, pp. 59–68. The association with Apollo which the Emperor fostered (cf. L. Cerfau and J. Tondriau, *La culte des souverains dans le civilisation gréco-romaine*, 1957, pp. 335–336) is significantly maintained in the proposed model for the celebration to be found in the festival of that god on the seventh of the month (L. Deubner, *Attische Feste*, p. 202; J. D. Mikalson, *Sacred and Civil Calendar*, p. 51) and in the decision, if line 24 offers sufficient indication, that the festival was to be equal in rank with that of the Pythian god. For the celebration of Augustus' birthday, a method of honoring the Emperor widely adopted, cf. the bibliography provided by Stamires, *op. cit.*, pp. 262–263, note 125.

Line 3. The proposer of the decree, Antipatros, son of Antipatros, of Phlya, was a notable figure in the Athens of this epoch, seven times στρατηγὸς ἐπὶ τοὺς ὁπλίτας. See T. C. Sarikakis, *The Hoplite General in Athens*, 1951, p. 41; S. Dow, *Prytaneis*, pp. 190–191; Stamires, *op. cit.*, pp. 249–251; *Agora* XV, 284, 290 + 292b (*SEG* XXVIII, 161, XXIX, 125), 292a; *SEG* XVII, 70 (*IG* II², 3539) and 71, XXIX, 170. Line 27. πεντε]τηρίς or Σω]τῆρι σ[– – – – Stamires.

Stamires argued that this decree was passed shortly before Augustus' second visit to Athens in the winter of 21/20, in disagreement with Graindor, who had placed it in or soon after 27/6, the *terminus post quem* being the grant to the Emperor of the title Augustus. Graindor supposed that the Athenians, who had jeopardized their relations with Octavian by taking the side of Antonius and Kleopatra in the war of Actium, would be in haste to make what amends they could. See further Geagan, *AJP* 100, 1979, pp. 59–68. On relations between Augustus and Athens at this time cf. also G. W. Bowersock, *Augustus and the Greek World*, 1965, pp. 106–108; Geagan, *ANRW* II (Principat), vii, 1, 1979, pp. 378–379, 418–419; J. H. Oliver, *Hesperia* 49, 1980, pp. 44–45 (with bibliography, note 35); E. A. Kapetanopoulos, Ἑλληνικά 33, 1981, pp. 222–223; M. C. Hoff, *Hesperia* 58, 1989, pp. 267–276.

A DOCUMENT CONCERNING JULIUS NIKANOR

337. Five fragments of a stele of Pentelic marble, forming part of the same monument as *IG* II², 1119 and the unpublished fragment E.M. 5245: that these fragments (with the exception of fragment *c* below, then not yet discovered) belong to the same stele was suggested by A. E. Raubitschek, *Hesperia* 23, 1954, pp. 318–319, no. 4, and accepted in the *editio princeps*. Raubitschek's inclusion of *IG* II², 1069 with the same group, also accepted in the *editio princeps*, has since that time been generally discounted; see below.

a. A fragment (I 6132 a) preserving the original rough-picked back of the stele but otherwise broken all around, discovered on January 24, 1949, among stones collected during 1938–1940 on the southern part of Kolonos Agoraios. On its right it joins the left side of fragment *b*.

b. *IG* II², 1119 (E.M. 9504), found on the Akropolis, preserves the right side and original back of the stele but is broken above, below, and on the left where it makes a join with fragment *a*.

c. A fragment (I 6132 b) preserving the original back of the stele but broken elsewhere, discovered in April 1958 among collected marbles in the area of the Panathenaic Way, north of the Eleusinion (S 17). It makes no join with any other piece.

d. E.M. 5245, a fragment similarly preserving the original back but broken elsewhere and making no join with any other piece.

e. A fragment (I 1059) broken all around and making no join with any other piece, discovered in summer 1933 among marbles collected east of the Tholos (I 11).

f. A fragment (I 6387) similarly broken on all sides and making no join with any other piece, discovered on May 26, 1951, in a Byzantine wall at the northeast corner of the Temple of Ares (L 7).

g. A fragment (I 179) of similar character, making no join with any other piece, discovered on March 1, 1932, in a Roman context near the northwest corner of the Metroon (I 9).

a: H. 0.27 m.; W. 0.36 m.; Th. 0.16 m.

b: H. 0.38 m.; W. 0.39 m.; Th. 0.16 m.

  a + b, as joined: W. 0.547 m.

c: H. 0.35 m.; W. 0.35 m.; Th. 0.16 m.

d: H. 0.39 m.; W. 0.33 m.; Th. 0.16 m.

e: H. 0.085 m.; W. 0.125 m.; Th. 0.053 m.

f: H. 0.08 m.; W. 0.164 m.; Th. 0.037 m.

g: H. 0.063 m.; W. 0.097 m.; Th. 0.032 m.

LH. 0.0155 m. (theta and omicron 0.012–0.013 m.)

Ed. B. D. Meritt, *Hesperia* 36, 1967, pp. 68–71, no. 13, with photographs pl. 23. See also *SEG* XIV, 79 (reference to Raubitschek's association of the fragments, for which see above) and XXIV, 143.

saec. I p., p. post.   NON-ΣTOIX.

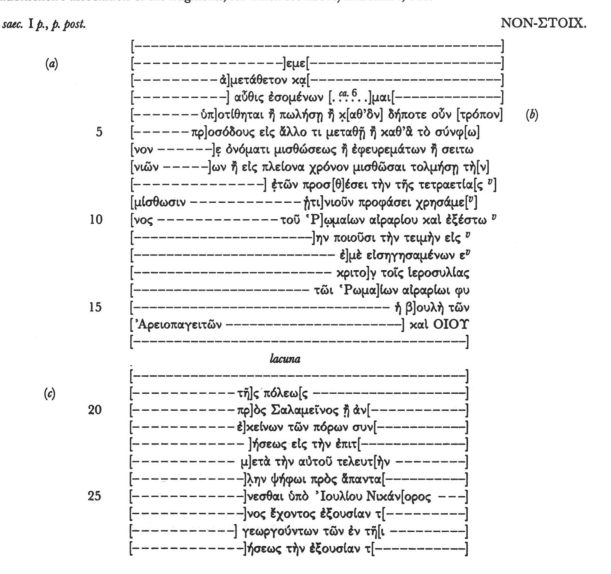

```
[----------------]ς ἀτελείας καὶ νῦν φυλ[----------]
30  [----------- Ἐλ]ευσῖνα ἐπὶ πράσει φε[-----------]
    [-----------]Σ[...]ΠΙΣΕ[-----------]
    [-----------------------------------]
```

lacuna

```
    [-----------------------------------]
(d) [-----------]οντ[..]ων χ[-----------]
35  [----------]ιων μετ'αὐτὸν τι[-----------]
    [---------- τ]εταγμένην ὀγδόηι [-----------]
    [----------]σωι καθάπερ καὶ εἶχον [-----------]
    [----------]γενημάτων οπ[-----------]
    [---------]όμε[ν]ος τῶν ε[-----------]
40  [---------]νων καὶ ὅτι ἀ[-----------]
    [-------]σκευὰς ἢ τ[-----------]
    [------]ομης ἐν τ[-----------]
    [------] ποτε π[-----------]
    [-----------------------------------]
```

```
    [-----------------------------------]
(e) [----------]ε ἐχ[-----------]
    [----------]ομενοι[-----------]
    [----------]τα ἀνετ[-----------]
    [----------]γραμμα[-----------]
5   [-----------------------------------]
```

```
    [-----------------------------------]
(f) [------------]εμε[-----------]
    [------------]πον ἢ παρε[-----------]
    [------------]ηματο[-----------]
    [-----------------------------------]
```

```
    [-----------------------------------]
(g) [------------]αμμε[-----------]
    [------------ ἐ]πιμελη[-----------]
    [------------]Σ[-----------]
    [-----------------------------------]
```

The lettering is of the "standard imperial" type, regular in form and neat in appearance. The fallibility of its use as a criterion of date is suggested by the attribution of fragment *b* by J. Kirchner to "init. s. III(?) p. Chr." and by the fact that with equal confidence the document could be assigned by various commentators to the latter part of the reign of Augustus, to the Claudian-Neronian period, and to the time of the emperors Nerva and Trajan. Characteristic of this inscription are especially (1) mu with angled external strokes and a projection upwards either of these or of the central strokes above their point of junction; (2) rho often but not always with the upright stroke projecting above the loop; (3) phi with a "pinched-in" oval, composing as it were two loops on either side of the upright stroke; (4) omega with downward-sloping "horizontals". The crossbar of alpha is generally straight; theta (which, with omicron, is smaller than the other letters) has a short cross-stroke in replacement of the central dot; the two upright strokes of pi are of equal length, and its horizontal stroke projects beyond both; the external strokes of sigma are parallel. There is some enlargement of "free ends" of strokes, and in some places this amounts to the writing of serifs.

Iota adscript is written in all relevant preserved instances except for the subjunctives in lines 4, 5, and 7, and perhaps also line 20 (see below). EI has taken the place of I in lines 6–7 (σειτω[νιῶν), 11 (τειμήν), and 20 (Σαλαμεῖνος) but not in line 30 (Ἐλ]ευσῖνα). For the practice in the 1st century A.D. see L. Threatte, *Grammar*, p. 198.

A copy of this enactment was set up in Eleusis (cf. line 30), now partly preserved as *IG* II², 1086, to which belongs also a fragment published by A. N. Skias, 'Εφ. 'Αρχ., 1895, col. 121, no. 34. It enables some restorations to be made in the composite fragment *a* + *b* and conversely may itself be supplemented from that source. Nevertheless, the interpretation of the entire dossier remains obscure.

When *IG* II², 1069, a fragment copied in the 19th century and now lost, was believed to form part of this monument, it provided its supposed upper left-hand corner and appeared to establish it as a decree in honor of C. Julius Nikanor, the "new Homer" and "new Themistokles" (appellations recorded in other texts, the references to which were usefully assembled by A. E. Raubitschek, *op. cit.*, pp. 317–319, and in some cases showing that they had been erased, as if the Athenians had come to repent of their extravagance). Moreover, it contained references to Caesar Augustus, to an archon Lakon, and to the priest of Drusus, Augustus' stepson. The name of the archon was not helpful, and a date for him was derived from the estimated date of the document, rather than *vice versa*; but the other references seemed to place both the document and Lakon's archonship between 9/8 B.C. and A.D. 13/14. Cf. P. Graindor, *Chronologie des archontes athéniens sous l'Empire*, 1920, pp. 59–62, no. 26. Thus the *editio princeps* of the Agora fragments was given by Meritt the dating "*aet. Augusti*".

That *IG* II², 1069 is to be dissociated from the other fragments was strongly hinted at by D. J. Geagan (*Athenian Constitution*, p. 23, note 43) and more fully argued by E. A. Kapetanopoulos ('Ελληνικά 33, 1981, p. 220). Without it, the remainder of the document lacks the character of an honorary decree and suggests, on the contrary, a contract of some kind (cf. D. Behrend, *Attische Pachturkunden*, p. 50, note 2). That being so, it may on strict definition not belong with the present collection of Agora *psephismata*; but it nevertheless seems both useful and advisable to retain it.

Discussion is therefore to be focussed on the identity and date of Julius Nikanor himself and on the place of Salamis (line 20) in the context of his career and of this document. With the support of *IG* II², 1069, both had appeared to direct attention towards the reign of Augustus. For earlier bibliography see Raubitschek, *op. cit.*, p. 317, note 2, and for epigraphical references cf. *SEG* XIV, 79, 90, 128; cf. also Geagan, *Athenian Constitution*, pp. 33–35, 140, *et alibi*. At a later stage of the controversy the Augustan date was still upheld by C. P. Jones, *Phoenix* 32, 1978, pp. 222–228. Dio Chrysostom (31.116) referred to the purchase of Salamis by Nikanor (assumed to be this Nikanor), in the context of criticism of an epigram about him, to be associated, it has been contended, with the deletion of his laudatory titles: and, since Strabo (9.1.10) referred to Salamis as being in Athenian possession in his own time, it was long thought that Athens had lost the island in the aftermath of the defeat at Sulla's hands and had recovered it as a gift from Nikanor, thanks to his purchase of it, late in Augustus' reign; cf. G. W. Bowersock, *Augustus and the Greek World*, 1965, p. 96; J. H. Kroll, Δελτ. 27, A', 1972 [1973], p. 103.

It is important to distinguish Julius Nikanor of Hierapolis in Syria, the Nikanor concerned here, from his homonym, the son of Areios, of Alexandria, who was indeed a contemporary of Augustus, as emphasized by L. Robert (*REG* 94, 1981, pp. 348–349; cf. Bowersock, *loc. cit.*, note 5; Jones, *Phoenix* 32, 1978, p. 226; Kapetanopoulos, *RF* 104, 1976, p. 375); for there had been an inclination to confuse them (cf., e.g., Raubitschek, *op. cit.*, p. 317). Accumulating evidence has pointed to a later date for the Hierapolitan, especially by reason of his appearance as στρατηγὸς ἐπὶ τὰ ὅπλα in a new fragment of *IG* II², 1723; see *SEG* XXVI, 166. The case argued by Kapetanopoulos in Δελτ. 30, A', 1975 [1978], p. 123 and *RF* 104, 1976, pp. 375–377 was developed at length by him in 'Ελληνικά 33, 1981, pp. 217–237. A date *ca.* 61/2 (the date of *IG* II², 1723) for the present text and for Nikanor's career has been adopted by Geagan (*ANRW* II [Principat], vii, 1, 1979, pp. 382, 420) and by T. L. Shear Jr. (*Hesperia* 50, 1981, pp. 365–367). The latter indeed suggested a date for this document earlier than 61, perhaps between 41/2 and 61/2; but the suggestion appeared to depend on a continuing association with it of *IG* II², 1069 (p. 366, note 49). Kapetanopoulos, originally proposing "shortly after 61/2" (*RF* 104, 1976, p. 375), was subsequently disposed to think in terms of a later date: "about A.D. 61–110, with the later years appearing as the most likely" ('Ελληνικά 33, 1981, pp. 218–223, 231). He further contended there that the Athenians never did lose possession of Salamis in the 1st century B.C. and that the remark of Dio Chrysostom contains an ambiguity suggesting that Nikanor bought the island from the Athenians rather than for them, the contract in the present document being perhaps concerned with that transaction. On the unfolding arguments see also *SEG* XXVI, 121, 166, XXVIII, 192, XXXI, 108.

A continuing span of activity for Nikanor's mature years from 61 to 110 seems doubtful, despite the evidence of the epigram *SEG* XXIX, 192 (on which see further Kapetanopoulos, *Prometheus* 13, 1987, pp. 1–10) and arguments drawn from it. A date for this document in the period covering the reigns of Nero and Vespasian is probably to be recommended.

Line 16. καὶ οἷου Meritt; καὶ ὁ 'Ιού|[λιος Νικάνωρ – – – –] Raubitschek, but see J. H. Oliver, *HSCP*, Supplementary volume 1 (*Athenian Studies Presented to W. S. Ferguson*), 1940, pp. 524–525. Line 20. ἢ ἀν[– – – – –] Meritt. Possibly ἢ ἀν [– – – –]. Line 22. Or ἐπὶ τ[– – –], as Meritt.

THE ARCHONSHIP OF FLAVIUS MACRINUS, A.D. 116/17

In his Περὶ Θαυμασιῶν καὶ Μακροβίων, Phlegon of Tralles (F. Jacoby, *FGrHist*, no. 257, fr. 36, section IX) dates a sex change that happened to a woman of Laodikeia in Syria by reference to the Athenian archon Makrinos and the Roman consuls L. (Fundanius) Lamia Aelianus and (Sex. Carminius) Vetus. Aelianus and Vetus were the *consules ordinarii* of A.D. 116; cf. E. M. Smallwood, *Documents Illustrating the Principates of Nerva, Trajan and Hadrian*, 1966, p. 7. The lack of coordination between the archon and consular years left it open whether Makrinos' term of office should be reckoned as 115/16 or 116/17; see P. Graindor, *Chronologie des archontes athéniens sous l'Empire*, 1920, pp. 116–123, no. 82. W. Kolbe, however, convincingly demonstrated that in such cases it was Phlegon's custom to equate the consuls with the archon who came into office in the course of their year and who functioned in the latter part of it (*AthMitt* 46, 1921, pp. 106–107). He therefore assigned Makrinos to 116/17, a date accepted by Graindor, *Athènes sous Hadrien*, 1934, pp. 27–29 and also p. 165, note 5 (in a reference to *IG* II², 2026, a list of epheboi dated to the same year). Kolbe's dating was adopted by J. Kirchner, *IG* II², *loc. cit.* (cf. *ad* II², 1737) and p. 792, J. H. Oliver, *Hesperia* 11, 1942, p. 84, J. A. Notopoulos, *Hesperia* 18, 1949, p. 13. For a comparable consuls/archon equation cf. p. 452 above, on the archonship of 112/11 B.C. But the choice between the years was left open by S. Follet, *Athènes au IIᵉ et au IIIᵉ siècle*, 1976, p. 507 (cf. pp. 26–29, 298). A. S. Henry, in quoting lines 1–2 of **338**, preferred the date 115/16 (*Prescripts*, pp. 97–98).

FRAGMENT OF A DECREE

338 (Pl. 30). A fragment from the upper right section of a stele of Hymettian marble (I 6149), broken all around except on the reverse side and shaped at the top into a pediment defined by two taeniae raised in relief to form the horizontal and raking cornices, discovered on April 26, 1949, in a late wall across the Great Drain southwest of the Market Square. The text is inscribed on what had previously been the back of the stele, presumably dressed down and remodeled for the purpose. The original front face carries a poletai record of leases relating to the mines at Laureion, approximately dated to the middle of the 4th century B.C., for which see M. Crosby, *Hesperia* 26, 1957, pp. 2–9, no. S2 and *Agora* XIX, P9.

H. 0.34 m.; W. 0.27 m.; Th. 0.09 m.
LH. 0.26 m.

Ed. M. Crosby, *Hesperia* 26, 1957, pp. 2 and 5, note 2, without photograph. See also *SEG* XVI, 103.

a. 116/17 p.   NON-ΣΤΟΙΧ. *ca.* 17–23

[ʼΕπὶ ἄρχοντος Φλαο]υίου Μακρί
[νου ʼΑχαρνέω]ς ἐπὶ τῆς
[·1–2΄· πρυτανεί]ας ἧς ἐγραμ
[μάτευεν ––––––––––––––]
5   [––––––––––––––––––]

Line 2 is more generously spaced than line 1, seven letters filling the space of nine in the line above; the last three letters in line 3 are crowded, although the earlier part of the line may well have been more generously spaced. It must be supposed that as in, e.g., *IG* II², 1773, 1776, or 1779 (*Agora* XV, 369, 378, and 342) the numeral of the prytany was expressed according to the alphabetic numeral system.

The writing is regularly formed and elegant in the "standard imperial" style. Serifs are added to the "free ends" of strokes. The strokes forming the apex of alpha and the central angle of sigma are crossed to provide decorative effect; the center horizontal strokes of epsilon and eta are detached from the adjacent upright strokes, made very short, and given serif decoration at each end. The crossbar of alpha is broken; the external strokes of mu and sigma are parallel, and the uprights of pi are of equal length. A scar on the stone makes upsilon in line 1 appear as psi.

The decline of public *psephismata* in post-Sullan Athens provides scanty material for comparative study, but what there is suggests that earlier formulas in the prescripts were inconsistently applied; see A. S. Henry, *Prescripts*, pp. 96–103. Indeed in some cases the prescript was dispensed with altogether. The notable features here are the placing of the participle ἄρχοντος before, rather than after, the name to which it refers and the addition of the archon's demotic, for which Henry (*op. cit.*, p. 97) compared *Agora* XV, 460, a prytany decree of the old style, of A.D. 209/10. For similar examples from prytany texts of the 2nd century A.D. sponsored by the prytaneis themselves see (e.g.) *Agora* XV, 331 and 333 (of 138/9), 364 (162/3), 369 (166/7). The same form of words is used in the decree of the Council of the Areopagos **339**.

DECREE OF THE COUNCIL OF THE AREOPAGOS

339. Seven fragments of a rectangular base of Pentelic marble, inscribed on two adjacent sides: four of the fragments join, two of them (*a* + *b*) as joined providing the width of one face (now Face B) of the monument, and these make up a considerable part of the text recorded in 1436 by Cyriacus of Ancona "near the Valerian Wall"; cf. E. W. Bodnar, *Cyriacus of Ancona and Athens* (*Collection Latomus* 43), 1960, pp. 40, 145–150. The stone Cyriacus saw was broken after his time and its fragments evidently scattered quite widely; about half of it has been recovered. He did not see, or at any rate record, what is now described as Face A. His text, partly confirmed by the one fragment (*a*) then known, formed the basis of J. Kirchner's publication *IG* II², 1104. This fragment, preserving the left edge of Face B and an uninscribed (or at best illegible) part of Face A but broken elsewhere, is in the British Museum, to which it was presented in the early 19th century by Lord Elgin. Fragments *b*, *c*, and *d* were identified by A. E. Raubitschek as part of Cyriacus' monument; fragment *b* (E.M. 3013) joins fragment *a* on the right of the latter and preserves the right edge of Face B together with part of the uninscribed Face C but is otherwise broken all around.

Fragments *c* and *d* both came to light during the excavations of the Agora: fragment *c* (I 3155) was discovered on December 17, 1935, in a wall of a modern house over the eastern end of South Stoa I (N–O 16); it preserves an inscribed part of Face A as well as part of the text of Face B and joins fragment *a* above the latter on its left end. Fragment *d* (I 5740) was discovered on March 27, 1939, in a Byzantine context west of the Panathenaic Way and southwest of the Eleusinion (S 22). It is broken all around and joins fragment *c* below the surface on the right of the latter. These four fragments were together designated fragment *a* by D. J. Geagan (see below), but the original designations have been retained here.

Fragments *e*, *f*, and *g* (Geagan *b*, *c*, and *d*) were also all found in the Agora, and all form part of Face A. Fragment *e* (I 5198), preserving also part of the uninscribed Face D and in depth extending as far as Face C (i.e., the entire width of Face B), was discovered on January 29, 1938, at the surface outside the Market Square in the area south of the Church of the Holy Apostles (P 19); it too was identified as part of this monument by Raubitschek.

Fragment *f* (I 6783) was discovered in May 1957 in modern house walls south of the Market Square and preserves part of the top of the monument and of the right section of Face A, together with an uninscribed area of Face B, but is otherwise broken.

Fragment *g* (I 7184 = **342A**), discovered on August 20, 1970, in a marble-pile area (N–Q 19–22), also preserves part of the top of the monument but is otherwise broken. It forms part of Face A and belongs on the left of fragment *f*, although making no direct join with it.

a: H. 0.122 m.; W. 0.403 m.; Th. 0.127 m.

b: H. 0.22 m.; W. 0.25 m.; Th. 0.215 m.

c: H. 0.10 m.; W. 0.189 m.; Th. 0.142 m.

d: H. 0.095 m.; W. 0.17 m.; Th. 0.11 m.

e: H. 0.15 m.; W. 0.39 m.; Th. 0.59 m.

f: H. 0.21 m.; W. 0.15 m.; Th. 0.45 m.

g: H. 0.214 m.; W. 0.19 m.; Th. 0.422 m.

The width of Face B, derived from fragments *a* + *b* and confirmed by the thickness of fragment *e*, is 0.59 m. On fragments *a–d* above, "width" refers to Face B, on *e–g* to Face A. It appears that Faces C and D were not inscribed, and the monument may have stood in a corner with those faces invisible.

Ed. *a–d*: *IG* II², 1104 (from Cyriacus' copy, confirmed in part by fragment *a*). *a–e*: E. W. Bodnar, *op. cit.*, pp. 145–150 (cf. p. 217), with drawings of *a–d* (Face B), p. 145; see also *SEG* XXI, 503. *a–f*: D. J. Geagan, *Hesperia* 42, 1973, pp. 352–357, with photographs of all fragments pls. 63 and 64. *f* and *g* only: Geagan, *Hesperia* 52, 1983, pp. 163–166, no. 4, with photograph of both fragments pl. 43; see also *SEG* XXXIII, 138. For the text of Face B adopted by J. H. Oliver, "The Athens of Hadrian" (in *Les empereurs romains d'Espagne*, 1965), pp. 123–132 (esp. 129–130), see *SEG* XXIV, 150.

a. 195/6 *p*.   NON-ΣΤΟΙΧ. *ca*. 40 (Face A),
                                                                          36–41 (Face B)

FACE A

(*g*)   [᾽Επ᾽ἄρχοντος Γα(ίου) ῾Ελβιδίου Σεκούν]δο[υ Παλλ]ηνέως, χηρυ   (*f*)

[χεύοντος ————————————————]ας ᾽Αμφί[ου το]ῦ ᾽Αμφίου ᵛ

[ἐξ Οἴου, . . .^{*ca*. 10}. . . δεκάτηι ὑ]στέρα[ι· ἔδο]ξεν τῆι ἐξ ᾽Α

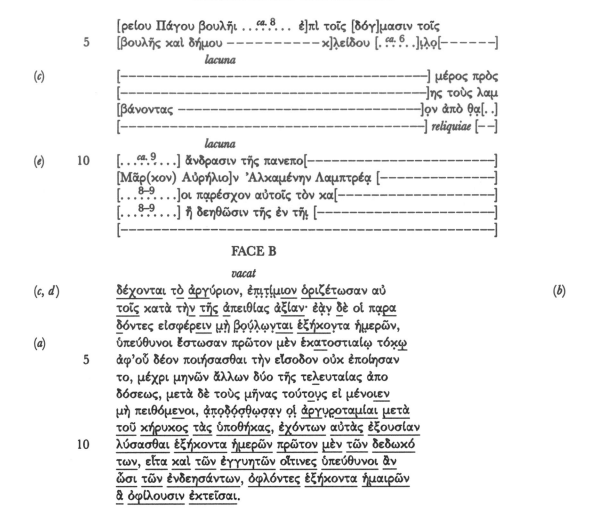

[ρείου Πάγου βουλῆι ...^{ca. 8}... ἐ]πὶ τοῖς [δόγ]μασιν τοῖς

5   [βουλῆς καὶ δήμου ----------x]λείδου [.^{ca. 6}.]ιλο[------]

lacuna

(c)   [----------------------------------] μέρος πρὸς

[----------------------------------]ης τοὺς λαμ

[βάνοντας ----------------------------]ον ἀπὸ θα[..]

[----------------------------------] *reliquiae* [--]

lacuna

(e)   10   [...^{ca. 9}...] ἄνδρασιν τῆς πανεπο[-----------------]

[Μᾶρ(κον) Αὐρήλιο]ν ᾿Αλκαμένην Λαμπτρέᾳ [------------]

[...⁸⁻⁹...]οι παρέσχον αὐτοῖς τὸν κα[------------]

[...⁸⁻⁹...] ἢ δεηθῶσιν τῆς ἐν τῆι [------------]

[----------------------------------]

FACE B

vacat

(c, d)   δέχονται τὸ ἀργύριον, ἐπιτίμιον ὁριζέτωσαν αὐ   (b)

τοῖς κατὰ τὴν τῆς ἀπειθίας ἀξίαν· ἐὰν δὲ οἱ παρα

δόντες εἰσφέρειν μὴ βούλωνται ἑξήκοντα ἡμερῶν,

(a)   ὑπεύθυνοι ἔστωσαν πρῶτον μὲν ἑκατοστιαίῳ τόκῳ

5   ἀφ᾿οῦ δέον ποιήσασθαι τὴν εἴσοδον οὐκ ἐποίησαν

το, μέχρι μηνῶν ἄλλων δύο τῆς τελευταίας ἀπο

δόσεως, μετὰ δὲ τοὺς μῆνας τούτους εἰ μένοιεν

μὴ πειθόμενοι, ἀποδόσθωσαν οἱ ἀργυροταμίαι μετὰ

τοῦ κήρυκος τὰς ὑποθήκας, ἐχόντων αὐτὰς ἐξουσίαν

10   λύσασθαι ἑξήκοντα ἡμερῶν πρῶτον μὲν τῶν δεδωκό

των, εἶτα καὶ τῶν ἐγγυητῶν οἵτινες ὑπεύθυνοι ἂν

ὦσι τῶν ἐνδεησάντων, ὀφλόντες ἑξήκοντα ἡμαιρῶν

ἃ ὀφίλουσιν ἐκτεῖσαι.

The above text is based upon Bodnar's drawings and Geagan's two articles. On Face B the words and letters recorded by Cyriacus and not now surviving are underlined; in lines 9–13 no account is taken of misreadings by him, sufficiently indicated by Bodnar and others. What survives on Faces A and B is so aligned that line 6 of Face A appears at the level of line 1 of Face B (both on fragment *c*): that part of Face B preserved on fragment *f* is uninscribed.

The writing may be described as "standard imperial" and gives the appearance of neatness and regularity: it was regarded as compatible with a Hadrianic date until the discovery of fragments *e–g* demonstrated that it belonged to the Severan period. On closer inspection of the individual letters, however, some lack of care and consistency is evident. The upright of tau, for example, is at times aslant, and the upright of phi, projecting above and below the line of writing, is placed off center to the right in relation to the circle it supposedly bisects. The central strokes of mu vary considerably in the angle at which they meet. Serifs or enlargement of "free ends" are applied intermittently; the crossbar of alpha is straight. Bodnar noted similarities with the hand of *IG* II², 1118.

Originally interpreted as an "edictum de vectigalibus", *IG* II², 1104 was assigned by Kirchner, following Boeckh (*CIG*), to the age of Hadrian. The identification of fragment *e*, with its reference to Alkamenes of Lamptrai, suggested a connection with the already known στρατηγός of 209/10 (*IG* II², 1077, lines 9, 14), and this is confirmed by the likely restoration of the name of the archon derived from fragments *f* and *g*. But the document may well represent the republication of a Hadrianic law, as urged by Oliver, *loc. cit.* For discussion of the contents, explained as a *lex praediatoria*, see Bodnar, *loc. cit.*, with earlier references. *IG* II², 1118 seems to deal with related issues; cf. Geagan, *Hesperia* 42, 1973, p. 357.

Face A: Line 1. Before the discovery of fragment *g*, S. Follet (*Athènes au IIe et au IIIe siècle*, 1976, p. 228, note 3) suggested three possible names for the archon to be restored here; cf. *SEG* XXXIII, 138. Fragment *g*, providing two letters of what must be the archon's name, narrowed the choice, for the archon of 195/6 alone suits the surviving data. Line 2. Amphias, son of Amphias. The name is uncommon, as Geagan noted (*Hesperia* 42, 1973, p. 356), except in a family of the deme Oion; cf. *IG* II², 2068, 2110, 2199. This makes the restoration in line 3 highly probable. In the lacuna Geagan (*Hesperia* 52, 1983, p. 165) suggested μετὰ τοὺς ἀργυροταμί]ας. Line 3. The month may well have been Mounichion. Line 4. Either συνκλήτωι (or συνηχθείση or κληθείση) attached to βουλῆι, or γνώμην (or ἀνέγνω) with punctuation after βουλῆι, Geagan, *loc. cit.*

Line 11. Alkamenes of Lamptrai. On his identity, career, and connections see Oliver, *Hesperia* 27, 1958, p. 39; Geagan, *Athenian Constitution*, pp. 172–173, *Hesperia* 42, 1973, p. 356, *ZPE* 33, 1979, pp. 96–97; Follet, *op. cit.*, pp. 86–87, 93–94.

DIVINE HONORS ACCORDED TO THE FAMILY OF THE EMPEROR SEPTIMIUS SEVERUS

340. Three fragments, two of which join, of a stele of Pentelic marble, the surface of which is somewhat mottled in appearance. Fragment *a* (I 6735) preserves the right edge and original rough-picked back of the stele but is broken elsewhere; at the bottom it makes a direct join with fragment *b*. It was discovered on June 18, 1955, in a Late Roman context near the northwest corner of the Temple of Ares (I 7). Fragment *b* (I 6170) similarly preserves the right side and back of the stele but is elsewhere broken; it was first observed by D. J. Geagan that it joins fragment *a* with the right section of its upper edge. It was discovered on May 3, 1949, in a long Late Roman Wall east of the Panathenaic Way (O 8). Fragment *c* (I 5855) preserves the original back but is otherwise broken all around and was discovered on June 1, 1939, in a modern wall west of the Panathenaic Way and south of the Eleusinion (R 22). That fragments *a* and *c* formed part of the same monument was first observed by A. G. Woodhead.

a: H. 0.37 m.; W. 0.26 m.; Th. 0.072 m.

b: H. 0.21 m.; W. 0.275 m.; Th. 0.072 m.

Height of combined fragments *a* + *b* 0.50 m.

c: H. 0.33 m.; W. 0.165 m.; Th. 0.075 m.

LH. 0.014 m. (phi and psi 0.03 m.)

Ed. *c* only: J. H. Oliver, *Hesperia* 10, 1941, pp. 84–85, no. 36, with photograph. *a* only: B. D. Meritt, *Hesperia* 33, 1964, pp. 200–201, no. 52, with photograph pl. 32; see also *SEG* XXI, 504. Fragment *b* is hitherto unpublished.

post a. 196 p. NON-ΣΤΟΙΧ. *ca.* 67

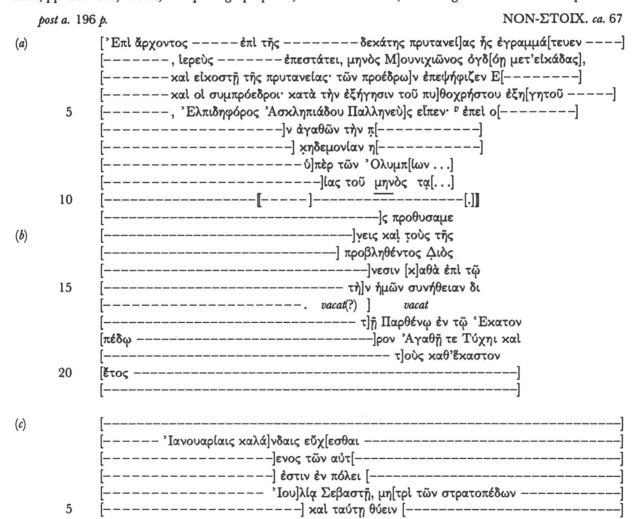

```
[------------- τὰ εἰσιτ]ήρια τῆι Ἀθηνᾷ [τῆι ----------------------------]
[------------------- κ]ατάρχεσθαι δὲ κα[ὶ τούτων τῶν θυσιῶν τὴν ἱέρειαν τῆς]
['Αθηνᾶς τῆς Πολιάδος καὶ τὰ γέρα] φέρεσθαι· τὰ δὲ λο[ιπὰ -----------------]
[--------------------]πεν δὲ τῇ καταρ[------------------------------]
[------------------ 'Ι]ουλίαν Σεβασ[τὴν ----------------------------]
[-----------------]‾αθησ[------------------------------------]
[----------------]ντα[------------------------------------]
[-------------------------------------------------------]
```
10

No direct connection can be made between fragments *a* + *b* and fragment *c*. The lettering is good Severan work but is not quite of the high quality of **341** and **342**, and there is some crowding. The very elongated upright strokes of phi and psi are particularly notable. Serifs are added to many of the "free ends" of strokes. There is slight curvature at times in the cross-stroke of nu and the strokes of upsilon and chi. In the triangular letters one of the angled strokes sometimes projects above the apex, and in alpha the crossbar is straight or slightly curved. At the end of line 11 of fragments *a* + *b* there is a ligature of mu and epsilon. The *rasura* in line 10, which a supra-lineate mark has escaped, presumably contained a reference to Geta Caesar and was made when his memory was condemned in A.D. 212.

The decree concerned sacrifices and ritual to be prescribed in honor of the imperial house and principally (cf. **341**) for the Empress Julia Domna. Hence the intervention of the Πυθόχρηστος ἐξηγητής in the context of what amounted to a *lex sacra*. Too little remains for the provisions to be at all clear, but they were to some extent amplified and amended in a later decree, **341**, the proposer of which was out of town when this decree was passed (see lines 9–11 of that text). See below, note on line 5.

Fragments *a* + *b*: Lines 1–5. The preamble is cast in a formula apparently regular for the period, evidence for which is not abundant, the restorations being based by Meritt on *IG* II², 1077 (*Agora* XV, 460). Cf. A. S. Henry (*Prescripts*, pp. 101–103), who however classes it as "unusual", a major point being that the ἱερεύς is presumed to have taken the chair (as in *Agora* XV, 460). The date, as Henry further noted, is postponed until after the reference to the ἐπιστάτης. At this time practice may perhaps best be described as fluid and arbitrary, without suppositions as to what is to be regarded as usual or unusual. For the exegesis of the Πυθόχρηστος ἐξηγητής see J. H. Oliver, *The Athenian Expounders of the Sacred and Ancestral Law*, 1950, pp. 160–161, no. I 52. Line 5. The proposer Elpidephoros, son of Asklepiades, of Pallene appears in **341** as author of a decree to which that text makes amendments and improvements. It is likely, as Oliver recognized in his publication of fragment *c*, that this is the decree there amended, and Elpidephoros' name is restored in consequence. The patronymic is derived from the *catalogus virorum nobilium SEG* XVIII, 61; see *SEG* XVIII, 30. The name Asklepiades recurs in the deme Pallene throughout the 2nd century A.D. in ephebic and other contexts (e.g., *IG* II², 2065, line 28, 2085, line 20).

Lines 11–12. προθυσαμε[νο–– reflects the προθύειν of **341**, lines 34–35. Line 16. The space may indicate a break between the detail of honors for the family in general and of those for Julia Domna in particular. Julia Domna was equated with Athena Polias in a manner expressed more fully in the revised proposals of **341**. For lines 18–20, cf. **341**, lines 11–13 and 22–25 (sacrifice on January 1st). There the archons perform a joint sacrifice to Bona Fortuna on Julia Domna's birthday.

Fragment *c*: Lines 5–9. Possibly these lines envisaged that the sacrifices in honor of Julia Domna were to be on a par with those in honor of Athena Polias, e.g., καὶ ταύτῃ θύειν [ὡς σωτείρᾳ τῶν Ἀθηνῶν τὸν ἐπὶ τοὺς ὁπλίτας στρατηγὸν ὅταν ποιῇ τὰ εἰσιτ]ήρια τῇ Ἀθηνᾷ. In **341** the improved suggestion is rather that the Empress is herself to be identified with, and not merely given parity with, the patron goddess of Athens. See Oliver's commentary on that text.

DIVINE HONORS ACCORDED TO THE EMPRESS JULIA DOMNA

341. A small fragment of a pedimental stele of Pentelic marble (I 5680, hereafter fragment *k*), broken on all sides save for the original smoothly polished back, which forms part of the monument *IG* II², 1076. It was discovered between February 13 and 18, 1939, in a modern context in the industrial section southwest of the Market Square. At its bottom edge it joins the united fragments *l* + *m* and belongs to the upper half of the stele on its left-hand side.

k: H. 0.087 m.; W. 0.086 m.; Th. 0.069 m.

k + *l* + *m*: H. 0.25 m.; W. 0.185 m.; Th. 0.07 m.

Stele overall: H. not less than 1.75 m.; W. *ca.* 0.85 m.; Th. 0.07 m.

LH. 0.017 m. (phi 0.044 m.)

Ed. *e–t*: J. H. Oliver, *HSCP*, Supplementary Volume I (*Athenian Studies Presented to W. S. Ferguson*), 1940, pp. 521–530, with photograph of all fragments then known to which a definite place in the monument could be assigned, fig. 1, and drawing on opposite page. See also J. and L. Robert, *REG* 59/60, 1946/1947, pp. 323–324, no. 101. Five new fragments added (four belonging to the top of the stele), with Oliver's fragments redesignated and lines renumbered in consequence, by R. S. Stroud, *Hesperia* 40, 1971, pp. 200–204, no. 53, with photographs of all fragments except *k*, *s*, and *t*, pl. 36, and drawing of the position of those fragments to which a definite place can be assigned, fig. 2; see also *SEG* XXXVII, 97.

The Agora fragment comprises no more than sixteen letters, in whole or in part, and is of value only in its context. A combination of Stroud's and Oliver's texts, comprehending the whole monument, is therefore reproduced below, with a conspectus of all the fragments as assembled by them. Oliver added the Agora fragment and another which he identified in the Epigraphical Museum (E.M. 3490, here fragment *p*) to the fourteen known to O. Broneer, whose publication in *Hesperia* 4, 1935 (pp. 178–184, no. 45) was the foundation of his study. Broneer had added fragments *m*, *n*, *s*, and *t* to the ten published in *IG* II², 1076 on the basis of A. von Premerstein's fundamental publication (*ÖJh* 16, 1913, pp. 249–270). The fragments may be listed as follows, designated as in Stroud's revision but, for convenience, with Oliver's designations added in brackets where apposite:

a. E.M. 5029, identified by Stroud (as also were *b*, *c*, and *d*) and preserving part of the top and smooth back of the monument. It contains the center of the pediment and part of line 1. There is no record of its provenience.

b. E.M. 12290, on its right joining fragment *c*, was discovered on April 14, 1937, on the North Slope of the Akropolis.

c. E.M. 3813, preserving the right end of the pediment with its akroterion, joins to the left fragment *b* and, below, fragment *d*. There is no record of its provenience.

d. E.M. 5700 joins fragment *c* above; it was discovered on the Akropolis at an unknown date.

e (*h¹*). E.M. 8369; *IG* II², 1076. From the upper right of the stele, it joins fragment *f* (below).

f (*h²*). E.M. 8370; *IG* II², 1076. It joins *e* (above) and *g* (below).

g (*g*). E.M. 8375; *IG* II², 1076. The center right of the stele, joining *f* (above) and *h* and *i* (below).

h (*d*). E.M. 8373; *IG* II², 1076. From the lower right of the stele, joining *j* (to right) and *g* (above).

i (*e*). E.M. 8379; *IG* II², 1076. From the same section, joining *g* (above) and *j* (below).

j (*f*). E.M. 8374; *IG* II², 1076. From the same section, joining *h* (to the left) and *i* (above).

k. Agora I 5680. See above.

l. E.M. 8376; *IG* II², 1076. From the upper left of the stele, joining *k* (above) and *m* (to the right).

m (*m*). E.M. 12751, discovered by Broneer on the North Slope of the Akropolis and published in *Hesperia* 4, 1935, pp. 178–184. From the left of the stele, joining *k* and *l* (to the left).

n (*j*). E.M. 4646, identified by Broneer, *loc. cit.*, with fig. 68. From the center left of the stele, joining fragment *o* (below).

o (*a*). E.M. 8371; *IG* II², 1076. From the same section, but lower, joining *n* (above), *p* (to the right), and *r* (below).

p (*o*). E.M. 3490, identified by Oliver and published by him at the same time as fragment *k* (see esp. pp. 522–527). On its left it joins fragment *o*.

q (*c*). E.M. 8377; *IG* II², 1076. From the same section, joining *o* and *r* (to the left).

r (*b*). E.M. 8372; *IG* II², 1076. From the same section, joining *o* (above) and *q* (to the right).

s (*k*). E.M. 3144, identified by Broneer, *loc. cit.*, with fig. 71. Of uncertain position.

t (*l*). E.M. 12731, discovered by Broneer on the North Slope of the Akropolis on September 19, 1932, and separately published by him, *Hesperia* 2, 1933, p. 412, no. 34, with drawing fig. 84, but correctly assigned in *Hesperia* 4, 1935, *loc. cit.*, with fig. 71. Of uncertain position.

u. E.M. 13028, identified by Stroud, *loc. cit.*, with photograph pl. 36, and discovered on the North Slope on April 8, 1937. It is broken on all sides including the back and makes no join with any other fragment.

For further description and bibliography (to that date) see Oliver, *op. cit.*, p. 521, notes 1 and 2, and p. 522, and for description and measurements of fragments *a–d* and *u* see Stroud, *loc. cit.* Cf. also L. Deubner, *Attische Feste*, pp. 236–237.

post a. 196 *p.* NON-ΣΤΟΙΧ. *ca.* 36–44 (lines 3–44)

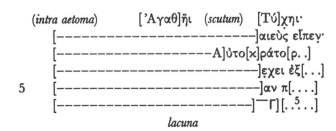

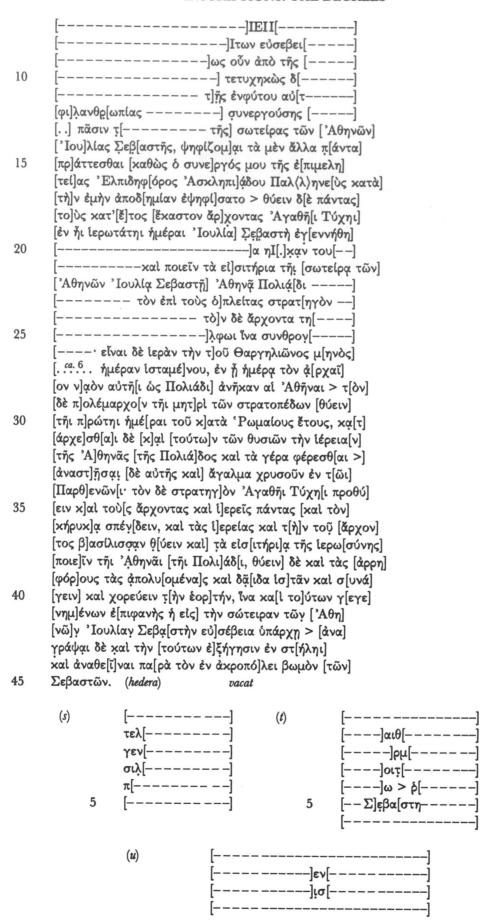

[--------------------]ΙΕΙΙ[--------]
[------------------]Ιτων εὐσεβει[-----]
[------------------]ως οὖν ἀπὸ τῆς [-----]
10 [------------------] τετυχηκὼς δ[------]
[---------------- τ]ῆς ἐνφύτου αὐ[τ------]
[φι]λανθρ[ωπίας --------] συνεργούσης [-----]
[..] πᾶσιν τ[-------- τῆς] σωτείρας τῶν ['Αθηνῶν]
['Ιου]λίας Σεβ[αστῆς, ψηφίζομ]αι τὰ μὲν ἄλλα π[άντα]
15 [πρ]άττεσθαι [καθὼς ὁ συνε]ργός μου τῆς ἐ[πιμελη]
[τεί]ας 'Ελπιδηφ[όρος 'Ασκληπι]άδου Παλ⟨λ⟩ηνε[ὺς κατὰ]
[τὴ]ν ἐμὴν ἀποδ[ημίαν ἐψηφί]σατο > θύειν δ[ὲ πάντας]
[το]ὺς κατ'[ἔ]τος [ἕκαστον ἄρ]χοντας 'Αγαθῆ[ι Τύχηι]
ἐν ἧι ἱερωτάτηι ἡμέραι 'Ιουλία] Σεβαστὴ ἐγ[εννήθη]
20 [-----------------------]α ηΙ[.]χαν του[--]
[-----------καὶ ποιεῖν τὰ εἰ]σιτήρια τῆι [σωτείρα τῶν]
['Αθηνῶν 'Ιουλία Σεβαστῆ] 'Αθηνᾶ Πολιά[δι -----]
[-------- τὸν ἐπὶ τοὺς ὁ]πλείτας στρατ[ηγὸν --]
[--------------- τὸ]ν δὲ ἄρχοντα τη[----]
25 [---------------]λφωι ἵνα συνθρογ[-----]
[----· εἶναι δὲ ἱερὰν τὴν τ]οῦ Θαργηλιῶνος μ[ηνὸς]
[. ca.6.. ἡμέραν ἱσταμέ]νου, ἐν ἧι ἡμέρᾳ τὸν ἀ[ρχαῖ]
[ον ν]αὸν αὐτῆ[ι ὡς Πολιάδι] ἀνῆκαν αἱ 'Αθῆναι > τ[ὸν]
[δὲ π]ολέμαρχο[ν τῆι μητ]ρὶ τῶν στρατοπέδων [θύειν]
30 [τῆι π]ρώτηι ἡμέ[ραι τοῦ κ]ατὰ 'Ρωμαίους ἔτους, κα[τ]
[άρχε]σθ[α]ι δὲ [κ]αὶ [τούτω]ν τῶν θυσιῶν τὴν ἱέρεια[ν]
[τῆς 'Α]θηνᾶς [τῆς Πολιά]δος καὶ τὰ γέρα φέρεσθ[αι >]
[ἀναστ]ῆσαι [δὲ αὐτῆς καὶ] ἄγαλμα χρυσοῦν ἐν τ[ῶι]
[Παρθ]ενῶν[ι· τὸν δὲ στρατηγ]ὸν 'Αγαθῆι Τύχη[ι προθύ]
35 [ειν κ]αὶ τοὺ[ς ἄρχοντας καὶ ἱ]ερεῖς πάντας [καὶ τὸν]
[κήρυκ]α σπέγ[δειν, καὶ τὰς ἱ]ερείας καὶ τ[ὴ]ν τοῦ [ἄρχον]
[τος β]ασίλισσαν θ[ύειν καὶ] τὰ εἰσ[ιτήρι]α τῆς ἱερω[σύνης]
[ποιε]ῖν τῆι 'Αθηνᾶι [τῆι Πολι]άδ[ι, θύειν] δὲ καὶ τὰς [ἀρρη]
[φόρ]ους τὰς ἀπολυ[ομένα]ς καὶ δᾷ[ιδα ἱσ]τᾶν καὶ σ[υνά]
40 [γειν] καὶ χορεύειν τ[ὴν ἑορ]τήν, ἵνα κα[ὶ το]ύτων γ[εγε]
[νημ]ένων ἐ[πιφανὴς ἡ εἰς] τὴν σώτειραν τῶ[ν 'Αθη]
[νῶ]ν 'Ιουλίαν Σεβα[στὴν εὐ]σέβεια ὑπάρχη > [ἀνα]
γράψαι δὲ καὶ τὴν [τούτων ἐ]ξήγησιν ἐν στ[ήληι]
καὶ ἀναθε[ῖ]ναι πα[ρὰ τὸν ἐν ἀκροπό]λει βωμὸν [τῶν]
45 Σεβαστῶν. (hedera)   vacat

(s)   (t)
[---------- ---]   [---- ----------]
τελ[---------- ---]   [----]αιθ[------ --]
γεν[---------- ---]   [-----]ρμ[------ --]
σιλ[-------- ---]   [----]οιτ[------ --]
π[---------- --]   [----]ω > ῥ[------]
5 [-------- ---]   5 [-- Σ]εβα[στη----]
                            [---- ----------]

(u)
[------------------ ----]
[--------- ---]εν[---- --------]
[---------- ---]ισ[---- --------]
[------------------ ----]

For earlier readings and restorations, and for full *apparatus criticus*, see Oliver, *op. cit.*, pp. 529–530. The writing is of great regularity and elegance, and the stele deserves recognition for its artistic quality as well as for its historical interest. Serifs are attached to the "free ends" of strokes. The crossbar of alpha is broken, and (as in **340**) one of the angled strokes of the triangular letters projects slightly beyond the junction forming the apex of the triangle. Theta has a short cross-stroke; in eta the horizontal stroke is detached from the two uprights and carries serifs. Mu, pi, and sigma are all in the imperial form, and the upright stroke of phi is so elongated as to make contact with the lines above and below. Iota adscript is intermittently written. A small, angular mark of punctuation appears in lines 17, 28, and 42, as well as in fragment *t*, and is restored in line 32.

For the subject matter of the document see the commentary on **340**, which (at least in respect of the honors prescribed for the Empress Julia Domna) is amended and expanded by this decree. On the polemarch's duties see D. J. Geagan, *Athenian Constitution*, pp. 11–12, with note 65. A. N. Oikonomides (*Bulletin of the American Society of Papyrologists* 21, 1984, pp. 179–180) saw reason to date this decree to 193–195 rather than as shown here; cf. *SEG* XXXIV, 184.

The pediment (in the center of which is a round shield) and akroterion (surviving on the right) are described by Stroud as in low relief. They appear to be delineated by simple grooving, with minimal additional working. The two words of line 1 are written within the pediment on either side of the shield; line 2 occupies the space between the two grooves which represent the floor of the pediment.

Line 13 *init.* [ἐν]J. and L. Robert; [. .] Oliver. Line 15. [πρ]άττεσθαι. For the usage cf. **336**, line 5. Line 16. *Lapis* ΠΑΛΗΝΕ. On Elpidephoros see **340**, commentary on line 5. Lines 17–18. Cf. **340**, lines 19–20.

Lines 30–32. Cf. **340**, fragment *c*, lines 7–8. Lines 34–35. Cf. **340**, fragment *c*, commentary on lines 5–9; Geagan, *Athenian Constitution*, pp. 60 and (on the function of the Hoplite General) 30. Lines 39–40. J. and L. Robert expressed doubts concerning σ[υνάγειν] καὶ χορεύειν τ[ὴν ἑορ]τήν. Line 43. ἐ]ξήγησιν rather than Oliver's εἰ]σήγησιν (εἰσ]ήγησιν *priores*)? Cf. **340**, fragments *a + b*, line 4.

DECREE IN HONOR OF C. FULVIUS PLAUTIANUS(?)

342. Eight fragments of a stele of Pentelic marble, four of which join to form a single piece and two of which (not included among the joining fragments) were found in the Agora (I 4853 a, b). Of the Agora fragments, both of which are broken on all sides save for the original smooth back, one (fragment *d*) was discovered on May 12, 1937, in a modern context east of the Post-Herulian Wall south of the Eleusinion (U 20). Traces of orange paint survive in the cutting of some of the letters. The other fragment (*e*) was discovered on May 21, 1937, in a fill of Early Byzantine date over the Eleusinion (T 19). Both were identified as belonging to a document of which J. H. Oliver recognized *IG* II², 1081/5 and 1116 as constituent parts, and to which he added three pieces in the Epigraphical Museum previously unpublished.

d: H. 0.258 m.; W. 0.165 m.; Th. 0.085 m.

e: H. 0.105 m.; W. 0.05 m.; Th. 0.085 m.

LH. 0.022 m. (phi 0.044 m.)

Ed. J. H. Oliver, *Hesperia* 10, 1941, pp. 85–90, no. 37, with photographs of all fragments. See also J. and L. Robert, *REG* 57, 1944, p. 204, no. 82. Lines 4–7 cited in *Agora* III, p. 30, no. 46 (for line 22 see also p. 174). The fragments, all fully described by Oliver, may be briefly listed as follows:

a. *IG* II², 1081/5; E.M. 9484. From the top of the stele.

b. E.M. 9483, broken all around except at the back and identified by Oliver. According to his reconstruction, it is from the left of the stele, on the same level as fragment *c*. In this position its lower edge maintains the line of fracture of the lower edge of *c*.

c. *IG* II², 1116; E.M. 5728 + 5831 + 8582 + 8583. Oliver identified nos. 5728 and 5831, adding them to the left of the other two fragments which compose the *IG* II² entry and which preserve the right side of the stele.

d. Agora I 4853 a. See above. Of uncertain position.

e. Agora I 4853 b. See above. Of uncertain position.

a. 203 *p.* (?)   NON-ΣTOIX. *ca.* 35–38

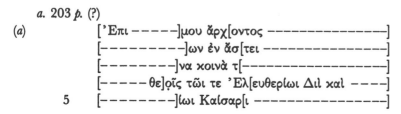

(a)   ['Ἐπι ─ ─ ─ ─ ─]μου ἄρχ[οντος ─ ─ ─ ─ ─ ─ ─ ─ ─ ─ ─ ─ ─ ─ ─ ─]
             [─ ─ ─ ─ ─ ─ ─ ─ ─]ων ἐν ἄσ[τει ─ ─ ─ ─ ─ ─ ─ ─ ─ ─ ─ ─ ─ ─ ─]
             [─ ─ ─ ─ ─ ─ ─]να κοινὰ τ[─ ─ ─ ─ ─ ─ ─ ─ ─ ─ ─ ─ ─ ─ ─ ─ ─]
             [─ ─ ─ ─ ─ θε]οῖς τῶι τε Ἐλ[ευθερίωι Διὶ καὶ ─ ─ ─ ─]
      5   [─ ─ ─ ─ ─ ─ ─]ίωι Καίσαρ[ι ─ ─ ─ ─ ─ ─ ─ ─ ─ ─ ─ ─ ─ ─]

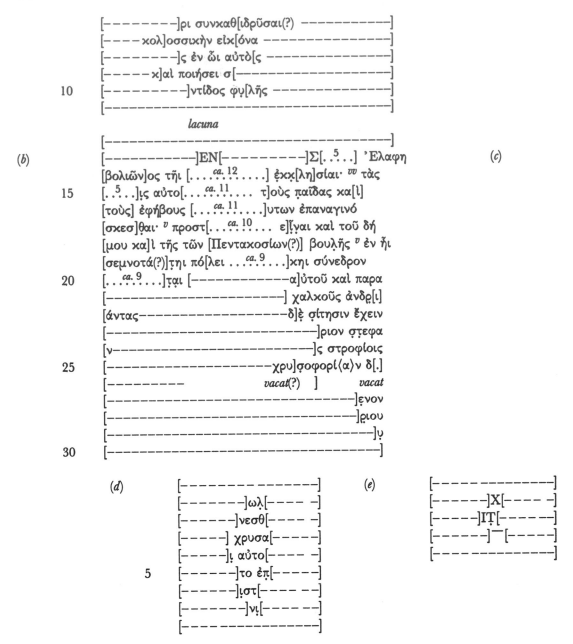

[----------]ρι συνκαθ[ιδρῦσαι(?) -----------]

[----χολ]οσσικὴν εἰκ[όνα ----------------]

[--------]ς ἐν ὧι αὐτὸ[ς ----------------]

[-----κ]αὶ ποιήσει σ[----------------]

10 [----------]ντίδος φυ[λῆς ---------------]

[------------------------------]

lacuna

[------------------------------]

(b) [-----------]ΕΝ[---------]Σ[..⁵..] Ἐλαφη (c)

[βολιῶν]ος τῆι [....*ca.* 12....] ἐκκ[λη]σίαι· ᵛᵛ τὰς

15 [..⁵..]ις αὐτο[...*ca.* 11... τ]οὺς παῖδας κα[ὶ]

[τοὺς] ἐφήβους [...*ca.* 11....]υτων ἐπαναγινό

[σκεσ]θαι· ᵛ προστ[...*ca.* 10... ε]ἶγαι καὶ τοῦ δή

[μου κα]ὶ τῆς τῶν [Πεντακοσίων(?)] βουλῆς ᵛ ἐν ἧι

[σεμνοτά(?)]τηι πό[λει ...*ca.* 9...]κηι σύνεδρον

20 [...*ca.* 9...]ται [-----------α]ὐτοῦ καὶ παρα

[----------------] χαλκοῦς ἀνδρ[ι

[άντας------------δ]ὲ σίτησιν ἔχειν

[-------------]ριον στεφα

[ν------------]ς στροφίοις

25 [------------χρυ]σοφορί⟨α⟩ν δ[.]

[--------   *vacat*(?)]   *vacat*

[----------------]ενον

[----------------]ριου

[----------------]υ

30 [----------------]

(d) [-------- --------]   (e) [----- --------]

[-------]ωλ[---- -]   [------]Χ[---- -]

[-----]νεσθ[---- -]   [----]ΙΤ[-----]

[-----] χρυσα[-----]   [------]⌐[-----]

[-----]ι αὐτο[---- -]   [----- --------]

5 [------]το ἐπ[-----]

[------]ιστ[---- --]

[-------]νι[---- --]

[--- ----------]

Line 15. αὐτο[ῦ .*ca.* 6.. πρὸς τ]οὺς παῖδας Oliver. Line 16. α]ὐτῶν Oliver. Lines 16–17. ἐπαναγινώ[σκεσ]θαι Oliver: the *corrigendum* was pointed out by L. Threatte, *Grammar*, p. 231; cf. *SEG* XXX, 83, where, however, Oliver's reading is reprinted *per errorem*. Line 17. προστ[άτην δ'αὐτὸν ε]ἶγαι Oliver. Line 23. *Lapis* ΦΟΡΙΛΝ. Oliver's text is elsewhere followed; he gives an *apparatus criticus* in respect of earlier editions. The lines end at irregular distances from the right edge, where vacant spaces have not been indicated.

The lettering is that of the "imperial style" at its neatest and most elegant. Oliver justly noted that the inscription "must have been one of the handsomest ever erected at Athens." There is some enlargement of the "free ends" of strokes, with occasional full serifs. The crossbar of alpha is straight; the center strokes of sigma are crossed to provide decorative effect; omega is in the uncial form, the sole example of this type among the Agora *psephismata* of this collection, although it is frequent enough in the less monumental contexts of prytany and ephebic decrees. Other letters have their regular imperial aspect, and the vertical stroke of phi is very elongated. Iota adscript is consistently written.

Oliver observed that the stones composing this stele were unweathered, one of them retaining traces of paint in the lettering, and he inferred that the monument had a short life as part of the Athenian scene. He argued that the colossal statue (line 7) could not have been that of an emperor, as had been the earlier and most natural interpretation, by reason of the grant of σίτησις in line 22; but if the decree does nevertheless refer to an emperor, his opinion was that Commodus was the honorand most likely to be concerned (with the restoration of the archon Philotimos in line 1). His contention that C. Fulvius Plautianus, the great praetorian prefect murdered by Caracalla in A.D. 205, was the person for whom the honors were decreed appeared to accord with the short life of the stele and its demolition, as well as with the extravagance of the honors and the opulence of the stele itself. Neither this suggestion nor the proposed restorations received the approval of J. and L. Robert (*loc. cit.*), whose comments were repeated without further discussion by S. Follet, *Athènes au IIe et au IIIe siècle*, 1976, p. 37.

If the decree does refer to Plautianus, of whom Oliver gave a short account, the following bibliographical references may be added to those supplied in his edition: G. Barbieri, *L'Albo Senatorio da Settimio Severo a Carino*, 1952, p. 63, no. 255; A. Birley, *The African Emperor, Septimius Severus*, 1988, *passim* (esp. p. 221, no. 32); F. Grosso, *Accademia Nazionale dei Lincei: Rendiconti*, 1968, pp. 7–58; L. L. Howe, *The Pretorian Prefect from Commodus to Diocletian*, 1942 (repr. 1966), pp. 69–70, no. 18; S. N. Miller, *CAH* XII, 1939, pp. 19–21; J. J. van Norren, "Plautianus" (diss. Amsterdam), 1953; A. Stein, *RE* VII, i, 1910, cols. 270–278, *s.v.* Fulvius (101); *PIR*^{2}, F 554.

For the competence of the δῆμος at this epoch, as suggested in this text, see D. J. Geagan, *Athenian Constitution*, pp. 87–90.

Line 22. On σίτησις see **310**, commentary on lines 49–50, and cf. A. S. Henry, *Honours*, p. 288, note 72.

APPENDIX: MATERIAL DISCOVERED SINCE 1967

342A. Decree of the Council of the Areopagos. For I 7184, discovered on August 20, 1970, see **339**.

CONCORDANCES

CONCORDANCES

1. PUBLICATIONS

A. *INSCRIPTIONES GRAECAE, EDITIO MINOR*

IG I²	*Agora* XVI
29	**3**
32	**1**
45	**7**
90	**16**
96	**19**
122	**18**
130	**12**
141	**10**
144	**20**
155	**20**
156	**18**
174	**10**

IG I³	*Agora* XVI
16	**2**
17	**1**
22	**5**
26	see **28**
29	**3**
31	**4**
44	**6**
46	**7**
50	**9**
62	**15**
70	**14**
76	**16**
86	**19**
90	**17**
91	**20**
95	**21**
121	**23**
122	**22**
125	**28A**
129	**8**

	Agora XVI
135	**24**
139	**12**
145	**10**
155	**11**
182	**18**
187	**13**
196	**27**
202	**26**
210	**28**
225	**25**
416	see **28**

IG II²	*Agora* XVI
11	**30**
14	**34**
17	**36**
20	**106A**
25	**40**
30	**41**
46	**35**
55, b	**15**
66	**20**
98	**46**
138	**55**
144	**47**
145	**52**
174	**28A**
181	**59**
272	**45**
305	**47**
318	**47**
319	**47**
334	**75**
369	**94**
372	**95**

	Agora XVI
407	**106 J**
414, b, c	**94**
463	**109**
514	**112**
535	**104**
564	**111**
635	**47**
643	**162**
662	**172**
691	**157**
760	**172**
778	**208**
791	**213**
851	**248**
898	**332A**
925	see **266**
933	**308**
937	**310**
954	**276**
1051	**335**
1058	**335**
1069	see **337**
1071	**336**
1076	**341**
1081/5	**342**
1104	**339**
1116	**342**
1119	**337**
1141	**44**
1176	**93**
1707	**332C**

IG XII, Suppl.	*Agora* XVI
pp. 200–201 (2)	**224**

B. *SUPPLEMENTUM EPIGRAPHICUM GRAECUM*

SEG III	*Agora* XVI
73	**41**

SEG X	*Agora* XVI
11	**2**
13	**1**
15	**4**
21	**3**
26	**6**
34	**7**

	Agora XVI
42	**8**
44	**9**
51	**10**
54	**11**
62	**12**
67	**15**
76	**14**
79	**18**
87	**17**
89	**16**

	Agora XVI
104	**19**
108	**20**
111	**21**
120	**25**
123	**24**
131	**18**
140	**23**
145a	**26**

SEG XII	*Agora* XVI
15	see **7**
22	**11**
33	**20**
87	**73**
91	**116**
92	**137**
93	**244**

SEG XIII	*Agora* XVI
7	**15**
42	**109**

SEG XIV	*Agora* XVI
40	**20**
50	**52**
58	**122**
59	**207**
64	**187**
65	**188**
69	**269**
73	**316**
75	**264**
76	**312**
79	**337**
81	**192**

SEG XV	*Agora* XVI
84	**36**
86	**40**
90	**48**
91	**47**
95	**73**
101	**185**

SEG XVI	*Agora* XVI
42	**36**
50	**56**
61	**169**
62	**172**
63	**186**
72	**228**
73	**239**
74	**259**
75	**260**
76	**290**
77	**262**
85	**258**
92	**284**
94	**292**
97	**295**
102	**319**
103	**338**

SEG XVII	*Agora* XVI
16	**38**

17	**35**
18	**47**
19	**50**
20	**51**
21	**56**
26	**73**
27	**74**
28	**138**
30	**290**
34	**336**
36	**235**

SEG XVIII	*Agora* XVI
4	**8**
10	**35**
12	**73**
13	**75**
17	**139**
18	**111**
23	**294**
31	**270**

SEG XIX	*Agora* XVI
3	**5**
5	**4**
48	**50**
52	**70**
53	**61**
54	**64**
55	**65**
58	**109**
62	**133**
63	**152**
65	**149**
66	**150**
68	**158**
70	**159**
72	**212**
75	**237**
78	**218**
81	**226**
83	**243**
90	**240**
94	**271**
95	**332**
98	**273**
100	**284**
102	**308**
103	**286**
104	**317**
105	**328**
106	**302**
107	**268**
117	**93**
119	**77**
123	**271**

124	**306**
125	**329**

SEG XXI	*Agora* XVI
9	**1**
11	**4**
29	**7**
32	**8**
39	**11**
45	**17**
49	**19**
50	**20**
57	**22**
219	**29**
220	**34**
230	**43**
237	**46**
245	**50**
246	**49**
255	**56**
257	**56**
258	**63**
259	**51**
269	**75**
288	**85**
290	**91**
298	**94**
300	**95**
303	**97**
306	**100**
310	**101**
312	**102**
316	**103**
318	**104**
319	**105**
333	**109**
334	**107**
336	**112**
340	**66**
342	**141**
343	**142**
344	**140**
345	**90**
346	**56**
347	**133**
348	**145**
358	**176**
359	**178**
360	**205**
361	**155**
362	**163**
367	**184**
370	**189**
371	**195**
380	**197**
388	**200**

389	**201**	96	**73**	*SEG* XXVI	*Agora* XVI
407	**267**	102	**94**	13	**17**
414	**248**	112	**111**	21	**18**
416	**232**	114	**131**	72	**106C**
417	**255**	116	**153**	93	**189**
418	**301**	119	**164**	94	**213**
419	**285**	134	**289**	96	**255H**
427	**290**	135	**310**	97	**248**
432	**265**	137	**327**	106	**263**
439	**272**	139	**326**	112	**308**
441	**275**	140	**317**	120	**333**
444	**274**	141	**335**		
447	see **279**	143	**337**	*SEG* XXVIII	*Agora* XVI
449	**281**	147	**322**	7	**15**
450a	**284**	150	**339**	46	**106A**
452	**292**			48	**37**
455	**295**	*SEG* XXV	*Agora* XVI	49	**106C**
456	**296**	4	**1**	60	**255D**
458	**304**	9	**4**	68	**229**
471	**318**	28	**11**	70	**189**
475	**311**	33	**17**	71	**248**
484	**257**	37	**20**	75	**255 J**
487	**331**	63	**41**	78	**265**
490	**313**	65	**75**	80	**299**
503	**339**	69	**85**	362	**232** note
504	**340**	73	**101**	363	see **299**
515	**80**	74	**102**	488	see **255 J**
516	**93**	78	**109**		
521	**93**	80	**122**	*SEG* XXIX	*Agora* XVI
522	**233**	82	**67**	13	**16**
526	**270**	84	**166**	82	**106A**
529	**151**	85	**162**	85	**36**
530	**161**	89	**181**	86	**106B**
531	**245**	90	**182**	87	**106C**
532	**223**	94	**187**	92	**129**
533	**231**	95	**189**	93	**164**
535	**324**	98	**190**	101	**165**
536	**325**	101	**198**	102	**255D**
		102	**199**	113	**213**
SEG XXII	*Agora* XVI	104	**215**	121	**332G**
10	**17**	106	**224**		
96	**104**	108	**225**	*SEG* XXX	*Agora* XVI
97	**105**	109	**234**	6	**10**
102	**263**	110	**251**	7	**11**
104	**278**	111	**256**	10	**15**
107	**305**	112	**261**	14	**21**
		113	**263**	59	**106C**
SEG XXIII	*Agora* XVI	114a	**284**	61	**56**
14	**7**	116	**292**	65	**106G**
58	**85**	118	**291**	69	**114**
60	**95**	124	**276**	72	**117**
67	**214**	126	**307**	77	**255 J**
		128	**323**	80	**333**
SEG XXIV	*Agora* XVI	129	**334**	83	**342**
6	**15**	141	**114**		
13	**28A**				

SEG XXXI	Agora XVI
21	**18**
58	**40**
63	**106C**
66	**46**
69	**56**

SEG XXXII	Agora XVI
16	**28B**
37	**106A**
54	**43**
55	**106C**
57	**48**
65	**51**
72	**106D**
74	**106F**
84	**78**
93	**95**
94	**106J**
96	**100**
107	**255B**
110	**255C**
113	**255E**
114	**255G**
117	**208**
118	**213**
124	**332B**
126	**219**
131	**332D**
133	**332E**
140	**106E**
150	**255F**
1705	see **114**

SEG XXXIII	Agora XVI
11	**18**
17	**28A**
67	**106A**
68	**37**
72	**106B**
	(and see **36**)
77	**106C**
96	**120**
102	**142**
104	**111**
105	**162**
117	**194**
133	**332G**
138	**339**
143	**93**

SEG XXXIV	Agora XVI
6	**1**
9	**4**
15	**7**
18	**9**

62	**106C**
64	**61**
76	**117**
77	**139**
79	**162**
90	**255H**
91	**222**
94	**332C**
95	**296**
101	**80**
184	see **341**

SEG XXXV	Agora XVI
57	**106C**
58	**55**
63	**72**
65	**45**
67	**76**
68	**75**
71	**79**
75	**92**
76	**135**
78	**122**
79	**143**
80	**144**
82	**154**
86	**170**
88	**255D**
90	see **196**
97	**293**

SEG XXXVI	Agora XVI
6	see **17**
10	**14**
140	**36**
141	**35**
145	**106C**
147	**47**
151	**73**
152	**75**
170	**213**
299	see **80**
1527	**7**

SEG XXXVII	Agora XVI
6	see **17**
9	**7**
65	**106A**
69	**106C**
79	**75**
83	**106J**
85	**109**
90	**162, 163**
91	**255D**
92	**332A**
97	**341**

100	**84**
393	see **255J**

SEG XXXVIII	Agora XVI
57	**56**
65	**73**
71	**172**
88	**204**
92	**211**
93	**210**
99	**213**
103	**332A**
104	**289**
106	**291**
108	**295**
112	**310**

SEG XXXIX	Agora XVI
61	**14**
62	**30**
63	**31**
64	**59**
67	**45**
68	**32**
74	**60**
76	**58**
78	**81**
80	**73**
87	**98**
88	**75**
92	**132**
94	**95**
97	**99**
98	**106**
100	**108**
102	**114**
103	**117**
104	**119**
105	**116**
106	**122**
107	**126**
112	**162, 163**
113	**146**
115	**168**
117	**156**
118	**176**
119	**193**
120	**188**
126	**219**
130	**208**
137	**332C**
138	**332D**
139	**296**
145	**84**
154	**257**
306	**105**

308	**18**	98	**242**	39	**35**		
324	**19, 20,**	99	**246**	41	**106C**		
	28A, 50,	100	**247**	49	**114**		
	55, 71,	103	**252**	50	**115**		
	92, 97	108	**287**	59	**261**		
329	**64, 102,**	109	**288**	1877	**106C**		
	114, 115,	110	**291**				
	121, 122,	114	**298**	*SEG* XLII	*Agora* XVI		
	151, 176	115	**305**	5	**1**		
		116	**196**	7	**4**		
SEG XL	*Agora* XVI	118	**314**	86	**106A**		
5	**9**	119	**315**	87	**41**		
68	**67, 137**	125	**84**	88	**106C**		
79	**106J**	290	**56**	92	**75**		
82	**114**			93	**133**		
86	**162, 163**	*SEG* XLI	*Agora* XVI	98	**255D**		
96	**232** note	8	**28A**	116	**277**		

[For an addendum too recently identified for inclusion in this volume (between **71** and **72**) see *SEG* XLII, 91.]

C. *HESPERIA* AND SUPPLEMENTS

Hesperia 2, 1933	*Agora* XVI		
156–158 (5)	**185**		
160–161 (7)	**227**		
412 (34)	**341**		
494–497 (12)	**4**		

Hesperia 3, 1934	*Agora* XVI
1 (1)	**26**
1–2 (2)	**147**
2–3 (3)	**42**
3 (4)	**148**
3–4 (5)	**85**
5–6 (6)	**113**
6–7 (7)	**124**
7 (8)	**206**
7–8 (9)	**191**
9 (11)	**204**
10 (12)	**254**
11 (14)	**236**
11 (15)	**303**
18–21 (18)	**291**
27–31 (20)	**295**
37–38 (25)	**330**
43–44 (32)	**87**
44–46 (33)	**160**

Hesperia 4, 1935	*Agora* XVI
32–34 (3)	**8**
34–35 (4)	**71**
35–37	**105**
37–38 (6)	**125**
41–42 (9)	**136**
178–184 (45)	**341**

525–561 (39)	**224**
562–565 (40)	**182**

Hesperia 5, 1936	*Agora* XVI
360–362 (3)	**1**
381–382 (5)	**21**
413–414 (11)	**78**
414–416 (12)	**124**
416–417 (13)	**174**
418–419 (14)	**190**
419–428 (15)	**261**
428–429 (16)	**263**
429–430 (17)	**291**

Hesperia 6, 1937	*Agora* XVI
442–444 (1)	**102**
444–448 (2)	**194**
448–453 (3)	**225**
453–454 (4)	**202**

Hesperia 7, 1938	*Agora* XVI
80–81 (8)	**16**
91–92 (11)	**33**
94–96 (15)	**86**
97–100 (17)	**167**
100–109 (18)	**181**
109 (19)	**175**
118–121 (23)	**208**
123–126 (25)	**218**
127–131 (27)	**322**
269–270 (4)	**18**
476–479 (31)	**102**

Hesperia 8, 1939	*Agora* XVI
1–3 (1)	**34**

5–12 (3)	**48**
12–17 (4)	**53**
26–27 (6)	**79**
27–30 (7)	**94**
30–34 (8)	**104**
35–41 (9)	**115**
42 (10)	**171**
42–44 (11)	**157**
44–45 (12)	**128**
65–69 (22)	**20**
173–175 (4)	**95**
223–224	see **101**

Hesperia 9, 1940	*Agora* XVI
66–72 (9)	**109**
80–83 (13)	**162**
83 (14)	**179**
85–86 (16)	**260**
104–111 (20)	**123**
111–112 (21)	**203**
313–314 (30)	**39**
321–324 (33)	**46**
325–327 (35)	**72**
327–328 (36)	**76**
332–333 (39)	**82**
333–334 (40)	**88**
334–335 (41)	**89**
335–339 (42)	**94**
345–348 (44)	**101**
348–351 (45)	**122**
351 (46)	**118**
352 (47)	**177**
352–354 (48)	**173**
355 (49)	**274**

Hesperia 10, 1941	*Agora* XVI
41 (9)	**83**
42 (10)	**77**
49–50 (12)	**91**
50–52 (13)	**92**
55–56 (19)	**120**
56–57 (20)	**130**
57–58 (21)	**183**
58–59 (22)	**249**
59–60 (23)	**250**
60–61 (25)	**297**
61–62 (26)	**321**
84–85 (36)	**340**
85–90 (37)	**342**
262–263 (66)	**40**
263–265 (67)	**44**
266 (68)	**52**
268–270 (69)	**103**
269	**101, 102**
270–273 (70)	**121**
279–280 (75)	**283**
328–330	see **20**
331–332	**18**

Hesperia 11, 1942	*Agora* XVI
230–231 (42)	**11**
241–242 (46)	**110**
265–274 (51)	**277**
278–280 (53)	**129**
281 (54)	**165**
282–287 (55)	**161**
287–292 (56)	**213**
293–298 (58)	**306**
298–299 (59)	**227**

Hesperia 13, 1944	*Agora* XVI
211–224 (2)	**15**
229–231 (3)	**54**
231–233 (5)	**96**
234–241 (6)	**100**
242–243 (7)	**164**
243–246 (8)	**127**
246–249 (9)	**209**
248	see **204**
249–251 (10)	**238**
251–253	see **225**
266 (20)	**295**

Hesperia 14, 1945	*Agora* XVI
82–83 (2)	**2**
83–85 (3)	**3**
85–86 (4)	**6**
86–87 (5)	**7**
87–93 (6)	**9**
94–97 (8)	**10**
115–119 (10)	**14**

119–122 (11)	**17**
122–127 (12)	**19**
127 (13)	**12**
128 (14)	**25**
128–129 (15)	**24**
129–132 (16)	**18**
132–133 (17)	**23**

Hesperia 15, 1946	*Agora* XVI
144–146 (6)	**265**
149–150 (9)	**220**
156 (13)	**231**
156–158 (14)	**180**
159–160 (16)	**131**
188–189 (34)	**113**
189 (35)	**87**
189–190 (36)	**206**
214–215 (43)	**230**
246–249 (77)	**2**

Hesperia 16, 1947	*Agora* XVI
153 (46)	**114**
159 (54)	**221**
160 (56)	**300**
163 (61)	**284**
164–168 (64)	**296**
188–191 (94)	**279**
191 (95)	**282**

Hesperia 17, 1948	*Agora* XVI
3–13 (3)	**216**
7–13	see **214**
22–23 (10)	**309**
54–57 (65)	**37**
114–136 (68)	**114**

Hesperia 21, 1952	*Agora* XVI
348–351	see **11**
355–359 (5)	**73**
367–368 (8)	**116**
371 (17)	**137**
378–379 (36)	**244**
380	see **7**

Hesperia 23, 1954	*Agora* XVI
233 (1)	**207**
239 (8)	**269**
240 (10)	**264**
241–242 (13)	**316**
242 (14)	**312**
242–243 (15)	**192**
287–296 (182)	**187**
296–309 (183)	**188**
318–319 (4)	**337**

Hesperia 26, 1957	*Agora* XVI
5 note 2	**338**

29–30 (2)	**172**
30–31 (3)	**290**
31–32 (4)	**262**
47–51 (7)	**292**
51–52 (8)	**36**
52–53 (9)	**56**
53–54 (10)	**169**
54–55 (11)	**186**
57–58 (12)	**228**
58–59 (13)	**239**
61 (15)	**258**
61–62 (16)	**259**
62–63	**260**
73	see **295**
77–78 (23)	**319**
207 (53)	**38**
207–208 (54)	**74**
208–209 (56)	**138**
209–210 (57)	**235**
221–225 (84)	**47**
225–229 (85)	**35**
229–231 (86)	**51**
231–233 (87)	**50**
260–265 (98)	**336**

Hesperia 28, 1959	*Agora* XVI
239–247	**75**
248–250	**35**
273–274 (1)	**294**

Hesperia 29, 1960	*Agora* XVI
1 (1)	**93**
1–2 (2)	**61**
2–4 (3)	**77**
5 (4)	**152**
5–6 (5)	**64**
6 (6)	**149**
7 (8)	**159**
7–8 (9)	**212**
10 (12)	**243**
10–11 (13)	**237**
12–13 (15)	**240**
15 (19)	**332**
15–16 (20)	**273**
17–18 (23)	**271**
18–19 (24)	**286**
19–20 (25)	**317**
20 (26)	**328**
21 (27)	**329**
50–51 (63)	**5**
51 (64)	**133**
51 (65)	**70**
51 (66)	**65**
52 (68)	**150**
52 (69)	**158**
54 (73)	**271**

54 (74)	**302**	40–41 (41)	**56**
54 (75)	**268**	41 (42)	**80**
76 (153)	**226**		
76–77 (154)	**308**	*Hesperia* 33, 1964	*Agora* XVI
78–80 (155)	**270**	170–171 (25)	**184**
80–81 (156)	**139**	193 (42)	**318**
81–82 (157)	**111**	195–196 (46)	**313**
417	**306**	200–201 (52)	**340**

Hesperia 30, 1961	*Agora* XVI	*Hesperia* 34, 1965	*Agora* XVI
207–208 (2)	**49**	89 (1)	**278**
208–210 (3)	**66**	89	see **263**
210 (4)	**141**	89–90 (2)	**305**
210–211 (5)	**142**		
211–212 (6)	**176**	*Hesperia* 36, 1967	*Agora* XVI
212–213 (7)	**178**	57–58 (3)	**15**
213–214 (8)	**195**	58–59 (4)	**153**
214–215 (9)	**197**	59–63 (6)	**310**
215–216 (10)	**201**	64 (9)	**289**
217–218 (13)	**267**	64–65 (10)	**327**
219–220 (16)	**248**	66–68 (12)	**335**
221–222 (18)	**301**	68–71 (13)	**337**
222–223 (19)	**257**	242–244 (51)	**326**
223 (20)	**311**		
227 (25)	**245**	*Hesperia* 37, 1968	*Agora* XVI
227–228 (26)	**223**	266–267 (2)	**41**
228 (27)	**231**	267–268 (3)	**67**
229 (28)	**324**	268–269 (4)	**166**
229–230 (29)	**325**	269–270 (5)	**198**
257 (58)	**145**	270 (6)	**199**
257 (59)	**63**	270 (7)	**251**
257–258 (60)	**151**	271 (8)	**215**
258 (61)	**205**	271 (9)	**234**
258–259 (62)	**155**	271–272 (10)	**256**
259 (64)	**200**	272–273 (11)	**276**
259 (65)	**232**	273 (12)	**307**
259 (66)	**255**	273–274 (13)	**323**
289–292 (184)	**97**	277 (15)	**334**

Hesperia 32, 1963	*Agora* XVI	*Hesperia* 38, 1969	*Agora* XVI
1–2 (1)	**43**	108	**162**
2 (2)	**56**	110–112	**190**
2–3 (3)	**140**		
3–5 (4)	**112**	*Hesperia* 39, 1970	*Agora* XVI
5 (5)	**163**	111–114	**28A**
12–13 (10)	**93**	308 (1)	**241**
14–15 (13)	**233**	311 (4)	**320**
15–16 (14)	**285**		
17 (16)	**272**	*Hesperia* 40, 1971	*Agora* XVI
20 (19)	**281**	101–108 (3)	**333**
20–21 (20)	**304**	162–173 (23)	**41**
23–24 (24)	**331**	200–204 (53)	**341**
33–36 (32)	**296**	280–301	**106A**
39 (38)	**22**		
39 (39)	**29**	*Hesperia* 41, 1972	*Agora* XVI
39–40 (40)	**90**	46–49 (II)	**276**

Hesperia 42, 1973	*Agora* XVI		
352–357	**339**		
Hesperia 43, 1974	*Agora* XVI		
157–188	**106C**		
322–324 (3)	**106H**		
464–465	**104, 105**		
Hesperia 44, 1975	*Agora* XVI		
379–380 (1)	**13**		
380 (2)	**28**		
380–381 (3)	**27**		
392–393 (20)	see **28**		
394–395 (23–25)	see **28**		
Hesperia 45, 1976	*Agora* XVI		
283–285 (1)	**255H**		
289–295	**18**		
Hesperia 47, 1978	*Agora* XVI		
49–57	**255 J**		
252–253 (4)	**229**		
253 (5)	see **232** note		
258–259	**248**		
264 (7)	see **299**		
264–265 (8)	**299**		
Hesperia 48, 1979	*Agora* XVI		
178–179 (2)	**332G**		
180–193	**106B**		
Hesperia 49, 1980	*Agora* XVI		
251–255 (1)	**106G**		
255–257 (2)	**117**		
258–288	**56**		
Hesperia 51, 1982	*Agora* XVI		
41–42 (1)	**28B**		
43–45 (3)	**106D**		
45–46 (4)	**106F**		
46–47 (5)	**106E**		
47–48 (6)	**106 J**		
48–50 (7)	**255F**		
50–51 (8)	**255G**		
52–53 (9)	**255B**		
53–54 (10)	**255C**		
54–56 (11)	**255E**		
56 (12)	**332B**		
60–62 (3)	**332D**		
62 (4)	**332E**		
Hesperia 52, 1983	*Agora* XVI		
163–166 (4)	**339**		

Hesperia 53, 1984	*Agora* XVI	315–316 (3)	**210**	92–93 (20)	**146**
370–374 (3)	**332C**	316–317 (4)	**211**	93–94 (21)	**156**
374–377 (4)	**296**			94–95 (22)	**168**
		Hesperia 58, 1989	*Agora* XVI	95–96 (23)	**193**
Hesperia 54, 1985	*Agora* XVI	71–72 (1)	**30**		
309–312 (1)	**55**	72–74 (2)	**31**	*Hesperia* 59, 1990	*Agora* XVI
312–313 (2)	**45**	74–75 (3)	**59**	463–466	**114**
313–314 (3)	**135**	75–78 (4)	**45**		
314–317 (4)	**143**	78–79 (5)	**32**	*Hesperia,*	*Agora* XVI
317–319 (5)	**144**	79–81 (6)	**58**	Supplement IV	
319–321 (6)	**154**	81–82 (7)	**60**	144–147	**275**
321–323 (7)	**170**	82–83 (8)	**81**		
324–325 (9)	**293**	84 (9)	**98**	*Hesperia,*	*Agora* XVI
		84–85 (10)	**132**	Supplement XV (Tracy)	
Hesperia 55, 1986	*Agora* XVI	85–86 (11)	**95**	70–71 (10, 11)	**326**
319–354	**47**	86 (12)	**99**		
		87–88 (13)	**106**	*Hesperia,*	*Agora* XVI
Hesperia 56, 1987	*Agora* XVI	88 (14)	**108**	Supplement XVII	see **255D**
47–58	**84**	88–89 (15)	**117**	(Shear)	
63–71	**332A**	89 (16)	**116**	96 (12)	**172**
		89–90 (17)	**122**		
Hesperia 57, 1988	*Agora* XVI	90–91 (18)	**119**		
308	**172**	91–92 (19)	**126**		

D. OTHER PUBLICATIONS

Agora XIX	*Agora* XVI	197	**275**	M. J. Osborne,	*Agora* XVI
L 1	**6**	198	**274**	*Naturalization* III/IV	
L 3	**41**			T 20	**52**
L 7	**75**	M. J. Osborne,	*Agora* XVI	X 31	**142**
L 8	**84**	*Naturalization* I, II			
L 13	**93**			W. K. Pritchett and	
L 16	**329**	D 8	**36**	B. D. Meritt, *Chronology*	*Agora* XVI
		D 9	**40**	7–8	**107**
D. Behrend,	*Agora* XVI	D 13	**54**	22–23	**214**
Attische Pachturkunden		D 25	**94**	23–27	**217**
51–52 (2)	**41**	D 26	**96**	100–101	**219**
55 (5)	**6**	D 29	**101**	117–118	**266**
63–67 (13)	**75**	D 62	**117**	119–121	**280**
86–88 (30)	**93**	D 63	**120**	127–128	**264**
99 (42)	**329**	D 64	**121**		
		D 67	**162**	*Staatsverträge* II, 1962,	*Agora* XVI
K. Clinton, *The Sacred*	*Agora* XVI	D 74	**172**	H. Bengtson, ed.	
Officials of the		D 77	**173**	150	**4**
Eleusinian Mysteries		D 82	**178**	187	**16**
24–27	**306**	D 91	**248**	196	**19**
		D 92	**255H**	223	**34**
HSCP, Suppl.	*Agora* XVI	D 94	**255**	235	**35**
vol. I, 1940		D 95	**255J**	267	**46**
521–530	**341**	D 100	**276**	279	**47**
		D 104	see **266**	294	**50**
B. D. Meritt,	*Agora* XVI	D 109	**332G**	296	**51**
Athenian Year		D 110	**267**		
105	**91**	D 111	**301**	*Staatsverträge* III, 1969	*Agora* XVI
156	**265**	D 119	**239**	H. H. Schmitt, ed.	
194–195 (2)	**189**	D 121	**316**	445	**115**

476	see p. 275	64–65 (2)	**247**	146–151 (24)	**11**	
487	**208**	75–76 (1)	**252**	313–324 (60)	**18**	
		104 (1)	**287**	336–349 (64)	**20**	
J. S. Traill, *Demos and Trittys*	*Agora* XVI	107 (5)	**288**	367–370 (69)	**21**	
		151–152 (1)	**298**	373–375 (71)	**22**	
85–87 (6)	**80**	152–154 (2)	**305**	376–378 (72)	**37**	
		176 (1)	**314**	393–395 (76)	**25**	
S. V. Tracy, *Attic Letter-Cutters*	*Agora* XVI	177 (2)	**315**	398–405 (78)	**36**	
				413–415 (82)	**59**	
50–51 (1–4)	**232** note	M. B. Walbank, *Athenian Proxenies*	*Agora* XVI	415–417 (83)	see **60**	
59–60 (2)	**242**			418–421 (84)	**23**	
64 (1)	**246**	123–129 (19)	**14**			

2. INVENTORIES

A. EPIGRAPHICAL MUSEUM NUMBERS

E.M.	*Agora* XVI	E.M.	*Agora* XVI	E.M.	*Agora* XVI
64	**47**	6565	**3**	7615	**335**
390	**36**	6588	**19**	7618	**335**
2402	**310**	6588α–ε	**19**	7719	**93**
2404	**310**	6599	**16**	7741	**44**
2505	see **18**	6616	**18**	8369–8377	**341**
2537	**104**	6627	**12**	8379	**341**
2604	**59**	6800	**1**	8582	**342**
2633	**45**	6847	**18**	8583	**342**
2658	**308**	6883	**30**	9483	**342**
2659	**112**	6900	**36**	9484	**342**
2673	**47**	6900α, β	**36**	9504	**337**
3013	**339**	6904	**41**	10396	**109**
3144	**341**	6905	**41**	12290	**341**
3490	**341**	6916	**41**	12572	**94**
3813	**341**	6953	**15**	12577	**22**
4646	**341**	6988	**55**	12731	**341**
5029	**341**	7091–7099	**47**	12751	**341**
5197	**10**	7101	**47**	12948	**18**
5245	**337**	7157	**111**	12964	**41**
5267	**335**	7184	**95**	13028	**341**
5314	**336**	7330	**157**	13371	**12**
5392	**16**	7332	**94**	13374	**18**
5700	**341**	7333	**94**	13446	**93**
5728	**342**	7493	**248**	13447	**93**
5831	**342**	7510	**248**	13770	**10**

B. AGORA INVENTORY NUMBERS

Inv.	*Agora* XVI	Inv.	*Agora* XVI	Inv.	*Agora* XVI
I 15	**185**	I 164	**291**	I 220	**206**
23	**204**	179	**337**	226	**85**
73	**295**	181	**148**	242	**191**
79	**227**	200	**154**	250	**113**
84	**254**	207	**26**	260	**236**
96	**185**	217	**160**	317	**4**
111	**42**	219	**124**	319	**303**

Inv.	*Agora* XVI	Inv.	*Agora* XVI	Inv.	*Agora* XVI
I 329	147	I 2025	47	I 3611	6
409	87	2105	276	3617	see 28
419	18	2115	283	3619	124
456	330	2155	266	3625	86
524	230	2161	130	3632	158
536	136	2165	307	3668	312
559	105	2173	144	3687	128
568	8	2211	297	3745 a, b	9
605	261	2351	333	3755	293
605 c	261	2361	225	3777	286
657	71	2373	240	3791	see 299
658	10	2409	72	3804 a	316
672	209	2426	45	3804 b	282
707	125	2440	93	3828	193
749	174	2446	244	3843	109
750	314	2453	323	3854	56
779	5	2455	192	3870	211
788	33	2527	250	3871 a, b	326
830	78	2545	13	3878	102
834	261	2580	45	3918	126
860	124	2609	137	3939	319
863	182	2619	336	3954	252
896	287	2636 a–m	115	3960	76
909	261	2688	83	3972	7
918	224	2701	128	4003	269
937	118	2719	65	4007	56
968	see 288	2720	99	4026	326
984	296	2752	94	4034	98
1036	241	2767	152	4071	91
1048	221	2768	see 288	4103	12
1051	190	2777	133	4113	46
1059	337	2806	20	4138	218
1218	16	2821	106	4140	56
1250	322	2841	171	4143	329
1273	183	2895	150	4144	265
1276	1	2898	149	4169	194
1299	300	2925	47	4181	177
1318	263	2986	198	4184	58
1330	246	2995	64	4185	243
1441	114	3028	268	4224	92
1497	210	3048	199	4234	299
1524	180	3055	51	4241	264
1541	120	3087	271	4250	280
1594	321	3142	251	4260	239
1611	25	3155	339	4266	181
1619	333	3233	168	4267	273
1674	21	3234	168	4317	167
1731	232 note	3238	194	4352	34
1832	175	3241	202	4377	328
1886	260	3364	79	4384 a, b	48
1906	161	3365	258	4389	306
1912	315	3367	135	4421	95
1966	249	3392	146	4439	77
2016	298	3460	179	4442	24

Inv.	*Agora* XVI		Inv.	*Agora* XVI		Inv.	*Agora* XVI
I 4477	55		I 5032	294		I 5487	32
4496	159		5036	121		5488	141
4503	see 288		5039	173		5495	201
4522	310		5090	222		5496	94
4526	212		5143	270		5504	60
4534	112		5147	15		5520	31
4536 a, b	213		5148	69		5526	156
4541	228		5165	277		5556	306
4546 a, b	3		5172 a, b	2		5559	214
4547	320		5173	62		5560	54
4564	44		5174	142		5588	41
4593	107A		5191	217		5589	238
4597	256		5198	339		5592	195
4605	237		5207	52		5597	232 note
4606	207		5212	68		5617	232
4608	255		5215	116		5626	100
4609	317		5224	253		5645	145
4615	247		5228	123		5651	267
4622	208		5234	72		5653	197
4633	36		5251	139		5655	103
4639	30		5254	57		5657	178
4646	61		5256	134		5664	245
4663	38		5257	59		5680	341
4725	see 109		5263	45		5691	231
4739	56		5271	81		5709	122
4768	39		5272	49		5713	63
4772 a, b	104		5278	47		5723	176
4798	310		5283	57		5733	56
4811	313		5295	111		5740	339
4812	162		5296	23		5751	47
4813	28		5310	302		5760	205
4816	27		5322	239		5761	284
4829	6		5326	203		5772	164
4848	157		5334	336		5773	131
4853 a, b	342		5344	275		5791	220
4875	332		5351	35		5792	132
4886	288		5354	70		5796	219
4899	74		5368	see 46		5803	47
4900	279		5372	108		5824	127
4902 a	88		5400	274		5826	14
4902 b	89		5401	110		5828	96
4906	138		5410	50		5836	155
4914	143		5424 a, b	271		5855	340
4920	310		5426	334		5871	248
4935 a–f	94		5439	129		5879	17
4954	40		5444	122		5884	107
4956	82		5446	229		5886	165
4960	126		5454	101		5887	223
4977	11		5458	226		5896	37
4985	35		5460	200		5923	170
4988	119		5463	117		5929	232 note
4991	235		5464	66		5964	see 28
5026	19		5469	308		5972	114
5030	53		5477	75		6003	309

Inv.	*Agora* XVI	Inv.	*Agora* XVI	Inv.	*Agora* XVI
I 6064	**216**	I 6691	**335**	I 6999	see **28**
6081	**290**	6696	**186**	7029	**215**
6090	**232** note	6700	**296**	7050	**106 J**
6096	**188**	6703	**169**	7065	**28A**
6100	**259**	6731	**189**	7070	**117, 255A**
6103	**289**	6735	**340**	7093	**255E**
6108	**325**	6743	see **28**	7110	**106E**
6132 a, b	**337**	6755	**29**	7121	**106B**
6149	**338**	6771	**272**	7134	**106F**
6155	**318**	6783	**339**	7137	**255B**
6156	**262**	6793	**84**	7163	**255C**
6170	**340**	6794	**56**	7169	**106A**
6234	**257**	6804	**77**	7178	**106H**
6267	**242**	6827	**233**	7180	**106C**
6275	**311**	6842	**80**	7182	**255 J**
6282	**324**	6843	**285**	7184	**339**
6314	**151**	6844	**163**	7197	**332A**
6367	**292**	6877 a, b	**56**	7199	**332A**
6372	**301**	6885	**331**	7226	**332B**
6387	**337**	6915 a–i	**56**	7235	**332E**
6421	**67**	6921	**140**	7254	**255H**
6434	**90**	6923	**22**	7259	**48**
6439	**93**	6968	**153**	7295	**255D**
6496	**97**	6974	**56**	7312	**255G**
6516	**116**	6977	**305**	7360	**106G**
6521	**43**	6978	**305**	7382	**28B**
6524	**73**	6979	**232** note	7400	**106D**
6529	**304**	6980	**305**	7421	**332G**
6533	**184**	6986	**278**	7453	**332D**
6560	**172**	6987	**166**	7492	**296, 332F**
6589	**281**	6989	**234**	7496	**332C**
6664	**187**	6995	**327**	7500	**255F**

INDICES

INDICES

The general practice of these indices follows that employed in *Hesperia* and *Agora* XV, but the particular character of this volume has invited a difference of treatment that will, it is hoped, prove of additional benefit to those who consult them. There are ten sections, and a note prefacing certain of them provides, where it is needed, guidance concerning their use and intention. Certain considerations however apply more widely.

1. All dates are B.C. unless identified otherwise.
2. Except in Index 10 references are to the number of a text: except in Index 9, where the information is of no consequence, the number of the relevant line or lines within the text follows that of the text.
3. Names fully restored in a given context, or of which only the first letter survives, have not been indexed, whatever the degree of certainty of the restoration.
4. Broken names of which only the latter part survives have not been indexed.
5. Doubtful letters are not indicated by under-dots, and spaces within the citations are not numbered.
6. Names have been entered in the nominative case, even if in their context they appear in an oblique case.
7. Ἀθηναῖοι and related words or phrases (e.g., Ἀθήνησι, ὁ δῆμος ὁ Ἀθηναίων) occur *passim* and have not been indexed.

1. NAMES OF MEN AND WOMEN

In the alphabetizing of multiple entries of the same name simple names come first. Then follow simple names with some qualification (e.g., "father of"). Next come names with patronymic but no demotic, then names with demotics (in the alphabetical order of these latter and whether or not a patronymic is included), and finally names of non-Athenians with their ethnics on the same principle. Occasionally an evident or possible family relationship has been more easily noted by a variation from the strict application of this formula. Restorations have for the most part been repeated as they appear in the texts, but the names of archons are always entered in their complete form irrespective of any restored element.

A

Ἄβρων Ἐπιγένου Ἁλαιεύς, taxiarchos in 281/80, 182₂₄

Ἀγάθαρχο[ς] Λαμπτρεύς, sitophylax in 256/5 or 254/3, 194₆

[Ἀ]γαθόδωρος, father of a γραμματεύς of *ca.* 170, 286₂

Ἀγαθοκλῆς, archon in 357/6: [Ἀγαθο]κλέος, 53₁

Ἀγάθων, named in list of dedicators 161/60, 296₁₁₈

[Ἀγ]νοκ[ράτ]ης Ἁλαι(εύς), contributor to a defense fund in 245/4 or 244/3, 213₆₅

Ἀγύρριος Καλλιμέδοντος Κολλυτεύς, proposer of a decree in 282/1, 181₉

[Ἀδείμ]αντος Ἀνδροσθέν[ους Λαμψακηνός], honored in 302, 122₂₂

Ἄδμητος, father of a man of Priene honored between 307 and 305(?), 111₃

Ἀθηνόδωρος, archon in 256/5 or 254/3, 194₅

Αἰ[----], contributor to a defense fund in 245/4 or 244/3, 213₄₉

Αἰ[----], another contributor to the same fund, 213₅₆

Αἰν[έας](?), γραμματεύς in 410–405, 23₂

Αἴνητος Δαήμονος Ῥόδιος, honored in 319/18, 101₂,₁₃,₃₀,₃₄

Αἰσ[----], named in list of dedicators, 296₃₄

Αἰσχίνης, concerned with colony finance, 439/8(?): [Α]ἰσχίνεν, 7(a)₃₀

Αἰσχίνης, father of Aristokrates γραμματεύς in 394/3, 36₁₃

Αἰ[σ]χίνης Νικομάχου Ἀναφλύστιος, chairman of an assembly in 271/70, 187₆

Αἰσχίνης (Οἰναῖος), father of Molottos the proposer of a decree in 241, 240, or 239, 216₈

Αἰσχίνης Ἀντικράτου Φαληρεύς, chairman of an assembly in 275/4, 185₅

Αἰσχρίων Εὐαινέτου Ῥαμνούσιος, γραμματεύς in 196/5, 261₂

[Αἰσ]χρων, 229₄

Αἰσχρων Παιανι(εύς), contributor to a defense fund in 245/4 or 244/3, 213₆₇

Αἰσχρων (Χαλκιδεύς), father of Archeleos of Chalkis honored in 306/5, 113₁₂

Αἰσχύλος (Περιθοίδης), father of Philistides a contractor for public works and of Euktemon a guarantor of the contract in 307/6, 109 IV₁₂₂,₁₂₅

Ἀλέξανδρος, archon in 174/3, 282₁, 283₁

Ἀλεξίας Ὑ[βάδης], 84₉₇

Ἄλεξις, archon in 173/2, 284₇

Ἀλε[ξ]ι[ς] Φυλάσι(ος), contributor to a defense fund in 245/4 or 244/3, 213₇₂

Ἀλκ[----], contributor to the same fund, 213₅₇

Ἀλκαμένης: [Μᾶρκος Αὐρήλιο]ς Ἀλκαμένης Λαμπτρεύς, 339₁₁

Ἀλκίμαχος (Μυρρινούσιος), father of Thoukritos the proposer of a decree in 226/5, 224₁₀

Ἀμεινίας (Ἀχαρνεύς), father of Chairestratos the γραμματεύς of 337/6, 73₂

[Ἀ]μεινίας Ξυπετ[αιών], military commander honored between 301 and 297, 129₄

Ἀμειψ[ίας], chairman of an assembly in 394/3, 36₂

Ἀμοι[----], contributor to a defense fund in 245/4 or 244/3, 213₆₅

Ἀμυν[όμαχος] Εὐκλέους Ἁλαιεύς, proposer of a decree in 148/7, 306₃

Ἀμφίλοχος Ξυπετα[ι]ών, chairman of an assembly in 319/18, 102₈

Ἄμφι[ος τ]οῦ Ἀμφίου [ἐξ Οἴου], named in a decree of A.D. 195/6, 339 A₂

Ἄμφιος (ἐξ Οἴου), father of the above, 339 A₂

Ἀν[----], father of the chairman of an assembly in 302/1, 124₉

Ἀν[---- Ἀν]τιοχεύς, proposer of a decree of a cult organization in 112/11, 324₄

Ἀν[----]ς, honored in 415/14, 21₅

Ἀναξικράτης, archon in 307/6, 107A₂

Ἀνδρον[---], honored in 353/2(?), 55₁₀

Ἀνδροσ[---], honored in 307/6, 107₁₀

Ἀνδροσθέν[ης] (Λαμψακηνός), father of Adeimantos of Lampsakos honored in 302, 122₂₂

[Ἀν]τίγονος Θε[----], honored in the mid 3rd century, 197₁(?): but the reference may be to Antigonos II Gonatas, king of Macedon

E

Λ

M

Μακρῖνος: [Φλάο]υιος Μακρῖ[νος], archon in A.D. 116/17, 338_1

Μεγαχλῆς Μενίππ[ου Ἀχαρνεύς], guarantor of a contract for public works in 307/6 and father of Menippos also a guarantor, 109 $IV_{123,124}$

Μέδων (Ἀφιδναῖος), father of Memnon the proposer of a decree in 302/1, 123_{11}

Μειδογένης Μείδωνος Ἀθμονεύς, πάρεδρος to the archon of 283/2, 181_{32}

Μ[ει]δοκράτης ἐκ Κο[λωνοῦ], surveyor of land at Oropos ca. 330(?), 84_{11}(?)

[Μειδοκρ]άτης Μει[δοκράτου Προβ]αλ(ίσιος), honored by the phyle Pandionis between 332 and 323, 80_5

Μειδοκράτης (Προβαλίσιος), father of the above, 80_6

Μείδων (Ἀθμονεύς), father of Meidogenes, πάρεδρος to the archon of 283/2, 181_{33}

Μελάνωπος, proposer of a decree in 359/8(?), 52_{13}

Μελάνωπος (ἐκ Κοίλης), father of a guarantor of a contract for public works in 307/6, 109 III_{129}

Μελησίας Ἀριστοκράτου Λαμπτρεύς, lessee of the theater at Peiraieus 324/3, $93_{29,39}$

Μέλητ[ος], chairman of an assembly ca. 435–430, 11_3

Μέμνων Μέδοντος Ἀφιδναῖος, proposer of a decree in 302/1, 123_{10}

Μέμνων (Ἀφιδναῖος), father of Spoudias the chairman of an assembly in 226/5, 224_7

Μενέδημος, archon in 179/8, 278_1

[Με]νεκρατ[– –], mentioned at the end of the 3rd century, 242_2

Μενεκράτης, father of [– – –]τας a contractor for public works in 307/6, 109 III_{123}

[Μενέ]μαχος Μενεστράτου Λαμπτ[ρεύς], γραμματεύς in 193/2, 262_1

Μενέστρατος (Λαμπτρεύς), father of the above, 262_2

Μενέστρατος Αἰξωνεύς, chairman of an assembly in 337/6, 73_4

Μένιππος (Ἀχαρνεύς), father of Megakles a guarantor of a contract for public works in 307/6, 109 IV_{123}

Μένιππος Μεγακλέους Ἀ[χ]α[ρνεύς], guarantor of the same contract, grandson of the above, 109 IV_{124}

Μενοι[– – –] (Μενοί[τιος] or Μενοι[τιάδης]), 141_6

Μέντωρ (Περιθοίδης), father of Lakrates the proposer of a decree in 181/80, 275_{12}

[Μη (or Ζη)]νόδωρος Εὐμένου Τρινεμε[εύς], honored ca. 135, 310_{42}

Μιχαλίων Φίλωνος Ἀλεξ[ανδρεύς], honored between 300 and 294, $164_{6,10}$

Μιχίων Θριάσι(ος), contributor to a defense fund in 245/4 or 244/3, 213_{36}

Μιχίων (Κηφισιεύς), father of Eurykleides the ταμίας τῶν στρατιωτικῶν of 245/4 or 244/3, 213_2

Μιχίων Κηφισι(εύς), son of the above, contributor to a defense fund in 245/4 or 244/3, 213_{35}

Μνήσαρχος, honored by a society of orgeones ca. 300, $130_{2,7}$

Μνησιγείτων, proposer of the decree honoring Mnesarchos above, 130_1

Μνησίε[ργος Μνησίου Ἀθμονεύς], proposer of a decree between 280 and 270, 183_4

Μνησίθεος, archon in 155/4, 297_1

Μολοττὸς Αἰσχίνου Οἰναῖος, proposer of a decree in 241, 240, or 239, 216_8

[Μορυ]χίδης, proposer of a decree in 451/50(?), 1_5(?)

Μοσχίων (Θημακεύς), father of Philiskos a taxiarchos in 272/1, 187_{40}

Μόσχος, cochairman of an assembly between 229 and 224, 222_6

[Μ]όσχος (Πλαταιεύς), father of Τ[– – – –] of Plataia honored a little earlier than 321/20, 96_4

[Μύ]ννιον, named in list of dedicators 161/60, 296_{59}

N

Νάνναχος (Εὐπυρίδης), father of Herakleon the γραμματεύς of 190/89, 264_2

Ναύκριτος (Λαμπτρεύς), father of Archedikos the proposer of a decree in 318/17, 104_{10}

Ναυσικράτη[ς], father of Thrasykles the ἀναγραφεύς of 321/20, 97_2

Ναυσιφάνης (Κυθήρριος), father of Lysikrates a taxiarchos in 272/1, 187_{38}

Νέων Δωροθέο[υ], chairman of an assembly ca. 86, 333_6

Νικ[– – – –], father of the chairman of an assembly in 190/89, 264_5

Νικαγόρας Ἐρχι(εύς), contributor to a defense fund in 245/4 or 244/3, 213_{47}

Νικάνωρ: Ἰούλιος Νικάνωρ, in a decree of the later 1st century A.D., 337_{25}

Νικάνωρ Νικοκ[λέους Ῥαμνούσιος(?)], sponsor of Kleomachides of Larisa honored in 139/8(?), $308(a)_7$

Νικήρατος Φλυε(ύς), contributor to a defense fund in 245/4 or 244/3, 213_{78}

Νικήρατος (Ἡρακλεώτης), father of a contractor for public works in 307/6, 109 III_{124}

Νικησίας Σιτ[άρχ]ου (Ἐρετριεύς), honored in 306/5, 113_{13}

Νικήτης Περγασῆ(θεν), contributor to a defense fund in 245/4 or 244/3, 213_{74}

Νικίας, archon in 282/1, 181_2

Ξ

O

T

Υ

Φ

X

Χαιρέστρατος Ἀμεινίου Ἀχαρνεύς, γραμματεύς in 337/6, 73₂

Χαιρεφῶν, archon in 219/18, 226₁, 227₁

Χαιρεφῶν Εἰτεαῖ(ος), contributor to a defense fund in 245/4 or 244/3, 213₆₂

Χαρίας, archon in 415/14, 21₄

Χα[ρίας Κ]ο[λ]λυτεύς, lessee of property at Oropos ca. 330, 84₁₀₈

Χ[αρ]ίδημος (Ἰκαριεύς), father of the guarantor of a contract for public works in 307/6, 109 III₁₂₈

Χαρίδημος (Ἐφέσιος), father of Nikophon of Ephesos honored between 224 and 221, 225₁₆

Χαρικλῆς, archon in 196/5, 261₁

[Χ]αρικ[λῆς], 25₁

Χαρῖνος, archon in 291/90, 169₁, 170₁

Χαρίσανδρος, archon in 376/5, 44₅

Χαρίσανδρος (Κικκυνεύς), father of a taxiarchos of 272/1, 187₄₆

Χίω[ν](?), honored ca. 430, 14₁₁

Χίων (Κορυδαλλεύς), father of a contractor for public works in 307/6, 109 I₁₂₅

Χρ[έ]μης Φαλ[η(ρεύς)], surveyor of land at Oropos ca. 330(?), 84₁₄(?)

Χρόμων, proposer of a decree between 440 and 430, 10₂

2. KINGS, EMPERORS, AND THEIR FAMILIES

Alexander III ("the Great"), king of Macedon: Ἀλεξάνδρου τοῦ βασιλέα, 101₁₆

Antigonos II Gonatas, king of Macedon: [τὸν βασιλέα Ἀντίγον]ον, 194₂₄; [Ἀν]τίγονος, 171₁(?)

Antiochos IV Epiphanes, king of Syria: τοῦ βασιλέως Ἀντιόχο[υ], 292₅; τοῦ βασιλέως, 292₉; [τοῦ βασιλέως Ἀντ]ιόχο[υ] (= Epiphanes?), 310₄₆

Antiochos VII Sidetes, king of Syria: τοῦ βασιλ[έως], 310₂₁; το[ῦ] βασ[ιλέως], 310₃₁; τ[οῦ βασ]ιλέω[ς], 310₂₆; [τοῦ βασιλέως Ἀντ]ιόχο[υ] (= Sidetes?), 310₄₆

Athenaios, brother of Eumenes II king of Pergamon: Ἀθηναίου, 291₁₆

Attalos (later king Attalos II), brother of Eumenes II king of Pergamon: Ἀττάλου, 291₁₅

Augustus, Roman emperor: [Αὐτοκράτορι Καίσα]ρι Σεβαστῶι, 336₄

Demetrios Poliorketes (see also Index 8, s.v. Σωτῆρες): βασιλέως Δημητρίου, 122₇; [Δ]ημητρίωι, 115(a)₂; [τ]οῦ βασιλέως (= Demetrios?), 144₁₀

Eumenes II Soter, king of Pergamon: [τ]οῦ βασιλέως Ε[ὐ]μένους, 291₁₄

Julia (Domna) Augusta, wife of Emperor Septimius Severus: [Ἰουλία] Σεβαστή, 341₁₉; [Ἰ]ουλίαν Σεβασ[τήν], 340(c)₁₀; τὴν σώτειραν τῶν [Ἀθηνῶ]ν Ἰουλίαν Σεβα[στήν], 341₄₂; [τῆς] σωτείρας τῶν [Ἀθηνῶν Ἰου]λίας Σεβ[αστῆς], 341₁₃; [Ἰου]λίᾳ Σεβαστή, μη-[τρὶ τῶν στρατοπέδων], 340(c)₄; τῆι [σωτείρᾳ τῶν Ἀθηνῶν Ἰουλίᾳ Σεβαστῆ] Ἀθηνᾷ Πολιά[δι], 341₂₁

Laodike III, wife of Antiochos III ("the Great"), king of Syria: τῆς βασιλίσσης Λαοδίκης, 275₉

Lysimachos, king of Thrace: [τῶι βασιλεῖ Λ]υσιμάχωι, 172₉; τὸν βασιλέα, 172₁₀; τὸμ β[ασιλέα], 172₁₃

Philokles, king of Sidon: [Φιλο]κλέα τὸν Σιδο[νίων βασιλέα], 173₈

Ptolemy III Euergetes I, king of Egypt: τὸν βασιλέα Πτολεμαῖον, 225₉

Seleukos IV Philopator, king of Syria: τὸν βασιλέα [Σέλ]ε[υκ]ον, 266₁₂; τοῦ βασιλέως Σελεύκου, 266₁₀

3. THE ATHENIAN PHYLAI

No completely restored items are included.

Αἰαντίς, 336₁; Αἰαν[τίς], 19₂; Αἰαντίδα, 86₁₁,₂₀; Αἰαντίδος, 86₅; Αἰαντίδο[ς], 182₁; Αἰ[αντίδος], 116₂; Α[ἰαντίδος], 91₁; Αἰαντιδῶν, 84₁₀

Αἰγηΐς, 36₁; Αἰγεῖδος, 261₁; Αἰγε[ΐδος], 165₂; Αἰγειδῶν, 84₁₀

Ἀκαμαντίς: Ἀκα[μ]αντ[ίς], 20₄; Ἀκαμαντίδος, 123₃, 187₄₅; Ἀκαμαντίδ[ος], 114₂₄; Ἀκαμαντ[ίδος], 96₁₄; Ἀκα[μαντίδος], 214₁; [Ἀ]καμαντίδος, 190₂, 279₁; [Ἀκαμαν]τίδος, 76₂

Ἀντιγονίς: Ἀντιγονίδος, 187₂; Ἀν[τιγον]ίδος, 124₃

Ἀντιοχίς, 21₂; Ἀντιοχ[ΐς], 4₃; Ἀντιοχίδος, 169₁; [Ἀντι]οχί[δος], 102₂

Ἀτταλίς: Ἀτταλίδος, 291₂; Ἀττ[αλίδος], 281₂

Δημητριάς: [Δημητ]ριάδος, 113₁

Ἐρεχθηΐς: [Ἐρ]εχθηΐς, 38₃; [Ἐρε]χθηΐς, 52₁; Ἐ[ρ]εχθεῖδα, 7(b)₅; Ἐρεχθεῖδος, 184₁, 187₃₉, 216₂; Ἐρεχθε[ῖδος], 266₂; [Ἐρεχθ]εῖδος, 260₂; [Ἐρεχ]θ[εῖδος], 154₁(?)

Ἱπποθωντίς: Ἱπποθωντίδος, 224₂, 308(a)₁; [Ἱπποθωντ]ίδος, 53₁; [Ἱπποθωντί]δος, 187₅₁

Κεκροπίς, 33₃; Κε[κροπίς], 13₂; Κεκροπὶς φυλή, 44₅; Κεκροπίδος, 186₃; Κεκροπίδ[ος], 104₂; Κεκροπί[δος], 78₂, 179₂; [Κεκ]ροπίδος, 172₁; [Κεκροπ]ίδος, 187₄₉; [Κεκροπ]ιδῶν, 105₉; φυλὴ Κεκροπιδῶν, 44₄; οἱ ἐπίλεκτοι Κεκροπιδῶ[ν], 105₄
Λεωντίς, 52₁₁; [Λεων]τίς(?), 30₄; Λεωντίδος, 73₁, 185₁, 187₄₃, 295₂; Λεωντίδο[ς], 188₁; Λ[εωντίδος], 97₃; [Λε]ων[τίδος], 171₁; [Λεω]ντίδος, 274₁

Οἰνηίς, 48₄; Οἰνε[ί]ς, 1₃; Οἰνηίδος, 181₂; Οἰνηί[δος], 85₁; [Ο]ἰνεῖδος, 187₄₇; [Ο]ἰνεῖ[δος], 94₃
Πανδιονίς: Πανδιονίδος, 187₄₁, 275₁₀; [Πανδ]ιονίδος, 219₁
Πτολεμαιίς: Πτολεμαιίδος, 319₁

4. DEMES AND OTHER SOCIAL GROUPS

No completely restored items are included.

Ἀγγελῆθεν, 53₃; Ἀγγ[ελῆθεν], 278₂; [Ἀ]ν[γελῆ]θεν, 54₄
Ἀγνούσιος: [Ἀγν]ούσιος, 222₆
Ἀζηνιεύς, 296₁₁₂; Ἀζ[ην(ιεύς)], 213₃₉; Ἀζη[νιε--], 269₃
Ἀθμονεύς: [Ἀθ]μον(εύς), 213₆₀; [Ἀ]θ[μο]ν[εύς], 188₇; Ἀθμονέα, 181₃₃
Αἰγιλιεύς: Αἰγιλ(ιεύς), 213₇₃
Αἰξωνεύς, 73₄, 182₂,₈, 216₆, 319₂; Αἰ[ξωνεύς], 185₆
Αλ[----], 296₃₇
Ἁλαιεύς, 20₃, 101₉, 213₄₅,₄₆, 306₄; Ἁλαιεύ[ς], 30₃; Ἁλαι(εύς), 213₆₅; Ἁλαιέα, 182₂₄
Ἁλιμούσιος, 307₂
Ἀλωπεκῆθεν, 224₄; Ἀλωπεκῆθε[ν], 335₅₈; Ἀλωπε[κῆθεν], 296₃₈; Ἀλωπ(εκῆθεν), 213₅₀,₆₈; Ἀλ[ωπεκῆθ]εν, 102₁₀; Ἀ[λωπεκῆθεν], 213₄; [Ἀλ]ωπεκ(ῆθεν), 187₅₆; [Ἀλω]πεκῆθεν, 208₆; [Ἀλωπ]εκῆθεν, 212₂
Ἀμ[φιτροπῆθεν], 19₁(?)
Ἀνα[----], 333₃
Ἀναγυράσιος, 123₉; [Ἀ]ναγυράσ[ιος], 125₆
Ἀναχαιεύς, 101₃; [Ἀ]ναχα[ιεύς], 23₃; Ἀν[αχ]αέω[ς], 103₂; Ἀ[ναχαι]έως, 102₃
Ἀναφλύστιος, 109 III₁₂₇, 187₇; Ἀναφλύ[στι]ο[ς], 222₁₀; [Ἀναφλύ]στιον, 194₆; Ἀ[να]φ[λ]υ[στιο--], 84₇₅; [Ἀν]αφλυσ[τιο--], 84₈₁
Ἀραφήνιος: Ἀρ[αφήνιος(?)], 296₁₀₄; Ἀραφην[ίου], 296₄₃; Ἀρ[α]φηνίου, 296₄₅
Αὐρίδης: Αὐρί[δην], 127₁₁
Ἀφιδναῖος, 86₃, 123₁₁, 172₅, 224₈; Ἀφιδναῖ[ος], 113₇; Ἀφιδναῖ(ος), 213₄₉; Ἀφιδ(ναῖος), 213₃₉; [Ἀ]φιδναῖος, 187₅₄; [Ἀφ]ιδνα[ῖος], 54₅; [Ἀφιδ]ναῖος, 218₃; Ἀφιδναῖ[ον], 127₁₂; Ἀφιδ[ναῖο]ν, 335₅₈; Ἀφιδ[ναῖον], 233₅
Ἀχαρνεύς, 73₃, 181₄; Ἀχαρνε[ύς], 113₉; Ἀχαρνε(ύς), 213₇₂; Ἀχαρ[νεύς], 116₉; Ἀχαρ(νεύς), 213₃₅; Ἀχ[αρνεύς], 110₃; Ἀ[χ]α[ρνεύς], 109 IV₁₂₄; [Ἀχαρ-νεύ]ς, 72₂; Ἀχαρνέα, 182₂₃, 194₆; Ἀχαρ[νέα], 335₆₀; [Ἀ]χαρνέα, 206₁₆; [Ἀ]χαρν[ε--], 269₄
Ἀχερδούσιος: Ἀχερ[δούσιος], 76₃

Βατῆθεν: [Β]ατ[ῆ(θεν)], 84₁₁(?)
Βουτάδης: Βο[υτάδην], 217₂₃

Γαργήττιος: Γαργήττιο[ς], 270₃; Γα[ρ]γήττ[ιο]ς, 188₅₂; Γαργήττιον, 153₅, 182₂₆

Δεκελεεύς, 105₃
Διομεεύς: Δι[ομειεύς], 296₅₇; [Δ]ιο[μ]ειεύ[ς], 107₃; [Δι]ο[με(εύς)], 84₁₂(?); [Διομ]εεύς, 110₅

Εἰρεσίδης, 225₂₃; Εἰρεσ[ίδης], 213₇₀; Εἰρεσ(ίδης), 213₄₀; [Εἰ]ρεσί(δης), 213₈₀; [Εἰρ]εσίδης, 199₄
Εἰτεαῖος: Εἰτεαῖ(ος), 213₆₂; Εἰτεαῖον, 335₅₉
Ἐλευσίνιος, 187₅₂; Ἐλευσίν(ιος), 213₆₁; Ἐλευσ(ί-νιος), 213₇₉; Ἐλε[υ]σίνιος, 181₈; Ἐ[λ]ευσίνιος, 361₄; Ἐλευσινία, see Index 8, s.v. Δημήτηρ
Ἐπικηφίσιος, 295₃
Ἐρχιεύς, 296₅₆; Ἐρχιε[ύς], 213₇; Ἐρχιε(ύς), 213₃₆; Ἐρχι(εύς), 213₃₃,₃₄,₄₇,₅₄,₅₈,₇₄; [Ἐ]ρχιε(ύς), 213₃₇; [Ἐ]ρχι(εύς), 84₁₁(?); Ἐρχ[ιέα], 217₂₂; Ἐρ[χ]ιέα, 194₂₀
Εὐμολπίδαι: Εὐμολ[πίδαι], 57₅; Εὐμ[ολπ]ίδαι, 306₁₁; [Εὐμολ]πίδας, 48₂₂; Εὐμολπιδῶν, 48₁₁, 56 A₃₈, 306₁₄; [Ε]ὐμολ[πιδῶν], 56 A₂₇; [Εὐ]μολπιδῶ[ν], 56 B(d)₉; [Εὐ]μολπιδ[ῶν], 56 A₃₁; [Εὐμολ]πιδῶν, 56 A₃₀; Εὐ-μολπ[ίδαις], 306₆; [Ε]ὐμολπίδαις, 56 B(f)₅; Εὐμολ-π[ιδ---], 56 B(h)₅
Εὐπυρίδης, 213₅₂, 216₃; Εὐπυ[ρίδης], 264₂; [Εὐπυρί]δης, 97₅, 217₃; Εὐπυρίδου, 296₂₇
Εὐωνυμεύς, 184₂, 185₂; Εὐων(υμεύς), 213₅₅; [Εὐωνυ]-μεύς, 188₅₄

Θημακεύς, 187₄₀; Θημαχ(εύς), 213₃₈,₇₈
Θοραιεύς: Θ[ορ]αιε[ύς], 96₂
Θορίκιος, 265₂; [Θ]ορικιο[--], 158₂
Θριάσιος, 308(a)₂; Θριάσι(ος), 213₃₆; Θριά[σ]ιος, 85₇; Θ[ριάσιος], 97₂; Θριά[σιον], 305₃₂
Θυμαιτάδης: [Θυμ]αιτάδης, 222₉; [Θυ]μαι[τάδης](?), 283₆

Φιλαίδης, 296_{113}; Φιλαί(δης), 213_{59}; Φιλ[αίδης], 270_1; [Φ]ιλαίδης, 84_{156}

Φλυεύς, 187_{50}; Φλυεύ(ς), 213_{79}; Φλυε(ύς), $213_{63,78}$; Φλυ(εύς), 213_{64}; Φ[λυεύς], 336_3

Φρεάρριος, 208_3; Φρεάρρι(ος), $213_{75,76}$; Φ[ρεάρριος], 162_3(?); Φρεάρριον, 275_{20}

Φυλάσιος, 213_{56}, 291_{13}, 296_{39}; Φυλάσι(ος), 213_{72}; Φυλά(σιος), 213_{66}; Φυλ[ά]σιος, 213_{58}; Φ[υλάσιος], 162_3(?); Φυλάσιο[ν], 291_{33}; Φυλ[άσιο]ν, 291_{50}

Χολαργεύς, 266_7; Χολαργεύ[ς], $308(a)_5$; [Χο]λα-[ρ]γεύ[ς], 170_{12}; Χολαργέα, 241_3; [Χο]λαργ[− −](?), $115(e)_{14}$

Χολλείδης, 296_{59}; Χολλείδην, 182_{22}

5. BUILDINGS AND LOCATIONS IN ATHENS AND ATTICA

See also Index 9, *s.vv.* "Council and Assembly, specified locations of" and "Locations of stelai".

Ἄρειος Πάγος, $73_{14,18,25}$; ἡ βουλὴ ἡ ἐξ Ἀρείου Πάγου, 73_{12}; ἡ βουλὴ ἡ ἐξ Ἀρήο[υ Πάγου], 322_{11}; [τῆς βουλῆς τῆς ἐν Ἀ]ρείωι Πάγωι, 333_{18}; [τῆς] ἐξ Ἀρείου Πάγου βο[υλ]ῆς, 335_8; τῆι ἐξ Ἀ[ρείου Πάγου βουλῆι], 339 A_3

Ἐλευσίς: [Ἐλ]ευσῖνα, 337_{30}; [ἐν Ἐλ]ευσῖνι, 322_9; [Ἐλευσι]νόθεν, 56 A_{48}; [Ἐλ]ευσιν[− − −], 56 $B(e)_8$; *see also* Index 4, *s.v.* Ἐλευσίνιος

Ἐλευσίνιον: τὸ [Ἐλευσίνιον], 94_5; τοῦ Ἐλευσινίου τοῦ ἐν ἄστει, 56 $B(a)_{23}$; ἐν τ[ῶι Ἐλευσινί]ωι, 306_9; [ἐν τῶι Ἐ]λευσ[ιν]ίωι, 306_{16}; [ἐν τῶι Ἐλευσ]ινίωι, 331_3

Ἡρακλεῖδαι: τὸ ἱερὸν τὸ τῶν Ἡρακλειδῶν, 68 A_3, 68 B_4

Θησεῖον: [παρ]ὰ τῶι Θησείωι, 41_{11}

Ἱππάδες (πύλαι), 109 IV_{128}

Ἰτωνίδαι πύλαι: τῶν [Ἰτων]ίδων πυλῶν, 109 III_{122}

Κεραμικὴ πύλη: [π]ύληι Κεραμικ[ῆι], $326(a)_2$

Κηφισός (river): τοῦ Κηφ[ι]σοῦ, 109 II_{122}; [τ]οῦ Κ[ηφισοῦ], 109 II_{124}

Λαύρειον: ἐπὶ Λαυρείοι, 17_{12}

Λευκοπύρα: Λευκοπ[ύρ]α, 84_{95}; Λευκοπυραῖος (τὸ Ἑρμαῖον [τὸ] Λευκοπυρ[α]ῖον), 84_{96}

Μητρῷον: εἰς τὸ Μητρῶιον, 275_{17}; [ἐκ τοῦ] Μητρώιου, 327_2; ἐν [τῶι] Μητρώιω, 322_4

Νέα: Νέας, $75_{14,42}$; Νέαι, 75_{15}; Νέα[ι], 75_{17}

Πειραιεύς, 181_{30}; Πει[ρ]αιᾶ, 176_4(?); [Πει]ραιεῖ, 315_3; ἐμ [Πε]ιραιεῖ, 322_9; [ἐμ Πειραι]εῖ, 261_{53}; [ἐμ Πειραιε]ῖ, 261_{34}; *see also* Index 9, *s.v.* Assembly, specified locations of

Σαλαμίς, 71(b); ἐς Σαλαμ[ῖνα], 41_{34}; Σαλαμεῖνος, 337_{20}; Σαλαμίνιος, 296_{58}; ὁ δῆμος ὁ Σαλαμινίων, 181_{44-45}

Σκιάς: ἐν τεῖ Σκιάδι, 275_{14}

Ὠρωπός: ἐ[ν Ὠρ]ω[πῶι], 84_{10}

6. PLACES AND PEOPLES BEYOND ATTICA

Ἀβδηρίτης: [Ἀβδη]ρίτης, 79_9

Αἰόλειον: hαιό[λειον], 16_{53}

Αἰτωλοί: Αἰτωλῶν, 48_8; [Αἰ]τω[λῶν], 48_{17}; Αἰτωλο[− − −], 48_{20}

Ἀλεξανδρεύς, 325_6; Ἀλεξανδ[ρέα], 316_1; Ἀλεξ[ανδρεία], 164_6; Ἀλεξανδ[ρέως], 325_3; [Ἀ]λεξανδρέως, 324_3

Ἁλικαρνασσεύς: [Ἁ]λικαρνα[σσεύς], 64_4

Ἀντιοχεύς: [Ἀν]τιοχεύς, 324_4, 325_4

Ἀπτεραῖος: Ἀπτε[ραῖον], 328_8

Ἀργεῖοι: Ἀργεῖο[ι], 19_{13}; [Ἀργεῖο]ι, 19_{15}; Ἀργ[εῖος], 19_5; [Ἀργ]εῖον, 19_6; Ἀργείοις, 19_{12}

Ἀρεθούσιοι: Ἀρεθουσίοις, 43_7

Ἀσία: εἰς τὴν Ἀσίαν, 101_{17}

Ἄφυτις, Ἀφυταῖοι: ἐν Ἄ[φυτι], 15_5; Ἀφυταῖοι, 15_{18}; Ἀφυταῖο[ι], 15_8; Ἀφυ[ταῖος], $15_{3,13}$

Βοιωτία, Βοιωτοί: [εἰ]ς τὴν Βοιωτί[αν], 84_{142}; Βοι-[ωτός], 34_5; [Β]οιωτούς, 182_{21}; Βοιωτῶν, 208_{11}; Βοιω[τῶν], 34_2

Βόσπορος: [εἰ]ς Βόσπορο[ν], 94_{31}

Βοττιαῖοι: Βοττια[ῖοι], $16_{27,39}$; [Β]οττιαῖοι, 16_{43}; [Β]οτ-τιαῖον, 16_{29}; [Βοτ]τια[ῖον], 16_{11}; [Βοττια]ῖον, 16_9; Βοττι[αῖοις], 16_{12}; [Βοττι]αῖοις, 16_{14}

Βρέα: Βρέαν, 7(b)$_{2,9}$; ἐμ Βρέαι, 7(a)$_{28}$

7. THE ATHENIAN MONTHS

The months are listed in their order in the Athenian calendar. References are given to days within each month as recorded in the enactment cited, these usually describing the date of a meeting of the assembly. Where that precise information is absent, the month is indexed in Greek as it appears in its context.

Ἑκατομβαιών: 11th 107_4; 17th 161_{13}; 18th 161_{13}; Ἑκατο[μβαιῶνος], 56 A$_{17}$

Μεταγειτνιών: 9th 187_4; 12th 208_3; 18th 226_3(?); 28th 182_3; 29th 224_4; Μετ[αγειτν]ιῶνι, 117_{12}

Βοηδρομιών: 9th 179_5; 11th 227_3; 12th 336_7; 18th 190_4; 29th 226_3(?); [Βοηδ]ρομ[ιῶνος], 107A$_5$; [Βο]η-δρομιῶνι, 160_{14}

Πυανοψιών: 8th, intercalated the third time (8^3) 305_3(?); 16th 306_1; 25th 123_5; Πυανοψιῶνος, 56 B(b)$_9$; [Πυα]νοψιῶνος, 290_2; Πυα[νοψιῶνι], 160_{15}

Μαιμακτηριών: 11th 101_5; 29th 97_5; 29th or 30th 289_2(?); Μαιμακτηρι[ῶνος], 292_2; [Μαιμα]κτηριῶ[νος], 321_3; [Μαιμακτηριῶ]νο[ς], 281_4(?)

Ποσιδεών: 9th 330_4; 11th 76_4; 28th 91_4(?); 29th 124_5, 180_3; [Π]οσιδεῶνος, 286_3; [Ποσιδ]εῶνος, 296_{44}

Γαμηλιών: 6th 100_5(?); 9th 181_4; 10th 100_5; 25th 275_{11}; 30th 104_4, 105_2; Γαμηλιῶνος, 113_4

Ἀνθεστηριών: 18th 295_3; 19th 171_4; 29th or 30th 263_4

Ἐλαφηβολιών: 9th 162_4(?), 184_3, 216_4, 217_3, 280_2(?), 308_3; 9th intercalated the fourth time (9^4) 188_3; 12th 102_4; 13th 95_4, 261_3; 18th 265_2; 19th 79_4; 22nd 162_4, 218_3; 30th 172_2, 213_5; Ἐλαφηβο[λιῶνος], 114_{21}; Ἐλαφ[ηβολιῶνος], 165_4; Ἐλαφ[ηβολι]ῶ[νος], 309_3; Ἐλαφη[βολιῶν]ος, 342_{13}

Μουνιχιών: 8th 100_5(?); 10th 125_4(?); 11th 266_4, 284_2; 21st 255C; 22nd or 23rd 340_2; 28th or 29th 276_1; 29th or 30th 167_4; Μουνιχιῶνος, 85_3, 213_{18}, 327_3; [Μο]υνι[χιῶνος], 288_2

Θαργηλιών: Θαργηλιῶνος, 341_{26}; Θαργηλι[ῶ]ν[ος], 67_3

Σκιροφοριών: 11th 186_5; 14th 67_3; 20th 324_3, 325_3; 21st 189_3; 26th 219_4; 29th 291_5; 29th or 30th 185_3; 30th 103_3, 116_5; [Σκιροφ]οριῶνος, 259_3

8. GODS, HEROES, AND FESTIVALS

Ἀγαθὴ Τύχη (as deity receiving cult), $114_{16,22}$, 340_{18}, $341_{18,34}$

Ἀθηνᾶ: Ἀθηνᾶν, 115(a)$_6$; Ἀθηναῖ, $75_{5,18}$; Ἀθην[αι], 153_2; Ἀθηνάα[ι], 36_{37}; Ἀ[θηναῖ], 75_{28}; Ἀθηναῖ τῆι Νίκηι, 75_{47}, 114_{16}; [Ἀ]θηνᾶς [τῆς Πολιά]δος, 341_{32}; Ἀθηναῖ [τῆι Πολι]άδ[ι], 341_{38}; [Ἀθηναῖ τῆι] Πολιάδι, 75_{47}; Ἀθηναῖ τῆι Σωτείραι, 186_{15}; Ἀθηναῖ τῆι Ὑγιείαι, 75_{34}; Νίκη (= Ἀθ.), 75_{45}; ἡ θεός (= Ἀθ.), 72_4, 47 A(f)$_2$, $75_{31,37,58}$; see also Παλλάς, Παρθένος, and Index 2, s.v. Julia Augusta

Ἀπόλλων: [Ἀπό]λλωνι, 336_9; Ἀ[πό]λλωνι τῶ[ι] Πυθίωι, 36_{37}; [τοῦ] θεοῦ (= Ἀπ.), 276_4

Ἄρτεμις: Ἀρτέμι[δ]ος Βουλαίας, 225_{19}

Ἀφροδίτη: Ἀφροδίτης, 296_{47}; Ἀ[φροδίτης], 325_8; [Ἀφ]ροδίτει, 202_5; [Ἀφροδίτην] τὴν Στρατονικ[ίδα], 209_7

Βασίλεια, 182_{10}
Βασίλη: τῆς Βασίλ[ης], 218_{10}
Βενδῖς: τεῖ Βενδῖδι, 329_3

Δηλόπτης: τῶι Δηλόπτε[ι], 329_3
Δημήτηρ: Δήμητρος, 123_{15}, 277_{12}; Δήμ[η]τρος τῆς Ἐλευσινίας, 48_9; see also Θεώ
Διονύσια: [Διονύσι]α, 7_{12}; Διονυσ[ίων τῶν μεγάλων], 208_{27}; Διονυσίων τῶν ἐν ἄστει, 224_{37}, 225_{10}; Δι[ονυσίων τῶν ἐν ἄστει], 238_8; [Διονυσίω]ν τῶν ἐν

ἄστει, 249_2; [Διονυσίων] τῶν ἐν ἄστει, 248_{12}; [Διονυσίων τῶν ἐν] ἄσ[τει], 261_{48}
Διόνυσος: τῶι Διονύσωι, 181_{12}; τὸ τέμενος τοῦ Διονύσου, 93_4; ἱμάτιον Διονυσι[ακόν], 296_{105}; θέατρον Διονύσου, see Index 9, s.v. Assembly, specified locations of

Ἐλευθέρια, 304_6
Ἐλευσίνια: Ἐλευσινίων, 225_{11}, 295_{15}; [Ἐ]λευσιν[ίω]ν, 248_{13}; Ἐ[λε]υσινίων, 249_4
Ἐρεχθεύς, 32_1(?)
Ἔχελος: [Ἐ]χέλου, 161_4; τῶι ἥρωι, $161_{14,16}$

Ζεύς: Διός, 340_{13}; ἐγ Διός, 9_8; τῶι Ἐλ[ευθερίωι Διί], 342_4; Διὶ τῶι [Σωτῆρι], 186_{14}; τῆς τοῦ Δ[ιὸς στοᾶς], 174_8; [τῆς τοῦ Διὸς] στοᾶς, 304_8; τῶι τεμένει τοῦ Δι[ός], 214_{23}

Ἥλιος: Ἥλιον, 115(a)$_6$
Ἡρῶναι: Ἡρώναις, 161_{14}
Ἥρως: see Ἔχελος

Θεός: τὸ[ι] θεõι, 12_8; see also Ἀθηνᾶ, Ἀπόλλων
Θεώ (= Demeter and Kore): τοῖν θεοῖν, 56 A$_{14,27,29,36,37,48}$; 56 B(a)$_{11,24}$, (e)$_3$
Θεοί: τοὺς θεούς, 225_8, 329_2; τοὺς θ[εούς], 250_7; το[ὺς] θεο[ύς], 214_{18}; [τοὺς] θεούς, 206_{12}, 240_8; [τοὺς θ]εούς, 330_3; [τοὺς θεο]ύς, 205_{10}; [τοὺς] θεούς (= μεγάλοι θεοί), 325_6; τοὺς [θεούς] (= μεγάλοι θεοί),

324₈; τῶν θεῶν, 261₂₉, 270₆; [τῶν θε]ῶν, 235₈; τοῖς θεοῖς, 271₄; τοῖς θεοῖ[ς], 299₉; [τοῖ]ς θεοῖς, 306₂₃; τοῖς ἄλλοις θεο[ῖς], 284₁₂; τοῖς [ἄλλοι]ς θεοῖς, 153₃; τοῖ[ς] δώδεκα θεοῖς, 41₂. Θεοί as superscript: *see* Index 9

Θεσμοφόροι: τῶν Θεσμοφό[ρων], 277₁; τῶν Θ[ε]σμοφόρων, 277₈; [τὰ]ς θεάς, 277₁₀

Κέκροψ: Κέκροπα λαός, 44₁
Κόρη: τῆς Κόρης, 48₁₀; τῆς Κόρη[ς], 277₁₂; [τεῖ Κό]ρει, 284₁₁; *see also* Θεώ

Μεγάλοι Θεοί: [τῶν] μεγάλων θεῶν, 325₇; *see also* Θεοί
Μυστήρια: [τῶν μεγάλων Μυστη]ρίων, 284₈; τοῖς μ[υσ]τικοῖς ἱε[ροῖς], 300₅

'Ολύμπιοι: τῶν 'Ολυμπ[ίων], 340₈
'Ολύμπιεια: [τοῖ]ς 'Ολυμπιείο[ις], 203₂

Παλλάς, 44₂

Παναθήναια: Παναθέναια τὰ μεγάλ[α], 7₁₂; Παναθήναια, 75₅₇; Παναθ[έναια], 19₂₄; [Παν]αθηναίων τῶν μικρῶν, 75₁₉; Παναθηναίων, 224₃₈, 295₁₅; Πανα[θη]ναί[ω]ν, 225₁₀; [Παναθ]ηναίων, 261₄₉; [Παναθηναί]ων, 249₃
Παρθένος: [τ]ῆ Παρθένῳ, 340₁₇
Ποσειδῶν: τῶι Ποσειδῶνι [τῶι 'Ιππίωι], 270₅
Πτολεμαῖα: Πτολεμαίων, 225₁₁; Πτολ[εμαίων], 261₄₉
Πύθιος: *see* 'Απόλλων

Σώτειρα: *see* 'Αθηνᾶ
Σωτήρ: *see* Ζεύς
Σωτῆρες (Antigonos Monophthalmos and Demetrios Poliorketes as recipients of cult): τοῖς Σωτῆρσιν, 114₂₂; [το]ῖς Σωτῆρσιν, 114₁₆; [τοῖς Σω]τῆρσιν, 115(*a*)₃

Χάριτες: [Χάρι]σιν, 270₄

9. SIGNIFICANT THEMES AND FORMULAIC PHRASES

In this section the citations refer only to the text in which the theme or phraseology occurs; line references are not included. Where the theme or phrase is not preserved on the stone but is a probable restoration the number of the text is shown in parentheses.

"Analiskomena fund" as source of expenditure on stelai (τὰ κατὰ ψηφίσματα ἀναλισκόμενα τῷ δήμῳ): 45(?), 48, 54, 60, 66, 79, 83, 88, 104, 111, 112, (115), 120, 121, 122, 123, 128, 137, 138, 139, 140, 164, 252. *See also* 255B.

Assembly (ἐκκλησία), specified locations or meetings of: ἐν Διονύσου, 79, 181; ἐν τῷ θεάτρῳ, 224, (242), (243), 262, 264, 265, 266, 273, (278), (284), (286), 295, (305), 308, 313, 332B, (335); ἐν τῷ θεάτρῳ μεταχθεῖσα ἐκ Πειραιέως, 319; ἐμ Πειραιεῖ, 124(?), 222, 259, 261, (282), 283, 290, 291, 292, (296); σύγκλητος ἐμ Πειραιεῖ στρατηγῶν παραγγειλάντων, 289; κατὰ ψήφισμα βουλῆς, 102; κατὰ τὴν μαντείαν τοῦ θεοῦ, 276

Citizenship, grants of: *see* Concordance 1. D. Other Publications, *s.v.* M. J. Osborne, *Naturalization*

Cost of stelai
  expressly specified
    10 drachmai, 181, 182, 187
    20 drachmai, 40, 73, (88?), 112, (120), (137), (138), (192)
    30 drachmai, 43, 54(?), 60, (66), (88?), 90, (111), (121), 123, (139), (140), 162, 164
    40 drachmai, (83)
    50 drachmai, (104)
  amount specified but not to be restored with probability: (115c), (122), (128), (129), (174)

stated as τὸ γενόμενον ἀνάλωμα: 177, 178, 193, 194, (200), 201, 214, (220), (221), 224, 225, 239, 248, (250), (253), 267, 291, 295, 296, 301, 310, 312

Cost and type of stephanoi
  gold, cost stated
    500 drachmai, 44, 54(?)
    1000 drachmai, 77, 86, 92, 99, 101, 111, 127, 141
  gold, cost stated but uncertain: (94), (112)
  gold, awarded κατὰ τὸν νόμον: 122, 141, 155, 157, 159, 163, 173, 181, 185, 187, 188, 194, 208, 224, 225, 238, 261
  gold, lacking further description: 79, 94, 115(*b*), 206, 240, 248, 310, 332E
  olive: 55, 104, 123, 129, 153, 175, 188, 221, 225, 233, (250), (276), (291), (298?), (316), 332G(?), 335
  myrtle: 228, 239, 277, 285
  ivy: 166
  type not identified: 174, 212, 249, 328

Council (βουλή), specified locations or meetings of: βουλὴ ἐμ βουλευτηρίῳ, 116, 260; βουλὴ ἐμ βουλευτηρίῳ σύνκλητος στρατηγῶν παραγγειλάντων, 276; βουλὴ ἐν τῷ 'Ελευσινίῳ, 331

"Economy design" in prescripts: 214, 216, 217. *See also* "Perfect design".

"Hortatory intention" (the encouragement of others to emulate the merits of honorands): 86, 98(?), 101, 112, 123, 131, 144, 157, 158(?), 164, 173, 181, 185, 187,

10. ARCHONSHIPS DISCUSSED

The references in this section are to pages of this volume. The names of the archons are accompanied by the year (or, in some cases, alternative years) to which their term of office has been assigned.

ILLUSTRATIONS

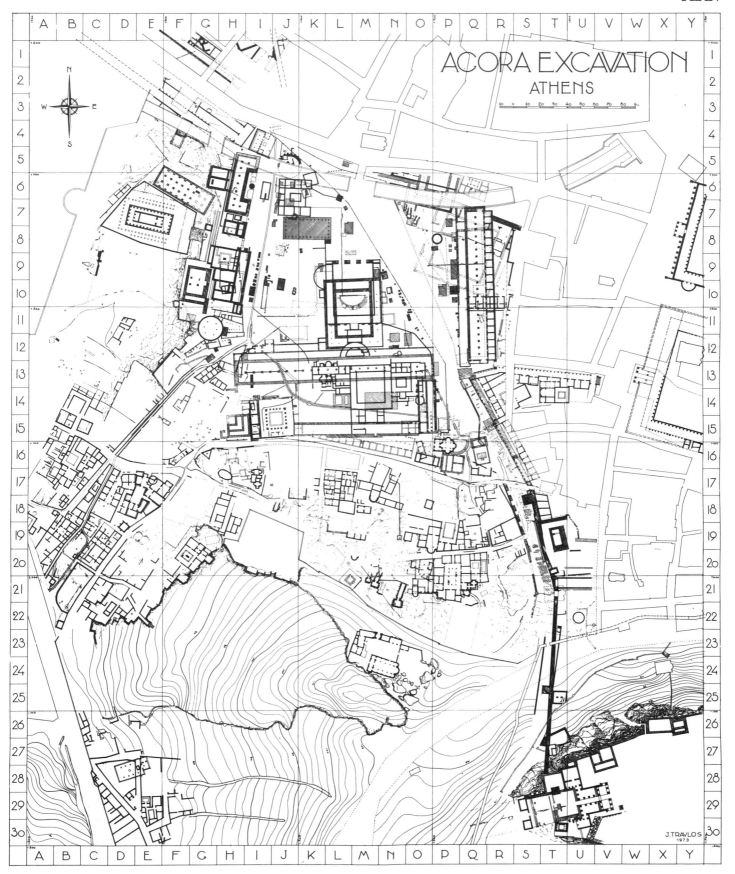

ACORA EXCAVATION
ATHENS

J.TRAVLOS
1973

Actual-State Plan of the Agora and Vicinity

PLATE 1

1, fragment *a*

PLATE 2

6, fragment *a*

6, fragment *b*

PLATE 3

17

26

24

PLATE 4

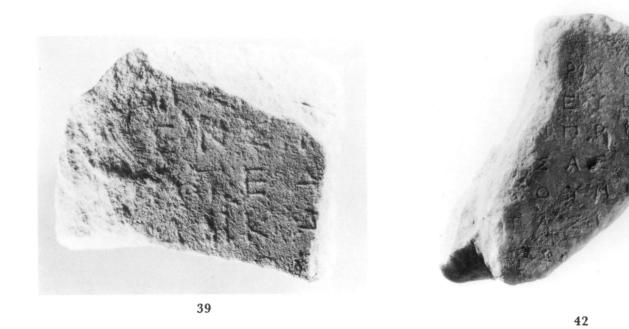

39

42

48

PLATE 5

54

PLATE 6

52

57

69

PLATE 7

62

75

76

PLATE 8

68, Face A   **68**, Face B

PLATE 9

86

PLATE 10

93, fragment *c*

93, fragments *a* and *b*

PLATE 11

96

105

PLATE 12

100

PLATE 13

107A

109

115, fragment *a*

PLATE 14

114, fragment *b*

114, fragment *a*

129

PLATE 15

134

PLATE 16

148

165

162, fragment *a*

PLATE 17

206

173

PLATE 18

PLATE 19

191

190

PLATE 20

194, fragment *a*

194, fragment *b*

PLATE 21

208

PLATE 22

222

220

PLATE 23

224

PLATE 24

227

PLATE 25

239, fragment *a*

239, fragment *b*

PLATE 26

242

246

PLATE 27

247

252

253

PLATE 28

261, fragment *a*

261, fragments *c* and *d*

PLATE 29

284

287

297

PLATE 30

298

303

314

338

PLATE 31

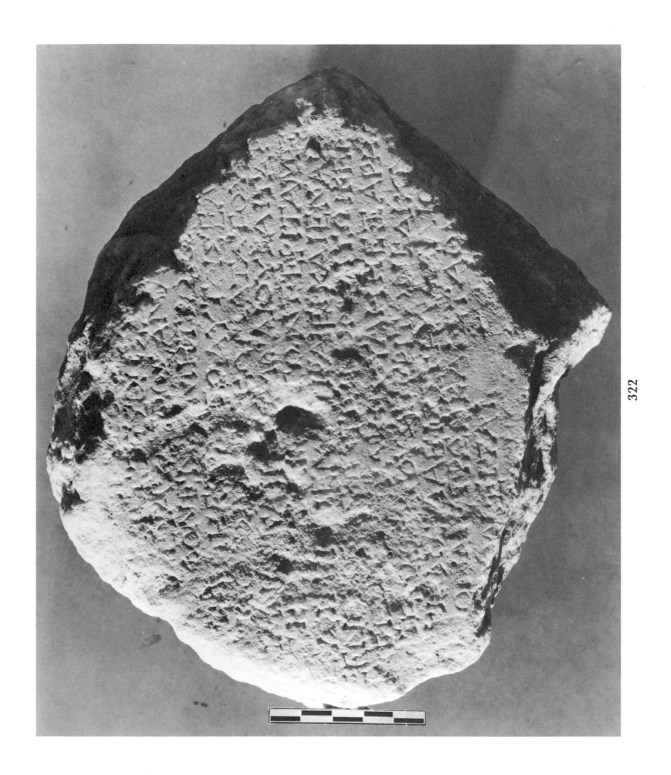

PLATE 32

330